The Class Struggle
in the Ancient Greek World

The Class Struggle in the Ancient Greek World

from the
Archaic Age to the Arab Conquests

G. E. M. DE STE. CROIX

Cornell University Press

ITHACA, NEW YORK

Frontispiece:
De Aardappeleters (The Potato Eaters)
by Vincent van Gogh
(Stedelijk Museum, Amsterdam):
see pages 209–10.

First published in 1981 by Cornell University Press.

International Standard Book Number 0-8014-1442-3
Library of Congress Catalog Card Number 81-66650

Printed in Great Britain.

Contents

Preface   ix

PART ONE

I Introduction
   i   The plan of this book   3
   ii 'The Ancient Greek World': its extent in space and time   7
   iii *Polis* and *chōra*   9
   iv The relevance of Marx for the study of ancient history   19

II Class, Exploitation, and Class Struggle
   i   The nature of class society   31
   ii 'Class', 'exploitation', and 'the class struggle' defined   42
   iii Exploitation and the class struggle   49
   iv Aristotle's sociology of Greek politics   69
   v   Alternatives to class (status etc.)   81
   vi Women   98

III Property and the Propertied
   i   The conditions of production: land and unfree labour   112
   ii The propertied class (or classes)   114
   iii Land, as the principal source of wealth   120
   iv Slavery and other forms of unfree labour   133
   v   Freedmen   174
   vi Hired labour   179

IV Forms of Exploitation in the Ancient Greek World, and the Small Independent Producer
   i   'Direct individual' and 'indirect collective' exploitation   205
   ii The peasantry and their villages   208
   iii From slave to *colonus*   226
   iv The military factor   259
   v   'Feudalism' (and serfdom)   267
   vi Other independent producers   269

PART TWO

V   The Class Struggle in Greek History on the Political
    Plane
    i   The 'age of the tyrants'   278
    ii   The fifth and fourth centuries B.C.   283
    iii The destruction of Greek democracy   300

VI Rome the Suzerain
    i   'The queen and mistress of the world'   327
    ii   The 'conflict of the Orders'   332
    iii The developed Republic   337
    iv   The Roman conquest of the Greek world   344
    v   From Republic to Principate   350
    vi   The Principate, the emperor, and the upper classes   372

VII The Class Struggle on the Ideological Plane
    i   Terror, and propaganda   409
    ii   The theory of 'natural slavery'   416
    iii The standard Hellenistic, Roman and Christian attitude to
         slavery   418
    iv   The attitudes to property of the Graeco-Roman world, of Jesus,
         and of the Christian churches   425
    v   The ideology of the victims of the class struggle   441

VIII The 'Decline and Fall' of the Roman Empire: an
      Explanation
    i   Intensified political subjection and economic exploitation of the
         lower classes during the early centuries of the Christian era   453
    ii   Pressure on the curial class   465
    iii Defection to the 'barbarians', peasant revolts, and indifference
         to the disintegration of the Roman empire   474
    iv   The collapse of much of the Roman empire in the fifth, sixth
         and seventh centuries   488

APPENDICES

    I   The contrast between slave and wage-labourer in Marx's
         theory of capital   504
    II   Some evidence for slavery (especially agricultural) in the
         Classical and Hellenistic periods   505
    III The settlement of 'barbarians' within the Roman empire   509
    IV   The destruction of Greek democracy in the Roman period   518

Notes   538

Bibliography (and Abbreviations)   661

Indexes   700

Preface

The main text of this book is intended not only for ancient historians and Classical scholars but also in particular for historians of other periods, sociologists, political theorists, and students of Marx, as well as for 'the general reader'. The use of Greek text and of anything in Latin beyond very brief quotations is reserved for the Notes and Appendices.

As far as I am aware, it is the first book in English, or in any other language I can read, which begins by explaining the central features of Marx's historical method and defining the concepts and categories involved, and then proceeds to demonstrate how these instruments of analysis may be used in practice to explain the main events, processes, institutions and ideas that prevailed at various times over a long period of history – here, the thirteen or fourteen hundred years of my 'ancient Greek world' (for which see I.ii below). This arrangement involves rather frequent cross-referencing. Some of those who are interested primarily in the methodology and the more 'theoretical', synchronic treatment of concepts and institutions (contained mainly in Part One) may wish for specific references to those passages that are of most concern to themselves, occurring either in other sections of Part One or in the more diachronic treatment in Part Two. Similarly, practising historians whose interests are confined to a limited part of the whole period will sometimes need references to a particular 'theoretical' portion in Part One that is specially relevant. (This will, I think, be clear to anyone who compares II.iv with V.ii-iii, for instance, I.iii with IV.ii, or III.iv with Appendix II and IV.iii.)

The book originated in the J. H. Gray Lectures for 1972/73 (three in number), which I delivered at Cambridge University in February 1973 at the invitation of the Board of the Faculty of Classics. I am particularly grateful to J. S. Morrison, President of Wolfson College, then Chairman of the Faculty, and to M. I. (now Sir Moses) Finley, Professor of Ancient History, for their kindness to me and the trouble they took to make the experience a delightful one for me and to ensure a large audience at all three lectures.

The J. H. Gray lectures were founded by the Rev. Canon Joseph Henry ('Joey') Gray, M.A.(Cantab.), J.P., born on 26 July 1856, Fellow and Classical Lecturer of Queens' College Cambridge for no fewer than 52 years before his death on 23 March 1932, at the age of 75. His devotion to his College (of which he wrote and published a history), to the Anglican Church, and to Freemasonry (he became Provincial Grand Master of Cambridgeshire in 1914) was equalled only by his athletic interests, in rowing, cricket, and above all Rugby football. From 1895 until his death he was President of the Cambridge University Rugby Football Club; and when that club, in appreciation of his presidency, presented him with a sum of no less than £1,000, he used the money to endow a special lectureship in Classics at Cambridge – 'thus making the gladiators of the football field into patrons of the humaner letters', to quote the admiring and affectionate obituary in *The Dial* (Queens' College Magazine) no.71, Easter Term 1932. The obituary refers to Gray's 'vigorous Conservative politics' and characterises him as 'an almost perfect incarnation of John Bull in cap and gown'. I am afraid he would have disapproved strongly of my lectures, and of this book; but I am comforted by another passage in the same obituary which speaks of his 'hearty goodwill to all men, even to individual socialists and foreigners'.

This book represents of course a very considerable expansion of the lectures, and it incorporates, almost in their entirety, two other papers, given in 1974: a lecture on 'Karl Marx and the history of Classical antiquity', to the Society for the Promotion of Hellenic Studies in London on 21 March 1974, published in an expanded form in *Arethusa* 8 (1975) 7-41 (here cited as 'KMHCA'); and another lecture, on 'Early Christian attitudes to property and slavery', delivered to the Conference of the Ecclesiastical History Society at York on 25 July 1974, also subsequently expanded and published, in *Studies in Church History* 12 (1975) 1-38 (here cited as 'ECAPS'). Parts of this book have also been delivered in lecture form at various universities, not only in this country but also in Poland (in June 1977), at Warsaw; and in the Netherlands (in April-May 1978), at Amsterdam, Groningen and Leiden. I have many friends to thank for their kindness to me during my visits to those cities, in particular Professors Iza Bieżuńska-Małowist of the University of Warsaw and Jan-Maarten Bremer of the University of Amsterdam.

I had intended to publish the Gray Lectures almost in their original form, with little more than references added. However, the comments received from most of those to whom I showed drafts convinced me that owing to the extreme ignorance of Marx's thought which prevails throughout most of the West, especially perhaps among ancient historians (in the English-speaking world at least as much as anywhere), I would have to write the book on an altogether different scale. As I did so my opinions developed, and I often changed my mind.

Friends and colleagues have given me some useful criticisms of the many successive drafts of chapters of this book. I have thanked them individually but now refrain from doing so again, partly because most of them are not Marxists and might not be happy at finding themselves named here, and partly because I do not wish to debar them from being asked to write reviews, as usually happens to those to whom an author makes a general acknowledgment.

I have incorporated very many essential brief references (especially to source material) in the text itself, placing them as far as possible at the ends of sentences. This, I believe, is preferable, in a work not intended primarily for scholars, to the use of footnotes, since the eye travels much more easily over a short passage in brackets than down to the foot of the page and back again. (Longer notes, intended principally for scholars, will be found at the end of the book.) I give this as a reply to those few friends who, out of sheer Oxonian conservatism, have objected to the abbreviation of titles by initial letters – e.g. 'Jones, *LRE*', for A. H. M. Jones, *The Later Roman Empire 284-602* – while themselves habitually using such abbreviations for various categories of references, including periodicals, collections of inscriptions and papyri, and so forth, e.g. *JRS*,

CIL, ILS, PSI, BGU. For me, the only alternatives still allowing the use of references in the actual text itself would have been to abbreviate with date or serial number, e.g. 'Jones, 1964' or 'Jones (1)'; but initial letters are as a rule far more likely to convey the necessary information to a reader who already either knows of the existence of the work in question or has looked it up in my bibliography (pp. - below), where all abbreviations are explained. I should perhaps add that titles abbreviated by initials represent books when italicised, articles when not.

My reading for this book, while concentrated above all on the ancient sources and the writings of Marx, has necessarily been very wide; but there are some 'obvious' works which I have refrained from citing – in particular, books which are specifically philosophical in character and which concern themselves primarily with abstract concepts rather than with the actual historical 'events, processes, institutions and ideas' (cf. above) that are the subject-matter of the practising historian. One example is G. A. Cohen's book, *Karl Marx's Theory of History, A Defence*, based on much greater philosophical expertise than I can command, but which I find congenial; another is the massive work in three volumes by Leszek Kolakowski, *Main Currents of Marxism: Its Rise, Growth and Dissolution*, which seems to me to have been vastly overpraised, however accurately it may delineate some of the disastrous developments of Marx's thought by many of his followers.

In an interview printed in *The Guardian* on 22 September 1970 the released Nazi war criminal Albert Speer said that in the Third Reich 'Each Minister was responsible for his own department, and for that only. Your conscience was quiet if you were *educated to see things only in your own field*; this was convenient for everybody.' Our educational system also tends to produce people who 'see things only in their own field'. One of the techniques contributing to this is the strict separation of 'ancient history' from the contemporary world. This book, on the contrary, is an attempt to see the ancient Greek world in very close relation with our own and is inspired by the belief that we can learn much about each by careful study of the other.

The dedication of this book expresses the greatest of all my debts: to my wife, in particular for the perfect good-humour and patience with which she accepted my concentration on it for some years, to the neglect of almost everything else. I also wish to record my gratitude to my son Julian for his valuable assistance in correcting the proofs, and to Colin Haycraft for agreeing to publish the book and accomplishing the task with all possible tact and efficiency.

September 1980   G.E.M.S.C.

PART ONE

I

Introduction

(i)
The plan of this book

My general aim in this book is first (in Part One) to explain, and then (in Part Two) to illustrate, the value of Marx's general analysis of society in relation to the ancient Greek world (as defined in Section ii of this chapter). Marx and Engels made a number of different contributions to historical methodology and supplied a series of tools which can be profitably used by the historian and the sociologist; but I shall concentrate largely on one such tool, which I believe to be much the most important and the most fruitful for actual use in understanding and explaining particular historical events and processes: namely, the concept of *class,* and of class *struggle*.

In Section ii of this first chapter, I state how I interpret the expression 'the ancient Greek world', and explain the meaning of the terms I shall be using for the periods (between about 700 B.C. and the mid-seventh century C.E.) into which the history of my 'Greek world' may conveniently be divided. In Section iii I go on to describe the fundamental division between *polis* and *chōra* (city and countryside) that plays such a vital role in Greek history after the 'Classical' period (ending at about the close of the fourth century B.C.) which – absurdly enough – is all that many people have in mind when they speak of 'Greek history'. In Section iv I give a brief account of Marx as a Classical scholar and emphasise the almost total lack of interest in Marxist ideas that is unfortunately characteristic of the great majority of scholars in the English-speaking world who concern themselves with Classical antiquity. I also try to dispel some common misconceptions about Marx's attitude to history; and in doing so I compare the attitude of Marx with that of Thucydides.

Chapter II deals with 'class, exploitation, and class struggle'. In Section i I explain the nature and origin of class society, as I understand that term. I also state what I regard as the two fundamental features which most distinguish ancient Greek society from the contemporary world: they can be identified respectively within the field of what Marx called 'the forces of production' and 'the relations of production'. In Section ii I define 'class' (as essentially a relationship, the social embodiment of the fact of exploitation), and I also define 'exploitation' and 'class struggle'. In Section iii I show that the meaning I attach to the expression 'class struggle' represents the fundamental thought of Marx himself: the essence of class struggle is exploitation or resistance to it; there need not necessarily be any class consciousness or any political element. I also explain the criteria which lead me to define Greek (and Roman) society as 'a slave economy': this expression has regard, not so much to the way in which the bulk of production was done (for at most times in most areas in antiquity it was free peasants and artisans who had the largest share in production), but to the fact that the propertied classes derived their surplus above all through the exploitation of unfree labour. (With this section goes Appendix I, dealing with the technical question of the contrast between slave and wage-labourer in Marx's theory of capital.) In Section iv I demonstrate that a Marxist analysis in terms of class, far from being the imposition upon the ancient Greek world of inappropriate and anachronistic categories suited only to the study of the modern capitalist world, is actually in some essentials much the same type of analysis as that employed by Aristotle, the greatest of ancient sociologists and political thinkers. In Section v I consider some types of historical method different from that which I employ, and the alternatives which some sociologists and historians have preferred to the concept of class; and I demonstrate (with reference to Max Weber and M. I. Finley) that 'status' in particular is inferior as an instrument of analysis, since statuses altogether lack the organic relationship which is the hallmark of classes and can rarely if ever provide explanations, especially of social change. In Section vi I consider women as a class in the technical Marxist sense, and I give a brief treatment of the early Christian attitude to women and marriage, compared with its Hellenistic, Roman and Jewish counterparts.

Chapter III is entitled 'Property and the propertied'. In Section i I begin with the fact that in antiquity by far the most important 'conditions of production' were land and unfree labour: these, then, were what the propertied class needed to control and did control. In Section ii I explain how I use the expression 'the propertied class': for those who were able to live without needing to spend a significant proportion of their time working for their living. (I speak of 'the propertied classes', in the plural, where it is necessary to notice class divisions within the propertied class as a whole.) In Section iii I emphasise that land was always the principal means of production in antiquity. In Section iv I discuss slavery and other forms of unfree labour (debt bondage, and serfdom), accepting definitions of each of these types of unfreedom which now have world-wide official currency. (Appendix II adds some evidence for slave labour, especially in agriculture, in Classical and Hellenistic times.) In Section v I deal with freedmen (an 'order' and not a 'class' in my sense), and in Section vi I discuss hired labour, showing that it played an incomparably smaller part in the pre-capitalist world than it does today and was regarded by members of the propertied class in antiquity (and by many of the poor) as only a little better than slavery.

In Chapter IV I discuss 'Forms of exploitation in the ancient Greek world, and the small independent producer'. In Section i I distinguish between 'direct individual' and 'indirect collective' exploitation, in such a way as to make it possible to regard even many peasant freeholders as members of an exploited class, subject to taxation, conscription and forced services, imposed by the State and its organs. I also explain that those whom I describe as 'small independent producers' (mainly peasants, also artisans and traders) were sometimes not severely exploited themselves and equally did not exploit the labour of others to any substantial degree, but lived by their own efforts on or near the subsistence level. At most periods (before the Later Roman Empire) and in most areas these people were very numerous and must have been responsible for the largest share in production, both in agriculture and in handicrafts. In Section ii I speak specifically of the peasantry and the villages in which they mainly lived. In Section iii ('From slave to *colonus*') I describe and explain the change in the forms of exploitation in the Greek and Roman world during the early centuries of the Christian era, when the propertied class, which had earlier relied to a great extent on slaves to produce its surplus, came more and more to rely on letting to tenants (*coloni*), most of whom at about the end of the third century became serfs. Most working freehold peasants were also brought into the same kind of subjection, being tied to the villages of which they were members: I call such people 'quasi-serfs'. (An Appendix, III, gives a large quantity of evidence for the settlement of 'barbarians' within the Roman empire, the significance of which is discussed in Section iii of Chapter IV.) In Section iv ('The military factor') I point out that in the face of external military threat it may be necessary for the ruling class of a society consisting mainly of peasants to allow the peasantry a higher standard of life than it would otherwise have attained, in order to provide a sufficiently strong army; and that the failure of the Later Roman Empire to make this concession induced in the peasantry as a whole an attitude of indifference to the fate of the Empire, which did not begin to be remedied before the seventh century, by which time much of the empire had disintegrated. In Section v I have something to say about the use of the terms 'feudalism' and 'serfdom', insisting that serfdom (as defined in III.iv) can exist quite independently of anything that can properly be called 'feudalism', and ending with a few words on the Marxist concept of the 'feudal mode of production'. In Section vi I recognise briefly the role of small 'independent producers' other than peasants. That completes Part One of this book.

In Part One, then, I am occupied largely with conceptual and methodological problems, in the attempt to establish and clarify the concepts and categories which seem to me to be the most useful in studying the ancient Greek world, above all the process of change which is so obvious when we look at Greek society over the period of thirteen to fourteen hundred years with which this book is concerned.

In Part Two I seek to illustrate the usefulness of the concepts and methodology I have outlined in Part One in explaining not only a series of historical situations and developments but also the ideas – social, economic, political, religious – which grew out of the historical process. In Chapter V ('The class struggle in Greek history on the political plane') I show how the application of a class analysis to Greek history can illuminate the processes of political and social change. In Section i I deal with the Archaic period (before the fifth century B.C.) and demonstrate how the so-called 'tyrants' played an essential role in the transition from hereditary aristocracy, which existed everywhere in the Greek world down to the seventh century, to more 'open' societies ruled either by oligarchies of wealth or by democracies. In Section ii I make a number of observations on the political class struggle (greatly mitigated by democracy, where that form of government existed) in the fifth and fourth centuries, showing how even at Athens, where democracy was strongest, bitter class struggle broke out in the political plane on two occasions, in 411 and 404. In Section iii I explain how Greek democracy was gradually destroyed, between the fourth century B.C. and the third century of the Christian era, by the joint efforts of the Greek propertied class, the Macedonians, and ultimately the

Romans. (The details of this process in the Roman period are described in greater detail in Appendix IV.)

Since the whole Greek world came by degrees under Roman rule, I am obliged to say a good deal about 'Rome the suzerain', the title of Chapter VI. After some brief remarks in Section i on Rome as 'The queen and mistress of the world', I give in Section ii a sketch of the so-called 'Conflict of the Orders' in the early Roman Republic, intended mainly to show that although it was indeed technically a conflict between two 'orders' (two juridically distinct groups), namely Patricians and Plebeians, yet strong elements of class struggle were involved in it. In Section iii I notice some aspects of the political situation in the developed Republic (roughly the last three centuries B.C.). In Section iv I briefly describe the Roman conquest of the Mediterranean world and its consequences. In Section v I explain the change of political regime 'From Republic to Principate', and in Section vi I sketch the nature of the Principate as an institution which continued under the 'Later Roman Empire' from the late third century onwards. In my picture of the Later Empire there is much less emphasis than usual upon a supposed change from 'Principate' to 'Dominate'; far more important, for me, is a major intensification of the forms of exploitation: the reduction to serfdom of most of the working agricultural population, a great increase in taxation, and more conscription. I give a characterisation of the position of the emperor in the Principate and the Later Empire and an outline sketch of the Roman upper classes, not forgetting the changes that took place in the fourth century.

Chapter VII is a discussion of 'The class struggle on the ideological plane'. After taking up some general issues in Section i ('Terror, and propaganda'), I proceed in Section ii to discuss the theory of 'natural slavery', and in Section iii the body of thought which largely replaced that theory in the Hellenistic period and continued throughout Roman times, appearing in Christian thought in an almost identical form. Section iv deals with the attitudes to property of the Graeco-Roman world, of Jesus, and of the Christian Church -- or rather, churches, for I insist that the term 'the Christian Church' is not a historical but a strictly theological expression. Jesus is seen as a figure belonging entirely to the Jewish *chōra*, who may never even have entered a Greek *polis*, and whose thought-world was thoroughly alien to Graeco-Roman civilisation. The chapter concludes with Section v, which attempts a reconstruction of part of the ideology of the victims of the class struggle (and of Roman imperialism), with some attention to 'Resistance literature' (mainly Jewish) and Christian apocalyptic. The best example that has survived is the fable, which is explicitly said by one of its practitioners to have been invented to enable slaves to express their opinions in a disguised form which would not expose them to punishment, although some of the examples turn out to speak not merely for slaves but for the lowly in general, and of course the fable could also be utilised by members of a ruling class to reinforce their position.

The final chapter, VIII, seeks to explain the 'decline and fall' of much of the Roman empire, leading ultimately to the loss of Britain, Gaul, Spain and north Africa in the fifth century, part of Italy and much of the Balkans in the sixth, and the whole of Egypt and Syria in the seventh – not to mention the Arab conquest of the rest of north Africa and much of Spain in the later seventh and the early eighth century. Section i shows how the ever-increasing exploitation of the vast majority of the population of the Graeco-Roman world by the all-powerful wealthy classes (a tiny minority) first depressed the political and legal status of nearly all those who were not members of my 'propertied class', almost to the slave level. Section ii describes the way in which, from just after the middle of the second century, the fiscal screw was tightened further up the social scale, on the 'curial class', the richer members of the local communities, who were in theory an 'order', consisting of the town councillors and their families, but in practice were virtually a hereditary class, consisting of all those owning property above a certain level who were not members of the imperial aristocracy of senators and equestrians. Section iii is a largely descriptive account of defection to the 'barbarians', assistance given to them, peasant revolts, and indifference to the disintegration of the Roman empire on the part of the vast majority of its subjects. The last section, iv, explains how the merciless exploitation of the great majority for the benefit of a very few finally led to the collapse of much of the empire – a process too often described as if it were something that 'just happened' naturally, whereas in fact it was due to the deliberate actions of a ruling class that monopolised both wealth and political power and governed solely for its own advantage. I show that a Marxist class analysis can provide a satisfactory explanation of this extraordinary process, which proceeded inexorably despite the heroic efforts of a remarkably able series of emperors from the late third century to near the end of the fourth.

★ ★ ★ ★ ★ ★

The fact that the whole Greek world eventually came under the rule of Rome has often obliged me to look at the Roman empire as a whole, and on occasion at the Latin West alone, or even some part of it. For example, in Chapter VIII 'barbarian' invasions, internal revolts, the defection of peasants and others, and similar manifestations of insecurity and decline have to be noticed whether they happened in the East or in the West, as they all contributed towards the ultimate disintegration of a large part of the empire. Even the settlements of 'barbarians' within the Graeco-Roman world – on a far greater scale than most historians, perhaps, have realised – need to be recorded (for the reasons discussed in IV.iii) although they occurred on a far greater scale in the Latin West than in the Greek East.

<h2 align="center">(ii)
'The ancient Greek world': its extent in space and time</h2>

For my purposes 'the Greek world' is, broadly speaking, the vast area (described below) within which Greek was, or became, the principal language of the upper classes. In north Africa, during the Roman Empire, the division between the Greek-speaking and Latin-speaking areas lay just west of Cyrenaica (the eastern part of the modern Libya), on about the 19th meridian east of Greenwich: Cyrenaica and everything to the east of it was Greek. In Europe the dividing line began on the east coast of the Adriatic, roughly where the same meridian cuts the coast of modern Albania, a little north of Durazzo (the ancient Dyrrachium, earlier Epidamnus); and from there it went east and slightly north, across Albania, Yugoslavia and Bulgaria, passing between Sofia (the ancient Serdica) and Plovdiv (Philippopolis) and joining the Danube at about the point where it turns north below Silistra on the edge of the Dobrudja, an area containing several cities on the Black Sea coast that belonged to the 'Greek' portion of the empire, which included everything to the south and east of the line I have traced.[1] My 'Greek world', then, included Greece itself, with Epirus, Macedonia and Thrace (roughly the southern part of Albania, Yugoslavia and Bulgaria, and the whole of European Turkey), also Cyrenaica and Egypt, and all that part of Asia which was included in the Roman empire: an area with an eastern boundary that varied from time to time but at its widest included not merely Asia Minor, Syria and the northern edge of Arabia but even Mesopotamia (Iraq) as far as the Tigris. There were even Greek cities and settlements[2] beyond the Tigris; but in general it is perhaps convenient to think of the eastern boundary of the Graeco-Roman world as falling on the Euphrates or a little to the east of it. Sicily too was 'Greek' from an early date and became romanised by slow degrees.

The time-span with which I am concerned in this book is not merely (1) the *Archaic and Classical periods* of Greek history (covering roughly the eighth to the sixth centuries B.C. and the fifth and fourth centuries respectively) and (2) the *Hellenistic age* (approximately the last three centuries B.C. in the eastern Mediterranean world), but also (3) the long period of *Roman domination* of the Greek area, which began in the second century and was complete before the end of the last century B.C., when Rome itself was still under a 'republican' form of government. How long one makes the 'Roman Empire' last is a matter of taste: in a sense it continued, as J. B. Bury and others have insisted, until the capture of Constantinople by the Ottoman Turks in A.D. 1453. The Roman 'Principate', as it is universally called in the English-speaking world ('Haut-Empire' is the normal French equivalent), is commonly conceived as beginning with Augustus (Octavian), at or a little after the date of the battle of Actium in 31 B.C., and as passing into the 'Later Empire' ('Bas-Empire') at about the time of the accession of the Emperor Diocletian in 284. In my view the 'Principate' from the first was virtually an absolute monarchy, as it was always openly admitted to be in the Greek East (see VI.vi below); and it is unreal to suppose, with some scholars, that a new 'Dominate' came into being with Diocletian and Constantine, although there is no harm in using, at any rate as *a chronological formula*, the expression 'Later Roman Empire' or 'Bas-Empire' (see VI.vi *ad init.*). Many ancient historians like to make a break somewhere between the reign of Justinian in 527-65 and the death of Heraclius in 641,[3] and speak thereafter of the 'Byzantine Empire', a term which expresses the fact that the empire was now centred at the ancient Byzantium, re-founded by the Emperor Constantine in 330 as Constantinople. My choice of a terminal date is dictated, I must admit, by the fact that my own first-hand knowledge of the source material becomes defective after the death of Justinian and largely peters out in the mid-seventh century: for this reason my 'ancient Greek world' ends not much later than the great book of my revered teacher, A. H. M. Jones, *The Later Roman Empire 284-602* (1964), which goes down to the death of the Emperor Maurice and the accession of Phocas, in 602. My own terminal point is the Arab conquests of Mesopotamia, Syria and Egypt in the 630s and 640s. In justification of keeping within the limits I have described I would plead that virtually everything in this book is based upon first-hand acquaintance with original sources. (In one or two places where it is not, I hope I have made this clear.)

I do believe that 'the ancient Greek world' is sufficiently a unity to be worth taking as the subject of this book: if my knowledge of the source material had been more extensive I should have wished to end the story not earlier than the sack of Constantinople by the Fourth Crusade in 1204, and perhaps with the taking of Constantinople by the Ottoman Turks and the end of the Byzantine empire in 1453. The alleged 'orientalisation' of the Byzantine empire was in reality slight.[4] Although the Byzantines no longer commonly referred to themselves as 'Hellenes', a term which from the fourth century onwards acquired the sense of 'pagans', they did call themselves '*Rhōmaioi*', the Greek word for 'Romans', a fact which may remind us that the Roman empire survived in its Greek-speaking areas long after it had collapsed in the Latin West – by something like a thousand years in Constantinople itself. By the mid-ninth century we find a Byzantine emperor, Michael III, referring to Latin as 'a barbarous Scythian language', in a letter to Pope Nicholas I. This contemptuous description of the Roman tongue exasperated Nicholas, who repeated the sacrilegious phrase five times over in his reply to Michael (A.D. 865), with indignant comments.[5]

There is a fascinating account of the Greek contribution to the Roman empire and the relationship of the two cultures in A. H. M. Jones's brief article, 'The Greeks under the Roman Empire', in *Dumbarton Oaks Papers* 17 (1963) 3-19, reprinted in the posthumous volume of Jones's essays edited by P. A. Brunt, *The Roman Economy* (1974) 90-113.

(iii)
Polis and *chōra*

In the Archaic and Classical periods, in Greece itself and in some of the early Greek colonies in Italy and Sicily and on the west coast of Asia Minor, the word *chōra* (χώρα) was often used as a synonym for the *agroi* (the fields), the rural area of the city-state, the *polis* (πόλις); and sometimes the word *polis* itself, in the special limited sense of its urban area, was contrasted with its *chōra* (see my ECAPS 1, nn.2-3). This usage continued in the Hellenistic period and under Roman rule: every *polis* had its own *chōra* in the sense of its own rural area. However, except where a native population had been reduced to a subject condition there was generally, in the areas just mentioned, no fundamental difference between those who lived in or near the urban centre of the *polis* and the peasants who lived in the countryside, even if the latter tended to be noticeably less urbane (less cityfied) than the former and in the literature produced by the upper classes are often treated patronisingly as 'country bumpkins' (*chōritai*, for example, in Xen., *HG* III.ii.31), an attitude which nevertheless allows them to be credited on occasion with superior moral virtues of a simple kind (see Dover, *GPM* 113-14). Both groups, however, were Greek and participated in a common culture to a greater or less degree.

It is hardly possible to give a general definition of a *polis* that would hold good for all purposes and all periods, and the best we can do is to say that a political entity was a *polis* if it was recognised as such. Pausanias, in a famous passage probably written in the 170s, in the reign of Marcus Aurelius, speaks disparagingly of the tiny Phocian *polis* of Panopeus, east of Mount Parnassus – 'if indeed you can call it a *polis*', he says, ' when it has no public buildings [*archeia*], no gymnasium, no theatre, no market place [*agora*], and no fountain of water, and where the people live in empty hovels like mountain shanties on the edge of a ravine' (X.iv.1). Yet Pausanias does call it a *polis* and shows that in his day it was accepted as such.

In those parts of Asia and Egypt into which Greek civilisation penetrated only in the time of Alexander the Great and in the Hellenistic period the situation was very different. In Asia, from at least the time of Alexander (and probably as early as the fifth century B.C., as I have argued in my *OPW* 154-5, 313-14), the terms *chōra* and *polis* had come to be used on occasion in a recognised technical sense, which continued throughout the Hellenistic period and beyond in Asia and Egypt: in this sense the *chōra* was the whole vast area not included in the territory administered by any Greek *polis*; sometimes referred to as the *chōra basilikē* (royal *chōra*), it was under the direct, autocratic rule of the kings, the successors of Alexander, and it was bureaucratically administered, while the *poleis* had republican governments and enjoyed forms of precarious autonomy which differed according to circumstances. (It will be sufficient to refer to Jones, *GCAJ*, and Rostovtzeff, *SEHHW*.) Under Roman rule the same basic division between *polis* and *chōra* continued, but the bulk of the *chōra* came by degrees under the administration of particular *poleis*, each of which had its own *chōra* (*territorium* in the Latin West). The cities in the narrow sense were Greek in very varying degrees in language and culture; native languages and culture usually prevailed in the *chōra*, where the peasants did not normally enjoy the citizenship of the *polis* that controlled them, and lived mainly in villages, the most common Greek term for which was *kōmai* (see IV.ii below). Graeco-Roman civilisation was essentially urban, a civilisation of cities; and in the areas in which it was not native, in which it had not grown up from roots in the very soil, it remained largely an upper-class culture: those whom it embraced exploited the natives in the countryside and gave little in return. As Rostovtzeff has said, speaking of the Roman empire as a whole:

> The population of the cities alike in Italy and in the provinces formed but a small minority as compared with the population of the country. Civilised life, of course, was concentrated in the cities; every man who had some intellectual interests . . . lived in a city and could not imagine himself living elsewhere: for him the *geōrgos* or *paganus* [farmer or villager] was an inferior being, half-civilised or uncivilised. It is no wonder that for us the life of the ancient world is more or less identical with the life of the ancient cities. The cities have told us their story, the country always remained silent and reserved. What we know of the country we know mostly through the men of the cities . . . The voice of the country population itself is rarely heard . . . Hence it is not surprising that in most modern works on the Roman empire the country and the country population do not appear at all or appear only from time to time in connexion with certain events in the life of the State or the cities' (*SEHRE*[2] I.192-3).

We can therefore agree wholeheartedly with the American mediaevalist Lynn White, when he says:

> Because practically all the written records and famous monuments of Antiquity were produced in cities, we generally think of ancient societies as having been essentially urban. They were, in fact, agricultural to a degree which we can scarcely grasp. It is a conservative guess that even in fairly prosperous regions over ten people were needed on the land to enable a single person to live away from the land. Cities were atolls of

civilisation (etymologically 'citification') on an ocean of rural primitivism. They were supported by a terrifyingly slender margin of surplus agricultural production which could be destroyed swiftly by drought, flood, plague, social disorder or warfare. Since the peasants were closest to the sources of food, in time of hunger they secreted what they could and prevented supplies from reaching the cities (Fontana *Econ. Hist. of Europe, I. The Middle Ages*, ed. C. M. Cipolla [1972], at 144-5).

Actually, as we shall see in IV.ii below, the opinion expressed in that last sentence is less true of the Roman empire (including its Greek area) than of other ancient societies, because of the exceptionally effective exploitation and control of the countryside by the imperial government and the municipalities.

A Greek (or Roman) city normally expected to feed itself from corn grown in its own *chōra* (*territorium*), or at any rate grown nearby: this has been demonstrated recently by Jones, Brunt and others, and is now beginning to be generally realised.[1] (Classical Athens of course was the great exception to this rule, as to so many others: see my *OPW* 46-9.) An essential factor here, the relevance of which used often to be overlooked, is the inefficiency and high cost of ancient land transport.[2] In Diocletian's day, 'a wagon-load of wheat, costing 6,000 denarii, would be doubled in price by a journey [by land] of 300 miles'; and, if we ignore the risks of sea transport, 'it was cheaper to ship grain from one end of the Mediterranean to the other than to cart it 75 miles' (Jones, *LRE* II.841-2; cf. his *RE* 37). Jones cites evidence from Gregory Nazianzenus and John the Lydian, writing in the fourth and sixth centuries respectively (*LRE* II.844-5). According to Gregory, coastal cities could endure crop shortages without great difficulty, 'as they can dispose of their own products and receive supplies by sea; for us inland our surpluses are unprofitable and our scarcities irremediable, as we have no means of disposing of what we have or of importing what we lack' (*Orat.* XLIII.34, in *MPG* XXXVI. 541-4). John complains that when Justinian abolished the public post in certain areas, including Asia Minor, and moreover taxes had to be paid in gold instead of (as hitherto) in kind, 'the unsold crops rotted on the estate . . . , and the taxpayer was ruined . . . , since he could not sell his crops, living far from the sea' (*De magistr.* III.61). This evidence, as Brunt has rightly observed, 'is perfectly applicable to every preceding epoch of the ancient world and to every region lacking water communications, for there had been no regress in the efficiency of land transport' (*IM* 704). I would add a reference to an interesting passage in Procopius, *Bell.* VI (*Goth.* II) xx.18, describing how, during a widespread famine in northern and central Italy in 538, the inhabitants of inland Aemilia left their homes and went south-east to Picenum (where Procopius himself was), supposing that that area would not be so destitute of food supplies 'because it was on the sea' (cf. IV.ii below and its n.29).

As I shall not have occasion to refer again to transport in the ancient world, I will give here a particularly striking – though rarely noticed – example of the great superiority of water to land transport even in late antiquity. In 359 the Emperor Julian considerably increased the corn supply of the armies on the Rhine and of the inhabitants of the neighbouring areas by having the corn which was already customarily shipped from Britain transported up the Rhine by river-boats (Libanius, *Orat.* XVIII.82-3; Zosimus III.v.2; Amm. Marc. XVIII.ii.3; cf. Julian, *Ep. ad Athen.* 8, 279d-80a). The fact that transport *against the current of the Rhine* was, as Libanius and Zosimus realised, much cheaper than carriage on wagons by road is impressive evidence of the inferiority of the latter form of transport. (It is convenient to mention here that the discovery in recent years of further fragments of Diocletian's Price-Edict of A.D. 301[3] has advanced our knowledge of the relative costs of land and water transport, a subject I cannot discuss here as it deserves.) I will add a reference to the vivid little sketch in Ausonius of the contrast between river-journeys by boat, downstream with oars and upstream with haulage (*Mosella* 39-44). It is also worth drawing attention to the repeated allusions by Strabo to the importance of river-transport in the countries where rivers were sufficiently navigable – not so much in the Greek lands, of course, as in Spain and Gaul (see esp. Strabo III, pp.140-3, 151-3; IV, pp.177-8, 185-6, 189). In 537 the Emperor Justinian recorded with sympathy the fact that litigants involved in appeals, who therefore needed to travel (to Constantinople), had been complaining that they were sometimes prevented from coming by sea owing to unfavourable winds or by land owing to their poverty – another testimony to the greater cost of land journeys (*Nov. J.* XLIX. *praef.* 2). Yet sea voyages could sometimes involve long delays, because of rough weather or unfavourable winds. The official messengers who brought a letter from the Emperor Gaius to the governor of Syria at Antioch at the end of A.D. 41 are said by Josephus (no doubt with some exaggeration) to have been 'weather-bound for three months' on the way (*BJ* II.203). In 51 B.C., when Cicero was travelling to Asia to taken over his province of Cilicia, it took him five days to sail from Peiraeus to Delos and another eleven days to reach Ephesus (Cic., *Ad Att.* V.xii.1; xiii.1). Writing to his friend Atticus after reaching Delos, he opened his letter with the words, 'A sea journey is a serious matter [*negotium magnum est navigare*], and in the month of July at that ' (*Ad Att.* V.xii.1). On his way home in November of the following year, Cicero spent three weeks on the journey from Patras to Otranto, including two spells of six days each on land, waiting for a favourable wind; some of his companions, who risked the crossing from Cassiope on Corcyra (Corfu) to Italy in bad weather were shipwrecked (*Ad fam.* XVI.ix.1-2).

In point of fact, even the availability of water-transport, in the eyes of Greeks and Romans, could hardly compensate for the absence of a fertile *chōra*. I should like to refer here to an interesting text, seldom or never quoted in this connection, which illustrates particularly well the general realisation in antiquity that a city must normally be able to live off the cereal produce of its own immediate hinterland. Vitruvius (writing under Augustus) has a nice story – which makes my point equally well whether it is true or not – about a conversation between Alexander the Great and Deinocrates of Rhodes, the architect who planned for Alexander the great city in Egypt that bore (and still bears) his name, Alexandria, and became, in Strabo's words, 'the greatest place of exchange in the inhabited world' (*megiston emporion tēs oikoumenēs*, XVII.i.13, p.798). In this story Deinocrates suggests to Alexander the foundation on Mount Athos of a city, a *civitas* – the Greek source will of course have used the word *polis*. Alexander at once enquires 'whether there are fields around, which can provide that city with a food supply'; and when Deinocrates admits that the city could only be supplied by sea transport, Alexander rejects the idea out of hand: just as a child needs milk, he says, so a city without fields and abundant produce from them cannot grow, or maintain a large population. Alexandria, Vitruvius adds, was not only a safe harbour and an excellent place of exchange; it had 'cornfields all over Egypt', irrigated by the Nile (*De architect.* II, *praef.* 2-4).

Now the civilisation of old Greece had been a natural growth ('from roots in the very soil', to repeat the phrase I used above); and although the cultured gentleman, living in or near the city, could be a very different kind of person from the boorish peasant, who might not often leave his farm, except to sell his produce in the city market, yet they spoke the same language and felt that they were to some extent akin.[4] In the new foundations in the Greek East the situation was often quite different. The upper classes, living in or very near the towns, mostly spoke Greek, lived the Greek life and shared in Greek culture. Of the urban poor we know very little, but some of them were at least literate, and they mixed with the educated classes and probably shared their outlook and system of values to a very considerable extent, even where they did not enjoy any citizen rights. But the peasantry, the great majority of the population, on whose backs (with those of the slaves) the burden of the whole vast edifice of Greek civilisation rested, generally remained in much the same state of life as their forefathers: in many areas the majority probably either spoke Greek not at all or at best imperfectly, and most of them remained for centuries – right down to the end of Graeco-Roman civilisation and beyond – at little above the subsistence level, illiterate, and almost untouched by the brilliant culture of the cities.[5] As A. H. M. Jones has said:

> The cities were . . . economically parasitic on the countryside. Their incomes consisted in the main of the rents drawn by the urban aristocracy from the peasants . . . The splendours of civic life were to a large extent paid for out of [these] rents, and to this extent the villages were impoverished for the benefit of the towns . . . The city magnates came into contact with the villagers in three capacities only, as tax collectors, as policemen, and as landlords (*GCAJ* 268, 287, 295).

This of course is as true of much of the Roman West as of the Greek East, and it remained true of the greater part of the Greek world right through the Roman period. The fundamental relationship between city and countryside was always the same: it was essentially one of exploitation, with few benefits given in return.

This is brought out most forcibly by a very remarkable passage near the beginning of the treatise *On wholesome and unwholesome foods* by Galen,[6] the greatest physician and medical writer of antiquity, whose life spanned the last seventy years of the second century of the Christian era and who must have written the work in question during the reign of Marcus Aurelius (161-80) or soon afterwards, and therefore during or just after that Antonine Age which has long been held up to us as part of that period in the history of the world during which, in Gibbon's famous phrase, 'the condition of the human race was most happy and prosperous' (*DFRE* 1.78). Galen, setting out to describe the terrible consequences of an uninterrupted series of years of dearth affecting 'many of the peoples subject to Roman rule', draws a distinction, not expressly between landlords and tenants, or between rich and poor, but between city-dwellers and country folk, although for his purposes all three sets of distinctions must obviously have been much the same, and it would not matter much to him (or to the peasantry) whether the 'city-dwellers' in his picture were carrying out their exactions purely as landlords or partly as tax-collectors.

Immediately summer was over, those who live in the cities, in accordance with their universal practice of collecting a sufficient supply of corn to last a whole year, took from the fields all the wheat, with the barley, beans and lentils, and left to the rustics [the *agroikoi*] only those annual products which are called pulses and leguminous fruits [*ospria te kai chedropa*]; they even took away a good part of these to the city. So the people in the countryside [*hoi kata tēn chōran anthrōpoi*], after consuming during the winter what had been left, were compelled to use unhealthy forms of nourishment. Through the spring they ate twigs and shoots of trees, bulbs and roots of unwholesome plants, and they made unsparing use of what are called wild vegetables, whatever they could get hold of, until they were surfeited; they ate them after boiling them whole like green grasses, of which they had not tasted before even as an experiment. I myself in person saw some of them at the end of spring and almost all at the beginning of summer afflicted with numerous ulcers covering their skin, not of the same kind in every case, for some suffered from erysipelas, others from inflamed tumours, others from spreading boils, others had an eruption resembling lichen and scabs and leprosy.

Galen goes on to say that many of these wretched people died. He is dealing, of course, with a situation which in his experience was evidently exceptional, but, as we shall see, enough other evidence exists to show that its exceptional character was a matter of degree rather than of kind. Famines in the Graeco-Roman world were quite frequent: various modern authors have collected numerous examples.[7]

There is one phenomenon in particular which strongly suggests that in the Roman empire the peasantry was more thoroughly and effectively exploited than in most other societies which rely largely upon peasant populations for their food supply. It has often been noticed (as by Lynn White, quoted above) that peasants have usually been able to survive famines better than their town-dwelling fellow-countrymen, because they can hide away for themselves some of the food they produce and may still have something to eat when there is starvation in the towns. It was not so in the Roman empire. I have just quoted a very remarkable passage in Galen which speaks of 'those who live in the cities' as descending upon their *chōra* after the harvest, in time of dearth, and appropriating for themselves practically all the wholesome food. There is a good deal of specific evidence from the Middle and Later Roman Empire to confirm this. Philostratus, writing in the first half of the third century a biography of Apollonius of Tyana (a curious figure of the late first century), could describe how at Aspendus in Pamphylia (on the south coast of Asia Minor) Apollonius could find no food on sale in the market except vetches (*oroboi*): 'the citizens,' he says, 'were feeding on this and whatever else they could get, for the leading men [*hoi dynatoi*, literally 'the powerful'] had shut away all the corn and were keeping it for export' (Philostr., *Vita Apollon.* I.15; cf. IV.ii and its n.24 below). And again and again, between the mid-fourth century and the mid-sixth, we find peasants crowding into the nearest city in time of famine, because only in the city is there any edible food to be had: I shall give a whole series of examples in IV.ii below.

We must also remember something that is far too often forgotten: the exploitation of the humbler folk was by no means only financial; one of its most burdensome features was the exaction of menial labour services of many kinds. A Jewish rabbi who was active in the second quarter of the third century of our era declared that cities were set up by the State 'in order to impose upon the people *angaria*' – a term of Persian or Aramaic provenance and originally relating to forced transport services, which had been taken over by the Hellenistic kingdoms (as the Greek word *angareia*, plural *angareiai*) and by the Romans (as the Latin *angaria*, *angariae*), and had come to be applied to a variety of forms of compulsory labour performed for the State or the municipalities;[8] 'the Middle Ages applied it to services (*corvées*) owed to the *seigneur*' (Marc Bloch, in *CEHE* I².263-4), and in fifteenth-century Italy we still hear of *angararii*, and of those bound by fealty in rustic vassalage to their lords, subject to *angaria* and *perangaria* (Philip Jones, in id. 406). An example familiar to most people today who have never heard the word *angaria* is the story of Simon of Cyrene, who was obliged by the Romans to carry the cross of Jesus to the place of execution: Mark and Matthew use the appropriate technical term, a form of the verb *angareuein* (Mk XV.21; Mt. XXVII.32). Only an understanding of the *angareia*-system can make fully intelligible one of the sayings of Jesus in the so-called Sermon on the Mount: 'Whosoever shall compel thee to go a mile, go with him twain' (Mt. V.41). Again, the word 'compel' in this text represents the technical term *angareuein*. (The passage deserves more notice than it usually receives in discussions of the attitude of Jesus to the political authorities of his day.) Readers of the Stoic philosopher Epictetus will remember that he was less positively enthusiastic than Jesus about co-operation with officials exacting *angareia*: he merely remarks that it is sensible to comply with a soldier's requisition of one's donkey. If one objects, he says, the result will only be a beating, and the donkey will be taken just the same (*Diss*. IV.i.79).

As it happens, it is in a speech *On angareiai* (*De angariis* in Latin, *Orat*. L) that the great Antiochene orator Libanius makes a particularly emphatic assertion of the absolute dependence of the cities upon the countryside and its inhabitants. (The word *angareia* does not actually occur in the speech, and *Peri tōn angareiōn* as its title may be due to a Byzantine scholar; but no one will dispute that *angareiai* of a particular municipal kind are the subject of the document.) Libanius is complaining to the Emperor Theodosius I in 385 that the peasants of the neighbourhood are being driven to desperation by having themselves and their animals pressed into service for carrying away building rubble from the city. Permits are given by the authorities, he says, which even allow private individuals to take charge of particular gates of the city and to impress everything passing through; with the help of soldiers they drive hapless peasants with the lash (§§ 9, 16, 27 etc.). As Liebeschuetz puts it, the animals of *honorati* (acting or retired imperial officials and military officers) 'were not requisitioned; other notables managed to get their animals excused even if with some difficulty. All the suffering was that of peasants. There is not a word about losses of land-owners' (*Ant*. 69). Although he has to admit that the practice has been going on for years (§§ 10, 15, 30), Libanius claims that it was illegal (§§ 7, 10, 17-20). He cleverly adduces the fact that a permit was once obtained from an emperor as proof that even the provincial governor has no right to authorise it (§ 22). He also asserts that visitors from other cities are aghast at what they see happening in Antioch (§ 8) – a statement there is no need to take seriously. Towards the end of the speech Libanius explains that the practice he is complaining about has a bad effect on the city's corn supply (§§ 30-1), an argument that might be expected to appeal strongly to the emperor. (We may compare the complaint of the Emperor Domitian, almost exactly three hundred years earlier, that the infliction on working peasants of burdens of the type of *angaria* is likely to result in failures of cultivation: *IGLS* V.1998, lines 28-30.) And then Libanius comes to his climax: he begs the *philanthrōpotatos basileus*,

> Show your concern not just for the cities, but for the countryside too, or rather for the countryside in preference to the cities – for the country is the basis on which they rest. One can assert that cities are founded on the country, and that this is their firm footing, providing them with wheat, barley, grapes, wine, oil and the nourishment of man and other living beings. Unless oxen, ploughs, seed, plants and herds of cattle existed, cities would not have come into being at all. And, once in existence, they have depended upon the fortunes of the countryside, and the good and ill that they experience arise therefrom.

Any foe to the well-being of working farmers and even of their animals, he goes on,

> is foe to the land, and the foe to the land is foe to the cities also, and indeed to mariners as well, for they too need the produce of the land. They may get from the sea increase of their store of goods, but the very means of life comes from the land. And you too, Sire, obtain tribute from it. In your rescripts you hold converse with the cities about it, and their payment of it comes from the land. So whoever assists the peasantry supports you, and ill-treatment of them is disloyal to you. So you must put a stop to this ill-treatment, Sire, by law, punishment and edicts, and in your enthusiasm for the matter under discussion you must encourage all to speak up for the peasants (§§ 33-6, in the translation of A. F. Norman's Loeb edition of Libanius, Vol. II).

I should perhaps add, not only that the practice against which Libanius is protesting is something quite separate from the burdensome *angareiai* exacted by the imperial authorities, mainly in connection with the 'public post', but also that Libanius himself sometimes takes a very different and much less protective attitude towards peasants in his other writings, notably when he is denouncing the behaviour of his own and other tenants, as well as freeholders resisting tax-collectors, in his *Orat*. XLVII (see IV.ii below).

The linguistic evidence for the separation between *polis* and *chōra* is particularly illuminating. Except in some of the western and southern coastal areas of Asia Minor, such as Lydia, Caria, Lycia, Pamphylia and the Cilician plain, where the native tongues seem to have been entirely displaced by Greek during the Hellenistic age, the great majority of the peasants of the Greek East and even some of the townsmen (especially of course the humbler ones) habitually spoke not Greek but the old native tongues.[9] Everyone will remember that when Paul and Barnabas arrived at Lystra, on the edge of a mountain district of southern Asia Minor, and Paul is said to have healed a cripple, the people cried out 'in the speech of Lycaonia' (Act. Apost. XIV.11) – a vernacular tongue which was never written down and which in due course perished entirely. (And this happened inside a city, and moreover one in which Augustus had planted a citizen colony of Roman veterans.)[10] Such stories could be paralleled again and again from widely separated parts of the Roman empire, in both East and West. And those who did not speak Greek or Latin would certainly have little or no part in Graeco-Roman civilisation.

We must not exaggerate the strictly ethnic and linguistic factors, which are so noticeable in the more eastern parts of the Greek area, at the expense of economic and social ones. Even in Greece itself, the Aegean islands and the more western coasts of Asia Minor, where Greeks had for centuries been settled and where even the poorest peasant might be as much a Hellene as the city magnate (if at a much lower cultural level), the class division between the exploiters and those from whom they drew their sustenance was very real, and it naturally deepened when the humble entirely lost the protection many of them had been able to obtain from a democratic form of government (see V.iii below). And in the 'Oriental' parts, newly brought within the great Hellenistic kingdoms, the clear-cut difference between 'Hellene' and 'barbaros' (Greek and native) gradually became transformed into a more purely class distinction, between the propertied and non-propertied. This is true even of Egypt, where the gulf between the Greeks and the native Egyptians had originally been as wide as anywhere, extending to language, religion, culture and 'way of life' in general. In Egypt, indeed, there was more interpenetration between the two elements than elsewhere, because until A.D. 200 cities were few (there were only Alexandria, Naucratis, Paraetonium and Ptolemais, and in addition Hadrian's foundation of Antinoöpolis in A.D. 130), and because far more Greeks settled outside the cities, in the country districts, often as soldiers or administrators, but with a strong tendency to gravitate towards the 'metropoleis', the capitals of the districts ('nomes') into which Egypt was divided. The exploitation of Egypt under the Ptolemies (323-30 B.C.) was not as intense as under the succeeding Roman administration, and the rents and taxes exacted from the peasantry were at least spent mainly at Alexandria and Naucratis, and at the other centres of population (not yet *poleis*) where men of property lived, and were not partly diverted (as they were later) to Rome. Nevertheless, the income of the Ptolemies was enormous by ancient standards, and the fellahin must have been pressed hard to provide it.[11] After 200 B.C. 'some natives rose in the scale and took Greek names, and some Greeks sank; Greek and native names occur in the same family. Some Greeks kept themselves aloof; but a new mixed race formed intermediate between Greeks and fellahin, and Hellene came to mean a man with some Greek *culture*' (Tarn, *HC*³ 206-7).[12] In Egypt, as elsewhere, 'being a Greek' was certainly very much more a matter of culture than of descent; but culture itself was largely dependent upon property-ownership. Before the end of the second century B.C., as Rostovtzeff says, 'From the social and economic standpoint the dividing line between the upper and lower class was no longer between the Greeks forming the upper, and the Egyptians forming the lower, but between the rich and poor in general, many Egyptians being among the first, many Greeks among the second'; but 'the old division into a privileged class of "Greeks" (which comprised now many hellenised Egyptians) and a subordinate class of natives remained as it had been' (*SEHHW* II.883). This is true, although some of the documents cited by Rostovtzeff might now be differently interpreted in some respects.[13] In the Roman period, with the growth of the *metropoleis* into something more nearly resembling Greek cities, where the landowners mainly lived, the propertied classes generally regarded themselves as Greeks and the peasants as Egyptians. In a letter surviving on papyrus from the third century of the Christian era, the writer does not want his 'brethren' to think of him as 'a barbarian or an inhuman [*ananthrōpos*] Egyptian' (*P. Oxy.* XIV.1681.4-7).

Marriages between city folk and peasants must have been very uncommon in all parts of the Greek world. Occasionally, no doubt, a peasant girl might be beautiful enough to attract a well-to-do city gentleman, but as a rule he would probably be far more likely to make her his mistress or concubine than his wife. There is, however, one delightful story, which I cannot resist telling, of love and marriage between two rich young city men and two lovely Sicilian peasant girls, who became known as the Kallipygoi. This is transmitted to us through Athenaeus (XII.554cde), from the iambic poems of Cercidas of Megalopolis and Archelaus of Chersonesus. (How much truth there is in it we have no means of knowing.) The two beautiful daughters of a peasant (an *anēr agroikos*), disputing which of them was the more callipygous, went out on to the highway and invited a young man who happened to be passing by to arbitrate between them. Inspecting both, he preferred the elder, with whom he then and there fell in love. His younger brother, when he heard about the girls, went out to see them, and fell in love with the younger. The aged father of the two young men did his best to persuade his sons to make more reputable marriages, but without success, and eventually he accepted the two peasant girls as his daughters-in-law. Having thus risen greatly in the world and become conspicuously rich, the two women built a temple to Aphrodite Kallipygos – a cult title which was not only most appropriate to the goddess of love and beauty but also made a charming allusion to the circumstances of the foundation. (One may feel that this is one of the cases in which paganism had a distinct advantage over Christianity.) Marriages of well-bred girls to peasants must also have been exceedingly rare. In Euripides' *Electra* the marriage of the princess Electra to a poor rustic who is not even given a name in the play – he is just an *autourgos* (a man who works his farm with his own hands) – is regarded even by the man himself as a grave and deliberate slight on the girl, and in his opening speech he alludes with pride to the fact that he has never taken her to his bed and she is still a virgin – tense and neurotic, as we presently discover.[14]

The contrast between superior city-dweller and unsophisticated countryman could even be projected into the divine sphere. In a collection of fables by Babrius we hear of a belief that it is the simple-minded (*euētheis*) among the gods who inhabit the countryside, while those deities who live within the city wall are infallible and have everything under their supervision (*Fab. Aesop.* 2.6-8).

In III.vi below I shall mention briefly the creation by wealthy benefactors in Greek and Roman cities of 'foundations' to provide distributions of money or food on special occasions, often graded according to the position of the recipients in the social hierarchy – the higher a person's social position, the more he was likely to get. Rustics, who in the Greek East would often not be citizens of their *polis*, would very rarely benefit from such a distribution. Dio Chrysostom can make one of his Euboean peasants adduce the fact that his father had once participated in a distribution of money in the local town as evidence that he was a citizen there (VII.49). The only inscription I have noticed that mentions countryfolk benefiting from a distribution instituted by a citizen of a Greek *polis* is one from Prusias ad Hypium in Bithynia, which speaks of handouts both to all those 'reckoned as citizens' (*enkekrimenois*) and to those 'inhabiting the country district' (*tois tēn agroikian katoikousin/paroikousin, IGRR* III.69.18-20, 24-6).[15]

★   ★   ★   ★   ★

To conclude this section, I cannot do better than quote two summaries by A. H. M. Jones of his researches into a thousand years of Hellenistic and Roman rule in the Greek East. One, from his first major work, *Cities of the Eastern Roman Provinces* (1937, 2nd edn 1971), deals specifically with Syria, which had previously been only on the fringe of the Greek world but was brought within it be degrees from the time of Alexander's conquests, from 333 B.C. onwards; but Jones's conclusions are equally, or almost equally, true of the other areas in western Asia, north Africa and south-east Europe which became hellenised only in Alexander's time or later. Summing up 'the results of the millennium during which Syria had been ruled by the Macedonian dynasties and by Rome', Jones says,

> On paper the change in the political aspect of the country is considerable. In the Persian period cities existed only on the sea-coast, the desert fringe, and two of the gangways between them through the central mountain barrier. By the Byzantine period practically the whole of Syria was partitioned into city states; only in a few isolated areas, notably the Jordan valley and the Hauran, did village life remain the rule. In reality, however, the change was superficial. It was achieved partly by assigning vast territories to the old cities of the coast and of the desert fringe, partly by the foundation of a small number of new cities, to each of which was assigned a vast territory. The political life of the inhabitants of the agricultural belt was unaffected; their unit remained the village, and they took no part in the life of the city to which they were attached. Economically they lost by the change. The new cities performed no useful economic function, for the larger villages supplied such manufactured goods as the villagers required, and the trade of the countryside was conducted at village markets. [16] The only effect of the foundation of cities was the creation of a wealthy landlord class which gradually stamped out peasant proprietorship. Culturally, the countryside remained utterly unaffected by the Hellenism of the cities; [17] the peasants continued to speak Syriac down to the Arab conquest. The only function which the cities performed was administrative; they policed and collected the taxes of their territories (*CERP*² 293-4).

And in a note later in the book Jones adds,

> The indifference of the villagers to the cities is, I think, well illustrated by the tombstones of Syrian emigrants in the West . . . . : they always record their village, but name their city, if at all, merely as a geographical determinant' (*CERP*² 469 n.92). [18]

The other passage is from p.vi of the Preface to Jones's *The Greek City from Alexander to Justinian* (1940). Summarising the conclusions in Part V of that book, Jones says that he discusses 'the contribution of the cities to ancient civilisation' and argues that

> Great as their achievement was, it was based on too narrow a class foundation to be lasting. On the economic side the life of the cities involved an unhealthy concentration of wealth in the hands of the urban aristocracy at the expense of the proletariat and the peasants. Their political life was gradually narrowed till it was confined to a small clique of well-to-do families, who finally lost interest in it. The culture which the cities fostered, though geographically spread over a wide area, was limited to the urban upper class. [19]

(iv)
The relevance of Marx for the study of ancient history

So complete has been the lack of interest in Marx displayed by nearly all ancient historians in the English-speaking world[1] that many who begin to read this book may wonder what relevance Marx can possibly have to the history of Classical antiquity. I have heard this lack of interest described as 'a conspiracy of silence'; but that would be to dignify it with a conscious element which in practice is absent: the reality is just silence. I know of nothing comparable as yet in the British Isles to the symposium on the programme of the American Philological Association in 1973, entitled 'Marxism and the Classics', or to the issue of the American Classical periodical *Arethusa*, vol.8.1 (Spring, 1975), with the same title.[2] (The article included in that volume, with the title 'Karl Marx and the history of Classical antiquity', pp.7-41, is virtually a series of extracts from earlier drafts of this book.) One often hears the view expressed that in so far as the ideas of Marx on history have any validity, they have already been absorbed into the Western historiographical tradition. One thinks here of the late George Lichtheim's description of Marxism as 'the *caput mortuum* of a gigantic intellectual construction whose living essence has been appropriated by the historical consciousness of the modern world' (*Marxism*[2] [1964 and repr.] 406). This is altogether untrue, above all in regard to the modern historiography of the Classical world.

Now the situation I have described is certainly due in part to a general ignorance of the thought of Marx, and a lack of interest in it, on the part of the vast majority of ancient historians and other Classical scholars in the English-speaking world. But I shall suggest later that this ignorance and lack of interest can be attributed partly to mistaken attempts in modern times, on the part of those who call themselves Marxists (or at least claim to be influenced by Marx), to interpret the essentials of Marx's historical thought both in general terms and in particular in relation to Classical antiquity. I like to remember that Engels, in a letter written to Conrad Schmidt on 5 August 1890, more than seven years after Marx's death, recalled that Marx used to say about the French Marxists of the late 1870s, 'All I know is that I am not a Marxist' (*MESC* 496). I think he would have felt much the same about *soi-disant* Marxists – not only French ones – of the 1980s. As the German poet Hans Magnus Enzensberger says, in his moving short poem, *Karl Heinrich Marx* –

> I see you betrayed
> by your disciples:
> only your enemies
> remained what they were.

(The translation of the poem by Michael Hamburger is reprinted in the Penguin *Poems of Hans Magnus Enzensberger* 38-9.)

Much modern Marxist writing in languages other than English seems recalcitrant to translation into English. I am inclined to apply to much of this writing some forceful remarks made by Graham Hough in a review in the *Times Literary Supplement* of two books on Roland Barthes. Approving a statement by Stephen Heath, that the language evolved by Barthes and his school 'has no common theoretical context with anything that exists in English', he continues:

> To transfer it bodily – simply to anglicise the words, which is not difficult – produces a wall of opacity that blocks all curiosity at the start. To adapt, to paraphrase, which can also be done and often looks inviting, runs the risk of denaturing the original and reducing disconcerting ideas to acceptable commonplace (*TLS* 3950, 9 December 1977, p.1443).

So it is, I feel, with much contemporary Marxist work, even in French and Italian, and still more in German and Russian.

More and more people in my adult lifetime have become willing to take some account of Marx's analysis of the capitalist world in the nineteenth and twentieth centuries. As I am a historian and not an economist, I shall do no more than mention the revival of serious interest in Marx's economics in Britain on the part of a number of leading economists of our generation (whether or not they would describe themselves as Marxists): Maurice Dobb, Ronald Meek, Joan Robinson, Piero Sraffa and others.[3] In the Foreword to the first edition of her *Essay on Marxian Economics* (1942) Joan Robinson remarked that 'until recently Marx used to be treated in academic circles with contemptuous silence, broken only by an occasional mocking footnote'. In the first paragraph of the Preface to the second edition (1966), she mentioned that when she was writing the original edition, a quarter of a century earlier, most of her 'academic colleagues in England thought that to study Marx was a quaint pastime . . . , and in the United States it was disreputable'. Matters are rather different now. Within the last few years sociologists too have rather suddenly become far more willing than they used to be to adopt a Marxist analysis of problems of contemporary society. I may perhaps be allowed to refer to one particularly impressive recent example: a book entitled *Immigrant Workers and Class Structure in Western Europe*, by Stephen Castles and Godula Kosack, published in 1973, the relevance of which for our present study will emerge in II.iii below. Even so, many people would, I think, agree with the opinion of a leading British sociologist. T. B. Bottomore (who is far from hostile to Marx), that 'while the Marxian theory seems highly relevant and useful in analysing social and political conflicts in capitalist societies during a particular period, its utility and relevance elsewhere are much less clear' (*Sociology*[2], [1971] 201). Those who hold such views may be prepared to concede that a very valuable contribution has been made by certain Marxist historians who have dealt mainly with the eighteenth and nineteenth centuries, for example Eric Hobsbawm, George Rudé and E. P. Thompson; but they may begin to feel that their premise has been somewhat weakened when they take notice of the work of an American Marxist historian, Eugene Genovese, who has produced work of outstanding quality on slavery in the antebellum South; and it is surely strained to breaking-point and beyond when they have to take account of Christopher Hill (formerly the Master of Balliol), who has done so much to illuminate the history of the sixteenth and seventeenth centuries, and Rodney Hilton, who has dealt with English peasants and peasant movements in the fourteenth century and earlier, in various articles and in two recent books, *Bond Men Made Free* (1973) and *The English Peasantry in the Later Middle Ages* (1975, the publication of his Ford Lectures at Oxford in 1973). We are already a very long way from nineteenth-century capitalism; and if we go still further back, into the Bronze Age and prehistory, in Europe and Western Asia, we can find archaeologists, in particular the late V. Gordon Childe, also acknowledging their debt to Marx. [See now VIII.i n.33 below.]

Anthropologists too, at least outside Great Britain, have for some time been prepared to take Marx seriously as a source of inspiration in their own discipline. French economic anthropologists such as Maurice Godelier, Claude Meillassoux, Emmanuel Terray, Georges Dupré and Pierre-Philippe Rey have operated to a high degree within a Marxist tradition, which they have developed in various ways.[4] Even the structuralists have often acknowledged a debt to Marx. Over twenty years ago Claude Lévi-Strauss himself referred to his 'endeavours to reintegrate the anthropological knowledge acquired during the last fifty years into the Marxian tradition'; and spoke of 'the concept of structure which I have borrowed, or so I thought, from Marx and Engels, among others, and to which I attribute a primary role' (*SA* 343–4).[5] American anthropologists have also become much more attentive to Marx in recent years: Marvin Harris, for example, in his comprehensive work, *The Rise of Anthropological Theory* (1969 and repr.), devotes some serious attention to Marx and Engels as anthropologists, including a chapter of over 30 pages ('Dialectical materialism', pp.217–49). And then, in 1972, came what I can only describe as a break-through in British anthropology. An anthropologist of the very first rank, Sir Raymond Firth, delivering the inaugural lecture of a new British Academy series in honour of Radcliffe-Brown, gave it a significant title: not merely 'The sceptical anthro-pologist?' (an allusion, of course, to Robert Boyle's *The Sceptical Chymist*) but also 'Social anthropology and Marxist views on society'.[6] I should like to quote part of the last paragraph of this lecture, because it urges social anthropologists to interest themselves in particular aspects of human societies which I think historians of Classical antiquity should also be studying, and which – like the social anthropologists to whom Firth is addressing himself – most of them are not studying. Firth says:

> What Marx's theories offer to social anthropology is a set of hypotheses about social relations and especially about social change. Marx's insights – about the basic signi-ficance of economic factors, especially production relations; their relation to structures of power; the formation of classes and the opposition of their interests; the socially relative character of ideologies; the conditioning force of a system upon individual members of it – [these insights] embody propositions which must be taken for critical scrutiny into the body of our science. The theories of Marx should be put on a par with, say, those of Durkheim or Max Weber. Because they imply radical change they are more threatening.

That last word is particularly significant. (I shall return to the 'threatening' nature of Marxist analysis in II.ii below.) Now Firth, I am sure, would not describe himself as a Marxist. Shortly before the paragraph I have quoted he expresses the opinion that 'much of Marx's theory in its literal form is out-moded': the examples he gives in support of this claim do not seem to me well formulated or cogent. But what I am primarily concerned to do at the moment is to make a plea for the relevance of Marx's general historical methodology to the study of ancient history. If it can make major contributions to history between the early Middle Ages and the twentieth century, and even in archae-ology and anthropology, then there is good reason to expect that it may be able to shed light upon Classical antiquity.

Apart from one negligible book which I shall mention later (in II.i below and its n.20), I know of no single work in English which consistently attempts *either* to analyse Greek history – or, for that matter, Roman history – in terms of Marxist historical concepts, *or* to expound those concepts themselves and explain why they are relevant for the purpose of such an analysis. In fact both these tasks need to be accomplished together at least once, within one pair of covers (as I am trying to do here), if the new start that I am advocating is to be made successfully. As I have said, most English-speaking ancient historians ignore Marx completely. If they do mention him, or Marxist historical writing, it is usually with ignorant contempt. An exception is a recent well-chosen selection of source material in translation for Greek economic and social history in the Archaic and Classical periods, first published in French by Michel M. Austin and Pierre Vidal-Naquet under the title of *Économies et sociétés en Grèce ancienne* (Paris, 1972 and 1973) and then, with some improvements, in English, as *Economic and Social History of Ancient Greece: An Introduction* (London, 1977). The introduction (mainly by Austin) devotes several pages (20 ff. in the English version) to the notion of 'class struggles'. Now, as I shall explain (in II.iii below), I disagree profoundly with the way these scholars have applied the Marxist concept of class conflict to the Greek world; but at least they are operating with categories that have become thoroughly associated with the Marxist tradition in historiography and are very often repudiated altogether or allowed only a very limited role by non-Marxists.

In languages other than English the situation is much better – although, as I indicated near the beginning of this section, many of the Marxist works on ancient history published on the Continent are as foreign to the English reader in their intellectual and literary idiom as in their actual language: they tend to take for granted a whole range of concepts to which most people in the English-speaking world are not accustomed and which they find largely unintelligible.[7] The word 'jargon' is often used in this context, if not always by those who have earned the right to use it by refraining from a different jargon of their own.

* * * * * *

At this point I must write briefly about Marx himself as a Classical scholar. He received, in school and university, at Trier, Bonn and Berlin, the thorough Classical education which was given to most young middle-class Germans in the 1830s. At the universities of Bonn and Berlin he studied law and philosophy, and between 1839 and 1841, among various other activities, he wrote, as his doctoral thesis, a comparison of the philosophies of Democritus and Epicurus. This work, completed in 1840–41, before Marx was 23, was not published in full even in German until 1927, when it appeared in *MEGA* I.i.1 (the first fascicule of Part i of Vol. I of the Marx-Engels *Gesamtausgabe*, published at Frankfurt and edited by D. Rjazanov) 1-144. It has not been republished in *MEW* I (the first volume of the complete *Werke* of Marx and Engels now in course of publication in East Berlin). An English translation (replacing an inferior earlier one) has recently been published in *MECW* I, the first volume of the new English edition of the Marx-Engels *Collected Works* (Moscow/London/New York, 1975), 25-107. Cyril Bailey, reviewing the original publication in the *Classical Quarterly* 22 (1928) 205-6, was greatly impressed with its scholarship and its originality: he found it 'of real interest to a modern student of Epicureanism' and ended by saying that such a student would find in it 'some illuminating ideas'. The thesis looks forward to a larger work (never actually written) in which Marx planned to 'present in detail the cycle of Epicurean, Stoic and Sceptic philosophy in their relation to the whole of Greek speculation' (*MECW* I.29). It is worth noticing that the Foreword to the thesis ends by quoting the defiant reply of Prometheus to Hermes, in Aeschylus' *Prometheus Bound* (lines 966 ff.), 'Be sure of this: I would not exchange my state of misfortune for your servitude', and adding that Prometheus (the Prometheus of Aeschylus) is 'the most eminent saint and martyr in the philosophical calendar' (*MECW* I.31). During this period Marx read extensively in Classical authors, in particular Aristotle, of whom throughout his life he always spoke in terms of respect and admiration which he employs for no other thinker, except perhaps Hegel. As early as 1839 we find him describing Aristotle as 'the acme [*Gipfel*] of ancient philosophy' (*MECW* I.424); and in Vol. I of *Capital* he refers to 'the brilliance of Aristotle's genius' and calls him 'a giant thinker' and 'the greatest thinker of antiquity' (60, 82n., 408) – as of course he was. Later, Marx returned again and again to read Classical authors. On 8 March 1855 we find him saying in a letter to Engels, 'A little time ago I went through Roman history again up to the Augustan era' (*MEW* XXVIII.439); on 27 February 1861 he writes again to Engels, 'As a relaxation in the evenings I have been reading Appian on the Roman civil wars, in the original Greek' (*MESC* 151); and some weeks later, on 29 May 1861, he tells Lassalle that in order to dispel the serious ill-humour arising from what he describes, in a mixture of German and English, as 'mein in every respect unsettled situation', he is reading Thucydides, and he adds (in German) 'These ancient writers at least remain ever new' (*MEW* XXX.605-6).

(This is a convenient place at which to mention that I normally cite *MESC*, an English translation of 244 of the letters of Marx and Engels, published in 1956, when it includes a letter I am quoting. I need not regularly refer to the German texts, since they print the letters in chronological order, and the dates will enable them to be found easily. The letters exchanged between Marx and Engels are published in four volumes, *MEGA* III.i-iv, 1929-31; there is a much larger collection , including letters written by Marx or Engels to other correspondents, in *MEW* XXVII-XXXIX.)

Scattered through the writings of Marx are a remarkable number of allusions to Greek and Roman history, literature and philosophy. He made a careful study of Roman Republican history in particular, partly from the sources and partly with the aid of the works of Niebuhr, Mommsen, Dureau de la Malle and others. I have not been able to discover any systematic study of Greek history by Marx after his student days, or of the history of the Graeco-Roman world under the Principate or the Later Roman Empire; but he frequently quotes Greek authors (more often in the original than in translation), as well as Latin authors, in all sorts of contexts: Aeschylus, Appian, Aristotle, Athenaeus, Democritus, Diodorus, Dionysius of Halicarnassus, Epicurus, Herodotus, Hesiod, Homer, Isocrates, Lucian, Pindar, Plutarch, Sextus Empiricus, Sophocles, Strabo, Thucydides, Xenophon and others. He could also make use of that charming little poem by Antipater of Thessalonica, in the Greek Anthology (IX.418), which is one of the earliest pieces of evidence for the existence of the water-mill (see II.i below). After his doctoral dissertation Marx never had occasion to write at length about the ancient world, but again and again he will make some penetrating remark that brings out something of value. For example, in a letter to Engels of 25 September 1857 he makes some interesting and perfectly correct observations: for example, that the first appearance of an extensive system of hired labour in antiquity is in the military sphere, the employment of mercenaries (how often has that been noticed, I wonder!), and that among the Romans the *peculium castrense* was the first legal form in which the right of property was recognised in members of a family other than the *paterfamilias* (*MESC* 118-19). In a footnote in the *Grundrisse* (not in the section on 'pre-capitalist forms of production'), written at about the same time as the letter from which I have just quoted, Marx has some acute observations on pay in the Roman army, which need to be put beside the remark in the letter:

> Among the Romans, the army constituted a mass – but already divorced from the whole people – which was disciplined to labour, whose surplus time also belonged to the State; who sold their entire labour time for pay to the State, exchanged their entire labour capacity for a wage necessary for the maintenance of their life, just as does the worker with the capitalist. This holds for the period when the Roman army was no longer a citizen's army but a mercenary army. This is here likewise a free sale of labour on the part of the soldier. But the State does not buy it with the production of values as aim. And thus, although the wage form may seem to occur originally in armies, this pay system is nevertheless essentially different from wage labour. There is some similarity in the fact that the State uses up the army in order to gain an increase in power and wealth (*Grundrisse*, E.T. 529n.; cf. 893).

It came naturally to Marx to illustrate what he was saying with some Classical simile, as when he wrote that the trading peoples of antiquity were 'like the gods of Epicurus, in the spaces between the worlds' (*Grundrisse*, E.T. 858; cf. *Cap.* III.330, 598), or when he spoke scornfully of Andrew Ure, author of *The Philosophy of Manufactures*, as 'this Pindar of the manufacturers' (*Cap.* III.386 n.75). I have heard quoted against Marx his remark that Spartacus (the leader of the great slave revolt in Italy from 73 to 71 B.C.) was 'the most splendid fellow in the whole of ancient history. Great general (no Garibaldi), noble character, real representative of the ancient proletariat'; so let me mention here that the statement was made not in a work intended for publication but in a private letter to Engels, of 27 February 1861 – in which, incidentally, he also described Pompey as 'reiner Scheisskerl' (*MEW* XXX.159-60=*MESC* 151-2).

A recent book by the Professor of German at Oxford University, S. S. Prawer, *Karl Marx and World Literature* (1976), has shown in detail how extraordinarily wide Marx's reading was, not only in German, French, English, Latin and Greek, but also in Italian, Spanish and Russian.

I shall have something to say in II.iii below on Marx's intellectual development in the 1840s.

I may add that Engels too was very well read and received a Classical education. A school-leaving report testifying to his knowledge of Latin and Greek survives, as does a poem he wrote in Greek at the age of sixteen.[8]

* * * * * *

However, it is not so much as the student of a particular epoch that I wish to regard Marx now, but rather as a historical sociologist: one who proposed an analysis of the structure of human society, in its successive stages, which sheds some illumination upon each of those stages – the Greek world just as much as the nineteenth and twentieth centuries.

Let me first mention and dismiss two or three common misconceptions. It is easy to discredit Marx's analysis of society by presenting it in a distorted form, as it is so often presented both by those who wrongly suppose themselves to be employing it and by those who are in principle hostile to it. In particular the thought of Marx is said to involve both 'materialism' and 'economic determinism'. Now the historical method employed by Marx was never given a name by him, but from Engels onwards it has been generally known as 'historical materialism'. (It seems to have been Plekhanov who invented the term 'dialectical materialism'.) It is certainly 'materialist', in the technical sense of being methodologically the opposite of Hegel's 'idealism' – we all know Marx's famous remark that Hegel's dialectic was standing on its head and 'needs to be turned right side up again if you would discover the rational kernel within the mystical shell' (*Cap*. I.20, from the Afterword to the second German edition, of 1873). But 'materialism' does not, and must not, in any way exclude an understanding of the role of ideas, which (as Marx well knew) can often become autonomous and acquire a life of their own, and themselves react vigorously upon the society that produced them – the role of Marxism itself in the twentieth century is a conspicuous example of this. As for the so-called 'economic determinism' of Marx, the label must be altogether rejected. We can begin with his alleged over-emphasis on the economic side of the historical process, which has even led to the application to his historical methodology – quite absurdly – of the terms 'reductionist' and 'monistic'. In fact the dialectical process which Marx envisaged allowed to other factors than the purely economic – whether social, political, legal, philosophic or religious – almost as much weight as very many non-Marxist historians would give to them. The alleged 'economism' of Marx is no more than the belief that out of all the elements which are operative in the historical process, it is 'the relations of production' (as Marx called them), namely *the social relations into which men enter in the course of the productive process*, which are the most important factors in human life, and which tend, in the long run, to determine the other factors, although of course these other factors, even purely ideological ones, can sometimes exert a powerful influence in their turn upon all social relations. In five of the letters he wrote between 1890 and 1894 Engels, while admitting that he and Marx had been partly to blame for an unavoidable over-emphasis on the economic aspect of history, stressed that they had never intended to belittle the interdependent role of political, religious and other ideological factors, even while considering the economic as primary. (The letters are those of 5 August, 21 September and 27 October 1890, 14 July 1893, and 25 January 1894.)[9] In an *obiter dictum* in one of his earliest works, the *Contribution to a Critique of Hegel's Philosophy of Law*, Marx declared that although material force can be overcome only by material force, yet 'Theory also becomes a material force as soon as it has gripped the masses' (*MECW* III.182). And Mao Tse-tung, in a famous essay 'On Contradiction' (dating from August 1937), insisted that in certain conditions theory and the ideological 'superstructure' of a society (revolutionary theory in particular) can 'manifest themselves in the principal and decisive role'.[10]

It is true that Marx himself occasionally writes as if men were governed by historical necessities beyond their control, as when (in the Preface to the original German edition of *Das Kapital*) he speaks of 'the natural laws of capitalist production' as 'self-assertive tendencies working with iron necessity' (*MEW*

XXIII.12. I have altered the misleading translation in *Cap.* I.8). Such expressions are rare: they probably derive from a conception of historical events in which a high degree of *probability* has been momentarily taken as *certainty*. In fact there is nothing in the least 'deterministic' in the proper sense in Marx's view of history; and in particular the role of *no single individual* is 'determined' by his class position, even if one can often make very confident *predictions* (of a statistical character) about the behaviour of the *collective* members of a given class. To give just two examples: if you have an income of more than, say, £20,000 a year, the statistical probability that you will normally hold right-wing views, and in Britain vote Conservative, is very high indeed; and if you do not belong to the lowest social class you will have a far better chance of achieving individual sainthood in the Roman Church – a sociological analysis in the early 1950s showed that of 2,489 known Roman Catholic Saints, only 5 per cent came from the lower classes who have constituted over 80 per cent of Western populations.[11] (Recent proclamations of sanctity, I understand, have not departed from this pattern.)

I believe that some light may be shed on the last question we have been considering (the 'determinism' of which Marx is often accused) by a comparison between Marx and the greatest historian of antiquity, Thucydides – probably the writer who, with the single exception of Marx, has done most to advance my own understanding of history. Thucydides often refers to something he calls 'human nature', by which he really means *patterns of behaviour* he believed he could identify in human conduct, partly in the behaviour of individual men but much more emphatically in that of human groups: men acting as organised *states*, whose behaviour can indeed be predicted far more confidently than that of most individual men. (I have discussed this in my *OPW* 6, 12 & n.20, 14-16, 29-33, 62, cf. 297.) The better you *understand* these patterns of behaviour, Thucydides (I am sure) believed, the more effectively you can *predict* how men are likely to behave in the immediate future – although never with complete confidence, because always (and especially in war) you must allow for the unforeseeable, the incalculable, and for sheer 'chance' (see *OPW* 25 & n.52, 30-1 & n.57). Thucydides was anything but a determinist, although he often speaks of men as being 'compelled' to act in a particular way when he describes them as choosing the least disagreeable among alternatives none of which they would have adopted had their choice been entirely free (see *OPW* 60-2). This common feature of the human predicament, I believe, is just what Marx had in mind when he said, in *The Eighteenth Brumaire of Louis Bonaparte*, 'Men make their own history, but they do not make it just as they please; they do not make it under circumstances chosen by themselves, but under circumstances directly encountered, given and transmitted from the past' (*MECW* XI.103).

In every situation in which one is making a judgment there are some factors which cannot be changed and others which can only be partly modified, and the better one understands the situation the less forced and unfree one's judgment becomes. In this sense, 'freedom is the understanding of necessity', Thucydides, by enabling his readers to recognise and understand some of the basic recurring features in the behaviour of human groups in the political and international field, believed – surely with reason – that his History would be for ever 'useful' to mankind (I.22.4). Similarly, what Marx wished to do was to identify the internal, structural features of each individual human society (above all, but not only, capitalist society), and reveal its 'laws of motion'. If his analysis is largely right, as I believe it is, then, by revealing the underlying Necessity, it increases human Freedom to operate within its constraint, and has greatly facilitated what Engels called 'the ascent of man from the kingdom of necessity to the kingdom of freedom' (*MESW* 426).

In the third volume of *Capital* there is a point at which Marx suddenly and quite unexpectedly bursts out into one of those emotional passages 'full of hope and splendour' – an apt phrase of Hobsbawm's (*KMPCEF* 15) – which look beyond the harsh realities of the present towards a future in which mankind is largely set free from the soul-destroying compulsion which still obliges the greater part of humanity to spend most of their time producing the material necessities of life. This passage, one of many in *Capital* that reveal the essential humanity of Marx's outlook, must seem less purely visionary and utopian, in our age of increasing automation, than it may have appeared to those who first read it in the 1890s. It occurs in Part VII of *Capital* III (p.820), in a chapter (xlviii) entitled 'The trinity formula', from which I also quote elsewhere. (The German text can be found in *MEW* XXV.828.)

> The realm of freedom actually begins only where labour which is determined by necessity and mundane considerations ceases; thus in the very nature of things it lies beyond the sphere of actual material production. Just as the savage must wrestle with Nature to satisfy his wants, to maintain and reproduce life, so must civilised man, and he must do so in all social formations and under all possible modes of production. With his development this realm of physical necessity expands as a result of his wants; but, at the same time, the forces of production which satisfy these wants also increase. Freedom in this field can only consist in socialised man, the associated producers, rationally regulating their interchange with Nature, bringing it under their common control, instead of being ruled by it as by the blind forces of Nature; and achieving this with the least expenditure of energy and under conditions most favourable to, and worthy of, their human nature. But it none the less still remains a realm of necessity. Beyond it begins that development of human energy which is an end in itself, the true realm of freedom, which, however, can blossom forth only with this realm of necessity as its basis. The shortening of the working day is its basic prerequisite. (Cf. Marx/Engels, *MECW* V.431-2, from the *German Ideology*, quoted in II.i below.)

Marx and Engels were certainly not among those who not merely speak loosely (as any of us may) but actually think seriously of History (with a capital 'H') as a kind of independent force. In a splendid passage in his earliest joint work with Marx, *The Holy Family* (1845), Engels could say,

> History does *nothing*, it 'possesses *no* immense wealth', it 'wages *no* battles'. It is *man*, real, living man who does all that, who possesses and fights; 'history' is not, as it were, a person apart, using man as a means to achieve *its own* aims; history is *nothing but* the activity of man pursuing his aims (*MECW* IV.93=*MEGA* I.iii.265).

★   ★   ★   ★   ★   ★

Except in so far as the concepts of class and class struggle are involved, I do not propose in this book to undertake any comprehensive discussion of Marx's general historical methodology,[12] which of course involves much more than class analysis, although that to my mind is central and its rejection entails the dismissal of most of Marx's system of ideas. Nor do I intend to say anything about such controversies as those concerning 'basis and superstructure',[13] or the so-called 'modes of production' referred to by Marx, in particular in the *German Ideology* (*MECW* V.32-5), in *Wage Labour and Capital* (*MECW* IX.212), in the section on pre-capitalist economic formations in the *Grundrisse* (E.T. 471-514, esp. 495),[14] and in the *Preface to A Contribution to the Critique of Political Economy* (*MESW* 182). Above all I can legitimately avoid any discussion of the desirability (or otherwise) of recognising an 'Asiatic' (or 'Oriental') mode of production, a notion which seems to me best forgotten.[15] When speaking (for example) of various parts of Asia at times before they had been taken over by the Greeks (or the Macedonians), I believe that it is best to employ such expressions as 'pre-Classical modes of production', in a strictly chronological sense.

It is not my purpose in this book to defend Marx's analysis of capitalist society or his prophecy of its approaching end (both of which in the main I accept); but I have so often heard it said that he did not allow for the growth of a managerial and 'white-collar' middle class[16] that I will end this final section of my Introduction with a reference to two passages in his *Theories of Surplus Value* which rebut this criticism – and are by no means irrelevant to the main subject of this book, because they serve to illustrate a feature of the modern world to which there was no real parallel in antiquity. Criticising Malthus, Marx says that 'his supreme hope, which he himself describes as more or less utopian, is that the mass of the middle class should grow and that the proletariat (those who work) should constitute a constantly declining proportion (even though it increases absolutely) of the total population'; and he adds, 'This in fact is the course taken by bourgeois society' (*TSV* III.63).

And criticising Ricardo, Marx complains that 'what he forgets to emphasise is the constantly growing number of the middle classes, those who stand between the workman on the one hand and the captalist and landlord on the other. The middle classes . . . are a burden weighing heavily on the working base and they increase the social security and power of the upper Ten Thousand' (*TSV* II.573=*MEW* XXVI.ii.576).

These passages may remind us of the fact that in the Greek and Roman world there was no proper parallel to our own 'white-collar', salaried, managerial class (we shall see why in III.vi below), except in the Roman Principate and Later Empire, when three developments took place. First, a proper *standing army* was established in the early Principate, with (for the first time) regular benefits on discharge as well as fixed pay, found by the state. Those who became what we should call 'regular officers', especially the senior centurions, might become men of rank and privilege. Secondly, an *imperial civil service* grew up gradually, consisting partly of the emperor's own slaves and freedmen and partly of free men who, at all levels, served for pay (and for the often considerable perquisites involved): this civil service eventually achieved considerable dimensions, although many of its members were technically soldiers seconded for this duty. The third group of functionaries consisted of the *Christian clergy*, whose upkeep was provided partly by the state and partly by the endowments and contributions of the faithful. I shall have more to say about all these three groups later (VI.v-vi and esp. VIII.iv). Exactly like the middle classes referred to by Marx, they were certainly 'a burden weighing heavily on the working base', and as faithful bastions of the established order they too – except in so far as sections of the army were drawn into civil wars in support of rival emperors – 'increased the social security and power of the upper Ten Thousand'.

To conclude this section, I wish to emphasise that I make no claim to be producing *the* 'Marxist interpretation of Greek history': it is *a* would-be Marxist interpretation. After reading by far the greater part of Marx's published work (much of it, I must admit, in English translation), I myself believe that there is nothing in this book which Marx himself (after some argument, perhaps!) would not have been willing to accept. But of course there will be other Marxists who will disagree at various points with my basic theoretical position or with the interpretations I have offered of specific events, institutions and ideas; and I hope that any errors or weaknesses in this book will not be taken as directly due to the approach I have adopted, unless that can be shown to be the case.

II

Class, Exploitation, and Class Struggle

(i)
The nature of class society

'The concept of class has never remained a harmless concept for very long. Particularly when applied to human beings and their social conditions it has invariably displayed a peculiar explosiveness.' Those are the first two sentences of a book, *Class and Class Conflict in Industrial Society*, by Ralf Dahrendorf, a leading German sociologist who in 1974 became Director of the London School of Economics and Political Science. And Dahrendorf goes on to quote with approval the statement by two prominent American sociologists, Lipset and Bendix, that 'discussions of different theories of class are often academic substitutes for a real conflict over political orientations'. I fully accept that. It seems to me hardly possible for anyone today to discuss problems of class, and above all class *struggle* (or class *conflict*), in any society, modern or ancient, in what some people would call an 'impartial' or 'unbiased' manner. I make no claim to 'impartiality' or 'lack of bias', let alone 'Wertfreiheit', freedom from value-judgments. The criteria involved are in reality much more subjective than is commonly admitted: in this field one man's 'impartiality' is another man's 'bias', and it is often impossible to find an objective test to resolve their disagreement. Yet, as Eugene Genovese has put it, 'the inevitability of ideological bias does not free us from the responsibility to struggle for maximum objectivity' (*RB* 4). The criteria that I hope will be applied to this book are two: first, its *objectivity and truthfulness* in regard to historical events and processes; and secondly, the *fruitfulness* of the analysis it produces. For 'historical events and processes' I should almost be willing to substitute 'historical facts'. I do not shrink from that unpopular expression, any more than Arthur Darby Nock did when he wrote, 'A fact is a holy thing, and its life should never be laid down on the altar of a generalisation' (*ERAW* I.333). Nor do I propose to dispense with what is called – sometimes with a slight sneer, by social and economic historians – 'narrative history'. To quote a recent statement in defence of 'narrative history' by the present Camden Professor of Ancient History at Oxford:

> I do not see how we can determine how institutions worked, or what effect beliefs or social structures had on men's conduct, unless we study their actions in concrete situations . . . The most fundamental instinct that leads us to seek historical knowledge is surely the desire to find out *what* actually happened in the past and especially to discover what we can about events that had the widest effect on the fortunes of mankind; we then naturally go on to inquire *why* they occurred (P. A. Brunt, 'What is Ancient History about?', in *Didaskalos* 5 [1976] 236–49, at 244).

Can we actually identify classes in Greek society such as I shall describe? Did the Greeks themselves recognise their existence? And is it profitable to conduct an investigation along these lines? Is our understanding of the historical process, and of our own society, illuminated and strengthened by thinking in terms of classes and of a 'class struggle' in the Greek world? When I find Lévi-Strauss saying, 'I am not a sociologist, and my interest in our own society is only a secondary one' (*SA* 338), I want to reply, 'I am a historian who tries also to be a sociologist, and my interest in our own society is a primary one.'

I am not going to pretend that class is an entity existing objectively in its own right, like a Platonic 'Form', the nature of which we merely have to discover. The word has been used by historians and sociologists in all sorts of different senses;[1] but I believe that the way in which Marx chose to use it is the most fruitful, for our own society and for all earlier ones above the primitive level, including Greek and Roman society. Now Marx never, unfortunately, gave a definition of the term 'class', and it is true that he uses it rather differently on different occasions, above all when he is speaking of actual historical circumstances, in which the nature of the particular classes involved could differ considerably.[2] Even when, at the very end of the unfinished third volume of *Capital*, pp.885-6 (cf. 618),[3] he was about to answer his own question, 'What constitutes a class?' he only had time to say that the reply to this question 'follows naturally from the reply to another question, namely: What makes wage-labourers, capitalists and landlords constitute the three great social classes?' – as indeed they did, at the period of which and during which he was writing. He did not live to write down his answer to even that prior question, which would have produced a definition of the classes of nineteenth-century capitalist society rather than of class in general; and whether he would then have gone on to give an explicit general definition of class, we cannot tell. But after collecting scores if not hundreds of passages in which Marx operates with the concept of class (sometimes without actually using that word), I have little doubt what essential form it took in his mind. (I can give only a preliminary sketch here: I shall attempt to provide a proper account in Section ii of this chapter and subsequently.)

Class as a general concept (as distinct from a particular class) is essentially a relationship; and class in Marx's sense must be understood in close connection with his fundamental concept of 'the relations of production': the social relations into which men enter in the process of production, which find legal expression to a large degree either as property relations or as labour relations. When the conditions of production, such as they are at any given time, are controlled by a particular group (when, as in the great majority of such cases,[4] there is private property in the means of production), then we have a 'class society', the classes being defined in terms of their relationship to the means and the labour of production and to each other. Some of the most important 'means of production' in the modern world – not only factories, but also banks and finance houses, even railways and aircraft – were of course absent in Classical antiquity, and so, to a great extent, was that wage labour which is an essential element, indeed the essential element, in the relations of production characteristic of a capitalist economy. (As we shall see in III.vi below, free wage labour played an infinitely less important part in the Greek and Roman world than it does today.) In the ancient Greek world the principal means of production was land, and the principal form in which labour was directly exploited was unfree labour – that of chattel slaves above all; but debt bondage was far more widespread than many historians have realised, and in the Roman empire agricultural labour came to be exploited more and more through forms of tenancy (at first involving mainly free men), which in the late third century were converted into legal serfdom. (I shall give precise definitions of slavery, serfdom and debt bondage in III.iv below.) In antiquity, therefore, wealth may be said to have consisted above all in the ownership of land, and in the control of unfree labour; and it was these assets above all which enabled the propertied class to exploit the rest of the population: that is to say, to appropriate a surplus out of their labour.

At this point I must introduce an important and difficult subject which needs careful treatment and can easily lead to serious confusion, and which I intend to deal with properly in Chapter IV below. I refer to the fact that a large part of production in antiquity was always carried on, until the Later Roman Empire (and to a certain degree even then), by small free producers, mainly peasants, but also artisans and traders. In so far as these numerous individuals neither exploited the labour of others (outside their own families) to any appreciable extent nor were themselves exploited to any marked degree, but lived not far above subsistence level, producing little surplus beyond what they themselves consumed, they formed a kind of intermediate class, between exploiters and exploited. In practice, however, they were only too likely to be exploited. As I shall explain in Chapter IV, this exploitation could be not only direct and individual (by landlords or moneylenders, for instance) but also indirect and collective, effected by taxation, military conscription or forced services exacted by the state or the municipalities.

It is very hard to assess the condition of these small free producers accurately. The vast majority were what I shall call peasants (see my definition in IV.ii below), a term covering a wide variety of conditions, which nevertheless can be convenient to use, especially where we are in doubt about the precise situation of the people concerned. In Chapter IV I shall try to show the wide variety of institutions involved, and how the fortunes of some groups might fluctuate very considerably according to their political and legal as well as their economic position.

* * * * * *

Other categories than those of class, in the sense in which I am using that concept, have of course been proposed for the analysis, or at least the description, of Greek society. I shall consider some of them in Section v of this chapter.

Historians, who are usually dealing with a single society, rarely trouble themselves with any reflections about their choice of categories: they are seldom aware of any problem in this respect; often it does not even occur to them that there is any need to go beyond the concepts employed by the members of the society they are studying. Indeed, a practising historian in the British – and American – empirical tradition may well say to us (as the author of a major recent book on the Roman emperor has virtually done: see the opening of Section v of this Chapter): 'Why on earth should we waste time on all this theoretical stuff, about class structure and social relations and historical method? Why can't we just go on doing history in the good old way, without bothering about the concepts and categories we employ? That might even involve us in the philosophy of history, which is something we prefer to abandon with disdain to philosophers and sociologists, as mere ideology.' The reply to this, of course, is that it is a serious error to suppose that unconsciousness of ideology, or even a complete lack of interest in it, is the same thing as absence of ideology. In reality each of us has an ideological approach to history, resulting in a particular historical methodology and set of general concepts, whether conscious or unconscious. To refuse – as so many do – to define or even to think about the basic concepts we employ simply results in our taking over without scrutiny, lock, stock and barrel, the prevailing ideology in which we happen to have been brought up, and making much the same kind of selection from the evidence that our predecessors have been making and for the same reasons.

Nevertheless, there are very great virtues in the traditional approach of the historian, the essence of which – the insistence on recognising the *specificity* of the historical situation in any given period (and even area) – must not be abandoned, or even compromised, when it is combined with a sociological approach. Indeed, anyone who is not capable (whether from a deficiency of intellect or from lack of time or energy) of the great effort needed to combine the two approaches ought to prefer the strictly historical one, for even mediocre work produced by the purely fact-grubbing historian may at least, if his facts are accurate and fairly presented, be of use to others capable of a higher degree of synthesis, whereas the would-be sociologist having insufficient knowledge of the specific historical evidence for a particular period of history is unlikely in the extreme to say anything about it that will be of use to anyone else.

The study of ancient history in Britain has long been characterised by an attitude to detailed empirical investigation which *in itself* is most admirable. In a recent reassessment of Rostovtzeff's great *Social and Economic History of the Roman Empire*, Glen Bowersock of Harvard University (who had himself been through the Oxford Greats School and was a graduate pupil of Sir Ronald Syme) has spoken of a general raising of eyebrows in Oxford when Rostovtzeff, who had come there in 1918 as an exile from his native Russia, 'announced that he would lecture on no less a subject than "The Social and Economic History of Eastern and Western Hellenism, the Roman Republic, and the Roman Empire"'. He adds, 'Together with the immodest grandeur of Rostovtzeff's topic went, perhaps inevitably, an occasional cloudiness of thought'; and he records Rostovtzeff's own remark in the Preface to his book, 'Evidently the English mind, in this respect unlike the Slavonic, dislikes a lack of precision in thought or expression.'[5] Now here we come right up against a problem which faces every historian: how to reconcile full and scrupulous attention to all forms of evidence for his chosen subject and a study of the modern literature relating to it with a grasp of general historical methodology and sociological theory sufficient to enable him to make the most of what he learns. Few if any of us strike exactly the right balance between these very different desiderata. It has been said that the sociologist comes to know 'less and less about more and more', the historian 'more and more about less and less'. Most of us fall too decisively into one or other of these categories. We are like Plutarch's truly pious man, who has to negotiate a difficult course between the precipice of godlessness and the marsh of superstition (*Mor.* 378a), or Bunyan's Christian in the Valley of the Shadow of Death, treading a narrow path between, on the right hand, 'a very deep Ditch . . . into which the blind have led the blind in all Ages, and have both there miserably perished', and on the left, 'a very dangerous Quagg, into which, if even a good Man falls, he can find no bottom for his foot to stand on'.

I feel much happier, in dealing with the history of the ancient Greek world, if I can legitimately make use of categories of social analysis which are not only *precise*, in the sense that I can define them, but also *general*, in the sense that they can be applied to the analysis of other human societies. Class, in my sense, is eminently such a category. Nevertheless, I realise that it is a healthy instinct on the part of historians in the empirical tradition to feel the need at least to *begin from* the categories and even the terminology in use within the society they are studying – provided, of course, they do not remain imprisoned therein. In our case, if the Greeks did not 'have a word for' something we want to talk about, it may be a salutary warning to us that the phenomena we are looking for may not have existed in Greek times, or at any rate not in the same form as today. And so, in Section iv of this chapter, I propose to *begin from* the categories employed by the ancient Greeks themselves, at the time of their greatest self-awareness (the fifth and fourth centuries B.C.), to describe their own society. It will immediately become obvious that there is a striking similarity between those categories and some of the features of Marx's class analysis: this is particularly clear in Aristotle's *Politics*.

* * * * * *

Let us now get down to fundamentals. I begin with five propositions. First, man is a social animal – and not only that, but, as Marx says in the *Grundrisse* (E.T. 84), 'an animal which can develop into an individual only in society'. (Although in the same passage Marx contemptuously and rightly dismissed the individual and isolated hunter or fisherman who serves as the starting-point for Adam Smith and Ricardo – or, for that matter, Thomas Hobbes – as an uninspired conceit in the tradition of Robinson Crusoe, it is impossible not to recall at this point Hobbes's famous description of the life of his imaginary pre-societal man, in *Leviathan* I.13, as 'solitary, poor, nasty, brutish, and short'.) Secondly, the prime task of man in society is to organise production, in the broadest sense, including both the acquisition from outside his society, by trade or forcible appropriation, of such necessary or desirable things as the society needs but cannot produce, or cannot profitably produce, within itself, and the distribution of what is produced. (In an area which is large or, like the Greek world, much split up by mountains or the sea, the nature of the transport system may be an important factor.) I shall use the term 'production' in this convenient, extended sense, as Marx commonly does.[6] It should hardly be necessary to add that production, in the very broad sense in which I am using the word, of course includes reproduction: the bearing and rearing to maturity of offspring (cf. Section vi of this chapter). Thirdly, in the very act of living in society and organising production, man necessarily enters into a particular system of social and economic relations, which Marx referred to as 'the relations of production' or 'the social relations of production'.[7] Fourthly, in a civilised society such as that of the ancient Greeks or ourselves, the producers of actual necessities must (for obvious reasons, to be noticed presently) produce a surplus beyond what they actually consume themselves. And fifthly, the extraction and perpetuation of such a surplus has led in practice to exploitation, in particular of the primary agricultural producers: this exploitation, with which the whole concept of class is associated, is the very kernel of what I refer to as 'the class struggle'. (I shall deal with it in Sections ii and iii of this chapter. As I shall there explain, when I speak about 'the class struggle' in the ancient world I am never thinking of a struggle on the political plane alone, and sometimes my 'class struggle' may have virtually no political aspect at all.)

I should perhaps add, for the benefit of those who are accustomed to 'structuralist' terminology, that I have not found it useful or possible to draw the distinction employed by Lévi-Strauss and his school between social *relations* and social *structure* (see e.g. Lévi-Strauss, *SA* 279, 303–4). I shall sometimes speak of a set of social relations *as* a social structure, or social formation.

I am of course thinking throughout in terms of the civilised societies of the last few thousand years, which, having developed technologically far beyond the level of primitive man, have aimed at providing themselves with a sufficient and stable supply of the necessities and luxuries of civilised life, and consequently have had to devote a very considerable volume of effort to ensuring that supply. Some anthropologists have argued that by reducing their wants to a minimum, primitives existing in a favourable environment may be thought happier than men in at least the earlier stages of civilisation, and may even enjoy a good deal of leisure; but for my purposes primitive society[8] is irrelevant, since its structure is totally different from that of Graeco-Roman antiquity (let alone the modern world), and any exploitation which may exist at the primitive stage takes place in quite different ways. Moreover, primitive society has not proved able to survive contact with developed modern economies – to put it in the crudest possible way, with Hilaire Belloc (*The Modern Traveller*, vi),

> Whatever happens we have got
> The Maxim gun, and they have not.

Now in a primitive food-gathering and hunting tribe the mere day-to-day provision of food and other immediate necessities and of defence against wild beasts and other tribes and so on may be virtually a whole-time job for all adult members of the tribe, at least in the sense that in practice they do not extend their economic activities much further.[9] In a civilised community, however, it is not possible for everyone to spend all his time on these basic activities: there must be at least some members of the community who have enough *leisure* – in the technical sense of being released from directly producing the material necessities of life – for governing and organising and administering a complex society; for defending it against outsiders, with whatever weapons may be needed; for educating the next generation and training them in all the necessary skills, over a period of perhaps ten to twenty years; for the arts and sciences (whatever stage of development these may have reached); and for the many other requirements of civilised life. Such people (or some of them) must be at least partly freed from the cruder tasks, so that they may fulfil their specialised functions. And this means that they will have to be maintained by the rest of the community, or some part of it, in return for the services they provide. The producers will now have to produce more than what they themselves consume – in other words, a *surplus*.[10] And 'the appearance of a surplus makes possible – which does not mean "necessary" – structural transformations in a society' (Godelier, *RIE* 274).

In view of the controversy which has been going on for years among economic anthropologists about the whole notion of a 'surplus', I feel it is necessary to make two observations on that concept. First, I use the term in a strictly relative sense and with (so to speak) an 'internal' application, to mean that part of the product of *an individual man's* labour of which he does not directly enjoy the fruit himself, and the immediate benefits of which are reserved for others. I would distinguish an 'external' application of the term surplus, namely the way in which the notion is employed by anthropologists such as Pearson, to mean something set aside by *the society as a whole*, or by those who make its decisions, as 'surplus to its needs', and made available for some specific purpose – feasts, war, exchange with other societies, and so forth.[11] Secondly, I agree with Godelier that there is no *necessary* connection between the existence of a surplus and the exploitation of man by man: there may at first be exchange considered profitable by both sides, with certain persons taking upon themselves services genuinely performed on behalf of the whole community[12] – its defence against attack from outside, for example.[13] The precise point in history at which exploitation should be conceived as beginning is very difficult to decide, and I have not made up my own mind. The question is not important for my present purposes, because exploitation began long before the period with which I am concerned in this book. Perhaps we could say that exploitation begins when the primary producer is obliged to yield up a surplus under the influence of compulsion (whether political, economic or social, and whether perceived as compulsion or not), at any rate at the stage when he no longer receives a real equivalent in exchange – although this may make it very difficult to decide the point at which exploitation begins, since it is hard to quantify, for example, military protection against agricultural produce (cf. IV.iv below). A much more sophisticated definition of exploitation (which may well be preferable) has been offered by Dupré and Rey on the basis of their anthropological fieldwork in west Africa: 'Exploitation exists when the *use* of the surplus product by a group (or an aggregate) which has not contributed the corresponding surplus of labour *reproduces the conditions of a new extortion of surplus labour* from the producers (RPTHC 152, my italics). Although even a good and fully socialist society must arrange for 'surplus labour' by some, to support the very young, the aged and the infirm, and to provide all kinds of services for the community (cf. Marx, *Cap.* III.847, 876), it would necessarily do so in such a way that no individual or group of individuals had a right to appropriate the fruits of that 'surplus labour' in virtue of any special control over the process of production through property rights, or indeed except at the direction of the community as a whole or its organs of government.

In every civilised society there has been a basic problem of production: how to extract a sufficient surplus ('sufficient' in a relative sense, of course) from the primary producers, who are not likely to relish their position at the base of the social pyramid and will have to be subjected to a judicious mixture of persuasion and coercion – the more so if they have come to see the favoured few as exploiters and oppressors. Now men's capacity to win for themselves the freedom to live the life they want to live has always been severely limited, until very recently, by inadequate development of the productive forces at their disposal.

> All emancipation carried through hitherto has been based on restricted productive forces. The production which these productive forces could provide was insufficient for the whole of society and made development possible only if some persons satisfied their needs at the expense of others, and therefore some – the minority – obtained the monopoly of development, while others – the majority – owing to the constant struggle to satisfy their most essential needs, were for the time being (i.e. until the creation of new revolutionary productive forces) excluded from any development (*MECW* V.431-2, from the *German Ideology*; cf. *Cap*. III.820, quoted in I.iv above).

If I were asked to name the fundamental features of ancient Greek society which most distinguish it from the contemporary world, I would single out two things, closely connected, which I shall describe in succession. The *first*, within the field of what Marx called 'the forces of production', is a technological distinction. The advanced countries of the modern world have immense productive power. But go back to the ancient world, and you go down and down the technological ladder, so to speak. The Greek world, compared with the modern one, was very undeveloped technologically, and therefore infinitely less productive.[14] Great advances in technology occurred long before the Industrial Revolution, in the Middle Ages and even the Dark Ages. These advances were far more important than most people realise, not only in the most essential sphere of all, that of sources of energy or 'prime movers' (which I shall come to in a moment), but in all sorts of other ways. To take only one example – I wonder how many people who have not only read Greek and Latin literature but have looked at Greek vase-paintings and at the reliefs on Greek and Roman monuments have noticed the absence from antiquity of the wheelbarrow, which at least doubles a man's carrying capacity, but only appears in Europe in the thirteenth century (in China it was known a thousand years earlier).[15] As for sources of energy, I will say only that animal power, in the form of the tractive effort of the horse and ox, was nothing like fully realised in Classical antiquity, in particular because of the extreme inefficiency of the ancient horse-harness;[16] and that only in the Middle Ages do we find the widespread utilisation of two important forms of energy which were very little used in antiquity: wind and water (cf. n.14 below). Wind, of course, was used for the propulsion of merchant ships, though not very efficiently and without the stern-post rudder;[17] but the windmill was not known in Europe before (or not much before) the early twelfth century. The water-mill[18] (*hydraletēs*) was actually invented not later than the last century B.C.: the earliest known mention is by the Greek geographer Strabo, in a reference to Pontus, on the south shore of the Black Sea, in the 60s B.C. (XII.iii.30, p.556). But the most fascinating piece of evidence is the delightful poem in the *Greek Anthology*, by Antipater of Thessalonica, to which I referred in I.iv above as being known to Marx: the poet innocently assures the slave mill-girls that now they have the water-nymphs to work for them they can sleep late and take their ease (*Anth. Pal.* IX.418: see *Cap.* I.408). There is a little evidence, both literary and archaeological, for the use of the water-mill in the Graeco-Roman world, but it was rare before the fourth and fifth centuries, and its full use comes a good deal later (see n.14 again). Marx realised that 'the Roman Empire had handed down the elementary form of all machinery in the water-wheel' (*Cap.* I.348).

That is the essential background to my second basic distinction between the ancient and the modern world, which is intimately connected with the first and indeed largely grew out of it. In the ancient world, as we have seen, the producers, as I am calling them (men engaged in essential economic activities), produced a very much smaller surplus than is necessary to sustain a modern advanced society. This remains vitally important, even if we allow for the fact that the average Greek had a far more restricted range of wants and demanded a much lower standard of living than the modern Englishman, so that the volume of production per head could be well below what it has to be today. But even if we make allowance for this the disparity is still very striking. As I have shown, the ancient world was enormously less productive than the modern world. Therefore, unless almost everyone was to have to work practically all the time, and have virtually no leisure, some means had to be found of extracting the largest possible surplus out of at any rate a considerable number of those at the lowest levels of society. And this is where we come face to face with the *second* of my two fundamental distinctions between the ancient and the modern world, one that occurs this time in the field of what Marx called 'the relations of production': the propertied classes in the Greek and Roman world derived their surplus, which freed them from the necessity of taking part in the process of production, nor from wage labour, as in capitalist society, but mainly from unfree labour of various kinds. The ancient world knew other forms of unfree labour than strict 'slavery' ('chattel slavery', if you like), in particular what I shall call 'serfdom' and 'debt bondage' (see III.iv below). But in general slavery was the most important form of unfree labour at the highest periods of Greek and Roman civilisation; and the Greeks and Romans themselves always tended to employ the vocabulary of actual slavery when referring to other forms of unfree labour.

I have indicated that it is above all in relation to its function of extracting the maximum surplus out of those primary producers who were at the lowest levels of ancient society that I propose to consider slavery and other forms of unfree labour in this book. In treating slavery in this manner I am looking at it in very much the way that both masters and slaves have commonly regarded it. (Whether the ancient belief in the efficiency of the institution of slavery in this respect is justified or not is irrelevant for my purposes.) Perhaps I may cite here the opening of the third chapter of one of the best-known books on North American slavery, Kenneth Stampp's *The Peculiar Institution* (p.86):

> Slaves apparently thought of the South's peculiar institution chiefly as a system of labour extortion. Of course they felt its impact in other ways – in their social status, their legal status, and their private lives – but they felt it most acutely in the lack of control over their own time and labour. If discontented with bondage, they could be expected to direct their protests principally against the master's claim to their work.

The feature of slavery which made it appropriate and indeed essential and irreplaceable in the economic conditions of Classical antiquity was precisely that the *labour* it provided was *forced*. The slave, by definition, is a man *without rights* (or virtually without effective rights) and therefore unable to protect himself against being compelled to yield up a very large part of what he produces. Dio

Chrysostom, in the early second century of the Christian era, reports an imaginary discussion about slavery in which there was general agreement about the basic definition of the slave's condition: that someone else 'owns him as master, like any other item of property or cattle, so as to be able *to make use of him at his pleasure*' (*Orat.* XV.24).

I suggest that the most profitable way of approaching the problem of unfree labour is to think of it in precisely the way in which I have introduced it, in terms of *the extraction of the largest possible surplus from the primary producers.* I think that in antiquity slavery probably did provide the best possible answer, from the purely economic point of view (that is to say, disregarding all social as well as moral factors), having regard to the low level of productivity, and also to the fact that *free, hired* labour was scarce, largely confined to unskilled or seasonal work, and not at all mobile, whereas slaves were available in large numbers and at prices the lowness of which is astonishing, in comparison with what is known of slave prices in other societies. But given these conditions – the poor supply of free, hired labour, the easy availability of slaves, their cheapness, and so on – I do believe that slavery increased the surplus in the hands of the propertied class to an extent which could not otherwise have been achieved and was therefore an essential precondition of the magnificent achievements of Classical civilisation. I would draw attention to the fact that the distinction I have just drawn is based not on a difference of *status*, between slaves *and free men*, but on a difference of *class*, between slaves *and their owners* – a very different matter. (I shall return to this difference later: see Sections iii and v of this chapter.)

It may not have been fully obvious that so far I have been preparing the ground for the definition of the terms 'class' and 'class struggle' which I shall offer in Section ii of this chapter. I had to make clear certain fundamental features of ancient Greek society. I have now explained one of these, the essential part played by what I am calling unfree labour; and I must now briefly mention another, the fact that by far the most important means of production in the ancient world was land. Wealth in Classical antiquity was always essentially landed wealth, and the ruling classes of all the Greek states, as of Rome itself, invariably consisted mainly of landowners. This is something which most ancient historians now realise; but the whole question, like that of slavery and other forms of unfree labour, will require a more extended discussion than I can give it at this point (see III.i–iii below).

★ ★ ★ ★ ★ ★

In seeking to use the concept of class as a method of historical analysis there are two quite different dangers that we must guard against: one, a matter of definition, is in the province of the sociologist; the other, a matter of identification, is a question strictly for the historian. After stating them together, I shall briefly discuss them separately. First, we must be quite sure what we mean by the term 'class' (and 'class struggle'), and not slide carelessly and unconsciously from one interpretation to another. Secondly, we must be careful to make a correct historical identification of any class we propose to recognise.

1. The first problem, that of definition, is of a sociological nature. Marx himself, as I said earlier, never gave a definition of class in general terms. Some may feel that no such general definition is possible, but I believe the one I shall

produce in Section ii below will serve well enough, although there may be some special cases in which a unique set of historical circumstances makes qualification necessary. Even if it could be shown that there are too many exceptions for my definition to be considered a general one, I would at least claim that it holds for the society, or rather series of societies, of the Graeco-Roman world, discussed in this book. I hope that others will improve upon it.

2. The second problem is purely historical: one must thoroughly understand the particular society one is considering, and know the evidence about it at first hand, before one can expect to identify its classes correctly and precisely. Some serious mistakes have been made in defining the actual classes existing in particular societies, and the results of employing unreal conceptions of those classes, not corresponding closely with reality, have sometimes been disastrous. Misconceptions about classes existing in historical societies have not, of course, been confined to Marxists, by any means, but since they make more use of class categories than other historians they are likely to commit even worse blunders if they start out with misconceptions about the classes they recognise. It has been a standard practice among ancient historians to refer to the governing classes of several Greek cities in the Archaic and Classical periods, in particular Aegina and Corinth, as 'commercial aristocracies' or 'industrial and merchant classes' (see my OPW 264-7, esp. n.61; cf. 216, 218-20, and Appendix XLI, esp. p.396). This extraordinary notion, for which there is not a shred of ancient evidence, was adopted without examination by Busolt, Eduard Meyer and other leading historians (even Max Weber was not entirely free of it), and it is still being reproduced today in some quarters. Not a few Marxists have started out from similarly mistaken positions. It is not surprising that attempts by George Thomson (essentially a literary scholar and not a historian in the proper sense) to expound the intellectual development of the Classical Greek world in Marxist terms have not succeeded in convincing historians or philosophers; for Thomson presents the development of Greek thought, and even of Greek democracy, in the sixth and fifth centuries as the consequence of the rise to power of a wholly imaginary 'merchant class'. Thomson even describes the Pythagoreans of Croton as 'the new class of rich industrialists and merchants', who 'resembled Solon in being actively involved in the political struggle for the development of commodity production'.[19] In my opinion, this is little better than fantasy. The one book I know in English which explicitly seeks to give an account of Greek history (before the Roman period) in Marxist terms is a prime example of the methodological catastrophe involved in giving a would-be Marxist account in terms of classes that are fictions and correspond to no historical reality. The author, Margaret O. Wason, pretends that in the seventh and sixth centuries, in most Greek states, there came to power a 'new bourgeois class', defined as 'the class of merchants and artisans which challenged the power of the aristocracy'. It is no surprise to find Cleon referred to in the same book as 'a tanner' (this of course reproduces Aristophanes' caricature; cf. my OPW 235 n.7, 359-61, 371) and as 'the leader of the Athenian workers'.[20]

I may add that it would similarly be absurd to speak of a 'class struggle' between Senators and Equites in the Late Roman Republic. Here I am in full agreement with a number of non-Marxist ancient historians of very different outlooks. As P. A. Brunt and Claude Nicolet have so conclusively demonstrated in the last few years, the Equites were part of the class of large landowners to which the Senators also belonged. As Badian has put it, for the Senate they were simply 'the non-political members of its own class'[21] – those who preferred not to take upon themselves the arduous and often dangerous life that a political career would involve. At certain times a purely political contest might develop between these two groups within the propertied class on specific issues, but this must not mislead us into seeing them as two separate classes having irreconcilable interests. I shall in fact speak sometimes of the Roman Senators (though not the Equites) as a class: the 'senatorial class'. It is possible that some other Marxists may prefer not to break down my 'propertied class' (for which see III.ii below) into two or more classes for certain purposes, as I do — for example, in the developed Principate and the Later Empire, primarily into the senatorial and curial classes, with the Equites perhaps as a kind of sub-class closely attached to the Senators, until in the late fourth and early fifth centuries they were entirely absorbed into the senatorial class (see VI.vi below, *ad fin.*). But in my set of definitions, early in Section ii of this chapter, I allow for *Rechtsstellung* (legal or constitutional situation) as a factor that can help to determine class in so far as it affects the type and degree of exploitation practised or suffered; and the constitutional privileges enjoyed by Senators surely did materially increase their capacity to exploit – just as the condition of being a slave, with its severe juridical disabilities, greatly increased the slave's liability to exploitation. But I could quite understand if some other Marxists, feeling that it was above all their great wealth which lay at the root of the Senators' privileged position, rather than the office-holding and the consequential legal privileges it brought them, preferred to treat the Senators merely as an 'order' (which they certainly were) rather than a class. Perhaps 'sub-class' would be a convenient term; but I have avoided it.

★ ★ ★ ★ ★ ★

I have only one more preliminary point to make before proceeding to a definition of my terms: I am deliberately avoiding, at this stage, discussion of the terms 'caste', 'order', 'estate' (*état*). Caste is a phenomenon which we do not encounter at all in the Greek or Roman world.[22] We do find what can legitimately be described as 'orders' (or 'estates') – that is to say, status-groups (*Stände*) which are *legally recognised* as such and have different sets of juridical characteristics (privileges or disadvantages). Such groups will be noticed when we have occasion to discuss them. I shall have something to say of 'status-groups' in general, and (in Section v of this chapter) of 'status' as an alternative concept to 'class'. But although I shall of course refer at times to particular 'orders' (citizens, slaves, freedmen, senators, equestrians, curials), I shall take no special account of 'orders' as such, treating them as a rule merely as a special form of status-group, except in so far as they materially affect the degree of exploitation concerned (cf. the preceding paragraph).

<h2 style="text-align:center">(ii)
'Class', 'exploitation', and 'the class struggle' defined</h2>

We can now attempt to define 'class', 'exploitation', and 'class struggle'. As I said in Section i of this chapter, I am not going to pretend that there is an objective entity, class, the nature of which remains to be discovered. I would also deny that there is any definition of class which is so generally agreed upon that we are all obliged to accept it or run the risk of being accused of perversity. The concept has been discussed *ad nauseam* by sociologists during the past few decades (cf. n.1 to Section i above). After working through a good deal of the literature, most of which seems to me almost worthless, I feel entitled to insist from the outset that the disagreement about the best way of using the expression 'class' has been so great that anyone who attempts an analysis of any society in terms of class is entitled to establish his own criteria, within very wide limits, and that our verdict on the definition he adopts ought to depend solely on its clarity and consistency, the extent to which it corresponds with the historical realities to which it is applied, and its fruitfulness as a tool of historical and sociological analysis. If in addition we find (as we shall in this case) that the notion of class in the sense in which we define it corresponds closely with concepts employed in the best sociological thought of the society we are examining (in our case, that of Aristotle especially: see Section iv of this chapter), then we shall be fortunate indeed.

I should like to quote here a statement by a leading British sociologist, T. B. Bottomore, raising questions which are all too unfamiliar to many historians. Speaking of the construction of general concepts by sociologists, he says:

> In some recent attempts to improve the 'conceptual framework' of sociology, and notably in that of Talcott Parsons and his collaborators, the whole emphasis is placed upon definition of concepts rather than upon the use of concepts in explanation. This is a retrograde step by comparison with the work of Durkheim and Max Weber, both of whom introduced and defined concepts in the course of working out explanatory theories. Weber's exposition of his 'ideal type' method deals more clearly with this matter than any later writing, and had his ideas been followed up sociology would have been spared much confused and aimless discussion. In essentials his argument is that the value of a definition (i.e. of a concept) is only to be determined by its fruitfulness in research and theorising (*Sociology*[2] [1971] 37, cf. 121).

I should not like it to be thought, however, that I regard Marx's concept of class as a Weberian 'ideal-type construct', in the sense that Weber himself took it to be. For me, as for Marx, classes and class struggles are real elements which can be empirically identified in individual cases, whereas for Weber all such 'Marxian concepts and hypotheses' become 'pernicious, as soon as they are thought of as empirically valid' (Weber, *MSS* 103, repr. in Eldridge, *MWISR* 228).

I propose first to state my definition of class and class struggle, and to explain and justify it in subsequent discussion. I believe that this definition represents the central thought of Marx as accurately as possible: this claim too I shall try to justify.

Class (essentially a relationship)[1] is the collective social expression of the fact of exploitation, the way in which exploitation is embodied in a social structure. By *exploitation* I mean the appropriation of part of the product of the labour of others:[2] in a commodity-producing society this is the appropriation of what Marx called 'surplus value'.

A class (a particular class) is a group of persons in a community identified by their position in the whole system of social production, defined above all according to their relationship (primarily in terms of the degree of ownership or control) to the conditions of production (that is to say, the means and labour of production)[3] and to other classes. Legal position (constitutional rights or, to use the German term, 'Rechtsstellung') is one of the factors that may help to determine class: its share in doing so will depend on how far it affects the type and degree of exploitation practised or suffered – the condition of being a slave in the ancient Greek world, for example, was likely (though far from certain) to result in a more intense degree of exploitation than being a citizen or even a free foreigner.

The individuals constituting a given class may or may not be wholly or partly conscious of their own identity and common interests as a class, and they may or may not feel antagonism towards members of other classes as such.

It is of the essence of a *class society* that one or more of the smaller classes, in virtue of their control over the conditions of production (most commonly exercised through ownership of the means of production),[4] will be able to exploit – that is, to appropriate a surplus at the expense of – the larger classes, and thus constitute an economically and socially (and therefore probably also politically) superior class or classes. The exploitation may be direct and individual, as for example of wage-labourers, slaves, serfs, 'coloni', tenant-farmers or debtors by particular employers, masters, landlords or moneylenders, or it may be indirect and collective, as when taxation, military conscription, forced labour or other services are exacted solely or disproportionately from a particular class or classes (small peasant freeholders, for instance) by a State dominated by a superior class.

I use the expression *class struggle* for the fundamental relationship between classes (and their respective individual members), involving essentially exploitation, or resistance to it. It does not necessarily involve collective action by a class as such, and it may or may not include activity on a political plane, although such political activity becomes increasingly probable when the tension of class struggle becomes acute. A class which exploits others is also likely to employ forms of political domination and oppression against them when it is able to do so: democracy will mitigate this process.

Imperialism, involving some kind of economic and/or political subjection to a power outside the community, is a special case, in which the exploitation effected by the imperial power (in the form of tribute, for instance), or by its individual members, need not necessarily involve direct control of the conditions of production. In such a situation, however, the class struggle within the subject community is very likely to be affected, for example through support given by the imperial power or its agents to the exploiting class or classes within that community, if not by the acquisition by the imperial power or its individual members of control over the conditions of production in the subject community.

There is one aspect of my definition of class which, I realise, may need clarification. Not all individuals belong to one specific class alone: some can be regarded as members of one class for some purposes and of another class for others, although usually membership of one will be much the most significant. A slave who was allowed by his master to accumulate a considerable *peculium*, and who (like Musicus Scurranus, mentioned in III.iv below, at its n.13) had even acquired under-slaves of his own, *vicarii*, might have to be regarded *pro tanto* as a member of what I am calling 'the propertied class'; but of course his membership of that class would necessarily be qualified and precarious and dependent on the goodwill of his master. A slave who was settled by his landowning master as tenant of a small farm, *quasi colonus* (see IV.iii § 12 below), would in strictly economic terms be in much the same position as a poor free peasant leaseholder, and we might be inclined to put him in the class of peasants (see IV.ii below); but his legal status would remain greatly inferior and his tenancy would be much more at the pleasure of the landowner, who could therefore exploit him more severely if he were so inclined. And a poor peasant who owned or leased a plot of land so small that he regularly needed to betake himself to a neighbouring city for part of the year to earn wages would be a member of two classes: small peasants and wage-labourers. I also maintain in Section vi of this chapter that women, or at any rate married women (and so the great majority of adult women in antiquity), must be regarded for some purposes as a distinct class, although membership of such a class (because of its consequences for property-ownership) would in a city like Classical Athens be far more important to a high-born woman than to a poor peasant, who would have had no opportunity to own much property had she been a man and whose membership of the class of women would therefore be of far less significance.

Of course I have no wish to pretend that class is the only category we need for the analysis of Greek and Roman society. All I am saying is that it is the fundamental one, which *over all* (at any given moment) and *in the long run* is the most important, and is by far the most useful to us, in helping us to understand Greek history and explain the process of change within it. In Section v of this chapter I shall briefly consider alternative approaches, particularly those which have the primary aim – as I have not, and as Marx did not (see Section v) – of establishing a scheme of 'social stratification' according to 'status'. Such activities are perfectly legitimate and may even have quite useful results, provided we keep them in their proper place and realise that they will not by themselves disclose the real secrets of history: the springs and causes of human behaviour and social change. I would say that social status, and even in the long run political power, tended to *derive from* class position in the first place (as indeed political status always did directly in the commonest form of Greek oligarchy in the Classical period, based on a property qualification), and that in the long run distinctions having any other basis than the economic tended to *decay in favour of*, and *ultimately to resolve themselves into*, distinctions based upon economic class. (We shall notice some examples of this process later: see V.iii and VIII.i and ii below.)

Let us be quite clear about one thing. Whereas descriptions of ancient society in terms of some category other than class – status, for instance – are perfectly innocuous, in the sense that they need have no direct relevance to the modern world (which will of course need to be described in terms of a completely different set of statuses), an analysis of Greek and Roman society in terms of class, in the specifically Marxist sense, is indeed (to use Firth's adjective: see I.iv above) something *threatening*, something that speaks directly to every one of us today and insistently demands to be applied to the contemporary world, of the second half of the twentieth century. If Marx's analysis, originally derived above all from the study of nineteenth-century capitalist society, turns out to be equally well adapted not merely to *describe* ancient society over a long period of many centuries but to *explain* its transformations and its partial disintegration (as we shall see it is), then its relevance for the contemporary world becomes very hard to ignore. Of course in some quarters it will be ignored. To quote Marx and Engels, addressing themselves sarcastically in 1848 to the ruling classes of their day:

> The selfish misconception that induces you to transform into eternal laws of nature and of reason the social forms springing from your present mode of production and form of property – historical relations that rise and disappear in the progress of production – this misconception you share with every ruling class that has preceded you. What you see clearly in the case of ancient property, what you admit in the case of feudal property, you are of course forbidden to admit in the case of your own bourgeois form of property (*MECW* VI.501, from the *Communist Manifesto*).

★ ★ ★ ★ ★ ★

I shall now glance briefly at the use of the conception of class (and class struggle) by Marx himself. I shall maintain that for five different reasons in particular there has been a widespread and serious misunderstanding of the part this idea played in Marx's thought. I believe that my definition represents his fundamental thinking more accurately than do the statements of some modern Marxist and non-Marxist writers who have taken different views from mine. My five reasons are as follows.

First, partly perhaps because of a much-quoted definition by Lenin, in his *A Great Beginning*, which (as Ossowski says, *CSSC* 72 and n.1) has been 'popularised by Marxist text-books and encyclopaedias', it has been customary to lay particular stress on relationship to the means of production as the decisive factor (sometimes as the one essential factor) in determining a person's class position. Although his formulation contains a profound truth, it will be seen from the definition of class given above that I regard it as a rather too narrow conception. Secondly, as is well known, Marx himself, although he made important use of the concept of class throughout his work, never gave a formal definition of it, and indeed employed it in very different senses at different times. Thirdly, Marx himself was concerned in his writings almost entirely with a capitalist society which had already undergone a considerable process of development: apart from one section of the *Grundrisse* (E.T. 471-514) which is specifically devoted to 'pre-capitalist economic formations' (see the excellent edition by Hobsbawm, *KMPCEF*), the statements in his work about pre-capitalist societies in general and the Graeco-Roman world in particular are all brief, and many of them are in the nature of *obiter dicta*. In these passages, as a rule, he takes no pains to be precise over terminology. Fourthly (and as a consequence of the facts I have just stated), when Marx spoke in particular about 'class struggle' he tended – thinking almost always, as he was, of nineteenth-century capitalism – to have in mind the kind of class struggle which was so noticeable in the mid-nineteenth century in the more developed capitalist countries: namely, open class struggle on the political plane. Thus when, for example, he spoke in *The Eighteenth Brumaire of Louis Bonaparte* of the French bourgeoisie as 'doing away with the class struggle for the moment by abolishing universal suffrage' (*MECW* XI.153), he simply meant that the law of 31 May 1850, by reducing the total number of electors from ten to seven million (id. 147), made it far harder for the French working class to carry on effective political struggle. And finally, in the work often wrongly taken to be the definitive statement of Marx's 'materialist conception of history', namely the *Preface to A Contribution to the Critique of Political Economy* (1858-9), we find only a passing reference to classes and none at all to class struggle. There is, however, a perfectly good explanation of this, well brought out by Arthur M. Prinz in an article in the *Journal of the History of Ideas* 30 (1969) 437-50, entitled 'Background and ulterior motive of Marx's "Preface" of 1859'. The *Preface* was to be published (through the good offices of Lassalle) in Berlin, and it was absolutely necessary for Marx to take careful account of the stringent Prussian censorship and abstain from anything that might be suspected of incitement to class hatred, at that time an actual offence punishable with imprisonment under para. 100 of the Prussian Penal Code. Marx, already well known to the Prussian censors, was now living in England and in no danger of prosecution himself; but he had to be circumspect if there was to be any hope of finding a publisher, for the same paragraph of the Penal Code also prescribed the penalty of confiscation for any offending work. Yet Marx had to publish in Germany, in order to make a bid for the intellectual leadership of the German socialist movement. The *Preface*, then, had to steer clear of class struggle. But when on 17/18 September 1879 Marx and Engels – thinking back to the *Communist Manifesto* and beyond – wrote to Bebel, Liebknecht and others, 'For almost forty years we have stressed the class struggle as the immediate driving power of history' (*MESC* 395), they were making a perfectly correct statement. Even in those considerable parts of Marx's writing which are concerned entirely with economics or philosophy rather than with the historical process he will sometimes show that the class struggle is ever-present in his mind, as when in a letter to Engels on 30 April 1868 he rounds off a long passage on economics with the words, 'Finally . . . we have as conclusion the class struggle, into which the movement of the whole *Scheiss* is resolved' (see *MESC* 250).

★　★　★　★　★　★

From reactions I have had to drafts of this chapter, I know that some people will protest against what will seem to them an excessive emphasis on collective entities, classes, at the expense of 'the individual'. To any such objection I would reply that my main aim in this book is to explain 'what happened in history' *on a large scale*: the history of the Greek world as a whole over more than 1,300 years – dare I use the rather repellent expression, 'macro-history'? But the history of 'macro-units' (of classes, as of states and alliances) needs to be explained in terms very different from those appropriate to the behaviour of individuals. Here I must hark back to I.iv above, where I explained how I have learnt from Thucydides about the patterns of behaviour of human groups in organised States. Elsewhere I have explained at length how Thucydides – rightly, in my opinion – recognised that the canons of interpretation and judgment applicable to the actions of States are fundamentally different from those we apply to the actions of individuals (see my *OPW* 7 ff., esp. 16-28). I now wish to advance the following propositions: that the factors governing the behaviour of classes (in my sense) are different again from either of the sets I have just mentioned; that the behaviour of a class as such (that of men *as* members of a class) may well be inexplicable in terms we can legitimately apply to their behaviour as individuals; and even that a given individual or set of individuals may behave *as* a constituent part of a class in a way that is quite different from the behaviour we are entitled to expect of him or them as individuals.

If in that last sentence we substitute 'a state' for 'a class', there may be little objection, since the moral standards generally accepted as governing the conduct of individuals are clearly quite different from those applied to the behaviour of states: a man who participated in the bombing of Hiroshima or Nagasaki, Berlin or Dresden, Vietnam or Laos, will not be accounted a mass murderer by most people, because he was acting in the interests – or at any rate on the orders – of his own state, against an 'enemy' state; and those who gave the orders suffered no criminal indictment, for in the event they were not the defeated. It would similarly be easy to find examples from the ancient world that would be universally considered morally atrocious behaviour on the part of individuals acting in their own personal interests, but were yet regarded as unobjectionable and even praiseworthy when employed in the service of the state. Most of the acts of odious injustice or unnecesssary cruelty committed by fourth-century Roman generals against 'barbarians' or rebels which are noticed, for example, by Ammianus Marcellinus (a Greek historian who wrote in Latin) are recorded without any sign of disapproval;[5] and the same historian could mention without comment the opinion of 'lawyers of old' that sometimes even the innocent may be put to death (XXVII.ix.5), and felt no need to shed any tears over the wholesale extermination of the children of the Maratocupreni, fierce and wily robbers (XXVIII.ii.11-14). I suspect, however, that many people would be far less willing to accept the propositions advanced at the end of the last paragraph in regard to classes, which I will now demonstrate.

That slaves who rebelled, or who could even be held guilty of failing to protect their masters from being assassinated by one of their own number, were treated with pitiless ferocity by the Romans is well known: I have given one or two prominent examples in VII.i below. The relationship of the Spartans to their Helots – very much a class relationship, of exploiter to exploited – was one of quite extraordinary hostility and suspicion. In III.iv below I draw attention to the remarkable fact that each set of Spartan ephors, upon taking office, made an official declaration of war on their work-force, the Helots, so as to be able to kill any of them without trial and yet avoid incurring the religious pollution such acts would otherwise have entailed. The Greeks on the whole showed less savagery than the Romans towards their slaves; but even in Classical Athens, where we hear most about relatively good treatment of slaves, all our literature takes the flogging of slaves for granted.

Literary sources in abundance from all over the Greek world show that this form of punishment for slaves was commonplace. An epitaph on the tomb of a virtuous matron, Myro (who may be an imaginary character), by the Hellenistic poet Antipater of Sidon, describes quite casually, as if it were the most natural thing in the world, the depiction on her tomb of (among other things) a whip, as a sign that Myro was a 'just chastiser of misdeeds' – though not, of course, a 'cruel or arrogant mistress'! (*Anth. Pal.* VII.425). No one will doubt that refractory slaves were repressed without mercy, at any rate in so far as this could be done without excessive damage to the interests of their masters, whose property they were (cf. III.iv below).

Whom among our main literary sources might we have thought less likely to order a slave to be flogged than Plutarch? – a man conspicuous, surely, for his humanity. But there is a nasty little story which has come down to us from Calvisius Taurus, a friend of Plutarch's, through Aulus Gellius (*NA* I.xxvi.4-9).

An educated slave of Plutarch's who knew his master's treatise *On freedom from anger* (*Peri aorgēsias*, usually referred to by its Latin title, *De cohibenda ira*) protested, while being flogged, that Plutarch was being inconsistent and giving in to the very fault he had reprobated. Plutarch was quite unabashed. Insisting that he was perfectly calm, he invited the slave to continue the argument with him – in the same breath ordering the flogger to continue applying the lash. The incident was quoted by Taurus, in reply to a question by Gellius at the end of one of his philosophical lectures, and with complete approval. But we need not be surprised in the least at Plutarch's action, if we can bring ourselves to see this particular slaveowner and his slave as 'but the personifications of the economic relations that existed between them' (Marx, *Cap*. I.84–5).

The class struggle between the propertied class and those who were relatively or absolutely propertyless was also accompanied at times by atrocities on both sides: see e.g. V.ii below. When we hear of particularly murderous behaviour by those who had the upper hand in a *stasis* (a civil commotion), we can be reasonably safe in concluding that the conflict was basically between social classes, even if our information about it is not explicit.[6]

I forbear to cite contemporary examples of the conduct of class warfare in ways which have been widely accepted as 'necessary' but which have involved behaviour that would be condemned by everyone as morally indefensible in actions between individuals.

(iii)
Exploitation and the class struggle

Since the title of this book refers not merely to 'class' in the ancient Greek world but to 'the class struggle', I must explain what I mean by that expression, more precisely than in the definition I have given in Section ii of this chapter. Now there is no denying that although 'class' is an expression any of us may use without a blush, 'class struggle' is a very different matter. Merely to employ the expression 'the class struggle', in the singular, evidently seems to many people in the Western world a deplorable concession to the shade of Karl Marx; and indeed, on hearing the title of this book (as of the lectures on which it is based) some of my friends have grimaced, like one that hears tell of a hobgoblin in whose very existence he cannot bring himself to believe, and have suggested that the plural, 'class struggles', would be less objectionable. But I wished to make it perfectly clear, by my choice of title, not only that my approach is based upon what I believe to be Marx's own historical method, but also that the process of 'class struggle' which I have in mind is not something spasmodic or occasional or intermittent but a permanent feature of human society above primitive levels. Marx did not claim to have invented the concept of class struggle,[1] but it was he and Engels who first made of it both a keen analytical tool to facilitate historical and sociological investigation and a powerful weapon for use by all oppressed classes.

The very existence of classes, in the sense in which (following Marx, as I believe) I have defined that term, inevitably involves tension and conflict between the classes. Marxists often speak of 'contradictions' in this context. As far as I can see, although Marx himself could speak of 'contradictions' between (for example) the relations of production and the forces of production, between the social character of production and private appropriation of its products by a few, and between private landownership and rational agriculture,[2] it is not at all characteristic of him to describe a situation of what I am calling class struggle as a 'contradiction': this terminology is more often found in Engels and especially in Lenin and Mao Tse-tung. I realise that Mao in particular has made some important contributions to this subject;[3] but I am not myself satisfied with any discussion I have seen in English of the concept of 'contradiction' in a Marxist context, and I feel reluctant to employ the term in a peculiar sense which has not yet established itself in the English language and become accepted into normal usage, as it doubtless has in French, for instance. I therefore prefer to speak of class 'struggles', 'conflicts', 'antagonisms', 'oppositions' or 'tensions', arising as (in a sense) the *result* of 'contradictions'. Here I think I am nearer to Marx's own usage – as when he says, for example, that the very existence of industrial capital 'implies class antagonism between capitalists and wage-labourers' (*Cap.* II.57); or when he and Engels write, in the *Communist Manifesto*, of 'modern bourgeois private property' as 'the final and most complete expression of the system of producing and appropriating products that is based on class antagonisms, on the exploitation of the many by the few' (*MECW* VI.498). Sometimes, when Marx writes of a 'Gegensatz' or 'Klassengegensatz', words which should be translated 'opposition' and 'class antagonism', the term in question will appear in a standard English translation as 'contradiction' or 'class contradiction': there are examples (as Timothy O'Hagan has pointed out to me) in *MECW* V.432, from the *German Ideology*, and in *Capital* III.386.[4]

As I have already indicated, Marx himself never gave any proper, systematic exposition of his theory of classes, or of class struggle, although these conceptions occur again and again in his works, and indeed occupy a central place in his thought, being omnipresent even when the specific term 'class' is not actually employed. *The Communist Manifesto*, drawn up by Marx and Engels in 1847-8, opens with the words, 'The history of all hitherto existing society ['that is, all *written* history', as Engels added to the English edition of 1888] *is* the history of class struggles.'

I believe that if Marx himself had tried to give a definition of class in the most general terms he would have produced one not very different from the one I have given in Section ii of this chapter. Marx began with a fundamental idea of civilised society of which class is the very kernel. It should be sufficient to single out four passages in *Capital* in which the central importance of class is made clear, although it is only in the first that the term 'class' is actually used. The first, which is very brief, is the one I have just quoted above, in which Marx says of 'industrial capital' (*Cap.* II.50 ff.) that its very 'existence implies class antagonism between capitalists and wage labourers' (id. 57). The second passage, which is also quite short, is as follows:

> Whatever the social form of production, labourers and means of production always remain factors of it. But . . . for production to go on at all they must unite. The specific manner in which this union is accomplished distinguishes the different economic epochs of the structure of society from one another (*Cap.* II.36-7).

The third passage is equally brief but contains an important implication that seems to me to have been too often overlooked. (I shall soon return to it.)

The essential difference between the various economic forms of society (between, for instance, a society based on slave labour and one based on wage labour) lies only in the mode in which surplus labour is in each case extracted from the actual producer, the worker (*Cap.* I.217).

Now 'surplus labour' and (in the case of commodity-producing societies) 'surplus value' are simply the terms Marx uses for the exploitation of the primary producers by those who control the conditions of production; and indeed, the sentence I have just quoted from *Capital* I is part of Section 1 of Chapter ix (Chapter vii in German editions), headed 'The degree of exploitation of labour-power' ('Der Exploitationsgrad der Arbeitskraft'), in which Marx – dealing, of course, specifically with capitalist society – says that 'the rate of surplus value is an exact expression for the degree of exploitation of labour-power by capital, or of the worker by the capitalist' (I.218 and n.1; cf. III.385 and many other passages). The passage I have quoted, therefore, is merely another way of saying that it is the precise form of exploitation which is the distinguishing feature of each form of society (above the most primitive level, of course), whether it is, for example, a slave society or a capitalist society (cf. *Cap.* I.539–40). And class, as I have indicated, is essentially the way in which exploitation is reflected in a social structure. As it happens, Marx often fails to employ the actual expression 'exploitation' (whether by means of the more colloquial word 'Ausbeutung' or the more technical 'Exploitation') in contexts where we might have expected it, preferring to speak in thoroughly technical language of 'extraction of surplus labour' or 'of surplus value'. He evidently regarded 'Exploitation' as being strictly a French word, for in the work now generally known as *Wages, Price and Profit*, written in English in June 1865 as an address to the General Council of the First International, Marx uses the words, 'the *exploitation* (you must allow me this French word) of labour' (*MESW* 215). But he uses the verb 'exploitieren' and the nouns 'Exploiteur und Exploitiertem' from at least 1844 onwards,[5] and 'Exploitation' is found in several of his works, including all three volumes of *Capital*.[6] 'Ausbeutung' and its verb 'ausbeuten' are relatively rare in Marx's writings, but they do occur now and again from 1843 onwards.[7] (I should perhaps add that most of *Capital* was written in 1863–5; Vol. I was prepared for publication by Marx himself in 1867, Vols II and III by Engels after Marx's death in 1883.)

The longest and most explicit of my four passages, which seems to me one of the most important Marx ever wrote, comes from Vol. III of *Capital* (791–2, Chapter xlvii, Section 2):

The specific economic form in which unpaid surplus labour is pumped out [*ausgepumpt*] of the direct producers determines the relationship between those who dominate and those who are in subjection [*Herrschafts- und Knechtschaftsverhältnis*], as it grows directly out of production itself and reacts upon it as a determining element in its turn. Upon this, however, is founded the entire organisation of the economic community which grows up out of the production-relations themselves, and thereby at the same time its specific political form. It is always the direct relationship of the owners of the conditions of production to the immediate producers – a relation always naturally corresponding to a definite stage in the development of the nature and method of labour and consequently of its social productivity – which reveals the innermost secret, the hidden foundation of the entire social structure and therefore also of the political form of the relations of sovereignty and dependence [*Souveränitäts- und Abhängigkeitsverhältnis*], in short, the corresponding specific form of the State. This does not prevent the same economic basis – the same as far as its main conditions are concerned – owing to innumerable different empirical circumstances, natural environment, racial peculiarities, external historical influences etc., from manifesting infinite variations and gradations of aspect, which can be grasped only by analysis of the empirically given circumstances. (I have slightly altered the standard translation, after studying the German text, *MEW* XXV. 799-800.)[8]

★ ★ ★ ★ ★ ★

I have waited until now to state one major part of my theory of class, because I wished to show that it is implicit in Marx's own writings, and this emerges most clearly from the last two passages in *Capital* that I have just quoted (I.217 and III.791-2). As I claim to have found the theory in Marx, I cannot of course pretend that it is new; but I have never seen it stated clearly and explicitly. My point is that the most significant distinguishing feature of each social formation, each 'mode of production' (cf. the end of IV.v below), is not so much *how the bulk of the labour of production is done*, as *how the dominant propertied classes*, controlling the conditions of production, *ensure the extraction of the surplus* which makes their own leisured existence possible. That was the view of Marx, which I follow. In the last of the four passages from *Capital* quoted above, this is made abundantly clear; and although the sense of the third passage (*Cap.* I.217) is perhaps not so immediately obvious, yet it is certainly saying the same thing, as can be seen a little more easily if we follow rather more closely the original German text (*MEW* XXIII.231): 'Only the form in which this surplus labour is extracted from the immediate producer, the worker, distinguishes the economic forms of society, for example the society of slavery from that of wage labour.' What I think has been often overlooked is that what Marx is concentrating on as the really distinctive feature of each society is not the way in which the bulk of the labour of production is done, but how the extraction of the surplus from the immediate producer is secured. Now as a consequence of this we are justified in saying that the Greek and Roman world was a 'slave economy', in the sense that it was characterised by *unfree labour* (*direkte Zwangsarbeit*, 'direct compulsory labour', in Marx's phrase: see below), in which actual slavery ('chattel slavery') played a central role. Our justification will be that that was the main way in which the dominant propertied classes of the ancient world derived their surplus, whether or not the greater share in *total* production was due to unfree labour. In point of fact, until round about A.D. 300 the small, free, independent producers (mainly peasants, with artisans and traders) who worked at or near subsistence level and were neither slaves nor serfs (cf. III.iv below) must have formed an actual majority of the population in most parts of the Greek (and Roman) world at most times, and must have been responsible for a substantial proportion of its total production – the greater part of it, indeed, except in special cases, above all Italy in the last century B.C., when masses of cheap slaves were available (cf. IV.iii below), and conceivably at Athens and a few other Greek cities in the fifth and fourth centuries B.C., when also slaves were very cheap. (I shall deal with the position of the peasantry and the other free independent producers in Chapter IV.) We can speak of the ancient Greek world, then , as a 'slave economy' (in my broad sense), in spite of the fact that it was always, or almost always, a minority of the free population (virtually what

I am calling 'the propertied class': see III.ii below) which exploited unfree labour on any significant scale, and that the majority – often the great majority – of free Greeks (and Romans) were peasants utilising hardly more than their own labour and that of their families and therefore living not very much above subsistence level.

It was precisely of these peasants that Aristotle was thinking when he spoke of the lack of slaves (the *adoulia*) of the propertyless (the *aporoi*) and said that it was because of this lack of slaves that they had to 'use their wives and children in the role of assistants' (*hōsper akolouthois: Pol.* VI.8, 1323^{a}5-6). Elsewhere he says that for the poor (the *penētes* – a word commonly used to indicate a less extreme degree of poverty than *aporoi*) 'the ox serves in place of a slave' (*oiketēs*, I.2, 1252^{b}12). The unspoken assumption is that the men of property will own and use slaves.

Continuing the exposition of the theory I have sketched, I wish to make explicit another fact that is never stated clearly enough: that an individual or a class can obtain a surplus in only a limited number of ways, which can be summarised under three main headings:

1. The surplus can be extracted by the exploitation of wage labour, as in the modern capitalist world.
2. The exploitation can be of unfree labour, which may be of (a) chattel slaves, (b) serfs, or (c) debt bondsmen, or a combination of any two or all three of these.
3. A surplus can be obtained by the letting of land and house property to leasehold tenants, in return for some kind of rent, in money, kind or services.

I need do no more than mention the possibility that a class which controls a state machine may collectively extract a surplus, either by internal taxation and the imposition of compulsory state services (for transport, digging canals, repairing roads and the like), or by a policy of imperialism, exploiting some other country by conquest followed either by immediate plunder or by the levying of tribute.

Now before the age of complete automation, which has not even yet arrived, the individual members of a dominant class can hardly obtain a *substantial* surplus except by the employment of 'free' wage labour or some form of unfree labour (nos. 1 and 2 above), supplemented by the taxation and compulsory services which they may exact collectively. For obvious reasons, resorting to the third of my numbered alternatives and letting land to free tenants is not likely to yield the same rate of surplus, even if the small producers are subjected to high rents as well as political control: to ensure a really large surplus for a long period, the bulk of the primary producers must either be made to give unfree labour, under the constraint of slavery or serfdom or debt bondage, or they must be driven to sell their labour power for a wage. In antiquity, since free wage labour was normally unskilled and was not available in any great quantity (see III.vi below), there was no alternative but unfree labour; and it was this source from which the propertied classes of antiquity derived their surpluses. The ancient Greek (and Roman) world was indeed a 'slave-owning society' or 'slave economy' (in my sense); *Sklavenhaltergesellschaft, Sklavenhalterordnung* are the familiar German words.

Marx refers again and again to the world of the Greeks and Romans, in its full development, as a 'slave economy' or 'slave system' (see e.g. *Cap*. III.332, 384–5, 594, 595); and he can say that 'slavery or serfdom [*Leibeigenschaft*] form the broad foundation of social production in antiquity and during the Middle Ages' (*Cap*. III.831). Above all I would draw attention to what seems to me his most technically correct statement on this subject: 'Direct forced labour [*direkte Zwangsarbeit*] is the foundation of the ancient world' (*Grundrisse* 156=E.T. 245). Yet he also realised the important role played, especially in the early stages of the Greek and Roman world, by peasant producers. Thus he could say that 'the form of free self-managing peasant proprietorship of land parcels as the prevailing, normal form constitutes . . . the economic foundation of society during the best periods of Classical antiquity' (*Cap*. III.806, cf. 595), and that 'peasant agriculture on a small scale and the carrying on of independent handicrafts . . . form the economic foundation of the Classical communities at their best, . . . before slavery had seized on production in earnest' (*Cap*. I.334 n.3).

Anyone to whom the statements I have just made about the character of Classical civilisation as a slave–owning society seem surprising can easily set his mind at rest by looking at other slave–owning societies. It will be sufficient to give just one example: the American Old South. I am not pretending that the Old South was in any sense 'typical'; but comparison with it will serve to establish my main point, which is that we are perfectly entitled according to common parlance to speak of a society as a 'slaveowning' one even though its slaves constitute much less than half the population and slaveowners are quite a small minority. A leading American historian, Carl N. Degler, records that in the Old South in 1860 'slaves made up less than a third of the population of the region; fewer than a quarter of the Southern families owned a single slave, let alone a gang of them'. And 'in the antebellum South less than 3 per cent of the *slaveholders*, something like six-tenths of 1 per cent of all Southern families, owned fifty or more slaves'.

Nevertheless, Degler insists (as do all other historians) on treating the Old South as a slave society in the full sense; and he points out the usefulness of a comparison with the situation in Classical antiquity. In his article, he was giving a much-needed lesson in historical method to an American ancient historian, Chester G. Starr, who failed to realise what can be learnt from comparative studies of slavery and who greatly underestimated the contribution of slavery to Classical civilisation.[9] Starr was prepared to say that slavery was not 'basic' to the ancient economy, on the ground apparently that slaves did not make up a majority of the labour force or do most of the work – a situation which of course was equally true of the Old South. Degler rightly replied that 'the really significant question about the place of slavery in antiquity is not "Did slaves do most of the work?" but "What role did they play in the economic process?" '. For my own part, I find Degler's question, although on the right lines, cast in so general a form that it is hard to give a succinct answer to it. I would make it much more specific, and ask, 'What role was played by slaves – or rather (as I would prefer to put it) by *unfree labour* – in supplying the dominant propertied classes with their surplus?' The answer is clear: a fundamental and – in the conditions of the time – an irreplaceable one.

It may be useful if I make a few quotations at this point from one of the major works of recent years on North American slavery, which I mentioned in Section i

of this chapter: Kenneth Stampp's *The Peculiar Institution*. Using the official
Federal Census figures, he points out that

> The [Old] South was not simply – or even chiefly – a land of planters, slaves, and
> degraded 'poor whites'. Together these three groups constituted less than half of the
> total southern population. Most of the remaining Southerners (and the largest single
> group) were independent yeoman farmers of varying degrees of affluence. If there
> were such a thing as a 'typical' antebellum Southerner, he belonged to the class of
> landowning small farmers who tilled their own fields, usually without any help except
> from their wives and children . . . [I myself would be tempted to say much the same of
> 'the typical Greek'!] . . . In 1860, there were in the South 385,000 owners of slaves
> distributed among 1,516,000 free families. Nearly three-fourths of all free Southerners
> had no connection with slavery through either family ties or direct ownership. The
> 'typical' Southerner was not only a small farmer but also a nonslaveholder (*PI* 29-30).

Of the slaveholders,

> 72% held less than ten [slaves], and almost 50% held less than five (*PI* 30).

And yet,

> Whatever the reason, most of the nonslaveholders seemed to feel that their interest
> required them to defend the peculiar institution [slavery as it existed in the Old South]
> (*PI* 33).

★　★　★　★　★　★

I have already dealt briefly (in I.iv above) with Marx as a Classical scholar and
with some aspects of his outlook and method. He formulated a large part of the
main outlines of his whole system of ideas, including the concepts of class and
exploitation, between the years 1843 and 1847, although of course many details
and refinements and even some major features emerged only later. Virtually all
the essential ideas comprised in what has come to be known as 'historical
materialism' (see I.iv above) appear in some form in the works, published and
unpublished, which were written during those years, especially Marx's 'Introduction to a contribution to the critique [then unpublished] of Hegel's philosophy
of law' and *Economic and Philosophic Manuscripts* (both of 1844), the *German
Ideology* (a joint work of Marx and Engels, of 1845-6), and *The Poverty of
Philosophy*, written by Marx in French in 1847. Hegelian as his cast of mind was
from the first in some ways, Marx did not by any means develop his ideas in a
purely theoretical manner: he was already proceeding in a completely different
way from Hegel. Shortly before he even began his serious study of economics
he read a large quantity of historical material: the notebooks he compiled while
staying at his mother-in-law's house at Kreuznach in the summer of 1843 show
him studying not merely political theorists such as Machiavelli, Montesquieu
and Rousseau, but a considerable amount of history, mainly recent – that of
England, France, Germany, Sweden, Venice and the United States. Details of
the 'Kreuznacher Exzerpte' are published in *MEGA* I.i.2 (1929) 98, 118-36. It is
a great pity that the English *Collected Works* contain only one brief extract from
the Kreuznach notebooks, about half a page in length (*MECW* III.130), and give
no idea at all of the scope of the works excerpted by Marx. Yet, as David
McLellan has said, 'It was his reading of the history of the French Revolution in
the summer of 1843 that showed him the role of class struggle in social development' (*KMLT* 95). I am myself convinced that another seminal influence in the

development by Marx of a theory of class struggle was his reading during his student years of Aristotle's *Politics*, a work which shows some striking analogies to Marx in its analysis of Greek society (see Section iv of this chapter). During 1844 and early 1845 Marx also read and excerpted many works by leading classical economists: Adam Smith, David Ricardo, James Mill, J. R. McCulloch, J. B. Say, Destutt de Tracy and others (see *MEGA* I.iii.409-583). In the Preface to the *Economic and Philosophic Manuscripts* of 1844 Marx insisted that his results had been obtained 'by means of a wholly empirical analysis based on a conscientious critical study of political economy' (*MECW* III.231). And in the *German Ideology* of 1845-6, just after the well-known passage sketching the series of 'modes of production', Marx and Engels declare that 'Empirical observation must in each separate instance bring out empirically, and without any mystification and speculation, the connection of the social and political structure with production' (*MECW* V.35; cf. 36-7, 236 etc.).

Another important influence was at work on Marx from soon after his arrival in Paris in October 1843: the French working-class movement. 'You would have to attend one of the meetings of the French workers,' Marx wrote in a letter to Feuerbach on 11 August 1844, 'to appreciate the pure freshness, the nobility which burst forth from these toil-worn men' (*MECW* III.355). And in the *Economic and Philosophic Manuscripts* he uses the same language. 'The most splendid results are to be observed when French socialist workers [*ouvriers*] are seen together . . . The brotherhood of man is no mere phrase with them, but a fact of life, and the nobility of man shines upon us from their work-hardened bodies' (id. 313). Again, in *The Holy Family* (a joint work with Engels, dating from 1845) Marx wrote, 'One must know the studiousness, the craving for knowledge, the moral energy and the unceasing urge for development of the French and English workers to be able to form an idea of the *human* nobility of this movement' (*MECW* IV.84). Marx also attended meetings of some of the German immigrant workers in Paris, of whom there were many tens of thousands, and got to know their leaders (McLellan, *KMLT* 87). His second article for the *Deutsch-französische Jahrbücher*, namely the brilliant 'Introduction to a contribution to the critique of Hegel's philosophy of law' (*MECW* III.175-87), written soon after his arrival in Paris, contains, in its concluding pages, his first clear expression of the view that the emancipation of capitalist society can come about only through the proletariat. The concept of class struggle appears explicitly in this article (see esp. id. 185-6); and in the *Economic and Philosophic Manuscripts*, although the actual term 'class' is not often used (see, however, id. 266, 270 etc.), we find frequent references to antagonistic relationships which Marx speaks of in the article just mentioned and elsewhere in terms of class struggle – and, interestingly enough for the ancient historian, these antagonistic relationships are not limited to those between capitalist and worker but include also those between landlord and tenant, landowner and farm labourer. Marx can say that 'the rent of land is established as a result of the struggle between tenant and landlord. We find that the hostile antagonism of interests, the struggle, the war [*den feindlichen Gegensatz der Interessen, den Kampf, den Krieg*] is recognised throughout political economy as the basis of social organisation' (id. 260=*MEGA* I.iii.69). He goes on to compare the hostility of interest between the landowner and his farm worker with that between the industrialist and the factory worker;

and he shows that the relationship between landowner and farm worker can equally be 'reduced to the economic relationship of exploiter and exploited' (*MECW* III.263, 267).

To those who have not studied the development of Marx's thought in the 1840s I should like to recommend two recent works in particular. There is a good brief sketch of the emergence of Marx's ideas in the economic sphere in Ronald L. Meek, *Studies in the Labour Theory of Value* (2nd edition, 1973) 121-56 (esp. 129–46); cf. 157-200 for later developments. And Richard N. Hunt, *The Political Ideas of Marx and Engels, I. Marxism and Totalitarian Democracy 1818-1850* (Pittsburgh, 1974; London, 1975) gives a very sympathetic account of the growth of the political ideas of Marx and Engels in the 1840s (see esp. 26-131).

★   ★   ★   ★   ★   ★

I have found that some people disapprove of my using the expression 'class struggle' for situations in which there may be *no explicit common awareness of class* on either side, *no specifically political struggle* at all, and perhaps even *little consciousness of struggle* of any kind. I concede that the term 'class struggle' is not a very happy one when used in my sense for such situations, but I do not see how we can avoid using it in this way: the opening sentence of the *Communist Manifesto* and the whole type of thinking associated with it have made this inevitable. To adopt the very common conception of class struggle which refuses to regard it as such unless it includes *class consciousness* and *active political conflict* (as some Marxists do) is to water it down to the point where it virtually disappears in many situations. It is then possible to deny altogether the very existence of class struggle today in the United States of America or between employers and immigrant workers in northern Europe (contrast the end of this section), and between masters and slaves in antiquity, merely because in each case the exploited class concerned does not or did not have any 'class consciousness' or take any political action in common except on very rare occasions and to a very limited degree. But this, I would say, makes nonsense not merely of *The Communist Manifesto* but of the greater part of Marx's work. Bring back exploitation as the hallmark of class, and at once class struggle is in the forefront, as it should be. This, of course, is highly objectionable to those who have an interest (or believe themselves to have an interest) in preserving the capitalist system: they can no longer laugh off the class struggle as a figment of the Marxist imagination or at most a deplorable and adventitious phenomenon which would surely disappear of its own accord if only everyone would simply agree on its non-existence.

★   ★   ★   ★   ★   ★

I wish now to examine the position of some modern writers who have seriously misconceived Marx's conception of class in one way or another, and consequently have either rejected his approach altogether or, if they have believed themselves to be utilising it (at least in some degree), have misapplied it. In most cases their mistakes have been due largely to the assumption that class struggle 'must be' something of an essentially political nature. I discuss them here only in so far as they have failed to understand Marx or have misinterpreted his position. In so far as they advance rival theories of their own I shall deal with them in Section v of this chapter.

I begin with M. I. Finley's *The Ancient Economy* (1973), which has made a real contribution to our knowledge of ancient social history, in spite of its serious defects, which include a cavalier rejection of Marx's whole concept of class as an instrument of analysis, for reasons I would have to describe as frivolous did they not reveal a surprising lack of knowledge of some of Marx's basic concepts, and of the place of the slave, compared with the free wage-labourer, in Marx's economic analysis. In Section v of this chapter I shall discuss Finley's attempt to substitute for Marx's class analysis a scheme of social 'stratification' in terms of what he himself calls 'a spectrum of statuses and orders' (*AE* 67-8); here I shall concentrate on his reasons for rejecting a Marxist approach in general. His statement, 'Invariably, what are conventionally called "class struggles" in anti-quity prove to be conflicts between groups at different points in the spectrum [of statuses and orders] disputing the distribution of specific rights and privileges' (*AE* 68), shows clearly that in Finley's mind 'class struggles' are primarily if not solely political in character: they concern 'the distribution of specific rights and privileges'. On p.49 Finley first purports to describe 'the Marxist concept of class', in the words, 'Men are classed according to their relation to the means of production, first between those who do and those who do not own the means of production; second, among the former, between those who work themselves and those who live off the labour of others'. He then claims that on Marx's analysis 'the slave and the free wage labourer would then be members of the same class, *on a mechanical interpretation* [my italics], as would the richest senator and the non-working owner of a small pottery'; and he adds, 'That does not seem a very sensible way to analyse ancient society.'[10] Marx would surely have been shocked, as many of us are, by these suppositions. Even on the most 'mechanical interpretation' of what Marx called 'the relations of production' (a concept which is wider and more complex than mere 'ownership of the means of production'),[11] the free wage-labourer, who has his own labour-power to sell, obviously occupies a completely different position from the slave, who is the property of his master, a mere 'animate tool' (*empsychon organon*), as Aristotle calls him.[12] And the slave (with working animals and the land itself) is placed specifically by Marx among the 'instruments of labour' which form an impor-tant category of the 'means of production' and are therefore a part of 'fixed capital' and of Marx's 'constant capital', whereas the free wage-labourer (part of 'circulating capital') constitutes Marx's 'variable capital' – a profound difference in Marx's eyes. The subject is perhaps rather complicated at first sight: I have therefore dealt with it fully in Appendix I, with copious references to the various works of Marx in which these questions are dealt with.

There can be no possible doubt, then, that in Marx's mind wage labour and slave labour belong to completely different categories, whether in a predomi-nantly 'slave society' or in a capitalist society which also uses slave labour. Moreover, in Marx's scheme of things, the *nature* and the *quantity* of exploitation – *how*, and how *much*, one exploits or is exploited – are among the decisive elements in fixing a man's position in the whole system of property-relations. Finley's very rich senator, as the owner of a vast quantity of landed property and the exploiter of a large amount of slave labour and/or numerous tenants or *coloni*, would be in a totally different category from the owner of a small pottery – or even, for that matter, a small peasant freeholder, a creature whom Marx often distinguished sharply from the great landowner, for example in his writings on nineteenth-century France, and most usefully (for our present purposes) in the *Economic and Philosophic Manuscripts of 1844*, where he says, 'The small landed proprietor working on his own land stands to the big landowner in the same relation as an artisan possessing his own tool to the factory owner', and 'In general, the relationship of large and small landed property is like that of big and small capital' (*MECW* III.264). Engels, too, in one of his most penetrating works, *The Peasant Question in France and Germany*, draws a careful distinction between big and middle peasants who do exploit the labour of others, and small peasants who do not (see esp. *MESW* 624-6, 634-9, and in more detail IV.ii below). It matters hardly at all, of course, on a Marxist analysis, whether a man who exploits the labour of others, by owning or employing slaves or serfs or hired hands, actually works beside them himself or not: his class position depends upon whether he is able to exploit, and does exploit, the labour of others; and if he does this, then whether or not he works himself will be almost irrelevant, unless of course he needs to work because he is able to exploit the labour of others to only a small degree.

The next misinterpretation of Marx's concept of class which I intend to discuss is that of Dahrendorf, who is certainly less casual about the thought of Marx than Finley and has at least taken some care in reconstructing it, but who is misled by much the same assumption as Finley: that for Marx class struggle is something entirely political.

Dahrendorf's position is explained at length in his important book, *Class and Class Conflict in Industrial Society*, which appeared in 1959 in a revised and expanded version (by the author himself) of the German original, *Soziale Klassen und Klassenkonflikt in der industriellen Gesellschaft* (1957). The opening chapter of this book, entitled 'Karl Marx's model of the class society', seeks (on pp.9-18) to reconstruct 'the unwritten 52nd chapter of Volume III of Marx's *Capital*', which has the title 'Classes' but breaks off after scarcely more than a page (*Cap*. III. 885-6), when Marx had done little more than ask himself 'the first question to be answered' – namely, 'What constitutes a class?' – and answer that 'the reply to this follows naturally from the reply to another question, namely: What makes wage-labourers, capitalists and landlords constitute the three great social classes?'. After that Marx proceeds to rebut the answer that he thought might be given 'at first glance': namely, 'the identity of revenues and sources of revenue', which he proceeds to specify as 'wages, profit and ground-rent respectively'. A few lines later, when he is in the act of arguing against this answer, the manuscript breaks off. Dahrendorf makes an attempt, most praiseworthy in principle, to complete the chapter: he prints a large number of quotations from Marx (in italics), and supplies a roughly equal amount of material on his own initiative. Much of this undertaking is conducted fairly and quite shrewdly, with little serious distortion until disaster comes suddenly and irretrievably, with the statement (p.16),

> The formation of classes always means the organisation of common interests in the sphere of politics. The point needs to be emphasised. Classes are political groups united by a common interest. *The struggle between two classes is a political struggle.* We therefore speak of classes only in the realm of political conflict.

I reproduce the italics by which Dahrendorf indicates (see above) that he is quoting from Marx himself, in this case a passage from just before the end of *The Poverty of Philosophy*, written early in 1847 in French, as *La Misère de la philosophie*. But the passage appears in a different light when it is read in context and as what it is: the last sentence at the end of the following paragraph (from which, for some reason, Dahrendorf cites elsewhere in his book only the third sentence, *CCCIS* 14):

> Economic conditions had first transformed the mass of the people of the country into workers. The domination of capital has created for this mass a common situation, common interests. This mass is thus already a class as against capital, but not yet for itself, In the struggle . . . this mass becomes united, and constitutes itself as a class for itself. The interests it defends become class interests. But the struggle of class against class is a political struggle (*MECW* VI.211=*MEGA* I.vi.226).

The context is the early development of large-scale industry under capitalism. I will only remark here that it would be absurd to pretend that for Marx the mass of workers under early capitalism is 'not a class' at all: it is merely that until it becomes united and self-conscious it is 'not a class *for itself*' (*pour elle-même*: the phrase is usually quoted in German, as *für sich*). When, earlier in *The Poverty of Philosophy* (*MECW* VI.177), Marx speaks of the stage of class struggle at which 'the proletariat is not yet sufficiently developed to constitute itself as a class [he surely means 'a class for itself'!], . . . the very struggle of the proletariat with the bourgeoisie has not yet assumed a political character', it is clear that in his mind proletariat and bourgeoisie already existed as classes and even that there was a class *struggle* between them, although it had 'not yet assumed a political character'.

Before we can see this passage in the proper light, it needs to be placed beside another, a famous paragraph a few pages before the end of *The Eighteenth Brumaire of Louis Bonaparte* (1852), following soon after the statement 'Bonaparte represents a class, and the most numerous class of French society at that, the *small-holding* [*Parzellen*] *peasants*'. After an intervening paragraph Marx sets out to explain how these small peasants in one sense did, and in another did not, form a class (the italics are mine):

> The small-holding peasants form a vast mass, the members of which live in similar conditions but without entering into manifold relations with one another. Their mode of production isolates them from one another . . . The isolation is increased by France's bad means of communication and by the poverty of the peasants . . . Each individual peasant family is almost self-sufficient . . . A smallholding, a peasant and his family; alongside them another smallholding, another peasant and another family. A few score of these make up a village, and a few score of villages make up a Department. In this way, the great mass of the French nation is formed by simple addition of homologous magnitudes, much as potatoes in a sack form a sack of potatoes. *Insofar as* millions of families live under economic conditions of existence that separate their mode of life, their interests and their culture from those of the other classes, and put them in hostile opposition to the latter, *they form a class*. *Insofar as* there is merely a local interconnection among these small-holding peasants, and the identity of their interests begets no community, no national bond and no political organisation among them, *they do not form a class*. They are consequently incapable of enforcing their class interests in their own name, whether through a parliament or through a convention. They cannot represent themselves, they must be represented. Their representative must at the same time appear as their master, as an authority over them, as an unlimited governmental power that protects them against the other classes and sends them rain and sunshine from above. The political influence of the small-

holding peasants, therefore, finds its final expression in the executive power subordinating society to itself (*MECW* XI.187-8).

I have quoted nearly the whole of this long paragraph because it is relevant, as we shall see in V.i below, to the appearance of the early Greek 'tyrants'.

Let us take these two passages, from *The Poverty of Philosophy* and *The Eighteenth Brumaire*, together. It is perfectly clear that Marx considered both the workers under early capitalism and the small French peasants of the mid-nineteenth century to be a class: he gives that title again and again to both groups, not only in the two works from which I have just been quoting but elsewhere. In both passages, the apparent contradiction between the two parts of the statement can be resolved quite satisfactorily by taking the question at issue as one of definition. If we define a class according to one set of characteristics, Marx is saying, the workers under early capitalism or the French peasants of his day would fall within the definition; but if we substitute another set of characteristics in our definition, they would then fall outside it. The fact that a class *in the most complete sense* ('for itself', or whatever) could be expected to fulfil the second definition, and that Marx felt it would otherwise lack something of *the full set of attributes that a class is capable of attaining*, must not blind us to the fact that for Marx a class could perfectly well *exist as such* before it developed the second set of characteristics – indeed, he says as much in both our passages: the workers *are already 'a class* as against capital'; the French peasants, who live under particular conditions of existence that give them a special mode of life, interests and culture, different from those of other classes, to whom they are in hostile opposition, *do 'form a class'*. It would be perverse to deny this. Again, Marx could say in 1847 that 'the German bourgeoisie already finds itself in conflict with the proletariat even before being politically constituted as a class' (*MECW* VI.332).

Sometimes, when Marx is dealing with a specific situation, he will speak loosely of class and class struggle as if these terms applied mainly or even only to overt political conflicts. Towards the middle of the fifth chapter of *The Eighteenth Brumaire* he can even say that 'the bourgeoisie had done away with the class struggle for the moment by abolishing universal suffrage' (*MECW* XI.153; cf. Section ii above). A number of other such passages could be collected. In the Preface to the second German edition (1869) of *The Eighteenth Brumaire* Marx could altogether forget the antithesis formulated near the end of that work, which I quoted a moment ago, and actually say, 'In ancient Rome the class struggle took place *only* within a privileged minority, between the free rich and the free poor [he means rich and poor *citizens*], while the great productive mass of the population, the slaves, formed the purely passive pedestal for these conflicts.' And in a letter to Engels dated 8 March 1855 he gives a brief general characterisation of the internal history of the Roman Republic as 'the struggle of small with large landed property, specifically modified, of course, by slave conditions' (*MEW* XXVIII.439): once more, the class struggle takes place only within the citizen class, for only Roman citizens could own land within the boundaries of the Roman State. But these are isolated remarks which are of trivial importance compared with the main stream of Marx's thought – concentrated, as I have shown, in the passages from *Capital* I, II and III quoted towards the beginning of this section, and exemplified also in very many other contexts.

It is open to anyone, of course, to reject Marx's categories, provided he makes it clear that that is what he is doing, as indeed Finley and Dahrendorf have done.

I need say little more about Dahrendorf's treatment of Marx's theory of class. I would emphasise that – astonishingly enough – it is not just class *struggle* which Dahrendorf wishes to confine to the political plane: Marx's classes *exist* for him *only in so far as they conduct political struggle*, as the passage I have quoted above (from *CCCIS* 16) demonstrates: for him, Marx's classes '*are* political groups', and he will 'speak of classes *only* in the realm of political conflict'. Yet Dahrendorf himself quotes several texts from Marx which falsify this, in particular the very important one from *Capital* III (791-2) which I have set out at length above, and the statement that 'the German bourgeoisie stands in opposition to the proletariat *before* it has organised itself as a class *in the political sphere*' (my italics) – which Dahrendorf tries to weaken by prefacing it with the misleading gloss, 'In a sense, class interests precede the formation of classes'! (*CCCIS* 14).

Among many other passages which might be cited in support of the position I am taking here on Marx's view of class is his letter to Bolte of 23 November 1871, the relevance of which has been pointed out to me by Timothy O'Hagan. Near the end of this letter, under the heading 'N.B. as to political movement', Marx says that 'every movement in which the working class comes out as a *class* against the ruling classes', for example in order to agitate for a general *law* enforcing the eight-hour day, 'is a political movement', whereas 'the attempt in a particular factory or even in a particular trade to force a shorter working day out of individual capitalists by strikes, etc., is a purely economic movement'. And in his final paragraph Marx speaks of the necessity for training, 'where the working class is not yet far enough advanced in its organisation to undertake a decisive campaign against the collective power, i.e., the political power of the ruling classes' (*MESC* 328-9). This makes it perfectly clear that in Marx's eyes the working class exists as such at the economic level, and that sections of it can carry on activities at that level in furtherance of their interests, over against their employers, before it develops sufficient organisation to enable it to become active in the mass at the political level.

*   *   *   *   *   *

On the very first page of the Preface to his major work, *The Making of the English Working Class*, E. P. Thompson, a contemporary English Marxist historian who has made a notable contribution to nineteenth-century social history, declares that '*Class happens when* [my italics] some men, as a result of common experiences (inherited or shared), feel and articulate the identity of their interests as between themselves, and as against other men whose interests are different from (and usually opposed to) theirs. The class experience is largely determined by the productive relations into which men are born – or enter involuntarily.'[13] For Thompson, clearly, it is the second half of Marx's statement at the end of *The Eighteenth Brumaire* which alone is significant; the first half has simply disappeared. Another leading English Marxist historian, E. J. Hobsbawm, in an essay entitled 'Class consciousness in history',[14] begins by explicitly recognising that Marx's uses of the term 'class' divide into two main categories, in one of which classes are above all 'groups of exploiters and exploited'; but he mistakenly sees this usage as belonging to 'what we might call

Marx's macro-theory', and he thinks that 'for the purposes of the historian, i.e., the student of micro-history, or of history "as it happened" . . . as distinct from the general and rather abstract models of the historical transformation of societies', it is the other category which is relevant: one which takes account of class consciousness. For the historian, he believes, '*class and the problem of class consciousness are inseparable* . . . Class in the full sense only comes into existence at the historical moment when classes begin to acquire consciousness of themselves as such'. I accept the last sentence (giving the words 'in the full sense' the greatest possible weight), but not the words I have italicised, which would make it seldom possible for us to speak of 'class' in the ancient world at all, except in relation to certain ruling classes. When Hobsbawm speaks of 'the historian', in the passage I have quoted, he is really thinking only in terms of the historian of modern times: of him alone is his statement true, if at all. I realise that Marx himself *in certain exceptional passages* (see the quotations above from *The Eighteenth Brumaire* and its Preface, *The Poverty of Philosophy*, and the letter to Engels) gives evidence of adopting something very like Hobsbawm's position; but, as I have shown, such an attitude is not really consistent with the fundamentals of Marx's thought. I myself used to pay much more attention to these exceptional passages than I do now.

It is doubtless also under the influence of these passages that a number of writers in French in recent years, who are not entirely out of sympathy with what they believe to be Marx's concept of classes and class struggle, have taken up a position which is essentially very far removed from that of Marx. Thus J.-P. Vernant, in an article entitled 'Remarques sur la lutte de classe dans la Grèce ancienne', in *Eirene* 4 (1965) 5-19, which has recently been translated into English,[15] took over an unfortunate distinction established in a paper published two years earlier by Charles Parain[16] between a 'fundamental contradiction' and a 'principal or dominant contradiction' (pp.6,12), and spoke of the opposition between slaves and their masters as the 'fundamental contradiction' of Greek slaveowning society but not its 'principal contradiction' (pp.17-19): the latter he saw in a class struggle inside the citizen body only, between rich and poor (p.17, cf. 11). Whether Parain or Vernant would allow Greek slaves to count as a class at all in Marx's sense is not clear to me. Quite apart from any dissatisfaction I may feel with the use of the word 'contradiction' in this sense (its use is certainly less well established in English than in French: see the beginning of this section), I must say emphatically that the distinction between 'fundamental contradiction' and 'principal (or dominant) contradiction' is mere phrase-making and conveys no useful idea.

Pierre Vidal-Naquet, in an article called 'Les esclaves grecs étaient-ils une classe?', in *Raison présente* 6 (1968) 103-12, follows Vernant in the main but goes still further away from Marx, with whom he seems ill acquainted. While admitting that 'the opposition between masters and slaves is indeed the fundamental contradiction of the ancient world' (p.108), but denying (like Vernant) that it is legitimate to speak of Greek slaves as participating in class conflicts, he explicitly refuses to accept the slaves as a class at all (see esp. his p.105). But Vidal-Naquet, in seeking to show that there is authority in Marx himself for his own denial that Greek slaves formed a class, has made a most misleading selective quotation from the passage near the end of *The Eighteenth Brumaire* which I cited at length earlier, on whether the mid-nineteenth-century French peasantry formed a class. He cites only the second half of the antithesis, in which Marx declares that *in respect of certain characteristics* the French peasants did not form a class; he ignores the first half, in which Marx says that because of certain other characteristics they *did* form a class! And, as I said earlier, Marx repeatedly refers to those peasants as a class; and the few passages in which he speaks loosely of class and class struggle in particular situations as if these terms applied only to *overt political* conflicts are of minor importance compared with the main stream of his thought.

Austin and Vidal-Naquet, in the recent collection of ancient texts in translation (with an interesting Introduction) to which I made a brief reference in I.iv above, have given an account of class and class struggle in the Greek world during the Archaic and Classical periods which to me is unsatisfactory in the extreme (*ESHAG* 20 ff.). They entirely reject Marx's class *analysis*, at least as far as the ancient Greek world is concerned (it is not clear to me whether they would accept it for any other period of history); but they hardly make it clear whether this is because they dislike his *whole concept* of class or whether it is because they think that concept is merely *inapplicable to the particular situation* existing in the Greek world. At no point, unfortunately, do they give a definition of class as they themselves wish to conceive it: this makes it hard to examine their argument rigorously. Certainly they reject, at least for the ancient Greek world, those two of their 'three fundamental representations' of the notion of a social class which they themselves identify as the contributions of Marx: namely, position in 'the relations of production', and 'class consciousness: community of interests, development of a common vocabulary and programme, and the putting into practice of this programme in political and social action' (*ESHAG* 21, cf. 22, 23). They are very sure that slaves 'did not . . . constitute a class', and that we must 'reject completely the conception often expressed according to which the struggle between masters and slaves was the manifestation of class struggle in antiquity' (*ESHAG* 22, 23). Here of course they are flatly contradicting Marx, who certainly regarded slaves as a class, involved in class struggles. They have failed to grasp the fundamental position which Marx states so clearly in the passages I have quoted from *Capital* near the beginning of this section, and which he and Engels take for granted throughout their works, from the *German Ideology* and the *Communist Manifesto* onwards. At the beginning of the *Manifesto*, for instance, the very first example given of class struggles is that between 'free man and slave' – in Classical antiquity, clearly (*MECW* VI.482). And in the *German Ideology* (*MECW* V.33) Marx and Engels can speak of 'completely developed class relations between citizens and slaves' in the ancient city-state. (I will merely remark here, and explain presently, that Marx and Engels ought, according to their own principles, to have spoken in both cases of class relations between '*slaveowners* and slaves'.) Non-Marxist writers are of course perfectly entitled to reject Marx's concept of class and substitute another – although one may hope that they will then provide their own definition. Austin and Vidal-Naquet, following Aristotle, are at any rate willing to accept the existence of what they call class struggles in the Greek world, in the sense of 'antagonism . . . between the propertied and the non-propertied'; and they go on to say that 'the antagonism between the propertied minority and the non-propertied majority was fundamental in Greek class struggles', although 'class struggles could be expressed between citizens only' (*ESHAG* 23, 24). Here, if we modify their terminology to make it refer only to 'active political class struggles', they are on the right track; and in their selection of texts they provide some useful illustrations.

Occasionally one comes across the further argument that slaves should not be treated as a class at all, in the Marxist sense, because their condition could vary so greatly, from the mine slave, worked to death, perhaps, in a few months, or the drudge who spent almost every waking hour toiling in the fields or the house, to the great imperial slave of the Roman period who, like Musicus Scurranus or Rotundus Drusillianus (mentioned in III.iv below), could acquire considerable wealth even before the manumission he might confidently expect. This is patently fallacious. Of course slaves can be treated for many important purposes as a class, in spite of all the differences between them, just as one can legitimately speak of a 'propertied class', in my sense (see III.ii below), even though some members of it would be hundreds or even thousands of times as rich as others. Even among senators the range of wealth in the early Principate was from HS 1 million to something like 400 million; and if many city councillors (to be counted generally as members of my 'propertied class'; cf. VIII.ii below) owned little more than the HS 100,000 which was the minimum qualification for a decurion in some Roman towns, then the richest Romans would have had fortunes thousands of times as large (cf. Duncan-Jones, *EREQS* 343, with 147-8, 243). The 'propertied class' certainly needs to be spoken of as such when, for example, it is being set over against propertyless wage-labourers or slaves. Similarly, slaves can be considered on occasion as a single class in relation to slaveowners, who exploited them (and who virtually coincided with my 'propertied class'), or in contrast to wage-labourers, who were exploited by members of the propertied class in a very different way; but of course the slaves sometimes need to be subdivided, just like the propertied class, when we wish to take account of factors that distinguished important groups or sub-classes among them. As I said in Section ii of this chapter, a slave who was permitted by his master to possess slaves of his own, *vicarii*, was also *pro tanto* a member of the propertied class, although of course his foothold within that class was very precarious and dependent upon his master's goodwill.

Now it may be that some people today will feel that to restrict Marx's notion of class struggle (as he occasionally did himself) to circumstances in which an *overt struggle on the political plane* can be shown to exist (as it cannot between masters and slaves in Classical antiquity) makes better sense and should be generally adopted. I am now[17] far from sharing this view. To me, the essence of the relationship of classes, in a class society founded on the existence of private property in the means of production, is the economic exploitation which is the very *raison d'être* of the whole class system; and, as I have insisted all along, Marx himself normally takes this for granted. If we adopt the view I am combating, we are obliged to take the expression 'the class struggle' in the very limited sense of '*effective and open* class struggle *on the political plane*, involving actual *class consciousness* on both sides'. Certainly, the slaves of the Greeks had no means of political expression: they were ethnically very heterogeneous, and they could often not even communicate with each other except in their master's language; they could not hope to carry on an *open political* struggle against their masters, therefore, except on very rare occasions when, as in Sicily in the late second century B.C., the circumstances happened to favour mass uprisings (see III.iv below and its nn.8, 15). But if the division into economic classes is in its very nature the expression of the way in which above all exploitation is effected – by which, that is to say, the propertied classes live off the non-propertied – then there is to that extent an unceasing struggle between exploited and exploiting classes, and in antiquity between masters and slaves *above all*, even if only the masters could carry it on effectively: they would always be united, and be prepared to act, as Xenophon says in the *Hiero* (IV.3), 'as unpaid bodyguards of each other against their slaves' (cf. Plato, *Rep.* IX.578d-9a, quoted in III.iv below). And in my picture the masters conduct a permanent struggle, if some-times an almost effortless one, in the very act of holding down their slaves. But in a sense even slaves who are kept in irons and driven with a whip can conduct some kind of passive resistance, if only by quiet sabotage and breaking a tool or two.[18] I also regard as an important form of class struggle the propaganda, whether sincere or tongue-in-cheek, which masters (or any exploiting class) may use to persuade slaves (or any exploited class) to accept their position without protest, even perhaps as being 'in their own best interests': the doctrine of 'natural slavery' is only the most extreme example of this (see VII.ii-iii below). There is even evidence of counter-propaganda by the slaves, replying to their masters. But the class struggle in the Greek world on the ideological plane is a particularly fascinating subject which I must reserve for extended treatment in VII below.

I wish now to draw attention to a minor methodological and conceptual error which sometimes occurs in the writings of Marx and Engels, in particular in two early works: *The Communist Manifesto*, of 1847-8, and the *German Ideology*,[19] written in 1845-6 but then (as Marx put it in 1859, in the short *Preface to a Contribution to the Critique of Political Economy*) 'abandoned to the gnawing criticism of the mice', as something through which he and Engels had achieved their 'main purpose: self-clarification' (*MESW* 183). The error in question may sound quite trivial and is certainly a mere slip; but if it is not noticed and corrected it may have serious methodological consequences. In both works Marx and Engels, speaking at the beginning of *The Communist Manifesto* of class struggle (*MECW* VI.482), and in the *German Ideology* (*MECW* V.432) of the 'opposition' (*Gegensatz*) within which society has hitherto always developed, mention among their pairs of contestants 'free man and slave', 'free men and slaves';[20] and in the *German Ideology*, as I have already stated, there is also mention of 'completely developed class relations' in the ancient city-state 'between citizens and slaves' (*MECW* V.33). In each case they should of course have spoken of '*slaveowners* and slaves'.[21] The contrast between slave and free, or slave and citizen, is of the highest importance *as a distinction of status or 'order'* (cf. Section v of this chapter), but it is not the right contrast to draw when one is thinking (as Marx and Engels were here) in terms of *economic class*: in that sense the correct opposition is between slave and *slaveowner*, for large numbers of free men in antiquity owned no slaves. There is no harm, of course, in speaking of class conflicts between 'the propertied class' and the slaves, because all Greeks or Romans who owned any substantial amount of property would own slaves.

* * * * * *

In support of taking class as above all the collective social expression of the fact of exploitation, rather than (at the opposite extreme) self-conscious and united political activity, I wish to adduce a contemporary phenomenon of very great interest: the large class of temporary migrant (or immigrant) workers who come to the countries of north-west Europe from, mainly, the lands bordering on the Mediterranean, and whose number in the years from about 1957 to 1972 was of the order of 9 million, a figure which by now has been greatly exceeded. This extraordinary movement, which has been described as 'colonisation in reverse', has recently been the subject of a detailed and excellent study, *Immigrant Workers and Class Structure in Western Europe* (1973),[22] by Stephen Castles and Godula Kosack, who point out (p.409) that it 'involves the transfer of a valuable economic resource – human labour – from the poor to the rich countries'. Immigrant workers normally occupy the lowest posts in the hierarchy of labour, which indigenous workers prefer to avoid and often can hardly be induced to undertake at all, and which carry the lowest rates of pay. Most of these migrants have no political rights and do not belong to trades unions, and they are normally unable to take any action in defence of their position. Even though industrial action may occasionally be open to them in principle, there is hardly any chance that they will indulge in it and thus place their whole position in jeopardy and risk arousing the unreasoning hostility of the natives (see Castles and Kosack, op. cit. 152 ff., 478–80). Immigrants are therefore more exposed to ruthless exploitation than the native workers, and they are often subjected to a degree of 'discipline' which the indigenous worker would not tolerate. This can have not merely economic but also social and political effects, extending far outside the circle of the immigrants themselves. As Castles and Kosack put it, 'Immigration helps to give large sections of the indigenous working class the consciousness of a "labour aristocracy" which supports or acquiesces in the exploitation of another section of the working class. In this way immigration helps to stabilise the capitalist order, not only economically, but also politically' (op. cit. 481, cf. 426–7) – a fact which has of course been noted with great approval by members of the ruling class in host countries. A similar movement of temporary immigrant workers into South Africa from the much poorer countries on or near her borders has also been taking place for some time, and this too has made the white South African working class into a 'labour aristocracy', organised in trades unions from which the black immigrants are rigorously excluded.[23]

We see here, then, another illustration of the principle we observed earlier: although the immigrant worker (like the ancient slave) is, almost by definition, precluded from playing any sort of political role, and in practice has little or no chance of taking even industrial action in his own defence, *the very existence* of a class of immigrant workers has important consequences not only in the economic sphere but also socially and politically. A definition of 'class struggle' in purely political terms, which can take account neither of the Greek slave nor of the immigrant worker, is therefore not even adequate on the political level, even though the immigrant or the slave himself cannot operate directly at that level. The only definition that does make sense, here as elsewhere, is one that proceeds from the *fact of exploitation*, and takes account of its nature and intensity.

This brings out a question of principle on which I feel obliged to register a

˙small disagreement with Castles and Kosack. In their opinion:

> Immigrant workers cannot be regarded as a distinct class . . . All workers, whether
> immigrant or indigenous, manual or non-manual, possess the basic characteristics of a
> proletariat: they do not own or control the means of production, they work under the
> directions of others and in the interests of others, and they have no control over the
> product of their work . . . Immigrant workers and indigenous workers together form
> the working class in contemporary Western Europe, but it is a divided class . . . We
> may therefore speak of two strata within the working class [with the indigenous
> workers forming the upper and the immigrants the lower stratum] (op. cit. 461-82,
> at 476-7).

The choice *in this particular case* between, on the one hand, two classes, and on
the other, a single 'divided class' or one possessing a 'higher stratum' and a
'lower stratum', is not in itself very important. There is a significant sense in
which immigrant workers and indigenous workers do form a single 'working
class'. However, the principle adopted by Castles and Kosack of disregarding,
as criteria of class, everything except relationship to the means of production is
too rigid. It would certainly involve our treating the slaves of the Greek world,
absurdly, as belonging to the same class as free hired workers and even many
poor free artisans and landless peasants.[24] Yet, as I have shown above, Marx and
Engels certainly wrote of slaves in antiquity as a class, even if on occasion they
could contrast them, unsuitably, with 'free men' rather than 'slaveowners' (see
above). Although I generally treat ancient slaves as a separate class, I realise that
for some purposes they may have to be considered as very close to hired labourers
and other poor free workers and as forming with them a single class (or group of
classes) of 'the exploited'. In my definition of class (in Section ii of this chapter) I
recognise that legal (constitutional) position, *Rechtsstellung*, is 'one of the factors
that may help to determine class', because it is likely to affect the type and
intensity of exploitation involved. The modern immigrant worker is not subject
to anything like such extreme constraints as the ancient slave, and whether we
should regard him as belonging to a different class from the indigenous worker
depends on the nature and purpose of the investigation we are conducting. Marx
certainly regarded Irish immigrants as 'a very important section of the working
class in England' in his day: see his letter to L. Kugelmann of 29 November 1869
(*MESC* 276-8, at 277), and compare his letter to S. Meyer and A. Vogt of 9 April
1870 (*MESC* 284-8), quoted by Castles and Kosack, op. cit. 461.

★　★　★　★　★　★

Anyone who finds the term 'class *struggle*' objectionable when used in the
sometimes quite unpolitical sense which for me is primary can try to find an
alternative. All I ask is that the situation I have depicted in my definition of class
– that is to say (to put it crudely), *exploitation by the propertied class of the
non-propertied* – be accepted both as the most fruitful way of employing the
expression 'class', at any rate in relation to the ancient world, and as the primary
way in which Marx and Engels conceived class when they were not thinking
mainly of the confrontation between the classes of mid-nineteenth-century
capitalist society. That society had characteristics very different from those of
the ancient world, above all in the fact that the lowest class, the proletariat, was
already beginning to acquire in some of the advanced countries (notably England)

a sense of unity and class interest which virtually never existed at all among the slaves of antiquity.

In short, I am fully prepared to be criticised for what some may think a clumsy and even potentially misleading use of the term 'class *struggle*', provided it is always recognised that class *is* a relationship involving above all things exploitation, and that in every class society it is indeed class – and not social status or political position or membership of an 'order' – which is *in the long run* the fundamental element.

(iv)
Aristotle's sociology of Greek politics

I am very far from being one of those historians who, by instinct or of set purpose, insist upon defining the society they are studying in the terms adopted by its own dominant class – as when Roland Mousnier, in a remarkably compact and well-written little book, *Les hiérarchies sociales de 1450 à nos jours* (Paris, 1969), wishes to see pre-revolutonary France as a 'société d'ordres', divided not into classes (these he will admit only in the capitalist era) but into 'orders' or 'estates', grades in society based not upon any role in the productive process but ultimately upon social function, and instituted in legally recognised categories. However, it happens that I am fortunate in being able to find in Greek thought an analysis of the society of the Greek *polis* which is quite remarkably like the one I would wish to apply in any event.

It is natural to begin with Aristotle, who was in a class by himself among the political theorists and sociologists of antiquity: he studied the politics and sociology of the Greek city more closely than anyone else; he thought more profoundly about these subjects and he wrote more about them than anyone. There could be no greater mistake than to suppose that because Aristotle was primarily a philosopher he was, like most modern philosophers, either incapable of, or uninterested in, extensive and accurate empirical investigation. Not only was he one of the greatest natural scientists of all time, especially in zoology (a field in which he had no rival in antiquity); he was also a social and political scientist of the very first rank. In addition to that masterpiece, the *Politics*,[1] he is also credited with having produced – doubtless with the aid of pupils – no less than 158 *Politeiai*, monographs on city constitutions, and several other works in the field of politics, sociology and history (see my AHP),[2] including a list of victors in the Pythian Games, compiled in collaboration with his young relative Callisthenes, for which they must have done research in the archives at Delphi. This is the earliest known archival research which is certain, although there is a late tradition that Hippias the 'sophist', of Elis, compiled an Olympic victor list (about 400 B.C.), which is generally accepted (as by Jacoby) but seems to me unreliable in the extreme: our only authority for its existence is a statement by Plutarch (*Numa* 1.6), more disparaging than most people realise, mentioning an *Olympionikōn anagraphē* 'which *they say* Hippias published late, having no source that obliges us to trust it'.[3] No fragments survive. The partially preserved Delphic inscription of the 320s B.C. which records the completion of the Pythian victor list by Aristotle and Callisthenes is a sufficient refutation of the view that Aristotle, as a philosopher, could not have been greatly concerned about brute facts in the sphere of the social sciences and would be likely to distort or invent them to suit his preconceived philosophical views. (The inscription from Delphi is Tod, *SGHI* II.187=*SIG*³ 275; cf. my AHP 57 n.44.) There is good reason to think that Aristotle was at least the part-author of the works with which he was credited in antiquity in the field of what we call history, sociology, law and politics, and that he planned, and worked upon during his lifetime with his pupil Theophrastus, a vast treatise on *Laws* (the *Nomoi*), which was eventually published by Theophrastus in no fewer than 24 Books (roughly three times the size of the *Politics*), and of which a few fragments survive.⁴ Aristotle's competence as an authority on the political life of the *polis* cannot be doubted: in this field, as I have indicated, he towers above everyone else in antiquity. He receives unqualified and justified eulogy from Marx, as 'a giant thinker', 'the greatest thinker of antiquity', 'the acme of ancient philosophy' (see I.iv above).

My concentration on Aristotle as the great figure in ancient social and political thought and my relative neglect of Plato will surprise only those who know little or nothing of the source material for fourth-century Greek history and have acquired such knowledge as they possess from modern books – nearly always very deferential to Plato. Aristotle, in the *Politics*, usually keeps very close to actual historical processes, whereas Plato throughout his works is largely unconcerned with historical reality, with 'what happened in history', except for certain matters which happened to catch his attention, inward-looking as it generally was. Certainly he had one or two powerful insights: in a recent article, Fuks (PSQ) has drawn attention to his obsessive conviction – justified, as I think – that the tense political atmosphere and acute civil strife of his day were the direct consequence of increasing contrasts between wealth and poverty. In particular Plato realised that an oligarchy – in the sense of a constitution resting on a property qualification, in which the wealthy rule and the poor are excluded from government (*Rep.* VIII.550cd) – will actually be two cities, one of the poor and the other of the rich, 'always plotting against each other' (551d): it will be characterised by extremes of wealth and poverty (552b), with nearly all those outside the ruling circle becoming paupers (*ptōchoi*, 552d). We may recall the picture of England in 1845 drawn by Benjamin Disraeli in his novel significantly entitled *Sybil, or The Two Nations*. Plato therefore gave much attention to the problems of property and its ownership and use; but his solutions were ill-conceived and misdirected. Above all, in the vitally important field of production he had nothing of the slightest value to suggest: in the *Republic* in particular he concentrated on consumption, and his so-called 'communism' was confined to his small ruling class of 'Guardians' (see Fuks, PSQ, esp. 76-7). But he was not willing, as Aristotle was, to study carefully a whole series of concrete situations, which might have upset some of his preconceived notions. He preferred to develop, as a philosopher, what his numerous admirers often call 'the logic of the ideas' – a 'logic' which, if it starts out from a faulty empirical base, as it often does, is only the more certain to reach faulty conclusions, the more rigorous it is. To take just one prominent example – Plato's account of democracy and 'the democratic man' in *Republic* VIII.555b-569c is a grotesque caricature of at any rate the one fourth-century democracy we know most about: that of Athens, which in Plato's day bore little resemblance to his unpleasant portrait of democracy, and moreover was particularly stable and showed nothing of the tendency to transform itself into tyranny which Plato represents as a typical feature of democracy (562a ff.). Yet Plato's fancy picture of the transformation of democracy into tyranny has often been treated as if it were a revelation of the innate characteristics of democracy – as of course it was intended to be. Cicero, giving in *De republica* I.65 (*fin.*) to 68 almost a para-phrased summary of Plato, *Rep.* 562a-4a, evidently regarded Plato's account as a description of what is likely to happen in actual practice. Yet Cicero, in the same work, can make one of his characters, Laelius, describe Plato's imaginary ideal state as 'remarkable indeed, no doubt, but irreconcilable with human life and customs' (*praeclaram quidem fortasse, sed a vita hominum abhorrentem et a moribus*, II.21). Aristotle's criticisms of the *Republic* (in *Pol.* II.1, 1261^{a}4 ff.) are far from showing him at his best, but at least he did grasp one vital fact: that even Plato's ruling 'Guardian' class (*phylakes*) could not be happy. 'And if the Guardians are not happy, who else can be?', he asks. 'Certainly not the *technitai* and the mass of the *banausoi*' (*Pol.* II.5, 1264^{b}15-24). As for the city pictured in Plato's *Laws*, described as his 'second-best State' (*Laws* V.739b-e; VII.807b), it is both so grimly repressive and so unworkable that even Plato's admirers usually prefer to let it drop out of sight.[4a]

The wildly exaggerated respect which has been paid down the ages to Plato's political thought is partly due to his remarkable *literary* genius and to the anti-democratic instincts of the majority of scholars. Plato was anti-democratic in the highest degree. It would not be fair to call him typically 'oligarchic' *in the usual Greek sense*, as I shall define it later in this section: he did not want the rich *as such* to rule. (Plato of course knew well that the standard form of Greek oligarchy was the rule of a propertied class: see e.g. *Rep.* VIII.550cd, 551ab,d, 553a; *Polit.* 301a.) But both Plato's 'best' and his 'second-best' States were iron-bound oligarchies, designed to prevent change or development of any kind, and permanently excluding from political rights every single one of those who actually worked for their living. Plato's arrogant contempt for all manual workers is nicely displayed in the passage from the *Republic* (VI.495c-6a) about the 'bald-headed little tinker', which I have given in VII.i below.

* * * * * *

Like so many other Greeks, Aristotle regarded a man's economic position as the decisive factor in influencing his behaviour in politics, as in other fields. He never feels the need to argue in favour of this position, which he could simply take for granted, because it was already universally accepted. For him even *eugeneia*, noble birth, involved inherited wealth as an essential element (see my *OPW* 373).[5] At times he employs what some modern sociologists (for instance Ossowski, *CSSC* 39-40 etc.) have called a 'trichotomous' scheme of division, into rich, poor and men of moderate wealth, *hoi mesoi*, an expression which it is better not to translate 'middle class' (the usual rendering), if only because of the peculiar modern connotation of that term. In an important passage in the *Politics* (IV.11, 1295^{b}1-96^{b}2) he begins by saying that in every *polis* – he is speaking only of the *citizen* population – there are three parts (*merē*): the rich (*euporoi*), the poor (*aporoi*, who need not be completely propertyless: see III.8, 1279^{b}19), and the *mesoi*; and he goes on to say that neither of the two extreme classes is willing to listen to reason and persuasion; they feel either contempt or envy for each other; they are likely either to be plotted against because of their great possessions or to covet the possessions of others and plot against them; they are either too unwilling to obey or too abject and mean-spirited to know how to command; and the result is a city consisting not of free men but as it were of masters and slaves, in which there occur civil dissensions and armed conflicts (*staseis . . . kai machai*) between rich and poor, and either the few rich set up a pure oligarchy (an *oligarchia akratos*) or the many poor set up an extreme democracy (a *dēmos eschatos*). The *mesoi*, he thinks, suffer from none of the disadvantages mentioned; and the greater the proportion of *mesoi*, the better governed the city is likely to be. (Did Aristotle perhaps have Athens particularly in mind here? It surely had more *mesoi* than most Greek states.) Shortly afterwards Aristotle returns to the same theme, insisting that it is the arbitrator (*diaitētēs*) who inspires the greatest confidence everywhere, and that the *mesos* is an arbitrator between the other two groups, who are again designated as rich and poor: neither of these two groups, he says, will ever willingly endure political subjection (*douleuein*) to the other, and they would not even consent to 'rule turn and turn about' (*en merei archein*), so deep is their distrust of one another (IV.12, 1296^{b}34–97^{a}7).

On the other hand, Aristotle also (and more often) resorts to a simpler 'dichotomic' model – which, by the way, is regularly adopted by Plato.[6] In Aristotle's dichotomy (as in Plato's and everyone else's) the citizens are divided into rich and poor, or into the propertied class (*hoi tas ousias echontes*) and those who have no property, or virtually none (*hoi aporoi*). Even in the passage from *Politics* IV which I summarised above Aristotle admits that the number of *mesoi* in most cities is small, and he regards outright oligarchy or democracy as only too likely to occur.[7] In general, it would be true to say that in Aristotle, as in other Greek writers (especially the historians), the nearer a political situation comes to a crisis, the more likely we are to be presented with just two sides: whatever the terminology used (and the Greek political vocabulary was exceptionally rich)[8] we shall usually be justified in translating whatever expressions we find by 'the upper classes' and 'the lower classes', meaning essentially the propertied and the non-propertied.

One could cite quite a large number of passages in which Aristotle takes it for granted – quite correctly – that the propertied class would set themselves up as an oligarchy whenever they were able to do so, whereas the poor would institute democracy (see my *OPW* 35, with the notes). Technically, of course, oligarchy (*oligarchia*) should be the rule of the Few (the *oligoi*), democracy the rule of the Demos, a term which sometimes means the whole people, sometimes specifically the lower classes, the poor (see my *OPW* 35 ff., esp 41-2). But in one remarkable passage (*Pol.* III.8, 1279^{b}16 ff., esp. 1279^{b}34–80^{a}3) Aristotle brushes aside the mere difference of number, which he says is purely accidental and due to the fact that the rich happen to be few and the poor many: he insists that the real ground of the difference between democracy and oligarchy is poverty and wealth (*penia kai ploutos*), and he goes on to explain that he would continue to speak in terms of 'oligarchy' and 'democracy' in the same way even if the rich were many and the poor few! (Cf. IV.4, 1290^{a}40–^{b}3, 17-20.)[9] When the propertied class can rule, they do, and that is oligarchy. Democracy is government by the majority, and the majority are in fact poor: democracy is therefore government by the poor, and the poor could be expected to desire democracy. (All this illustrates Aristotle's firm belief, to which I have already drawn attention, that a man's political behaviour will normally depend upon his economic position.)

Aristotle also takes it for granted – as did Greek thinkers generally, including Plato – that the class which achieves power, whether it be the rich or the poor, will rule with a view to its own advantage (cf. *Pol.* III.7, 1279^{b}6-10). He remarks that those who have a greater share of wealth than others tend to conceive themselves as absolutely superior (V.1, 1301^{a}31-3); and he regards it as a foregone conclusion that those who have very great possessions will think it actually unjust (*ou dikaion*) for men having no property to be put in a position of political equality with property-owners (V.12, 1316^{b}1-3).[10] Indeed, he says, men of oligarchical inclinations define justice itself in terms of 'what is decided by [those possessing] a preponderant amount of property' (VI.3, 1318^{a}18-20). So completely did Aristotle see oligarchy and democracy as rule by the rich (over the poor) and rule by the poor (over the rich) respectively that in one striking passage he remarks that neither oligarchy nor democracy could continue without the existence of both rich and poor, and that if equality of property (*homalotēs tēs ousias*) were introduced the constitution would have to be something different from either (V.9, 1309^{b}38-10^{a}2). It is just after this, incidentally, that he records the interesting fact that 'in some States' (he is apparently referring to oligarchies) of his day the oligarchically-minded (*hoi oligarchikoi*) 'take the oath, "I will bear ill-will towards the common people [the *dēmos*], and I will plan against them all the evil I can"' (1310^{a}8-12). Needless to say, Aristotle did not approve of such behaviour. Elsewhere in the *Politics* he remarks, 'Even when the poor have no access to honours they are willing to remain quiet provided no one treats them arrogantly or robs them of their property' (IV.13, 1297^{b}6-8; cf. V.8, 1308^{b}34-9^{a}9; VI.4, 1318^{b}11-24). But he goes on at once to qualify this: 'It does not come about easily, however, for those who have political power are not always gracious' (1297^{b}8-10; cf. 1308^{a}3 ff., esp. 9-10). He realised that if the poor are to be kept contented, magistrates, especially in oligarchies, must not be allowed to profit unduly from office (V.8 and VI.4, quoted above). Yet he could also admit that *all* constitutions which he was prepared to describe as 'aristocratic' are so oligarchical that the leading men are unduly oppressive (*mallon pleonektousin hoi gnōrimoi*: V.7, 1307^{a}34-5).

The categories employed by Aristotle were already very well established. Earlier in the fourth century Plato, Xenophon, the Oxyrhynchus historian and others had taken them for granted, and in the fifth century we find them not only in Thucydides, Herodotus and others (notably the writer of the Pseudo-Xenophontic *Athēnaiōn Politeia*, often referred to as 'the Old Oligarch'),[11] but even in poetry. I am thinking in particular of the passage in the *Supplices* of Euripides (lines 238-45; cf. my *OPW* 356 and n.1), where Theseus is made to say that there are three kinds of citizen: the greedy and useless rich (the *olbioi*); the covetous poor, easily led astray by scurvy demagogues (*ponēroi prostatai*); and 'those in the middle' (*hoi en mesōi*), who can be the salvation of the city – Aristotle's *mesoi*, of course. Here, as in Aristotle and elsewhere, these people are quite clearly men of moderate *opinions* or *behaviour*, although both Euripides and Aristotle evidently expected that moderate opinions and behaviour would be the natural consequence of the possession of a moderate amount of property – a delightfully realistic view, which may however seem distressingly Marxist to those who today speak of 'moderates' when they mean right-wingers. (I shall not go back behind the fifth century in this brief review of Greek political terminology: I propose to say something about the seventh and sixth centuries later, in V.i below.)

It is a fact of the utmost significance that the earliest known example – and the only certain example before Alexander the Great – of divine cult being paid to a living man by a Greek city was the direct result of bitter class struggle on the political plane. The cult in question was instituted in honour of the Spartan commander Lysander by the narrow oligarchy (it is referred to as a 'decarchy', or rule of ten men) which he had installed in power at Samos in 404 B.C., after destroying the Samian democracy and 'liberating' the island from its alliance with Athens, to which the democracy had clung firmly even after the defeat of Athens in the Peloponnesian war had become certain, with Lysander's victory over the Athenian fleet at Aegospotami in the autumn of 405. (The existence of the cult of Lysander at Samos, sometimes doubted, has become certain since the discovery of an inscription referring to the festival of the Lysandreia: see my *OPW* 64 and n.5.)

I have just been showing that Aristotle's analysis of political activity in the Greek city started from the empirically demonstrable premise, which he shared not only with other Greek thinkers but also with Marx, that the main determining factor in the political behaviour of most individuals is economic class – as of course it still is today.[12] (Naturally Aristotle realised, as Marx did, that there will be exceptions to this rule, but he knew that they were not numerous enough to deprive it of its value as a generalisation.) I shall presently show that Aristotle also, in an even more interesting way, took the same fundamental approach as Marx towards the analysis of a citizen body; but before I do this I should like to demonstrate the value of the kind of analysis I have just been giving of Greek political and sociological thinking (utilising the same basic categories as Aristotle – and Marx) by showing how well it explains the origin of the so-called 'theory of the mixed constitution'. This theory played an important part in Greek (and Roman) political thought: the 'mixed constitution', in the writings of Polybius, Cicero and others, became a kind of Weberian 'ideal type';[13] but by then the theory had developed into something rather different from what it had been in its initial phase, in the late fifth century and the fourth. By far the earliest surviving expression of the notion that the mixed constitution is a desirable one is in a much-discussed passage in Thucydides (VIII.97.2), praising the so-called 'constitution of the Five Thousand' at Athens in 411-410 B.C. as just such a mixture.[14] The mixed constitution was evidently admired by Plato,[15] but the best theoretical justification of it is to be found in Book IV of Aristotle's *Politics*.[16]

In a striking passage earlier in his great work, Aristotle recognises that if the lower classes (the *dēmos*) are totally deprived of political rights and are not even allowed to have the necessary minimum power of electing the magistrates and calling them to account, they will be in the position of 'a slave and an enemy' (II.12, 1274^{a}15-18; cf. III.11, 1281^{b}28-30). Indeed, in a particularly realistic chapter (no.11) in Book III Aristotle accepts perhaps more explicitly than anywhere else in his surviving works the distinguishing characteristic of Greek democracy: the necessity for *the whole citizen body* to be sovereign in the deliberative, legislative and judicial spheres (1282ᵃ29 ff., esp. 34–ᵇ1), including of course the two activities already mentioned to which Aristotle again attaches the greatest importance, namely electing the magistrates and calling them to account (*hairesis* and *euthyna*, 1282ᵃ26-7). The reasoning that lies behind this conclusion is based on the recognition that while each individual may be a worse judge than the experts (*hoi eidotes*, 'those who know'), the judgment of all collectively is better, or anyway no worse (1282ᵃ16-17; cf. III.15, 1286ᵃ26-35, esp. 30-3). However, Aristotle also felt instinctively that if the poor are all allowed to vote in the Assembly they will be able to swamp it and outvote the propertied class; and indeed – blandly ignoring what actually did happen at Athens, where property rights were very carefully preserved – he says that if the majority are allowed to do exactly as they like, they will confiscate the property of the rich (*Pol.* VI.3, 1318ᵃ24-6; cf. III.10, 1281ᵃ14-19). Democracy, in Aristotle's view, can only too easily become (if I may be forgiven a momentary lapse into highly anachronistic and inappropriate terminology) the dictatorship of the proletariat! So it is necessary to give the propertied class extra weight, so to speak, in such a way as to make up for their built-in numerical inferiority and bring them to something like a balance with the non-propertied. Aristotle has various suggestions as to how this might be done: for example, you might decide to fine the rich for non-attendance in the courts at the same time as you pay a certain number of the poor for attending (*Pol.* IV.9, 1294ᵃ37-41; 13, 1297ᵃ36-40; cf. 14, 1298ᵇ23-6).

This reveals clearly the climate of thought which originally produced the theory of the mixed constitution: you start by assuming, as Aristotle always does, that the propertied and the non-propertied are naturally opposed classes whose interests are very hard to reconcile, and you then manipulate the constitution in such a way as to compensate for the numerical inferiority of the upper class and produce a balance between rich and poor, which can be expected to have the important virtue of stability, and which you can hold out as a judicious mixture of oligarchy (or aristocracy) and democracy – with kingship thrown in for good measure if you happen to have important magistrates like the kings of Sparta or the Roman consuls. After Aristotle the theory of the mixed constitution changed its character: as it became more and more unnecessary to take serious account of democracy (in the full sense) as a possible political form, so interest in the mixed constitution came to centre mainly in formal constitutional elements and the relative powers of Assembly, Council (or Senate) and magistrates. In Cicero's eyes it was the best way of reconciling the masses to aristocratic rule and thus ensuring political stability and the security of property-ownership.[17] Discussion has lately concentrated on the later phase; what I have been trying to do is to show how the theory first emerged and the place it occupied in the thought of Aristotle. I would describe it as being in its origin a means of ensuring a balance in the political class struggle.

There are traces at many points in Aristotle's work of his belief that the conflict of interests between propertied and non-propertied is fundamental and inescapable, and that even if a fully 'mixed' constitution cannot be achieved, attempts ought at least to be made to reconcile that conflict of interests as far as possible both by constitutional rules and by sensible behaviour in practice. Perhaps the most useful series of passages to quote here is *Politics* V.8 (esp. 1308ª3-11, 1308ᵇ25-31, 1308ᵇ34-9ª9, 1309ª14-32).

It would be easy to sneer at Aristotle's recommendations for the reconciliation of the irreconcilable – 'mixed constitution' and all. This however would be wrong, for in the class society for which Aristotle was prescribing the conflicts were indeed inescapable, and no radical transformation of society for the better was then conceivable. In the later Middle Ages the ending of feudal restrictions and the full transition to capitalism offered real hope of betterment for all but a few; and in our own time the prolonged death-throes of capitalism encourage us to look forward to a fully socialist society. For Aristotle and his contemporaries there were no prospects of fundamental change that could offer any expectation of a better life for even a citizen of a *polis*, except at the expense of others. The greatness of Aristotle as a political and social thinker is visible to us not only in his recognition (which even Plato shared: see above) of the structural defects of existing Greek *poleis*, automatically creating an opposition between propertied and non-propertied, but also in his generally practicable and often very acute ideas for palliating as far as possible the evil consequences of those defects – ideas which at least compare very favourably with the utterly impracticable fantasies of Plato.

Aristotle was a great advocate of the sovereignty of law (*nomos*), a subject to which he returns again and again. Yet in one of the many passages in which he honestly faces difficulties he admits that law itself can be 'either oligarchic or democratic' (*Pol.* III.10, 1281ª34-9, at 37); and at the end of the next chapter he explains that the nature of law depends upon the type of constitution (*politeia*) within which it functions (11, 1282ᵇ6-11). Also, as Jones pointed out some years ago and Hansen has recently demonstrated in detail,[18] Aristotle is demonstrably unfair to what he is pleased to call 'extreme democracy' – for when many of us would prefer to speak of 'radical democracy' or 'full democracy', Aristotle uses the expressions *eschatē dēmokratia* or *teleutaia dēmokratia*.[19] Over and over again Aristotle treats this form of democracy as one in which there is characteristically and habitually an overriding of law (or the laws) by decrees (*psēphismata*)[20] passed by the *dēmos* or *plēthos* in Assembly,[21] and in one case he speaks specifically of the *plēthos* of the *aporoi*, the mass of the propertyless (*Pol.* IV.6, 1293ª9-10), a notion which is implicit in all these passages. Aristotle must have regarded the Athenian constitution, at any rate in the fourth century,[22] as a form of 'extreme democracy', yet his treatment of that kind of constitution, even if it applied to some other Greek democracies, was certainly not true of the Athenian form (see V.ii below, *ad init.*, § E, and its n.12). Nor, I may say, can we accept in relation to Athens, where property rights were carefully preserved, Aristotle's assumption that it was characteristic of Greek democracies to despoil the rich of their property (see *Pol.* III.10, 1281ª14-24; and VI.3, 1318ª24-6; cf. 5, 1320ª4-14). All we can admit is that some condemnations in the courts, involving the confiscation of the property of wealthy men, were – in the eyes of some critics of the democracy – prompted at least partly by a desire to enrich the State at the expense of opulent individuals. How true Aristotle's strictures were of other Greek democracies we have no means of telling. He may well have generalised from a few notorious cases.

★ ★ ★ ★ ★ ★

I now come to what I regard as the most important and interesting part of this section: the fulfilment of my promise to demonstrate another way in which Aristotle's analysis of the citizen body of the Greek *polis* bears a remarkable resemblance to the method of approach adopted by Marx. Aristotle understood the reason why there are different types of constitution (different *politeiai*): it was because each citizen body was composed of different parts, *merē*, made up of households or families (*oikiai*) having widely differing characteristics,[23] and the constitution would express the relative strength of the different elements. As anyone who has studied the *Politics* carefully will know, Aristotle has various different ways of classifying the inhabitants of the Greek city-state. In Book IV, chapter 4, in particular, he tries to give a detailed list of the constituent parts of the citizen body, the *merē poleōs* (1290^{b}38-1^{a}8, 1291^{a}33-^{b}13). The categories with which he begins are the very ones I have specified (in Section ii of this chapter) as the defining characteristics of class in Marx's sense: Aristotle starts off with four groups defined according to their role in production – working farmers (*geōrgoi*), independent artisans (*to banauson*), traders (*to agoraion*, including both *emporoi*, who were essentially inter-state merchants, and *kapēloi*, petty local dealers),[24] and wage-labourers (*to thētikon*). Precisely the same four groups appear in Book VI (7, 1321^{a}5-6), but there they are the constituent parts of the *plēthos*, the masses; and in IV.4 too it soon becomes evident that the *geōrgoi* are indeed (as I have called them above) *working* farmers, and not 'gentlemen farmers' who were really absentee landlords or employers of slave labour, for after Aristotle has mentioned his first four groups he wanders off into a mixture of economic, political and military categories, and as one of these (his no.7) he mentions the *euporoi*, the rich, the well-to-do property owners (1291^{a}33-4). This is not one of Aristotle's clearest pieces of analysis: it contains a very long digression of nearly a page in length (1291^{a}10-33), and some people think there must be a lacuna in the text. But eventually, after listing nine or ten categories, he realises that he has got himself into a hopeless mess, and he pulls together what he has been saying by remarking that there is just one distinction which will sort everyone out: no one can be both poor and rich. And so he returns once more to his fundamental distinction between rich and poor, propertied and propertyless: *euporoi* and *aporoi* (1291^{b}7-8). He ends this section of his work by reiterating that there are two basic forms of constitution, corresponding to the distinction between *euporoi* and *aporoi*, namely oligarchy and democracy (1291^{b}11-13). And in a later Book of the *Politics* he says emphatically that the *polis* is made up of 'two *merē*: rich and poor' (*plousioi kai penētes*, VI.3, 1318^{a}30-1).

It is of the greatest interest, and entirely consistent with Aristotle's fundamental principles of sociological classification, that he was able to discriminate between different types of democracy *according to the role played in production* in each individual case by the majority of the lower classes (the *dēmos*), whether as farmers, artisans or wage-labourers, or as some mixture of these elements (see *Pol.* VI.1, 1317^{a}24-9 and other passages),[25] whereas he can draw distinctions only on technical, constitutional grounds in three different passages discussing forms of oligarchy,[26] all of which would of course be ruled (as he takes for granted) by landowners (cf. III.iii below). Austin and Vidal-Naquet, while admitting that Aristotle is 'constantly reasoning in terms of class struggles', maintain – apparently as a criticism of what they regard as Marxism – that 'modern representations of class struggles' are inappropriate here and that 'one will search in vain for the place held by different groups in the relations of production as a criterion of ancient class struggles' (*ESHAG* 22). This is literally correct – but why should anyone wish to apply categories that are highly relevant in capitalist society to a pre-capitalist world in which they are indeed inappropriate? Austin and Vidal-Naquet at this point seem to overlook the fact that the great majority of citizens in all Classical Greek States were involved in *agricultural* production in one way or another. Artisans in the fourth century were neither numerous nor important enough to exert any real influence as a class; foreign trade was probably often (as certainly at Athens) in the hands mainly of non-citizens;[27] and internal trade, although some citizens participated as well as many metics, gave little opportunity of acquiring wealth or political power. Aristotle realised that it was above all property-ownership or the lack of it which divided citizen bodies into what I am calling classes: he had no need to tell his Greek audience that property was overwhelmingly landed (cf. III.i-iii below).

The Aristotelian categories perhaps tend to be less refined than those of Marx. Except in one or two passages such as *Pol.* IV.4, quoted above, Aristotle is mainly thinking in quantitative terms, classifying citizens according to the amount of property they owned, whether large or small (or sometimes mid-dling), whereas Marx's analysis, except when he is speaking loosely, is usually more qualitative and concentrates more explicitly on relationship to the means and the labour of production. To put it in a different way: Marx perhaps concentrates more on the beginning and the structure of the process of production, Aristotle more on its results. But there is less difference than might appear. The very term Aristotle and others often use for the propertied class, *hoi tas ousias echontes*, employs a word, *ousia*, which is characteristically, though not exclusively, used of landed property (cf. the Latin word *locupletes*). As I have said, land and slaves were the principal means of production in antiquity, and land was always regarded as the ideal form of wealth. And Aristotle, in his analysis of the political community, certainly does come closer to Marx than any other ancient thinker I know: one one occasion, as we have seen, he begins his classification of the constituent parts (the *merē*) of a citizen body by distinguishing the citizens according to the functions they perform in the productive process; he ends up with a basic dichotomy between propertied and property-less; and he always takes a man's economic position to be the main determinant of his political behaviour.

Now it is true that Aristotle may sometimes impose upon earlier events inappropriate categories drawn from the experience of his own day; but it is not legitimate to say (as some scholars have done) that whereas his picture of class differences and class struggle in Greek cities may be true of the fourth century, it need not be accepted for earlier periods. Fifth-century writers, as I have shown, give a very similar picture; and when we go back to contemporary sources in the Archaic Age, the poets Solon and Theognis in particular, we find some very clear examples of overt political class strife, although of course the classes were then rather different from what they had become by the fifth century (see V.i-ii below).

Aristotle does record the fact that some Greeks believed the fair regulation of property to be the most important of all matters, because they thought that all *staseis* (civil disturbances) had their origin in questions of property (*Pol.* II.7, 1266^a37-9). Plato, of course, is the most obvious example (see Fuks, PSQ, esp. 49-51). And Aristotle goes on (1266^a37-7^b21) to discuss some of the views of Phaleas of Chalcedon (a thinker of unknown date, presumably of the late fifth or early fourth century), who, he says, was the first to propose that citizens should own equal amounts of property – in fact, as he explains later, of land (1267^b9-21). Among various criticisms of Phaleas, Aristotle advances the view that it is no use confining a prescription for equal distribution of property to land; wealth, as he points out, can also consist of 'slaves and cattle and money', and one should either leave wealth entirely unregulated or else insist on complete equality or the fixing of a moderate maximum amount. This is the place to mention the remarkable opinion expressed by Diodorus (II.39.5), in connection with his idealised Indian society: 'It is foolish to make laws on a basis of equality for all, but to make the distribution of property unequal.' (Against gratuitous emendation of this passage, see my *OPW* 138 n.126.)

I fully realise that some people will feel irked by my unqualified and general acceptance of Marx's concept of class struggle, with its emphasis on economic differentiation as the fundamental element, rather than social prestige or status or political power; they may still be disinclined to accept Marx's picture as a generally valid description of human societies. But it should at least be clear beyond dispute by now that anyone who holds such opinions has no right to complain of my accepting Marx's categories in the analysis of ancient Greek society. Far from being an anachronistic aberration confined to Marx and his followers, the concept of economic class as the basic factor in the differentiation of Greek society and the definition of its political divisions turns out to correspond remarkably well with the view taken by the Greeks themselves; and Aristotle, the great expert on the sociology and politics of the Greek city, always proceeds on the basis of a class analysis and takes it for granted that men will act, politically and otherwise, above all according to their economic position. The Marxist character (in the sense I have indicated) of Aristotle's sociology has not escaped notice. The Aristotelian scholar J. L. Stocks remarked in 1936 of one statement in Book IV of the *Politics* that 'it might be a quotation from the Communist Manifesto'! (*CQ* 30.185). Stocks's article, by the way, is entitled '*Scholē*' (the Greek word for 'leisure'), a concept of considerable importance in Aristotle's thought which I find it more convenient to deal with in III.vi below, on hired labour. In recent years, in the Antipodes and across the Atlantic, some writers on the ancient world have contrived to forget Aristotle's class analysis – which I dare say they regard as dangerously Marxist – or to pretend that it can be ignored, especially for the centuries earlier than the fourth. They have managed to persuade themselves that the conflicts in Greek society can be explained exclusively in terms of factions grouped around aristocratic families – factions which of course existed and could indeed cut across class lines, although to treat them as the basic elements in Greek politics and the rise of democracy is to fly in the face of the evidence, especially for Athens in the early sixth century onwards (see V.i and ii below). I shall waste no further time on these idiosyncratic notions; but I cannot resist referring to the delightful expression, 'Aristotelian-Marxist explanations of Greek social and political development', in a recent article by D. J. McCargar, who is prudently disinclined to reject such explanations entirely, especially – for Athens – in the period beginning with Cleisthenes (508/7).[28]

I should perhaps just mention (since it has recently been reprinted) a very feeble attempt made by Marcus Wheeler, in an article published in 1951, to dissociate Aristotle's theory of *stasis*, or civil disturbance, from Marx's concept of class struggle.[29] The summary of Wheeler's arguments at the end of his article reveals his inability to make a deep enough analysis of either Aristotle or Marx.

There is positively no comfort in Aristotle, or in any other Greek thinker known to me, for those who (like Finley recently: see the next section of this chapter) have rejected class as the principal category for use in the analysis of ancient society and have preferred 'status'. It is hard to find even a good Greek equivalent for 'status'; but since Max Weber defined his 'status situation' (*ständische Lage*) as those aspects of a man's life that are determined by 'social estimation of honour' (*WuG*[5] II.534=*ES* II.932=*FMW* 186-7), I think we may accept *timē* ('honour', 'prestige') as the best Greek translation of 'status'. Now Aristotle of course knew very well – as did other Greek writers, including Thucydides (I.75.3; 76.2, etc.) – that *timē* was of great importance to many Greeks. For some, indeed, Aristotle realised that *timē* was a principal ingredient in happiness (*EN* I.4, 1095^{a}14-26); and those he calls 'men of refinement and affairs' (*hoi charientes kai praktikoi*) – in contrast with the masses, who 'betray themselves as utterly slavish, in their preference for a life suitable for cattle' – could be expected to set great store by *timē*, which he himself considered to be 'virtually the goal of political life' (I.5, 1095^{b}19-31), 'the greatest of external goods' (IV.3, 1123^{b}15-21), 'a prize for excellence' (*aretē*, 1123^{b}35), 'the aim of the majority' (VIII.8, 1159^{a}16-17). But it is essential to observe that Aristotle's discussions of *timē* are kept almost entirely for his ethical works.[30] He would have had scant patience with those modern scholars who have wanted to use status as a yardstick in political and general classification – for that, Aristotle chose class, expressed in terms of property.

* * * * * *

I think I have now made at least a partly sufficient reply to statements such as that of Bottomore, quoted in I.iv above, that 'while the Marxian theory seems highly relevant and useful in analysing social and political conflicts in capitalist societies during a particular period, its utility and relevance elsewhere are much less clear'.

I have not thought it necessary to examine here any Greek 'political thought' – if we can dignify it with that name – of the Hellenistic and Roman periods.[31] I shall notice some of this disagreeable stuff later, when I have occasion to do so (see e.g. V.iii, VI.vi and VII.i below), but there is really no point in my dragging it in here. The whole concept of democracy – that great, fertile innovation of Classical Greek political thinking (as it was, notwithstanding its limitation to citizen bodies) – now became gradually degraded, as I shall show in V.iii below. *Dēmokratia* came to mean little more than some form of constitutional rule as opposed to tyranny, or else a measure of independence for a city, as opposed to outright control by a Hellenistic monarch; and there could no longer be any honest political thought on a realistic basis. Serious political activity, such as it was, became confined more and more completely to the propertied classes.

(v)
Alternatives to class (status etc.)

We must now consider whether there is any more fruitful method of analysing human societies, according to different principles from those I have been advocating.

I must begin by putting myself at the opposite extreme from those I may call 'antiquarians', who renounce, explicitly or by implication, any wish to provide an organic picture of a historical society, illuminated by all the insight that we in modern times can bring to bear upon it, and deliberately confine themselves to reproducing as faithfully as possible some particular feature or aspect of that society, strictly in its own original terms. Such a person may often prove very useful to the historian, by drawing attention to particular sets of evidence and collecting a great deal of information which the historian can then transform into something significant. An outstanding example of this kind of antiquarian activity, which is yet presented in the opening sentence of its Preface as 'an essay in historical interpretation', is Fergus Millar's recent large book, *The Emperor in the Roman World* (1977), which begins by proclaiming in its Preface (xi-xii) a series of methodological principles to most of which the historian ought to feel hostile. Asserting that he has 'rigidly avoided reading sociological works on kingship or related topics, or studies of monarchic institutions in societies other than those of Greece and Rome', Millar goes on to say that 'to have come to the subject with an array of concepts derived from the study of other societies would merely have made even more unattainable *the proper objective of a historian, to subordinate himself to the evidence* and to the conceptual world of a society in the past' (my italics). And he congratulates himself on not having 'contaminated the presentation of the evidence from the Roman empire with conceptions drawn from wider sociological studies'. For Millar, 'the emperor "was" what the emperor did', an opinion given twice (xi and 6), the first time as a pendant to the 'conscious principle' he says he has followed, 'that any social system must be analysed primarily in terms of the specific patterns of action *recorded* of its members'. Another of his 'conscious principles' is that we must 'base our conceptions *solely* on . . . attitudes and expectations *expressed* in those ancient sources which provide our evidence'. And Millar believes himself to be describing 'certain *essential* elements', 'certain *basic* features of the working of the Roman empire', patterns which 'are of *fundamental* importance in understanding what the Roman empire was' (my italics in each case).

Perhaps the most serious of all the mistaken assumptions behind this 'programme' is that there is an objective entity, '*the* evidence', to which the historian has merely to 'subordinate himself'. The volume of the surviving evidence for the Roman empire is enormous (inadequate as we may often find it for the solution of a particular problem); and all the historian can do is to *select* those parts of the evidence which he considers most relevant and significant. To pretend to oneself that all one has to do is simply to reproduce 'the' evidence is all too likely to result, and in Millar's case has resulted, in a mainly superficial picture, and one that *explains* little or nothing of importance. Moreover, to 'base our conceptions' as Millar advocates, *solely* on the attitudes and expectations *expressed* in those ancient sources which happen to survive is to deprive ourselves of all the insights that come from penetrating beneath that very limited series of 'attitudes and expectations' and, where they reveal false comprehension and even self-deception, as they so often do, demonstrating the realities which they serve to conceal. (Compare what I have said in Sections i and iv of this chapter about 'beginning from' the categories and even the terminology in use among the ancient Greeks.) Again, before interrogating the evidence one needs to decide what are the most fruitful questions to ask. By altogether abjuring, not only all material which is not made explicit in the surviving sources, but also the comparative method and all those forms of analysis which have been developed in the study of sociology and of other historical societies, Millar has greatly impoverished himself and has failed even to become aware of many of the most fruitful questions. Particularly when our information from the ancient world is scanty or non-existent, as for example in regard to the peasantry (see I.iii above and IV.ii below), we may gain much insight from comparative studies. I would suggest that the passage I have summaried in IV.ii below from William Hinton's book, *Fanshen*, sheds light in a way no Greek or Roman source can equal upon the acceptance by poor peasants of the exploitation they suffer at the hands of a landlord class. However, it would be ungracious not to record that Millar's book is a notable piece of antiquarian research, an outstanding and invaluable repository of detailed and accurate information on those limited aspects of the Principate in which he happens to be interested. One would have had little to complain about had the Preface been omitted and the book given the more modest and more accurate title, 'Communication between the Roman Emperor and his Subjects'. If I have dwelt too long upon the book's limitations it is because they are all too characteristic of much contemporary writing about ancient history, though never made so explicit elsewhere.

I find myself not merely unwilling but unable to make use, for present purposes, of the wide range of theories of social stratification often grouped together (sometimes inappropriately) under the name of 'functionalism',[1] the main distinguishing characteristic of which is the attempt to explain social institutions above all in terms of their role in maintaining and reinforcing the social structure. Among the leading sociologists and anthropologists who can be placed at least to some extent in this group are Durkheim, Malinowski, Radcliffe-Brown, Talcott Parsons, and R. K. Merton. I cannot see that the functionalist approach can help to explain any of the phenomena we shall be examining, least of all the process of social change which is very noticeable in parts of our period. A paper of great insight by Ralf Dahrendorf, 'In praise of Thrasymachus' (in his *ETS* 129-50), has traced functionalist theory as far back as the Socrates of Plato's *Republic* (I.336b-354c), who, in his debate with Thrasymachus, develops (as Dahrendorf puts it) an 'equilibrium theory' of social life, based upon an assumed consensus, in opposition to the 'constraint theory' of Thrasymachus, and who thus 'became the first functionalist' (*ETS* 150). As Dahrendorf says, 'An equilibrium approach cannot come to terms with certain substantive problems of change . . . Equilibrium theories lend themselves to explaining continuity alone, and even this only with respect to the most formal aspects of the political system' (*ETS* 143).

A methodology in the study of economic history which resembles that of the functionalists in anthropology has been emerging in recent years, partly under the stimulus of economists, especially in the United States. (I am sure that those who are in principle hostile to Marxism will make great efforts to develop it still further.) I refer to those works which seek to minimise class conflicts in society and (if they notice them at all) treat such conflicts as less significant than those features which can be conceived, with or without distortion, as promoting social cohesion and 'rationality'. It is hard to choose examples among such works, for some of them may bear little resemblance to each other except their common 'functionalist' approach. I shall begin by singling out a recent book and two articles by D. C. North and R. P. Thomas,[2] enthusiastic practitioners of the 'New Economic History' (as its devotees like to call it), whose picture of the major economic developments that took place in the Middle Ages depends partly upon the assumption that 'Serfdom in Western Europe was essentially not an exploitative arrangement where lords "owned" labour as in North America, or as it developed in Eastern Europe', but 'essentially a contractual arrangement where labour services were exchanged for the public good of protection and justice'. I need say no more about these authors' fancy picture of serfdom as a voluntary contract, as it has been sufficiently demolished by Robert Brenner in a very able article, 'Agrarian class structure and economic development in pre-industrial Europe' in *Past & Present* 70 (1976) 30-75. This deals admirably with various types of 'economic model-building' which try to explain long-term economic developments in pre-industrial Europe primarily in terms either of demography (Postan, Bowden, Le Roy Ladurie, and North and Thomas) or of the growth of trade and the market (Pirenne and his followers), disregarding class relations and exploitation as primary factors.[2a] And Brenner's case against North and Thomas in particular can be strengthened. No one acquainted with the sources for Later Roman history would try to pretend that the serfdom of the Roman colonate, of the fourth and following centuries, was anything but thoroughly 'exploitative', for in the Later Roman world, over all, there was no such failure of State power as may have driven some mediaeval peasants to 'choose' subjection to a lord as a less unpleasant alternative than being at the mercy of all and sundry. We do find in the Later Empire a certain amount of resort to 'patronage', as something temporarily preferable to helpless independence in the face of fiscal oppression or barbarian incursions (see below), but in general it would be ridiculous to treat the colonate as anything but an instrument for reinforcing the subjection of the peasant to fiscal extortion and landlord control (see IV.iii and VI.vi below). And if the serfdom of the colonate is thus understood, the case for treating mediaeval serfdom as a voluntary contract benefiting peasant as well as lord is greatly weakened.

Another good example of the 'functionalist' tendencies I have just described is the very able little book by Sir John Hicks, *A Theory of Economic History*, published in 1969 and representing an expansion of lectures delivered from 1967 onwards. This is more directly relevant to subjects I deal with in this book, in that it purports to delineate the general features of what Hicks calls 'the lord-and-peasant system' (*TEH* 101 ff.), which would include not only the Late Roman colonate but a good deal of earlier rural life in the Greek world. Dr Pangloss would have been delighted with Hicks's account of this system. It was 'very ancient', he says, 'and very strong. It was strong because it met a real need. Lord and peasant were necessary to each other, and the land, the same land, was necessary to both. The peasant was necessary to the lord, since it was from a share in the peasant's produce that he derived his support; and there was a corresponding way in which the lord was necessary to the peasant. Whatever the burden that was laid upon him, he got something in return; and what he got in return was vital. What he got was Protection' (*TEH* 102). This system is at once hypostatised and takes on a life of its own: Hicks speaks of it as if it could be itself a living force. 'It did not only persist; it recreated itself, under suitable conditions, when there had been a move away from it' (*TEH* 104). When it involves the cultivation of a lord's 'demesne land' by the forced labour of the peasants, Hicks can remark blandly that 'a lord-and-peasant system that moves in this direction would generally be regarded as moving towards a more complete condition of serfdom' (*TEH* 105). And when there is a shortage of labour, 'it is competition for labour that must be stopped. The labourer, or peasant-labourer, must be tied to the soil, or re-tied to the soil; in a more exact sense than before, he must be made a serf' (*TEH* 112). Hicks's characters, it will be observed – 'the lord', 'the peasant' and other such abstractions – are mere creatures of his system; and in all their acts they obediently conform to the types of behaviour expected of them by orthodox neo-classical economists, if not by historians. The absurdity of this idyllic picture of the 'lord-and-peasant system', like· that of North and Thomas, which I have criticised above, is equally revealed, of course, by the serfdom of the Later Roman colonate, where 'protection' by the landowner was only rarely involved, and not at all at the inception of the colonate and for some time afterwards. It is a pity that Hicks was not acquainted with the source material for the Later Roman Empire, especially the passages quoted in III.iv and IV.iii below to demonstrate that in the eyes of the Roman ruling class the serf *colonus* was in a condition so close to slavery that only the vocabulary of that institution, technically inappropriate as it was, proved adequate to describe his subject condition. Perhaps it would be too cheap a sneer to say that we may be tempted to interpret the Protection which Hicks and others see the lord as extending to the peasant in a rather different sense from that intended by him: as a 'protection racket' indeed, in most cases – even if it could sometimes be taken seriously by peasants (for an example from fourteenth-century France, see IV.iv below, *ad fin.*). But at least we may be allowed to feel regret that Hicks could not have had these matters properly explained to him by the peasants of Long Bow village after their eyes had been opened at the meeting in Li Village Gulch in January 1946 and they had come to understand the real nature of landlordism (see IV.ii below).

The intellectual origins of the theory that involves conceiving mediaeval serfdom as a voluntary contractual arrangement are not traced back by North and Thomas beyond 1952.[3] I should like to suggest that an important formative influence in establishing the background of thought in which such theories may flourish was a short book written nearly half a century ago by a young English economist who was soon to become very prominent: Lionel Robbins, *An Essay on the Nature and Significance of Economic Science* (1932, second edition 1935). Robbins carefully isolates economics from contamination by such disciplines as history or sociology or politics, by defining it (on p.16 of his second edition) as 'the science which studies human behaviour as a relationship between ends and scarce means which have alternative uses'. Individuals make a series of choices, which for the purpose of the theory have to be treated as free choices, in flagrant disregard – as Maurice Dobb pointed out in 1937[4] – of the class relations which in reality largely determine such choices. (The significance of 1932, a year of acute capitalist crisis in England, as the date of publication of the first edition of Robbins's book is too obvious to need emphasis.) From that position, it is but a short step to serfdom as a nice, contractual relationship – and if serfdom, then why not slavery, which, as its defenders from George Fitzhugh onwards proclaimed (see VII.ii below), provides a security for the slave to which the individual wage-labourer cannot aspire?

★ ★ ★ ★ ★ ★

If we now turn to Max Weber's sociological approach to ancient history, we can find elements of real value, even if in the end we feel dissatisfied with the categories he employs, as unclear and unhelpful.[5] If I may speak as a historian – sociologists not thoroughly trained as historians who have ventured outside their own familiar world into earlier periods of history have often made disastrous mistakes and have sometimes produced conclusions of little or no value, simply because of their inability to deal properly with historical evidence. Weber not only possessed rare intellectual quality; he was trained in Roman law and history, and his earliest work, after his doctoral thesis, was a Roman *Agrargeschichte* (1891).[6] It is a pity that British ancient historians today, with few exceptions, seem to be little interested in Weber. Even Rostovtzeff, who did not miss much, had not read[7] the very interesting lecture Weber delivered and published in 1896, 'Die sozialen Gründe des Untergangs der antiken Kultur' (see IV.iii below), which seems to me Weber's best piece of historical writing, and of which English translations, as 'The social causes of the decay of ancient civilisation', have now become easily available.[8] I must admit, however, that Weber, who wrote about Greek society as well as Roman, evidently knew much less at first hand about the Greek world than the Roman, and that he was much less at home when dealing with Greek history.[9] It is also an unfortunate fact that the English reader who is not already well versed in sociological literature and terminology is likely to find Weber hard to read in the original German.[10] (There are many different English translations, varying from excellent to very poor; the notes provided with them vary even more, some being worse than useless.)[11] At times Weber can be lucid enough, even for quite long stretches; but often he lapses into an obscurity which does not always repay the repeated re-readings it invites. In particular, his use of various forms and combinations of the German word ' Stand' can be a source of confusion – even, I think, for the German reader. Talcott Parsons, whose translations of Weber are excellent, could say in a footnote to one of them:

> The term *Stand* with its derivatives is perhaps the most troublesome single term in Weber's text. It refers to a social group the members of which occupy a relatively well-defined common status, particularly with reference to social stratification, though this reference is not always important. In addition to common status, there is the further criterion that the members of a *Stand* have a common mode of life and usually more or less well-defined code of behaviour. There is no English term which even approaches adequacy in rendering this concept. Hence it has been necessary to attempt to describe what Weber meant in whatever terms the particular context has indicated (Weber, *TSEO* 347-8 n.27).

The whole footnote is an attempt to explain how Parsons has come to translate Weber's 'ständische Herrschaft' by 'decentralised authority' – a rendering which nicely illustrates the difficulty he is trying to explain. (My reason for dwelling upon Weber's use of the word *Stand* will shortly become apparent.)

Under Weber's powerful influence above all, it has become an accepted practice on the part of sociologists to concern themselves with what is usually referred to as the 'social stratification' of human societies, under one or more of three aspects: *economic*, in terms of class; *political*, in terms of authority or domination or power; *social*, in terms of status or honour or prestige. I must add at once, with all possible emphasis, that Marx shows not the least interest in social *stratification*, a spatial metaphor which I think he scarcely ever employs in connection with his concept of classes, even as the metaphor it is. (Any such expression as 'the stratification of classes', in *Cap*. III.885, is very rare.) He uses the term 'the middle class' (or 'middle classes', or some variant) quite frequently, in the sense in which it had come to be regularly employed by his day, as a synonym for 'the bourgeoisie' or 'the capitalist class'; but he rarely refers to 'upper' or 'lower' classes, although in the *Eighteenth Brumaire*, for example, he can refer to 'the social strata situated above the proletariat' in France (*MECW* XI.110). My own practice in this book is the reverse: I avoid using the term 'middle class' in relation to the ancient world, because of its inevitable modern colouring, but I often find it convenient to speak of 'upper' and 'lower' classes. Near the beginning of *The Communist Manifesto* Marx and Engels did speak of the existence, in 'earlier epochs of history', of 'various *orders*, a manifold gradation of social *rank*' (*MECW* VI.482-5); but in spite of the occurrence of a few phrases of that kind in their works, it would be a great mistake to conceive the Marxist class analysis as an attempt to construct a scheme of 'social stratification'. Neglect of this cardinal fact has led to much misunderstanding of Marx. Although of course it is perfectly possible to produce a series of such schemes of stratification for the ancient world at different periods, the result, however true to reality, will not provide an instrument of historical analysis and explanation in any way comparable with the application of the Marxist concept of class. At this point, however, I wish to glance briefly at theories of social stratification couched primarily in social or political terms.

That the primary and most useful kind of classification was social status was in effect the position of Max Weber (according to my understanding of it), and it has recently been explicitly re-stated in relation to the Greek and Roman world by M. I. Finley. Let us first concentrate on Weber. It was said of him (with some exaggeration) by the German sociologist Albert Salomon that he became a sociologist in a long and intense dialogue with the ghost of Karl Marx![12] He was not altogether hostile to Marx (whom he never ventured to disparage), and he was prepared to concede 'eminent, indeed unique, heuristic significance' to Marx's concepts, considered as a form of his own 'ideal types', but he refused to allow them any empirical reality.[13] According to the American sociologists, H. H. Gerth and C. Wright Mills, in their Introduction to a well-chosen set of extracts from Weber's writings, 'Throughout his life, Max Weber was engaged in a fruitful battle with historical materialism. In his last course of lectures in Munich at the time of the Revolution [1918], he presented his course under the title, "A positive critique of historical materialism"' (*FMW* 63). How far Gerth and Mills were justified in adding at this point, 'Yet there is a definite drift of emphasis in his intellectual biography towards Marx', I leave to others to decide. I have certainly not been able to discover anywhere in Weber's works any serious discussion of Marx's concept of class – an omission which I find very strange.

I must say, it would have been a rare pleasure to attend the lecture Weber gave on socialism to the officer corps of the Austro-Hungarian Royal Imperial army in Vienna in July 1918, in which Weber actually described *The Communist Manifesto* in terms of the greatest respect:

> This document, however strongly we may reject it in its critical theses (at least *I* do), is in its way a scientific achievement of the first rank [*eine wissenschaftliche Leistung ersten Ranges*]. That cannot be denied, neither may one deny it, because nobody believes one and it is impossible to deny it with a clear conscience. Even in the theses we nowadays reject, it is an imaginative error which politically has had very far-reaching and perhaps not always pleasant consequences, but which has brought very stimulating results for scholarship, more so than many a work of dull correctness.[14] (I resist the temptation to continue the quotation.)

I shall try to represent those of Weber's views that are immediately relevant as fairly as I can; but the reader who fears that his stomach may be turned by the horrible jargon that is characteristic of so much sociological theorising and by the repellent welter of vague generalisation that infects even a powerful intellect like Weber's in such circumstances had better skip the next few paragraphs.

Weber gave more than one explanation of what he meant by *Stand* and *ständische Lage*, which can here be translated 'status group' and 'status situation'. He discusses classification in this social sense as well as in economic and political terms in two passages in his posthumously published *Wirtschaft und Gesellschaft* (both very difficult, but now easily available in good English translations),[15] and he also deals with the subject of *Stände* elsewhere, for example in an essay on the 'world-religions' written in 1913,[16] and in one of his works on India dating from 1916.[17] Although Weber, I think, never says so expressly, it seems clear to me that he regarded 'status situation' as the most significant kind of classification, even if, in accordance with his general principles, he did not actually make it the necessary determinant of 'class situation' (*Klassenlage*, a term he used in quite a different sense from Marx),[18] and indeed said that status situation might be 'based on class status directly or related to it in complex ways. It is not, however, determined by this alone . . . Conversely, social status may partly or even wholly determine class status, without, however, being identical with it'.[19] For Weber, status groups were normally 'communities' (*Gemeinschaften*), and men's status situation includes 'every typical component of the life fate of men that is determined by a specific, positive or negative, social estimation of *honour* [*soziale Einschätzung der Ehre*]', involving 'a specific *style of life* [*Lebensführung*]'.[20] In his opinion, 'the decisive role of a "style of life" in status "honour" means that status groups are the specific bearers of all "conventions". In whatever way it may be manifest, all "stylisation" of life either originates in status groups or is at least conserved by them'.[21] And 'status groups are stratified according to the principles of their *consumption* of goods as represented by special "styles of life"'.[22] We can therefore agree with the opinion expressed by Reinhard Bendix, one of Weber's greatest admirers, that 'Weber's approach conceived of society as an arena of competing status groups, each with its own economic interests, status honour, and orientation toward the world and man. He used this perspective in his analysis of the landed aristocracy, the rising bourgeoisie, the bureaucracy, and the working class in imperial Germany. He used the same perspective in his comparative sociology of religion' (*MWIP* 259-63, at 262). And in its constant attention to 'social stratification' twentieth-century sociological theory has broadly followed Weber. As S. N. Eisenstadt put it in 1968, 'The central concept in later sociological analysis of stratification, largely derived from Weber, is that of prestige' (*Max Weber On Charisma and Institution Building*, Introduction, p.xxxiii).

Yet Weber could also admit, in the essay on world-religions to which I have already referred, that 'Present-day society is predominantly stratified in classes, and to an especially high degree in income classes.' (In the previous sentence he had distinguished between 'propertied classes' and 'primarily market-determined "income classes"'.) He went on, however: 'But in the special *status* prestige of the "educated" strata, our society contains a very tangible element of stratification by status.' Shortly afterwards he added, 'In the past the significance of stratification by status was far more decisive, above all for the economic structure of the societies.' A little earlier in the same passage he had defined 'class situation' as 'the opportunities to gain sustenance and income that are primarily determined by typical, *economically* relevant, situations'; and he had said that 'A "status situation" can be the cause as well as the result of a "class situation", but it need be neither. Class situations, in turn, can be primarily *determined by markets*, by the labour market and the commodity market' (Gerth/Mills, *FMW* 301: see n.16 to this section).

This is confusing, and the confusion hardly resolves itself when we put this passage together with the two in *Wirtschaft und Gesellschaft* referred to above, which contain Weber's formal discussion of economic, social and political classification. Here, in the earlier passage (no.1 in n.15), under the general heading of 'Concepts' (*Begriffe*), we are first told that 'a class is any group of persons occupying the same class situation (*Klassenlage*)', and we are then introduced to various different types of class: the 'property class' (*Besitzklasse*), the 'acquisition class' (*Erwerbsklasse*), and the 'social class' (*soziale Klasse*); after some unilluminating remarks, especially on the significance of property classes, both 'positively privileged' and 'negatively privileged', we suddenly encounter 'the "middle" classes' (*Mittelstandklassen*). The discussion that follows, mainly of 'acquisition classes' and 'social classes', consists of a string of poorly connected observations. We then move on to 'social status' – I have already quoted one or two sentences from Weber's account of this. No kind of organising principle seems to be at work, and the various kinds of class evidently overlap in all sorts of ways. Things are at first a little better – though not much – when we reach the second main passage (no.2 in n.15), at the very end of *Wirtschaft und Gesellschaft*. Here we do at least find a definition of 'class':

> We may speak of a 'class' when (1) a number of people have in common a specific causal component of their life chances, in so far as (2) this component is represented exclusively by economic interests in the possession of goods and opportunities for income, and (3) is represented under the conditions of the commodity or labour markets (Gerth/Mills, *FMW* 181).

And a little later we are told that

> Always this is the generic connotation of the concept of class: that the kind of chance in the *market* is the decisive moment which presents a common condition for the individual's fate. 'Class situation' is, in this sense, ultimately 'market situation' (*FMW* 182).

We begin to see a little light at the end of the tunnel, although we are still very much in the dark as to how many classes Weber would recognise and at what points he would draw the boundaries between them. Slaves, because their 'fate is not determined by the chance of using goods or services for themselves on the market' (*FMW* 183), are a status group (*Stand*) and not a class at all 'in the technical sense of the term' – according, that is to say, to Weber's definition of class.

The faint light continues to glow, although still very much in the distance, when we go on in the next paragraph to learn that 'According to our terminology, the factor that creates "class" is unambiguously economic interest, and indeed, only those interests involved in the existence of the "market".' So far, so good: at least this is intelligible. But alas! we then find ourselves in a particularly luxuriant and stifling Weberian thicket: 'Nevertheless, the concept of "class-interest" (*Klasseninteresse*) is an ambiguous one: even as an empirical concept it is ambiguous as soon as one understands by it something other than the factual direction of interests following with a certain probability from the class situation for a certain "average" of those people subject to the class situation' (still *FMW* 183). For the next page or two things get better again, and there are some interesting observations; the only one that I need notice is, 'The "class struggles" of antiquity – to the extent that they were genuine class struggles and not struggles between status groups – were initially carried on by indebted peasants, and perhaps also by artisans threatened by debt bondage and struggling against urban creditors . . . Debt relationships as such produced class action up to the time of Catiline' (*FMW* 185). And in the last few pages of *Wirtschaft und Gesellschaft* one firm statement stands out from the medley, the second half of which I have already quoted above in dealing with Weber's status groups: 'With some over-simplification, one might say that "classes" are stratified according to their relations to the production and acquisition of goods; whereas "status groups" are stratified according to the principles of their *consumption* of goods as represented by special "styles of life"' (see *FMW* 193). Weber makes a very similar statement to that last one in an essay on Indian society, first published in 1916, to which I have already referred: '"Classes" are groups of people who, from the standpoint of specific interests, have the same economic position. Ownership or non-ownership of material goods or of definite skills constitute the "class-situation". "Status" is a quality of social honour or a lack of it, and is in the main conditioned as well as expressed through a specific style of life' (*FMW* 405: see n.17 to this section).

A proper comparison of Weber's categories with those of Marx would take us too far from our main subject, but certain features of this comparison leap to the eye, and of these I shall single out three:

1. Weberian 'status' stratification plays no significant role in the thought of Marx, who (as I said earlier) shows no interest in social stratification as such. In so far as classes happen to be status groups and are stratified accordingly, it is their *class relationship* that matters to Marx, rather than any *stratification* according

to status. Is this a defect in Marx? The answer to this question depends on the value we attach to 'social statification' as an instrument of historical or sociological analysis. But – and this is my first point – Weber in fact makes virtually no signficant *use* of his 'status groups' in *explaining* anything. Although I have read many of Weber's works, I cannot claim to know them all, and it may be that I have missed something; but my statement is certainly true of the great bulk of his writings, whether on the society of his own day or on Classical antiquity or on China – or even on the rise of capitalism, in what is perhaps his most famous work among historians, *The Protestant Ethic and the Spirit of Capitalism*.[23] Only in writing of India does Weber attribute a central explanatory role to one peculiar, and indeed unique, form of 'closed status group', the caste.

2. Weber's use of the term 'class', as is evident from my citations above, is totally different from that of Marx. (As I have already observed, I have not myself found in Weber any discussion of Marx's concept of class; and I may add that after consulting many works by his disciples I have not been able to discover any reference to such a discussion.) To me, Weber's notion of class is exceedingly vague and inherently incapable of precise definition. According to one of his own statements, quoted above, classes can be 'stratified'; but even if classes are (according to another such statement) 'groups of people who, from the standpoint of specific interests, have the same economic position' (a highly indefinite specification), *how are the boundaries of classes to be ascertained*? That is the essential question, and my second point is that Weber fails to provide an answer to it. Individuals, certainly, can be regarded as 'stratified', after a fashion, according to 'economic position' in general; but if we are to have stratified *classes* we need to be able to define their respective *boundaries* in some way, even if we are prepared to allow for some indeterminate borderline cases and do not wish to have hard-and-fast lines of demarcation. 'A class', after all, 'is a class is a class', and we must be able to define different classes.

3. But it is my third contrast between the categories of Weber and Marx which is by far the most important. The 'status groups' and even the 'classes' of Weber are not necessarily (like Marx's classes) in any *organic relationship* with one another; and consequently they are not dynamic in character but merely lie side by side, so to speak, like numbers in a row. Class in Marx's sense, as I said at the beginning of my definition in Section ii of this chapter, is essentially a relationship, and the members of any one class are necessarily related *as such*, in different degrees, to those of other classes. The members of a Weberian class or status group *as such*, on the other hand, need not have any necessary relationship to the members of any other class or status group *as such*; and even where a relationship exists (except of course where the classes or status groups concerned happen to be also classes in Marx's sense), it will rarely involve anything more than efforts by *individuals* to rise up in the social scale – a feature of human society so general and obvious that it hardly helps us to *understand* or *explain* anything except in the most trite and innocuous way. I have no wish to minimise the importance which may sometimes attach to certain features of status *in a static situation* – that is to say, when we are looking at a society as it is at a given point in time, and not in a historical perspective, as a developing organism. For example, members of a status group near one extreme of a stratified social scale may seldom if ever marry members of another such group at the opposite end of the scale; and in India membership

of one particular type of closed status group, namely caste, may even involve contamination for members of one caste who are involved in certain kinds of contact with members of another. I would insist, however, that when we are concerned with *social change*, these and similar status elements have at best a negative importance: they may help to account for the absence of such change, but they can never explain why it takes place.

Perhaps I can best bring out the difference between thinking in terms of class and status categories respectively by considering slaves. Is it more profitable to regard them as a class in the Marxist sense, in which case we must oppose them to slaveowners, masters; or is it more useful to treat them as a status group (indeed, as an 'order', a juridically recognised form of status), in which case they must be opposed either to free men in general or to some special category of free men, such as citizens, or freedmen? The question surely answers itself, if we believe that the most significant feature of the condition of slaves is the virtually unlimited control which their masters exercise over their activities, above all of course their labour (cf. III.iv below). Between slaves and free men (or citizens, or freedmen) there is no relationship of involvement, but rather a technical difference – however important it may be in some contexts. Slaves and wage-labourers, slaves and poor peasants, slaves and petty traders are not *significantly related* as are slaves and slaveowners. (I find it strange that Marx and Engels could speak carelessly of relations between free men and slaves, or citizens and slaves, when they were clearly thinking of relations between slaveowners and slaves: see above.)

Recently Sir Moses Finley has explicitly rejected a Marxist analysis in terms of economic class and has reverted to a classification by status which seems to me virtually identical with Weber's, although I think he does not so identify it himself. Now it may be that Finley had some better reason in mind for discarding a class analysis, but in his book, *The Ancient Economy* (p.49), he gives only one argument, which, as I showed in Section iii of this chapter, rests on a serious misunderstanding of what Marx meant by 'class'. (It is unfortunately all too characteristic of contemporary Western historiography of the ancient world that one of the few practitioners who has taken the trouble to examine some of the concepts and categories with which he operates should have failed to grasp even the basic elements of Marx's thought.) As for exploitation (which does not even appear in Finley's Index, but does raise its head feebly once or twice), it is treated by Finley only in connection with conquest and imperialism (e.g. *AE* 156-8); but both 'exploitation' and 'imperialism' are for him 'in the end, too broad as categories of analysis. Like "state", they require specification' (*AE* 157), which they never receive from him; and after a couple of paragraphs they are dropped again.[23a]

It is fascinating to observe the way in which Finley (*AE* 45) introduces his analysis of ancient society – ultimately, as I have said, in terms of 'status', after he has rejected a classification primarily according to either 'orders' or 'class'. He makes it plain from the outset (reasonably enough, in view of the nature of our evidence) that he is going to begin by concentrating on those at the top end of the social scale: 'they alone,' he says, 'are at present under consideration.' But who are these people? He actually defines them as 'the *plousioi* of antiquity'. But, as he himself has already made it clear (*AE* 41), 'a *plousios* was a man who was rich enough to live properly on his income (as we should phrase it)': he is the characteristic member of my 'propertied class' (III.ii below). Finley begins his analysis, then, by accepting a definition in terms of economic class, and specifically with those I am calling 'the propertied class' – an unconscious admission of the inadequacy of his own chosen categories. One remembers here the reluctant admission of Weber, in the midst of his discussion of 'status honour': 'Property as such is not always recognised as a status qualification, but in the long run it is, and with extraordinary regularity' (*FMW* 187).[24]

Of course I admit that ancient society can be *described* (though hardly 'analysed' and certainly not 'explained') in the manner advocated by Weber and Finley; but Finley's description, compared with one based upon Marx's class categories, is as inadequate as Weber's and is open to much the same objections. I am certainly not at all attracted by Finley's unfortunate metaphor (which has already been given a wide currency, by himself and others) of 'a spectrum of statuses and orders' (*AE* 68, cf. 67): I am much happier when he says that 'rich Greeks and Romans' (and presumably not only rich ones) were 'members of criss-crossing categories' (*AE* 51). But 'criss-crossing categories' represent a kind of classification which is the very opposite of a 'spectrum' (or 'continuum')[25] and, I must say, more appropriate to Greek and Roman society, if we want to think in terms of 'social stratification'. Indeed, the characteristics according to which we may wish to classify ancient Greeks and Romans were sometimes complementary, sometimes the reverse: political rights (citizen or non-citizen), social prestige and economic position, for example, might reinforce each other in a particular case or they might not – Lysias and his brother Polemarchus may have been among the richest men in late-fifth-century Athens, and in 404 they are certainly said to have owned the largest number of slaves which can be reliably credited to any Greek of the Classical period,[26] but in Athens they were metics (resident foreigners) and enjoyed no political rights; and some of the wealthiest men known to us in the late Roman Republic and early Principate were freedmen, whose strictly social status was much lower than it would have been had they not been born in slavery. (See the useful Appendix 7, 'The size of private fortunes under the Principate', in Duncan-Jones, *EREQS* 343–4: here five of the first sixteen men are freedmen, the first four of them imperial freedmen.)

Status, as conceived by Finley (following Weber), is often convenient enough as a pure means of classification; and again, I have no wish to deny its usefulness for some purposes. As an analytical tool, however, it has, when compared with Marx's concept of class, the same fatal weaknesses as the corresponding set of categories in Weber.

First, as Finley himself admits, it is inescapably 'vague', because the word 'status' has (as he puts it, *AE* 51) 'a considerable psychological element'. In defining a man's status we are always obliged to take into account other people's estimation of him – a factor not at all easy to evaluate even in our own contemporary world, and surely impossibly difficult in antiquity, from which only a small fragment of the necessary evidence has survived. I think I know what Finley means when he describes 'status' as 'an admirably vague word' (*AE* 51), but I do not share his belief in the utility of its vagueness.

Secondly, and much more important, status is a purely descriptive category, with no heuristic capacity, no such explanatory power as the dynamic Marxist concept of class provides – because (as I said earlier, when criticising Weber) there can be no organic relationship between statuses. I realise that Finley himself believes that 'at the upper end of the social scale, the existence of a spectrum of statuses and orders . . . explains much about economic behaviour'; he goes on to assert that 'the same analytical tool helps resolve otherwise intractable questions about the behaviour at the lower end' (*AE* 68). I cannot myself see how his 'spectrum of statuses and orders' *explains* anything whatever, at either end of the social scale. Anyone who makes such a claim must surely be prepared to prove it by giving a number of examples – as I am doing throughout this book, to illustrate the value of a Marxist analysis. Finley does nothing of the sort. The only example I can find in his book is the one he goes on at once to give, and this is a false example, which does nothing to establish his position. 'Helots revolted,' he says, 'while chattel slaves did not in Greece, *precisely because* the helots possessed (not lacked) *certain rights and privileges*, and *demanded more*' (*AE* 68, my italics). This is clearly false. The Helots – mainly the Messenian helots rather than those of Laconia, who were far fewer in number (*Thuc.* I.101.2: see III.iv n.18 below) – revolted, ultimately with success, not because they had 'rights and privileges' or because they 'demanded more', but because they alone, of all Greek 'slaves', were a single united people, who had once been the independent *polis* of 'the Messenians' (Messene, as we should call it), and who could therefore take *effective action in common*, and because they wanted to be *free* and an independent entity (the *polis* of 'the Messenians') once more, whereas the slaves of virtually all other Greek states were, as I have put it elsewhere, 'a heterogeneous, polyglot mass, who could often communicate with each other only [if at all] in their masters' language, and who might run away individually or in small batches but would never attempt large-scale revolts' (*OPW* 89-94, esp. 90). I have looked in vain elsewhere in Finley's book for any actual use of his 'spectrum of statuses and orders' to 'explain economic behaviour' or to 'help resolve otherwise intractable questions about the behaviour at the lower end' of the spectrum. And his sentence that follows the one I have quoted above about the helots, 'Invariably, what are conveniently called "class struggles" in antiquity prove to be conflicts between groups at different points in the spectrum disputing the distribution of specific rights and privileges', is simply beside the point if classes and class struggle are understood in the way I am advocating.

There is a very real difference in historical method between a Weber-Finley type of approach and that which I am advocating in this book. I can only say, again, that the method I am adopting makes it possible to offer an *explanation* in situations where Finley is obliged to stop short with *description*. I can best illustrate this, perhaps, from Finley's attempt to give what he himself calls an 'explanation' of 'the "decline" of slavery' during the Roman Principate and its replacement to a considerable extent by the colonate (*AE* 84-5 & ff.) – a process I have discussed in IV.iii below. In VIII.i below I have tried to make clear the radical difference between the explanation (which is no explanation) given by Finley and that which I offer in this book.

The acceptance of class criteria as the essential ones can also enable us to overcome triumphantly the dilemma with which Finley found himself confronted when he set himself to answer the question, 'Was Greek civilisation based on slave labour?' – the title of a paper (mentioned in n.25 to this section) to which I shall refer in its reprinted form, in *SCA = Slavery in Classical Antiquity* (1960), ed. Finley, 53-72. Under the influence of his unfruitful notion that we do best to 'think of ancient society as made up of a spectrum of statuses' (*SCA* 55), Finley found himself unable to make proper sense of his own question, even after he had gone part of the way to answering it, with a cautious and grudging 'If we could emancipate ourselves from the despotism of extraneous moral, intellectual, and political pressures, we would conclude, without hesitation, that slavery was *a basic element* [my italics] in Greek civilisation' (*SCA* 69). But he then shies away from the question altogether: the word 'basic', he believes, 'has been pre-empted as a technical term by the Marxist theory of history'; and he declares that 'neither our understanding of the historical process nor our knowledge of ancient society is significantly advanced by . . . repeated statements and counter-statements, affirmations and denials of the proposition, "Ancient society was based on slave labour"'. He concludes by throwing up his hands and substituting a totally different question from that of his title: 'not whether slavery was the basic element, or whether it caused this or that, but how it functioned' – an enormous and entirely open-ended question, to which of course there can never be any summary answer, or anything approaching a complete one, so that we are absolved from any obligation to provide more than fragments of an answer. Let us discard the 'spectrum of statuses, with the free citizen at one end and the slave at the other' (*SCA* 55), as a tool of analysis, and begin again, with class instead of status. We can then formulate the specific question I posed in Section iii of this chapter: did the propertied class obtain its surplus mainly by the exploitation of unfree (especially slave) labour? It is by giving an affirmative reply to this question that we are also able to answer, in the most effective way possible, the question to which Finley eventually found himself unable to give a confident reply: 'Was Greek civilisation based on slave labour?'

I am very far from wishing to discard social status as a *descriptive* category. Of course it has important uses in relation to the Greek world, especially in cases where it partakes of some legal recognition and can therefore be considered as constituting an 'order' in the technical sense: a juridically defined category, invested with privileges, duties, or disadvantages. Before the Greek cities came under Roman rule, by far the most important form of status was the possession of citizenship (very much an 'order'), which gave access not merely to the franchise and the possibility of political office, but also to the ownership of freehold land in the area of one's *polis*. (We cannot be absolutely sure that this was true of every Greek city, but it certainly applied to Athens and a good many others, and it is likely to have been the universal rule in the Classical period.) Citizenship was normally obtained by birth alone; special grants (usually for services rendered) were rare in the Archaic and Classical periods but became more common in Hellenistic times. Non-citizens at Athens could take land on lease (see e.g. Lys. VII.10) but could not own land in freehold unless they had been specially granted the right of *gēs enktēsis* by the sovereign Assembly[27] – a privilege which seems to have become more frequent from the late fifth century onwards but was probably not extended very widely. The situation at most other cities is less well known, but it looks as if Athens was not untypical in this respect. In the Hellenistic period the practice of granting to non-citizens (individually, or collectively as members of some other community) the right to own land within the territory of the *polis* gradually grew, and in due course this right seems to have become widely available and to have been extended in particular to all Roman citizens.[28] During the Hellenistic period there was also a great expansion of *isopoliteia*, the mutual exchange of citizenship between cities, and this practice continued in the Roman period: it was so strong that a Roman attempt to forbid it in Bithynia-Pontus by the 'Lex Pompeia' was being widely disregarded by the end of the first century (Pliny, *Ep.* X.114: see Sherwin-White, *LP* 724-5). Some prominent men became not only citizens but councillors of several other cities: there is much evidence for this, both epigraphic (e.g. *IGRR* IV.1761; *MAMA* VIII.421.40-5) and literary (e.g. Pliny, loc. cit.; Dio Chrys. XLI.2,5-6,10). This situation sometimes caused problems concerning liability for local magistracies and liturgies (compulsory municipal burdens), and the Roman government was obliged to legislate about it from the second century onwards (see Sherwin-White, *LP* 725).

The possession or lack of political rights would not *of itself* determine a man's class, in the sense in which I am using that term, so that in an oligarchy a man who had the civil rights of citizenship, but lacked the franchise and access to office because he had not quite a sufficient amount of property, would not necessarily, on my scheme, have to be put in a different class from his neighbour, a fraction richer, who just succeeded in scraping into the oligarchic *politeuma* (the body of those possessing full political rights). The non-citizen, however, the *xenos* who lacked even the civil rights of citizenship, would certainly fall into a different class, if he was not one of those rare foreigners who had been granted full *gēs enktēsis* by the State, for without this essential right of property he would be unable to own the one form of wealth upon which economic life mainly depended.

Another 'order' may be seen in those 'resident foreigners' who had official permission to reside in a particular *polis* for more than a brief period, and whose official status was sometimes (as at Athens) carefully regulated: these 'resident foreigners' are usually referred to nowadays as 'metics' (from the Greek word *metoikoi*),[29] and that is how I shall speak of them, although the term *metoikoi* was not universal in the Greek world even in the Classical period, and it largely died out in the Hellenistic age. (Other expressions found in Greek cities in place of *metoikoi* include *synoikoi, epoikoi, katoikoi,* and later predominantly *paroikoi*.)[30] I shall mainly ignore metics in this book, since the great majority of them who were neither political exiles nor freedmen would be citizens of some other city, living *by choice* in their city of residence; and even today such people do not normally have citizen rights in the country they happen to reside in. (Political exiles were men deprived of citizenship; and Greek freedmen, unlike Roman freedmen, seem virtually never to have been granted citizenship on manumission, a fact which I shall try to explain in III.v below.) Since the metic who was a citizen of *polis* A but preferred to live in *polis* B could normally return to A and exercise political rights there if he wished, there is no need for me to pay any special attention to him. It is often assumed nowadays that, in the fifth and fourth centuries B.C. anyway, the merchants who carried on the external trade of a given city would mostly be metics living in that city; but this is a misconception, as I have shown elsewhere (*OPW* 264-7, 393-6; cf. II.iv n.27 below).

When the Greek cities came under Roman rule, the possession of Roman citizenship (until that was extended in about A.D. 212 to virtually all free inhabitants of the Roman empire) created a new 'order', the importance of which is nicely illustrated in the story of St. Paul in Acts XXI-XXVI (see VIII.i below). In due course Greeks gradually penetrated into the equestrian and even the senatorial order, the imperial nobility (see VI.vi below). The 'curial order' (which became to all intents and purposes a class), another feature of the Roman period, I shall deal with in VIII.ii below. Certain kinds of individual prowess such as military ability, literary or forensic skill, and even athletic proficiency (cf. *OPW* 355), could sometimes enable a man to rise beyond the status into which he was born, or at least enhance his 'ständische Lage'; but these and other such forms of personal quality require no particular attention here, since their possession would merely facilitate the 'upward social mobility' of the individuals who possessed them.

★　★　★　★　★　★

I do not think that any historian or sociologist who is concerned with the ancient world will want to analyse its social structure in terms that are basically political. The substitution of such a method for a Marxist analysis in terms of economic class has certainly been argued for the modern world, most eloquently perhaps by Dahrendorf, some of whose views I have discussed in Section iii of this chapter. His position is well summarised in the Inaugural Lecture which he delivered at Tübingen and was published in English in 1968:[31] '[Social] stratification is merely a consequence of the structure of power.' (This lecture of course needs to be read with Dahrendorf's other works, in particular his book, *Class and Class Conflict in Industrial Society*, 1959, mentioned in Section iii of this chapter.) I find Dahrendorf's conclusions quite unconvincing for modern society,[32] and they are certainly even more defective when applied to the ancient world: I doubt if any ancient historian would feel inclined to follow them. As I have said before, I am not myself much interested in 'social *stratification*', and Marx certainly was not. But the view we are considering, that social stratification depends primarily on political power, has an important element of truth in it, which emerges clearly when the theory is re-stated in a less exaggerated form. Access to political power may have very important effects upon the class struggle: a class in possession of economic power will use its political authority to reinforce its dominant economic position; and on the other hand an exploited class which is able to exercise some degree of political influence will seek to protect itself against oppression. That extraordinary phenomenon, Greek democracy, was essentially the political means by which the non-propertied protected themselves (see V.ii below) against exploitation and oppression by the richer landowners, who in antiquity always tended to be the dominant class (see III.i-iii below). In the seventh century and earlier, before the emergence of democracy, there was probably a great deal of the kind of exploitation of the poor by the rich which we find in Solon's Attica at the opening of the sixth century (see V.i below). In a Greek democracy, however, making its decisions – probably for the first time in human history (see *OPW*

348-9) – by majority vote, the poor, because they were the majority, could protect themselves to a certain extent. They could sometimes even turn the tables on the rich, not only by obliging them to undertake expensive liturgies (especially, at Athens and elsewhere, the trierarchy), but also by occasionally confiscating their property when they were convicted in the courts. Such measures were a form of redistribution which might be loosely compared with the progressive taxation imposed by modern democratic governments. Thus political conflicts in Greek states would tend to reflect opposed class interests, at least in some degree; but this was by no means always the case, any more than it is today, and more often there was nothing like a one-to-one correspondence of political and economic factors; sometimes, indeed, there may be little visible alignment of class divisions with what we know of a particular political contest in Greek history. At crises, however, even at Athens (in 411 and 404, for example: see V.ii below), political factions might largely coincide with class divisions.

At Athens and some other cities in the fifth and fourth centuries B.C. there was an astonishing development of real democracy, extending to some extent right down to the poorest citizens: this is a good example of exceptional political factors operating for a time in such a way as to counterbalance economic forces. But, as I shall explain in V.iii below, the basic economic situation asserted itself in the long run, as it always does: the Greek propertied classes, with the assistance first of their Macedonian overlords and later of their Roman masters, gradually undermined and in the end entirely destroyed Greek democracy.

It goes without saying that when one people conquers another its leading men may often, if they wish, appropriate the whole or some part of the land and other wealth of the conquered. Thus Alexander the Great and his successors claimed the whole of the *chōra* of the Persian empire, on the ground – whether true or false (cf. III.iv below) – that it had all belonged ultimately to the Great King; and they proceeded to make massive land grants to their favoured followers, whose dominant position in the areas concerned then had a 'political' origin, being derived from a royal grant. The Romans sometimes appropriated part of the land of a conquered people as *ager publicus populi Romani*, public land of the Roman People: it would then be leased out to Roman citizens. And in the Germanic kingdoms set up from the fifth century onwards by Visigoths, Ostrogoths, Vandals, Franks and others, in what had once been parts of the Roman empire, in Gaul, Spain, north Africa and Britain, and later in Italy itself, the rights of the new landowners and rulers were again derived from conquest. But all these examples are of highly exceptional cases, involving conquest by outsiders. Corresponding internal phenomena can be found in the seizure of wealth by those who had first gained power not as a result of their economic position but as adventurers (especially *condottieri*) or revolutionaries, who consolidated their rule by appropriating the property of citizens in general or of their political adversaries. But again all such cases are exceptions. That in the regular course of events it was political power which regularly determined social stratification is an idea which seems to me to lack all confirmation from the history of the ancient world.

★ ★ ★ ★ ★ ★

There are two other positions I ought to mention. The first is that represented by L. V. Danilova, in an article originally published in Russian in 1968 and in an English translation, as 'Controversial problems of the theory of precapitalist societies', in *Soviet Anthropology and Archaeology* 9 (1971) 269-328, which first came to my notice as a result of Ernest Gellner's article, 'The Soviet and the Savage', in the *Times Literary Supplement* 3789 (18 October 1974) 1166-8. Danilova's general theory, which she admits to be contrary to the prevailing Soviet view, is that in pre-capitalist societies control of the conditions of production is not the principal way in which exploitation is secured by a ruling class, and that it is 'direct relations of dominance and subjection' (a phrase which doubtless owes its origin to Marx's *Herrschafts- und Knechtschaftsverhältnis*: see Section iii of this chapter) which are 'the basis of social differentiation'. As regards the Greek and Roman world and western Europe in the Middle Ages, this view seems to me to have nothing in its favour, and I shall therefore waste no time on it here. It is also clearly contrary to the views of Marx, although Danilova tries to justify it in Marxist terms.

The other position I want to mention here may appear at first sight to be very different from the Marxist class analysis I am presenting, but turns out in the end to be reconcilable with it. This involves regarding the ancient Greek world as a 'peasant society' or even 'peasant economy', in the sense in which those terms have been used by A. V. Chayanov, A. L. Kroeber, Robert Redfield, Teodor Shanin, Daniel Thorner and many others. In IV.ii below I discuss 'the peasantry' in antiquity. Although I do not find the concept of an overall 'peasant *economy*' useful in relation to the Greek and Roman world, it is true that those we may legitimately call 'peasants' (provided we define them as I do in IV.ii below) were actually a majority of the population in vast areas of the ancient world, and for long periods in many places were responsible for a major share of total production. Recognising the existence of 'peasants' or 'the peasantry' is entirely compatible with my general approach, provided a class analysis is applied throughout, as it is in IV.i-iii below.

To conclude this section, I wish to make it clear that I am not denying all value to the approaches I have been criticising. Some of them, indeed, can be very useful, if in a limited way, and some of their practitioners have made valuable contributions to knowledge. A much-quoted aphorism which can be traced back to Sir Isaac Newton and even to Bernard of Chartres reminds us that however limited our own capacities we can see farther than others by 'standing on the shoulders of giants',[33] those great men of the past whose insights can give us a new vision. But it is not only the giants of the past whose shoulders may offer us a platform for new vistas: standing on the shoulders even of dwarfs, if hardly as rewarding, may at least raise us a little above those around us who are content to stand only on their own feet. (I say this, of course, without imputing dwarf-like characteristics to any of the writers I have been examining here.)

(vi)
Women

The *production* which is the basis of human life obviously includes, as its most essential constituent part, the *reproduction* of the human species.[1] And for anyone who, admitting this, believes (as I do) that Marx was right in seeing position in the whole system of production (necessarily including *re*production) as the principal factor in deciding class position, the question immediately arises: must we not allow a special *class* role to that half of the human race which, as a result of the earliest and most fundamental of all divisions of labour, specialises in reproduction, the greater part of which is biologically its monopoly? (Under 'reproduction' I of course include in the role of women not merely parturition but also the preceding months of pregnancy, and the subsequent period of lactation which, in any but the advanced societies, necessarily makes the care of the child during the first year and more of its life 'woman's work'.)

Marx and Engels, it seems to me, failed to draw the full necessary conclusion. Engels, in the Preface to the original German edition (*Der Ursprung der Familie, des Privateigenthums und des Staats*) of the work I refer to by its English title, *The Origin of the Family, Private Property and the State*, written in 1884 (the year after Marx's death), acknowledged specifically that 'the production *and reproduction* of immediate life' is, 'according to the materialistic conception, the determining factor in history'. And he went on at once to emphasise its 'twofold character: on the one hand, the production of the means of subsistence, of food, clothing and shelter and the tools requisite therefor; on the other, the production of human beings themselves, the propagation of the species'. Marx and Engels, who were always talking about the division of labour in production, did speak casually, in the *German Ideology* (1845-6) of procreation as involving 'the first division of labour', but for them, 'the division of labour . . . was originally nothing but the division of labour *in the sexual act* [*im Geschlechtsakt*]' (*MECW* V.44, my italics); and this seems to me to miss the main point – as indeed Engels appears later to have realised, for when, two-thirds of the way through the second chapter of *The Origin of the Family*, he quoted this very passage (as appearing in 'an old, unpublished manuscript, the work of Marx and myself in 1846'), he changed the wording slightly, to 'The first division of labour is that between man and woman *for the production of children* [*zur Kinderzeugung*]', and he added, 'The first *class antagonism* [*Klassengegensatz*] which appears in history coincides with the development of the antagonism between man and woman in monogamous marriage, and the first *class oppression* [*Klassenunterdrückung*] with that of the female sex by the male' (my italics: *MESW* 494-5). And in the same early work from which Engels quoted, Marx and Engels said that 'the nucleus, the first form, of property lies in the family, where wife and children are the slaves of the husband. This latent slavery in the family, though still very crude, is the first form of property; but even at this early stage it corresponds perfectly to the definition of modern economists who call it the power of disposing of the labour-power of others' (*MECW* V.46). Yet Marx and Engels seem hardly to have realised what far-reaching consequences ought to have been drawn from this particular specialisation of role, within their own system of ideas above all. Engels' *Origin of the Family* deals with the subject, to my mind, very inadequately. (It is perhaps a pity that this work of Engels has had such great influence on Marxist thought: although a brilliant and very humane study, it is too dependent on limited and secondhand information in both anthropology and ancient history, and its general picture is far too unilinear.) I propose to take perfectly seriously the characterisation of the role of women, or anyway married women (I leave these alternatives open), *as a class*, which is implied in the *German*

Ideology, and for a brief moment, in the passage I have quoted, becomes explicit in the second chapter of *The Origin of the Family*.

Now the effective property rights of women have often been restricted in practice. Sometimes this has applied to all the women of a given society, sometimes particularly to the married women, whose property rights have often been more limited (or even more limited) than those of the rest of their sex, as for example in modern England until the Married Women's Property Acts of 1882 and after began to effect a change. A few years ago the fact suddenly dawned upon me that Athenian women in the fifth and fourth centuries B.C. – apart perhaps from a handful of expensive prostitutes, like Neaera and her circle (Ps.-Dem. LIX) and Theodote (Xen., *Mem.* III.xi, esp. § 4), who of course were not citizens – were quite remarkably devoid of effective property rights and were apparently worse off in this respect than women in many (perhaps most) other Greek cities of the period, Sparta in particular, or for that matter in Hellenistic and Roman Athens (see my OPRAW). A suggestion I then made that the question of property rights of Greek women was worth investigating on a much larger scale has already been taken up, in a Harvard thesis and a book by David Schaps,[1a] and I hope there will be further studies. There are all too many interesting questions in this field which I myself certainly cannot answer, and I doubt if anyone can – at least (if the evidence is avilable) until much more research has been done.

Meanwhile, this is the thesis I propose. In many societies either women in general, or married women (who may be regarded in principle as monopolising the reproductive function),[2] have rights, including above all property rights, markedly inferior to those of men; and they have these inferior rights as a direct result of their reproductive function, which gives them a special role in the productive process and makes men desire to dominate and *possess* them and their offspring. In such societies it is surely necessary, on the premises I have accepted, to see the women, or the wives (as the case may be), as a distinct economic class, in the technical Marxist sense. They are 'exploited', by being kept in a position of legal and economic inferiority, so dependent upon men (their husbands in the first place, with their male kin, so to speak, in reserve) that they have no choice but to perform the tasks allotted to them, the compulsory character of which is not in principle lessened by the fact that they may often find real personal satisfaction in performing them. Aristotle, in a perceptive passage which I have quoted in Section iii of this chapter, could speak of the propertyless man (the *aporos*), who could not afford to buy slaves, as using his wife and children in their place (*Pol.* VI.8, 1323a5-6).

Needless to say, if we think of women (or married women) as a class, membership of such a class may or may not be the prime criterion of a woman's class position. (As I have explained in II.ii above, it is perfectly possible for many individuals to belong to more than one class, and it may then be necessary to determine the essential óne, membership of which is paramount for them.) I suggest that in our present case the relative importance of a woman's member-ship of the class of women (or wives) will depend to a high degree upon whether her economic and legal condition is very different from that of her menfolk. In Classical Athens I would see the class position of a citizen woman belonging to the highest class as largely determined by her sex, by the fact that she belonged to the class of women, for her father, brothers, husband and sons would all be property owners, while she would be virtually destitute of property rights, and her class position would therefore be greatly inferior to theirs. The humble peasant woman, however, would not in practice be in nearly such an inferior position to the men of her family, who would have very little property; and, partly owing to the fact that she would to some extent participate in their agricultural activities and work alongside them (in so far as her child-bearing and child-rearing permitted), her membership of the class of poor peasants (cf. IV.ii below) might be a far more important determinant of her class position than her sex. Even less, perhaps, would the class of a non-citizen town-dwelling prostitute or *hetaira* be decided primarily by her sex, for her economic position might be virtually identical with that of a male prostitute or any other non-citizen provider of services in the city. We must of course realise that to place a woman in a separate class from her menfolk would often cut right across the usual criteria of 'social stratification', so far as the property-owning classes are concerned: within a single family the husband might be in the highest class, while his propertyless wife, in respect of the distinction I have just been making, might rate very low indeed; but in life-style she would rank according to the status of her husband. Since those elements in a woman's position which derive from her being virtually the possession of another are very precarious and unstable, I would tend to discount the husband's position as a factor in the real status of the wife, important as it may seem on the surface, and put more emphasis on any dowry which the women can rely on receiving and controlling, in accordance with custom. But this needs a great deal of further thought.

* * * * * *

I believe that I am justified in including these brief and oversimplified remarks on the position of women in the ancient Greek world – at any rate in the Classical period, of which I am now mainly thinking, as I know too little in detail as yet of the property rights of Greek women in the Hellenistic and Roman periods, before Roman law became in theory the universal law of the Mediterranean world, in the third century.[3] Greek wives, I have argued, and therefore potentially all Greek women, should be regarded as a distinct economic class, in the technical Marxist sense, since their productive role – the very fact that they were the half of the human race which supported the main part of the burden of reproduction – led directly to their being subjected to men, politically, economically and socially. Not only were they generally deprived of even the most elementary political rights; they were also, as a rule, allowed only very inferior property rights, and they suffered other legal disabilities; a woman's marriage was entirely at the will of her *kyrios* (normally her father, or if he were dead, her eldest brother or nearest male relative),[4] who, in at least some Greek states, could also withdraw her from her marriage and give her to another husband;[5] and in very many other ways she was at a disadvantage compared with her menfolk. An Athenian woman could not inherit in her own right, from her father at least: if he died without leaving a natural or adopted son, she as *epiklēros* was expected to marry the nearest male relative (who would divorce any wife he might have already), and the property would pass to their male children, thus remaining in the family.[6] Many (perhaps most) other Greek states seem to have had customs that were similar in at least some degree.

Marriage was every Greek woman's normal lot, so that it was as wife and mother that she lived above all. The only group of women who were in a completely different category were prostitutes (often slaves or freedwomen, and virtually never of citizen status), the very ones who removed themselves from the 'class' of women as far as possible by minimising their reproductive function. In Classical Athens at least they may have had in practice a greater control of property than citizen women, and the same may have been true of other states.

I would suggest that where, as at Athens, women are largely deprived of property rights, one good result may follow. If property is fairly widely distributed in the first place, and if (as in all or nearly all Greek states) marriage is patrilocal, so that the girl leaves her father's clan and family and, taking with her whatever she possesses either as dowry or in her own right, goes to join her husband's family, then to keep women propertyless may well help to prevent property from accumulating rapidly in the hands of the richer families. If women can inherit property in their own right they will, in a society where marriage is patrilocal and inheritance patrilineal, remove it from their father's family into their husband's; and of course a father who has (in default of sons) an heiress daughter will naturally, if he is able to give her in marriage outside his kin, find her the richest husband he can, for her own protection. At Sparta, the fact that daughters could inherit in their own right and that the *patrouchos* (the Spartan equivalent of the Athenian *epiklēros*) did not have to marry the next-of-kin must have played a major part in bringing about the concentration of property in a few hands which reduced the number of adult male Spartan citizens (the *homoioi*) from eight or nine thousand to hardly more than a thousand by the date of the battle of Leuctra in 371 B.C. (see my *OPW* 137-8, 331-2, cf. 353-5). At Athens, as I have already explained, there could be no such thing as a daughter inheriting in her own right, and the *epiklēros* had to marry the next-of-kin and thus keep the property in the family. This would help to preserve family property, and would work against automatic accumulation by the already rich through the processes of marriage and inheritance; and the resulting greater equality of property among citizen families is likely to have been one of the factors making for the exceptional strength and stability of the Athenian democracy.

The whole situation is to me a good illustration of the validity of Marx's class analysis, in that it is *the woman's place in production* which was directly responsible for her special status, and in particular created a tendency (observable in many other societies) for her to be denied those property rights which were available to men, and indeed to become herself an object of property rights on the man's part, so that both she and her children could be secured as possessions by her husband. However, woman's inferior social, economic, legal and political position, although a probable and very frequent consequence of her position in the productive process, is not of course a necessary consequence. Even in some modern capitalist societies (in England, for example, since 1975) her rights are the same, or nearly the same, as those of her brothers, although she is still likely to find it more difficult to exercise many of them. And in some early societies, especially perhaps those depending on a light form of agriculture which is particularly well suited to be women's work, she has enjoyed rights superior in some respects to those of men, including the capacity to transmit property (or some forms of property) primarily in the female line (matrilineality, *Mutterrecht*). But in a patrilineal society where dowry and not 'bride-price' or 'indirect dowry' prevails, a woman can be seen as a positive danger to the family into which she is born, for (as we have already noticed) when she marries she will take property out of the family. In such a society we can expect to find the woman's property rights restricted in some degree; Classical Athens was merely an extreme case. Plato, in the *Laws*, went so far as to forbid dowries altogether (V.742c; cf. VI.774c).

In the Greek world a baby girl probably always had a worse chance than a baby boy of surviving, or at least of being reared by its own parents. Exposure of infants, of course, has often been resorted to as a means of population control: by the rich or the moderately well-off in order to prevent the division of inheritances, and even more by the poor in their struggle for survival (see V.i and its n.6 below). There is a great deal of evidence for exposure, scattered through Greek literature.[7] It was no doubt an exaggeration characteristic of Comedy when Poseidippus the Athenian dramatist (writing around the 280s and 270s B.C.) made one of his characters assert that 'Everyone rears a son even if he is poor [*penēs*] but exposes a daughter even if he is rich [*plousios*].' (Cf. Terence, *Heautontim.* 626-30.) However, there are indications that exposure of girls was indeed more common than of boys. In particular, in a famous papyrus of 1 B.C. an Egyptian named Hilarion (who seems to have been a wage-labourer) writes from Alexandria to his wife Alis at Oxyrhynchus, telling her that if she has a child she is to rear it if a boy but expose it if a girl (*P. Oxy.* IV.744=*SP* I.294-5, no.105).

★   ★   ★   ★   ★   ★

I now turn to a brief treatment of Christian marriage as an institution and Christian attitudes towards women and on sexual matters, subjects which I believe to be very relevant to the class position of Greek women, because of the influence Christianity has had in depressing the status of women. We must not forget that the ancient Greek world, according to my definition of it (I.ii above), was at least partly Christian during the later centuries of its existence and had become predominantly Christian well before the end of my period. Early Christian marriage has not been fully investigated by historians (as distinct from theologians) in the light of its Hellenistic, Jewish and Roman counterparts.[8] We often hear Christian marriage praised today; but its admirers, in my experience, very seldom grasp the fact that in its origins it was more backward and more oppressive towards women than most varieties of marriage in the Graeco-Roman world: in particular, (1) as in Jewish marriage, the subjection of the woman to her husband was both more strongly emphasised than in other systems and given a divine origin not found elsewhere; and (2) an unhealthy attitude to sex and marriage can be seen in some of the books of the New Testament, regarded by the dominant form of early Christianity as divinely inspired, the very Word of God.

I propose to deal with the second point first, although I regard it as the less important of the two. Christianity did not have the healthy acceptance of sex and marriage which was in the main a feature of Judaism,[9] but treated marriage as a second-best to virginity. Since this attitude is too often discussed as if it were characteristic of St. Paul only, I will begin with the passage in the *Apocalypse* in which the 144,000 (all male Israelites), who are called 'the firstfruits unto God and to the Lamb' and who are represented as sealed on their foreheads with the divine name, are described as 'they which were not defiled [*ouk emolynthēsan*] with women, for they are virgins' (Rev. XIV.1-5, esp. 4, with VII.2-8). However, it is true that the most powerful influence exerted upon early Christianity towards disparaging sex and even marriage was the seventh chapter of St. Paul's *First Epistle to the Corinthians* (I Cor. vii.1-9, 27-9, 32-4, 39-40, esp. 2, 9).[10] To say that marriage, for St. Paul, was a 'necessary *evil*' would be to go a little too far; but we must begin by recognising that for him the married state was clearly inferior to virginity. It is an indisputable fact that the *only* purpose of marriage specifically mentioned by Paul is the avoidance of fornication ('because of acts of fornication': I Cor. vii.2);[11] and it is only if the unmarried and widows 'cannot be continent' that they are to marry, 'for it is better to marry than to burn [with sexual desire]' (verse 9). Indeed, Paul suffered from an aversion to sex as such: he opens his disquisition on sex and marriage in I Cor. vii with the emphatic generalisation, 'It is good for a man not to touch a woman' (verse 1). If this is, as some have maintained, a quotation from a Corinthian letter to him, written perhaps from an exaggeratedly ascetic standpoint, and if Paul is answering, in effect, with a 'Yes, but . . . ', let us at least be clear that he is saying 'Yes'! And a little later he says, 'It is good for the unmarried and widows to abide even as I' (verse 8). Paul was very complacent about his own continence: he could actually say, 'I would that all [and by *pantas anthrōpous* he almost certainly means 'all men and women'] were even as I myself' (verse 7). Apologies have often been made for Paul on the ground that he was thinking in eschatological terms, in daily expectation of the Second Coming; but I cannot myself see that this excuses him in any way. (We have even been presented recently with the concept of 'the eschatological woman';[12] but of this theological fantasy the less said the better.)

I come now to the most important aspect of the attitude of the early Christians to women and marriage: their belief – which, as we shall see, was firmly rooted in the Old Testament – that wives must be subject to their husbands and obey them. In most of the passages I shall be quoting it is wives specifically who are addressed, rather than women in general; but of course in the ancient Greek world virtually all girls could be expected to marry – the 'maiden aunt' and even the 'spinster' are phenomena unknown to antiquity. Aristophanes, *Lysistrata* 591-7 provides 'the exception that proves the rule'. (I think I should add that when in I Cor. vii.25 St. Paul says he has 'no commandment from the Lord concerning virgins', we must not be tempted to say that virgins are fortunate indeed, for I am among those who believe that the passage may have a much more limited application than may appear at first sight.)[13] I cannot of course set out all the relevant evidence here and will merely concentrate on the most important passages. In I Cor. xi.3 and Ephes. V.22-4 a striking parallel is drawn between the relation of the husband to the wife and that of God to Christ and of Christ to man (I Cor. xi.3) or to the Church (Ephes. V.23), upon which is based the command to the wife not merely to *reverence* her husband (the word used in Ephes. V.33 is *phobētai*: literally, 'let her go in dread') but to be *subject* to him in the most complete sense: the word *hypotassesthai*,[14] which is used of this relationship in Ephesians (V.22,24), Colossians (III.18), Titus (II.5), and I Peter (iii.1), is the word also used in the Epistles for the subjection of slaves to their masters (Tit. II.9; I Pet. ii.18), of ordinary people to State power (Rom. XIII.1; Tit. III.1), of Christians to God the Father (Hebr. XII.9; James IV.7; cf. I Cor. xv.27-8), and of the Church to Christ (Ephes. V.24, where the relationship Church : Christ = wives : husbands is explicit; cf. 23). In I Timothy ii.11 the woman is to 'learn in silence, in all subjection' (*en pasēi hypotagēi*). The forceful metaphor employed both in I Cor. xi.3 and in Ephes. V.23 is that of the 'head', *kephalē* in Greek. 'The head of every man is Christ; and the head of the woman is the man; and the head of Christ is God' (I Cor. xi.3). 'Wives, submit yourselves unto your own husbands, as unto the Lord. For the husband is the head of the wife, even as Christ is the head of the Church; and he is the saviour of the body. But as the Church is subject unto Christ, so let wives be to their own husbands in everything' (Ephes. V.22-4).

At this point, unfortunately, I am obliged to turn aside in order to deal with a highly technical question concerning the metaphor of the 'head' (*kephalē*), to which I have just referred, since desperate attempts have recently been made by theologians to play down the notion of authority which it certainly conveys. And this will also raise, for some people, the problem of the genuineness of the various 'Pauline' epistles. I will deal briefly with the latter point first. There can be no doubt that St. Paul regarded his own rulings on the subjects of women, sex and marriage as directly inspired by God, even when he knew of no tradition of a statement by Jesus on a particular point.[15] This places in an exceedingly difficult position those Christians who are reluctant to reject authoritative statements in their sacred books entirely but are nevertheless sufficiently responsive to modern humanist – not only feminist – criticism to find some of the 'Pauline' statements intolerable as they stand. Those statements, it is felt, cannot mean what they say: although for centuries they have been accepted by virtually all Christian churches as divinely inspired, in their literal and natural sense, they must now be given a very different interpretation. I know of no historian who would be prepared to countenance such exegesis, but it does seem to have an appeal to some theologians, as we shall see. One expedient is to exclude certain texts always accepted until recently as written by Paul himself but now regarded by many New Testament scholars as pseudo-Pauline (or 'deutero-Pauline', a nice euphemism) and the work of later writers.[16] One can then pretend that there are no real 'difficulties' except perhaps I Cor. vii and xi.3-15 – although what we need to do is to see what these texts meant to contemporaries, and of course the 'deutero-Pauline' material is very relevant to such an enquiry, providing as it does some evidence of how contemporaries interpreted the 'genuine' epistles. As it happens, I am myself far less interested in the views of Paul himself than in what I may call 'Pauline Christianity', which is mainstream early Christianity, basing itself upon all the epistles attributed to Paul, as well as the other books of the New Testament.

The meaning of *kephalē* (head) in I Cor. xi.3 (and the 'deutero-Pauline' Ephes. V.23) is central. In 1954 an acute analysis by Stephen Bedale[17] established that in some contexts in the Epistles, when *kephalē* is used metaphorically (as it rarely is outside the Septuagint and the New Testament),[18] its essential idea may be that of priority, origin, beginning. However, Bedale admitted, honestly and correctly, that the word in its metaphorical sense (like *archē*, which can also signify either 'rule' or 'beginning') 'unquestionably carries with it the idea of "authority"', even if 'such authority in social relationships derives from a relative priority (causal rather than merely temporal) in the order of being'.[19] (Here Bedale was apparently thinking of woman's imagined origin from man – Eve from Adam – pictured in Genesis II.18-24.) Dealing with the 'headship' of the male in I Cor. xi.3 (primarily in the sense of 'origin'), Bedale adds, 'In St. Paul's view, the female in consequence is "subordinate" (cf. Ephes. V.23). But this principle of subordination which he finds in human relationships rests upon the order of creation.'[20] It is absolutely impermissible to go beyond this and to treat *kephalē* in our passages as meaning *only* 'source' and not *also* 'authority'.[21] And whatever may be intended by the 'head' metaphor, the very fact that the *relationship* of man (or husband) to woman (or wife) is *equated* in I Cor. xi.3 with that of Christ to man and God to Christ, and in Ephes. V.23 with that of Christ to the Church, makes the relationship of woman to man one of total subordination: this is entirely consistent with the other New Testament evidence which I quoted above.

Some Christians in the modern world have been inclined to lay much of the blame, not only for the unhealthy attitude to sex but also for the subjection of wives to their husbands in early Christian thought and practice, upon the peculiar psychology of St. Paul, who of course was deeply influenced by his devout Jewish upbringing (for which see Acts XXII.3) and also conceivably by the fact that in Tarsus, his home town, women were veiled in public (Dio Chrys. XXXIII.48-9). I must make it clear, therefore, that in reality the subjection of the wife to the husband was part of Christianity's inheritance from Judaism, *necessarily* including (as we shall see) a thorough-going conception of the dominance of the husband, which Christianity actually intensified. This is a very important question which requires emphasis. In these days, when most Christians venerate the Old Testament far less than did the early Church, and the opening chapters of Genesis are taken literally and seriously by none but the most ignorant and bigoted Fundamentalist, we may need to make a conscious effort to remember three features of the account of the creation of man and woman, and of the 'Fall' and its consequences, in Genesis II-III, which more enlightened Christians often prefer to forget. (1) First, and most important in its practical influence upon Christian marriage, is the fact that in Gen. III.16 God himself is made to proclaim the authority or lordship of the husband over the wife. No such religious sanction for male dominance existed in Greek or Roman paganism.[22] A passage in Josephus is explicit about the inferiority of the wife to the husband 'in all respects', according to the Jewish Law. 'Let her therefore be submissive [*hypakouetō*], not for her humiliation but so that she may be controlled [*archētai*], for God gave power [*to kratos*] to the husband' (*C. Apion.* II.201). Interpolation has been suspected, but in any event this passage is an adequate description of the position of the first-century Jewish wife (see e.g. Baron, *SRHJ* II².236). Philo uses even stronger language than Josephus: in *Hypoth.* 7.3 he says that in Jewish law, 'with a view to their rendering obedience in all respects', wives must 'be *slaves* to' their husbands – the actual word *douleuein* is used. (I think I should take this opportunity just to mention a particularly nasty passage in Philo, justifying the Essenes for refraining from marriage on the ground that wives are unpleasant in various ways and a source of corruption – I shrink from reproducing his invective: *Hypoth.* 11.14–17.) (2) Secondly, there is the extraordinary fact that in Gen. II.21–4 the woman is not brought into existence independently and at the same time as the man, like all the rest of Creation (including, apparently, female animals!), but was made after man and from one of his ribs. This of course reverses the actual order of things: man is now born of woman, but the first woman is depicted as having been taken from man and created specifically to be his 'help meet' (Gen. II.18,20). As St. Paul put it, 'For the man is not of the woman, but the woman of the man; for neither was the man created for the woman, but the woman for the man' (I Cor. xi.8–9; cf. Mk II.27 for a very similar use of the Greek preposition *dia*). This particular myth in Genesis has long been a powerful buttress of male 'superiority'. There is, of course, every reason to think that Jesus himself and all his followers, including Paul, accepted the myth in its literal sense, as if it represented historical fact; we are not dealing with a mere Pauline aberration. And in face of this, it is grossly dishonest to pretend that Paul could have had any other view than the one he expresses, in favour of the subjection of the wife to the husband.

Both the aspects of the Genesis story that I have just described were part of the Jewish legacy to the Christian conception of marriage, which overall was certainly nearer to the Jewish than to the Roman or even the Hellenistic variety. (3) A third feature of the Genesis myth, equally accepted as fact by the early Christians, was the greater responsibility of the woman for the 'Fall'. She eats the forbidden fruit first and persuades the man to follow her example (Gen. III.1–6, 12 and esp. 16–17), with the result that God gives her a special punishment: having to endure pain in childbearing (III.16, where the authority of the husband over her is also laid down). Because of Christian soteriology, in which the 'Fall' played an essential part, the leading role attributed to the first woman, which appears only occasionally in Jewish writings (e.g. Ecclus. XXV.24), naturally figured more prominently in Christian than in Jewish theology. In this respect Christianity made an unfortunate use of its Jewish inheritance. For the writer of I Tim. ii.11–14 the facts that 'Adam was first formed, then Eve', and that 'Adam was not deceived, but the woman being deceived was in transgression' (cf. II Cor. xi.3: 'the Serpent beguiled Eve') are the justification – indeed, the sole explicit justification – for the order to the woman to 'learn in silence with all subjection', and not to 'teach, nor to usurp authority over the man, but to be in silence' (cf. I Cor. xiv.34–5).

Some recent writers have made much of the fact that many of St. Paul's converts who are named in the New Testament were women; but this has no significance at all in the present context. A large number of female converts was only to be expected, since religion formed 'the major outlet for female activity in the Roman world', as Averil Cameron has pointed out in an article, 'Neither male nor female', to be published in *Greece & Rome* in 1980, which she has been kind enough to show me.[22a] And of course there is not the least sign that any of these women occupied a place of authority or even importance in their local churches. Nor need the historian take any serious account of that text so often quoted by theologians, Galatians III.28: 'There is neither Jew nor Greek; there is neither bond nor free; there is neither male nor female; for ye are all one in Christ Jesus' (cf. Coloss. III.11 for a similar text, not mentioning the sexes). I have discussed both these passages near the beginning of VII.iii below. They have a purely spiritual or eschatological meaning and relate only to the situation as it is 'in the sight of God', or 'in the next world'; they have no significance whatever for this world, where the relations in real life between man and woman, or master and slave, are not affected in any way. Precisely as the slave who is a good man ceases, in Hellenistic philosophical thought, to be 'really' a slave at all (see VII.iii below), so the slave becomes 'Christ's freedman' merely by becoming a Christian; and the woman achieves oneness with the man, the Jew with the Greek, in exactly the same way. The situation of none of them *in this world* is altered in the slightest degree; and of course the whole train of thought provides a convenient excuse for *doing* nothing whatever to *change* the situation of the disadvantaged, for, theologically, they have *already* achieved everything.

Now it would not have been at all surprising to find the early Christians simply adopting the Jewish and/or Hellenistic social practice of their day, in regard to sex and marriage as in other ways, but we find them taking a position which was even more patriarchal and oppressive than that of most of their contemporaries. Distinctly more enlightened ideas were common in the world around them. Roman marriage in particular had developed beyond other systems in the rights it allowed to women, whether married or not. (The existence of the Roman *patria potestas* does not disprove my assertion.)[23] I think Schulz was right in regarding the Roman law of husband and wife as the supreme example in Roman jurisprudence of humanistic sentiment, and in attributing the later decay of some of its most progressive features to the much more male-dominated thought-world of the invading German 'barbarians' and of the Christian Church (*CRL* 103-5). The Roman law of marriage, by the way, showed remarkable tenacity in resisting the modifications (the abolition of divorce by consent, for example) desired by the Church and the Christian emperors from Constantine onwards: this has been very well brought out by A. H. M. Jones (*LRE* II.973-6, with III.327-8 nn.77-82). As we all know, the Christian churches have tended until very recently either to forbid divorce altogether or at best (as in England until very recently, and in Scotland still) to permit it only upon proof of a 'matrimonial offence' by one party against the other – a disastrous notion, productive of much unnecessary suffering, not to mention frequent collusive divorces.

Apprehensive and irrational ideas about the regularly occurring 'uncleanness' of woman during her reproductive years might have been expected to have some effect on early Christianity, since such ideas were not uncommon in the pagan Greek and Roman world (see IV.iii § 10 below) and were particularly strong in Judaism. In Leviticus XV, representing in its present form one of the latest strands of the Torah (however ancient its origins), great stress is laid upon the pollution incurred by contact with a menstruating woman or even anything she has touched (Levit. XV.19-33; cf. Isai. XXX.22). Intercourse with such a woman is a capital crime for both parties (Levit. XX.18).[24] Many people who fail to understand the strength of feeling often associated with beliefs about ritual pollution may be astonished when they read one of the finest passages in the Old Testament, in which Ezekiel gives what I have called elsewhere 'an explicit and emotional repudiation of the whole idea of joint family responsibility for crime' (so firmly embedded in the older strata of the Hebrew Scriptures),[25] and discover that 'coming near to a menstruous woman' is placed in the same category as idolatry, adultery, the oppression of the poor, the taking of usury and so forth, as a serious crime justifying punishment (Ezek. XVIII.1 ff., esp. 6). The 'Mosaic' legislation on the subject of 'uncleanness' was taken very seriously indeed by the rabbis. To go no further than the *Mishnah* – one whole tractate, *Niddah*, occupying some 13 pages (745-57) in the standard English translation by Herbert Danby (1933), is devoted entirely to menstruation and the pollution it entails, and the subject is noticed in numerous passages in other tractates. (There are some nice rulings, e.g. on how large a blood-stain which a woman finds on herself may be set down to a louse: the answer is 'of the size of a split bean', *Nidd.* 8.2. Contrary to what might be suggested by considerations of hygiene, irrelevant here, the assumption of infestation may thus *remove* suspicion of 'uncleanness'!) It is to Christianity's credit that in the end it was not much influenced by superstitious ideas of this particular kind, at any rate in the West. In some of the Greek-speaking communities, however, there remained a deep-seated feeling that woman's regular 'uncleanness' made it wrong for her, while so afflicted, to take communion and even perhaps to enter a church. The earliest official exclusions of women in this condition from communion, so far as I know, are by two patriarchs of Alexandria: Dionysius (a pupil of Origen), around the middle of the third century, and Timothy, *c*. 379-85, whose rulings became canonical in the Byzantine Church and were confirmed by the 'Quinisext' Council *in Trullo* at Constantinople in 692.[26] The Trullan Canons, passed by Eastern bishops only, were rejected in the West; but to this day the Orthodox churches, including the Greek and the Russian, refuse communion to women during menstruation.

It is true that the Christians were in theory more insistent than the great majority of pagans upon the necessity for men as well as women to abstain from sexual intercourse outside marriage (from 'fornication'); but there were pagans who condemned adultery by husbands as much as by wives (see below for Musonius Rufus), and a statement by the Roman lawyer Ulpian, that it is 'most inequitable that a husband should exact chastity from his wife when he does not practise it himself', is preserved in the *Digest* (XLVIII.v.14.5). What evidence there is from the Later Roman Empire suggests to me that the Christian churches were hardly more successful than the pagans in discouraging 'fornication'; and the conspicuous prevalence of prostitution in Christian countries down the ages shows that mere prohibitions of conduct regarded for religious reasons as immoral, even if backed by threats of eternal punishment, may have little effect if the structure of society is not conducive to their observance. And the irrational hatred of sex in its physical manifestations (with the grudging exception of marriage) which was so characteristic of early Christianity from St. Paul onwards sometimes led to an asceticism which bordered on the psychopathic. The modern reader of some of the letters and other works of St. Jerome (an over-sexed man who was bitterly ashamed of his natural feelings) may be deeply moved by the unnecessary suffering caused in this highly gifted individual by a set of insane dogmas which he never questioned, and the observance of which sometimes created in him a deep agony of mind which could hardly be vented except in some excessively ferocious and even scurrilous tirade against a religious adversary (a Helvidius or a Vigilantius) who had dared to say something

Jerome could interpret as a disparagement of the Virgin Mary or of virginity in general.[27]

As a wholesome corrective of the popular Christian view, repeated over and over again in modern times, that the early Church introduced an entirely new and better conception of marriage and sex, it is worth reading some of the fragments that have been preserved of the Stoic philosopher of the second half of the first century, Musonius Rufus – perhaps the most attractive, to my mind, of all the later Stoics. He was a Roman of the equestrian order (see Tac., *Hist.* III.81), but he probably did most of his teaching in Greek, and although he is not reliably credited with any written works, a certain amount of his doctrine is preserved (almost entirely by Stobaeus) in some fairly substantial Greek fragments compiled by an unknown pupil, whose name is transmitted to us merely as Lucius. The English reader can enjoy the benefit of a complete text (virtually the standard one by O. Hense, 1905), with a good facing English translation and a useful introduction, as part of an article (also published separately) entitled 'Musonius Rufus. "The Roman Socrates"', by Cora E. Lutz, in *YCS* 10 (1947) 3-147.[28] Musonius is both more rational and more humane that St. Paul in his attitude to women, sex and marriage, and he is exceptionally free from the male-dominated outlook, desiring the subjection of women to their husbands, which was common enough in antiquity but was stronger among the Jews than among many pagans (the Romans above all) and was implanted in Paul by his orthodox Jewish upbringing (see above). According to Musonius: (1) in marriage 'there must be above all perfect companionship and mutual love of husband and wife', in sickness and in health; (2) 'all men consider the love of husband and wife to be the highest form of love'; (3) husbands who commit adultery are doing wrong just as much as wives, and it is very objectionable for them to have sexual relations with their slave-girls; (4) marriage is an excellent thing, and even the philosopher should accept it gladly; and (5) girls should receive the same kind of education as boys, extending to philosophy.[29] Although Musonius sees the sphere of activity of a woman as different in some ways from that of a man, he never suggests that she is in any way inferior to him or that she ought to be subjected to him or dominated by him. Most of the individual statements attributed to Musonius which I have just quoted can be paralleled in other Greek and Latin authors, but I fancy that their combination is exceptional.

If we want an explanation of the failure of the Christian churches to effect in practice any noticeable change for the better in moral or social behaviour, even in those spheres (such as the prohibition of fornication for men as well as women) in which it advocated a higher standard than that commonly accepted in the Graeco-Roman world, we may find it in the conclusion of a parable to which I shall have occasion to refer again later (VII.iv below), that of Lazarus. When the rich man suffering the torments of hell begged that Lazarus might be enabled to go and preach to his five brothers and save them from sharing his dreadful fate (for surely they would listen to one risen from the dead), the reply was, 'They have Moses and the prophets, let them hear them . . . If they hear not Moses and the prophets, neither will they be persuaded, though one rose from the dead' (Lk. XVI.27-31). In order to generalise this statement, we must substitute, for 'Moses and the prophets', 'the general climate of orthodox opinion in society': if men are not swayed by that, Jesus is saying, even one who has risen from the dead is not likely to move them. Hence we should not expect Christian preaching itself to make much difference to men's behaviour, as distinct from their purely spiritual life – nor did it.

★   ★   ★   ★   ★   ★

I need hardly add that very much more can be done than in most modern societies to reduce the male dominance which has been characteristic of the great majority of civilised societies, subjecting a high proportion of women to the exploitation and oppression which are (as we have seen) normal consequences of class conflict. Of course, the brainwashing process we all go through in child-hood has played a powerful role here: a particular stereotype has commonly been foisted upon females from infancy onwards, and naturally the vast majority have largely accepted it, as if it were an inevitable biological necessity rather than a social construction which could be changed.[30]

★   ★   ★   ★   ★   ★

I trust that this section will serve to exculpate me from any crime I may have committed in the eyes of feminists by sometimes speaking of the slave, serf, peasant etc. as a 'he' rather than a 'he/she' (or 's/he').

III

Property and the Propertied

(i)
The conditions of production: land and unfree labour

In the ancient world the principal 'means of production', in the sense in which I am using that term, were land and unfree labour. The latter expression should really include, in addition to chattel slavery and serfdom and debt bondage (to be discussed in Section iv of this chapter), all kinds of compulsory labour services exacted from the exploited classes by local city governments or a royal or Roman imperial administration; but I find it more convenient to discuss these labour services performed for governmental authorities (forms of 'indirect collective exploitation', as I am calling them: see IV.i below) in the next chapter, which deals principally with the peasantry. The ownership of land and the power to exact unfree labour, largely united in the hands of the same class, together constitute, therefore, the main keys to the class structure of the ancient Greek communities. Free wage labour, which plays the essential part in capitalist production, was relatively unimportant in antiquity (see Section vi of this chapter). In a sense, as Marx insisted, the hired labourer is not fully free, as he has virtually no alternative to selling his labour-power for wages; his 'surplus labour' (as Marx calls it), from which the employer derives his profit, is given without an equivalent, and 'in essence it always remains forced labour, no matter how much it may seem to result from free contractual agreement' (*Cap.* III.819). Just as 'the Roman slave was held by fetters, the wage-labourer is bound to his owner by invisible threads. The appearance of independence is kept up by means of a constant change of employers, and by the *fictio juris* of a contract' (*Cap.* I.574). Yet the disappearance of legally, economically or socially unfree labour and its replacement by wage labour entered into under a contract which can have a good deal of free choice in it is a very real step forward. 'It is one of the civilising aspects of capital that it enforces surplus-labour in a manner and under conditions which are more advantageous to the development of the productive forces, social relations, and the creation of the elements for a new and higher form than under the preceding forms of slavery, serfdom etc.' (*Cap.* III.819). Whether this entails our attributing to the *ancient* hired labourer a position superior to that of the slave or serf is a doubtful point, to which we shall return in Section vi of this chapter.

In a brilliant passage in *Wages, Price and Profit*, ch. ix (reappearing in a slightly different form in *Capital* I.539–40), Marx draws attention to the most obvious difference in the exploitation of the slave, the serf and the wage labourer. The slave's labour has the appearance of being totally unpaid; he works all the time for his master and receives in return only enough to allow him to live – and perhaps to reproduce himself. 'Since no bargain is struck between him and his master, and no acts of selling and buying are going on between the two parties, all his labour seems to be given away for nothing.' With the serf liable to labour rent, or the peasant subjected to the *corvée*, who works for so many days on the field which is regarded as his own possession, and for so many days on his lord's field, the reality emerges clearly: 'the paid and unpaid parts of labour are sensibly separated.' The position of the wage-labourer, like that of the slave, can also give rise to confusion: all the labour given by the hired worker has the appearance of being paid, even that 'surplus labour', as Marx called it, out of which comes the employer's profit, the 'surplus value' yielded up by the worker. 'The nature of the whole transaction is completely masked by the intervention of a contract and the pay received at the end of the week. The gratuitous labour appears to be voluntarily given in the one instance, and to be compulsory in the other [the case of the slave or serf]. That makes all the difference.' I will add only that 'the intervention of a contract' similarly masks the exploitation by a landlord of a leasehold tenant who is not tied to his plot but is free to leave it and go elsewhere, to negotiate a lease on better terms with another landlord, if he can, or to take service as a wage-labourer. [*Wages, Price and Profit* ix = *MESW* 210-12.].

How were the propertied classes of the Greek and Roman world to obtain their surplus? Letting land (and houses) to free tenants was always practised in some degree; but (as I have shown in II.iii above) it would naturally yield a lower rate of exploitation than working the land directly, with unfree labour, wage labour, or a combination of the two. Now wage labour was, as I have said already (and will demonstrate in detail in Section vi of this chapter), of little account in antiquity, in particular because it was generally unskilled and not plentifully available. Therefore, there was simply no way in which the propertied classes of the Greek world could obtain a substantial surplus directly except through unfree labour – a most powerful argument for the role played by such labour in the economy of all the Greek states, which is too often neglected. It is very interesting to find that Aristotle, in a passage near the beginning of the *Politics* (I.4, $1253^{b}33-4^{a}1$), can imagine only one alternative to using slaves – and that is *complete automation*: that of the statues endowed with life by Daedalus or of the tripods made by the god Hephaestus, which Homer had described as running on wheels of their own accord to Olympus! (*Iliad* XVIII.376). Much the same idea is amusingly expressed by the Athenian comic poet Crates (fr. 14-15, *ap.* Athen. VI.267e-8a). There were also, it is true, ways in which the propertied class could obtain part of its surplus indirectly, even while a very large number of humble Greeks, including most of those I am calling 'peasants' (see IV.i-iv below), were still in a condition of freedom and could not easily be exploited directly to any intense degree: this indirect exploitation, which mainly took the form of taxation and compulsory services, is rather a difficult subject, best left until Chapter IV, in which I shall be dealing with the peasantry and other small, free, independent producers. When, in the Later Roman Empire, there was apparently a considerable increase in the exploitation of the small free producers, the use of slave labour in the strict sense was in principle less necessary; but the Greek and Roman world always remained what we may loosely call a 'slave society', with unfree labour continuing to be a main source of exploitation, and when it became necessary for the screw to be tightened upon the peasantry, a large number of them were reduced to a form of serfdom.

Contrary to what is sometimes said, a great deal of slave labour was employed in agriculture, which was by far the most important sector of the ancient economy (see Sections iii and iv of this chapter and Appendix II below).

In the Greek and Roman world wealth was never measured by general income in money, nor were taxes ever levied upon money income. When wealth was quantified it was as capital, and when direct taxes were levied they were either a proportion of a crop (a tenth or whatever), always collected by tax-farmers (*telōnai, publicani*), or they took the form of a capital levy, as in the case of the Athenian *eisphora* and the *tributum* paid by citizens in the early Roman Republic. Very occasionally we hear of a political qualification being assessed in terms of agricultural produce, again in kind: the Athenian Pentacosiomedimnoi (though not, in my opinion, the other Solonian *telē*)[1] were so assessed. Only in Egypt, under the Roman Principate, is there any evidence of income expressed in money being given official recognition as a qualification for the performance of liturgies (public duties); and it is significant that in this case the income was purely from landed property.[2] A recent theory that the four Solonian *telē* at Athens were later based on money incomes is an impossible one, as I have already demonstrated elsewhere.[3] A conclusive argument against any assessment in terms of money income is provided by the extremely primitive nature of ancient accounting, which was incapable of distinguishing properly between what is nowadays kept apart as 'capital' and 'income', let alone enabling a merchant or even a landowner to arrive at a concept of 'net profit', without which the taxation of money income is unthinkable. There seems to have been no really efficient method of accounting, by double or even single entry, before the thirteenth century. (I have discussed Greek and Roman accounting in detail, and have said something about the emergence of modern accounting in the Middle Ages, in my GRA = *Studies in the History of Accounting*, edited by A. C. Littleton and B. S. Yamey [1956] 14-74.)

(ii)
The propertied class (or classes)

The most important single dividing line which we can draw between different groups of free men in the Greek world is, in my opinion, that which separated off from the common herd those I am calling 'the propertied class', who could 'live of their own' without having to spend more than a fraction of their time working for their living. (Expressions like 'live of their own' were sometimes used in English political writings of the seventeenth century and later; but my impression is that they usually signified not the ability to live entirely without working at all – the sense in which I am using the word – but the capacity to live an 'independent' life, on the land or by some form of handicraft or other occupation, without entering into the employment of another by taking wage-service under him; cf. Section vi of this chapter, *ad fin.*, and its nn.48-51.)

Although small peasants and other free men such as artisans and shopkeepers, *working on their own account*, without much property of their own, must always have formed a substantial proportion of the *free* population of the Greek world, and indeed were probably a majority of the *whole* population until about the end of the third century of the Christian era, they would normally have to spend most of their time working for their livelihood, with their families, at somewhere near the subsistence level, and would not be able to live securely and at leisure, as members of the upper class. (I deal very briefly with these small, free producers in IV.ii and vi below.) By and large, a comfortable, leisured existence could be secured only by the possession of property (primarily in land: see Section iii of this chapter), which alone gave the upper classes that *command over the labour of others* which made it possible for them to live the good life, as the Greeks saw it, a life not constrained by the inescapable necessity of working for one's living, a life which could be devoted to the pursuits considered proper for a gentleman: politics or generalship, intellectual or artistic pursuits, hunting or athletics. Isocrates (VII.45), writing in the mid-fourth century B.C., characteristically brackets together 'horsemanship, athletics, hunting and philosophy' as the very proper avocations fostered by the Athenians in the good old days, enabling some men to develop outstanding qualities and others at least to avoid most evils. (For the prestige that might be derived from athletic prowess, see my *OPW* 355.)[1] For the present we can largely forget about the small peasant, the artisan and their like, who formed the very backbone of many Greek states: we shall come to them in Chapter IV below. Our concern here is with the propertied (*hoi euporoi, hoi tas ousias echontes*, and many similar expressions), who alone had the leisure (*scholē*, or in Latin *otium*), a prerequisite of what was then considered to be the good life, as I have defined it. The dividing line between such people and the more or less propertyless masses below them was created by the possession of sufficient *property* to make it possible for them 'to live with discretion an unconstrained life of leisure' (or 'to live a leisured life liberally and temperately'), *scholazontes eleutheriōs hama kai sōphronōs*, as Aristotle put it (*Pol.* VII.5, 1326[b]30-2). Most Greeks would have put less emphasis on the restraint which Aristotle and his like thought so important. Heracleides Ponticus, a contemporary of Aristotle, declared in his treatise *On pleasure* that pleasure and luxury, which relieve and reinforce the mind, are the characteristics of free men; labour (*to ponein*), on the other hand, is for slaves and humble men (*tapeinoi*), whose minds accordingly become shrunken (*systellontai*).[2]

These men, liberated from toil, are the people who produced virtually all Greek art and literature and science and philosophy, and provided a good proportion of the armies which won remarkable victories by land over the Persian invaders at Marathon in 490 and at Plataea in 479 B.C. In a very real sense most of them were parasitic upon other men, their slaves above all; most of them were not supporters of the democracy which ancient Greece invented and which was its great contribution to political progress, although they did supply almost all its leaders; and they provided little more than the commanders of the invincible navy organised by Athens which kept the Greek cities of the Aegean secure against Persia. But what we know as Greek civilisation expressed itself in and through them above all, and it is they who will normally occupy the centre of our picture. I may add that they were a distinctly smaller class than the combined hoplites (heavy-armed infantry) and cavalry, the *hopla parechomenoi*, who must always have included at the lowest hoplite level a certain number of men who needed to spend a certain amount of their time working for their living, generally as peasant farmers. As I hope I have made clear already (in II.iii above), a man's position as a member of the propertied class depends in principle upon whether he *needed* to work in order to maintain himself. If he was not obliged to do so, then whether he actually did or did not spend time on such work himself (supervising the labour of those he exploited on his agricultural land, for instance) is irrelevant for his class position.

I have spoken of 'the propertied class', in the singular, as if all those whose level of existence was above the minimum just mentioned formed a single class. In a sense they did, as opposed to all the rest (*hoi polloi, ho ochlos, to plēthos*); but of course there were very considerable differences inside this 'propertied class', and it will often be necessary to think of its members as subdivided into a number of classes. As compared with the slave, the hired labourer, the full-time artisan, even the peasant who did little more than scrape a living from a small farm worked by himself and his family, we are surely justified in seeing as members of a single 'propertied class' such men as the owner of a large or even medium-sized farm, worked by slaves under a slave bailiff (*epitropos*, in Latin *vilicus*), or leased out at a rent (in which case it would necessarily yield a lower profit); the proprietor of a workshop of, say, 20-50 slaves, supervised by a slave manager; the lessee of mines in the Laurium district of Attica, worked by slaves, and similarly supervised by a manager who would himself be a slave (or conceivably a freedman); the owner (*nauklēros*) of a merchant ship or two[3] which he hired out to traders (*emporoi*) or used for trading himself, manning them with slaves (and of course rarely if ever travelling himself for purely business reasons); the owner of a fair quantity of money capital which he lent out at interest, partly perhaps on mortgage of land (a perfectly safe investment, but bringing in no great return), or, at a much higher rate of interest, on bottomry bonds (a form of transaction known from at least the end of the fifth century B.C., which I have recently described in detail in my AGRML). On the other hand, all those I have just described would be worlds apart from a great Roman senator who owned hundreds of acres and of slaves, and who was even more emphatically a member of the 'propertied class'; but *the scale on which exploitation of the labour of others takes place* must also be taken into account in assessing a man's class, as well as the type of production concerned, and the senator could only be considered a member of the same 'propertied class' as the much smaller figures I have mentioned when they are being collectively contrasted with the exploited classes and the peasantry. I shall sometimes speak of 'the propertied classes', sometimes of 'the propertied class': the latter expression will be particularly appropriate when we are thinking of all the men of property as a single entity, over against the non-propertied.

The Greek propertied class, then, consisted essentially of those who were able to have themselves set *free* to live a civilised life by their command over the labour of others, who bore the burden of providing them with the necessities (and the luxuries) of the good life. This *freedom* of the Greek propertied class is what Aristotle has principally in mind in some very interesting passages, of which I shall single out one here: the concluding sentence of the discussion in *Rhetoric* I.9, 1367[a]28-32, of the concept of *to kalon* – the noble, perhaps; but there is no precise English equivalent. In this passage the word *eleutheros*, literally 'free', is applied in the peculiar sense in which Aristotle and other Greeks sometimes used it, to the gentleman, the man who is fully free from all constraining toil, as opposed to the *aneleutheros*, who works for another's benefit. Aristotle remarks that at Sparta it is *kalon* to have long hair, and he adds, 'for it is the mark of a gentleman [an *eleutheros*], since it is not easy for a man with long hair to do work appropriate to a hired labourer' (*ergon thētikon*). And he goes straight on to give, as another example of *to kalon*, 'not carrying on a menial craft [a *banausos technē*], for it is the mark of a gentleman not to live for the benefit of another' (*to mē pros allon zēn*). Finley mistranslates this passage, 'The condition of a free man is that he not live under the constraint of another.'[4] However, in view of Aristotle's other uses of the phrase in question and similar ones[5] there is not the slightest doubt that he means what I have stated in the text above; and in the context the distinction is between the vulgar artisan and the gentleman; slavery and the slave are never mentioned there. (But Finley goes on to say, quite correctly, that Aristotle's 'notion of living under restraint was not restricted to slaves but was extended to wage labour and to others who were *economically* dependent'.)

 It is desirable at this point to issue a warning. In most of the universities of this country and others in the Western world and the Antipodes, the expression 'Greek history' is likely to be taken to apply to the history of Old Greece from the eighth to the fourth century B.C., and above all to the mainland states, especially Athens and (to a less extent) Sparta. This may be natural enough, because of course a large proportion of the surviving literary evidence (as of those parts of the archaeological and epigraphic evidence which have been collected and published in a form accessible to non-specialists) relates to Old Greece in general and to Athens in particular. Right up to the end of the undergraduate stage this situation is likely to persist, even if in specialist studies interest happens to shift away from the Archaic and Classical periods – which, however, can still be made to yield fresh material, by archaeologists and others, and the economic and social history of which still offers great opportunities to anyone whose training has not been too narrowly confined within the tradition of strictly historical research, and who is not content to remain indifferent (like so many ancient historians) to the techniques developed by sociologists, anthropologists and economists. But we must never forget – and this is the 'warning' of which I spoke a moment ago – that even in their great days, in the fifth and fourth centuries B.C., the Greeks of the mainland inhabited a very poor country, with little natural wealth, agricultural or mineral, and that the predominance of the great states, Sparta and Athens, was due to military or naval strength, resting upon an organised system of alliances: Sparta's Peloponnesian League, or the Delian League which grew into an Athenian empire, and was succeeded in the fourth century by the much weaker Second Athenian Confederacy.[6] It is of mainland Greece that Herodotus was thinking when he made Demaratus say that Greece and poverty had always been foster-sisters (VII.102.1).

 What many people still fail to realise is that some of the most important cities on the west coast of Asia Minor and its offshore islands were already, by the early fourth century, on the way to becoming more wealthy than the cities of mainland Greece – just as Syracuse, under the rule of its remarkable tyrant, Dionysius I, in roughly the first three decades of the fourth century, achieved greater strength than any of the contemporary cities on the Greek mainland, and built up a small empire of its own in Sicily and south Italy. The Asiatic cities scarcely ever enjoyed political power and independence in the same way as

Athens and Sparta in their palmy days: situated as they were on the fringe of the great Persian empire, they were from the late sixth century to the late fourth (when they were finally 'liberated' by Alexander the Great) either under Persian control or subject to strong influence and pressure from Persian satraps or native dynasts, except when they were under Athenian dominance in the fifth century. I have remarked upon this situation elsewhere (*OPW* 37-40): it deserves much more detailed investigation than it has yet received. Here I will only say that I can remember the shock of surprise with which I first realised the significance of the information given by Xenophon (especially in *HG* III.i.27-8; cf. *OPW* 38-9) about the vast wealth of the family of Zenis of Dardanus and his widow Mania, who collected the revenues of a large area in the Troad on behalf of the Persian satrap Pharnabazus in the years around 400 B.C. We can hardly doubt that the bulk of the fortune of this family will have been invested in land, whether it was within the territory of Dardanus and other Greek cities or whether it formed part of the adjacent Persian empire; but there is good evidence from Xenophon that their 'thesaurised' *movable* wealth, stored (after the murder of Mania by her son-in-law Meidias) in a treasury in the fortress town of Gergis above the Scamander valley, is likely to have been worth between 300 and 400 talents,[7] a far larger fortune (even without the family's landed property, likely to have been more valuable still) than any which can be confidently attributed to any inhabitant of mainland Greece before the Roman period. It is true that according to Plutarch (*Agis* 9.5; *Gracch.* 41.7) the fortune of the third-century Spartan King Agis IV (which he is said to have distributed among his fellow-citizens) included 600 talents of coined money, apart from a quantity of agricultural and pasture land; but this is probably a great exaggeration. The Athenian Hipponicus, son of Callias, often said to be the richest Greek of his day (around the 420s), was credited with property (in land and personal effects) to the value of only 200 talents (Lys. XIX.48). We do hear of some larger fortunes alleged to exist in the fourth century B.C., but all the figures are again unreliable. Alexander Isius of Aetolia, who had the same reputation as Hipponicus a little over two centuries later, is said by Polybius (XXI.xxvi.9,14) to have possessed property to the value of 'more than 200 talents'. Fortunes such as those of Zenis and Mania, I suggest, were possible only for the few fortunate Greeks who enjoyed the favour of the Great King or one of his satraps. We know of some other such families in the fifth and fourth centuries, in particular the Gongylids and Demaratids and Themistocles, all of whom received vast estates in western Asia Minor from the King in the fifth century (see *OPW* 37-40).

The wealth of the Great King was enormous by Greek standards, and some of his satraps were many times richer than any Greek of their day. We happen to know that Arsames, a great Persian noble who was satrap of Egypt in the late fifth century B.C., owned land in no less than six different areas between Susa and Egypt (including Arbela and Damascus), and in Lower and Upper Egypt too.[8] This need not astonish us, for although the Achaemenid rulers of the Persian empire seem not to have exacted excessive tribute, according to ancient standards, from the satrapies of their empire, but to have allowed the local ruling class a considerable share in the surplus extorted from the primary producers, yet there were evidently all sorts of opportunities for satraps to make large personal gains, quite apart from the tribute.

Alexander the Great, who conquered the whole Persian empire between 334 and 325, and his successors, who divided up his vast kingdom between them, were able to make gifts of very great value to their followers, in money and land. There is a nice little illustration of how such rewards had grown even before Alexander had completed his conquests in the fact that whereas Dionysius I, tyrant of Syracuse, made a present of 100 minae (10,000 drachmae, or $1^2/_3$ talents) to his mercenary captain Archylus for being the first man over the wall in his siege of Motya in Sicily in 398 (Diod. XIV.53.4), Alexander in 327, at the siege of 'the Sogdian rock', offered to the first man who scaled the wall a reward of no less than 12 talents (Arr., *Anab*. IV.18.7) – probably a greater sum than the whole fortune of any except a handful of Athenians in Alexander's day. The great estates handed out to some of the 'King's friends' in Asia Minor, Syria and Egypt must have made their owners far richer than any mainland Greek had ever been.[9] It is no surprise to find that Plutarch, in the very work (referred to above) in which he speaks of King Agis IV of Sparta as owning 600 talents in coined money apart from his land, also makes Agis say that the satraps and servants of Kings Ptolemy and Seleucus 'possessed more than all the kings of Sparta combined' (*Agis*. 7.2).

In the Hellenistic and Roman periods the leading families of the cities of Asia enjoyed greater wealth than ever[10] and were among the strongest supporters of Roman rule. Largely because of their conspicuous wealth they began to enter the Roman Senate in the early Principate, albeit slowly; but the senatorial families they provided steadily increased in number in the second century, and by the reign of Hadrian 'orientals' seem to have been almost on an equality with westerners in their chance of becoming senators and even reaching the highest posts, of praetor and consul. Recent research, admirably summarised by Habicht in 1960,[11] has led to a marked revaluation of the evidence and a realisation that to speak loosely of 'Greek' or 'oriental' senators[12] can effect a blurring of some important distinctions. First, we must separate from genuine 'Greeks' the descendants of Roman (or Italian) families transplanted to the eastern provinces and now inhabiting either Augustan military colonies (Pisidian Antioch, Alexandreia in the Troad) or towns with important groups of Italian settlers, such as Pergamum, Attaleia in Pamphylia, Ephesus, and Mytilene.[13] Secondly, as Habicht has rightly emphasised, we must not fail to notice among the 'oriental' senators a very important group of members of the old dynastic families of Asia Minor and Syro-Palestine in the late Republic and early Principate, sometimes possessed of immense wealth and much inter-connected by marriage: among these are descendants of the Attalids of Pergamum; of Galatian tetrarchs and the Galatian King Deiotarus; of Archelaus and Polemo, the kings of Cappadocia and Pontus; and of King Herod of Judaea. Thirdly, the appreciable number of men who can be identified as immediate descendants of new 'oriental' senators must not themselves be counted as 'new' senators, for they were members of the senatorial order equally with the older senatorial families and could normally expect to become senators in their turn: this is particularly important when we are comparing reigns or periods and trying to see how many *new* Greeks entered the Senate during each of them.

The largest fortunes we hear of in the Roman empire, however, always remained those of Western senators, even in the Later Empire, until in the fifth century the governing class in the West lost many of their possessions through barbarian conquest of areas where some of their great estates lay: North Africa, Spain, Gaul, and Britain.[14] In the early Principate, in particular, some Romans acquired immense wealth through the munificence of the emperors, especially Augustus, who after the civil wars could dispose of confiscated property on a vast scale. An Italian *novus homo* who became suffect consul in B.C. 16, L. Tarius Rufus, described by Pliny the Elder as a man 'of exceedingly low birth' (*infima natalium humilitate*, NH XVIII.37), acquired through the generosity of Augustus, according to Pliny, a fortune of 'about a hundred million sesterces' (well over 4,000 Attic silver talents), which he proceeded to dissipate by unwise purchases of agricultural lands in Picenum, although he remained 'in other respects a man of old-fashioned parsimoniousness' (*antiquae alias parsimoniae*).[15] But it is the Western senators of around A.D. 400 who are credited with the most enormous fortunes of all. A famous fragment of the historian Olympiodorus, of Egyptian Thebes (fr. 44, Dindorf or Mueller), gives some figures for alleged annual incomes in both the richest and the middling senatorial grades. These are almost beyond belief: even senators of second-order wealth (*deuteroi oikoi*) are said to have had incomes of 1,000 to 1,500 pounds of gold; they turn out to include the great orator Q. Aurelius Symmachus (consul in 391), who is placed among 'the men of middle fortunes' (*tōn metriōn*). The richest senators are said to enjoy incomes of 4,000 pounds of gold, plus about a third as much again in the value of what they receive by way of agricultural produce in kind. (Does this perhaps imply that about three quarters of the rents of Western senators at this period were paid in gold and about one quarter in kind?) Those who held certain offices were expected to spend lavishly on public entertainments, the 'games', and we hear of vast sums being spent on a single celebration: 1,200, 2,000, and even 4,000 pounds of gold.[16] We have no way of verifying these figures, but they ought not to be rejected out of hand.[17] I should say that we can perhaps take 1,000 pounds of gold as not far short of HS 4½ million during the early Principate (1 lb. gold = 42–45 aurei = HS 4,200–4,500).

I have given some of the figures for the reputed wealth of the great men of later periods in order to place in better perspective the relatively mean little estates possessed by even the 'aristocracy' of Classical Greece.

(iii)

Land, as the principal source of wealth

Wealth in the Greek world, in the Archaic, Classical and Hellenistic periods, as in the Roman empire throughout its history, was always essentially wealth in land, upon which was conducted the cultivation of cereals (providing the main source of food) and of other agricultural products, especially those of the olive and the vine, and also the pasturing of cattle, sheep and horses. The ruling classes of all the Greek states were always primarily landowners; the oft-repeated notion that the governing classes of places like Aegina and Corinth were merchants, a 'Kaufmannsaristokratie', is an invention of modern scholarship (cf. my OPW 266-7, esp. n.61). A citizen merchant who did happen to make his pile and aspired to lead the life of a gentleman would have to retire and buy land. 'Agricultural land [*agros*],' says Amphis, a comic poet of the fourth century B.C., 'is the father of life to man; land alone knows how to cover up poverty.'[1] For a positive panegyric of *geōrgia* (Latin *agricultura*), in the sense of '*gentleman*-farming', *owning* a farm (and taking a merely supervisory interest in it), we can turn to the *Oeconomicus* of Xenophon, a man of unimpeachably orthodox and traditional opinions, who wrote the work in question at some time between the second and fourth decades of the fourth century B.C.[2] Farming, in the sense I have indicated, is to Xenophon the noblest of pursuits, the pleasantest and most agreeable way of gaining a living; it fortifies the body and instils valour (cf. IV.iv below); to the prudent man who is prepared to take a keen interest, nothing is more profitable; and above all it is easy to learn and it affords most opportunities for the useful employment of leisure for the real gentleman, the *kalos kagathos* (on whom see *OPW* 371-6); it is 'most important both as an occupation [an *ergasia*] and as a branch of knowledge [an *epistēmē*]'.[3] Xenophon, like other authors, may speak at times as if his farmer would actually take part in the work of the farm, but it is always understood that in so far as he does this he does it for pleasure and for the sake of the physical and moral benefits such exercise can bestow, and not because economic necessity obliges him to work. Xenophon makes the great Spartan commander Lysander express astonishment at the very idea that the Persian prince Cyrus could himself have laid out his magnificent park (*paradeisos*) at Sardis and actually done some of the planting with his own hands, until Cyrus tells him that it was his principle never to dine until he had exerted himself strenuously in 'some activity of war or agriculture' (*Oecon.* IV.20-5, only partly repeated in Cic., *Cat. mai.* 59). Even a Roman emperor and his heir apparent might choose to get themselves into a healthy sweat by helping to gather in the grapes, as we hear of Antoninus Pius and Marcus Aurelius doing on one occasion in the mid-140s.[4]

I believe that the standard attitude to farming of the Greek and Roman propertied classes was that expressed by Cicero in the *De oratore*, as part of a long passage (I.234-57) in which he argues that just as an orator needs no detailed acquaintance with the civil law, the *ius civile*, but can easily pick up whatever he needs to know for a particular case he is conducting, so the landowner can be content with 'what is a matter of common knowledge' (*hac communi intelligentia*, 249): the nature of sowing and reaping, the pruning of vines and other trees, the time of year and the manner in which such things are done. Such knowledge is quite sufficient for giving instructions to one's general manager (*procurator*) or orders to one's overseer (*vilicus*).

We hear again and again in Latin writers of some leading figures in the early Roman Republic who are represented as afflicted by what Horace calls 'cruel poverty' (*saeva paupertas*: *Od.* I.xii.43): they own very small farms (some of the sizes given are ridiculous) and actually take part themselves in working them. Among those who turn up most often are L. Quinctius Cincinnatus (dictator 458) and M'. Curius Dentatus (consul 290, 275, 274). The former, we are told, was actually at the plough when informed that he had been nominated Dictator.[5] Yet it is sometimes made clear in the tradition that such men were simply amusing themselves. Cicero, for example, in a passage in his treatise on old age (*Cat. mai.* 51-60), first says he is going to speak of the 'pleasures' of farmers (*voluptates agricolarum*, § 51); after mentioning Curius and Cincinnatus he uses of their agricultural activities the words *oblectabant* ('they delighted in them') and *delectatione* ('with enjoyment'); and he goes on to show that the sort of farmer he has in mind is a well-to-do master (*dominus*), whose farmhouse (*villa*) is well-stocked (*locuples*) and whose storehouse is full of wine and oil and other provisions (§ 56). Quite different were the small farmers who actually had to work alongside their slaves: they do not form part of what I am calling 'the propertied class'. On the borderline of that class would be those who needed to work with their slaves only occasionally. They may have been quite a large group in the Greek states of the Classical and Hellenistic periods. (We may compare the situation in the American Old South, as described by Stampp, *PI* 34-5.) As Peter Garnsey has well said, speaking of the Roman 'peasant cult' of the Late Roman Republic, 'The idealisation of the peasant patriarch was then, as in the twentieth century, primarily an expression of the nationalist ideology of the ruling class of a militarist State' (*PARS* 224).

In a treatise of Cicero's which was considered an important part of the education of the eighteenth-century English gentleman – 'Tully's *Offices*', it was then generally called – there is a much-quoted statement, *De offic*. I.151, which is just as characteristic of the outlook of the Greek as of the Roman propertied class: indeed, it is probably derived from the Rhodian Stoic philosopher Panaetius, of the second century B.C. (Here I agree with Brunt's valuable article, *ASTDCS*, although I would be inclined to allow Cicero a rather larger contribution in some respects than would Brunt and some others.) The life of the merchant, we are told, if he operates on a very large scale, is not entirely contemptible; and Cicero warmly commends the merchant who, 'sated (or rather, satisfied) with his profits, retires from the harbour to the fields . . . But still,' Cicero concludes, 'of all means of acquiring wealth there's nothing better, nothing more profitable, nothing sweeter, nothing more worthy of a free man, than *agricultura*' – which here also means, of course, not *working* a farm but *owning* one; just as, 'in the writings of the physiocrats, the *cultivateur* does not stand for the actual tiller of the soil, but for the big farmer' (Marx, *Cap*. III.604). Veyne and Finley have expressed the fundamental idea admirably: 'In antiquity land ownership on a sufficient scale marks "the absence of any occupation"' (see Finley, *AE* 44 and 185 n.19). The life of the landowner is a life of leisure (cf. Cic., *De offic*. I.92). The peasant farmer who has to work his own land is a very different creature. In a fragment of the Athenian comic poet Menander, a line which says that 'farming is slave's work' is preceded by one which explains that 'it is deeds of war by which a man ought to prove his superiority' (fr. 560, ed. A. Koerte, II².183). For 'deeds of war', others might substitute politics or philosophy, athletics or hunting (cf. Section ii of this chapter). Cicero quotes a passage from a play of Terence (from a Greek original by Menander), produced in 163 B.C., in which a character, Chremes, refers to such acts as digging, ploughing and carrying as what Cicero calls *illiberalis labor*, 'ungentlemanly toil' (*De fin*. I.3) – and indeed in the play itself Chremes strongly advocates leaving all such work to one's slaves (*Heaut*., Act I, Sc.i). In Italy in the reign of Nero farming was regarded by the upper classes as a demeaning employment, a *sordidum opus* (Colum., *RR* I. praef. 20). The essential thing is that one should not *need* to work for one's daily bread.

The characteristic members of my 'propertied class', then, are essentially Machiavelli's 'gentry' (*gentiluomini*), defined by him in his *Discourses on the First*

Decade of Livy (I.55) as 'those who live in idleness on the abundant revenue derived from their estates, without having anything to do either with their cultivation or with other forms of labour essential to life'.[6] But Machiavelli continues at once, 'Such men are a pest [*pernizioni*] in any republic and in any province'; and a little later he adds, 'Where the gentry are numerous, no one who proposes to set up a republic can succeed unless he first gets rid of the lot'! (He excepts from his strictures the *gentiluomini* of the Venetian Republic, who 'are so in name rather than in point of fact, for they do not derive any considerable income from estates: their great wealth is based on merchandise and movable goods'.) The contrast between Machiavelli's outlook and that of a wealthy Greek or Roman is interesting: Machiavelli, writing in the first quarter of the sixteenth century, foreshadows the economically far more progressive mentality of the bourgeois society that was about to emerge.

It was axiomatic in the Greek and Roman world that the gentleman should own his land and not be a lessee of it, a mere tenant. Xenophon can make Socrates speak of the man who is concerned only with his beloved's appearance as 'like one who has rented a piece of land: his concern is not that it may become more valuable but that he himself may get the greatest possible amount of produce out of it; whereas the man whose aim is affection (*philia*) is more like one who owns his own farm, for he strives with all his might to make his beloved of greater worth' (*Symp.* VIII.25). Among all the ancient thinkers I know who belonged (like Xenophon and Cicero) to the propertied class, I have found but one who not only recommends the gentlemanly intellectual, the would-be philosopher, both to supervise the work on his farm and actually to take part in it personally and work with his own hands, but who also explicitly says that it does not matter whether the farm is his own property or not. This is the Roman equestrian and Stoic philosopher of the late first century, Musonius Rufus, whose relatively enlightened views on marriage I had occasion to refer to in II.vi above. In his disquisition, 'What means of livelihood befits a philosopher?', a fragment of which is preserved by Stobaeus, there is a veritable paean of praise of farming and the pastoral life. Musonius says that the earth repays many times over the effort that is put into her and gives an abundant supply of the necessities of life to the man who is willing to work; and he adds, in a charming phrase, that 'she does this in such a way as to preserve dignity and without giving any offence'.[7] One may suspect that Musonius was indulging in a flight of fancy and idealising a situation of which, as a Roman equestrian, he had had no real, direct, personal experience, except perhaps by occasional free choice. However, he is at least trying to deal with the real world, unlike that curious Epicurean enthusiast, Diogenes of Oenoanda, a figure known to us only through the very long inscription he put up in his native city in Lycia (south west Asia Minor) around A.D. 200: a recently published fragment of this depicts a future Golden Age in which – if the text has been correctly restored – everyone will take part not only in the study of philosophy but in agricultural and pastoral activities.[8]

When Plotinus, a leading philosopher of the third century of the Christian era, is discussing what makes men rich or poor (*Enn.* II.iii.14), the first cause of wealth that he notices is inheritance; and when he turns to riches acquired by labour (*ek ponōn*), his one example is 'from farming'; the only other means of acquisition he notices is not trade or industry, but 'finding a treasure'. There is one notorious example of this: Ti. Claudius Atticus (the father of the great sophist, Herodes Atticus), at the very end of the first century, found a large sum of money in his house at Athens; although, as Rostovtzeff says, this was in reality 'not a treasure but probably money hidden by Herodes' grandfather, Hipparchus, in the troublous times of Domitian's persecutions (of which Hipparchus was himself a victim)'.[9] At the other end of the social scale, Horace in one of his *Satires* imagines a poor wage-labourer (a *mercennarius*) finding by good luck a silver treasure (an *urna argenti*) which enables him to buy the farm on which he works (*Sat.* II.vi.10-13).

Here and there, of course, a poor man might acquire property through the exercise of some exceptional personal skill, as a soothsayer or doctor or poet or politician, or, in the Roman period, as an advocate or (especially in the Later Empire) a soldier, although his chances of rising high in some of these ways (politics and advocacy in particular) would be small if he had not received a proper education from a well-to-do father in the first place. A political career always offered the greatest possibilities of profit, to those who were qualified for it, but politics was arduous and very risky, and at the highest levels anyway it was a full-time job and therefore open only to a man who was well-off already; and in the Classical period, unless one had inherited political *aretē* (competence and 'know-how') by being born into the right sort of family, one would have little chance of rising to the top.

Occasionally – less often, I believe, than is generally supposed – a man might rise from poverty to riches through trade or manufacture. Personal participation in trade or industry, however, would so seriously affect one's life-style that one could hardly hope to be accepted in the best society; and there are many denunciations of such activity in the literary record. Philostratus, writing in the second quarter of the third century of the Christian era, was anxious to exculpate the Athenian orator Isocrates, who had lived some six centuries earlier, from the charge of being an *aulopoios* ('oboe-maker' would be a less misleading translation than the usual 'flute-maker') levelled at him by the comic poets (see my *OPW* 234-5 and n.7). Philostratus will admit that Isocrates' father Theodorus was an *aulopoios*, but he insists that 'Isocrates himself knew nothing about *auloi* or anything else connected with banausic activity, nor would he have been honoured with the statue at Olympia if he had worked at any mean occupation' (*Vita soph.* I.17; I am tempted to recall Arist., *Pol.* VIII.6, 1341^a18-$^b8$, a diatribe against the *aulos*). The practised advocate Libanius, in the late fourth century, knew even better how to defend a man on such a charge. When the Senate of Constantinople refused to admit the wealthy Thalassius of Antioch to its ranks because he was said to be a cutler, Libanius retorted that Thalassius, like the father of Demosthenes, simply owned slaves who made knives (*Orat.* XLII.21); and that made all the difference, because by leaving one's slaves to work under the supervision of a manager (who would himself be a slave or freedman) and living on one's landed property one could enjoy the life-style of a gentleman as well as anyone else, even if (as would rarely happen) the larger part of one's income came from the slave artisans. That was precisely the situation of the prominent fifth- and fourth-century Athenian politicians like Cleon and Cleophon and Anytus who are satirised by Aristophanes and other comic poets as tanners and leather-sellers and cobblers and potters and cattle-dealers and lyre-sellers: since politics, at any rate at the top level, was a full-time occupation in a Greek city, if one was a politician one would not go in personally for trade or industry (see *OPW* 234-5, 357, 371). It would only be among the snobs like Aristophanes that one would then 'lose face' because one's fortune (or, more likely, that of one's father or even grandfather: see *OPW* 235 n.7) originally came from industry or trade. Not a few of those among Aristophanes' audience who laughed at his nasty little jokes about the 'demagogues' he so detested must have been tradesmen of one sort or another and are not likely to have felt demeaned by their calling (cf. IV.vi below) – although of course they would probably all have been glad to escape from the practice of a trade and settle down as landowners if they could. The ideas of a dominant class (at least if it is not a conquering, alien race) are always accepted in some measure by those it exploits, and most of all (as modern experience shows) by those who are near the top level of the exploited and see themselves as about to rise into the ruling class. And most of the words used in Greek to express social qualities and distinctions were heavily loaded with the moral overtones which had always been associated with them (cf. VII.iv below), so that the poorer Greek would find it hard to avoid expressing himself in the very terms which proclaimed his unworthiness.

The situation I have depicted remained true of the Greek world (as of the Latin area of the Roman world) throughout its existence. Marx noticed that 'the secret history of the Roman Republic is the history of its landed property' (*Cap.* I.81 n.1, on p.82). In Rostovtzeff's remarkably full survey of the evidence, in his great work on the social and economic history of the Roman empire, there are several statements which may give a misleading impression if taken by themselves, to the effect that, for instance, 'The main source of large fortunes, now [A.D. 69-192] as before, was commerce' (*SEHRE*[2] 153, cf. 157); or, 'Commerce, and especially foreign and interprovincial maritime commerce, provided the main sources of wealth in the Roman empire [in the first two centuries of the Christian era]' (ibid. 172). And the second of these statements continues immediately, 'Most of the *nouveaux riches* owed their money to it [commerce].' In these and other cases, where Rostovtzeff speaks as if commerce were the main source of Roman wealth, he has in mind *new* fortunes, cases of upward social mobility, in which men rose from below into the propertied class. In this he may well be mainly right. But in the continuation of both the passages I have just quoted, as elsewhere, Rostovtzeff shows he recognised that large profits made by commerce would not be re-employed in commerce so much as invested in something quite different: land above all, also perhaps mortgages, moneylending, even industry (ibid. 153, 172, 218; cf. 17, 57-8, 223-6 etc.). He knew that commerce took second place to agriculture in the economic life of the empire even in the early Principate (ibid. 66), that agriculture was of 'capital importance', that 'it is no exaggeration to say that most of the provinces were almost exclusively agricultural countries', and that 'the largest part of the population of the empire was engaged in agriculture, either actually tilling the soil, or living on an income drawn from the land' (ibid. 343); the rural population had 'enormous importance . . . for the empire in general', far exceeding the city population in number; and indeed 'the country people who tilled the soil formed an enormous majority of the population of the empire' (ibid. 345-6). In his section on the African provinces in the period A.D. 69-192 he can say that 'in every case where we can trace the origin of the large fortunes of wealthy municipal nobles, we find them to have been derived from ownership of land' (ibid. 331). Even what looks at first sight like 'wealth derived from industry' may turn out on closer examination to be wealth derived from ownership of the land on which the industry was carried on. This was half realised by Tenney Frank several decades ago. Referring to the great development of the brickyards on the estates near Rome of the Domitii (beginning with the sons of Domitius Afer, the famous orator, who died in A.D. 58 and whose great-granddaughter was the mother of the Emperor Marcus Aurelius), he said, 'And yet the wealth of this family was probably not thought of as coming from "industry" so much as from a careful exploitation of the resources of their landed estates.'[10] This is perfectly true. But Frank went on to describe this as 'practically the only instance in a thousand years of Roman history in which wealth *derived from industrial success* contributed to political distinction' (ibid., my italics), a statement we can now recognise to be incorrect, for recent researches by a team of Finnish scholars at Rome have shown that there is no reason to suppose that the Domitii and similar landowners whose names appear (as owners of *praedia* or even *figlinae*) on brick-stamps had any direct connection with brick-making.[11]

For the period of the Roman Principate and Later Empire I need do no more than refer to Rostovtzeff's great work, cited above, to A. H. M. Jones's *magnum opus* (*LRE*), and to two valuable papers by Jones, one on 'The economic life of the towns of the Roman Empire', 1955, and the other on 'Ancient empires and the economy: Rome', 1965, published 1969 (both are now conveniently reprinted in Jones, *RE* 35-60 and 114-39). In the Later Roman Empire there is if anything an even greater volume of evidence than in earlier periods for the overwhelming predominance of agriculture in the economic life of the empire – in the eastern provinces as much as in the Latin West, although the concentration of landed property in a few hands seems to have been much less marked in the East. This predominance of agriculture over trade and industry can now be taken for granted. I propose, however, to give here some half a dozen interesting pieces of evidence (which are not all as well known as they should be) from the legal codes: these concern mainly the position of decurions, the members of the local Town Councils, about whom I shall have a good deal to say in VIII.ii below. These legal texts are particularly valuable because virtually all men of substantial property who were not exempted through being *honorati* (members of some superior grade in society) were by now obliged to become members of their Council and thus assume the sometimes heavy financial and administrative burdens involved.

Callistratus, a Roman lawyer of the first half of the third century, is quoted in the *Digest* (L.ii.12) as saying that 'those who deal with goods and sell them' (*qui utensilia negotiantur et vendunt*) are not excluded from the decurionate or from municipal office, and should not be disdained as 'viles personae', even though they are liable to be flogged by the aediles. Nevertheless, he says he thinks it unbecoming (*inhonestum*) for such persons to be received into a municipal Council, especially in those states which have a supply of *viri honesti*: it is only a deficiency of the latter which makes it necessary to allow the former to have access to a *dignitas municipalis*.

The Emperor Julian in 362 exempted decurions from the *collatio lustralis* (*chrysargyron* in Greek), a tax payable during most of the fourth and fifth centuries by *negotiatores*, a term which by then had come to mean 'tradesmen' in the widest sense, including manufacturers, artisans, merchants, shopkeepers, moneylenders etc.[12] In so doing he added to his edict the words 'unless perchance it should prove that a decurion is engaging in trade in some way' – as if this were an unlikely contingency. (The law is *CTh* XII.i.50 = XIII.i.4: 'nisi forte decurionem aliquid mercari constiterit'.) In a constitution of 364, relating to the payment of the same tax, the Emperors Valentinian I and Valens subject even 'the more powerful men' (*potiores*) to the *collatio lustralis* 'if indeed they make a practice of trading' (*si tamen his mercandi cura est*); and they add that any such member of the *potiores* 'either ought not to involve himself in trade' or ought to be the first to pay the tax (*CTh* XIII.i.5) – evidently such men were exceptional.

Another imperial constitution, of 370, opens with the words, 'If any trader [*negotiator*] should purchase farms and be called to his local Council as the holder of landed property', and ends by saying that such a man is to be 'subject to the compulsory public burdens of that Council to which he gave himself of his own accord by converting the use of his money into the profit of agricultural land' (*CTh* XII.i.72). In 383 the emperors thought it necessary to pass a special law permitting the enrolment on the city Councils of the Danubian province of [Lower] Moesia[13] of 'men from among the common people, rich in the possession of slaves', to prevent them from evading their financial obligations: these men are evidently owners of workshops who would otherwise have escaped enrolment because of having little or no land (*CTh* XII.i.96: Clyde Pharr badly mistranslates this text, *TC* 356). Finally, by a constitution of 408 or 409, Honorius altogether forbade 'those who are decidedly noble by birth or resplendent with honours or notably rich in property to carry on trade, to the detriment of the cities, so that the intercourse of buying and selling may be easier between commoner and merchant' (*CJ* IV.lxiii.3).[14] Decurions were not even expected to take the kind of salaried post known as *procuratio*, managing someone else's property as bailiff: for a decurion to accept such a post is described in a constitution of 382 as 'the most infamous baseness', involving 'servile obsequiousness' (*CTh* XII.i.92 = *CJ* X.xxxii.34). But this is a subject which falls to be treated under the general heading of 'hired labour' in Section vi of this chapter and its n.4.

In addition to the evidence cited above from the legal sources, it is worth mentioning the inscription recording the fact that Q. Sicinnius Clarus, imperial legate of Thrace, when constituting the posting station of Pizus as an *emporion* in 202, said he had put in charge of this and other newly founded *emporia* (all below the rank of city) 'not commoners engaged in trade but toparchs [district magistrates] who are city councillors'[15] – probably of Augusta Traiana, the modern Stara Zagora in Bulgaria.

A decisive argument for the predominance of landed wealth over commercial wealth in the Greek and Roman world is that in the Later Empire even the *navicularii* (*nauklēroi* in Greek), who were responsible for government shipments, mainly of corn to Rome (and after 330 to Constantinople as well), were primarily landowners, to whose estates was attached the *navicularia functio*, the burden of making the prescribed shipments.[16] We even hear from Callistratus, in the *Digest* (L.vi.6.6 & 9, citing rescripts of Marcus and Verus, and of Antoninus Pius), of men who as early as the mid-second century enrolled themselves in the *corpus naviculariorum*, purely in order to obtain the valuable immunity they would thereby receive from other public burdens, although some of them actually owned no ships at all! (It was to *navicularii* alone, by the way, and not – as recently stated by Cardascia and Garnsey[17] – to *negotiatores* or *negotiantes* in general, that Constantine and Julian gave the honour of equestrian status, by laws which have not survived but are referred to in a subsequent constitution of Gratian and his co-emperors in 380: *CTh* XIII.v.16.*pr.*) Finally, tax-farmers (*publicani, telōnai*), who continued in the Roman Empire to farm most indirect taxes (such as customs and market dues, and taxes on inheritances, slave manumissions and auction sales), must not be thought of as a group distinct from landowners: they had in fact to give security in freehold landed property for the due performance of their obligations.

In his fascinating story of the very able Antoninus, who 'defected' to Persia in 359, Ammianus begins by calling him a 'wealthy merchant' (*opulentus mercator*) and goes on to tell how he then took a not very exalted civil service post as an accountant under the military governor of the province of Mesopotamia: this was evidently a potential rise in status, and it led in due course to the honorary rank of *protector* (Amm. Marc. XVIII.v.1 ff.; cf. VIII.iii below).

★　★　★　★　★　★

What I have been saying about the minor role of commerce and industry in the fortunes of the propertied classes of the Greek world throughout its existence is almost universally true, but there are of course exceptions. I am thinking not so much of *individuals*: the vast majority of those who rose into the propertied class by their own efforts in trade or industry would be certain to become landowners when they could. I have in mind a handful of *cities*, the dominant class of which either certainly or probably included a substantial proportion of merchants. They are not easy to find and may not have amounted to more than one or two. I am not concerned here with the Latin West, where Rome's port Ostia (which had only a small *territorium*) stands out as perhaps the one Western city in which far more wealth came to the local notables from commerce than from land.[18] Lugdunum, Arelate and Narbo, the three great *emporia* of Roman Gaul, and also Augusta Treverorum (Trèves, Trier), were certainly in a sense commercial towns, in that a large volume of goods passed through them; but the governing class in each case (the magistrates and decurions) seem to have been almost entirely landowning, while a high proportion of those who acquired wealth through trade and industry seem to have been freedmen or foreigners.[19] The leading 'commercial city' of the whole empire, Alexandria, undoubtedly had some rich merchants among its citizens, but I know of no evidence whether they accounted for any substantial proportion of its governing class: I should be astonished if they did. One of its citizens, Firmus, is said by one very base source, the *Historia Augusta* (*Firmus* 3.2-3), both to have been a merchant and to have aspired to the imperial power, in some kind of unsuccessful revolt against the Emperor Aurelian (in 272). If both these statements are correct, Firmus would certainly be unique; but the first may not be true, and the second is probably at least a great exaggeration. The whole story, indeed, may be fictitious (see Bowman, PRIH 158). Otherwise, I know of no specific evidence for rich merchants at Alexandria except in three late hagiographic sources, which – for what they are worth – speak of fortunes that work out at about 275, 70 and 50 lb. gold (see Jones, *LRE* II.870-1; *RE* 60, 150). But even the largest of these, from the *Historia Monachorum* 16 (in *MPL* XXI.438c), if expressed in the way it might have been in the early Principate, would have come out at not very much more than HS 1 million, the minimum qualification of a Roman senator, and neither of the other two would have reached the equestrian qualification of HS 400,000.

In the East, the one certain example of a city which must surely have had a governing class consisting at least partly of merchants is Palmyra, which was of no great importance until well into the last century B.C., but then grew rapidly into a prosperous commercial city, until its period of affluence was ended by its sack by Aurelian in 272. Palmyra gained much of its wealth from its control of a considerable part of the profitable caravan trade with the East.[20] Petra may well have been another such town, on a rather smaller scale, and I suppose there may have been one or two more.[21]

Mention of Palmyra and of its vital role in the Eastern trade reminds one of the customs duties, sometimes heavy, which were levied there and at some other places on the eastern frontier of the empire on all imports and exports. There is a nice little story in Philostratus' *Life of Apollonius of Tyana* (I.xx) about a journey to the East made by Apollonius, who left the Roman empire at Zeugma on the Euphrates. The tax-collector took Apollonius up to the notice-board and asked him what he had to declare. Apollonius replied with a string of feminine nouns: 'Temperance, Justice, Virtue, Chastity, Courage, Perseverance'. The tax-collector took these to be female slaves, who were sometimes given such names and on whom export duty would have to be paid – we know that the duty on prostitutes at Coptos in Egypt in A.D. 90 was as much as HS 108 or 27 denarii each (*OGIS* 674.16-17: 108 Egyptian drachmae). So he demanded a list of the girls. 'Ah,' said Apollonius, sententious as ever, 'it is not slave-girls I am taking out, but ladies to whom I am slave (*despoinas*).'

* * * * * *

We need not doubt that Greek (and Roman) landowners took care to dispose of the products of their estates in ways as profitable to themselves as possible. Naturally, this will normally have involved arranging for its transport to the nearest market, but we have extraordinarily little evidence about this kind of activity. I cannot believe that members of the propertied class (in my sense) would themselves take their produce even to their city market if they could help it, let alone transport it across the sea, or otherwise indulge personally in commerce.

Solon may be taken as a test case, for modern works constantly state it as a fact that he went on sea journeys as a merchant both as a young man and after the passing of his laws in 594/3 B.C. The source most usually quoted for the latter statement is Aristotle (writing nearly three centuries later), who certainly speaks of Solon's voyage to Egypt after 594 as 'combining business with pleasure': he went, says Aristotle, *kat' emporian hama kai theōrian* (*Ath. pol.* 11.1). However, it is very interesting to find that our earliest witness by far, namely Herodotus (I.29.1), when giving both a pretext and a cause for the later voyage (to Egypt and elsewhere), says not a word about trade: Solon's pretence was that he wanted to see the world, the real reason was that he wished to avoid being pressed to repeal his laws. And I suggest that Aristotle's expression, *kat' emporian hama kai theōrian*, has not been correctly understood: precisely what it means can best be discovered from its occurrence in a text of the early fourth century B.C., Isocrates XVII (*Trapeziticus*) 4 – the only other example of the phrase that I have been able to find. The speaker, a young man from the 'Pontic kingdom' in the Crimea, says that when he sailed to Athens, his father, financing his journey, sent with him two ships loaded with corn; and here it is very significant that the expression used is precisely the same as the one Aristotle was later to use for Solon's travels: the young man went *hama kat' emporian kai kata theōrian*, the single 'commercial' activity being undertaken for the enlargement of his experience rather than an economic purpose. The phrase in question, identical (except for the word–order) in Isocrates and Aristotle, may have been a familiar expression in the fourth century, since it is likely that any Greek who was sailing about from one place to another in the Mediterranean world might take some of the products of one place to sell at a profit in another, as a means of paying for his travels. One of the stories in Diogenes Laertius (VI.9) about Antisthenes tells of another 'Pontic youth' who financed a stay at Athens with a shipload of another commodity that was regularly exported from the Pontus to Athens: salt fish. And even Plato is said by Plutarch to have financed his visit to Egypt by selling olive oil there (*Solon* 2.8). As for Solon, Plutarch (who was writing nearly seven centuries afterwards) almost agrees with Herodotus when he says that Solon's real motive for sailing away from Athens after 594 was the hope that the Athenians would grow to accept his laws, but he rejects Herodotus in favour of some unknown writer when he maintains that Solon gave out that he was leaving Athens on account of his *nauklēria*, which ought to mean business interests as a shipowner (*Sol.* 25.6). Plutarch also quotes a statement by the unreliable Hellenistic biographer Hermippus that when Solon was a young man he tried to repair his family fortunes, largely dissipated by his father's many acts of charity (a nice moralising touch!), by going in for commerce (*emporia*); against this, perhaps remembering Herodotus, Plutarch says we are also told that Solon travelled 'for the sake of gaining experience and knowledge [*polypeiria* and *historia*] rather than money-making [*chrēmatismos*]' (*Sol.* 2.1; cf. *Mor.* 410a). Evidently the participation of Solon in commerce was a story that grew with the years and the telling.

It is essential to realise that just as Hesiod had represented trade as a *pis aller* for the peasant who was unable to make a living from the land (see V.i below), so in Solon trade heads the list of activities to which a man may be driven who is propertyless (*achrēmōn*) and under the compulsion of poverty (*peniē*, fr. 1.41 ff.); and clearly the merchant's life in Solon's mind is a hard and dangerous one. After the trader comes the agricultural labourer who hires himself out by the year (fr. 1.47-8): this is the sole reference we have from early Attica to such people except for the name of the lowest of Solon's four property-groups, the *thētes*, a word which normally means wage-labourers. Next in the list we have the artisan; and then – incongruously, to our way of thinking – the poet, the seer, and the doctor. Actually, Solon does not speak slightingly of any of these people, even of the trader or the labourer or the artisan: in this he is exceptional.

His own basic outlook is surely that of the landed gentleman (see esp. frr. 1.3–16; 13; 14.1–3; 24.1–7).

It is probably as a result of the elaboration in the Hellenistic period of such tales as those I have mentioned above concerning Solon that Plutarch (*Solon* 2.6–8) was ready to contrast what he took to be the conditions of the Archaic age with those that obtained later and in his own day, and declare that '*in those times* [the Archaic period] work was no disgrace' (these four words are a quotation from Hesiod, *WD* 311), a trade or craft (a *technē*) brought no stigma (*diabolē?*), and commerce (*emporia*) was in good repute, as it gave a man familiarity with foreign countries, friendship with kings and a wide experience of affairs; some [merchants] became founders of great cities, as Protis of Massalia.[22] And then Plutarch, before concluding with the remark about Plato which I have already quoted, adds, 'They say that Thales and Hippocrates the mathematician went in for commerce' – but the surviving sources referring to Hippocrates' alleged activity as a merchant (*emporos*) are even later than Plutarch (see Diels-Kranz, *FVS*[5-11] no.42.2,5), and the only story preserved about Thales' alleged 'commercial activities' is the one familiar from Aristotle, about how Thales secured a monopoly by hiring all the olive-presses of Miletus and Chios on one particular occasion, with the justified expectation of securing a large profit, in a year which he foresaw would produce an exceptional crop of olives! (*Pol.* I.11, 1259[a]5–21; cf. Diog. Laert. I.26). Plutarch is able to cite no good evidence of any kind for his statement about the situation of traders in the Archaic period.

We also happen to know that in the first half of the sixth century Charaxus of Lesbos, son of Scamandronymus and brother of Sappho the poetess, sailed to Naucratis in Egypt; and according to Strabo (who of course lived more than half a millennium later) Charaxus brought to Naucratis a cargo of Lesbian wine, *kat' emporian* (XVII.i.33, p.808; cf. Athen. XIII.596b–d). If that is true, Charaxus may have been deliberately trying to obtain a higher price for his wine by cutting out the middle-man; or he may simply have been 'seeing the world', and the sale of the wine may have been merely incidental and a means of financing his voyage – there is no evidence to show whether the journey was a single or a repeated one. It is characteristic of the sources for early Greek economic history, by the way, that we only hear of this visit of Charaxus to Naucratis because Charaxus, while in Egypt, happened to become enamoured of a famous courtesan, named Doricha (or Rhodopis, but this may have been her nickname), a *mésalliance* for which he was apparently reproached by his sister in a poem known to Herodotus (II.134–5, esp. 135.6) but not to us, and perhaps sympathised with in some fragments recovered not long ago among the Oxyrhynchus papyri (5 and 15b Page: see Page, *SA* 45–51; contrast Gomme, in *JHS* 77 [1957] 258–9). Gomme, in his attack on Page's interpretation of Sappho, frr. 5 and 15b, takes very seriously the words *kat' emporian* in Strabo, and feels able to add scornfully, 'so much for the family of "noble birth and high fashion"' (a phrase of Mure's). But the family surely was an aristocratic one, and we have seen from Isocrates and Aristotle what *kat' emporian* is capable of meaning in such contexts.

What is referred to as 'trade' or 'commerce' in the Archaic period and even rather later may prove on inspection to be something very different from the activities now connoted by such expressions. Take for example the story quoted by Athenaeus (VI.232ab) from Theopompus (*FGrH* 115 F 193), concerning events that occurred in the 470s B.C. Architeles the Corinthian, who had by degrees bought up a large quantity of gold, sold it to the emissaries of Hiero, the tyrant of Syracuse, adding a handful of gold by way of gift. In return, the grateful Hiero sent Architeles a shipload of corn and many other gifts as well. This transaction partakes not only of trade in the proper sense, but also of the ancient practice of gift-exchange between aristocrats. I may add that I know of no specific reference to the conduct of 'the corn-trade of the city of Corinth', in the proper sense, except the statement of Lycurgus (see *OPW* 265) that the Athenian Leocrates, some time after 338 B.C., settled as a metic at Megara, and while living there shipped corn from Epirus to Leucas and thence to Corinth. (That Corinth did sometimes import corn from the West is made very probable by the reference in Thuc. III.86.4 to the export of corn from Sicily to the Peloponnese; for Lechaeum, the western port of Corinth, is perhaps the most likely place to which such corn would go.)

Pericles is said by Plutarch (*Per.* 16.4) to have sold the whole produce of his estate on a single occasion each year, as if this were exceptional; devoted as he was to politics, he did this, we are told, with the aim of wasting as little time as possible on such things, and through an able slave, Evangelus. This may be true, but once more it is the kind of thing Hellenistic biographers were fond of inventing.

I agree with a recent statement by Pleket that 'it is on predominantly local markets that urban landowners will have sold their products (corn, oil, wine)', using as intermediaries 'either their freedmen or independent *negotiatores*'.[23] However, I think that in the latter part of the same paragraph, beginning, 'Perhaps we are all brought up too much with the idea that the aristocracy in antiquity was an *exclusively* landed élite', Pleket puts too much emphasis on the 'commercial interests of landowners', which were very minor. Our evidence about the way in which landowners dealt with the produce of their estates is too scanty for us to be able to produce a confident picture, though we may agree with Pleket that in the Later Roman Empire the widespread decline of trade is likely to have forced many landowners to take more active steps to promote the sale of their crops. The essential fact is that these landowners always remained primarily landowners, and that any 'commercial' activities they might indulge in never became more than a minor and wholly subsidiary part of their activities. It is of little significance that Rufinus of Pergamum (as Pleket notes) had a shipowner in his service (an *idios nauklēros*): that must have been quite a common phenomenon. According to Libanius, a rich man could be expected to possess ships, along with land and gold and silver (see Liebeschuetz, *Ant.* 75 and n.7). We may also remember Myrinus of Zeleia in Phrygia, *pragmateutēs* (Latin *actor*) of a landowning noblewoman, Claudia Bassa, who according to his own epitaph not only collected his mistress's rents for thirty-five years but also undertook journeys on her behalf to numerous distant places, including Italy, Dalmatia, Istria, Liburnia and Alexandria.[24] And since, as I have mentioned above, the *navicularii* (the government shippers – of corn in vast quantities, by the way, from Africa and Egypt to Rome and Constantinople) were landowners first and foremost, whose estates were saddled with the burden of this duty, they at least would all have to own ships, which of course they could use for their own purposes, in so far as they were not required for government transport.

(iv)
Slavery and other forms of unfree labour

Although ancient slavery has been examined again and again, from many different points of view, I believe that I am justified in making yet another attempt to give a general treatment of the subject, if only because of three methodological characteristics of the account I shall present.

First, I hope that I have at least moved the discussion on to a different plane by conducting the investigation in terms not merely of slavery in the narrow sense ('chattel slavery') but of *unfree labour*,[1] in its different forms, of which slavery in the strict sense is only one, and not always the most important in the sphere of actual production – although, for reasons I shall explain towards the end of this section, I believe it always played a very significant role.

Secondly, the situation we have to examine, as I see it, is one in which *the propertied class* (defined in Section ii of this chapter) extracts the greater part of its *surplus* from the working population by means of *unfree labour*. That is a very different matter from trying to show that in Greek (and Roman) antiquity *the bulk of production* was done by slaves, or even (at least until the Later Roman Empire) by slaves, serfs and all other unfree workers put together – I am sure it was not: in my opinion, the combined production of free peasants and artisans must have exceeded that of unfree agricultural and industrial producers in most places at all times, at any rate until the fourth century of the Christian era, when forms of serfdom became general in the Roman empire. I have already explained, in II.iii above, why I believe that the significant thing we have to concentrate on is not the overall role of unfree compared with free labour, but the role played by unfree labour in providing the dominant propertied classes with their surplus, a very different question and a much more restricted one, not so entirely open-ended as the other. In this, I am certainly following the central thought of Marx, for whom the fundamental difference between the various forms of society lay in 'the mode in which surplus labour is in each case extracted from the actual producer', 'the specific economic form in which unpaid surplus labour is pumped out of the direct producers' (*Cap.* I.217; III.791, cited more fully in II.iii above). And in the opinion of Marx, expressed most clearly in the *Grundrisse* (156), 'Direct forced labour [*direkte Zwangsarbeit*] is the foundation of the ancient world' (E.T. 245) – a statement which must certainly be interpreted in the light of the passages from *Capital* which I have just noticed. I accept this. I think it would not be technically correct to call the Greek (and Roman) world 'a *slave* economy'; but I should not raise any strong objection if anyone else wished to use that expression, because, as I shall argue, the propertied classes extorted the bulk of their surplus from the working population by means of unfree labour, in which slavery, in the strict technical sense, played at some periods a dominant role and was always a highly significant factor.

Thirdly, I have tried to avoid the very common mistake of denying the existence, or minimising the extent, of slave labour in situations where all we have a right to assert is that there is no, or little, *evidence* for it. The point here is that we often have no right to *expect* such evidence. Our knowledge of the large-scale use of slaves in production (especially in agriculture, which matters most) depends mainly upon a mere handful of literary texts, even for Athens in the fifth and fourth centuries B.C. and Italy and Sicily in the late Republic and early Principate, where we know that slavery was particularly widespread. (I shall have much more to say on this topic later, both in this section and in Appendix II.)

I quoted, in II.iii above, statements by Aristotle about the poor or property-less free man who was obliged to use an ox, or his wife and children, as a substitute for slaves. But in this section I am not concerned with such people, who of course were themselves liable to be exploited by the propertied classes to a greater or less degree, in ways I shall describe in IV.i below. Here I am dealing with the propertied class and the unfree labour from which they derived the bulk of their surplus; the poor free man is prominent in this section only in so far as he fell into debt bondage or serfdom.

*   *   *   *   *   *

The resources of different languages – Greek, Latin and the various modern languages – differ greatly in the categories of unfree labour which they make it possible to distinguish by name; but as it happens there is a set of definitions of the three main categories I propose to recognise – namely chattel slavery, serfdom and debt bondage – which today has a very special status. This set of distinctions is enshrined, for 'slavery', in Article 1(1) of the Slavery Convention of 1926, organised by the League of Nations; and, for 'serfdom' and 'debt bondage', in Article 1 of the Supplementary Convention on the abolition of slavery, the slave trade, and institutions and practices similar to slavery. (The Supplementary Convention resulted from a conference at Geneva organised by the United Nations in 1956 and attended by representatives of no fewer than forty-eight nations.) There is a particularly well-informed account of the whole subject by C. W. W. Greenidge, *Slavery* (London, 1958), who gives the full texts of the two Conventions in his second and third Appendices (pp.224 ff.) and a summary of their respective first Articles on pp.25-6.

It would be perverse to disregard internationally established practice unless there is a valid reason for doing so, as there is not in this case, and I shall follow it as far as possible, except that I shall not treat as a separate category the 'forced labour' which, for reasons of state in the modern world, has been set apart from 'slavery and other institutions and practices akin to slavery'. As Greenidge puts it (accepting the definitions in the Conventions of 1926 and 1956), 'Slavery is the exaction of involuntary labour by one individual from another individual to whom the latter belongs, whereas forced labour is the exaction of involuntary labour from an individual to a government, i.e. a collectivity, to punish or discipline the person from whom the labour is exacted' (*Slavery* 25). According to the modern definitions in the Conventions referred to above, those who in the ancient world were mine slaves belonging to individual owners and those who were criminals condemned by the Roman state to convict labour in the mines (*ad metallum*, always in perpetuity) would have to be put in two different categories: the first would be in 'slavery', the second in 'forced labour'. In antiquity there would hardly have been more than a technical difference between the two groups, not significant for my purposes, and I shall therefore treat 'forced labour' as a form of slavery. (I shall devote only a single brief paragraph to convict labour in antiquity.) I may add that compulsory labour services such as the *angariae* (see I.iii above and IV.i below), which were performed either by free individuals or by village communities for a Hellenistic monarch or the Roman state, or for a municipality (including any Greek city), are dealt with in this book under the heading of 'indirect collective exploitation', in IV.i below.

My own general category of 'unfree labour' divides naturally under the three headings which follow, established by the international Conventions referred to above: (*A*) Slavery, (*B*) Serfdom, and (*C*) Debt bondage. At this point I shall merely describe them briefly, deferring discussion of each until later in this section.

A. Slavery is defined in the 1926 Convention as 'the status or condition of a person over whom any or all of the powers attaching to the right of ownership are exercised'. I accept this definition of 'chattel slavery' (as it is often called) for the ancient as well as the modern world, the more willingly since what it stresses is not so much the fact that the slave is the *legal property* of another as that 'the *powers attaching* to the *right of ownership* are *exercised over him*' – for the essential elements in the slave's condition are that *his labour and other activities are totally controlled* by his master, and that he is virtually without rights, at any rate enforceable legal rights. In Roman law, enslavement was regarded as closely resembling death (Ulpian, *Dig.* L.xvii.209; *Nov. J.* XXII.9).

It will be useful if I quote at this point a paragraph from the very thorough study of '*Paramonē* clauses' by A. E. Samuel in 1965. After considering in detail a large number of documents connected with (*inter alia*) manumission, Samuel makes a statement which some might think over-legalistic and framed in rather too absolute terms, but which nevertheless contains an important truth:

> Legal freedom in Greece is essentially a concept of property. The sole meaning of freedom is that a man has jurisdiction over his property and family, and the concept of manumission is the concept of change of property; a man no longer is property, but has it. A man's activities can be limited by restrictions, and he can be subject to burdensome obligation, and these matters do not affect his freedom. If a man can own property, he is free, and if he is free, he can own property. That is the meaning of manumission (RPCAD 295).

B. Serfdom is defined in the 1956 Convention as 'the tenure of land whereby the tenant is by law, custom or agreement bound to live and labour on land belonging to another person and render some determinate services to such other person, whether for reward or not, and is not free to change his status'. I must add one qualification: 'render some determinate services', in the conditions of antiquity (especially the Later Roman colonate, for which see IV.iii below), need not necessarily mean more than the paying of a determinate rent, in money or kind or share of crop. It is necessary to recognise that the serf is a peasant (see IV.ii below) who does not own, or does not fully own, but at least possesses (as the slave and normally the bondsman do not) the means of production of his livelihood, usually on a hereditary basis, and who is responsible for providing his own maintenance (clothing and food) from his own productive efforts (as the slave cannot normally be), but who is not a fully free man: he is to a considerable extent under the control of his lord, and he is 'bound to the soil' (to the particular farm on which he labours or to his village), often by law, though sometimes only by custom or contract, or (see below) by a treaty made on submission to conquest. (To quote Marc Bloch, speaking of the early Middle Ages, 'Neither the barbarian laws nor the Carolingian capitularies contain a line that forbids tenants to desert their land, or the master to tear them from it. It is the lord's business to keep his tenants, legally or illegally,' *CEHE* I².260.) The question of the precise manner in which Late Roman *coloni* of different types and in different areas were bound to the soil can be left to IV.iii below. I should perhaps mention here that binding to the soil (to farm or village) was not limited purely to *tenants* living and labouring 'on land belonging to another person' (to quote the 1956 Convention), but that working peasant *freeholders* could also be bound, although with them it was always their village to which they were tied: we may call such people 'quasi-serfs' (see IV.iii below). Since there is evidently in some people's minds a groundless connection between serfdom and 'feudalism', I must make it clear that although in some or most societies to which the term 'feudal' has been applied (or misapplied) the labour of serfs has been prominent, serfdom can exist and has existed (as in the Later Roman Empire) quite independently of anything that is likely to be called (or miscalled) 'feudal' (cf. IV.v below). At this point I need add only that most, if not all, of the serf peoples we encounter in the Greek world before the Hellenistic period entered that condition as a result of conquest by invaders who settled in their territory (cf. Lotze, *MED*, esp. 69-79; and see, later in this section, 'II. Serfdom'). We hear in several of these instances (Sparta, Thessaly, Pontic Heraclea) of treaties or compacts made between conquerors and conquered, regulating in some degree the future position of the conquered and in particular preventing them from being sold abroad. We must not, however, treat conquest by alien invaders as the necessary genesis of serfdom: as we shall see (in IV.iii below), that of the Later Roman colonate, for example, had a totally different origin.

   C.   *Debt bondage* is defined in the 1956 Convention as 'the status or condition arising from a pledge by a debtor of his personal services or those of a third person under his control as a security for a debt, where the value reasonably assessed of those services rendered is not applied towards the liquidation of the debt or the length and nature of those services are not respectively limited and defined'. In the Greek (and Roman) world there were many different forms of debt bondage, not all of which, perhaps, are fully covered by the definition I have just quoted.
   The position of the defaulting debtor in antiquity was always very precarious. He might often be actually enslaved, legally or illegally – a permanent change of status. There is a convenient distinction in German between 'Schuldhaft', corresponding to one form of what I call 'debt bondage', and 'Schuldknecht-schaft', actual enslavement for debt. We must be careful to distinguish between the two. I would call the man concerned a 'debt bondsman' only if he did not technically become a slave (a distinction of great importance in principle) and if his condition in practice was such that he might (at least in theory) hope eventually to become free again: the possibility of a limitation in time of his quasi-servile status is for me a characteristic mark of the bondsman as opposed to the slave. (Here my usage differs from that of some others, e.g. Finley: see his SD 164 n.22.) But there was no general technical term in Greek for such a man: see the opening pages of Finley, SD, who has much to say that is interesting,

especially on the myth of Heracles' service to Omphale, and on various forms of debt bondage and debt slavery in the ancient Near East, with ample bibliography.

Debt bondage was evidently widespread throughout the Greek world, and we must not be misled by the fact that the one Greek city we know most about, Athens, abolished the institution in the Archaic period. This happened when the legislation that accompanied the *seisachtheia* of Solon (his cancellation of debts), as early as 594/3 B.C., put an end – of course only at Athens – to debt bondage as well as enslavement for debt in the full sense. I think that those who study Greek history too often fail to realise what a radical reform this was, and how adroitly the new law was framed: Solon did not merely (as people often say) 'forbid *enslavement* for debt'; he went so far as to forbid 'pledging the body as security' (*mē daneizein epi tois sōmasin*), and thereby ruled out all forms of debt bondage too.[2]

I am aware that I ought perhaps to have made a more careful separation between the type of debt bondage in which the debtor actually works for the creditor and that which involves confinement in a prison, whether private or official (cf. the Latin expression quoted under heading III below: *vel privata vel publica vincula*), and also between debt bondage resulting from 'personal execution' and that which can only be effected by order of a court of law. To have made the necessary qualifications, however, would have lengthened the treatment of the subject unduly.

* * * * * *

The definitions I have accepted of my three categories of unfree labour are, I think, the ones most people would accept for the ancient world. I admit that they do not always have precise equivalents in modern languages, but I think that sufficiently close approximations can usually be found. And the three do correspond to definite situations which we find existing in antiquity, even if the edges of each category are, so to speak, blurred: a bondsman who has not the least hope in practice of freeing himself is virtually a slave; a slave who is settled as tenant of a piece of land, with a 'cabin' and a 'wife' and family ('quasi colonus', as the lawyers put it: see IV.iii below), is in practice far nearer to a serf than to an ordinary agricultural, industrial or mine slave; and so on.

One contemporary historian of the ancient world, Sir Moses Finley, has a strong but unreasonable objection to the use of the word 'serf' in relation to the Greek and Roman world. He is perfectly justified in protesting against the rigid reduction of the ancient work-force to 'only three possible categories: slaves, serfs and free wage-earners' (*AE* 65; cf. SSAG 178-9), and he has himself done much to illuminate intermediate and special categories (see especially his SSAG, SD and BSF). Of course we must not treat these three categories as real entities, divided by sharp lines: there were many intermediate or special situations contributing to what Finley is fond of calling a 'spectrum' or 'continuum' of different statuses which in practice shaded imperceptibly into each other (see II.v above). Yet it seems to me that to decline to draw firm lines inside this 'spectrum' is as capricious as refusing to speak of the colours red, blue, yellow and the rest, simply because any precise lines of division of the colour-spectrum must be to some extent arbitrary, and different people would draw them at slightly different points. Even Finley is perfectly prepared to speak of 'slaves', among whom great variations of condition existed, and of 'wage-earners', another term which included very different kinds of status. He also often uses the term 'peasants', a far broader category (defined in *AE* 105); he even has a 'peasant spectrum' (*AE* 104). Yet although his 'peasants' often cry out for a term that will distinguish the broad group I have defined as 'serfs', he refuses to use the word which almost everyone else applies to them and of which there is now an internationally agreed definition. The reason for this is simply that he insists gratuitously upon confining the term 'serf' to the European mediaeval serf within the feudal system: this is clear from his *AE* 189 n.5 (especially the reference to Marc Bloch in *CEHE* I².253-4) – where, incidentally, he specifies several features of serf status, every single one of which can be found (as he seems not to be aware) in forms of the Late Roman colonate. Pierre Vidal-Naquet has also stated, equally without good reason, that to speak of serfs is to create 'une confusion avec l'époque du moyen-âge européen' (RHGE 40 n.6). To this I would make a twofold reply. First, there were serfs (in my sense, the one now officially accepted throughout much of the modern world) long before the European Middle Ages; and secondly, what we must fear is not 'confusion' with the mediaeval world, but the failure to notice features that appear in closely related (though not identical) forms in Graeco-Roman antiquity and in the Middle Ages. I may add that the often very acute discussion by Lotze (*MED*) of a famous passage in Pollux (III.83) which I shall notice presently is also marred by an unwillingness to treat serfdom (in my sense) as a general phenomenon: for Lotze, 'Hörigkeit' must be specifically *'feudale* Hörigkeit' (*MED* 60 ff., at 64-8, 77, 79) – an unnecessary restriction which is not found, for instance, in Busolt (see *GS* I.272-80; II.667-70 etc.).

Before proceeding further we must acknowledge the fact that the categories into which we are dividing unfree labour are not those which were employed by the Greeks or the Romans. They were inhibited from recognising what we call serfdom and debt bondage as distinct categories, because they divided mankind into just two groups: free and slave. This was just as true when the Emperor Justinian issued his *Institutes* in A.D. 533 as in Classical Greek times. According to the *Institutes*, all *homines* (an expression which here, as almost everywhere else, includes women as well as men) are *liberi aut servi*, either free or slave (I.iii.*pr.*). No intermediate or mixed status is recognised. There follows in *Inst. J.* I.iii.4-5 the statement that there are no differences of legal status (*condicio*) among slaves, whereas there are 'many differences' among the free; the next sentence speaks only of a division into free-born and freedmen. The main statement of principle reproduces the very words of another work: the *Institutes*, written nearly four centuries earlier, of the jurist Gaius, who probably originated in the Greek East (Gai., *Inst.* I.9).

There are various words in Greek – such as *pais* ('boy') and its variants, or *sōma* ('body') – which are used on occasion in the sense of 'slave', besides the more standard terms: *doulos, andrapodon, oiketēs*; and there are other expressions in Latin apart from *servus* and *mancipium*, the regular technical terms. All these words could be used loosely and even purely metaphorically. But for 'serf' and 'serfdom' there are no strict technical equivalents in Greek or Latin, and serfdom is not visible on a large scale in most areas of the Greek world until the Later Roman Empire, although there were certainly subject peoples in particular localities who qualify as serfs under my definition or virtually any other. Nor were there standard technical expressions for 'bondage' and the 'bondsman', although this institution was known throughout the Greek world, as I have already indicated. The fundamental division into 'free and slave' is invariable in ancient sources, and I know of only one literary statement in either language which explicitly recognises the existence of a set of intermediate or mixed categories: this is a brief and isolated passage (generally believed to be derived from Aristophanes of Byzantium) in the *Onomasticon* of Julius Pollux, a Greek from Naucratis in Egypt who taught rhetoric at Athens in the late second century, in the reign of Commodus, and who refers to those 'between free and slave' (*metaxu eleutherōn kai doulōn*, III.83). As it stands, it is a very disappointing statement: our text simply gives a short list of local peoples, amounting to some six or seven items, beginning with the Spartan Helots, who were certainly State serfs (see my *OPW* 89-94, and below), and continuing with a miscellaneous collection of other local peoples, probably of very different statuses varying mainly between what we should call freedom and serfdom. (The original work may well have been more informative – our version of the *Onomasticon* represents only a Byzantine epitome.) The passage has often been discussed. The conclusion of Lotze, in his monograph on it, is that we should set apart, as essentially free men, two of Pollux' categories, the Argive Gymnetes and the Korynephoroi (elsewhere Katonakophoroi) of Sicyon, and see the remainder as peoples of 'unfree' condition, in a kind of 'Kollektivsklaverei' to their conquerors, akin to (but distinct from) 'feudale Hörigkeit' (*MED* 79): these are the Spartan Helots, the Klarotai and Mnoïtai of Crete, the Thessalian Penestai, and the Mariandynoi of Heraclea Pontica. To these he would add some peoples of similar condition known to us from other sources: the Killyrioi or Kyllyrioi (or, later, Kallikyrioi or Killikyrioi) of Syracuse, the Woikiatai of East Locris, and perhaps the Bithynians in the territory of Byzantium.[3] With this I largely agree, except that I would unhesitatingly put the 'unfree' peoples in my category of serfs, and bring in certain other serfs who need to be, but seldom are, mentioned in this connection (see under the heading 'II. Serfdom' below).

Undoubtedly there did exist in the Greek world a whole range of statuses between full slavery and complete freedom. But what I want to emphasise here is the fact, well brought out by the Pollux passage, that the only mixed or intermediate categories to which the Greeks were prepared to give full recognition were a few individual cases which had established themselves in customary law and were treated as *local exceptions* to the general rule that everyone was either slave or free. A Greek confronted with some peculiar serf-like status might apply to it by analogy a term that was in strictness appropriate only to some different but better-known example, as when the word *penestai*,[4] the technical term for the subject population of Thessaly, is used for the peasants of Etruria by Dionysius of Halicarnassus (*AR* IX.v.4; cf. II.ix.2); or when the verb *heilōteuein*, corresponding to the noun Helot, is applied to a group of dependent people in some other area, or their condition is likened to that of the Helots (see again 'II. Serfdom' below). How long these local variations continued is hard to say. The Pollux passage is timeless: it does not say when these statuses existed, or whether they had lasted down to Pollux' own day (or the third/second centuries B.C., the date of Pollux' probable source, Aristophanes of Byzantium) or disappeared earlier. I suspect that in fact by Pollux' time they were all almost certainly things of the distant past, as the Spartan Helots certainly were (see below and n.19). If so, we have a significant piece of evidence in favour of the argument I shall advance later in this section (under heading 'II. Serfdom'), to the effect that when an area in which forms of serfdom existed was taken into the Greek or Roman world, those forms tended to decay and ultimately to disappear.

I must mention here that I shall not be separately discussing on its own the longest treatment of slavery to be found in any ancient author: Athenaeus VI.262b-275b, a mere rag-bag of fragments from Greek writers, assembled higgledy-piggledy and with no real discrimination or judgment, yet most valuable as a quarry (if used with discretion), because of some of the passages from earlier authors which it preserves. I will only refer to a recent article which contains much bibliographical material, partly arising out of the Athenaeus passage: Vidal-Naquet, RHGE (1972).

★ ★ ★ ★ ★ ★

It is now time to look at each of our three categories of unfree labour in turn.

I. SLAVERY. It seems to me beyond dispute that the magnificent achievements of the Greeks were partly due to the fact that their civilisation was founded to a considerable degree on a slave basis. That slave labour was indeed regarded by the Greeks in general as essential to their way of life is something I hope I can take for granted, without having to go to the trouble of proving it by citing a great deal of evidence. 'Of property,' says the author of the Pseudo-Aristotelian *Oeconomica* I (an early Peripatetic, perhaps Theophrastus), 'the first and most necessary kind is that which is best and most appropriate to household management [*oikonomikōtaton*]: namely, the human variety [*anthrōpos*]. Therefore we must first provide ourselves with industrious slaves [*douloi spoudaioi*]' (I.5,1344ª23-5). Immediately after this the author proceeds to distinguish the two main species of slave: the ordinary worker (*ergatēs*) and the *epitropos*, the manager or overseer. (We must not forget that the vast majority of the overseers we come across in antiquity were themselves slaves or ex-slaves: their essential role must not be overlooked.) I have referred in Section i of this chapter to a fascinating passage in the *Politics* in which, to replace slaves, Aristotle can think only of the self-moving statues of the legendary artificer, Daedalus, or the automated tripods of the god Hephaestus (I.4,1253ᵇ35-4ª1). A little earlier Aristotle had said that a complete household consisted of 'slaves and free', and had described master and slave, with husband and wife, and father and children, as 'the primary and simplest elements of the household' (I.3,1253ᵇ5-7, 14 ff.). Polybius speaks of slaves, equally with cattle, as being among the essential requirements of life (*anankaiai tou biou chreiai*, IV.38.4). But I do not feel I need pursue this matter further. Slavery was a fact of Classical Greek life, and from the strictly economic point of view (the efficient satisfaction of material wants) it was useful, indeed indispensable (cf. II.i above). I do not see how the brilliant civilisation of the Classical period could have come into existence without it. I should like to quote here a fine passage in Marx:

> In the development of the richness of human nature as an end in itself . . . at first the
> development of the capacities of the human species takes place at the cost of the

majority of human individuals and even classes . . . ; the higher development of individuality is thus only achieved by a historical process during which individuals are sacrificed; for the interests of the species in the human kingdom, as in the animal and plant kingdoms, always assert themselves at the cost of the interests of individuals (*TSV* II.118).

Now we must not confuse the situation in Greek cities, even Athens, with that at Rome, with which I wish briefly to compare it. There are two separate points to be made here. First, the upper classes of Rome in its great days had an immensely larger area from which to draw their surplus than was ever available to the rulers of any Greek city (even fifth-century Athens), and when Rome became an imperial power its upper classes were infinitely richer than their Greek counterparts – and remained so on the whole even when individual Greeks began to enter the Roman senatorial class: see Section ii of this chapter, especially its nn.11-13, also VI.iv below for emphasis on the vastly greater scale of exploitation by the Romans of their provinces in the late Republic than by the Athenians of the subject states of their 'empire' in the fifth century B.C. The second important distinction between many Greek cities and Rome is that owing to the absence of any real political democracy in the Roman world, the humbler free men were much more at the mercy of the men of power than were the poorer citizens of a Greek democracy. But democracy, when it really works (as it did, for the citizens, at Athens and some other Greek cities), has certain very important consequences: it gives the whole citizen population extensive and enforceable legal rights, and so gives the humbler and poorer citizen an opportunity of protecting himself against at any rate the more extreme forms of ill-treatment by the powerful. I am sure that a rich Athenian of the fifth or fourth century B.C. who wanted to grab the land of his humble neighbour would not dare to adopt the methods described in the fourteenth satire of Juvenal and other sources, which included sending in cattle to trample down the unfortunate man's crops and thus ruin him and compel him to part with his land cheaply.[5]

In a city like Athens, however, just because it was a democracy and the poorer citizens were to some extent protected against the powerful,[6] the very most had to be made out of the classes below the citizens. Now metics (free foreigners residing in the city) could not be milked intensively: they paid a small tax to the state, but if the screw was put on them too hard they would simply go elsewhere. The essential fact about the slave, however, was that the screw could be put on him in any way the master liked, because he was *without rights*: as I mentioned earlier in this section, that is one of the distinguishing features of the slave's condition; mere ownership of the slave as a chattel, a piece of property, is in the long run less significant, as a feature of his condition, than the *unlimited control over his activities* which his master enjoys.[7] Even that windbag Dio Chrysostom could define slavery as the right to *use* another man at pleasure, like a piece of property or a domestic animal (XV.24). We need not be surprised, then, if we find a more intense development of slavery at Athens than at most other places in the Greek world: if the humbler citizens could not be fully exploited, and it was inexpedient to try to put too much pressure on the metics, then it was necessary to rely to an exceptional degree on exploiting the labour of slaves. This *explains* 'the advance, hand in hand, of freedom and slavery' in the Greek world, noted by Finley (*SCA* 72) but left by him as a kind of paradox:

entirely without explanation. (Finley is handicapped here, as elsewhere, by his refusal to think in terms of class categories and by his curious disinclination to recognise exploitation as a definable characteristic of a class society: see his *AE* 49, 157.)

The master might find that he got more out of his slaves by very harsh treatment: mine slaves, in particular, often seem to have been worked to death in quite a short period.[8] The Pseudo-Aristotelian *Oeconomica* I (5, 1344ª35) allots to slaves just three things: work, punishment and food. (It is interesting to find precisely the same list, in reverse order, in Ecclus. XXXIII.24; cf. 26, and XXIII.10.) But in some kinds of work, especially skilled work, it might pay the master better to treat his slaves well, and even perhaps set them up on their own, as *chōris oikountes*.[9] As well as giving them the stick (literally, as well as metaphorically), he might even dangle before their eyes the carrot of ultimate manumission. But whatever the method employed, it was he, the master, who decided what it was to be. I have mentioned already (near the end of II.ii above) that the flogging of slaves was generally taken for granted. I dare say that except when slaves were dirt cheap (after a profitable war, for instance) most masters would not treat their slaves in too inhuman a manner and work them swiftly to death, for they were human capital and precious for that reason if for no other. Some masters might take particular care of slaves who became ill; but others of course might follow the advice of that typical old Roman landowner, Cato, by cutting down the rations of sick slaves or selling off those who were elderly or diseased, just like decrepit oxen, old tools, and 'anything else that is superfluous'.[10] (One may well wonder who would buy old or sick slaves!) In Varro's book on agriculture we read that in *gravia loca* (presumably malarious districts) it is better to use *mercennarii*, hired hands, rather than slaves. (Columella would have such lands let out to tenants, and similarly those too far away to be regularly supervised by their owner.)[11] Slaves are apt to be thought less expendable than hired labourers: this is well illustrated by a story told by the American writer, F. L. Olmsted, in an account of his journey on the steamboat *Fashion* up the Alabama River in 1855. He saw some bales of cotton being thrown from a height down into the ship's hold: the men throwing the bales down were negroes, the men in the hold were Irishmen. Olmsted remarked on this to the mate of the ship. 'Oh,' said the mate, 'the niggers are worth too much to be risked here; if the Paddies are knocked overboard or get their backs broke, nobody loses anything.'[12] The slave, representing an investment by his master, might at least expect to receive enough food to keep him alive and working; if he were manumitted, this supply might immediately dry up. Epictetus, an exslave who had thoroughly acquired the outlook of a master, took pleasure in pointing out that the slave who thinks only of gaining his freedom may be reduced, when he is manumitted, to 'slavery much more severe than before'; he may experience the pangs of disappointed love and 'long for slavery again' (it seems to be assumed that slaves would never fall in love); and the wretched man will remember too how in slavery he was fed and clothed and received medical attention, and he will realise that mere freedom has made him no better off (*Diss.* IV.i.33 ff., esp. 35-7; another part of the same passage is quoted in VII.iii below).

It might be thought that slaves before they were freed could never have been of much account. Certainly the position of the slave was always exceedingly precarious. But some slaves of rich masters were allowed to prosper and even acquire slaves of their own, *vicarii* in Latin. During the Roman Principate and Later Empire, imperial slaves were naturally in the best position to do well for themselves, even before they became freedmen. There are two particularly nice illustrations of this. One is an inscription of the reign of Tiberius (*ILS* 1514 = E/J² 158), set up to a provincial member of the *familia Caesaris*, Musicus Scurranus, a mere *dispensator* (cashier) in the *fiscus* (the provincial treasury) of Gallia Lugdunensis.[13] The inscription bears the names of no fewer than fifteen men and one woman 'from among the number of his *vicarii*, who were with him at Rome when he died'. All these slaves of a slave, except the woman, are careful to mention their respective functions in Musicus' household: there are three personal servants (*a manu*), two 'gentlemen of the bedchamber' (*a cubiculo*), two men who looked after Musicus' silver plate (*ab argento*), two footmen (*pedisequi*), two cooks, a doctor, a business manager (*negotiator*), a man who controlled the household expenditure (*sumptuarius*), and a valet (*a veste*); the function of the woman, Secunda, is not specified. Musicus evidently had other *vicarii* – how many, we do not know. The other illustration of the possession of wealth by an imperial slave is the Elder Pliny's account of Rotundus Drusillianus, who a little later occupied a similar position to Musicus Scurranus, that of *dispensator*, in the province of Hither Spain in the reign of Claudius (*NH* XXXIII.145). He is said to have had a silver dish (a *lanx*) weighing 500 lb., to manufacture which a special workshop had to be constructed, and eight companion pieces (*comites eius*), weighing 250 lb. each – a total of 2,500 lb. of silver. Before dismissing this offhand as a mere yarn we should do well to remember that Musicus had needed more than one under-slave to look after his silver plate! These rather surprising examples of wealthy imperial slaves bring out the fact that in the imperial household, at any rate, some slaves were of higher status than some freedmen: this has recently been stressed in relation to the imperial *dispensatores* (and incidentally their *vicarii*) by Weaver (*SAS*, ed. Finley, 132). In the Later Roman Empire the eunuch *cubicularii* of the Sacred Bedchamber became personages of great influence (see Section v below). They all began their careers as slaves until the Emperor Leo ordered them to be freed on admission to the imperial household (*CJ* XII.v.4.*pr.*,6, of *c.* 473). Finley is certainly right in saying that 'much the greatest opportunity for social mobility lay among the imperial slaves'; and we need not limit this, as he does, to 'the first century of our era' (BSF 244), although it was most conspicuous then.

There was no doubt a certain sense of backstairs importance and of hierarchy inside slave households, as there has so often been among the servants of the upper classes in more modern times. When Libanius, professor of rhetoric at Antioch during most of the second half of the fourth century, was petitioning the Council of Antioch to supplement the meagre salaries of his Assistant Lecturers, by giving them some lands to farm, he pictured them as living in unendurable squalor: some of them, he said, had only three slaves, others two, others not even that – slaves who got drunk and were insolent to their masters 'because they belonged to such small establishments' (*Orat.* XXXI.9-11). Frederick Douglass, himself a former slave in the Old South, remarked that 'to be a slave, was thought bad enough; but to be a *poor man's* slave was deemed a disgrace indeed'; and another ex-slave, Steward, said he had 'heard of slaves object to being sent in very small companies to labour in the field, lest that some passer-by should think that they belonged to a poor man, who was unable to keep a large gang' (Stampp, *PI* 338-9). We certainly hear from time to time in antiquity of slaves being owned by men described as 'poor' (*penētes*), like Chremylus in the *Plutus* of Aristophanes (see lines 29, 254, with 26, 1105), or at least as very lowly people. And Sidonius Apollinaris speaks in the third quarter of the fifth century of the Bretons as trying to entice away the slaves (*mancipia*) belonging to a man in his part of Gaul whom he describes, in his lordly way, as 'humilis obscurus despicabilisque' (*Epist.* III.ix.2). However, we must remember that the various terms in Greek and Latin which are usually translated 'poor' can sometimes refer to quite well-to-do people: an extreme example is Demosthenes XVIII.108, where we find applied to the 1,500 particularly wealthy Athenians who between 357 and 339 were saddled with paying for the trierarchy not merely the word *penētes* but even *aporoi*, a term normally kept for those who had no property at all, or virtually none.

In the Classical and Hellenistic periods, contrary to what is sometimes said (e.g. by A. H. M. Jones, SAW in *SCA* [ed. Finley] 3, and *AD* 13), a great deal of slave labour in many Greek states (including Athens) was employed on the land, which, as we have seen (in Section iii of this chapter), was always by far the most important sector of the ancient economy. I have had to relegate the evidence to Appendix II, not because the subject is unimportant, but because it consists mainly of small scraps which would be uninteresting and indeed often unintelligible to all but Classical scholars.

Even after the use of slaves in agriculture had declined (a process we shall trace in IV.iii below), many were still so engaged. The legal writers represented in the *Digest* have much to say about slaves and relatively little about hired labour; letting to tenants is much in view, but perhaps not quite as much as we might have expected. It is simply impossible to make even an informed guess about the proportion of agricultural work done by slaves and free peasants respectively. My impression is that, over all, direct cultivation by slaves was steadily giving way to letting to tenants during the first three centuries of the Christian era, although perhaps at very different rates in different parts of the Roman empire. But, as I shall show in IV.iii, the fact that land is leased must certainly not be taken to exclude its being made to yield a greater profit to the landowner and/or the tenant by the use of slaves, who may belong to the lessee or may be supplied by the landlord as part of what the Roman lawyers called the *instrumentum* (the equipment) of the farm. Sometimes, perhaps, the absence of specific evidence for slave labour may suggest that relatively few slaves were being used; but it is very rarely that the evidence can legitimately be pressed in that way, since in most areas at most periods large numbers of slaves could easily be present without leaving behind any recognisable sign of their existence. In particular, above all where the evidence for slaves and freedmen is mainly epigraphic (as it often is), we must expect to find two complicating factors: slaves employed in managerial capacities, especially of course those who emerged as freedmen, are likely to be heavily over-represented (in epitaphs, for instance); and among ordinary slaves, agricultural ones are less likely to appear than domestics or those engaged in some form of manufacture. In this connection it is useful to glance at the excellent article by Stéphane Gsell, ERAR (which I may have no occasion to mention elsewhere, since it deals entirely with Roman Africa), pointing out that the slaves revealed to us by the African inscriptions were not, in general, humble agricultural workers: these, as he says, 'disparaissaient sans laisser aucune trace' (ERAR 402). In some periods, especially the Middle and Later Roman Empire, we may find reason to conclude, at least for many areas, that slaves and freedmen were indeed relatively few and were concentrated at the top end of the working scale, fulfilling mainly managerial functions. This, however, must not lead us to depreciate the importance of slavery in production,[13a] but rather the reverse, for there could be nothing of greater interest to the propertied classes than making the largest possible profit out of their landed estates, and the direction and control of the labour on those estates must always have been a matter of the first importance. A good steward was highly valued. As I show in Section vi of this chapter and in Appendix II below, it was assumed in Classical Athens that the overseer of a farm would necessarily be a slave; and the same is probably true of the rest of the period with which this book deals. Free Greeks and Romans disliked taking permanent employment as managers (see again Section vi of this chapter). In the Roman agricultural writers the *vilici* (stewards or bailiffs) and their subordinates are assumed to be slaves, and I have no doubt that they were so in reality. (I have not tried to collect the epigraphic evidence, but as far as I am aware it confirms the literary sources.) Needless to say, competent *vilici* would be required to supervise hired labourers just as much as slaves, in so far as such men were used – mainly at the peak periods of agricultural activity, but also occasionally for special jobs (see Section vi of this chapter). Sometimes in the Roman period slave (or freedmen) managers are found in control of slaves; in other cases they seem to be mainly supervising *coloni*: see IV.iii below and its n.54. As I point out there, such men were playing a role of great importance in providing the propertied classes with their incomes. In the Later Roman Empire slaves (and freedmen) certainly remained prominent as stewards or bailiffs or overseers or agents (*actores* now, or *procuratores*; in Greek, *pragmateutai* or *epitropoi*), and indeed are an actual majority among men in that capacity who are referred to in the literary, legal and papyrological sources for the Later Empire,[14] even when their masters' lands are mainly let to *coloni* rather than worked by direct slave labour. Slavery, then, was still fulfilling an essential role in production at the very time when it is generally supposed to have been 'in decline' – as indeed it was in some degree, at lower levels.

At the same time, domestic slavery continued on a large scale in the Later Roman Empire in the households of members of the propertied classes, and it was accounted a great misfortune by many of the well-to-do (by no means only the very rich) not to be able to possess a full number of domestic servants. Two examples will suffice. I have referred above to the well-known speech in which the leading teacher of rhetoric at Antioch in the late fourth century sought to arouse pity for the sad plight of some of his assistants, who were so under-paid, according to him, that they could afford only two or three slaves, if that (Liban., *Orat.* XXXI.9-11). The other text is rarely if ever noticed, no doubt because it comes from the *Acta* of the Church Council of Chalcedon, which are read by few but ecclesiastical historians, and perhaps not in bulk by many of them, since a large part of the contents is (or ought to be) rather painful reading for those who wish to believe that the deliberations and decisions of orthodox bishops may be expected to reveal the workings of the Holy Spirit. At the third session of the Council, on 13 October 451, four documents were presented attacking Dioscorus, the Monophysite Patriarch of Alexandria, whom the Catholics were determined to discredit and depose. Three of the four complainants made great play with accusations that Dioscorus had reduced them to beggary. One, a priest named Athanasius, asserted that as a consequence of Dioscorus' persecution of him he had had to give a bribe of no less than 1,400 pounds of gold to Nomus, the powerful *magister officiorum* of Theodosius II, to prevent himself from being kept in prison indefinitely, and that he had been robbed of all his other property as well, with the consequence that he was driven to live by begging, with 'the two or three slaves [*mancipia*] that remained' to him! (*Acta Conc. Oec*. II.iii.2.36-7 = 295-6, ed. E. Schwartz; Mansi VI.1025-8).

It is not my intention here to give anything like a complete account, even in outline, of slavery in the ancient Greek world – a subject on which the bibliography is already enormous. (See the *Bibliographie zur antiken Sklaverei*, ed. Joseph Vogt [Bochum, 1971], containing 1,707 items, to which many additions could now be made.) Slavery will of course come up in various ways in other parts of this book, especially IV.iii below. But I think I ought at least to explain why at Athens and in the other Greek cities where slavery was already highly developed in the Classical period we never hear of slave revolts – although a few such revolts did develop in various parts of the Mediterranean world in the Hellenistic period, particularly in the 130s-70s B.C.[15] The reason is simple and obvious: the slaves in each city (and even in many cases within single families and farms and workshops) were largely imported 'barbarians' and very heterogeneous in character, coming from areas as far apart as Thrace, South Russia, Lydia and Caria and other parts of Asia Minor, Egypt, Libya and Sicily, and sharing no common language or culture. The desirability of choosing slaves of different nationalities and languages was well recognised in antiquity, and it is stressed by several Greek and Roman writers as an indispensable means of preventing revolts: see Plato, *Laws* VI.777cd; Arist., *Pol.* VII.10, 1330^{a}25-8; Ps.-Arist., *Oecon*. I.5, 1344^{b}18; Athen. VI.264f-5a; Varro, *RR* I.xvii.5. Serfs in any given area, on the other hand, would normally be of a single ethnic stock, likely to retain a measure of uniformity and common culture, and for that reason could be expected to feel some solidarity and be more collectively troublesome to their masters, especially if they were in a position to receive help from their masters' enemies. As we shall see presently, the Helots of the Spartan area (particularly the Messenians) and to a less extent the Thessalian Penestai were a perpetual danger to their lords.

We often hear of the flight of individual slaves; but if they were of real value to their masters they would not perhaps, in normal times, have much chance of achieving their freedom, as their masters would use all available means of recapturing them. Dio Chrysostom could take it for granted that a man buying a slave would enquire 'if he ever ran away and would not remain with his former master' (XXXI.42). One particular Greek slave of Cicero's, Dionysius, an educated man whom his master used as a reader (*anagnōstēs*), and who had absconded in 46 B.C. with a number of valuable books from Cicero's library, puts in an appearance in no fewer than four letters in our collection of Cicero's correspondence (*Ad Fam.* XIII.lxxvii.3; V.ix.2; xi.3; xa.1). Vatinius, commanding in Illyricum, where Dionysius was last seen at Narona, promised Cicero that he would not give up until he had secured the man; but whether he was able to do so we do not know. We occasionally hear of the flight of slaves *en masse*, but only, I think, in time of war. By far the most famous text is Thucydides VII.27.5, speaking of the desertion of 'more than 20,000 slaves' from Attica during the Spartan occupation of Decelea in the late fifth century B.C. (I have said something about this in Appendix II below.)

In the background, always, was the fact that fellow-citizens could be relied upon, in Xenophon's phrase, to act as unpaid bodyguards of one another against their slaves (*Hiero* IV.3). There is a fascinating passage in Plato in which this theme is expanded (*Rep.* IX.578d-9a). Socrates, with the monotonously enthusiastic assent of Glaucon, is developing his ideas on the subject of tyranny. He speaks of rich men in cities who resemble the tyrant in owning many slaves and yet live in security and are not at all afraid of them. The reason (supplied for once by Glaucon) is said to be that 'the whole city protects each single individual'. Socrates agrees, and he goes on to invite Glaucon to contemplate the case of a man owning fifty slaves or even more, suddenly wafted away by some god, with his wife and children and all his slaves and other property, to some desert place, where there is no free man to assist him. And what is likely to happen then? Why, the man will be terrified of an uprising of his slaves in which he and his family will be massacred. He will therefore be obliged to fawn upon some of the slaves and, against his own wishes, to give them their freedom, as the only possible means of escaping destruction. And it is only now, if you please, and not before, that the precious pair see the slaveowner as having become a *kolax therapontōn*, a parasite on his own servants!

II. SERFDOM. There are essential differences between the slave and the serf, for 'serfdom is not slavery; it is a status intermediate between slavery and complete freedom' (Greenidge, *Slavery* 24). For a slave to become a serf represents a real rise in status. The serf, in my sense, although 'not free to change his status' (according to the 1956 Convention), is not in theory, like the slave, his lord's property. I would prefer, however, to concentrate on the more practical side of the condition of the ancient serf, for the precise nature of his legal status is often unclear to us, owing to the nature of the evidence, and was sometimes a matter of dispute in antiquity, and the terminology used in our sources can on occasion be misleading. For example, although the Spartan Helots were certainly serfs rather than slaves in my scheme (see below), they are sometimes referred to specifically as slaves, as when they are called 'the slave population' (*hē douleia*) in the official treaty of alliance between Sparta and Athens in 421 (Thuc. V.23.3). And a Greek writer could easily apply the terminology of slavery to that part of the indigenous population of Asia which worked the land, often in serfdom and sometimes referred to as the *laoi*. Thus Strabo could say of the *laoi* of Iberia in the Caucasus (roughly the modern Georgia) that they were 'slaves of the kings' (*basilikoi douloi*, XI.iii.6, p.501). Again, as we shall see later, Theodosius I could declare in the early 390s that serf *coloni*, although legally free men, 'should be regarded as slaves of the very land to which they were born' (which of course did belong to their masters), and Justinian was perplexed by the similarity of the legal powers exercised over both groups by the *dominus* and the *possessor*, as the master and the landlord are called respectively. No, in distinguishing the condition of the serf from that of the chattel slave I think we shall do better to concentrate on two characteristics that have not yet been mentioned.

First, the services which could legally be required of the serf were limited, at least in theory, either by legal enactment (a Roman imperial edict, for example) or by a compact entered into by his people, perhaps long ago, with conquering invaders, whose serfs they became (see below). Needless to say, the position of the serf has always been precarious: a local potentate might not scruple to disobey an imperial law; and how is a conquering people to be compelled to abide by its undertakings, even if given by treaty under oath? But the serf was never entirely without rights, as the slave might be. Secondly (and even more important, though often overlooked), serfs, because they were 'bound to the soil', could marry and have a fairly secure family life, whereas the slave, who could not legally 'marry' at all, had no redress if his master decided to sell him separately from the woman he regarded as his 'wife' and their offspring, until some time in the fourth century, when first *originarii* (whom I would identify with those described in the East as *adscripticii*, or *enapographoi* in Greek) and then, in *c.* 370, all those agricultural slaves who were 'enrolled in the tax register' rose to a quasi-serf position, in that it became illegal to sell them separately from the land they worked.[16] Next to the prospect of freedom itself, perhaps, nothing can be more important to those who are unfree than the knowledge that their family life at least is secure. The break-up of a slave family is the most effective of all threats against its members. As an ex-slave in the American Old South reminded sceptics, 'The agony at parting must be seen and felt to be fully understood' (Stampp, *PI* 348). A man there who claimed to have witnessed the sale of such a family only once said he 'never saw such profound grief as the poor creatures manifested' (Genovese, *RJR* 456). Genovese has collected much evidence about the deep attachments created among slaves in the Old South by their establishment of family life, which was in general allowed, even though slave 'marriages' were never legally recognised as such by any state (ibid. 452-8), any more than they were in antiquity (including the Christian Later Roman Empire). Indeed, the slaves were actually encouraged to create and maintain family relationships, which were commonly believed by their owners to make them more tractable – more 'attached to the plantation' and 'better and less troublesome workers' (ibid. 452, 454). As the author of the Pseudo-Aristotelian *Oeconomica* saw it, the children of slaves are as it were their hostages for good behaviour (see IV.iii, § 4 below). Thus, paradoxically, a feature of the serf's condition (his being 'bound to the soil') which is one of its greatest derogations from freedom will also – as compared with chattel slavery – work to his advantage if it prevents the master from separating him from the land on which he works or resides, with his family, as in the Later Roman colonate. Neglect of this vital feature of the serf's condition is noticeable in several recent treatments of the forms of subjection in antiquity (e.g. Lotze, *MED* 63 ff., esp. 67). Even the free peasant who became a serf would at least be secure against eviction, in theory at any rate.

The possibilities of variation in the condition of serfs are considerable, and we must not make the mistake of thinking that certain other peoples resembled the

Spartan Helots closely, either in their legal status or in their actual condition, simply because certain Greek writers came near to identifying them (see the next paragraph). It is hard to decide, in respect of most of the serf peoples we happen to know about, whether they went on living (as some did) in their traditional villages and thus enjoyed a relatively congenial form of dependence, or whether they lived on individual farms owned by the masters to whom they belonged, or to whom they were allocated, as the Helots, or most Helots, certainly did (see Lotze, *MED* 38).

The Helots of the Spartan area are by far the best known Greek serfs before the colonate of the Later Roman Empire. Their condition was so celebrated in the Greek world that – to give but four examples – the verb corresponding to their name, *heilōteuein*, could be used to convey an impression of the unfree status of another conquered people, the Mariandynoi of Heraclea Pontica (Strabo XII.iii.4, p.542); the Hellenistic historian Phylarchus felt that he could best convey the condition of the Bithynians subject to Byzantium by saying that the Byzantines 'exercised mastery [*desposai*] over the Bithynians as the Spartans over the Helots' (*FGrH* 81 F 8, *ap.* Athen. VI.271bc);[17] Theopompus, writing in the fourth century B.C., could say of the Illyrian Ardiaioi (Vardaei has been suggested as an emendation) that they 'owned 300,000 dependants [*prospelatai*] like Helots' (or 'as if Helots', *FGrH* 115 F 40, *ap.* Athen. X.443b = VI.271de); and the aged Isocrates, writing to Philip II of Macedon in 338 B.C. (*Ep.* III.5), could relish the prospect that Philip would 'compel the barbarians to *heilōteuein* to the Greeks'. (Isocrates, of course, was thinking of the non-Greek inhabitants of Asia.) Actually, we know of no precise parallels to the condition of the Helots, which was much debated in the Classical period (see Plato, *Laws* VI.776c), and a certain amount of oversimplification is involved by forcing it into any general category; but for convenience I shall treat them as the 'State serfs' they undoubtedly were. I need add nothing here to what I have said elsewhere about the Helots (*OPW* 89-93), but I should perhaps repeat the most extraordinary of all pieces of evidence about the relationship between the Helots and their Spartan masters, which comes from no less an authority than Aristotle (fr. 538, *ap.* Plut., *Lycurg.* 28.7). Every year, on taking office, the principal magistrates of Sparta, the ephors, made a formal declaration of war upon the Helots, so that they became enemies of the state, *polemioi*, and could be killed as occasion required, without bringing on the Spartans the religious pollution involved in putting to death, otherwise than by due process of law, anyone who was not officially a *polemios*. Declaring war on one's own work-force is an action so unparalleled (as far as I know) that we need not be surprised to find the relationship between Spartans and Helots unique in the Greek world.

When we speak of Helots and the hostility between them and the Spartans we are justified in thinking primarily (though not entirely) of the Messenians, who greatly outnumbered the Laconian Helots.[18] The Messenians were not only a single people: until the late eighth century they had been *hoi Messēnioi*, an autonomous political unit which had recently become, or was in process of becoming, an independent Greek *polis*, in the very area where they subsequently laboured for their Spartan masters. They had, therefore, a natural feeling of kinship and unity. After Messenia was liberated and became an independent *polis* again, in 369 B.C., the only Helots left were the Laconian ones, many of whom were liberated subsequently, especially by Nabis in the early second century B.C. By the end of the Roman Republic at the latest the status of Helot had ceased to exist, for Strabo, who calls the Helots 'State slaves, in a sense' (*tropon tina dēmosioi douloi*), says that they existed 'until the Roman supremacy' (VIII.v.4, p.365), and this can only mean the second century B.C. (or conceivably the first) – for Strabo would have used quite a different expression had the Helots remained such down to the time at which he was writing, the early first century of the Christian era.[19]

The other main serf people of mainland Greece, the Penestai of Thessaly,[20] also gave their masters much trouble in their efforts to free themselves, according to Aristotle (*Pol.* II.9, 1269ᵃ36-7; cf. only Xen., *HG* II.iii.36). The subject Cretans whom Aristotle compares to the Helots and Penestai were much less of a problem: Aristotle attributes this in one place to their comparative isolation from the outside world (*Pol.* II.10, 1272ᵇ16–22) and in another to the fact that Cretan cities, although they often fought with one another, never entered into alliances with each other's disaffected *perioikoi* (as he calls them, *Pol.* II.9, 1269ᵃ39-ᵇ2), whereas the Spartan Helots and Thessalian Penestai received help from states which were at enmity with their masters (ibid. 1269ᵇ2-7).

When we hear of alleged *douloi* who were regularly used as soldiers, we are justified in regarding them as serfs rather than slaves. According to the Hellenistic historian Agatharchides of Cnidus, individual Dardanians (an Illyrio-Thracian people) possessed a thousand or more such *douloi*, who in time of peace farmed the land and during war fought in regiments commanded by their masters (*FGrH* 86 F 17, *ap*. Athen. VI.272d). This may remind us of certain Demosthenic passages (cited in n.20) which show large bodies of Thessalian Penestai fighting under the command of their master.

I have explained above that until the Later Roman Empire we can identify only isolated *local* forms of serfdom in the Greek world. Pollux, in the famous passage I have quoted, mentions only quite early forms, which (as I have suggested) had probably long since ceased to exist. Only one of his peoples 'between slave and free', the Mariandynoi, lived in Asia, and they had been subjected not by one of the new Hellenistic foundations but probably as far back as the sixth century B.C., soon after the Milesians founded their colony at Heraclea. We do, however, have evidence of the existence of serfdom during the Hellenistic period at various places in Asia Minor and Syria – mainly, though not quite exclusively, in the area which was hellenised only in the time of Alexander onwards. Unfortunately, although this subject has been much discussed over the last two generations, nothing like agreement has yet been reached, mainly because there is surprisingly little clear evidence, and many scholars have not taken a broad enough view but have generalised from the few fragments of evidence on which they have concentrated. The whole question is much too complicated to be discussed at length here, and I shall present only a summary of the views I hold, which I may be able to justify in detail elsewhere.

I must begin this brief discussion of Hellenistic serfdom by insisting that we must never be surprised to find very great variations in land tenure from one area to another and even within a given small area. How wide such variations can be within a single country, even today, emerges particularly well from a standard work on land tenure in modern Iran, before the reform of 1962: Ann

K. S. Lambton, *Landlord and Peasant in Persia* (1953, enlarged repr. 1969). A reading of at least chapters 13-18 and 21-2 of that book might do something to lessen the over-confidence of modern scholars who do not hesitate to generalise about land tenure in Seleucid Asia Minor and Syria or the Pergamene kingdom on the basis of a handful of isolated and often fragmentary texts. Again, if we look for comparison at mediaeval Europe we can find numbers of local exceptions to almost any rule we try to formulate. If our evidence were as bad for fourteenth-century England as it is for Hellenistic Asia Minor, and we happened to possess only the records (very well analysed by Eleanor Searle) of Battle Abbey in Sussex, dealing with the manor of Marley after its creation in 1310, we might have imagined that a manorial estate at that time consisted of nothing but 'demesne land', worked entirely by free wage-labour, with no sign of serfdom or even of labour-rents (then still almost universal in southern England), and that it practised full 'convertible husbandry', which did not in fact become standard practice for some generations.[21]

The Achaemenid kings of Persia (with their satraps)[22] and their Macedonian successors created new forms of property ownership, mainly by distributing large areas of land to their favourites and (on very different terms) to some of their soldiers; but there is every reason to think that they allowed ancient customs to persist, to some extent at least, as far as those who actually worked the land were concerned; and this would allow many local peculiarities to survive. I should like, in passing, to register a doubt concerning the view, so popular in modern times, that the Achaemenids claimed to be actual owners of all the land in their kingdom, in a sense more real than the modern fiction of the ruler's 'eminent domain'. In mid-ninth-century Israel, certainly, the king enjoyed no such rights: this emerges clearly from the splendid story in I Kings xxi, in which King Ahab covets Naboth's vineyard but is unable to compel him to transfer it to himself, even by sale or exchange, until the evil Queen Jezebel contrives to have Naboth judicially murdered, whereupon it seems that his property is forfeited to the king – with fatal consequences to that wicked man.[23] Whether or not the Achaemenid monarchs claimed to be the owners of all the land in the Persian empire, it was natural for the Macedonian kings, from Alexander onwards, to assert their rights of conquest in the East and to regard themselves as invested with the ownership of all 'spear-won territory' (see e.g. Diod. XVII.17.2) outside the area of those Greek cities which they were graciously prepared to recognise as such (cf. V.iii below).[24] Even within the vast area of 'king's land', however, there existed several different varieties of tenure (see Kreissig, LPHO, esp. 6-16); and below the holders who occasionally appear in our sources it is likely that ancient forms of tenure mainly persisted at first.

If, when interpreting the epigraphic evidence for land tenure in Asia in the Hellenistic period, we allow the Greek to mean what we have every right to expect it to mean, there is not the slightest doubt that serfdom, in one form or another (not necessarily always the same), is among the variety of tenures with which we are confronted. There are a few documents recording the sale or gift of land which include its occupiers in the sale or gift and yet give reason for thinking that some at least of these occupiers, especially those called *laoi* or *basilikoi laoi* (the native population), were not slaves. Now it may well be that the conveyance of land with its occupants makes it highly probable that those occupants, if not slaves, are serfs, bound to the soil, whether to a particular farm or to their village community. (As we shall see later, we find both these types of restriction of peasant movement in the Later Roman colonate.) But I do not think we can be absolutely certain that these people are indeed serfs, in cases in which we have no further evidence of their condition: they may have been mentioned with the land simply because they were the more or less hereditary tenants, who could be *expected* to continue working the land as before and who would therefore constitute a most valuable asset, at any rate if agricultural labour was not otherwise easily obtainable. To borrow a technical expression from English law – they might be thought to constitute a kind of 'goodwill' in the land: to make an important contribution to its value by creating a high probability that it would not lack families to work it, just as the 'goodwill' that goes with a shop in modern England, for example, may greatly increase its selling value. However, at least one famous mid-third-century inscription, a sale of land by the Seleucid King Antiochus II to his divorced queen, Laodice, does make it virtually certain that the *laoi* who are sold with the land were indeed serfs. The king's letter says that he has sold to Laodice for 30 talents, free of royal taxation, Pannoukome (or the village of Pannos) with its land, 'and any in-habited places [*topoi*] that may be in it, and the *laoi* that belong to it, with all their households and with the income of the [current] year,²⁵ . . . and similarly any persons from this village being *laoi* who have moved away to other places' (Welles, *RCHP* 18.1-13). It is a fact, certainly, that some of the *laoi* are said to have gone to live elsewhere, very probably in a place of greater security (cf. *RCHP* 11.22-5); but there can be no reasonable doubt (in spite of recent assertion to the contrary)²⁶ that the document records an out-and-out sale to Laodice, in terminology which is as explicit as it could be, and that the *laoi* of the village in question were included in the sale, even if some of them had moved away – Laodice, having acquired title to them, is obviously to have the right to recall them, if she so desires, to the village, which now belongs to her and to which they are evidently regarded as bound.

A famous Vienna papyrus of 260 B.C. (*PER* Inv. 24552 gr. = *SB* V.8008),²⁷ aimed at giving some protection against indiscriminate enslavement to the inhabitants of Syria and Palestine, then subject to Ptolemy II, refers to the purchase of *sōmata laïka* (lines 2, 22) by private individuals, and provides that if the *sōmata* in question were *oiketika* when acquired they can be retained, but that if *eleuthera* they are to be taken away from their purchasers (unless sold to them by agents of the king), and that in future *sōmata laïka eleuthera* must not be sold or given in pledge except in specified circumstances arising in fiscal matters. The Greek word *sōmata* (literally 'bodies') is very often, though not always, used of slaves; the noun *oiketēs*, from which *oiketika* is derived, is uncommon in Ptolemaic papyri but when it is used seems almost always to designate slaves; and the adjective *laïka* comes from *laos*, a word reserved for indigenous inhabitants, 'natives' (cf. I.iii n.13 below). According to Bieżuńska-Małowist this ordinance is dealing with 'une main-d'oeuvre libre mais dépendante'; and in Rostovtzeff's view it was probably directed 'against the endeavours of certain people to enslave free workmen, chiefly by transforming Oriental bondage resembling slavery into regular slavery of the Greek type'; he adds that 'this may be the basis of the distinction made in the Vienna papyrus between the *sōmata laïka eleuthera*

(Oriental bondage) and the *sōmata onta oiketika'*.[28] On the other hand, the former group (the *eleuthera*) may well have been, or at least included, those who were completely free. We do not yet have enough information about land tenure in Syria in the third century to be precise.

It also seems probable that what I call serfs are referred to in inscriptions mentioning *oiketai* (or *oiketeia*, e.g. *SIG³* 495.112-13)[29] and in other epigraphic and literary sources.[30] Among inscriptions I wish to mention only the famous one of Mnesimachus, inscribed on a wall of a temple of Artemis (Cybele) at Sardis in western Asia Minor, probably around 200 B.C., and recording a conveyance – not, as used to be supposed, a mortgage – of Crown land near Sardis by Mnesimachus, to which he did not have an indefeasible freehold title.[31] The inscription mentions both 'the *laoi* and their households with their belongings' (who seem to be described as 'attached to the plots' and are apparently liable to rents in money and labour), and also *oiketai*, who are usually taken to be slaves. I will only add that in Ptolemaic Egypt we hear of peasants, often *basilikoi geōrgoi* ('cultivators of Crown land'), who were undoubtedly free in the technical sense that they were not slaves and cannot properly be described as serfs either, but were subject to very strict controls and supervision to a greater extent than any other non-serf peasants I have come across in the Greek world.[32]

There is, however, even better evidence of the existence of serfdom in Hellenistic Asia, which is sometimes neglected by those who study the subject,[33] perhaps because it comes mainly from the beginning of the Roman period, in the pages of the Greek geographer Strabo, who lived at Amaseia in Pontus, on the southern shore of the Black Sea, and who wrote under Augustus and Tiberius. Certain passages in Strabo prove conclusively the existence of what I am calling serfdom on some of the temple estates in Asia Minor; and other evidence to the same effect is furnished by some remarkable inscriptions of the kings of Commagene (in north-eastern Syria), of the middle and late first century B.C. This evidence relates specifically to what are called 'hierodules' (*hierodouloi* in Greek),[34] literally 'sacred slaves', and perhaps best described in English as 'temple-servants'. My own belief is that the generic form of tenure of these hierodules (which I shall describe immediately), far from being exceptional and limited to temple-lands, is very likely to be one of the most ancient kinds of land tenure in Asia, which happens to have survived long enough to allow us to find a specific description of it simply because the land was sacred and belonged to temples, and was therefore not subject to the normal vicissitudes of private ownership, which might involve fragmentation (as a result of inheritance, as well as sale) and alteration of the terms of occupation. I must add that my position is not at all the same as that of Sir William Ramsay, who believed that all or most of Asia Minor once consisted of temple-states, the lands of many of which were confiscated by the Hellenistic kings. Ramsay's theory has been thoroughly refuted by Jones (*GCAJ* 309-10 n.58). What I have suggested is quite different: that the examples of 'sacred' serfdom which we find existing in the temple-estates in the late Hellenistic period are likely to be survivals of forms of serfdom that had earlier been widespread in Asia.

I find it particularly significant that in at least two of the main texts mentioning hierodules we hear of a feature of their condition which is also found in the case of three other peoples identified as serfs in the Classical period: Spartan Helots,

Thessalian Penestai, and Mariandynoi of Heraclea Pontica.[35] This feature is that they cannot be sold off the land on which they reside. Strabo says that when Pompey (in 64-63 B.C.) made his favourite Archelaus priest of the important temple of Ma (or Enyo) at Comana in Pontus, he made him ruler of the whole principality and master of the hierodules who lived there, to the number of at least 6,000, 'except that he was to have no power to sell them' (XII.iii.32-6, esp. 34, p.558). This, I think, is likely to have been a recognition of a long-existing situation. Inscriptions from Commagene, including the famous one set up by Antiochus I of that country on the Nimrud Dagh (in south-eastern Turkey), are even more specific: they not only provide (in the words *mēte eis heteron apallotriōsai*) that the hierodules and their descendants are not to be alienated but also forbid their reduction to slavery (*mēte . . . katadoulōsasthai*), thus providing conclusive proof that the hierodules, in spite of their name, were not technically slaves (see esp. *IGLS* I.1 = *OGIS* I.383, lines 171-89).[36] Strabo mentions several other sets of hierodules, including 'more than 6,000' at Comana in Cappadocia, of whom the priest of Ma was *kyrios*, master (XII.ii.3, p.535), and 'almost 3,000' in a settlement belonging to the temple of Zeus of Venasa in Morimene (also in Cappadocia, id. 6, p.537). These temples, and others in the more remote parts of Asia Minor,[37] had evidently preserved the ancient way of life on their estates. On the lands of some other temples serfdom had decayed, no doubt owing to Greek or Roman influence. The temple of Men Ascaënus in the territory of Pisidian Antioch, for example, had once had a number of hierodules, but this situation had come to an end in Strabo's own time (XII.viii.14, p.577; and see Levick, *RCSAM* 73, 219). There were also fewer hierodules in Strabo's day than in earlier times at the temple of Anaïtis at Zela in Pontus, where the priest had once been 'master of everything' (*kyrios tōn pantōn*); Strabo describes the Zela of his own day as 'for the most part a small town [*polisma*] of hierodules' (XI.viii.4, p.512; XII.iii.37, p.559). There are also many temple estates in Asia Minor (and at least one in northern Phoenicia), recorded by Strabo or known from other sources (almost entirely epigraphic), where hierodules are not specifically mentioned but where they, or other serfs, are very likely to have existed.[38] Outside Asia, and especially in Egypt, we hear of temple-servants who may well have been serfs, but the evidence is rather obscure.[39] I am ignoring here other types of hierodules, such as the sacred prostitutes whom we hear of in some places in the Greek East (Pontic Comana, for instance), and even in Greece itself (at Corinth) and in Sicily (at Eryx).[40]

The material I have adduced proves beyond question that forms of serfdom existed in Asia in Hellenistic times, almost certainly as a survival from earlier regimes. It is essential to realise, however, that these forms of serfdom tended to dissolve as a result of contact with the more advanced Greek and Roman economy (above all, no doubt, when the land came into the ownership or under the control of Greeks or hellenised natives or of Romans), and after a few generations virtually ceased to exist, except as part of very conservative complexes such as the temple estates I have discussed above and in remote areas little affected by the Graeco-Roman economy, like Iberia/Georgia (see above). Until the introduction of the Later Roman colonate (for which see IV.iii below) serfdom failed to maintain itself in the Greek world (or, as we shall see presently, in the rest of the Roman empire), and when it disappeared in a particular area, there is no sign that it was re-established.

It has been claimed recently by some Marxist scholars, especially (in their different ways) Kreissig and Briant,[41] that the dependent condition in Asia which I call serfdom (as does Kreissig, though not Briant) is a form of production basically different from the Hellenic one, and that in the Hellenistic kingdoms we should recognise the existence of what Marx himself and some of his followers have called the 'Oriental' or 'Asiatic' mode of production. I cannot do better than cite part of the last paragraph of Kreissig's latest article, which is conveniently written in English and is a most useful collection of material on Hellenistic land tenure. According to his view, in the forms of tenure he specifies, which include by far the greater part of the land in Hellenistic Asia, 'the laoi-system, dependent labour in the form of serfdom, overwhelmingly predominates . . . In the most basic section of production, in agriculture, the Orient in Hellenistic times is profoundly Oriental, not at all Greek. 'Hellenism' was confined to elements of social superstructure' (LPHO 26).

I cannot accept this as it stands, for the following reasons:

1. The existence of an 'Oriental' or 'Asiatic' mode of production seems to me a useless and even misleading conception, evolved by Marx on the basis of what can now be seen as a seriously defective knowledge of the Oriental world (though based on the best sources available in his day), and far too imprecise to be of any value in historical or sociological analysis. I cannot believe that anyone who has read the works of Perry Anderson and Daniel Thorner cited in I.iv n.15 below could still wish to cling to this outmoded notion. Pre-Classical modes of production (cf. I.iv above) need to be characterised quite differently and much more specifically.

2. Even if we assume for the moment that an 'Oriental/Asiatic' mode of production is a concept worth employing, there is a decisive argument against seeing the serfdom of Hellenistic Asia as an example of it, which takes the form of a *reductio ad absurdum*. Around A.D. 300, with the introduction of the Later Roman colonate, serfdom reappeared, this time imposed and maintained by the Roman imperial government and on a much larger scale than ever before, increasing both in geographical scope and in severity as time went on, and becoming the predominant mode of production. As we shall see (in IV.iii below), all working tenants and even working freeholders were originally bound to the land, some to their actual plots, others to their villages. This was serfdom indeed, not fundamentally different, as a mode of production, from some of the earlier forms we have noticed in Greece and Asia. If we were to treat the serfdom of the early Hellenistic period as 'non-Hellenic', as an 'Oriental/Asiatic' mode of production, then we should be ineluctably driven to consider the Later Roman Empire as having that mode of production – a notion which is patently ridiculous.

3. Kreissig himself admits that in an area such as Priene, 'an old Greek colony and not a new settlement of the Hellenistic period in Asia Minor, . . . chattel slavery . . . would have been quite normal' (LPHO 25). But before Alexander's conquests a very large part of the best land in western and south-western Asia Minor had been taken over by Greek colonists, who from the ninth century onwards founded walled settlements that grew into cities; and we can surely

suppose – badly informed as we are about methods of exploitation of agricultural land in Asia Minor – that the citizens of all the cities founded in Archaic and Classical times would have made use of slaves for agriculture when they could. The obvious exceptions would be cases where a pre-existing system of serfdom, or one that could be introduced at the conquest of the land, gave something like equal possibilities of exploitation; but the only certain pre-Hellenistic example we have of this in Asia, noticed by the Greeks as peculiar, is Heraclea Pontica (see above). (Of course there may have been other pre-Hellenistic instances of serfdom, but I know of no certain evidence of any, except perhaps the Pedieis in the territory of Priene.)[42] A goodly part of the coastal areas of Asia Minor (its most fruitful and populated regions) would therefore have to be removed from the category of an 'Oriental/Asiatic' mode of production, even if we were prepared to concede its existence in principle; and the existence of this area would be bound to have a powerful effect upon neighbouring districts.[42a]

4. As for the remainder of Asia Minor and Syria, Kreissig and others have hardly made sufficient allowance for the fact that serfdom there in the Hellenistic period was a very transitory phase, which evidently began to wane as soon as it was exposed to Greek (or Roman) influence. After going through all the evidence cited by Kreissig and Briant, I would emphasise that it is concentrated in the earliest part of the Hellenistic period, especially the late fourth century and the first half of the third, and that it is rare in the second century and ceases entirely thereafter, save in such exceptional cases as age-old temple estates or districts little exposed to Greek or Roman influence. After Strabo's time, until the introduction of the Later Roman colonate, there is virtually no evidence of the continued existence of serfdom, even in remote areas (cf. Rostovtzeff, *SEHHW* I.512), although of course our evidence is too poor to enable us to say confidently that it died out altogether. I conclude, therefore, that in the absence of special circumstances serfdom tended to decline in each area as soon as it came under Greek (or Macedonian) or Roman rule and was directly exposed to Greek or Roman influences – which spread by degrees farther and farther into Asia. However, although serfdom was not a major or necessary part of the original Graeco-Roman system of production, it was by no means entirely alien to that system: it certainly existed, as we have seen, as a *local* institution, at various places within the Greek world, sometimes maintaining itself for centuries in an area where it had become traditional. As I shall explain in IV.iii below, when the rate of exploitation achieved by slavery had become greatly reduced, and the Roman empire, if it was to survive, had to bear heavy additional burdens (especially a much enlarged army and civil service), serfdom was introduced from above on a grand scale, in the form of the Later Roman colonate. The existence of serfdom in the Hellenistic East, therefore, even in the fairly brief period during which it retained its importance, should not lead us to deny that that area was subjected to the standard Graeco-Roman method of production. Outright slavery, as the mode of production most favoured by the Greek and Roman propertied classes, must always have exercised a pervasive influence, even in areas where as yet it did not actually predominate. The vast wealth of the 'King's friends' of the Hellenistic period (cf. III.ii above & its nn.9-10 below), and of the leading citizens of many Greek cities at that time (including some of

those newly founded by the kings), must naturally have led to a rapid expansion of the area dominated by the Classical mode of production, in which slavery played a vital role; and slavery and the exploitation of free peasants who had emerged from serfdom then became the principal means by which the propertied classes acquired their surplus.

I must again insist that we know too little about systems of land tenure in Asia to be able to describe with confidence the methods by which the working agricultural population was exploited, either before or after they came under the direct control of Greek cities. In particular, we simply do not know what happened to the native population of each area, the *laoi* (no doubt consisting largely of serfs), when they were first taken over fully into the Greek economy. Even the moment at which we should conceive that change as happening is uncertain, but perhaps we should see it as essentially the transfer of the peasants concerned from 'king's land' (and probably the lordship of a native dynast or of a Hellenistic courtier who allowed the old system of exploitation to continue) to a Greek city. Not only were many new cities founded by the Hellenistic kings and the Roman emperors in Asia; many ancient villages and military cleruchies were eventually promoted to the status of cities;[43] lands were sometimes (how often, we cannot tell) transferred to favourites of the kings, with permission to 'incorporate' them in the territory of a city (see esp. Welles, *RCHP* 10-13 and 18-20);[44] and land could also be sold or given to a city by a king: we know of a sale to Pitane by Antiochus I, and of a gift by Ptolemy II to Miletus (*OGIS* 335.133 ff.; *SIG*³ 322, § 38).

What, then, happened to the serf when he emerged from that condition? Again, the answer is that we do not know: we can only speculate, in deciding between certain alternatives. In principle, the alternatives are that when his condition changed he was likely to become either an outright slave or a free leasehold tenant – or conceivably a freeholder, but I would imagine that this was very rare at the initial stage, although the descendants of some ex-serfs might manage to acquire ownership of land eventually. Many Greeks who took over agricultural land from indigenous Asiatic owners must have been strongly tempted to treat serfs – to whose condition they would be unaccustomed – as chattel slaves, when they felt they could get away with it. And I agree with Rostovtzeff: 'I see nothing to prevent the kings, the chief priests, or the feudal [sic] lords of Bithynia, Pontus, Cappadocia, Galatia, and Paphlagonia from selling under one pretext or another some of their serfs to an agent of the Roman *publicani* [tax-farmers] or to a Delian slave dealer' (*SEHHW* III.1515 n.49). Let us concede, then, that some proportion – but an unknowable proportion – of former peasant serfs were reduced to full slavery.

On the other hand, many scholars have held that when former 'king's land' was absorbed by a city (whether ancient or newly founded) and became part of its territory, its *chōra*, those of the existing *laoi* who had been serfs ceased to be so and became free *paroikoi* or *katoikoi* of the city – not its citizens, and therefore possessing no political rights in it, but recognised free inhabitants. This was the view Rostovtzeff expressed in different places, with varying degrees of confidence, and it has often been stated as an undoubted fact by others.[45] A forthright expression of it is by Tarn, who says that 'the peasants *might* sometimes still be serfs, . . . but generally they became free hereditary 'settlers' (*katoikoi*), paying taxes to the city, and their villages sometimes began to acquire a kind of corporate life . . . The Greek city then was a boon to the Asiatic peasant and tended to raise his status' (*HC*³ 134-8, at 135).

The most persuasive argument for this theory, to my mind, is the absence of evidence for serf tenures in Roman Asia after Strabo's time and the apparent presence of large numbers of free peasants. Positive evidence of the conversion of serfs into free *paroikoi* or *katoikoi*, however, seems scarcely to exist. One inscription which is often quoted as evidence for this process, namely the letter of a Hellenistic king to Priene, of the third century B.C. (Welles, *RCHP* 8), seems to me of no value whatever in this connection: its interpretation, by Welles and others (even Kreissig, *LPHO* 24), seems to me greatly over-confident.[46] Again, in 133 B.C. the city of Pergamum gave its citizenship to all its registered *paroikoi* and certain other persons (mainly military), and at the same time promoted to the class of *paroikoi* various other groups, including public slaves (*dēmosioi*), the descendants of freedmen, and 'adult or youthful *basilikoi*' (*OGIS* 338.10-19, 20-6).[47] As in the inscription of Priene just mentioned, there is no mention of *laoi*. But who are the *basilikoi*? Some take them to be slaves, others serfs. I suspect that the ambiguous term *basilikoi* was used deliberately, to cover both statuses and any doubtful or intermediate cases.

Serfdom, then, did virtually disappear from Hellenistic and Roman Asia, but we have no means of telling how many ex-serfs became slaves and how many achieved a fully free status. I would guess that incorporation of their land in the territory of a city did tend to lead, in the long run, to a theoretically freer status, as most scholars have believed. This might be expected to enable them to make a rather more effective resistance to exploitation; but, on the other hand, they would still enjoy no political rights, and indeed their former position as serfs may have given at least some of them some traditional privileges (a limit, for example, on the rents or labour-services that could be demanded of them) which would no longer apply when they achieved a technically free status. Indeed their incorporation in what was to a certain extent a market-economy and a money-economy may well have led to increasing exploitation of them and to an increase in economic and social differentiation among them.

I need make only a brief mention of what I may call 'the Roman area': that part of the Roman empire which was not Greek according to my definition in I.ii above. Serfdom was not native to the original Roman area either, although some form of it may well have existed in Etruria (see above, and n.4 below). The Romans may have preferred to treat as free at least some of those coming under their control who were in some form of serfdom: I give three probable examples in a note,[48] one from Sicily, admittedly a Greek area in my sense.

It is time now to turn to the Later Roman colonate. It was only at the end of the third century of our era that legislation began to be introduced, subjecting to forms of legal serfdom the whole working agricultural population of the Graeco-Roman world. In outline, leasehold tenants (*coloni*) became serfs, bound either to their actual farms or plots or to their villages and almost as much subject to their landlords as were slaves to their masters, even though they remained technically *ingenui*, free men rather than slaves; working peasant freeholders too were tied, to their villages. There were appreciable differences between different groups among the working agricultural population and between different areas: for the details, which need not concern us here, see IV.iii below.

As I have said before, neither in Greek nor in Latin had there been any general technical word for 'serf' or 'serfdom'; but the Latin word *coloni*, which had originally been used in the sense of 'farmer' or 'colonist' and during the Principate had increasingly come to mean 'lessee' of agricultural land, was commonly used from the reign of Constantine (the early fourth century) onwards to refer to men I call serfs. From A.D. 342 (*CTh* XII.i.33) the term *colonatus* begins to appear, in the sense of the tied colonate (see IV. iii below). By the mid-fifth century we find the Latin term *adscripticii* (*enapographoi* or *enhypographoi* in Greek) employed to designate those *coloni* who according to my definitions were strictly serfs (see IV.iii again). Even when the serf colonate was in full swing, however, the government found it difficult if not impossible to express the legal condition of the *coloni* satisfactorily without resorting to the terminology of slavery, which, as it realised, was not properly appropriate. (I shall deal with this subject rather more fully in IV.iii § 21 below.) The Emperor Justinian could show some exasperation at the difficulty he found in distinguishing between slaves and *adscripticii* (*CJ* XI.xlviii.21.1, A.D. 530). Earlier, in a constitution of *c*. 393, relating to the civil diocese of Thrace, the Emperor Theodosius I, while admitting that its *coloni* were legally 'of free status' (*condicione ingenui*), could qualify that statement by adding that they 'must be *regarded* as slaves of the very land to which they were born' (*servi terrae ipsius cui nati sunt aestimentur*), and he could speak of their *possessor* as exercising over them 'the power of a master' (*domini potestas, CJ* XI.lii.1.1). I need hardly add that of course it was impossible at law for land to own slaves or anything else: a fiction of that sort would surely have shocked a jurist of the Classical period of Roman law (the second and early third centuries), who would have condemned it as the legal nonsense it was. There were other attempts, which I shall record in IV.iii below (§ 21), to represent the land as endowed with some mysterious legal personality of its own, and exercising compulsion. I may add that in mediaeval Europe we encounter from time to time assertions that everyone is either free or a *servus* (see e.g. Hilton, *DSME* 9); but by then the word *servus* would often mean something more like 'serf' than 'slave'.

One cannot help remembering here the brilliant passages in two very early works of Marx, the *Contribution to the Critique of Hegel's Philosophy of Law* (1843) and the *Economic and Philosophic Manuscripts* (1844), describing the inheritor of an entailed estate as the property of that estate, inherited by the land, 'an attribute fettered to it', indeed 'the serf of landed property'! (*MECW* III.106, 266). But Marx, of course, was fully conscious of the paradox: he was writing in a very theoretical way and with great irony, while the Roman emperors were simply giving lame excuses for a situation which they knew to be anomalous under Roman law but were trying to justify.

I have gone into some detail on the question of the legal status of the *coloni* of the Later Empire, as seen by the Roman government, because it brings out most forcibly the dominant role that slavery in the strict sense always played in the minds of the Roman ruling class. They may grudgingly admit that their *coloni* are *ingenui* and not slaves; but they are driven by the subject condition of the *coloni* to apply to them all but the strictly technical terms of slavery – never simply *servi* or *mancipia*, but *servi terrae* and similar expressions, which from the strictly legal point of view are mere metaphors. The very fact that Graeco-Roman society was still, so to speak, permeated with slavery and dominated by its ideology, I would suggest, strongly affected the institutions of serfdom that developed from the fourth century onwards (cf. the last part of IV.iii below).

I think it will be helpful if I speak briefly at this point about the use in Greek texts of the word *perioikoi*, often translated 'serfs', as for example in Ernest Barker's version of Aristotle's *Politics* and even in W. L. Newman's commentary thereon.[49] This translation is wrong: the essential characteristic of the *perioikos* was not at all that he was unfree (what we call a slave or serf), but that he was *without political rights in the state*. He would not be a slave, but he might not be a serf either. It was the Spartan *perioikoi* whom a Greek of the Classical period would naturally think of first, when he heard the term *perioikoi* used, and everyone knew roughly what the status of the Spartan *perioikoi* was: they were certainly not unfree and they had a certain amount of self-government in their settlements, which on occasion can even be called, inaccurately, *poleis* (see my *OPW* 345-6); but of course they had no political rights in the Spartan State.[50] Other communities of *perioikoi* are known to have existed in Greece itself in the territory of Argos, Elis and Thessaly, and outside the Greek mainland in Cyrene and Crete.[51] Aristotle wished the lands of his ideal State to be cultivated, if not by slaves, then by *barbaroi perioikoi* (*Pol.* VII.10, 1330²25-31; cf. 9, 1329²24-6); but since he goes on to speak of them as if they might all 'belong to' private owners or to the community, I am sure he would not have conceived them as necessarily in a state of freedom: surely in his mind they would be more like serfs. Aristotle was acquainted with Asiatic peoples who were in some form of serfdom or quasi-serfdom to their Greek conquerors, such as the Mariandynoi of Pontic Heraclea, whom I have mentioned above. (He had evidently studied the history of Heraclea Pontica.)[52] And Aristotle would doubtless think it perfectly natural for Greeks to accept the existence of serfdom in any non-Greek country they conquered. Similarly, when Isocrates, after complaining that the Spartans have compelled their neighbours (the Messenians) to *heilōteuein*, speaks of it as in their power to join with Athens in 'making all the barbarians into *perioikoi* of the whole of Hellas' (IV.131), he is surely thinking of a status comparable to that of the Spartan Helots rather than that of the Spartan *Perioikoi* – compare his letter to King Philip II of Macedon (which I quoted above when discussing the Helots), anticipating that Philip would compel the native inhabitants of Asia to *heilōteuein* to the Greeks (*Ep.* III.5).

Before leaving the subject of serfdom I must mention that the definition I have adopted (from the 1956 Convention) of serfdom and the serf may not appear at first sight identical with that which Marx seems to have had in mind when he used those terms, or German words of which they are legitimate English translations. In reality my conception is very similar to his: it merely lacks one element which sometimes, but not always, figures prominently in his view of serfdom. The immediate impression that emerges from some of the writings of Marx is that for him the outstanding characteristic of serfdom was 'labour rent' (*Arbeitsrente*): the obligation upon a man who is 'in possession of his own means of production' to perform a substantial amount of labour on his lord's land. This is true in particular of Marx's main discussion of 'labour rent', in *Capital* III.790-4 (=*MEW* XXV.798-802), from which I have quoted elsewhere – it is one of the most important passages Marx ever wrote. At one point there he seems to be giving a brief description of serfs as 'those subject to enforced labour' (*Cap*. III.793). Whenever Marx wrote of serfdom, he was probably thinking primarily of a typical situation in Europe, involving, as he puts it, 'the peasant serf, such as he, I might say, until yesterday existed in the whole East of Europe. This peasant worked, for example, three days for himself on his own field or the field allotted to him, and the three subsequent days he performed compulsory and gratuitous labour on the estate of his lord (*Wages, Price and Profit* ix, in *MESW* 211; cf. *Cap*. III.790).

I feel myself that the existence of 'labour rent' would tend to make the tenant more subservient to his landlord, especially in an economy where slave labour was not uncommon, for the tenant would be working directly under the orders of the landlord or his agent (*actor, procurator*) and might well become, in the eyes of the overseer, hardly distinguishable from a slave.

Now if 'labour rent', in the form of substantial personal service on the lord's land, is indeed an essential characteristic of the serf, then serfdom could hardly be said to have existed at all in antiquity, for there is no proof of the yielding of 'labour rent' on any substantial scale in the whole Greek or Roman world until a very late date, in the sixth century, when the Ravenna papyri disclose the existence of regular labour services for several days a *week*, whereas at other times and places in the ancient world we find at most only a few days' service a *year*, as in a famous series of inscriptions from north Africa (see IV.ii below and its nn.16-19). Yet, after all, the giving of actual labour service does not seem to have been, for Marx, a necessary feature of serfdom, for he can say of the man he calls, in English, a 'self-sustaining serf' ('a direct producer who is not free', but is subject to a 'direct relation of lordship and servitude') that his 'lack of freedom may be reduced from serfdom with enforced labour [*Leibeigenschaft mit Fronarbeit*] to a mere tributary relationship', presumably the payment of an ordinary rent in money or kind (*Cap*. III.790). And after distinguishing the serf from the slave (who 'works under alien conditions of production and not independently') he says of the serf that 'conditions of personal dependence are requisite, a lack of personal freedom, no matter to what extent, and being *tied to the soil* as its accessory, bondage [*Hörigkeit*] in the true sense of the word' (ibid. 791, my italics; *MEW* XXV.799). Similarly, in the *Economic and Philosophic Manuscripts* of 1844 Marx could say of the serf that he is 'the adjunct of the land' (*MECW* III.266), and in *Wage Labour and Capital* that he 'belongs to the land' (*MECW* IX.203). In the *Grundrisse* he speaks of the worker 'in the serf relation' as 'an appendage of the soil [*Zubehör der Erde*], exactly like draught-cattle' (368 = E.T. 465). In the first volume of *Das Kapital* (*MEW* XXIII.743) Marx describes the emergence of the wage-labourer under capitalism as taking place after he had ceased being 'attached to the soil' and '*leibeigen oder hörig* to another person'. (The standard English translation misleadingly renders the German words I have just quoted by 'slave, serf or bondsman', *Cap*. I.715.) Although Marx sometimes uses the terms *leibeigen* and *hörig* in a general sense of being subject to and dependent upon someone else and under his control, the words 'attached to the soil' (*an die Scholle gefesselt*) prove beyond question that he was thinking here of the man I am calling a serf. So I think Marx would have accepted the man I have defined as a serf under that designation. Indeed, in a footnote in Vol. I of *Capital* (717-18 n.2), referring to the situation in Silesia in the late eighteenth century, he can use the expression 'diese serfs' which in *MEW* XXIII.745 n.191 is explained as 'Leibeigenen'. For such a condition he normally employs the term *Leibeigenschaft*, but sometimes *Hörigkeit*, apparently as an alternative name for the same status.[53] A passage in which he dwells upon the condition of the serf of mediaeval and modern times is *Cap.* I.235-8 (=*MEW* XXIII.250-4). Here he speaks again and again of *Leibeigenschaft* and *Fronarbeit*. I need only add that of course we must not take the use of the words 'serf' and 'serfdom' to imply any necessary connection with feudalism, even if we regard feudalism as necessarily involving forms of serfdom (cf. IV.v below). This point is made explicitly in a letter from Engels to Marx dated 22 December 1882. After expressing his pleasure at the fact that he and Marx are in agreement on the history of *Leibeigenschaft*, Engels continues, 'It is certain that *Leibeigenschaft* and *Hörigkeit* are not a peculiarly mediaeval-feudal form; we find them everywhere, or nearly everywhere, in places where conquerors have the land cultivated for them by the old inhabitants, e.g. very early in Thessaly.' Engels was of course thinking of the Penestai, of whom I have spoken briefly above. He and many others, he adds, had been misled by this about *Mittelaltersknechtschaft* (mediaeval servitude): 'one was much too inclined to base it simply on conquest'. (This letter of Engels is unfortunately omitted from *MESC* in the English version I normally refer to, of 1956; but it can be found on pp.411-12 of an earlier English edition, of 1936, which has a different selection of letters. The German text is in *MEGA* III.iv.587 and *MEW* XXXV.137.)

III. DEBT BONDAGE. I said earlier that debt bondage was a common phenomenon in the Greek world and we must not make the mistake of supposing that many other cities followed the example of Athens and abolished it entirely. As far as I know, we cannot name any other single city which certainly did away with debt bondage, and it is quite likely that many allowed even actual enslavement of defaulting debtors. The Sicilian Greek historian Diodorus, who visited Egypt and wrote his account of it (with much second-hand material) in the second third of the last century B.C., inspires no confidence when he attributes Solon's reform of the Athenian debt laws to borrowing from the legislation of the late-eighth-century Pharaoh Bocchoris; but he is surely speaking from his knowledge of the contemporary world when he declares that *most* Greek lawgivers, although they forbade the taking of indispensable articles such as weapons and ploughs as securities for debt, nevertheless allowed the debtors themselves to become *agōgimoi* (I.79.3-5), a technical term which would cover liability to both debt bondage and actual enslavement (Plut., *Sol.* 13.4). We happen to know that one Alexandrian citizen could not be a slave to another (*P. Hal.* 1.219-21). Some other Greek cities evidently had the same rule as early Rome, that a citizen who was enslaved must be sold abroad (at Rome, 'trans Tiberim'); but we cannot be sure that this rule was universal (see Finley, *SSAG* 173-4). I think it virtually certain that forms of debt bondage existed at all times in the great majority of Greek cities. We often hear of laws being passed by Greek cities, dealing with problems of indebtedness: Asheri, *LGPD* (1969), discusses forty known examples in the half-millenium between 594/3 and 86/5 B.C.

Just as Latin words like 'servitus' and 'servire' were sometimes used (as we shall see presently) to mean either the merely temporary 'servitude' of a free man in debt bondage or the condition of a peasant serf who was 'free' only in the sense that he was not technically a slave, so in Greek we find applied to those in debt bondage words (even *doulos*) which ought to be reserved for the slave, as well as those which are most often applied to slaves (e.g. *sōmata*, literally 'bodies'). A fragment of Menander shows how wary we must be. Daos, in the *Hero*, asked if the girl he loves is a *doulē* (a slave), replies, 'Well, yes, in a sort of way' (*houtōs, hēsychēi, tropon tina*); and he goes on to explain that she and her brother are serving to work off a debt (*Hero* 18-40, esp. 20). This is evidently conceived as happening in Attica, for the setting of the play is the Athenian deme of Ptelea (line 22); but we must remember that all Menander's plays were produced in the generation following the destruction in 322 of the fifth/fourth-century Athenian democracy, when forms of debt bondage could well have crept in and even received at least tacit legal recognition (cf. V.iii below).[54] Some of our texts from the Classical period, if taken literally, suggest that in some Greek cities the consequence of defaulting on a debt might be actual enslavement or the sale of one's children (see e.g. Lys. XII.98; Isocr. XIV.48; Ar., *Plut.* 147-8).[55] I doubt if Aristophanes, in the *Acharnians* (729-835), would have represented his Megarian as actually trying to sell his two daughters (who would then, of course, become the slaves of the buyer) unless such things were known to happen in the Greek world, even perhaps in places where they were contrary to law. According to Herodotus, writing in the third quarter of the fifth century, the Thracians – who were of course a non-Greek people, and incidentally provided Classical Greece with more slaves than any other 'barbarian' race – had a custom of selling their children abroad (V.6.1); and over six hundred years later Philostratus attributes to the Phrygians of Asia Minor (by then largely hellenised) a similar practice of selling their children (*Vita Apollon.* VIII.7). In both cases the sales are represented as outright; and although nothing is said of debt, we may suspect that usually the children would be sold as a substitute for the enslavement or debt bondage of the parents. (Diodorus says that the Gauls would give Italian merchants a boy, *pais* – as a slave, of course – in exchange for a jar of wine; but he gives as a reason not debt but the Gauls' love of wine and the 'accustomed avarice' of the Italian merchants, V.26.4.)

Arrest and imprisonment for debt seem to have been common in the cities of the Achaean League in the mid-second century (Polyb. XXXVIII.xi.10, B.C. 147-6). At Temnos in Asia Minor, in the last century B.C., we hear from Cicero of a man named Heracleides becoming 'addictus' to his surety, Hermippus, who had had to discharge his debt (Cic., *Pro Flacc.* 42, 46-50, esp. 48-9). Although 'addictio' was also an institution of Roman law (mentioned below), entitling a creditor to seize his judgment debtor and imprison him or (in practice) make him work for him, it seems equally likely that this case would have been regulated by the local law of Temnos. The practice of seizure and imprisonment for debt was still rife in Egypt in A.D. 68, as shown by the famous edict of Tiberius Julius Alexander, the Roman Prefect, to which I shall return presently. And Plutarch, around A.D. 100, could speak of debtors being actually sold by their creditors (*Mor.* 829e), and of others who fled for sanctuary to the temple of Artemis in Ephesus (828d), evidently to save themselves from seizure. The passages I have just referred to come from an invective against borrowing, usually known by the Latin translation of its title, *De vitando aere alieno* (*Mor.* 827d–832a). In this work Plutarch (828f) shows a pathetic inability to grasp the significance for the poor man of the law of Solon to which I have already alluded. At one point, too, he can remark that 'nobody lends to the poor man' (830d), while at another he says, 'Do you possess nothing? Don't borrow, for you won't be able to repay' (829f). In a passage which is almost unique in Greek literature in proffering advice to the very poor man on how to maintain himself (830ab), Plutarch tells him to gain a living by teaching reading and writing (*grammata didaskōn*); by acting as *paidagōgos*, which involved taking children to school, an action normally performed by slaves; by being a door-keeper (*thyrō-rōn*), another activity almost monopolised by slaves; or by going in for sailing (*pleōn*) or the coasting trade (*parapleōn*) – anything rather than becoming a borrower, for Plutarch well knew what that was likely to lead to. (I shall return to this passage in Section vi of this chapter, dealing with hired labour.)

Those who are familiar with the New Testament will remember the Parable of the Unmerciful Servant, in Mt. XVIII.23-34, where Jesus, thinking as he always did in terms of the *chōra* of Palestine (see VII.iv below), is giving a vivid picture of the kind of thing that might well happen to someone who defaulted on a debt to a member of the family of Herod. The 'slave' (he is called *doulos* in the Greek), who owes his master, a king, the enormous sum of 10,000 talents, is very nearly sold up, with his wife and children; but he pleads for mercy, and his master remits the debt. The servant subsequently puts a 'fellow-slave' who owes him a mere 100 denarii under guard (or 'in prison'); but he himself ends up being 'delivered to the tormentors' until he has cleared off his own debt to his master. (The picture is complicated, from a strictly juristic point of view, by the fact that both the royal servants are called 'slaves'; but I think we need not bother about that.) The first servant is originally condemned by the king to be sold, with his family: this is permanent enslavement (*Versklavung, Schuldknechtschaft*). The second servant has temporary debt bondage (*Schuldhaft*) imposed upon him, by a powerful member of the king's household acting on his own authority: this is a form of what is often called 'personal execution'; and we may contrast this with Mt. V.25-6 and Lk. XII.58-9, contemplating the possibility of the enforcement of a debt through formal judicial process, leading to official imprisonment.[56] The first servant seems eventually to suffer debt bondage too, with torture thrown in; and here we need not consider too closely whether it is a form of 'personal execution' or an official condemnation by the king. In the Gospels, then, we can see three different sets of circumstances resulting from a debtor's default: outright enslavement, and debt bondage resulting either from 'personal execution' or from legal process. (There is, by the way, some interesting material on this subject in the Old Testament, above all Nehem. V.1-13, which reminds us of Solon's *seisachtheia*; also II Kings iv.1; Prov. XXII.7, and other references in Finley, SD 179 n.65.)

I am sure that there were many other places in the Greek East at about the beginning of our era where conditions would have been very similar to those described in the Parable of the Unmerciful Servant (and elsewhere in the Bible), especially in areas ruled for a long time by kings or dynasts which had recently been incorporated, or were soon to be incorporated, in the Roman empire. It is not clear to me what lies behind the claim by the Roman client king, Nicomedes III of Bithynia, in 104 B.C., that 'most of the Bithynians had been carried off by [Roman] *publicani* and were serving as slaves in the [Roman] provinces' – an allegation which led the Roman Senate to decree that no citizen of an 'allied' state should be held as a slave in a Roman province (Diod. XXXVI.3.1-2). Perhaps, as Badian has suggested, the *publicani* had made loans to Nicomedes, and he had pledged some of his subjects to them as security (*PS* 87-8). In Ptolemaic Egypt, for which we have much information from the papyri, there is clear evidence both for outright enslavement for debt and for debt bondage;[57] but in the Roman period the latter seems to have replaced the former. It is difficult to generalise about Greek cities, because the evidence is so scanty, but it does look as if debt bondage largely superseded outright enslavement for debt during the Hellenistic period.[58]

★   ★   ★   ★   ★   ★

So far, in speaking of debt bondage (and of actual enslavement for debt), I have been dealing with the Greek world in the Classical and Hellenistic periods. In Roman law, to which I must now turn (because it ultimately prevailed throughout the Greek world), the position of the defaulting debtor was in early times very bad indeed. His creditors might keep him in chains; and ultimately, according to the most probable interpretation of a laconic provision of the *Law of the Twelve Tables* (III.6), they might cut his body in pieces and divide the parts among themselves (*FIRA* I².33-4; there is an English translation in *ARS* 10, cf. 14). Other interpretations have been suggested; but the ancient writers who are known to have mentioned this law, even if they were shocked by it, all took it in the literal sense (which I have accepted): Quintilian, Tertullian, Cassius Dio, and especially Aulus Gellius, who may well be conveying the opinions of a leading second-century jurist, Sextus Caecilius Africanus, represented by Gellius as praising the wholesome severity of the law in question (*NA* XX.i.19, 39-55). The wealthy Roman regarded a defaulting debtor who had been driven to borrow because of dire need, rather than for some speculative or luxurious purpose, almost as a kind of criminal. Alternatively a debtor, in early Roman times, might become subject to the mysterious *nexum*, an institution of the early Roman law (much discussed in modern times) whereby, most probably, a debtor in effect committed himself totally to his creditor as security, 'giving his labour [or 'labour power'] into servitude', as Varro put it (*suas operas in servitutem, LL* VII.105); with the result that his creditor, if he defaulted (and perhaps even before that), could seize him, by the procedure known as *manus iniectio* or otherwise (possibly without even resorting to legal process), and deal with him as he wished, on default selling him as a slave and perhaps even putting him to death.[59] Historians are often content to say that *nexum* was abolished by the Lex Poetelia of (probably) 326 B.C. – and so indeed it may have been, in its full original form; but the position of the defaulting debtor remained precarious in the extreme. Modern Roman lawyers and historians usually say very little about his plight. I have found no account in the last half-century to equal the fundamental study by Friedrich von Woess in 1922 (PCBRR), which showed beyond doubt that in practice what is commonly called 'personal execution' – that is to say, seizure by a creditor – always remained in the forefront as a means of coercing a defaulting debtor. This was also the position taken some thirty years earlier by Ludwig Mitteis, in his great work (quoted here as *RuV*), *Reichsrecht und Volksrecht in den östlichen Provinzen des römischen Kaiserreichs* (1891) 418-58 (esp. 442-4; 450 on the Principate; and 450-8 on the Later Empire).[60]

Von Woess understood particularly well the nature of the Roman state and its law, as an instrument of the propertied classes; for the propertyless, he realised, the state 'couldn't care less': 'Der antike Staat ist ein Klassenstaat, der nur für die führenden Schichten Interesse hat, das Schicksal der Besitzlosen ist ihm herzlich gleichgültig' (PCBRR 518).

Well before the end of the Roman Republic a procedure had been devised known as *bonorum venditio*: the 'selling up' of the whole of an insolvent debtor's property.[61] This, however, was not at all a benefit to the debtor, but rather an added penalty, as it did nothing to prevent 'personal execution' against the debtor himself or his being subsequently sued for anything that might still remain owing, and it also involved disgrace, *infamia*, and was regarded as a great misfortune (see esp. Cic., *Pro Quinct.* 48-51, characteristically exaggerated as the passage is).

The procedure known as *cessio bonorum*, instituted by Julius Caesar or Augustus,[62] enabled some few debtors to escape 'personal execution' (and *infamia*) by ceding all or most of their property towards discharge of their debts, and thus avoid being 'adjudged' to their creditors and dragged off to prison.[63] The earliest surviving imperial constitution I can find which refers to *cessio bonorum* shows that that is precisely what the alternative was: the cession of property is a *beneficium*, a privilege, *ne iudicati detrahantur in carcerem* (*CJ* VII.lxxi.1, of A.D. 223). But *cessio bonorum* was permissible, it seems, only for a man whose default was not blameworthy and was due to misfortune: fire, theft and shipwreck are mentioned (Seneca, *De benef.* VII.xvi.3; *CTh* IV.xx.1: see esp. von Woess, PCBRR 505-10). Papyri show that it might be avilable in principle even to a 'poor' man;[64] but such a person would surely be much less likely than a man of substance to be granted the privilege, and *ex hypothesi* it would be of no use to the propertyless.

A greater privilege, the appointment (by the praetor in Rome or by the provincial governor) of a special *curator*, to carry out *distractio bonorum*, the sale of enough of the debtor's property to satisfy his creditors, was available, at least before Justinian's day, only to an insolvent who was a person of great consequence, a *clara persona*: the examples given by Gaius, in *Dig.* XXVII.x.5, are a senator or his wife. It did not involve *infamia*.

Recent standard works on Roman law, however much they may disagree about the technical details of *manus iniectio, addictio,* and the *actio iudicati*, leave no doubt that in the Roman world 'personal execution' never ceased to exist. As Schulz says, 'The plaintiff was permitted to take the defendant home and to keep him there until the judgment was fulfilled . . . This execution on the person existed throughout the whole classical period [of Roman law, roughly the second century and the first half of the third], though it is but rarely mentioned in our sources. Some rules of classical law remain unintelligible if one does not remember this form of execution' (*CRL* 26-7).[65]

We hear of men referred to in Latin as *obaerarii* or *obaerati* in several different parts of the Graeco-Roman world who are evidently being made to labour under burdensome conditions as a result of having defaulted on debts (which of course may include rents);[66] and a number of isolated texts strongly suggest that creditors often imposed very harsh conditions on defaulting debtors (including tenants), making them work almost like slaves in order to discharge their liabilities.[67] Later evidence shows the prohibition of imprisonment of private debtors in the well-known edict of Tiberius Julius Alexander, prefect of Egypt in 68, to have been essentially a piece of propaganda for the new regime of the Emperor Galba and a mere flash in the pan:[68] 'personal execution' in Egypt in particular remained 'ineradicable' and 'pertinacious', as Mitteis insisted (*RuV* 55, 59, 447-50). Much would depend on the relative social position of creditor and debtor, always an important factor in the Roman world[69] and one which played an even greater role in the Later Empire (cf. VIII.i below). In a court case in A.D. 85 the prefect of Egypt expressed horror at the conduct of a creditor named Phibion: 'You deserve to be flogged,' he said, 'for keeping in your custody a man of quality (*euschēmōn*) and his wife' (M. *Chr.* 80 = P. *Flor.* 61 II.59-61).

Quintilian, writing his handbook on oratory in the late first century, could speak of debates on whether a man is a slave if at the time of his birth his mother was 'addicta' (serving a creditor as a bondswoman), and whether 'an *addictus*, whom the law orders to be in servitude [*servire*] until he has paid his debt', is a slave or not (*Inst. orat.* III.vi.25; VII.iii.26). (Of course there could be no possible doubt about the answers, from the proper legal point of view: the first man was born free, *ingenuus*, and the second was free also; but the very fact that such questions could be thought worthy of oratorical debate is significant.) And when Quintilian thinks it necessary to point out that 'being a slave is different from being in a state of servitude' (*aliud est servus esse, aliud servire*), it is the bondsman, the *addictus*, whom he is setting beside the slave (V.x.60). A fragment, from the second century, of one of those curious rhetorical declamations in which orators displayed their often perverse ingenuity refers to an *addictus* in servitude to a money-lender, and asserts that 'an *addictus* never hopes for freedom' (Calpurnius Flaccus, *Declam.* 14, ed. G. Lehnert, 1903, pp.13-14). The statement is strictly untrue, of course, both literally and juridically, and is even falsified in the imaginary case given by the orator; but it may well give a fair impression of the situation of many *addicti* who realised that they had little or no hope of escaping from servitude. Two of the declamations which have come down to us under the name of Quintilian (for which see Michael Winterbottom, in *OCD*[2] 317) also deal with the *addictus*. One, in the 'major' series (Ps.-Quintil., *Declam.* III.17), describes an unfortunate debtor, known to us from a passage in Livy (VIII.28.1-9), as 'an *addictus* and scarcely a free man'. The other, from the 'minor' set (Ps.-Quintil., *Declam.* 311), again raises the question whether an *addictus* is a free man or a slave, under the guise of a disputed claim by an *addictus* that he has been freed from his status by a clause in his deceased creditor's will, manumitting all his 'slaves'. Fortunatianus, in an *Ars Rhetorica* written probably as late as the fourth century, when giving a list of twenty-one different ways in which a particular person can be described, including name, age, sex, place of origin, 'fortuna' (rich or poor) etc., gives under the heading 'condicio' (legal status) the examples 'servus, addictus' (II.1, p.103, ed. C. Halm, *Rhet. Lat. Min.*, 1863). In Gaius' *Institutes* (III.199) we find a casual reference to the fact that just as there can be theft (*furtum*) of members of one's family (a child in *potestas* or a wife in *manus*) or of one's *auctoratus* (a man bound under contract as a gladiator), so there can be theft of one's judgment debtor, a *iudicatus*, who is evidently assumed to be giving useful service in working off his debt. Salvius Julianus, one of the greatest of the Roman lawyers, who wrote in the second third of the second century, could contemplate a situation in which 'someone carries off a free man by force and holds him in chains' (*Dig*. XXII.iii.20); and Venuleius Saturninus, writing about the same time, could speak of the use of 'private or public chains' (*vel privata vel publica vincula*, *Dig*. L.xvi.224). In the early third century yet another jurist, Ulpian, writes of the man who, although not strictly 'in servitute', is put in chains by a private individual (*in privata vincula ductus*, *Dig*. IV.vi.23.*pr*.). At about the same period Paulus speaks of the man who casts someone into prison, to extract something from him (*Dig*. IV.ii.22): the passage seems to me to imply that the prison (*carcer*) is a private one. 'Private imprisonment by powerful creditors was an evil which the State, in spite of repeated enactments, was not strong enough to uproot' (Jolowicz and Nicholas, *HISRL*[3] 445). Some of the situations described above may, of course, have been created by indiscriminate acts of violence by powerful men; but they make much better sense if the perpetrators were creditors, as Jolowicz and Nicholas rightly assume in the passage I have just quoted.

It is true that the creditor who seized his judgment debtor had no *explicit legal right* to make him *work* off his debt. But what would be the point of merely seizing a defaulting debtor and incurring the expense of keeping him in idleness, except perhaps when he was believed to have concealed assets? The *addictus* or *iudicatus* to whom the word *servire* could be applied in popular speech (see above) must normally have been 'constrained' to work for his judgment creditor, if only to save himself from the even more unpleasant alternative of incarceration and chains, with only just enough food to keep him alive.

Most of the texts concerning 'personal execution' that I have quoted so far come from the Principate. In the Later Empire the position of the lower classes deteriorated further, and laws passed to give some protection to the humble were if anything disregarded with even greater impunity by the powerful, the *potentes* or *potentiores*, whom the Severan lawyer Callistratus evidently had in mind when he wrote (in the early third century) of the man who is 'kept in chains, *potentiore vi oppressus*' (*Dig*. IV.vi.9), and again when he recorded that taking refuge at a statue of the emperor was permitted, as an exception, to a man 'escaping from chains, or who had been detained in custody by *potentiores*' (*Dig*. XLVIII.xix.28.7). A constitution of Diocletian and Maximian dated 293 insisted that pledges for debt should consist only of property and not of 'sons, or free men' (*CJ* VIII.xvi.6). Another constitution of the same emperors in the following year stated that 'the laws do not permit *liberos* to be in servitude [*servire*] for debt to creditors' (*CJ* IV.x.12). Whether these *liberi* are to be conceived as *free men* who had become the bondsmen of their creditors (or had even tried to sell themselves into slavery), or whether they are *children* whose parents are being forbidden to commit them to bondage (for the Latin word could refer to either category), is hardly clear (see e.g. Mitteis, *RuV* 363-4, 451 and n.3, 456). In the Later Empire, in spite of a series of imperial laws positively forbidding the existence of private prisons (*CJ* IX.v.1 and 2, A.D. 486 and 529),[70] large landowners openly maintained such prisons, where defaulters could be coerced, along with other undesirables and criminals. More is known about this practice from Egypt than elsewhere (see Hardy, *LEBE* 67-71). One papyrus reveals that on a particular day in *c.* 538 there were no fewer than 139 persons in the estate prison of the Apion family at Oxyrhynchus (*PSI* 953.37,54–60): many if not most of them are likely to have been debtors.

We may conclude, then, that 'personal execution' continued unabated throughout the Principate and Later Empire,[71] at least to the time of Justinian;[72] that measures such as *cessio bonorum* benefited mainly the propertied classes; and that attempts by the imperial government (such as they were) to assist the weak foundered on the defiance of the *potentes*.

'Debt bondage' in antiquity, as I have defined it, would include at any rate the more burdensome form of the condition (which I can do no more than mention here) often known technically as *paramonē* ('indentured labour' is perhaps the nearest English equivalent for at least some of its varieties), which itself varied considerably not only from place to place and time to time but also from transaction to transaction, and might arise in very different ways, for example as a condition of manumission from slavery, or as a result of defaulting on a debt or even incurring one, as well as embodying a contract of service or apprenticeship.[73] Juridically, the person subject to the obligation of *paramonē* was undoubtedly 'free' rather than a slave, but his freedom in some cases was so circumscribed as to be very like that of the judgment debtor in Roman law, the *addictus*, who (as we have seen) could be said to be 'in a state of servitude' (*servire*), although not technically a *servus*. It may well be that Dio Chrysostom had one of the more onerous forms of this institution in mind when he spoke of 'myriads of free men selling themselves to be slaves according to a contract' (*douleuein kata syngraphēn*), sometimes on very harsh terms (XV.23). I suspect, too, that something very like *paramonē* may possibly have been involved in the case of the boys and girls described by Cassiodorus as standing around at the great fair in Lucania (in southern Italy), to be 'sold' by their parents, to their own profit, passing 'from the labour of the fields into *urbana servitia*' (*Var.* VIII.33, written about 527).

Before I leave the topic of debt bondage I wish to mention briefly a subject which can hardly be discussed in any detail without going into highly technical questions: I mean the sale of oneself or of one's children into slavery. This of course falls in strictness under the head of 'chattel slavery' rather than 'debt bondage', and it has already come up once or twice in this section; but since self-sale or sale of children would virtually always in practice be the result of extreme poverty and very probably of debt, and is often associated with the pledging of individuals for debt, it is convenient to refer to these practices here. The situation before the Roman conquest of the Greek world is so poorly known that it is best for us to confine ourselves to the Roman period, merely noticing that the enslavement of free men seems to have been possible in many places in the Greek East before they became subject to Rome (see above, and Mitteis, *RuV* 357-72). In legal theory a free person could not in general become a slave on Roman territory. But certain exceptions existed at various times even in strict law, quite apart from the enslavement resulting from certain types of sentence for crime, such as condemnation to the mines or quarries. In particular, the sale of newborn children (*sanguinolenti*)[74] was sanctioned at least from Constantine's time (*Fragm. Vat.* 34, of A.D. 313) and perhaps earlier (*CTh* V.x.1, of 319 or 329, referring to the 'statuta priorum principum'). Whether or not the sale of older children was ever legally permitted, it certainly occurred as a result of poverty and debt: this is clear above all from a series of constitutions issued between the early fourth century and the mid-fifth (see esp. *CTh* XI.xxvii.2; III.iii.1; *Nov. Val.* XXXIII) and from various literary sources and papyri; and we also know that adults in need sometimes sold themselves into slavery.[75] A passage not often quoted in this connection is *I Clement* lv.2 (usually thought to have been written at the end of the first century):

> We know that many among us [presumably the Christians of Rome] have handed themselves over into bondage [*eis desma*], in order to ransom others. Many have given themselves into slavery [*eis douleian*], and with the price paid for themselves have fed others.

The implication of the word used, *epsōmisan*, is I think that it was their starving children who needed to be fed. (Of course, this text and some similar ones may in reality refer to some form of *paramonē*: see above.)

The unfree labour characteristic of the pre-Classical Near East and illustrated particularly in numerous cuneiform documents seems to have included a high proportion of cases of what was really debt bondage rather than slavery of the Greek and Roman type; but that is a subject with which I cannot concern myself in this book.[76] Anyone who wishes to make a direct comparison between what I am calling debt bondage and ordinary chattel slavery can read a useful, if idealised, account in Philo, *De spec. leg.* II.79-85, of Hebrew debt bondage, as contemplated by Deut. XV.12-15; cf. Exod. XXI.2; Levit. XXV.39-43; Jerem. XXXIV.14. Philo is trying to make the point that men in this kind of bondage, who must be set free at the end of six years' service, although called slaves, *douloi*, are really in the position of hired labourers; he uses both the standard technical terms, *thēs* and *misthōtos* (cf. Section vi of this chapter). That concludes my treatment of the subject of debt bondage.

★　★　★　★　★　★

Convict labour was never very important in the Greek or even the Roman world,[77] and it is only in the Later Roman Empire that we hear much of it. It appears most often in the condemnation of men of low status *ad metallum*: that is to say, to serve in perpetuity in the State mines or quarries (see Jones, *LRE* II.838). In the so-called 'Great Persecution', in the early years of the fourth century, we know from Eusebius that many Christians were condemned to the copper mines of Phaeno in the south of Palestine, many others to the porphyry quarries of the Eastern Desert of Egypt, and others again to mines in Cilicia.[78] In the fourth century minor criminals from districts in Italy and from Sardinia were sometimes condemned to work in the Roman bakeries (*CTh* IX.xl.3,5-7) – where the bakers used to supplement their inadequate supply of convicts, according to the ecclesiastical historian Socrates, by setting up taverns and brothels on the ground floors above their bakeries, from which unsuspecting customers were precipitated below, and put to work at baking for the rest of their days, until the Emperor Theodosius I in *c.* 390 put a stop to the practice (*HE* V.xviii.3-8).

★ ★ ★ ★ ★ ★

Returning to the subject of slavery proper, I should like to stress something of which so far I have given only the briefest mention. The nature of our evidence for antiquity is often such as to tempt us to draw misleading conclusions about the *absence* of certain phenomena, when all we have a right to do is to note the absence of *evidence for* those phenomena; and so it is here. The nature of the evidence for ancient slavery is such that we are likely to find slave labour (outside the domestic scene, anyway) greatly under-represented in our sources, as indeed are all forms of labour. The evidence for the employment of slaves in production in antiquity can be very scanty even for places and times at which we know it was widespread and essential. Even where the fundamental part played by slave production cannot be denied, as for parts of the Greek mainland and some of the Aegean islands during the Classical period and (to a less extent) the Hellenistic age, we should have scarcely any mention of the use of slaves in Greek agriculture outside Attica were it not for the fact that historians (Thucydides, Xenophon, Polybius) make incidental mention of such slaves in accounts of military campaigns, if as a rule only when recording captures and booty: see Appendix II. Indeed, but for a few scattered texts in the Athenian orators and a handful of inscriptions we should have hardly any specific evidence of the central role played by slaves in production even in Attica itself, to set beside the general (and often vague) references to slavery in Plato, Aristotle, Xenophon's *Oeconomicus* and other literature. For many areas of the Greek world in most periods no sources exist from which we can expect specific evidence of the employment of slave labour. I believe that this has not been sufficiently realised. When there is little or no relevant literature or epigraphic material from which we can expect to derive enlightenment about the labour situation – as, for instance, in most of the Greek world outside Egypt in the Hellenistic period – we must be particularly careful not to jump to the conclusion that unfree labour was of little significance.

To give only one example – we have no right to expect any mention, even in our best-preserved building accounts, of the many slaves who must have been working under the craftsmen and transport-contractors who undertook the various pieces of work (mainly quite small) referred to in the inscriptions concerned. Some of the building accounts mentioned in Section vi below and its nn.20-3, for instance those for the Erechtheum and the temple of Eleusis in Attica, name a number of slaves, all of whom I would take to be *chōris oikountes* (see above and n.9). To treat such slaves as the only ones involved in the building operations is an error of which scholars have too often been guilty. Anyone entering into a State building contract might, and often would, make use of slaves in carrying out the works for which he had undertaken responsibility; and of course there would be no occasion for any of these slaves to be mentioned in the inscriptions. No slaves are referred to in some of the building accounts, including those recording the works at Epidaurus in the fourth century (discussed at length by Burford, *GTBE*); but it would be ridiculous to suppose that there were no slaves working there. And the slaves engaged in the Athenian building operations are likely to have been far more numerous than those who are mentioned by name in the inscriptions.

Those who are inclined to infer from the scarcity of references to agricultural slave labour that the bulk of the agricultural work on the farms of the well-to-do was not done by slaves should ask themselves what evidence there is for any other kind of labour! As I have indicated earlier in this section (under 'II. Serfdom'), there must have been many serfs and quasi-serfs in those Asiatic areas which came under Greek (or Macedonian) control from Alexander's time onwards; and of course a large part of the working peasant population of the whole Roman empire was brought into some kind of serfdom, at different times in different areas, in the late third century and later (see IV.iii below). But serfdom, I have suggested above, tended not to persist under Roman rule before the institution of the Later Roman colonate. *How then, if not by slave labour, was the agricultural work done for the propertied class? How, otherwise, did that class* (a landowning class above all: see III.ii-iii above) *derive its surplus?* The only alternatives are by wage-labour or by leasing. But there is good reason to think that wage-labour existed on only a small scale, apart from seasonal activities such as harvesting and vintage and olive-picking, and the hiring of slaves (see Section vi of this chapter). And leasing (see IV.iii below) cannot be expected to yield nearly as much profit as working land directly with slave labour – provided of course the landowner can acquire not only ordinary working slaves but also a thoroughly competent steward, assisted where necessary by 'slave-drivers'. (The steward, as we saw above, would himself be a slave, or perhaps a freedman, and all the slave-drivers would be slaves.) The view held by Roman agriculturalists of the late Republic and early Principate was that one should let a farm to a tenant only when one cannot work it properly oneself with slaves – either because the climate is too bad or the soil too poor – or when it is too far away for regular personal supervision by the owner (see Colum. I.vii.4-7, discussed in IV.iii below). Therefore, provided the cost of purchasing or rearing the slaves and their overseers was not too great, slavery, *as a means of extracting a surplus*, was superior to any other method of exploitation; and surely, when Greeks or Romans who were used to slave-worked agriculture in their own countries went to settle in Asia Minor or Syria, they would use slaves to work their farms when they could. An exception might be furnished by some local form of serfdom, or of quasi-serfdom, in so far as the workers concerned could be kept in that condition by their Greek masters; but it looks as if these local peculiarities were usually not long-lasting, serfdom (as I have said) not being an institution that flourished under Greek or Roman rule until the introduction of the Later Roman colonate.

* * * * * *

Some may question my justification for having used the portmanteau term, '*unfree* labour', on the ground that it is objectionably broad. Is there not an important difference, it may be said, according to Marxist categories or indeed any acceptable ones, between slave production and serf production? The serf has at least *possession* of the means of agricultural production, which is legally recognised in some degree although it may not amount to *ownership*, or even to Roman *possessio* – which, incidentally, not even a free leasehold tenant enjoyed under Roman law. The position of the serf is therefore different in an important way from that of the slave. Was there not, then, a profound change in the conditions of production, as between the earlier period of slavery and the period of widespread serfdom which (as we shall see in IV.iii below) began round about

A.D. 300 and eventually covered a large part of the Graeco-Roman world?

My answer begins with the assertion that 'unfree labour', in the broad sense in which I use that expression, is a most useful concept, in contrast with the 'free' wage-labour which is the basis of capitalist society. Slavery and serfdom are in many respects similar, and societies in which they are the dominant forms of production will be fundamentally different from capitalist society, founded on wage-labour. In the Greek (and Roman) world it is particularly hard to separate slavery and serfdom because, as I have demonstrated, neither the Greeks nor the Romans recognised serfdom as a distinct institution, and neither had a general word for it. I have illustrated in this section the perplexity shown by Roman emperors from the fourth to the sixth centuries in dealing with serf *coloni*, who were (as the emperors well knew) technically 'free men' (*ingenui*) as opposed to slaves (*servi*), but whose condition in practice was really more like that of slaves. The solution adopted by some of the fourth-century emperors, it will be remembered, was to regard the serf *coloni* as in some sense slaves of their land; but this conception was as questionable from the legal point of view as regarding the judgment debtor who had become *addictus* as being in a form of slavery to his creditor.

There is surely no doubt at all that in the Greek (and Roman) world, when forms of unfree labour appear, it is commonly slavery in the strict sense which is in the forefront. Serfdom occurs, in the Classical Greek world, only in local forms, each of which is treated as a unique case. Only in the Later Roman Empire does it appear on a large scale, and there is really no word for it until 'colonatus' is coined in the mid-fourth century (see above). Even then, we sometimes hear of large slave households, though mainly in the West (see IV.iii below). The relative numbers of serfs and slaves cannot be estimated with any degree of confidence, although by now there were undoubtedly far more serfs than slaves, at any rate.if we discount domestic slaves, whose role in production would be indirect only. There is, however, a great deal of material in the Roman law-books which to my mind proves conclusively that even chattel slavery remained very important in the Greek and Roman world, right down to the time when Justinian published his great *Corpus Iuris Civilis* in the early 530s. I suspect that the continued existence of slave and freedman managers (see above), even when slavery was far less important at lower levels than it had been, may be partly responsible for the frequent references to slavery in the *Corpus*.

It therefore seems realistic to me to describe slavery as the dominant form of ancient 'unfree labour', not in the quantitative sense that the propertied class actually derived its surplus at most times mainly from the labour of chattel slaves, but in the sense that slavery, with debt bondage (a condition which hardly differed from slavery in practice except in being chronologically limited), was *the archetypal form of unfree labour* throughout Graeco-Roman antiquity, so that not only the occasional early forms of serfdom like that of the Spartan Helots but also the widespread Later Roman colonate had to be expressed in language derived from slave terminology, whether technical (Helots as the Spartan *douleia*) or not (*coloni* as 'slaves *of the land*' or 'in servitude' to it). I suggest that such a society, where slavery in the strict sense is omnipresent in the psychology of all classes, is something very different from one in which slavery proper is unknown or unimportant, even if it is serfdom which then provides the propertied class with much of its surplus.

★ ★ ★ ★ ★ ★

A very recent publication has revealed that we now have explicit evidence of a vase-painter at Athens who was a slave and was even prepared so to describe himself on one of his products. On a black-figure *kyathos* (a ladle in the form of a cup) dating from the 520s B.C. and discovered at Vulci, a man named Lydus records that he painted the vase and that his name was 'Lydus, a slave [*dōlos*], a Myrineus' – meaning that he came from Myrina, an Aeolic Greek city on the coast of Lydia in western Asia Minor.[79]

★ ★ ★ ★ ★ ★

Freedom was the great hope of every slave. Some could be almost certain of manumission. For others, who had little or no chance of it, there was only one way of escape from slavery: death. That in death the slave gained his freedom is a not uncommon theme in slave epitaphs (see e.g. *Anth. Pal.* VII.553). To end this Section I quote one of the most moving of all ancient epitaphs. It is on the slave Narcissus, a farm overseer (*vilicus*) in the territory of Venafrum in Italy, who died at the age of twenty-five, and who is made to say that his freedom, denied to him as a youth by law, has been made eternal by an untimely death (*CIL* X.i.4917):[80]

Debita libertas iuveni mihi lege negata
Morte immatura reddita perpetua est.

(v)

Freedmen

The slave of a Roman citizen, if manumitted formally by his master in one of the ways legally prescribed, became a Roman citizen. The manumitted slave of a citizen of a Greek city seems never to have achieved, as an automatic result of manumission by his master, more than metic status, as he certainly did in Classical Athens. In all Greek states, as far as we know, only a decision of the sovereign body could confer citizenship upon a freed slave, as upon anyone else who was not born a citizen; and such decisions were uncommon. There is an interesting letter of King Philip V of Macedon to the Thessalian city of Larissa, now dated 215 B.C., pointing out that if they were to follow the Roman instead of the Greek practice they would be able to increase significantly the size of their citizen body (*SIG*³ 543 = *IG* IX.517, lines 26 ff.: there is an English translation in Lewis and Reinhold, *RC* I.386-7). The Rhodians, in their heroic resistance to the famous siege by Demetrius Poliorcetes in 305-4, were unusually generous in granting citizenship as well as freedom to those slaves (purchased by the state from their masters) who had fought well during the siege (Diod. Sic. XX.84.3; 100.1). At Athens, citizenship was occasionally conferred by a special grant of the Assembly upon ex-slaves for services rendered, as upon Pasion in the first quarter of the fourth century B.C. and upon his former slave Phormio in 361/0 (see Davies, *APF* 427 ff., esp. 430, 436). By the Antonine period there were apparently freedmen at Athens who had managed to become not only citizens but members of the Council: these were expelled by order of Marcus Aurelius. (Freedmen, although not their sons born after their manumission, were as a rule disqualified from becoming city councillors.) Marcus did not exclude the sons of freedmen (born after the manumission of their fathers) from serving on the

Athenian Council. As for the august Areopagus, he wished it were possible to allow only those whose fathers *and grandfathers* had been born in freedom to become members (an 'ancient custom' which he had earlier, it seems, during his joint reign with Verus in 161-9, tried to reimpose); but since this rule had become impossible to enforce, he later consented to allow the admission of those whose fathers and mothers had been born in freedom. (These provisions of Marcus have come to light only recently, in an inscription first published in 1970, which has aroused some discussion: see Appendix IV below, § 2.)

As far as I know, there is only one statement in any ancient author which attempts to explain the surprising generosity of the Romans towards slaves manumitted by their masters, in accepting them as Roman citizens, and it is too rarely quoted. It occurs in the *Roman Antiquities* of Dionysius of Halicarnassus, a leading Greek literary critic, who wrote at Rome at the end of the last century B.C. Dionysius, drawing attention to the difference between Greek and Roman manumission, emphasises the great advantage obtained by Romans who were very rich (*euporōtatoi*) in having large numbers of citizen freedmen who were bound to assist them in their public life and who would be clients (*pelatai*, the Greek word corresponding to the Latin *clientes*) of their descendants also (*Ant. Rom.* IV.22.4 to 23.7, esp. 23.6).[1] Probably no Greek state had anything approaching the Roman *clientela* (see my SVP, also VI.iii and v below), the institution of patronage and clientship, which (among its many ramifications) made of the freedman a *cliens* of his former master and his descendants. (We know much about the relationship of the Roman freedman to his ex-master,[2] little about that of his Greek counterpart.)

My remarks on freedmen will be highly selective, as it is not my purpose to give a general account of them. Admittedly, there have been few useful studies of Greek freedmen since A. Calderini's book, *La manomissione e la condizione dei liberti in Grecia*, published as long aso as 1908, but we have had three books on Roman freedmen in recent years in English alone.[3] All I want to do here is to emphasise that the question whether a man was a slave or a Roman freedman or a freeborn Roman or Greek might be far less important than the question *whose* slave or freedman he was or had been and what financial condition he had reached. I have spoken before (II.v), with disapproval, of the elevation of 'status' – useful as it can be as a descriptive and secondary classification – to a position superior to that of class as an instrument for the effective analysis of Greek society. This consideration applies with exceptional force in the present context, at any rate to the centuries in which some or all Greeks were under Roman rule (and above all to the third and following centuries C.E., when virtually all free Greeks were also Roman citizens), since being a Roman freedman ('libertinus') was *strictly a one-generation condition*, and any children born to a freedman after manumission were *ingenui*, free-born, and subject to none of the considerable legal and social disabilities attaching to actual freedmen,[4] even though they would remain clients of their father's former owner and his heirs. One freedman's son, C. Thoranius, is said to have entered the Roman Senate under Augustus (Dio Cassius LIII.27.6); and P. Helvius Pertinax, who was twice consul (*c.* 175 and 192), and emperor for a few weeks in 193, may also have been the son of a freedman.[5] Had I been dealing with the Latin West instead of the Greek East, it would have been necessary to say something of the prominent role played by the descendants of freedmen in municipal life in many cities, but nearly all our evidence for this comes from the West, especially Italy.[6]

'A freedman is a freedman is a freedman' is hardly a more helpful assertion, therefore, than 'a slave is a slave is a slave'. At one extreme, especially in the late Roman Republic and early Principate, there were freedmen of wealth and influence far greater than that of most *equites* and even some senators of their day. (I need have no hesitation in paying attention to these men, as many of them were of Greek origin, in the widest sense.) Demetrius, the powerful freedman of Pompey, is said to have died worth 4,000 talents, which would be HS 96 million in Latin terms (Plut., *Pomp.* 2.9; cf. 40.1). Augustus' freedman and procurator Licinus, who is accused of behaving with odious injustice during his 'rule' of his native Gaul, evidently amassed great wealth.[7] And the three greatest of all imperial freedmen, in the reigns of Claudius (41-54) and Nero (54-68), are said by Pliny the Elder (*NH* XXXIII.134) to have been – among 'many' liberated slaves! – even richer than Crassus, one of the great millionaires of the late Republic, who is particularly remembered for his remark that a man could not count as rich (*locuples*) unless he could maintain a whole army out of his own income, and who must have been worth more than HS 200 million (over 8,000 talents).[8] Narcissus and Pallas, two of Pliny's three outstanding imperial freedmen, are each credited with up to HS 400 million (over 16,000 talents),[9] and Callistus, the third, cannot have been far behind (see Duncan-Jones *EREQS* 343, no.10). Such figures tend to be exaggerated in literary sources; but if in fact any of these men did possess anything like HS 400 million, then he may have been even richer than Seneca, whose wealth was said to reach HS 300 million (or 12,500 talents): see Tac., *Ann.* XIII.42.6; Dio Cass. LXI.10.3 (75 million drachmae). If we set aside the imperial families of the early Principate, which of course were incomparably richer than any others, we can say that in the late Republic and the Principate only Pompey the Great is credited in the surviving sources with wealth greater than that of Pallas and Narcissus: Pompey's fortune, confiscated at his death, may have been of the order of HS 700 million (or nearly 30,000 talents).[10] However, Narcissus and Pallas were the most extreme examples that could be found at any time during the Principate, and several of the other most notorious freedmen also belonged to the same period (roughly the second third of the first century of the Christian era) – Felix the brother of Pallas, for instance, who became the husband of three successive Eastern princesses; as procurator of Judaea, he 'exercised a royal power in the spirit of a slave' (Tac., *Hist.* V.9) and incidentally is said to have kept St. Paul in prison for two years, hoping he would be bribed to release him (Acts XXIV, esp. 26-7).

Soon after this time imperial freedmen were gradually ousted from the higher offices in the imperial civil service, from which the vast fortunes of Pallas and his like had come, and these offices, in the late first and early second centuries, were taken over by equestrians.[11] The one important office that imperial slaves and freedmen never lost was that of *cubicularius*, 'chamberlain', always freed after *c.* 473 (see Section iv above). The *cubicularii*, who were all eunuchs, were in charge of the imperial bedchamber of the emperor and empress (the 'Sacred Bedchamber', *sacrum cubiculum*), and since castration was illegal within the Roman empire they had virtually all begun life (in theory anyway) as imported 'barbarian' slaves; but the scope of their activities extended very widely, in particular to imperial audiences. In the Later Empire very great political influence was sometimes exerted by the *cubicularii*, especially of course the Grand Chamberlain, *praepositus sacri cubiculi*.[12] The Emperor Julian, writing an open letter to the city of Athens in 361, could speak of the benevolence towards him of the late Empress Eusebia before his accession as having been manifested 'through the eunuchs in her service', just as he attributed primarily to the machinations of the Emperor Constantius' accursed chief eunuch (*ho theois echthros androgynos*, as he calls him), whose name happened to be Eusebius, the fact that the emperor could keep him for six months in the same city (Milan), without seeing him more than once (*Ep. ad Athen.* 5, p.274ab). The official *Acta* of the first Council of Ephesus in 431 happen to preserve a remarkable letter from the Alexandrian archdeacon Epiphanius to Bishop Maximian of Constantinople, giving a list of the bribes lavished on members of the imperial court of Theodosius II and Pulcheria in the early 430s by St. Cyril, the Patriarch of Alexandria, in his determination to see that the contradictory decisions of the rival parties at the Council should eventually be turned to the advantage of himself and the Catholics, against Nestorius and his followers. The highest figure recorded in this list, 200 pounds of gold (14,400 solidi), was paid to Chryseros, a *praepositus sacri cubiculi*, who also received many other costly presents, and several others among the *cubicularii* received at least 50 pounds of gold, as did two of Pulcheria's *cubiculariae* ('Women of the Bedchamber').[13] More than one of the eunuch imperial freedmen *cubicularii* achieved distinction in military commands, above all of course the great Narses, *sacellarius* and *praepositus*, a supremely successful general under Justinian.[14]

It was not only freedmen of the *familia Caesaris* who acquired riches. Pliny the Elder, as we saw a moment ago, could speak of 'many' freedmen (not merely Callistus, Pallas and Narcissus) as being richer than Crassus. Pliny himself in the same passage (*NH* XXXIII.134-5) gives details of the will of a freedman, C. Caecilius Isidorus, who died in 8 B.C.: according to Pliny, the man said that although he had lost a great deal in the civil wars he was leaving 4,116 slaves, 3,600 yoke of oxen, 257,000 other cattle, and HS 60 million in cash (2,500 talents), and he ordered HS 1,100,000 (over 450 talents) to be spent on his funeral. (At least some of these figures are probably exaggerated, perhaps grossly so.)[15] I must not omit to mention the delightful account in Petronius (*Sat.* 45-77) of the enormous property of the *imaginary* freedman Trimalchio, who is represented as being worth HS 30 million (1,250 talents): he is made to say that he was left 'a fortune worthy of a senator' (*patrimonium laticlavium*) by his former master's will and that he had greatly increased it by his own efforts. Among Trimalchio's friends are depicted several other wealthy freedmen: one is said to be worth HS 800,000 and another a million (*Sat.* 38), and there is a reference to yet another freedman who had died leaving HS 100,000 (*Sat.* 43). Now I would not deny that quite a number of freedmen may have been really well-to-do, and a few perhaps very rich indeed – although I think that in order to attain great wealth a freedman who had not been a member of the *familia Caesaris* would need (like Trimalchio) to receive a very substantial legacy from his former master, and this would be anything but a frequent occurrence. But, apart from the altogether exceptional imperial freedmen, I see little *evidence* for *large* fortunes in the hands of freedmen. It would be a mistake to see in Martial's expression, *libertinas opes* (V.13.6), any implication that freedman status and wealth went naturally together: in this poem, Martial – who calls himself 'a poor man' (*pauper*), although an honorary equestrian – is expressing his scorn for a rich freedman, Callistratus, and the word *libertinas* is the one clue he gives to the man's status.

I feel that far too much reliance has been placed on the fictitious *cena Trimalchionis* in Petronius: its inventions have too easily been accepted as facts and its deliberately comic exaggerations treated as if they were typical. Even Rostovtzeff could write at some length about Trimalchio as if he were a real person instead of an imaginary character; he calls him 'one type of this age' (the Julio-Claudian), although later in the same passage he does add, 'I am inclined to think that Petronius chose the freedman type to have the opportunity of making the *nouveau riche* as vulgar as possible' (*SEHRE*² I.57-8). Finley, who refers to Trimalchio in at least ten different places in his *Ancient Economy*, treats him as if he were not only a *real* person but a *representative* one: 'Trimalchio,' he says, '*may* not be a *wholly typical* ancient figure [my italics], but he is not wholly untypical either' (*AE* 36, cf. 38, 50-1, 61, 78, 83). And later he says, 'Once again we turn to Trimalchio for the bald truth' (*AE* 115-16) – but in reality we find once more a ludicrous series of comic exaggerations.[16]

Surely the great majority of freedmen, at the time of their manumission, will have been men of at best very modest wealth, even if a fair number of them were comfortably off, and a few quite rich. Many of them must have been poverty-stricken wretches who were either allowed to buy their freedom with every penny they had managed to accumulate as their *peculium* during slavery, or were left at their master's death with the gift of freedom and nothing else. A children's nurse who was manumitted on retirement might not be far off the poverty-line, but the Younger Pliny settled on his old nurse a 'little farm' worth HS 100,000 (*Epist.* VI.iii.1) – perhaps of about 25-30 acres (see Sherwin-White, *LP* 358). Nearly all those freedmen who accumulated really large fortunes will have done so because they had been the slaves of very rich men, or had belonged to the *familia Caesaris*. A delightful funerary inscription (*ILS* 1949) from near Rome, which no one able to read simple Latin should miss, records the benefits received from M. Aurelius Cotta Maximus, who was consul in A.D. 20, by one of his freedmen, Zosimus, who after manumission had acted as his official attendant, *accensus*. (The man's name is Greek, whether or not he himself was of Greek origin.) Cotta had more than once given him the equivalent of the equestrian census, HS 400,000 (*saepe libens census donavit equestris*); he had brought up his sons and given dowries to his daughters, 'as if he himself were their father'; he had obtained for one son the honour of a military tribunate (the usual first step in an equestrian career); he ended by paying for the inscription, in elegiac couplets, which he either wrote himself or entrusted to someone who understood how necessary it was to stress Cotta's munificence.

It appears from a famous inscription of the year 133 B.C. that freedmen (*exeleutheroi*) and their descendants in the important Greek city of Pergamum were in a condition inferior to other non–citizen residents, here called *paroikoi*, for while those already registered as *paroikoi* were to receive the citizenship (in the emergency confronting the city), the descendants of freedmen (though not, apparently, freedmen themselves) were merely to become *paroikoi*, and this was clearly regarded as an improvement in their status (*IGRR* IV.289 = *OGIS* 338, lines 11-13, 20-1).

In a Greek city in the Roman period we can expect to find freedmen of Roman citizens having much the same social rank (other things being equal) as other freedmen, outside the local citizen body. Thus in the donations of Menodora at Sillyum in Pisidia, prescribing hand-outs to be given in a series of grades, according to social position (see Section vi of this chapter, just after its n.35), we find *ouindiktarioi* (Roman freedmen duly manumitted *per vindictam*) put on the same level as *apeleutheroi* (Greek freedmen) and *paroikoi* (residents without local citizenship), and below the citizens (*poleitai*) of Sillyum (*IGRR* III.801.15-22).[17]

I know of no reliable evidence from any part of the Greek world (or the Roman world)[18] that could enable us to draw trustworthy conclusions about the comparative frequency of manumission at different periods or in different areas, or the ages at which it took place. The evidence, even that of inscriptions, is always too 'weighted' to give us anything like a 'random sample' and is useless for statistical purposes.

Finally, I must reiterate that the financial condition of the freedman really mattered more than his technical legal status, which *died with him* (and with those of his children who had been born in slavery and manumitted with him), while his children born after his manumission counted as free-born and could inherit the bulk of his property.[19]

(vi)
Hired labour

I have already pointed out that the single most important organisational difference between the ancient economy and that of the modern world is that in antiquity the propertied class derived its surplus mainly from unfree labour (especially that of slaves) and only to a very small degree from hired labour (wage-labour), which was generally scarce, unskilled and not at all mobile. We must also remember that many hired labourers (in Greek, *misthōtoi* or *thētes*; in Latin, *mercennarii*)[1] will have been slaves hired out by their masters.

I can illustrate what I have just been saying about the prevalence of slave labour and the comparative insignificance of hired labour by summarising three of the delightful little Socratic dialogues included in Xenophon's *Memorabilia*, which demonstrate very nicely how small a role was played by wage-labour in Classical Athens. They are all lifelike conversations, bearing in this respect little resemblance to the dialogues – often, no doubt, of far greater philosophical profundity – in which Socrates just argues down some unfortunate Platonic stooge. In the first of these, the charming conversation between Socrates and the high-class call-girl Theodote (*Mem.* III.xi, esp. 4), Socrates, with assumed innocence, quizzes the girl about the source of her income. She was obviously well-off, as she had nice furniture and a lot of good-looking and well-set-up slave girls. 'Tell me, Theodote,' Socrates says, 'have you a farm [an *agros*]?' 'No,' she says. 'Then have you a house that brings in rents [an *oikia prosodous echousa*]?' 'No, not that either.' 'Then haven't you some craftsmen [*cheirotechnai tines*]?' When Theodote says that she has none of these, Socrates asks where she does get her money from, as if he had exhausted all possible alternatives. She answers, very prettily, that she lives on the generosity of her friends. Socrates politely congratulates her on having such a satisfactory asset. The conversation goes on, and Socrates makes such an impression on the simple Theodote that she even asks him to go into partnership with her: he is to be her associate in the chase for lovers, *synthēratēs tōn philōn* (a metaphor drawn from Xenophon's own favourite recreation, hunting). When Socrates evades this, Theodote says she hopes that at any rate he will come up and see her some time; but he turns that aside too, and the conversation ends with Socrates telling Theodote to come and see him – although he is rather cavalier about it: he says he will welcome her provided he has with him no other girl-friend of whom he is fonder still. (I like this dialogue. It is not often that one finds Socrates in what one might call a heterosexual attitude.) The point of this story that particularly concerns us is in the nature of the three questions which Socrates puts to Theodote. They suggest – and here they are entirely in accord with all the other evidence – that anyone at Athens who did not work for a living might be expected first to own a farm (which of course he would either work with slaves under an overseer or let outright); or secondly to own a house, which he would let either as a whole or in sections (there were many tenement houses, *synoikiai*, in Athens and the Peiraeus);[2] or thirdly to have slave craftsmen, who might work either under an overseer, or on their own as *chōris oikountes* (see Section iv of this chapter).

The second dialogue from the *Memorabilia* (II.vii, esp. 2–6) is a conversation between Socrates and one Aristarchus in 404/3, under the tyranny of 'the Thirty' in Athens. Aristarchus, once a rich man, is now at his wits' end to know how to maintain a household of fourteen free persons, mainly female relatives temporarily abandoned by their menfolk, who had gone off to join the democratic Freedom Fighters on the barricades in the Peiraeus. Aristarchus of course is getting nothing from his land, and he is receiving no rents from his house property either, because so many people have fled from the city, nor can he sell or pawn his movable goods, because there are no buyers or lenders. Socrates gives him excellent advice – quite different, surely, from what Plato's Socrates would have recommended. He begins by citing examples of several men with large households who have prospered exceedingly: Ceramon, who has become rich in some unspecified manner, through the earning power of his slave workmen; Nausicydes, who has done so well out of making *alphita* (barley groats)[3] that he has large herds of swine and cattle and often undertakes expensive liturgies (civic services); and some other people who live luxuriously – Cyrebus, by being a baker, Demeas and Meno and 'most of the Megarians' (he clearly means most of the *well-to-do* Megarians), by making various kinds of clothes. 'Ah, but, Socrates,' objects Aristarchus, 'they have many *barbaroi* as slaves and make them work for them, whereas my household are free and my kith and kin.' 'Well, and if they are,' retorts Socrates, 'do you think they should do nothing but eat and sleep?' Eventually Aristarchus is persuaded to put his womenfolk to work; he borrows money and buys wool. They enjoy the work so much that they even refuse to have a break at their dinner-hour, and their one complaint is that Aristarchus himself is the only person in the house who eats the bread of idleness – a criticism which Socrates rebukes with an improving fable about the dog which protects the sheep against wolves. This passage shows

that in Xenophon's opinion the average upper-class Athenian of his day automatically assumed that a really profitable manufacturing business would be
slave-worked. We can agree that this assumption did exist, and was justified,
and that manufacture without slaves would only be on a very small scale. The
prosperous *technitai* we shall encounter presently in Aristotle would normally
have obtained their wealth by making use of slave labour, like Socrates' Megarians and the rest. The passage also shows that an Athenian belonging to the
propertied class would not think it proper for his own family to do any manual
work, except of course the sort of spinning and weaving and so forth *for the
benefit of the family itself* which Greek women were expected to do – and Roman
women, even (down to the early Principate) of the highest social class. We are
told that the Emperor Augustus normally wore (though only when at home!)
clothes made by his sister, wife, daughter or grand-daughters, and that he had
his daughter and grand-daughters trained in spinning and weaving (*lanificium*,
Suet., *Aug.* 73; 64.2). The women of Aristarchus' family were doing something
quite different from that: they were producing things *to be sold on the market as
commodities*. Needless to say, the story provides no evidence about the habits or
outlook of the humbler Athenian, who must often have done manufacturing
work of this kind, with his whole family: there is no reason to think he
considered such work degrading, although no doubt he was glad to get clear of
it when he could, if there were an opportunity for him to rise into the upper
class. But at present we are mainly interested in the fact that the labour exploited
by the propertied class is that of slaves.

My third passage from the *Memorabilia* (II.viii, esp. 3–4) is a conversation
Socrates had with Eutherus, described as an old comrade of his and therefore no
doubt a member of a respectable propertied family. It is after the end of the
Peloponnesian war in 404 B.C. Eutherus tells Socrates that he has lost his
property abroad and now, having nothing on the security of which he can
borrow, has been obliged to settle down in Attica and earn his living by working
with his hands – *tōi sōmati ergazomenos*, 'working with his body', as the Greeks
put it. Socrates points out that he will soon be an old man and advises him to take
a permanent job as overseer or bailiff to some landowner, supervising operations and helping to get in the harvest and generally looking after the property.
Eutherus' reply is very interesting: I think it would have been made by any
Greek citizen who belonged to what I am calling the propertied class and
perhaps by a good many quite humble men too. He says, 'I just couldn't stand
being a slave' (*chalepōs an douleian hypomeinaimi*). What Eutherus cannot endure
is the idea of being at another's beck and call, of having to submit to dictation
and reproof, without the option of being able to walk out or to give as good as he
got. If one is making or selling things oneself or even – as Eutherus had been
doing – working for hire on short-time jobs, one can at least answer back, and at
a pinch betake oneself elsewhere. To take the sort of permanent employment
which most people nowadays are only too glad to have is to demean oneself to
the level of the slave: one must avoid that at all costs, even if it brings in more
money. Of course a really poor Greek, even a citizen, might sometimes have
been glad to find such a post, but only, I think, as a last resort. When we meet
identifiable bailiffs or business managers in the sources, they are always slaves or
freedmen: see Appendix II below. It is true that at the very opening of Xenophon's

Oeconomicus (I.3-4) the possibility of becoming someone else's overseer is raised, but only as a hypothetical point, as an illustration of the fact that what you do for yourself you can also do for others. But in the later chapters, XII-XV, which are thoroughly practical and discuss the choice and training of an overseer or bailiff (an *epitropos*), it is taken for granted that he will be a slave (see esp. *Oecon.* XII.2-3; XIII.6-10; XIV.6,9).

The last of the three Socratic dialogues of Xenophon which I have just recounted brings out very well the low estimate of wage-labour in Classical Greece; and things were no different in Hellenistic and Roman times. Nearly eight hundred years later there is a fascinating constitution of Gratian and his co-emperors (mentioned in Section iii of this chapter and dating from A.D. 382), which in the most stringent terms forbids the entrusting of property by way of *procuratio* to a decurion (a member of a city Council), who would thus become what we should call a bailiff or salaried manager. The emperors speak of a decurion who accepted such a post as one who, 'undertaking the most infamous baseness, heedless of his liberty and his lineage, ruined his reputation by his servile obsequiousness' (*CTh* XII.i.92 = *CJ* X.xxxii.34).[4]

★ ★ ★ ★ ★ ★

The first appearance in antiquity of hired labour on a large scale was in the military field, in the shape of mercenary service. (As I mentioned in I.iv above, this interesting fact was noticed by Marx and is referred to in his letter to Engels of 25 September 1857: *MESC* 118-19.) I need do no more than just mention this topic here, as the subject of Greek mercenaries has often been dealt with (see V.ii n.16 below). Among the earliest pieces of evidence for Greek mercenaries – serving, however, not inside the Greek world but for the Egyptian Pharaoh Psamtik II in Nubia – is the inscription M/L 7, scratched on the leg of a colossal statue of Rameses II in front of the temple at Abu Simbel.

★ ★ ★ ★ ★ ★

It is Aristotle, needless to say, who gives the most useful analysis of the position of the hired man, the *thēs*, as Aristotle usually calls him. The term often found in other authors and in inscriptions is *misthōtos* (the man who receives *misthos*, pay); but Aristotle for some reason never employs this word, although he does use its cognates.[5] It does not seem to have been sufficiently realised that in the eyes of Aristotle (as of other Greeks) there was an important qualitative difference between the *thēs* or *misthōtos*, who is specifically a hired man (a wage-labourer), and the independent skilled artisan or craftsman who works on his own account (whether employing slaves or not) and is commonly called a *technitēs* or *banausos* (occasionally a *banausos technitēs*) – although I must admit that in some contexts Aristotle, when he is speaking loosely (e.g. in *Pol.* I.13, 1260^{a}36-^{b}1), can use *banausos/technitēs* for a larger category, including the *thēs*. (I deal with the skilled man, the *technitēs*, in IV.vi below.) Unfortunately Aristotle does not give a full theoretical discussion of this difference, but it emerges very clearly when several passages in the *Politics, Rhetoric,* and *Nicomachean* and *Eudemian Ethics* are put together.[6] Aristotle does not say in so many words that the labour given by the hired man is characteristically unskilled and poorly rewarded, while that of the *banausos/technitēs* tends to be skilled and better rewarded; but this is sometimes implied, especially in a passage in which Aristotle distinguishes the labour of the *banausoi/technitai* from that of the men who are 'unskilled and useful only with the body' (*Pol.* I.11,1258^{b}25-7). This is understandable: of course a skilled man would always work on his own (and even exploit slave labour) when he could, whereas the unskilled man would scarcely ever be able to do that. For some Greeks, including Xenophon, the word *technitēs*, most often used for the independent craftsman, had acquired such a necessary primary connotation of skill that it could even be used of skilled slaves, as in *Mem.* II.vii.3-5. (The term *cheirotechnai* is used in precisely the same sense, of skilled slaves, in Thucydides VII.27.5, to describe the majority of the 'more than 20,000 slaves' who escaped from Attica during the final stages of the Peloponnesian war: see Appendix II below.) When he was not just making things for sale on his own account, the skilled artisan (or, for that matter, the man who possessed some equipment of his own that could be useful in transport, for instance) would normally perform work for others by entering into specific contracts. Our evidence for such activities comes mainly from inscriptions recording public works (see below), where the 'contractor' (as we should call him) is most often referred to as a *misthotēs*, but sometimes (outside Athens) he is *ergolabos, ergolabōn* or *ergōnēs*, and sometimes he receives no technical name, as at Epidaurus (where it is simply said that he 'undertook', *heileto*, a particular task) or in fifth-century Athens. I deal with such men in IV.vi below: their class position is distinct from that of *misthōtoi*, who hire themselves out in a general way and not (as a rule) for specific jobs or those requiring skill or equipment.

Here it is interesting to recall a remark made by Plato, who was just as contemptuous as Aristotle of hired labourers and placed them (as did Aristotle) at the very bottom of his social scale (*Rep.* II.371de; cf. *Polit.* 290a; *Laws* XI.918bc; and V.742a, where the *misthōtoi* are slaves or foreigners). In *Rep.* II.371de Plato describes his *misthōtoi* as servants who are altogether unfit to associate with his citizens on an intellectual level but have enough physical strength to labour; and he goes on to speak of them, very accurately, as 'those who sell their labour power' (*hoi pōlountes tēn tēs ischyos chreian*: very literally, 'those selling the use of their strength') – a phrase which should remind us immediately of a major step forward taken by Marx in formulating his theory of value, when he came to realise, in 1857-8, that one must speak of the worker's selling to his employer not his *labour* but his labour *power* (or capacity): see the Foreword by Martin Nicolaus to his English translation of Marx's *Grundrisse* (1973) 20-1, 44-7. Marx refers on two occasions to a phrase in Thomas Hobbes (*Leviathan* I.x) which already embodied the idea he wished to express: 'The value, or worth of a man, is as of all other things, his price; that is to say, so much as would be given for the use of his power' (*Cap.* I.170 n.2; and *Wages, Price and Profit*, ch.vii). But he does not seem to have noticed the significance of the passage in Plato's *Republic* which I have quoted, and I have never seen it cited in this connection. In antiquity, most wage-labourers were unskilled men, not contracting to do specific pieces of work for another (as the skilled independent artisan may do), but hiring out their general labour power to others in return for pay; and it looks as if they tended to be severely exploited.

As we should expect from Aristotle, his disapproval of the *thēs* is an integral part of his sociology and is deeply rooted in his philosophy of life. For him, there could be no civilised existence for men who did not have *leisure (scholē)*,[7] which was a necessary condition (though not of course a sufficient condition) for becoming a good and competent citizen (see esp. *Pol.* VII.9, 1329ª1-2), and indeed was the goal *(telos)* of labour, as peace was of war (VII.15, 1334ª14-16) – although of course there was 'no leisure for slaves' *(ou scholē doulois)*: Aristotle quotes a proverb to that effect (1334ª20-1). Now the overriding necessity for leisure excludes the citizens of Aristotle's ideal State from all forms of work, even farming, not to mention craftsmanship. But in an ordinary city he realises (in passages from Books IV and VI of the *Politics*, discussed in II.iv above)[8] that 'the masses' *(to plēthos)*[9] can be divided into four groups *(merē)* according to the kind of work they perform: farmers, artisans, traders, and wage-labourers *(geōrgikon, banausikon, agoraion, thētikon)*, with the wage-labourers *(thētikon)* clearly forming a group different from that of the independent artisans *(banausi-kon)*; and although (as I have already mentioned) his language elsewhere is sometimes ambiguous, in that it is hard to tell whether he is identifying the *thēs* with, or distinguishing him from, the *banausos/technitēs*, yet in some other passages he again shows that he does have two distinct groups in mind, especially when he says that in oligarchies the existence of high property-qualifications makes it impossible for the *thēs* to be a citizen, while a *banausos* may be, 'for many of the *technitai* are rich' *(Pol.* III.5, 1278ª21-5).[10] By the exercise of his skill, then, and no doubt by exploiting slave labour in addition, the *banausos/technitēs* may even gain enough property to enter the wealthy class, but this is denied to the (unskilled) *thēs*.

However, the essential fact which, in Aristotle's eyes, makes the hired man a less worthy figure than the ordinary artisan is not so much his comparative poverty (for many independent artisans are likely to be poor too) but his 'slavish' dependence upon his employer. This would apply equally, of course, to the day-labourer and to the permanent bailiff, even if a gentleman like Xenophon's Eutherus might feel that working in the former capacity was not quite so 'slavish' because he would retain more freedom of movement. Near the end of the *Politics* (VIII.2, 1337ᵇ19-21) Aristotle contemplates acts which are done for other people and do not have certain saving characteristics (some of which he specifies): any such act he stigmatises as both *thētikon* (appropriate to the hired labourer) and *doulikon* (appropriate to the slave); clearly the two adjectives had a very similar colouring in his mind.[11] To allow your life to revolve around anyone except a friend is *doulikon*, slavish, Aristotle says in the *Nicomachean Ethics* (IV.3, 1124ᵇ31-5ª2), and he adds that 'this is why all flatterers are *thētikoi*', they have the characteristics of hired men. In Section ii of this chapter I quoted Aristotle's remark in the *Rhetoric* (I.9, 1367ª28 ff.) that at Sparta the gentleman wears his hair long, as a mark of his gentlemanly status, 'for it is not easy for a man with long hair to do work appropriate to a hired labourer' *(ergon thētikon)*, and also the statement that follows, that 'it is the mark of a gentleman not to live for the benefit of another'.

There is one curious feature of Aristotle's attitude to the wage-labourer which is worth mentioning. For him (see *Pol.* I.13, 1260ª36-ᵇ6) the slave is at least a 'partner in life' *(koinōnos zōēs)* with his master, whereas the *banausos technitēs* (here certainly including the *thēs*, of whom Aristotle may be mainly thinking) is 'further removed' *(porrhōteron)* from his employer and 'subject only to what may be called a limited servitude'. Now Aristotle expects the master to impart to his slave a certain amount of *aretē* (in this case, moral virtue); but nothing is said about the necessity for any such process for the benefit of the workman who – rather strangely, to our way of thinking – is evidently conceived by Aristotle as deriving less benefit from his relationship to his employer than the slave may be expected to obtain from his association with his master. Here again no distinction is drawn between the temporary or long-term wage-labourer or independent craftsman: none of them, in Aristotle's eyes, has a relationship with the master as close as that of the slave.

★ ★ ★ ★ ★ ★

The lot of the hired man is almost invariably presented throughout Greek and Roman history in an unpleasant light. The one striking exception I know is Solon, fr. 1.47-8 (Diehl = 13.47-8 West), where the farm labourer hired by the year is depicted no more unfavourably than other propertyless men, constrained by poverty (line 41): the sea trader, the artisan, the poet, the doctor or the seer. When Homer was making the shade of Achilles compare his existence in the underworld with the most unpleasant kind of life he could think of on earth, the occupation he pictured was that of *thēs* to a poor and landless man (*Od.* XI.488-91);[12] and Hesiod shows what sort of treatment the agricultural labourer could expect at about the beginning of the seventh century B.C. when he advises the farmer to put his *thēs* out of doors when summer comes (*Works and Days* 602). When Euripides' Electra is speculating dolefully, before she has re-encountered her brother Orestes, about his present miserable existence in exile, she imagines him working as a hired labourer (*Electr.* 130-1 uses the word *latreueis*, and lines 201-6 have *thēssan hestian*). We have seen with what disfavour Xenophon expected an Athenian gentleman to regard taking even a rather superior form of permanent service for wages, as a bailiff; and the fourth-century Attic orators speak of being driven to work for wages as if it were a fate second only to slavery in unpleasantness (Isocr. XIV.48; Isae. V.39). In one speech by Demosthenes (LVII.45) the fact that many citizen women in a time of emergency had become 'wet-nurses and wool-workers and grape-harvesters' is given as an illustration of the way in which poverty may compel free individuals to do 'many servile and base acts', *doulika kai tapeina pragmata*. Euthyphro, in Plato's dialogue of that name, is pictured as farming with his father in Naxos and employing a dependant of theirs as a hired labourer (*pelatēs . . . ethēteuen ekei par' hēmin*): when the wretched man kills one of the slaves on the farm in a drunken quarrel, Euthyphro's father binds him and throws him into a ditch, where he dies (*Euthyphro* 4c, cf. 15d). When Isocrates was speaking of fifth-century Athens as having the tribute of the allies displayed on the stage of the theatre at the festival of the Dionysia, he evidently felt that it made the idea more painful and wounding when he described the silver as 'brought in by hirelings' (*misthōtoi*, VIII.82). Demosthenes, too, uses the term *misthōtos* for 'political hireling' in a bitterly contemptuous way (IX.54, and esp. XIX.110). Hired labourers are commonly depicted as doing rough or unskilled work, or tasks considered characteristic of slaves (see e.g. Ar., *Birds* 1152-4; Ps.-Dem. XLIX.51-2; Poll. VII.131). And when there is evidence about their pay, it is very low, as in the two long and important Athenian building-inscriptions of the late fourth century

B.C. relating to Eleusis (*IG* II².1672-3, on which see below): at this time, skilled artisans like bricklayers and plasterers are receiving 2 or 2½ drachmae per day, while the hired labourers (*misthōtoi*) get only 1½ drachmae.[13] (The daily keep, *trophē*, of the public slaves employed in the same operations was half a drachma per day.)[14] At Athens, men wishing to be hired – like the agricultural labourers in the Parable of the Vineyard, in Mt. XX.1-16 – congregated in a recognised place, known as Kolonos Agoraios (or Ergatikos or Misthios), apparently at the west end of the Athenian Agora. This is known only through a fragment of Old Comedy and the scholiasts and lexicographers: the evidence has been very well set out by Alexander Fuks.[15] Hired labour at the peak periods of agricultural activity (harvesting, vintage, olive-picking) must have been quite common everywhere; but I have come across surprisingly few passages in Greek literature which mention the employment of hired labour in any form of agricultural work in the Classical period,[16] and it is worth remembering that men so engaged might well turn out to be slaves, hired out by their masters, as they certainly are in Ps.-Dem. LIII.20-1. No doubt there was also a good deal of mutual assistance among farmers, although I do not recall in Greek literature any parallel to the mention of such exchanges by two Latin authors of the mid-second century of the Christian era: Apuleius, *Apol.* 17.1 (*an ipse mutuarias operas cum vicinis tuis cambies*), and Gellius, *NA* II.29.7 (*operam mutuam dent* – from an Aesopic fable, of which Ennius made a version, in Latin tetrameters, id. 20). A prosperous farmer might wish to employ his poorer neighbours as hired workers at peak periods, as apparently in Cato, *De agr. cult.* 4 (*operarios facilius conduces*).

In antiquity it was not only in the Greek and Roman world that the hired man was despised and likely to be ill-treated. In Judaea in the Persian period (the fifth or fourth century B.C.) the prophet Malachi threatened divine punishment on those who oppress 'the hireling in his wages', mentioning in the same breath those traditionally helpless figures of Israelite society, 'the widow and the fatherless' (Mal. III.5; cf. Deut. XXIV.14-15; Lev. XIX.13). When Alexander the Great in 323 sent Miccalus of Clazomenae from Babylon with a large sum of money (500 talents), to procure experienced additional crews from Phoenicia and Syria for an expedition into the Persian Gulf, we are told by Arrian that his instructions were to 'hire some and buy others' (*Anab.* VII.19.5). Evidently hired men and slaves could be expected to serve side-by-side. I must not take time to mention other evidence from the 'pre-Classical' world. (I have referred at the end of this section to the passages in the New Testament that mention hired labour.)

For the Hellenistic period, where the sources for economic history are more documentary than literary, and regional differences can be very great (not only between Greece, Asia Minor, Syria and Egypt, but between individual areas within those countries), the evidence about wage-labour is hard to disentangle from that concerning the activity of artisans or even of peasants who occasionally take service as hired labourers.[17] But over fifty years ago a brilliant essay by W. W. Tarn, 'The social question in the third century',[18] which Rostovtzeff described as 'the best treatment of the social and economic conditions of Greece and the Greek islands in the third century B.C.' (*SEHHW* III.1358 n.3), showed good grounds for thinking that in the early Hellenistic age, while a few Greeks became richer, the condition of the masses probably became appreciably worse; and of course in such conditions hired labourers are bound to suffer. (I accept this conclusion, even though I am far less confident than Tarn about the validity and the implications of many of his figures.)

In the Roman Principate and Later Empire the evidence is again very hard to interpret, and again the situation undoubtedly varied greatly from area to area. We seldom hear of hired labour except in agriculture, where it was highly seasonal, and in building, where it was casual and irregular (see below).[19] As a rule, the situation of such hired workers as we find seems to be very humble indeed, even if occasionally an isolated one manages, by a combination of good luck and hard work (he would certainly need both), to rise in the world and enter the propertied class, like the unknown man who is the subject of a famous third-century metrical epitaph from Mactar in Africa (modern Tunisia): he came from a poor family, but partly by acting as foreman of gangs of reapers at harvest-time, he succeeded in becoming a prosperous landowner himself and a member of his local Council (*ILS* 7457 = *CIL* VIII.11824; there is a translation in MacMullen, *RSR* 43). But this man was probably a very rare exception. I doubt if he is much more 'typical' than the unnamed bishop who is said by John Moschus to have worked with his hands as a labourer in the rebuilding of Antioch after the great earthquake of 526 (*Pratum spirit.* 37, in *MPG* LXXXVII.iii.2885-8). There was also a story mentioned by Suetonius (who says his efforts to verify it had been unsuccessful) that the great-grandfather of the Emperor Vespasian (who reigned from 69 to 79) had been a contractor (*manceps*) responsible for bringing gangs of agricultural labourers from Umbria into the Sabine country (*Vesp.* 1.4); but the story did not allege that the man rose in this way from poverty. No doubt a certain amount of such migratory labour existed in various parts of the Greek world, as well as in the West, and there will undoubtedly have been a number of miserably poor Greeks like the Italian *mercennarii* whose employment Varro, as we have seen (in Section iv above), advises in areas too unhealthy for precious slaves to be risked there. And Varro's recommended practice of employing hired men even in healthy districts for occasions of heavy work, such as the harvest and the vintage, must have been general in the Graeco-Roman world. I should mention here that in the same passage Varro states that many *obaerarii*, who must be men in some kind of debt-bondage, were still employed in his day on farms in Asia Minor and Egypt as well as Illyricum (*RR* I.17.2-3; cf. Section iv of this chapter and its nn.66-7). I cannot resist mentioning also the passage in which Columella, discussing the rearing of thrushes (*turdi*), says that some people gave them dried figs which were pre-chewed; but, he adds, 'when the number of thrushes is large, it is hardly expedient to do this, because it costs not a little to hire people to chew the figs (*nec parvo conducuntur qui mandant*), and they themselves tend to swallow a fair quantity because of the nice taste' (*RR* VIII.10.4). We must surely suppose that there were large numbers of poor peasants and artisans who supplemented their meagre incomes by taking temporary hired posts when they needed to do so and the work was available; and some unskilled men will doubtless have been obliged to earn their living primarily in that way. But this would be a *pis aller*, to be resorted to only if one were unable to make a living either on the land or as a skilled craftsman or semi-skilled worker. A pathetic illustration of the desperately poor condition of some hired agricultural labourers is given by Strabo (III.iv.17, p.165), preserving the account by Poseidonius of a story told him by a

Massiliot friend about an estate of his in Liguria. Among a number of labourers, male and female, whom the Massiliot had hired for digging ditches was a woman who left her work to give birth to a child and came straight back to her work on the same day, as she could not afford to lose her pay. (I do not think this story loses its force when we compare it with Varro's statement that women in Illyricum 'often' give birth during a brief pause in their agricultural work and then return with the child so nonchalantly that 'you would think the woman had not given birth to it but had found it', *RR* II.x.9.) In the Roman period, as in earlier times, the hired man might well be unable to obtain payment of his meagre wages (cf. Dio Chrys. VII.11-12). A well-known passage in the New Testament, James V.4, rebukes rich men for fraudulently withholding the wage of the labourers (*ergatai*) who have been harvesting or mowing their fields. And in the *Spiritual Meadow* of John Moschus, dating from the early seventh century, we hear the complaint of a man who claims to have been working as the hired agricultural labourer of a rich man for fifteen years, without receiving his pay; but such long service under a single employer is, I believe, unparalleled (*Pratum spirit.* 154, in *MPG* LXXXVII.iii.3021-4).

Although I do not agree in all respects with the analysis of Francotte, in his book on Greek industry, I think that he is broadly right when he says that the description of a man as *misthōtos* indicates 'une condition sociale inférieure . . . C'est un ouvrier de rang subalterne, un "mercenaire", un "journalier"' (*IGA* II.150 ff., at 157).

★   ★   ★   ★   ★

Public works may have been an important source of employment of hired labour (as well as the more skilled activity of craftsmen) in some Greek cities, but here the evidence of the literary sources is scanty and very unhelpful, and the modern literature is far from satisfactory. We have a considerable quantity of epigraphic material for public building works from Epidaurus, Delos and other places,[20] but the most instructive detailed evidence comes from Athens in the fifth and fourth centuries B.C., above all from a series of accounts of the early 320s, relating to the works in the temple at Eleusis – the only ancient source I know which provides unimpeachable evidence in a single set of documents not merely for a wide range of prices, including that of corn (both wheat and barley, sold by public auction), but also for the wages of men specifically called *misthōtoi*, for the cost of maintenance of public slaves (*dēmosioi*), and for contract work, remunerated sometimes at 'time-rates' (often calculated by the day, occasionally by the month) and sometimes at 'piece-rates', all in the same chronological and geographical context.[21] For the ancient economic historian this is one of the most valuable sources from Greek antiquity. Most of the work here, as well as in the great majority of other cases of which we know anything, was done by a series of what we should call 'contractors' (*misthōtai*), and not many *misthōtoi* in the strict sense are visible (see above, and n.13), although of course some wage-labour may have been employed by those contractors who did not do all the work for which they were responsible either by themselves or with the aid of their slaves. Going back to what I said earlier in this section, when dealing with Aristotle's treatment of hired labour, I must draw attention again to the fundamental distinction between the general labourer, the *misthōtos* (plural *misthōtoi*) in the proper sense (Aristotle's *thēs*: see above) and the *misthōtēs* (plural *misthōtai*) or 'contractor'. I want to emphasise that we shall only confuse our-selves if, with some modern writers, we take the principal dividing line to be that between piece-worker and time-worker, or if we assume that the payment of something called *misthos* places the recipient among *misthōtoi*.²² The essential dichotomy is between the general labourer, the *misthōtos*, who hires out his labour power for unskilled or at best partly skilled work, in a general way, and the man I am calling a 'contractor' (*misthōtēs, ergolabos, ergōnēs* etc.: see above), who undertakes *a specific task*, always (or virtually always) involving either skill or at least the possession of equipment of some kind, such as oxen or asses or carts for traction or transport, block-and-tackle (*trochileia*) or the like, and probably slaves.²³ As I have indicated, the use of the word *misthos*, which (when it does not happen to mean 'rent') we can nearly always translate by the equally imprecise 'pay', does not help us to distinguish between *misthōtēs* and *misthōtos*: it can be used in either case, and even for what we should call a 'salary' given to an architect or some other relatively dignified person – in which case it is normally calculated by the day, even if actually paid at a much longer interval. The state or its officials (in Athens, usually the Poletai) would 'farm out' contracts, sometimes for very small sums. Often this procedure is described by some such phrase as *misthousi ta misthōmata* (as in Arist., *Ath. Pol.* 47.2; Hdts II.180, and many other texts); but the expression *misthōmata* can have different shades of meaning, and in one of the late-fifth-century inscriptions from the Athenian Erechtheum the use of the phrase '*misthōmata* and *kathēmerisia*' probably distinguishes between payments made at piece-rates and day-rates respectively (*IG* I².373.245-6). *Misthōtos* is a passive formation, *misthōtēs* an active, and the basic distinction is remarkably like that which modern Roman lawyers have established between what is called in Latin *locatio conductio operis* and *locatio conductio operarum* (see below).

There is a much-quoted passage in chapter 12 of Plutarch's *Life of Pericles*, purporting to describe the organisation of the great public works initiated by that statesman at Athens, in the third quarter of the fifth century B.C., and representing them as undertaken deliberately to provide employment for the whole citizen population (to 'make the whole city *emmisthos*', 12.4), including 'the unskilled and banausic masses' (12.5). Most of the workers Plutarch then proceeds to specify would have had to be skilled, but according to him each separate craft had its own mass of unskilled men (*thētikos ochlos kai idiōtēs*) working in a subordinate capacity, and the prosperity of the city was thus shared out widely among the whole population (12.6). Certainly, any *misthōtēs* con-tracting for a major piece of work may have utilised *misthōtoi* as well as slaves. However, the whole passage is highly rhetorical in character and – as Meiggs and Andrewes have independently demonstrated recently – is likely to be so exaggerated as to have little or no connection with the reality.²⁴ Such reliable evidence as we have (mainly from inscriptions) suggests that even at Athens metics and other foreigners (as well as slaves) participated in public works to a considerable degree; and in those few other cities for which we have similar information (and which would normally be less able to supply all the craftsmen needed) the role of non-citizens seems to have been greater still: this makes it unlikely that the main purpose of such works was to 'provide employment' for citizens. Certainly a city was regarded as prosperous, and felt itself to be prosperous, when there was an exceptional amount of productive activity going on inside its walls, as for example at Ephesus in 407 and again in 395, when large-scale military preparations were being undertaken there by Spartan commanders, in the first case by Lysander (Plut., *Lys.* 3.3-4) and in the second by Agesilaus (Xen., *HG* III.iv.16-17); but city revenues were seldom enough to allow for very much enterprise of this kind. In all such cases it was doubtless the local artisans, the *technitai*, who were the main beneficiaries, and when there was more work on hand than they could cope with there was very likely to be an influx of foreign craftsmen.[25] In the eyes of Isocrates (VIII.21), when Athens had been 'full of merchants and foreigners and metics' it had enjoyed twice the revenue it received at the time he was writing (*c.* 355 B.C.), when – according to his exaggerated picture – such people were absent.

Anyone who wants to make out that the hiring of free labour in construction works played a major part in the economic life of ancient cities should ask himself how, in that case, the men concerned were able to live at all when – as often happened – there was little or no public building going on. It is worth noticing the attitude of Aristotle, who was well aware that 'tyrants' in particular had been responsible for major public works, but never attributes these to a desire to provide a better livelihood for the urban poor. On the contrary, in one passage he gives it as a characteristic of tyrants that they (like oligarchs) treat the common people (the *ochlos*) badly and 'drive them out of the city' into the countryside (*Pol.* V.10, 1311^{a}13-14). A little later (id. 11, 1313^{b}18-25) he develops the theory that the tyrant is anxious to keep his subjects poor, an objective for which he sees two reasons: for the first, the interpretation is doubtful (as the text may be unsound: see Newman, *PA* IV.456-7); the second is the desire to keep people so occupied that they will have no leisure to go in for plots! (cf. *Ath. pol.* 16.3). The illustrations Aristotle gives are the Egyptian pyramids and the public works undertaken by three sets of Greek tyrants (all in the Archaic age): the Corinthian Cypselids, Peisistratus of Athens, and Polycrates of Samos. All these measures, he adds, have the same results: poverty and the lack of leisure. Now the whole of Aristotle's argument assumes that the works concerned will have been carried out, not by *corvées* but by the voluntary labour of free men, citizens indeed – nothing is said of slaves, although of course their use as assistants is not excluded. Most people nowadays would naturally assume that the *purpose* of the works in question was at least partly to give employment to the citizens who were engaged in them. I think that this motive may well have been present, at least in some cases; but *in Aristotle's mind* it played no part at all: for him, the citizens were being given work in order to keep them poor and too much occupied to have any inclination to plot against their tyrant. Why the tyrant should desire his subjects to be poor may not be immediately obvious to us. Xenophon at any rate seems to have thought that the more poverty-stricken the subjects of a tyrant were, the more submissive (*tapeinoteroi*) he could expect to find them (*Hiero* V.4). But in order to understand Aristotle fully here, we must look at a silly passage in Plato's *Republic* (VIII.566e-7a), which Aristotle is thoughtlessly transcribing, and muddling unnecessarily at the same time by introducing the notion of public works. Plato sees the tyrant as beginning with demagogic measures such as the cancellation of debts and the distribution of land to the *dēmos* (elements which do not occur in Aristotle); then, if peace is secured, the tyrant constantly stirs up foreign wars, 'so that the *dēmos* may be in need of a leader' – an idea which is repeated word for word by Aristotle (1313^b28-9). In Plato, the way in which the tyrant impoverishes the people is by making them pay financial levies (cf. Arist., 1313^b25-8): this it is which makes them poor and obliges them to spend all their time working, so that they are disinclined to plot. The public buildings which Aristotle drags in are not properly worked into the argument, which is clearer and better without them – if otherwise equally feeble – in Plato. We may feel that Aristotle is far from his best in the passages I have just quoted, but I do not think we can afford to ignore the complete absence from his work and that of all his contemporaries (including Plato) of any suggestion that public works were ever undertaken to provide a livelihood for the urban poor. The few other passages describing public building in Greek authors, with the single exception of Plutarch, *Pericles* 12 (discussed in the preceding paragraph), also contain no hint of any desire to create employment. Indeed, there is nothing about the provision of employment by means of public works in the whole of the literature of the fifth and fourth centuries B.C., as far as my knowledge goes. This is certainly true even of the treatises addressed to (or put into the mouths of) tyrants: the *Hiero* of Xenophon, and Isocrates II (*To Nicocles*), III (*Nicocles*), and IX (*Evagoras*).[26] Isocrates, in one of his most unpleasant speeches, the *Areopagiticus* (VII), giving at one point a ludicrously idealised picture (§§ 15 ff.) of 'the good old days' at Athens (meaning the early fifth century: see § 16), pretends that while the poor regarded the wealth of the rich (which they scrupulously respected) as a means of prosperity (*euporia*) for themselves, the rich behaved benevolently towards the poor, leasing land to some of them at moderate rents, sending out others on commercial journeys, and providing resources for others 'to engage in other kinds of activity' (*eis tas allas ergasias*, § 32). But in this case too there is no mention of public works (although of course Isocrates was well aware of the public building that had gone on later in the fifth century, § 66), for the acts of kindness are represented as those of wealthy individuals (cf. § 55); and I may add that the word *ergasia* has just been used, in § 30, in relation to agricultural work. Later in the speech we are told that the Athenians in the same period impelled the poor 'towards farming and trading operations' (§ 44), and that many citizens 'never entered the city even for festivals' (§ 52). Keeping the poor in the country, away from the city, is a course urged upon oligarchs by the author, doubtless Anaximenes, of the Pseudo-Aristotelian *Rhetoric to Alexander*, who points out that if the *ochlos* congregates in the city it will be more likely to unite and put down the oligarchy (2.19, 1424^b8-10).

The literary passage which gives the most detailed and convincing account of a large-scale piece of public construction in the Classical period is Diodorus XIV.18, dealing with the fortification of Epipolae with a wall 30 stades in length (about 3⅓ miles or between 5 and 6 km.), undertaken by the great tyrant Dionysius I of Syracuse at the very end of the fifth century. We hear of 60,000 able-bodied *countrymen* organised in 30 labour teams, each with a master-builder (*architektōn*) in charge of one stade (nearly 600 feet), six builders (*oikodomoi*) under him, each responsible for one plethron (nearly 100 feet), and 200 unskilled labourers assisting each *oikodomos*. Other men quarried the necessary stone and transported it to the site, with 6,000 yoke of oxen. (There is no mention of slave labour.) In so far as we can rely upon the narrative in Diodorus, the passage provides evidence against the existence of a sufficient pool of free labour for major construction work inside even this exceptionally large Greek city, since the mass of the workers are represented as being brought in from the country-side. The whole project is said to have been undertaken in a great hurry, and finished in twenty days. Prizes were offered to each category within the team which finished first. I may say that we hear of no attempt by Dionysius to provide regular employment for his subjects, although he did carry out a certain amount of public building (see Diod. XV.13.5). When in 399 Dionysius built warships and made large quantities of weapons and missiles (again organising the work very thoroughly), he collected great numbers of craftsmen (*technitai*), not only from the cities he himself controlled but also, by providing high pay, from Italy, Greece and even the area dominated by Carthage (Diod. XIV.41-2); and again the work was done as quickly as possible.

Only in one case, apart from Diodorus XIV.18.4 (mentioned in the preceding paragraph), are we given a definite figure, reliable or not, for the number of men involved in a major building project: Josephus says that 'over 18,000 *technitai*' were engaged on finishing the Second Temple in Jerusalem in A.D. 64, two years before the outbreak of the great Jewish revolt (*AJ* XX.219). According to Josephus, on the completion of the temple the 18,000, who had been dependent on this work for their daily bread, were now 'out of work and lacked pay' (*argēsantes . . . kai misthophorias endeeis*); and Agrippa II, who had been financing the work, now agreed to have the city paved with white marble (evidently to provide work), although he refused to have the east portico raised in height, as the people had demanded (ibid. 220-3). Josephus can be very unreliable over figures, and I would expect the 18,000 to be a vastly exaggerated estimate. I imagine that a good many of the men concerned ought to be regarded as independent craftsmen rather than men who regularly hired themselves out, even if in this case they mainly worked for daily wages – which Josephus says they received if they had done only one hour's work (cf. Mt. XX.1-15). Probably a good many of them had come into Jerusalem from the countryside of Judaea, Galilee and even farther afield, and would expect to go home again when the work was finished. The economic situation in and around Jerusalem was now very strained, with a great deal of serious poverty: this of course contributed greatly to the enthusiasm of the revolt.

In the whole Graeco-Roman world, it was probably in Rome itself that there was the highest concentration of free men, including freedmen. Anyone accustomed to modern cities would naturally tend to assume that these men would have made themselves available in large numbers for hired labour. In fact there is no evidence at all for *regular* hired labour of any kind at Rome. A certain proportion of the free poor lived to some extent on hand-outs provided by wealthy families whose clients they were – thus bringing themselves within 'the sound section of the populace, attached to the great houses', whom Tacitus, in his patronising way, compares favourably with the *plebs sordida*,[27] frequenting (in his picture) the circus and theatres (*Hist.* I.4). But the great majority of the *plebs urbana* must have been shopkeepers or traders, skilled craftsmen (or at least semi-skilled artisans), or transport-workers using ox-carts, asses or mules. We know that there were large numbers of such people (an actual majority of them probably freedmen or the children of freedmen, by the late Republic), because of the mass of inscriptions which have survived, mainly either epitaphs of individuals or documents connected with one or other of the scores of what are often, if misleadingly, called 'craft-guilds' (one form of *collegia*), which flourished at Rome, and to which, incidentally, slaves were only rarely admitted.[28] Now even some of these skilled and semi-skilled workmen might be driven at times to take service for hire as general labourers, although as a rule they would not do that, but perform their specialised tasks for particular customers. And of course the unskilled would very often hire themselves out generally. We are obliged, therefore, to assume the existence of a great deal of *short-term* hiring at Rome – a very precarious form of livelihood. Here it is worth taking into consideration the one literary work we possess which describes in painstaking detail a whole system of public works: the *De aquis* (*On the Aqueducts*) of Sextus Julius Frontinus, written at the very end of the first century. Frontinus speaks several times of slave workers (II.96, 97, 98, 116-18) and gives particulars of two large slave-gangs, one belonging to the state and the other to the emperor, totalling together no fewer than 700 men (II.98, 116-118), but never refers to free wage-labour. He also contemplates the possibility that certain works may need to be undertaken by private contractors (*redemptores*, II.119,124). There is nothing at this point to indicate whether the contractors would make use of slaves or of free workers; but Frontinus also mentions that in former times, before Agrippa organised the care of the aqueducts systematically (II.98), contractors had regularly been used, and the obligation had been imposed upon them of maintaining permanent slave-gangs of prescribed sizes for work on the aqueducts both outside and inside the city (II.96). There is no reference anywhere in Frontinus to the employment of free wage-labour in any form. On the other hand, we must remember that Frontinus is dealing entirely with the permanent maintenance of existing aqueducts; he says not a word about the type of labour involved in their original construction, a short-term job in which free artisans and transport-workers and hired labourers must surely have been involved, as well as slaves. (It is in the *De aquis*, by the way, that Frontinus, with all the philistine complacency of a Roman administrator, depreciates, in comparison with the Roman aqueducts he so much admired, not only 'the useless Pyramids' but also 'the unprofitable [*inertia*] though celebrated works of the Greeks' [I.16] – he no doubt had in mind mere temples like the Parthenon.)

Brunt has maintained that 'demagogic figures' at Rome are 'continually associated with public works'.[29] There does seem to be some truth in this, and I see no objection to attributing to some of the Roman *populares* a desire to provide work for poor citizens living at Rome. But I feel far from certain about this. Neither from the Late Republic nor from the Principate, at Rome *or anywhere else*, do I know of any explicit evidence of an attempt to recruit a labour force from poor citizens as a means of providing them with sustenance – except of course for the passage in Plutarch's *Life of Pericles* 12.4-6 (quoted above), which I would take (with Andrewes: see above and n.24) to be a reflection of conditions nearer to Plutarch's own time than to fifth-century Athens. It hardly encourages one to feel confidence when the only piece of literary evidence on such a major subject turns out to be an imaginary description of Classical Athens in the fifth century B.C.! Moreover, when Polybius speaks of the interest of the Roman *plēthos*[30] in State contracts (for the construction and repair of public buildings, and for the farming of taxes), he is thinking only of those rich men who in the Late Republic formed the equestrian order, for when he proceeds to specify the various groups concerned in these activities and the profits[31] (*ergasiai*) they involved, he lists only the contractors themselves, their partners and their sureties; there is no mention of small sub-contractors (who would be artisans of various kinds), let alone men who were hired and worked for wages (Polyb. VI.xvii.2–4). This must not be taken to disprove some involvement of free labour in public works; but it does suggest that such labour did not play a major part. (Cf. also what I say below about Dio Chrysostom's *Euboean Oration*, VII.104–152.)

I find it hard to take seriously that unique and much-quoted text, Suetonius, *Vespasian* 18.2, in which the emperor refuses to make use of a new invention by a certain *mechanicus*, designed to facilitate the transport of heavy columns to the Capitol, on the ground that it would prevent him from 'feeding the populace' (*plebiculam pascere*).[32] The obvious implication is that such work was done, and Vespasian wished it to continue to be done, by the paid labour of citizens, which the adoption of the invention would have made unnecessary, thus depriving the citizens concerned of their livelihood. My reason for declining to accept this story as true is that Vespasian – who was no fool – could have had no possible motive for refusing to take up the invention *at all*, even if it would have saved a great deal of indispensable labour *at Rome*, for of course it could have been most usefully employed elsewhere in the empire, especially for such things as military fortifications, however impolitic it might have been to bring it into use at Rome itself. For this reason alone the story must surely have been an invention. Moreover, the emperors did not in fact regularly dole out food, money or anything else to the poor at Rome (or anywhere else) at any time *in return for labour*, and we never hear of any attempt to recruit a labour force from the poorer citizens as a means of providing them with sustenance. Vespasian, like most of the earlier emperors, certainly carried out a large programme of public building at Rome; but as far as I am aware we have not a single scrap of evidence about the type of labour employed in these works. I would guess that they were mainly organised through contractors, both large and small (*redemptores, mancipes*), who will have used gangs of slaves (if perhaps not often on the scale of the 500 with which Crassus is credited by Plutarch, *Crass.* 2.5), and will also have done a good deal of what we should call 'sub-contracting' to independent artisans and transport-workers, as well as employing much casual labour for unskilled work. I am tempted to say that employment on public works cannot regularly have played a major part in the life of the humbler Roman, for the programme of public building varied a great deal in quantity from time to time, and in particular, whereas Augustus had been responsible for a tremendous amount of construction and reconstruction, there was hardly anything of the kind in the reign of his successor, Tiberius, which lasted for 23 years (14–37). Had the lower classes at Rome depended to any large degree on employment in public works, they simply could not have survived such periods when little or no building was going on. However, even if the story about Vespasian which we have been discussing is almost certainly a fiction, it was accepted as true by

Suetonius, writing probably within half a century of Vespasian's death in 79, and it must have sounded plausible to at least some of his contemporaries. The same will be true of Plutarch, *Pericles* 12.4–6 (see above), if indeed it comes, as I believe, from the Roman period (see above), and probably the original source, as well as Plutarch, was influenced by conditions at Rome. We must presumably conclude, therefore, that the labour of humble free men did play a real part – how large, we have no means of telling – in the organisation of public works at Rome in the first century, although hired labour, in the strict sense, is likely to have played a far smaller role than that of skilled and semi-skilled men performing specific tasks. But the city of Rome, of course, is a very special case.

I for one find it impossible to accept the motive attributed by Dio Cassius (LXVI [LXV].10.2, in the abridgment of Xiphilinus) to Vespasian's action in being the first, at the rebuilding of the Capitoline temple, to bring out a load of earth: he hoped, according to Dio-Xiphilinus, to encourage even the most distinguished men to follow his example, 'so that the service [*diakonēma*] might become unavoidable by the rest of the populace'. (This motive does not appear in the earlier account by Suet., *Vesp.* 8.5.) There were certainly no *corvées* at Rome. Therefore, *if* we want to take the text seriously, we must suppose that the labour to be furnished by the citizens would necessarily be voluntary and unpaid, for Vespasian is seen as expecting the actions of 'the most distinguished men' to encourage 'the rest of the populace' to come forward; and it seems to me absurd to imagine 'the most distinguished men' as offering their services for hire. Yet it is surely unlikely in the extreme that large numbers of poor men would have wished to offer their labour for nothing, even towards the construction of a temple, and indeed many could scarcely have afforded to do so. The text, then, hardly makes sense. If, on the other hand, we seek to avoid the absurd conclusion I have just outlined by supposing that the poor were being expected to offer their services for pay, then the argument becomes most uncomfortable for those who believe that public works were largely carried out by the labour of poor free citizens, for it is a necessary implication of the story that not many poor citizens could have been induced to come forward but for the emperor's initiative! I should therefore prefer to adopt a suggestion made to me by Brunt: that we should ignore the motive suggested by Dio, and see Vespasian's act as something akin to the laying of a foundation-stone by royalty in the modern world. (As he points out, there is a close parallel in Suet., *Nero* 19.2; cf. also Tac., *Ann.* I.62.2.)

In the Roman provinces, including those of the Greek East, a good proportion of major public building by the cities during the Principate came to depend upon imperial munificence. Unfortunately, we are as badly informed about the types of labour employed on building in the provinces as we are for Rome and Italy – except of course when the work was carried out by the army, as happened frequently from at any rate the second half of the second century onwards.[33]

One may well wonder how it was possible for the poor in great cities to maintain themselves at all. Certainly at Rome[34] and (from 332 onwards) at Constantinople the government provided a limited quantity of food free (mainly bread, with oil and meat also at Rome) and in addition tried to ensure that further corn was made available at reasonable prices. It is clear from a passage in Eusebius (*HE* VII.xxi.9) that a public corn dole (*dēmosion sitēresion*) was being distributed at Alexandria near the beginning of the sole reign of Gallienus (the early 260s); and Egyptian papyri, mostly published very recently, have now revealed that corn doles also existed at Hermopolis at the same date, at Oxyrhynchus a few years later, and a whole century earlier at Antinoöpolis. All the evidence is given by J. R. Rea in his publication of *The Oxyrhynchus Papyri*, Vol. XL (1972). At Oxyrhynchus, from which we have much more evidence than anywhere else, the rules governing admission to the list of privileged recipients (partly chosen by lot) were complicated and are not entirely clear; but there is little doubt that it was reasonably well-to-do local citizens who were the chief beneficiaries and that the really poor would have little chance of benefiting (cf. Rea, op. cit. 2–6,8). Freedmen seem to have qualified only if they had performed a liturgy, and therefore had at least a fair amount of property (ibid. 4, 12). The distribution at Alexandria was subsidised by the government, at least in the fourth century (cf. Stein, *HBE* II.754 n.1), when there is reason to think that Antioch and Carthage (the next largest cities of the Mediterranean world after Rome, Constantinople and Alexandria) also received State subsidies of corn (see Jones, *LRE* II.735, with III.234 n.53; Liebeschuetz, *Ant.* 127–9). A serious riot in such a city might result in the suspension or reduction of the corn distribution: this seems to have happened at Constantinople in 342 (Socr., *HE* II.13.5; Soz., *HE* III.7.7), at Antioch after the famous 'riot of the statues' in 387 (Liebeschuetz, *Ant.* 129), and at Alexandria as a consequence of the disturbances that followed the installation of the Chalcedonian patriarch Proterius in *c.* 453 (Evagr., *HE* II.5). The evidence so far available may give only a very inadequate idea of the extent of such corn doles. As Rea has said, 'We have relatively very little information about what begins to bear the appearance of an institution widespread in the cities of Egypt' (op. cit. 2). Whether such doles existed outside Egypt and the other places named above we have at present no means of telling. We hear of subsidies in corn (and wine) granted by the emperors from Constantine onwards to some Italian cities of no very great size, such at Puteoli, Tarracina and Capua; but these were very special arrangements intended to compensate the cities concerned for the levies in kind (of wood, lime, pigs and wine) which they were obliged to furnish for the maintenance of the city of Rome itself and its harbour at Portus (see Symm., *Rel.* xl, with Jones, *LRE* II.702–3, 708–10). Apart from this there are only isolated examples of imperial munificence to individual cities, which may or may not have been long-lasting, as when we are told that Hadrian granted Athens *sitos etēsios*, which may mean a free annual subsidy of corn, of unknown quantity (Dio. Cass. LXIX.xvi.2). There is evidence from many parts of the Greek world for cities maintaining special funds of their own for the purchase of corn and its supply at reasonable prices: as early as the second half of the third century B.C. these funds became permanent in many cities (see e.g. Tarn, *HC*[3] 107–8). The food liturgies at Rhodes may have been unique (Strabo XIV.ii.5, p.653). In the Hellenistic and Roman periods wealthy men sometimes created funds in their cities out of which distributions of food or of money (*sportulae* in Latin) could be made on certain occasions; but, far from giving a larger share to the poor, these foundations often discriminated in favour of the upper classes.[35] In his book on Roman Asia Minor, Magie speaks of what he believed to have been 'the only known instance . . . of what is now thought of as a charitable foundation . . . : the gift of 300,000 denarii by a wealthy woman of Sillyum [in Pamphylia] for the support of destitute children' (*RRAM* I.658). In the inscription in question (*IGRR* III.801) there is however no justification at all for speaking of '*destitute children*'; and the rest of the inscription, with two others relating to the woman concerned, Menodora, and her family (ibid. 800, 802), shows clearly that these people made their gifts strictly in conformity with social rank, according to a hierarchical order in no fewer than five or six grades, in which councillors come first, and after that 'elders' (*geraioi*), members of the local Assembly (*ekklēsiastai*), and then ordinary citizens; below these are *paroikoi* (resident strangers, who would have been called 'metics' in Classical Athens) and two varieties of freedmen (cf. Section v of this chapter and its n.17), and finally the wives of the three leading grades, who (in the two inscriptions in which they are noticed) receive either the same amount as the freedmen etc. or rather less. In each case the councillors receive at least twenty times as much as the freedmen. (A convenient summary of the figures, which are not perfectly clear in the inscriptions, is given by T. R. S. Broughton, in Frank, *ESAR* IV.784-5.)

* * * * * *

I am concerned in this book with the Roman world only in so far as the Greek East came to be included in it, and I shall have little to say about strictly Roman wage-labour, a good, brief, easily intelligible account of which will be found in John Crook's *Law and Life of Rome* (1967).[36] A certain amount of free hired labour in the Roman world can be detected, for instance, in mining and various services, often of a menial character, as well as in agriculture, where we have already noticed the employment of *mercennarii*: see above on the Mactar inscription, and Section iv of this chapter. The situation does not seem to have changed much in the Later Roman Empire, during which the greater part of our information comes from the Greek East (see Jones, *LRE* II.792-3, 807, 858-63). Many technical problems arise in connection with what we should now call 'professional' posts (see below). Cornelius Nepos, writing in the third quarter of the last century B.C., could remark on the fact that the status of *scribae* (secretaries) conveyed much more prestige (it was *multo honorificentius*) among the Greeks than among the Romans, who considered *scribae* to be *mercennarii* – 'as indeed they are', adds Nepos (*Eum.* 1.5). Yet secretaries employed by the State, *scribae publici*, who were what we should call high-level civil servants and might serve in very responsible positions as personal secretaries to magistrates, including provincial governors, were members of what has been rightly called an 'ancient and distinguished profession' (Crook, *LLR* 180, referring to Jones, *SRGL* 154-7). Statements of this kind make it easier to accept a later apologia, one's instinctive reaction to which might have been derision: Lucian, the second-century satirist from Samosata on the Euphrates, who wrote excellent literary Greek although his native tongue was Aramaic,[37] was at pains to excuse himself for accepting a salaried post in the Roman imperial civil service, although in an earlier work (*De merc. cond.*) he had denounced other literary gentlemen for taking paid secretarial posts in private employment; and the excuse is that his own job is in the service of the emperor (*Apol.* 11-13) – that is to say, the State.

There was a parallel in Roman thinking, and to some extent even in Roman law (which of course applied in theory to the whole empire from *c.* 212 onwards), to the distinction drawn by Aristotle between the hired man and the independent craftsman: the earliest text I know that brings it out clearly is part of a much-quoted passage in Cicero's *De officiis* (I.150), referring to 'the illiberal and sordid ways of gaining a living of all those *mercennarii* whose labour (*operae*), not their skill (*artes*), is bought; their very wage is the reward of slavery (*ipsa merces auctoramentum servitutis*)'. Here again we find the notion, prevalent among upper-class Greeks, that general wage-labour in the strict sense (not the specific labour of the independent craftsman) is somehow servile.[38] Even if Cicero is closely following Panaetius of Rhodes (see Section iii of this chapter), the sentiments he expresses at this point are thoroughly characteristic of the Roman propertied class.

At this point I must briefly mention a technical and difficult question: the distinction which most modern 'civilians' (Roman lawyers) draw between two different forms of the contract known to the lawyers of Rome as *locatio conductio* – essentially 'letting out', 'lease', 'hire'. (The rest of this paragraph can easily be skipped by those with no stomach for technical details.) The simplest form of this contract, with which we are all familiar, is *locatio conductio rei*, letting and hiring out a thing, including land and houses. Two other forms of *locatio conductio*, between which I now wish to discriminate, are *locatio conductio operis (faciendi)* and *locatio conductio operarum*:[39] a distinction does seem to have existed between them in Roman times, although it was never made as explicitly by the lawyers as by Cicero in the passage I have just quoted, and was always a socio-economic rather than a legal distinction. We must begin by excluding many 'professional services', in the modern sense: in Roman eyes they were simply not in the category of things to which the contract *locatio conductio* could apply.[40] This is a very thorny subject, which has been much discussed by Roman lawyers: I agree with the opinion that the texts do not allow us to construct a coherent overall picture, because the status of the various so-called *operae liberales* (a modern expression not found in the sources)[41] underwent considerable changes between the Late Republic and the Severan period – a few leading teachers and doctors, for example, achieved a notable rise in status, while some surveyors (*mensores, agrimensores*) sank. Broadly speaking we can say that professions like oratory and philosophy were perfectly respectable because they involved in theory no direct payment for the service rendered (except of course to 'sophists' and philosophers who held State appointments as professors), while doctors, teachers and the like, who did receive such payments, were thereby mainly disqualified from the high degree of respect which nowadays is accorded to their professions, until in the first two centuries of the Principate a few of their most prominent members, especially teachers of literature and rhetoric at the highest level, achieved a very dignified position. The derogatory term *mercennarius* is never used in connection with *locatio conductio operis* but is attached only to the man who 'had hired out his labour', *operas suas locaverat* (Dig. XLVIII.xix.11.1 etc.); and this form of contract can scarcely be distinguished from *locatio conductio sui*, where a man 'had hired himself out' (see e.g. *Dig.* XIX.ii.60.7: 'si ipse se locasset'). Hiring out one's labour (*operae*) was in itself discreditable, and Ulpian could say that the incurring of a certain specific legal stigma by a man who hires himself out to fight with wild beasts in the arena depends not on his having actually indulged in that particular practice but in having hired himself out to do so (*Dig.* III.i.1.6). It is merely a curious anomaly that in *locatio conductio operarum* the workman (the *mercennarius*) who contracts for the 'letting out' (of his services) and who does the work (the *operae*) and receives the payment should be the *locator*, whereas in *locatio conductio operis* the *locator* is the man who 'puts out' the *job* to the *conductor* (we might call the latter 'the contractor'), who does the work (the *opus*) and receives the payment. (In *locatio conductio rei*, the *locator* is what we should call, in the case of land, the 'lessor', and of course it is he who receives the payment.) The legal technicalities, complicated as they are, should not be allowed to hide from us the very real difference which Cicero had in mind when he distinguished the relatively respectable man who allowed his *skill* to be purchased (for a particular job) and the *mercennarius* who in selling the general disposition of his labour power received as his hire 'the reward of slavery'.

In case it is objected that all the evidence I am citing comes from upper-class circles, and that only the well-to-do would regard wage-labour as a mean and undesirable activity, I must insist that there is every reason to think that even humble folk (who of course were far from despising all work, like the propertied class) really did regard hired labour as a less dignified and worthy form of activity than one in which one could remain *one's own master,* a truly free man, whether as a peasant, trader, shopkeeper, or artisan – or even a transport-worker such as a bargee or donkey-driver, who could hardly be classed as a skilled craftsman. I am tempted to suggest that in Greek and Roman antiquity being a fully free man almost necessarily involved being able, in principle, to utilise slave labour in whatever one was doing! Even a petty retailer (a *kapēlos*) who was prospering might buy a slave to look after his shop or stall; a carter or muleteer might aspire to have a slave to attend to his animals. But the *misthōtos*, who would be paid the very minimum for giving his employer the full use of his labour-power, would never be able to employ a slave out of his miserable wage; he alone was not a properly free man.

As I hope I have made sufficiently clear, the status of the labourer was as low as it could well be – only a little above that of the slave, in fact. Even in their own eyes, I feel sure, men who hired themselves out would have had a minimum of self-regard. Corax, a fictitious character who in the *Satyricon* of Petronius is hired as a porter and is called a *mercennarius* (mistranslated 'slave' by Rouse in the Loeb edition of 1913, corrected to 'hireling' in a revised edition in 1969), strongly objects to being treated as a beast of burden and insists (in correct technical terminology: see above) that what he has hired out is the service of a man, not a horse (*hominis operas locavi, non caballi*).[42] 'I am as free as you are,' he says to his employer, 'even if my father did leave me a poor man' (117.11-12). But it is implicit in the story that Corax knows he is not behaving like a free man. I would accept that as a true picture of such men in general. I find it significant that Plutarch, when advising the propertyless man on how to maintain himself (*Mor.* 830ab), makes no reference to taking hired service in a general way. The occupations he suggests (which I have reproduced in Section iv of this chapter, while discussing debt bondage) do include two unskilled activities, ordinarily performed by slaves, which the poor free man could undertake only for a wage: acting as *paidagōgos*, to take children to school, or as a doorkeeper, *thyrōrōn* (cf. Epict., *Diss.* III.26.7). For the former, he might be paid at what we should call piece-rates; for the latter, only time-rates seem appropriate. But each of these tasks, however unskilled and humble, is one that has a narrowly defined sphere of action and does not allow for the man who is hired to be used as a general labourer. For Plutarch, and surely for most Greeks, I suspect that this would make a great difference. Undertaking this kind of post would at least put one on the borderline between the provider of skilled services and the general hired labourer in the full sense; and we ourselves might be inclined to think that Plutarch's individual would be crossing the line and could best be classified with the hired man. But perhaps, for Plutarch, the specificity of the services he recommends would have prevented the men concerned from sinking into the category of mere hirelings. The only other passage I know in Greek literature which shows any concern about the provision of a livelihood for the urban poor is in Dio Chrysostom's *Euboean oration*, VII.104–152; and the greater part of this is devoted to discussing occupations in which the poor must *not* be allowed to indulge, either because they minister to the unnecessarily luxurious life of the rich or because they are useless or degrading in themselves (109–11, 117–23, 133–52). Ideally, Dio would clearly like to settle the urban poor in the countryside (105, 107–8); the only identifiable occupation he recommends for those in the city is to be craftsmen (*cheirotechnai*, 124), although in another place (114), with what we can recognise as a literary allusion (to a speech of Demosthenes, LVII.45), he does say that a man ought not to be sneered at merely because his mother had been a hireling (*erithos*) or a grape-harvester or a paid wet-nurse, or because his father had been a schoolmaster or a man who took children to school (*paidagōgos*). I must add that there is never the slightest hint of public works undertaken in order to 'give employment' in any of the dozen or so orations of Dio delivered in his native city of Prusa (XXXVI, XL, XLII–LI), although there are several references in these speeches to public building and Dio's own responsibility therefor.[43] One passage in particular, XLVII.13–15, makes it perfectly clear that the aim of all such works was simply to make the city more handsome and impressive – an activity in which many cities of Asia Minor indulged to excess in the first and second centuries. In all Dio's references to his goodwill towards the *dēmos, dēmotikoi, plēthos* (e.g. in L.3–4; XLIII.7, 12) there is never any reference to public works; and his claim to have pitied the common people and tried to 'lighten their burdens' (*epikouphizein*, L.3) would have been quite inappropriate to such activities.

Surely, in any slave society a low estimation of hired labour is inevitable, in the absence of very special circumstances: few free men will resort to it unless they are driven to do so by severe economic pressure, and they will suffer in their own estimation and that of everyone else by doing so. Wages will tend to be low: among the factors that will help to keep them down may well be a supply of 'spare' slave labour, with masters possessed of slaves they cannot profitably use letting them out for hire dirt cheap rather then have them on their hands, doing nothing profitable. In the antebellum South, where to work hard was to 'work like a nigger', and poor whites could be said to 'make negroes of themselves' by wage-labour in the cotton and sugar plantations, there were many exhortations to the yeoman farmer and the urban and rural proletarian not to feel demeaned by working with his own hands – 'Let no man be ashamed of labour; let no man be ashamed of a hard hand or a sunburnt face.' But the very fact that such assurances were so often delivered is a proof that they were felt to be necessary to contradict established attitudes: this point has been well made by

Genovese (*PES* 47-8, with the notes, 63-4), who emphasises the presence in the Old South not merely of 'an undercurrent of contempt for work in general' but in particular of 'contempt for labour performed for another' – precisely the situation of the ancient *misthōtos* or *mercennarius*. The poison of slavery, in a 'slave society' – one in which the propertied class draws a substantial part of its surplus from unfree labour, whether of slaves or of serfs or of bondsmen (cf. II.iii above) – works powerfully in the ideological as well as in the social and economic spheres. It has often been remarked that in the Greek and Roman world there was no talk of 'the dignity of labour', and that even the very concept of 'labour' in the modern sense – let alone a 'working class' – could not be adequately expressed in Greek or Latin.[44] (I do not imply, of course, that labour is depreciated only in what I am calling a 'slave society': see below.)

It has often been said that in the Greek and Roman world the 'competition' of slave labour must have forced down the wages of free, hired workers and would be likely to produce 'unemployment', at any rate in extreme cases. 'Unemployment', indeed, is often imagined to be the necessary consequence of any great increase in the use of slave labour in a particular place, such as Athens in the fifth century B.C. But we must begin by understanding that *un*employment, in anything like the modern sense, was virtually never a serious problem in the ancient world, because, as I have shown, *employment*, again in our sense, was not something sought by the vast majority of free men; only those who were both unskilled and indigent would normally attempt to take service for wages. I shall deal presently with the question how far slavery affects the position of these hired labourers proper; for the moment I wish to concentrate on the artisan or skilled craftsman (the *technitēs*), including the man who was semi-skilled and had some equipment (see above), engaged in transport and the like. Such a man, in the ordinary way, obtained a rather different kind of 'employment': he performed specific jobs for his customers, for which he would be paid at 'piece rates', according to what he did, except perhaps when he was working on what we should call a 'government contract', in public works, when he might be paid at 'time rates', by the day. (The best-known evidence for such payments comes from the accounts relating to the Athenian Erechtheum in the late fifth century B.C. and the temple at Eleusis in the late fourth century, references for which will be found in n.21 below.) A sudden influx of working slaves might of course reduce the craftsman's chances of finding people needing his services and willing to give him jobs to do; and to this extent the slaves might be said to 'compete with free labour' and in a very loose sense to 'create employment'. However, it would be simple-minded to say that a man who made use of several slaves in his workshop 'must have' under-sold the small craftsman who worked on his own in the same line: the larger producer in antiquity, not being exposed to the psychological pressures, the ambitions and the opportunities of a rising capitalist entrepreneur, might be more likely to sell at current standard prices and pocket the additional profit he might expect from the exploitation of the labour of his slaves – here I am rather inclined to agree with Jones, even if he was able to give only one illustration, which does nothing to establish his case (*SCA*, ed. Finley, 6).[45] Above all, we must remember that the size of a slave workshop, unlike a modern factory, would not increase its effectiveness in proportion to the number of its workers: it is machinery which is the decisive factor in the modern world, allowing the larger workshop to produce more cheaply and thus to undercut the smaller one (other factors being equal) and drive it out of business. The ancient workshop had no machinery of any kind. It would be valued, apart from any freehold premises in which it happened to be carried on, solely in terms of the slaves employed in it and any raw materials of value, as in Dem. XXVII.4 ff. (esp. 9-10), where the orator – anxious as he is to put as high a value as he possibly can on his father's estate – values the two workshops controlled by the elder Demosthenes (one his own, the other held as security for a debt) in terms of nothing but the raw materials in them (ivory, iron, copper and gall) and their 52 or 53 slaves.[46] Demosthenes speaks of the slaves as if they virtually *were* the 'factory' in each case. Increasing the number of slaves in an ancient workshop would do nothing to improve its efficiency. In fact, as soon as it became large, problems of discipline would be likely to arise. So the ancient artisan was not nearly as likely to be 'driven off the market' and into 'unemployment' by 'slave competition' as we might have been tempted to think, on the basis of misleading modern analogies.

Having sufficiently distinguished the skilled craftsman and his like, I now return to the wage-labourer proper, who hired out his general services for wages. I suggest that such men might indeed have their wages forced down and even suffer unemployment, owing to the 'competition of slave labour', in one set of circumstances particularly. I refer to a situation in which slaveowners were hiring out their slaves on a considerable scale: we know this did happen (see Section iv of this chapter), but how prevalent the practice was we cannot tell. If in these conditions the demand for hired labour was not greater than those free men wishing to perform it were able to fulfil, then some of the free men would be likely to fail to obtain work, even if the slaves' masters offered them at wages no lower than would be given to the free; and if the masters were willing to hire out their slaves at cut rates, then the free men's chances of getting employment would be much reduced.[47]

I know of only one isolated passage in all Greek or Roman literature which gives even a hint of any feeling on the part of free men that slaves were 'taking the bread out of their mouths'. This passage occurs in a quotation by Athenaeus (VI.264d; cf. 272b) from the Sicilian Greek historian Timaeus of Tauromenium, who wrote in the late fourth century B.C. and the early decades of the third (*FGrH* 566 F 11a). According to Athenaeus, Timaeus said that Mnason of Phocis (a friend of Aristotle's) bought a thousand slaves, and was reproached by the Phocians for thus 'depriving as many citizens of their livelihood'. So far, so good, perhaps – although the number of slaves is suspiciously high, especially for a rather backward area like Phocis. But Timaeus (or at any rate Athenaeus) then goes on, 'For the younger men in each household used to serve their elders'; and this seems to me a complete *non sequitur*. I cannot help thinking that Athenaeus has misquoted Timaeus, or that something has gone wrong with the text. Even if one is content to accept the passage as true and meaningful, there is no parallel to it, as far as I know. Otherwise there are only a few general remarks such as Appian's that the Roman poor in the Republic spent their time in idleness (*epi argias*), as the rich used slaves instead of free men to cultivate the land (*BC* I.7).

Even in societies in which unfree labour is a thing of the past, or nearly so, wage-labourers have often been despised by the propertied class, and sometimes they have been deeply distrusted even by would-be reformers on the ground that those who receive wages (especially domestic servants) are too dependent upon their employers to be able to think and act of their own volition, and for that reason are unworthy to be entrusted with democratic rights. The English Levellers of the seventeenth century have been described as 'the one genuinely democratic party thrown up by the Puritan revolution' (Woodhouse, *PL*², p.[17] of Introduction); yet some of them[48] wished to exclude from the franchise all apprentices and 'servants', as well as 'those that take alms', on the ground that 'they depend upon the will of other men and should be afraid to displease [them]. For servants and apprentices, they are included in their masters and so for those that receive alms from door to door' – thus Maximilian Petty, in the second 'Putney Debate', on 29 October 1647 (Woodhouse, *PL*² 83). The conjunction of beggars with servants and apprentices is significant.[49] There is no doubt that James Harrington, the very interesting and influential political writer of the third quarter of the seventeenth century, divided the population into two classes: Freemen or Citizens who can, and Servants who cannot, 'live of themselves' or 'live upon their own'.[50]

The desire to discriminate politically against those who work for wages continued well beyond the seventeenth century. I cannot follow it further here than to say that it is still very visible in some works of Immanuel Kant, written in the 1790s, where we may find some interesting reminiscences of the distinctions drawn in Roman law referred to above. Kant wished to confine the franchise to those who were their own masters and had some property to support them. A man who 'earned his living from others' could be allowed to qualify as a citizen, in Kant's eyes, only if he earned it 'by *selling* that which is his, and not by allowing others to make use of him'. Kant explains in a note that whereas the artist and the tradesman, and even the tailor and the wig-maker, do qualify (they are *artifices*), the domestic servant, the shop assistant, the labourer, the barber, and 'the man to whom I give my firewood to chop' do not (they are mere *operarii*). He ends his note, however, with the admission that 'it is somewhat difficult to define the qualifications which entitle anyone to claim the status of being his own master'! (I suspect that Roman law may have been among the influences at work on Kant's thought here. The distinction he draws may remind us irresistibly of that between *locatio conductio operis* and *operarum* which I drew attention to above as a social and economic differentiation. Kant was prepared to give it legal and constitutional effect, even though he was unable to define it satisfactorily.) In a work published four years later Kant returned to this theme, asserting that 'to be fit to vote, a person must have an independent position among the people'; and now, without attempting a more precise definition of his 'active citizen', he gives four examples of excluded categories which 'do not possess civil independence', such as apprentices, servants, minors and women, who may 'demand to be treated by all others in accordance with laws of natural freedom and equality' but should have no right to participate in making the laws.[51]

★   ★   ★   ★   ★   ★

I must end this chapter by re-emphasising a point I have made elsewhere in this book: that if free hired labour played no very significant part at any time in the economy of the Greek world, then the propertied classes must have extracted their surplus in other ways, primarily through *unfree labour* (that of slaves, serfs and bondsmen) performed 'directly' for individuals (a subject I have already dealt with in Section iv of this chapter), but also 'indirectly' to some extent, in the form of *rent* (in money or kind) from leases, or else from *taxation*, or *compulsory services* performed for the state or the municipalities (which I propose to deal with in the next chapter).

It may not be out of place if I add a note[52] listing all the references to hired labour in the New Testament, of which the only ones of particular interest are Mt. XX.1-16 (the 'Parable of the Vineyard', referred to above) and James V.4.

IV

Forms of Exploitation in the Ancient Greek World, and the Small Independent Producer

(i)
'Direct individual' and 'indirect collective' exploitation

So far, in discussing the forms of class struggle in the ancient Greek world, I have spoken mainly of the *direct individual* exploitation involved in the master-slave relationship and other forms of unfree labour, and in wage-labour. I have done little more than mention such relationships as those of landlord and tenant, and mortgagee and mortgagor, involving the payment of rent or interest instead of the yielding of labour, and (except in I.iii above) I have similarly said little or nothing about the *indirect collective* exploitation effected through the various organs of the state – a term which, when applied to the Hellenistic and Roman periods, must be taken to include not only imperial officials (those of the Hellenistic kings and of the Roman Republic and Empire) but also the agents of the many *poleis* through which the Greek East came more and more to be administered. Broadly speaking, all those among the exploited classes who were of servile or quasi-servile condition (including serfs and bondsmen) and also hired labourers, tenants and debtors were subject to what I have called *direct* exploitation by *individual members* of the propertied class, although – even apart from the slaves of the emperors and other members of the imperial household, the *familia Caesaris* – there were a certain number of public slaves (*dēmosioi, servi publici*) owned by the Roman state or by particular *poleis*. The forms of exploitation which I have called *indirect*, on the other hand, were applied by the state (in ways I shall describe presently) for the *collective* benefit of (mainly) the propertied class, above all to persons of at least nominally free status who were small independent producers: of these a few were either traders (merchants, shopkeepers or petty dealers) or else independent artisans (working not for wages, but on their own account; cf. Section vi of this chapter and III.vi above), but the vast majority were peasants, and most of what I have to say about this category of small independent producers will be concentrated on the peasantry – a term which I shall define in Section ii of this chapter.

Ideally, it might have been best to deal separately with the kinds of exploitation effected by landlords and mortgagees (taking the form of rent or interest) together with other kinds of what I have called 'direct individual' exploitation; but since they applied almost entirely to those I am calling 'peasants', I have found it convenient to treat them in this chapter, with forms of 'indirect collective' exploitation.

By 'indirect and collective' forms of exploitation I mean those payments or services which were not rendered from individual to individual but were exacted by the authority of the state (as defined above) from a whole community (a village, for example) or from individuals. They would normally take one of three main forms: (1) taxation, in money or in kind; (2) military conscription; or (3) compulsory menial services such as the *angariae* I mentioned in I.iii above. Taxation, of course, was usually the most important of these forms of exploitation. After working out the position I have just stated, I came across a statement in Marx which proves that he too distinguished between what I am calling 'direct individual' and 'indirect collective' exploitation, specifically in regard to taxation. In the earliest of his three major works on recent French history, *The Class Struggles in France* (published as a series of articles in the *Neue Rheinische Zeitung* during 1850), Marx says of the condition of the French peasants of his day that 'Their exploitation differs only in *form* from the exploitation of the industrial proletariat. The exploiter is the same: *capital*. The individual capitalists exploit the individual peasants through *mortgages* and *usury*; the capitalist class exploits the peasant class through the *State taxes*' (*MECW* X.122).

Now except in a democracy, like that of Athens in the fifth and fourth centuries B.C., which extended political rights to the lowest levels of the citizen population, the state would be in effect simply the instrument of the collective property-owners, or even of a restricted circle among them – a Hellenistic king and his henchmen, for instance, or a Roman emperor and the imperial aristocracy. 'To the wider vision of the historian,' Sir Harold Bell once wrote, 'one ruler may differ greatly from another; to the peasant the difference has mainly been that the one chastised him with whips and the other with scorpions.'[1] Quite apart from direct exploitation of slaves, bondsmen, serfs, hired labourers, tenants, debtors and others by individual property-owners, such a state would provide for 'its own needs' by taxation, the exaction of compulsory services, and conscription. Taxation took many different forms in the Greek world.[2] In the cities before the Hellenistic period it may often have been quite light, if only because the lack of anything resembling a modern civil service made it difficult if not impossible to collect small sums in taxes profitably from poor people (that is to say, from the great majority of the population), without the intervention of tax-farmers (*telōnai* in Greek, Latin *publicani*), who seem to have been very unpopular with all classes. We have hardly any information about taxation in the Greek cities in the Classical period, except for Athens,[3] where the poor were in practice exempt from the *eisphora*, the only form of direct taxation, and were probably little affected by indirect taxes other than the import duties and harbour dues. (It is a melancholy fact, characteristic of our sources of information for Greek – even Athenian – economic history, that our fullest list of taxes for a single city in any literary source should occur in Comedy: Aristophanes, *Wasps* 656-60!) The total burden of taxation in the Greek cities and their territories certainly increased in the Hellenistic and Roman periods. According to Rostovtzeff, 'the Hellenistic period did not introduce any substantial changes into the system which had been firmly established for centuries in the Greek cities' (*SEHHW* III.1374 n.71). With emphasis on the word 'substantial', this can be accepted, but the evidence consists mainly of small scraps; the only individual source of any real significance is an inscription from Cos, *SIG*[3] 1000 (which has been fully discussed in English).[4] But most of the Greek cities were sooner or later subjected to some form of taxation by Hellenistic kings, and eventually the vast majority had to pay taxes to Rome. In Asia, of course, the Hellenistic kings inherited the Persian system of taxation, first organised by Darius I at the end of the sixth century B.C.; and although in the Hellenistic period many Greek cities were exempt from this, the peasants on land not included in the territory of a city must always have been subject to this burden. In Egypt, the Ptolemies reorganised the age-old taxation system of the Pharaohs, and the elaborate arrangements they devised were later inherited by the Romans.[5] Modern historians have largely ignored the tiresome question of taxation in the Hellenistic and Roman periods, no doubt mainly because of the very unsatisfactory source material. Rostovtzeff is a prominent exception. A glance at the relevant index of his *SEHHW* (III.1741-2) will show nearly three columns filled with entries under 'Tax collectors . . . taxation . . . taxes' (and see the column and a half in the index to his *SEHRE*[2], II.815). Further epigraphic discoveries may well extend our knowledge of this subject, as they have done in the past. For instance, it was from an inscription discovered not long ago in Bulgaria that the first example came to light of a poll-tax (of one denarius per head) collected by a local city from some of the inhabitants of its area, with the express permission of the emperor, for its own benefit (*IGBulg.* IV.2263, lines 6-8).[6]

Taxation greatly increased in the Middle and Later Roman Empire,[7] falling most heavily on the peasantry, who had least power to resist – as I shall explain in VIII.iv below, the rich man had a far better chance of escaping, or minimising payment. The small producer might also be compelled to perform all kinds of compulsory services at the behest of the state, at first mainly in those parts of the Greek world (especially Egypt and Syria) which had once formed part of the Persian empire and in which there survived indefinitely forms of obligatory personal service such as the *corvée* (for repairing canals etc.) or the transport duties which were the original *angariae* (see I.iii above and its n.8 below).

Among the forms of what I have called 'indirect collective exploitation' we must not fail to notice conscription. In the Greek cities, military service in the cavalry or the heavy-armed infantry (the hoplite army) was a 'liturgy' expected mainly of those I am calling 'the propertied classes' (see III.ii above), although I believe that hoplite service sometimes (perhaps often) went down rather below that level and affected some of those who normally had to do a certain amount of work for their living. Light-armed troops and naval forces were recruited from the non-propertied, and some cities even used slaves, among others, to row their warships (see e.g. Thuc. I.54.2; 55.1). I suspect, however, that conscription of the poor for such purposes was rather rare, at any rate unless pay (or at least rations) were given. And I think there is reason to believe that at Athens in particular those below the hoplite class (the Thetes) were conscripted only temporarily, in emergencies (as in 428, 406 and perhaps 376), until 362, when – as I think – conscription of Thetes for the fleet was introduced and became much more frequent.[8]

The feature of military conscription which is particularly relevant here is that it will have represented no really serious burden upon the well-to-do, who did not have to work for their living and whom military service would merely divert from other occupations – often more profitable, it is true. For all those below my 'propertied class', conscription, diverting them from the activities by which they earned their daily bread, could be a real menace, and those who were furthest from belonging to the propertied class would presumably suffer most. Marx, who knew his Appian, quotes in a footnote to Vol. I of *Capital* (pp.726-7 n.4) part of the passage in which Appian describes the growth of great estates and the impoverishment of the Italian peasantry during the Republic (*BC* I.7), and adds the comment, 'Military service hastened to so great an extent the ruin of the Roman plebeians.' (Appian, indeed, in that passage gives the freedom of slaves from conscription as the reason why Roman landowners 'used slaves as cultivators and herdsmen', rather than free men.) With the inception of the Roman Principate (and indeed even earlier, from the time of Marius, in the late second century B.C.) conscription came to be replaced to some considerable extent by voluntary recruitment, although it continued to a greater degree than many historians have realised (see Section iv of this chapter and its n.1 below).

(ii)
The peasantry and their villages

Although the peasantry represents 'an aspect of the past surviving in the contemporary world', yet it is 'worth remembering that – as in the past, so in the present – peasants are the majority of mankind'! Thus Teodor Shanin, in his Introduction (p.17) to the valuable Penguin volume on *Peasants and Peasant Societies* which he edited in 1971.[1] In the present generation, partly as a result of the recent proliferation of studies of backward or exploited countries (the so-called 'developing countries'), there has been a remarkable growth of interest in what some people like to refer to as 'peasant economies' or 'peasant societies', and a *Journal of Peasant Studies* began to appear in 1973. A great deal of information has been collected about peasants; but just as this branch of studies had to rely largely in time past upon historians untrained in sociology and with little or no regard for wider sociological issues, so now it is in danger of becoming mainly the province of sociologists who have an insufficiently historical approach or are not qualified by their training to make the best use of historical material – in particular that from the ancient world, much of which is very hard for anyone but a trained Classical scholar and ancient historian to use profitably.

Now I admit that a very large part of the Greek (and Roman) world throughout most of its history would satisfy some of the currently popular definitions of a 'peasant *economy*' or 'peasant *society*', notably one that is widely accepted today, that of Daniel Thorner, presented to the Second International Conference of Economic History at Aix in 1962, as a paper entitled 'Peasant economy as a category in economic history', published in 1965 in the Proceedings of the conference[2] and reprinted in Shanin's Penguin reader mentioned above (*PPS* 202-18: see esp. 203-5), where we also find a number of alternative definitions and discussions of the concepts of 'peasant economies' (e.g. 99-100, 150-60, 323-4) and 'peasants' (104-105, 240-5, 254-5, 322-5). The ancient historian needs to be able to operate occasionally with the concept of a 'peasant economy', at least for comparative purposes, and he may sometimes find this category really useful in dealing with Greek and Roman society. On the other hand, he will also want to isolate the specific features which differentiate the various phases of ancient Greek (and Roman) society from peasant economies – or other peasant economies. My own inclinations are rather of the second variety, and although I shall certainly make use (after defining it) of the category of 'peasants', I shall rarely think in terms of a 'peasant *economy*'. I agree with Rodney Hilton, who in the publication of his 1973 Ford Lectures at Oxford has pointed out that 'this concept "peasant economy" could embrace most of human history between "tribal" (American, "folk") society and the completion of industrial transformation in modern times. It could certainly apply to most European mediaeval states' (*EPLMA* 7-8). If we feel the necessity to classify the particular society we are studying, in order to group it with certain broadly similar societies and to distinguish it from those in other groups, then for most purposes I think we shall find it more profitable to place the ancient Greek world, in its successive – and in some ways very different – phases, within the field of 'slave society' rather than 'peasant society', although of course operating mainly with the former concept does not by any means exclude the use of the latter in appropriate situations. Perhaps I should repeat here what I have said before (e.g. in II.iii and III.iv above): for my purposes, the fact that the propertied classes of the Greek and Roman world derived the bulk of their surplus from the exploitation of unfree labour makes it possible for us to consider that world as (in a very loose sense) a 'slave economy' or 'slave society', even though we have to concede that during a large part of Greek and Roman history peasants and other independent producers may not only have formed the actual majority of the total population but may also have had a larger share (usually a much larger share) in production than slaves and other unfree workers. Even when, by the fourth century of the Christian era at the very latest, it is possible to be fairly sure that production by chattel slaves in the strict sense has dropped well below the combined production of free peasants, peasant serfs, and miscellaneous artisans and other free workers of all kinds, whether working on their own account or for wages (see III.vi above), the unfree labour of the serfs is a major factor, and permeating the whole society is the universal and unquestioning acceptance of slavery as part of the natural order (cf. III.iv above and Section iii of this chapter). As I shall demonstrate in VI.vi and VII.iii below, Christianity made no difference whatever to this situation, except perhaps to strengthen the position of the governing Few and increase the acquiescence of the exploited Many, even if it did encourage individual acts of charity.

The townsman through the ages has always regarded the peasant's lot as unenviable, except on those occasions when he has allowed himself some sentimental reflection upon the morally superior quality of the peasant's life (see the first paragraph of I.iii above). Edward Gibbon, congratulating himself in his autobiography on having been born into 'a family of honourable rank and decently endowed with the gifts of fortune', could shudder as he contemplated some unpleasant alternatives: being 'a slave, a savage or a peasant' (*Memoirs of my Life*, ed. G. A. Bonnard [1966] 24 n.1).

To my mind, the most profound and moving representation in art of 'the peasant' is Vincent Van Gogh's *De Aardappeleters* (*The Potato Eaters*), painted at Nuenen in Brabant in April-May 1885, a reproduction of which forms the Frontispiece to this book. Apart from preliminary studies, two versions (as well as a lithograph) exist, of which the one in the Van Gogh Museum in Amsterdam is undoubtedly finer than the earlier one in the Kröller-Müller Museum at Otterlo near Arnhem. As Vincent himself said, in a letter to his brother Theo, written on 30 April 1885, while the picture was still being painted:

> I have tried to emphasise that those people, eating their potatoes in the lamplight, have dug the earth with those very hands they put in the dish, and so it speaks of *manual labour*, and how they have honestly earned their food. I have wanted to give the impression of a way of life quite different from that of us civilised people.[3]

(I am sure it would not be possible to find a parallel to that statement in the whole of the literature that survives from the Greek and Roman world.) The quality that impresses one most about Van Gogh's peasants is their endurance, their solidity, like that of the earth from which they draw just sufficient sustenance to maintain life. In at least four of his letters Van Gogh quotes a description of Millet's peasants which certainly applies to his own: 'Son paysan semble peint avec la terre même qu'il ensemence.'[4] The Potato Eaters are poor, but they are not evidently miserable: even if the artist shows infinite sympathy with them, he depicts in them no trace of self-pity. These are the voiceless toilers, the great majority – let us not forget it – of the population of the Greek and Roman world, upon whom was built a great civilisation which despised them and did all it could to forget them.

★   ★   ★   ★   ★   ★

People today are apt to take it for granted that peasant production is inefficient, compared with modern large-scale agriculture, 'agribusiness', because the latter can farm a vast acreage with very little labour on the spot and can therefore undersell the peasant and drive him off the land. However, on the basis of a different method of calculation, taking into account the vast quantities of fossil fuels, manufactured fertiliser and machinery that 'agribusiness' needs to consume, there are those who maintain that peasant production is more efficient, ecologically and in the long term. I do not pretend to be able to decide this issue.

★   ★   ★   ★   ★   ★

We must formulate a definition of 'peasants', 'peasantry'. I have found the one given by Hilton (*EPLMA* 13) most illuminating, and my own follows it closely. He is prepared to accept the 'peasantry' as a useful category not only in connection with the period he is concerned with (roughly the century after the Black Death of 1347/8-51) but also as applying to peasants 'in other epochs than the Middle Ages and in other places than Western Europe'. The definition he proceeds to give is based on treating the peasantry as 'a class, determined by its place in the production of society's material needs, not as a status group determined by attributed esteem, dignity or honour' (*EPLMA* 12). That is precisely the way in which I wish to treat the ancient Greek peasantry. My definition, then, adapted from Hilton's, is as follows:

1. Peasants (mainly cultivators) possess, whether or not they own, the means of agricultural production by which they subsist; they provide their own maintenance from their own productive efforts, and collectively they produce more than is necessary for their own subsistence and reproduction.

2. They are not slaves (except in the rare case of the *servus quasi colonus*, dealt with in Section iii of this chapter) and are therefore not legally the property of others; they may or may not be serfs or bondsmen (within the definitions in III.iv above).

3. Their occupation of land may be under widely differing conditions: they may be freeholders, lessees (at a rent in money, kind or shares, and combined or not with labour services), or tenants at will.

4. They work their holdings essentially as family units, primarily with family labour, but occasionally with restricted use of slaves or wage-labour.

5. They are normally associated in larger units than the family alone, usually in villages.

6. Those ancillary workers (such as artisans, building and transport workers, and even fishermen) who originate from and remain among peasants may be considered as peasants themselves.

7. They support superimposed classes by which they are exploited to a greater or less degree, especially landlords, moneylenders, town-dwellers, and the organs of the State to which they belong, and in which they may or may not have political rights.

It will be seen that the peasantry, as I have defined them, partly overlap the categories of unfree labour which I have laid down in III.iv above: all serfs are peasants, and so are most agricultural bondsmen, but slaves are not – although the 'slave *colonus*' whom I describe in § 12 of Section iii below must be allowed for some purposes to count as a peasant. At their highest level, peasants begin to merge into my 'propertied class' (as defined in III.ii above); but in order to do so they must *exploit the labour of others* outside the family, by making use of slaves, serfs, or hired labourers, and as soon as they do that to any significant degree, and become able to live without being obliged to spend any substantial amount of their time working for their living, they cease, according to my definition, to count among peasants and must be treated as members of the propertied class. Only by exploiting the labour of others could a peasant family hope to rise into the propertied class.

One of the best analyses I know of a particular peasantry is that given by Engels in 1894 in an article entitled 'The peasant question in France and Germany'. (An English translation is included in *MESW* 623-40.) Engels knew much more about peasants at first hand than most academic historians. As he wrote in some travel notes late in 1848, he had 'spoken to hundreds of peasants in the most diverse regions of France' (*MECW* VII.522). In the article written in 1894 he distinguishes three broad groups of peasants, with one, the 'small' peasant, set apart qualitatively from the other two, and carefully defined as 'the owner or tenant – particularly the former – of a patch of land no bigger, as a rule, than he and his family can till, and no smaller than can sustain the family' (*MESW* 625). The other two groups, of 'big' and 'middle' peasants, are those who 'cannot manage without wage-workers' (637), whom they employ in different ways (624-5); the bigger ones go in for 'undisguised capitalist production' (638). It is roughly along these lines that I would divide ancient Greek peasants, although of course the labour which the 'big' and (to a less extent) the 'middle' peasant would employ in the Greek world would more often be that of slaves than of hired hands. It will be seen that clause 4 of the definition of peasants I have given above excludes Engels' 'big' peasants altogether: they are part of my 'propertied class', and my 'peasants' are mainly his 'small' ones, with some of the 'middle' variety.

Another analysis of a peasant situation which shows a deep understanding of its class constituents is that of William Hinton, in his remarkable book, *Fanshen. A Documentary of Revolution in a Chinese Village* (1966 and repr.). At the very outset of the Chinese revolution in each area it was necessary to break down the conformist assumptions generated in the minds of the peasants by centuries of landlord rule.[5] The ancient historian can find extraordinary interest in Hinton's description of a meeting held in January 1946 in Li Village Gulch to decide upon the nature of the agrarian reform to be undertaken in the Fifth District of Lucheng County in the Province of Shansi, which included the village of Long Bow, the particular object of Hinton's study. The main practical question to be decided was whether rent should continue to be paid to landlords. But the meeting opened with a consideration of certain fundamental questions, beginning with 'Who depends upon whom for a living?'. Many peasants assumed that of course it was they who depended upon the landlords: 'If the landlords did not let us rent the land,' they said, 'we would starve.' Many who had been driven by poverty to work as hired labourers for landlords were prepared to accept their situation as part of the natural order, provided they were not actually cheated but were fed and paid according to their contract. Gradually the peasants came to realise that it was the landlords who depended for a living upon them and their labour, and they grasped the fact that 'the exploitation inherent in land rent itself' was 'the root of all the other evils' (*Fanshen* 128-30). I may add that the criteria for analysing class status in the countryside, forming part of the Agrarian Reform Law of the Chinese People's Republic (and set out in Appendix C to Hinton's book, 623-6), are well worth studying: the categories recognised there are again defined primarily by the extent to which each individual exploits others or is himself exploited. When there is no one interested in opening the peasant's eyes to his oppressed condition, he will often accept it, whether with resignation or with resentment; and his lords, who would like to believe that he is perfectly contented, may even persuade themselves that he really is. When the Pearce Commission reported in 1972 that the majority of the African population of Rhodesia (now Zimbabwe), amounting to five or six million, refused to accept the sham constitutional reforms offered to them by the British Conservative government and Smith's Rhodesia Front, and designed to prolong the rule of the quarter of a million whites, the British and even more Smith and the Front were astounded. 'No one could henceforth believe that Smith governed with African support, or on any other basis than *force majeure*' (Robert Blake, *A History of Rhodesia* [1977] 405).

I do not wish to elaborate on the differences one could proceed to establish between ancient Greek and, for example, mediaeval English peasants. In doing this one would of course wish to introduce those varying political and legal characteristics which my definition, couched as it is primarily in economic and social terms, deliberately omits. Yet even then one must admit that the differences between various kinds of peasants inside the Greek world or within mediaeval England were in some important respects more significant than the differences at each corresponding level between the societies. I would suggest that the free English yeoman who held a small plot of land in free socage and the Athenian small peasant of the fifth or fourth century B.C. had more in common in some ways than the yeoman with the villein, or the Athenian with one of the abject villagers of Aphrodito in Egypt who grovelled before their local bigwig in a petition of A.D. 567, quoted later in this section.

It may be asked why I have singled out the peasantry as a class. The answer is that those I have defined as 'the propertied class' (or classes: see III.ii above) often derived part of their surplus, and sometimes a very substantial part, from peasants, either by direct and individual exploitation (principally through rent and interest) or in the mainly 'indirect and collective' way I have described in Section i above. In some places, at some periods, by far the greater part of a rich man's income might be derived from unfree labour; but even at the very time when we have most reason to expect precisely that situation, namely the Italy of the Late Republic, we find Domitius Ahenobarbus raising crews for seven ships in 49 B.C. from his 'slaves, freedmen and *coloni*', who are shortly afterwards referred to as his '*coloni* and *pastores*' (Caes., *BC* I. 34, 56); and some members of the propertied class, especially in the Later Roman Empire, derived much of their surplus from nominally free *coloni* rather than slaves (see Section iii of this chapter).

There might be very great variations – political and legal, as well as economic – in the condition of peasants over the vast area and the many centuries of my 'ancient Greek world'. In an independent Greek democracy which was its own master, the non-propertied classes would at least have a chance of reducing to a minimum any direct exploitation of themselves by the State on behalf of the propertied class (cf. II.iv above and V.ii below). Under an oligarchy they would be unable to defend themselves politically, and when they became subject to a Hellenistic king or to Rome they might find themselves taxed for the benefit of their master, and perhaps subjected to compulsory personal services as well. In the Greek East (see I.iii above) the peasantry derived little or no benefit from the costly theatres, baths, aqueducts, gymnasia and so forth which were provided for the enjoyment mainly of the more leisured section of the city population, partly out of local taxation and the rents of city lands, partly out of donations by the local notables, who of course drew the greater part of their wealth from their farms in the countryside (see III.ii-iii above), We can still think in terms of 'exploitation' of the 'small independent producer', even in cases where no particular individual appears in the capacity of direct exploiter (see Section i of this chapter).

Of course the great majority of our 'small independent producers' were what I am calling peasants. Some might be tempted to draw firm distinctions between a number of different types of peasant. Certainly in principle one can distinguish several categories even among the peasants, according to the forms of tenure by which they hold their land, for example:

1. Freeholders who had absolute ownership of their plots.

2. During the Hellenistic period, men who in practice were virtually absolute owners for the duration of their lives, but who held their land on condition of performing military service, and who could not transmit it directly to their heirs without the endorsement of the king. (In practice, such lots often became eventually equivalent to freeholds.)[6]

3. Tenants who either (*a*) held on lease, for their lives or (much more commonly) for a term of years (which might in practice be renewable at the option of one party or the other or both), or (*b*) were what English lawyers call

'tenants at will', subject at any time to the possibility of being ejected or of having their terms of occupation made more onerous (e.g. with a higher rent). These tenants, of either class, would fall into four broad groups, according to the nature of the landlord's return, which might be (i) a fixed rent in money, (ii) a fixed rent in kind, (iii) a share of the crop (the Roman *colonia partiaria*, modern *métayage* or share-cropping), or (iv) labour services. Combinations of these alternatives were of course possible: in principle, a share of the crop could be combined with a fixed rent in money or kind or both; a rent could be made payable partly in money and partly in produce at a predetermined price (as in *Dig.* XIX.ii.19.3); and labour services could be exacted in addition to rent in money or kind – although in point of fact there is surprisingly little evidence in ancient literature, legal texts, inscriptions or papyri for labour services on anything more than a very small scale (about six days a *year*) until we reach the sixth century, when a Ravenna papyrus speaks of several days' service a *week* on the 'home farm' in addition to rent in money (*P. Ital.* 3: see below). I will add only that in some cases payment of rent in money rather than kind might make things much more difficult for the tenant, who would be obliged to sell his crop in order to pay his rent, and might have problems where the crop could not easily be disposed of on the spot or at a nearby market.

This is a convenient place at which just to mention the form of leasehold tenure known as *emphyteusis*, under which land (usually uncultivated or derelict) was leased for a long term or in perpetuity at a low rent (often nominal at first).[7] But emphyteutic tenures, which became widespread in the Later Empire, from the fourth century onwards, raise very complicated problems of Roman law. In most cases the lessees would probably not be small peasants (but see the end of IV.iii n.50 below).

Some people might be tempted to say that peasants who hold their land in freehold, as absolute owners, 'must always have been' in a better position than leaseholders. I would concede that there is a small measure of truth in this, if we add, 'other circumstances being equal'; but as a generalisation it will not stand, as there were too many countervailing factors. In the first place, the properties of freehold peasants would often tend to become smaller by subdivision among sons and might well end up as units too small to work economically, whereas a landowner leasing out property could choose what size was most profitable (cf. Jones, *LRE* II.773-4). And in many circumstances – for instance, in areas with poor soil or subject to exceptionally high taxation, or after successive crop failures or devastation by enemy raids or maltreatment by government officials – a tenant might well suffer less than a freeholder, especially perhaps if the tenant was a share-cropper (*colonus partiarius*), and even more if his landlord was a powerful man who was willing to give him some protection. The freeholder's farm was a far more valuable piece of property than mere rented land and could therefore be used as a security for debt – and become subject to foreclosure on default. Debt was always the nightmare of the small freehold peasant, especially since the laws affecting defaulting debtors in antiquity (see under heading *III* of III.iv above) were often very harsh and might involve personal enslavement or at any rate some measure of bondage while the debt was being worked off – sometimes an indefinitely long process. Impoverished debtors sometimes agitated not only for a moratorium on interest payments or for limitation or reduction of the rate of interest (which could be very high), but for the total cancellation of all debts: in Greek, *chreōn apokopē*; in Latin, *novae tabulae*. This demand was sometimes supported by radical reformers in antiquity, and it was frequently joined with the advocacy of a general redistribution of land, *gēs anadasmos*, the other main plank in the platform of radicals on the political Left. (For recent works on both these phenomena see V.ii n.55 below.) In the Greek world there were two occasions in particular on which we happen to be quite well informed about these demands and the degree of success they achieved: at Athens in 594/3 B.C. the lawgiver Solon granted a complete cancellation of debt (known as his *seisachtheia*) but refused to redistribute the land (see V.i below and its n.27); and at Sparta in 243-242 B.C. King Agis IV procured a general cancellation of debts but was prevented from going on to the redistribution of land he had also planned (see V.ii n.55 below). Similar measures, and agitations for them, are recorded not only from the Greek world but also from the Near East, in particular the reform brought about in Judaea by the prophet Nehemiah, probably in the 440s B.C., described in Nehemiah V.1-13:[8] this provides the nearest parallel I know (even if not a very close one) to the debt-cancellations by Solon and Agis.

The possibility of foreclosure by a mortgagee and the consequent forfeiture of his land made the humble freeholder's position much less superior to that of the leasehold tenant than it might seem at first sight. And a tenant, the 'mere' tenant of a landlord, might have a weapon of sorts, if he and his neighbours could act in concert: the *anachōrēsis* or *secessio*, an 'exodus' which was essentially a strike, taking the form of a collective departure (preferably to a nearby temple where asylum could be claimed) and a refusal to resume work until grievances were remedied. The evidence comes largely from Hellenistic and Roman Egypt, where the practice was evidently common[9] and was resorted to even by the tenants of royal land, the 'king's peasants'. Tenants might indeed be able to draw some advantage from the fact that the landlord's interest (even if concentrated on exploiting them as much as possible) was not entirely hostile to their own, and they might actually receive some measure of protection from a powerful landlord, who might even be the Roman emperor himself, and who in any event might at least be willing, in his own interest, to try to prevent his tenants' efforts to cultivate the land from being thwarted by the depredations of officials or soldiers – always a terror to the peasantry in the Roman empire.

It is worth while to give a few examples of the plight of peasants, out of many possible ones, in the shape of four very well known inscriptions (texts and English translations of which are easily available),[10] recording the bitter complaints of peasants against ill-treatment by government officials. Three are in Greek, but I shall begin with one in Latin, the most famous, from the first years of the reign of Commodus (*c*.181), found at Souk el-Khmis in north Africa (modern Tunisia), and referring to the *saltus Burunitanus*, an imperial estate let out to head lessees, *conductores*, who had sub-let to small peasants, *coloni*. (Although this document relates to a Western area, far outside my 'Greek world', it has attracted so much attention and records such a characteristic situation that I think it well worth mentioning.) The inscription records a petition by the *coloni* to the emperor, complaining of collusive action to their detriment between their head lessee and the imperial procurator, who was responsible to the emperor for managing the estate. (This situation is likely to have been very common throughout the Greek and Roman world.) The *coloni*, describing themselves as 'most unhappy men' and 'poor rustics', object that more than the proper share of their crops and the prescribed number of days of labour services (six per year) have been exacted from them and that the procurator has sent in troops and had some of them seized, and tortured, fettered or flogged, simply because they had dared to make a complaint to the emperor. (R. M. Haywood, in Frank, *ESAR* IV.96-8, gives a text and English translation.)[11] The other three inscriptions all record petitions in Greek, to the first two of which are appended imperial replies in Latin. A petition (of A.D. 244-7) to the Emperor Philip from the villagers of Arague in the Tembris valley in Phrygia (in western Asia Minor), who describe themselves as 'the community [*koinon*] of the Aragueni' and as tenants of the emperor, mentions an earlier petition to the emperor before his accession, when he was praetorian prefect, and reminds him how deeply his divine soul had been troubled by their plight, although it appears that the only evidence they had for this touching disturbance of soul was that Philip had sent on their petition to the proconsul of Asia, who had done nothing (or at any rate, nothing effective) about it – they were still, they said, being plundered by rapacious officials and city magnates against whom they had no redress. (This inscription can conveniently be consulted in Frank, *ESAR* IV.659-61, where there is a text with English translation by T. R. S. Broughton.)[12] In another petition (of A.D. 238), from Scaptopara in Thrace to the Emperor Gordian III, the villagers, who seem to be freeholders, make a very similar complaint, adding, 'We can stand it no longer. We intend to leave our ancestral homes because of the violent conduct of those who come upon us. For in truth we have been reduced from many householders to a very few' (*IGBulg*. IV.2236; there is an English translation in Lewis and Reinhold, *RC* II.439-40).[13] Most interesting of all is an inscription from Aga Bey Köy, near the ancient Philadelphia in Lydia (in western Asia Minor), to be dated perhaps at the very beginning of the third century, in the reign of Septimius Severus. (There is a text with English translation by Broughton in Frank, *ESAR* IV.656-8.)[14] Here the peasants, who are tenants of an imperial estate, actually threaten that unless the emperor does something to stop the dreadful exactions and oppression by government officials from which they are suffering, they will desert their ancestral homes and tombs and go off to private land (*idiōtikē gē*) – in other words, become the tenants of some powerful landlord who can give them the protection they need, a practice we hear of as actually happening elsewhere, notably in mid-fifth-century Gaul, from the Christian priest Salvian (see below).

As between the various forms of tenancy, much would depend upon the terms of the individual letting. Rents in money or kind might be relatively high or low, labour services (if exacted) might differ widely, and share-cropping tenancies might vary a good deal in the division of the crop between landlord and tenant: half-and-half was common, but the landlord's share (often depending on the nature of the crop) might be as much as two-thirds and was hardly ever less than one-third. Perhaps share-cropping was preferable as a rule from the tenant's point of view, in bad times at any rate; but this would depend upon the shares allocated to each party, and these would naturally differ according to how much the landlord provided of the slaves, animals, tools, corn and other elements in what the Roman lawyers called the *instrumentum* (the equipment) of the farm (for which see § 18 of Section iii of this chapter). As the second-century jurist Gaius put it, 'The share-cropper [*colonus partiarius*] has a sort of partnership, and shares both profit and loss with his landlord' (*Dig.* XIX.ii.25.6). In the event of a near-total crop failure even the share-cropper, who would then have to give his landlord virtually nothing, would himself soon be left with nothing to eat, and he would be just as much at the mercy of his landlord, or some usurious lender, as any tenant who defaulted in payment of a fixed rent. In a moderately bad year the share-cropper's position, and whether or not he was driven to borrow from his landlord or a moneylender, would depend as much on the size of his plot as on the share of the crop he was allowed to keep – this is often overlooked.

I think that the most important factor in the peasant's position must often have been the labour situation in his locality – or, to be more precise, the supply of labour in relation to the area of cultivable land. Landlords needed labour to cultivate their lands. There is little evidence for hired labour on any considerable scale, except at harvest times, when it must have been very common; but it cannot have been available in large quantities at other times: see III.vi above, where I have also mentioned some texts which speak of neighbours helping each other out. If slaves were expensive or difficult to obtain (as they evidently were in at any rate some areas during the Principate and Later Empire), then there would be some competition among rich landlords for the services of tenants. Plagues, conscription, and the capture of agricultural workers by 'barbarian' raiders would naturally improve the situation of those who were left, as the Black Death improved the position of agricultural workers in fourteenth-century England. But as early as the beginning of the second century, long before the Graeco-Roman world began to suffer seriously from pestilences or major 'barbarian' invasions, we hear from Pliny the Younger of a scarcity of tenants on his estates in north Italy: see his *Ep.* VII.30.3 (*rarum est invenire idoneos conductores*), and III.19.7, where *penuria colonorum* must mean 'scarcity' and not 'poverty' of tenants[15] (cf. *raritas operariorum* in Pliny, *NH* XVIII.300). We also find Pliny making large reductions in his rents (IX.37.2) and contemplating more (X.8.5).

In an interesting article published in the *Journal of Peasant Studies* in 1976, Peter Garnsey advanced the view that 'the only substantial class of peasant proprietors for which there is documentary evidence in the late Empire consists of military men' (PARS 232). This I think needs qualification: it seems to be founded partly on the belief that in the fourth century assignations of land to veterans on discharge were 'tax-free' (ibid. 231). This is an appallingly difficult question; but since I accept the views of A.H.M. Jones on the matter of *iugatio/capitatio* (*RE* 280-92; *LRE* I.62-5, 451-4), I would regard the tax-exemption of the veteran as normally limited to the *capita* of himself and his wife (and his parents, if living), and not extending to their *iuga* of land (see esp. Jones, *RE* 284). And this was a purely personal privilege, not extending to children. The words 'easque *perpetuo* habeant immunes' in *CTh* VII.xx.3.*pr.* must refer only to the lifetime of the veteran (cf. Ulpian, in *Dig.* L.xv.3.1): I see nothing in *CTh* VII.xx to contradict this, and there is no trace of further privilege for veterans' sons in *CTh* VII.xxii or elsewhere – indeed, during the fourth century the sons were expected to serve in the army. But on these questions I do not wish to seem dogmatic.

★   ★   ★   ★   ★   ★

I turn now to a brief consideration of *labour rents*, an expression I use for convenience for those *labour services due regularly* under the terms of a tenancy instead of, or as a supplement to, rent in money or kind. (Labour *services*, as I use that expression, could include not only the regular labour *rents* I am considering here but also labour demanded *occasionally* from tenants, whether legitimately or not, and resembling the *angariae* which I have referred to elsewhere, especially in I.iii above.) Labour rents seem to have played a surprisingly small part in the Greek and Roman world. I say 'seem to have played', because it is just possible, although in my opinion unlikely, that labour rents were in reality far more widespread than our surviving evidence suggests. As far as I know, only one writer in recent times, John Percival, has seriously examined this difficult question and suggested that labour rents may have been a great deal more common than most of us suppose.[16] I have nothing new to contribute to the discussion, and I can do no more here than state the position as it is generally known.

Only in a mid-sixth-century Latin papyrus from Ravenna, dealing with an estate belonging to the Church of Ravenna, do we find labour rents exacted on a scale resembling the situation in many mediaeval manors, up to three days per week (*P. Ital.* 3, I.3.2-7). Apart from a few texts which may or may not refer to labour rents,[17] it is only in three of a well-known set of African inscriptions of the second and early third centuries that labour rents figure prominently, and here they are on a very much smaller scale: in two of these inscriptions the tenants have to perform six days' labour per year (two days at each of the seasons of ploughing, harvesting and hoeing), and in the third (and most fragmentary) their obligation is apparently to supply twelve days' labour per year (four days on each of the same three occasions).[18] It is of course only for the benefit of a landlord's 'demesne' or 'home farm' that labour rents are desirable, and it looks as if it was rare in the Greek and Roman world for such a holding to exist, surrounded by farms let to peasants whose labour is utilised.[19] I agree with A. H. M. Jones that the institution of labour rents was 'relatively rare' in the Later Empire (*LRE* II.805-6), and I believe that the same is true of the Principate, although a few days' service each year, as revealed by the African inscriptions I have just mentioned, may well have been exacted much more often than our evidence reveals.

★   ★   ★   ★   ★   ★

A thorough investigation is needed of the ways in which agricultural production was organised in the various parts of the Graeco-Roman world. I believe that the best way of approaching this subject is through the forms of land tenure, always with the primary aim of discovering *how exploitation was effected*, and to what extent – a point of view which has all too often been absent from modern work in this field. A vast amount of evidence is available, not only from inscriptions and papyri and the legal and literary sources (including among the last the ecclesiastical ones), but also from archaeology, although those who have done the actual excavating have too seldom been interested in the kind of problem

I have in mind. Since there is a great deal of material in legal texts, especially the *Digest*, the co-operation of Roman lawyers should be particularly helpful. (I hope to pursue this undertaking with the aid of some Oxford colleagues and pupils.) In any such research it is desirable to employ, for comparative purposes, some of the ample evidence about mediaeval and modern peasantries which historians have collected about individual societies, commonly without regard for wider sociological issues, and in which sociologists have recently become very interested, often (as I said at the beginning of this section) with an insufficiently historical approach. But the main desideratum is a concentration upon the precise conditions in each individual area at different periods: only upon the basis of a whole series of regional analyses can any secure general conclusions be arrived at. Such studies have certainly begun here and there,[20] but all too rarely has sufficient attention been paid to the type and degree of exploitation involved – to the class struggle, in fact.

I should like to mention at this point a series of passages in which Marx dealt with the question of rent: I have listed in a note[21] a few I happen to have come across. Some of these apply specifically to rents within a capitalist system, governed by an economy very different from that which we find in the ancient world; but some are of general significance.

*   *   *   *   *   *

In I.iii above I referred to some evidence suggesting that in the Roman empire the mainly city-dwelling class of landowners was able to exploit the peasantry and appropriate their products more completely and ruthlessly than most landlords have succeeded in doing – so much so that during famines it was often the cities alone in which food was available, rather than the country districts in which it was grown. I quoted a horrifying description by Galen of the effects of several years of famine in what must be the countryside of Pergamum, and a description by Philostratus of how on one occasion of dearth the landowners had got possession of all available grain, which they intended to export, leaving no food but vetches for sale on the market. We hear occasionally of intervention by the authorities to prevent this kind of profit-making from exceeding all bounds and driving many poor people to starvation. Among the best-known examples is one from Pisidian Antioch in the early nineties of the first century, where an inscription has revealed that the govenor, L. Antistius Rusticus, intervening at the request of the city magistrates, ordered everyone to declare how much grain he had, and forbade charging more than 1 denarius for each modius – twice the ordinary price (A/J 65a = *AE* [1925] 126*b*).[22] I also alluded in I.iii above to the fact that many times between the mid-fourth century and the mid-sixth we hear of peasants flocking into the nearest city during a famine, in order to obtain edible food, available there and nowhere else. I shall now give seven examples of this situation about which we happen to have some reasonably reliable information.

1. In 362-3 there occurred in the area of Antioch on the Orontes a famine about which we have perhaps more information than any other in antiquity.[23] Its cause was partly harvest failure in Syria, partly the arrival at Antioch in July 362 of the emperor and his court and part of his army, preparatory to the disastrous Persian expedition of March 363. Our sources here include some good contemporary ones: above all the Emperor Julian (who was present in person),

the orator Libanius (a leading citizen of Antioch), and the great historian Ammianus Marcellinus, in whose narrative one particular passage, XXII.xiv.1-2, is especially fascinating for its condemnation of Julian's attempt to fix maximum prices, in terms that would commend it to most contemporary Western economists. The influx of country folk is mentioned by Julian himself (*Misopogon* 369cd). On this occasion, as on others, there is evidence that the local landowners callously hoarded grain for sale at inflated prices; and when Julian arranged for some special imports, from Chalcis and Hierapolis and even Egypt, and fixed a low price, they bought up the grain cheap and either hoarded it or sold it at a profit in the countryside where Julian's maximum price could more easily be evaded.

2. A few years later, probably in 373, we hear from Sozomen and Palladius of a famine in Mesopotamia, in Edessa and its neighbourhood, when the starving poor, tended by the famous ascetic Ephraim (who induced the rich to disgorge), included people from the surrounding countryside.[24]

3. During a severe food shortage at Rome, perhaps in 376,[25] there was a general demand for the expulsion from the city of all *peregrini*, which in this context means all those whose official domicile was not actually Rome itself; and it is clear from our one account of this incident, in St. Ambrose, *De offic. ministr.* III.(vii).45-51, that numbers of country folk would have been involved (see esp. §§ 46,47). Ambrose puts into the mouth of the City Prefect of the time an eloquent speech, addressed to 'the men of rank and wealth' (*honorati et locupletiores viri*), pointing out that if they allow their agricultural producers to die of starvation, the result will be fatal to their corn supply – a piece of evidence that an appreciable part of the corn supply of the city still came from the neighbouring country districts. The speech goes on to say that if they are deprived of their peasants, they will have to buy cultivators – slaves, of course – to replace them, and that will cost them more! A subscription is raised, corn is purchased, and the situation is saved.

4. Shortly afterwards, probably during the urban prefecture of the orator Symmachus in 384,[26] there was another food shortage at Rome, and all *peregrini* were duly expelled. It is clear from the passage I quoted in the preceding paragraph from St. Ambrose (§§ 49,51) that many country people were driven out. The saint expresses great indignation that the Romans should eject the very people who provide their sustenance.

5. There was another famine in 384-5 at Antioch, where the supply of corn had been deficient for a couple of years. A speech of Libanius mentions that the country people had come into the city to obtain food because there was none in the countryside (*Orat.* XXVII.6,14).[27]

6. There was a serious famine at Edessa in 500-1, caused by a terrible plague of locusts in March 500. There is an account of this famine in §§ 38-44 of the very interesting *Chronicle* (surviving only in Syriac) written probably *c.* 507 by the ascetic generally known today as Joshua the Stylite, who at many points in his work gives precise figures for grain and other prices, and does so in this case.[28] Joshua twice mentions the crowds of peasants who came into Edessa to procure food (§§ 38,40).

7. In the Ostrogothic kingdom of Italy, in 536-8, grain from the state granaries at Ticinum and Dertona was sold to the starving people of Liguria, and a third of the stores in the warehouses of Tarvisium and Tridentum was also sold to the inhabitants of Venetia. (Both Liguria and Venetia had been ravaged by the Alamanni.) The first of the three relevant letters in the collection of Cassiodorus (*Var.* X.27; XII.27, 28), giving orders for the opening of the granaries, remarks that it would be shameful for the cultivators to starve while the royal barns were full.[29] Again, the exploitation of the peasantry had been severe and effective.

There are some other examples of state granaries plentifully filled with corn while many starved, as in Rome during the siege by Totila and the Ostrogoths in 546, when famine conditions prevailed in the city. The only ample supply was in the hands of Bessas the Roman commander, who made a large personal profit by selling to the rich at the exorbitant price of 7 solidi for the modius, while first the poor and eventually almost everyone, we are told, fed on boiled nettles, many dying of starvation. Bessas continued to profit from selling grain to the rich, until in December 546 Totila suddenly captured the city, and Bessas' ill-gotten gains fell into his hands.[30]

I imagine that large distributions of food by rich men who were charitably inclined were unknown (see my ECAPS 24-5 ff.) until at least the fourth century, when many of the wealthy were converted to Christianity; and even from then onwards they are likely to have been very rare. The only actual example I have discovered is beyond the scope of this book: Luke, the future stylite saint, is said to have distributed 4,000 modii of corn (as well as animal-fodder) to the starving poor from his parents' granaries in Phrygia, probably during the great famine of 927-8 (*Vita S. Lucae Styl.* 7).[31]

The landowner who was more prosperous than the 'peasant' (as I have defined him: see above) would find it easier to take the advice of Hesiod and lay up an ample store of corn (*WD* 30-2). Ausonius, writing over a thousand years after Hesiod, remarks that he always laid in two years' supply of produce: without this, he says, hunger is near (*De hered.* 27-8).

* * * * * *

The characteristic unit in which peasant life was organised was the village, the most common Greek word for which was *kōmē*.[32] Of these *kōmai*, many were situated inside the territory of some city; and some belonged to a handful of absentee landlords, or even entirely to a single proprietor, to whom the villagers paid rents. On the other hand, there were also villages of freehold peasant proprietors. It is impossible to form any idea of the proportion of villagers who were freeholders at any time or in any area of the Greek (or Roman) world, except at certain periods in parts of Egypt from which useful papyrological evidence happens to have survived. The bibliography is vast,[33] and I cannot attempt to give even a summary account, since many important questions are still in dispute, and on some issues I have not yet made up my own mind. I shall confine myself here to a few remarks, mainly about peasant villages in the Later Roman Empire.

Some villages, at least in Syria and Asia Minor, had what appears to have been a democratic form of organisation, headed by a general meeting of the villagers; and – strange as it may seem – it looks as if this democratic form of organisation may actually have survived in some villages, in parts of Syria at any rate, after all the genuinely democratic elements had perished from the constitutions of the cities throughout the empire (see Jones, *GCAJ* 272).[34] The villages had magistrates of their own, sometimes no doubt hereditary, but often elected. (The usual term for the 'head man' of a village, *kōmarchos*, turns up in relation to Armenia under Persian rule as early as 400 B.C. in Xenophon's account of the northward march of the 'ten thousand' across the interior of Asia Minor: Xen., *Anab.* IV.v.10, and 24 to vi.3.) Some of them certainly had a general meeting of villagers which passed decrees like the Assembly of a city: this is referred to in inscriptions by a variety of terms, including the *kōmē*, those *apo (tēs) kōmēs*, the *kōmētai*, the *koinon tēs kōmēs*, the *dēmos* or *ekklēsia* or *syllogos* or *synodos*, or even the *ochlos*.[35] (The last is rather surprising as an official term, for it had often been used in earlier times in a pejorative sense, to refer to the 'rabble'!) I agree with Jones, against some other scholars, that a council (*boulē*) was the distinguishing mark of a city and is not found in villages,[36] which, however, sometimes had a council of elders, called a *gerousia*,[37] as of course did many cities. Virtually all our information about village administration comes from inscriptions and is very different to interpret; in particular it is often hard to date the inscriptions. All I can do here is to express the hope that further research will be conducted in this field, in particular (as I said above) with a view to discovering how and to what extent exploitation of the village population was effected. The appearance and the unexpectedly long survival of democratic organisation within the villages is a topic which would also be particularly well worth studying. The development of villages into cities, a not uncommon event, is one of the aspects of village history which has already received a good deal of attention.

In the Later Empire, with which I am now mainly concerned, taxation bore very heavily upon the villages, the great majority of which paid their taxes to collectors appointed by the local city. But in the fourth century some of the bigger landlords (*potentiores possessores*, *CTh* XI.vii.12) acquired the valuable privilege of *autopragia*: the right to pay their taxes (or at least a considerable part of them) direct to the provincial governor; and they would then be responsible for collecting the taxes due from their tenants. The earliest evidence I have come across of this practice consists of three imperial constitutions, of 383, 399 or 400, and 409 (*CTh* XI.vii.12 and 15; and xxii.4); the last of these uses language suggesting that the practice was already widespread (*quae vulgo autopractorium vocatur*), and in the fifth and sixth centuries it may have done much to increase the power of the great men.[38] During the fifth century the right of *autopragia* was extended to certain villages – how many, we cannot say: only one (as far as I know) can be identified with certainty, Aphrodite (later Aphrodito) in the nome of Antaeopolis in the Thebaid (Upper Egypt), about the affairs of which in the sixth century we happen to be exceptionally well informed.[39]

Now we must not assume that an 'autopract' village (one enjoying the right of *autopragia*) would necessarily be in a better position than one inhabited by the tenants of one or more landowners, at any rate if the latter were men of influence, able to protect their own *coloni*. Some of the great men seem to have resented the grant of *autopragia* to villages, and their hostility might be more effective than the always precarious rights enjoyed in theory by villagers. The need for even an autopract village to adopt the most abject and grovelling attitude towards important officials is worth illustrating, in a historical perspective.

It will surprise no one to find a humble individual tenant in sixth-century Egypt addressing a petition to his landlord, the wealthy and powerful Apion, in the most submissive and cringing terms:

> To my good master, lover of Christ, lover of the poor, all-esteemed and most magnificent Patrician and Duke of the Thebaid, Apion, from Anoup, your miserable slave [*doulos*] upon your estate called Phacra (*P. Oxy.* I.130).

That is the way in which any *colonus* in the Later Roman Empire might find it prudent to address a great and powerful man, and it must not be assumed that only native Egyptians would be likely to address their superiors in such terms: it is simply that Egypt is the one area from which papyri survive, recording petitions of such a kind. Indeed, as Sir Harold Bell has remarked (*EAGAC* 125), there is a striking contrast between petitions like that of Anoup and earlier Egyptian ones of the Ptolemaic period, like one which he quotes, from a minor village official, of the year 243 B.C., preserved in *P. Hibeh* 34:

> To King Ptolemy, greeting, from Antigonus. I am being unjustly treated by Patron, the superintendent of police in the lower toparchy.

And Bell comments, 'It is a minor official in a village of Middle Egypt petitioning the all-powerful King Ptolemy III Euergetes; yet he addresses the king without servility or verbiage, as man to man.' I will add another petition, of 220 B.C., from an even more humble person, a working woman:

> To King Ptolemy [IV Philopator], greeting from Philista, daughter of Lysias, resident in Tricomia [a village in the Fayum]. I am wronged by Petechon. For as I was bathing in the baths of the said village, and had stepped out to soap myself, he, being the bathman in the women's rotunda and having brought in the jugs of hot water, emptied one(?) over me and scalded my belly and my left thigh down to the knee, so that my life was in danger . . . I beg you, O king, if it please you, as a suppliant who has sought your protection, not to suffer me, a woman who works with her hands, to be thus lawlessly treated

– and so forth (Hunt and Edgar, *SP* II no.269 = *P. Enteuxis* 82 = *P. Magd.* 33).

Let us now go forward again nearly eight hundred years and return to the mid-sixth century of the Christian era, to look at a petition from the village of Aphrodito (mentioned above), dated A.D. 567, which is the subject of a most instructive discussion by Bell (*EVAJ*), and has also been studied by other scholars (see n.39 again). The submissive and even servile attitude of the villagers would have been unthinkable in a petition made by a city at any period of Graeco-Roman antiquity. It is true that the petition was drafted by one Dioscorus, son of Apollōs, a notary and man of affairs who had unfortunate literary pretensions and 'achieved the distinction, for what it was worth, of being the worst Greek poet whose works have come down to us' (Bell, *EAGAC* 127-8).[40] But such a person should have known exactly the right language to use to a great man.

> To Flavius Triadius Marianus Michael Gabriel Constantine Theodore Martyrius Julian Athanasius, the most renowned general and consular and most magnificent Patrician of the Prefect Justin, Duke and Augustal of the Thebaid for the second year. Petition and supplication from your most pitiable slaves,[41] the wretched small-owners and inhabitants of the all-miserable village of Aphrodito, which is under the Sacred

Household and your magnificent authority. All justice and just dealing for ever illuminate the proceedings of your pre-eminently excellent and magnificent authority, which we have long expected as the dead in Hades once awaited the coming of the Christ, the everlasting God. For after him, our master God, the Saviour, the Helper, the true and merciful Benefactor, we set all our hopes of salvation upon your Highness, who are among all men praised and bruited abroad, to help us in all our emergencies, to deliver us from the assault of unjust men, and to snatch us out of the unspeakable sufferings, such as no paper can contain, which have from the beginning befallen us at the hands of Menas, the most illustrious *scriniarius* and pagarch of Antaeopolis. We humbly recall your all-wise, most famous and good-loving intelligence, but it reaches such a height of wisdom and comprehension (beyond the limited range of words to express) as to grasp the whole with complete knowledge and amendment [the sense is a trifle obscure here]; whence without fear we are come to grovel in the track of your immaculate footsteps and inform you of the state of our affairs

– which the villagers then at last proceed to do (*P. Cairo Masp*. I.67002, in Bell's translation, EVAJ 33; cf. *EAGAC* 126).

As this complaint was directed against misbehaviour by the pagarch (the imperial official in charge of the area, under the provincial governor), it is relevant to recall that in an imperial rescript to the *dux* (the military governor) of the Thebaid, as a result of a complaint from the very same village some sixteen years earlier (*c*. 551), Justinian had remarked of the then pagarch Theodosius that 'his intrigues [*peridromē*] proved stronger than our commands'! (*P. Cairo Masp*. I.67024.15-16). I have much more to say about misconduct by Roman officials in VIII.iv below.

I can do no more than just mention here two very interesting forms of rural patronage, which were more formalised than the innumerable resorts we come across in Later Roman sources to that form of protection, often involving what is called 'suffragium' (see my SVP, esp. 45). One of these two types of rural patronage appears in the second half of the fourth century and the fifth, partly as a result of the growth under Diocletian and Constantine and their successors of the practice of giving the military command in a particular area (a province, or more usually a group of provinces) to an individual separate from the provincial governors and known as the *dux*. This division of authority was cleverly utilised and turned into a weapon of class struggle by many peasants, at least in Egypt and Syria (from which all our evidence comes): groups of peasants, and sometimes whole villages collectively, placed themselves under the patronage of their *dux* (or some other powerful man), and with his help – sometimes involving the use of his soldiers – resisted demands made upon them for rent or taxes or both. This practice was resorted to by peasant freeholders as well as by tenant farmers, *coloni*. Both could use it against tax collectors (usually decurions and their agents, who were responsible to the provincial governor; cf. VIII.ii-iv below), and tenants in addition against their landlord and his rent collectors. How effective this device could be in both cases is well illustrated by Libanius' *Oration* XLVII, *De patrociniis*, and by a series of imperial laws fulminating against such practices (*CTh* XI.xxiv; *CJ* XI.liv).[42] Unfortunately for the peasants, the patronage of a great man was not something that could be acquired for nothing, and the wretched creatures may often have had to pay dearly for it. In the East, though apparently not in the Western part of the empire (see Jones, *LRE* II.775 ff., at 777-8), the government legislated against patronage and threatened to inflict heavy penalties on the patrons concerned (see *CTh* XI.xxiv.2 ff.; *CJ* XI.liv.1-2). The second of my two developed forms of rural patronage appears most clearly in Salvian, a Gallic priest writing in the second quarter of the fifth century. Here we see something that makes us think of what was to occur in many places during the Middle Ages: peasant freeholders threatened by extortionate taxation (on which Salvian lays most stress), or by barbarian incursions, surrendered themselves to some great neighbour, who could give them protection – of course, at the cost of their land, which was ceded to the patron, the peasants becoming his *coloni* (*De gubernat. Dei* V.38-45). Both types of patronage I have been describing could involve a heavy price. However, some peasants evidently thought the price worth paying, as a protection against even more burdensome exactions. The patronate, oppressive as it must often have been, seemed to many desperate men better than unprotected freedom (especially dangerous to freeholders), accompanied by the unchecked activities of the dreaded finance officials, soldiers, billeting officers, and those who imposed compulsory labour. (I shall return in Chapter VIII below, Sections iii and iv, to the exploitation of the peasantry in the Greek world in the Later Roman Empire.)

Outright land-grabbing by the powerful at the expense of the humble, whether as a result of direct appropriation or of foreclosure on what we should call mortgage, is a phenomenon that can be seen from time to time, but is not the sort of thing of which our sources take much notice. Except in those Greek democracies where the poor man could obtain effective protection from the courts of law (cf. V.ii-iii below), the process must have gone on throughout antiquity. Administrators of ecclesiastical property were no exception: a letter of Pope Gregory the Great to the *rectores* of the estates of the Roman Church in Sicily in 591 orders the restitution of 'the properties of others which had been seized by Church administrators' (*de rebus alienis ab ecclesiasticiis defensoribus occupatis*: *Ep*. I.39a, § II). Such ecclesiastical administrators might also subject hapless *coloni* to severe exploitation and unjust treatment, from which only the bishop could save them, if he cared to exercise his authority in the cause of mercy, or even justice. Cheating tenants by the use of fraudulent measures was very common. In A.D. 603 we find Pope Gregory writing to a notary, Pantaleo, of his indignation at the discovery that certain *coloni Ecclesiae* had been obliged to hand over their produce according to a *modius*-measure containing no fewer than 25 *sextarii* instead of the proper 16: he expresses his pleasure at the news that Pantaleo has now broken up the iniquitous measure 'et iustum fecisse' (*Ep*. XIII.37). It would be interesting to know how many *sextarii* the new 'modius iustus' contained, in view of Gregory's order, in another letter (to Peter, a Sicilian subdeacon, *Ep*. I.42), that the *rustici Ecclesiae* were not to be compelled to hand over their produce according to a *modius*-measure containing more than 18 *sextarii*! Again, the charming *Life of St. Theodore of Sykeon* (an almost exact contemporary of Pope Gregory) describes how the peasants of the estates of the Church of Anastasiopolis in Galatia were constantly harried by Theodosius, a leading man of the city who had been appointed chief administrator of the Church lands, to the point at which they were driven to resist him by force. St. Theodore, now bishop of Anastasiopolis (in the last years of the sixth century), threatened to sack Theodosius, who persisted strenuously until he was persuaded to yield obedience to his bishop, by one of those miracles which are more frequent in the hagiography of the Early Church than they are likely to have been in reality.[43] One other document is worth quoting here, although it relates to a private estate and not to Church property: it is a letter written by St. Augustine (*Ep.* 247), in sorrow and anger, to a landowner who was one of his flock, rebuking him for allowing his agents (*actores*) to oppress his tenants (*coloni*, § 1; *rusticani homines*, § 3), apparently by extracting their rents twice over. Augustine refers repeatedly to the tenants as 'poor and needy men' (*miseri et pauperes . . . , miseri et egeni homines*, § 1; *homines miseri*, § 4). I will only add a reference to a famous passage from a sermon by St. John Chrysostom, of which there is a convenient translation in C. E. Stevens's chapter in *CEHE* I².123–4: this illustrates vividly the merciless treatment of their peasants by the landowners of Antioch.[44]

(iii)
From slave to *colonus*

In this book I have singled out a propertied class in the ancient Greek world the members of which were leisured, in the sense that they were not obliged to devote themselves to the labour of providing for their own sustenance to any appreciable degree, even if they sometimes occupied themselves for short periods in the productive process in a supervisory capacity (see III.ii–iii above). I have also emphasised more than once that such a propertied class can exist only if its members exploit the labour of others, whether as unfree labour or as wage-labour, to the extent necessary to provide themselves with a surplus sufficient to support their leisured existence. I have argued (in II.iii and III.iv above) that we may speak of the Greek (and Roman) world as (in a loose sense) a 'slave economy' or 'slave-owning society', because the propertied class derived the bulk of its surplus from unfree labour, mainly that of slaves, although various forms of what we may properly call serfdom were also known, and debt bondage too was widespread (see III.iv above). In thus characterising the ancient Greek world loosely as a 'slave economy', however, I have not ignored the fact that there were always large numbers of free men and women, mainly peasants, living not much above the subsistence level, who were exploited by the ruling class to a greater or less degree, to some extent individually and directly (the leasehold tenant by his landlord and the freeholder by his mortgagee, for example), but partly through what I have called 'indirect and collective' forms of exploitation, such as taxation, military conscription, and compulsory services (see Sections i and ii of this chapter).

I have now to discuss the important change which came over the Graeco-Roman world by slow degrees during the first three centuries of the Christian era: a change in *the forms of exploitation*, involving no sudden or radical alteration until the end of the third century but a slow progression, in very varying degrees and at very different speeds in different areas. The subject is extraordinarily complicated and difficult, and every assertion, if it is to be strictly accurate, needs to be hedged about with qualifications. But I have no space here to give anything like a full-scale account, and I propose to plunge straight into the heart of the matter and make a series of statements designed to convey the essentials of the process I have in mind, without many of the qualifications which are ideally necessary. 'Those who are unfamiliar with the mass of literature dealing with the vexed question of the origin of the "colonate" heaped up by the industry and ingenuity of scholars since the time of Savigny will probably turn with impatience from a fresh attempt to give a satisfactory answer', said Henry Francis Pelham in his Inaugural Lecture as Camden Professor of Ancient History at Oxford, as long ago as 1890: see Pelham's *Essays* [on the spine: *Essays on Roman History*] (1911) 275. I wish to emphasise that what follows is an oversimplification, and that there were far more differences (above all in the rate of change) between areas than I am able to bring out here. I hope to be able to deal with the subject in a more satisfactory way in a few years' time. To make cross-referencing easier, I shall proceed by numbered paragraphs.

★   ★   ★   ★   ★   ★

1. We know all too little of the details of the economy of the vast majority of Greek states in the Classical period, to which I must go back for a moment. At that time, at Athens and most of the other leading states of which we know anything, it was slaves principally who provided the propertied class with its surplus (see III.iv above and Appendix II below); but purely local varieties of serfdom existed here and there (especially the Helots of the Spartan area and the Thessalian Penestai), and free peasants also contributed, more especially no doubt in non-democratic cities, where the poor man would have far less chance of protecting himself against the depredations of the powerful and could more easily be exploited by the ruling class (see II.iv above and V.ii-iii below). Now the most extraordinary fact about Greek (and Roman) slaves is their cheapness:[1] in particular, at Athens, one could apparently buy an average slave in the late fifth century (and probably most of the fourth) for 200 drachmae or less – not much more than half what an artisan would earn in a year. Later, prices were not nearly so low. The comparison with American slaves in the Old South before the Civil War (about whom, of all slave populations, we know most) is astounding: in the first six decades of the nineteenth century 'prime farm hands' could be sold for several hundred dollars, going up in the 1850s to not far short of $2,000; and a skilled artisan such as a blacksmith could fetch $2,500. Agricultural slaves were commonly hired out, over the year, at between ten and twenty per cent of their market value, artisans often at 25 per cent (Stampp, *PI* 414-18). At the same period the annual cost of feeding a slave could be put at between $7.50 and $15.00; and the total yearly cost of maintaining him 'seldom exceeded $35.00, and was often considerably less than this' (ibid. 406-7). The fact that mid-nineteenth-century American slaves were relatively many times as costly to buy as fifth/fourth-century Athenian ones was of course due primarily to the large and expanding foreign market for American cotton. (For the remarkable growth in the world demand for cotton between 1820 and 1860, and its important effects on the economy of the Old South, see esp. Gavin Wright, as cited in n.8 below.)

The great majority of Greek slaves in the Classical period were imported 'barbarians', among whom Thracians were particularly prominent.

2. In those parts of Asia Minor and Syria which were brought into the Greek world from the late fourth century onwards, with the conquests of Alexander and the many city-foundations of that monarch and his successors, slavery already existed; but the institution was not nearly as developed as in the Greek

world, and it seems likely that a far larger place was occupied than in Old Greece by other forms of exploitation: occasionally outright serfdom and debt bondage, but also exploitation of free or semi-free peasants through rent and tributary payments and a variety of compulsory services: *angariae* and the like (see I.iii above). I see no reason why the process which had begun in the Hellenistic period should not have continued in these eastern districts when they became Roman provinces – sometimes after periods as 'client kingdoms', a condition which was very likely to increase the grip of the propertied classes on the peasantry. Even if actual serfdom steadily receded in the Hellenistic and Roman periods (as I have argued it did: see III.iv above), the increased exploita- tion of the peasantry which would be the necessary result of Roman tribute and other new exactions (including the often large profits made by provincial governors and their staffs, and Roman or local tax-farmers) must have driven some small peasants into outright slavery or debt-bondage and converted others from freeholders into tenants or landless labourers, some of whom might tend to drift into the towns. The Greek propertied classes certainly went on drawing considerable profits from the peasantry in rents, taxes and services, even if many of them were made to disgorge part of these profits for the benefit of the Romans. Greeks and Romans coming to Asia who were accustomed to employ slave labour at home would naturally make use of it in their new abodes, except perhaps where a native population was already by custom subjected to very severe exploitation, thereby making it hardly worth while to import slave labour. There seem to be no figures from Asia for large slave households to equal the 200 slaves and freedmen ascribed to Python of Abdera in Thrace in 170 B.C. by Diodorus XXX.6 – a figure which (for what it is worth) presumably includes only male slaves of military age, for they are said to have taken part in defending the city against the Romans.

Egypt, Ptolemaic and Roman, is a special case: here chattel slavery never seems to have played a very important role in production, at least agricultural production; but the peasants, who formed the vast majority of the population, were apparently in a very subject condition and, although they were technically not slaves and most of them could not be described strictly as serfs, many of them seem to have been in a condition near to serfdom (see III.iv above). The general impression we derive is that much labour in Egypt was not fully free. The very fact that there was relatively little chattel slavery is likely to have necessitated a higher degree of exploitation of the humbler free men.

3. In the late Roman Republic a series of foreign wars and civil wars provided an ample supply of cheap slaves for the Mediterranean slave markets: the Greek island of Delos in particular was such a market, and we are told by Strabo, probably with much exaggeration, that 'tens of thousands of slaves' could be imported there and exported again on the same day (XIV.v.2, p.668). With the beginning of the Augustan Principate (*c*.30 B.C.) and the relative peace that followed, from the reign of Tiberius (14–37) onwards, the number of slaves that were simply *appropriated from outside the Graeco-Roman economy, or brought within it by purchase at very cheap rates*, soon began to decline, even if from time to time an occasional slave-haul either brought in a new batch of 'barbarian' captives or (as on the suppression of the Jewish revolt in A.D. 70) reduced to slavery men

who had previously been Roman subjects of free status. The Graeco-Roman world certainly acted as a magnet, attracting to itself anyone capable of work who was enslaved or captured in war in a neighbouring area. Thus we hear from Tacitus of an auxiliary Roman cohort of German Usipi who, after being sent to Britain, mutinied in 83 and went off on a piratical expedition around the island (during which they even resorted to cannibalism), but were eventually captured on the north coast of Europe, 'sold to traders, and after passing though the hands of various masters, were brought across to the left bank of the Rhine', thus entering the Roman world as slaves (Tac., *Agric.* 28, esp. § 5: 'per commercia venumdati et in nostram usque ripam mutatione ementium adducti').

4. There had always been some breeding of slaves, even in Italy as well as in the Greek areas. The author of the Pseudo-Aristotelian *Oeconomica* I (5, 1344^{b}17-18) had actually advised allowing slaves to breed, but for him the usefulness of the practice lay in the fact that it was a means of providing hostages from the slaves themselves, in the form of their children! Similarly, planters in the American Old South 'did everything possible to encourage the slaves to live together in stable units; they realised that a man was easier to control if he had a wife and children to worry about' (Genovese, *RB* 12).

I know of no decisive proof that after the fifth and fourth centuries B.C. the breeding of slaves in the Greek area began to play a steadily increasing role; but that is the inference I would draw from the scanty evidence, which includes more frequent references to home-bred slaves (most usually *oikogeneis,* Latin *vernae*). The best piece of evidence I know is that of the Delphic manumission inscriptions,[2] as analysed by Westermann, *SSGRA* 31-3. (I have not been able to make a fresh analysis, taking into account some inscriptions published after the appearance of Westermann's book in 1955;[2a] and having regard to the serious unreliability of that book at many points[3] I would emphasise that the figures given here should be treated as approximate only.) If, with Westermann, we separate these inscriptions into three groups, covering roughly half a century each, namely 201-153 B.C, 153- *c.*100 B.C., and *c.*100- *c.*53 B.C., we find a marked increase in the proportion of home-bred slaves in the second group (153- *c.*100) as compared with the first, and a further increase in that proportion in the third group (*c.*100 - *c.*53) as compared with the second. I will give the figures for home-bred slaves for each period, for what they are worth, first as a percentage of those manumitted slaves in their group whose origins (as home-bred or not) are known, and then, in brackets, as a percentage of all manumitted slaves in their group (including those of whose origin nothing is known):

(1) B.C. 201-153: 32% (13%)
(2) B.C. 153- *c.*100: 63% (47%)
(3) B.C. *c.*100 - *c.*53: 89% (51%).

On the basis of these figures we are presumably justified in inferring an increase in the proportion of home-bred slaves owned by those who manumitted their slaves at Delphi, and who came mainly from Delphi itself or (in the first of the three periods) from cities nearby.[4] We must of course remember that the area in question was something of an industrial backwater, not to be compared with the larger cities such as Athens and Corinth, although perhaps for that very reason it is not untypical of the agricultural areas of Greece. And it would be very wrong to draw any conclusions about the total number of slaves in the respective periods, even within the restricted area of Delphi and its neighbourhood, for the practice in manumission may well have changed in various ways during the years in question. However, I feel sure that the proportion of home-bred slaves in mainland Greece did grow during the second and first centuries B.C., if only for the reason shrewdly pointed out by Westermann (*SSGRA* 34), that there must have been 'a westward movement of most of the *marketed* slaves' between the mid-second century and the mid-first, into the Roman rather than the Greek area.

In 146 B.C., according to Polybius (XXXVIII.xv.3), Diaeus, the general of the Achaean League, sent out orders to the cities which were members of the League, telling them to free and arm (for the forthcoming war with Rome) and send to Corinth those of their slaves who had been born and brought up in their homes (*oikogeneis kai paratrophoi*) and were of military age, to the number of 12,000. This figure was given by Diaeus himself;[5] he made an assessment on each city separately, ordering that those which had insufficient home-bred slaves should fill up their quotas from their other *oiketai* (ibid. 4-5). The figure of 12,000 is a striking testimony to the increase in the breeding of slaves which, as I have suggested, had been going on in Greece during the third and second centuries, and was to continue. As we shall see presently, this breeding of slaves is the decisive factor in the development we are considering: a gradual change in the forms of exploitation in the Graeco-Roman world, involving heavier pressure upon the free population, and the greatly increased use of letting to tenants in place of the direct working of the estates of the well-to-do by slave labour.

5. I must make it clear at this point that my argument is not affected by the conclusions of Michael H. Crawford, in his very interesting and able article in *JRS* 67 (1977) 117-24 (esp. 123). It is true, as he points out (121), that Italy had suffered severe losses of slave manpower in the revolt of Spartacus in 73-71 B.C. (when over 100,000 slaves are said to have been killed);[6] that Pompey's suppression of piracy in the eastern Mediterranean in 67 B.C. must virtually have ended the kidnapping and slave-raiding organised by the pirates; and that in 63 B.C. the inclusion of vast new areas within the Roman empire will have made them no longer available, in theory anyway, as a source of slaves. I accept his suggestion that the large numbers of Republican coins found in hoards in the lower Danube basin in modern times (something like 25,000 in Romania alone) may well be connected with the slave-trade and should be dated to the middle or late 60s onwards, with a slackening off in the 50s, presumably due to Caesar's mass enslavements in Gaul (perhaps of the order of half a million),[7] and a renewed increase in the 40s and 30s. However, the fact remains that any slaves coming in at this time from the Danube area were not war-captives of the Romans and will have had to be bought (and the costs of their transport for a considerable distance paid for) by the traders who brought them to their destinations, and therefore ultimately by the purchasers who used them. We have no information of any kind about the prices at which they were eventually sold. They can have done no more than fill a gap in the supply of slaves. I may add that many enslavements of war captives *en masse* must have profited

above all the Roman generals whose booty they had become, and who would have sold them off at the highest price they could get. But one would expect relatively low original prices for slaves sold in thousands or even in hundreds; and of course the sums involved would remain within the Roman economy, by which the slaves were simply appropriated.

6. It is here that I wish to draw, in three stages, an important conclusion, strangely neglected in every modern discussion I have seen (even Weber's, mentioned in § 13[a] below), but (it may be thought) obvious enough once it is stated. I shall first summarise this conclusion and then discuss various parts of it.

(a) If slaves are to be induced to breed in large quantities, they certainly cannot be kept in barracks, as were many agricultural slaves in antiquity, not only (as is well known) in late Republican Italy but also – to some extent – in Classical Greece, for example at Athens: see e.g. Xenophon, *Oecon.* IX.5, where the male and female slaves have separate quarters (the *andrōnitis* and *gynaikōnitis*) and cannot breed without their master's permission. Indeed, if they are to enjoy the relatively stable family life which (as slave societies have often found) is most conducive to reproduction on a large scale, they should ideally be settled in small 'cabins' and allowed to become what we should call – if only they were free rather than servile – tenants, peasant families (cf. § 12 below).

(b) Treating slaves in this way, however, is likely (and this is my essential point, which has been generally overlooked) to *lower the rate at which they can be exploited*, for the female slaves at least will have part of their time and energy diverted from normal work to bearing and rearing children, and – what is more important – with high rates of mortality, many slave mothers will die in childbirth, and those of the children (a large proportion, in antiquity) who do not live to an age at which they can give a good day's work will be a dead loss (see § 8 below). A domestic servant-girl could be thought a nuisance if she had a child to nurse (Hesiod, *WD* 602-3). For breeding purposes it is necessary, too (if stable family units are desired), to establish a fairly equal sex-ratio, in place of the large excess of male slaves which seems to have been a feature of many slave-importing societies, notably Italy in the late Republic – doubtless because more profit could be made out of males than females. *Breeding slaves inside the economy*, then, instead of mainly bringing them in from outside, either cheap or even (as a consequence of the enslavement of war captives) virtually gratis, *necessarily imposes a greater burden on the economy as a whole*, especially in a society like that of ancient Greece (and Rome), with a high infant and maternal death-rate (cf. § 8 below).

(c) The inevitable consequence is that *the propertied class cannot maintain the same rate of profit from slave labour*, and, to prevent its standard of life from falling, is likely to be driven to *increase the rate of exploitation of the humbler free population* – as I believe the Roman ruling class now actually did, by degrees: see below, and VIII.i-ii.

7. Perhaps I should make it clear at this point (although it is obvious enough) that we need not concern ourselves with the general question whether slaves can in principle be 'profitably' bred inside an economy – that is to say, whether an economy which has to breed all or most of its slaves can go on flourishing. That

question simply does not arise here, because we are dealing throughout with one particular economy, and what we are considering is the *relative* profitability, *for that economy*, of importing cheap slaves, and breeding them internally. The general question I have referred to is not one that can be answered *a priori*: much may depend on particular circumstances, above all the relation of the economy in question with the outside world. In certain places (some of the islands in the West Indies, for instance) the impossibility of importing slaves may have been responsible for a marked decline in the economy, and even the disappearance of slavery. Opinions differ about the healthiness of the economy of the American Old South just before the Civil War, but at least it is clear that the antebellum South had large overseas markets for its major products: cotton above all, in the nineteenth century; earlier (on a much smaller scale) tobacco, and to a less extent sugar.[8] The Graeco-Roman world as a whole certainly had no large predominance of exports over imports. Indeed, by the early Principate it was importing luxury articles from the East on quite a large scale: pepper and spices, pearls, silken clothing, ivory too from Africa and amber from Germany. According to statements mady by Pliny the Elder in two different passages, the trade in luxuries created an annual drain in cash of HS 50 million to India and as much again to China and Arabia combined (*NH* VI.101; XII.84). The payment of subsidies to 'barbarian' chiefs and kings, mainly in gold, grew to great proportions in the fifth century; and even before that the Roman government became anxious enough about the outflow of gold to issue in 374 (or a few years later) a constitution forbidding payments to 'barbarians' in gold (for slaves in particular, it seems), and adding that if any gold happened to be discovered among them, it ought to be 'got away from them by some subtle stratagem' (*subtili auferatur ingenio*: *CJ* IV.lxiii.2). All this, however, is irrelevant to my present theme.

8. A major recent work tries to calculate the point at which the average planter in the American Old South about 1850 'broke even' on his investment in slaves: that is to say, reached the point at which he began to make a profit on his total expenditure, after making all necessary allowances, including of course the premature death of many slave children. It is of great interest that according to this calculation the critical point was the attainment by the slave of the age of 27 – to which, incidentally, fewer than half the slaves at that time survived, although the general life expectation of United States slaves then 'exceeded the break-even age by more than a half decade' (Fogel and Engerman, *TC* I.153-7). A direct comparison with the Graeco-Roman world can hardly be attempted, as there are too many unknowns there: the expectation of life of the ancient slave; the standard of life he was allowed by his master; the comparative incidence of disease, and so forth. But at least we can say with some confidence that whatever the figures were for the ancient world, they were probably even worse, and certainly no better, than those for the American Old South. I agree with Keith Hopkins's conclusion that in the Roman empire

> life expectancy at birth was probably under 30, with infant mortality above 200 per thousand; for this has been generally true of pre-industrial populations and correlates with the predominance of agriculture, low average income, and scarcity of doctors and of useful medical knowledge, which together distinguish the Roman empire and other pre-industrial societies from modern industrial societies (PASRP 263).[9]

The American figure, even if it is too high, may serve as a warning that in a slave economy which has to rely entirely, or even mainly, on internal breeding of slaves, and moreover has no such extensive export markets for its products as had the antebellum South, the margin of profit on the exploitation of slave labour may be much narrower than we might be tempted to assume. And in any event, the expectation of life of the Greek or Roman slave is likely to have been below the average for the population as a whole, and well below that of the American slave *c.* 1850; and the 'break-even age' will then have been correspondingly high.

It would be interesting to know at what age a young slave in the Graeco-Roman world was generally believed to change from being a burden on his master to being an asset, who could more than earn his keep. The only specific evidence that I know on this question is a rule appearing in the collection of laws codified in 654 in the Visigothic kingdom in Spain and south-west Gaul and known as the *Leges Visigothorum*: this deals with the infant abandoned by his parents to someone else to bring up and known in the Greek world as a *threptos*. [10] Such a child, until Justinian changed the law, became in effect the slave of the person who brought him up. [11] The Visigothic law allowed the child to be reclaimed on payment of one gold solidus per year for the cost of his maintenance, up to a maximum of ten: after the age of ten the child was supposed to have earned his keep (*quia ipse, qui nutritus est, mercedem suam suo potest compensare servitio,* IV.iv.3). [12] We may compare this law with two issued by Justinian, in 530 and 531 (*CJ* VII.vii.1.5-5b; VI.xliii.3.1), putting values (for technical reasons arising out of bequest and manumission) on various groups of slaves, in which those under ten years of age are treated separately and valued at ten solidi (or thirty, if eunuchs). A statement by Ulpian shows that Roman lawyers considered a slave to have some value provided he was not physically feeble or unable to provide services for his master, and was at least five years old; but it was also stipulated that in establishing the slave's value (in certain legal actions) 'necessary expenses' should be deducted (*Dig.* VII.vii.6.1,3).

9. It is difficult to trace the details of the introduction of slave-breeding on a large scale in the Greek and Roman world. In this field I am obliged to have regard mainly to Italy, because I know of no sufficient evidence from any other area; but I believe I am entitled to treat the process that took place there as characteristic in some degree. We can surely at least assume that if a diminution in the supply of slaves from outside the economy became noticeable in Italy itself, it is likely to have been felt more strongly in other parts of the Graeco-Roman world. Indeed, in areas other than Italy (and Sicily) the process of transition from using mainly imported 'barbarian' slaves, procured by capture or purchase, to breeding the bulk of them at home is likely to have taken place rather earlier and to have gone further than in Italy, unless perhaps slaves happened to be available in exceptionally large quantities nearby, owing to the presence of a major slave-market such as Delos (see above). In areas where slaves had not been available in large quantities and at low prices, of course, the process I am describing may have been very much less marked, because slave-worked estates are not likely to have predominated to anything near the same degree as in Italy, and a larger share of total production will have been in the hands of peasants, whether serfs, leasehold tenants or small freeholders.

I must mention at this point, for the benefit of those unacquainted with the Roman fiscal system, that Roman territory in Italy long enjoyed a special privilege: exemption from the payment of land tax and poll tax. *Tributum*, in the original sense of the word (an occasional capital levy), was levied in Italy down to 168 B.C. only. After that, Roman land in Italy paid no land tax (*tributum soli*), and poll taxes (*tributum capitis*) were levied only in the provinces. A few Roman towns in the provinces received a grant of *immunitas* (a privilege also retained by only a handful of Greek cities), and even fewer enjoyed the special privilege of 'Italian rights' (*ius Italicum*), putting them on the same footing as Italy itself. For some time under the Principate these privileges were very valuable, and land in Italy (and in the few provincial cities with their territories enjoying *immunitas* or *ius Italicum*) must have yielded an exceptionally large profit to its owners and thus have had an inflated value. But by degrees *tributum* became insignificant compared with the growing system of requisitions in kind (*indictiones* etc.), theoretically in return for payment but becoming increasingly uncompensated; and by the late third century, when Diocletian abolished the privileges of Italy and of the cities possessing *immunitas* or *ius Italicum*, those privileges had become relatively unimportant.[13]

10. It looks as if women and children were not widely used as slaves in Italy during the Republican period, and in particular were not put to use in Italian agriculture nearly as much as they were in the American Old South or in the West Indies or Latin America. Conclusions by Jonkers and Brunt, from the legal texts and the Roman agronomists, strongly suggest that after the end of the Republic the sex-ratio among slaves began to grow more equal, and that slave-breeding played a much larger part in the economy.[14] One factor that may have militated to some small extent against the general use of female slaves in the actual operations of agriculture in the Graeco-Roman world was the existence, even in the highest circles, of superstitious ideas about women in general. Columella believed, for example, that if a woman during menstruation touched a shrub of rue it would wither, and that young cucumber shoots could be killed if such a woman so much as looked at them (*RR* XI.iii.38, 50). The Egyptian Greek writer Bolus of Mendes, in the third century B.C., some of whose works circulated under the name of Democritus (cf. ibid. VII.v.17), did little to restore the balance by describing how a menstruating woman could kill caterpillars by simply walking around the infested plant three times with loose hair and bare feet (ibid. XI.iii.64). In Greek and Roman literature, women are generally seen as busying themselves in the house, while the men work in the fields: Columella has an impassioned statement of this view (*RR* XII.Praef.1-7), taken directly from Xenophon's *Oeconomicus* (VII.23-42, esp. 23, 30), which had been translated into Latin by Cicero; and he proceeds to describe at length (XII.i.1 to iii.9) the duties of the slave housekeeper (*vilica*, generally mated with the slave overseer, the *vilicus*). Yet an isolated passage in Columella seems to me to prove that he expected women slaves to be working in the fields provided it was not raining and the weather was not too cold or frosty (XII.iii.6). (I need make no apology for referring so often to the Roman agricultural writers, since their advice was largely based upon handbooks either written in Greek or dependent

on Greek sources – this is true to some extent even of the work of Mago the Carthaginian, translated into Latin by order of the Roman Senate: see Col., *RR* I.i.10, 13 etc.)

Although I realise that it can be dangerous to use isolated literary texts to prove a historical progression, I think that if we look at statements bearing on slave breeding made successively by the first three leading Roman agricultural writers whose works survive, namely Cato, Varro and Columella, we shall see a faithful reflection of the actual developments in Italy. Cato, who died in 149 B.C., never refers to the breeding of slaves in his handbook on agriculture; and indeed he never so much as mentions female slaves in that work, except when he speaks of the slave housekeeper, the *vilica* (*De agricult.* 10.1, 11.1, 56, 143), whom he contemplates giving as a 'wife' to the overseer, the *vilicus*, also a slave. Plutarch, however, in his *Life of Cato*, says that he used to allow his male slaves to have sexual intercourse with their female fellow-slaves for payment (to himself, of course: *Cato mai.* 21.3); and these encounters must have resulted in occasional conceptions, for we also hear from Plutarch that Cato's wife used to suckle the babies of her slave-girls, in the hope that this would make them well-disposed towards her own son, their future master (ibid. 20.5). Varro, writing more than a hundred years later, in 36 B.C., contemplates the breeding of slaves in two contexts only. First, he seems willing to allow *pastores* (shepherds and herdsmen) to have mates. If they are living in the farm-complex itself (the *villa*), then, as Varro charmingly remarks, 'Venus Pastoralis' will be satisfied if they have a slave-mate there. He also records a prevalent view that if the *pastores* are more remote and live in huts on their own, it is no bad thing to provide them with women, who will be able to share their work (*RR* II.x.6 ff.; cf. i.26). But Varro first discusses the purchase of *pastores*, which he seems to consider the normal method of procuring them (x.4-5). Secondly, when he is writing about slaves doing agricultural work on the farm itself, he advises giving female fellow-slaves as mates to overseers only (*praefecti*, slave-drivers), to bear them children and thus make them 'more reliable and more attached to the farm' (*firmiores et coniunctiores*: *RR* I.xvii.5). In the same passage, however, Varro happens to remark that slaves from Epirus (a Greek-speaking area) were valued more highly than any others at the time because of the family relationships (*cognationes*) they were able to develop. Evidently whole families of Epirot slaves were already being sold as units and would give exceptionally good service if permitted to retain that unity. A leading equestrian of the last century B.C. (110-32), T. Pomponius Atticus, the friend and correspondent of Cicero and a very rich man who owned large numbers of slaves, is said by his friend and biographer, Cornelius Nepos, to have kept not a single slave who was not born and trained in his own house (*domi natum domique factum*): Nepos takes this as a demonstration of Atticus' *continentia* and *diligentia*, and it was evidently exceptional at the time (*Att.* 13.3-4). Later writers who refer to slave-breeding in the Republic may be introducing anachronistically a feature of the economy of their own day, as when Appian, speaking of the middle period of the Republic, says that 'the ownership of slaves brought the rich great profit from the many children of the slaves, whose number increased without hindrance because they were exempt from military service' (*BC* I.7).

Columella, writing about a hundred years later again, in the 60s or 70s of the first century of the Christian era, is keen to have home-bred slaves: he advocates rewarding female slaves for bearing children and adds that he himself has been accustomed to give exemption from all work to any woman who has born three sons, and for any further ones, freedom (*RR* I.viii.19; cf. Salvius Julianus, in *Dig.* XL.vii.3.16, cited below). Nothing is said about daughters, who seem to be excluded, as the word I have translated 'children' is *natos* (the masculine form, although I think that form could include girls as well as boys), and the three or more who will earn for the woman exemption or freedom are *filii* (masculine again). It is just possible that offspring of either sex are meant, but had Columella intended to include girls he would surely have spoken of *liberi*. Petronius, whom many would see as a contemporary of Columella, wrote in his comic account of the wealth of the imaginary freedman Trimalchio of '30 boys and 40 girls' (slaves, of course) born in a single day on his estate at Cumae (*Satyr*. 53): the story is significant, however exaggerated the numbers may be. I will only add that it might indeed be necessary, as Columella contemplates, to reward female slaves who actually bore children. In an imaginary dialogue in the second of Dio Chrysostom's two discourses *On slavery and freedom* (written probably in the later years of the first century) it is assumed that slave women who became pregnant would tend to resort to abortion or infanticide (sometimes even with the consent of the men concerned), 'so as not to have trouble in addition to their slavery, by being obliged to rear children' (XV.8) – which of course, as Dio had no need to remind his audience, might then be taken away from them and sold to another master. As late as the early third century there was no general practice of buying female slaves with the deliberate purpose of breeding from them (Ulpian, *Dig.* V.iii.27.*pr.*: 'non temere ancillae eius rei causa comparantur ut pariant'); and therefore their offspring were not technically regarded as 'profits' (*fructus*) of the estate (ibid.).[14a] Nevertheless, such offspring were inherited with the estate, which they 'increased', as were *fructus* (ibid., with 20.3). And a woman slave who had become sterile or was past the age of fifty was regarded as distinctly less valuable (Paulus, *Dig.* XIX.i.21.*pr.*), for 'conceiving and bringing to birth a child' was regarded as 'the most important particular function of women' (Ulpian, *Dig.* XXI.i.14.1).

Further useful evidence is provided by the legal sources. Of a large number of legal texts mentioning the offspring of slave-girls or home-bred slaves, very few go back to the lawyers of the Late Republic or the time of Augustus. This of course does not prove anything by itself, because the great bulk of the jurists cited in the *Digest* belonged to the Antonine or Severan periods (A.D. 138-193-235). However, Brunt, with all due caution, is prepared to infer that 'slave-breeding assumed greater economic importance after Augustus' (*IM* 708); and we may surely agree at least that by the second century of our era it was playing a much larger role than in the last century B.C. In the second and third centuries the lawyers sometimes use the correct technical expression for the 'consorts' of slaves, *contubernales*, but sometimes refer to them as 'wives', *uxores*, which in strict law they could never be, although the term may often have been applied to them in popular speech, as by Cato, *De agric.* 143.1, quoted above. Ulpian in *Dig.* XXXIII.vii.12.33 uses the right word, *contubernales*, but in 12.7 of the same title he actually refers to the consorts as *uxores* – a surprising lapse by a jurist, unless it had become very common for slaves to have permanent consorts, to such an extent that even a lawyer could refer to them loosely as 'wives'.[15] A particularly interesting text from Salvius Julianus, writing probably in the 150s, contemplates a case in which a man provided in his will that his slave woman should be free 'if she bore three slaves', but she was prevented from doing so by his heir either giving her some 'medicamentum' to prevent conception or procuring abortion (*Dig.* XL.vii.3.16). I may add that children born to town-slaves in a man's urban *familia* might be reared on his country estate: see *Dig.* XXXII.xcix.3 (Paulus); L.xvi.210 (Marcianus).

11. I hope I have now established that, in so far as it is permissible to speak of a 'decline' of slavery during the Principate, what we must concentrate on is the fact that as a result of slaves being to a large extent bred within the economy instead of being brought into it under exceptionally favourable conditions, the *rate of exploitation* of the slave population as a whole must have diminished, to allow for the diversion of effort to producing and rearing children, including a considerable number who would not survive to become useful to their owners. The increased cost of slaves imported from outside the economy would also diminish their profitability.

12. We have now admitted the necessity for slave-breeding in the Principate and the desirability of encouraging slaves to breed by establishing them in conditions conducive to the rearing of families. It need not surprise us, there-fore, to find actual evidence, from as early as the last century B.C. onwards, of slaves settled as virtual tenants of agricultural plots – a situation which might have been widespread without its making an appearance in our sources, but which we happen to know about from quotations in Justinian's *Digest* from some of the earlier lawyers whose works are cited there, including two of the very earliest: Alfenus Varus, consul in 39 B.C., and his younger contemporary, M. Antonius Labeo, who flourished under Augustus. Alfenus wrote of a man who leased a farm to his slave for cultivation (*quidam fundum colendum servo suo locavit*: *Dig.* XV.iii.16), and mentioned the possibility of such a lease as if it were a normal occurrence (XL.vii.14.*pr.*). Labeo (and also Pegasus, who was at work in the 70s of the first century), as quoted by Ulpian, wrote of a *servus qui quasi colonus in agro erat*, 'a slave who was on agricultural land as if he were a tenant' (*Dig.* XXXIII.vii.12.3). The same situation is also referred to by Q. Cervidius Scaevola, a leading jurist of the second half of the second century (XXXIII.vii.20.1, with 18.4; cf. XX.i.32), and I would see it reflected again in two other texts of Scaevola: Dig. XXXIII.viii.23.3 (*coloni praediorum* who are slaves) and vii.20.3 (where the *reliqua* due from *vilici*, as well as *coloni*, may well be, or at least include, rents). All the texts in question mention this situation quite casually, as if it were well known, and I suggest that it was probably very common indeed from the first century onwards. In such cases the tenant, considered from the strictly legal aspect, was still a slave; but from the economic point of view the slave was properly a tenant, and he might even employ slaves of his own (*vicarii*, mentioned by Scaevola, for example, in *Dig.* XX.i.32), as an ordinary free *colonus* might (see e.g. *Dig.* IX.ii.27.9,11; XIX.ii.30.4). Ulpian could con-template a slave as occupier (*habitator*) of a house (*Dig.* IX.iii.1.8); he goes on to define a *habitator* as one who occupies a house that is his own or leased to him, or which he is occupying by favour (*vel in suo vel in conducto vel gratuito*, § 9).

In the late fourth century slave tenants were apparently still common, for an imperial constitution of 392 (*CTh* XVI.v.21), ordering the punishment as criminals of those who allowed heretical meetings to take place on lands they owned or leased, decrees that a lessee (*conductor*) guilty of any such heinous offence is to pay a large fine if a free man, but, if he is 'the offspring of servile dregs' (*servile faece descendens*) and is contemptuous of the fine because of his poverty and his low condition, he is to be flogged and deported. (I realise, of course, that the Latin phrase I have quoted need not necessarily imply more than servile birth, and was presumably used to cover both slaves and freedmen.) A century later, in the 490s, a slave of the Roman Church named Ampliatus, who had been *conductor* of some of its land, is mentioned in a letter (fr. 28) of Pope Gelasius (A.D. 492-6).[16] If such tenancies of slaves were found to be to the master's advantage, they would doubtless be continued indefinitely, and the slave-*colonus*, if not manumitted in his master's lifetime, might well be freed by his master's will (as in *Dig.* XXXII.xcvii, Paulus). The situation I have been discussing has long been known, of course, and good use has been made of some of the texts I have quoted by various modern historians, including for instance Marc Bloch (in *CEHE* I².251-2), although he is concentrating entirely on the Latin West, whereas we are primarily interested in the Greek East. The 'hutted slave', *servus casatus*, so much in evidence by the time of Charlemagne, is not known under that designation in the Roman empire: the term *casatus* is unknown before the Middle Ages, and the *casarii* who are bracketed with *coloni* in a constitution of 369 are as likely to be free 'cottagers' as 'hutted slaves' (*CTh* IX.xlii.7 = *CJ* IX.xlix.7). But Pope Pelagius I, in a letter giving instructions about an inheritance, part of which could be claimed by his Church (*Ep.* 84, of A.D. 560-1),[17] advises his agent, Bishop Julian of Cingulum, that a 'rusticus vel colonus' is preferable to an 'artifex et ministerialis puer' (§ 1), and warns him not to release 'those who can become *conductores* or *coloni*' (§ 3) and not to give away 'such men as may be able to occupy cottages or to become cultivators' (*qui vel continere casas vel colere possunt*, § 2) – where the words 'continere casas' come near to calling these men 'servi casati'.

The *servus quasi colonus* was well known among the German tribes as early as the first century, for Tacitus describes the condition of such a man as the characteristic form of German slavery. Each slave, he says, lives on his own, and the master imposes on him liability for a fixed quantity of corn or cattle or clothing, 'as on a *colonus*', or 'as if he were a *colonus*' (*ut colono*: *Germ.* 25.1). We can accept this without misgiving: it was probably the best way of preventing the slave from escaping to his home, which might be quite near (see Thompson, *SEG* 22-3, 18-19 = *SCA* [ed. Finley] 196-7, 192-3).

According to a much-quoted letter of Pliny the Younger, written in the first years of the second century, he himself nowhere used chained slaves (*vincti*, elsewhere also *compediti, alligati*), nor did anyone else in the part of Italy to which he is referring (*Ep.* III.xix.7). Sherwin-White, in his commentary on Pliny's letters, has shown that the area in question must be on the edge of Tuscany, where Pliny had an estate in the upper valley of the Tiber, at Tifernum Tiberinum (*LP* 254). A passage in the poet Martial, probably written within a decade before this letter of Pliny's, contemplates the prospect of 'the fields of Tuscany resounding with countless fetters' (*et sonet innumera compede Tuscus ager*,

IX.xxii.4); but this may not refer to a real contemporary situation. In the early 70s the Elder Pliny had deplored large-scale cultivation by *vincti*, housed in prison-like barracks (*ergastula*): this, he says, is the worst kind of farming, and one could well believe that it makes Mother Earth herself unwilling and indignant! (*NH* XVIII.21,35-6). However, Columella (writing probably a few years earlier) does refer occasionally to chained slaves: and although two of these passages rather suggest that the men concerned (*ergastuli mancipia*, I.viii.16-17; *mancipia vincta*, XI.i.22) will be in that condition as a special punishment, Columella also speaks of vineyards as being '*very often* cultivated by fettered slaves' (*vineta plurimum per alligatos excoluntur*, I.ix.4; cf. I.vi.3; vii.1; also I.*praef*.3; iii.12). Evidently the use of chain-gangs in agriculture was on the decline even in Italy in the time of the two Plinys but had not entirely died out by the beginning of the second century.

13. I wish to mention at this point three works which have made a particularly valuable contribution to our understanding of Roman land tenure and the rise of the colonate in its earlier form, before it was converted into serfdom.

(*a*) The first is a brilliant lecture delivered by Max Weber in 1896 and published in the same year. It remained unread even by Rostovtzeff (see *SEHRE*[2] II.751 n.9), who did not miss much; but in recent years it has become easily available in good English translation in no fewer than three different paperbacks, under the title, 'The social causes of the decay of ancient civilisation' (see II.v above and its n.8 below), and Mazzarino has described it (with some exaggeration) as 'really the most fundamental work and the greatest work of genius which has ever been written on the economic crisis of antiquity' (*EAW* 140). Weber's interesting approach to his problem is from the point of view of the supply of labour. He points out, as I have done, that the slave-barracks which had flourished in certain areas in the Late Republic were anything but self-reproducing, and that when the external supply of slaves began to some extent to dry up, 'the effect on the slave-barracks must be the same as that of exhaustion of the coal-deposits on the blast-furnaces'. When that happened, Weber adds, 'we have reached the turning-point in the development of ancient civilisation'. But his sketch of the decline of slavery and the development of the colonate, perfectly valid as far as it goes,[18] fails to bring out the complex of connected processes which I explained in § 6 above: *the fall in the rate of exploitation of slave labour* consequent upon the widespread extension of slave-breeding, and also *an increased exploitation of humble free men*, as a material result of the fact that the propertied classes were determined to maintain their relatively high standard of life and had all the political control necessary to enable them to depress the condition of others.

(*b*) The second work is a long essay by Fustel de Coulanges, 'Le colonat romain', in his *Recherches sur quelques problèmes d'histoire* (Paris, 1885) 1-186. Fustel has a great deal to say on the development of the colonate that is still of real interest. He lays particular stress on the fact that *coloni* often went deeply into debt, like the tenants of the Younger Pliny, some of whom seem to have got into a hopeless position, with their arrears (*reliqua*) ever mounting and their securities forfeited (Pliny, *Ep.* III.19.6-7; IX.37.1-3; cf. VII.30.3; IX.36.6; X.8.5). There are many references in the works of the Roman lawyers cited in the *Digest* to 'rents outstanding from tenants' (*reliqua colonorum*). These would surely include rents merely *due* after the testator's death, and not only rents then already *over*due, in arrear (for no text I have noticed distinguishes between the two); but of course they would also include any arrears, such as the *reliqua* that so worried Pliny (*Ep.* III.19.6; IX.37.2). More recent work has shown that Fustel was mistaken on certain technical questions of Roman law: in particular, he was wrong in believing that a fixed rent was essential for the Roman contract of lease, *locatio conductio* (see e.g. Clausing, *RC* 161-2; Thomas, *NM*). Nevertheless, his work is very useful in its demonstration of the humble status, and the precariousness of the legal and economic position, of the *coloni* of the Principate. Horace, as the very opposite of 'kings', had chosen 'strengthless *coloni*' (*inopes coloni: Od.* II.xiv.11-12). Later we see them dominated by their landlords even in religious matters: in 251 St. Cyprian could praise African landlords who had preserved their Christian 'inquilini et coloni' from the act of public sacrifice demanded by the Emperor Decius (*Ep.* LV.xiii.2), and around the year 400 masterful landowners in North Africa took it upon themselves to convert their *coloni* from Donatism to Catholicism (August., *Ep.* 58.1) or vice versa (Aug., *C. Litt. Petil.* II.184, 228).

(*c*) The last of the three works is an article by Bernhard Kübler (SCRK, esp. 580-8) which brings out better than anything else I know the very weak position of the lessee under the Roman contract of *locatio conductio*. It is worth drawing attention here to something recently pointed out by Elizabeth Rawson: 'the rarity, among the upper class [of Late Republican Rome], of renting, which may be connected with the unfavourable position at law of a tenant' (*SRP*, ed. Finley, 87).

And here, going back to what I said under the heading 'III. Debt bondage' in III.iv above about 'personal execution' for debt, I must point out that rent in arrear, a breach of the contract of *locatio conductio* between landlord and tenant, would constitute a debt for which the landlord would be entitled to 'personal execution' against the defaulting tenant, as against any other debtor. I can now add an important consideration to one I advanced in III.iv above (in the paragraph just before the one containing n.70), to the effect that the *addictus* or *iudicatus*, who could have slave-terminology applied to him in popular usage, may often have been obliged in practice to work for his creditor. Is it not very likely indeed that in such a situation a landlord would often offer to keep his tenant on the same land, *under more burdensome conditions than could normally be exacted from a willing tenant*, and that the tenant would *prefer to accept such conditions*, rather than risk being turned into an *addictus* and simply kept in a prison, or taken away elsewhere to work off his arrears? We know from a statement in the treatise of Callistratus, *De iure fisci*, preserved in the *Digest* (XLIX.xiv.3.6), that by the second quarter of the second century a practice had grown up of forcing the lessees of public land to renew their tenancies if no one else could be found to take the property at the same rent. (Tax farmers, too, were similarly made to renew their contracts.) Hadrian, rebuking such a procedure, refers to it as 'a thoroughly inhuman *custom*' (*valde inhumanus mos*), from which we must conclude that it had already occurred on numerous occasions. And according to a provision of the Emperor Philip in 244 the retention of 'unwilling lessees or their heirs' after the expiration of a lease had 'often' been forbidden by imperial rescript (*CJ* IV.lxv.11). It is indeed easy to believe that private landlords, as well as imperial agents, often attempted to keep their tenants on the land after their leases had expired, although of course they had no right to do so – unless, I would emphasise, the tenant was in debt to the landlord: see the reference at the beginning of this paragraph to III.iv above, dealing with 'personal execution' for debt. I would assume that in the case which is being dealt with in *CJ* IV.lxv.11 the tenant concerned was not in that situation, but that had he been indebted to his landlord for rent or the repayment of a loan, and unable to discharge the debt, the law which was being stated would simply have been inapplicable.

14. There was one factor in particular, noticeable in Italy, which we might expect to operate almost as strongly in the Greek East: the additional time and effort which a landowner working his estate directly with slave labour would have to expend in order to get the best results, compared with the landlord who leased out his land, and the impetus this would give to leasing. Even a landowner who did go in for letting to tenants might occasionally be involved in tiresome supervisory activities, as we find from some of the letters of Pliny the Younger.[19] But, over all, farms which were leased would normally have required less attention from their owners, and this would have partly discounted the higher profits to be expected from land worked directly with slaves. It was always considered highly desirable for the landowner to be present in person on a directly worked estate for much of the year, as ancient writers often stressed.[20] Columella bewails the disinclination of many of the landowners of his day (the mid-first century), and of their wives, to remain on their estates and take a personal interest in them (*RR* I.*praef*.12-15; I.iv.8; XII.*praef*.8-10). The ladies, he says, regard a few days spent at a country house as 'a most sordid business' (*sordidissimum negotium*). The obvious solution for such people was to let their lands on lease as much as possible; and this was all the more likely since many large landowners in the West (and to some extent in the Greek East) owned estates scattered around in many different places, which they could hardly have supervised closely in person, even if they had wished to do so. My own impression is that until the Late Republic wealthy Romans perhaps tended to have fairly concentrated landholdings (even the thirteen farms of Sextus Roscius were 'almost all along the Tiber': Cic., *Pro Sex. Rosc. Amer.* 20), but that in the Late Republic, and still more during the Principate and Later Empire, they were likely to own property more and more widely diffused – in the Later Empire above all we hear of Romans owning estates in many different provinces. This would of itself encourage leasing, for reasons I have just made clear. Certainly, we ought not simply to take it for granted, in the absence of sufficient evidence, that leasing became much more common than it had been in the Republic: here I agree with Brunt, who has made a useful collection of texts relating to leases in Italy in Republican and Augustan times (ALRR 71 nn.27-33).[21] Nevertheless, it does look to me as if leasing did grow, at the expense of direct working. I think that many of the farms distributed to discharged veterans may have been dealt with in this way. Horace's Ofellus is a case in point: his farm has been confiscated and handed over to a veteran, whose *colonus* he has become (*Sat.* II.ii.2-3, 112-15, 127-35). We also hear of men selling their farms on condition of taking

them back on lease, a practice contemplated in *Dig.* XIX.i.21.4 (Paulus) and XVIII.i.75 (Hermogenianus). I must add here that letting land to a tenant does not by any means imply a cessation of slave labour (see below and nn.52-8).

15. If up to now I have concentrated too much on evidence from Italy, it is because (as I said earlier) we have much more explicit evidence from there than from the Greek East for the developments I have been describing, during the Principate. In some of the Balkan provinces of the Roman empire we find numerous slaves down to about the middle of the second century; but later the proportion of slaves in the population seems to have declined very considerably. This has been shown for Dalmatia by Wilkes and for Noricum by Géza Alföldy.[22] In most of the Greek world, however, above all in Egypt, slave production had never reached as high a level as it did in Italy in the last century or two of the Republic, and in particular there were nothing like as many great estates as existed in Italy, Sicily and north Africa – *latifundia*, as they have generally been called in modern times, although in antiquity that expression is quite late and rare. In the last years of the Republic, Varro could speak of a large farm as a *latus fundus* (*RR* I.xvi.4), but the earliest occurrence that I know of the actual word *latifundium* is in Valerius Maximus (IV.iv.7), who wrote in the 30s, in the reign of Tiberius, and who refers ironically to *magna latifundia*.[23]

Large estates, of course, could be either slave-worked, or let to tenants, or both. As it happens, we have literary evidence from the first century for large numbers of tenant-farmers in the West, Africa particularly. Seneca, in a letter written in the early 60s, speaks of 'thousands of *coloni*' working the land of (it seems) single owners in Sicily and Africa (*Ep.* CXIV.26). And the Roman surveyor Agennius Urbicus (whose date is uncertain), probably reproducing the *De controversiis agrorum* of Sextus Julius Frontinus, written in the 80s or 90s, speaks of individuals in Africa as owning estates (*saltus*) 'no smaller than the territories of cities, many of them indeed much bigger; and individuals have on their estates no small number of humble people [*non exiguum populum plebeium*] and villages of the size of towns around their villa'.[24] The same general features were at work in the Greek world; and I would say that for my present purposes the main difference between Italy and the Greek East was merely that the change from large-scale slave production to what I may call 'peasant production' (principally in the form of the letting of land in small parcels to tenants) was less noticeable because in the Greek East peasant production already played a relatively larger role. I must admit that I have not yet been able to collect sufficient evidence for the different areas separately. Figures of any sort for slave households in the Greek world in the Roman period are non-existent, except for statements of a rhetorical character like that in St. John Chrysostom, *Hom. in Matth.* 63.4, in *MPG* LVIII.608 (Antiochene landowners possessing one or two thousand *andrapoda*). I know of no estimate of the number of slaves in the territory of any Greek city in the Roman age apart from a casual and surely quite unreliable one by Galen, in the second half of the second century, to the effect that his own city, Pergamum, had 40,000 citizens, plus 'wives and slaves' to the number of 80,000, from which we may presumably infer that Galen – who could hardly have *known* the number of slaves at Pergamum – estimated that number at about 40,000 (*De cogn. curand. animi morbis* 9, in Galen's *Opera Omnia* V.49, ed. C. G. Kühn, 1825).

16. Although I could not yet prove it against sceptical opposition, I believe that the condition of the peasantry throughout much of the Roman empire, including its Greek areas, deteriorated markedly during the first three centuries of the Christian era – just as the position of slaves improved somewhat, especially if they became tenants *de facto* (see § 12 above). This depression in the status of the peasantry (and indeed of all the free poor) was facilitated by a deterioration in their legal rights (in so far as they had any), in ways I shall describe in VIII.i below, and, in the Greek world, by the final extinction of democracy (see V.iii and Appendix IV below). The various processes (economic, legal and political) were closely related; but the legal and political aspects are better evidenced and can be more precisely described, and I have found it convenient to treat them separately, setting them apart from the economic side, which is a perfect jumble of small scraps of material from different areas of the empire which were developing in diverse ways and at unequal speeds, even if the final result – achieved by no means simultaneously everywhere – was very much the same over the whole vast area. The one thing I should most like to know, but have not yet been able to discover to more than a small extent, is the relative weight in the early and middle Principate of the three main burdens imposed upon the peasant (see Section ii of this chapter), of rent, compulsory services (such as *angariae*), and taxation, and how these changed over the years.

17. We are not yet quite ready to take account of the enserfment of most of the free working agricultural population of the Roman empire, which took place from the end of the third century onwards. Before we do that, there are two major connected problems, unnoticed as yet in this book, which we must briefly examine. The first problem, which gradually forced itself on my attention while I was working on the emergence of the Later Roman colonate, is the very large question of the settlement of *barbari* within the empire. This was discussed in part as long ago as the 1840s, by Zumpt and Huschke (see Clausing, *RC* 44-9, 57-61, 77-89); a very brief but more up-to-date account of it was given by Otto Seeck (*GUAW* I⁴.i.407; ii.591-2), when formulating an important theory which I shall discuss in connection with the second of the two problems I have just mentioned, and in the past few years particular aspects of it have attracted attention; but I know of no recent overall account. The subject is much too large to be dealt with properly in this book: it raises a host of highly technical questions, such as the nature of the *laeti* and *gentiles*, and it involves consideration of epigraphic and archaeological evidence, as well as a great many literary passages, some of them hard to assess. I have, however, set out in Appendix III, with a few comments, all the relevant evidence I know that seems to me important for the settlement of *barbari* in the empire from the first century to the late sixth. This will at least give some idea of the extent of these settlements, which will, I think, astonish most people, and may be useful to those who wish to pursue the matter further. I need make no apology for directing some attention to these issues, although they affect the Western part of the empire much more than the Greek East, for the introduction into the empire of what were certainly very large numbers of *barbari* as settlers, amounting to many hundreds of thousands in all, is obviously something that must be seriously taken

into account when we are considering the question of the 'decline and fall' (cf. Chapter VIII below), especially if, like so many recent writers, we regard as an important aspect of that process a 'shortage of manpower' – whether in the absolute sense, of a general decline in population, or (as I would much prefer) in the relative sense, of a diversion of manpower from productive tasks, in agriculture above all, to spheres of activity which, however important they might be in themselves, were not directly concerned with production, like the army and the imperial civil service.[25] I shall return to this subject in § 19 below, after taking up the second of the two problems I mentioned at the beginning of this paragraph.

18. My second problem arises out of a particular text in the *Digest*, which seems to me important in any attempt to trace the emergence of the serfdom of the Later Roman colonate. The text, *Dig*. XXX.112.*pr*., is an extract from the *Institutes* of Aelius Marcianus, one of the last of the great jurists of the 'Classical' period of Roman law, who was probably writing around 220.[26] It falls into two parts: a brief statement by Marcianus himself, followed by a reference to a joint rescript of the Emperors Marcus Aurelius and Commodus. This rescript can be very closely dated, between 177, when Commodus became co-Augustus with his father, and the death of Marcus on 17 March 180. The text is as follows:

(a) If anyone bequeaths *inquilini* without the lands to which they are attached [*sine praediis quibus adhaerent*],[26a] the bequest is legally invalid [*inutile*];
(b) But the question whether a valuation [*aestimatio*] ought to be made [*sc*. of what the heir should pay the legatee as an equivalent, in compensation] is to be decided in conformity with the wishes of the testator, according to a rescript of the deified Marcus and Commodus.

Interpreted according to its natural sense, the passage implies that the first of the two points it makes, namely (a) above, was already settled law, and what the emperors were deciding in 177-180 was that in the event of an ineffectual bequest of *inquilini* without the lands to which they were attached, the value of such a bequest might have to be estimated (so that the heir could compensate the legatee to that extent for the failure of the bequest). In any event, we can be certain, if we accept the text as it stands, that by 180 at the latest it was settled law that those '*inquilini*' who were regarded as attached to particular lands could not be bequeathed separately from those lands. (I must make it clear that our text deals not with *inquilini* in general but with a particular type of *inquilini*.)[27]

The very use of the term *inquilini* in such a way may seem to some to create a problem in itself, for it is often supposed that right through the Principate, in legal texts, the word *inquilinus* normally means 'a tenant living in a rented dwelling' (thus Berger, *EDRL* 503), a man who leases a house, rather than the tenant of a farm or plot of land, who is a *colonus*. However, I think we must assume that the word *inquilinus* is being used in its less technical sense of tenants of land of any sort (cf. Justin XLIII.iv.5). Unfortunately, the fact that the word *praedia* is used is not decisive. It tells us only that we are dealing with some form of landed property: in principle, either *praedia urbana*, of which buildings are an important element, or *praedia rustica*, essentially agricultural land, whether it has buildings on it or not (see e.g. *Dig*. VIII.i.1; 14.*pr*.; ii, esp. 2, with iii, esp. 1 and 2; iv.6.*pr*. and 1; iv.12).

What is extraordinary about this text is that the *inquilini* in question are described as *attached* to the 'praedia', in the words 'praediis quibus adhaerent'. One explanation of this text has been offered which, if correct, would offer a neat and tidy solution and would not leave us with any disquiet about possible further consequences. This is the theory of Otto Seeck, first published in 1900 as part of an article on the colonate (*RE* IV.i.483-510, at 494-7), and set out again in his account of the Later Roman colonate contained in his massive history of the decline of the ancient world (*GUAW* I⁴.i.404 ff., esp. 405-7, with ii.585-90). Seeck suggested that the *inquilini* of our text, far from being *inquilini* of the traditional type, were *barbari* settled by the Emperor Marcus, mainly in frontier areas of the Roman empire, after his Marcomannic wars (for which see VIII.ii below); that these settlers are the *laeti* we encounter from the time of Diocletian onwards, who were indeed Germans settled on lands within the empire (later referred to once as 'terrae laeticae'), apparently with the twin obligations of cultivation and military service; and that the attaching to the land of these men is a natural corollary of their settlement, and foreshadowed the serf-colonate of the Later Empire. The date of our rescript is, *prima facie*, an argument in Seeck's favour, for settlements of *barbari* on an appreciable scale were certainly made in the 170s (see Appendix III below, § 7), and the circumstances referred to by Marcianus must have arisen at that very time, if they were the subject of a rescript of the late 170s. It is perfectly conceivable that a landowner on whose estates Germans were settled (whether they are to be identified with the later *laeti* or not) should attempt to bequeath them separately from the lands originally provided for them. Unfortunately we are not told the reason why the bequest of the *inquilini* in question was held to be invalid. If the men were indeed Germans (*laeti* or not), then it may be that they were held to be inseparable from the lands on which they had originally been placed, and that they could be bequeathed, if at all, only with that land. (I shall leave aside for the moment the question what law was being applied if they were not German *laeti* or the like.) Seeck's theory has been accepted (with or without modifications) by some scholars and rejected by others;[28] but I have not seen any additional argument of any weight in its favour, nor have I discovered any convincing argument against it. If it is true, the theory provides us with an interesting anticipation of the Later Roman serf-colonate, which (as we shall see in §§ 20 ff. below) certainly tied a very large part of the working agricultural population of the Roman empire to the land in one way or another. The one argument of some weight against Seeck is that there is no further evidence of 'barbarian' settlers tied to their lands for over a century: the earliest relevant text would be the reference to *laeti* in the Latin Panegyric IV (VIII), of 1 March 297, mentioned in Appendix III below, § 14a. (I reject as fictitious the inalienable plots of land in *Hist. Aug., Alex. Sev.* 58.4 – which of course purports to refer to lands granted to Roman soldiers, not *barbari*.)

Two problems seem to me to have been generally overlooked by those who do not accept Seeck's theory. First, how could any ordinary *inquilini,* as early as the 170s, be said to be 'attached to lands' in any sense at all? And secondly, how could any landowner at that date feel himself entitled to bequeath his *inquilini* – with or without land to which they were mysteriously 'attached'? If Seeck is right, these problems do not arise; but if we reject or doubt his theory they cannot simply be ignored, as by several of Seeck's critics. I know of no evidence that tenants (*coloni* or *inquilini*) in general were ever thought capable of being bequeathed by will during the Principate; although of course when the serf colonate was introduced, in the Later Empire, and tenants could not be separated from the land they leased, they could – and indeed must – pass with the land by bequest or inheritance as well as sale. As far as I can see, tenants during the Principate certainly did not form part of the *instrumentum* of a farm – the equipment of the farm, which might be specifically mentioned in a lease or bequest, or might be held to go with the farm automatically if it were leased or bequeathed by the owner, with or without the words 'cum instrumento' or 'instructum'. The Roman lawyers were at pains to define precisely what was included in the *instrumentum*, both in *Dig*. XIX.ii.19.2, in that part of the work which deals with the contract of *locatio conductio* (including what we call the leasing of land) and, at greater length, in another part dealing with legacies (XXXIII.vii), for farms were often – perhaps usually – bequeathed with their *instrumentum*. Slaves, of course, could form part of the *instrumentum*; but the slave-*colonus*, discussed in § 12 above, was held not to be part of the *instrumentum* of the farm of which he was regarded as the lessee (*Dig*. XXXIII.vii.12.3), and *a fortiori* an ordinary free *colonus* or *inquilinus* would certainly not be. It is true that some writers (including Jones: see below) have taken the *inquilini* of Marcianus to be slaves; but had they been slaves it is surely inconceivable that a bequest of them apart from the land on which they happened to be working would have been declared invalid. Leonhard saw them as 'grundhörige Sklaven' (*RE* IX.ii [1916] 1559, s.v. *inquilini*). But slaves bound to the soil are a category which never appears, as far as I know, before the fourth century, perhaps as late as *c.* 370 (see III.iv above and its n.16 below). It does not solve our problem, therefore, to regard the *inquilini* of Marcianus as slaves; and I feel sure that Marcianus himself would not in any event have referred to slaves as 'inquilini'. Inexplicable to me, too, is Piganiol's statement (*EC*² 307 n.2): 'Au IIIᵉ siècle, tout *colonus* peut être dit *inquilinus* (cette observation explique le texte de Marcien)' – of course it does nothing of the sort. Even A. H. M. Jones showed uncharacteristic imprecision when dealing with the text we have been examining: I am not quite sure what he means by saying that the persons described as *inquilini* 'must be slaves, or they could not be left by will, but are attached to land and are only alienable with it'; the sentence that follows may be an imperfect recollection of Seeck, although he is not mentioned (see *SAS*, ed. Finley, 291-2).

It is possible, I suppose, that Saumagne was right in thinking that the text of Marcianus has suffered interpolation and that originally it did not contain the words 'without the lands to which they are attached' (ROC 503 n.3). To this one instinctively objects that in such circumstances there could be no *aestimatio* (see above), for how could a valuation be placed upon free men? As we read in the *Edictum Theodorici* 94, 'Homo enim liber pretio nullo aestimatur'. (The same objection would apply to any attempt merely to delete 'quibus adhaerent'.) But a valuable footnote of Fustel de Coulanges (see n.28 again) may provide an answer to our objection: the valuation in the *aestimatio* could be based on the amount of rent which the legatee would have received had the bequest of the *inquilini* been valid. If we are willing to suppose interpolation in *Dig*. XXX.112.*pr.*, it may be that this is the solution of our problem. If we reject this and also Seeck's theory, I can suggest only one possible interpretation of the text of Marcianus. As far as I can see, tenants (*coloni* or *inquilini*) were relevant to the *instrumentum* only in so far as they owed rent: the *reliqua colonorum* are certainly a normal part of the *instrumentum*. May it not be that the *inquilini* of Marcianus had defaulted in payment of their rents (or had committed some other breach of their contract of tenancy), and that their landlord had then reduced them to some kind of debt bondage? As we saw in III.iv above, a man could be regarded as having property in his judgment debtor (*iudicatus*), sufficient to make removal of him theft (*furtum*: Gai., *Inst.* III.199). Could the tenants of the testator in Marcianus's passage have been *iudicati*? If so, he might indeed have felt himself entitled to bequeath them – although it is then hard to see why the bequest should have been held to be invalid. It is a great pity that we are not given the reason for this decision. I would regard Seeck's theory as quite possibly correct, but I would leave the whole question open, with the two alternatives I have mentioned as other possibilities. [See, however, n.26a.]

19. A glance through Appendix III will give some idea of the astonishing extent of 'barbarian' settlement. One aspect of the subject, on which quite a large literature has grown up recently, is the *laeti*, and their connection (if any) with the so-called 'Reihengräberkultur' (in north-eastern France and the Low Countries) and with other categories of *barbari* such as *gentiles* and *foederati*.[29] The earliest mention of *laeti*, as I said above, is in 297; they are noticed several times by Ammianus during the reign of Constantius II and by other writers such as Zosimus and Jordanes; we possess the texts of laws referring to them from 369 to 465; they turn up in the *Notitia dignitatum*, mainly in the Prefecture of the Gauls; and there even seem to be references to them in a Ravenna papyrus, as late as the mid-seventh century (*P. Ital.* 24, lines 1, 21, 46-7), and in some even later texts.[30] A detailed discussion of the condition of the *barbari* settled in the Roman empire is beyond the scope of this book, and I shall limit myself to two observations upon them. First, it is clear that the terms of their settlements might differ very widely;[31] and secondly, their installation inside the empire, which from a strictly *cultural* point of view may have contributed to the *decline* of the empire, must certainly, when considered from its *economic* aspect, be regarded as a contribution (however temporary the effect in each case) to the *preservation* of the empire. I shall deal briefly with each of these points in turn.

As for the terms of settlement, we can broadly distinguish among the settled *barbari* two main groups: those who became mere tenants or *coloni*, and those who presumably received land in freehold. There is very little positive evidence, but I would guess that the vast majority of *barbari* who came in after capture by or surrender to Roman generals would have become mere tenants (often perhaps of imperial estates), whereas many (probably most, if not all) of those who entered the empire by voluntary compact would have received land in free-hold,[32] or at least in some beneficial tenure such as emphyteusis (for which see Section ii of this chapter). Of course, where lands were granted to a king or chief and his tribe, the condition of individuals might vary widely: the chief and perhaps some of his retainers might become freeholders and lease out parcels to more humble men. Unequivocal evidence is rare, but, of the settlements listed in Appendix III below, no.23 refers specifically to *coloni*, and in several other cases the settlers certainly seem to have been mere tenants.[33] Except perhaps in a few cases, where an emperor had been obliged to grant land (which might indeed be in the possession of the *barbari* concerned already), it is likely that the lands remained subject to imperial taxation, as well as involving liability to military service; occasionally the tributary status of the recipients of land is specifically mentioned.[34] [For *hospitium/hospitalitas* see n.34a.]

My second observation (see the last paragraph but one above), pointing out that any cultural 'barbarisation' effected by these settlements must have been balanced by short-term economic advantages, needs clarification. I shall say nothing about the process of 'barbarisation', which has often been discussed. The economic benefits seem to me far more important, when we remember the decline in the rate of exploitation of slave labour resulting from the difficulty the Graeco-Roman world had, from the early Principate onwards, in obtaining slaves gratis or at very cheap rates from outside the economy, and the breeding of slaves within the economy which consequently came to predominate (see § 6 of this section). The 'barbarian' settlements, I suggest, must have had a highly beneficial economic effect (if temporary in each case) which has not been taken into account by historians but becomes immediately obvious when we realise that all those in which the settlers became mere tenants, and (if to a less extent) the majority of those involving freeholders, provided *both recruits for the army and an adult work-force, the cost of producing which had not fallen upon the Graeco-Roman economy*. (Recruiting could of course continue indefinitely, but in each case there would be only one generation of workers not produced inside the economy.) I have already emphasised that breeding slaves within the economy involved much loss of labour, not merely because the whole process of breeding necessitates giving slaves improved conditions of life and because the mothers do less work during pregnancy and lactation, but because of the very high rates of maternal and infant mortality which prevailed in antiquity (see §§ 6[b] and 8 of this section). The 'barbarian' settlements, then, produced exactly what the Roman economy most needed: adult farmers (many of them potential soldiers), the cost of whose birth and nurture had been met entirely outside the economy, and who would normally provide some surplus, either in the form of rent, or produce they did not themselves consume, or at least by way of taxation; and many of those who were disinclined to do agricultural work would be ready to serve as soldiers in the Roman army. It is true that sometimes – especially in some of the cases in which a block grant of lands may have been made in freehold – little or no surplus in taxes, rent or produce might be derived by the State from a particular settlement; and here and there we actually hear of the emperor agreeing to pay the 'barbarians' a subsidy. But in any event the new settlers would provide much-needed recruits for the army, and the great majority probably at least paid tax on their lands. Those who became *coloni* would of course provide a much more substantial surplus. After recording the despatch of 'bands of barbarian captives' to 'deserted lands destined for them to cultivate', an enthusiastic panegyrist of Constantius I in 297 rejoices because

> Now the Chamavus ploughs for me, and so does the Frisian . . . ; the barbarian cultivator lowers the cost of food. And if he is summoned to the military levy he responds, and is smartened by discipline . . . ; he congratulates himself on serving under the title of soldier (*Paneg. Lat.* IV[VIII].ix.3).

How large a surplus could be extracted from a whole tribe of Germans settled together on land which had become their freehold is unclear; but we should not underestimate the quantity of agricultural production which might be expected of them and would naturally be reflected in the rate of taxation. (The question of the agricultural and pastoral activities of the Germans is treated with admirable succinctness and clarity in two small books of E. A. Thompson: *EG*, 1965, and *VTU*, 1966.)[35] Even in Julius Caesar's day the Germans, although then primarily pastoralists, did practise agriculture in varying degrees, if at a rather primitive level. And at the time Tacitus was writing (roughly the first two decades of the second century)[36] the role played by agriculture in the economy of many German tribes, at any rate those most influenced by contact with the Roman world, had appreciably increased: even agricultural slavery was known (Tac., *Germ.* 25.1: see § 12 above). We must not suppose that the work-shy characteristics vividly depicted by Tacitus were general among the Germans: it is only the leading men whom he describes as lounging about in peace-time, doing nothing, concentrating on sleep and food, and leaving the care of their homes and fields to 'the women and the old men and the weakest members of the family' (*Germ.* 15.1; cf. 14.4, 26.1-2, 45.4, 46.1). Changes in the economy of the various Germanic peoples depended largely on the extent of their exposure to Roman influence. Evidence is scarce and mainly archaeological, but there does happen to be some good literary evidence for a considerable increase in the use of slaves by two groups of exceptionally advanced Germanic peoples: the Marcomanni and Quadi (across the middle Danube) in the second and third centuries, and the Alamanni (east of the upper and middle Rhine) in the fourth century; and in the latter case at any rate it is clear that slaves were employed in agriculture, if only by some of the leading men (see Thompson, SEG 26-9 = *SCA*, ed. Finley, 200-3). And the Visigoths and Ostrogoths, who play a major part in the story of 'barbarian' settlements in the second half of the fourth century and throughout the fifth, seem to have been predominantly agriculturalists even before the Huns, in their great westward movement in the 370s, conquered the Ostrogoths and drove the Visigoths to seek shelter across the Danube in Roman territory. Of the settlements recorded in Appendix III below, only one or two seem to have been of peoples who were nomadic or semi-nomadic and would consequently not have been capable of yielding to the Romans any kind of surplus, even by way of taxation, except perhaps the produce of their flocks and herds; but I doubt if this applies to any except the Hunnic tribes, such as the Kotrigurs (Appendix III, no.30d; cf. 26) – among the Germans, even the exceptionally 'barbarous' Heruls seem to have been partly agricultural (ibid. 29b and 30a).

20. We now reach the point at which a very considerable part of the hitherto free working agricultural population is legally bound to the soil, in one way or another. I have no doubt at all that this began to occur towards the end of the third century, as part of the great reform of the system of regular taxation introduced by Diocletian (284-305), and became universal during the fourth century. The nature of this innovation is rarely stated properly. In my opinion the only account of it which fully brings out its essential character (and therefore one of the most illuminating contributions made to the study of ancient history in

modern times) is that of A. H. M. Jones; but even some of those who refer to his treatment of the subject have failed to understand it thoroughly.[37] Not merely leasehold tenants but *the whole of the working agricultural population* throughout the Roman empire, inscribed in the tax registers, were tied to the land on a hereditary basis and thus entered into serfdom – or (as far as peasant freeholders were concerned) what I am calling 'quasi-serfdom' (see below). It seems that the *peasant freeholder* (peasant proprietor, the absolute owner of his land)[38] who was entered in the census in that capacity, however small his plot and whether or not he also happened to lease land from someone else, was tied to his *village*,[39] while the peasant who was *only a leasehold tenant* was tied to the actual *farm or plot* he rented, as a *colonus, provided* his name appeared in his landlord's census return. (The landlord in the latter case would normally be a freeholder, but he might be only a head lessee, as explained in § 22 below, e.g. the *conductor* of an imperial or ecclesiastical estate, who might often be a wealthy man.) The fact that different systems of registration in the census were adopted in different parts of the empire brought about complications, and it may be that I am over-simplifying if I notice only the two broad groups I have mentioned. But in some – probably most – areas, including at any rate Asia Minor and the Aegean islands, Thrace and Illyricum, there is reason to think that landowners entered on their returns the names of all their tenants who were not also proprietors of freehold land. In some other areas, however, including at least Egypt (for which we have some solid evidence) and probably Palestine and some of the provinces in the Prefec- ture of the Gauls, the names of leasehold tenants were apparently not entered in the census returns of the landowners from whom they leased their plots, but only under their villages, even if they owned no freehold land in addition to their rented plots; and in these areas the tenants seem to have been tied, not to their leasehold farms or plots, but to their villages, as were all peasant freeholders.[40] The overall situation, if I have analysed it correctly (and I am not quite certain of this), can be summed up as follows:

1. The peasant who owned any *land in freehold* was entered in the census return under his village and was *tied to his village*, whether he also had land on lease or not.
2. The situation of the peasant who owned no freehold land, but was a *leaseholder only*, differed according to the area in which he lived: it seems that
   (*a*) in some areas (including at least Egypt, and probably Palestine and some of the provinces in the Prefecture of the Gauls) he was, like the freeholder, entered in the census return under his village and *tied to his village*; but that
   (*b*) in other areas (perhaps in most, and certainly in Asia Minor, the Aegean islands, Thrace and Illyricum) he was entered on his landlord's census return, and he was then *tied to the actual farm or plot he rented*. (Only these last, I believe, were properly *adscripticii*, although the expression may sometimes have been used of members of my group 2(*a*) also.)

These far-reaching reforms amounted to the enserfment of a large part of the working agricultural population of the empire, in order to facilitate the increased exploitation of them – through taxation above all, not to mention forced services and military conscription – which had become necessary to maintain the Roman empire in the form in which it was reorganised by Diocletian and

Constantine. That reorganisation was of course seen by its authors as necessary, in the common interest of all, for the very preservation of the empire, imperilled as it was now, as never before, by 'barbarian' threats, by the increased power of Persia under the Sassanids, and by internally destructive rivalries for control of the imperial power (see Chapter VIII below, especially Section iv). However, the propertied classes were determined to maintain, and were able to maintain, their dominance and their economically privileged situation; and the greater a man's wealth and the more exalted his rank in the social and political hierarchy, the more likely he would be to succeed in preserving and even strengthening his position, even if a certain number of prominent individuals had to be sacrificed in the process. The great reorganisation was therefore primarily for the benefit of the propertied classes as a whole; and for them, or at any rate their upper crust, it worked wonders for a time (cf. VIII.iv below). We now enter upon the period commonly called the 'Later Roman Empire', in which the emperors, from Diocletian onwards, assumed an even more exalted position, enabling them (if they were competent enough) to exercise still greater control, in the collective interest of the governing class. But, as I have explained in VI.vi below, it is a mistake to imagine a fundamental change in the nature of imperial rule, from 'Principate' to 'Dominate', with the inception of the Later Empire. The Princeps (as he was still often called) had always been in practice a virtually absolute monarch, and the most significant feature of the changes that came about with the Later Empire was an intensification of the forms of exploitation, among which the introduction of widespread serfdom was perhaps, in the long run, the most important element.

21. I think Jones was right in believing that the law binding peasants to their villages or farms was 'primarily a fiscal measure, designed to facilitate and ensure the collection of the new poll tax, and not specifically aimed at tying tenants to their farms'; but that 'landlords found the law useful in holding their tenants and reclaiming them if they left', and the emperors extended the original measure for their benefit (see especially *CJ* XI.li.1, of Theodosius I), and increased the dependence of tied *coloni* on their landlords by a series of laws over the fourth and fifth centuries (Jones, RC, in *SAS*, ed. Finley, 293-5; cf. Jones, *RE* 406-7; *LRE* II.796-801). Peasant freeholders, however, although they always remained numerous, at any rate in the Greek East, were of no particular interest to the landlord class, and the laws binding them to their villages seem to have been little enforced, except when villages themselves took action (as we see in *P. Thead.* 16-17) to stop mass desertions – which were probably rare, for peasant freeholders would seldom be driven to the length of abandoning their ancestral properties.

As regards tenants the position was exceedingly complicated. The tied 'colonate', in the sense of tenants bound to the plots they leased (and not simply to their villages), was naturally a matter of keen interest to the landlord class: it was extended to Palestine by a law of Theodosius I (quoted above), and probably to Egypt well before 415, when we first hear of tenants called *coloni homologi* (*CTh* XI.xxiv.6.*pr.*,3), who apparently included tenants on estates, although they were actually registered in their villages. Even tied coloni, however, although serfs according to my definition (in III.iv above), remained theoretically free in status: they were not technically slaves. Before the second half of the fourth century the term *colonatus* had come into use for the serf colonate. Its earliest appearance is usually dated to 382 (*CTh* XIV.xviii.1 = *CJ* XI.xxvi.1), perhaps on the strength of the *Thesaurus Linguae Latinae*, in which that is the earliest text cited; but the term *colonatus iure* occurs as much as forty years earlier, in *CTh* XII.i.33, where it is already used as a technical term. At this point I must revert to the fact (already mentioned under heading II of III.iv above) that from the later fourth century onwards the emperors tended to use for the serf colonate the terminology of slavery, inappropriate as it was, in a way which the great lawyers of the earlier centuries would surely have scorned. In a constitution of *c.* 395, relating to the civil diocese of Thrace, the Emperor Theodosius I, while admitting that its *coloni* were technically 'of free status' (*condicione ingenui*), could add the sinister phrase that they 'must be regarded as slaves of the very land to which they were born' (*servi terrae ipsius cui nati sunt aestimentur*), and could allow their *possessor* to exercise over them 'the power of a master' (*domini potestas: CJ* XI.lii.1.1). A few years later the Eastern Emperor Arcadius declared that it was 'almost the case' that serf *coloni* (here called *coloni censibus adscripti*), although admittedly *liberi*, seemed to be 'in a kind of servitude' (*paene est ut quadam servitute dediti videantur: CJ* XI.l.2.*pr.*, probably to be dated 22 July 396: see Seeck, *RKP* 132, 291). Between 408 and 415 Theodosius II, in a vivid phrase, referred to 'all those whom Fortune holds bound by the chains of their inherited fields' (*omnes quos patrimonialium agrorum vinculis fortuna tenet adstrictos: CJ* XI.lxiv.3) – a curious phrase, paralleled in an earlier constitution of Gratian and his colleagues, in 380, speaking of 'persons owed to the law of the fields' (*iuri agrorum debitas*), to which they are to be brought back (*CTh* X.xx.10.1 = *CJ* XI.viii.7.1). In a constitution of 451 the Western Emperor Valentinian III ruled that the children of a free woman and a slave or *colonus* must remain as *coloni* (*colonario nomine*) under the control and ownership (*in iure et dominio*) of those on whose lands they were born, except in the case of a woman who had beforehand been given formal notice (*denuntiatio*) that she might not enter into such a union, in which event the children were treated as slaves: there is a reference to the former being held by *nexus colonarius*, the latter by the *condicio servitutis* (*Nov. Val.* XXXI.6; cf. *CTh* IV.xii.4–7). From the mid-fifth century onwards we begin to hear of a particular kind of serf *coloni* known as *adscripticii* (*enapographoi* or *enhypographoi* in Greek),[41] who in the West are called *tributarii, originales* or *originarii*, and whose status began to verge towards that of slaves. (Their precise nature is still disputed, but I believe the account given by Jones to be substantially right: *LRE* II.799–803; RC, in *SAS*, ed. Finley, 298–302; *RE* 417.) In 530 the Emperor Justinian found some difficulty in distinguishing between *adscripticii* and slaves: 'What difference can be detected,' he says, 'between slaves and *adscripticii*,when each of them has been placed in the power of his master (*dominus*), who can manumit the slave with his *peculium* and alienate the *adscripticius* with his land?' (*CJ* XI.xlviii.21.1). A few years later Justinian could describe it as 'contrary to human nature' (*inhumanum*) to defraud the land of its *adscripticii*, 'its very limbs [*membra*], as it were': the *adscripticius* 'must remain and adhere to the land' (*remaneat adscripticius et inhaereat terrae:* ibid. 23.*pr.,* of the early 530s).[42] Significantly, Justinian treated marriages between *adscripticii* and free persons as governed by the rules of Roman law regulating unions between free men or women and slaves (*CJ* XI.xlviii.24, very probably of 533; *Nov.J.* CLXII.1–3, of 539). The legal issue was not really settled even yet, and Justinian, as so often, kept changing his mind (see Jones, in *SAS*, ed. Finley, 302 n.75); but whatever the legal situation might be, the emperor was determined that every single *colonus* should be made to remain on the land on which he was born – that, he says, in a very curious phrase, is what the very name of *colonus* signifies (*Nov.J.* CLXII.2.1, of 539).

One of the most interesting documents we possess, dealing with the Later Roman colonate, is a very short letter of Sidonius Apollinaris to his friend Pudens, which must have been written in the 460s or 470s (*Ep.* V.xix). Its terminology is worth special attention. The son of Pudens' nurse, a dependant of Pudens, had raped the daughter of Sidonius' nurse. Pudens had begged Sidonius not to punish the man, and Sidonius now agrees on condition that Pudens releases him from his *originalis inquilinatus* and thus becomes his *patronus* instead of his *dominus*: this will enable the ravisher, as a *cliens* of Pudens instead of a *tributarius*, to take on the character of a *plebeius* instead of a *colonus* (*plebeiam potius . . . personam quam colonariam*) and thus to achieve *libertas* and marry the woman, who was already free (*libera*). The man, although not a slave, and of course not requiring to be manumitted, cannot be regarded as fully free until Pudens, his 'master', recognises him as no longer a *colonus, inquilinus, tributarius,* but now a free *plebeius* and a *cliens*.

22. In §§ 20 and 21 I have been speaking of what I have called 'the *working* rural population', who in the late third century were bound to the land (freeholders to their villages, and those who were only tenants and had no freehold land of their own either to their villages or to their particular farms or plots), although for reasons I have already mentioned much less pressure was put upon the freeholders – provided they duly paid their taxes. Historians (and lawyers) not sufficiently familiar at first hand with the literary as well as the legal evidence for the colonate are apt to think of the long series of laws we are now discussing as affecting only leasehold *tenants*; but this is quite wrong, because by no means all leaseholders were bound, in the fourth century and later, and at the beginning of the process most if not all working peasant *freeholders* were bound too, in the areas in which the serf colonate was introduced. This mistake is made, for example, by Finley, who speaks of the Codes as providing evidence that 'from Diocletian at the end of the third century, *tenants* were tied, not free', and adds that 'with the *disappearance* of the free tenant [presumably with Diocletian] went the *disappearance* from the legal texts of the classical Roman tenancy contract' (*AE* 92, my italics). This formulation is most misleading as it stands. In the first place, in so far as it has any validity at all it applies only to the Latin West, not to the Greek East. In at least some parts of the Greek East there were even among working peasants (as can be seen from the papyri) a considerable number of tenants, including some apparently quite humble ones, who were not 'tied' but took leases for short terms.[43] Finley's statement was perhaps taken from the one work he refers to: an article by a distinguished Roman lawyer (Ernst Levy, RPGL, 1948) which hardly makes it sufficiently clear that it is concerned almost entirely with the West alone, and moreover shows altogether inadequate knowledge of the non-legal sources, even for the West (see the next paragraph). A book by Levy, published eight years later, is explicitly devoted to the West and does draw a contrast with the East on the very point we are considering (*WV* 251-75, esp. 251 n.476); but again it shows unawareness of important literary and papyrological evidence. The overall picture of Later Roman leasing from

the strictly legal point of view is rather better presented by Max Kaser (*RP* II[2] [1975] 400-8). Although paying too high a compliment to Levy's book by referring to it as 'grundlegend', he does at least draw a series of contrasts between West and East. However, even he, in my opinion, exaggerates and antedates the decline in the West of the Classical Roman contract of lease, *locatio conductio*, in his almost exclusive reliance on legal sources.

In fact people we may conveniently refer to as 'head lessees', who did not themselves work the land they held (often either imperial domain, leased from the *res privata*, or else Church property), but let it out to working tenants, *coloni*, were not tied to the land at all: these are the *conductores* (in Greek, *misthōtai*) who still turn up frequently in the Codes and Novels, in papyri, and in literary sources. Leasing according to the traditional pattern, without involving any enserfment (see e.g. *CJ* XI.xlviii.22.*pr*.,1, of A.D. 531), continued even in the West into the late sixth century and beyond: there is ample evidence for this, well summarised by Jones, *LRE* II. 788-92 (with III.252-5 nn.44-50; and see 97 n.13). The lessees concerned varied greatly in status. In a papyrus from the Ravenna collection dated 445-6 (*P. Ital.* 1) we find that some of the *conductores* who took leases from a retired high official (a former Grand Chamberlain) were able to pay very high annual rents, amounting to hundreds of solidi (up to 756), for blocks of estates (*massae*) in Sicily.[44] These were evidently men of substance; but at the opposite extreme we come across *conductores* who were actually slaves. I have already referred to Ampliatus, who appears in a letter of Pope Gelasius in the 490s as a slave-*conductor* of the Roman Church.[45] There is also the enterprising man Clarentius, claimed by Pope Pelagius I (*Ep.* 64) in 559 as the son of a female slave of his Church (who would therefore himself be legally a slave of that Church): he is said by Pelagius to have acquired a *peculium* of his own, including a small farm (*agellus*), and even to have had the audacity to pass himself off as a *curialis*;[46] he was to be returned to the ecclesiastical *massa* whence he originated. The most interesting literary evidence of all is provided by the letters of Pope Gregory the Great (590-604), showing that the vast estates of the Church of Rome, the *patrimonium Petri*, were still very often let to *conductores*, who sublet to *coloni*.[47] In 592 there were no fewer than four hundred of these *conductores* on the estates of the Roman Church in Sicily alone (*Ep.* II.38);[48] and the same system of exploiting its lands was employed by that Church in other areas, notably Gaul. A letter of Gregory's written in 595 is addressed 'To the [head] lessees of the estates or farms [of the Roman Church] throughout Gaul' (*conductoribus massarum sive fundorum per Galliam constitutis*): *Ep.* V.31. (Among many other interesting letters of Gregory there are two, *Ep.* II.38 and V.7, of A.D. 592 and 594 respectively, which contemplate the possibility of bribing Jewish tenants to convert to Christianity by offering them reductions, up to one third, of their rents, *pensiones* – which, incidentally, were paid in gold: sums of from one to four solidi per year seem to have been common.) Further literary evidence for Late Roman *conductores* is not hard to find: see e.g. Symm., *Ep.* IV.68; IX.52; and later (between *c*.507 and *c*.536) Cassiod., *Var.* I.16; II.25; V.39; VIII.33; XII.5 (of which V.39 relates to Spain, the others either to Italy in general or to Apulia or Lucania and Bruttium). I may add that I could cite over thirty laws, mostly issued in the West, from the Theodosian Code and the fifth-century Novels, which speak of *conductio* or *locatio, conductores* or *locatores*, and the rents (*pensiones*) payable under these contracts, not to mention other texts.[49] It is indeed impermissible to speak of the disappearance of the contract of *locatio conductio*, even in the West, in the period covered by this book. And peasant freeholders, although over all a declining group, especially in the West, still survived in considerable numbers throughout the Later Empire, at any rate in the Greek East;[50] and, as we have seen, many of them were also 'tied' to their villages. (That freeholders as well as tenants were tied has often been over-looked; but it was noticed, for Egypt, by Gelzer, although not very clearly stated, in a book published seventy years ago, *SBVA*, 1909, which remained unknown to Jones: see n.37 again.)

23. Apart, then, from landowners and 'head lessees' who belonged to my 'propertied class' (III.ii above) and are not to be reckoned among those I have called the '*working* agricultural population', we can recognise four broad groups among the non-slave working agricultural population:[51] (1) peasant freeholders, of whom an unascertainable and varying (perhaps decreasing) proportion were tied to their village communities; (2) free leasehold tenants; (3) those tenant serfs who were yet technically of free status, and (4) *adscripticii*, serfs who by the sixth century at least had become scarcely distinguishable from slaves. It is impossible to make even an informed guess about the relative proportions of these groups, which will have varied greatly from place to place and from time to time. Some people today might wish to confine the term *colonus* to my third and fourth groups, who alone were 'serfs' in the strict sense (see III.iv above). The sources, however, even the legal texts, sometimes use the word *coloni* more loosely, in my opinion, in such a way as to include at any rate those of my first group who were in fact tied to their villages, and perhaps all or virtually all working peasants (cf.Stein, *HBE* II.207-8, esp. 208 n.1). Tied freeholders, of course, do not in strictness fulfil my definition of serfs; but, as I have explained in III.iv above, if they paid heavy taxation they were not really in a very different position from serf-tenants, and I refer to them as 'quasi-serfs'.

Agricultural slaves, while legally retaining their servile status, benefited during the fourth century from a series of imperial enactments (for which see III.iv § II above and its n.16 below). These culminated about 370 in a law which forbade selling them apart from the land where they were registered in the census (*censiti*: *CJ* XI.xlviii.7.*pr.*), and thus raised them in effect to a serf-like condition. If manumitted, they would have to remain on the land they had been cultivating, as *adscripticii*. Pope Gregory the Great, who was determined to enforce the laws forbidding Jews to possess Christian slaves, gave orders that the Christians owned by Jewish tenants on the estates of the Roman Church at Luna in Etruria should, after being freed, remain on the same land and perform 'all those services which the laws prescribe concerning *coloni* or *originarii*' (*Ep.* IV.21, of A.D. 594).

* * * * * *

Before I leave this section I must face a problem (perhaps of greater interest to Marxists than to others) which I have so far ignored. It concerns the inter-mediate period, if I may call it that, between the general use of *slave labour* as the principal way in which the propertied class obtained its surplus, and large-scale *serfdom*, which (as we have seen) did not come into existence until the very end of the third century and in some areas was not complete until the late fourth century (as in Palestine) or even the early fifth (as perhaps in Egypt). This 'intermediate period' may be conceived as beginning at very different times in different areas, and it may be that some people will deny its existence altogether. But I believe that most historians who interest themselves in problems of this sort would be prepared to see it as coming into existence at some time during the first two centuries. We must then face the difficulty: during this 'intermediate period', must not a rather large proportion of the propertied class have derived its surplus more (perhaps much more, in some places) from letting its land to free tenants than from working it directly with slave labour? And if so, have we any justification for continuing to speak of that surplus as being derived from the exploitation of '*unfree* labour' at all, before the introduction of serfdom at the beginning of the Later Roman Empire?

My answer to this question can be divided into three parts.

(i) First, leasing land to a free tenant must as a rule yield a smaller profit to a landowner than working it directly with slaves, since the tenant will need to provide himself and his family with a livelihood out of the produce of the land, before he can pay rent or taxes. Leasing is simply not considered as a desirable method of exploiting one's land by the Roman agricultural writers, unless the land is situated in an unhealthy district, where the landowner would be ill-advised to risk employing valuable slaves, or at such a distance that he cannot give the necessary regular supervision (Colum., *RR* I.vii.4,6–7). Therefore, landowners eager for profit would be unlikely to resort to leasing, unless they could not obtain the necessary slave labour, or could not exploit a particular piece of land adequately because it involved more personal supervision than they were willing or able to give it, or because they could not procure efficient stewards.

(ii) Next, the use of slaves must not be thought of as necessarily or even ordinarily absent when land in antiquity was leased. A leasehold tenant might have his own slaves, in which case he would in principle be able to derive a greater profit from the land and as a result pay a higher rent. Far more often, it seems, at any rate in the early Principate, slaves were supplied by the landlord as part of the *instrumentum* (the equipment) of the farm; and of course, if a tenant works a farm with slaves provided by the landowner, the latter profits from the labour of the slaves, because he can charge the tenant a higher rent. I referred in § 18 above to the two main passages in the *Digest* defining the *instrumentum* of a farm. One, from Ulpian, describes what items are 'customarily' supplied by way of *instrumentum* when a farm is leased, so as to become the subject of a legal action if they are not included (*si quis fundum locaverit, quae soleat instrumenti nomine conductori praestare*: *Dig*. XIX.ii.19.2); but of course any items might be added or excluded by explicit agreement. (This is so, even if the words 'nisi si quid aliud specialiter actum sit' are an interpolation.) The *Digest* texts, which also speak of bequests of a farm 'supplied with slaves' (*instructus*[52] *cum mancipiis*, etc.), show that slaves (although not mentioned in *Dig*. XIX.ii.19.2) were frequently contained in the *instrumentum*, and they might evidently in some cases be quite numerous and varied and include bailiffs or supervisors (*vilici et monitores*), as well as various specialists (*Dig*. XXXIII.vii.8.*pr.*,1), with their 'consorts' (*contubernales*: ibid. 12.33; cf. 27.1), who in other texts, as we saw at the end of § 10 above, are actually called 'wives' (*uxores*). We often hear of bequests of landed property that include 'rents outstanding from tenants', *reliqua colonorum* (see §§ 13[b] and 18 above); and sometimes slaves are mentioned as well (e.g. *Dig.* XXXIII.vii.27.*pr.*,1) – although in the latter case we need not assume that part of the land is being worked directly, for the slaves may simply be those handed over to tenants; and when we find another text referring to 'farms furnished with their overseers and rents outstanding from tenants' (*fundos . . . instructos cum suis vilicis et reliquis colonorum*: ibid. 20.*pr.*; cf. XX.i.32), the overseers, mentioned alone without other slaves, surely have the function of supervising cultivation by tenants. Dorothy Crawford has drawn attention to the fact that '*vilicus*-management' on the imperial estates which she has studied in many parts of the Roman empire 'often went together with leasing' (in *SRP*, ed. Finley, 50). Installing such men as overseers would be all the more necessary when the tenants were share-croppers. When Pliny the Younger was faced with declining returns from his north Italian farms and was thinking of going over to what came to be called *colonia partiaria* (share-cropping, *métayage*), he realised that he would have to put in some of his own slaves as overseers (*operis exactores, custodes fructibus*: *Ep.* IX.xxxvii.2-3). Earlier he had brought slaves from his city household, *urbani*, to supervise his *rustici*, during a vintage (xx.2): these *rustici* may be either tenants or (as I think much more probable) slaves.[53] And in one of the most important of his many letters referring to his estates, Pliny speaks of the resources of the tenants on an estate he had acquired as having been gravely reduced by the fact that the previous owner had on several occasions forfeited their securities ('sold their pledges', *vendidit pignora*, III.xix.6), thus in the long run increasing their arrears. The *pignora* evidently included slaves, for Pliny now regrets that he himself will have to provide the tenants with efficient and expensive slaves (ibid. 7). Pliny goes on to speak of the value of the estate in question as having been reduced from five to three million sesterces: he attributes this to what he conceives as a prevailing recession (*communis temporis inquitas*) and the current *penuria colonorum* – an expression which (as I said in Section ii of this chapter) must refer to the shortage of available tenants rather than to their poverty. Certainly Pliny complained in another letter of the difficulty he was having in finding 'suitable tenants' (*idoneos conductores*, VII.xxx.3).

There are many indications that slaves were being used to an appreciable degree in agriculture throughout the Principate and beyond, though no doubt much less in Egypt (as always) than in other parts of the Greek world. For example, in Hadrian's law concerning the sale of oil produced in Attica about A.D. 125 we find it taken for granted that a slave or freedman will be in charge of production (*IG* II².1100 = A/J 90, lines 15-18). A law issued by Constantine in 318 seems to assume that a decurion will have both urban and rural slaves (*mancipia, urbana* and *rustica*: *CTh* XII.i.6). Even in the handful of surviving census records of the late third or early fourth century from which it is possible to make some estimate of the relative sizes of the free and slave labour forces in two or three places in Asia Minor and the Aegean, slaves do appear; and if in some areas they seem to constitute but a small porportion of the registered agricultural population, they also turn up elsewhere in households of 20 or more (see Jones, *RE* 228-56, esp. 242-4; cf. 296-7 = *SAS*, ed. Finley, 292). And when in many imperial constitutions of the fourth and fifth centuries we hear of overseers (*actores* and/or *procuratores*, occasionally *vilici*), they often appear to be conceived as slaves.[54] (Cf. III.iv above and its n.14 below.) It is seldom if ever possible to tell whether these men are supervising the employment of direct slave labour: probably many if not most of them would spend at least part of their time controlling the activities of humble *coloni*. In view of the reluctance of free Greeks and Romans in general to take long-term hired service (see III.vi above) and the disinclination of many members of the propertied class in late antiquity to spend time supervising their estates (see above), the function of slave (and freedman) overseers was essential, and I would see them as playing a very important role in the economy, perhaps far more so than has been generally realised. (On the traditional functions of a *vilicus*, see Toynbee, *HL* II.576-85.) If we speak of a 'decline of slavery' in the early centuries of the Christian era, we must not forget that slaves (and freedmen) always played a major part at the highest level, in providing the propertied class with their incomes.

I suspect, too, that we may tend to underestimate the actual number of slaves usefully employed in the Later Empire. Occasionally mass enslavements might occur, usually as a result of war. Perhaps the most remarkable example is the defeat of the horde of Goths and others led by Radagaisus across the Danube and into north Italy in 405-6 (see e.g. Stein, *HBE* I[2].i.249-50), when we are told that some of the captured barbarians were sold off at one solidus per head – perhaps about one-twentieth of the usual price of slaves about this time (see Jones, *LRE* II.852; III.286 n.68). A generation earlier, in 376-7, when vast numbers of Visigoths were allowed to cross the Danube and settle in Roman territory (see Appendix III below, § 19b), the Roman officials Lupicinus and Maximus are said by Ammianus to have taken advantage of their inability to obtain sufficient food by selling them dogs to eat, in exchange for humans, who thereby became slaves: one dog would be given in exchange for a slave, who might even be the son of a leading Goth (Amm. Marc. XXXI.iv.11). In the *Expositio totius mundi et gentium*, a survey of much of the Roman empire, of very uneven value (written in 359, according to its latest editor, Jean Rougé, *SC* 124, 1966), we find but two references to slaves, both using the technical term *mancipia*. In its ch. 60 Mauretania is said to be an area which exports slaves, and in ch. 57 Pannonia is described as 'in part, rich also in slaves' (*terra dives . . . ex parte et mancipiis*). These statements may well be true, in the sense that in both areas there were at the time numbers of 'barbarian' captives: in Pannonia at any rate, if we can date the work in 359, the Emperor Constantius II, as Rougé points out, had just brought to a successful conclusion his campaigns against the Sarmatians. A letter of St. Augustine, written at the end of the second decade of the fifth century, speaks of 'innumerable barbarian peoples', as yet ignorant of the Gospel, from among whom captives are taken and enslaved by the Romans and are then given religious instruction (*Ep.* 199.46). [See also Evagr., *HE* V.19 (*c.* A.D. 581).]

In one case, from the first decade of the fifth century, in which we happen to have many details (whether accurate or not) of the estates of a particular person, St. Melania the Younger (or of Melania and her husband Pinianus), we hear in one source (the Latin *Life,* § 18)[55] of her owning sixty farms or hamlets (*villulae*), each with 400 agricultural slaves (*servi agricultores*), and in another source of her offering freedom to her slaves, a gift accepted by 8,000 who wanted it (Pallad., *Hist. Lausiac.* 61). Many other texts in the fifth and sixth centuries mention agricultural slave households in smaller numbers.[56] It is worth noticing in particular the will of St. Remigius, bishop of Rheims, which gives an exceptionally detailed picture of the landed property of a moderately well-to-do Gallo-Roman of the first half of the sixth century. This, I believe, can be taken as fairly representative of the estates of a substantial section of the men of moderate wealth throughout the empire, in the Greek lands as well as the Roman West. The will, in its shorter form (which unlike the longer one can be accepted as genuine),[57] disposes of fifteen parcels of land in the territory of Rheims and of 81 named individuals (52 men and 29 women), some of them with families, amounting to roughly a hundred persons in all, partly *coloni* and partly slaves, constituting the work-force of the land. (The farms and their workers seem to have made up virtually the whole of Remigius' property.) Fifteen or sixteen of the individuals bequeathed are evidently slaves, twelve are called *coloni*; of the others it is uncertain whether they are *coloni* or slaves.[58] Although a majority of the work-force in this case are likely, I think, to have been *coloni*, it is quite possible that not many fewer than half consisted of slaves, some of them slaves of the *coloni*.

(iii) Finally, I would again emphasise the universal and unquestioning acceptance of slavery as part of the natural order of things, which during the Principate still pervaded the whole of Greek and Roman society – and of course continued in the Christian Empire just as in earlier times (see VII.iii below). Slavery continued to play a central role in the psychology of the propertied class. And here I would refer again to what I said earlier about debt bondage: every humble free man must always have been haunted by fear of the coercion, amounting to slavery in all but name, to which he might be subjected if he ever defaulted on a debt to a rich man – including the payment of rent, of course, as I have pointed out above.

I therefore see no serious difficulty in the objection I have discussed, and I feel justified in re-stating what I said near the end of III.iv above: that slavery was indeed the archetypal form of unfree labour throughout Graeco-Roman antiquity.

I have said nothing in this section about hired labour, a subject treated at some length in III.vi above (see esp. its n.19 below on the Roman period).[59]

(iv)
The military factor

There is one aspect of the situation of the peasantry in the ancient world which I have no space to discuss properly but which needs to be carefully examined; and I offer some reflections for consideration. One view of the decline of Roman power, especially in the West – which might commend itself, *prima facie*, to some self-styled Marxists in particular – is as follows. It is an established fact that the next great advance in Europe, namely capitalist society, was to develop not on the basis of communities of small, free, independent peasants but out of urban elements growing up inside feudal regimes the economic base of which had always been a peasantry mainly held in a very subject condition, often outright serfdom. As Max Weber put it, 'At the time of the decline of the Roman Empire the future belonged to the development of large landownership'

(*RA* 264). Therefore, it could be maintained, the enserfment of the Late Roman peasant was ultimately, in the long view of history, beneficial to human progress, since it facilitated, over several centuries, a new and better form of society which could never have developed spontaneously out of a largely peasant economy. As those who are fond of this detestable phrase might like to put it: '*History was on the side of* the great landowner, with his serfs, not of the small, free, independent peasant.'

There may be some truth in this view, but it ignores an element in society to which I rarely have occasion to pay serious attention in this book, but which must now be allowed to come to the fore: military efficiency. When a society is dangerously threatened from the outside, as the Greeks and Romans were on various occasions, its very survival may depend upon its military prowess. Here, in individual cases, factors peculiar to the situation may sometimes be decisive: sheer weight of numbers, technological efficiency, an unforeseeable disaster like a plague, or the death of a gifted leader (Attila's in A.D. 453 is an obvious example). But many of us – and not only Marxists – would say that military success, at least in the long term, is largely dependent upon economic and social as well as political factors. It was certainly the growth of a free and fairly substantial peasantry in Greece in the Archaic and Classical periods which produced the hoplite armies that frustrated the might of the Persian empire at Marathon and Plataea (B.C. 490 and 479). The success of Greek over Persian fleets in a few decisive engagements (above all, of course, Salamis in 480) was due above everything else to the indomitable fighting spirit of their sailors and marines; and no one will doubt that this spirit was inseparably bound up with the *polis*, a political community of free men based upon fairly widely diffused landownership and access to political rights by the whole citizen body or at least the more well-to-do members of it. The successful armies of Philip II and Alexander the Great were highly professional, but were based upon a sudden great access of landed wealth, in varying degrees, to the formerly insignificant Macedonian peasantry and aristocracy, producing not only cavalry which was more than a match for that of the Persian aristocracy, but also excellent infantry, in which the Persians of the Achaemenid period (mid-sixth to late fourth century B.C.) were entirely wanting. The irresistible military power of Rome in her great days was similarly founded upon a free peasantry, at first conscripted, then, especially during the Principate, furnishing recruits in large measure voluntarily to a standing professional army (although conscription was still often employed).[1]

For some three and a half centuries before the mid-third century of the Christian era there had been no major external threats to Rome: after initial disasters, the German tribes which invaded Gaul and Italy in the last years of the second century B.C. were effectively destroyed, and although the Parthians could cause anxiety, they were no more than an intermittent nuisance to Syria and Palestine. The German Marcomanni and Quadi were very troublesome in the reign of Marcus Aurelius, in the 160s and 170s (see VIII.iii below), but they were eventually contained. Then, from the mid-third century onwards, barbarian pressure on the frontiers of the empire became severe, if in fits and starts; and the Sassanid kingdom in Persia (A.D. 224–636) became a much stronger force than the Parthians had ever been and presented a real threat to some of the eastern provinces. The defeat and capture of the Emperor Valerian by Shapur I in 260 was a milestone in the relations between the Graeco-Roman world and its Iranian neighbours – to whom at least one great historian, Ammianus Marcellinus (a Greek from Antioch who chose to write in Latin), much as he disliked them, never once applies the term 'barbari' which he uses for every other external adversary of the Roman empire.[2] Military efficiency now became a matter of life and death to Graeco-Roman civilisation. By the end of the fourth century the Roman armies had probably grown to well over half a million men, considerably greater than the figure in the early Principate (cf. VIII.iv and its nn.9-10 below); and from the reign of Diocletian onwards there was once more regular conscription, although by the time of Justinian recruitment seems to have become mainly voluntary once more.[3] The army of course was a very great burden on the economy of the Roman empire (cf. VIII.iv below).

★   ★   ★   ★   ★   ★

Before proceeding further, I wish to state the main thesis of this section in summary form.

1. As I have just shown, from the second quarter of the third century onwards pressure on the frontiers of the Roman empire became much greater and tended to go on increasing, and the defence of the frontiers therefore became a matter on which the empire's survival rested.

2. In the circumstances of the time, the necessary standing army had to be raised largely from the peasantry.

3. In order to provide sufficient recruits of strong physique and potentially good morale, it was therefore essential to maintain a reasonably properous and vigorous peasantry.

4. On the contrary, as land, during the early centuries of the Christian era, became increasingly concentrated in the hands of a few owners (throughout most of the West and also, to a less extent, over a large part of the Greek East), the condition of a substantial proportion of the agricultural population became more and more depressed, until before the end of the third century most working peasants (as we saw in the preceding section of this chapter) were subjected to forms of serfdom or quasi-serfdom.

5. In the *strictly economic* sense, this may or may not have been a progressive development. (Whether or not it promoted the efficient use of scarce resources is a question that deserves investigation, but which I do not yet feel able to answer confidently.)

6. *Socially* and *militarily*, however, the process I have described was very harmful, since the peasants became increasingly indifferent towards the maintenance of the whole imperial system, most of the burden of which fell heavily upon them; and the morale (and probably the physique) of the army deteriorated, with the result that much of the empire disintegrated by stages between the early fifth century and the mid-seventh.

7. The maintenance of a relatively prosperous peasantry, sufficiently numerous to provide the large number of recruits needed for the army and willing to fight to the death in defence of their way of life (as the free Greeks and

the early Romans had been), might have made all the difference and might have preserved the unity of the empire very much longer.

*   *   *   *   *   *

The statement I have made in § 7 above becomes more than a mere hypothesis when we look at what happened in the Byzantine empire, where the success of the imperial armies against invading Persians, Avars, Arabs, Bulgars and other Slav peoples, Magyars, and Seljuk and Ottoman Turks, from the time of Heraclius (610-41) onwards, depended to a considerable degree on the condition of the peasantry which still provided the bulk of the recruits. I need say no more on this subject here, as it has been admirably dealt with by the great Byzantine historian Ostrogorsky.[4] The tenth and eleventh centuries were the decisive period: after the death of Basil II 'the Bulgar-Slayer' (976-1025), the landed magnates (the *dynatoi*) finally triumphed, and the army gradually disintegrated.

Much the same situation has existed down the ages, until the nineteenth century. As Max Weber said,

> The need for recruits was the reason why the mercantilist rulers during the epoch of 'enlightened despotism' curbed big enterprise in agriculture and prevented enclosures. This was not done for humanitarian reasons and not out of sympathy with the peasants. The individual peasant was not protected – the squire could drive him out without any scruples by putting another peasant in his place. But if, in the words of Frederick William I, 'a surplus of peasant lads' was to be the source of soldiers, such a surplus had to exist. Therefore, any reduction in the number of peasants through enclosures was prevented because it would endanger the recruitment of soldiers and depopulate the countryside (SCDAC 270).[4a]

It was also Weber who pointed out, in one of his most inspired passages, that in Renaissance Europe there was one conspicuous exception to this situation: England, the exception which – we may legitimately say, for once – proves the rule.

> The free labour force necessary for conducting a modern factory . . . was created in England, the classical land of the later factory capitalism, by the eviction of the peasants. Thanks to its insular position England was not dependent on a great national army, but could rely upon a small, highly trained professional army and emergency forces. Hence the policy of peasant protection was unknown in England, although it was a unified State early on and could carry out a uniform economic policy; and it became the classical land of peasant eviction. The large labour force thus thrown on the market made possible the development first of the putting-out and the domestic small master systems and later of the industrial or factory system. As early as the sixteenth century the proletarianising of the rural population created such an army of unemployed that England had to deal with the problem of poor relief (Weber, *GEH* 129 = *WG* 150).[4b]

I do not wish to be dogmatic on this subject; but it does seem to me that societies which depend largely upon armies recruited from their peasants are much more likely to be destroyed or at least damaged by invaders from outside if they allow the bulk of their peasants to be so oppressed and exploited that they lose interest in the maintenance of the regime under which they live. Naturally, a society in which wealth is mainly in land is likely to be dominated by its great landowners. Sometimes, however, such a society – at any rate if political control of it is concentrated, as in the Roman and Byzantine empires, in the hands of a single ruler who knows that he is personally responsible for the fate of his whole kingdom – may be forced to acquiesce in measures designed to protect the peasantry upon which, as its potential soldiers, its very survival depends. The policies of several of the Byzantine emperors, above all Romanus I Lecapenus and Basil II, were strongly in favour of the independent peasants and against the appetite of the magnates for ever-increasing acquisition of great estates; and indeed there is intermittent legislation by the Roman emperors from the third century onwards, attempting to curb the activities of the *potentiores* which were seen as a threat to the security of the empire as a whole (see n.4 again, also VIII.iv and its n.43 below).

For the man who actually had to work with his own hands (the *autourgos*, as the Greeks called him), farming was universally believed to provide the ideal training for the military life: this is explicit in Xenophon and other writers, including Cato, Pliny the Elder and Vegetius.[5] On the other hand, 'the mass of artisans and those with sedentary occupations' (*opificum vulgus et sellularii*) were thought to be the least suited of all to military service; and in Republican Rome it was only on exceptional occasions that they would be called up, as in 329 when a Gallic incursion was thought to be imminent (Livy VIII.20.3-4). I know of no parallel to the attempted levy of soldiers from the urban slave households of Roman senators in the crisis of 398, revealed by Symmachus, *Ep.* VI.58, 64. Vegetius, writing probably near the end of the fourth century of our era, innocently reveals the essential contribution made by the poverty of the peasant to his military qualities: the more frugal one's life, the less one fears death! ('Ex agris ergo supplendum robur praecipue videtur exercitus; nescio quomodo enim minus mortem timet qui minus deliciarum novit in vita': *De re mil.* I.3.) Poverty and frugality, however, are relative; and below a certain limit poverty can become deleterious and insupportable, and may even lead to a decline in population, as many historians think it did in the Middle and Later Roman Empire (see e.g. Jones, *LRE* II.1040-5).

Now we must surely admit that the attitude of the peasantry in both Eastern and Western parts of the Roman world during the Later Empire in the face of barbarian irruptions and conquests was extraordinarily passive and indifferent. I must say, I have only come across one case in the Graeco-Roman world in which the government is actually seen ordering the inhabitants of the country-side to confine their attentions to agriculture and leave all military action to the army: this was in the summer of 536, when Justinian's forces from Sicily under Belisarius were moving into southern Italy, and a Gothic army had been mobilised against them in Lucania and Bruttium. Cassiodorus, as praetorian prefect of the Ostrogothic kingdom of Italy during the brief reign of Theo-dohad, admitted the depredations of the Goths against the peasants but ordered the local governor to restrain rash initiatives on the part of the *possessores* (*continete possessorum intemperantes motus*: *Var.* XII.5). He strictly forbade in-dividual lessees of great estates (*singuli conductores massarum*) and the important landowners (*possessores validi*) to take up arms and concern themselves with the fighting: they were to take pleasure in the thought that others were fighting the foreign enemy on their behalf. Evidently the government was afraid of armed assistance being given to Belisarius; but I would not care to say whether the people Cassiodorus was most nervous about were the mass of peasants or the landowning class – the language I have quoted certainly suggests the latter, for elsewhere Cassiodorus normally uses the words *possessores* and *conductores* for landowners and head lessees (see e.g. *Var.* II.25; V.39; VIII.33).

Jones justifiably speaks of 'the passive inertia of the civil population, high and low, in the face of the barbarian invasions', and gives many examples. As I shall demonstrate, he is too inclined to ignore or discount some of the evidence showing that many humble folk in the Roman empire might evince a positive preference for barbarian rule, as being less oppressive than that of the emperors (cf. VIII.iii below). But in the main he is certainly right in emphasising that 'the peasantry were in general apathetic and docile' (*LRE* II.1061; cf. IV.ii above). They usually remained passive, although if they were formally conscripted into the army, or were pressed into service either against the barbarians (often on the initiative of local notables) or by the barbarians against an imperial army, they might fight obediently enough until released.[6] (Discipline in the Roman army was virtually always such that once a recruit was enrolled he was completely obedient to his commanders: see below.) On one occasion, during the conflict in 546 between Justinian's forces and the Ostrogoths in Italy under Totila, we even hear of peasants being impressed into both armies and fighting a battle against each other.[7] Perhaps the most striking example of what seems to be spontaneous military action by peasants is attributed to some villagers of the region of Edessa in Mesopotamia by the contemporary *Chronicle* of 'Joshua the Stylite' (§§ 62-3). We are told that in 503 the villagers greatly impressed the Roman general Areobindus by making sorties from the city against the invading Persian army, after Areobindus had ordered the garrison not to take aggressive action. The outlines of the story may well be correct (see esp. § 63 *init.*), even though miraculous happenings tend to creep into the chronicler's narrative when he is dealing with the holy city of Edessa (see §§ 5 and 60 for the reason).

The view expressed by some scholars that the peoples subject to Rome were forbidden to manufacture and possess arms has recently been attacked by Brunt (DIRDS).[8] He is clearly right to point out that it would anyway not have been possible to stop the manufacture of arms in village smithies; and that apart from occasionally prescribing disarmament as a temporary move immediately after a capitulation or in very special circumstances, Rome was quite willing to allow a certain amount of armed force to remain at the disposal of the local ruling classes, who were 'left to control the masses and share in their exploitation', and who in return were mainly very loyal to Rome. 'There was no good reason for Rome to impose disarmament on any subject communities whose local governments could be counted on to show fidelity' (ibid. 270, 264). It is certainly relevant that we do not seem to hear of any state arms factories before the reign of Diocletian, at the end of the third century; and it was only in A.D. 539, by Justinian, that the manufacture and sale of arms was made a complete state monopoly (*Nov.J.* LXXXV). However, apart from local police forces (264 and nn.15-16) Brunt seems to be able to produce no specific evidence for any 'local militia', even for the early Principate, the period from which all his material comes. I certainly know of no such evidence for the third century or after, apart from small local levies of *burgarii* and the like to defend fortified places;[9] and in the Later Empire, as far as I can see, there was nowhere any regular 'local militia'. Jones may not be justified in saying of the Later Empire that 'the civil population was in fact, for reasons of internal security, forbidden to bear arms'; but I entirely agree with his continuation, that what was more important was the general 'attitude of mind . . . Citizens were not expected to fight, and for the most part they never envisaged the idea of fighting' (*LRE* II.1062). Allowing the possession of weapons does not necessarily ensure that men will be organised, and trained in the use of weapons. In Cyrenaica in the early fifth century, when it was being attacked by the nomads of the interior, Synesius could get together hundreds of spears and swords (*lonchai* and *kopides*) and a certain number of axes, but no body-armour (*hoplōn problēma*), for the militia he was organising to resist the barbarian raiders (*Epist.* 108; and see n.6 to this section). Nearly half a century later Priscus could represent the Greek whom he met in the camp of Attila (see VIII.iii below) as speaking of a general prohibition on the use of arms by Romans except in the regular army. The general view was certainly that the defence of the empire was a matter for the professional army alone; and, as I have indicated, the civil population mainly regarded fighting as something with which it was simply not concerned.

I would take seriously a passage in the speech which Cassius Dio (writing perhaps towards the end of the second decade of the third century) makes Maecenas address to Augustus, when advising him to create and isolate a standing army: 'If we allow all adult males to possess arms and practise the military arts, they will continually be the source of disturbances and civil wars', whereas if arms are confined to professional soldiers, 'the toughest and the strongest, who are generally obliged to live by brigandage [a significant admission!],[10] will then support themselves without harming others, and the rest will all live in security' (LII.xxvii, esp. §§ 3-5; contrast vi.5, from the speech of Agrippa; and cf. V.iii and its n.40 below).

The limitation of arms in practice to a standing professional army, and to it alone, was a natural consequence of the very nature of the Roman empire, as an instrument of class domination. Recruits for the army, as I have said, always came primarily from the peasantry, even if from the early fifth century onwards the government, desperate to maintain agricultural manpower, had to exclude *coloni adscripticii*, tenants tied to their plots: see Jones, *LRE* II.614, with III.184 n.14. (It will surprise no one that it was the great senatorial landowners who were able to offer the most stubborn and successful opposition to the levying of recruits from their estates, even in an emergency such as the revolt of Gildo in Africa in 397.)[11] As I shall argue (in VIII.iii-iv below), the indifference of the mass of humble people (most of them peasants) to the maintenance of the imperial machine, under which they suffered merciless exploitation, was a prime cause of the collapse of much of the Roman empire in the West in the fifth and sixth centuries and the loss of many Eastern provinces to the Arabs in the seventh.

I would add that the army of the late Roman Republic, Roman Principate and Later Empire[12] developed a most remarkable discipline and *esprit de corps* of its own: the rank-and-file soldiers became entirely detached from their origins and were usually the obedient instruments, if not of their emperors, then of their actual officers. Except when an emperor could command general loyalty, and at rare times such as the year 69 when there was a widespread collapse of discipline, all the soldiers accepted the hierarchical principles on which Roman society was conducted and would often follow their commanders with complete fidelity into insurrection and civil war, when that was what their commanders ordered, just as into foreign wars. The civil wars of the third and fourth centuries were invariably contests for the imperial throne (see VIII.iii below). Among the few mutinies we hear of that were not primarily attempts to secure the imperial title for some favoured officer, it is those of the armies on the Danube and the Rhine at the beginning of the reign of Tiberius (A.D. 14) of which we have the most lively and instructive account, in the *Annals* of Tacitus (I.16-30, 31-8).[13] The speech of Percennius, the leader of the mutiny in Pannonia, is vivid and compelling in its description of the lands given to veterans on retirement, after thirty or forty years' service, as 'stinking swamps or mountain wastes' (I.17.5). And the ferocious discipline to which the common soldiers were subjected is nicely illustrated in the account of the centurion Lucilius, who had gained the nickname 'Bring me another' (*cedo alteram*) from his habit of breaking his vine-stick on a soldier's back and calling for another and another (I.23.4). Lucilius was murdered by the mutinous soldiers; Percennius, needless to say, was executed, with other leading mutineers (I.29.4; 30.1).

★ ★ ★ ★ ★ ★

I think we should admit that when in Europe the most effective form of defence against attacks from outside (by Arabs, Turks, Magyars, Northmen and others) was found to lie not so much in the simple foot-soldier, but rather in a much more expensive military figure, the mounted and armoured knight, there would be a case, on military grounds, for a sufficiently increased exploitation of the primary producers to permit the maintenance of such figures in sufficient quantity to repel invaders. The mediaeval knight, burdensome to his society as he was, certainly played a role in preserving the heritage of Graeco-Roman civilisation in Europe against outside attack, whether we think that heritage worth preserving (as I do) or not. His role, that of doing the required *fighting*, and the accompanying one of the priest and monk, whose essential function was to do the *praying* that was generally believed to be a necessity, were accepted willy-nilly by the great mass of the people whose function was *working*; but the latter might feel they had cause for bitter complaint when the fighters ceased to give them any real protection. Rodney Hilton has recently drawn attention to the fury of the French peasants after the battle of Poitiers (1356) against the nobles 'as a whole, for not having fulfilled their duty of protection, which tradition and mutual obligation demanded of them' (*BMMF* 131). I should not wish, therefore, to assert the necessity in all circumstances for a pre-capitalist society to maintain a solid free peasantry as the basis of its military power. An even greater military burden might have to be shouldered. Nevertheless, efficient cavalry forces can in principle be maintained, in the same way as infantry, by a state which levies general taxation, rather than by allowing mounted knights to support themselves individually by the surplus labour of peasant serfs (or slaves) on specific estates. And in any case I do believe that the accumulation by a landed aristocracy of vast estates, greater than would be necessary to maintain efficient cavalry forces, is a development which can seldom if ever – and certainly not in the Later Roman Empire – be regarded as a progressive feature.

This whole subject, and the extent to which military considerations have been allowed (and should be allowed) to predominate over others in given societies, would be worth careful consideration over a very long period. I am of course thinking only of military strength designed for use in defence against attacks from outside, not for internal police duties.

(v)
'Feudalism' (and serfdom)

This seems a convenient place to deal briefly with the subject of 'feudalism'. Throughout this book I have studiously avoided using the terms 'feudal', 'feudalism', in reference to any period or area of ancient society. These words are often used by ancient historians (even some of the most distinguished: Jones, Rostovtzeff, Syme)[1] in a slipshod way, a habit which can only be deplored. Unfortunately there is still no complete agreement among historians, even of mediaeval Europe, as to how the essential features of their 'feudalism' should be defined,[2] but at least they can point to certain societies which they and virtually everyone else would not hesitate to recognise as 'feudal'. There are a few mediaevalists, on the other hand, who would prefer to avoid the term 'feudalism' altogether. According to a recent writer in the *American Historical Review*, 'The tyrant feudalism must be declared once and for all deposed and its influence over students of the Middle Ages finally ended'![3] At the opposite extreme, we find a symposium published in 1956 with the title, *Feudalism in History*, investigating the question how far feudalism can be discovered in all sorts of different historical circumstances, not only in western Europe but in Japan, China, Ancient Mesopotamia and Iran, Ancient Egypt, India, the Byzantine empire, and Russia; a 'comparative study of feudalism' by the editor, Rushton Coulborn, wishes to see feudalism treated as 'primarily a method of government, not an economic or a social system', and with the relation of lord and vassal as its essential feature.[4] We must of course leave it to the historians of other countries (Japan and China, for instance) to decide for themselves whether certain societies in their area of study can usefully be described as 'feudal' (or 'semi-feudal' or 'quasi-feudal'), provided only that they make it perfectly clear what these terms mean to them.

There are, I suppose, two principal characteristics of a society which most often lead to its being designated 'feudal' by those in the English-speaking world who are not specialists in European mediaeval history: one is the existence of something resembling the military fief of European feudalism, and the other is the presence of serfdom on a large scale. In the former case there may sometimes be little harm in making use of some such term as 'quasi-feudal'; but the existence of serfdom alone certainly does not justify the employment of any such expression,[5] since forms of serfdom have existed in many societies which have little or no resemblance to those European mediaeval ones which have the best right to be called 'feudal'. I wish to make it clear that throughout this book any reference to 'serfs' or 'serfdom' (see especially heading II of III.iv above) must not be taken to imply any necessary or even probable connection with anything which can properly be described by terms such as 'feudal' or 'feudalism'.

There is a short definition of feudalism which I think many Western European mediaevalists would accept, and which was adopted in one place even by Marc Bloch: 'the system of vassalage and of the fief' (*CEHE* I².265-6). Pollock and Maitland suggested that 'feudo-vassalism' would be a more serviceable expression than 'feudalism'.[6] But Bloch never for one moment forgot the economic foundation of feudalism; and indeed the formula I have just quoted occurs in a chapter entitled 'The rise of dependent cultivation and seignorial institutions', in which Bloch goes on at once to speak of the seignorial system as closely related to feudalism. And in his great work, *Feudal Society* (described by M. M. Postan, in the opening sentence of his Foreword to the English translation, as 'now the standard international treatise on feudalism'), Bloch actually begins his list of 'the fundamental features of European feudalism', occupying some eight lines, with 'A subject peasantry' (II.446).

However, many other Western mediaevalists, when they are speaking of feudalism, feel they can afford to treat the whole edifice independently of the sub-structure which sustained it, and define it entirely with reference to those free men who were each other's lords or vassals, united by bonds of fealty and the creation of benefices in the form of fiefs. When Ganshof declared, 'The way in which the word [feudalism] is used by historians in Soviet Russia and in other countries behind the Iron Curtain seems to me to be absolutely irrelevant',[7] I feel sure it was their Marxist disinclination to forget the 'subject peasantry' which he found particularly tiresome. Postan, in his Foreword to the English edition of Bloch's *Feudal Society* to which I have already referred, has a fascinating paragraph on what he describes as

> an Anglo-Soviet occasion when the two principal speakers, the Russian and the English, gave carefully composed disquisitions on feudalism which hardly touched at a single point. The English speaker dwelt learnedly and gracefully on military fiefs, while the Russian speaker discoursed on class domination and exploitation of peasants by landlords. Needless to say the Russian disquisition was packed tight with familiar Marxist furniture: the state as a vehicle of class rule, 'commodity exchange' as a solvent of feudalism, feudal economy as an antecedent of early capitalism. Yet for all its dogmaticism and ancient verbiage, the Russian use of the term appeared to bear more directly on the intellectual enterprise of history than the conventional connotation adopted by the English speaker (p.xiii).

Although I have little sympathy for the kind of mediaevalist I mentioned at the beginning of the last paragraph, I do feel that since the word 'feudalism' has some value as a generic name for a set of European mediaeval institutions of a peculiar kind, characterised in particular by vassalage and the fief, even though resting largely upon a basis of some kind of dependent labour (most characteristically serf labour), it is a pity to weaken it by extending the vocabulary of feudalism (including *féodalité, féodale, Lehnwesen, lehnbar* etc.) too widely. As I have already insisted, serfdom can exist and has existed in societies which have little or nothing in them that can properly be called 'feudal'. In the Hellenistic kingdoms, for example, where forms of serfdom certainly existed, only a minor role was played by the military *katoikiai* and other settlements of soldier-cleruchs which provide the nearest analogy to the fief in the Hellenistic world and have led some of the best scholars to speak of 'feudal' tenures; and there was certainly no necessary connection between the military settlements and serfdom. It seems to me regrettable, therefore, that some Marxists seem to want to call a society 'feudal' merely because it rested on a basis of serfdom. Wolfram Eberhard could even say that 'Marxist scholars' (whom he does not identify) 'tend to call feudal any society in which a class of landowners who at the same time also exercised political power, controlled a class of farmers and often also a class of slaves' (*Hist. of China*[4] 24).

It may be rather a pity that Marxists have been saddled by Marx himself with a terminology in which the name of 'feudalism' is given to the 'mode of production' *in Western Europe* out of which capitalism emerged. Terms such as 'the feudal mode of production' are perhaps too deeply rooted in Marxist writing to be replaced by any such alternative as 'the mediaeval Western European mode of production'. But Marxists ought to remember – as they too often fail to do – that Marx and Engels described feudalism at one point in the *German Ideology* as 'the *political* form of the mediaeval relations of production and intercourse' (*MECW* V.176); and at all costs they must avoid using the terminology of feudalism in such a loose way that it could be made to fit, for example, the society of the Later Roman Empire. The usage of which Eberhard complains (if he is not misrepresenting his 'Marxists') would extend, indeed, to most pre-capitalist societies, including the greater part, if not the whole, of Graeco-Roman antiquity! Of course there are borderline cases, such as Hittite society in Asia in the second millenium B.C.: I need refer only to R. A. Crossland's admirably compressed summary, in which he says that 'The Hittite state was a feudal society, in the sense that a large sector of its economy was organised to provide a trained army, and that there were in it social divisions based on tenure of land under the obligation to perform military service for the king.'[8] I shall not myself presume to lay down a definition of feudalism. There have been several recent discussions of the subject in English. If what is wanted is a Marxist analysis of the expression 'feudal *mode of production*' which would limit that term strictly to the society of mediaeval Western Europe, to which alone (I think) Marx applied the expression, then I would prefer Perry Anderson's (*PAF* 147-53). Rodney Hilton has produced a much briefer characterisation, in a single-page 'Note on Feudalism' (*TFC* 30), which would allow, for example, for the fact that Marx could speak at one point of Japan as having a 'purely feudal organisation of landed property' (*Cap.* I.718 n.1) – the only time, I believe, that Marx applied the terminology of feudalism to any country outside Europe. The brief definition of feudalism given in a single paragraph by Witold Kula (*ETFS* 9) is less specific: he is thinking primarily of Poland in the sixteenth, seventeenth and eighteenth centuries.

(vi)
Other independent producers

I intend to be brief about my 'other independent producers', who are a very heterogeneous collection rather than a single category, and of course must not be treated as belonging to a single class. My reasons for dealing with these 'independent producers' in a separate section are to indicate broadly how I think their class position should be determined, and to mention a few relevant facts about them.

I begin by excluding two exploited classes with which I have dealt already: first, hired labourers in the strict sense (see III.vi above); and secondly, those ancillary workers – artisans, building and transport workers, fishermen and others – who originate from the peasantry and remain among it, and are treated here as part of the peasantry (see Section ii of this chapter). Manual workers who cannot properly be regarded as part of the peasantry (because, for example, they live in a town) form the bulk of those I am considering in this section, with traders and those who provide transport and other services of various kinds. Perhaps the largest single group would be artisans or craftsmen[1] (*Handwerker*: the German word has a somewhat broader scope). Traders of different sorts, from the merchants who carried on commerce between cities (*emporoi*) to small local dealers and shopkeepers (*kapēloi*), would be a group of perhaps equal importance. A fair number in almost every section would be freedmen (see III.v above). The status and the class position of all these people would usually be closely related, but not always: here, it is only the latter with which I am concerned, and for me the main determinant of an individual's class position in antiquity is the extent to which he exploits the labour of others (mainly slaves, but also occasionally hired men) or is himself exploited. At its highest level my present category – like that of peasants – will merge with my 'propertied class': the criterion for membership of that class, as I have already made plain (in III.ii above), is the ability to live a life of leisure without actually working oneself to provide one's daily bread. And it is likely that any of my 'independent pro-ducers' who acquired sufficient wealth to enable them to live the life of a gentleman would make the necessary change of life-style, although others might aim higher and prefer to continue their trade or business activity until, for example, in the Roman period, they qualified for the equestrian order. (In my scheme of things the second set of individuals, as much as the first, would already have entered the 'propertied class', although their social status would be relatively lower until they ceased their 'banausic' activity.)

Most of the individuals I am now considering would be quite humble men, who could normally raise themselves into my 'propertied class' only in one of two ways: either by displaying some extraordinary skill, or by becoming able to exploit the labour of others. Among those we should call 'artists' (the ancients did not normally distinguish them from craftsmen), we hear of a handful who made their fortunes, although the few figures we find in the literary sources are seldom very plausible – the HS 1 million, for instance, which Lucullus is said by Varro to have promised the sculptor Arcesilaus for making him a statue of Felicitas (Pliny, *NH* XXXV.156), or the twenty talents' weight of gold which Alexander the Great is supposed to have paid the painter Apelles for depicting him wielding a thunderbolt in the temple of Artemis at Ephesus (ibid. 92). Certainly the great Athenian sculptor Praxiteles, whose life probably spanned the first six decades of the fourth century B.C., must have become wealthy, for in the 320s we find his son Cephisodotus appearing as a trierarch and as one of the most conspicuously rich Athenians of his day (see Davies, *APF* 287-8).[2] Ordinary skilled craftsmen might have to be prepared to travel about a good deal if they did not live in a large city where there would always be plenty of work. We often hear of Greek architects, sculptors, builders and the like moving from city to city where major projects were in progress (see Burford, *CGRS* 66-7, with examples and references). When Dionysius I, the famous tyrant of Syracuse, planned to attack the Carthaginian area in 399 B.C., he is said by Diodorus to have brought together *technitai* to make weapons of war, not only from the considerable portion of Sicily which he controlled but also from Italy, where there were many Greek cities, from Greece itself, and even from the

Carthaginian dominions (XIV.xli.3-6).

Doctors, in the earlier periods of Greek history, were also placed in much the same category as other 'craftsmen': in Homer the doctor is grouped among *dēmioërgoi*, with the seer, the carpenter and the minstrel (*Od.* XVII.382-5); and in Plato he is put on the same level as the shipwright (*Gorg.* 455b). Only one Greek doctor before the Hellenistic period appears in literature as having earned large sums of money by his professional skill: the famous physician Democedes of Croton, as early as the sixth century B.C., is said to have been paid in three successive years a talent by Aegina, 100 minae (1²/₃ talents) by Athens (at this time under the tyrant Peisistratus), and two talents by Polycrates, the tyrant of Samos (Hdts III.131.2). In case anyone feels that Democedes was really giving a form of hired labour, I had better explain that what the Aeginetans and Athenians and Polycrates were really paying for was Democedes' valuable presence in their cities; he may well have made additional earnings from his patients. In the Hellenistic and Roman periods the status of the more successful Greek doctors (though hardly of doctors as a whole) certainly rose; and we have numerous texts that speak of them with respect, in particular the 'public physicians'[3] employed by cities and at the royal courts; in the Roman period the title of 'chief doctor' (*archiatros* in Greek) was widespread. The greatest of all Greek doctors, Galen,[4] whose life covered the last seven decades of the second century, was personal physician to the Emperor Marcus Aurelius.

Talented *hetairai* (courtesans) and other providers of essential services sometimes did very well for themselves. Among traders, the petty local ones called *kapēloi* would rarely if ever make substantial sums; but *emporoi*, inter-city merchants (who might also be called *nauklēroi* if they were ship-owners),[5] must sometimes have made fortunes, if not nearly as often as many modern scholars have supposed.[6] But the great majority of the people I am dealing with in this section are likely to have lived not very far above the poverty-line, unless and until they could manage to acquire a slave or two, as I think a fair number may have done when conditions were favourable and slaves were cheap. There is a very revealing remark in Sallust, describing the common people whose votes, in his opinion, had been mainly responsible for the election of Marius (a *novus homo*) to the consulship of 107 B.C. (but see VI.v n.60 below): he describes them as 'artisans and countrymen all, whose *assets and credit* were *embodied in their hands* (*opifices agrestesque omnes, quorum res fidesque in manibus sitae erant: BJ* 73.6). In this the craftsman and the poor peasant bore a strong resemblance to each other.

Those I am dealing with in this section are all, by definition, not members of the 'propertied class', apart of course from the few who managed to rise into it. We must then ask, How were they exploited, and to what extent? This is not at all an easy question to answer. The great majority of these individuals will have shared an important characteristic with those peasants who were freeholders: as a rule they were not subject to *direct* exploitation by *individual* members of the propertied class (cf. Section i of this chapter), except in so far as they got into debt to rich men. They were unlike hired labourers in that their principal asset, their skill ('embodied in their hands'), was under their own control; in addition, some of them will have owned simple tools and the like, but the only items in this category which are likely to have been really important are those that belonged to some transport-workers: mules, donkeys and oxen, carts and wagons. Exploitation of members of all the groups with which I am dealing in this section will probably not as a rule have been severe, unless it took place in an *indirect* form, through taxation or compulsory menial services.

As we saw in Section i of this chapter, taxation in the Greek cities in the Classical, Hellenistic and Roman periods is a very difficult subject, about which little that is significant is known, owing to the fragmentary and chaotic nature of the evidence; but I believe that detailed investigation might well reveal a heavier incidence of taxation on these groups than has been generally realised. In the Later Roman Empire there is at least one general tax on such people about which we have some definite evidence: the *chrysargyron* or *collatio lustralis*, imposed by Constantine in the early fourth century upon *negotiatores* in a broad sense, including for this purpose not only traders but also fishermen, moneylenders, brothel-keepers and prostitutes, as well as urban craftsmen who sold their own products, though not rural craftsmen (whom I have classified among peasants: see above). The tax was payable at first in gold or silver, but from the 370s onwards in gold only. It is probably the fact that this tax was payable once every four years which made its incidence appear so heavy. At any rate, there are harrowing descriptions by the orator Libanius, the historian Zosimus and the ecclesiastical historian Evagrius of the hardships which the collection of this tax was believed to impose: parents are even said to have been driven to sell their children into slavery and fathers to prostitute their daughters in order to raise the necesary money to pay the tax.[7] We have only a single figure for the amount raised by this tax: in the last years of the fifth century, 140 lb. gold was being collected every fourth year at the important city of Edessa in Mesopotamia (Josh. Styl. 31). This works out at 2,520 solidi per year – not a large sum, certainly, compared with what peasants had to pay (see Jones, *LRE* I.465), but enough to cause distress, or at least bitter complaints. The tax was still being paid in Italy under the Ostrogothic kings in the sixth century; but it was abolished in the East by the Emperor Anastasius in 498 (*CJ* XI.i.1, dated by Josh. Styl. 31).

I cannot resist mentioning here one amusing fact, arising out of the payment of the *chrysargyron* by the brothel-keepers of Constantinople. The trade of the procurer (the *leno*) was forbidden in 439 in Constantinople by the Emperor Theodosius II; but the wording of the imperial constitution by which this was done (*Nov. Theod.* XVIII) begins with a fascinating preamble (§ 1), showing that it had been necessary for the chief promoter of this measure, Florentius (who had just been Praetorian Prefect of the East), to make a settlement of property (undoubtedly in land) the income of which would be sufficient to compensate the state for the loss of revenue from the tax consequent upon the hoped-for disappearance of the *leno* from Constantinople! The Novel in question, written in the degenerate rhetorical Latin of the fifth century, is well worth reading as a whole. It begins by expressing satisfaction that no one need now doubt the historical traditions of 'eminent men putting the interests of the state before their own wealth': the opening words are, 'Let historical works earn credence from contemporary example' (*fidem de exemplis praesentibus mereantur historiae*). Not for another two or three decades, by the way, were brothels prohibited everywhere, by a constitution of the Emperor Leo (*CJ* XI.xli.7) – which of course was widely disregarded. As the lawyer Ulpian had said more than two centuries earlier, in a passage reproduced in Justinian's *Digest*, 'brothels are maintained on the property of many men of quality' (*multorum honestorum virorum*, V.iii.27.1).

Specialised workers of various kinds – not only craftsmen but also merchants, shipowners, ferrymen, fishermen, moneychangers, gardeners and many others – became more and more addicted, partly under Roman influence, to collective associations, often referred to in modern times, misleadingly, as 'guilds'. The normal Latin word for one of these is *collegium*.[8] In Greek a great variety of collective terms is found;[9] it is also very common for the men concerned simply to refer to themselves as 'the ferrymen', 'the bakers', 'the shoemakers', 'the wool-workers', and so forth. Some of these associations may have been little more than 'burial-clubs'; and there is very little evidence of their having acted like modern trades unions to improve their members' pay or conditions of work; but there are a few scraps of evidence for such activities in one or two places in the Greek East, extending even to the organisation (or the threat) of what we should call strikes. An interesting article by W. H. Buckler (LDPA) presented all the important evidence available down to 1939; MacMullen in 1962-3 added a few scraps (NRS). Of the four documents printed and discussed by Buckler I shall single out two. Buckler's no.1 (LDPA 30-3) shows the provincial governor intervening at Ephesus, in the late second century, at a time of 'disorder and tumult', to discipline 'the bakers', who had been holding allegedly factious meetings and refusing to bake sufficient bread. Buckler's document no.4 (LPDA 36-45, 47-50, republished as *IGC* 322, and finally as *Sardis* VII.i [1932] no.18), an inscription precisely dated to 27 April 459, is much the most interesting: it shows 'the builders and artisans [*oikodomoi kai technitai*] of Sardis' making an elaborate compact with the *ekdikos* (*defensor*) of the city, a government official belonging to the department of the Master of the Offices. In order to put an end to strikes and the obstruction of building work, the association guarantees (among other things) that any work contracted for by any of its members will be properly carried out, and even undertakes to pay an indemnity in certain cases of default, and to accept liability for payment of fines out of its common property. Although the word *misthos* does occur in line 23, it does not refer (as so often elsewhere: see III.vi above) to the wages of hired labour but to the payment to workmen of their 'contract price': this is clear from the technical terms *ergodotēs* and *ergolabēsas*, used several times for the employer who 'gives out the work' and the artisan who 'undertakes the work' respectively; and when in line 35 the word *misthos* occurs again, it is used in the sense of 'indemnities' to be paid as mentioned above by the association. These 'builders and artisans' are all craftsmen, not hired labourers.

A constitution of the Emperor Zeno, issued in 483 to the City Prefect of Constantinople (*CJ* IV.lix.2), forbade anyone to create a monopoly (*monopolium*), on pain of confiscation of property and permanent exile, or to hold illicit meetings for the swearing of oaths and the making of agreements fixing minimum prices (ibid. *pr.*,2) – evidently such things had recently been happening. Building and other workers were forbidden to refuse work on contracts begun but not finished by others (ibid. 1), and the officials of other associations were threatened with huge fines, of 50 lb. gold, if they dared to enter into a conspiracy to increase prices (ibid. 3).

★   ★   ★   ★   ★   ★

There is a much-quoted passage in Plutarch's *Life of Pericles* (2.1-2) which some people today may find astonishing: in Plutarch's eyes no young gentleman, just because he had seen the Zeus of Pheidias at Olympia or the Hera of Polycleitus at Argos (two of the most-admired ancient statues) could possibly want to *be* Pheidias or Polycleitus.[10] Such statements in the mouth of a 'real Roman' might not seem so surprising, it will be said; but was not L. Mestrius Plutarchus, the Roman citizen (albeit a newly-made, first-generation one), also very much a Greek? The answer is that in the Roman period the Greek as well as the Roman propertied classes felt a greater gulf between themselves and all those (including *technitai*, and therefore 'artists') who engaged in 'banausic' occupations than had the leading Greeks of the Classical period, at least in Athens and some other democracies. Had Pheidias and Polycleitus sculpted purely as amateurs, had they enjoyed large private incomes and received no payment for their artistic work, Plutarch and his like would have found nothing contemptible about them. It was the fact that they could be considered to have *earned their living* by actually working with their own hands that made them no fit model for the young Graeco-Roman gentleman. Plutarch says elsewhere that the Athenian painter Polygnotus showed he was no mere *technitēs* by decorating the Stoa Poikile at Athens *gratis* (*Cimon* 4.7).

Since in a class society many of the values of the governing class are often accepted far down the social scale, we must expect to find disparagement of craftsmen, and therefore even of artists, existing in the ancient world not only among the propertied Few. In particular, anyone who aspired to enter the propertied class would tend to accept its scale of values ever more completely as he progressed towards joining it. Yet it would be absurd to suggest that the lower classes as a whole dutifully accepted the social snobbery and contempt for the 'banausic' that prevailed among the well-to-do. Many Greeks (and western Romans) who might be called 'mere artisans' by superior people even today were evidently very proud of their skills and felt that they acquired dignity by the exercise of them: they referred to them with pride in their dedications and their epitaphs, and they often chose to be pictured on their tombstones in the practice of their craft or trade, humble as it might be in the eyes of their 'betters'.[11] To say that 'the ancient Greeks' despised craftsmen is one of those deeply misleading statements which show blindness to the existence of all but the propertied Few. It might have shocked even the humble Smikythe, who, in an inscription of four words accompanying an early-fifth-century dedication at Athens, took care to record her occupation: she was a *plyntria*, a washerwoman (*IG* I².473 = *DAA* 380).[12] It would certainly have shocked the families of Mannes the Phrygian, who was made to boast on his tombstone in late-fifth-century Attica, 'By Zeus, I never saw a better woodcutter than myself' (*IG* I².1084),[13] and of Atotas the Paphlagonian, whose fine Attic monument of the second half of the fourth century, describing him as 'Atotas, miner' (*metalleus*), bears two elegiac couplets advertising the *Selbstbewusstsein* of the proud technician, with not only a conventional claim to distinguished heroic ancestry but also the boast that no one could compete with him in *technē* (*IG* II².10051).[14] In a dedication of A.D. 149, also in elegiac couplets, probably from Perinthus in Thrace, the sculptor Kapiton and his assistant Ianouarios (who inscribed the verses) prided themselves on being 'skilled in craftsmanship' (*sophotechnēïes*).[15] They were using a very rare word; but the *sophia* in *technē* which they were claiming, whatever it might be called (most often just *technē*), had a long history that we can trace for many centuries, in literature and inscriptions, right back into the Archaic age. The name Technarchos ('master of *technē*'), revealed by a graffito of about the last decade of the sixth century B.C. in the temple of Apollo at Spartan Amyclae, suggests that around the middle of the sixth century an artisan could hopefully give his son a name that would suit a master craftsman, proud of his calling.[16] And very many makers and painters of vases in the sixth century B.C. and later, especially at Athens, proudly inscribed their names on their products, followed by the word '*epoiēsen*' (for the maker) or '*egrapsen*' (for the painter).[17]

PART TWO

V

The Class Struggle in Greek History
on the Political Plane

(i)
'The age of the tyrants'

In this chapter I propose to concentrate mainly on the ways in which the class struggle in Greek history manifested itself on the political plane.

After the Dark Age which succeeded the Mycenaean civilisation, our earliest contemporary picture of Greece is that of the poet Hesiod, in the *Works and Days*, written from the standpoint of a Boeotian countryman, in the late eighth century B.C. or at the beginning of the seventh.[1] Here the lot of the farmer is presented as hard, with unceasing toil.[2] But we must not think of anything resembling the miserably poor 'Potato Eaters' whom Van Gogh portrayed with such heartrending sympathy (see IV.ii above and its nn.3-4 below). In fact, Hesiod is writing for reasonably well-to-do freehold farmers,[3] who are assumed to have a number of slaves,[4] as well as the occasional hired hand, the *thēs*,[5] and various kinds of cattle. When the poet advises his reader to have only one son – or, if he has more, to die old (*WD* 376 ff.) – one remembers that this theme, the desirability of transmitting one's property undivided to a single heir, has often obsessed members of a privileged class, especially perhaps those who are on the lower edge of that class and whose descendants may fall below it if they inherit only a part of the ancestral estate.[6] The mentality is very different from that of a peasant serf in a 'labour rent' system such as that of Poland from the sixteenth century to the eighteenth (as analysed with great acuteness by Witold Kula), where the peasant's obligation to perform the traditional amount of labour for his lord was paramount, and he could not hope to rent additional land and profit from the sale of its produce unless he could find additional labour inside his own family, with the result that 'in this economic system, in which the families of rich peasants are those which have the most members, they are not larger because they are richer, but on the contrary, richer because larger'.[7]

Access to political power in Hesiod's Boeotia, as in all other Greek states of which we know anything at this time, is clearly the exclusive preserve of a hereditary aristocracy, described by Hesiod as 'gift-devouring princes' (*dōro-phagoi basilēes*),[8] who scorn justice and give crooked judgments. The outlook of these blue-blooded gentlemen is superbly expressed in the *Theognidea*, poems probably put together at a later time, around a nucleus of genuine poetry written by Theognis of Megara at some time between the mid-seventh century and the mid-sixth.[9] But now, in Theognis' world, the situation is very different from what it had been in Hesiod's time. The old secure days of aristocracy are gone. The poet himself, a class-conscious aristocrat if ever there was one, had been driven into exile and his lands confiscated: for this he cries bitterly to Zeus for vengeance, praying that he may drink the blood of those who have his lands.[10] For Theognis, society is divided into just two groups, his terminology for which (as always in ancient Greece)[11] is an inextricable mixture of the social and the moral. On one side are Theognis and his like, who are quite literally the Good (the *agathoi* or *esthloi*), and on the other side are the Bad (the *kakoi* or *deiloi*).[12] Everything depends on birth: in one of his most emotional pieces the poet bewails the corruption of heredity that comes from intermarriage between the Good and the Bad (lines 183-92).[13] In mating rams and asses and horses, he says, men look for thoroughbreds; but now, provided he gets a large dowry, a 'good' man (he means of course a man of blue blood) does not hesitate to marry the 'bad daughter of a bad father' – a *kakēn kakou*, the daughter of what I have sometimes heard called 'a pleb'. The result is that *ploutos emeixe genos*: perhaps 'wealth confounds heredity' (190, cf. 192). Correspondingly, a woman will not disdain a 'bad' husband, provided he is rich (187-8). A nice illustration would be the marriage of Pittacus of Mytilene in Lesbos, described (perhaps quite unfairly) by the aristocratic poet Alcaeus as a *kakopatridēs* (a man with a low-born father),[14] to a girl from the arrogant Penthelid family of the same town – who, according to Aristotle, were in the habit of going round striking people with clubs, an unfortunate trait which led to their being attacked (and some of them killed) by a certain Megacles and his associates (*Pol.* V.10, 1311^{b}26-8).[15] Mere wealth, without good birth, remains a trivial quality for Theognis; and he is being bitterly sarcastic when he apostrophises Wealth (Plutus) as 'the fairest and most desirable of all the gods', and says, 'With you a man becomes Good (*esthlos*) even if he's really Bad' (1117-18). As for the 'demos' (δῆμος), the lower classes (the great majority of the population), who had been taking the wrong side in this acute class strife, the right way to treat them is to kick them hard, prod them with a sharp goad, and put a harsh yoke on their necks – then you will not find a *dēmos* anywhere so *philodespotos*, one that so loves its master (847-50).[16] Theognis must have thoroughly approved of the way Odysseus treats the low-class agitator Thersites in Book II of the *Iliad* (211-78): he thumps him into silence, and of course everyone applauds (see VII.i below).

In the poems of Theognis we see bitter class struggle with a vengeance. What had happened to cause the remarkable change since Hesiod's day? The answer, in a word, is the Tyrants.[17] Between the mid-seventh century and the late sixth (and later still in Sicily) many Greek cities, dominated until now by hereditary aristocracies, experienced a new form of personal dictatorial rule, by the so-called tyrants (*tyrannoi*). Attempts have of course been made to deny any important class basis to the rule of the tyrants and to pretend that they were no more than isolated adventurers, greedy for power and profit. Take any one Greek city on its own, and it may be difficult to prove that its tyrant was anything more than a self-seeking, power-hungry despot. But one might as well try to represent the English Reformation as nothing more than the consequence of King Henry VIII's annoyance with the Pope for refusing to help him get rid of Catherine of Aragon. Certainly, each Greek tyranny has some features peculiar to itself, as does the Reformation in each of the various countries of Europe; but in either case it is when one looks at all the examples together that the general picture begins to become clear. When the rule of the Greek tyrants ended, as it usually did after quite a short period, of a generation or two,[18] hereditary aristocratic dominance had disappeared, except in a few places, and had been succeeded by a much more 'open' society: political power no longer rested on descent, on blue blood, but was mainly dependent upon the possession of property (this now became the standard form of Greek oligarchy), and in many cities, such as Athens, it was later extended in theory to all citizens, in a democracy. This was a change of fundamental importance and it provides a good example of the process I am trying to illustrate.

The classes I would recognise here are on the one hand the hereditary ruling aristocrats, who were by and large the principal landowners and who entirely monopolised political power, and on the other hand, at first, all other classes, sometimes together called the 'demos' – an expression now often used in a much wider sense than in the fifth and fourth centuries, to mean roughly 'commoner' as opposed to 'aristocrat'. At the head of the demos there were likely to be some men who had become prosperous themselves and who aspired to a political position commensurate with their economic status.[19] Those of the tyrants who were not (as some were)[20] renegade aristocrats themselves may have come from this class: we rarely have any reliable information about the social origins of tyrants, but in some cases they do appear to be commoners of some wealth and position: an example (though probably not a characteristic one) is Phalaris of Acragas in Sicily, in the second quarter of the sixth century, who is said to have been a tax-farmer and then a contractor for building a temple.[21] (There was once a widespread view, propagated in particular by Percy Ure,[22] and taken over by George Thomson and others, that many tyrants were, so to speak, 'merchant princes', who had made their fortune in commerce; but in fact this cannot be proved for any single tyrant, and the most one can say is that some tyrants may have been the sons or grandsons of men who had had successful trading ventures and had then acquired the necessary social standing by turning themselves into landowners; cf. III.iii above.) A few of these prosperous commoners may even have achieved the ultimate social *cachet* of providing themselves with a warhorse (roughtly the equivalent of a Rolls-Royce)[23] and thus becoming *hippeis* ('knights'); but in my opinion the great majority of the *hippeis* would normally be members of the ruling nobility. Below the leading group of men I have mentioned came the mass of well-to-do and middling peasants: those who are often referred to as 'the hoplite class', because they provided the heavy-armed infantry (*hoplitai*) of the Greek citizen armies of the seventh and following centuries, who played a notable part in defeating the invading Persian armies at Marathon (490) and Plataea (479), and by whom the inter-city warfare that was endemic among the Greek states was largely conducted. Membership of the hoplite class depended entirely upon the ownership of a moderate amount of property, sufficient not merely to provide a man with a full 'panoply' (complete military equipment, including body-armour and shield), the only qualification that is sometimes mentioned by modern writers, but also to ensure him and his family an adequate livelihood even if he had to go abroad on campaign or stay on guard away from his farm for weeks or even months on end. A man who had too little property to become a hoplite served only in the fleet (if there was one) or as a light-armed soldier, using a bow or sling or dagger or club rather than the spear, the gentleman's weapon (cf. my *OPW* 372-3). In the literature of the fifth and fourth centuries the term 'demos' is often used particularly of this 'sub-hoplite' class. Some of them would be poor peasants (freeholders or lease-holders), others would be artisans, shopkeepers, petty traders, or men who earned their living in what was then considered (as we have seen: III.vi above) to be the meanest of all ways open to free men: namely, as hired labourers – *misthōtoi* or *thētes*. (The last expression, used in a specialised sense, was actually the technical term at Athens for those who were too poor to be hoplites.)

There was a very simple reason why tyranny was a necessary phase in the development of many Greek states: institutions suited to maintaining in power even a non-hereditary ruling class, let alone a democracy, did not exist (they had never existed) and had to be created, painfully and by experience, over the years. As far as we know, democracy had never before been established in a thoroughly civilised society, and the Greek *poleis* which developed it had to build it up from the very bottom: they had both to devise the necessary institutions and to construct an appropriate ideology – a brilliant achievement of which I shall have something more to say later (Section ii below). Even non-hereditary oligarchy, based entirely on property ownership and not on right of birth, was something new and untried, lacking a traditional pattern which could be utilised without potentially dangerous experiment. Until the necessary institutions had been devised there was no real alternative to aristocracy but the dictatorship of a single individual and his family – partly according to the old pattern of Greek kingship, but now with a power that was not traditional but usurped. Then, as the tyrant and his successors (from his own family) brought new men into positions of responsibility, and political *aretē* (competence and 'know-how') gradually seeped down into at least the upper layers of the social strata below the nobility, a time came when the propertied class (or even the whole body of citizens) found that they could dispense with the tyrant and govern by themselves. As Glotz so admirably put it:

> The people regarded tyranny only as an expedient. They used it as a battering-ram with which to demolish the citadel of the oligarchs, and when their end had been achieved they hastily abandoned the weapon which wounded their hands (GC 116).[24]

The metaphor of the 'battering ram' must not of course be taken to imply that the whole process was conscious and directed by the demos – in the sense explained above, of those outside the ruling aristocracy – towards securing power ultimately for themselves. The movement might often begin as a simple revolt by the demos, or (more usually) some sections of it, against oppression and exploitation, simmering possibly for years and breaking out only when a willing and capable leader presented himself – a leader, perhaps, whose aims eventually turned out to be mainly selfish. The motives of the tyrants have often been scrutinised; but this is a singularly pointless quest, since with hardly an exception we have no real evidence except later traditions, often at least partly fictitious, and inferences from actions, which will support different hypotheses.

There is one political figure in the age of the tyrants about whom we know much more than any of the others: Solon the Athenian, at the beginning of the sixth century (he was archon in 594/3), whose political outlook and activities can be seen clearly in some of their aspects in his own excellent poems, consider-able fragments of which have survived.[25] There is no doubt at all about Solon's perfectly serious conception of his own role, as a would-be impartial arbitrator in a situation of severe class strife, who was pressed by the demos to make himself tyrant, but refused.[26] Although Solon also refused to make a general redistribution of land, as demanded by the impoverished lower classes, he did take the extraordinary step of cancelling all debts, and he forbade for the future not merely enslavement for debt but also any kind of debt bondage, by the simple expedient of prohibiting the giving of the body as security[27] – a much-needed reform affecting Athens alone, of course: we have no idea how many other Greek states, if any, followed the example of Athens here (see III.iv above and its n.2 below). Other leading political figures who were less reluctant than Solon to take unconstitutional power need not necessarily have had less worthy motives, although no doubt many of them will have been primarily concerned with gaining political power. Cylon, who staged an abortive coup at Athens nearly thirty years before Solon's archonship, failed completely: either the discontent had not yet reached fever-pitch, or the Athenians knew enough about Cylon to reject him. Peisistratus later completed Solon's work at Athens by enforcing (if with a certain amount of 'fiddling')[28] the new constitution of Solon – admirable and progressive in its day – which (in my opinion) the old aristocracy of Eupatrids had been sabotaging.[29]

A subject for investigation that is decidedly more promising than the motives of individual tyrants is the social basis of their power. Here again the evidence is far from satisfactory and its interpretation is much disputed, recently in particular in regard to the extent to which the tyrants received support from the hoplite class. I think I have said enough above to indicate how I would set about solving such a problem. The fact is that the situation must have varied greatly from *polis* to *polis*. In some cases the tyrant might be installed mainly or entirely by superior force from outside, either by a more powerful city, or (as in Asia from the late sixth century to the late fourth) by the king of Persia or one of his satraps or a local dynast.[30] In other cases the tyrant may have come to power with the aid of a mercenary force,[31] and may have maintained himself in power for some time by its aid. In the absence of any such external pressures, the tyrant would have to rely upon discontented sections of the demos. My own feeling is that the lowest classes (the poorest peasants, the landless labourers, the humbler artisans and the like) would not at this early date have formed a source of strength effective enough to bring to power a tyrant who was not acceptable to the bulk of the hoplite class, whose role, if it came to armed conflict, would surely at this period have been decisive.[32] Many humble citizens in some *poleis* are anyway likely to have been clients of nobles or to have had such a dependent relationship to them that they could do little to oppose them. I myself have no doubt at all that a considerable proportion of the hoplite class in many *poleis*, especially at its lower levels, must have given support to tyrants. This thesis, first argued in detail by Andrewes (*GT*, 1956) but criticised by Snodgrass in 1965, is now sufficiently established, in my opinion, by Paul Cartledge's excellent article, 'Hoplites and heroes', in *JHS* 97 (1977) 11-27.[33]

For Aristotle, there was an essential distinction between the two Greek forms of *monarchia* (one-man-rule), namely *basileia*, traditional kingship according to established forms of law, and *tyrannis*, the rule of a tyrant. They differed in their very origin. Kingship, says Aristotle, 'came into existence for the purpose of helping the better classes [*hoi epieikeis* – just another name for the propertied class] against the demos' (the common people), whereas tyrants arose 'from among the common people and the masses, in opposition to the notables [*hoi gnōrimoi*], so that the demos should not suffer injustice at their hands . . . The great majority of the tyrants began as demagogues, so to speak, and won confidence by calumniating the notables' (*Pol.* V.10, 1310^{b}9-16). A little later he says that the king 'wishes to be a guardian of society, so that those who possess property may suffer no injustice and the demos may not be subjected to arrogant treatment', whereas the tyrant does just the opposite and in practice considers only his own interests (1310^{b}40-11^{a}2). The tyrants, who had fulfilled their historic role long before Aristotle's day and by his time were often the oppressive and despotic figures he conceives most tyrants to have been, receive almost uniformly hostile treatment in our surviving sources. One single figure emerges only slightly tarnished:[34] the Athenian tyrant Peisistratus, who receives some positive encomia from Herodotus, Thucydides and Aristotle (see n.28 again).

I must not leave the subject of Greek tyranny without recalling some passages in Marx, inspired by the seizure of power in France by Louis Napoleon in December 1851: these are cited in II.iii above.

(ii)
The fifth and fourth centuries B.C.

Before the end of the sixth century virtually all the tyrants had disappeared, except in Sicily, and in the Greek cities of Asia and the offshore islands in which many tyrants ruled as Persian quislings.[1] The two centuries that followed, the fifth and fourth,[2] were the great age of Greek democracy, when democratic constitutions of various kinds, successful or unsuccessful in different degrees, were introduced, often by violent revolution, and sometimes with the intervention of an outside power. The regimes they displaced were usually oligarchies of wealth: political rights had been confined not merely to a Few (the *oligoi*) but to the *propertied* Few (cf. II.iv above). At its broadest, such an oligarchy might extend to the whole class of the *hopla parechomenoi* (those able to afford to serve as cavalry or hoplites: see Section i above), who may perhaps have accounted for something between one-fifth and one-third of all citizens in most cases (see esp. Ps.-Herodes, *Peri Politeias* 30-1, discussed in my *OPW* 35 n.65). If the property qualification for the exercise of political rights was put rather higher, the oligarchy might consist of what I have defined as 'the propertied class' *par excellence* (see III.ii above): those who could live off their own property without having to work for their living. And of course the membership of the oligarchy might be more restricted still; at its narrowest it might even be confined to a few leading families, forming a hereditary *dynasteia*. I think one could say that, broadly speaking, the narrower the oligarchy, the smaller the chance of its surviving for a long time, except in special circumstances, such as the backing of an outside power.

Classical Greek democracy[3] is far too large a subject for me to discuss in any detail here, and I shall content myself with a very brief summary of its principal characteristics, as we can see them both in contemporary (and often hostile) specifications of *dēmokratia*[4] and in what we know of its practice.[5] Unfortunately, we have so little information about other Greek democracies that I am obliged to treat the Athenian democracy as if it were typical, as it evidently was not, although it was certainly the most respected and illustrious of Greek democracies, and the most highly developed one of which we have any knowledge.

A. (i) The first and most characteristic feature of *dēmokratia* was rule by majority vote of all citizens, determined in a sovereign Assembly (*ekklēsia*, normally voting by show of hands) and large popular lawcourts, *dikastēria*, consisting of dicasts (*dikastai*) who were both judges and jurors, voting by ballot and inappellable. Even many Classical scholars have failed to realise the extraordinary originality of Greek democracy, which, in the fundamental sense of *taking political decisions by majority vote of all citizens*, occurred earlier than in any other society we know about: see my *OPW* 348 (Appendix XXIV).

(ii) *Dēmokratia* was the rule of the 'demos' (δῆμος), a word used in two main senses, to mean either the whole citizen body (and its Assembly), or the poor, the lower classes. Since the majority of citizens everywhere owned little or no property, the propertied class complained that *dēmokratia* was the rule of the *dēmos* in the narrower sense and in effect the domination of the poor over the rich. In so far as this was true, democracy played a vital part in the class struggle by mitigating the exploitation of poorer citizens by richer ones – a fact that seldom receives the emphasis it deserves. (I have discussed this subject sufficiently in II.iv above.)

(iii) Only adult males were citizens in the full sense, and women had no political rights. When I use the term 'citizen', therefore, it must be understood to include adult males only.

(iv) We must never forget, of course, that Greek democracy must always have depended to a considerable extent on the exploitation of slave labour, which, in the conditions obtaining in the ancient world, was if anything even more essential for the maintenance of a democracy than of any more restricted form of constitution. (I have explained the reason for this in III.iv above: see the third paragraph of its § I.) However, even though we may regard slavery, *sub specie aeternitatis*, as an irredeemably evil feature of any human society, we must not allow the fact of its existence under Greek democracy to degrade that democracy in our eyes, *when we judge it by even the highest standards of its day*, for Greek states could not dispense with slavery under any other constitutional form either,[6] and virtually no objection was ever raised in antiquity to slavery as an institution (see VII.iii below).

B. The great aim of democrats was that their society should achieve as much freedom (*eleutheria*) as possible.[7] In strong contrast with many twentieth-century societies which boast of their freedom but whose claim to have achieved it (or even to aim at it) may be denied and derided by others, the opponents of Greek democracy fully accepted the fact that freedom was indeed the goal of democrats, even when they disparaged that goal as involving license rather than real liberty. Plato, one of the most determined and dangerous enemies that freedom has ever had, sneers at democracy as involving an excess of freedom for everyone – citizens, metics, foreigners, slaves and women and (a brilliant conceit) even the animals in a democracy are simply 'full of *eleutheria*'! (*Rep.* VIII.562a–4a). Since public debate was an essential part of the democratic process, an important ingredient in democratic *eleutheria* was freedom of speech, *parrhēsia*.[8]

C. Because under democracy every citizen had an equal vote, political equality (*isotēs*) was, so to speak, a built-in feature of Greek *dēmokratia*.[9] Greek democrats would say that their society was characterised by *isonomia* (perhaps 'equality before the law', although not a 'correct translation', conveys the essential idea best to a modern reader) and *isēgoria*, the equal right of everyone to speak his mind freely.[10] There was no pretence, however, of economic equality.

D. It was a fundamental principle of democracy that everyone who exercised any power should be *hypeuthynos*, subject to *euthyna*, the examination of his conduct (and audit of his accounts) which every official had to undergo, at Athens and most if not all other democracies, at the end of his term of office, normally one year.[11]

E. Democrats believed deeply in the rule of law, however much they might be accused by their opponents of habitually overriding their laws by decrees (*psēphismata*) passed *ad hoc* and *ad hominem* – an accusation that was conspicuously untrue of Classical Athens, even if the strictures of Aristotle and others under this head may have been justified in relation to some other democracies.[12]

Since it is alleged by some ancient sources and even by some modern scholars that Greek democrats believed in making appointments to office by lot rather than by election, I must emphasise that this is true only of minor offices and of those not involving military command. The issue is well put by the author of the Pseudo-Aristotelian *Rhetoric to Alexander*, which we may as well now call (with its latest Teubner editor, M. Fuhrmann, 1966) Anaximenes, *Ars Rhetorica*:

> In democracies it is necessary for the minor magistrates (the majority) to be appointed by lot, for this avoids civil strife, but for the important ones to be elected by the whole citizen body (2.14, 1424^{a}17-20).

And the same work goes on to say that even in oligarchies it is desirable to appoint to most offices by lot, reserving only the greatest ones for 'a secret vote under oath and with strict precautions' (2.18, 1424^{a}40-^{b}3).

*   *   *   *   *   *

The evidence that survives from the fifth and fourth centuries is very fragmentary, and although a large proportion of it relates to Athens, there is also a scatter of evidence for scores of other *poleis*, each different in some respects from every other. Generalisation is exceedingly difficult and oversimplification is an ever-present danger. I have, however, done my best to examine virtually all the important evidence that is in any way relevant (far more than I have found it possible to cite), and I now propose to make a series of general statements concerning the class struggle in the fifth and fourth centuries, based upon the specific evidence I have mentioned.

1. In an ancient Greek *polis* the class struggle in the basic economic sense (see my definitions, in II.ii above) proceeded of course without cessation in so far as it was between property-owners and those workers whose labour provided them, directly or indirectly, with their leisured existence: that is to say, chattel slaves in the main, but in a few places principally serfs (see III.iv above); some hired labourers, relatively few in number (see III.vi above); those unfortunates

who were obliged by need to borrow at interest and (probably in the great majority of *poleis* other than Athens) might become debt bondsmen on default; and more indirectly their tenants. This struggle was of course very one-sided: it expressed the master's dominance, and its essence was his exploitation of the labour of those who worked for him. I know of no parallel to the mass liberation of the Messenian Helots (see III.iv above, § II, and its n.18 below), who in 370-369 obtained their freedom with the aid of powerful outside intervention at a time of unprecedented Spartan weakness, and became once more the independent *polis* of Messene.

2. There were, however, very many Greeks who owned little property and no slaves: the majority of these will have fulfilled my definition of 'peasants' (see IV.ii above), and a good number of others will have been artisans or traders (IV.vi). Collectively, these people were the 'demos', the common people, and they must have formed the great bulk of the citizen population in the vast majority of Greek *poleis*. How did this demos participate in class struggle? If class is a relationship of exploitation, then the answer to this question must depend upon the extent to which the members of a particular demos were either exploited or, although in danger of falling into that condition, were successful in avoiding it by political class struggle. What happened in practice would depend largely upon the result of this political class struggle, which (as we shall see) was essentially for control of the state. We must look closely at the nature of this struggle, and how it was related to the state. It is convenient and profitable to deal with this topic here, in relation to the fifth and fourth centuries, since before that period our knowledge is insufficient, and after it the Greek *poleis* were mainly no longer their own masters but were subject to a greater or less extent to the dictation of a suzerain, whether a Hellenistic king or the Roman government (see Section iii of this chapter). Moreover, I can discuss the subject in the very terms used by contemporary thinkers, Aristotle and Plato above all.

When I speak of control of the 'state' I am referring to what the ancient Greeks called the *politeia* – literally, the 'constitution', the fundamental laws and customs governing political life; but the Greek word has on occasion something very like the force of the modern expression, 'way of life'. Isocrates describes the *politeia* as the very soul of the city (the *psychē poleōs*, VII.14). Aristotle declares that when the *politeia* changes, the city is just not the same city (*Pol*. III.3, 1276^{b}3-4). For him, the body of citizens having full political rights,[13] the *politeuma*, is 'master in all respects of the *polis*; *politeuma* and *politeia* are identical' (III.6, 1278^{b}10-11), the two words 'signify the same thing' (1279^{a}25-6). The constitution *is* the ruler or rulers, who may be One man, or a Few, or the Many: each of these ought to rule in the interests of all members of the community but in practice will often not do so (1279^{a}27-39), for Aristotle makes it plain in numerous passages that what one must expect in practice is that the rulers will rule in what they regard as their own personal or class interest. (It is worth remarking here, by the way, that Aristotle and other Greek intellectuals did not regard the preservation of the rights of property as a main function of the state,[14] in the way that so many later thinkers have done, in particular Cicero, who fervently believed that states exist primarily in order to protect private property rights (*De offic*. II.73, cf. 78, 85; I.21), and of course Locke and the many other political theorists of more modern times who have held similar views.[15]

We can accept the fact that what we call 'the state' was for the Greeks the instrument of the *politeuma*, the body of citizens who had the constitutional power of ruling. And as I have already shown (in II.iv above), the Greeks habitually expected an oligarchy to rule in the interests of the propertied class, a democracy mainly in the interests of the poorer citizens. Control of the state, therefore, was one of the prizes, indeed the greatest prize, of class struggle on the political plane. This should not surprise even those who cannot accept the statement in the *Communist Manifesto* that 'political power, properly so called, is merely the organised power of one class for oppressing another' (*MECW* VI.505).

3. Class struggle on the political plane, then, was above all in most cases for control of the state. If in a Greek *polis* the demos could create and sustain a democracy that really worked, like the Athenian one, they could hope to protect themselves to a high degree and largely to escape exploitation. The only long-lived example of really successful democracy which can be cited with confidence is Athens between 507 and 322/1, when the democracy was securely in power except for two brief oligarchic revolutions in 411 and 404-3 (see below and nn.29-34). Many other democracies existed, but our knowledge of them is slight.

4. When, on the other hand, the propertied class were able to set up an oligarchy, with a franchise dependent on a property-qualification, the mass of poor citizens would be deprived of all constitutional power and would be likely to become subject in an increasing degree to exploitation by the wealthy. In II.iv above I quoted a number of statements by Greek writers who took this for granted. As Plato says, an oligarchy becomes 'two cities', of Rich and Poor respectively, for in oligarchies some have great wealth, others extreme poverty, and almost everyone outside the ruling class is a pauper (*Rep.* VIII.551d, 552bd). Oligarchy, Plato adds, is a form of constitution that 'abounds with many evils' (544c). As happened under the Roman oligarchy in Italy (see III.iv n.5 below), 'the powerful' in Greek oligarchies must often have been able to usurp possession of most of the best land, legally or illegally. Aristotle mentions that the leading men (the *gnōrimoi*) of Thurii, a Greek city in southern Italy, were able to profit by absorbing 'the whole countryside, contrary to law, for the constitution was too oligarchic' (*oligarchikōtera*): the eventual result was a violent revolution (*Pol.* V.7, 1307ᵃ27 ff., esp. 29-33). Aristotle goes on at once to generalise about 'aristocratic' constitutions: since they are oligarchical, he says, the *gnōrimoi* grasp more than their share (*pleonektousin*, 1307ᵃ34-5). No doubt in most Greek oligarchies the law of debt was harsh, allowing forms of debt bondage, if not actual enslavement for debt (cf. III.iv, § III above). Even if they retained personal freedom, defaulting borrowers might lose their property altogether and be forced to become either tenant-farmers or wage-labourers, or they might resort to mercenary service, an escape-route available only to the most able-bodied.[16] In oligarchies there may well have been forms of compulsory labour for those without sufficient property to make financial contributions to the state or to serve in the hoplite army (cf. the *angareiai* we so often encounter in the Hellenistic and Roman periods: see I.iii above and its n.8 below). And with the courts of law staffed exclusively by magistrates and other members of the ruling class, it will often have been difficult for a poor man even to obtain his legal rights (such as they were) against members of the oligarchy – in whose eyes justice, as Aristotle

realised, was likely to be equated with the interests of the propertied class: they normally felt themselves to be absolutely superior and entitled to make all political decisions at their own will (see II.iv above).[17]

5. An oligarchy, once securely in power, might survive for quite a long time if it remained vigilant and above all united, and if its members did not abuse their political power too grossly. (In II.iv above I have quoted some of Aristotle's remarks on this subject.) Few examples are known of long-lived oligarchy. One of the most obvious is Corinth, for nearly two centuries from the fall of the Cypselid tyranny (probably *c.* 582) until the democratic revolution in 392. The most enduring oligarchy of all was Sparta (see my *OPW* 124-49), where successful revolution was unknown after the setting up of the 'Lycurgan' constitution in (probably) the mid-seventh century until the coup effected by King Cleomenes III in 227, when there began a troubled period of two or three generations of civil strife. Economic distress often drove the impoverished to attempt revolution, with the aim both of capturing control of the state and of effecting some kind of reallocation of property – most frequently in the form of a redistribution of land (*gēs anadasmos*), or the cancellation of debts (*chreōn apokopē*), or both these measures (see below, with n.55). There is an important proviso to be added: no democratic revolution had much chance of success, or of leading to a stable democracy, unless the impoverished masses received leadership from some members of the governing class. According to a neglected passage in Aristotle, however, light-armed forces and naval crews – drawn entirely from the lower classes and therefore uniformly democratic in outlook – were very numerous in his day, and since in civil conflicts 'light-armed troops easily overcome cavalry and hoplites' (he is not thinking of pitched battles, of course), the lower classes (the *dēmoi*) got the better of the wealthy (the *euporoi*: *Pol.* VI.7, 1321[a]11-21). I may say that the only way in which oligarchy could be transformed into democracy was by revolution: I know of no single case in the whole of Greek history in which a ruling oligarchy introduced democracy without compulsion and by a simple vote.

6. Conditions favouring successful revolution of either sort (from oligarchy to democracy or vice versa) were most likely to arise when (as very often happened) an outside power was called in by the would-be revolutionaries. This might be an imperial state (Athens or Sparta), or a Persian satrap or other Asiatic grandee (see my *OPW* 37-40), who could at the very least produce mercenaries or money with which to hire them. Almost invariably, intervention by democratic Athens was in favour of democracy, by oligarchic Sparta or a Persian monarch or satrap in favour of oligarchy or tyranny.[18]

7. Of course it was only adult male citizens of a *polis* who could indulge effectively in class struggle on the political plane, except in very special circumstances, such as the democratic restoration at Athens in 403, after the rule of the 'Thirty', when metics and other foreigners (and even slaves) participated, and some of them were rewarded with citizenship.[19] And we must not forget that land – by far the most important means of production and form of wealth, as we have seen (III.iii above) – could be owned only by citizens and by those few foreigners to whom the exceptional right of *gēs enktēsis* had been granted by

the state, as an honour or in return for useful services. Probably metics (resident foreigners) could take land and houses on lease in most states, as they evidently could at Athens (see Lysias VII.10; cf. XII.8 ff., 18-19);[20] but any profit they could make out of it would be greatly reduced by the rent they would have to pay to their citizen landlords. In a sense, therefore, the citizens of a Greek state could be considered a distinct class of landowners, according to my definitions (in II.ii above), over against foreigners, although of course they themselves would be divided into different classes in confrontation with each other, in a more significant way. I will only add that anyone who feels that metics ought to be given more attention here will find the subject sufficiently dealt with in II.v above and its nn.29-30 below: most metics who were not freedmen would be citizens of another *polis*, living voluntarily for a time in a city not their own, probably – whether or not they were political exiles – with the intention of returning home in due course. And surely metics could not be exploited intensively: if they were, they would simply move elsewhere.

*   *   *   *   *   *

I said earlier that much of the evidence for the history of Greece in the fifth and fourth centuries relates primarily or exclusively to Athens. Athens was anything but typical – I have explained why in *OPW* 34 ff. (esp. 46-9). Yet I propose to concentrate on that city, simply because the evidence for it is so much more plentiful than for any other.

The constitution of Cleisthenes in 508/7 gave to Athens what the Greeks regarded as full democracy, in the sense that, although property-qualifications were required for the holding of certain offices,[21] every citizen had a vote in the sovereign Assembly, both in its deliberative and legislative capacity (in which it was known as the *ekklēsia*) and in its judicial capacity, when it was the *hēliaia*, divided for most purposes – if not until later, perhaps even 462/1 – into *dikastēria*, 'jury-courts'. Apart from the organs of state at Athens itself there were numerous and important local political functions, democratically organised,[22] in the 'demes' (roughly 150 in number) into which the citizen population was divided. No very important changes were made before the destruction of the democracy in 322/1 (for which see Section iii of this chapter and its n.2 below), but there were certain modifications, both in the constitutional structure and in its practical working, which made it distinctly more democratic, to our way of thinking, during the fifth century. Apart perhaps from the 'reforms of Ephialtes' in 462/1, of the precise nature and details of which we know far less than many modern scholars pretend, much the most important reform was the introduction by degrees, between the middle of the fifth century and its closing years, of pay for the performance of political tasks: at first sitting in the jury-courts, and on the Council (*boulē*) which prepared business for the Assembly, and later (after 403) for attending the Assembly.[23] Although the rates of pay were low (less than the wages of an artisan), this reform enabled even the poorer citizens to play a real part in the political life of the city if they so desired. I would emphasise (since the contrary has recently been asserted, in defiance of the evidence, by Sir Moses Finley) that political pay was certainly not peculiar to Athens but was introduced in a number of other democracies by at any rate the fourth century: this is perfectly clear from a series of passages in Aristotle's *Politics*, even if Rhodes is the only other city we can actually name for the fourth century – see my PPOA.[24]

Political leadership at state level was long monopolised by a fairly small circle of 'political families'; but Athens' acquisition of an empire in the fifth century created a large number of new openings which made it necessary for this circle to be widened; and in the last thirty years of the fifth century we encounter a group of 'new men', often unfairly satirised by upper-class writers such as Aristophanes and the other comic poets as jumped-up tradesmen, 'sellers' of this, that or the other (see my *OPW* 359-62).[25] The politicians who played a leading role were often referred to as 'demagogues' (*dēmagōgoi*), originally a neutral term meaning 'leaders of the demos' but one which soon came to be used most frequently in a disparaging sense. The most famous of these 'demagogues', Cleon, who played a leading role in the late 420s, was a full-time professional politician, very different from the vulgar 'tanner' or 'leather-seller' ridiculed by Aristophanes (and depicted in a very different light, if an almost equally hostile one, by Thucydides). Some other 'demagogues' are known to have been similarly travestied, and there are good reasons for thinking that the time-honoured picture of most of these men is very unreal (see my *OPW* 234-5, esp. n.7).

I have explained at length elsewhere why members of the Athenian upper class such as Aristophanes and Isocrates should have detested Cleon and his fellow-demagogues (*OPW* 355-76). To put it in a nutshell – these demagogues were *dēmotikoi* (the equivalent of the Roman *populares*): they often took the side of the lower classes at Athens against their 'betters', or they acted in some way or other that was considered inimical to the best interests of the Athenian upper class or some of its members. However, the political class struggle at Athens was on the whole very muted in the period we are discussing (I shall notice the two prominent exceptions presently), and the internal political conflicts recorded in our sources seldom arise directly out of class struggle. This is very natural and precisely what we might have expected, for the democracy was firm and unshakeable and it satisfied the aspirations of the humbler Athenians. The Assembly and in particular the courts must have given the poorer citizen a considerable degree of protection against oppression by the rich and powerful. Here it is worth remembering that the control of the courts by the demos was regarded by Aristotle as giving the demos control of the constitution (*Ath. pol.* 9.1 *fin.*). The democracy was also remarkably indulgent to the rich, whose financial position was secure and who were not heavily taxed (even if we allow for occasional hardship resulting from the *eisphora*, a capital levy sometimes imposed in wartime), and who had ample opportunity for achieving honour and esteem, above all through public service. The fifth-century 'empire',[26] from which the leading Athenians profited most (Thuc. VIII.48.6),[27] had for a time reconciled many rich men to the democracy, which was widely recognised to be an integral part of the foundation on which the empire rested. It is unique among past empires known to us in that the ruling city relied very much on the support of the lower classes in the subject states (see my *OPW* 34-43) – in striking contrast with other imperial powers, which have commonly aimed to secure the loyalty of royal houses, aristocracies, or at least (as with Rome: see Section iii of this chapter) the upper classes among the peoples they ruled. The miserable failure of the two oligarchic revolutions of the late fifth century, which I shall briefly describe presently, discouraged any further attempt to attack the democracy, even after the fall of the Athenian empire in 404.

Between 508/7 and the destruction of the democracy by the Macedonians in 322 there were only two episodes in which class struggle at Athens erupted in violent *stasis*, civil strife. (I need only mention in passing two abortive oligarchic conspiracies in 480-79 and 458-7, and the assassination of the radical-democratic leader Ephialtes in 462-1.)[28] The oligarchy of the Four Hundred in 411, which lasted for only about four months, was altogether a product of fraud:[29] the pretence, known to be false by the revolutionaries by the time they put their plans into effect, that if a form of oligarchy were introduced at Athens some desperately-needed financial help for the war against Sparta might be forth-coming from Persia through the agency of Alcibiades. The whole thing was planned from the start by men who were among the wealthiest Athenians: the trierarchs (Thuc. VIII.47.2) and 'the most influential people' (*hoi dynatōtatoi*, 47.2 [twice], 48.1), 'the best people' (*hoi beltistoi*, 47.2). The Samian *dynatōtatoi* joined in the plan (63.3; cf. 73.2, 6). The preparatory moves were carried through amid serious uneasiness on the part of the demos (54.1; cf. 48.3), allayed only by the belief (emphasised by Thucydides) that the demos would be able, when it wanted, to vote away any oligarchic constitutional measures that might have been imposed as a temporary expedient – a vital consideration which is seldom given sufficient emphasis.[30] In the weeks before the climactic stage of the revolution there were a number of assassinations (the first we hear of at Athens for fifty years) and a deliberate campaign of terror (65.2 to 66.5); and the actual decisions setting up the oligarchy were taken, *nem. con.* (69.1), at a meeting of the Assembly convened at Colonus, well outside the walls, to which – since the Spartans had now set up a fortified post at Decelea, only a few miles away – the hoplites and cavalry must have marched out as an army, with few if any *thētes* (sub-hoplites) present. Meanwhile the fleet (the *nautikos ochlos*: Thuc. VIII.72.2), based at Samos, remained staunchly devoted to democracy: the passages in Thucydides which bring this out vividly are among the most moving in his work (VIII.72.2; 73.4-6; 75-77; 86.1-4). The oligarchy soon collapsed, and then, after about eight months with a 'mixed constitution',[31] the full democracy was restored.

In 404 the narrow oligarchy of the Thirty was forced upon Athens by the victorious Spartan commander, Lysander, some weeks or even months after the capitulation of Athens at the end of the Peloponnesian war, during which period the Athenian oligarchs had evidently found it impossible to force through a change of constitution on their own.[32] The victory of the democratic Athenian Resistance in 403, made possible by a sudden, complete change of policy at Sparta (for which see my *OPW* 143-6), is one of the most remarkable and fascinating episodes in Greek history, which often fails to receive the attention it deserves, although a whole book has been devoted to it by the French historian Cloché.[33] The Athenian demos was surprisingly magnanimous in its victory, and it receives high praise for this from many quarters, notably Aristotle, *Ath. pol.* 40. (The demos even refunded to Sparta money which had been borrowed by the Athenian oligarchs to pay for the garrison supplied by Sparta, said to have amounted to a hundred talents.)[34]

The two episodes I have just described are clear examples of a struggle *to control the state*, between the mass of the Athenians and a few 'top people', with many of the hoplites inclined to waver – as one would expect of *mesoi* (see II.iv above) – but eventually coming down firmly on both occasions in favour of democracy. (In most other cities democracy had evidently not gained anything like such a firm hold on the mind of the hoplite class.)

In the fourth century, with the fortunes of Athens first rising and then falling again, it was taken for granted by virtually all citizens that there was no practicable alternative to democracy for Athens, and for roughly two generations the upper classes evidently gave up hope of any fundamental constitutional change and concentrated on immediate issues, above all on foreign policy, now a rather bewildering problem for the Athenians, who often had cause to wonder where their real interests lay – whether to fight Sparta, or to accept her as an ally against Athens' immediate neighbour Thebes, now growing ever more powerful; how much effort should be devoted to regaining control of the Thracian Chersonese, at one of the two main bottle-necks on Athens' vital corn-supply route from the Crimea (see *OPW* 45 ff., esp. 48-9); and whether to try to reconquer Amphipolis, the key to the timber supply of the area around the River Strymon and the strategic point that controlled the crossing of the Strymon itself. Once or twice we hear of a division on foreign policy at Athens on class lines, between rich and poor (see *Hell. Oxy.* VI[I]3; Ar., *Eccl.* 197-8); but on most issues, home and foreign, there is no clear evidence of any such division: there is not the least reason to expect it at this period.

A decisive change began, almost imperceptibly at first, with the rise of Macedon, in the person of King Philip II, from the early 350s, at the very time when the power of Athens and her 'Second Confederacy' had begun to decline.[35] The role of Philip is something that can be more conveniently treated a little later: all I want to emphasise here is the fact that Philip was a highly despotic ruler, with an unlimited thirst for personal power, and naturally no friend to democracy; and that it was all too likely that if he gained control of Athens he might feel it desirable to install a government of oligarchic partisans – as in fact he did at Thebes after his victory over that city and Athens at the battle of Chaeronea in 338 (Justin IX.iv.6-9). It took quite a long time for the Athenians to appreciate the underlying realities of the situation, but I think there is reason to believe that Demosthenes suddenly grasped the truth late in 352,[36] and soon came to understand that it was the humbler Athenians who were most likely to respond to appeals for an all-out resistance to Macedon, for the simple reason that if Philip gained power over Athens, he might well decide (though in fact he did not) to destroy the democracy – in which event they, the poorer Athenians, would necessarily be disfranchised, as indeed they actually were in 322/1 (see below). In fact it was no part of Philip's plan to treat Athens roughly, if he could avoid it, as he did; and as it happened Philip's son and successor Alexander the Great had no occasion to interfere with the Athenian constitution. But when the Athenians led a major Greek revolt against Macedon on Alexander's death in 323, and in the following year were utterly defeated and compelled to surrender, the Macedonian general Antipater put an end to the democracy; and after 322 Athens was subjected to a whole series of interventions and constitutional changes and was never able to decide her own destiny for very long (see Section iii of this chapter; also Appendix IV, § 2, and its n.5).

Perhaps the most obviously noticeable failure of Athens in the fourth century was her inability to find the sums of money (very large, by Greek standards of public finance) required to maintain the naval forces which she needed, to a far greater extent than any other Greek state, in order to pursue what I might call her 'natural' foreign policy. I have already, in *OPW* 45-9, explained why Athens was driven by her unique situation, as an importer of corn on an altogether exceptional scale, towards a policy of 'naval imperialism', in order to secure her supply routes. (I have also, in the passage just mentioned, listed the principal occasions on which Athens came to grief, or nearly so, when interruption of her corn supply was threatened.) Athens' whole way of life was involved; and what is so often denounced, as if it were sheer greed and a lust for domination on her part, by modern scholars whose antipathy to Athens is sharpened by her promotion of democratic regimes in states under her control or influence, was in reality an almost inevitable consequence of that way of life. In the fifth century the tribute from the empire made it possible for Athens to maintain a large fleet. After 405 the whole situation changed: because of the rudimentary character of all Greek public finance, and their own failure to innovate in this sphere, the Athenians were perpetually unable to provide the funds necessary to man their essential fleets. Contributions from their allies in the so-called 'Second Athenian Confederacy' of 378/7 ff. could not just be demanded by the Athenians (as in the fifth-century empire) but had to be requested, and voted by the allies in their *synedrion*. In the long run these contributions were not adequate, and Athenian commanders sometimes resorted to what were virtually piratical measures in order to make good the deficiencies. I think that by no means all historians sufficiently realise how desperately serious was Athens' lack of state funds in the fourth century. I have collected a great deal of evidence on this subject, which, since I know of no single presentation of it, I will give here in a note.[37]

But it is time to take a more general view of fourth-century Greece and its future.

* * * * * *

As I shall show in Section iii of this chapter, Greek democracy, between the fourth century B.C. and the third century of the Christian era, was gradually destroyed – because it did not just die out, let alone commit suicide: it was deliberately extinguished by the joint efforts of the Greek propertied classes, the Macedonians and the Romans.

Greece and Poverty had always been foster-sisters, as Herodotus put it (VII.102.1); but poverty in the fourth century seems to be a more pressing evil than in the fifth. The seventh, sixth and fifth centuries had been an age of steady economic development, with a distinct increase of wealth in at least the more progressive cities; and from the meagre information available one gets the impression that there had been a marked rise in the standard of life of practically all sections of the population. There had certainly been a genuine economic expansion, made possible by the growth of commerce, of small-scale industry, and of a money economy, and greatly assisted by the early movement of colonisation, in the eighth and seventh centuries. The export of Greek oil, wine, pottery, metal work and other agricultural and industrial products grew to surprising dimensions, reaching a climax probably in the second half of the fifth century.[38] On the political plane the whole period was characterised by a movement towards the attainment of political rights by an ever-increasing proportion of the citizen community. In the fifth century the Athenian 'empire' undoubtedly promoted the creation, or the strengthening, of democracy in many other Greek cities (see n.26 again). In the fourth century this development stopped, and indeed in some places was reversed. The status of democracy in the fourth century, except at Athens and probably not many other *poleis*, was always precarious, and it was perpetually on the defensive. In both the economic and the political spheres, then, the tide of development had turned by the beginning of the fourth century, and a slow regression had begun. As regards the details of economic life in the fourth century we are still very badly informed, except to some extent in regard to Athens; but my own impression is that there was widespread and serious poverty among the mass of the people, at the same time as the few rich were perhaps growing richer. I do not myself think that we have nearly enough evidence to be certain whether or not the first trend (the impoverishment of the Many) greatly outweighed the second (the enrichment of the Few) and produced a real total impoverishment of Greece as a whole. Rostovtzeff, in his great *Social and Economic History of the Hellenistic World* (published some forty years ago), argued that the economic decline of many Greek cities from the end of the fifth century onwards was mainly due to the contraction of the foreign market for Greek exports, as local production began to grow at the periphery of the Greek trading area: he traces the growth of ceramic industries, coinage, jewellery and metal working, the manufacture of textiles, and the culture of the vine and olive, in districts as far apart as Italy, Thrace, Syria, the Crimea and south Russia, all of which until the latter part of the fifth century provided markets for the products of Greece itself, but thereafter became increasingly able to supply their own needs, often by crude local imitations of the former Greek imports.[39] Athens was altogether exceptional in needing to import the greater part of her food supply (see my *OPW* 46-9), as well as all her timber and metals (except silver and lead, which were supplied by the famous mines at Laurium in south-east Attica); but many other Greek cities will have been dependent in some degree upon imports, even of corn when their own crops failed or were deficient (as often happened), and if their exports declined seriously, they would have difficulty in paying for necessary imports.

How far this theory of Rostovtzeff's (recently endorsed in the main by Claude Mossé)[40] provides even a partial explanation of the situation I have described, I am not sure; and in any event the whole question needs to be re-examined by someone with a far greater command than mine of the archaeological evidence. I certainly know of no single passage in any Greek literary source which gives the slightest hint that any of the Greeks realised that the market for Greek goods was contracting against them, or which betrays any awareness of a need to increase exports. Moreover, can we be sure that the production of the commodities which used to be exported (wine and oil as well as manufactured goods) was not offset to some extent by an increase in the growth of cereals? Except during the great grain shortage that began at the end of the 330s, the price of cereals does not seem to have risen very much in the fourth century, relative to other prices. My own impression, for what it is worth, is not so much that Greece as a whole was poorer in the fourth century as that the wealthy class was now able to appropriate a greater share of the small available surplus than in the late fifth century – though probably less so in democratic Athens than in most other states. If so, the real cause of Greek decline is much more deeply rooted in the nature of the Greek economic and social system than Rostovtzeff's theory would allow.

I should like to draw particular attention to the very large and increasing number of men who took service as mercenaries, not only in Greek armies but also with non-Greeks, especially the king of Persia and his satraps – in the second half of the fourth century especially they numbered many tens of thousands.[41] We have a series of statements in the fourth-century sources, above all Isocrates, to the effect that it was inability to make a living at home which drove these men to become mercenaries, and others to wander far from home in search of a livelihood.[42] Writers of oligarchic sympathies sometimes abuse the mercenaries bitterly. According to Plato they are about the most overbearing, unjust, violent and senseless of men.[43] Isocrates represents them as bands of fugitives, vagabonds, criminals and robbers, 'the common enemies of all mankind',[44] and he says bluntly that they would be better dead (V.55). Isocrates was anxious that these men should at all costs be prevented from banding together against those of their fellow Greeks who, like himself, lived in some affluence, and seizing their property by force.[45] The obvious solution, urged early in the fourth century by Gorgias and Lysias, and most persistently by Isocrates himself over a period of some forty years,[46] was a grand Greek crusade against the Persian empire, which would wrest from the barbarians enough land in Asia to provide a comfortable livelihood for these men and any other Greeks who were in need. But when the crusade was in fact undertaken a few years after the death of Isocrates, by Alexander the Great and his Macedonians, the reality was very different from Isocrates' dream.

★   ★   ★   ★   ★   ★

In the political sphere, democracy barely held its own in the fourth century, and in many cities outside Athens the class warfare which had already become widespread in the last quarter of the fifth century became more acute. Since a very large part of the surviving evidence for the political history of the fourth century relates specifically to Athens, where (as I said earlier) the class struggle on the political plane was probably much milder than in any other Greek city, it is easy for us to overlook the parlous condition of tension and strife in many of the other cities. Oligarchic and democratic leaders had no hesitation in calling in outside powers to help them gain the upper hand over their adversaries. A particularly interesting example is the situation at Corinth in 387/6, just after the 'King's Peace' or 'Peace of Antalcidas'. Corinth had recently ceased to exist as an independent polis, having beeen absorbed by the neighbouring democracy of Argos.[47] When the Spartan King Agesilaus appeared before the walls of Corinth, 'the Corinthians' – that is to say, the democratic faction which was now in control at Corinth – at first refused to dismiss the Argive garrison which ensured the maintenance of the existing democratic regime at Corinth (Xen., HG V.i.33–4). Although they knew that if the garrison withdrew and Sparta regained control of the city, Corinth would be reconstituted as an independent polis, they realised that this would also involve the reimposition of the former oligarchy – and they regarded that as a more unpleasant alternative than accepting the non-existence of Corinth as an independent polis, and remaining a mere part of Argos! An equally extreme example, this time involving oligarchs instead of democrats, is the surrender of the Cadmeia (the Acropolis of Thebes) to the Spartan general Phoebidas in 382 by the oligarchic Theban faction led by Leontiadas, a devoted partisan of Sparta. Leontiadas then headed a small oligarchy, thoroughly subservient to the Spartans, who installed a garrison on the Theban Cadmeia to keep the puppet regime in power. It is interesting to hear from Xenophon that the Thebans now 'gave the Spartans even more service than was demanded of them' (*HG* V.ii.36) – just as the Mantinaean landowners, when Sparta destroyed the walls of their city and broke it up into its four original villages, were so glad to have an 'aristocracy' and be no longer troubled by 'burdensome demagogues', as under their democracy, that they 'came for military service with the Spartans from their villages far more enthusiastically than when they were under a democracy' (ibid. 7).

In such incidents we see Sparta[47a] as the great supporter of oligarchy and the propertied classes: this was the situation throughout the first three or four decades of the fourth century, until Sparta lost her pre-eminent position in Greece (see my *OPW* 98-9, 162-4). In the early fourth century, Xenophon in particular always takes it for granted that when there is a division within a city on class lines, the rich will naturally turn to Sparta, the demos to Athens.[48] Among several illustrations of this we can certainly include the case of Phlius, which has been badly misunderstood in one important respect in a detailed recent study by Legon.[49]

Some cities seem to have been able for quite long periods to preserve at least a certain superficial harmony, but in others there were outbreaks of *stasis* (civil strife), sometimes assuming a violent and bloody form, reminiscent of the terrible events at Corcyra in 427, of which Thucydides has left us such a vivid account (III.70-81; IV.46-8), and which he himself regarded as one of the opening episodes in a new age of intensified civil strife (III.82-3, esp. 82.1). One of the most sanguinary of the many fourth-century outbreaks of *stasis* was the *skytalismos* at Argos in 370, when 1,200-1,500 of the upper classes were said to have been massacred by the demos – an event which caused such horror when it was announced to the Athenian Assembly that a purificatory sacrifice was immediately performed (Diod. XV.57.3 to 58.4; Plut., *Mor.* 814b).

Tyranny, a phenomenon which had become very much rarer in the fifth century than in the seventh and sixth, now occurred again in several cities: its reappearance suggests an intensification of political class strife. It is a great pity that we cannot reconstruct what happened in particular at Heraclea Pontica: the real situation is almost totally obscured by abusive rhetoric in the sources, especially the local historian, Memnon (*FGrH* 434 F 1), who wrote several centuries later, during the early Roman Principate. Part of the essential truth does come out in a rather unlikely source, Justin (XVI.iv-v, esp. iv.2, 10-20), where we learn that class strife had led to a revolutionary situation, with the lower classes clamouring for a cancellation of debts and a redistribution of the lands of the rich; that the Council, evidently the organ of oligarchic rule, sent for the exiled Clearchus, believing that he would make a settlement in their favour; but that he in fact took the side of the lower classes, who made him tyrant (364-352/1 B.C.). He evidently pursued a radical policy, in opposition to the interests of the rich: it is hidden from us behind a welter of abuse in Justin, Memnon and others.[50] The 'wickedness' of Clearchus surprised Isocrates (*Epist.* VII.12), whose pupil he had once been, as he had also been Plato's (Memnon, F 1). In the same letter in which Isocrates refers to Clearchus he shows (§ 8, cf. 4) in what circumstances he would be prepared to accept a tyrant as a *kalos kagathos*, an expression we might here translate as 'a high-minded gentleman' (cf. *OPW* 371-6): he praises Cleomis of Mytilene because he has provided for the security of the property of the citizens; he has not made any confiscations; and when he has restored exiles he has given them back their property and compensated those who had purchased it!

Another interesting figure, a contemporary of Clearchus, is Euphron of Sicyon, who receives much abuse in our two main sources for the 360s, Xenophon and Diodorus,[51] as having made himself tyrant of Sicyon in 367 by taking the side of the demos against those of the citizens whom Xenophon often describes indifferently as 'the richest' (*plousiōtatoi*, *HG* VII.i.44) or 'the most powerful' (*kratistoi*, iii.1) or simply 'the best' (*beltistoi*, iii.4,8), from whose property he is said to have made wholesale confiscations (i.46; iii.8; Diod. XV.70.3). Euphron is also said by Xenophon to have proclaimed that he would set up a constitution under which all would participate 'on equal and similar terms' (*epi isois kai homoiois*, *HG* VII.i.45). But, for Xenophon and Diodorus, Euphron is a tyrant, and Xenophon is disgusted at the fact that the Sicyonians, after he had been murdered at Thebes, buried him in their Agora and honoured him as a 'founder of the city' (iii.12), evidently giving him the cult proper to heroes. (Euphron's grandson, also named Euphron, was specially honoured by the Athenians for his friendship and assistance to Athens in the difficult days of the Lamian war and the oligarchy that followed, for which see Section iii of this chapter and its n.2.)[52]

The Athenian democracy, secure and impregnable as it was against purely internal attack, came under constant sniping. In some of our sources, and in the judgment of many modern writers, this situation is seen mainly through the eyes of the wealthy, from whom all the surviving propaganda comes – hence the opinion so often held that in the fourth century the unfortunate rich were dreadfully plundered and exploited and taxed by the merciless and greedy poor. That was certainly what many of the rich said. Listen, for example, to the piteous complaints of Isocrates (XV.159-60; cf. VIII.128):

> When I was a boy [this would be the 420s], being rich was considered so secure and honourable that almost everyone pretended he owned more property than he actually did possess, because he wanted to enjoy the prestige it gave. Now, on the other hand, one has to defend oneself against being rich as if it were the worst of crimes . . . ; for it has become far more dangerous to give the impression of being well-to-do than to commit open crime; criminals are let off altogether or given trivial punishments, but the rich are ruined utterly. More men have been deprived of their property than have paid the penalty of their misdeeds.

But when we put generalisations of this sort on one side and consider such specific factual evidence as we have, we find that the situation is totally different. For example, we shall not take very seriously the gloomy passage I have just quoted from Isocrates when we discover that the orator himself, although a very rich man by ancient standards, had borne a quite remarkably small share of state burdens.[53]

As I have already indicated, outside Athens the political class struggle in the fourth century often became very acute. Rich and poor would regard each other with bitter hatred, and when a revolution succeeded there would be wholesale executions and banishments, and confiscation of the property of at least the leaders of the opposite party. The programme of Greek revolutionaries seems largely to have centred in two demands: redistribution of land, cancellation of debts (*gēs anadasmos, chreōn apokopē*). These twin slogans, characteristic of an impoverished peasantry, had appeared at Athens in the early sixth century, in the time of Solon, as we saw earlier (Section i above). They are not much heard of in fifth-century Greece[54] but became ever more insistent in the fourth. At Athens, where the democracy put the poor in a position to exercise a certain amount of political control and thus to protect themselves in some degree against exploitation and oppression, we scarcely hear of them again after the early sixth century. Elsewhere they became the permanent nightmare of the propertied class.[55] The mid-fourth-century writer Aeneas, generally known as Aeneas 'Tacticus', who wrote not long after 360 (and who may well be the Arcadian general Aeneas from Stymphalus mentioned in Xenophon's *Hellenica*),[56] affords some interesting evidence of the fear by the propertied class of revolution prompted by the burden of debt: among the measures he recommends to cities under siege is a reduction or cancellation of interest and even of the principal (XIV.1-2); and in general he shows a positive obsession with the danger that the city will be betrayed to the enemy by political malcontents within.[57] Sometimes a leading political figure might take up the cause of the poor and put at least part of their programme into effect, at the same time perhaps seizing power himself as a tyrant. (We noticed one or two examples of this earlier: Clearchus of Heraclea and Euphron of Sicyon – if indeed Euphron is to be classed as a 'tyrant'.) But these explosions were futile: even when they did not result in an irresponsible and ultimately repressive tyranny, they merely effected a temporary levelling, after which the same old process started again, intensified by the rancours of civil war.

In the long run there could be only one satisfactory solution, from the point of view of the propertied classes in general: the acceptance of a powerful overlord who could quell by force any further attempts to change the existing scheme of things – and perhaps lead the Greek crusade against Persia long advocated by Isocrates and others (see above), which – it was thought – might provide land and a new hope for those who could no longer make a living at home. It was this solution which was ultimately adopted when Philip II of Macedon had defeated Athens and Thebes at the battle of Chaeronea in 338. Not that by any means all wealthy Greeks welcomed this development: at Athens in particular it looks as if not very many did. The desire of each Greek *polis* for that absolute political independence which in reality few of them ever enjoyed for very long died hard. But the remarkable support which Philip obtained, in the shape of what would nowadays be called 'Fifth Columns' in the Greek states, shows that many leading citizens understood that they had within their walls more dangerous and irreconcilable enemies than the Macedonian king. The affections of some of Philip's Greek partisans were of course bought with handsome gifts.[58] We have, for example, a fascinating vignette showing one of Philip's Arcadian supporters,

Atrestidas, returning from the king's court with some thirty Greek women and children, enslaved by Philip on his capture of Olynthus in 348 and given by him as a present to Atrestidas, doubtless for services rendered or expected – a story which is the more valuable in that it is not a Demosthenic fiction but goes back to a speech of Philip's admirer Aeschines, who had told the Athenians how he had burst into tears at the sight (Dem. XIX.305-6). But men may require no bribes to induce them to pursue courses that are anyway congenial to them (as indeed some Greeks realised),[59] and even at Athens there were a number of rich and influential citizens who needed no persuasion to support Philip. They included Isocrates, the leading publicist and rhetorician of his time, and Speusippus, who had succeeded his uncle Plato as head of the Academy on Plato's death in 348/7.[60] A recent article by Minor M. Markle has well explained the political attitude of these two men and those who thought as they did: 'Support of Athenian intellectuals for Philip', in *JHS* 96 (1976) 80-99. Pointing out, with Momigliano, that Philip could expect support in Greece from the oligarchically-inclined only, Markle demonstrates admirably why men like Isocrates and Speusippus were prepared to accept Philip's hegemony over Greece: the king could be expected to support the propertied classes and to favour a regime of a more 'hierarchical and authoritarian' type than existed in democratic Athens (ibid. 98-9). And indeed the League of Corinth, the almost[61] Panhellenic league which Philip organised in 338/7 and his son and successor Alexander renewed in 335, explicitly guaranteed the existing social order: city constitutions were 'frozen', and there was an express prohibition of the redistribution of land, the cancellation of debts, the confiscation of property, and the freeing of slaves with a view to revolution (Ps.-Dem. XVII.15).

After Athens and Thebes had been defeated by Philip in 338, Philip installed an oligarchy of three hundred of his partisans at Thebes (Justin IX.iv.6-9), backed by a Macedonian garrison;[62] but he treated Athens with great mildness and made no attempt to suppress the Athenian democracy – he had no need to, and it had always been his aim to appear not only 'completely Greek' but also 'most friendly towards Athens' (*hellēnikōtatos* and *philathēnaiotatos*: Dem. XIX.308); and above all he himself, and even Alexander in the 330s, needed the Athenian fleet to secure their communications with Asia. However, as we shall see early in Section iii of this chapter, the Athenian democracy was changed to an oligarchy by the Macedonians in 322/1, and thereafter, although at times it revived, it was never again secure. If the fears felt by men like Demosthenes that the Macedonian king might well destroy the Athenian democracy were not realised in Philip himself, they were justified by the events that took place less than twenty years after his victory over Athens.

The results of Alexander's vast conquests in the East in the late 330s and the 320s were ultimately very far-reaching. They had less direct, immediate effect upon the old Greek world, but it was subjected to the suzerainty of a series of Macedonian kings, who controlled the foreign policy of the Greek states in various degrees but sometimes left them a considerable degree of precarious civic autonomy (see Section iii of this chapter). By far the most important indirect result of Alexander's conquests was a great spread of Greek civilisation into Asia (and Egypt), with the foundation of very many new cities by Alexander himself and his successors, a process which continued in the Roman period. The consequence was a remarkable Hellenisation of the Near East, or rather of its upper classes, extending far into Asia, with Greek cities dotted all over the map from Turkey to Afghanistan, although by the beginning of the Christian era there were not very many cities that can genuinely be called Greek east of Syria and Asia Minor.

As early as 380 B.C. Isocrates (IV.50) had declared that being a Greek was not a matter of race (*genos*) but rather of mental attitude (*dianoia*), and that the name 'Hellenes' was given to those who shared a particular culture (*paideusis*: the process of education and its effects) rather than a physical relationship (a *koinē physis*). That Greek civilisation was indeed a matter of culture rather than 'race' or 'nationality' comes out most noticeably in the vast eastern area which became Hellenised only from the late fourth century B.C. onwards, because in this area a striking difference can be observed from the first between two worlds, one superimposed on the other: those of the city and the countryside, the *polis* and the *chōra*. As I have already discussed this subject (I.iii above), I shall only repeat here that in the newly Hellenised East the world of the *polis* was largely Greek-speaking, with Greek city-life and Greek civilisation generally prevailing, if sometimes much affected by a native culture, and that this world existed (a fact too often forgotten) through its ability to exploit the world of the *chōra*, inhabited almost entirely by peasants living in villages, who spoke mainly their native languages and shared to only a small degree, if at all, in the benefits of Greek civilisation.

(iii)
The destruction of Greek democracy

I have now to describe the gradual extinction of Greek democracy, a subject often ignored or misrepresented in the books which becomes fully intelligible only when explained in terms of a class analysis.

In the early Hellenistic period the lower classes, especially among the city-dwellers (who would naturally find it easier to attend the Assembly), may still have played quite an important part in the life of their city, at least in the older Greek cities of the East as well as in some of those of Greece itself – unfortunately, we have not much information on this point, and much of it is epigraphic and scattered over a wide area and has never been properly collated and analysed. Very soon, however, there developed all over the Greek world a tendency for political power to become entirely concentrated in the hands of the propertied class. This development, or rather retrogression, which seems to have begun early in the Hellenistic period, was still by no means complete when the Romans took over, in the second century B.C. The Romans, whose governing class always detested democracy, intensified and accelerated the process; and by the third century of the Christian era the last remnants of the original democratic institutions of the Greek *poleis* had mostly ceased to exist for all practical purposes.

The earlier stages of this transformation are difficult to trace: not much firm evidence survives and it is often capable of more than one interpretation. I shall presently single out three aspects of the process: the growth of royal, magisterial, conciliar or other control over the citizen assemblies; the attachment to magistracies of liturgies (the performance of expensive civic duties); and the gradual destruction of those popular law courts, consisting of panels of dicasts (*dikastēria*, in which the dicasts were both judges and jury), which had been such an essential feature of Greek democracy, especially in Classical Athens. All these were devices invented for the express purpose of getting round the fact that outright oligarchy, the open limitation of political rights to the propertied Few, was still likely to meet with strong resistance from the lower classes, and had been discredited in many places by Alexander's time by its bad record in practice, notably at Athens. In fourth-century Athens even would-be oligarchs found it politic to pretend that they too wanted democracy, only of course it must be the good old democracy of the good old times, not the vicious contemporary form which led to all sorts of unworthy and wicked men gaining power for their own nefarious ends, and so forth – the odious Isocrates furnishes some excellent examples of this kind of disguised right-wing propaganda, notably in his *Areopagiticus* and his treatise *On the Peace*.[1]

As I shall not have occasion to describe it elsewhere, I must not omit to mention briefly the destruction of the Athenian democracy in 322/1, at the end of the 'Lamian war',[2] by Antipater, who may be described as the Macedonian viceroy of Greece. When the Athenians received the news of Alexander's death (which had occurred at Babylon in June 323), they soon led a widespread Greek revolt, which they themselves referred to proudly as a 'Hellenic war', against Macedonian domination; but in 322 they were utterly defeated and compelled to surrender, and the Macedonians turned the constitution of Athens into an oligarchy, limiting the exercise of political rights to the 9,000 citizens (out of, probably, 21,000) who possessed at least 2,000 drachmae (Diod. XVIII.18.4–5, with Plut., *Phoc*.27.5; 28.7, on which see n.2 below). The figure of 2,000 drachmae may have been roughly equivalent to the property level that would enable a man to serve as a hoplite. After 322/1 Athens was subjected to a whole series of interventions and constitutional changes and was never able to decide her own destiny for very long. There was a short-lived restoration of democracy under the aegis of the Macedonian regent Polyperchon in 318, but in the following year Antipater's son Cassander regained power over Athens and installed a less restricted oligarchy, excluding from political rights all those who possessed a property qualification of less than 1,000 drachmae (Diod. XVIII.74.3). At the head of this oligarchy was Demetrius of Phalerum, who was virtually tyrant in the Macedonian interest, having been appointed overseer or superintendent of Athens (probably *epimelētēs*, perhaps *epistatēs*) by Cassander under the terms of the treaty made when Athens capitulated to him in 317.[3] Pausanias calls Demetrius a *tyrannos* outright (I.xxv.5-6); according to Plutarch his regime was 'nominally oligarchical but in reality monarchical' (*Demetr*. 10.2). Yet the term oligarchy still had a rather unpleasant sound, and Demetrius himself claimed that he 'not merely did not destroy the democracy but actually reinforced it' (Strabo IX.i.20, p.398). There was then, to quote W. S. Ferguson's *Hellenistic Athens* (95), 'a new era of internal and external conflict for Athens, which continued almost without intermission for 46 years. Seven times the government changed hands [in 307, 303, 301, 294, 276, 266, and 261], and on as many occasions the constitution was in some degree altered . . . Four times the institutions were modified, and a new government established, through the violent intervention of a foreign prince [in 303, 294, 276, and 261]. Three uprisings were bloodily suppressed [303, 295, and 287/6], and the city sustained four blockades [304, 296-4, 287, and 265-1], all with equal heroism, but twice unsuccessfully [294, and 261].' After further vicissitudes the story virtually comes to an end with the heroic and futile resistance to the Roman general Sulla, which ended with the sack of Athens in March 86 (see Appendix IV, § 2, and its n.5 below).

The relation of the Hellenistic kings – or, for that matter, of the Romans at first – to the Greek cities within their realms is hard to define with precision,[4] because each side tended to see the relationship differently, although a king, especially when he needed the support of the cities, was often willing to pander to their *amour propre* by using the diplomatic terminology they preferred. 'It was rarely that a king so far forgot himself as to issue commands to a city; he was usually scrupulous to give advice and offer suggestions' (Jones, *GCAJ* 111). While Alexander the Great was actually in the process of conquering Asia Minor and those of the Aegean islands which had been taken over by the Persians or by pro-Persian parties, he did not hesitate to issue some peremptory orders to the cities; when he discovered that the democrats were in general on his side, while many oligarchs and would-be oligarchs were prepared to fight to the death for Persia, he prescribed democracies everywhere (see my *OPW* 40 n.76). But since he was 'liberating' the Greek cities of Asia from Persian domination, he was quite prepared, when a city was firmly under his control, to avoid speaking of a 'gift' of freedom and to use a technical term which signified 'recognition' (literally, 'giving back'): instead of the verb *didōmi* ('I give'), he used *apodidōmi* or some similar word (see the list at the end of n.12 of Magie, *RRAM* II.828). The difference between these two formulae emerges best from negotiations in the late 340s between Athens and Philip II of Macedon concerning Halonnesus, which the Athenians refused to accept as a 'gift' from Philip, insisting that he should 'recognise' the island as theirs (Ps.-Dem. VII.2-6) – with the result that Philip kept Halonnesus. The essential thing to notice here is that it lay entirely with Philip to decide whether he should 'give' Halonnesus to Athens or 'recognise' it as hers. Similarly, it was purely a matter for Alexander to decide what formula he would use in regard to the freedom of the Asian cities. He was usually prepared to 'recognise' the freedom of Greek cities he 'liberated' from Persia; but the velvet glove could be stripped off when necessary to reveal the iron hand beneath. When Alexander in 324 issued a decree or edict (*diagramma*) prescribing the return of exiles[5] he of course had all the Greek cities in mind; but the decree will simply have used the expression, 'I restore' (or, more probably, 'We restore', *katagomen*, the royal plural; cf. Diod. XVIII.8.4; 56.4; Tod, *SGHI* II.192.10, 17), without addressing a direct order to the cities, and it was therefore possible for them to pass their own decrees recalling their exiles and to pretend to themselves that it was they who were issuing the orders, even if the mask occasionally slipped, as when the Tegeates referred to 'those whom it pleased the city to restore' in a decree which makes repeated reference to the *diagramma* of Alexander as something binding on the city (Tod, *SGHI* II.202, esp. 58-9).

The successors of Alexander behaved towards the cities in whatever ways they thought their own interests dictated; and it is just as mistaken as in the case of Alexander to press the use of words like *apodidōmi* as if they had some genuine legal, constitutional significance, apart from propaganda.[6] If I had to choose a single text to illustrate the realities of the situation, it would be the statement of Antiochus III, at a conference with Roman envoys at Lysimacheia in 196 B.C., that 'those of the cities of Asia which were autonomous ought to acquire their freedom by his own grace [*charis*] and not by an order from Rome' (Polyb. XVIII.li.9; cf. App., *Syr*. 3). A little earlier Antiochus had sent ambassadors to Lampsacus, to insist that if they were to gain their liberty it must be in circumstances which would make it perfectly clear that they had obtained it from himself 'and not usurped it themselves at an opportune moment' (*libertatem non per occasionem raptam*, Livy XXXIII.xxxviii.5-6). 'Freedom' (*eleutheria*), in the mouth of a king, signified very much what 'autonomy' (*autonomia*) had always meant. As Bickerman has shown in his fundamental study of that conception in the fifth and fourth centuries B.C., 'Toujours le terme *autonomia* indique que la cité n'est pas la maîtresse absolue de sa politique', and 'L'indépendance d'une cité autonome est nécessairement imparfaite' (APT 330, 337). Claire Préaux has rightly said of Alexander's actions in regard to the cities of Asia, 'C'est sans aucun doute agir comme un maître sur des villes sujettes: l'autonomie, quoiqu'elle s'appelle "liberté", n'exclut pas la sujétion'.[7] And so it was with all the Hellenistic kings.

As for the internal affairs of cities under their control, whether theoretically free or not, the kings might or might not interfere directly. Some cities were left almost entirely to themselves. In others a king might reserve the right to appoint one or more of the regular magistrates, or install an overseer (e.g. an *epistatēs*: see n.3 again) of his own choice, with or without a garrison (sometimes paid for by the city concerned); and a city might sometimes be made to feel that it would be impolitic to pass decrees on a certain range of matters without first obtaining the consent of the king or his overseer (see n.4 again). The imposition of a garrison (by no means a rare event) could be particularly destructive to a democracy, if the garrison commander (who was exceedingly unlikely to be a democrat) felt obliged or inclined to intervene politically; and even if he did not, the menacing presence of the garrison was bound to have a deleterious effect on internal democratic politics.

At this point I must jump ahead for a moment and (in a single paragraph) glance at the relationship of Rome to the Greek cities within the area she dominated. With some Rome made actual treaties acknowledging their freedom: they were 'free and federate states', *civitates liberae et foederatae*. Others received freedom by a unilateral grant: they were *civitates liberae*. The great majority (except in Old Greece, where the cities were from the first declared 'free') were subject to the provincial governor like any other 'native' community: for them there was no corresponding technical description. I have no doubt that A. H. M. Jones was right in saying that 'freedom was, it would seem, to the Roman government what it was to the Hellenistic kings, a privileged status granted by itself to cities under its dominion, and the principal element in it was exemption from the authority of the provincial governors . . . Rome took over the royal concept of freedom; she too by a free city meant not an independent sovereign state, but a state subject to her suzerainty enjoying by her grace certain privileges . . . But there was an infinite gradation of privilege, and some subject cities – those of Sicily for instance – enjoyed rights hardly inferior to those of some free cities' (Jones, CLIE 112, 106, 109). As for the 'federate states' (*civitates foederatae*), they 'differed only in the sanction of their privileges: those of free cities were in theory as well as in fact revocable at will, those of federate, being guaranteed by a sworn instrument, were in theory irrevocable' (ibid. 113). But 'in effect the difference was not very great, for free cities were not arbitrarily degraded and if a federate city offended Rome it could generally be found that it had violated the terms of its *foedus*, which thereupon became void' (Jones, *GCAJ* 117). And although federate states continued occasionally to be created as late as the early Principate, Suetonius mentions that Augustus deprived of their liberty several cities which were federate but were 'heading for ruin through their lawlessness' (*Aug.* 47) – in other words, as Jones puts it, 'internal disorders were a good enough excuse for cancelling a *foedus*' (*GCAJ* 131, cf. 132). An apt illustration of the Roman attitude to *civitates foederatae* much weaker than themselves is the statement of Appius Claudius to the Achaean League in 184 B.C., reported by Livy (XXXIX.37.19): he strongly advised them, he said, to ingratiate themselves with Rome 'while they still had the power to do so of their own free will' (*voluntate sua facere*); the alternative was that they would soon have to do as they were told, against their will (*inviti et coacti*). The Achaeans, needless to say, were afraid to disobey, and they merely allowed themseles the luxury of a 'general groaning' (*omnium gemitus*: id. 20).

In Jones's great work on the Greek city in the Hellenistic and Roman periods, from which I have already quoted, we read that 'whatever devices the kings might invent to secure their control over the cities, there was one which they could not use, the formal limitation of political power to a small class; . . . the kings felt obliged to support democracy in the cities and were thus unable to create and effectively support monarchist parties which should rule in their interest; the few attempts made – notably by Antipater and Cassander [in 322 ff.] – to establish oligarchies of their supporters roused such violent discontent that this policy became utterly discredited' (*GCAJ* 157-60, 111). Apart from the short-lived oligarchies just mentioned, Jones could produce only one exception to his rule: Cyrene, to which the first Ptolemy dictated a moderately oligarchical constitution (replacing a more extreme oligarchy) in the last quarter of the fourth century, perhaps in 322/1.[8] But I think there are likely to have been other exceptions. For instance, in an inscription of Ptolemais in Upper Egypt, of the third century B.C., we hear that disorders had occurred at meetings of the Council and Assembly, especially at the elections of magistrates; and with a view to remedying this situation the decree (of Council and Demos) proceeds to restrict the choice of those eligible for the Council and the courts of law to a select list of *epilektoi andres* (*OGIS* 48.9-11, 13-16). I find it hard to believe that the reigning Ptolemy had not intervened on this occasion, even if he tactfully left it to the organs of city government to provide against repetition of the disturbances (and cf. Jones, *GCAJ* 104). Also, it is only fair to mention that in many *poleis* of the newly hellenised East, unlike Old Greece (and the long-settled Greek fringe of Asia Minor), the citizens themselves were often an exclusive oligarchy among the permanent free inhabitants, a large part of the old native population (essentially the poorer classes) being excluded from citizenship (see Jones, *GCAJ* 160-1, with 335 nn. 10-11).

As for the new cities founded by Alexander and the Hellenistic kings, it is only rarely that we have any details of their original constitutions, but there is reason to think that full political rights were never extended to anything like the whole free population, even where (as at Egyptian Alexandria) the constitution was at first of the standard Greek type, with a Council and Assembly.[9] Some of the disfranchised (like the Jews of Antioch and Alexandria and Berenice Euesperides, and the Syrians of Seleuceia on the Tigris) were organised in special *ad hoc* bodies known as *politeumata*, through which their affairs were administered;[10] but probably in most cases the natives in the countryside, who cultivated the lands of the citizens, had no political rights of any kind, except to a small degree in their villages, and remained to a considerable extent outside the ambit of Graeco-Roman culture, which always remained essentially urban. As I have explained in I.iii above, the relationship of those who dominated the Greek cities to the natives outside is best described as one of exploitation, with few benefits given in return. As a matter of fact, there are traces even in Aristotle's *Politics* of a situation in which 'those around the countryside' (*hoi kata tēn chōran*) can be expected not to possess the franchise. In *Pol.* VII.14, 1332^{b}27-32, they are seen as likely to join in a body in revolutions begun by those citizens who do not possess proper political rights. An example of such a situation might be the revolt against the Gamoroi of Syracuse, perhaps in the late 490s (see Dunbabin, *WG* 414-15), by the *dēmos* of Syracuse and their 'slaves', as Herodotus calls them (VII.155.2) – in fact the Killyrioi, who were serfs: see III.iv above and its n.3 below.

I have mentioned three principal oligarchic devices by which democracy was in practice frustrated after the fourth century B.C. The first (control of the Assembly by royal officials, magistrates, Council or otherwise) is obvious enough and requires little comment. Assemblies continued to meet in most if not all cities, and sometimes quite large numbers of citizens might attend the sessions, as we know from a handful of surviving decrees (mostly of about the early second century B.C.) which give the actual numbers present and voting. On three occasions at Magnesia on the Maeander attendances of 2,113, 3,580 and even 4,678 are mentioned; an inscription found on the island of Cos records a decree of the Assembly of Halicarnassus passed by a vote (unanimous or *nem. con.*, like most of the others) of 4,000; other figures are smaller.[11] I might add that all or most of the decrees just mentioned are honorific in character, as indeed are the majority of the city decrees inscribed on stone which have survived from the Hellenistic and Roman periods.

The second device, the assimilation of magistracies to liturgies by attaching special burdens to the performance of magistracies, is much more interesting and deserves discussion. Aristotle, in that part of his *Politics* which is devoted to advising oligarchs how to run a state of which they are in control, has this remarkable passage:

> To the most important magistracies should be attached liturgies, in order that the common people may be willing to acquiesce in their own exclusion from office and may sympathise with those who have to pay so high a price for the privilege. Those who enter into office may also be reasonably expected to offer magnificent sacrifices and to erect some public building, so that the common people, participating in the feasts and seeing their city embellished ,with offering and buildings, may readily tolerate a continuance of this constitution [oligarchy]. The leading citizens, too, will have visible memorials of their own expenditure. But this is not the policy pursued by oligarchs today – they do the very opposite: they covet profit as well as honour (*Pol.* VI.7, 1321^{a}31-42).

This passage (which seems to have escaped general notice) is of very great interest, because it describes something that did happen in the Hellenistic period, when magistracies and liturgies often became to some extent assimilated. (One wonders how many 'thinking' members of the ruling class in the fourth century shared Aristotle's sentiments!) There was seldom, it seems, any constitutional requirement that magistrates should perform liturgies, but this became the custom in many cities, which no one would dare to flout. This has been referred to as 'a tacit convention whereby the people elected rich men to magistracies, and they as magistrates contributed freely to the public services under their charge' (Jones, *GCAJ* 167, cf. 168); but this does not take account of the passage from the *Politics* which I have just quoted and obscures the fact that the whole process was partly an adroit expedient by the wealthy class to keep the poorer citizens out of office without having to pass invidious legislation to that end, and even more to serve as a substitute for the one thing the wealthy Greeks would never tolerate: a legally enforceable taxation system under which the burden of maintaining the state would fall mainly upon those who derived most benefit from it and were best able to bear that burden. It is fascinating to read the passage in Dio of Prusa's Rhodian speech, expressing horror at the very thought that 'a time might ever come at which it would be necessary for each individual citizen to pay a levy from his private means' (Dio Chrys. XXXI.46). Dio congratulates the Rhodians on never having done such a thing except when their city was in extreme danger.

The third significant oligarchic device by which democracy was gradually extinguished was the abolition of the popular *dikastēria* mentioned above, on which in a full Greek democracy all citizens were entitled to serve, just as they were able to attend the Assembly. This, the judicial aspect of the decline of Greek democracy, has received even less attention than the political aspect of the same process: the decline of the popular assemblies. This is partly because the evidence is so deplorably scanty, but also because modern scholars tend to forget how extraordinarily important the popular courts were for the main-tenance of proper democracy. (Clear separation of the 'political' and the 'judicial' is a very modern phenomenon.) My own collection of the evidence is very incomplete, and I do not feel able to give a coherent account; I shall merely mention some of the more interesting material later in this section.

The seventh, sixth and fifth centuries, as I said earlier, had been characterised by a movement towards the attainment of political rights by an ever-increasing proportion of the citizen community. By the Hellenistic age, the upper classes had learnt that it was unwise to make legally enforceable concessions by granting too wide a range of *political rights*. Instead, they offered to the lower classes a certain amount of *charity*, to be granted or withheld at their own pleasure. When things were not going well for them the charity could be cut down, without anyone having the right to complain. They were prepared on occasion to enforce upon recalcitrants among their own number the performance of expensive tasks which were really necessary; but inessential offices involving some outlay could at a pinch, in very hard times, or when no one could be persuaded to shoulder the burden, be conferred upon some obliging god or hero, who could scarcely be expected to make the customary expenditure.[12] One of the worst features of this whole process was surely its demoralising effect on both sides.

It was only in the Roman period, however, that the last remaining vestiges of

democracy were gradually stamped out of the Greek cities. (The evidence for
this is very fragmentary and scattered, and I can do no more here than give an
oversimplified outline.) It was the regular aim of the Romans to place the
government of provincial cities under the sole control (subject of course to the
Roman governor) of the propertied classes. This was effected in various ways,
partly by making constitutional changes, but even more by giving steady
support to the rich and encouraging them to assume and retain control of local
political life, as of course they were only too ready to do. Livy puts it perfectly in
a nutshell, in a speech he gives to Nabis, the tyrant of Sparta, in 195 B.C., which
almost certainly derives from Livy's main source for this period, Polybius.
Addressing the Roman general, T. Quinctius Flamininus, Nabis says, 'Your
[the Romans'] wish is that a few should excel in wealth, and that the common
people should be subject to them' (*paucos excellere opibus, plebem subiectam esse
illis, vultis*, XXXIV.xxxi.17). And, as Plutarch said in the reign of Trajan, the
Romans were 'very eager to promote the political interests of their friends'
(*Mor.* 814c).[13] We know enough about this process to be confident of its general
outlines, but the particulars are difficult to display in a palatable shape for the
general reader, even in summary form, and I have therefore relegated the details
to Appendix IV. I will refer at this point only to a single series of incidents, from
one small town in the northern Peloponnese, which may not be in themselves at
all typical of what happened in Old Greece after its final conquest by Rome in
146 B.C. ('typical', in the sense that we might expect many similar occurrences
elsewhere), but which certainly brings out very well the significance of the
Roman conquest and the effect this could have upon the class struggle in Greek
cities. In the Achaean town of Dyme, probably in 116-114 B.C., there was a
revolution, evidently caused in part by the burden of debt, for it began with the
burning of the public archives and the cancellation of debts and of other
contracts. This was suppressed, with or without the aid of the Roman proconsul
of Macedonia (who now had a general oversight of Greece, not yet organised as
a separate province); two of the revolutionary leaders were immediately condemned to death by the proconsul and another was sent to Rome for trial. Our
only evidence for these events is an inscription recording a letter of the proconsul, Q. Fabius Maximus, to the city of Dyme, which complains bitterly of
'disorder' (*tarachē*), a 'disregard of contractual obligations and cancellation of
debts' (*chre[ōkopia]*), and twice speaks of the revolutionary legislation as carried
'in violation of the constitution given to the Achaeans by the Romans'[14] – a
reference to the oligarchies imposed by the Roman general L. Mummius in
various parts of central Greece and the Peloponnesus, when in 146 he had
crushed the revolt of the Achaeans and their allies. Much more often, I imagine,
any local disturbance would be nipped in the bud by the action of the city
magistrates themselves, who would usually be anxious to avoid attracting the
attention of the provincial governor by making an appeal to him. Thus we find
an inscription of Cibyra (on the borders of Phrygia and Caria in the province of
Asia), apparently of the second quarter of the first century of the Christian era,
honouring a conspicuously wealthy citizen named Q. Veranius Philagrus who,
after the serious earthquake of A.D. 23, had not only reclaimed for the city 107
public slaves who had somehow escaped from their condition (perhaps at the
time of the earthquake), but had also 'suppressed a great conspiracy which was

doing the greatest harm to the city' (*IGRR* IV.914.5-6, 9-10).

Dio Cassius, writing in the early third century, puts into the mouth of Maecenas a speech addressed to Augustus, to which I shall return later in this section. One of the policies Maecenas is made to advocate is the total suppression of city Assemblies. The *dēmoi*, says Maecenas, should not be sovereign in any respect (*mēte kyrioi tinos*), nor should they be allowed to meet together in *ekklēsia* at all, for they would come to no good conclusions and they would often create disturbances (LII.xxx.2). I agree with Jones (*GCAJ* 340 n.42) that this is 'not true even of his [Dio's] own day but must represent the policy which he himself would have favoured'. We have little explicit evidence for constitutional changes brought about directly or indirectly by Roman action; but we can trace the imposition – in Greece itself in the second century B.C., and later elsewhere – of property qualifications for at any rate magistracies and membership of the Council, and in some cases the courts, if not for access to the Assembly (see Appendix IV below, § 2); the gradual turning of Councils (*boulai*) into little models of the Roman Senate, with ex-magistrates having life membership; and the exercise of such control over the popular Assemblies that by slow degrees they eventually died out entirely. By at any rate the end of the second century of the Christian era the Assemblies of the Greek cities had either ceased to meet or at least lost all effective power, and the Councils, which had orginally been chosen annually (as a rule) from the whole body of citizens or at least a large part of it, often by lot, had been transformed into permanent, largely hereditary, and more or less self-perpetuating bodies, sometimes enrolled by censors chosen by and from their own number, the councillors (*bouleutai, decuriones* in Latin) being drawn only from the wealthier citizens and, with their families, eventually forming the privileged curial order, by which and from which in practice all magistrates were chosen. (I shall have more to say about the curial order in VIII.i and ii below.) Paulus, the Severan jurist, can say that non-decurions (*plebeii*) are excluded from local magistracies, because they are debarred from *decurionum honores*, the offices open only to decurions (*Dig.* L.ii.7.2). He is speaking specifically of the duumvirate, the principal magistracy in very many towns of the Roman West, but his statement would apply equally, *mutatis mutandis*, to Greek cities. And of course a city Council might suffer interference from the provincial governor in its choice of magistrates. Legal texts speak of a Roman governor giving directions to a local Council (*ordo*) to elect a certain man as a magistrate or to confer on him some office or liturgy (*honor vel munus*: Ulpian, in *Dig.* XLIX.iv.1.3); and it is contemplated that the governor may himself be present at the meeting of the Council in question (id. 4). A proconsul, says Ulpian elsewhere, ought not to agree to the election of a duumvir by mere 'low-class clamour' (*vocibus popularium*), in place of the regular legal procedure (*Dig.* XLIX.i.12).

I know of no detailed description of this process which to my mind sufficiently brings out its deliberate, purposive character. The 'Greats' pupils I used to teach at Oxford, who study one period of Greek history and one of Roman, with quite a large gap in between, were often puzzled by the way in which Greek democracy, so vigorous in the fifth century and even in the fourth, has by the beginning of the Roman Principate become but a shadow of its former self. The books sometimes note this as a fact in passing, but most of them make no attempt to supply an explanation of it, and when it is noticed at all it tends to be recorded as something that 'just happened'. Characteristic is the statement of Hugh Last, in *CAH* XI.458-9: 'In the East democracy had been in decline even before Rome came to throw her influence on the side of the more substantial elements, and in Rome itself circumstances had combined to make oligarchy the one possible alternative to monarchy. In the municipalities the same forces were at work . . . Rome showed no enthusiasm for democracy.' I on the other hand would see the whole process as part of the class struggle on the political plane: the Greek propertied classes, with the assistance first of their Macedonian overlords and then of their Roman masters, gradually undermined and in the end entirely destroyed Greek democracy, which before the end of the Principate had become extinct. Of course the suppression of Greek democracy was gratifying to the Romans; but it is clear that the Greek propertied classes did not merely acquiesce in the process: they assisted in it – and no wonder, because they themselves, after the Romans, were the chief beneficiaries of the system. An important letter of Cicero's congratulates his brother Quintus because he has made sure, during his government of the province of Asia, that the municipalities have been administered by the deliberations of the leading men, the *optimates* (*Ad Q.fr.* I.i.25; cf. *De rep.* II.39, and passages from the *Pro Flacco* quoted below). Pliny the Younger, writing in *c.* A.D. 107-8 to his friend Caelestrius Tiro, who was then proconsul of Baetica (southern Spain), reminds him of the necessity to preserve distinctions of rank and dignity (*discrimina ordinum dignitatumque*). 'Nothing,' he declares, with a characteristically Roman perversity, 'is more unequal than equality' (*Ep.* IX.v.1,3; cf. II.xii.5). Doubtless Pliny was familiar with the curious oligarchical argument for the superiority of 'geometrical' over 'arithmetical' proportion, which was known to Cicero (see VII.i below & its nn.10-11). The 'greatest and most influential men of every city' are said by Aelius Aristeides, in the mid-second century, to act as guards of their native places for the Romans, making it unnecessary for them to be garrisoned (*Orat.* XXVI.64). Those of the principal propertied families of the Greek world who were prepared to accept Roman domination wholeheartedly and co-operate with their masters sometimes flourished remarkably. In Asia, with its great natural wealth, they might become immensely rich and aspire to membership of the imperial nobility, the Roman Senate (cf. III.ii above). Even in Old Greece, with its comparative lack of resources, they might at least achieve great prestige locally by holding office through several generations, like the four leading families of Roman Athens recently studied by Michael Woloch, which held a high proportion of the most important magistracies (as well as some major priesthoods) in the period 96-161; and occasionally they might eventually enter the senatorial class, like the family of Flavii from the insignificant little city of Thespiae in Boeotia, whose history from the third century B.C. to the third of our era has been ably reconstructed by C. P. Jones.[15] A man who could claim to have expended much of his fortune for the benefit of his city (as some did, eager for the prestige it could bring) might sometimes receive from the city a real 'golden handshake': in the reign of Domitian, 40,000 drachmae/denarii (nearly 7 talents) were given to Julius Piso, by a decision of the Council and Assembly of Amisus, on the southern shore of the Black Sea. Trajan had issued instructions to Pliny, as his special governor of Bithynia-Pontus, forbidding such gifts; but he gave a special exemption to Piso because his present had been made to him more than twenty years earlier (Pliny, *Ep.* X.110-111). And at about the end of the third century the lawyer Hermogenian regarded it as settled law that pensions (*alimenta*) might be decreed to ruined councillors, especially if they had 'exhausted their patrimony through munificence towards their native place' (*Dig.* L.ii.8) – a claim which was by no means infrequent (see Dio Chrys. XLVI.3 etc.).

In the earlier period of Roman rule – indeed, even occasionally in the early second century of the Christian era – the Assemblies of some Greek cities could evidently still show signs of life and vigour. Cicero, in the speech he delivered in 59 B.C. when successfully defending L. Valerius Flaccus, who was being prosecuted for extortion during his governorship of the province of Asia in 62-1, indulges in some bitterly contemptuous abuse of the Assemblies of the Greek cities of Asia, contrasting what he represents as their disorderly character with the dignified procedure of a Roman Assembly. Parts of this speech (*Pro Flacc.* 9-24, 57-8, 63) ought to be – as they rarely if ever are – prescribed reading for those who are studying the history of political institutions. Cicero pours scorn on Greek popular Assemblies, whose very procedure in passing their decrees (*psēphismata*) after general debate and by the holding up of hands he repeatedly derides (§§ 15, 17, 23): he says that these Greek Assemblies are excitable, rash, headstrong, tumultuous (§§ 15-19, 23, 24, 54, 57, 58) and that they are dominated by men of no account, 'uneducated men' (*imperiti,* § 58), cobblers and belt-makers (§ 17), artisans and shopkeepers and all such 'dregs of the state' (§ 18), rather than by the 'rich *bien-pensants*' (*locupletes homines et graves,* § 18), the 'leading men' (*principes,* §§ 54, 58; *optimates,* §§ 58, 63) for whom Cicero and his like, as we have seen, always wished to reserve the monopoly of political power in subject states. Cicero actually attributes the 'fall' of Greece (he uses the word *concidit,* § 16) to 'this one evil: the immoderate liberty and license [*licentia*][16] of their Assemblies'; and just afterwards he shows that he has Classical Athens particularly in mind (§ 17). None of this need surprise us, of course, for Cicero's speeches, letters and treatises are full of abuse of the lower classes at Rome itself (cf. VI.v below). And it should not escape our notice, by the way, that Cicero, who represents Greeks in general (even when he is not artfully denigrating them by calling them Asiatics, Phrygians, Mysians, Carians, Lydians: §§ 3, 17, 37-8, 40-1, 60, 65, 100) as totally untrustworthy witnesses, 'men to whom an oath is a joke, testimony a game' (§ 12; cf. 9-10, 36, 37), can bluntly tell his jury that decisions in a lawsuit ought to be rendered according to 'the welfare of the state, the safety of the community, and the immediate interests of the Republic' (*quid utilitas civitatis, quid communis salus, quid reipublicae tempora poscerent,* § 98) – that is to say, the interests of the propertied class. The merits of the particular case are in comparison unimportant.

The difference between being a genuinely free Greek city in the fifth or fourth century B.C. and a city subject to Roman rule can best be conveyed by a few quotations from a work of Plutarch, the *Politika parengelmata* ('Political precepts', or 'Precepts of statecraft'), usually refered to by the Latin translation of its title, *Precepta gerundae reipublicae* (*Moralia* 798a-825f), written in about the first decade of the second century of the Christian era, in the earlier years of the reign of Trajan. Plutarch had been asked by a young friend, a citizen of Sardis (813f, with 825d), to give him advice for a political career – or at least, that is the ostensible occasion for the composition of the work. (The young man is obviously a member of my 'propertied class'; the alleged poverty discussed in *Mor.* 822def is simply the absence of ostentatious wealth: see 823abc etc.)[17]

'Nowadays, when the affairs of the cities do not include leadership in war, or the overthrow of tyrannies, or the making of alliances, what opening for a conspicuous and splendid career could one find?' Well, reflects Plutarch, 'there remain public lawsuits and embassies to an emperor, which require a man of ardent temperament and one with courage and intelligence'! (805ab). He suggests various ways of doing good turns to friends (809a). He protests against being laughed at when he is seen (as he says he often may be) supervising the measuring of tiles or the transport of concrete or stones, as a magistrate of his native town of Chaeronea (811bc). And then he really comes to the point: 'When you take up some magistracy,' he says, 'you must say to yourself, "You who rule are a subject, and the state you rule is dominated by proconsuls, the agents of Caesar", . . . whose boots you see above your head.[18] You should imitate those actors who . . . listen to the prompter and do not take liberties with rhythms and metres beyond those permitted by those in authority over them, for a failure in your part now brings not just hissing or mockery or jeering, but many have experienced "the terrible avenger: the axe that cleaves the neck"' (a quotation from some unidentified Greek tragedy), and others have been exiled to islands (813def). Let others do their rabble-rousing with the common herd, Plutarch advises, 'stupidly advocating imitation of the deeds and designs and actions of their ancestors, which are out of proportion with present opportunities and conditions' (814a). 'Leave it to the schools of the Sophists to prate of Marathon and the Eurymedon and Plataea and all the other examples which make the masses swell with pride and prance' (814bc). 'The politician should not only show himself and his state blameless towards our rulers; he should also have some friend among those men of the greatest influence, as a firm bulwark of his administration, for the Romans themselves are very eager to promote the political interests of their friends' (814c). Plutarch is scornful about the highly profitable procuratorships and provincial governorships 'in pursuit of which most men in public life grow old at the doors of other men's houses, neglecting their own affairs' (814d). He insists that the politician, while making his native land amenable to its rulers, ought not to humble it unnecessarily, 'or, when the leg has been fettered, go on to place the neck under the yoke, as some do when they refer everything, great or small, to our rulers, and thus bring the reproach of slavery upon us, or rather, altogether destroy its constitutional government, making it dazed and timid and powerless in everything' (814ef). 'Those who invite the rulers' decision on every decree or meeting or privilege or administrative act are obliging their rulers to become their masters [*despotai*] more than they themselves wish to be: the principal cause of this is the greed and contentiousness of the leading men, who . . . call in their superiors, and as a result the Council and Assembly and courts and every magistracy lose their authority. One should placate the ordinary citizens by offering them equality[19] and the powerful by corresponding concessions, and thus control affairs *within the constitution* and dispose of difficulties' (814f-5b). 'The statesman will not allow to the common people any high-handed treatment of the citizens or any confiscation of the property of others or distribution of public funds, but will firmly contest aspirations of that sort with persuasion, instruction and threats – although harmless expenditures may on occasion be permitted' (818cd). Plutarch proceeds to cite some instructive precedents for the making of concessions to the people to divert their feelings into harmless channels (818def, cf. 813b). One remembers here that Pliny the Younger, writing to a friend in 107, describes a certain leading citizen of Ephesus, Claudius Aristion, as *'innoxie popularis'*, which should perhaps be translated 'inclined towards the common people, but harmlessly so' (*Ep.* VI.xxxi.3). Above all, says Plutarch a little later, civil strife (*stasis*) must never be allowed to occur: its prevention should be regarded as the greatest and noblest function of statesmanship (824bc). After all, he goes on, war has been done away with, and 'of liberty the common people have as much as our rulers grant them; and perhaps more would not be better for them' (824c). The wise statesman will aim at bringing about concord and friendship (*homonoian . . . kai philian*); he 'will lay stress on the weakness of Greek affairs, in which it is better for prudent men to accept one benefit: to live quietly and in harmony, since Fortune has left us no prize to compete for . . . What sort of power is it which a small edict of a proconsul may abolish or transfer to someone else, and which, even if it should last, has nothing worthy of enthusiasm?' (824def).

It is anything but an inspiring picture. Not that Plutarch and his like were at all basically dissatisfied with Roman rule:[20] the Greek propertied class had greatly benefited from it politically, when everything is taken into account (cf. VI.iv-vi below). They had even managed to preserve some of their self-respect, if with the loss of some of the nobler qualities of the Classical period.

As Rostovtzeff and others have seen,[21] there is an interesting correspondence between the work of Plutarch which I have just been discussing and certain speeches delivered by Dio Chrysostom,[22] mainly in the last decades of the first century and the first decade or so of the second. Particularly striking are Dio's advice to his native city (Prusa in Bithynia, north-west Asia Minor) to give up its futile quarrels with its neighbours, 'for leadership and power are vested in others' (meaning of course the Romans); and his apt comparison of such squabbles with 'the strife of fellow-slaves [*homodouloi*] with one another for glory and precedence'! (Dio XXXIV.48, 51). Dio could warn his fellow-citizens to be particularly careful not to give offence to the neighbouring city of Apamea, a Roman citizen colony, which, as long as it behaves itself, he says, can enjoy prestige and influence (*timēn tina kai dynamin*) with the proconsuls (of Bithynia: XL.22; cf. XLI.9). Even the status of a 'free city' was a very precarious one and might be lost by some act to which the Roman government objected (see below and n.23).

It seems likely, from some of the passages quoted above from Cicero's *Pro Flacco* and similar evidence, that as late as the mid-first century B.C. the poorer classes among the citizen population of a Greek democracy might derive some protection against exploitation and oppression by the rich from the control they could exercise on occasion over their popular Assembly – in which, so long as there was no property-qualification for the exercise of basic political rights, they would form a majority if enough of them could manage to attend. The local notables, however, could normally rely on receiving Roman support, and if an Assembly were driven by exceptional circumstances to act too strongly against their (or the Romans') interests, the result might be what Plutarch calls 'a small edict of a proconsul', inflicting a penalty on the city (see above, and Appendix IV below, § 3B). And if the people dared to come together in a spontaneous Assembly, like the Ephesians who gathered in tumult to defend their precious goddess Artemis against St. Paul (and are said to have shouted their rhythmic civic slogan for a whole two hours), the city might well be punished by the governor, as the town clerk contemplated on that occasion (Acts XIX.21-41, esp. 40). This might involve withdrawal of the right to hold Assemblies (see Dio Chrys. XLVIII), or, in the case of a 'free city', the cancellation of that status – a step of which we know several examples,[23] and which Augustus (as we saw earlier) is said by Suetonius (*Aug.* 47) to have taken even in regard to cities which were actually *civitates foederatae*. 'Nothing in the cities escapes the notice of the provincial governors,' remarked Dio of Prusa at the end of one of his speeches (XLVI.14), delivered perhaps in the 70s, before the Assembly of his home city, when a band of his fellow-citizens had threatened to burn down his house and stone him, in the belief that he was partly to blame for a grain shortage (cf. below). It is interesting, by the way, to notice the threatened resort to 'lynch law', which indeed we find at intervals throughout the period of Roman rule in the Greek world, even in the Later Empire, when there are some striking examples of murderous riots, usually occurring as a result of famines, although in the fourth century onwards it is often Christian fanaticism which is responsible.[24] (I shall return presently to the subject of riots.)

By the age of Dio Chrysostom and Plutarch the Greek popular Assemblies, the very nerve-centre of Classical Greek democracy, were already in full decay, although some of them still met and might even occasionally discuss important matters, as is evident from the works of Dio and Plutarch themselves. Gradually, however, they died out altogether, as their functions became too trivial to be worth preserving. There is a great deal of scattered evidence of general Assemblies continuing to function in Greek cities well into the third century, but by then it is never possible to detect evidence that they are acting with any independence, let alone deciding policy. One of the latest decrees that have survived at any length, that passed at Athens in *c.* 230 in honour of M. Ulpius Eubiotus Leurus (and first published in 1941), records the making of a manual vote for and against the resolution; but the issue was entirely non-contentious, for the vote was unanimous – and no wonder, for Eubiotus, a man of consular rank, had given the city 250,000 drachmae (= HS 1 million) and much free wheat during a famine.[25] I know of no recent general discussion of the evidence for the functioning of Greek Assemblies in the Roman period, a subject well worth studying in detail.

Curiously enough, we happen to know from an edict of Constantine that in Roman Africa the elections of city magistrates were still being ratified by popular vote – no doubt a pure formality – as late as the 320s (*CTh* XII.v.1). Far more characteristic of the whole Graeco-Roman world by the late third century is the situation we see depicted in an imperial letter (in Latin, and probably of the time of Diocletian, A.D. 284 ff.) regarding the raising of Tymandus in Pisidia (southern Asia Minor) from the rank of village to that of city (*FIRA*[2] I.454-5, no. 92 = *MAMA* IV.236 = *ILS* 6090). Great emphasis is placed on an assurance given by the inhabitants that they will be able to provide a sufficient supply of decurions (town councillors), and reference is made to the fact that they will now have 'the right of meeting in council (*coeund[i i]n curiam*) and of passing decrees' etc., and will have to create magistrates, aediles and quaestors – there is no hint anywhere of a general Assembly. Well over a century earlier, in A.D. 158, a recently discovered letter of the Emperor Antoninus Pius to a city (perhaps Parthicopolis) in the Strymon valley in the province of Macedonia, at the site of the modern Sandanski in Bulgaria, had authorised a Council of 80 members, emphasising the dignity or repute (*axiōma*) which the citizens would derive from the size of such a Council – which, incidentally, seems to have been below rather than above average size (*IG Bulg.* IV.2263).[26]

With one possible exception, from Pisidian Antioch (noticed in Appendix IV below, near the end of § 3*B*), the last meeting I have been able to discover of the public Assembly of a Greek city of which we have any detailed record took place within a few years either side of A.D. 300 at Oxyrhynchus in Egypt – an area where, of course, proper city life never developed in the way it did in most of the Greek world. We happen to possess part of the shorthand record of this meeting, which graphically conveys the utter futility of the political life of the cities under the Later Roman Empire. The people, for some reason which is not apparent, are bent on passing a decree that very day in honour of Dioscorus, their *prytanis* (the Chairman of the Town Council, we might call him), during a visit from the provincial governor and the principal financial officer of the province, the Katholikos. This is the record (which I have abbreviated slightly), consisting of little more than acclamations (*P. Oxy.* I.41 = Hunt and Edgar, *SP* II.144-7, no. 239):

> Bravo Prytanis, bravo the city's boast, bravo Dioscorus, chief of the citizens! under you our blessings still increase, source of our blessings! . . . Good luck to the patriot! good luck to the lover of equity! source of our blessings, founder of the city! . . . Let the Prytanis receive the vote, let him receive the vote on this great day. Many votes does he deserve, for many are the blessings we enjoy through you, Prytanis! This petition we make to the Katholikos about the Prytanis, with good wishes to the Katholikos, for the city's founder (the Lords Augusti for ever!), this petition to the Katholikos about the Prytanis, for the honest man's magistrate, the equitable magistrate, the city's magistrate, the city's patron, the city's lover of justice, the city's founder. Good fortune, governor! good fortune, Katholikos! Beneficent governor, beneficent Katholikos! We beseech you, Katholikos, concerning the Prytanis. Let the Prytanis receive the vote; let him receive the vote on this great day!

The Prytanis seems to have been seriously embarrassed and he speaks with deprecation:

> I welcome, and with much gratification, the honour which you do me; but I beg that such demonstrations be reserved for a legitimate occasion when you can make them securely and I can accept them without risk.

But this dignified reply only stimulated the people to further transports of enthusiasm – perhaps it was all part of a time-honoured ritual.

> Many votes does he deserve . . . (Lords Augusti, all-victorious for the Romans; the Roman power for ever!). Good fortune, governor, protector of honest men . . . We ask, Katholikos, for the city's Prytanis, the city's lover of justice, the city's founder . . . and so on, interminably.

I have said nothing here about the Gerousia which appears in many Greek cities, especially during the Roman period, because there is nothing to show that it ever had any political or administrative functions: it enjoyed prestige and influence but was strictly a social organisation; and the same applies to the associations of youths: Epheboi and Neoi.[27]

The most significant result of the destruction of Greek democracy was the complete disappearance of the limited measure of political protection afforded to the lower classes against exploitation by the propertied, which became intensified in the early centuries of the Christian era (as I shall explain in VIII.i below) and was one of the prime causes of the disintegration of a large part of the Roman empire between the fifth and seventh centuries (see VIII.iii and iv below). Modern historians have shown little concern with this aspect of the disappearance of democracy; and when they have noticed the disappearance at all, their interest in it has usually been submerged by attention to the super-session of 'city-state' or 'republican' forms of government (which of course may be either democratic or oligarchic) by the monarchy of the Hellenistic kingdoms or of the Roman Principate. Both these characteristics appear in Finley, *The Ancient Economy*, where attention is focused not on the destruction of demo-cracy (a process that is noticed nowhere in the book) but on 'the replacement of the city-state form of government, with its intense political activity, by a bureaucratic, authoritarian monarchy' (that of the Roman Principate). Finley sees that process as making a 'major contribution' to the developments I have set out in VIII.i below, which are described by him as producing 'a cumulative depression in the status of the lower classes among the free citizens' (*AE* 87; I should perhaps add that the passage is indexed in *AE* 217, with only three others, under 'government, democratic', although it makes no specific reference to democracy).

★ ★ ★ ★ ★ ★

I said earlier that I would return, before the end of this section, to the decay of the popular lawcourts (*dikastēria*) which had been characteristic of Greek demo-cracy in its great days. They evidently died out partly in the Hellenistic age and totally in the Roman period. One drawback of the *dikastēria* of Classical Greek democracy needs to be emphasised: both to make them representative, and to make bribery expensive and therefore more difficult, they needed to be *large*. But they could not be really large without the participation of many citizens outside the propertied class; and to make this possible it was necessary to *pay* the dicasts, or at least some of them. It has recently been claimed that Athens was the only city to give dicastic pay; but this is certainly false, and probably many democracies did provide pay (if only for limited numbers of dicasts), although the only other cities we can name with confidence which did this are Rhodes and Iasus, and only at Rhodes have we any ground for thinking that dicastic pay continued well into the Roman period (see my PPOA, with V.ii above and its n.24 below).[28]

As part of the general decline of democracy during the Hellenistic period, the popular courts, like the Assemblies, evidently came more and more into the hands of the propertied class, although it is rare for us to be able to find any such specific evidence as that which I quoted above from a third-century inscription from Ptolemais in Egypt (*OGIS* 48), confining the choice of dicasts, as of councillors, to a chosen few. In the absence of sufficient evidence (which I believe does not exist) I would assume both that the participation of the poorer citizens in such dicastic courts as continued to exist became increasingly rare, and that in many cities legal cases came to be tried more and more extensively by small boards of magistrates, even where words like *dikastērion* continued to be used, as they did generally.

I agree with Jones that in the sphere of jurisdiction the Romans 'interfered far more systematically than had the kings' (*GCAJ* 121-3, cf. 119). During the Republic and early Principate different rules obtained in different provinces, and moreover the position of an individual city might vary to some extent according to whether or not it was a 'free' or 'free and federate' state (but see above for the precarious nature of these statuses, especially the former). Our best information during the Republican period is from Sicily (ibid. 121-2, and see Appendix IV below, § 1 *ad fin.*). We also know something of the position in Cyrenaica in the early Principate (see Appendix IV, § 5). In both provinces we find the collective body of resident Romans (*conventus civium Romanorum*, of whom I shall have more to say in Appendix IV) providing judges for lawsuits. From the language used by Cicero in letters written while he was governing the province of Cilicia in 51-50 B.C., pluming himself on his generosity in allowing the Greeks to try their own cases, it seems that the cities of that province had no guaranteed constitutional rights of jurisdiction, and that the position was probably the same in the province of Asia (Cic., *Ad Att.* VI.i.15; ii.4).[29] Otherwise, most of our evidence comes from documents giving special privileges, including resort to Roman courts, to Greeks who were prominent pro-Romans, such as Asclepiades of Clazomenae and others in 78 B.C. and Seleucus of Rhosus in 41.[30] I believe that Jones may well be right (at any rate for some areas) in thinking it 'possible that the Romans abolished the jury system, which was already moribund, and substituted for it in the cities an arrangement like their own civil procedure, whereby a judge was appointed to try each case, perhaps by the local magistrates' (*GCAJ* 123). At any rate, I can see no sign of dicastic courts still functioning widely, although they continued for a time at Rhodes and perhaps a few other places (see below).

In the Principate interference with Greek judicial autonomy was intensified, with several 'free cities' losing their privileged status; and we now begin to find specific mention of the transfer of cases to the emperor's court,[31] a practice which became more and more widespread. Sometimes we find the court of the provincial governor mentioned;[32] and sometimes we may suspect that our source is referring to the governor's court rather than that of the city (see perhaps Plut., *Mor.* 805ab). Even if there is a clear reference to a city court,[33] we can hardly ever be sure that the case will be tried by any larger body than a board of magistrates[34] or a panel of judges drawn from the more well-to-do citizens[35] – and this is true, unfortunately, even in examples where the word *dikastērion* is used.[36] In particular, we find many times some such expression as *metapempton dikastērion*, in the sense of a small panel of judges (one or more) sent by one city to try legal cases in another, by special request.[37] I think it is significant when we find Hadrian's well-known law regulating the production of olive oil in Attica decreeing that certain offenders are to be prosecuted in the Athenian *Assembly* (see n.34 again) – the Assembly still existed, but the old Athenian *dikastēria* had presumably disappeared entirely by now (cf. Appendix IV below, § 2). As far as

I know, it is only at Rhodes that there is any real evidence for the survival of something like the old *dikastēria* into the second century of the Principate (and incidentally for pay being given to *dikastai* who served in the courts there: see my PPOA). There is, however, at least one other possible exception, namely Tarsus (see Dio Chrys. XXXIII.37). When Dio Chrysostom (XXXV.15) includes *dikazontes* in his list of the various people who can be expected to attend the judicial sessions at Apamea (Celaenae) in Phrygia, he is certainly not referring to mere local 'jurymen' of that city, for the occasions he is describing were the regular visits of the provincial governor, to preside over a court trying cases from the whole judicial *conventus* of which Apamea was the official centre. Dio's *dikazontes* must be members of the governor's *consilium* (his panel of advisers, *assessores*) and/or those men appointed by the governor to try less important cases who later (from the early third century onwards) became known as *iudices pedanei* and who might have their own *assessores*.[38]

Before the end of the third century the local courts seem to have died out completely, and all jurisdiction was now exercised by the provincial governor or his delegates. (No doubt many governors were glad to allow local magistrates to try minor cases.) This development 'bore hard on the provincials, and in particular on the humbler classes, who had often to travel to the metropolis of the province to obtain justice and could not afford the gratuities expected of litigants by the governor and his officials. Moreover, when as was often the case their grievance was oppression by these very officials, they had little chance of satisfaction if they obtained a hearing' (Jones, *GCAJ* 150). The institution of *defensores civitatum* or *plebis* (in Greek, *ekdikoi* or *syndikoi*) in the fourth century is not likely to have made a great difference (cf. VI.vi below).

I have said nothing here of the *dikastai* who appear, though rarely, in inscriptions (mainly of the Hellenistic period) in roles not normally associated with dicasts: performing administrative functions, acting as witnesses to documents, moving decrees, and even perhaps filling eponymous offices,[39] since I do not think they are in any way relevant to the subject we are examining.

The whole process I have been describing, in which, under Roman rule, the legal and constitutional position (the *Rechtsstellung*) of poorer citizens became steadily worse, with the loss of those democratic elements that still remained, deserves to be considered side by side with the marked deterioration in the *Rechtsstellung* of humbler *Roman* citizens during the first two centuries of the Christian era, which I describe in VIII.i below. Both processes must have facilitated the exploitation of the poor: in the one case Greeks, in the other Romans.

*   *   *   *   *   *

The most important long-term effect of the destruction of Greek democracy, as I have already indicated, was the removal from the poor (who formed the vast majority of the population of the Graeco-Roman world) of all protection against exploitation and oppression by the powerful, and indeed of all effective opportunity of even voicing their grievances by constitutional means. If they lived in the country, as most of them did, they could do little, when things became intolerable, but take to flight or to brigandage – unless of course they could find some great landowner who would give them a measure of protection in return for their becoming virtually his serfs (see IV.ii above). I have quoted in IV.iv above the interesting passage in which Dio Cassius takes it for granted that the most vigorous elements in the empire would tend to live by brigandage (LII.xxvii.3-5). When Fronto thought he was going to become proconsul of a relatively peaceful province, Asia, in *c.* 155, one of the first things he did was to send to Mauretania, on the other side of the empire, for a man he happened to know, Julius Senex, who was particularly skilled at dealing with brigands or bandits, *latrones* (*Ep. ad Ant. Pium* 8.1, ed. M. P. J. van den Hout, p.161). In Italy brigandage was evidently rife in the fourth and fifth centuries: a series of imperial constitutions of the second half of the fourth century attempted to deal with this condition (*CTh* IX.xxx.1-5), and an edict of 409 actually forbade anyone except an ordinary rustic to put his sons out to nurse with shepherds on pain of being treated as an accomplice in brigandage (ibid. xxxi.1). But it would be superfluous to cite more of the plentiful evidence concerning brigandage (or banditry), which has often been discussed in modern times, for instance by MacMullen, *ERO* ch. vi and Appendix B, and Léa Flam-Zuckermann, in an article in *Latomus* (1970).[40] Doubtless most of those called brigands in antiquity were indeed essentially robbers, who had no wish to change the social order and were concerned only with their own personal advantage. Some, however, may well have been much more like what we should call social revolutionaries, with at least the rudiments of an ideology different from that of the ruling class of their day: a good example is the Italian Bulla, in the Severan period (see VIII.iii below). It is salutary to recall that in the series of 'suppression' and 'encirclement' campaigns waged by the Kuomintang against the Chinese Communists from 1927 onwards, the term regularly applied to the Communists by the government was 'bandits'. In VIII.iii below I quote the statement of Ulpian, in *Dig.* I.xviii.13.*pr.*, about the importance to a *latro* of having local assistance, from *receptores*.

The poor townsman, or the peasant who lived near enough to a city, had more effective means of making his protests known: he could riot, or, if his city was large enough to have a hippodrome (circus), an amphitheatre or a substantial theatre, he might be able to organise a demonstration there. I need say nothing here about the very marked quasi-political role played during the Principate and the Later Empire by demonstrations in these places of public entertainment, sometimes in the very presence of the emperor himself, as this subject has been admirably dealt with in the Inaugural Lecture by Alan Cameron as Professor of Latin at King's College London in 1973, entitled *Bread and Circuses: the Roman Emperor and his People*, and also – up to a point – in his book, *Circus Factions: Blues and Greens at Rome and Byzantium* (1976). Such demonstrations could often take place, of course, quite apart from the presence of the emperor or even the provincial governor.[41] Those organised (roughly from the mid-fifth century to the reign of Heraclius) by the circus factions, the 'Blues' and 'Greens' mainly, were often futile affairs, sometimes apparently no more 'political' in intent than an outbreak of 'aggro' at a modern football match, for the factions as such had no specifically political characteristics – although I believe they may have acquired a political significance more often than Cameron would allow: this question, for me, remains open.[41a] Outright abuse of an emperor, in the circus in particular, was not unknown. John the Lydian preserves an exceptionally entertaining example: a lampoon in four elegiac couplets, posted up in the hippodrome at Constantinople in the early years of the sixth century (*c.* 510–15), attacking the Emperor Anastasius at a time when his financial policy was being carried out through Marinus the Syrian, and indeed was probably inspired by Marinus, who was praetorian prefect of the East from 512 to perhaps 515. Anastasius is named; he is addressed as *basileu kosmophthore*, 'World-destroying emperor'; he is accused of 'money-grubbing' (*philochrēmosynē*); Marinus is named only as Scylla to his Charybdis (*De Magistr.* III.46). The most famous example of a major disturbance arising out of the games is the so-called 'Nika Riot' at Constantinople in 532: it began as a demonstration against certain oppressive officials, developed into a revolution against the Emperor Justinian, and ended in a frightful massacre by Belisarius and Mundus and their 'barbarian' troops of vast numbers of the common people, estimated by even the most conservative of the sources – no doubt with the usual exaggeration – at thirty to thirty-five thousand (see e.g. Stein, *HBE* II.449–56).

That, one cannot help remarking, is the sort of price that may have to be paid for the total suppression of proper democratic rights. Occasionally we hear of milder demonstrations, like the one at Alexandria mentioned by Philo, who says he saw an audience rising to its feet and shouting with enthusiasm at the mention of 'the name of freedom' in the *Auge*, a play of Euripides now lost to us (*Quod omn. prob. lib.* 141). That remark of Philo's may make us think of some passages in Dio Chrysostom's insufferably verbose speech to the Alexandrians, which contains a series of animadversions, sometimes hard to interpret, on the public behaviour of the citizens (*Orat.* XXXII, *passim*, esp. 4, 25–32, 33, 35, 41–2, 51–2, 55: for the date, see VIII.iii n.1 below).

One of the last references, during the period covered by this book, to a popular movement inside a major city is made by the historian Evagrius in his *Ecclesiastical History* (completed in 594), concerning the situation at Antioch in 573, in the reign of Justin II, when a Persian army under a commander called in Greek Adaarmanes was invading and plundering Syria. (The work of Evagrius, our only surviving narrative source for the whole of the period it covers, 431–594, is not limited to the history of the Church, which is its major subject.) Antioch had never fully recovered from its sack by the Persians in 540: although rebuilt by Justinian, it had suffered further disasters, including two earthquakes, in 551 and 557, and more than one outbreak of plague. In 573 it seems that only the countryside and suburbs of Antioch were devastated by the Persians, although much of the population had fled. But before the city was abandoned, according to Evagrius (who may have been present at the time), 'the *dēmos* rose, with the aim of starting a revolution' (*epanestē neōterōn pragmatōn arxai thelōn*); and he adds the enigmatic remark that this is 'an event that *often occurs* [*hoia philei gignesthai*], especially in circumstances such as this' (*HE* v.9 *fin.*, p.206.11–13, ed. Bidez/Parmentier; and see Downey, *HAS* 561–2, with 533–59).

It is no wonder that the imperial government was suspicious of any kind of combination or association among the lower orders in the Greek East. The Emperor Trajan refused to permit the formation of a fire-brigade in the city of Nicomedia in Bithynia (which had just suffered from a disastrous fire, and had no organised body to deal with such things), on the express ground that any association in the province was bound to take on a political character and lead to disturbances (Pliny, *Ep.* X. 33–34). Indeed, there seems to have been a marked absence from the Greek East of organised fire-brigades such as there were in the

West. For the same reason, Trajan was also nervous about allowing new *eranoi* (friendly societies, or mutual benefit societies) in Bithynia-Pontus (ibid. 92-3).[42]

One popular form of riot was to lynch a detested official, or burn down the houses of local bigwigs who were held responsible for a famine or some other misfortune. In the late first century the common people of Prusa in Bithynia threatened to burn down the house of Dio Chrysostom, and to stone him, on the ground that he was one of those mainly responsible for a famine. We possess the speech he delivered on that occasion in the Assembly of Prusa, which I have already mentioned above: he claims that he is not to blame for the famine, as his land produced only enough grain for his own needs and was otherwise given over to vine-growing and the pasturing of cattle (*Orat.* XLVI.6,8-13); he also reminds his audience that the Romans are watching them (§ 14). On other occasions the victims of popular indignation[43] may even have been innocent of at any rate the particular offence with which they were being charged – as when Ammianus tells us of a Roman noble of the third quarter of the fourth century, the father of the great orator Symmachus, whose beautiful house across the Tiber was burnt down by the people because of a baseless rumour to the effect that he had said he would rather use his wine for quenching lime-kilns than sell it at the price they expected (XXVII.iii.4). But I do not think we need waste very much sympathy on most of the magnates whose houses were destroyed in this way. The situation at Antioch in Syria, about which, in the late fourth century, we know more than any other city in the Greek East, may throw some light on this matter. I should explain first that the food supply of Antioch seems to have come mainly – as we should expect – from the neighbouring area, the plains of the lower Orontes,[44] and that it was the Council of the city, dominated by substantial landowners, which was always regarded as responsible for the corn supply, a sizeable proportion of which is likely to have come from the estates of the rich proprietors themselves. Their prime concern was evidently selling their corn at the highest possible price, even in time of famine. They were accused by the Emperor Julian of stock-piling it in their granaries during the famine at Antioch of 362-3 (*Misop.* 369d). A little later St. John Chrysostom denounced them for throwing whole sacks of grain into the river rather than let the poor have it cheap; and speaking of one particular landowner who had publicly bewailed the end of a threatened scarcity because of the loss he would sustain through the consequent fall in prices, the Saint spoke with some sympathy of demands to have his tongue cut out and his heart incinerated, and (with an apt reference to Proverbs XI.26) declared roundly that he ought to have been stoned! (*In Ep. I ad Cor., Hom.* XXXIX.7-8, in *MPG* LXI.343-4). These passages should not be written off entirely, although Chrysostom may well be exaggerating, as usual (cf. Petit, *LVMA* 117 n.5).

I need not describe here the famine at Antioch in 362-3, which I have already mentioned in IV.ii above: it did not give rise to outbreaks of violence, but this was entirely due to the personal presence of the Emperor Julian for some seven months and the exceptional measures he took to reduce the famine (see IV.ii and its n.23). It is, however, worth drawing attention to the demonstrations which took place on the emperor's arrival in July 362, both in the hippodrome (Liban., *Orat.* XVIII.195) and in the theatre (Julian, *Misop.* 368c), with rhythmical shouts of 'Plenty of everything: everything dear' (*panta gemei, panta pollou*). I will only add that there is but a brief and vague account of these events in Ammianus, who, although one of the best historians the ancient world produced, was himself a member of the propertied class of Antioch and sympathised strongly with the councillors. Ammianus merely tells us disparagingly that Julian, without good reason and out of zest for popularity, tried to lower prices, 'a thing which sometimes, when not done in a fitting manner, is apt to produce scarcity and famine' (XXII.xiv.1; cf. XIV.vii.2) – Ammianus was evidently what would be regarded today in the capitalist world as an orthodox economist! But he does give us rather more details concerning a somewhat similar situation at Antioch in 354 (XIV.vii.2,5-6).[45] The Caesar Gallus, who was ruling the East, realised that a corn shortage was at hand and advised the councillors of Antioch to fix a lower price – inopportunely, as Ammianus believed (§ 2, *vilitatem intempestivam*). The councillors of course objected, whereupon Gallus ordered the execution of their leading members, some of whom were put to death (Liban., *Orat.* I.96), although the majority were saved by the intervention of Honoratus, the Comes Orientis. The common people begged the Caesar to help them. According to Ammianus, Gallus virtually accused Theophilus, the provincial governor (*consularis*) of Syria, of being responsible for the crisis: he was torn to pieces by the crowd, and the people also burnt down the house of a rich Antiochene, Eubulus – who, as we happen to know from Libanius, only just escaped stoning (*Orat.* I.103). The way the riot is referred to by Julian (*Misop.* 363c, 370c), and the failure of the authorities to take any very severe measures (except against a few humble people),[46] suggest that Theophilus and Eubulus between them had perhaps been conspicuously responsible for allowing the threat of famine to develop. Thus was a rough sort of justice sometimes done in the Later Empire – but at what a cost!

Justice through ordinary channels was virtually out of the question for the poor man by now, unless of course he could obtain the help of some powerful protector, at a price, in the way I have described elsewhere (SVP) and in IV.ii above. Emperors like Julian, and some imperial officials, might be well-intentioned, but if so they were likely to be defeated by the intrigues of the *dynatoi* or *potentes*, the great landlords. Even the autocratic Justinian, in a rescript dealing with a case of oppression by a government official in Egypt, which I have described in IV.ii above, could say apologetically, 'The intrigues of Theodosius proved stronger than our commands' (*P. Cairo Masp.* I.67024.15-17). In a constitution of 536 the same emperor complains that in Cappadocia (central Asia Minor) many small possessions and even the greater part of the imperial estates have been appropriated by the great landowners, 'and no one has protested, or if he has, his mouth has been stopped with gold' (*Nov.J.* XXX.v.1). The best-intentioned emperors could do little to protect the humble. Julian, one of the best of all the emperors in this respect, is said by Ammianus (XVI.v.15) to have deliberately refrained, when he was commanding in Gaul, from giving remissions of *arrears* of taxes, although he reduced the amount of tax for the future, because he well knew that everywhere the poor were invariably obliged to pay their taxes at once and in full, and that remissions of arrears could benefit only the rich. (And see VIII.iv below.)

*　*　*　*　*　*

The Greek term *dēmokratia* became steadily more devalued during the process

I have been describing. It is possible to distinguish two phases in this development: the first began quite early in the Hellenistic period; the second is not
evidenced (as far as I know) until the mid-second century of the Christian era
and may not have evolved much earlier than that. During the third and second
centuries B.C. *dēmokratia* increasingly came to signify no more than an internally
self-governing republic,[47] whether democratic or oligarchic, and it could be
used merely for the very limited degree of autonomy accorded by Rome to
complaisant Greek cities, or to celebrate a restoration of constitutional republican
government. The best early illustration of this that I can find is the bilingual
dedication by the Lycian League to Capitoline Jupiter at Rome, probably of the
160s B.C. (*IGRR* I.61).[48] The Lycians themselves refer in Greek to the restoration of their 'ancestral democracy' (*hē patrios dēmokratia*), equating it in Latin
with their 'ancestors' liberty' (*maiorum leibertas*). By the last century B.C. this
sense of *dēmokratia* seems to have become the standard one. The Romans, of
course, had no word of their own for 'democracy' and never resorted to a
transliteration of the Greek word. When Cicero, for example, is speaking in his
De republica of democracy in the original Greek sense, he usually substitutes for
dēmokratia either *liber populus* or just *populus* (e.g. I.42-9, 53, 55, 69; cf. 66-8,
where Cicero is partly paraphrasing Plato, *Rep.* VIII.562a ff.), and on one
occasion he says that a state in which the people are all-powerful is called a *civitas
popularis* (I.42). The original meaning of *dēmokratia* is still occasionally found in
Greek until well into the Principate,[49] although this is more usually expressed
now by some other word, such as *ochlokratia* ('mob-rule').[50]

I do not know when the Greek word *dēmokratia* was first used for the
constitution of the Roman Republic, but it seems likely that this happened by
the last century B.C., or anyway by the first century of our era, when the
dēmokratia of the Republic could be contrasted with the *monarchia* of the Principate.
This was a perfectly natural usage, given the previous Hellenistic developments:
it was simply an application to Rome of the terminology already in use for
Greek cities. The earliest texts I happen to know in which the Roman Republic is
clearly seen by an author writing in Greek as a *dēmokratia* are of the late first
century: Josephus, *AJ* XIX.162,187, and Plutarch, *Galba* 22.12. Josephus tells
us that the soldiers who made Claudius emperor on the assassination of Caligula
did so because they realised that a *dēmokratia* (which here can only mean a
restoration of the Republic) could never have sufficient control of the great
affairs of state, and anyway would not be favourable to themselves (id. 162).
And Plutarch says that the oaths sworn to Vitellius as emperor in 69 by the army
in Upper Germany were given in breach of oaths sworn but a short time before
'to the Senate' – in fact, to 'the Senate and People of Rome' (22.4), which
Plutarch describes as *dēmokratikoi*. One could certainly translate *dēmokratikoi*
here 'republican', especially since the very giving of those oaths had been an open
repudiation of the existing emperor, Galba, if not of the Principate itself. Greek
writers of the first, second and third centuries commonly refer to the Roman
Republic as a *dēmokratia*, in contrast with the Principate, which is almost always
an outright *monarchia*,[51] under a *basileus* (cf. VI.vi below). Occasionally they
apply to the Republic some other term than *dēmokratia*. For Strabo, in a passage
written early in the reign of Tiberius (before the death of Germanicus in 19), the
Republican constitution was a mixture of monarchy and aristocracy (*politeian . . .*

miktēn ek te monarchias kai aristokratias), characterised in his mind – as were also its leaders – by *aretē*, a word conveying approval not only of its efficiency but also of its moral qualities (VI.iv.2, pp.286,288; cf. Dion. Hal., *De antiq. orator.* 3). Appian, in the second quarter of the second century, often refers to the Roman Republic as a *dēmokratia* (see n.51 again), but in his *praef.* 6 it is an *aristokratia* (cf. VI.vi below). Dio Cassius, for whom *dēmokratia* is the standard term, sometimes describes the late Republican constitution as descending into, or at least disturbed by, *dynasteiai* (a term he seems to use as a milder form of *tyrannis*);[52] and for Herodian, writing in the mid-third century, the Roman Republic as a whole was a *dynasteia*, a word he probably used to mean a close hereditary oligarchy (I.i.4), very much as Thucydides and Aristotle had done (Thuc. III.62.3; Arist., *Pol.* IV.5, 1292^{b}7-10, etc.).

I have spoken of two phases in the devaluation of the term *dēmokratia*. In the first, as we have just seen, it came to be used for almost any type of constitutional, republican government, however oligarchic. The second represents the ultimate degradation of the concept of *dēmokratia*: from at least the Antonine age onwards the term could actually be used of the Roman Principate.[53] In the oration *To Rome* of Aelius Aristeides, from the reign of Antoninus Pius in the mid-second century, the Roman empire as a whole is claimed as the ideal *dēmokratia*, because all the people have willingly resigned their powers of ruling into the hands of the one man best fitted to rule: the emperor![54] And about A.D. 220 Philostratus, writing an imaginary dialogue between the Emperor Vespasian and some Greek philosophers, makes his hero, Apollonius of Tyana, after loftily dismissing constitutions as unimportant (his own life, he says, is in the power of the gods), declare that 'the rule of one man who is always looking after the common good *is* a democracy [*dēmos*]' (*Vita Apollon.* V.35).[55] What Aristeides and Philostratus are really praising, of course, is monarchy. Much the same line of thought is expressed in the extraordinarily interesting speech with a dramatic date of 29 B.C. which Dio Cassius puts into the mouth of Maecenas, addressing Augustus in reply to Agrippa's advocacy of a form of constitution called *dēmokratia* and represented by Agrippa not only as the traditional Greek but also as the Roman Republican form of government.[56] Maecenas is made to claim that 'that freedom of the mob [the *ochlos*] becomes the bitterest servitude of the best, and involves both in a common ruin', while under the regime he advocates (an outright monarchy) everyone will achieve, paradoxically, '*dēmokratia* which is genuine [*tēn dēmokratian tēn alēthē*] and freedom which is secure' (LII.xiv.4-5). And the Emperor Marcus Aurelius (161-80) could apply to his own rule, if not the actual word *dēmokratia*, a whole array of terms which had meant something very real in the great days of Greek democracy but were now largely empty. In *Medit.* I.6 he says he has learnt to endure free speech (*parrhēsia*).[57] In I.14 he applies to his own rule the concept of a constitution preserving equality before the law (a *politeia isonomos*), administered according to equality and with equal liberty of speech (*isotēs* and *isēgoria*). But of course these are merely attributes of a monarchy (*basileia*, the most dignified name for that institution), which, he thinks, honours above all things the freedom of its subjects (*tēn eleutherian tōn archomenōn*, I.14).

★   ★   ★   ★   ★   ★

There is one text I wish to mention, which never seems to be brought into any discussion by historians of the later uses of the word *dēmokratia*, perhaps because it occurs in a work of much greater literary than historical interest: the last surviving chapter of the partly preserved treatise in Greek, *On the sublime* (*Peri hypsous*, or *De sublimitate*), a piece of literary criticism which used to be attributed to 'Longinus' or 'Dionysius' (and often to Cassius Longinus in the mid-third century) but is now generally agreed to be the work of an otherwise unknown author, writing in one of the first three centuries and perhaps most probably in the first, or the first half of the second. The writer states a problem put to him by 'a certain philosopher', who may of course be a creature of his own imagination – a common literary device. The 'philosopher' stresses the world-wide dearth of great literature, and asks whether it is right to accept 'the oft-repeated view [*ekeino to thryloumenon*] that *dēmokratia* is the effective nurse of great achievements [or, 'of great men'], and that literary genius flourished almost exclusively under it and perished with it'. *Dēmokratia* is then virtually equated with freedom (*eleutheria*) and contrasted with the 'slavery' which is represented as universally prevailing (44.1-3). By 'slavery', of course, political subjection is meant; and it is described as 'douleia *dikaia*', an adjective I find puzzling: is it 'legalised, legal, legitimate', or 'deserved, justified', or 'just'? (I think that perhaps 'deserved [or 'just'] political subjection' gives the best sense.) The reply by the author of the treatise is bitterly disappointing: it hardly notices the 'philosopher's' statement and, in a very traditional manner, characteristic of the Stoics among others, attributes the prevailing 'frivolity' (*rhathymia*) to avarice and the pursuit of pleasure, and all the evils accompanying such qualities (44.6-11).

What the 'philosopher' says is of great interest. The general view of literary scholars today is that it is the introduction of the Roman Principate which is represented as the transformation of *dēmokratia* and *eleutheria* into 'slavery'.[57a] Yet the literary scholars, best represented by D. A. Russell (whose edition of *On the sublime* can now be regarded as the standard one),[58] fail to bring out the startling paradox presented by the passage in question. It might be possible to maintain that *Latin* literature of the highest quality flourished best in the Republic and did not long survive its extinction.[59] But although the author of our treatise dedicated it to a man with a Roman name, Postumius Terentianus, and must have been writing at least partly, if not mainly, for educated Romans, he is not interested in the slightest in Latin literature, which, apart from a passing reference to Cicero (12.4), he entirely ignores – as did the vast majority of Greek men of letters, including even Dionysius of Halicarnassus, who lived at Rome from 30/29 B.C. onwards, and who never notices Latin authors except when he has occasion to use them as historical sources. Even Plutarch, an omnivorous reader, did not take up the study of Roman literature until he was well into middle age (Plut., *Demosth*. 2.2). Our author is concerned exclusively with *Greek* literature. And I do not see how it could possibly be maintained that it was the institution of the Principate that had crippled Greek literature, which was surely little affected for the worse by the fall of the Roman Republic. A very much better case could be made for saying that Greek literature, apart from Homer and the early poets, did indeed rise and fall with *dēmokratia* – in the original and proper sense! Certainly the largest number of references in the treatise *On the sublime* to works which evoked the admiration of the author are to those written in the fifth and fourth centuries B.C.; there is little or no enthusiasm for Hellenistic literature.[60] The author reports the opinion I have been discussing (that of the 'philosopher') as 'widely held' – unless, as is possible, *ekeino to thryloumenon* in 44.2 has a pejorative sense: Rhys Roberts's translation, in his edition (of 1899), is 'the trite explanation'. Could the statement about the decay of great literature after Republican times have originated with Romans, thinking primarily about Latin literature in general, or perhaps oratory in particular, and after much repetition by them, could it have gained currency among Greeks? Or did the statement originate among Greeks, who realised that the period of the greatest development of Greek literature was precisely that in which real democracy had flourished? I must say, I should be rather surprised if there were many literary men in the Roman period who had opinions of the latter sort; and I would imagine that the view expressed by Longinus' 'philosopher' originated among Greeks during the Hellenistic period and was tenacious enough to retain a few adherents even under Roman rule. Dionysius of Halicarnassus, one of the leading literary critics of antiquity, opens his work, *On the ancient orators*, by dating the beginning of the end of 'ancient, philosophic rhetoric' (by which he means essentially the Attic style) to the death of Alexander the Great, in 323 B.C. (*De antiq. orat.* 1). It evidently did not occur to him that a more powerful influence might have been exerted by the destruction of the Athenian democracy in the following year!

* * * * * *

Two very puzzling references to *dēmokratiai* (in the plural), for which I have never been able to find a parallel, or an explanation, occur in the works of Hippolytus, Pope (or Antipope) of Rome and martyr: one is in section 27 of that curious work, *On the Antichrist*, which seems to have been written very near the year 200, and the other is in a slightly later work, the *Commentary on Daniel* II.xii.7.[61] (For the Book of Daniel itself, see VII.v and its n.4 below.) Of the image depicted in Dan. II.31 ff. it is the toes (verses 41-2) which are singled out by Hippolytus as symbolising democracies – I cannot understand why, since they play no significant or independent role in Daniel (or in the Apocalypse) and are not given any particular explanation there, unlike the ten horns, interpreted as ten kings, with which they could be equated. (It is interesting, by the way, to find Porphyry, the great pagan scholar and anti-Christian polemicist, giving – as is now universally admitted – a far better interpretation of Daniel's beasts than any of the early Christian Fathers. I need do no more here than refer to G. Bardy, in the *Sources chrétiennes* edition of Hippol., *Comm. in Dan.*, mentioned in n.61, at pp.23-4, 271 note *a*.)

* * * * * *

Real democracy had always been anathema to the upper classes of the Graeco-Roman world. By the time of the Later Empire it had become a vaguely-remembered bogey, now – happily – extinct, but still something that a rich man might shudder at. It was probably in 336[62] that the historian and bishop, Eusebius of Caesarea, delivered his *Triakontaëtērikos* (or *Oratio de laudibus Constantini*), a panegyric announcing for the first time the full theory, including the theology, of the new Christian monarchy of Constantine, on the thirtieth anniversary of that emperor's accession. (I shall have a little more to say about this speech in VI.vi below, and see its n.77.) Eusebius contrasts with Constantine's *monarchia* the *ex isotimias polyarchia*, 'the rule of the Many, founded on equality of privilege'. He may well mean any form of rule other than monarchy, but *isotimia* suggests democracy above all. And he declares that such *polyarchia* is mere 'anarchy and civil strife' (*anarchia kai stasis*).[63] This was very much what Plato had thought about democracy. But in the seven eventful centuries between Plato and Eusebius democracy had perished utterly. Its spirit had been partly broken before the end of the fourth century B.C., and its institutions had then been gradually stamped out by the combined efforts of the Greek propertied classes, the Macedonians and the Romans. In Byzantine writers from at least the early fifth century onwards, the word *dēmokratia* and its verb *dēmokratein* can denote 'mob violence', 'riot', even 'insurrection'.[64] The democracy which revived in the modern world was something new, which owed little directly to Greek *dēmokratia*. But by the very name it bears it pays a silent but well-deserved tribute to its ancient predecessor.[65]

VI

Rome the Suzerain

(i)
'The queen and mistress of the world'

This book is concerned primarily with what I am calling 'the Greek world' (see
I.ii above) and not with Rome. But Rome became the mistress of the whole
Greek world by stages during the last two centuries B.C. (roughly between 197
and 30: see Section iv of this chapter), and my 'Greek world' was therefore ruled
by Rome and part of the Roman empire for more than half the period of thirteen
to fourteen hundred years dealt with in this book. Moreover, the portion of the
Roman empire which preserved its unity and its character as an urban civilisation longest was actually the Greek portion, in the sense of the area within which
Greek was spoken by the upper classes (see I.ii–iii above). It is therefore necessary for me to say something about the Romans and their empire, and its effects
upon the Greek world.

We commonly, and rightly, speak of 'Graeco-Roman' civilisation; and
indeed the Greek contribution to the culture of the Roman empire was very
great, and actually dominant in many parts of the intellectual and artistic field. If
we ignore two or three Roman contributions in the realm of technology we can
say that the Romans of the Latin West showed a conspicuously higher genius
than the Greeks in two spheres only, one practical and the other intellectual.
First, they excelled in *ruling* (both themselves and others) in the interests of their
own propertied class, above all its richest members. Vergil expressed this
perfectly when he made the shade of Anchises (the mythical ancestor of the
Roman race) tell the Romans to leave the practice of metal work and sculpture,
of oratory and of astronomy to others who can manage such arts better (he
means of course the Greeks) and to concentrate on ruling:

> Let it be your work, Roman, to rule the peoples with your sway – these shall be your
> arts: to impose the habit of peace, to spare the conquered and put down the proud
> (*parcere subiectis, et debellare superbos: Aen.* VI.847-53).

The proud, the *superbi*, were simply those who refused to submit to Roman
domination; and beaten down they were, by 'the queen and mistress of the
world' (Frontinus, *De aquis* II.88), whose people was 'the lord of kings, con-
queror and commander of all nations' (Cic., *Pro domo suo ad pontif.* 90). The full
force of the verb 'debellare' emerges nicely from a passage in Tacitus (*Ann.*
II.22.1), where Germanicus sets up a trophy of his victory over some Germans
in A.D. 16, with an inscription recording that the peoples between Rhine and
Elbe had been *debellati* by the army of Tiberius; the preceding chapter (21.3) tells
how Germanicus had given his soldiers instructions to be 'steadfast in slaughter;

no prisoners were to be taken; nothing but the extermination of the race would put an end to the war' (cf. I.51.1-2). Vespasian, whose son Titus sacked Jerusalem in A.D. 70 with the most appalling carnage, is called by Tertullian 'Iudaeorum debellator' (*Apol.* 5.7). Let us never forget that the Roman passion for 'ruling' was anything but disinterested or motiveless: the intensely practical Roman governing class ruled because that was the best means of guaranteeing the high degree of exploitation they needed to maintain. (How far the *acquisition* by the Romans of much of their empire was due to this factor is a different question.) I fully agree with A. H. M. Jones:

> If I may venture a generalisation on the economic effects of the Roman empire I would say that its chief effect was to promote an ever increasing concentration of land in the hands of its governing aristocracy at the expense of the population at large (*RE* 135).

The other sphere (the intellectual one) in which Roman genius displayed itself was the *ius civile*,[1] the 'civil law', a term with a whole range of meanings (depending mainly on the context) which I shall use in a fairly broad sense, to mean the private law regulating relations between Roman citizens. (Only a small minority of even the free population of the 'Greek world', in my sense, was affected by the *ius civile*, of course, until the *Constitutio Antoniniana*, in A.D. 212, extended the Roman citizenship to nearly the whole free population of the empire: see VIII.i below.) I must immediately make it clear that I do not mean at all that the Romans had what we call 'the rule of law': in fact that was conspicuously lacking from large areas of the Roman legal system, including particularly what we should call criminal and constitutional law (together making up 'public law'), the very spheres most people today will mainly be thinking of when they use the expression 'the rule of law'. The opinion I have just expressed about Roman law is so different from the admiring one often heard that I may be excused if I repeat and amplify some views I have expressed briefly elsewhere,[2] with some citation of writers on Roman law who will command far greater authority than I can.

In the standard work of H. F. Jolowicz, *Historical Introduction to the Study of Roman Law* (now available in a third edition, revised by Barry Nicholas, 1972), the section on *criminal* jurisdiction in the Principate points out that the Roman 'criminal system never passed through a stage of strict law', and that here 'the "rule of law" . . . was never established' (401-4, at 404). As for the *constitutional* sphere, I show in Section vi of this chapter how autocratic was the rule of the emperors, not only in the Later Empire but also (if with more attempt to conceal the reality) in the Principate, from the very beginning. Even the operation in practice of the *civil* law was deeply affected by the new forms of legal process which were introduced in the early Principate and gradually came to supersede the 'formulary system' that had flourished during the last few generations of the Republic. It is difficult even to give these new processes a collective name, but perhaps 'the system of *cognitio*'[3] will serve. Introduced for some purposes (*fideicommissa*, for example) as early as the reign of Augustus, and always of course dominant in the provinces, this procedure had become universal even in Italy and Rome itself by the late third century, in civil as well as criminal cases. It was sometimes referred to by the Romans as 'cognitio *extraordinaria*', even long after it had become standard practice. The *Institutes* of Justinian (published in

533) could refer to the older forms of process which had long been obsolete as 'iudicia ordinaria', in contrast with the 'extraordinaria iudicia' introduced by 'posteritas' (*Inst.J.* III.xii.*pr.*), and in another context could use the expression 'as often as a legal decision is given *extra ordinem*', adding 'as are all legal decisions today'! (*quotiens extra ordinem ius dicitur, qualia sunt hodie omnia iudicia*: IV.xv.8). Mommsen, in his *Römisches Strafrecht* of 1899 (still a standard work), characterises the *cognitio* system as being essentially 'a legalised absence of settled form' and remarks that it entirely eludes scientific exposition (340, cf. 340-1, 346-51). In practice it gave the magistrate trying the case a very large measure of discretion, and its general extension justifies such statements as those of Buckland that 'civil procedure was superseded by administrative action' and that there was an 'assimilation to administrative and police action' (*TBRL*[3] 662-3). It is true, as Buckland insisted, that the civil procedure was 'still judicial' and that 'the magistrate must abide by the law' (loc. cit.); but the magistrate had very wide powers, and as far as criminal procedure is concerned even so doughty a champion of Roman legalism as Fritz Schulz admitted, in two separate passages (*PRL* 173, 247), that the rule 'nullum crimen sine lege, nulla poena sine lege' ('no criminal charge except by a law, no punishment except by a law') was always unknown to Roman law. If I am devoting more attention here to legal procedure and less to legal principle than might be expected, it is because the Roman lawyer, unlike his modern counterpart in most countries, 'thought in terms of remedies rather than of rights, of forms of action rather than of causes of action' (Nicholas, *IRL* 19-20), so that the nature of legal procedure was all-important.

The Roman *ius civile* was above all an elaborate system, worked out in extraordinary detail and often with great intellectual rigour, for regulating the personal and family relationships of Roman citizens, in particular in regard to property rights, a peculiarly sacred subject in the eyes of the Roman governing class. (I have said something in VII.iv below of the obsession of Cicero – not himself a lawyer, of course, although he was the leading advocate of his day – with the inviolable nature of property rights and his belief, shared no doubt by most of his fellows, that their preservation was the main reason for the foundation of states.) The admirable intellectual characteristics of Roman law, however, were confined within a far narrower field than many people realise. Quoting with approval a statement by Bonfante about the great importance of the law of succession within Roman law as a whole, Schulz comments, 'The Roman law of succession is indeed the focus of the Roman "will to law"' (*CRL* 204); and later he repeats this statement, adding that it is

> in particular true of the law of legacies, and whoever wishes to obtain a vivid and impressive picture of classical jurisprudence must needs study this domain of Roman law. However, this achievement of the classical lawyers reveals their limitations as well as their greatness . . . One cannot help wondering whether it was really justifiable to spend so much time and labour on these difficult and tortuous questions, the practical importance of which was so slight (*CRL* 314).

Mentioning various fields in which Roman lawyers showed little or no interest, he goes on to say that they

> refrained from discussing any issues in which public administrative law was involved. On the whole classical jurisprudence remained within the magic circle described by the

Republican lawyers. These were *iuris consulti*, i.e. lawyers who gave *responsa*, legal opinions, and advice when consulted by parties. Their sphere of interest was, therefore, inevitably limited, but questions on legacies were just the matters most frequently brought before them, since their clients mainly, if not exclusively, belonged to the *beati possidentes* [the rich]. In this respect the classical lawyers remained true to the Republican tradition. Absorbed in the spinning of their fine network, they not only neglected other issues which were of much greater importance, but they apparently failed to realise how complicated the law of legacies grew under their hands. The magnificent achievement of classical jurisprudence, here as elsewhere, was dearly purchased (*CRL* 314–15).

Later in the same book Schulz acknowledges that the Roman lawyers 'hardly touched upon those questions which seem vital to us' (*CRL* 545), such as the protection of workers, or of 'the poor lessees of flats or agricultural land'. (I have already referred, in IV.iii above, to the severity of the Roman law of leasing, *locatio conductio*.) But when Schulz says again that 'The lawyers wrote and worked for the class of the *beati possidentes* to which they themselves belonged and their social sense was ill developed' (ibid.), we may be tempted to comment that the 'social sense' of these lawyers was all too well developed: they were thinking, as we ought to expect, in terms of the interests of the class to which they themselves and their clients belonged. Law, indeed, has 'just as little an independent history as religion' (Marx and Engels, *German Ideology* I.iv.11, in *MECW* V.91).

One other feature of Roman law needs to be mentioned here: the discrimination on grounds of social status, based to a high degree upon distinctions of class in my sense, which I describe in VIII.i below. These manifested themselves chiefly, it is true, in the criminal field (where, as I have pointed out, Roman law remained a rather disreputable affair); but they also entered into the administration even of the *ius civile*, in the sense in which I am using that term, for instance by attaching greater weight to the evidence given by members of the upper classes. As I explain in VIII.i below, the inbuilt disposition of Roman law to respect and favour the propertied classes became more explicitly institutionalised during the Principate. Thus, as A. H. M. Jones has said, 'There was one law for the rich and another for the poor',[4] although in the purely civil sphere 'it was not so much the law that was at fault, as the courts' (*LRE* I.517,519). Jones's account of the practical administration of justice in the Later Empire provides by far the best available summary (*LRE* I.470–522).

I will conclude this brief sketch of the Roman legal achievement with a reference back to the statement by Friedrich von Woess which I quoted in III.iv above: the Roman state was a 'Klassenstaat', interested only in the upper classes; for the propertyless it 'couldn't care less' (*PCBRR* 518).

★ ★ ★ ★ ★ ★

According to the Elder Pliny (in many ways one of the most attractive of all Latin writers), 'the one most outstanding of all peoples in the whole world in *virtus* is without doubt the Romans' (*NH* VII.130). It is an isolated remark, followed by some pessimistic reflections on happiness, *felicitas* – with, unfortunately, no explicit expression of opinion on how the Romans compared with other races in that respect. *Virtus* has a whole range of meanings in Latin: sometimes 'virtue' is a legitimate translation; sometimes the word will mean particularly 'courage' or 'manly excellence'. Here I would be prepared to translate 'moral qualities'. Imperial powers – the British until recently, the Americans today – are easily able to fancy themselves morally superior to other peoples.

Romans often pretended that their empire had been acquired almost against their own will, by a series of defensive actions, which could be made to sound positively virtuous when they were represented as undertaken in defence of others, especially Rome's 'allies'. Thus according to Cicero, in whom we can often find the choicest expression of any given kind of Roman hypocrisy, it was in the course of 'defending their allies', *sociis defendendis*, that the Romans became 'masters of all lands' (*De rep.* III.23/35).[5] The speaker in the dialogue, almost certainly Laelius (who often represents Cicero's own views),[6] goes on to express opinions – basically similar to the theory of 'natural slavery' – according to which some peoples can actually benefit from being in a state of complete political subjection to another (cf. VII.ii below, with my ECAPS 18 and its n.52). Anyone innocent enough to be disposed to accept the view of Roman imperialism that I have just mentioned can best enlighten himself by reading Polybius, who was an intimate of some of the leading Romans of his day (roughly the second and third quarters of the second century B.C.) and well understood the Roman will to conquer the known world, even if in his mind it was more clear and definite than we perhaps have reason to believe. (I give the main Polybian passages in a note.)[7]

In fairness to Cicero, we must not fail to notice that on several occasions in his letters and speeches he shows a real awareness of the hatred Rome had aroused among many subject peoples by the oppression and exploitation to which she had exposed them: he speaks of *iniuriae, iniquitas, libidines, cupiditates, acerbitas* on the part of the leading Romans who had governed them (cf. Tac., *Ann.* I.2.2, and the passages cited in n.19 to Section v of this chapter).

But nearly all that I would have wished to say about Roman imperialism in the late Republic (and much more) has been admirably expressed by Brunt in an important recent article (LI), the purpose of which was 'to explore the conceptions of empire prevalent in Cicero's day'. I agree with Brunt that the Romans had managed to persuade themselves that their empire was 'universal and willed by the gods';[8] and I particularly like his statements that 'the peculiar Roman conception of defensive war . . . covered the prevention and elimination of any *potential* menace to Roman power' (LI 179), and that Rome's 'reactions to the possibility of a threat resembled those of a nervous tiger, disturbed when feeding' (LI 177).

*   *   *   *   *   *

I do not wish to give the impression that the Romans were habitually the most cruel and ruthless of all ancient imperial powers. Which nation in antiquity has the best claim to that title I cannot say, as I do not know all the evidence. On the basis of such of the evidence as I do know, however, I can say that I know of only one people which felt able to assert that it actually had a divine command to exterminate whole populations among those it conquered: namely, Israel. Nowadays Christians, as well as Jews, seldom care to dwell upon the merciless ferocity of Yahweh, as revealed not by hostile sources but by the very literature they themselves regard as sacred. Indeed, they contrive as a rule to forget the very existence of this incriminating material.[9] I feel I should mention, therefore, that there is little in pagan literature quite as morally revolting as the stories of the massacres allegedly[10] carried out at Jericho, Ai, and Hazor, and of the Amorites and Amalekites, all not merely countenanced by Yahweh but strictly ordained by him. (See in general Deut. XX.16-17, cf. 10-15. For Jericho, see Josh. VI-VII, esp. VI.17-18, 21, 26; VII.1, 10-12, 15, 24-5; for Ai, VIII, esp. 2, 22-9; for Hazor, XI, esp. 11-14; for the Amorites, X, esp. 11, 12-14, 28-42; for the Amalekites, I Sam. xv, esp. 3, 8, 32-3.) The death penalty might be prescribed, as at Jericho, even for appropriating part of the spoil instead of destroying it: 'He that is taken with the accursed thing,' said Yahweh to Joshua, 'shall be burnt with fire, he and all that he hath' (Josh. VII.15); and when Achan transgressed, he *and his sons and his daughters* (not to mention his cattle and other possessions) were stoned to death and burnt (id. 24-5). When Yahweh, at the request of Joshua, was said to have prolonged a particular day, by making the sun and moon 'stand still', it was for no other purpose than that the people should 'avenge themselves upon their enemies', the Amorites (X.12-14); Yahweh even joined in the slaughter by 'casting down great stones from heaven upon them' (id. 11) – just as Apollo was believed to have saved his temple at Delphi from molestation by the Persians in 480, with thunder and lightning and earthquake (Hdts VIII.35-9). Joshua then reduced one Amorite city after another: he 'left none remaining, but utterly destroyed *all that breathed*, as the Lord God of Israel commanded' (Josh. X.40; cf. Deut. XX.16). And few narratives are more blood-curdling than that of the Prophet Samuel 'hewing Agag [the King of the Amalekites] in pieces before Yahweh in Gilgal' (I Sam. xv.32-3). The Midianites too, we are told, were mercilessly slaughtered: after the men had all been killed, Moses rebuked the Israelites for sparing the women; he only consented to let virgins live (Num. XXXI, esp. 14-18). The Greek and Roman gods could be cruel enough, in the traditions preserved by their worshippers, but at least their devotees did not seek to represent them as prescribing genocide.[11]

The Gibeonites are shown as escaping total destruction by Israel only because they had previously deceived Joshua and the leading Israelites into making a sworn treaty to spare their lives, by pretending they came from afar (Josh. IX, esp. 15, 18, 20, 24, 26). Their fate was to be perpetual servants of the Israelites: their 'hewers of wood and drawers of water' (id. 21, 23, 27) – texts often quoted today as a Scriptural justification of *apartheid*.

The Romans, although refusing (like so many Greek cities) to recognise unions between their own citizens and foreigners as lawful marriages or their issue as Roman citizens, showed nothing like the ferocious hatred of such unions which we find in another revolting Old Testament story, that of Phineas, the grandson of Aaron, in Numbers XXV.1-15: he kills Zimri the Israelite and his Midianitish wife Cozbi, spearing the woman through the belly, and thereby earns the warm approval of Yahweh and the cessation of a plague that had caused 24,000 deaths.[12]

(ii)
'The conflict of the orders'

This is not the place for an outline history of Rome or even of the class struggle there; but (cf. Section i) I cannot avoid discussing some features of Roman history. First, although the Greek world was very little Romanised in speech or culture, it was deeply influenced socially as well as politically by being brought within the Roman empire. I have already explained briefly (in V.iii; and see Appendix IV below) the political changes which came about by degrees after the Roman conquest of the various parts of the Greek world (on the whole continuing, but greatly intensifying, a process which had already begun under the Hellenistic kings), and I must not neglect to give a brief sociological analysis of the Roman community. And secondly, the class struggle in Rome itself presents some very interesting features, which may illuminate the Greek situation by contrast as well as by analogy. From the very beginning of the Roman Republic (the traditional date of which is 509/8 B.C.) we find what is in reality to a large extent a political class struggle, although not technically so (I shall explain this distinction in a moment): this is the so-called 'conflict of the orders', between Patricians and Plebeians. (This is one of the two main interlocked themes with which the historian of early Rome is obliged to concern himself, the other being of course the territorial expansion of the Roman state.) Historians are very far from having reached agreement on the origin and nature of the distinction between the two 'orders', and several very different theories have been put forward; but my own starting-point is a view of the origin of the differentiation between the orders not unlike one skilfully developed in 1969 by Bickerman:[1] the Patriciate arose from the holding of public office, and became in practice the hereditary privilege of those who, by the end of the Regal period that preceded the Republic, had been able to sustain membership of the Senate – increasingly in practice the ruling power in the Republic, although in theory it was only an advisory body and its decisions (*senatus consulta*) were never 'laws' as were those of the supreme Assembly, the *comitia populi Romani*. By the foundation of the Republic the Patricians had succeeded in becoming a closed 'order', a group in the state having a special constitutional position (involving a monopoly of office), one that it had arrogated to itself, not one originally created by any 'law'. This led to the emergence of the *plebs*, the Plebeians, consisting in principle of everyone who was not a Patrician: the 'first plebeian secession' and the creation of tribunes of the plebs (traditionally in 494) and of an Assembly of the collective plebs (the *concilium plebis*), presided over by their tribunes, mark the appearance of the Plebeians as an organised body. During the 'conflict of the orders', from 494 to 287 on the traditional chronology, the Plebeians gradually gained access to virtually all political offices and to the Senate, and in 287 the Lex Hortensia placed *plebiscita*, the decrees of the plebeian Assembly (*concilium plebis*), on an equal footing with the laws (*leges*) passed by the *comitia populi Romani*, the Assembly of the Roman People.

In what follows I can hardly avoid some over-simplification. The sources are notoriously defective and misleading. The modern literature is vast; but as the subject is only marginally relevant to the main theme of this book I shall hardly refer to any modern work except P. A. Brunt, *SCRR* = *Social Conflicts in the Roman Republic* (1971), which is perhaps the best brief introduction to Roman Republican history for the beginner. (The third chapter of that book, pp.42-59, is devoted to 'Plebeians versus Patricians, 509-287'.)

I have already described the 'conflict of the orders' very briefly in what I believe to be the correct technical terms before attempting to bring out its underlying realities. It is only too easy for those who insist on accurate technical definition of the terms 'Patricians' and 'Plebeians' to say blandly that they have nothing to do with property or economic position, or class in my sense (as defined in II.ii above). Technically, this is quite correct: we are dealing here, not with 'classes' but with 'orders', juridically recognised categories of citizens. But of course the Patricians were able to gain access to, and ultimately to mono-polise, political power at Rome *because* they were by and large the *richest* families – in the mainly agrarian society of early Rome, the *largest landowners* above all. (Here some of Bickerman's analogies from mediaeval European communes are useful, although some of the towns he refers to had a high proportion of wealthy merchants among their great men, as Rome never did.) The richer a family was, the more chance it would have, other things being equal, of gaining political influence. Of course not quite *all* the wealthiest families would acquire patrician status, and *some* of the families which did so may not have been among the very richest; but the equation, Patricians = largest landowners, must have been broadly true over all, and when a family did become patrician and thus gained access to the small circle that enjoyed political privilege, it would naturally have every opportunity to consolidate and improve its own position *vis-à-vis* Plebeians. The Patricians, of course, were always few in number: 'after 366 only twenty-one clans [*gentes*] are attested, of which some were tiny, and not more than another score before that date' (Brunt, *SCRR* 47). Some of the Patricians, however, had large numbers of humble plebeian 'clients' (*clientes*): men bound to them by personal ties involving obligations on both sides which it was considered impious to disregard. (I shall return in Section iii of this chapter to the enduring importance in Roman history, from the earliest times to the Later Empire, not so much of this particular institution alone as of the whole system of patronage of which the *clientela* in the strict and technical sense was the origin and the nucleus.) The Roman annalists of the Late Republic assumed that in the 'conflict of the orders' the Patricians received much support from their clients; and I accept this, as do most modern historians (see e.g. Brunt, *SCRR* 49).

The Plebeians were not at all, as on the whole the Patricians were, a homo-geneous group. Their leaders were mainly rich men who could aspire to the highest positions in the state, even the consulship, and were interested mainly in gaining access to office and to the Senate (the *ius honorum*) and thus to political power and the chance of strengthening their own position. The rank-and-file had totally different objectives, which can be broadly summarised under three heads: (1) political, (2) juridical, and (3) economic. In (1) the political field they would normally support the aspirations of their leaders to state office, in the hope (vain, as events were to prove) that plebeian oligarchs would treat the mass of plebeians better than patrician oligarchs would. Their two main objectives in the political field, however, were very different: they wanted recognition of their own Assembly (the *concilium plebis*) as a supreme legislative body equal with the *comitia populi Romani*; and they wanted a strengthening of the powers of their own peculiar officers, above all those of their tribunes, about whom I shall have something to say in the next paragraph. In (2) the juridical field, they wanted the laws (and the rules of procedure, the *legis actiones* etc.), originally unwritten and locked up in the breasts of the patrician magistrates, to be published, as they were in *c.* 450, in the form of the 'Twelve Tables' (but the *legis actiones* only in 304); and they wanted their right of appeal against legal decisions of a magistrate (the *provocatio*) affirmed, in the teeth of patrician opposition – laws on this point, according to the tradition, had to be re-enacted more than once. In (3) the economic field, which for the mass of the Plebeians was probably even more important than the other two, they wanted three things: relief from the very harsh Roman law of debt, involving enslavement of defaulters (cf. III.iv above); distributions of land, either in the form of colonies in conquered territory or *viritim* (by individual distributions); and finally a less oppressive enforcement of the obligation to perform military service, which remained a very serious burden right down to the last years of the Republic, as Brunt in particular has demonstrated in his *Italian Manpower* (esp. 391 ff.; cf. his *SCRR* 11-17, 66-8). Rome was continually at war, and the bulk of her army was Plebeian. (Marx noted that it was 'wars through which the Roman Patricians ruined the Plebeians, by compelling them to serve as soldiers, and which prevented them from reproducing their conditions of labour, and therefore made paupers of them': *Cap.* III.598-9.) The most effective weapon the Plebeians could use, therefore, as they realised from the very start, was the *secessio*, the strike against conscription: the sources refer to no fewer than five occasions when this weapon is said to have been used with effect, three of which (in 494, 449 and 287) are probably genuine.[2]

The tribunes (*tribuni plebis*) were a most extraordinary feature of the Roman constitution, demonstrating the deep conflict of interests inside the body politic. The first tribunes were created, according to the tradition, as a result of the earliest plebeian 'secession' in 494, when it was not so much that the Patricians accepted their existence (as a sort of anti-magistracy) and their inviolability (*sacrosanctitas*, later given legal recognition) as that the Plebeians took a collective oath to lynch anyone who attacked them! At first, one might say, they stood to official state magistrates almost as shop stewards to company directors; but gradually, although they never acquired the insignia and trappings of state magistrates, their position became more and more assimilated to that of 'magistrates of the Roman People' in almost all respects, except of course that they were drawn from Plebeian families only, and that they could not preside in the *comitia populi Romani* but only in the *concilium plebis* (see above). Their powers included the right of vetoing any act of the *comitia* or of a magistrate (*intercessio*); rescuing any Plebeian – later, any citizen – menaced by a magistrate (*ius auxilii ferendi*); and, as part of their right to exercise *coercitio*, the ability to arrest and imprison any magistrate, even the consuls themselves. The tribunes' power of veto extended to obstructing military levies; and on at least two occasions in the middle of the second century they went so far as to arrest and imprison consuls who persisted with a call-up – not only in 138 B.C., represented by Cicero as the first time such a thing had happened (*De leg.* III.20; cf. Livy, *Per.* 55), but also earlier, in 151 (Livy, *Per.* 48). It is worth mentioning that the tribunes' power to summon meetings was not limited to the *concilium plebis*: they also had the right to summon and preside over *contiones*, public meetings not designed (as were the *comitia* and *concilium plebis*) for legislation or official elections, but corresponding rather to the pre-election meetings of British political parties, or (it has been suggested) to the modern 'press conference'.[3] This power of convening *contiones* was vitally important, because according to Roman constitutional law any meeting not presided over by a magistrate (or a tribune) was an illegal assembly. No speeches or debates took place in an official assembly (*comitia* or *concilium plebis*), the business of which was confined to voting. Great importance might therefore attach to *contiones*, at which the people could be informed, for instance, about the nature of legislation about to be proposed by a tribune in the Assembly, and their reactions tested.

I have been trying to show that the conflict which was ended in theory in 287 was conducted, so to speak, on two levels. Formally, it was a struggle between the two 'orders'; but it was *also* in a very real political sense a class struggle, the participants in which were on the one side a fairly solid group consisting of a good proportion of the principal landowners and on the other side a much less unified collection of men with very different interests, but the great majority of whom were seeking to protect themselves against political oppression or economic exploitation or both. The political class struggle, however, was masked – as class struggles so often have been – by the fact that it was formally a struggle between 'orders', and was therefore led on the Plebeian side by men who were qualified to become members of the oligarchy in every respect save the purely technical, legal one, that they were not Patricians but Plebeians. It is legitimate to see the 'conflict of the orders' as involving a series of tacit bargains between the two different Plebeian groups: first, the leaders, who had no important economic grievances or demands and whose aims were purely political (and usually, no doubt, selfish), concerned with the removal of a strictly legal disqualification for offices which they were otherwise well qualified to hold; and secondly the mass of Plebeians, who hardly suffered at all *as Plebeians*, because the legal disqualifications of Plebeians as such were for posts the vast majority of them could not hope to fill in any event. Thus it was in the interest of each of the two main groups within the Plebeians to join with the other: the mass of the Plebeians would help their leaders to achieve office so that they might be more influential as their protectors, and the leaders would obtain the essential help of the masses for their own advancement by holding out the hope that they would ensure the fulfilment of their aspirations for an improvement in their condition. The 'conflict of the orders' was *both* a conflict between 'orders' *and* a class struggle, in which – exceptionally, as far as Roman history is concerned – the lower classes, or at least the upper section of the lower classes,[4] played at times quite a vigorous part.

The historical tradition relating to the period of the 'conflict of the orders' is highly corrupt, and a great many of the elaborate details in the long accounts of Livy (down to 293 B.C.) and Dionysius of Halicarnassus (to 441 B.C.) must be fictitious; even the main features of the events they purport to record are sometimes open to grave suspicion. But there are several narratives which, even if they contain some fiction, are likely to give valuable clues about the nature of the 'conflict of the orders'. One in particular is most illuminating about the heterogeneous character of the plebs: this is Livy VI.39 (esp. §§ 1-2, 8-12), on the 'Licinio-Sextian rogations', revealing how different were the attitudes of Licinius and Sextius, the tribunes, who were mainly intent on gaining access to the consulship (still being denied to all Plebeians as such), and the mass of their followers, who were much more concerned about reforms of an economic character, dealing with land and debt. In fact Licinius and Sextius and their like satisfied their political ambitions and entered the ruling class, whose outlook they soon came to share fully. However, it was then 'harder for the poor to find champions' (Brunt, *SCRR* 58), and their situation had to become acute before such champions were available once more and a fresh series of political conflicts could break out, from 133 B.C. onwards.

It is also salutary to read the accounts in Livy and Dionysius of the murder or judicial murder of a number of prominent political figures, whether Patrician or Plebeian, who were felt by the leading Patricians to be too sympathetic to Plebeian grievances: these accounts reveal that the Roman ruling class was prepared to kill without mercy anyone who seemed likely to prove himself a genuine popular leader and perhaps fulfil the role of a Greek tyrant of the progressive type (cf. V.i above). Such a man could be conveniently accused of aspiring to make himself king, *rex* – in the precise sense of the Greek *tyrannos*. Cicero was fond of mentioning three famous examples of such men who in the early Republic 'desired to seize *regnum* for themselves': Spurius Cassius, Spurius Maelius, and Marcus Manlius Capitolinus, whose traditional dates are 485, 439 and 384, and whose stories have recently been well re-examined by A. W. Lintott.[5] We should remember, in this connection, that Cicero, for example in *Laelius* 40, also denounced Tiberius Gracchus for trying to seize *regnum* for himself and indeed 'for a few months' succeeding; and that the tribune C. Memmius, a *popularis* (see Section v of this chapter), could speak sarcastically in 111 B.C. of the restoration to the plebs of its proper rights as being in the eyes of his opponents a *regni paratio*, a plot to make oneself *rex* (Sall., *BJ* 31.8). Parts of the narratives concerning the three men I have mentioned may well be fictitious, a retrojection from the Late Republic, but I would accept the broad outlines; and in any event the attitude of Livy, Cicero and their like to these men is significant. It is indeed worth paying careful attention to the ruthless attitude of the Roman oligarchs to anyone they believed to be threatening their privileges – a posture which is treated most sympathetically by Livy and the other sources, and often apologised for by modern historians. To come out openly on the side of the unprivileged against the ruling oligarchy was a dangerous thing to do.

(iii)
The developed Republic

The result of the 'conflict of the orders' was to replace the originally patrician oligarchy by a patricio-plebeian oligarchy, differing very little in outlook and behaviour. It is a characteristic feature of exclusive oligarchies that their numbers tend to fall steadily (see the second paragraph of V.i above and its n.6 below), and the Roman Patricians were no exception to this rule. They remained technically an 'order', retaining a few minor constitutional rights as well as great social prestige, but the influential position of their members was now based rather upon the wealth which most of them possessed than upon their status as Patricians, which in itself gave them few political privileges. Even at this stage, however, we can observe a phenomenon which is noticeable throughout Roman history: the governing class, although it grudgingly consented to a gradual broadening of its basis, somehow managed to remain very much the same in character. The patrician oligarchy became patricio-plebeian: by the early second century B.C. the Senate was already predominantly plebeian – and of course it was the Senate (as I indicated in the first paragraph of the preceding section) which was in practice the 'government' of Rome: its members were men who had originally been elected to state office, and they all had life-tenure. The exaggerated respect which men of great distinction always enjoyed at Rome was manifest in the very procedure of the Senate, where debates were dominated by those of consular status (consuls and ex-consuls). The oligarchy thus remained very much an oligarchy, even though a handful of 'new men' did gain admission to its ranks, usually because they either had outstanding oratorical ability, like Cicero, or because they enjoyed the patronage of leading members of the oligarchy.

After the end of the 'conflict of the orders' and the disappearance of most of the specifically patrician privileges, a new concept slowly emerged: that of *nobilitas*, 'nobility'. The *nobiles*, unlike the Patricians, were never strictly an 'order' in the modern sense, a juridical class (that is to say, they never enjoyed any constitutional privileges in virtue of their *nobilitas*); but they were a well-recognised social class, and their combined political influence was so great that in practice they could make it difficult for anyone else to hold the highest office, the consulate. The precise definition of a *nobilis* has been much disputed, and I am not satisfied that even now the problem has been completely resolved: we must take into account the fact that there was no strict 'legal' or 'constitutional' definition and that our surviving literary sources often have a private axe to grind. Most historians now seem to accept the view of Matthias Gelzer, first published in 1912, that in the Late Republic the term *nobiles* included only consular families – descendants of consulars, men who had held the consulship.[1] The exclusiveness of the nobility is expressed (with some exaggeration) in a much-quoted passage by Sallust: they handed on the consulship, he says, from one to the other (*consulatum nobilitas inter se per manus tradebat: BJ* 63.6; cf. *Cat.* 23.6).

Now senators became such in virtue of having been elected to state office – from about 80 B.C. onwards, the office of quaestor. They therefore owed their position indirectly to popular election, even if the Assembly which elected them, the *comitia centuriata*, was dominated by the wealthy (see below and n.9). Once they had become senators, they held their dignity for life, and of course they were often able to advance their sons (provided they did not have too many) to the position they themselves had held; but membership of the Senate was never *legally* hereditary during the Republic, nor did the families of senators yet enjoy any special legal rights. Before the law, in all important respects, all citizens were in theory equal. (There was much less juridical equality in practice.) During the last century of the Republic we find a new social group emerging and becoming very prominent: the equestrians (*equites*, or *equester ordo*). I must not take time to trace the curious evolution of this body, originally the citizen cavalry (for *eques* means literally 'horseman'; hence the common translation, 'knights'), in later times specially associated with state contracts and above all the farming of taxes, and from the time of Gaius Gracchus (B.C. 123-122) onwards given one special constitutional function and one only: that of providing at first all, and later some, of the *iudices* or commissioners of the *quaestiones*, the standing tribunals which judged certain important cases (both criminal and civil, according to our classification) in the Late Republic. The qualification for membership of this class (the equestrians) was a financial one: the possession of property of a certain minimum value – in the last years of the Republic and in the Principate, HS 400,000. (The senators, on the average, were of course even richer than the equestrians, but during the Republic, strangely enough, there seems not to have been in theory a still higher financial qualification for becoming a senator.) Like the senators, the equestrians enjoyed certain *social* privileges: wearing the gold ring, sitting in special seats at the theatre. But, apart from the additional 'weighting' given to their votes in the *comitia centuriata* by their exclusive possession of no fewer than eighteen centuries, their only *political* privilege (an important but strictly limited one) was serving as commissioners on the *quaestiones*. Before the courts of law they, like the senators, were not in theory in a better position than the ordinary citizen. And their families had no privileges at all; nor was equestrian status hereditary, in theory, although of course in practice the property which gave access to the *ordo equester* tended to pass from father to son, and if there was only one son his chances of succeeding to his father's rank would be high.[2]

For some reason I find it hard to understand, a great deal of fuss has been made by some modern scholars about alleged important conflict between senators and equestrians as such. Occasionally the two orders might come into conflict temporarily: above all, the composition of the *quaestiones* was a matter of contention between them *c.* 122-70 B.C. Yet the famous remark attributed to Gaius Gracchus by Cicero (*De leg.* III.20), to the effect that in giving the *quaestiones* to the equestrians he had 'thrown daggers into the forum', is – as Badian has rightly said – 'obviously (if genuine) a rhetorical exaggeration' (*PS* 65). Again, late in 61 B.C. the Senate at first refused to grant the request of the *publicani* (the leading section of the equestrians) for a considerable reduction of the amount they were liable to pay under the contract by which they had secured the right to collect the tithes of the rich province of Asia.[3] But even on that occasion the disagreement was only temporary: to quote Badian again, 'The affair of the Asian contract did not cause a split between the Senate and the *publicani*' (*PS* 112). In reality no long-lasting or deep-seated hostility ever developed between Senate and *equester ordo*. I entirely agree with the opinion of Brunt, in his excellent paper on the Equites in the late Republic, first published in 1965,[4] which opens with the words 'A conspicuous feature of politics in the late Republic is the discord between Senate and Equites' but in the same paragraph decides that 'It might seem that there was more to unite the orders than to divide them. In fact the area of conflict was in my view more restricted than is often supposed. The Equites [in the broad sense] did not constitute an united pressure group with economic interests opposed to those of the Senate; it is only the publicans who can at times be seen in this light. Moreover the disputes that occurred . . . died away precisely in the crucial period, the age of Pompey and Caesar' (ELR 117-18 = *CRR*, ed. R. Seager, 83-4). This, of course, is precisely what we ought to expect, if we take a Marxist view and regard class struggle as the really fundamental kind of antagonism in society, for on this view senators and equestrians cannot be regarded as two different classes, and therefore no class struggle could develop between them. In fact the two groups were very homogeneous: the equestrians, although on the whole less rich than the senators, were essentially those among the very rich Romans who did not aspire (or had not yet aspired) to a career in politics, involving the holding of magistracies. Three good examples of leading members of the *equester ordo* who openly preferred the career open to equestrians, with its virtual certainty of large profits, to the more risky advantages of a political career as senators are T. Pomponius Atticus, the lifelong friend of Cicero; C. Maecenas, the friend of Augustus and patron of literary men; and M. Annaeus Mela, the brother of Seneca and Gallio and father of the poet Lucan.[5] Against the old view of the equestrians as primarily 'business men', it has been demonstrated beyond doubt by Brunt, Nicolet and others that, like senators, they were essentially land-owners, who might make large profits out of finance and moneylending (not 'trade': they hardly ever appear in the role of merchants) but would normally invest those profits in land (see n.4 again). The allegedly rooted opposition between senators and equestrians is a myth developed by historians in modern times on the basis of a few ancient texts which provide far too flimsy a basis. Compared with the fundamental opposition of interest between landowners and financiers (the latter virtually always also landowners) on the one hand, and peasants and artisans (not to mention slaves) on the other, the internal squabbles within the dominant class, whether between senators and equestrians or between other groups, could be no more than superficial disagreements about the division of the spoil of the world.

Senators and equestrians, then, were the two orders, *ordines*. When it is used in a strict and full political sense, the term *ordo*,[6] in the late Republic, commonly denotes only the *ordo senatorius* and the *ordo equester*. We hear of 'uterque ordo', each of the two orders; and when Cicero speaks of the *concordia ordinum*,[7] or harmony of the orders, as his political ideal, he means simply senators and equestrians. In our terminology the *plebs* was an 'order' in the early Republic, as against the Patricians, but the supposed 'ordo plebeius' seems not to have been an expression that was ever used in the Late Republic. (The word 'ordo', however, is sometimes used more loosely and applied, for example, not only to *scribae* and *praecones* but even to freedmen, ploughmen, graziers, or merchants.)

Rome, of course, was never a democracy or anything like it. There were certainly some democratic elements in the Roman constitution, but the oli-garchic elements were in practice much stronger, and the overall character of the constitution was strongly oligarchical. The poorer classes at Rome made fatal mistakes: they failed to follow the example of the poorer citizens in so many of the Greek states and demand an extension and improvement of political rights which might create a more democratic society, at a time when the Roman state was still small enough to make a democracy of *polis*-type (if I may call it that) a practical possibility. Above all, they failed to obtain (probably even to demand) a fundamental change in the very unsatisfactory nature and procedure of the sovereign Assemblies, the *comitia centuriata* and *comitia tributa* (*concilium plebis*).[8] These allowed no debate (see the preceding section of this chapter); they were subject to all kinds of manipulation by the leading men, and they employed a system of group voting, which in the case of the centuriate Assembly (the most important one) was heavily weighted in favour of the wealthy, although ap-parently rather less so after a reform in the second half of the third century B.C.[9] Instead of working towards thoroughgoing constitutional reforms, the Roman lower classes tended to look for, and put all their trust in, leaders whom they believed to be, so to speak, 'on their side' – men who in the Late Republic were called *populares* (*dēmotikoi* in Greek) – and to try to put them in positions of power. One explanation of this failure, I believe, was the existence at Rome, in a whole series of insidious forms, of the institution of patronage and clientship, from which most of the Greek cities (Athens especially) seem to have been largely free, but which played a very important part in Roman social and political life, and which came gradually to pervade the Greek world after it had been brought under Roman rule. I have discussed the subject in outline, right through to the Later Empire, in SVP = 'Suffragium: from vote to patronage', in the *British Journal of Sociology* 5 (1954) 33–48,[10] and I shall have something more to say about it in Section v of this chapter; but it is necessary to explain a few matters here, in order to clarify the role played by patronage in the class struggle.

Patronage in Roman society took many forms. Those not already well acquainted with the subject will find a good summary of them by A. Momigliano in *OCD*[2] 791, *s.v.* 'Patronus' (and see 252, *s.v.* 'Cliens'). From the earliest times until the Later Empire we hear of formal clientship, the *clientela*, a social institution very difficult to describe accurately. It first appears among the so-called 'Laws of the Kings' (*leges regiae*), its foundation being attributed to Romulus by Dionysius of Halicarnassus (*Ant. Rom.* II.9-10); and we find it referred to in two of the surviving laws in the *Twelve Tables* of 451–450 B.C., one section of which provides that a patron who acts fraudulently towards his client is to be 'accursed' (VIII.21: *sacer esto*).[11] Cicero could say that the Plebeians were originally clients of the Patricians (*De rep.* II.16),[12] and doubtless many of them were – if so, this would have been a complicating factor in the 'conflict of the orders', for of course the very existence of the *clientela*, in its complete form, tended to make the *clientes* dependent upon and subservient to their *patroni*. One special form of the *clientela* became, from its very nature, most strictly formulated, and it alone is the subject of frequent attention in the Roman lawbooks: this was the relationship of the freedman to his former master, who became his *patronus* and to whom he owed a whole series of obligations. Other forms of clientship and patronage could be ill-defined, and my own feeling is that the nature of the bond might differ widely in individual cases. It could be very strong: as late as the end of the fourth century of the Christian era we hear from Ammianus that the vastly rich praetorian prefect, Sextus Petronius Probus, 'although he was magnanimous enough never actually to order *a client or slave* of his to do anything illegal, yet if he found that one of them had committed a crime, he defended the man in defiance of justice and without any investigation or regard for what was right and honourable' (XXVII.xi.4).

There is a significant parallel in the field of foreign affairs. Rome acquired by degrees a number of what are often called nowadays 'client states'; and many modern writers have believed that the Romans conceived their relationship to them in terms of their age-old institution of *patrocinium* and *clientela* – although, as Momigliano has said, 'It is a controversial point whether the relations of certain vanquished states with Rome are to be described as clientship' (*OCD*[2] 252); and of course the terms actually used to describe that relationship would normally be 'friends', 'allies', 'treaty-partners' (*amici, socii, foederati*). Sherwin-White has rightly observed that 'To speak of "client states" is to use a metaphor. It is not a term of international law for the Romans. There are in fact no client states', although 'clientship and patronage came to form the background of the Roman attitude towards them' (*RC*² 188).[13] As a matter of fact, when Sherwin-White himself tries to illustrate what he sees as an explicit declaration of the doctrine of the relationship of Rome to her allies as a form of *clientela* (*RC*² 187-8), the word used by the Roman Senate (in 167 B.C.) is not in fact *clientela* but a quite different metaphor: *tutela*, the term used by Roman lawyers for the 'guardianship' of minors and women (Livy XLV.18.2). There is, however, at least one case in which the words *patrocinium* and *clientela* are used (or represented as being used) by a leading Greek state to describe its relationship to Rome. In Livy (whose source is doubtless Polybius), the ambassadors from Rhodes in 190 B.C., after speaking of their country's *amicitia* with Rome, and her having undertaken the preservation of their *libertas* against royal domination, go on to speak of Rome's *patrocinium* over them and of their having been received into the *fides* and *clientela* of the Romans (XXXVII.liv.3, 15-17). I must add that it was by no means only the Roman state as such and some of its subjects that developed relationships to which the metaphor of clientship might be thought appropriate: individual Romans, especially conquering generals, became hereditary *patroni* of cities and even whole countries which they had captured or benefited – for example, traditionally Fabricius Luscinus (from 278 B.C.) of all the Samnites, and certainly M. Claudius Marcellus (from 210 B.C.) of the whole of Sicily.[14]

I believe that the existence in Roman society of forms of patronage and clientship with very deep roots had great political as well as social consequences. Even during the Republic, when political activity by the lower classes was still possible in some degree, many individuals, out of obedience to their patrons or in deference to their known attitude, must have been diverted from participating actively in political class struggle, and even induced to take part on the side of those having interests directly opposed to their own. One of the proverbs in the collection of Publilius Syrus,[14a] a late Republican, declares that 'To accept a favour [*beneficium*] is to sell one's freedom' (61); and another asserts that 'To ask a favour [an *officium*] is a form of servitude' (641)! Under the Principate, as we shall see in the last two sections of this chapter, such political influence as the lower classes had had soon largely disappeared, and the ways in which patronage could be valuable to a great man changed. With the virtual cessation of election from below, and indeed the gradual drying up of all initiative from below, as political authority became concentrated in the hands of the Emperor, the new role of patronage assumed great importance, above all through the dignity and influence it brought to the patron, through his ability to recommend – and often make sure of procuring appointment – to all sorts of posts that could be both honorific and lucrative (see Sections v and vi of this chapter). And the *venale suffragium* (purchased patronage) which the emperors vainly attempted to suppress (see Section v) surely derived part of its tenacity from the fact that it was a natural development from that *suffragium* – that patronage – which a patron would give gratis to his client. I demonstrate in Section v, from a very revealing passage in Tacitus (*Ann.* I.75.1-2), that for the great men of the early Principate the absolutely unfettered exercise of their patronage rights, *for good or ill*, was an essential ingredient in *libertas* itself.

It would be easy to discount the pervasive influence of patronage and clientship if we were to notice only the relatively rare occasions on which it is specifically mentioned as such, with the characters concerned actually referred to as 'patroni' and 'clientes' or the use of the technical terms 'patrocinium' and 'clientela'. There were in fact many situations where a relationship which was in reality that of patron and client in some form would not be so called, for fear of giving offence. In Section v of this chapter I explain that a real gentleman would expect to be called his patron's 'friend' (*amicus*), not his 'client', even if that patron was the emperor himself. We know of innumerable occasions from the late Republic onwards when great men busied themselves in the interests of those in a less substantial position than themselves, above all in writing letters of recommendation on their behalf. Many such letters speak of the man recommended as an 'amicus'; very few say anything that enables us to tell whether he was technically a 'cliens' – and it hardly matters. The very humble Egyptian, Harpocras, for instance, on whose behalf as many as four letters passed between Pliny and Trajan (see my SVP 41 and n.5): was he a formal client of Pliny's? Again, does it matter? What does seem clear is that patronage was capable of extension well beyond the circle of those who were technically clients, and that patronage in this extended sense increased rather than lessened in importance in the Principate and the Later Empire. In IV.ii above (and see its n.42 below) I have briefly described two forms of rural patronage which are visible in the fourth and fifth centuries, one of them in Syria and Egypt and the other in Gaul. Here again we see the institution manifesting itself in new forms. A price always had to be paid for it, but in Syria particularly we see villagers turning the practice to their own advantage and using it as a weapon of class struggle, if an expensive one.

*   *   *   *   *   *

I shall resist the temptation to expatiate at length on one particularly fascinating subject: the manipulation of the Roman state religion by the ruling class in such a way as to procure political advantage. If I may be allowed to quote what I have already written elsewhere (RRW 69):

> The Greek historian, Polybius, writing in the late second century B.C., speaks admiringly of the Roman attitude in religious matters (VI.lvi.7-12). But when he gets down to details he says that what maintains the cohesion of the Roman commonwealth most of all is *deisidaimonia*, the Greek word which is normally used (as by Plutarch, *Mor.* 377f-8a; cf. 164e-71f) as the equivalent of the Latin *superstitio* or our 'superstition', and is employed in general in a derogatory sense. (The way Polybius introduces it here shows that he realised this.) Perhaps we would do best to translate it here as 'fear of the supernatural'. At any rate, Polybius approves the deliberate utilisation of this fear, explicitly in order to control the masses. The Roman upper classes shared Polybius' low opinion of the common people and felt no compunction at all about using religion in the service of politics and government: this was taken for granted as a necessity by many writers, including Cicero, Livy, Seneca, and above all the great authority on Roman religion, Varro, against whom St. Augustine later delivered a devastating polemic.[15]

A religious weapon that could be held in reserve for an extreme emergency was the use of the auspices (*auspicia*), which might be employed to invalidate the election of some magistrate disliked by the oligarchy,[16] or to put an end to popular Assemblies that were about to pass legislation objectionable to the oligarchy (especially of course agrarian reforms), or to annul such legislation retrospectively.[17] It was surely of such powers that C. Memmius was thinking, when in his tribunate in 111 he spoke of all things at Rome, 'divine as well as human', as having been under the control of a few (Sall., *BJ* 31.20: *divina et humana omnia penes paucos erant*). Let us note the value placed upon the auspices by that most articulate of all members of the Roman governing class, Cicero. For him, in speech after speech, the *leges Aelia et Fufia*, which facilitated the use and abuse of the auspices in the interests of the governing class, were 'laws of the greatest sanctity'; they were 'very beneficial to the state', 'bulwarks and walls of tranquillity and security'; they were 'the firmest bastions of the state against the frenzy of the tribunes', which they had 'often hampered and restrained'; and as for their repeal in 58, by a law promoted by Cicero's enemy Clodius, 'is there anyone who does not realise that by this one bill the entire State has been subverted?'.[18] In one of his so-called 'philosophical' works, containing legislation for his ideal state, Cicero is insistent that his magistrates should have the auspices, so that plausible methods may exist of hindering unprofitable assemblies of the people; and he adds, 'For the immortal gods have often restrained, by means of the auspices, the unjust impetuosity of the people'! (*De leg.* III.27). It was through the auspices that the oligarchs may have felt they had the immortal gods most effectively in their pockets.

(iv)

The Roman conquest of the Greek world

At this point I propose to give a very brief account of the way in which nearly the whole of the Greek world was incorporated into the Roman empire. Later in this chapter I shall return to Rome itself and give a short sketch of the developments in Roman society from the Late Republic onwards.

In just under a century and a half after the end of the 'conflict of the orders' Rome acquired a large part of the Mediterranean world. Of the Greek area, Rome took over Sicily first: it became, in Cato's words, 'the granary of the state, the nurse of the *plebs Romana*' (Cic., *II Verr.* ii.5). Over Macedon and Greece itself Rome established control in the early second century, although Macedon was not formally annexed as a province until 146 B.C., and for another century or more most of the cities of mainland Greece were in theory free; Greece was perhaps not organised as a separate province (called Achaia) until 27 B.C., but remained until then what we might call a Roman 'protectorate'. Rome's conquest of Macedon and Old Greece has been described over and over again,[1] and I have nothing new to say about it. Rome's treatment of the Greeks was usually rather less cruel and ruthless than of other peoples she conquered; but in 167 a vast number of Epirots (150,000, according to Livy) were enslaved by L. Aemilius Paullus, in pursuance of official senatorial policy;[2] and in 146 Corinth was pillaged and destroyed by L. Mummius. As I have explained in V.iii above (and Appendix IV, § 2 below), Rome made sure that Greece was kept 'quiet' and friendly to her by ensuring that the cities were controlled by the wealthy class, which now had mainly given up any idea of resistance to Roman rule and in fact seems to have welcomed it for the most part, as an insurance against popular movements from below. The extent of Roman interference in Greece at this time cannot be estimated, as there is so little evidence. In V.iii above I have referred to one single inscription which happens to have survived, from the little

Achaean town of Dyme, as showing what could happen if there were any revolutionary movement from below; the action taken by Rome on that occasion may have been only one of a series of such interventions, or it may have been an isolated case and such action may rarely have been 'necessary'. At any rate, the Roman governor of Macedonia could evidently intervene anywhere in Greece when there was a threat to the Roman-backed order.

The remainder of the Greek world came under Roman rule by stages (which there is no need to specify in detail here), beginning with the rich and important Attalid kingdom in north-west Asia Minor, centred at Pergamum, which was bequeathed to Rome by the will of its last king, Attalus III (who died in 133 B.C.), and was organised as a province in 129, after a major revolt, led by one Aristonicus, about which we are badly informed, but which seems to have developed (however it may have begun) into a class war by many of the poor and underprivileged, including serfs and slaves, against the Romans and the upper classes of the prosperous Greek cities of the area (see Appendix IV below, § 3 *init*.). There was another anti-Roman outbreak in Asia in 88 B.C., instigated by Mithridates VI of Pontus, when a large number of Romans and Italians in the province were massacred – 80,000 according to two of our sources, 150,000 according to Plutarch, who was probably using Sulla's Memoirs; but even the lower figure must be vastly exaggerated.[3] Rome then gradually absorbed by degrees the remaining western and southern coastal areas of Asia Minor (in which the Greek cities of Asia were concentrated), also Cyrenaica, Crete, Syria and Cyprus, and finally (in 30 B.C.) Egypt, which had been a Hellenistic kingdom ever since its conquest by Alexander the Great in 332. Although the Roman take-over of Asia Minor and the other areas just mentioned did not involve any major war of conquest after 129 B.C., Rome's wars against Mithridates VI (between 88 and 65) and her own civil wars (especially between 49 and 31) resulted in a series of exactions in which the cities were forced to pay over enormous sums, even apart from the regular taxation, and to supply naval and military forces. As Broughton has said, 'The Roman Republic had exploited in peace and pillaged in war the human and material resources of the eastern provinces until all their available reserves were exhausted.'[4] Sheer rapacity as a factor in Rome's expansion has recently been re-emphasised by W. V. Harris and by M. H. Crawford, both reacting against a tendency in modern times to play down this aspect of Roman imperialism.[5]

I shall have nothing to say here of the further conquests made by Rome during the Principate and Later Empire; but of course cities founded by Alexander and his successors which were at least in some respects 'Greek', east of Syria and the upper Euphrates (the eastern frontier of the Roman empire under Augustus) and as far east as the Tigris, came into the Roman empire and went out of it again, according to whether Rome ruled the district in which they were situated, forming at times parts of Roman provinces named Mesopotamia, Armenia, Osrhoene, Assyria.[6]

Since attention has so often been focussed upon the exploitation by the Athenians in the fifth century B.C. of the subject states of their 'empire', it will be useful for us to remind ourselves that the exploitation of the Roman empire was on an entirely different scale of magnitude. (For the latter, I need do no more than refer to the facts given succinctly in Jones, *RE* 114 ff., and Badian,

RILR[2], especially chapter vi.) Whether or not the original tribute of the so-called Delian League (which became the Athenian 'empire') was 460 talents, the figure given by Thucydides (I.96.2), it seems to have been running at less than 400 talents a year in the period immediately before the Peloponnesian war of 431-404 (see the notes on M/L 39, at its pp.87-8), although of course it was greatly increased in 425, almost certainly to a theoretical figure of over 1,400 talents (see M/L 69). Scores of city-states in the Aegean area were involved. Now we happen to know from a letter of Cicero's (*Ad Att.* V.xxi.7), written during his proconsulship of the province of Cicilia with Cyprus in 51-50 B.C., that his predecessors had been in the habit of exacting no less a sum than 200 talents a year (equivalent to HS 4,800,000) from the municipalities of Cyprus alone (not at that time a particularly rich area, and only a minor part of the combined province) as a personal bribe, in return for graciously giving exemption from the liability to billet soldiers. This exaction was of course an additional burden on the Cypriots, over and above the official tribute they had to pay to the Roman state. I do not know how common it was for governors to exact payment from cities in return for exemption from billeting, but there is certainly evidence for the practice in Cyrenaica in the early years of the fifth century, some four hundred and fifty years after Cicero's day: see Synesius, *Ep.* CXXX, ed. R. Hercher, *Epistologr. Graeci*, 1873 (= CXXIX★ in *MPG* LXVI.1512BC).

Provincial governors, then, must sometimes have done very well for themselves and profited greatly, in cash and in kind, out of illegal (or at least unauthorised) exactions, even if no one else equalled the enormous sum which, according to Cicero (*I Verr.* 56), Verres extorted from Sicily during his governorship there in 73-71 B.C., amounting to no less than HS 40 million (or over 1,600 talents). Tax-farmers might also make large profits – although probably as a rule on an altogether lower scale: as Badian has said, 'The exactions of the *publicani* would become bearable under good governors, intolerable only under bad' (*PS* 113). Too many modern writers have failed to distinguish the *illegal* exactions I have referred to from the sums which governors ordinarily expected to make out of the money which passed through their hands *legally* in the course of their ordinary administration. Certainly, they (and their quaestors) had to account, though only at the end of their terms of office, for what they had received and spent; but – at any rate before Julius Caesar's *Lex Julia* of 59 B.C. – accounts could evidently be absurdly brief, for Cicero quotes in one of his speeches against Verres the official record of the accounts handed in by Verres in respect of his quaestorship in 84 B.C., when he was attached to the consul Cn. Papirius Carbo in Picenum:

> I received HS 2,235,417. I spent on army pay, corn, legates, the proquaestor and the praetorian cohort HS 1,635,417. I left at Ariminum HS 600,000. The account rendered to P. Lentulus and L. Triarius, urban quaestors, in accordance with the decree of the Senate (Cic., *II.Verr.* i.36-7).

If I may continue with a quotation from what I have already written elsewhere –

> It is true that this account was handed in during a confused and revolutionary period, and that Cicero inveighs bitterly against the extraordinary impudence of a man who could hand in accounts as brief as this – 'Is this rendering accounts? Did you or I, Hortensius, or anyone else ever submit accounts in this fashion? What have we here?

What impertinence! What audacity! What parallel is there for this among all the accounts that have ever been rendered?' Nevertheless, some thirteen or fourteen years had passed, and Verres' accounts had evidently been accepted (GRA 46).

We need feel no surprise at all, then, when we find that Cicero, who boasts so often of his own rectitude and would have been careful not to do anything actually illegal during his proconsulship of Cilicia, makes it clear in his correspondence that he himself derived from his governorship a personal profit of no less than HS 2,200,000 (his own figure, in *Ad fam.* V.xx.9; *Ad Att.* XI.i.2), or a little over 90 talents. He himself describes this profit, no doubt quite correctly, as made 'legitimately' ('salvis legibus', *Ad fam.* V.xx.9). He had even incurred the resentment of his staff ('ingemuit nostra cohors'), by paying back into the Treasury another HS 1,000,000 which they felt ought to have been divided among them (*Ad Att.* VII.i.6).

★   ★   ★   ★   ★   ★

The Roman state itself, as such, did not profit very much from the taxation of most of its provinces, in the Late Republic and Early Principate (cf. Section v of this chapter), and perhaps only Asia and Sicily produced a really handsome surplus, if military and administrative expenditure is set off against tribute. But here one is reminded of some penetrating statements made by Marx about British rule in India, in one of the series of remarkable papers which he and Engels wrote for the *New York Daily Tribune* between 1851 and 1862, when Marx was London Correspondent of that paper – there were nearly 500 articles in all (McLellan, *KMLT* 285-7). The paper I have in mind was printed as a leading article in the issue of 21 September 1857. (Until it appears in due course in *MECW*, it can be read in *Karl Marx on Colonialism and Modernization*, ed. Shlomo Avineri [New York, 1968, 1969] 235-9.) What Marx says here about the way the British profited from India applies to a less extent to Rome's rule over much of her empire:

> The present state of affairs in Asia suggests the inquiry, What is the real value of their Indian dominion to the British nation and people? Directly, that is in the shape of tribute, or surplus of Indian receipts over Indian expenditures, nothing whatever reaches the British Treasury. On the contrary, the annual outgo is very large . . . The British Government has been at the expense, for years past, of transporting to and from and keeping up in India, in addition to the forces, native and European, of the East India Company, a standing army of 30,000 men. Such being the case, it is evident that the advantage to Great Britain from her Indian Empire must be limited to the profits and benefits which accrue to individual British subjects. These profits and benefits, it must be confessed, are very considerable.

Marx goes on to specify the individual beneficiaries and the amounts they received: apart from the stockholders in the East India Company, doctors, retired pensioners, and various ecclesiastical figures (bishops and chaplains), to whom of course there were no corresponding Romans, there were in India numerous British civil servants and military officers, not to mention 'other European residents in India to the number of 6,000 or more, employed in trade or private speculation'. And Marx concludes,

> It is thus evident that individuals gain largely by the English connection with India, and of course their gain goes to increase the sum of the national wealth. But against all this

a very large offset is to be made. The military and naval expenses paid out of the pockets of the people of England on Indian account have been constantly increasing with the extent of the Indian dominion. To this must be added the expense of Burmese, Afghan, Chinese and Persian wars. In fact, the whole cost of the late Russian war may fairly be charged to the Indian account, since the fear and dread of Russia, which led to that war, grew entirely out of jealousy as to her designs on India. Add to this the career of endless conquest and perpetual aggression in which the English are involved by the possession of India, and it may well be doubted whether, on the whole, this dominion does not threaten to cost quite as much as it can ever be expected to come to.

★   ★   ★   ★   ★   ★

Cults of the City of Rome, in the form of the goddess Roma (a Greek invention, of course) or festivals called *Romaia*, were set up in many Greek cities, especially in Asia Minor, for much the same reasons as the numerous cults of Hellenistic kings[7] and of other benefactors (cf. Section vi of this chapter) – sometimes in the hope of future benefits, or from sheer apprehension, sometimes out of genuine gratitude or goodwill. The earliest known of these cults, instituted at Smyrna in 195 (see Tac., *Ann*. IV.56.1), involved not merely a cult statue but an actual temple: it was a clear 'appeal for intervention and protection'.[8] Cults of individual Roman generals and proconsuls began at the same time in Greece itself, with Flamininus[9] (cf. Appendix IV below, § 2), and eventually became very common all over the Greek world: even the infamous Verres had his festival, the Verria, at Syracuse (Cic., *II Verr*. ii.51-2, 114, 154; iv.24, 151).

A few Greek cities lying to the east of the Mediterranean area were either absorbed into the Roman empire when the districts in which they were situated were made into Roman provinces during the Principate, or else they remained outside the empire altogether, or for long periods. Most of those which entered the Roman empire not at all or only for short periods were usually under the suzerainty of the Parthian empire and the Persian (Sassanid) empire which succeeded it in A.D. 224;[10] but some, like Edessa, came under native dynasts.[11] A certain amount of historical evidence is available about a few of these eastern Greek cities, notably Dura Europus on the Euphrates, a Macedonian foundation where the upper class long remained Greek in a real sense, although the language generally spoken there was evidently the native Aramaic and Syriac and the lower classes must have been more Syrian than Greek.[12] But for my purposes there is so little evidence that I shall henceforth mainly ignore those eastern Greek cities which were not permanently absorbed into the Roman empire (see, however, Appendix IV below, § 7).

I can do no more than just mention here one very interesting and fruitful feature of Rome's ultimate policy towards Greek cities (and other states) which she absorbed: her adoption of the principle of 'dual citizenship' (as it is sometimes called), allowing a man to be a citizen both of Rome and of one or more of her subject communities. This process has recently been elucidated, notably by A. N. Sherwin-White (*RC*²).[13] As late as the second quarter of the last century B.C., Cicero's friend and correspondent T. Pomponius Atticus felt unable to accept the citizenship of Athens when it was offered to him, because he believed that this would involve the loss of his Roman citizenship (Nepos, *Vita Attic*. 3.1). A similar view is expressed in two speeches by Cicero, dating respectively from 69 and 56 B.C.: *Pro Caecina* 100, and *Pro Balbo* 28-31; the latter (§ 30) shows that some other Romans had not been as cautious as Atticus. However, by a development of the peculiar Roman notion of *civitas sine suffragio*, associated with the status of the *municeps*, the Romans had already reached the stage at which a member of an Italian *municipium*, at any rate, could be regarded as in all respects a Roman. This is admirably expressed in a famous passage in Cicero's *De legibus* (II.5, written probably in the late 50s or mid-40s), a text and translation of which are conveniently printed in Sherwin-White, *RC*² 154. And before the end of the same century, in the early years of the Principate, we find a similar doctrine applied to the Greeks of Cyrenaica; the idea was soon generalised to include all communities under Roman rule (see n.13 again).

I must not take time to discuss the further consequences of Roman imperialism for the class struggle in the Greek world. As we saw in V.iii above, those local Greek upper classes who remained faithful to Rome could normally rely upon Rome's assistance in maintaining their position *vis-à-vis* the working population, with the result that oppression and exploitation of the lower classes must have increased. Greek democracy was gradually extinguished utterly, the Romans ensuring a continuance of the process which had already begun under Macedonian rule; and of course this made it increasingly difficult, and ultimately impossible, for the humble to offer effective resistance to the powerful save by extra-legal means such as rioting and the lynching of unpopular officials. Rome always exacted tribute, except from the limited circle of Greek *civitates liberae et immunes*, whose status was precarious even if they were *civitates foederatae* (see V.iii above). If a Greek city which came under Roman rule was already exploiting its working population as far as it was safe to do so, the tribute, and of course the additional exactions made by Roman officials and tax-farmers, will have had to come out of the pockets of the propertied class, at least in part; but no doubt the burdens on the peasantry were as a rule simply increased, to cover the tribute and the other Roman burdens.

The effect of Roman rule on the position of those peasants in Asia who were serfs or quasi-serfs (see III.iv above) is not known. We have very little evidence about the condition of the peasants in the Asiatic provinces, and I have no mind to add to the speculations, often over-confident, in which some scholars have indulged; but it is an obvious guess that while some poor peasants fell into debt bondage or even actual slavery, others improved in status, legally at any rate, owing to the fact that Roman law did not recognise serfdom as an institution – although no doubt Roman magistrates, like Macedonians and Greeks, would have been willing to preserve local forms of subjection and dependence.

An interesting sidelight on the arrogance of some Romans towards their Greek subjects (if the story is true, as it is likely to be) is the rebuke Cicero says he received from Verres' successor as governor of Sicily in 70 B.C., L. Caecilius Metellus, for making a speech at all to the Council of Syracuse, and in particular for making it in Greek: this Metellus described as intolerable (*id ferri nullo modo posse*: Cic., *II Verr.* iv.147).

* * * * * *

Throughout the rest of this book, as here, I often speak of the Roman 'empire', using the word (as virtually everyone normally does) in an essentially geographical sense, to mean the Roman and – after the Roman conquest – the

Graeco-Roman *world*: the whole *area of Roman rule*, including Italy and Rome itself. (On the rare occasions on which I refer to the Roman 'Empire', with a capital E, I mean the *period* during which the Graeco-Roman world was ruled by an emperor or emperors: that is to say, the Principate and the Later Empire.) I realise, of course, that 'empire', and particularly 'imperialism', are often used in a very different sense, to refer to situations in which one political entity (whether strictly territorial or not) exercises dominion over others. However, except for the period discussed in this section, during which Republican Rome was conquering the Greek world, I have paid little attention to Roman 'imperialism', in the strict sense of rule by those who were technically 'Romans' (*cives Romani*) over those who were not (*peregrini*, including Greeks). Had I done so it would have complicated the picture unnecessarily. During the Principate the Roman citizenship was gradually diffused in some degree, if very unevenly, over much of the Graeco-Roman world, until in the early third century it was extended to virtually the whole free population (see VIII.i below); but we are not sufficiently informed about most of the details, and it would be impossibly difficult to determine how the class struggle (the main theme of this book) was affected, in particular cases or overall, by the distinction between *civis* and *peregrinus*, especially since some leading Greeks who were Roman citizens rose into positions in the imperial administration and even into the Senate (see III.ii above and its nn.11-13 below), while many others, although members of the propertied class, did not even possess the citizenship. Those who are interested in Roman 'imperialism' in the sense I have just been describing will find little or nothing that is relevant to that subject in the rest of this book.

(v)

From Republic to Principate

I now return to Rome itself. In the last century of the Republic (between 133 and 31 B.C.) there was a series of political convulsions. These began with attempts at reform, partly in the interests of the lower classes, which were fiercely resisted by the great majority of the senatorial oligarchy, and ended in a series of civil wars which finally left Augustus the undisputed master of the Roman world. The system of government he founded, under the pretence, as we put it nowadays, of 'restoring the Republic',[1] is generally known as the 'Principate', a term (derived from the Latin word *princeps*) to which I shall return later, in the next section of this chapter. Perhaps more has been written on the end of the Republic and the foundation of the Principate in recent times than on any other topic in Roman or Greek history; yet problems still remain on a very large number of issues, even some central ones. The whole question is much too large and complicated to be summed up adequately in a few generalisations, and of course this is a matter of Roman rather than Greek history; but parts of the Greek world were drawn into the civil wars of 44-31 B.C., and since the whole Greek area was subject to Rome under the Principate (continued in the Later Empire) I cannot avoid a brief explanation of how that regime arose.

Sir Ronald Syme, who has made so many distinguished contributions to the study of Roman history, gave to his first great book, which described the foundation of the Principate, the title, *The Roman Revolution* – somewhat of a misnomer, one may feel. In the conflicts he describes there, in which (as he puts it, on p.8), 'Italy and the non-political orders in society triumphed over Rome and the Roman aristocracy', his gaze is concentrated entirely upon what the advertisements of the London *Times*, a few years ago, liked to call 'Top People'. It is not that Syme and his pupils are actually hostile to those he himself describes (in his *Colonial Elites*, p.27) as 'the slaves and serfs and the voiceless earth-coloured rustics', conveniently forgotten altogether by most of those who pass judgment on the past: it is rather that for this school what *matters* in Roman history is the activities of the leading men alone. One of Syme's outstanding pupils, Ernst Badian, has gone so far as to assert that the study of the Roman Republic *is* 'chiefly the study of its ruling class' (*RILR*[2] 92, the last sentence of the book). Another able pupil of Syme's, T. D. Barnes, has recently stated that, especially in a badly documented period like the age of Constantine, 'the reconstruction of the families and careers of individuals is a *necessary preliminary* to *any worthwhile social* or political history' (*JRS* 65 [1975] 49, my italics) – although of course the only individuals about whose 'families and careers' we are likely to know much, and indeed the only ones who can be said to have had 'careers', are those at the top of the social scale; and if the reconstruction of their families and careers is a necessary *preliminary*, then 'worthwhile social history' of the ancient world throughout much of its existence might have to be indefinitely postponed. Prosopography, the study of individuals, has become, in the hands of its practitioners (those I have just mentioned and many others), the study of prominent individuals, their careers, their families, and their alleged political connections; it has reached a very high level of expertise and has made a major contribution to the study of ancient history. In Roman history it can be traced back to F. Münzer, *Römische Adelsparteien und Adelsfamilien* (1920). Parallel investigations in modern English history by Sir Lewis Namier (especially in *The Structure of Politics at the Accession of George III*, the first edition of which appeared in 1929) seem to have had no direct influence on the early development of Roman prosopography.[1a]

Perhaps the treatment of Tiberius Gracchus, tribune in 133 B.C., may serve as an illustration of the approach I am criticising. Tiberius enters the pages of Syme's *The Roman Revolution* twice (12, 60). 'A small party,' we are told, 'zealous for reform – or rather, perhaps, from hostility to Scipio Aemilianus – put up the tribune Ti. Sempronius Gracchus.' And again, 'These prudent men soon refused further support to the rash, self-righteous tribune when he plunged into illegal courses.' But Momigliano, reviewing *The Roman Revolution* in the *Journal of Roman Studies* (1940), has rightly objected that 'very few revolutions are explained by their chiefs. The study of the leaders is necessary, but by itself is not enough'; and Brunt has protested that 'It is a fundamental misunderstanding of the crisis of 133 to explain it primarily in terms of factional feuds'; Gracchus was concerned with social problems: the impoverishment of the citizens, the growth of slave estates, the decline of the peasantry which had always been the backbone of the Roman economy (*SCRR* 77). The motives of the Gracchi and of the other great *populares* of the Late Republic are comparatively unimportant, and they can rarely be reconstructed with any confidence. What makes these men figures of real historical significance is the fact that they provided the essential leadership without which the struggles of the lower classes could hardly have emerged at all at the political level. As Brunt says, 'Their personal motives, which it may be hard to determine, are less significant than the real grievances and genuine discontents on which they could play' (*SCRR* 95).[2] Only once in the Late Republic, as far as I know, do we hear of those in weakness and poverty being warned that they ought not to put their trust in the promises of rich and prosperous men, and that only a man who was poor himself would be a faithful defender of their interests. This, according to Cicero, was said by Catiline ('that nefarious gladiator', as he calls him) in a speech made in 63 at a private gathering in Catiline's own house and later openly avowed by him in a session of the Senate (Cic., *Pro Mur.* 50-1). In a moving letter to Catulus, preserved by Sallust, Catiline asserted that it had been his habitual practice to uphold the interests of the poor in public life (*publicam miserorum causam pro mea consuetudine suscepi: Cat.* 35.3). If this is true, it becomes even easier to understand the extreme detestation with which Catiline was finally regarded by Cicero and his like, and the vilification to which they subjected him.

The *populares* of the Late Republic, who appear so often in the literary sources, were not an organised faction or party or even a compact body of men having substantially the same outlook on major political issues, as on the whole their opponents the *optimates* were, at least at times of crisis.[3] They were simply prominent individual politicians who had what we should call a 'popular following', in the sense of support from the poorer classes (whether urban or rural or both), and who adopted policies that were disliked by the oligarchy, usually because they were in one way or another unfavourable to the wealthier classes. Some of the politicians concerned were clearly motivated by real concern about the menacing social developments in Italy; others may have taken the courses they did mainly because they felt that this was the best way to advance their own careers. There are certain features of the policies of the *populares* which tend to appear again and again: agrarian measures of one kind or another, including above all the distribution of land to the poor or to army veterans, whether in individual lots or in the form of colonies; the supply of corn to poor citizens living at Rome, either free or at a low price (*frumentationes*); the relief of debt; and defence of the democratic elements in the constitution, such as they were, especially the privileges of the tribunes and the right of appeal (*provocatio*). All these policies were anathema to the oligarchs.

The *populares*, then, served, *faute de mieux* and sometimes no doubt against their will, as leaders of what was in a very real sense a political class struggle: a blind, spasmodic, uninformed, often misdirected and always easily confused movement, but a movement with deep roots, proceeding from men whose interests were fundamentally opposed to those of the ruling oligarchy, and who were not concerned (as were sometimes the equestrians, whom I shall mention later) with the mere exclusiveness, corruption and inefficiency of the senatorial government but with its rapacity and its utter indifference to their interests.[4] I submit that the sudden growth of perhaps not very remarkable men such as Saturninus, Sulpicius Rufus, Catiline and Clodius[5] (not to mention the Gracchi) into figures of some historical importance is more easily understandable if we recognise the existence among the poorer classes in the Roman state, especially perhaps the much-abused 'city mob' of Rome itself, of a permanent current of hostility to senatorial misrule and exploitation – hostility which might be repressed for quite long periods by a mixture of sternness and condescending patronage, and which is both minimised and vilified in the oligarchical tradition, but which nevertheless remained a potent force in Roman politics, available to any leader who incorporated in his programme one or more of the few simple policies I outlined at the end of the last paragraph, which would be regarded as the hallmarks of a real *popularis*. But except in so far as they tried to promote the power of the popular Assembly at the expense of the Senate and magistrates[6] (as for example did Tiberius Gracchus, Saturninus and perhaps Glaucia, and even Julius Caesar in his consulship in 59 B.C.), it would be misleading to call the *populares* 'democrats'. As their name implied, they were essentially those who either were, or represented themselves as being or were believed to be, in some respects 'on the side of the common people', against the ruling oligarchy. Cicero defines them as those who wished to please the *multitudo* in what they said and did; he contrasts them with the *optimates*, who behaved in such a way as to win the approval of 'the best men', *optimus quisque*, and act in their interests (*Pro Sest.* 96-7). The Greek equivalent for *populares* was *dēmotikoi*, a word which (unlike *dēmokratikoi*) had no necessarily democratic connotation: it could be used even of a 'tyrant' who was thought to favour the masses in some way, and indeed Appian describes Julius Caesar, a highly autocratic figure, as *dēmotikōtatos* (the superlative form of the word, *BC* I.4), just as Aristotle says that the Athenian tyrant Peisistratus was considered *dēmotikōtatos* (*Ath. pol.* 13.4; 14.1). It is the activities of the *populares* which are important for us, not their lineage or their motives or their ambitions or their moral characters. As I have already indicated, their motives, which have so often been minutely scrutinised, are of very secondary importance. The questions we have to answer are: what historical role did these men play, and what social forces gave them their strength? In point of fact most of them, as we should expect, came from the most prominent families. Catiline was a Patrician, and so was Clodius, until he turned himself into a Plebeian by making a *transitio ad plebem* in 59 B.C., in order to qualify himself as a tribune. All this is understandable. Depressed classes have often been obliged to seek leaders from among the ranks of their rulers, until they have obtained sufficient experience and political capacity to stand on their own feet – a condition to which the Roman masses never attained.

There is plenty of evidence to show that a large number of the common people, both in Rome itself and in Roman Italy, regarded the *populares* as their leaders, supported them, and often revered their memories when they were done to death – as many of them were: in particular Tiberius Gracchus, Gaius Gracchus, Saturninus and Glaucia, Sulpicius Rufus, Marius Gratidianus, Catiline, Clodius and Caesar.[7] Much of the evidence for the relationship between the lower orders and some of the leading *populares* is virtually ignored nowadays: for example, certain statements made by Plutarch about the Gracchi. When Tiberius Gracchus was proposing his agrarian bill in 133, the Roman people chalked up slogans on porches, walls and monuments, calling upon Tiberius to give them back their old possessions (Plut., *Ti.Gr.* 8.10). Gaius Gracchus, during his second tribunate in 122 B.C., left his house on the fashionable Palatine hill and went to live near the Forum, with the conscious aim of arousing the regard of the poor and humble who mostly lived in that area (*C.Gr.* 12.1). He also gave offence to fellow-magistrates by pulling down some private stands around the Forum which they had erected there in anticipation of being able to hire out the seats to spectators at a gladiatorial show the next day; Gaius claimed that the poor should be able to see the show for nothing (*C.Gr.* 12.5-7). After the death of Gaius (in 122) the Roman people demonstrated their respect for the brothers by setting up statues of them, regarding the places where they had been murdered as sacred and bringing first-fruits of everything there; many came to sacrifice and worship at these places, as if they were visiting shrines of gods (*C.Gr.* 18.2-3; cf. *Ti.Gr.* 21.8). Cicero in 70 B.C., in one of his speeches against Verres, invites the judges to consider how he might have excited the feelings of the ignorant multitude by producing 'a son of Gracchus or of Saturninus, or of some man of that sort' (*II Verr.* i.151).[8] Seven years later there was a popular outcry when Cicero, in one of his speeches, gloried in the killing of Saturninus (*Pro Rabir. perd. reo* 18). A form of cult was paid to Marius Gratidianus (praetor in *c.* 85 B.C.), with a statue set up to him in each district (*vicus*) of Rome, at which candles were burnt, and incense and wine were offered.[9] Catiline's tomb was decked with flowers on the condemnation in 59 of C. Antonius (Cic., *Pro Flacc.* 95), the fellow-consul of Cicero in 63, who had been the nominal commander of the army that finally crushed Catiline and his followers. Caesar was highly regarded by the Roman lower classes, who also revered him after his death and – mistakenly – transferred their allegiance to his designated heir and adopted son, Octavian, the future Emperor Augustus.[10]

Again, Clodius and Milo are commonly represented by modern historians as rival gangsters who employed bands of gladiators and desperadoes to intimidate their political adversaries. Clodius may or may not have been a man of more disreputable character than the average politician of his day. But when he was murdered by Milo's ruffians early in 52, the Roman people showed their anger and distress by violent demonstrations, in the course of which they actually burnt down the Senate House.[11] They gave no recorded sign of disapproval when Milo shortly afterwards was forced into exile, nor did they ever make any general demonstration of political enthusiasm, as far as I know, in favour of any Optimate leader.[12] I do not believe that the Roman lower classes deserve the vituperation they have received from Roman (and Greek) writers, especially Cicero, from whom so much of our historical tradition about Late Republican political life derives. If indeed they were to some extent demoralised and depraved, it was largely because the oligarchy had made it impossible for them to be anything else, and perhaps preferred them to be so, as our own ancestors preferred to keep the English labouring classes ignorant and uneducated and without a voice in the government until well on in the nineteenth century. What chance did the humble Roman have of acquiring a sense of political responsibility? The unfortunate thing is that we can virtually never feel we are seeing things as they really were: our sources normally present us with a mere stock caricature. This has descended from (above all) Cicero, through Plutarch, Amyot and North, direct to Shakespeare, through whose eyes we see the Roman populace as a pack of bloodthirsty *sans-culottes*, hooting and clapping their chopped hands and throwing up their sweaty nightcaps and uttering such a deal of stinking breath that we shudder at the very thought of them. Their fickleness, too, is well exemplified in some 130 famous lines of Shakespeare's *Julius Caesar*, in which Antony turns them from thoughtless acquiescence in

Caesar's murder to a frenzy of 'Burn! fire! kill! slay!'. I suspect that acceptance, often perhaps unconscious, of this bitterly contemptuous attitude to the lower orders at Rome lies at the very root of the perversion of Roman history which has dominated most modern accounts. Recently, a different picture has begun to emerge, notably in books and articles by Brunt and Yavetz, and now Helmuth Schneider (see the works cited in n.2). Some influence has been exerted here by Marxist historians of other periods, in particular Hobsbawm and Rudé.[13] But the standard picture is still virtually the one presented by Cicero and his like, for whom the lower classes at Rome are the *sordes urbis et faex*, dirt and filth (Cic., *Ad Att.* I.xvi.11), the *misera ac ieiuna plebecula*, a starving, contemptible rabble (ibid.), the *sentina urbis*, the bilge-water or dregs of the city (*Ad Att.* I.xix.4); they are *to aporon kai rhyparon*, the indigent and unwashed (Dion. Hal., *Ant. Rom.* VIII.71.3).[14] When they show radical tendencies they are habitually described by Cicero as the *improbi*, the wicked, and contrasted with the *boni*, the decent folk – that is to say, the oligarchs and their adherents. Here we are reminded again that the Greek and Roman world (as I explain at the beginning of VII.iv below) was positively obsessed with wealth and status, the latter depending largely on the former. Sallust, who often weakens his picture with facile moralising, sometimes realised the truth, as when he wrote: 'Every man who was most opulent and most capable of inflicting harm passed for a "bonus" *because he defended the existing state of affairs*' ('quisque locupletissimus et iniuria validior, *quia praesentia defendebat*, pro bono ducebatur'): *Hist.*, fr. I.12, ed. B. Maurenbrecher, 1893 – a passage which does not appear either in the Loeb edition of Sallust or in the Teubner text by A. Kurfess (3rd edition, 1957 & repr.).

The complicated political machinery of Rome was such that it would never have been possible for the poorer classes to attain the relatively united front which the oligarchy could easily achieve through the Senate, always dominated (as I have said) by a handful of senior consulars. The citizen population was much less concentrated than in any Greek *polis*, and when a large part of Italy was enfranchised after the 'Social War' of 91-87 the Assemblies (the *comitia* and *concilium plebis*) became even less representative.[15] Nothing like a genuinely representative form of government emerged (cf. Section vi of this chapter, *ad init.*, and its n.2). All major political decisions were taken entirely at Rome, normally in practice by the Senate, which remained immensely powerful, although sometimes the Assemblies, which were still mass-meetings of the Roman People (or of the collective *plebs*), could pass measures contrary to the wishes of the faction dominant in the Senate.

In addition to the vastly greater area inhabited by Roman citizens in the Late Republic, which made attendance at the Assembly virtually impossible for the great majority, except on rare occasions, there was another factor which was responsible for making the whole complexion of politics at Rome entirely different from that of any Greek state of any period: namely, Rome's position as a great imperial power. Enormous wealth, by the standards of those days, came to Rome as the result of her great wars in the third, second and first centuries B.C. The story has often been told and the available figures given.[16] There is more than enough contemporary evidence to convict the Romans – or rather, their propertied classes (magistrates, tax collectors and business men) – of plundering the provinces on a vast scale. Diodorus, a Greek-speaking Sicilian historian of the last century B.C., who at times shows some signs – exceptional in a Greek or Roman writer – of sympathising with the oppressed,[17] remarks that the Phoenicians had a talent for discovering sources of wealth, the Italians 'a genius for leaving nothing for anybody else'! (V.38.3; cf. Sallust's 'letter of Mithridates to Arsaces', quoted in VII.v below). Another *obiter dictum* by Diodorus, critical of the Romans, is in XXXI.27.5: 'among the Romans no one readily and willingly gives any of his property to anyone'. There is much evidence for the inordinate appetite of leading Romans for wealth and luxury. Four letters written by Cicero to his friend Atticus in the first half of 60 B.C. complain bitterly about the selfishness of those very rich men – *piscinarii* (fishponders), as he contemptuously calls them (*Ad Att.* I.xix.6; xx.3) – who are fools enough to think that even when the State is done for they will still have their fishponds (*piscinae*, I.xviii.6; II.ix.1), the 'leading men' (*principes*) who 'think themselves in heaven if they have bearded mullets coming to hand in their fishponds, while they neglect everything else' (II.i.7). These were no mere men of private leisure: most of the known *piscinarii* are mainly 'leading men' indeed. Only P. Vedius Pollio, the friend of Augustus, was a mere equestrian (and a freedman's son): he it was who had the habit of punishing his slaves by throwing them alive into his pool, to be devoured by his lampreys.[18] There are also some striking general statements by Cicero, who will hardly be accused of harbouring either prejudice against the Roman ruling class or radical ideas on the subject of Roman imperialism: I can do no more here than give references to some of them in a note.[19] I will quote only the opinion of Tacitus: that the provinces did not object to the change from Republic to Principate, 'for they distrusted the rule of Senate and People because of the struggles between the men of power and the greed of officials, against whom the laws, crippled by violence, intrigue, and especially by corruption, gave them no help' (*Ann.* I.2.2; cf. Sections i and iv of this chapter). Not only did vast sums in booty and war indemnities and taxation accrue to the Roman state 'legitimately'; the Roman military commanders (who took a considerable share of the booty)[20] made immense private fortunes, and so did many of the provincial governors. It is true that the majority of the provinces – perhaps all except Asia and the three great islands: Sicily, Sardinia and Corsica – must have cost at least as much to 'pacify' and garrison as they yielded *to the State* in tribute; but virtually every provincial governor expected to make at least a small fortune out of even a single year in office. When Cicero made a profit of HS 2,200,000 (a little over 90 Attic talents) out of his governorship of Cilicia and Cyprus in 51-50 B.C., he nevertheless felt – probably with justification – that he had acted with complete propriety (see Section iv of this chapter). The soldiers collectively profited from the distributions made to them out of booty, even if the rank-and-file received only modest sums individually. (Brunt has given a full list for the years 201-167: *IM* 394, Table IX.) And the poor at Rome, the *plebs urbana*, benefited indirectly in various ways, for instance from the public works which the profits of empire made possible, and above all from the regular supply of cheap corn from Sicily, Sardinia and Africa.[21]

The results of Roman imperialism, over all and in the long run, need to be assessed by an analysis in terms of class. This has sometimes been done even by those who are far from being Marxists. For example, my own teacher A. H. M. Jones (who to my knowledge never read Marx or took the slightest interest in

Marxism) gave a perfectly acceptable class analysis in his paper on Rome to the Third International Conference of Economic History at Munich in 1965, recently reprinted in his *Roman Economy*. After referring to the impoverishment of the provinces in the Late Republic ('most clearly demonstrated by the virtual cessation of civic building in this period in the provinces'), he went on to say that it was senators and equestrians in Italy who profited from the empire.

> But they did not use their newly acquired wealth for any economically productive purpose; they spent it either on luxury goods or on the acquisition of land. Their demand for luxuries encouraged a one-way traffic of imports into Italy, which provided employment for provincial craftsmen and profits to merchants both pro-vincial and Italian. Their acquisition of land led to the pauperisation of many of the Italian peasantry. The Italian lower classes lost rather than gained by the empire. Many of them lost their land and were recompensed only by cheap corn if they migrated to Rome, or meagre pay in the army (*RE* 124).

Now the *plebs urbana*, simply because of their permanent presence at Rome, had some political influence as voters in the Assembly, and the senatorial oligarchy had to take account of them, in so far as they could function as a 'pressure group'. If necessary, they could riot. 'Riots at Rome fill a large place in the pages of Cicero, but their effect on the course of events was limited; the government could in the end always repress urban disorder, if it could com-mand a loyal soldiery' (Brunt, ALRR 70). The soldiers and veterans, however, were a very different matter, and potentially a very much more serious source of danger to the oligarchy: in the end they helped to bring down the Republic. Perhaps the single most important factor here was that a large and increasing proportion of discharged veterans had little or no property to support them when they returned to their homes. (I have referred at the end of IV.i above to the part played by conscription in the ruin of part of the Italian peasantry.) Sometimes in a man's absence on military service his parents or children would be driven out by an influential neighbour (Sall., *BJ* 41.8). There is much evidence for the forcible dispossession of the poor by the rich during the Late Republic, which has been set out by Brunt in a valuable Appendix to his *Italian Manpower* (551-7, 'Violence in the Italian countryside').[22]

Great emphasis is often placed on what has been called 'Marius's creation of a client army' (Birley, TCCRE 260 n.3): the enlistment by Marius as consul in 107, for the Jugurthine war, not only of members of the five property-classes who were traditionally liable to regular conscription for the legions, but also of volunteers from among those who had too little property to qualify for the classes. These were the so-called *proletarii* or *capite censi* – 'the poor, who contributed little or nothing to the welfare of the state', as Hugh Last characteristi-cally put it (in *CAH* IX.134). In fact *proletarii* had sometimes been recruited before, although mainly in times of emergency; but Marius' action set a precedent, and 'after Marius recruiting officers ceased to inquire into the property qualifications of citizens, before enrolling them in the legions' (Brunt, *IM* 35, cf. 82). 'Marius himself does not seem to have perceived that he had secured the means to dominate the state as the patron of his troops . . . Only in retrospect could it be discerned that penniless soldiers could become the pliant instruments of an unscrupulous commander. Thus the censure of Marius' conduct [by Sallust in particular] is anachronistic; it implies, however, that Marius set a precedent that later magistrates had followed and that a proletarian army overturned the oligarchic Republic' (ibid. 406-7). 'We may well believe that Marius' main motive was to preserve his following among the people by sparing those who did not wish to serve and attracting the penniless with prospects of rich booty [cf. Sall., *BJ* 84.4]; yet with the steady decline of the peasantry the change he made was surely inevitable sooner or later' (ibid. 407, cf. 410).

Of course the senatorial government, even in its own interest, ought to have provided at least the poorer legionaries with land on discharge; but distributions of land of any kind, whether to ordinary poor citizens or to army veterans, were always detested by the oligarchy.[23] Consequently the loyalty of discharged veterans, and of soldiers who knew they would otherwise be left without means on discharge, was deeply engaged to commanders who could be relied upon, in the teeth of senatorial opposition, to make land grants available to their veterans, by laws promoted in the Assembly by or on behalf of the commanders, as by Caesar in 59. These land grants were sometimes facilitated by large-scale confiscations from political opponents defeated in civil wars, a tactic resorted to above all by Sulla the Optimate and by the triumvirs of 43–42 B.C. (see below). This gave the commanders irresistible strength. 'In refusing to satisfy the needs even of those "miseri" whom they were obliged to arm, the Republican ruling class displayed not only a lack of social sympathy which is conspicuous in their policy as a whole, but also a lack of prudence that was fatal to their power and privileges', . . . [for] 'the wretchedness of the population from whom the army was recruited enabled leaders whose primary concern was their own enrichment or aggradisement to threaten and finally to subvert the Republic' (Brunt, ALRR 84).

It was Augustus who took the essential step towards creating a permanent standing army, above all by setting up in A.D. 6 a special treasury for financing grants to discharged veterans, the *aerarium militare*, fed by two new taxes, the more important of which was much resented by the senators (see below). The army now became decreasingly Italian. As Brunt has well said (*IM* 130), the burden of conscription in Italy that Augustus had reduced 'Tiberius finally lifted; for it was under Tiberius that the levy in Italy fell into disuse, once the programme of foreign expansion had been given up. The *Pax Augusta* really began in A.D. 17. But it was made inevitable by the exhaustion of Italian manpower. The exhaustion was not strictly numerical, but moral. Italy could still have mobilised great armies. But too many Italians had been fighting for too long; *il faut en finir*. In all the literature of the time the words most characteristic of the new spirit of the age were not any of those famous commemorations of Rome's imperial mission and martial glories, but Propertius' "nullus de nostro sanguine miles erit"' – 'You'll get no soldier of my blood' (II.vii.14).

It is worth mentioning that during the period of intermittent civil war after the assassination of Caesar in 44 we often hear of attempts by the common soldiers (and sometimes the junior officers) to bring about a reconciliation between their implacable leaders.[24] The *plebs urbana*, so much despised by many historians, also demonstrated in favour of peace and reconciliation on more than one occasion.[25]

In its primary sense, as the way in which exploitation of the slaves and the lower orders was conducted by the owners of property (cf. II.ii above), the class struggle in the Late Republic proceeded with few of those checks on the activities of the powerful which Greek democracy had so carefully provided. In the political sphere, the Middle Republic (say 287-133 B.C.) saw few bitter conflicts: this was the great age of expansion, and of unparalleled enrichment for the oligarchs and their hangers-on, with the ruling class on the whole remarkably united. The political struggles of the late Republic (133 ff.) which ended in the establishment of the Principate by Augustus became possible only because serious splits began to develop within the ruling class – most but by no means all of which arose out of personal ambition rather than attempts at reform. That a governing oligarchy is unlikely to be overthrown as long as it preserves unity within its own ranks is one of those perceptive observations now regarded almost as truisms, as a result of the writings of Lenin and Mao Tse-tung. But this very observation was made as early as the fourth century B.C. by both Plato and Aristotle. To recapitulate what I have said elsewhere, in relation to Classical Sparta (*OPW* 91) – the Greeks realised the simple fact (stated as such by Plato's Socrates) that changes in a state begin from dissensions among the ruling class, and that the constitution can hardly be upset as long as that class is united, small as it may be (Plato, *Rep.* VIII.545d). Provided the rulers are not at variance among themselves, the rest will not be at odds with each other (V.465b). Aristotle speaks in much the same vein: an oligarchy which preserves harmony inside itself will not easily be overthrown from within (*Pol.* V.6, 1306ª9-10). There were occasional earlier signs of disagreement within the Roman ruling class[26] (cf. Section ii of this chapter), but only with the tribunate of Tiberius Gracchus in 133 B.C. did a serious breach begin to develop (see Cicero, *De rep.* I.31; etc. Cf. Sall., *BJ* 42.1; *Hist.* I, fr.17). There were now some members of the governing class who could see that reforms were necessary, however much the remainder of the oligarchy might resent them. There were also members of the oligarchy who could not resist the opportunities for self-advancement which were thrust into their hands by the growing discontent of the masses, especially the soldiers and veterans whose situation I have described above.

Most modern scholars present a very different picture from the one I am giving here.[27] Badian, for example, in a recent article on the tribunate of Tiberius Gracchus, is very scornful about the atmosphere of class strife which pervades the accounts of Appian and Plutarch: he places 'little trust in their chatter about the opposition between "the rich" and "the poor"' over Tiberius' agrarian law; to him, 'it is no more than a stereotype of *stasis* – a purely literary device of little use to the historian' (TGBRR 707). But this ignores much earlier testimony, indeed that of Cicero himself, who, in one of his most serious and – since it resulted in a unanimous verdict in favour of the man he was defending (*Ad Q. fr.* II.iv.1) – most successful speeches, sees the agrarian law as supported by the *populus*, because it seemed to be strengthening the poor (the *tenuiores*), and opposed by the Optimates, because it would 'arouse discord' and the rich (the *locupletes*) would be deprived of their long-held possessions (*Pro Sest.* 103). There is much other evidence to the same effect in Sallust (writing in the late 40s and early 30s), for the Gracchi and the decades that followed.[28]

The new period in Roman history which opened in 133 is commonly regarded as more violent and bloody than that which preceded it; but the real difference is that Rome itself now experienced at first hand on a few occasions the cruel violence and unnecessary bloodshed which had characterised so many Roman actions in their foreign conquests. In the preceding generation there had been several atrocious deeds by Roman generals, including the methodical massacre or enslavement of tens of thousands of Epirotes in time of peace, carried out by L. Aemilius Paullus in 167 (see Section iv of this chapter and its n.2 below), the vindictive destruction of Carthage in 146, and the treacherous slaughter or enslavement of the Lusitanians by Servius Sulpicius Galba in 150: the first two of these acts can be considered part of official Roman policy; the third was due to the initiative of the general concerned but went unpunished.[29] Men habituated to such excesses abroad were not likely to behave in a strictly constitutional manner at home, once the threat to their dominance (or even their property) became really serious – nor did they. The first bloody episode at Rome was the murder in 133 of Tiberius Gracchus and (according to Plutarch, *Ti.Gr.* 19.10) more than three hundred of his followers. After that things went gradually from bad to worse, until a prolonged series of civil wars on a massive scale ended with the victory of Octavian, the future Augustus, at the battle of Actium in 31 B.C. The Principate of Augustus and his successors (see the next section of this chapter) was one of the most remarkable constitutional constructions ever devised by man, and it was supremely successful in maintaining social stability, in the sense of the dominance of the Roman propertied classes. Without under-taking a description of this extraordinary political edifice (a task far too large for this book), I must try to explain, in this section and the following one, how it achieved such stability, and continued to work so successfully not only under a political genius like Augustus (one of the ablest political figures known to human history) but even under some third-rate emperors, and survived two major outbreaks of civil war, in 68-70 and 193-7, before partly disintegrating in the mid-third century under 'barbarian' attacks and military coups, only to revive again under Diocletian, from 284-5 onwards. The Later Empire, which is usually taken to begin with the accession of Diocletian in 284, was essentially a continuation of the Principate, even if the personal power of the Emperor, which had steadily increased all along, was now more open and undisguised than it had been at the outset (see the next section of this chapter).

In order to obtain the power he craved, Augustus did not hesitate to use as much force as might be necessary: he crushed all opposition without mercy, and he obtained enormous wealth, far greater than that which any other Roman had ever owned. He was, however, by nature and instinct a thorough conservative, who wanted the minimum of change in the Roman world, enough only to secure his own position of dominance and that of his family. Those who were willing to follow him unquestioningly he would accept as his instruments, whether they were blue-blooded aristocrats or *nouveaux riches*. Once he had created a regime that satisfied him there must be no further changes. 'In the civil wars he had fought against the *nobiles*. Victorious, and now a legitimate ruler, he became their friend and patron' (Syme, *RPM* 7). A remark of his is preserved by Macrobius (*Sat.* II.iv.18), which reminds us of the definition of a *bonus* given by Sallust, quoted above. 'Whoever does not want the existing state of affairs to be changed,' said Augustus, 'is a good citizen and good man.' (This statement also resembles Lord Blake's definition of a British Conservative, given in Section vi of this chapter.) Above all, property rights were to be secure, in so far as they represented no threat to him and his dynasty. Restoration of the inviolability of property ownership by Augustus is emphasised, along with the renewal of agriculture, of religion and of general security, by Velleius Paterculus, whose history was finished in A.D. 30, under Tiberius: 'rediit . . . certa cuique rerum suarum possessio' (II.89.4).

During the period between the murder of Caesar in March 44 and the battle of Actium in 31 some other tendencies emerged, besides threats to property, which might have deeply disturbed the senatorial oligarchy. Attention is usually concentrated nowadays, naturally enough, upon the use of military force for their own ends by the leading men, Octavian and Antony in particular. But there were also signs of initiative on the part of the soldiers themselves, which might have seemed ominous to the senators. It was not until A.D. 68, with the proclamation of Galba by the legions under his command in Spain, that – in the famous phrase of Tacitus – the secret of empire (*imperii arcanum*) was divulged, that a Princeps could be created elsewhere than at Rome (*Hist.* I.4). Even earlier than that, of course, the installation of Claudius as emperor in 41 had been the work of the Praetorian Guard. But as early as the autumn of 44 B.C. Octavian had marched on Rome with a private army of Julius Caesar's veterans from Campania, an act he repeated in the summer of 43 with eight legions and auxiliaries of which he was the official commander. Just before the second occasion a deputation consisting of four hundred centurions was sent to the Roman Senate, to demand for the legionaries a promised donative and for Octavian the consulship, which had become vacant through the death of the two consuls of 43. There are indications in our narrative sources, Appian and Dio Cassius, that the appearance of the centurions exasperated the senators, some of whom, we are told, could not endure the soldiers' assumption of free speech (*parrhēsiazesthai*).[30] And we must not forget other signs of initiative on the part of soldiers and junior officers and of the *plebs urbana* between the years 44 and 38 (for which see above and nn.24-5).

It was not only that revolutionary movements from below were now made impossible, and that initiatives by members of the lower classes ceased. In the years 43-42, before Octavian (Augustus) acquired supreme power, there had been several attempts to levy taxes in Italy, which had known no direct taxation (except in emergency) from the end of the Third Macedonian war in 168 B.C. until after the death of Caesar in 44. The levies of tax that we hear of in 43, 42, 39 and 33-32 were less productive than might have been expected, because they were strongly resisted by the rich. Self-assessment was still the rule, as it always had been, and in 43 and 42 we hear of fraudulent under-assessment, punished by complete confiscation when proved; there was general resistance to the introduction of taxes on slaves and on inheritances in 39; and during 32, when freedmen worth more than HS 200,000 were ordered to contribute an eighth of their total property and other men a quarter of the annual produce of their lands, there were disturbances throughout Italy.[31] It was largely because of the stubborn resistance to regular taxation that the triumvirs (Antony, Octavian and Lepidus) resorted at the end of 43 to wholesale proscriptions, resulting in the confiscation of the entire property of some hundreds of very rich men. As Syme has said, 'The proscriptions may not unfairly be regarded as in purpose and essence a peculiar levy upon capital' (*RR* 195; cf. Dio Cass. XLVII.6.5). But the proceeds were disappointing, and the triumvirs proceeded to proclaim a levy on 1,400 of the richest women, a figure soon reduced to 400 after energetic protests by the leading women; this tax was then supplemented by another on everyone, whether a citizen or not, who owned at least HS 400,000 (the *census* of a Roman *eques*): each of these men had to contribute a whole year's income to the expenses of the forthcoming war and lend to the state 2 per cent of his property.[32] All this was exceedingly alarming to the propertied classes of Rome and Italy. Octavian at the end of 36 remitted all unpaid taxes (App., *BC* V.130), and when he achieved supreme power he made it clear that large-scale exactions were at an end. The relief and gratitude of the propertied classes were naturally boundless. Only once did Augustus impose new taxation of any significance: this was in A.D. 6, when he created the *aerarium militare* ('military treasury'), to provide not for ordinary army pay but for the settlement of veterans on discharge. Augustus started it off with a large donation of HS 170 million from his own private fortune (Aug., *RG* 17.2) and the promise of further annual contributions, and he arranged for it to be regularly fed by the proceeds of two new taxes: one on inheritances (at 5 per cent, with exemptions) and the other on sales by public auction. It is interesting to note that the inheritance tax was received with much ill-will: there was agitation in the Senate for its abolition, and seven years later Augustus was driven to let it be thought that he was going to substitute a tax 'on fields and houses', a prospect which thoroughly alarmed the senators and made them abandon their outcry for the ending of the inheritance tax! (The story is well worth reading, in Dio Cass. LV.24.9 to 25.6, and LVI.28.4–6.)[33]

Although it would be technically incorrect, I am tempted to say that Augustus, as it were, took the collective *plebs* (especially at Rome itself) into his personal *clientela* (cf. below), procuring as the outward symbol of this a grant to himself of the tribunician power (cf. Tac., *Ann.* I.2.1; III.56.2) – as a Patrician, he could not actually become a tribune himself. With his unique combination of *auctoritas* and *potestas* (on which see the next section of this chapter), he knew that he had all the power he needed, at least from 19 B.C. onwards; further constitutional powers were unnecessary and would only make it more difficult for the great men to accept his fiction of a 'restored Republic'. But the poorer classes, loyal to him as the heir of the greatest of the *populares*, Julius Caesar, feared above all else a restoration of the oppressive senatorial oligarchy and would have been only too glad to have still greater powers conferred upon Augustus.[34] Their loathing of the old regime is well brought out in the description by Josephus of the murder of Gaius (Caligula) and the installation of Claudius as emperor in A.D. 41. Whereas the senators regarded the emperors as *tyrannoi* and their rule as *douleia* (political subjection, literally 'slavery'), says Josephus (*AJ* XIX.227-8), the people (the *dēmos*) saw in the emperors a restraint on the rapacity (*pleonexia*) of the Senate (cf. § 224) and for themselves a refuge (*kataphygē*; cf. Thuc. VIII.48.6!). Similarly, when in the following year the governor of the province of Dalmatia, L. Arruntius Camillus Scribonianus, raised a revolt, with the declared aim of restoring the Republic[35] and the ancient condition of 'freedom', his soldiers at once deserted him, as they suspected, according to Dio Cassius, that they would again have 'trouble and strife' (LX.xv.2-3).

* * * * * *

How was Augustus able to induce the Roman governing class to accept his rule? Let us be specific and speak of 'the senatorial order', for the equestrians obviously stood to gain more than they lost. How, then, did Augustus reconcile the senators to the Principate? I would say that the Roman aristocracy wanted five things above all: (1) Peace, (2) Prosperity, (3) Position, (4) Patronage, and (5) Power; and that it was only the last of these that Augustus was unwilling to allow the senators to pursue to their hearts' content.

(1) *Peace*, internal peace, after the years of civil war, was of course everyone's desire; but the Roman governing class had a special reason for wanting it. Bitter experience must have forced most of them to realise that in the absence of one supreme ruler, concentrating power in his own hands, a new struggle for mastery was all too likely to develop, almost certainly involving further civil war; and if this occurred the victor might well be another Julius Caesar, or even some much more radical dictator, far less concerned than Augustus to preserve the *status quo*. Tacitus, a senator through and through, reluctantly conceded that after the battle of Actium in 31 B.C. it was in the interests of peace (*pacis interfuit*) that all power (*potentia*, a word with sinister undertones) should be conferred on one man (*Hist.*I.1); he knew that *pax* and *princeps* were inseparable (*Ann.* III.28.3: *iura quis pace et principe uteremur*).

(2) As for *Prosperity*, it hardly needs to be stressed that the Roman governing class longed for it. They wanted to be rich, to indulge whatever tastes they might have for luxury, to enjoy unrestricted opportunities of acquiring new wealth, through provincial governorships and in other ways. Augustus was very ready to gratify these desires, within limits; but he regarded himself, and was generally regarded, as responsible for the empire as a whole, and if he allowed members of the governing class to plunder too freely, as in the past, there might be trouble, which it would fall to him to put down. It was therefore desirable to put some check on the more flagrant forms of extortion and oppression and illegality, even in the provinces.[36] 'I want my sheep shorn, not shaved,' said Tiberius reprovingly to Aemilius Rectus, the equestrian Prefect of Egypt in A.D. 14, who had sent him more than the prescribed amount in taxes (Dio Cass. LVII.x.5). Augustus and many of his successors would have applauded the fascinating passage, reproduced in Section vi of this chapter, from the *Discourses on the First Decade of Livy* (I.55), in which Machiavelli recognises the necessity, in a state containing over-powerful *gentiluomini* of the kind he so detested (bearing a striking resemblance to the Roman landed aristocracy; cf. III.iii above), for a monarch with 'absolute and overwhelming power', to restrain the excesses of 'the powerful'.

(3) The senators also wanted *Position* (a term I use as roughly equivalent to *dignitas*), and hereditary position at that: they wanted to monopolise the magistracies, priesthoods and other dignities which conferred such immense prestige among the Romans, and to hand them on to their sons after them, as in the 'good old days'. (It is difficult for us to realise how highly the Romans valued the mere 'dignitas' attaching to membership of the Senate and to holding the great offices of state, above all of course the consulship, even when these offices no longer

automatically provided a large sphere of liberty of action.) Here the senators did not lose much. The emperors promoted new men to the Senate (who were often sneered at as men of low birth, 'obscuro loco nati'),[37] but only in limited numbers; and the recognised senatorial aristocracy continued at first to mono- polise virtually all the highest offices, even if the choice of candidates for them was to some extent in the emperor's hands – even under Augustus we hear of some cases in which the consulship is said to have been given or offered to a particular man by the emperor;[38] and Pliny the Younger, when he became consul in A.D. 100, could acknowledge in his official speech in the Senate, addressed to that 'optimus princeps', Trajan, that the choice of consuls was now the emperor's.[39]

(4) The senators wanted their rights of *Patronage*, sanctified by the ancient Roman custom of the 'clientela' (see the end of Section iii of this chapter), to continue as of old. These rights too were maintained, although at the highest level they came under increasing imperial control – I shall return to this impor- tant subject very shortly.

(5) The senators also, of course, wanted the *Power* they had always enjoyed. The reality of power, however, was the one thing the emperors could not afford to grant to them, although they might choose to give a carefully controlled share in it to those individuals who had proved their loyalty and their fitness to be imperial advisers and legates in command of provinces and their legions. The army was the emperor's concern, and the great bulk of the armed forces were stationed in provinces governed by his legates, appointed directly by himself (cf. the next section of this chapter).

I now return to the subject of *Patronage*, which deserves much fuller treatment than I can give it at this point. (I have already discussed it at some length in my SVP: see Section iii of this chapter and its nn.10-12.) The *clientela*, as I have explained, was a very ancient and central feature of Roman society, and the exercise of patronage by the great men (by no means limited to their *clientes*) was a major factor in political and social life[40] – and incidentally much more pervasive and effective even in the judicial system than has been generally realised (see my SVP 42-5).[41] Patronage, indeed, must be seen as an institution the Roman world simply could not do without, once the genuinely democratic elements in the constitution (circumscribed as they had always been) were on the point of disappearing altogether. This is seldom sufficiently realised. Under any political system, many appointments to positions involving the exercise of authority must be made somehow. Democratic process allows them to be made *from below*; but if it ceases to exist, everything has to be done *from above*. At Rome election from below became less and less important, even in the last years of the Republic, and early in the Principate it came to occupy only a minor place.[42] When nearly everything was done from above, however, and appointment largely replaced election, patronage of course became all-important. A Roman emperor made most of the top appointments himself, from among men whom he would personally know. He, on the recommendation of his immediate subordinates, or those subordinates themselves, would appoint to the less exalted posts; and so the process went on, right down the line, to the humblest local officials. Everything now depended on favour, recommendation, patronage – on *suffragium*, in the new sense which that word had begun to have by at least the early second century, replacing its original sense of 'vote' (see my SVP). The *clientela* never entirely lost its importance; but as time went on, more and more was done by what the emperors, in attempting unsuccessfully to forbid it, called *venale suffragium*, patronage that was openly bought (see SVP 39–42) – for it was inevitable that the giving of favours by *patroni* to their *clientes* should be supplemented by the purchase of such favours by those outside the useful circle of clients.

It need not surprise us that the Latin word which had originally meant 'vote', namely *suffragium*, had by the beginning of the second century come to bear the more usual meaning of 'patronage' or 'influence' or (in the eighteenth-century sense) 'interest'. There are many fascinating texts which illustrate the working of patronage under the Principate (see SVP 37–9, 40–4), and in the Later Empire it assumed an even more important and more sinister role (cf. SVP 39–40, 44–8). The Greeks accommodated themselves by degrees to this Roman institution, which they could not now afford to do without, and in due course they became thoroughly habituated to it. As Liebeschuetz has demonstrated, a leading Greek orator of the late fourth century like Libanius might have to spend a vast amount of time soliciting favours from or for his friends (*Ant.* 192 ff., esp. 193). Libanius sometimes admitted that the practice could be objectionable, but he simply could not afford, placed as he was, to refuse to do what everyone expected of him, since 'the giving and taking of favours played an essential part in social relationships at Antioch and, indeed, throughout the empire' (*Ant.* 195–7). Even men holding no office conferring any *power*, political or military, might be felt to be persons of the greatest *influence* if they were friends of the really great men, the emperor above all. There is a most revealing picture in Eunapius' *Lives of the Sophists* (written in or after 396) about Maximus of Ephesus, a leading pseudo-philosopher, renowned as a wonder-worker, who was an intimate of the Emperor Julian. When Maximus was summoned to the court at Constantinople by Julian in 362, he became the centre of attention at Ephesus and was courted by everyone, including 'the leading members of the city Councils'; the common people too thronged around his house, jumping up and down and shouting slogans, and even the women came in crowds through the back door to beg favours of his wife. Maximus went to Julian in great pomp, 'revered by the whole province of Asia' (Eunap., *VS* VII.iii.9 to iv.1).[43] The more Christian the empire became, the more powerful was the influence of bishops and priests, and even of monks and 'holy men'. As early as the 330s we hear of a Novatian holy man, Eutychianus, living near the Mysian Mount Olympus in north-west Asia Minor, who became famous as a healer and miracle-worker: he successfully interceded with Constantine for the pardon of an accused officer; and indeed that emperor is said to have generally acceded to requests made by him (Sozomen, *HE* I.xiv.9–11).

Since the very apex of the great pyramid of patronage was, needless to say, the emperor, we must expect to find him subject, far beyond anyone else, to an extreme degree of solicitation, not only by those he condescended to call his 'friends', his *amici* (see below), but also by more ordinary people with ambitions as well as grievances, and of course by cities. (Here I need only refer to the recent book by Fergus Millar, *ERW*, which – in spite of a title that promises too much – I had occasion to recommend in II.v above as an exceptionally useful collection of information on the subject of communication between the Roman emperor and his subjects, in the period with which it deals, 31 B.C. to A.D. 337.)

To avoid exposing myself to an obvious objection, I must point out that an emperor would not inflict upon any of his great men the indignity of being *called* his 'cliens'. Cicero remarks that men who see themselves as rich and honourable gentlemen regard being patronised or called 'clientes' as 'mortis instar' (*De offic.* II.69) – as we would say, 'a fate worse than death'. Therefore, the man whom the ruler delighted to honour with his personal recognition would be styled his *amicus*, his 'friend'[44] – the high-sounding title which everyone has heard of, because the Jews are said to have cast it in Pilate's teeth at the trial of Jesus, crying out to him, 'If thou let this man go, thou art not Caesar's friend' (Jn XIX.12). But *amicitia* between an emperor and one of his subjects, even when it happened to involve warmth of feeling on both sides, could never be a relationship approaching equality. It would of course be technically incorrect to say that it was that of *patronus* to *cliens*, but in reality it would often resemble that relationship rather than what we should call genuine friendship.

At times some senators could feel bitter at the loss of the old *libertas*. It is usually admitted nowadays that under the Principate the word *libertas*, in the mouth of a member of the Roman governing class like Tacitus, meant essentially *libertas senatus*, the freedom of the Senate (see e.g. Wirszubski, *LPIR* 137, 163). I would go so far as to say that in the Late Republic the situation was very much the same. Cicero and his like might well qualify assertions of the liberty of the Senate, the organ of the ruling class, to do exactly as it pleased, by some such phrase as 'within the law' – for they of course (and this is the cardinal fact) had *made the law*, fashioning it and administering it in such a way as to ensure their own dominance, and they could hardly suffer by its observance. 'The Roman constitution was a screen and a sham', as Syme has put it (*RR* 15); but to its authors and beneficiaries, the Roman ruling class, it was authentic Law and Order. If the common herd acted of their own volition against the interests of their rulers, that would be not *libertas* but *licentia*, mere licence: a charge of illegality would almost certainly be brought against it. How nicely the senatorial concept of *libertas* was tailored to fit the senatorial interest, in particular the exercise of their patronage rights, emerges best from a passage in Tacitus' *Annals* (I.75.1-2). After describing how the mere presence of the Emperor Tiberius in a court of law (where he would be sitting as an adviser, *assessor*, to the officiating praetor)[45] ensured that the judgments given were uninfluenced by bribery or the entreaties of the powerful (*adversus ambitum et potentium preces*), Tacitus comments that while this aimed at justice, it destroyed *libertas* (*sed dum veritati consulitur, libertas corrumpebatur*). To be real, for Tacitus, the *libertas* of senators must not be precarious, as it had now become: for an emperor to prevent the praetor from giving judgments in court in favour of his own and his friends' protégés was something that corrupted the free essence of oligarchic political life, even when such initiatives were scrupulously directed *only against* the giving of judgments procured by bribery or favour! One is reminded of a parallel in the *Confessions* of Augustine (VI.[x].16). The saint's young friend Alypius (later bishop of Thagaste in Africa) was acting in the same capacity (*assessor*) in a fiscal case at Rome in 383-4, and again the judge would not have dared to resist the demand of a powerful senator for a decision in his favour contrary to law, had not Alypius insisted on justice being done, remaining impervious – to everyone's amazement – to the man's bribes and even his threats. I fancy that many readers of the *Confessions* may fail to realise that the situation depicted by Augustine, although of course even more common in the Later Empire, could easily occur in the early Principate nearly 370 years earlier.

It was once urged upon me in a letter from an eminent Roman historian, in defence of Tacitus, that the point of the passage from the *Annals* which I have just been discussing is simply that Tiberius, 'by being present, prevented judges from judging freely, as they were embarrassed (who would not be?) by his presence'. But that is not at all what the passage actually says, and, as we shall see in a moment, there is conclusive evidence against it. The presence of Tiberius may well have embarrassed the praetor; and Tacitus could easily have said this, but he has not done so. Tacitus was a master of the ambiguous phrase, and his perfectly explicit statement here should not be disregarded, in favour of a presumed but unstated implication. Tacitus claims most specifically that the presence of Tiberius actually prevented judgments – *unjust* judgments – from being given in response to bribes or the representations of the men of power:[46] it was precisely this, not a general 'embarrassment' of the praetor, which 'destroyed *libertas*'. And indeed there is positive evidence in favour of the picture I have presented. Dio Cassius (LVII.vii.2-5), dealing – as is Tacitus, in the passage I have quoted – with the early years of the reign of Tiberius, says that the emperor took great care when judging cases himself to impress on his assessors that they were to speak their minds quite freely: Dio is most emphatic about this, and he even adds that Tiberius would often express one opinion *and his assessors another*, and that Tiberius sometimes accepted their view, without harbouring any resentment. We may feel, then, that in the passage I have been discussing Tacitus has given himself away: he, as a member of the Roman ruling class, felt no reason to conceal his deep conviction that the ability to exercise, *whether for good or ill*, the proper degree of patronage to which a great man's position in society entitled him was indeed an essential ingredient in *libertas*. In the same way, he shows in two separate passages his instinctive feeling that senators who were financially embarrassed had a right to expect subventions from the emperor, without being obliged to give the sordid details of their financial situation: *Ann.* II.38.1 and 7-10 (cf. Section vi of this chapter and its n.101 below).

Modern historians have too often suffered from an unfortunate tendency to see the Roman concept of *libertas* either in much the same terms as the Roman ruling class saw it, or as something 'vague' and hardly worth taking seriously. The former tendency is exemplified in a very appreciative review by Momigliano, in *JRS* 41 (1951) 146 ff., of a much-praised book on *libertas* by Wirszubski (*LPIR*, 1950) – which, by the way, never discusses (and, unless I have missed something, ignores entirely) the passage from Tacitus' *Annals* (I.75.1-2) that I have emphasised above.[47] Momigliano reduces the interpretations that have been offered of *libertas* to two 'mutually exclusive' ones. According to the one he accepts, which he commends Wirszubski for adopting, 'Libertas is a juridical notion which, if properly analysed, proves to be identical with the notion of

Civitas' (Roman citizenship);[48] and he quotes Mommsen to that effect. He then proceeds to express disapproval of 'the other interpretation', according to which 'Libertas is a vague word which usually conceals egoistic interests'. This latter interpretation he attributes particularly to Syme, from whom he quotes two passages: 'Liberty and the Laws are high-sounding words. They will often be rendered, on a cool estimate, as privilege and vested interests' (*RR* 59); and '*Libertas* is a vague and negative notion – freedom from the rule of a tyrant or faction. It follows that *libertas*, like *regnum* and *dominatio*, is a convenient term of political fraud' (*RR* 155). Wirszubski, actually, is driven in the end almost into Syme's camp. After quoting a few examples of 'vindicatio in libertatem', used in *conflicting* senses, he admits that this phrase 'was a much used political catchword and *became as vague as libertas itself*' (*LPIR* 104, my italics).

This obscures the real issues. Syme's view is certainly the more realistic; and indeed he himself continues the passage from which I have just quoted (*RR* 155) by saying, '*Libertas* was most commonly invoked in defence of the existing order by individuals or classes in enjoyment of power and wealth. The *libertas* of the Roman aristocrat meant the rule of a class and the perpetuation of privilege.' This is perfectly true. And we can agree with Syme's commendation of a famous passage in Tacitus, to the effect that 'Nobody ever sought power for himself and the enslavement of others without invoking *libertas* and such fair names' (*RR* 155, quoting Tac., *Hist.* IV.73). At the same time, we need not discount *libertas* itself, with Syme, as *merely* 'a vague and negative notion' and 'a convenient term of political fraud'. 'Vague' is not at all the right word for the majority of the most interesting uses of the term 'libertas'. In most cases the meaning of 'libertas' is *specific* enough: the point is that it is capable of expressing very *different* and even *contradictory* notions. Certainly one particular kind of 'libertas', in which Wirszubski and Momigliano and others are mainly interested, and which they seem to regard as the most genuine one, can be treated as a 'primarily juridical notion' and made the subject of fairly precise analysis: this is the kind of 'libertas' of which Cicero was the great expositor.[49] Juridical analysis is not out of place here, for, as I have pointed out above, Cicero and his like (from the early Republic onwards) had *made the law*, and they would seldom if ever be disadvantaged by appealing to it. For Cicero himself, indeed, the constitutional law of Rome, at any rate before the Gracchan period, was the best that had ever existed in practice (see Cic., *De leg.* II.23; cf. *De rep.* II.53, 66). But in the Late Republic there was a totally *different kind* of 'libertas'; and to those who held it the Optimate version of *libertas*, that of Cicero & Co., was *servitus* ('slavery', political subjection), while their 'libertas' was stigmatised by Cicero as mere *licentia* ('licence', lawlessness)[50] – a word used also by the Roman rhetorician Cornificius as the equivalent of the standard Greek word for freedom of speech, *parrhēsia* (Quintil., *Inst. orat.* IX.ii.27; cf. V.iii above and its n.57 below). This is not the place to go into detail, and I can hardly do more than refer to one particular group of texts. Wirszubski never even mentions the very significant fact that when Clodius procured the exile of Cicero in 58 B.C., for having executed the Catilinarians without trial in 63 as consul (an act which Cicero of course saw as a necessary defence of his kind of 'libertas'), he also obtained a vote for the destruction of Cicero's grand house on the Palatine (purchased in 62, for HS 3½ million) and the erection on part of its grounds of a shrine to Libertas[51] – the personification of the very quality which, in the eyes of his opponents, Cicero had attacked! In his speech, *De domo suo ad pontifices*, Cicero equates Clodius' Libertas with the 'servitus' of the Roman People (§§ 110-11) and calls Clodius' statue of Libertas the image not of 'libertas publica' but of 'licentia' (§ 131); elsewhere he speaks of Clodius' shrine as a 'templum Licentiae' (*De leg.* II.42). The 'libertas' which was opposed to the Optimate variety can also be found in other texts.[52]

As for the Optimate version of Libertas, to which Cicero subscribed, I suggest that it corresponds well with the opinion of a speaker who is represented as addressing his hearers as

> if not equal all, yet free,
> Equally free; for orders and degrees
> Jar not with liberty, but well consist.

I fear, however, that some may deprecate my quoting this passage (*Paradise Lost* V.791-3) in the present context, for it comes from a speech by Satan, which Milton describes as delivered 'with calumnious art Of counterfeited truth' (770-1), to a concourse of demons.

Augustus himself was usually tactful enough to avoid stressing his own dominance in such a way as to remind senators publicly of what some of them regarded as their subjection, their *servitus* (literally, 'slavery'); and those of his successors who were 'good emperors' (that is to say, emperors of whom the Senate approved) persevered for some generations in the same tradition. In the early Principate the senator might well feel irked by his 'servitus', but under a 'good emperor' he would normally feel bound to suppress such dangerous emotions. I doubt if the Younger Pliny, for instance, was concealing any real qualms when composing in A.D. 100 the panegyric of Trajan to which I have referred above – to the modern reader at first sight, perhaps, a loathsomely dishonest document; but Pliny was surely expressing what he felt to be perfectly sincere sentiments of loyalty and gratitude when he declared that now 'the Princeps is not above the laws, but the laws are above the Princeps' (65.1); cf. Section vi of this chapter. In the same speech Pliny rejoices in the fact that Jupiter can now take things easy, since he has bestowed upon the emperor 'the task of performing his role towards the whole human race' (80.4-5). Most revealing of all, perhaps, is the passage (in 66.2-5) that begins, 'You order us to be free: we shall be' (*iubes esse liberos: erimus*). The words that follow show that this freedom is essentially a freedom of speech, a faculty that was particularly welcome to senators. The contrast Pliny proceeds to draw with the situation in the recent past under Domitian shows that even freedom of speech was indeed within the gift of the emperor. (Pliny's *Panegyricus* has recently been printed, with a good English translation, by Betty Radice, at the end of Vol. II of the improved reissue in the Loeb edition of Pliny's *Letters*, 1969.) Pliny's more intellectually sophisticated contemporary Tacitus could occasionally be very bitter about the Principate, but he was realist enough to understand that it was an absolute necessity, if an unfortunate one.

It would have been interesting to have Cicero's opinion, both public and private (there would have been a great difference), of the Principate of Augustus, which he did not live to experience. He did live through the much more undisguised dictatorship of Julius Caesar, which he survived by less than two years. He conformed in public, sometimes (in his speech *Pro Marcello*, for instance) displaying a feigned enthusiasm which belied his true feelings; but in private, writing to his intimate friends, he could express himself with great bitterness. It was not just *libertas* which in his eyes he and his senatorial colleagues now lacked; even their *dignitas* was gone, for, as he said in a letter (*Ad fam.* IV.xiv.1), how could one possess *dignitas* when one could neither work for what one believed in nor advocate it openly? Would Cicero, then, have followed the example of those famous Roman Stoics, especially Thrasea Paetus and Helvidius Priscus, who in the 60s and 70s of the first century came out in open verbal opposition to Nero or Vespasian, and paid for their temerity with their lives? Perhaps. But Brutus, who knew Cicero well, could say in a letter to their friend Atticus that Cicero did not reject *servitus* provided it involved the reception of honours (*servitutem, honorificam modo, non aspernatur*: Cic., *Ep. ad Brut.* I.xvii.4; cf. 6; xvi.1, 4, 8). This was the attitude of the great majority of senators. The Emperor Tiberius, it was said, used to utter a bitter exclamation in Greek every time he left the Senate House, describing the senators as 'men ready for slavery' (Tac., *Ann.* III.65.3; cf. I.7.1, 12.1 etc.). A famous phrase of Cicero's, *cum dignitate otium*,[53] perfectly expresses the political ideal which he held in common with his fellow-Optimates; and whether or not Cicero himself would have found it realised in the Principate of Augustus, I have no doubt that most senators would have done. The precise meaning of the phrase *otium cum dignitate* has been much disputed. I accept Brunt's revealing paraphrase: 'an ordered state in which men were valued according to their rank in a hierarchical social structure' (*SCRR* 124; the whole passage, pp.124-6, is well worth reading).[54]

It is misleading, I believe, to regard the political change from Republic to Principate as a 'Roman *Revolution*' – the title of Syme's great work, to which I have referred above.[55] It has been claimed that what happened was 'a triumph of Italy over Rome' (Syme, *RR* 453), and that 'Italy and the non-political orders in society triumphed over Rome and the Roman aristocracy' (*RR* 8) – but if that is true in any sense at all, it is so *only if we ignore the vast majority of the population, who had no share in any such 'triumph'*! Just as the Patricio-Plebeian oligarchy of the Middle Republic was in most important ways very little different from the Patrician oligarchy it succeeded, so the governing class of the Principate retained (or acquired) most of the characteristics of their Late Republican predecessors. There was very little change in the economic system and not much in the general social complexion of Italy, except that the governing class was now drawn increasingly from the Italian towns instead of only from Rome itself, a process which had already begun under the Republic. Soon men of provincial origin entered the Senate, at first mainly from southern Gaul and Spain, but in the second century (after a trickle in the first) from the richer Greek provinces, Asia above all (see III.ii above and its nn.11-12), and also from Africa. Even emperors were sometimes of 'provincial origin', in the sense that they came from families (sometimes old Italian ones) resident in a province: Trajan was born at Italica in Spain, near the modern Seville, and so probably was Hadrian; Septimius Severus came from an equestrian family of Lepcis Magna in Africa.

How much real change there was between Republic and Principate even in the political field is disputed. I myself would see it as essentially the completion of a pyramid of power and patronage, involving the placing of a coping stone – admittedly a very large and heavy one – on top of the whole oppressive edifice. The *direct political role of the class struggle* in this change was, in my opinion, perhaps not a central one; but the very existence of the poorer classes, as a potential reservoir of unrest and a source from which soldiers might be recruited by an aspiring dynast, was a factor of fundamental importance in ultimately inducing the upper classes of Italy to accept as supreme ruler a man they knew to be by inclination entirely on their side against any conceivable kind of revolution from below. The Roman lower orders had rarely played any very important part in politics, except as members of the faction supporting an individual politician whom they believed to be a *popularis*; and in the period of transition to the Principate they were on the whole only too content to leave their own political destinies completely in the hands of Octavian/Augustus, whom – as the heir of the great *popularis*, Julius Caesar – they mistakenly regarded as their champion (see above). By the time the Principate was fully consolidated, it was too late. The Greeks, who had already become accustomed to Hellenistic kingship, usually saw less reason to conceal the reality of imperial power behind republican phraseology, and to them the emperor was a king, *basileus* (see the next section of this chapter). They had of course no option but to accept the Principate, which for them represented more gain than loss.

There has been much sneering talk about the Roman lower classes being content with 'bread and circuses' – a phrase of Juvenal's, whose derisive 'panem et circenses' (X.81) has echoed down the centuries,[56] (I am afraid that even Marx could see the situation in those terms, as when he spoke in a letter of the dispossessed peasants of the late Roman Republic as 'a *mob* of do-nothings more abject than the former "poor whites" in the South of the United States'.)[57] I myself find it hard to understand why so many of those who have written about the Roman world have thought it discreditable to the humble Roman that his prime concern should have been bread. I see no reason to think that the attitude of the common people was unpleasantly materialistic or degraded just because they thought first of filling their bellies. In any event, the 'bread' (see III.vi above) was received regularly by only a very limited number of the *plebs urbana* at Rome itself (and in the Later Empire at Constantinople); food and cash doles were provided now and again at other cities, on a small scale (and often with the humble entitled to a smaller share than the more distinguished citizens; cf. III.vi again); nor did the rural poor anywhere receive any such official dole. And the number of those who could attend 'circuses', even at Rome, as Balsdon has demonstrated,[58] was relatively small in relation to the size of the population of the capital. The Inaugural Lecture by Alan Cameron, entitled *Bread and Circuses: the Roman Emperor and his People* (1973), to which I referred in V.iii above, would be most instructive reading for those brought up on the traditional picture of the obsession of the 'Roman mob' with 'free bread and circuses'. As Cameron says (pp.2-3), 'That notorious idle mob of layabouts sponging off the state is little more than a figment of middle-class prejudice, ancient and modern alike.' And he adds, 'It was not the people's fault that, being in origin religious festivals, public entertainments were provided free' – as indeed they always had been. In point of fact the circus and the theatre sometimes played an important quasi-political role during the Roman Principate and Later Empire,[59] a subject I have already touched on in V.iii above. It was certainly the *plebs urbana*, rather than the far greater number of peasants, who were in the best position to make their influence felt at Rome, if only as a kind of 'pressure group'. Their outstanding characteristic was that they were mainly very poor. It could be said of the workmen and peasants who agitated for the election of Marius as consul for 107 B.C.[60] that 'their assets and credit were embodied in their hands' (Sall., *BJ* 73.6). In 63 Sallust describes the Roman *plebs* as having no resources beyond their food and clothing (*Cat* 48.2; cf. Cic., *IV Cat.* 17); and when he writes of attempts made to rescue one of the revolutionaries of that year, P. Cornelius Lentulus Sura, by 'his freedmen and a few of his clients', he refers to their efforts as directed towards 'workmen and slaves' (*opifices atque servitia*: *Cat.* 50.1), as if the two groups might be expected to have much the same interests. It is impossible for us to tell how much fellow-feeling there was between the slaves at Rome and the *plebs urbana*, a fair proportion of whom are likely to have been freedmen. On one occasion, certainly, in A.D. 61, the common people of Rome made a violent if ineffective protest against the mass execution of the slaves of Pedanius Secundus (Tac., *Ann.* XIV.42-3: see VII.i below), but I know of no other important evidence.

(vi)
The Principate, the emperor and the upper classes

The Roman Principate was an extraordinary and unique institution. Gibbon hit it off admirably: the system of imperial government, as instituted by Augustus, can be defined as

> an absolute monarchy disguised by the forms of a commonwealth. The masters of the Roman world surrounded their throne with darkness, concealed their irresistible strength, and humbly professed themselves the accountable ministers of the Senate, whose supreme decrees they dictated and obeyed (*DFRE* I.68).

(Anyone who reads Dio Cassius LII.31.1-2 will find an apt reflection of it in that passage of Gibbon's.)

One of the essential features of Greek democracy in the Classical period, as I said in V.ii above, was that it made every holder of power *hypeuthynos*, 'subject to audit' (*euthyna*), subject to examination and control by the whole citizen body or some court of law to which it delegated its supreme authority.[1] This was true both in theory and in practice. With the Hellenistic kingdoms and the Roman Principate we have already arrived at the opposite extreme – for what king or emperor will deign to make himself accountable, or how can accountability in any form be forced upon him? In his orations *On kingship*, Dio Chrysostom, writing in the early years of the second century (and thinking above all of the Roman emperor), specifically defines kingship (*basileia*) as rule that is 'not subject to account': the king and his monarchy are *anhypeuthynos* (III.43; LVI.5); the king is 'greater than the laws' (III.10), 'above the laws' (LXXVI.4); indeed, law (*nomos*) *is* the king's decree, his *dogma* (III.43). That was not the constitutional theory of the Principate, but it is a correct description of its practice. It could be said by a contemporary (albeit in a satirical skit) that Claudius, the third of the emperors after Augustus, 'used to put men to death as easily as a dog sits down' (Seneca, *Apocoloc.* 10).

I am not suggesting, of course, that the vast Roman world could ever have been ruled by anything resembling a democracy of the Greek type, which relied essentially – to put it crudely – on government by mass meeting, and could not have been applied to a large area without at any rate a development of representative and federal institutions far beyond anything the Greeks ever imagined.[2] Nor did the Greeks suffer any *further* loss of 'freedom', in any sense, when the Roman Republic foundered and the whole empire became subject to a single master who was 'not subject to account'. They had lost their freedom already, many of them well over a hundred years earlier, even if they enjoyed various degrees of internal autonomy (see V.iii and VI.iv above). Many modern scholars have seen the change from Republic to Principate far too much in terms of Rome and the Italian ruling class. The provinces had always been subject to rule that was 'not subject to account' *by them*, and there is no reason to think that the vast majority of their inhabitants resented the change. In the preceding section of this chapter I quoted the opinion of Tacitus (*Ann.* I.2.2) that the provinces, having learnt to distrust 'the rule of Senate and People', did not object to the introduction of the Principate of Augustus.

The Principate may be said to have lasted for some hundreds of years, for there was no essential change in its monarchical character (as I believe) so long as its centralised control remained – in the West, only until some time in the fifth century. How long one allows the 'Later Roman Empire' to have continued in the Greek East is a matter of taste; but even if one prefers to speak of a 'Byzantine Empire' from some date in, say, the sixth century or the first half of the seventh, the despotic character of the regime was fundamentally the same, very different as its external aspect was in some ways. It has long been customary for English-speakers to make a break between 'Principate' and 'Dominate', at the accession of the Emperor Diocletian in 284-5.[3] I believe that any such distinction, based upon a supposed fundamental (or at least significant) *change in the nature of imperial rule* at the end of the third century, is misleading, because it takes appearance for reality. I do not deny that the outward forms of imperial rule and the terminology in which that rule was expressed did change by degrees during the first few centuries in the direction of even greater autocracy; but the emperor was always in reality an absolute monarch, however much he or his supporters might pretend the contrary – a pretence which, I would say, was by no means always insincere. I myself certainly find it convenient to distinguish between 'Principate' and 'Later Empire' ('Haut-Empire' and 'Bas-Empire'). To draw such a line is useful not only as a way of distinguishing two different chronological epochs: new elements did indeed enter in with the reigns of Diocletian and Constantine, but those which were formative and of major and lasting importance were not so much a transformation in the position of the ruler as *an intensification of the forms of exploitation*. The Later Roman colonate, reducing a large proportion of the free working peasants to serfdom; a new taxation system of far greater intensity and – in principle – efficiency; and a more extended use of conscription for the army: these were the features distinguishing 'Later Roman Empire' from 'Principate' which mattered most to most people and were of the greatest importance in the long run, and it was they which *necessitated* a further growth in the authority and prestige of the emperor, to reinforce the increased dominance of the ruling class. I shall briefly mention below the further exaltation of the emperor in the sixth and seventh centuries, in response to intensified pressure on the empire from outside.

My purpose in this book is to reveal the realities of life in the Greek (and Roman) world, mainly as they affected the vast majority of the population, rather than the much more pleasant features of that life which the ruling classes commonly perceived or imagined. In dealing with the nature of imperial rule, therefore, I am far less interested in the subtle ways in which, for example, the self-satisfied Roman picture of the good ruler differed from, or resembled, the equally unreal Hellenistic portrait of the ideal king, or the variations that took place over the centuries in the sophisticated concepts of monarchy produced by philosophers and rhetoricians. Such questions (including the problems of 'ruler-cult') are well worth pursuing, and they have been exhaustively studied – if rarely with as much common sense and clear-sightedness as one could desire – in such monumental works as Fritz Taeger's *Charisma. Studien zur Geschichte des antiken Herrscherkultes* (2 vols, 1957 & 1960, nearly 1,200 pages), and Francis Dvornik's *Early Christian and Byzantine Political Philosophy: Origins and Background* (2 vols, 1966, nearly 1,000 pages), not to mention many others. Anyone who wants to read a brief and clear statement, setting out most sympathetically the benevolent intentions of the emperors, as expressed in their own propaganda, can hardly do better than read M. P. Charlesworth's Raleigh Lecture on History for 1937, where we are told of the imperial propaganda that 'Perhaps it would be fairer to call it not propaganda but the creation of goodwill. For it was very sober and truthful propaganda, and it was not far divorced from fact. The great emperors of the second century were very much in earnest, very much aware of their responsibilities; what they announced, the benefits they described, were real and positive; they did bring peace, they did erect great buildings and harbours, they did secure calm and quietude and happiness . . . Their propaganda was not promises for the vague future, but a reminder of genuine achievement' (Charlesworth, VRE 20-1).

By contrast, I am primarily concerned to show how imperial rule contributed to maintain a massive system of exploitation of the great majority by the upper classes.

In the long run, nothing was more important to the empire than the emperor's ability to direct foreign policy and to exercise effectively the supreme military command which always belonged to him. It was not absolutely necessary for him to take the field in person; but being under the direct command of an emperor who was a successful commander-in-chief could have an inspiring effect on the troops, and an emperor who knew something of military operations at first hand was more likely to make an informed choice of generals. Many emperors conducted military campaigns in person. Tiberius and Vespasian were successful generals before they became emperors; Trajan and Marcus Aurelius commanded in the field during their reigns; later, especially in the two centuries from Septimius Severus (193 ff.) to Theodosius I (who died in 395), many emperors spent much of their time on campaign. In this book I can do no more than emphasise, without going into detail, the very great importance of the emperor's role in all branches of what we call foreign affairs, including relations with outside powers and client states, general foreign policy, diplomacy, strategy and military operations – not to mention the organisation of the army, and the taxation needed to provide for its requirements. I find it strange that a recent large-scale account of *The Emperor in the Roman World* (1977), by Fergus Millar, should virtually ignore financial policy and taxation, and make only a perfunctory mention of the emperor's role 'as a commander and in relation to the army, and his complex diplomatic relations with foreign powers and dependent kings' among 'many other elements which would need to be taken into account in any complete analysis even of the functions of an emperor, let alone of the entire cultural, social and political system within which he lived' (*ERW* 617-18). For Millar, 'the emperor was what the emperor did' (*ERW* xi & 6); but he has not sufficiently taken into account the loaded character of our evidence for 'what the emperor did'. Indeed, he gives what is almost a *reductio ad absurdum* of his own position when he admits that 'If we follow our evidence, we might almost come to believe that the primary role of the emperor was to listen to speeches in Greek'! (*ERW* 6). Allowing himself to be over-influenced by his own selection from the particular kinds of evidence that happen to have survived, Millar can speak of 'the *essential passivity* of the role expected of the emperor', and can say that 'the emperor's role in relation to his subjects was *essentially* that of listening to requests, and of hearing disputes'; he can even suggest that 'general edicts were in fact a relatively minor part of imperial business', simply because few general edicts are preserved on stone before the end of the third century (*ERW* 6, 256-7, my italics). Certainly, we must not expect to find emperors concerned to *change* their world, in the way that many modern governments are. Innovation was something the Roman upper classes always dreaded, and when it did take place it was likely to be dressed up as a return to ancestral tradition, the *mos maiorum* – as indeed the Principate of Augustus was represented as a restoration of the Republic. We can agree with Millar that 'the nature of the emperor's personal activities, and of the physical and social contexts in which they were conducted, was such as to exclude the initiation of change as a normal and expected function' (*ERW* 271). For this there was the best of reasons: the Roman ruling class as a whole perfectly fulfilled the definition of a Conservative (of the British variety) given recently by a leading academic figure in the Conservative Party, Lord Blake, Provost of The Queen's College, Oxford. Blake, reviewing in the *Times Literary Supplement* a biography of Balfour, quoted Balfour's answer to a question from Beatrice Webb: 'I am a Conservative. I wish to maintain existing institutions.' And Blake adds an opinion with which we can all wholeheartedly agree: 'This is, after all, much the best reason for being a Conservative, and it is undoubtedly the reason why the vast majority of Conservatives vote as they do' (*TLS* 4031, 27 June 1980, p.724. Cf. Augustus, quoted by Macrob., *Sat.* II.iv.18, as cited in Section v of this chapter). I must add, in defence of Millar, that he never tries to introduce any limitation on the autocratic nature of the emperor's position, from the beginning to the end of the period with which his book deals (from the battle of Actium to the death of Constantine, 31 B.C. to A.D. 337). However, he makes no attempt to explain the social basis of the Principate, or how the office was transmitted, or even why a monarchy, so repugnant to the Roman aristocratic tradition, had become necessary.

★ ★ ★ ★ ★ ★

The words commonly used in Latin to designate the emperor and his rule, namely *princeps* and *principatus*,[4] were not official titles[5] but were terms familiar from the Late Republic, referring to the outstanding prestige, dignity and influence achieved by a – or the – leading man (or, with *principes* in the plural, leading men), normally of consular rank, and they were carefully chosen by Augustus to avoid any monarchical taint. In his account of his own achieve-'ments, his *Res Gestae*, Augustus referred to his own reign by the phrase 'when I was Princeps' (*me principe*).[6] He also drew an important distinction between his *auctoritas*[7] and his *potestas* (*RG* 34.3).[8] The latter word denotes legal powers constitutionally conferred: it can legitimately be translated 'power'. For *auctoritas* there is no English equivalent: perhaps a combination of 'prestige' and 'influence' best conveys its meaning. In the *Res Gestae* (34.3) Augustus chose to emphasise his pre-eminent *auctoritas* and to play down, not quite honestly, his *potestas*, which in reality was equally pre-eminent. A sentence in Cicero's speech against L. Calpurnius Piso Caesoninus (of 55 B.C.), describing an incident that had occurred at the end of 61, illustrates perfectly the contrast between the two qualities. Q. Caecilius Metellus Celer, who was merely consul designate (for 60) and thus enjoyed no *potestas*, but was a man of great prestige, prevented the performance of some games ordered by a tribune in defiance of a ruling of the Senate. 'That which he could not yet bring about by *potestas* [legal power],' Cicero says, 'he achieved by *auctoritas*' (*In Pis.* 8). The *auctoritas* of a Roman was his ability to command respect and obedience by the accumulation of personal qualities (including of course distinguished ancestry) and his own record of achievement, irrespective of constitutional powers. In this respect no Roman ever surpassed Augustus.

As we shall see presently, the Greeks very soon came to use for the emperor – and even to address him by – their word for legitimate king, *basileus* (and their term for his monarchy was *basileia*); but in Latin the corresponding words, *rex* and *regnum*, were studiously avoided during Republic and Principate, except as a term of abuse, as when Cicero denounces Tiberius Gracchus for aiming at *regnum* (see the end of Section ii of this chapter), or writes of the regime in which Sulla had been personally dominant as the 'Sullanum regnum' (*Ad Att.* VIII.xi.2; IX.vii.3). According to Cicero, after the expulsion of Tarquin (when the Republic was created) the Roman people could not even bear to hear the title of 'king' (*nomen regis audire non poterat: De rep.* II.52; cf. III.47) – a statement which was certainly true of the Roman ruling class, about whose attitude alone we have adequate information. They used *rex* only for foreign kings (whether of independent states like Parthia or their own vassals), or as the virtual equivalent of the Greek *tyrannos*. I know of only one prominent exception to this rule during the Principate: Seneca, who in his *De clementia*, addressed to Nero in A.D. 55-6 (and much influenced by Hellenistic ideas), repeatedly uses *rex* and *regnum* in a good sense, coupling together *rex* and *princeps*, in the singular or plural, writing the word *rex* as a clear synonym for *princeps* or *imperator*, and using *rex* of the emperor himself without actually addressing him by that ill-omened title.[9] In his *De beneficiis* Seneca goes so far as to say that the best condition of a State is under a just king (*cum optimus civitatis status sub rege iusto sit*, II.xx.2).[10] I can only endorse what Miriam Griffin has said on this subject in her book on Seneca,[11] merely adding that one may feel that had Seneca lived half a century earlier or later, under Augustus or Trajan, he might well have used *rex* and its cognates more sparingly; he might have avoided drawing a contrast between *reges* and *tyranni* (as in *De clem.* I.xi.4; xii.3; *Epist. mor.* 114.23-4) and have preferred to speak instead of an opposition between *principatus* and *dominatio,* as the Younger Pliny did in A.D. 100 in his *Panegyricus* (45.3), from which I have quoted in the preceding section of this chapter.[12]

In the end, however, *rex* and *regnum* became permissible descriptions of imperial rule in the Latin West, as *basileus* and *basileia* had always been in the Greek East (see the next paragraph). By the year 400 the poet Claudian, repudiating the notion that the rule of a superior Princeps was *servitium* (total political subjection, literally 'slavery'), could go on to say, 'Never is liberty appreciated more than under a good *rex*' (*Stil.* III.113-15).[13] And if we are tempted to dismiss Claudian as an Alexandrian Greek writing in Latin and in verse, we can turn to a Western Christian writer of the same period (the last years of the fourth century and the first of the fifth), Sulpicius Severus of Aquitaine, who very often uses the term *rex* of an emperor, as an alternative to *imperator* and *princeps,* all three expressions once appearing in a single short sentence (*Chron.* II.42.6; cf. *Vita S. Martin.* 20.1-7 etc.). I do not know when an emperor is first recorded as referring to his own rule as *regnum* in an official context, but there is a clear example in the Emperor Majorian's address to the Roman Senate in 458 (*Nov. Major.* I.1). According to his opening words, it is the Senate and the army which have made him *imperator;* and in the next sentence he can also use the terms sanctified by tradition, referring to his rule as a *principatus* and to the state as the *res publica.* Yet in that second sentence he can also speak of his *regnum* (in the institutional sense, not the geographical), a word which can now be used without shame, not only by the emperor himself but also by his panegyrist – or 'poet, if we may degrade that sacred name', as Gibbon put it (*DFRE* IV.13) – according to whom 'ordo omnis *regnum* dederat, plebs, curia, miles, Et collega simul'. The panegyrist, or poet, is Sidonius Apollinaris (*Carm.* V.387-8), later a bishop, and described by Stein as 'pour nous le dernier poète et prosateur latin de l'Antiquité' (*HBE* I².i.369).

The standard title the Greeks commonly employed for the emperor was *autokratōr,* the normal Greek translation of the Latin *imperator.* This is interesting in itself, as the Greek term, although not so highly charged with military significance, emphasises the arbitrary element in the power of the holder of *imperium,* in a way that *imperator* hardly does, and *princeps* of course not at all. The Greeks also referred to the emperor as their *basileus,* their king. The poet Antipater of Thessalonica refers to Augustus as his *basileus* in a poem (*Anth. Pal.* X.25) probably written as early as 9 B.C. (or perhaps a few years later).[14] It is sometimes said that *basileus* is not used of the emperor in prose before the second century;[15] but this is false. Strabo, writing under Tiberius, seems to me to be using *basileus* in one passage for the emperor (XVII.i.12, p.797); and even if this is wrong, there is no doubt that Josephus, in his *Jewish War* (dating from the 70s, and originally written in Aramaic), applies this term to emperors on several occasions.[16] Dio Chrysostom also uses the noun *basileus* and the verb *basileuein* of the Roman emperors,[17] in particular in a speech that is very probably to be dated in the early 70s and anyway not later than the 80s (XXXI.150, 151).[18] New Testament texts, too, sometimes refer to the emperors as *basileis.*[19] During the second and third centuries the use of *basileus* and its cognates for the emperors became increasingly common.[20] A particularly interesting passage is Appian, *Praef.* 6 (cf. 14): the Roman Republic, we are told, was an *aristokratia* until Julius Caesar made himself *monarchos*, while preserving the form and name (the *schēma* and *onoma*) of the *politeia* (the *res publica*: we can translate 'the Republic'). This form of rule, under one man, Appian saw as persisting until the time at which he was writing, the second quarter of the second century. The Romans, he continues, call their rulers not *basileis* but *autokratores* (Appian means of course 'not *reges* but *imperatores*'), 'although in fact they are *basileis* in all respects'. Greeks addressing an emperor in their own language would often call him 'basileus'; and the second-century jurist Maecianus, in a passage preserved in the *Digest*, records a petition from Eudaemon of Nicomedia to the Emperor Antoninus Pius (138-161), addressing him as 'Antoninos basileus' and opening with the words 'Kyrie basileu Antonini', 'My lord King Antoninus' (*Dig.* XIV.ii.9).[21] By the early third century we begin to find emperors referring to their own rule as *basileia*, when writing to Greeks (see Millar, *ERW* 417, 614), but for several centuries they did not formally adopt *basileus* as their official title. Synesius of Cyrene, addressing the Eastern Emperor Arcadius in 399 in a treatise *On kingship* (*Peri basileias*, in Latin *De regno*), could still say that the emperors, while deservedly addressed as *basileis*, preferred to style themselves *autokratores* (§ 13, in *MPG* LXVI.1085). Only with Heraclius, in the early seventh century, do we find a new imperial titulature in which that emperor and his son first describe themselves (in Greek) as *pistoi en Christōi augoustoi* ('Augusti, faithful believers in Christ') and then, from 629 onwards, as *pistoi en Christōi basileis*.[22] Those who can understand Greek may derive much amusement from a reading of the first six chapters or sections (only five pages long) of that curious work by John the Lydian usually known by its Latin title, *De magistratibus populi Romani*, written just after the middle of the sixth century, in the reign of Justinian.[23] John was a Latin enthusiast, eager to show off his command of that language and his grasp (which was in fact very feeble) of the early history of Roman institutions, from the time of Romulus (if not Aeneas!) onwards. He usually employs the Greek word *basileus* in the sense of the Latin *princeps*, and as the opposite of *tyrannos*. For the early kings of Rome, who to him were *tyrannoi*, he uses a Greek transliteration, *rēx* (ῥήξ), which had come into occasional use in Greek in the fourth century.

★   ★   ★   ★   ★   ★

The empire centred in the emperor. His role was always primary, but from the mid-third century onwards, when barbarian irruptions began to threaten the very fabric of the empire, and the social evils the regime bred within itself became more apparent and more evidently harmful, the personal ability of the emperor, above all in the military sphere, became a matter of far greater importance. First-century Rome was strong enough to 'carry' a Caligula or a Nero, and second-century Rome a Commodus; Rome of the late third and fourth centuries could afford no such dangerous luxuries, especially as the emperor was now even more of a master than ever, The need produced the men: for a little over a hundred years, from the accession of Diocletian in 284 to the death of Theodosius I in 395, a succession of mainly very able and sometimes heroic figures occupied the imperial throne. For Graeco-Romans like Ammianus

Marcellinus (in the late fourth century), needless to say, no alternative to the rule of an emperor was conceivable. As Ammianus says (XIX.xii.17), 'The safety of the legitimate Princeps, the champion and defender of good men, on whom depends the safety of others, ought to be protected by the united efforts of everyone', and 'no right-thinking man could object' to the fact that in investigations of the crime of treason (*maiestas*) Roman law allowed not even the greatest men their usual exemption from torture, now inflicted as a matter of routine on members of the lower classes involved in legal process (see VIII.i below). Unnecessary haughtiness in an emperor might be out of place, and when the emperor was commanding his troops in the field he could behave as any great general should, and need not put too much distance between himself and his men. Ammianus evidently counts it a virtue in the Emperor Julian that when he and his army were in great difficulties in the last stages of their Persian campaign in 363 Julian 'had no dainties provided for his dinner, after the manner of royalty [*ex regio more*], but a small serving of pottage under the low poles of a tent' (XXV.ii.2). On all other occasions complete dignity was essential; and it is interesting to find Ammianus praising Constantius II (of whom he is often very critical) because he 'maintained in every way the prestige of the imperial majesty, and his great and lofty spirit disdained popularity' (XXI.xvi.1), and criticising his beloved Julian because when he heard of the arrival of the 'philosopher' Maximus of Ephesus, whom he greatly admired, he jumped up in the middle of a lawsuit he was trying and ran to receive and kiss the man (XXII.vii.3). At the end of his sumptuous narrative of the entry of Constantius II into Rome in 357, Ammianus makes what may appear at first sight to be an ironic commentary on the personality and behaviour of the emperor:

> Saluted as Augustus, he never stirred when the roar thundered back from the hills and shores: he showed himself to be the very same man, and just as imperturbable, as when he was in his provinces. For he both stooped when passing through lofty gates (although he was very short) and, as if his neck were fastened, he kept his gaze straight ahead and did not turn his face to right or left; and – as if he were a sculpted figure – he was never seen to droop his head when his carriage-wheel jolted, or to spit, or to wipe or rub his face or nose or move his hand. Although this was a studied attitude on his part, yet these and certain other features of his inner life were indications of no ordinary endurance, or so it was given out, granted to him alone (XVI.x.9-11; cf. XXI.xvi.7).

There is no real irony in this passage: Constantius was behaving exactly as a Roman emperor should. The atmosphere had undoubtedly changed since the first century, when imperial arrogance and even aloofness could be stigmatised as alien to the *civilitas* expected of a Princeps; but the essential reality , as opposed to outward show, remained much as it always had been. To their credit, the Roman emperors, in the period covered by this book, never described themselves in the ludicrously grandiloquent way that was characteristic of their Persian counterparts. In Ammianus' version of their correspondence in 358, King Shapur II of Persia and the Emperor Constantius II could call each other 'brother'; but Shapur, in his arrogant letter to Constantius, styles himself 'king of kings, partner of the stars, brother of the sun and moon', whereas Constantius, in his haughty reply, is content to describe himself as 'victor by land and sea, perpetual Augustus' (XVII.v.3,10).

* * * * * *

Occasionally in modern books one encounters the seriously false notion that there was a *necessary* and deep-rooted conflict between the emperor and 'the Senate' or 'the aristocracy'. There is a recent example in an article by Keith Hopkins (EMRE = *SAS*, ed. Finley, 103-20), which speaks again and again of 'tension', 'conflict' or 'hostility' between the emperor and the senatorial aristocracy collectively (*SAS* 107, 112, 113, 116, 119), even of the emperor's 'battle against aristocrats', and of all the emperors as 'necessarily engaged with the aristocracy in a struggle for power' (*SAS* 115, 112). Hopkins complains that there is 'a tendency among modern historians to minimise this conflict'; and while candidly admitting that 'of course it is difficult or impossible to *prove* its importance', he thinks there is 'massive evidence for it' (which he does not produce) in Tacitus, Suetonius, Dio Cassius and the *Historia Augusta* (*SAS* 107).

This theory is essentially false. There are two major elements of truth in it and two only. First, any serious revolt against an emperor would nearly always be *led* by a *member or members* of the aristocracy, for only such men would have enough wealth, prestige and influence to have any chance of success. But no substantial part of the senatorial aristocracy is ever found taking part in a revolution against an emperor without lining up at the same time behind some other claimant to the imperial throne, more often than not a senator himself. Never again after the assassination of Gaius in 41 do we hear of any serious consideration being given, even by the Senate, to the idea of 'restoring the Republic'.[24] And secondly, the emperor, like no one else, was personally responsible for the whole empire and was liable to face assassination or a military revolt if things went too badly wrong; and he might therefore be obliged to put a curb on excessive oppression or exploitation by individual holders of key posts, such as provincial governors – of whom the most important, of course, would be senators (see below).

The truth is, therefore, that although an *individual emperor* might act in such a way as to make the senatorial aristocracy detest him, their remedy for such a situation was always to try to *replace him by another emperor*. It is permissible, then, to speak of 'tension, conflict or hostility' (see above) between *an* emperor, or *some* emperors, and the aristocracy, but not between *the* emperor and the aristocracy. It is a mistake to pay too much attention to the few emperors like Gaius (Caligula), Nero, Domitian, Commodus and Caracalla – who were driven not only by an autocratic disposition but also by extreme tactlessness, and some of them by objectionable personal qualities – and to forget that the vast majority of senators would gladly accept, provided it was made sufficiently *honorifica* (as it usually was), a status which their republican ancestors might have stigmatised as *servitus* (cf. Section v of this chapter, e.g. on Brutus' opinion of Cicero). Serious opposition in principle to the rule of the emperors as such died out, as far as we know, early in the Principate, and thereafter we find nothing more deep-seated than criticism of an individual ruler, at most with the aim of replacing him with a more acceptable one. As we shall see later, when considering the question of imperial succession, the Senate did not even aspire to play a decisive role in the process of choosing the next emperor, and, until the seventh century, it did so in practice on only two occasions, in 275 and 518 (see below). In general the Senate would accept with resignation, sometimes even with enthusiasm, an emperor who treated them with tact (especially gratifying if it amounted to assumed deference), gave them jurisdiction over their own members, and only executed those who were guilty of open rebellion. To give just one example of imperial tact – it is entirely characteristic of Augustus that in the famous series of edicts of the last years B.C. found at Cyrene (E/J² 311) he should use peremptory language[25] when laying down the law concerning procedure in the province, but substitute the polite phrase 'Governors of Crete and Cyrene will be acting fairly and conveniently in my eyes if . . . ',[26] when in effect giving orders directly to the proconsul, who was of course a senator.

Certain imperial freedmen in the early Principate and soldiers or eunuchs in the Later Empire might acquire great importance *as individuals*, but in the long run the imperial system could rely upon the support of the senators *as a class*: the great majority of the emperors realised this and received that support. Even a man like Stilicho, who for more than a decade before his death in 408 virtually acted as regent for the Western Emperor Honorius (to whom he was completely loyal), did his best to enlist the co-operation of the Roman Senate, in spite of the fact that it despised him as a jumped-up nobody, the son of a Vandal officer. He did so, as Alan Cameron has said, 'quite simply because the co-operation of a body of men who between them absorbed a major part of the resources of Italy, Gaul, Spain and Africa was essential for the administration of the western provinces' (*Claudian* 233). The Eastern senators, of Constantinople, were never quite as much of a force in government or administration as their Western colleagues, at Rome;[27] but the emperors treated them with studied politeness, and Theodosius II in 446, by an edict retained in Justinian's Code, went so far as to assure their *gloriosissimus coetus* that all new legislation would first be submitted for their approval (*CJ* I.xiv.8). Only in the latter part of the third century, by a process already noticeable under Gallienus in the 260s and culminating in the reign of Diocletian and his colleagues (under whom the great majority of provincial governorships were held by equestrians), is there any trace of a deliberate policy of excluding senators from positions of power;[28] and Diocletian's policy was reversed under Constantine and his sons, with the result that (as we shall see towards the end of this section) the senatorial order grew apace and by the early fifth century had become the sole imperial aristocracy.

*　*　*　*　*　*

It is interesting to read the remark of Suetonius that the Emperor Domitian – notoriously a 'bad emperor' (that is to say, an emperor the Senate disliked) – 'took such care in coercing the city magistrates and provincial governors that never at any time were they more moderate or more just. Since Domitian's time we have seem most of them guilty of all crimes' (*Dom.* 8.2). Now Suetonius was basically very hostile to Domitian, and he is speaking here of his own times and from his own personal observation: he was probably in his late twenties at the assassination of Domitian in 96, and he continued to live under Nerva, Trajan and Hadrian, who were officially 'good emperors' (Nerva and Trajan in particular). Brunt, in his detailed and accurate account of the prosecutions of provincial governors during the early Principate (CPMEP), doubts the statement of Suetonius;[29] but I see no very good reason to follow him here: the second part of Suetonius' statement at any rate will seem quite credible to anyone who has studied the letters of the Younger Pliny, a rather older contemporary of Suetonius and, like his friend Tacitus, a distinguished consular. It is all too clear from these letters that the Senate tended to adopt an extremely indulgent attitude to some of the members of its order who had committed even the most shocking crimes during their administration of provinces – even to the notorious Marius Priscus, who as proconsul of Africa in 97-8 (under the Emperor Nerva) had been guilty of appalling cruelty (*immanitas* and *saevitia*: Pliny, *Ep*. II.xi.2). Although prosecuted by Tacitus and Pliny on behalf of some of the provincials concerned in 99-100, before a Senate presided over by the *optimus princeps* Trajan, as consul (ibid. 10), Marius received only the very light sentence of *relegatio* (banishment, but without loss of property or civil rights) from Italy, and payment into the Treasury of a particular bribe of HS 700,000 he had taken for having a Roman knight flogged and strangled (ibid. 8, 19-22). In such a case the provincials themselves received no redress whatever, beyond such satisfaction as they might derive from observing the punishment (mild as it was); yet Pliny, counsel for the province, shows no sign of dissatisfaction. It is interesting to compare the attitude of the satirist Juvenal, who occupied a much less exalted position in Roman society: he sympathises with the province Marius had plundered because, though victorious, it could only mourn – 'At tu, victrix provincia, ploras' (*Sat*. I.45-50; cf. VIII.87-145). In another letter Pliny describes with much self-satisfaction his activities in A.D. 97, shortly before the beginning of Trajan's reign, when he began an attack on a praetorian senator, Publicius Certus. Here he makes a most illuminating remark: resentment had been felt against the senatorial order 'because, although severe against others, the Senate spared senators alone, *as if by mutual connivance*' ('dissimulatione quasi mutua': *Ep*. IX.xiii.21). His claim to have freed the Senate from this invidious position by his attack on the not very important Certus is of course a ludicrous exaggeration. But not even a 'good emperor' like Trajan, whose relations with the Senate were particularly cordial, could allow unlimited plundering by a proconsul like Marius Priscus – or Caecilius Classicus, who governed Baetica, also in 97-8, and had boasted in a letter to his girl-friend (*amicula*) at Rome of having made a cool HS 4 million profit by 'selling' provincials: in his own words, read out by Pliny, *parte vendita Baeticorum* (*Ep*. III.ix.13). Such unabashed rapacity will make any reader of Machiavelli's *Discourses on the First Decade of Livy* remember the passage that stresses the desirability of having a single ruler, responsible for the whole State, to restrain the depredations of Machiavelli's over-mighty *gentiluomini*, who so often remind us of the Roman upper classes (cf. III.iii above and its n.6 below):

> Where the material is so corrupt laws do not suffice to keep it in hand; it is necessary to have, besides laws, a superior force, such as appertains to a monarch, who has such absolute and overwhelming power that he can restrain excesses due to ambition and the corrupt practices of the powerful (I.55).

I am not suggesting Domitian's reputation as a 'bad emperor' was due in any important way to a refusal to allow senatorial governors to plunder their provinces, or that it was a characteristic of 'bad emperors' to be exceptionally solicitous for the welfare of their provincial subjects, although I feel that any such courses of action by an emperor would be likely to contribute to his achieving that reputation.

I have represented the emperor's role as being above all the reinforcement of the whole social and political system and making it a stronger and more efficient instrument for the exploitation of the great majority. There is no inconsistency between this and the approving reference I have just made to Machiavelli. It was very necessary for the emperors to repress *individuals* who greatly overstepped the mark and indulged in acts which, if allowed to continue and spread, might disturb and endanger the whole system. Even slaves could receive some legal protection against intolerable treatment, sometimes for the express reason that this was ultimately *in the interests of masters* collectively (see VII.iii below and its nn.6-7). Similarly, an emperor could express solicitude for taxpayers on the ground that they needed to be protected against greedy officials, *in order to be able to pay their taxes in full* (see e.g. *Nov.J.* VIII, esp. *praef., pr.,* 1; cf. my SVP 47-8).

I shall mention only one or two examples of the many imperial pronouncements we happen to know which seek to protect the poor and weak against oppression by the rich and powerful. In the fourth century we find the post of *defensor* (sometimes *defensor civitatis*, or *defensor plebis*), which from early in the joint reign of Valentinian I and Valens at least (*c.* 368 ff.) was intended to afford protection to the ordinary provincial, although of course it largely failed to fulfil its intended function.[30] The *Third Novel* of the Emperor Majorian, in 458, is an interesting belated attempt to restore the importance and usefulness of the *defensores*. And I may recall what I have said earlier about a series of ineffectual attempts made by the emperors to abolish or restrict certain forms of rural patronage (see IV.ii above, *ad fin.*; and, briefly, my SVP 45 and n.2). Now it has been said that the earliest surviving enactment in which an emperor is known to have denounced the oppressive patronage rights exercised by the *potentiores* (the 'over-powerful') is a constitution, *CJ* II.xiii.1.*pr.,* of the Emperor Claudius II Gothicus (A.D. 268-70).[31] However, we must not infer from this that the great men did not begin seriously to abuse their power until the mid-third century. All we have a right to say is that the activities of the *potentiores* were not felt *by the government* as a serious threat until the central power was greatly weakened in the second quarter of the third century by a new wave of 'barbarian' invasions and civil wars (cf. VIII.iii below and my SVP 44). I mentioned in Section v of this chapter the passage in which Sallust speaks of a neighbouring *potentior* driving off the land the parents or children of a peasant absent on military service during the Late Republic (*BJ* 41.8); and there are other references from the Late Republic and Early Principate to actual or potential oppression of the poor and humble by *potentes, potentiores* or *praevalidi*.[32] Numerous examples of imperial rescripts, responding to specific complaints of maltreatment, survive from long before 268 (see e.g. Millar, *ERW* 240-52). For the sinister role of the *potentiores* in the Later Empire, see VIII.iv and its n.43 below. I must add that some of the Christian churches which were great landlords, especially of course the Church of Rome (see IV.iii and its n.47), might figure prominently among the *potentiores*: unless restrained by their bishop, they could probably ill-treat their tenants more or less as they pleased (see the end of IV.ii above).

* * * * * *

The position of the Emperor has been conceived in very different ways in modern times, and indeed there were basic contradictions at the very heart of the official version of it. I shall begin by summarising what are to a considerable degree the opinions of Jones (*LRE* I.321-6) – which are all the more striking in that they refer particularly to the Later Empire. The emperor was (1) the direct successor of a line of elected Republican magistrates; (2) his very sovereignty was derived (it was said) from a voluntary surrender to him by the People of their own sovereign power; (3) if he were to be more than a mere usurper, a 'tyrant', his assumption of power had to be approved by at least Senate and Army; (4) his position did not pass automatically by hereditary succession; and (5) above all, perhaps, he was expected to submit himself to the laws. The Greeks had always proudly contrasted their own freedom with the 'slavery' (as they conceived it) to the Great King of all members of the Persian empire, including even the satraps – who might well have been astonished, I suspect, at being so described. When the satisfied Roman or Greek depicted his own position, he might characterise it as a middle status between the slavery of the Persian to his king and the lawless licence of the German 'barbarian'. Pope Gregory the Great distinguished 'barbarian kings' (*reges gentium*) from Roman emperors in that the former were masters of slaves, the latter of free men (*Ep.* XI.4; XIII.34).[33]

That is the brighter side of the picture. I shall maintain that in reality it is deeply misleading. My own position is much nearer to that of Mommsen: I am not referring to his much-quoted but unhelpful notion of a 'dyarchy' between Princeps and Senate, but to his description of the Principate as 'autocracy tempered by legally permanent revolution, not only in practice but also in theory' (*Röm. Staatsr.* II³.ii.1133).[34] Against each of the five elements I have mentioned there were factors operating in an opposite direction, which I shall describe, and illustrate mainly from Greek authors, in the sense of men originating in the Greek East, whether they wrote in Greek or – like the historian Ammianus Marcellinus and the poet Claudian – in Latin.[35]

(1) For some two centuries, from Augustus onwards, the conception of the Princeps as the heir of the Republican magistrate may have had some faint shadow of reality, but by the third century – and some would say, long before that – the ancestry was far too remote for anyone to be able to take it seriously. The Princeps, although not officially numbered among the gods of the Roman state until he was dead and had been formally consecrated *divus* by the Senate (see below), already in his lifetime was credited with a kind of divinity in dedications and celebrations by many of his subjects; and from Diocletian's reign onwards he became a more remote and lofty figure, surrounded with greater pomp and approached by his subjects with the ceremony of *adoratio*, 'adoring the purple', in place of the traditional *salutatio*. (If some of the ritual reproduced that of the Persian court, the process of development was none the less an internal one.) The imperial treasury was now referred to as the *sacrae largitiones*, the imperial bedchamber as the *sacrum cubiculum*: 'sacred', in such contexts, had come to mean 'imperial'. The acceptance of Christianity by Constantine (and all his successors except Julian) meant that a firm line had to be drawn between emperor and God; but the person of the emperor, as God's vice-gerent on earth, became if anything even more sacred (see below).

Again, (2), in reality, the alleged transfer of power by the People to the Princeps was virtually a fiction from the first, for the prerogative of the People to play a formative part in the process of law-making, and its exercise of sovereign power, hardly survived the Republic and soon came to be exercised by the Senate. Certainly, according to a famous and much-quoted extract in the *Digest* from the *Institutes* of Ulpian (the great Severan lawyer who died in 223), 'whatever the Princeps decides *has the force of law*' (*legis habet vigorem*), and this is based explicitly upon the allegation that by a *lex regia* the *populus* confers on the Princeps all its own *imperium* and *potestas* (*Dig*. I.iv.1.*pr*.; repeated in *Inst.J.* I.ii.6). And Ulpian goes on to say that any pronouncement by the Princeps (the most general term is *constitutio*) in one of the recognised forms (which he specifies) is admitted to *be* law (*legem esse constat: Dig*. I.iv.1.1; repeated in *Inst.J.*, loc. cit.). Similarly, the *Digest* quotes a statement from the mid-second-century legal manual of Pomponius to the effect that 'what the Princeps himself enacts must be observed *as if it were a law*' (*pro lege: Dig*. I.ii.2.12). An interesting point is made in the *Institutes* of Gaius (of about the mid-second century): 'It has never been doubted,' says Gaius, 'that a *constitutio* of the Princeps takes *the same place as a law*' (*legis vicem*), 'since the emperor himself receives his supreme power [*imperium*] through a law' (I.5) – Ulpian's 'lex regia', of course.

In the Capitoline Museum at Rome there is the surviving portion of a famous bronze tablet, discovered (built into an altar in the Church of St. John Lateran) and displayed in the 1340s by Cola di Rienzi, which gives us our one surviving example of such a 'lex regia': this is the so-called 'Lex de imperio Vespasiani' (*ILS* 244 = *FIRA*² I.154-6, no.15 = E/J² 364; there are translations in *ARS* 149-50, no.183; Lewis and Reinhold, *RC* II.89-90, etc.). This document, of A.D. 70, has been discussed and reinterpreted again and again: I accept in all essentials the masterly analysis by P. A. Brunt, in *JRS* 67 (1977) 95-116 (with a text, 103), according to which the 'lex' conferred on Vespasian all the powers customarily voted to a Princeps, and much of it went back to the accession of Tiberius in 14. Although this enactment calls itself a 'lex' (line 29), its language is that of a resolution of the Senate, a *senatus consultum*, and evidently the essential part of its passage was its origin in the Senate, its perfunctory endorsement in the Assembly (the *comitia*) being regarded as relatively unimportant, although only that could technically make it a *lex*.[36] In a passage in the *Digest* which may be described as naïve or realistic, according to taste, the legal writer Pomponius remarks that *senatus consulta* had come to take the place of *leges*, enacted by the *comitia* or *concilium plebis*, because it was so difficult for the large number of citizens to meet together! (*Dig*. I.ii.2.9).[37] We may note Brunt's shrewd observation that the real reason why a *senatus consultum*, early in the Principate, came to be regarded as having the force of law, just like a comitial decision – and, for that matter, the opinions of authorised legal experts, the *responsa prudentium*[38] – was that it could be taken to have the authority of the Princeps behind it (Brunt, op. cit. 112).

Unfortunately the 'Lex de imperio Vespasiani' is incomplete: we lack the opening portion, and we cannot say how long this was or what it contained. But the powers it confers on the emperor are very wide, limitless indeed: see especially clause VI, lines 17-21, where the same powers are said to have been granted to Augustus and his successors. This makes it unnecessary to discuss the complicated question what is meant by various statements in the legal and literary sources to the effect that the Princeps is 'freed from the laws'. I will only say that although the 'Lex de imperio Vespasiani' specifically exempts the emperor from a certain number of laws only (lines 22-5; cf. 25-8, clause VII), and although the legal texts all seem to relate to the laws of marriage, inheritance and testament, there are statements by Dio Cassius which show that in his day (the first half of the third century) the Princeps was evidently regarded as freed from all laws (LIII.18.1-2; 28.2-3).[39] Some will say that he was 'expected' to obey the laws, subject to his right to change them; but I cannot myself attach significance to this, there being no effective sanctions to enforce any such expectation.

The last piece of 'statute law' that we know to have been voted by the Assembly (the *comitia* or *concilium plebis*) is an agrarian law of the Emperor Nerva (*Dig.* XLVII.xxi.3.1, A.D. 96-8);[40] and there is no reason to think that legislative assemblies lasted long into the second century. Electoral asemblies certainly survived much longer, into the early third century indeed, for Dio Cassius speaks of them as existing in his own day (XXXVII.28.3; LVIII.20.4), although it is clear that their role was unimportant and that from some time in the second century they had done no more than formally endorse a single list of candidates. The purely formal enactment by the *comitia* of the senatorial 'leges de imperio', although we have no positive evidence after the first century, probably continued at least as long as the electoral asemblies: both presumably died out during the half-century of general anarchy that ended only with Diocletian (see Brunt, op. cit. 108). I would suppose that the *Historia Augusta* is being merely inventive when it purports to describe an assembly in the Campus Martius (a *comitia centuriata*, therefore) on the accession of the Emperor Tacitus in 275; and in any event, the assembly is represented mainly as giving vent to acclamations (*Vita Tac.* 7.2-4). By now, and indeed two centuries earlier, the way the common people expressed their feelings was not in any sovereign Assembly but by a noisy demonstration in a place of public entertainment: the theatre or amphitheatre, or (in a city which had one) the hippodrome[41] (see V.iii above).

Even so good a historian as Norman Baynes could take seriously the role of the People in legitimising the rule of an emperor: 'The necessity for the accla-mation of the People, if the claimant to the throne is to be constituted the legitimate ruler of the Roman empire,' he says, 'lives on throughout East Roman history. Even under the Palaeologi that tradition is preserved' (*BSOE* 32-3).[42] To speak like this is to treat constitutional fiction with undue respect; and in any event the statement needs to be modified so as to refer to 'the acclamation of *even a minute fraction* of the People' – for under the Principate there soon ceased to be any democratic institutions whatever through which any significant fraction of the People could be consulted and express their will, had there been any wish to ascertain it, as of course there was not! As we saw near the end of V.iii above, a fulsome speech in praise of Rome by a Greek orator of the mid-second century, Aelius Aristeides, solemnly declared that the Roman empire was a kind of ideal democracy, because all the people had willingly surrendered their right to rule into the hands of the man best fitted to rule: the emperor (*Orat.* XXVI.60, 90, cf. 31-9). But this was merely the final corruption of political thinking, the result of a long process by which the original demo-cratic institutions of the Greek cities, and the democratic elements in the Roman constitution (such as they were), had been deliberately stamped out by the joint efforts of the rulers of the Roman world and the Greek and Roman propertied classes (see V.iii above and Appendix IV below). Much rhetoric was devoted by the emperors and their propagandists to claims that they ruled by the universal *consensus* of men (Augustus, *Res gestae* 34.1; cf. 25.2), or even of men and gods (Val. Max., *praef*.; Tac., *Hist.* I.15 etc.). Augustus' claim (*Res gestae* 34.1) that by 28/7 B.C. he had gained 'complete control of everything by the consent of everyone' had much to justify it: he certainly lived more than forty years after reaching the summit of power, and died in his bed. Later, the absurd fiction that the consent of the people had actually been given to the rule of the Princeps served only to conceal the reality and make the constitutional propriety of the regime an even more flagrant deception. Yet lip-service was repeatedly paid to it, even by those who knew its falsity. The historian Herodian, writing around the middle of the third century, could say openly near the beginning of his work that with Augustus the Roman hereditary oligarchy (*dynasteia*) became a *monarchia* (I.i.4). Yet when he is putting speeches into the mouths of new emperors, or referring to the messages of ambassadors sent by such an emperor or by the Roman Senate, he will solemnly speak of 'the Roman People' as having control of the imperial office (II.8.4; IV.15.7; VII.7.5; VIII.7.4–5).

As for (3) the need for a 'legitimate' emperor to obtain the approval of Senate and Army, it was often only a small fraction of the army whose *acclamatio* created an Augustus, a Caesar, or one who turned out to be a mere 'usurper'.[43] As Mommsen put it, 'Any armed man had the right to make anyone else, if not himself, emperor'! (*Röm. Staatsr.* II³.ii.844). It was the event only that decided between legitimacy and usurpation: an emperor demonstrated his legitimacy by successful maintenance of his power against other candidates, as became clear during the struggle for power in 68-9, in the 190s, and again and again afterwards. Magnentius (A.D. 350-3) failed to secure himself in power and is therefore remembered as a 'usurper', and an inscription set up at Rome in 352 could refer to Constantius II as the suppressor of his 'pestiferous tyranny' (*ILS* 731). But surviving milestones inscribed in Italy while it was under the control of Magnentius not only give him the title of 'Augustus' but call him 'liberator of the Roman world, restorer of liberty and the commonwealth, preserver of the soldiers and the provincials' (e.g. *ILS* 742). As late as 458 Majorian could announce to the Senate of Rome, with some truth, that he had become *imperator* 'by the judgment of your election and the decision of the most gallant army' (*Nov. Major.* I.1). The endorsement of an imperial accession by the Senate was certainly invested with great significance in the early Principate, as a mark of legitimation; and Tacitus and Dio Cassius are careful to record it on each occasion, while ignoring the subsequent proceedings in the Assembly which (as we have seen) had already come to be a pure formality. Yet there is a fine irony in the way Tacitus describes the accession of Nero in 54: 'The decisions of the Senate,' he says, 'followed the voice of the soldiers' (*Ann.* XII.69.3).[44] And in the military anarchy of the mid-third century the endorsement of a new Princeps by the Senate, now more than ever dictated by 'the voice of the soldiers', became meaningless except as a useful mark of prestige. In the fourth century, significantly, the careful Ammianus does not even bother to record the senatorial endorsements of imperial accessions, although he happens to show that the Roman Senate was decidedly averse to Julian's rise from Caesar to Augustus in 360-1, which it was powerless to arrest (XXI.x.7). But Symmachus, for whom we may say that the Senate was a way of life, must have been speaking with his tongue sadly in his cheek when on 25 February 369 he delivered a eulogy of Valentinian I, an emperor chosen by the army and meekly accepted by the Senate (see Amm. Marc. XXVI.i-ii). Symmachus actually describes the army as a *castrensis senatus*, a 'Senate under arms', and he adds, 'Let those who bear arms decide to whom the supreme command of the army is to be committed' (*Orat.* I.9). On only two or three occasions before the seventh century did the Senate itself as such create emperors, and only the last of these choices was really effective. In 238 it elected Balbienus and Pupienus, who lasted only a little more than three months before being murdered by the praetorian guard. In 275, if we can believe two unreliable sources, the army actually invited the Senate to nominate a successor to Aurelian.[45] Whether or not this is true, the man who became emperor was an elderly senator, Claudius Tacitus: he performed quite creditably for a few months but was then murdered. And in 518 the Senate – not of Rome but of Constantinople – chose Justin I; but this time the Senate was probably manoeuvred into its decision by Justin and his associates.[46] Nerva, who reigned from 96 to 98, is often regarded as the Senate's choice; but all that we can say for certain about this is that Nerva was as acceptable to the Senate as anyone.

(4) No other aspect of the Principate brings out better the extraordinary conflict in its very essence between theory and practice than the question of the succession.[47] That an emperor could not in theory guarantee the succession even of his own son was easily circumvented, by placing the designated heir in such a strong position that no one could safely challenge him. The Princeps could adopt his intended successor as his son if he had no son of his own. Augustus himself thus ensured the succession of Tiberius: on the death of Augustus in A.D. 14, an oath of allegiance was immediately taken to Tiberius, as his inevitable successor, from the consuls downwards (Tac., *Ann.* I.7.3),[48] even before Tiberius received confirmation of his position by formal votes in the Senate (id. I.11-13). This example was often followed. Within little more than a decade in the fourth century Valentinian I, by an interested choice which was far from universally approved, made his brother Valens an Augustus (364), as Ammianus puts it, 'with the consent of all, for no one ventured to oppose him' (XXVI.iv.3); Gratian was created Augustus by his father Valentinian at the age of eight, in 367 (XXVII.vi.4); and on the sudden death of Valentinian in 375 the army chiefs had his son Valentinian II declared Augustus although he was no more than four years old (XXX.x.1-5). Dynastic sentiment was easily aroused in the army in favour of the family of an emperor who, like Augustus or Constantine, had been conspicuously successful; and this sentiment could extend even to young daughters of the imperial house, from whose leadership military victories could not be expected (see Amm. XXVI.vii.10; ix.3). The dynastic principle conveniently worked equally well in favour of adopted sons: in accordance with Roman custom, they would be regarded no differently from sons who had been begotten. But there was one hidden defect in the system: a Princeps with a son of his own who was unfitted to succeed him could not very well disinherit him and adopt someone else. (I do not know of a single case in which this happened.) Not only would it have been repugnant to Roman custom; the natural son would automatically have commanded the allegiance of the army, or a large part of it, and he would have been a serious threat to any

other would-be emperor (cf. Philostr., *Vita Apollon.* V.35, ed. C. L. Kayser I.194, lines 16–25). A Commodus or a Caracalla could not be prevented from succeeding, and their respective fathers, Marcus Aurelius and Septimius Severus, could not avoid designating them as their successors.

Among our sources, two documents provide particularly good indications of senatorial attitudes to the succession: the speech Tacitus puts into the mouth of the Emperor Galba when adopting Piso in 69, and Pliny's panegyric of Trajan, delivered in 100. Tacitus makes Galba declare that he, unlike Augustus, is choosing a successor not from within his own family, but from the whole state (*Hist.* I.15); the empire is no longer something to be inherited within a single house, but selection has replaced the rule of chance that governed hereditary succession under the Julio–Claudian dynasty; and now that adoption can reveal the best man, a sort of freedom is being achieved (*loco libertatis erit quod eligi coepimus*: I.16). Pliny too appears at first to be an enthusiast for adoption, the manner in which Trajan had come to power in succession to Nerva (*Paneg.* 5.1 and 6.3 to 8.6, esp. 7.5–6). At one point he goes so far as to say that a man who is to be emperor 'ought to be chosen from among everyone' (*imperaturus omnibus eligi debet ex omnibus*: 7.6). Yet, almost at the end of the speech, he can utter a prayer that Trajan's successor will be, in the first place, a man begotten by him; only if this is denied him by Fate does Pliny contemplate his adopting, under divine guidance, some worthy man! (94.5).

The Senate's attitude to the succession could hardly be better expressed than by A. H. M. Jones:

> Senators did not go so far as to claim the right of electing the emperor, though they were insistent that they only could confer upon him his constitutional prerogatives. Their desire was that the emperor should select his successor from the whole body of the House, and be guided in that choice by its sentiments. Their objection to the hereditary succession was partly a matter of principle, but was more due to their suspicion that a prince, bred in the purple, would be less amenable to their influence and less respectful of their dignity than a man who had been brought up in the traditions of the House (*LRE* I.4–5).

Finally, and most important, (5), although the pretended subjection of the emperor to the laws was a principle to which everyone, including of course the emperor, paid lip-service, and he himself might be considered to be acting like a 'tyrant' if he broke the law to gratify his own desires, yet, as in each of the first four contexts in which I have been examining the imperial power, theory might equally bear little relation to the harsh reality. Monarchy was now an institution the Roman upper classes could not do without, and those who profited by the existing state of affairs, like the emperors themselves, were naturally tempted to idealise it. Let us remind ourselves of a statement made in A.D. 100 by Pliny the Younger (quoted in the preceding section of this chapter): 'You order us to be free: we shall be' (*Paneg.* 66.4; cf. 67.2). And when we read Pliny's claim that 'the Princeps is not above the laws, but the laws are above the Princeps' (65.1), we must not fail to note that Pliny has just given himself away by congratulating Trajan on having *voluntarily* submitted himself to 'laws which no one intended for a Princeps' (*ipse te legibus subiecisti, legibus, Caesar, quas nemo principi scripsit*, 65.1). Throughout the Principate and Later Empire we find equally naïve congratulations being offered to emperors (sometimes by themselves) because they are not despots but have *made themselves* 'subject to law'. In the early third century (according to Justinian) the Severans, Septimius and Caracalla (whom no one would count among the less autocratic emperors), had 'very often' boasted that although they were 'freed from the laws' they nevertheless 'lived by the laws' (*Inst.J*. II.xvii.8). A little later, Severus Alexander remarked sententiously that although the 'lex imperii' freed the emperor from the sanctions of law, nevertheless nothing so befitted the exercise of sovereignty as to live by the laws (*CJ* VI.xxiii.3, A.D. 232). In 348-9 Libanius expressed his enthusiasm that the Emperors Constantius II and Constans, although they were 'masters of the laws' (*kyrioi tōn nomōn*), had 'made the laws masters of themselves' (*Orat*. LIX.162).⁴⁹ As late as 429, in a constitution addressed to the praetorian prefect of Italy, the Emperor Valentinian III could say grandly that 'for an emperor to profess himself bound by the laws is a sentiment worthy of the majesty of a ruler, so much does our authority depend on that of the law; indeed, to submit our Principate to the laws is something greater than the exercise of sovereignty itself' (*CJ* I.xiv.4).⁵⁰

In a speech delivered in 385, Libanius, addressing the Emperor Theodosius I in the standard Greek way, with the traditional word for a monarch ('*Ō basileu*'), could say to him, 'Not even to you is everything permitted, for it is of the very essence of monarchy [*basileia*] that its holders are not allowed to do everything' (*Orat*. L.19). On this occasion, however, he was speaking in the most general and abstract way: he would never have dared to tell an autocrat like Theodosius that he could not carry out something specific he had a mind to do. The reality emerges clearly in another speech by Libanius, the funeral oration he wrote for Julian some time after his death in 363: Julian, he says, 'had it in his power to override the laws, if he wanted to, and ran no risk of being brought to justice and paying the penalty for it' (*Orat*. XVIII.184). The emperor 'has at the tip of his tongue the power of life and death,' says Ammianus (XXIX.i.19; cf. XVIII.iii.7); but all the historian can do is to hope that this absolute monarch will not behave arbitrarily or despotically. (He often touches on this theme: see e.g. XXIX.ii.18-19; XXX.iv.1-2.) An imperial constitution of 384-5 forbids dispute concerning any exercise of the imperial judgment, on the ground that 'it is a form of sacrilege [*sacrilegii instar*] to doubt whether he whom the emperor has chosen is worthy' (*CTh* I.vi.9 = *CJ* IX.xxix.2).⁵¹ This pronouncement may well have been evoked by a dignified protest from Symmachus, as City Prefect, about the poor quality of some of his subordinates (chosen by the emperor and not by himself) – men whom, as he tactfully put it, 'the multifarious preoccupations of Your Clemencies made it impossible to test'! (*Rel*. xvii).

As an emperor could punish, so he could also pardon, and graciously allow some 'freedom of speech'. In the second century Favorinus of Arles, the Gallic hermaphrodite who became a Greek sophist, had been accustomed to maintain, explicitly as a paradox, that he had 'quarrelled with an emperor and was nevertheless alive'; and Philostratus, recording this, compliments the emperor concerned, Hadrian, for 'quarrelling on terms of equality, ruler as he was, with a man he could have put to death' (*Vit. soph*. I.8). Ammianus tells a revealing story concerning Julian's behaviour in the 350s, while he was still only a Caesar – at this time a title indicating a junior partnership in the imperial dignity, subordinate to the Augustus, then Constantius II. Reproached for an act of clemency, Julian replied that even if his *clementia* was objectionable in the eyes of the law (*incusent iura clementiam*), it was proper for an emperor of very mild disposition to rise superior to laws other than his own (*legibus praestare ceteris decet*, XVI.v.12). Ammianus is clearly admiring Julian's conduct. And apart from punishing and pardoning according to his own will, an emperor could in practice, above all, make and unmake laws, generally or even *ad hoc*, at his own pleasure, for he was now the sole independent source of law. If I have space for only one example of an *ad hoc* alteration of the law for the ruler's personal benefit, it must be the constitution (*CJ* V.iv.23), drawn up 'in sonorous and circumlocutory Latin',[52] procured in the 520s by one of the most conservative and traditionally-minded of all the Roman and Byzantine emperors, Justinian I, while he was still only 'the power behind the throne' (of Justin I). This edict changed the Roman marriage law in a way that can have had no other object than to permit Justinian to contract an otherwise unlawful marriage with the ex-actress Theodora. Yet the emperors were if anything more clearly 'freed' from the marriage laws than from any others.[53]

I realise that some people, especially perhaps constitutional lawyers, are impressed by the notion that the emperor was in theory 'subject to the laws', and many even wish to discuss the question whether the better emperors did not really 'live by the laws', and the causes and consequences of this phenomenon. For me such questions are too unreal to merit discussion, even apart from the feeling many of us may have that some of the oppressive and cruel laws of the Roman Empire would have been more honoured in the breach than in the observance.

To sum up – an emperor was subject in reality to one sanction and one only: that of force. This of course meant that he needed to obtain the willing adherence of those whose discontent with his rule he could not simply ignore or suppress: they included mainly the highest layers of the propertied class, and perhaps some army officers below that level. An emperor might be assassinated, or he might be removed by an armed coup; and if this happened it would be claimed that he was a 'tyrant' who had received his just deserts, although of course what had made him a 'tyrant' was simply his inability to maintain his rule (see under [3] above). To provide against such contingencies the emperor had his own personal bodyguard (in addition to the praetorian guard), and he was also the supreme commander-in-chief of the Roman army – from the very first, in practice. If in the early Principate there were troops not in theory under the emperor's direct command, in Africa for instance, the municipal authorities of Lepcis Magna could think it prudent, when setting up an inscription commemorating a victorious campaign against the Gaetulians in A.D. 6 'under the military command' (*ductu*) of the proconsul of Africa, Cossus Cornelius Lentulus, to refer to the proconsul as commanding 'under the auspices of Caesar Augustus', a recognition that militarily he was the emperor's subordinate (E/J[2] 43 = AE [1940] 68). In a poem addressed to Augustus, celebrating the German victories of Tiberius and Drusus in 15 B.C., Horace had already described the men, the resources and the plans involved as the emperor's (*Od.* IV.xiv.9-13,33-4,41-52). In his *Res gestae*, of course, Augustus could speak of all the campaigns in his principate as conducted under his own auspices, and of the Roman army and fleet as 'my army' and 'my fleet' (see Wickert, PF 128-31). And the military oath (*sacramentum*) seems always to have been sworn to the reigning emperor (see below). Indeed, in a very striking phrase which he puts into the mouth of the emperor usually known to us as Pupienus (in 238), Herodian could say that the military *sacramentum* (in Greek, *stratiōtikos horkos*) was a *semnon mystērion* of Roman rule – words for which there is hardly an equivalent in English: perhaps a 'sacred talisman', 'august symbol', 'lofty secret' (VIII.vii.4). Thus the emperor was in a very real sense a 'military dictator'. But I would not myself place too much stress on the strictly military aspect of his rule, even though it was prominent in his official title in Latin of *imperator*, taken indeed as a *praenomen* by Augustus and by later emperors from Vespasian to Diocletian, who in their descriptions of themselves normally began, 'Imperator Caesar . . .' (The official Greek equivalent of *imperator* was *autokratōr*, a word far less strictly military in its connotation: see above.) My main reason for playing down the '*military* dictatorship' of the Roman emperors is that they could not afford to use their armies regularly as a means of internal control, and that when the system worked properly they did not need to, apart from suppressing an occasional revolt. The system normally had the full backing of the upper classes. As I insisted above, however much individual emperors – Tiberius, Gaius, Claudius, Nero, Domitian, Commodus, and others later – might antagonise 'the Senate' or 'the aristocracy', there was no necessary or permanent conflict between them.

As I have alluded more than once to official panegyrics delivered to emperors (normally in their presence), I should add that I agree with Alan Cameron that they are not the easiest of documents to interpret and that they need to be considered from several points of view. I particularly like Cameron's conclusion: 'What mattered more than the content was the form and execution. The panegyrist was applauded and rewarded, not, in general, for what he said, but for how he said it' (*Claudian* 36-7). This situation would have delighted Isocrates, an anti-intellectual who deeply believed in paying attention and respect to form in preference to content, and who must bear some share of responsibility for the deplorable fact that this attitude became standard in the Greek as well as the Roman world. (For Isocrates, see esp. V.ii n.53 below.) During the Hellenistic and Roman periods Greek education became ever more exclusively literary, and its crowning rewards were reserved for rhetoric.

★   ★   ★   ★   ★   ★

The modern literature on various aspects of the ideology (including the theology) of the Roman Principate is abundant, but much of it seems to me too subjective to be rewarding, above all when it is based to a considerable extent upon interpretations of iconographic evidence, especially that of coin-types. I am not referring so much to coin-*legends*: we all know that, as Charlesworth put it, 'Coins proclaim "The Loyalty of the Armies", *FIDES EXERCITUUM*, at the very time when armies are rebelling; or "The Unity of the Armies", *CONCORDIA EXERCITUUM*, when they are turning their swords against each other'! (VRE 22). I am often astonished at the confidence with which some modern scholars use coin-types to identify the policy and mentality of an emperor. Surely, we can hardly ever be certain, in the absence of other evidence (often unavailable), that a particular coin-type is even to be taken as representing the outlook of the emperor in whose name it was issued. As I shall show in a moment, there is reason to think that emperors did occasionally order particular motifs to be stressed on coins; but even then they are unlikely to have issued very detailed specifications, and it would have been left to the imperial officials who gave orders for the minting of the coins to carry out the emperor's instructions. And we do not even know who these officials were! In the vast majority of cases, I suggest, it was these men who chose the types and legends, in accordance with what they believed, rightly or wrongly, to be the emperor's wishes; and they had good reason to avoid over-subtlety. A little over twenty years ago A. H. M. Jones, in his contribution (recently reprinted) to a volume of essays dedicated to the distinguished Roman numismatist, Harold Mattingly, expressed his own scepticism:

> It is questionable whether the elaborate messages which some numismatists deduce from coin types were intended to be conveyed by them, and still more questionable whether they were generally understood. In the Middle Ages we are better informed by literary sources on the significance of pictorial representations; we know that the symbolism was simple to the point of crudity. We are hardly justified in postulating a very much greater subtlety in the average inhabitant of the Roman empire (NH 15 = RE 63).[54]

And Jones then recalls the statement by the late-sixth-century ecclesiastical historian John of Ephesus that the female figure on the solidi of the Emperor Justin II (565-578), which was in fact – although John does not say so – a personification of Constantinople, was felt to resemble the pagan goddess Aphrodite; Justin's successor Tiberius Constantine prudently substituted a cross.[55] This certainly shows how even a standard coin-type could be misunderstood.

Jones also made much of the absence of literary evidence that importance was attached to coin-types and legends (NH 14 = RE 62). This I think is right, even if we take account of a few literary passages (not noticed by Jones) that speak of an emperor's desire to strike coins expressing a particular motif. In the whole field with which I am concerned I myself know of only four such passages, although of course there may be many more. In one, Augustus issues a silver coin bearing the zodiacal sign under which he was born, that of Capricorn (Suet., *Div.Aug.* 94.12); and in another, Nero strikes coins (and orders statues) representing himself in the dress of a singer to the cithara (a *citharoedus*: Suet., *Nero* 25.2). Both these statements are confirmed by actual coins. In a third passage Constantine, according to Eusebius, orders himself to be portrayed on his solidi in an attitude of prayer, with eyes uplifted (*Vita Const.* IV.15); Eusebius adds that these coins were in general use. Now it is perfectly true that many Constantinian solidi from 324 onwards do display such a portrait; but whether Eusebius was right in supposing that the type was deliberately chosen by Constantine with pious intent is another matter, for the attitude in the portrait can be paralleled from Hellenistic times onwards, and the view has been expressed by numismatists that 'the coins were not designed to express any Christian attitude or virtue'.[56] The fourth literary passage is the continuation (not quoted by Jones) of the one from John of Ephesus to which I have referred in the preceding paragraph (*HE* III.14). The Emperor Tiberius Constantine, we are told, declared that his substitution of a cross for the female figure (representing Constantinople) which could be mistaken for Aphrodite was dictated to him in a vision – the only example, as far as I know, of divine intervention in this field, and perhaps the most useful surviving testimony to imperial concern with coin-types.[57] It is worth noticing here that in A.D. 365, according to Ammianus, the 'usurper' Procopius tried to advance his claim to the imperial throne by – among other forms of propaganda – having his gold coins circulated in Illyricum: the point stressed by Ammianus is that they 'bore his portrait' (they were *effigiati in vultum novi principis*, XXVI.vii.11). Of course the name of the aspiring emperor was inscribed on the coins as well; but from what Ammianus says we can infer that people could be expected to notice the portrait too. On the other hand, Ammianus does not trouble to record the interesting legend, *REPARATIO FEL. TEMP.*, which apparently was borne by all the gold coins of Procopius, as part (it has been suggested)[58] of his claim to connection (by marriage) with the Constantinian dynasty, which had come to an end on the death of Julian only two years earlier, and coins of which had been inscribed *FEL. TEMP. REPARATIO* from 347 onwards.

One might perhaps have expected the anonymous author of that curious little pamphlet, the *De rebus bellicis* (probably of the late 360s or early 370s), to express some views about the usefulness of coin types and legends; but although he realised that rulers did put their own portraits on their coins (which, he believed, had earlier been made of earthenware and leather as well as gold, silver and bronze!), he thought they did so merely for their own glorification and to inspire awe (I.2,3, in Thompson, *RRI* 93-4, with the English translation, 109; cf. 26-31).

The texts I have quoted show that emperors could and sometimes did personally order the striking of particular types; but in each case the type is a very obvious one, and Jones's point remains: would there ever have been an intention to convey any elaborate or subtle message; and if so, would it have been understood? And above all, as I have pointed out, we can virtually never be sure whether a particular motif should be attributed to an emperor, rather than to the unknown official responsible for issuing the coin.

* * * * * *

I have scarcely mentioned what I might call 'the theology of Roman imperial rule', a subject with which I must deal more briefly than it deserves. It is of course very relevant to the class struggle in the Roman empire, because religious reinforcement of the emperor's position could and did strengthen the whole gigantic apparatus of coercion and exploitation. This topic divides neatly into two parts: the pagan and Christian Empires. On the pagan side it is the so-called 'imperial cult' which has usually been the centre of attention.[59] (It is hard to define the expression 'imperial cult' otherwise than as the performance of acts of cult in honour of the emperors and sometimes their families:[60] this of course did involve some kind of 'religious worship', or at least the formal attribution of some kind of divinity to the person receiving cult; but what most people today would regard as the 'religious' element was often negligible.) For the benefit of those who know little of Roman history I must just mention the well-known fact that although a Roman emperor was worshipped in his lifetime at lower levels (so to speak), by provincial assemblies, cities, bodies of all kinds, and individuals, he never became an official god of the Roman state until after his death, when the Senate might or might not grant him a state cult and the title of *divus*, 'the deified'. (The course taken by the Senate would largely depend upon the attitude of the succeeding emperor.) At the other extreme from deification, a dead emperor might suffer a *damnatio memoriae*, amounting to a general condemnation of his reign, a cancellation of his acts, the destruction of his statues, and the erasure of his name from public monuments. The eventual giving or withholding of divine honours, and the confirmation or cancellation of his *acta*, represented a kind of control over the emperor's behaviour while he ruled, in so far as he took such considerations into account: I would not rate them as having much independent weight with most emperors, who would anyway be much concerned that the Senate, as the representative organ of the imperial aristocracy, should regard them favourably.

The imperial cult cannot be properly understood, at any rate in the Greek East (where it originated), without tracing it back, through the Hellenistic cults expressing gratitude to distinguished benefactors, right into the Classical period. In II.iv above I have remarked on the significance of the earliest certain case at present known to us of a cult by a Greek city of a living individual: that of Lysander at Samos in 404, a clear manifestation of political class struggle. Although of course it was kings above all who were in the best position to confer benefits, it is misleading – however convenient – to speak of the earlier cult of benefactors as '*ruler*-cult'; and it took centuries for such cult to become officially limited to one particular set of rulers: the Roman emperors. We must accept the fact that many of the earlier cults of benefactors, whether kings or not, were spontaneous expressions of gratitude. As Tarn said, in a brilliant passage:

> The cult-names of the earlier kings – Soter the Saviour, Euergetes the Benefactor – express the fact that they were worshipped for what they *did*; . . . the typical function of kingship was held to be *philanthrōpia*, helpfulness to subjects . . . The Olympians conferred no personal salvation, no hope of immortality, little spirituality; and as guardians of the higher morality they were mostly sad misfits. And one had to take so much on trust: one might believe in the power and splendour of Zeus, but one could see the power and splendour of Ptolemy. The local god could not feed you in a famine; but the king did . . . Apollo could not help the managers of his temple at Delos to get in his debts from the islands; Ptolemy, when appealed to, sent his admiral, who got them in at once. Had not then a king powers denied to a god? So at least men thought (*HC*[3] 49-55, at 53).

On the other hand, men and women also knew well that in some of their predicaments – illness in particular – what they wanted was supernatural or magical assistance: in such cases they commonly directed their prayers not to even the most powerful king but to the appropriate deity or other superhuman figure. If we feel inclined to limit our use of terms such as 'religion', 'worship', 'piety' to occasions on which the supernatural is involved, we shall agree with Arthur Darby Nock:

> The touchstone of piety in antiquity is the votive offering, made in recognition of supposed deliverance in some invisible manner from sickness or other peril. This we do not find directed to rulers dead or living (*CAH* X.481).

In A.D. 14, just before the death of Augustus, we hear that the crew and passengers of an Alexandrian ship which had just arrived at Puteoli approached the emperor in the white clothing and garlands that were appropriate for worship, burning incense to him and praising him extravagantly: 'It was through him they lived, through him they sailed the sea, through him they enjoyed their liberty and fortunes' (Suet., *Div. Aug.* 98.2). As Habicht has observed,[61] the Alexandrians were expressing their gratitude to the emperor for worldly benefits, such as being able to sail the seas and carry on trade in peace and security; in a storm, however, they would have appealed for help not to Augustus but to the Dioscuri, the twin gods often invoked by navigators in time of need.[62]

In an able article published in 1957 Nock examined possible exceptions to his statement, quoted above, and showed that the few certain cases are very special ones (DJ = *ERAW* II.833-46). His generalisation remains broadly true. Perhaps the incident that is most worth recalling here is the display of miraculous powers of healing by Vespasian at Alexandria in 70, a few months after he had been proclaimed emperor – the first of a new dynasty – by the legions of Egypt and Syria but before he had gone to Rome. His miracles, described by Tacitus, Suetonius and Dio Cassius,[63] included the healing of a blind man – with the aid of spittle, a feature shared with some of the miracles of Jesus (Jn IX.6; Mk VIII.23; cf. VII.33). Vespasian himself was a rather reluctant performer, but his staff persuaded him: as Suetonius says, Vespasian had not yet proved himself as emperor and he still lacked prestige and the capacity to inspire awe (*auctoritas et quasi maiestas quaedam*: *Vesp.* 7.2). A miracle or two might therefore be a valuable demonstration of his qualities. But he was not acting entirely by his own power: the god Sarapis had already given an indication that Vespasian could be expected to exercise miraculous gifts on his behalf, as Tacitus (*Hist.* IV.81) and Suetonius say; and according to the doctors, when consulted, Vespasian had an opportunity of demonstrating that he was the chosen human instrument of the gods.[64] (There are many other illustrations of the widespread occurrence in antiquity of events accepted as miracles: many readers may particularly enjoy the *Philopseudes* of Lucian.)[65]

As early as the third century B.C. ruler-cult had begun to be systematised and to lose much of its original spontaneity. Many Roman governors of provinces in the Greek area could aspire to receive cult – even, in Sicily, a Verres (see Section iv of this chapter). During the Principate the imperial cult was soon introduced into the West (where it had no such natural roots as in the Greek East), by the imperial government at the provincial level, and at lower levels mainly by the influence of Greeks and Greek cities.[66] Coins issued in the reign of Aurelian and later give the emperor the titles of *deus* and *dominus*, god and lord.[67] But many scholars now realise that the imperial cult is not nearly as important as it used to be thought, at any rate as a religious rather than a political phenomenon. One of the main reasons for the inflated impression of the imperial cult in the minds of at any rate those who do not know the evidence for Roman history at first hand is the supposed importance of the worship of the emperors in the persecutions of the early Christians; but this notion is quite false and is now being generally abandoned (see my *WWECP* 10, with 32-3 nn.26-34 = *SAS*, ed. Finley, 216-17; and most recently Millar, *ICP*).[67a]

I shall try here only to show how Christian thinking on the subject of the emperor's role was anticipated (as in so many other matters) by pagan conceptions. Out of a mass of small pieces of evidence – not cohering into a single whole, and often, indeed, conflicting with each other – I shall select three: two literary and one iconographic, combining to present the emperor as the viceroy on earth of the king of the gods. I have chosen these pieces because they all come from the reign of Trajan (98-117), one of the few emperors who earned the enthusiastic approval of the Senate. Earlier, in the 90s, the poet Martial could speak of the Emperor Domitian as Jupiter, or as 'our Thunderer', an epithet assimilating him to Jupiter; and another poet, Statius, could make the Sibyl invoke Domitian as a god and say that 'Jupiter orders him to rule the happy earth on his behalf'.[68] However, Domitian in his later years was an autocratic emperor, who (we are told) wished men to address him as *dominus et deus*, 'Lord (or Master) and God'.[69] Flattery which might be regarded as untypical and (if not from Statius) insincere, when addressed to Domitian, can often be accepted as spontaneous and characteristic when its object is Trajan, the *optimus princeps*. My first piece of evidence is a literary passage in Latin already referred to in Section v of this chapter: Pliny the Younger's notion of a delegation by Jupiter to Trajan of 'the task of performing his role towards the whole human race' (*Paneg.* 80.5; cf. 1.5 for Jupiter's choice of Trajan). The second is part of a speech delivered to Trajan in Greek by Dio Chrysostom (probably very close in time to Pliny's *Panegyric*), one of seven orations by Dio dealing with kingship (or tyranny or both).[70] Here we find the same basic idea as in Pliny, of a delegation of power to the ruler by the greatest of the gods – Zeus in this case, of course, and in a generalised form, referring however not to a particular ruler, or to any king whatever, but specifically to good kings, whose concern is the welfare of their subjects (I.11-12). And finally, the same conception appears in the same reign in an official monument in Italy: the 'Arch of Beneventum', commissioned by the Roman Senate as a compliment to Trajan (see *ILS* 296), and finished in the last years of his reign, between 114 and 117. I shall quote what a leading Roman archaeologist, I. A. Richmond, had to say in 1950 about the sculptures of the Arch of Trajan:

> Jupiter, the omnipotent protector of the Roman state, is shown preparing to hand his thunderbolt, the symbol of executive power, to Trajan himself. This awesome conception is not advanced at all in the form of a claim to identity with Jupiter. In the other half of the scene Trajan is shown as solemnly accompanied in his round of duties by the protector deities of the Roman state. The delegation of power is the declaration of confidence in Trajan by the supreme Deity in a fashion which presents the Roman Emperor as his vice-gerent upon earth. A claim to divine right is thus transformed into a proclamation of divine recognition.[71]

A Roman historian of the last generation from whom I have already quoted, M. P. Charlesworth (who apparently saw the object handed to Trajan by Jupiter as a globe[72] rather than a thunderbolt), also referred to the sculptures on the Arch of Beneventum as illustrating 'the father of the gods stretching out his right hand to give to Trajan the symbol of power'; and he added, 'and that act is repeated on many coin-issues. Sometimes the ruler receives the symbol of power . . . from his deified father, sometimes from Jupiter himself, but there can be no doubt that he is the chosen of the gods, sent to care for things on earth by divine *Providentia*, and he in turn exercises his *Providentia* in various ways for the good of mankind' (VRE 15-16).

This, I suggest, is the particular form of pagan imperial theology which most nearly anticipates its Christian counterpart: it is mainly for this reason that

I have noticed it here, not because it was of any great significance in its own time – I do not think it was.[72a] However, the concept of the reigning emperor as the *chosen* lieutenant of the gods, or of God, has one serious drawback, which does not apply when emperors in general are seen merely as enjoying divine *support*. In the latter case the existing emperor need only be accorded obedience so long as he is a *good* ruler (however the quality of goodness is defined), and he can be overthrown as soon as he begins to act like a tyrant, whereas acceptance of a given ruler as specifically chosen by divine will leaves no logical basis for a subsequent claim that he has ceased to rule well and therefore ought to be removed – for of course God, and even the pagan gods, must be assumed to have had foreknowledge of his behaviour when appointing him! To acclaim the emperor as the divine choice, then, means that in principle one is (if I may use the phrase) stuck with him, for good or ill. Perhaps it was partly a realisation of this that prevented the notion of divine choice of an emperor from playing any significant part in the ideology of monarchy during the Principate: it crops up occasionally, but only as one theme among many in literature and art. Far more important was the notion (incompatible in principle with divine choice, as I have shown) that the Princeps was entitled to reign only so long as he was a 'good emperor' – that is to say, so long as he was accepted by the upper classes, represented above all, of course, by the Senate. An anecdote illustrating this point of view is recorded by Dio Cassius: Trajan, when first handing the official sword of office to his praetorian prefect, unsheathed it, held it out, and said, 'Take this sword, so that you may use it for me if I rule well, but if I rule badly, against me' (LXVIII.16.1², ed. Boissevain III.203-4).[73]

The Christians, on the other hand, were committed (I shall suggest) by their own sacred Scriptures to accepting the emperor as God's chosen representative.[74] To them, of course, any form of cult of the emperor himself was impossible; nor could they continue those ingenious developments of the notion of a particular deity as the *comes* (the associate) of the emperor which arose first in the late 180s and then again from the mid-third century onwards (see Nock, EDC = *ERAW* II.653-75) – for although calling some divine being (god, hero or *daimōn*) the emperor's *comes* did not necessarily imply his subordination to the emperor, it was obviously not a practice to which the Christian God could be accommodated. It was perfectly natural that the Christians should wish to find a theological justification for the new Christian monarchy of Constantine and his successors. (I shall say nothing of possible Old Testament precedents and influences, since the Israelite conceptions of kingship were a jumble of conflicting ideas, including a strong anti-monarchical strain, deriving from the Prophets; and modern scholars have advanced extraordinarily diverse opinions about them, often constructed on the basis of a highly selective use of texts.)[75] The Christians accepted the disastrous Pauline principle that 'The powers that be are ordained of God' (Rom. XIII.1-7; Titus III.1; cf. I Pet. ii.13-17, and I Tim. ii.1-2: see my ECAPS 14 n.41). Thus, 'the union with the Christian Church, from the time of Constantine, gave the system a religious veneer, and stamped subjection as resignation to the will of God' (F. Oertel, in *CAH* XII.270). There was now every reason why the Christians should revive the idea – existing earlier, as we have just seen, in the Principate, but not then of any real importance – of a divine delegation of supreme earthly power to the monarch.

The whole structure was presented by the historian and bishop, Eusebius of Caesarea, to Constantine, who had boasted earlier of the Unconquered Sun (*sol invictus*) as his *comes* but was now perfectly prepared to abandon all such relics of paganism. Constantine was more than ready to receive such ideas: during the winter of 313-14 he had written a remarkable letter to Aelafius, almost certainly the vicar (the vice-prefect) of Africa, towards the end of which he claimed that God had, 'by his celestial will, committed the government of all earthly things' to his control (Optatus, Append. III).[76] The theology of the Christian Empire can be seen almost in its full development in the portentous address by Eusebius to Constantine, the *Triakontaëtērikos* (or *Oratio de laudibus Constantini*), probably of 336, which I mentioned at the end of V.iii above (and see its nn.62-3 below). It is a most extraordinary document. Its stupefying, inflated, verbose, bombastic rhetoric – expected at that date, on a very solemn occasion – makes it wearisome reading today, whether in Greek or in English; but it should not be missed. Anyone who has no stomach for such stuff in any quantity should at least read the passages I have cited in a note.[77] Here we find the emperor, as God's vice-gerent, invested, mortal as he is, with a supernatural aura, by no means inferior to the lofty status to which pagan emperors had aspired by accepting cult themselves or associating themselves with gods in one way or another. The Christian emperors lost none of the majesty or authority of their pagan predecessors. Indeed, the imperial power now took on a deeper theological colouring than it had ever had in the Principate. As Nock has said, 'The climax of imperial dignity was reached under Christianity' (EDC 105 = *ERAW* II.658). The Emperor Justinian, on 15 December 530, in the constitution (beginning *Deo auctore*) giving instructions for the compilation of the *Digest*, opens by referring to himself as 'governing under the authority of God the empire delivered to Us by the Celestial Majesty'.[78]

A particularly fascinating document emanating from the Later Roman Empire – now displaying many of the characteristics we associate particularly with the developed 'Byzantine Empire' – is the poem in praise of Justinian's successor, Justin II, *In laudem Iustini Augusti minoris*,[79] describing the inauguration of Justin in November 565 and written within a year or two of that event by Flavius Cresconius Corippus, who was himself present in Constantinople at the time. This is worth more than an incidental mention, especially as the poem and its author are not to be found in the patrologies or in such works as the *Oxford Classical Dictionary*[2] and the *Oxford Dictionary of the Christian Church*[2], or even – perhaps because Corippus wrote in Latin – in Dvornik's massive *Early Christian and Byzantine Political Philosophy* (mentioned near the beginning of this section). The admirable publication of the poem by Averil Cameron in 1976, with an English translation and commentary (see n.79), was an event which seems to have escaped the notice of most Greek and Roman – as opposed to Byzantine – historians. For our present purposes, the most important part of the poem (which is in four books) is the inaugural speech Corippus puts into the mouth of the new emperor (II.178-274), delivered in the presence of the full Senate (177), which immediately 'bowed down and adored the emperor, praising his pious speech' (II.276). The emperor begins by emphasising the God-given character of his rule (178-85), and he then develops an elaborate symbolism, uniting Emperor, Senate and People in a single body, while preserving of course their hierarchical order, by referring to the emperor as the head (the *caput*) of the body politic (197-200, 205, 214), the senators as its breast and arms (200-16, the *proxima membra: pectus* and *brachia*), and the mass of people (the *plebes*) as 'the feet and minor parts' (*pedes . . . et membra minora*, 216-18). A delightful touch follows, to round off the idyllic picture: the Imperial Treasury, the *fiscus*, is the belly, which 'nourishes the body' (*venter alit corpus*, 249-51). Later in the same book there is a curious and unique passage in which Corippus actually speaks of the emperor who conducts himself properly as a *deus*, a god (422-5). This passage is immediately followed by two lines (427-8) declaring that Christ has given all power to 'the lords of the earth' (the *terrarum domini*: the emperors are meant); Christ is omnipotent, and the emperor is his very image (*Ille est omnipotens, hic omnipotentis imago*). Justin was to reinforce this symbolism by his construction inside the palace of a new 'Golden Chamber' (*Chrysotriklinos*) for ceremonial use, with the emperor's throne placed beneath a mosaic of Christ enthroned,[80] thus visibly emphasising his role as God's vice-gerent – which, as we have seen, was first set out explicitly by Eusebius but was implicit in St. Paul's maxim that 'The powers that be are ordained of God'.

Thus, near the end of the period with which this book is concerned, in the second half of the sixth century (and in the seventh), there occurred, as I said near the beginning of this section, a further exaltation of the emperor. This is not difficult to explain. Greater burdens than ever were being imposed upon the Byzantines by the enormous military efforts demanded of them by Justinian and his successors, which nevertheless led to a series of disasters, culminating in the subjugation by the Persians during the first three decades of the seventh century of Mesopotamia and parts of Syria and Egypt; and although Heraclius seemed to have restored the situation by 630 (the year in which he triumphantly returned to Jerusalem the 'True Cross', now recaptured from the Persians), the greatest disasters that had ever befallen the Eastern empire were now to take place, in the form of the Arab conquests (for which see VIII.iii below). Throughout this period the rulers of the empire realised that the greatest possible amount of cohesion would be needed to survive the continuing enmity of Persia and the assaults of 'barbarians' from all directions, and they felt that their survival depended upon divine help. The emperors, through whom – if through mortals at all – God's aid might be expected to manifest itself, and who alone could unify the *Rhōmaioi* (as the Byzantines called themselves), were naturally impelled to increase their own dominance by every available means, and the upper classes had no reason to do other than assist in this process, now that their own privileged position was in grave danger from *barbaroi* on all sides. We must see the aggrandisement of the emperor as only one among many elements – political, religious, ceremonial, liturgical, iconographic and others[81] – designed to secure the cohesion of the empire and the aid of the Almighty. One very significant feature was the marked growth in the cult of icons and relics, and in particular the cult at Constantinople of the Virgin, the *Theotokos* (the Mother of God), whose robe and girdle – relics in which inestimable value and power were believed to reside – had been acquired by the city in the fifth century (see Baynes, *BSOE* 240-60) and who appears in the early seventh century as above all the principal channel of intercession with God. Her intervention was believed to have saved Constantinople from the Avars in 619 and most conspicuously on the occasion of the menacing attack by Avars and Persians in 626 (in the absence of the Emperor Heraclius), when the Virgin herself was thought to have made a personal appearance, sword in hand, in front of the church dedicated to her at Blachernae, far up the Golden Horn.[82] The emperors took their full share in this growth of piety and superstition,[83] and there seems to be no evidence that the educated, in this universally credulous age, were overborne (as some have supposed) by a wave of 'popular feeling' from below: indeed, 'the upper classes, if anything, led the way'.[84] Alan Cameron has well demonstrated how, from the late sixth century onwards and especially in the reign of Heraclius in the first half of the seventh, the Circus Factions (the Blues and the Greens) were given an increasingly important role in imperial ceremonial (*CF* 249-70, 298). We must see this as 'a very positive effort towards social integration'.[85] Similarly, the emperors 'had much to gain in terms of social control from formalising the cult of the Theotokos and transforming it into a special guarantee of safety for the city'; and we may see the whole process as 'an attempt by the governing class to impose control'[86] through the use of appropriate and meaningful ritual and symbolism. The lower classes always obediently followed the leadership of their bishops in religious matters (cf. VII.v below). Political or military revolt was anyway out of the question for them altogether, and few signs of positive recalcitrance on their part can be detected now, except for example in desertions to the Arabs by Egyptian Monophysites, embittered by the persecution they received at the hands of 'orthodox' Chalcedonians (see VIII.iii below).

In their enthusiastic reaction to the coming to power of a line of Christian emperors from Constantine onwards, Eusebius and many of his fellow-bishops saw no need to limit the delegation of divine authority on earth to a *good* emperor, as even Dio Chrysostom had done (see above), so confident were they that they could commit themselves completely to Constantine. Perhaps at first they simply took it for granted – if they thought about the matter at all – that the emperors would continue to be God's men. Their whole theory of divine choice, however, going back (as I have shown) to St. Paul, necessitated their acceptance of the monarch, if not as God's reward to them, then as the instrument of God's will, working usefully in its customarily mysterious way for their improvement through chastisement.[87] (I cannot enter here into the various arguments they devised to give themselves a free hand in strictly religious matters against emperors who in their eyes were not carrying out the will of God.) The emperors repaid their bishops' loyalty by condemning and persecuting 'heretics' and 'schismatics'; and in A.D. 545, by his *Novel* CXXXI.1, Justinian went so far as to give the force of law to the Canons of the four General Councils of the Church that had already taken place and were recognised by the Catholics as oecumenical (Nicaea, 325; Constantinople I, 381; Ephesus I, 431; Chalcedon, 451). Justinian tactfully ignored the Second Council of Ephesus, in 449, which had a hardly less good claim than some others to be regarded as oecumenical except that 'the wrong side' won: it has come to be known as the *latrocinium* or 'Robber-Synod' (cf. what I say below about the Council of Chalcedon).

How little the Christian emperors lost by accepting the new theological formulation of their position is well illustrated by a passage from the Latin military handbook written by Vegetius, probably in the late fourth century. He reveals that soldiers on recruitment swore (if I may translate literally) 'by God and Christ and the Holy Spirit, and the Emperor's Majesty, which, by God's will, ought to be beloved and venerated by the human race'; and he adds, 'For when the emperor receives the name of Augustus, faithful devotion must be given to him, *as if to a deity present in the flesh* [*tamquam praesenti et corporali deo*] . . . For the civilian or the soldier serves God when he loves faithfully him who reigns with God's authority' (II.5).

There is one other strain in the ideology of monarchy in antiquity that deserves a brief mention here, not because it is of any real importance in itself, but because some scholars have recently brought it into the foreground and have invested it with a significance which in reality it did not acquire until the high Middle Ages: I refer to the notion of the wise and good king as *nomos empsychos* (*lex animata*, 'law endowed with a soul', 'living law').[88] As early as the fourth century B.C. Xenophon had recorded the view that the good ruler was 'law endowed with the power of sight' (*blepōn nomos*, 'seeing law': *Cyrop*. VIII.i.22). Aristotle spoke of the cultivated and free man as 'a law unto himself' (*EN* IV.8, 1128ª31-2); and in the *Politics* he said that if there were a man so vastly superior to all the rest as to be beyond comparison with them, he could be likened to 'a god among men' and not subject to any law: such men indeed are 'law themselves' (III.13, 1284ª3-14; cf. 17, 1288ª15-19). The concept of the good king as *nomos empsychos* certainly emerged during the Hellenistic period, for Musonius Rufus, the Stoic philosopher of the second half of the first century of the Christian era, could refer to this notion as held by 'the men of old' (*hoi palaioi*); but the earliest certain appearance of the phrase in surviving Greek literature may be the one in Philo, *De vita Mosis* II.4 (early first century). The expression crops up only occasionally in the Principate and Later Empire, and it is absent from the *Triakontaëtērikos* of Eusebius; but it did not disappear in the Christian Empire, and we find it, for example, in the legislation of Justinian , who could speak in 537 of his own monarchy as *nomos empsychos* (*Nov.J.* CV.ii.4).[89] And now, in all seriousness, this is the direct gift of God. (Anyone who wishes to read English translations of some relevant passages in Plutarch, Musonius, 'Diotogenes' and Themistius will find them in Barker, *AC* 309-10, 365, 378.)

To the Byzantines the emperor's autocracy was, in the words of the seventh-century 'Poet Laureate' George of Pisidia, a *theostērikton kratos*, a power whose foundation is God himself (see Baynes, *BSOE* 32-5, 57-8; cf. 168-72). Such statements are not necessarily the product of anything that deserves to be dignified with the title of 'political *thought*'. Norman Baynes believed that to say 'there is no discussion of political theory' by the Byzantines is 'a misapprehension', and that 'Byzantine literature is interpenetrated by political thought, i.e. by the theory of East Roman monarchy' (*BSOE* 32). This seems to me to take the stuff too seriously. George's phrase, 'How fair a rule is monarchy with God for guide', is a representative specimen of it (ibid. 58; cf. 34-5 and n.25).

* * * * * *

When only one supreme figure remained in the Graeco-Roman world, the accretion of unchallengeable prerogatives in his hands proceeded inexorably. In the Christian Empire, apart from armed revolt, the only possible challenge to his authority that he might need to take seriously was an appeal over his head to that God whose viceroy on earth he was; and this kind of challenge was confined to religious matters. Even there, as I shall demonstrate elsewhere, an emperor who had a mind to interfere could enforce his will upon the clergy to a much greater extent, even in the doctrinal sphere, than ecclesiastical historians have generally been willing to admit. In recent years scholars have begun to bring out the powerful role played by Constantine in Church matters, first in the Donatist affair in north Africa (especially Numidia) and then in the Arian and other controversies which convulsed some of the churches of the Greek East. Fergus Millar, whose collection of useful information on the subject of communication between Roman emperors and their subjects I have referred to in this section and in II.v above, has brought out particularly well (*ERW* 584-90) the extent to which Constantine's earliest intervention in Church affairs, in the Donatist schism, was due to direct and repeated appeals made to him, especially by the Donatists. (His treatment of the Arian controversy, *ERW* 590-607, is much less satisfactory, perhaps because it illustrates unsolicited active intervention by the emperor, a theme that is less congenial to Millar.)[90] Once upon a time ecclesiastical historians could see Constantius II (337-361) as the emperor who began the 'interference' in Church affairs that led to 'Caesaro-Papism'; and this point of view is still sometimes heard. But this is due almost entirely to the fact that Constantius was not – in the eyes of those who became and remained the dominant faction[91] – a fully orthodox Catholic emperor; and 'inteference' in ecclesiastical matters, like 'persecution' (see VII.v below), merits its pejorative title, in the minds of many ecclesiastical historians even today, only when conducted by those having what they regard as heretical or schismatic tendencies[91a] – an emperor who coerced heretics or schismatics was simply helping to 'preserve the peace of the Church'. Now Constantine, converted to Christianity in his maturity, did not strongly fancy himself in the role of theologian. This emerges with particular clarity from the first document emanating from him in the Arian controversy: the long, emotional and moving letter he wrote in 324 to Alexander, the bishop of Alexandria, and Arius (given in full by Eusebius, *Vita Constant.* II.64-72), where he makes light of the super-subtle theological issues involved, treating them with great asperity as questions creating unnecessary discord which ought never to have been raised in public. Constantine was mainly prepared to let the bishops decide doctrine, but when a strong majority opinion emerged, or (as at the Council of Nicaea) seemed to him to be emerging, he was eager to support it powerfully, in pursuance of his fixed and overriding determination to secure peace and harmony,[92] and if necessary (as at Nicaea) to punish dissident clergy with exile.[93]

All subsequent emperors were brought up as Christians, and some of them had strong theological views of their own, which they were sometimes prepared to force upon the churches. Above all, since it was the emperor who decided whether, when and where to summon a 'General Council of the Church' and (a vital point) who should preside over it, an emperor who wished to do so could sometimes stack the cards decisively against ecclesiastical opponents and assert his will to a large degree even in doctrinal matters. This appears with startling clarity in the proceedings of the Council of Chalcedon in 451. Those who have innocently accepted statements in such 'standard works' as Altaner's *Patrology*, and even the first edition (1958) of the *Oxford Dictionary of the Christian Church*,[94] to the effect that it was papal legates who 'presided over the Council of Chalcedon' will need to be told that this is a gross misrepresentation of the true situation, and that in fact the Council was presided over by an extraordinarily high-powered lay commission of important imperial officials and distinguished senators (mostly *gloriosissimi*, and the rest *magnificentissimi*) appointed by the Emperor Marcian himself, who thus ensured in advance that its decisions would be in accordance with his own will and that of the influential Empress Pulcheria, both of whom happened to be orthodox. (It is precisely because the Monophysite bishops, with the single exception of Dioscurus of Alexandria, were overawed, and the Council produced a series of 'orthodox' decisions, that our ecclesiastical historians have failed to notice the way in which it had been thoroughly 'fixed' in advance.)

Emperors might sometimes deal harshly with bishops, exiling them from their sees: this practice was begun by Constantine himself. And emperors could on occasion issue rebukes to bishops who they felt were causing trouble. Not many authentic imperial replies to episcopal pretensions have been preserved. One that stands out is the letter (surviving in the *Collectio Avellana*) written by Justinian in 520, when he was not yet emperor (although already the power behind the throne), to Pope Hormisdas, politely but peremptorily ordering him to refrain from unnecessary dealings with dangerously controversial matters.[95] The last sentence reads, 'We shall not permit [*non patiemur*] a further religious controversy to be raised in our state by anyone, nor does it become Your Sanctity to listen to those who are quarrelling about superfluous questions.' In Justinian, indeed, as Ostrogorsky has well said, 'the Christian Church found a master as well as a protector, for though Christian he remained a Roman to whom the conception of any autonomy in the religious sphere was entirely alien. Popes and Patriarchs were regarded and treated as his servants. He directed the affairs of the Church as he did those of the state . . . Even in matters of belief and ritual the final decision rested with him' (*HBS*[2] 77).

Bishops, needless to say, sometimes felt obliged to oppose emperors whom they believed to be acting wrongly in theological or ecclesiastical matters. The earliest document I know in which a bishop orders an emperor not to meddle in ecclesiastical affairs (*ta ekklēsiastika*) is the letter written by the aged Bishop Ossius (Hosius) of Cordoba to Constantius II in 356, preserved by Athanasius (*Hist. Arian.* 44).[96] The emperor is warned that God has given to him the kingship but to 'us' – the bishops – the affairs of the Church; and appeal is made (for the first time in this context, I believe) to Matthew XXII.21: 'Render unto Caesar the things which are Caesar's, and unto God the things that are God's.' I cannot see this, with Frend (*EC* 165), as in any sense 'the first statement of the Western theory of the Two Swords': as far as I know, this theory was only just beginning to emerge in the works of Peter Damian in the eleventh century (*Serm.* 69; cf. *Ep.* IV.9) and did not achieve its definitive expression until the Bull, *Unam sanctam*, of Boniface VIII in 1302, where both Swords (the *temporalis* or *materialis gladius* as well as the *spiritualis*) are seen as ultimately under the control of the Church, itself ruled monarchically by the Pope. The nearest expression of opinion that I know to this in the early Christian centuries is the letter of Pope Gelasius I to the Emperor Anastasius I in 494, where the world is said to be ruled principally by the *auctoritas sacrata* of priests and the *regalis potestas*, with superiority in 'things divine' belonging to the former, above all to the bishop of Rome (*Ep.* XII, esp. 2).[97]

It was not only their spiritual patrimony, the heritage of St. Peter, which gave the bishops of Rome their extraordinary prestige and influence. In the fifth century and later they had no such powerful imperial master close at hand as had the bishops of even the greatest Eastern sees: Constantinople, Alexandria and Antioch, who sometimes had to pay a heavy price, in ecclesiastical terms, for the virtually unqualified way in which most Christian bishops had expressed their loyalty to the first Christian emperor and his successors. Strong-minded and intrepid bishops might occasionally denounce emperors for favouring those whom they themselves regarded (and who regarded them) as heretics or schismatics, sometimes employing the kind of intemperate abuse which is all too characteristic of the religious controversy of the age. The most bitter denunciations of an emperor that I have come across in the early Christian centuries are those of Constantius II in 356–61 by Lucifer, the bishop of Calaris (Cagliari in Sardinia): he ransacked the Scriptures for the most lurid parallels and images.[98] (Apposite appeals to the Old Testament, to settle an argument, could always be relied on to gratify the faithful: among many examples, see e.g. Evagrius, *HE* IV.38, p.187.17-27, ed. Bidez/Parmentier.) Lucifer, however, is not a major figure in the history of early Christianity, and I prefer to quote from the great St. Athanasius, the patriarch of Alexandria. For Athanasius, writing after the death of Constantius II, that emperor was an outright heretic (*De synod.* 1), 'the most irreligious Augustus' (12), who continued in heresy to his death (31). A few years earlier (probably in 358), while Constantius was still ruling, but in a work intended not for publication but for private circulation among the monks of Egypt, Athanasius could call him the patron of impiety and emperor of heresy (*Hist. Arian.* 45), compare him with the Pharaoh of the Exodus (30, 34, 68), and say that he tried to emulate Saul in savage cruelty (67); Constantius was 'a modern Ahab' (45, cf. 53, 68), the 'second Belshazzar of our times' (45), who made promises to heretical bishops as Herod did to the daughter of Herodias (52), and was 'more bitter than Pilate' (68); he was 'godless and unholy' (45), 'the forerunner of Antichrist' (46, 77, 80), indeed the very image of Antichrist (74). And with all this, Constantius is said to be dominated by eunuchs (38, cf. 67: Athanasius of course means Eusebius) and is allowed no mind of his own at all (69)! The fancy picture that Athanasius draws in *Historia Arianorum* 52, in which the Church makes all its own decisions and the emperor never interferes in its affairs, no doubt represents the ideal situation which the bishops would have desired – except, of course, when they needed, in crushing their rivals, to invoke the aid of 'the secular arm', a weapon they were delighted to use when it was available to them and not to their opponents. But the fantasy bore no resemblance to the reality, which has been well described by Henry Chadwick in his excellent first volume of the 'Pelican History of the Church':

> As the fourth century advanced, it became increasingly the tendency for the final decisions about church policy to be taken by the emperor, and the group in the church which at any given time swayed the course of events was very often that which succeeded in obtaining the imperial ear (*The Early Church* 132).

* * * * * *

I wish to add a very brief sketch of the sociology of the Roman upper classes during the Principate and Later Empire. With the foundation of the Principate there were important changes. 'Nobilitas' lost its importance as a kind of unofficial qualification for high office (see Section iii of this chapter), although the term 'nobilis' long continued to be used as a kind of technical term in much the same sense, for consuls and their descendants, until the Later Empire, when it apparently came to be applied to city prefects and praetorian prefects as well as ordinary consuls (but not suffect consuls) and their descendants.[99] The two 'orders' were transformed. The *ordo senatorius* was extended to include the families of senators to the second or third generation, and became a hereditary governing class; and every senator had to possess property of the value of at least (probably) HS 1,000,000 (one million sesterces).[100] Sometimes an emperor would subsidise a senatorial family which had fallen below the necessary minimum of wealth, either because of its spendthrift habits or because it was too prolific in the male line: several such imperial subsidies, running into millions of sesterces, are recorded in the early Principate;[101] and in the early sixth century, according to John Lydus, the Emperor Anastasius bestowed upon the ex-consul Paulus (son of Vibianus, a consul of 463) a gift of two thousand pounds of gold – one thousand to pay off a debt due to the honorary consul Zenodotus and another thousand for himself (*De mag.* III.48). The *ordo equester,* now greatly enlarged, became a sort of secondary nobility, although its privileges were personal and not hereditary and did not extend to the families of the men concerned. State offices, now greatly increased in number, were limited to these two classes, except that at first the emperor's freedmen (and even his slaves) might hold posts which ultimately came to be reserved for equestrians. To qualify for the highest offices one had to enter the Senatorial Order, either by being born into it or by special grant from the emperor, given in the form of permission to wear the *latus clavus,* the broad purple stripe on the *tunica,* which was the distinguishing mark of the senator, as the narrow purple stripe of the equestrian. In course of time, during the second and third centuries, senators came to be known by the honorary title of *clarissimi* (already an untechnical honorific title in the Late Republic), while equestrians, according to the dignity of the office they held, were (in ascending order) *egregii, perfectissimi* or *eminentissimi,* the last title being reserved, from the third century onwards, for the praetorian prefects, the highest equestrian officers.

By degrees the *ordo equester* became entirely a secondary aristocracy of *office,* all members of which were, or had been, holders of certain official posts. Even in the Late Republic a man had been able to describe himself loosely (as Cicero did) as 'born in equestrian status'.[102] Although an equestrian could not hand on his own rank automatically to his son, he could hand on the property which entitled the son to offer himself for equestrian posts conferring that rank – or at least, he could do so provided he did not have too many sons! (The division of a *census equestris* of precisely HS 400,000 between two brothers is amusingly dealt with in one of Martial's poems: 'Do you think two can sit on one horse?', he asks derisively, V.38.) This situation remained fairly stable until about the middle of the third century; but during the later third century and the fourth there were great changes, which I can do no more than summarise in a sentence or two. Broadly speaking, we can say that the sphere of influence of the equestrians increased greatly during the later third century, at the expense of the Senate, and provincial governorships which had formerly been reserved for senators came to be held by members of the *ordo equester*, especially those possessing military experience. However, the *ordo equester*, lacking an organ (such as the Senate) through which to make collective decisions, never acquired a corporate character or unity of purpose, but remained a collection of individuals. In the fourth century, from Diocletian and Constantine onwards, equestrian status became increasingly detached from office, because the emperors issued numerous honorary *codicilli*, granting the privileges of one or other of the several equestrian grades (which now existed separately, and not as part of a single 'equester ordo') to those who held no office. Then, during the third quarter of the fourth century, the highest of the former equestrian posts began to confer senatorial status. Thus the Senate, which by now had more than trebled in size (a separate Senate existing at Constantinople), absorbed the higher levels of the equestrian order; but this process was not completed until the last years of the fourth century or the early years of the fifth. [103]

In their own eyes and those of their toadies, the senators constituted the very summit of the human race. Nazarius, a leading rhetorician of his day, declared in a panegyric in honour of Constantine and his first two sons in 321 that Rome, the very apex of all races and the queen of lands, had attracted to her *curia* (her Senate House) the best men (*optimates viri*) from all the provinces, and the Senate now consisted of 'the flower of the whole world' (*Paneg. Lat.* X[IV].35.2). The great orator Symmachus described the Roman Senate in a letter written in 376 as 'the better part of the human race' (*pars melior humani generis: Ep.* I.52). Rutilius Namatianus, in the poem recording his journey from Rome up the west coast of Italy towards Gaul late in 417, [104] praised the Senate (whose *curia* he dignifies with the word *religiosa*) for its reception of all who are worthy to belong to it; and – pagan as he was – he compared it to the *consilium* of the *summus deus* (*De red.* I.13-18). And in the panegyric he delivered to the Western Emperor Avitus on 1 January 456, Sidonius Apollinaris could say, addressing Rome herself, 'The world has nothing better than you; you yourself have nothing better than the Senate' (*nil te mundus habet melius, nil ipsa senatu: Carm.* VII.503). It was entirely natural for St. Augustine – when he was considering 'the cause of the greatness of the Roman empire', why God should have wished that empire to be so great and so long-lasting, and attacking the astrologers – to choose the Senate, the *clarissimus senatus ac splendidissima curia*, as the most suitable simile for the starry heavens, which of course he saw as subject entirely to the will of God, much as the Senate (although he does not make the point explicitly here) was subject to the emperor (*De civ. Dei* V.i). Until the fourth century there were only about six hundred senators at any one time. The equestrians were far more numerous; but the two orders together could hardly have formed as much as one tenth of one per cent of the total population of the empire.

I cannot do better than end this section with a text that shows how powerfully people's minds were affected in the Later Roman Empire, down to the very roots, with notions of rank and hierarchy. The grades of precedence which existed in this world were projected into the next. The heavenly sphere, of course, went from the Godhead at the top, down through archangels, angels, patriarchs, apostles, saints and martyrs, to the ordinary blessed dead at the lower end. I do not think the relative positions of the middle strata were very clearly defined, but I would imagine that an archangel and even an ordinary angel, in a heavenly *ordo salutationis*, would take precedence of any mere human, except of course for the Virgin, who occupied an anomalous position, unique among females, analogous to that of an Augusta in the Roman imperial hierarchy. It is perhaps less often realised that the diabolic sphere might equally be conceived as organised in an order of rank, reproducing that of the terrestrial and the heavenly regions. I need only quote one piece of evidence for this. Palladius, writing his *Historia Lausiaca* in 419-20, records some interesting information he had received from a number of leading Egyptian monks (Cronius, Hierax and others), intimates in their youth of the great Antony, the first (or one of the first) of the Christian hermits and a man of unrivalled prestige among the early monks, who had died in 356. According to Antony, a man possessed by an authoritative demon (an *archontikon pneuma*) was once brought to him to be cured; but the holy man refused to deal with him, on the ground that 'he himself had not yet been counted worthy of power over this commanding rank' (*tagma archontikon: Hist. Laus.* xxii, ed. C. Butler, p.73.10-14). He advised that the man be taken to Paul the Simple, who eventually drove out the demon: it became a dragon 70 cubits long, and disappeared into the Red Sea. (This was a dragon larger even, perhaps, than the one disposed of, with little difficulty, by Donatus, bishop of Euroea in Epirus, for the removal of the corpse of which eight yoke of oxen were required, according to Sozomen, *HE* VII.26.1-3.) I may add that Antony, the original source of the story in the *Historia Lausiaca*, was an Egyptian peasant, who, although his family had been quite well-to-do (see Athan., *Vita Ant.* 1, 2), was illiterate and unable to speak Greek (id. 1, 16, 72, 74, 77; Pallad., *Hist. Laus.* xxi, pp.68-9). When Paul the hermit died, it was to Antony that two lions came, to dig the hermit's grave (Jerome, *Vita Pauli* 16).

VII

The Class Struggle on the Ideological Plane

(i)
Terror, and propaganda

In this chapter I propose to illustrate the way in which the class struggle was conducted on the ideological plane. For any overt expression of the point of view of the oppressed classes there is unfortunately very little evidence indeed: we shall look at some of it in Section v below. The nature of the evidence is such that we must resign ourselves to spending nearly all our time on the ideological class warfare (if I may call it that) of the dominant classes.

I shall waste little time on the simplest form of psychological propaganda, which merely teaches the governed that they have no real option anyway but to submit; this tends to be intellectually uninteresting, however effective it may have been in practice, and consists merely of the threat of force. It was particularly common, of course, in its application to slaves. 'You will not restrain that scum except by terror,' said the Roman lawyer, Gaius Cassius, to the nervous senators during the debate on whether there should be the traditional mass execution of all the 400 urban slaves of Pedanius Secundus, the Praefectus Urbi, who had been murdered by one of his slaves in A.D. 61. The execution was duly carried out, in spite of a vigorous protest by the common people of Rome, who demonstrated violently for the relaxation of the savage ancient rule (Tac., *Ann.* XIV.42-5) – which, by the way, was still the law in the legislation of the Christian Emperor Justinian five centuries later.[1] In Pliny's letters we hear of the similar murder in the first years of the second century of the ex-praetor Larcius Macedo (*Ep.* III.xiv.1-5). The slaves were quickly executed. Pliny's comments are worth quoting, especially since he describes Macedo (himself the son of a freedman) as 'an overbearing and cruel master' (§ 1). 'You see,' he says nervously (§ 5), 'how many dangers, insults and mockeries we are liable to. No master can be safe because he is indulgent and kindly, for masters perish not by the exercise of their slaves' reasoning faculty but because of their wickedness' (*non iudicio . . . sed scelere*). There are other indications in the literature of the Principate that slaveowners lived in perpetual fear of their slaves (see e.g. Griffin, *Seneca* 267, citing Sen., *De clem.* I.xxiv.1 etc.). The latest literary reference I have come across to masters' fear of being murdered and robbed by their slaves is in one of St. Augustine's sermons, in the early fifth century (*Serm.* CXIII.4, in *MPL* XXXVIII.650). Slave revolts, of course, were mercilessly punished: we hear from Appian (*BC* I.120) of the crucifixion of the six thousand captured followers of Spartacus along the Via Appia from Rome to Capua, on the suppression of the great revolt of B.C. 73-71. To avoid such a fate, rebellious slaves often either fought to the death or killed each other.[2] In case it is objected, quite rightly, that such cruelties were Roman rather than Greek, let me emphasise the way in which the Greek geographer Strabo deals with the Spanish Celtiberians, who, on being captured and crucified by the Romans, still *epaiōnizon*, went on shouting for victory from the cross: this, to Strabo, was merely another proof of their *aponoia* and *agriotēs*, their senselessness and savagery (III.iv.18, p.165). However, I must admit that Strabo's mind had been thoroughly infected with admiration of Roman imperialism (see e.g. VI.iv.2 *fin.*, p.288; XVII.iii.24 *init.*, p.839). The passage I have just quoted reminds one of another, in Sallust, where the admitted heroism and steadfastness of the revolutionaries who followed Catiline to their deaths in 63 B.C. is seen only as evidence of their pig-headedness and their urge to destroy both themselves and the state, amounting to 'a disease like a plague which had usurped the minds of most citizens' (*Cat.* 36.4-5).

The Greeks, among whom sheer cold-blooded cruelty towards the victims of their civilisation – slaves, criminals, and conquered peoples – was on the whole much less pronounced than among the Romans, naturally acquired many of the characteristics of their Roman masters, including even a taste for gladiatorial displays, which are known to have occurred in the Greek East from at least 70 B.C.,[2a] when the Roman general Lucullus provided such combats on a great scale; they were subsequently presented by Greek notables who could afford the expense, and they became very popular.[3] Even female gladiators appeared. Louis Robert's bitter comment is very apt: 'La société grecque a été gangrenée par cette maladie venue de Rome. C'est un des succès de la romanisation du monde grec.' Mommsen wrote with equal detestation of this 'abominable entertainment', describing it as a 'cancerous affliction'.[4]

In matters where evidence lasting over thousands of years is available from many different human societies, it is often very dangerous to generalise; but at least it seems to be true of many slave societies that ruthless treatment of the slave (if only as a last resort, and combined with rewards for the obedient and faithful slave) is most likely to maintain that institution in being and make it serve its purpose best. There is more than a little truth in the remark of the ex-slave Frederick Douglass, 'Beat and cuff your slave, keep him hungry and spiritless, and he will follow the chain of his master like a dog; but feed and clothe him well, – work him moderately – surround him with physical comfort, – and dreams of freedom intrude. Give him a *bad* master, and he aspires to a good master: give him a good master, and he wishes to become his *own* master' (see Stampp, *PI* 89). On the other hand, it has recently been claimed (if, as some have plausibly argued, with much exaggeration) that even in the American Old South the slaveowners relied very much upon incentives and rewards, as well as punishment (Fogel and Engerman, *TC* 41, 147-53, 239-42; cf. 228-32) – and yet they made far less use than the Greeks and Romans of what one might think to be the supreme incentive to the slave to obey his master's wishes: manumission (ibid. 150-1). Genovese's just appraisal of the evidence for American slave revolts – which is surprisingly scanty – and other forms of resistance has well shown how slaves may in certain circumstances be induced to accommodate themselves in some degree to the system that exploits them (*RJR* 587-660, esp. 587-98, 613-21, 648-57). And of course slaves who are allowed to rear families thereby become subject to one of the most telling forms of control which a master can have over them: the threat of breaking up the family (see III.iv above, § II).

A more sophisticated form of ideological class struggle was the attempt of the dominant classes to persuade those they exploited to accept their oppressed condition without protest, if possible even to rejoice in it. According to Aristoxenus of Tarentum, a pupil of Aristotle, it was laid down by the Pythagorean school that just as rulers ought to be humane, *philanthrōpoi*, as well as versed in the science of ruling, so ideally their subjects ought not only to obey them but to like them – to be *philarchontes*.[5] Another interesting word which is by no means uncommon is *philodespotos*, 'master-loving'. In the Archaic age the aristocratic poet Theognis believed that if you kick the 'empty-headed *dēmos*' (the mass of the people) hard enough you can reduce it to that desirable condition (lines 847-50; cf. V.i above and its n.16). A Syrian public slave at Sparta in the Roman period could even be given the name Philodespotos.[6] 'An essential function of the ideology of a ruling class is to present to itself and to those it rules a coherent world view that is sufficiently flexible, comprehensive and mediatory to convince the subordinate classes of the justice of its hegemony.'[7] Governing classes have often been successful in achieving this aim. As Rodney Hilton has said, 'For the most part, in so far as one has evidence at all, the ruling ideas of medieval peasants seem to have been the ideas of the rulers of society as transmitted to them in innumerable sermons about the duties and the characteristic sins of the various orders of society' (*EPLMA* 16). Those who disapprove of the techniques I am referring to may call them 'brainwashing'; those who employ them will reject such terms with righteous indignation and may prefer to speak of a process of enlightenment by which those who serve the community in a humble capacity are enabled to achieve a more profound understanding of social reality. Those of us who teach in universities often think in such terms, for a university, in a class society like ours, is among other things a place where the governing class seeks to propagate and perpetuate its ideology.

The most common form of the type of propaganda we are considering is that which seeks to persuade the poor that they are not really fitted to rule and that this is much better left to their 'betters' ('the best people', *hoi beltistoi*, as Greek gentlemen liked to call themselves): those who have been *trained* for the job and have the *leisure* to devote themselves thoroughly to it. In the ancient Greek world this demand is sometimes made quite unashamedly on behalf of the propertied class as such.[8] Sometimes it is limited to an even smaller circle: of this tendency there are two outstanding examples. First, there is the claim made by aristocrats that the essential qualification for ruling is noble birth (of which property is of course an inevitable accompaniment: see II.iv and its n.5). Of this kind of mentality we have already noted some examples, from Theognis in particular (see V.i above). Secondly, when government by a *dynasteia* of one or more well-born families had become almost extinct over a large part of the Greek world, we begin to find the assertion, familiar to everyone from Plato above all, that ruling should be the prerogative of those who have the right kind of intellectual equipment and have received a proper philosophical education. In practice, needless to say, virtually all such men would be members of the propertied class. Plato would no doubt have denied, as many of his modern admirers have done, that he was advocating oligarchy according to the normal meaning of that term (which he knew very well; cf. II.iv above); but this is true only in the sense that he did not wish access to political power to be given to the *whole* propertied class *as such*. (In *Laws* V.742e; 743a-c he first declares, in a rather qualified way, that a man cannot be both good and very rich, and then goes on to say explicitly that anyone who is outstandingly rich cannot be outstandingly good, and cannot be happy either! Plato himself, of course, was not one of the richest Athenians.) In fact Plato would have entrusted all political power to those men who were in his opinion intellectually qualified for ruling and had received a full philosophical education – and such men would necessarily have to belong to the propertied class. For Plato, any kind of work that interfered with the leisure necessary for the practice of the art of government was a disqualification for membership of his governing class: this is true both of the ideal state pictured in the *Republic* and of the 'second-best' state described in the *Laws*, and also of the more theoretical discussion of the art of ruling in the *Politicus* (or *Statesman*).⁹ The notion that manual work, because it 'weakens the body' (as Greek gentlemen evidently supposed), therefore *weakens* the mind, may have been a commonplace of the Socratic circle: it is very clearly expressed in Xenophon, *Oecon.* IV.2, and there is no reason to think that it was invented by Plato. But Plato has this conception in an intensified form: for him, manual work can actively *degrade* the mind. This comes out very well in a fascinating passage in the *Republic* (VI.495c-6a), describing the fearful consequences which are likely to follow if 'unworthy interlopers' meddle with such high affairs as philosophy – and therefore government, reserved by Plato for gentlemen philosophers. Unpleasant as it is from beginning to end, this is a dazzling piece of invective. Plato thinks it deplorable

> when any poor creature who has proved his cleverness in some mechanical craft sees here an opening for a pretentious display of high-sounding words and is glad to break out of the prison of his paltry trade and take sanctuary in the shrine of philosophy. For as compared with other occupations, philosophy, even in its present case, still enjoys a higher prestige, enough to attract a multitude of stunted natures, whose souls a life of drudgery has warped and maimed no less surely than their sedentary crafts have disfigured their bodies. For all the world they are like some bald-headed little tinker (*chalkeus phalakros kai smikros*), who, having come into some money, has just got out of prison, had a good wash at the baths, and dressed himself up as a bridegroom, ready to marry his master's daughter, who has been left poor and friendless. Could the issue of such a match ever be anything but contemptible bastards? And, by the same token, what sort of ideas and opinions will be begotten of the misalliance of Philosophy with men incapable of culture? Not any true-born child of wisdom; the only right name for them will be sophistry. (I have made use of Cornford's translation.)

It was of course the development of Greek democracy, especially in its Athenian form, where it depended very much on 'bald-headed little tinkers' and their like, that impelled Plato, an arch-enemy of democracy, to launch this tirade against the sort of person on whom it was so dependent. But Plato was well aware of the realities of the political class struggle of his own day: he knew only too well that (as he says in the *Republic*, IV.422e-3a) there was in each Greek city a basic division into two groups, hostile (*polemia*) to each other: the one of the poor, the other of the rich (cf. II.iv above). The two states he depicts in the *Republic* and the *Laws* were both designed, among other ends, to overcome this fundamental disunity.

The physical defects Plato attributes to his tinker remind one irresistibly of the earliest portrait which we have in Greek, and perhaps in any language, of the popular 'agitator': that of Thersites, who dares to speak out against King Agamemnon in the assembly of the Greek army besieging Troy, in Book II of the *Iliad* (lines 211-78). Thersites is all for sailing home and leaving Agamemnon and his noble friends to find out for themselves how dependent they really are on the rank and file; and he makes great play with the large share of spoils, in gold and bronze and women, that the king receives from the host. But Homer is not at all on his side; he represents the bulk of the army (*hē plēthus*, line 278) as disapproving strongly of his seditious speech and as breaking into applause and laughter when the great Odysseus thumps him on the back and shoulders with his golden sceptre and makes him subside weeping into his seat (lines 265-78). And Homer has carefully caricatured this proto-demagogue: he describes Thersites not merely as 'an irrepressible man who, when he felt inclined to bait his royal masters, was never at a loss for some vulgar quip, empty and scurrilous indeed, but well calculated to amuse the troops', but also as 'the ugliest man that had come to Troy; he had a game foot and was bandy-legged; his rounded shoulders almost met across his chest, and above them rose an egg-shaped head, which sprouted a few short hairs'. (I have used Rieu's translation of lines 212-19.) I might add that the aristocratic society for which the Homeric poems were composed would have regarded Odysseus' brutal treatment of Thersites as perfectly right and proper, and characteristic of a great man. A little earlier in the same book of the *Iliad* (II.188-206) we find the same hero's courteous behaviour to chieftains and leading men contrasted with his violence and contumely towards commoners ('men of the *dēmos*') who ventured to take independent action: such men he bludgeoned and abused, admonishing them to shut up and defer to their betters. The speech Homer gives him ends with the famous words, 'A multitude of chieftains is no good thing; let there be one lord, one ruler' (lines 204-5).

There is much other material of this kind which I wish I had space to quote, notably from Aristophanes (cf. my *OPW* 355 ff.). There is even a passage in Jewish literature which, under the influence of Hellenistic thought, asserts – in terms which would have warmed the hearts of Plato and Aristotle – that only the man who has leisure can achieve wisdom; the agricultural worker, the carpenter, the seal-maker, the smith and the potter, whose pursuits are admittedly essential for civilised life, are unfit to participate in public deliberation or exercise judicial functions. The whole passage, Ecclus. XXXVIII.24-34, is well worth reading.

I shall content myself with just two more pieces of anti-democratic propaganda. The first, a very abstruse and rarefied type of argument, was developed out of the mathematical and musical theories of Archytas of Tarentum, a Pythagorean of the first half of the fourth century B.C., who seems to have been the first to develop, in a work on music, the notion of three different kinds of proportion, two of which, the arithmetical and the geometric, are material for our purposes, arithmetical proportion being represented by the progression 2, 4, 6, 8, and geometric by 2, 4, 8, 16. It may well have been Archytas himself, rather than Plato, who first applied the notion of distinct arithmetical and geometric proportion to politics: it certainly appears with this application in Plato and Aristotle, and also (in a debased form, as we might expect) in Isocrates; and there are echoes of it in later times, down to at least the twelfth century. The whole subject is a very difficult one, but it has been illuminated by a most penetrating recent article by David Harvey,[10] whose interpretation I fully accept. I cannot do better than summarise his account, which explains very well how arithmetical proportion was alleged by anti-democrats to be 'a paradigm of a democracy; the geometric, of a 'better' form of constitution'. The equality exalted by democracy was said to be a kind of arithmetical proportion in which each number (representing a man) stands at an equal distance from its neighbour (2, 4, 6, 8, etc.). But this, it was claimed, fails to take account of the real value of each number (each man) and therefore introduces flagrant inequality, for the higher up the scale, the smaller the ratio at each step; hence, in political terms, the better the man, the less his worth is rewarded. Geometric proportion, which is not employed by democracy, is much fairer, in that the ratio at each step up the scale (2, 4, 8, 16 etc.) always remains the same; hence, in political terms, what each man receives is always equal to his worth.

I am afraid that the theory stated thus baldly and without the complicated intellectual scaffolding which surrounds it in Plato and Aristotle looks even feebler than it really is; but Harvey is certainly right in his judgment that the whole construction is essentially a subtle attempt to avoid an honest statement of the real oligarchic belief that 'Inequality is a splendid thing', by substituting a statement of the form, 'Inequality is true equality'. So flawed is the very basis of the argument that I do not think it is unfair to quote an unintentionally comic version of it in Plutarch (*Mor.* 719bc = *Quaest. conviv.* VIII.ii.2):

> Lycurgus expelled from Sparta arithmetical proportion, as being democratic and favourable to the rabble (*ochlikos*), and introduced geometric proportion, which is suited to sober oligarchy and law-abiding kingship. For the former distributes equality in numbers, while the latter distributes what a man deserves, by proportion; it does not mix up everything together, but it makes a clear distinction between good men and bad; . . . they get what befits them in accordance with how much they differ in virtue and vice. God applies this proportion to things: it is called Justice and Nemesis . . . God nullifies as far as possible the equality which the majority pursue, which is the greatest of all injustice, but he preserves that which is in accordance with worth, defining it geometrically, according to law and reason.

No one acquainted with Cicero's writings on political theory, which owe much to Plato, will be surprised to find reflections of the theory which we have just been discussing in his *De republica* (I.43, 53; II.39-40), where, as Elaine Fantham has put it, the 'moralistic language only thinly veils the fact that Cicero is approving a constitutional device to give political power to the wealthy in proportion to their wealth – no surprise perhaps in view of his respect for property and those dignified by its ownership in actual political life'.[11]

My other specimen of anti-democratic propaganda, which must come from the very end of the fifth century or the beginning of the fourth, is a brilliant little piece of pamphleteering which came to the notice of Xenophon and was inserted by him in his *Memorabilia* (I.ii.40-6). I think this is one of the best anti-democratic arguments produced in antiquity – better, anyway, than anything in Plato. Its thesis is that when the mass of the common people (*to plēthos*) enacts decrees by majority decision, against the will of the propertied class (they are specifically *hoi ta chrēmata echontes*), it is simply acting like a tyrant, and its decrees are not *nomos*, law, but *bia*: force, coercion, violence, often presented in Greek thought as the very opposite of law (see e.g. Xen., *Cyrop.* I.iii.17). Decision by majority vote, a method which in the eyes of Greek democrats (perhaps the first inventors of it: see my *OPW* 348-9) evidently had a peculiar sanctity, is treated as not different in kind, when it involves the coercion of a propertied minority, from the coercion of the majority by the Few or by a tyrant. In this little dialogue Pericles, the great democrat, is made to look a fool by the young freelance aristocrat, Alciabiades – who, in the speech Thucydides puts into his mouth at Sparta (VI.89.3-6), describes democracy as 'an acknow-ledged folly'. I have translated this passage as literally as possible.

> They say that Alcibiades, when he was less than twenty years old, had a con-versation about laws with his guardian, Pericles, the leading man of the city.
> 'Tell me, Pericles,' he said: 'can you explain to me what a law is?'
> 'Certainly I can,' replied Pericles.
> 'Then explain to me, do. For whenever I hear people being praised for being law-abiding citizens, I think that no one can really earn that praise who doesn't know what a law is.'
> 'There's no particular difficulty about your wanting to know what a law is, Alci-biades. Laws are what the mass of the citizens decree, meeting together and taking counsel, and declaring what can be done and what can't.'
> 'Do they think one ought to do good or evil?'
> 'Good, of course, my boy, not evil.'
> 'But . . . if it's not the masses, but a few, as happens under an oligarchy, who come together and enact what is to be done – what do you call that?'
> 'Everything the sovereign power in the city decrees to be done, after taking counsel, is called a law.'
> 'Even if . . . a tyrant who rules the city makes decrees for the citizens – is that a law too?'
> 'Yes, whatever a tyrant as ruler enacts, even that is called a law.'
> 'But . . . coercion (*bia*) and the negation of law – what is that, Pericles? Isn't it when the stronger compels the weaker to do what he wants, not by persuasion, but by force?'
> 'Yes, I suppose so,' said Pericles.
> 'Then whatever a tyrant compels the citizens to do by decree, without persuading them, is the negation of law?'
> 'Yes, I agree,' said Pericles. 'I take back what I said, that everything a tyrant decrees without persuasion is a law.' (Of course he is done for now: having incautiously allowed himself to be led *up* the garden path he is going to be led *down* it again, to his own confusion.) Alcibiades goes on,
> 'But when the Few make decrees, using not persuasion but force – are we to call that coercion or not?'
> 'I should say,' replied Pericles (he has evidently not seen the red light even yet), 'that whatever anyone compels anyone else to do, whether by decree or otherwise, without persuasion, is coercion rather than law.'
> 'Then . . . everything the masses decree, not persuading the owners of property but compelling them,[12] would not be law, but coercion?'
> 'Let me tell you, Alcibiades,' said Pericles, 'when I was your age I too was very clever at this sort of thing; for I used to think and talk about the very things you now seem to be interested in.'
> 'Ah, Pericles,' said Alcibiades, 'if only I had known you when you were at your very cleverest in such matters!'

The techniques of psychological class warfare which I have been describing – far from crude as they are – become even more subtle and interesting when we find the governing and exploiting class seeking to persuade not merely the exploited classes but also itself that its dominance is both justified in principle and benevolent in practice. Let us briefly consider, then, some of the ways in which the Greek (and Roman) magnates salved their consciences and avoided those feelings of guilt which can sometimes afflict even the most complacent Dives when he sees Lazarus hungrily eyeing the crumbs that have fallen from his sumptuous table. The theory of 'natural slavery' is the perfect example of this kind of thing.

(ii)
The theory of 'natural slavery'

I begin with two kindred themes: the distinction between Greek and 'barbarian', and the ideology of slavery. Early in Greek history we encounter the dichotomy of the human race into Hellenes and *barbaroi* – strictly, Greeks and non-Greeks, but I shall sometimes use the term 'barbarian' as the translation of the corresponding Greek and Latin words, as it is so convenient in practice, if often technically incorrect.

Plato, like the vast majority of his contemporaries, took it for granted that it was right and proper for Greeks to enslave 'barbarians', whom he calls their 'natural enemies'.[1] In the funeral oration which he puts into the mouth of Aspasia (a parody of the standard Athenian speech delivered on such an occasion), he makes her say that war against fellow-Greeks should be pursued 'until victory', but against barbarians 'to the death' (*mechri nikēs, mechri diaphthoras, Menex.* 242d). He also believed that all those whom he describes as 'wallowing in great ignorance and baseness' *ought* to be reduced to a condition of *douleia*[2] – the standard Greek word for 'slavery', which in this context may mean either that or merely 'complete political subjection'. Those who are not inhabited by divine wisdom, he thought, are actually better off when controlled by those who are (*Rep.* IX.590cd). As Vlastos demonstrated more than thirty years ago in a brilliant article,[3] slavery exercised a profound influence on some of Plato's basic philosophical concepts. Although Plato never explicitly formulated the doctrine of 'natural slavery', it is implicit in his thinking (as Vlastos again has shown);[4] but the earliest surviving writer to give a formal statement of it is Aristotle, whose discussion of the question is by no means as clear as could be desired.[5]

Aristotle, for whom the slave is essentially an 'animate tool' (*empsychon organon*: see II.iii above and its n.12), says most explicitly that some men are slaves by nature,[6] although he has to admit that not all those who are in practice slaves or free men are by nature slave or free respectively.[7] For the 'slave by nature' he thinks it is *better* that he be subjected to a master; for such a man slavery is both beneficial and just.[8] He does not actually say that all barbarians are slaves by nature, but he quotes current Greek opinions to that effect without expressing disapproval.[9] We can certainly say that in Aristotle's view 'barbarians are slaves by nature', provided we remember that for him what is according to nature is not necessarily what occurs in every case: 'it is what occurs *as a general rule (epi to poly)* that is most in accord with the course of nature', as he himself puts it in one of his great zoological works.[10] And in Book VII of the *Politics,* after prescribing for the lands of the Greek proprietors in his ideal state to be tilled by slaves (who are evidently conceived as barbarians), he goes on to suggest as an inferior alternative the use of barbarian *perioikoi*[11] – that is to say, men who would not be actual slaves (though they might be what I have called serfs), but who would certainly not enjoy any of the rights of citizenship in his *polis* (cf. III.iv above and its nn.49-52 below).

The essence of the views held by Plato and Aristotle on 'natural slavery' was nicely expressed, more vividly than by either of them, in a book by the Virginia slaveowner, George Fitzhugh, published in 1854: 'Some men are born with saddles on their backs, and others booted and spurred to ride them; *and the riding does them good*'![12] (Fitzhugh must have been quoting, and contradicting, some famous words spoken on the scaffold in 1685 by the English radical, Richard Rumbold.)[13] His book, bearing the title (remarkable at that date) of *Sociology for the South, or the Failure of Free Society*, is perhaps the best of the ripostes by the slaveowners of the Old South against what seemed to them the more impersonal and inhuman treatment by the Northern farm owners of their hired labourers. ('Slaves,' Fitzhugh maintained, 'never die of hunger; seldom suffer want.') In his Preface, after apologising for having employed in his title 'the newly-coined word Sociology', he continues, 'We could, however, find none other in the whole range of the English language, that would even faintly convey the idea which we wished to express.' Speaking for the Virginia slaveowners, he says he will show 'that we are indebted to domestic slavery for our happy exemption from the social afflictions that have originated this philosophy'.

One passage in the *Politics* that is particularly interesting is the one in which Aristotle gives the advice that all slaves should be offered the reward of ultimate emancipation: he promises to give his reasons later, but unfortunately never does so.[14] If we read this advice with earlier passages explaining how the slave can benefit from his association with his master,[15] we may see a fairly precise parallel, at the individual level, with the theory of the 'tutelage of backward nations', one of the main planks in the ideology of modern Western imperialism. But the statement in the *Politics* which corresponds best with the outlook of later Greek (and Roman) intellectuals is that in which Aristotle denies the very name of slave to the man who does not deserve to be in a condition of slavery – or, as we might say, denies that the man who does not deserve to be in slavery is 'really' a slave at all.[16] This, and not the theory of 'natural slavery', became the standard view of thinking slaveowners in Hellenistic and Roman times, as we shall see in Section iii of this chapter. Even before Aristotle wrote there had been protests against the hypothesis of 'natural slavery'[17] and even against the assumption that barbarians are naturally inferior to Greeks[18] – although of course the great majority of Greeks and Romans always took it for granted that they were generally superior to 'barbarians', and this attitude hardly changed in Christian times. As late as the beginning of the fifth century of our era the devoutly Christian poet Prudentius could say that there is as great a distance between the world of Rome and that of the 'barbarians' (*tantum distant Romana et barbara*) as between bipeds and quadrupeds, humans and dumb brutes, Christians and pagans (*C. Symm.* II.816-19).[19]

The theory of 'natural slavery' indeed is not at all prominent in antiquity after Aristotle's time, and when it does reappear it is mainly applied to peoples rather than individuals. This may be in a merely rhetorical context, as when Cicero stigmatises Jews and Syrians as 'peoples born for slavery' (*De prov. cons.* 10), but we also find it seriously stated by a speaker (Laelius) in Cicero's dialogue, *De republica* (III.24/36, cf. 25/37), that a nation can benefit from being in a state of complete political subjection – (*servitus*, literally 'slavery') – to another (see my ECAPS 18 and n.52). There were, however, some distant but powerful echoes of the 'natural slavery' theory in much later times, when it played a highly significant role in Christian Spain in the controversy concerning the rightfulness of enslaving negroes, and the Indians of the Caribbean and Central and Southern America, in the fifteenth century onwards. It was, I believe, a Scottish professor at Paris, John Major, who in 1510 first applied the Aristotelian doctrine of natural slavery to the American Indians.[20] And at the great debate ordered by Charles V at Valladolid in 1550, to decide whether Christian Spaniards might lawfully wage war upon Indians and enslave them, before even preaching the Faith to them, Aristotle's doctrine was accepted in principle by both the leading disputants: the great scholar Juan Ginés de Sepúlveda and the Franciscan friar Bartolomé de las Casas. The principal point of disagreement, it seems, was simply the factual question whether or not the Indians were 'natural slaves'; it was hardly questioned that negroes were. (The main book in English on this topic, by Lewis Hanke, on which I am mainly relying here, bears the delightful title, *Aristotle and the American Indians*!) It is things like this which give point to the remark of Engels that ancient slavery, even after its disappearance, left behind its 'poisonous sting' (*OFPPS* ch.viii: see *MESW* 560).

Anyone who is astonished at the acceptance of a doctrine so intellectually disreputable as that of natural slavery should reflect not only upon modern racist parallels but also upon certain other conceptions which are equally disreputable from the intellectual point of view but are widely accepted today because they are so convenient from the point of view of a ruling class. I suggest as one parallel the extension of the expression 'the Free World' to include countries like South Africa and a number of South and Central American dictatorships, while excluding all the Communist countries.

I have said nothing here about the position most opposed to the theory of 'natural slavery': that slavery was not merely 'not according to Nature' (*ou kata physin*) but actually 'contrary to Nature' (*para physin*). For this position, for which we have evidence from the fourth century B.C., from Philo of Alexandria in the early part of the first century of the Christian era, and in the Roman lawyers of the second to the sixth century, see the next section of this chapter.

(iii)
The standard Hellenistic, Roman and Christian attitude to slavery

From the Hellenistic period onwards, Greek and Roman thought on the subject of slavery, with hardly an exception, provides a set of uninspired variations on a single theme: that the state of slavery – like poverty and war, or liberty, riches and peace – is the result of accident, of Fortune rather than of Nature,[1] and that it is a matter of indifference, affecting externals only (see e.g. Lucret. I.455–8); that the good and wise man is never 'really' a slave, even if that happens to be his actual condition, but is 'really' free; that it is the bad man who is 'really' a slave, because he is in bondage to his own lusts – a wonderfully comforting set of doctrines for slaveowners. (I fancy that such austere philosophical notions are of greater assistance in the endurance of liberty, riches and peace, than of slavery, poverty and war.) An early example of the line of thought I have just described, from the first half of the fourth century B.C., is Xenophon's statement that some are slaves to gluttony, others to lechery or drink or to foolish and costly ambitions (*Oecon.* I.21-2); among many later formulations, see the brief one in Augustine, *De civ. Dei* IV.3. And of course it was easy for those who held this position to conclude that where the 'bad man' was a slave, his condition was, for him, a blessing in disguise. Ingenious developments can be found of this or that aspect of the general theory, and of course some authors emphasise one aspect of it, others another; but there is a dreary similarity of sentiment over all. I think the fourteenth Oration of Dio Chrysostom is probably the most entertaining example I know of this kind of perverse ingenuity. Interesting statements of principle regarding slavery are rare: I would single out that of Chrysippus (the leading Stoic of the second half of the third century B.C.), that the slave should be considered as a sort of permanent hired labourer, in Seneca's Latin a *perpetuus mercennarius* (see n.17 to Section ii of this chapter).

It is often said that Christianity introduced an entirely new and better attitude towards slavery. Nothing could be more false. Jesus accepted slavery as a fact of his environment (see my ECAPS 19 n.54), just as it is accepted in the Old Testament; and his followers accepted and adapted the prevailing Graeco-Roman view which I have just described. (From now until the end of Section iv of this chapter I shall be very selective in giving references, especially to modern works: those not given here will be found in my ECAPS.) The significance of the much-quoted text in Colossians (III.11), 'There is neither Greek nor Jew, circumcision nor uncircumcision, barbarian, Scythian, bond nor free', is better understood in the light of the parallel text in Galatians (III.28): 'There is neither Jew nor Greek, there is neither bond nor free, *there is neither male nor female*; for ye are all one in Christ Jesus.' There is 'neither bond nor free' in exactly the same sense as there is 'neither male nor female': these statements are true *in a strictly spiritual sense*: the equality exists 'in the sight of God' and has no relation whatever to temporal affairs. The distinction between slave and master in this world is no more seen as needing to be *changed* than that between male and female. (As I have explained in II.vi above, the relation of a wife to her husband, in the Pauline view, bears a very strong resemblance to that of a slave to his master!) For St. Paul, Jesus had set all his followers free – from the flesh and all its works. The exhortation to the Christian slave to regard himself as 'Christ's freedman' in the same sense that the Christian who is a free man is 'Christ's slave' (I Cor. vii.22) may well have afforded him greater spiritual comfort than the pagan slave could obtain from the familiar philosophic view that if he was a good man he was 'really' free already; but it was basically the same view. Christian masters are briefly enjoined to treat their slaves fairly (see ECAPS 19 n.56), but there are many similar exhortations in pagan writers, e.g. Seneca (esp. *Epist.* XLVII: see the full treatment of Seneca's attitude to slavery in Griffin, *Seneca* 256-85, 458-61). And the yoke of slavery is fastened even more firmly upon Christian slaves as the emphasis on obedience to their masters becomes even more absolute. Certain phrases in the Pauline Epistles (see ECAPS 19 n.57), such as that in Ephesians (VI.5), exhorting slaves to obey their masters 'with fear and trembling, in singleness of heart, as unto Christ', had sinister implications which were fully brought out in two post-Apostolic works, the *Epistle of Barnabas* (XIX.7) and the *Didache* (IV.11): they explicitly tell the slave that he must serve his master 'as a counterpart of God' (*hōs typōi theou*), 'in reverence and fear'. I know of nothing that goes as far as that in pagan literature. St. Augustine even uses the *apostolica auctoritas* of St. Paul to rebuke the presumption of any Christian slave who might fondly imagine himself entitled to appeal to the provision in Exodus XXI.2 for the release of the Hebrew slave after six years' service. No, says Augustine (remembering Ephesians VI.5), the apostolic authority commands slaves to be subject to their masters, 'that there be no blasphemy of God's name and doctrine' – a remark (however faulty its logic) that is significant of Augustine's whole position on social matters (*Quaest. in Heptat.* II.77; and see further below on Augustine's attitude to slavery).

Whatever the theologian may think of Christianity's claim to set free the soul of the slave, therefore, the historian cannot deny that it helped to rivet the shackles rather more firmly on his feet. It performed the same social function as the fashionable philosophies of the Graeco-Roman world, and perhaps with deeper effect: it made the slave both more content to endure his earthly lot, and more tractable and obedient. St. Ignatius, in his *Epistle to Polycarp* (IV.3), is anxious that Christian slaves should be neither despised nor 'puffed up' (*mē physiousthōsan*); that they should 'serve the more, to the glory of God'; and that they should 'not wish to be set free at the public cost, lest they become slaves of lust'. (I confess that I find the last phrase somewhat inconsequential, nor can I see exactly how an even more intense degree of labour on the part of the slave can enhance the glory of God.) The Fifth Canon of the Council of Elvira (in the late third century or the early fourth) punished with no more than seven years' excommunication even the intentional flogging to death by a woman of her slave girl[2] – doubtless one who had accepted the sexual attentions of the woman's husband. Later episcopal decisions decree flogging as a penalty for ecclesiastical offences by a slave, female as well as male, when free men and women suffer some less degrading punishment: a fine or a period of excommunication.[3] And baptism seems to have been refused to a slave by at least some churches without the consent of his master, perhaps at first only if a Christian one, but later even if a pagan (see ECAPS 21 nn.59-60).

The situation changed not at all when Christianity succeeded to the seats of power in the fourth century, and the Christian Church – or rather, churches – assumed a position even in the public life of the Roman empire of the fourth and following centuries which I can only compare, functionally, with the role of what Eisenhower (in the final broadcast of his Presidency, on 17 January 1961) called 'the military-industrial complex' in the United States today. (One should normally speak of the Christian 'churches' in the plural, rather than 'the Church', because the latter expression is a strictly theological and not a historical concept: see Section v of this chapter. But perhaps the term 'the Church' is too convenient to be abandoned entirely by the historian.)

St. Augustine at least admitted that slavery was an evil in principle, but with that extraordinary perverse ingenuity which never ceases to astonish one, he saw it as God's punishment upon mankind for the sin of Adam (*De civ. Dei* XIX.15-16, cf. 21).[4] (These are among the many passages justifying the astringent comment of Gibbon on the *City of God*, of which Colin Haycraft has reminded me, that Augustine's 'learning is too often borrowed, and his arguments are too often his own': *DFRE* III.211 n.86.) It evidently did not occur to Augustine that it might be thought blasphemous to attribute to an all-just Deity such a singularly indiscriminate method of collective punishment. In thus suggesting that 'justly was the burden of servitude laid upon the back of transgression', Augustine represented slavery as something divinely ordained, and gave the institution an even weightier justification than it had ever received from pre-Christian thinkers since the days when theories of 'natural slavery' were abroad. Indeed, Augustine and Ambrose went so far as to think that slavery could actually be good for the slave, an instructive form of correction and a blessing even – for, as Ambrose put it, 'the lower the station in life, the more exalted the virtue' (see ECAPS 21 nn.63-4). I have not been able to find in any early Christian writer anything like a demand for the abandonment of slavery or even for a general freeing of existing slaves. Passages in early Christian literature which are sometimes cited as containing attacks on the institution of slavery can be shown on inspection not to have any such implication (see ECAPS 21-2).

Although the Christians laid great emphasis on the importance of mono-gamous marriage and the sinfulness of sexual intercourse outside it (if with no great success, it must be said: see II.vi above, and Jones, *LRE* II.972-6), the Christian Empire did not provide for legal marriage between slaves, any more than the pagans had done. This need not surprise us. The antebellum South was deeply religious, but no single state legislature ever tried to legitimise slave unions and thus give them a greater chance of permanency, and they always remained subject in practice to the master's whim.[5]

Legislation giving a small measure of protection to slaves in certain respects was passed at various times by the Roman emperors, as when Claudius pro-vided that a sick slave exposed by a master should, if he recovered, become free and enjoy 'Latin rights'.[6] However, it is sometimes made explicit that enact-ments in favour of slaves have also in view the protection of the interests of masters in general, which might suffer if a few exceptionally cruel masters were allowed to behave with 'saevitia' and inflict intolerable indignities and injuries on their slaves.[7] (Probably it was reflections on these lines which made Augustus refuse – apparently – to allow the usual mass execution of the slaves of Hostius Quadra when they murdered him: the man is vividly described by Seneca as degraded, a *portentum*, a *monstrum*; *NQ* I.xvi.1,3,6.) Again, there are parallels from the Old South, as when the Supreme Court of South Carolina in 1849 upheld the conviction of a slaveowner for not giving his slaves enough to eat, on the ground that the law had to be enforced for the sake of 'public sentiment, . . . and to protect property from the depredation of famishing slaves' (Stampp, *PI* 217-18).

In the Christian Roman Empire, slaves were generally debarred from all grades of holy orders; serf *coloni* were similarly excluded, either entirely or unless their masters consented to their ordination. On this, Church and State were agreed, and there was legislation on the subject from 398 onwards.[8] It could of course be argued in defence of these disqualifications that a slave would be unable to consecrate his whole time to the service of God: this argument is found in a letter written in 443 by one of the greatest of the early popes, St. Leo I. More powerful, I suspect, was another argument advanced in the same letter:

Persons whom the merit neither of their birth nor of their character recommends are being freely admitted to holy orders, and those who have not been able to obtain their freedom from their owners are raised to the dignity of the priesthood, as if servile vileness could lawfully receive this honour . . . There is a double wrong in this matter, that the sacred ministry is polluted by such vile company, and the rights of owners are violated, in so far as an audacious and illicit usurpation is involved (*Ep.* IV.1, in *MPL* LIV.611).

As Gaudemet remarks, commenting on a letter of Pope Gelasius I (A.D. 492-6) in this connection, 'Le respect absolu du droit de propriété privé et de structures sociales cependant peu conformes à la doctrine évangelique, était ainsi nettement affirmé' (*EER* 139).

In the Roman lawyers (apparently pagan to a man), from the second or third century of the Christian era to the sixth, we sometimes find the admission that slavery was contrary to nature or to natural law – *contra naturam, iuri naturali contraria*: see *Inst.J.* I.ii.2; *Dig.* I.v.4.1 (Florentinus, third quarter of the second century); XII.vi.64 (Tryphoninus, *c.* 200); and I.i.4 (Ulpian, first quarter of the third century); and cf. L.xvii.32 (Ulpian).[9] Slavery indeed seems to have been regarded by at least some of the lawyers as the only feature of the *ius gentium* that did not also form part of *ius naturale* (see Jolowicz and Nicholas, *HISRL*[3] 106-7). This is a line of thought that can be traced right back to the unnamed thinkers of the fifth or fourth century B.C. who are said by Aristotle to have declared that slavery, because it was based on force, was contrary to nature and wrong (*Pol.* I.3, 1253[b]20-3; 6, 1255[a]5-12) – not merely 'not according to nature' (*ou kata physin*) but '*contrary* to nature' (*para physin*), a significant difference, not sufficiently brought out by modern writers (cf. my *OPW* 45). This line of thought may or may not have descended to the Roman lawyers through some of the Stoics. Certainly, apart from the Roman lawyers, the only identifiable Greek or Latin author I know in whom we find a reflection of the argument that slavery can be 'contrary to nature' is Philo, the Hellenised Jew who wrote at Alexandria during the first half-century of the Christian era. In one work he speaks with evident admiration of the Jewish sect of the Essenes, who (he says) do not have a single slave; they denounce slaveowners, he adds, for being unjust in destroying equality (*isotēs*) and impious in transgressing the precept of Nature, the *thesmos physeōs* (*Quod omn. prob. liber* 79; cf. *hoi tēs physeōs nomoi*, ibid. 37). In another work he similarly describes the 'Therapeutai' – who must surely have been either imaginary or a sect of the Essenes – as believing that the ownership of slaves was altogether contrary to nature, *para physin* (*De vita contempl.* 70); and again we have the interesting assumption that equality is the ideal: Philo speaks of the injustice and greed of 'those who introduce inequality, the origin of evil' (*tēn archekakon anisotēta*). It is perfectly clear, however, that Philo himself did not by any means reject slavery altogether. His own basic position was that which I have described as the standard one in Hellenistic and later thinkers: that the good man, even if he happens to be enslaved, is 'really' free, while the bad man, the man who is worthless or senseless – in Philo's Greek, the *phaulos* or *aphrōn* – is always 'really' a slave. Philo wrote two whole treatises on this theme, of which we possess only the second, usually referred to by its traditional Latin title, *Quod omnis probus liber sit*; the other, intended to prove 'that a *phaulos* is a slave' (see *Quod omn. prob. liber* 1), has fortunately not survived. The treatise we do possess is actually the earliest full-length statement of the theory to survive complete, for the still earlier Stoic and other writings on the subject now exist, if at all, only in fragments. It is perfectly possible to demonstrate from Philo himself that what I have described as the standard view of slavery from Hellenistic times onwards can be assimilated to the old theory of 'natural slavery', provided slavery, for the worthless man, is treated as a benefit. In one of his fanciful attempts to establish borrowings by Greek authors – in this case, Zeno the founder of Stoicism – from the Jewish Scriptures, Philo recalls Genesis XXVII.40, where Isaac tells Esau that he is to 'serve' his brother Jacob. In the Septuagint, used by Philo, the verb in this passage is a form of *douleuein*, the commonest Greek term for serving as a slave. Isaac believed, Philo continues, that what seems to be the greatest of evils, namely slavery (*douleia*), is the highest possible good for a fool (an *aphrōn*), since his being deprived of liberty prevents him from doing wrong unscathed, and his character is improved by the control he experiences (*Quod omn. prob. liber* 57). Plato and Aristotle (see Section ii of this chapter) would have warmly approved: to them, such a man was a slave 'by nature'.

Some Stoics – the ex-slave Epictetus, for example – may occasionally have spoken as if they actually disapproved in principle of possessing slaves (see my ECAPS 22 n.72). But this is all ultimately unreal, part of the smokescreen of plausible ideas by which the more fastidious thinkers of antiquity concealed from themselves the unpalatable truth about a ruthless world of which they were trying to make the best they could, according to their lights. The unreality of all this talk emerges most clearly from Epictetus' description of the ex-slave who ends up by becoming a senator: he is then subject, says Epictetus, to 'the fairest and sleekest slavery of all'! (*Diss*. IV.i.40, p.360, ed. H. Schenkl, 1916). If being a senator was slavery, it was slavery in a Pickwickian sense, a kind of slavery which the vast majority of the population of the Graeco-Roman world would have embraced eagerly enough.

In early Christian thought I have been able to find nothing that goes even as far in rejecting slavery as the purely theoretical statements to the effect that it is 'contrary to nature', made by the early thinkers mentioned in Aristotle's *Politics*, by the Essenes as reported by Philo Judaeus and by some of the Roman lawyers. The farthest that I think any early Christian writer goes is to admit – as does Pope Gregory the Great (590-604), when freeing two of the many slaves of the Roman Church – that 'it is right that men whom nature from the beginning produced free and whom the *ius gentium* has subjected to the yoke of slavery should be reinstated by the benefit of manumission in the liberty to which they were born' (*Ep*. VI.12). Yet even Gregory ordered no large-scale manumissions, except of Christian slaves owned by Jews. I cannot speak from personal knowledge of Christian literature much after the sixth century, but I know of no fundamental change in the attitude of the Christian churches to slavery for well over a thousand years after the fall of the Roman empire in the West, and there was certainly no absolute condemnation of slavery as an institution by any Christian writer during the Middle Ages: statements I have seen quoted from Theodore the Studite, Smaragdus Abbas and others always have some particular limited application (see ECAPS 24 and n.76). I dare say it is only my own ignorance, but I know of no general, outright condemnation of slavery, inspired by a Christian outlook, before the petition of the Mennonites of Germantown in Pennsylvania in 1668[10] – a sect (not far removed from the

Quakers) whose sixteenth-century founder was an Anabaptist and who were outside the main stream of Christianity. Christian writers have often emphasised attempts by Christians to prevent or at least discourage enslavement; but these efforts were rarely if ever extended for the benefit of those outside the Christian fold, and writers who have drawn attention to them have often failed to mention that condemnation of the sin of enslaving Christians is commonly accompanied by the tacit admission that enslaving non-believers is permissible, and even praiseworthy if enslavement is followed by conversion to the Faith – a conversion which perhaps in some cases could hardly be attained by other means.[11] Christianity, therefore, actually came to play a very positive role in the slave trade of the fifteenth to the eighteenth century. Boxer has remarked upon 'the dichotomy which bedevilled the Portuguese approach to the black Africans for so long – the desire to save their immortal souls coupled with the urge to enslave their vile bodies', with the result that 'a close connection speedily grew up between the missionary and the slave-trader' (*PSE* 98, 101). Papal bulls of Nicholas V and Calixtus III in the 1450s record with approval the way in which captured negro slaves had been brought to receive baptism and embrace the Catholic faith; they gave the Portuguese, as a reward for their efforts in this field, a monopoly of navigation and trade over a large area between the Gold Coast and India; and they expressly authorised the king of Portugal to reduce to slavery all unbelievers inimical to Christ (see Boxer, *PSE* 20-3). In the American Old South Christianity was regarded by slaveowners as an invaluable method of social control. As Kenneth Stampp has said, not only did pious masters feel an obligation to care for the immortal souls of their slaves and to look after their spiritual life; 'many of them also considered Christian indoctrination an effective method of keeping slaves docile and contented' (*PI* 156-62, at 156). The Bible, needless to say, was pressed into service in favour of slavery, as it so often has been, notably in the great argument over Abolition in the eighteenth and nineteenth centuries in the U.S.A. The negro, it was widely believed, inherited Noah's curse upon Canaan, the son of Ham (Gen. IX.25-7), and some would even have made him the inheritor of God's curse on Cain (Gen. IV.10-15). Those who knew their Aristotle could easily buttress his theory of natural slavery with an argument supposedly founded on the Bible.[12] If I have ventured far beyond the ancient world in tracing the attitude of the Christian churches towards slavery, it is because I wish to emphasise that we need feel no surprise at all at what we find in the writers of the early Christian centuries.

At this point I must mention one thing that has long puzzled me. I realise that on Christian principles a good case can perhaps be made for accepting the condition of slavery *for the slave,* in the way that Stoics and Epicureans accepted it, as well as St. Paul and so many of the other early Christians, as something external and unimportant. This is so, even for those who might not go all the way with Cardinal Newman when he declared that according to the teaching of his church 'it were better for sun and moon to drop from heaven, for the earth to fail, and for all the many millions who are upon it to die of starvation in extremest agony, as far as temporal affliction goes, than that one soul, I will not say, should be lost, but should commit one single venial sin, should tell one wilful untruth, though it harmed no one, or steal one poor farthing without excuse' (see ECAPS 23 n.74). But what of slavery as it affects the master? Surely the Christian who prays not to be 'led into temptation' should proceed to renounce the total irresponsible domination over fellow human beings which belongs to the master of slaves and is only too likely to lead him (as we know it often did) into the gravest temptation, to commit acts of cruelty and lust? I do not know when this was first realised; but it was evident to the genius of Tolstoy, who in a remarkable passage in *War and Peace* makes Prince Andrey tell Pierre that what is most evil about serfdom is its effect upon those masters who have the power to punish their serfs as they please, and who, in doing so, 'stifle their remorse and become hardened'. (The conversation occurs in Book V, during Pierre's visit to Andrey at Bogucharovo.) I can only conclude that what prevented the Christian Church from admitting the dangerous, brutalising effect of slavery (and serfdom) upon masters was the irresistible force of the class struggle: the absolute necessity for the dominant classes of the Graeco-Roman world to maintain those social institutions upon which their whole privileged position depended, and which they were not willing, or even able, to forego.

(iv)
The attitudes to property of the Graeco-Roman world, of Jesus, and of the Christian churches

From ideas about slavery we pass to a closely related subject: attitudes to property. In V.i above I have briefly discussed the way in which property, from the seventh century B.C. onwards, largely replaced nobility of birth as the foundation of political power and of social respectability in the early Greek states, as in early Rome (for which see VI.ii above). Throughout most of Greek history, except perhaps in a few democratic states in the fifth and fourth centuries B.C., the bulk of the propertied classes would have agreed with Tennyson's *Northern Farmer. New Style* that 'the poor in a loomp is bad'. Origen says this most emphatically: the majority of the destitute (*hoi ptōchoi*) have most worthless characters (they are *phaulotatoi ta ēthē*, *C. Cels.* VI.16). The Graeco-Roman world was obsessively concerned with wealth and status; and wealth was by far the most important determinant of status. Ovid put it beautifully in three words: *dat census honores*, 'it is property that confers rank' (*Amores* III.viii.55). The Elder Seneca, writing in the late 30s B.C., could represent Porcius Latro, a famous orator, as exclaiming that nothing in human affairs shows up a man's virtues more clearly than wealth: 'It is property [*census* again] that raises to the rank of senator, property that differentiates the Roman *eques* from the plebs, property that brings promotion in the army, property that provides the qualification for the judges in the forum' (Seneca, *Controv.* II.i.17; and cf. Pliny, *NH* XIV.5). The Greeks, from archaic times through the Classical and Hellenistic periods and on into the Roman age, habitually expressed political complexion and social status in a fascinating vocabulary which is an inextricable mixture of socio-economic and moral terminology, with two sets of terms applied more or less indiscriminately to the propertied and the non-propertied classes respectively. (For what follows, see my ECAPS 10-11, and its nn.29-32.) On the one hand we have not only words which mean property-owning, rich, fortunate, distinguished, well-born, influential, but also, as alternatives for virtually the same set of people, words having a basically moral connotation and meaning literally the good, the best, the upright, the fair-minded, and so forth. And on the other hand we find applied to the lower classes, the poor, who are also the Many, the mob, the populace, words with an inescapably moral quality, meaning essentially bad. Even Solon, often regarded as the founder of the Athenian democracy, could say in one of his poems that he had made laws equally for the *kakos* and the *agathos* – for the 'lower class' and the 'upper class', of course, rather than 'the bad' and 'the good'; but nothing could alter the social fact that the upper class *were* 'the good', the lower class 'the bad'. The Roman governing class was as thoroughly devoted to property as the most wealth-conscious of the Greeks. No surviving Greek writer is quite as explicit about the overriding importance of property rights as Cicero, the earliest known to me in a long line of thinkers, extending into modern times, who have seen the protection of private property rights as the prime function of the state. To mention only a few of the most interesting passages in Cicero – in the *De officiis*, after asking what greater mischief there could be than an equal distribution of property (*aequatio bonorum . . . , qua peste quae potest esse maior?*), he goes on to declare that States were established above all with the aim of preserving property rights (II.73, cf. 78, 83-5; I.21); and in the *De legibus*, after some very grandiose talk about the greatness of law (I.14) and how it is the highest Reason implanted in Nature (§§ 18,23), an eternal principle governing the entire universe,[1] indeed the very mind of God (II.8), he qualifies this by saying that of course he does not include under the name of law certain 'pernicious and unjust orders of the people, . . . many pernicious, many pestiferous enactments which no more deserve the name of law than the rules that brigands make for themselves' (§§ 11,13). And all three sets of laws he singles out as least deserving the name of law were – we might have guessed – primarily agrarian in character, and sought to effect those distributions of land which the Roman Optimates always regarded as a potential threat to the very basis of their power. In one of his speeches Cicero launches into a panegyric of the *ius civile*, the civil law – which I mentioned in VI.i above as one of the two greatest achievements of the Romans, their only outstanding one in the intellectual field. In the speech in question, *Pro Caecina* (67-75), Cicero emphasises that if the *ius civile* is subverted, no one can possibly feel certain of his own property (70); and that if it is neglected or treated carelessly, no one can be sure that he owns anything or will inherit from his father or leave anything to his children (73).

An interesting sidelight on the Greek and Roman respect for wealth and social position is the fact that 'charitable' foundations and bequests which provided for distributions in money or kind to a local population often divided the hand-outs into two or more categories, with the larger gifts going to those of higher social rank – councillors are the group in favour of whom discrimination is most often exercised (see III.vi above and its n.35).[1a]

In the rest of this section I shall concentrate on one particular aspect of ancient Greek ideas about property: namely, the way in which the ideas of the early Christians on this subject were moulded by social forces far beyond their control into something very different from those of the Founder of their religion. This again was a direct effect of the class situation in the Graeco-Roman world – of the class struggle. Unless Christianity was to become involved in a fatal conflict with the all-powerful propertied classes, it had to play down those ideas of Jesus which were hostile to the ownership of any large quantity of property; or, better still, it could explain them away.

We must begin with the central fact about Christian origins, to which theologians and New Testament scholars have never (as far as I am aware) given anything like the emphasis it deserves: that although the earliest surviving Christian documents are in Greek and although Christianity spread from city to city in the Graeco-Roman world, its Founder lived and preached almost entirely outside the area of Graeco-Roman civilisation proper. Here we must go back to the fundamental distinction which I drew in I.iii above between the *polis* (the Greek city) and the *chōra* (the countryside) – because, if we can trust the only information about Jesus which we have, that of the Gospels (as I believe in this respect we can), the world in which Jesus was active was entirely that of the *chōra* and not at all that of the *polis*. Apart from Jerusalem (a special case, as I shall explain presently), his mission took place exclusively in the *chōra*, in its villages (*kōmai*), in the rural area (the *agroi*) of Palestine. Mainly it was conducted altogether apart from *polis* territory, in areas of Galilee and Judaea administered not by cities but directly by Herod Antipas the 'tetrarch' or by the Roman governor of Judaea; but it is highly significant that on the rather rare occasions when we do find Jesus active inside *polis* territory, it is never in the *polis* itself, in the sense of its urban area, but always in its country district. As we shall see, whenever we have any specific information (as distinct from vague general statements) the terms used are such as to point unmistakably to the countryside – the *kōmai, kōmopoleis, agroi, chōra*, also the *merē, horia, paralios, perichōros*. There is of course a great dispute about how much reliable historical information can legitimately be extracted from the narratives of the Gospels, even the Synoptics. But I would emphasise that in so far as we can trust the specific information given us by the Gospels there is no evidence that Jesus even entered the urban area of any Greek city. That should not surprise us: Jesus belonged wholly to the *chōra*, the Jewish countryside of Galilee and Judaea.

Palestine, which had been ruled from Egypt by the Ptolemies for over a hundred years after the death of Alexander the Great in 323 B.C., became around 200 part of the Seleucid kingdom. Just before the middle of the second century Judaea achieved a considerable degree of independence for nearly a century; but from 63 B.C. onwards the whole of Palestine and Syria was always effectively under Roman control, although Judaea (and Samaria) did not actually become a Roman province until A.D. 6 and Galilee and Peraea until 44.[2] In Palestine the native language at the beginning of the Christian era was Aramaic, which was spoken throughout the countryside and also by a good proportion of the inhabitants of many of the cities. (Some vernacular Hebrew was apparently spoken in Judaea, but very little in Galilee, in which most of the preaching of Jesus took place, and Jesus must have preached almost entirely in Aramaic.)[3] By the time of Jesus, Palestine contained a number of genuine *poleis*, some of which were much more Hellenic in character than others.[4] With the exception of Tyre and Sidon, which I shall mention presently, the cities on the coast (Caesarea, Ascalon, Gaza and others) were too far from the main scene of Jesus' activity to be mentioned in the Gospels, and we can ignore them here. The cities we need to notice are, first, Sepphoris and Tiberias, the only two in Galilee; next Samaria, between Galilee and Judaea, recently re-founded by Herod the Great as Sebaste (but never mentioned under that name in the New Testament); thirdly the well-marked cluster of ten genuine cities administering a large area known as Decapolis, to the east and south-east of Galilee and the north-east of Judaea; and finally one or two cities at the periphery of the area within which Jesus moved: Caesarea Paneas, founded in 2 B.C. by Herod's son, Philip the tetrarch, some 25 miles to the north of the Lake of Galilee (and referred to in Mark and Matthew as Caesarea Philippi), and the ancient Phoenician towns of Tyre and Sidon, of which Tyre lay on the coast, due west of Caesarea Paneas, with Sidon to the north of it.

Now the word *polis* is often used by Greek authors (and in the Septuagint) in a loose sense, of places which were not true cities but simply large villages or market-towns which were described more correctly by other expressions such as *mētrokōmiai, kōmopoleis*. In the Gospels, Luke especially, the term *polis* is used on dozens of occasions for individual named places which were not technically cities at all: Nazareth, Capernaum, Nain, Chorazin, Bethsaida, Sychar of Samaria, Ephraim, Arimathea, Bethlehem – and Jerusalem. The last is a special case. From the early Hellenistic period onwards, Greek authors such as Hecataeus of Abdera and Agatharchides of Cnidus (*ap.* Jos., *C.Apion.* I. 197-8, 209) could call Jerusalem a *polis*; but that was never a correct description either in reality or in the strict technical sense, and it is best to regard Jerusalem as essentially the administrative capital of Judaea, of the *ethnos* (the 'nation') of the Jews.[5] Of the other places called 'poleis' in the Gospels we might wish to call Bethsaida a 'town'; none of the others was really more than a village. And although much of the activity of Jesus is said in the Gospels to have taken place in desert areas or by the shore of the Lake of Galilee or elsewhere in the country districts, we are sometimes told in very general terms that Jesus went through *poleis* (Mt. XI.11; cf. Lk. IV.43), or *poleis* and *kōmai* (Mt. IX.35; Lk.XIII.22), or *kōmai, poleis* and *agroi* (Mk VI.56). But in such contexts the word *poleis* must be understood in the very loose and untechnical sense in which the Evangelists (like some other Greek authors) habitually use it. As I said earlier, whenever we have a specific reference to a visit by Jesus to one of the genuine *poleis*, it is in every single case made clear that it was the country district of the *polis* concerned to which Jesus went. (Perhaps I should say again that I am omitting here many references which can be found in my ECAPS, esp. 5-8.)

Let us begin with Samaria. We can forget the bogus *polis* of Sychar (Jn IV.5), a mere village of course, and the passage in Matthew (X.5) in which Jesus tells his disciples *not* to go 'into a *polis* of the Samaritans'. That leaves us with only two passages in Luke: in XVII.11 Jesus merely goes 'through the midst of Samaria and Galilee', and in IX.52 he sends messengers 'to a *kōmē* of the Samaritans' to prepare for his coming, which in fact never took place – Jesus went to another *kōmē* (IX.55). There is never a mention of Sebaste, the city founded by Herod, which was a pagan town, with no large proportion of Jewish settlers, and the only genuine *polis* in the Samareitis.

The Decapolis (see above) crops up in two passages in Mark and one in Matthew, and the manner of its appearance is significant. In Mt. IV.25 crowds *from* Decapolis (which had a large *chōra*) and elsewhere follow Jesus. In Mk VII.31, Jesus comes from the borders of Tyre, through Sidon, to the Lake of Galilee, via (as the text has it) 'the midst of the boundaries (or 'territory') of

Decapolis'. But it is Mk V.20 which brings out most clearly what I am trying to emphasise: that in these cases Jesus is clearly in the country district attached to a *polis* and not in the actual *polis* itself. It needs to be taken with its whole context: the story of the demoniac out of whom was cast the legion of devils (Mk V.1-20; Mt. VIII.28-34; Lk. VIII.26-39), whether this is to be located at Gadara or Gerasa, both of which were cities of the Decapolis. (For an alleged 'Gergesa', see ECAPS 6 n.15). In all three Synoptics Jesus is in the *chōra* of the city, and the incident is pictured as taking place beside the Lake of Galilee; the demoniac comes out of the city (Lk. VIII.27) and indeed was always 'in the tombs and in the mountains' (Mk V.2-5); afterwards the swineherds go into the city (Mt. VIII.33), and they tell the story in 'the *polis* and the *agroi*' (Mk V.14; Lk. VIII.34), whereupon people ('the whole *polis*': Mt. VIII.34) come out to Jesus (Lk. VIII.35) and beg him to go away – in Lk. VIII.37 it is 'the whole multitude of the *perichōros* of the Gerasenes' who do this. When Jesus tells the former demoniac to go home and publish the news of the divine work, he proclaims it, in Luke (VIII.39), 'throughout the whole *polis*', and in Mark (V.20) 'in the Decapolis'.

The situation is exactly the same on the two occasions on which Jesus is said to have visited the territory of cities outside his main area of action. It is not in Caesarea Philippi itself that he is found, but in its *kōmai* (Mk VIII.27) or *merē* (Mt. XVI.13); and when he visits Phoenicia it is to the *merē* or *horia* of Tyre and Sidon that he goes (Mt. XV.21-2; Mk VII.24, 31), and he is there approached by a woman 'from those *horia*'. When multitudes come to him on another occasion from Tyre and Sidon, it is from their *paralios* (coastal district, Lk. VI.27). There is one reference in Matthew (XI.21) and Luke (X.13) to the doing of 'mighty works' in Tyre and Sidon; but (and this nicely confirms what I have been saying) this is simply part of the reproach to the 'cities' (in reality, *kōmai*) Chorazin and Bethsaida (and Capernaum) that *if* the mighty works which had actually been done in them had been performed instead in Tyre and Sidon, they would have repented!

It will have been noticed that I have said nothing so far about the first two Palestinian cities which I put at the head of my list above: Sepphoris and Tiberias, the only two real cities of Galilee, which had been founded by Herod Antipas (see ECAPS 7 n.17). There is the best of reasons for this: just as we hear nothing in the Gospels of Sebaste (the *polis* of the Samareitis), so we hear not a word of Sepphoris, and Tiberias is mentioned only in the Fourth Gospel (Jn VI.1,23; XXI.1), and then not in its own right but only in connection with the lake that bore its name, better known to us as the Lake of Galilee. Yet Sepphoris was only about four miles from Jesus' home village of Nazareth, and Tiberias is on the shore of the Lake of Galilee at almost the nearest point to Nazareth. One can understand that Jesus would not wish to enter Sebaste, a predominantly pagan city; but both Sepphoris and Tiberias were thoroughly Jewish in population and religion, even if their civic institutions (those of Tiberias at any rate) were of the standard Greek pattern, and even if Sepphoris was to be exceptionally pro-Roman during the great Jewish revolt of A.D. 66-70 (see ECAPS 7 nn.18-19). Yet it need not surprise us to find no record of Jesus' presence in either of these cities: they were both regarded with hatred by the Galilaeans in Josephus' army in 66 (see ECAPS 8 n.20), and Jesus would no doubt have seen them as belonging to an alien world. In Mark I.38 it is the nearby *kōmopoleis* (the substantial villages) of Galilee in which he contemplates preaching: that represents the reality.

I dare say that some New Testament scholars may object that I have made far too much of topographical evidence in the Gospels which they themselves are in general reluctant to press. To this I would reply that I am not using any of the Gospel narratives for any topographical purpose: it is a matter of indifference to me whether, for example, the pericope containing the 'confession of Peter' (Mk VIII.27ff.; Mt. XVI.13ff.) is rightly located near Caesarea Philippi rather than anywhere else. Nor have I drawn any conclusions from uses of the word *polis*. My one purpose has been to demonstrate that the Synoptic Gospels are unanimous and consistent in locating the mission of Jesus entirely in the countryside, not within the *poleis* proper, and therefore outside the real limits of Hellenistic civilisation. It seems to me inconceivable that this can be due to the Evangelists themselves, who (as we have seen) were very likely to dignify an obscure village like Nazareth or Capernaum (cf. ECAPS 8 n.22) with the title of *polis* but would certainly not 'down-grade' a locality by making it a country district if in their source it appeared as a *polis*. I conclude, therefore, that in this respect the Evangelists accurately reflect the situation they found in their sources; and it seems to me that these sources are very likely indeed to have presented a true picture of the general locus of the activity of Jesus. I may add that although I have not been able to find the point I have just been making emphasised by even a single modern New Testament specialist, it did not entirely escape the notice of the greatest scholar of the early Church, St. Jerome. As Henry Chadwick has now kindly pointed out to me, Jerome remarks in his *In Esaiam* xii, p.507 (the commentary on Isaiah XLII.1ff., in *MPL* XXIV.437), that 'if we read that Jesus was within the boundaries [*termini*] of Tyre and Sidon or the confines [*confinium*] of Caesarea Philippi, which is now called Paneas, nevertheless we must note that it is not written that he entered into the actual cities [*ipsas civitates*]'.

Jesus, then, lived and taught within an area which was neither Greek nor Roman, but wholly Jewish. This is best brought out, in my opinion, in the admirable recent book by Geza Vermes, *Jesus the Jew. A Historian's Reading of the Gospels* (London, 1973: see esp. its 48-9). As I mentioned earlier, Galilee, within which by far the greater part of the activity of Jesus apparently took place, was not even a Roman province during his lifetime: it was still a Roman 'client kingdom', until 39 part of the tetrarchy of Herod Antipas, the son of Herod the Great. Of course Jesus was well aware of the Roman imperial power that had already engulfed Judaea as a tributary province and could easily swallow up the remaining petty client kingdoms of Palestine whenever it wanted to. But he may well have had virtually no direct contact with the Roman imperial administration before his final arrest and trial, on the pretence that he was a political agitator, indeed a 'Resistance leader' – a charge which was certainly false, even if his followers may have included a few men with revolutionary associations.[6] Even the 'publicans' (*publicani* in Latin, *telōnai* in Greek) who crop up in the Gospels, such as Matthew (or Levi the son of Alphaeus), will have been employed by Herod Antipas, the tetrarch, and not by the Roman governor of Judaea – who by the way at this date, as we know from a recently discovered inscription, had the title not of Procurator but of Praefectus.[7] How much contact Jesus had with

Greek culture it is not possible to say, but it is likely to have been minimal.[7a]

The main element in the preaching of Jesus was the message, 'Repent, for the Kingdom of Heaven is at hand'. The meaning of this is that the end of the whole present dispensation is near: God will intervene and bring to a speedy end all the powers of this world. In preparation for these earth-shaking events men must repent of their sins and obey the law of God. In another sense of the expression 'Kingdom of Heaven' (or 'Kingdom of God'), that Kingdom is within man's power to grasp *now*: if he repents and follows the right way of life, he can to that extent enter into the Kingdom even before the final cataclysm.[8] Various consequences follow from this. One of the most important is that the possession of wealth is a positive hindrance to entering into the Kingdom. 'It is easier for a camel to go through the eye of a needle than for a rich man to enter the Kingdom of God,' said Jesus, after the man seeking eternal life who 'had great possessions' had gone away disconsolate on being told to sell all that he had and give it to the poor (Mk X.17-31; Mt. XIX.16-30; Lk. XVIII.18-30). This story, by the way, is commonly referred to nowadays as that of 'The Rich Young Man', and that is certainly what Matthew calls him; but Mark and Luke make it clear that in their minds young is what he is not, for they make him claim to have kept the commandments Jesus recommends 'from my youth up'! There is one respect in which Matthew's account differs radically from that in the other two Synoptics: Matthew (XIX.21) inserts into the command of Jesus the qualification, 'If you would be perfect' (*ei theleis teleios einai*) which is not in Mark (X.21) or Luke (XVIII.22): in them the command to sell all is unqualified. As we shall see presently, it is in Matthew's formulation that the passage is invariably quoted by the early Fathers.

Nothing better conveys the contrast between Jewish and Graeco-Roman attitudes to questions of wealth and poverty than the account given in chapter IV of Luke's Gospel of the public preaching of Jesus at Nazareth. (The point I am interested in does not occur in parallel accounts in the other Synoptics.) Jesus reads from the sixty-first chapter of Isaiah, opening with the words, 'The spirit of the Lord is upon me, because he has anointed me to preach the gospel to the poor' (Lk.IV.18). Now the word for 'poor' used here by Luke, as in the Septuagint version of Isaiah, is *ptōchoi*, a very strong word indeed, which very often in Greek means not just the poor but the down-and-out, the destitute, the beggar – Lazarus in the parable is a *ptōchos* (Lk. XVI.20, 22). Classical scholars will remember the appearance of Poverty (*Penia*) as a character in the *Plutus* of Aristophanes (lines 415-612), and how angry she becomes when Chremylus refers to Penia and Ptocheia as sisters: no, says Penia, the *ptōchos* has nothing, whereas her man, the *penēs*, may toil and scrape, but he has enough to live on (lines 548-54).

I must just mention here that although the word *ptōchoi* does also appear in the Septuagint version of Isaiah LXI.1, it there translates a Hebrew word which is sometimes better rendered – as indeed it is in the Authorised Version – by 'the meek'. But this takes us into irrelevant questions, which I am anyway not competent to deal with, of the various shades of meaning of the Hebrew words expressing poverty, lowliness and the like. Some of these are as ambiguous as the English word 'humble', which can be purely social or purely moral or a mixture of the two. The only point I need make here is that in the Hebrew terminology, unlike the Greek, poverty and a lowly station in life are often associated with the moral virtues.

Luke is also the only Evangelist to give us the Parable of Lazarus (XVI.19-31) – who, as I have just said, is specifically a *ptōchos*, here quite rightly translated 'beggar'. Expositors seldom bring out the fact that the terrible fate of the rich man in the parable (Dives, as we usually call him) is clearly seen as a direct result of his great wealth, for he feels (verses 27-8) that Lazarus alone will be able to teach his five surviving brothers how to avoid a similar fate. In Luke's account of the Beatitudes, too, there is a very interesting divergence from Matthew's version. In Matthew (in the so-called 'Sermon on the Mount', chapters v-vii) Jesus is made to say, 'Blessed are the poor *in spirit* [*hoi ptōchoi tōi pneumati*: we might say, 'humble at heart'], for theirs is the kingdom of heaven'; and 'Blessed are those who hunger and thirst *after righteousness*, for they shall be filled' (V.3, 6); but Luke's corresponding version (in the 'Sermon on the Plain', VI.17-49) has simply 'Blessed are ye poor [*ptōchoi,* without qualification], for yours is the kingdom of God', and 'Blessed are ye that hunger now [not 'hunger *after righteousness*'], for ye shall be filled' (VI.20-1). In both cases, of course, the fulfilment of the blessings is intended eschatologically: they will be realised not in this world but only in the Age to come. And even the Lucan version is echoing the large number of passages in the Old Testament (especially in the Psalms, Isaiah, Proverbs and Job) in which the poor and lowly as such are treated with special reverence – several different Hebrew expressions are involved. In the thought-world of Palestinian Judaism, out of which Jesus came, it was not so much the rich and influential from whom the moral virtues were to be expected (as in the Graeco-Roman world), but the poor. An illuminating recent treatment of the Beatitudes by David Flusser (see ECAPS 12 n.33a) shows interesting connections with some of the literature of the Dead Sea Sect. Although Flusser is sure that it is Mt. V.3-5 which 'faithfully preserves the saying of Jesus and that Lk.VI.20 is an abbreviation of the original text', he nevertheless insists that 'Matthew's "poor in spirit" also has a social content'.

There is just one other New Testament passage, again in Luke alone, which I wish to mention: the Magnificat (Lk.I.46-55, esp. 52-3).[9] Here we find an interesting variant on the eschatological conception we have noticed already, according to which in the Age to Come the poor and hungry will be satisfied. We are still within the realm of eschatology, but the desired result is now conceived – in one form of the tradition of Jewish Apocalyptic – as having been in some mysterious way achieved already. 'He *hath* put down the mighty from their seats and *hath* exalted them of low degree. He *hath* filled the hungry with good things and the rich he *hath* sent empty away.' In the Greek the 'mighty' are the *dynastai*, and Thomas Hardy took his title, 'The Dynasts', explicitly from this passage (see ECAPS 14 n.40). In fact nothing of the sort had actually happened: the Dynasts were now more firmly in control than ever, as the Roman Principate began its long era of power. The picture in the Magnificat, in which the events are represented as having in a mystical sense occurred already, was a pleasantly harmless one from the point of view of the Dynasts, who certainly cashed the blank cheque St. Paul later wrote them when he said, 'The powers that be are ordained of God' and enjoined strict obedience to the civil authorities: Rom. XIII.1-7; Titus III.1; cf. I. Pet. ii.13-17; I Tim. ii.1-2. (On the nature of the 'powers' to whom every soul is commanded to be subject, in Rom. XIII.1, see ECAPS 14 n.41.)

It is worth mentioning here that the Greek word *tapeinoi*, which is used in the Magnificat for 'them of low degree' (in opposition to 'the mighty', the *dynastai*) and has in Classical Greek literature, with very rare exceptions, a thoroughly pejorative sense (mean, lowly, poor, weak, base), appears as a personal name in a Greek papyrus emanating from a Jewish sectarian community at Nahal Seelim in Palestine about A.D. 130: one of the 'brethren' there is actually called Tapeinos,[10] a term which may have had much the same significance in the local community as it evidently did for the composer of the Magnificat.

I need not cite any of the other evidence from the Gospels showing that the possession of any substantial amount of property was regarded by Jesus as a positive evil, if only because it was all too likely to ensnare its possessor and divert him from the task of seeking the Kingdom of God. I am tempted to say that in this respect the opinions of Jesus were nearer to those of Bertolt Brecht than to those held by some of the Fathers of the Church and by some Christians today.

Within a generation the message of Jesus had been transformed into what is sometimes described (perhaps not unfairly) as Pauline Christianity. This process cannot be understood by the historian (as distinct from the theologian) unless it is seen as the transfer of a whole system of ideas from the world of the *chōra* to that of the *polis* – a process necessarily involving the most profound changes in that system of ideas. And in my opinion it is in this process of transformation that the most serious problems of 'Christian origins' arise.

I shall waste little time on the so-called 'communism' of the earliest Apostolic community, which appears only momentarily in the opening chapters of Acts (II.44-5; IV.32-7; V.1-11; cf. Jn XII.6; XIII.29), while the Christian Church was a single small body, and then ceases altogether, to reappear only within single monastic communities from the early fourth century onwards. This situation, which was already characteristic of certain Essene and other communities among the Jews, is entirely absent from the remainder of the New Testament; and even in the early chapters of Acts it is clear that communal ownership was not complete, and in any event had nothing to do with communal production. Later references which have sometimes been taken wrongly as evidence of a continuance of community of property are no more than idealisations of a situation in which charity is conceived as complete, as when Tertullian says, 'All things are in common among us, except our wives' (*Apol.* 39.11), or when Justin boasts that Christians share all their property with one another (*I Apol.* 14.2).

*   *   *   *   *   *

I turn now to the attitude of the early Christian Fathers to the question of property ownership.[11] There are considerable differences of emphasis, but I think it would be true to say that with hardly an exception all the orthodox writers seem to have no serious qualms in accepting that a Christian may own property, under certain conditions, the most important of which are that he must neither seek it avidly not acquire it unjustly; that he ought not to possess a superfluity but only a sufficiency; and that what he does have he may use but must not abuse; he must hold it as a kind of trustee (if I may be permitted to use that peculiar technical term of English law) for the poor, to whom he must give charity. (Of many possible examples I will cite only Jerome, *Epist.* 130.14, to the very wealthy Demetrias.) It is upon the necessity of almsgiving that there is most insistence: the whole conception of course descended direct to Christianity from Judaism; and here the Christian churches do seem to have gone far beyond the ordinary pagan standard. (There are some interesting remarks about the absence of similar organised activities among the pagans, in the works of the Emperor Julian: see ECAPS 25 n.81.)

I shall return in a moment to the question of almsgiving, which is worth special attention, and I shall also have something to say on the question of sufficiency or superfluity of property. But I must first add a rider to what I have said about the general early Christian view of property ownership. The words of Jesus to the rich man seeking eternal life, which I discussed earlier, were not entirely disregarded; but it seems that the unqualified version of Mark and Luke was conveniently forgotten and the words of Jesus were always quoted in Matthew's formulation (XIX.21), in which the direction to sell all and give to the poor was prefaced by the qualification, 'If you would be perfect'. Out of scores of passages I have come across in the Fathers I have not found one that even notices the discrepancy between the Matthaean text and that of Mark and Luke.

So complete was the refusal to recognise the existence of any other version than that of Matthew that when Clement of Alexandria, in his *Quis dives salvetur?*, sets out Mark's narrative of the whole story *in extenso* in his own text, explicitly as his source, he inserts Matthew's 'if you would be perfect' at the point that corresponds to Mt. XIX.21, without any indication that these words are not in Mark! (See ECAPS 26 n.82 for references to the standard text of Clement and the good Loeb edition by G. W. Butterworth.) St. John Chrysostom is even at pains to put the conditional clause in the forefront and to make out that Jesus did *not* merely say to the rich man, 'Sell what you have': he actually rubs it in, expanding the words of Jesus into 'I lay it down for your determination. I give you full power to choose. I do not lay upon you any necessity' (*Hom. II de stat.* 5). Thus, by quoting the statement of Jesus in its qualified, Matthaean form, the Fathers were able to make use of the standard distinction between 'precept' and 'counsel': the command to sell all became literally 'a counsel of perfection'. (Among very many examples, I will cite only Aug., *Epist.* 157. 23-39.) And I think it would be true to say that after the rise of monasticism in the fourth century there was a tendency to take 'If you would be perfect' to refer essentially to the adoption of the monastic life: thus when Jerome presses on his rich friend Julian the desirability of ridding himself of all his possessions (again of course on the basis of the Matthaean text we have been considering) he is clearly advising him to become a monk (*Epist.* 118, esp. §§ 4, 5, 6, 7; cf. *Epist.* 60. 10).

We can now return to almsgiving. There is an enormous amount of evidence of the high value attached to almsgiving by early Christian thinkers which it would be superfluous to quote, and I shall concentrate on two passages, one from a Latin and one from a Greek Father, both of which emphasise the expiatory character of almsgiving and thus demonstrate the Jewish roots of Christian thinking in this field. Optatus, in his polemical work against the Donatists (III.3), had occasion to allude to almsgiving when speaking of the visit of certain imperial emissaries (Macarius and others) to Africa in 347, in order to make charitable distributions provided by the Emperor Constans. He first claimed, on the strength of Proverbs XXII.2, that it was God who had made both the poor and the rich (a significant and characteristic use of the Christian religion to justify an oppressive social order), and he then proceeded to explain that God had a very good reason for establishing this distinction: it would of course have been perfectly possible for him to give to both classes at once, but if he had done so, the sinner would have had no means of atoning for his faults (*si ambobus daret, peccator quae sibi succurreret invenire non posset*). To drive his point home, Optatus now quotes what was for him another inspired and canonical work, Ecclesiasticus (III.30): just as water quenches fire, so do alms atone for sin (*sic eleemosyna extinguit peccatum*; Optatus might also have quoted Tobit IV.10; XII.9). Later, the theology of almsgiving – if I may call it that – may have become more subtle, but whenever almsgiving is being discussed, the notion that it can be an atonement for sin is seldom absent. This is conspicuously true of the second example I said I would give of the Christian concept of almsgiving, from a Greek Father. This comes from the work by Clement of Alexandria, usually referred to by its Latin title, *Quis dives salvetur?*, which is actually the earliest treatise to provide a detailed justification of property ownership by Christians, and is perhaps the most important work of its kind. Clement puts most eloquently the argument that almsgiving can actually purchase salvation, and he exclaims, 'What a splendid commerce! What a divine trading!' (32.1; cf. 19.4-6). Needless to say, almsgiving often played an important part in penance (see ECAPS 27 n.89). Too often, however, it seems to have been resorted to, contrary to the admirable prescription of Jesus in Matthew VI.1-4, as a means of self-advertisement: there is a good example in Paulinus of Nola, *Epist.* 34. 2, 7, 10.

The early Christian attitude to property ownership, then, developed into something very different from that of Jesus – as of course it was bound to do, not merely because, as time went on, the eschatological nature of the concepts of Jesus gradually lost its original force, but (and this is much more important) because such a development was imposed on the Church by irresistible social pressures. The orthodox Christian position that I have outlined was held with only minor variations by virtually all the great names among both the Greek and Latin Fathers (see ECAPS 28-31). So far I have found only three partial exceptions among the non-heretical writers: Origen, St. Basil and St. Ambrose. Of these, much the most interesting is Ambrose, certainly in the social sense one of the most exalted of the early Christian Fathers – he was a member of the senatorial aristocracy, the son of a Praetorian Prefect of the Gauls, and himself, at the time of his appointment to the bishopric of Milan in 374, the governor of the province of Aemilia and Liguria, of which Milan was the capital. (I know of scarcely any other early Father who could be considered his social equal, except Paulinus of Nola.) Now Ambrose is far from consistent in his attitude to property rights; and some recent Continental commentators, in their anxiety to rescue him from any such heinous offence as a belief in 'communism' (one monograph, published in 1946 by J. Squitieri, is entitled *Il preteso comunismo di San Ambrogio!*), have given rather perverse interpretations of some of his writings.[12] The fact is that in certain passages Ambrose shows great uneasiness on the whole question of property rights. Yet he can allegorise away the statement of Jesus contained in all three Synoptics (Mk X.25; Mt. XIX.24; Lk. XVIII.25) that it is easier for a camel to pass through the eye of a needle than for a rich man to enter the kingdom of God; he can say that not all poverty is holy nor all riches necessarily a source of crime, and that in good men riches can be a prop of virtue; and of course he accepts almsgiving as the great panacea through which the taint of riches can be removed: thus alone can riches become 'the ransom of a man's life' and 'the redemption of the soul', for 'almsgiving purges from sin'. And so, when Ambrose says that God intended the whole earth and its produce to be the common possession of all men, and continues, 'sed avaritia possessionum iura distribuit', he nevertheless goes on to accept the existing situation, provided the property owner gives to the poor. His attitude is perhaps best brought out in a passage in the *De Helia et ieiunio* (76), where he tells the sinner to redeem himself from his sins with his own money, thus using one poison to subdue another – wealth itself is a poison, but almsgiving, which redeems from sin, turns wealth into sin's antidote!

St. Augustine seems not to have been troubled about property rights. With characteristic ingenuity he extracts an argument in his favour even from the Parable of Lazarus: Lazarus, we are told, went to Abraham's bosom; well, Abraham was rich! (*Epist.* 157.23-4; cf. *Serm.* XIV.4 etc.). As this and many other passages show, the level of argument in this field is not always high, and some may feel some sympathy for the Pelagian who turned one of Augustine's favourite weapons against him by advocating a figurative interpretation of Abraham in the Parable (see ECAPS 31 n.112). Sometimes in the fourth century the poor are warned that they must not think they can take the initiative and *demand* even the necessary minimum of subsistence from those Christians who had vast possessions. Two centuries earlier Irenaeus, citing the Scriptural parallel of the Israelites 'spoiling the Egyptians' at the time of the Exodus (Exod. III.21-2; XI.2; XII.35-6), had expressed some sympathy for the man who, after being compelled to give years of forced labour to another, makes off with some small portion of his property (*Elench.* IV.30.1-3). But now Gregory of Nyssa is careful to show that no such initiative can be justified by an appeal to the 'spoiling of the Egyptians' in Exodus as a precedent (*Vita Moys.* 2).

If we may ignore some passages in early Judaeo–Christian writings, it is only in the mouths of heretics that we find an unqualified denunciation of private property ownership. Usually, of course, we know nothing of their arguments, all our information being derived from orthodox condemnations of their views. In this category are four or five strains of heretical thought from the second, third and fourth centuries, which I have already sufficiently identified elsewhere (ECAPS 32-3). I have been able to discover only one single surviving work which argues at length that the mere possession of wealth creates a tendency to sin and that it really is best to divest oneself of all one's possessions: this is a work probably written in the first decade of the fifth century, the *De divitiis*, either by the heresiarch Pelagius himself or by one of his disciples. (It was first published in 1890 and has been much discussed in recent years: see ECAPS 33-4 and nn.124-5.) I will only say that although this remarkable treatise does recommend divesting oneself of all property (thus 'transferring it from earth to heaven'), it does not actually condemn 'sufficientia', and it regards even wealth not as an actual sin but as something that is very likely indeed to result in sin. The most radical passage goes so far as to treat the existence of the few rich as the reason why there are so many poor, and continues, 'Get rid of the rich and you won't find any poor' (12.2)! There is, however, not a word to suggest that this desirable end can be achieved by anything but religious persuasion; and – rather strangely, perhaps – there is no appeal to the 'primitive communism' (if I may call it that) of the earliest Apostolic community at Jerusalem, and indeed no advocacy at all of community of property, even as a theoretical ideal. I know of no evidence that any Pelagian ever advocated the reform of secular institutions. I will only add that this work, the *De divitiis*, in spite of some over-ingenious arguments and the usual inflated rhetoric, seems to me a far better approximation to the thought of Jesus, as expressed in the Synoptic Gospels (Luke especially), than at any rate the principal work on the orthodox side, Clement's *Quis dives salvetur?*, from which I quoted earlier. Clement does not scruple to make use of the argument (ch. 13) that only if a man possesses some property can he do the things the Lord requires: feed the hungry and give drink to the thirsty, clothe the naked and entertain the homeless – as Zacchaeus and others entertained the Lord himself (Lk. XIX. 1-10). 'What sharing (*koinōnia*) would be left among men,' he asks, 'if nobody had anything?' (This at least is not quite as feeble as the passage in which Aristotle, *Pol*.II.5, 1263^{b}5-14, pretends that the very great delight of doing a kindness to friends or guests or comrades is possible only when there is private ownership of property – as if generosity or liberality could be expressed only in the form of material benefits.) But Clement's principal weapon in this controversy, as so often elsewhere, is a resort to the allegorical method of interpretation which had been invented by pagan Greek scholars in the Classical period and perfected by Hellenistic Judaism in regard to the Old Testament (Philo provides some extraordinary examples); this type of exegesis flourished extravagantly at Alexandria in particular (see ECAPS 35 n.128). The Fathers of the Church soon realised that any inconvenient statement in Holy Writ could easily be allegorised away; and they sometimes go to the most extreme lengths in their ingenious applications of this technique.[13] Anyone to whom exercises of this sort are not already too tiresomely familiar may derive some innocent amusement from the passage in which St. Augustine, in one of his anti-Manichaean works (*Contra Faust. Manich.* XXII.48-59), deals with the awkward problem of Rachel and the mandrakes, in Genesis XXX.14-18. (At the climax of this fascinating story, it will be remembered, the Patriarch Jacob, trudging in from the fields in the evening after a hard day's work, is greeted by the older and more ill-favoured of his two wives with a confident, ' "Thou must come in unto me, for surely I have hired thee with my son's mandrakes". And he lay with her that night,' the result being Issachar.) But it would be wrong to end this glance at allegorical interpretation of Scripture by the Christians on a note of levity. Such interpretation could also have dire consequences, as when St. Augustine, in yet another of his allegorical flights, dishonestly perverted the sense of the words 'compel them to come in' which occur in the Parable of the Great Supper in Luke's Gospel (XIV.16-24) to justify the persecution of religious dissent, interpreting the 'highways and hedges' (in the command to 'go out into the highways and hedges and compel them to come in') allegorically as 'heresies and schisms', thereby furnishing mediaeval persecutors with a bogus Scriptural foundation for their activities, of which they did not hesitate to make use.[14]

The early Christian attitude to property ownership, as I have described it, is open to criticism from more than one direction, quite apart from its departure from the teachings of its Founder. I shall single out two respects in which it can now be seen to be unsatisfactory: first, the exceedingly important role it allotted to almsgiving; and secondly, its notion that a sufficiency of wealth was harmless enough, even if a superfluity was dangerous.

Until quite recently, charity (in its most material form, almsgiving) was accepted by the great majority as an entirely admirable thing; and it is only in our own generation that a large number of people have begun to criticise powerfully the whole principle of organised charity within the community as a remedy for social evils, not only because it provides the giver with a moral justification for his privileged position but also because it is increasingly felt by the recipient as something degrading, as a derogation of human dignity – a feeling with which, I must say, I myself entirely sympathise. (In the conception of the 'Welfare State', such as it is, everyone contributes if he can; and he receives what he does receive not as charity but as a social right – a fundamentally different principle.) The almsgiving upon which the early Christians so prided themselves, therefore, appears to many of us nowadays in a very much less attractive light than it did in its own time and for centuries afterwards. It was obviously very desirable as a means of preserving the social order, by mitigating the last extremes of poverty which might lead to revolutionary outbreaks. But it was something much more than that: it also enabled the propertied class not merely to retain their wealth without any feelings of guilt, but even to glory in it, investing it with a moral aura derived from using a small proportion of it (fixed entirely at their own discretion) for 'good works' that would help to ensure their own salvation. If charity had not been part of the patrimony inherited by Christianity from Judaism, and recommended by Jesus himself, the Church would surely have been driven to invent it.

My other criticism of the early Christian position concerning property ownership is that the concept of a 'sufficiency' of property, whenever it was introduced, was always left vague and was no better defined than by some such imprecise formula as 'non plus quam necesse est', with the result that anyone except perhaps the ancient equivalent of the multi-millionaire could feel that he had no superfluity. Pliny the Younger could claim that he had no more than a 'modest fortune' ('Sunt quidem omnino nobis modicae facultates', *Epist.* II.iv.3), yet he cannot have been worth much less than HS 20 million and counts among the two or three dozen richest Romans we happen to know about during the Principate,[15] event if his assets were hardly more than a fifteenth or a twentieth part of those attributed to the richest men of all, who may have owned 300 or even 400 million – and who themselves did not approach the great imperial families in wealth. The great fortunes became greater still in the fourth and fifth centuries, and in those days it was even easier for the well-to-do to feel that they were possessed of only 'modest fortunes'. Four lines in a poem by Gregory of Nazianzus are worth quoting: 'Cast away all and possess God alone, for you are the dispenser of riches that do not belong to you. But if you do not wish to give all, give the greater part; and if not even that, then make a pious use of your superfluity' (*tois perittois eusebei, Carm. Theol.* II.33.113-16). The effect of such advice on most rich men can easily be imagined.

*   *   *   *   *   *

It is time to sum up. Why did early Christianity so signally fail to produce any important change for the better in Graeco-Roman society? Why did slavery and kindred forms of unfree labour such as the colonate persist, without Christians even realising that they were evil in themselves and that they tended to brutalise both slaves and masters? Why, after the empire became officially Christian, in the fourth century, did the extremes of wealth and poverty throughout the Roman world (and especially in the West) become even greater, with enormous riches concentrating in the hands of the senatorial class, and taxation becoming decidedly more oppressive? Why did torture become even more prevalent and punishments even harsher, with the barbarous practice of mutilation added?

The standard answer to all these questions (most of which are dealt with elsewhere in this book) is familiar to all of us: Jesus himself and the early Christians were concerned exclusively with the relations between man and man, or man and God, and not at all with social, economic or political *institutions* – with the relations between men and men, if I may use that expression. That does not seem to me a very good answer, even as far as it goes, for although the New Testament writers (like the early Fathers) concentrate on questions of individual morality and make no attempt to prescribe a general code of economic or political behaviour, they do make a series of statements on political and economic questions which the Church duly accepted as canonical and inspired: St. Paul's disastrous 'The powers that be are ordained of God', which I quoted earlier, is only one among many such pronouncements. One form of what I have called 'the standard answer' is that we must think in terms of the salvation or reformation of 'the individual' – a tiresome modern abstraction which might almost be designed to mislead: this often becomes apparent if we replace it by what it really means, 'all individuals', or 'each and every individual'. Those who say that it is 'the individual' and not social institutions which need to be changed for the better are in practice advocating that reform be postponed until all individuals, or at any rate the great majority, have undergone the necessary improvement – a clever and covert argument for keeping things as they are. Students of Greek thought are fortunate, in that this obfuscating notion of 'the individual' rarely appears in antiquity, and indeed can hardly be expressed in Greek, or for that matter in Latin.

But can the traditional Christian position which I have outlined provide a satisfactory answer to my questions, even if it is adjusted in such a way as to shed those unpleasant features of early Christian thought such as the acceptance of slavery and of political autocracy which so many Christians today are unwilling to endorse? This of course is a matter of opinion. I will only say that in my opinion it was precisely the exclusive concentration of the early Christians upon the personal relations between man and man, or man and God, and their complete indifference, as Christians, to the institutions of the world in which they lived, that prevented Christianity from even having much effect for good upon the relations between man and man. I suggest that the relations *between man and man* in any organised human society are severely conditioned by the relations *between men and men* – between different States, and between different groups (classes above all) within States, relations governed as a rule by criteria very different from those which can be applied between man and man. It has often been realised that Christianity has been conspicuously unsuccessful in preventing war between nations. It took the Church a long time to evolve a doctrine of the 'Just War', although incidentally even the early Roman Republic had had a doctrine of the 'bellum iustum', derived from the principle of fetial law: that no war was acceptable to the Roman gods unless it was a defensive war, waged to protect Rome or her allies – itself nicely criticised by Cicero as the means by which the Romans gave their aggression the appearance of legitimacy (see ECAPS 36-7 and nn.130-1). And the doctrine of the Just War has never come to very much, because any country that goes to war can always justify itself easily enough in its own eyes. As for the class struggle, I cannot see that the Christian churches have done much more than either deplore it in principle or ignore its very existence; and all too often they have explicitly underwritten the existing social and economic order in its crudest form. To quote a well-known Anglican hymn[16] –

> The rich man in his castle,
> The poor man at his gate,
> God made them, high or lowly,
> And order'd their estate.

Pope Pius XI's encyclical, *Quadragesimo anno*, of 1931, admits that the class struggle had been a serious danger forty years before, but then proceeds to speak of this danger as having been largely dispelled by Leo XIII's *Rerum novarum* – an opinion which has hardly been confirmed by the events of the years since 1931: not even the growth of Fascism, while it lasted, could validate that claim. There have, needless to say, been a few striking individual exceptions within the churches who have broken right away from their official policy, from John Ball in 1381 to Camilo Torres in our own time.[17]

When the early Hebrew prophets, or Plato and Aristotle, tried to formulate a vision of the good society, they thought first in terms of the Israelite nation or of the Greek city: for Plato and Aristotle the society as such had first to be good, to have good institutions, before men could lead the good life within it. Their successors, in both cases, tended to despair of creating a good society: for them, either the individual man (the Stoic, in particular) had to discover how best to live his personal life in an indifferent if not hostile world, or else there was a Good Time Coming, but it would be achieved by some supernatural agency. In the latter case one could comfort oneself by imagining (as in Jewish Apocalyptic) that in some mysterious way the desired result had been achieved already: the passage in the Magnificat which I quoted earlier provides a good example. The use of the future tense – 'He *will* put down the Dynasts, exalt the humble, feed the hungry, and send the rich empty away' – might have created a very different atmosphere: it might have pointed to social change instead of acceptance of the existing order. But the institutions of society were (as I have put it) the relations of *men and men*; and the Christian as such was therefore not concerned with them, and there was nothing to prevent him from being a complete political conformist. I have already referred to St. Paul's order to Christians to obey the political authorities, as 'powers ordained of God': he equated resistance to them with resistance to the ordinance of God, necessarily involving condemnation.

At the present time there is a debate going on among Christians whether (to use the language I have employed) it may not be absolutely necessary to reform the relations between men and men – in particular the relations between States and between classes within States – in order that the relations between man and man may not be for ever distorted and damaged. Among these relations between men and men, I would suggest that a central role is played by property-relations, including in particular ownership of property and the way in which production is organised. Those of us who watch the debate within the churches from the outside may feel that careful study of what actually happened in the early Christian centuries, both in the field of ideas and in actual social life, might well shed some light on current problems and controversies, and as a result might have a powerful influence upon the future of man.

(v)
The ideology of the victims of the class struggle

Let us turn now to something very different: the ideology and propaganda of the other side in the class struggle – of the exploited and the oppressed, of the slaves above all. The difficulty here is the scantiness of the evidence, even for the humbler *citizens*. For the great period of Greek history, the fifth and fourth centuries B.C., there is certainly some democratic propaganda, insisting on the fitness of the poor citizen, as well as the rich, to share in ruling the state: this might be compared with some of the arguments advanced in seventeenth-century England, notably the Leveller contributions to the Putney Debates in 1647. (These debates, preserved in the Clarke Papers, are most conveniently read in Woodhouse, *PL²*.)[1] To the Greek historian those debates should be exceptionally interesting, for the great question at issue was precisely that which divided Greek oligarchs and democrats: ought political rights to be strictly confined (as desired, for example, by Cromwell and Ireton) to men of sub-stantial property? 'All the main thing that I speak for,' said Ireton, 'is because I would have an eye to property' (Woodhouse, *PL²* 57).[2] But even some of the Levellers (though probably not the great majority) took the line that hired labourers and servants, as being too dependent upon their masters, ought not to enjoy the franchise (see III.vi above, *ad fin.*). Most of the surviving Greek literature that I have in mind here either pleads the cause of democracy (among citizens alone, of course) or merely, with Solon, urges the powerful to abate their exclusive and arrogant claims and recognise, in Colonel Rainborough's famous words at Putney, that 'the poorest he hath a life to live, as the greatest he' (see Woodhouse, *PL²* 53). Virtually all this Greek material has what we might almost call a middle-class flavour, and indeed much of it comes from the *mesoi* (the men of moderate wealth) so beloved by Aristotle and others, of whom Solon is an outstanding example. Needless to say, hardly anyone ever thinks of the mass emancipation of slaves unless they have volunteered for military or naval service during a 'national emergency'.[3] Aristophanes in the *Frogs* (lines 190-1, cf. 33-4, 693-4) makes Charon refuse to ferry a slave over the Styx unless he was one of those who 'fought in the naval battle' – that of Arginusae, in 406, in which a number of Athenian slaves helped to row the ships of the Athenian fleet (as they never did at normal times) and were rewarded with their freedom.

Some of the literary material from the Greek world in which we can recognise the heartfelt cry of the oppressed may be thought not strictly germane to the subject of this book, because it is only incidentally a product of class struggle: some of it is essentially a protest against *foreign imperialism*; some of it is primarily a *religious* protest; and some of it is both these things, like the Book of Revelation and some other Apocalyptic literature, Jewish as well as Christian, including the Book of Daniel, dating from 167-163 B.C. (probably 166-164) and the earliest surviving piece known to me in any language which can justifiably be described as 'resistance literature'.[4] But I myself would certainly not agree to exclude most of the literature I have just referred to. When imperialism leads directly to exploitation of a conquered people, or at any rate the primary producers among them, for the benefit of the foreign rulers, that is a situation closely resembling class struggle; and, as I have indicated in my definition of class and class struggle (II.ii above), effects are likely to be produced upon the class struggle within the oppressed community – as certainly happened, for example, in Seleucid Palestine and even more in Roman Palestine, where some members of the Jewish propertied class were hand-in-glove with their Roman masters, and the great Revolt of A.D. 66-70 was directed partly against the native Jewish oppressors.[5] Nor can protests which are primarily religious in form (like the Books of Daniel and Revelation) be excluded from a consideration of the outlook of an exploited class as such, at any rate if one of the reasons for their very existence is the oppressiveness of the imperial power, as in the two cases I have just mentioned. Rome, under the guise of 'Babylon', is ferociously attacked in Revelation (e.g. II.13; VI.9-10; XII-XVIII; XIX.2), and is said to be 'drunk with the blood of the saints and with the blood of the martyrs of Jesus' (XVII.6); and when she 'comes in remembrance before God', he 'gives unto her the cup of the wine of the fierceness of his wrath' (XVI.19) – splendid, blood-curdling stuff, in which the impotent fury of the oppressed, unable as they are to revenge themselves, finds satisfaction in the certainty of divine vengeance.

For nearly a century scholars have devoted a great deal of attention to the so-called 'Acts of the Pagan Martyrs of Alexandria', which survive only in Egyptian papyri of the period of the Roman Principate published in modern times.[6] The form of most of these papyri is a copy, or rather a pretended copy, of the official records of the trials of prominent Alexandrians, who are most sympathetically treated by the compilers, while the harshness of the Roman emperors towards the great metropolis of Egypt is implicitly rebuked. These documents emanated from the leading circles at Alexandria, who were themselves, of course, members of an exploiting class, and I mention them here merely because they do constitute indignant propaganda against an imperial power and have aroused so much scholarly interest. Some of them – the *Acta* of Isidore and Lampon, and of Hermaiscus – are also bitterly anti-Jewish: they provide, I suppose, the earliest surviving examples of popular anti-Semitic propaganda. Anti-Semitism was endemic at Alexandria in the early Roman Principate, for the Jews there had received various privileges from Julius Caesar and Augustus, which aroused resentment and jealousy on the part of the Alexandrians. (There is an excellent account of the position of the Jews in Egypt in the Hellenistic and Roman periods by V. Tcherikover, *C. P. Jud.* I.1-111.) Other anti-imperialist propaganda (anti-Greek or anti-Roman) has been assembled by recent writers: it includes some of the *Sibylline Oracles*, in Greek hexameters, the so-called *Oracle of the Potter*, surviving in Greek papyri from Egypt, and the *Demotic Chronicle*, a text in Egyptian demotic; from farther East come the *Oracle of Hystaspes*, a Persian work surviving only in some paraphrases in Latin by the Christian writer Lactantius, and the *Bahman Yasht*, another Persian text, in a Pahlevi translation.[7] Most of this material seems very strange to us today. Anyone who wishes to read some specimens might begin with *Orac. Sibyll.* III.350-5, 356-80; and V.155-78, 386-433, prophesying the doom of Rome (cf. VIII.37-49, 81-106, 165), and four other passages from the *Sibyllines*, IV.115-39; and V.137-54, 214-27, 361-85, containing prophecies associated with the 'false Neros' who appeared in the twenty years after Nero's death in 68.[8]

I must not fail to mention three remarkable documents in Latin (one a literary letter, the other two literary speeches) which reveal some recognition by members of the Roman governing class of the mentality of Rome's victims – it would be going much too far to speak of genuine 'sympathy' (cf. IV.iv n.13). The only one which relates to the eastern part of the Roman empire is the 'letter of King Mithridates [VI Eupator of Pontus] to King Arsaces' [of Parthia], composed by Sallust and surviving as a fragment of his *Histories* (IV.69). Mithridates attributes to the Romans 'a deep-seated desire for domination and rule' as their 'one inveterate motive for making war on all nations, peoples and kings' (§ 5); the letter calls them 'the plague of the world' (*pestis orbis terrarum*, § 17), accuses them of having become great 'by daring deceit and adding war to war', and declares that they will destroy everything or perish in the attempt (§§ 20-1). In a phrase which no doubt reflects Sallust's own belief, the king is made to say, 'Few men desire liberty; a large proportion are content with just masters' (*pauci libertatem, pars magna iustos dominos volunt*, § 18). The other two documents are speeches in Tacitus, relating to the western part of the empire, which also show some recognition of the mentality of the oppressed. The first is that of the fiercely anti-Roman British chieftain Calgacus (*Agric.* 30-2), who is depicted addressing his men before the battle of the 'mons Graupius' (perhaps not far south of Inverness) in A.D. 83 or 84. It contains defiant statements about 'liberty' which, in Tacitus, are hardly more than Roman clichés, and must have been written with quiet derision on his part; but one remark has echoed down the ages: when the Romans, says Calgacus, 'create a desolation, they call it peace' (*ubi solitudinem faciunt, pacem appellant,* 30.6). The other speech, in *Annals* I.17, is the one I have referred to near the end of IV.iv above, by a leader of the the mutiny of the Pannonian legions in A.D. 14, named Percennius, described by Tacitus as a former leader of one of the theatrical factions and represented by him as a noxious demagogue (see esp. IV.iv n.13). The real detestation felt by Tacitus for any 'agitator' who pleased the lower orders in the provinces by uttering sentiments hostile to Rome or its rulers emerges nicely from the brief but concentrated invective of *Hist.* IV.68 against Julius Valentinus, a leading man of the Treveri, who at an assembly during the Gallic revolt of A.D. 70 'heaped insults and odium upon the Roman people'. Tacitus scorns to itemise these, and contents himself with remarking that they included 'all the charges commonly levelled against great empires', which – if he is not merely dismissing them with contempt – he presumably regarded as too familiar to need specification. I shall do no more than record in a note[9] a few examples of other speeches, usually describing subjection to Rome as slavery, which are put by Tacitus or Dio Cassius into the mouths of leaders of rebellion against Rome.

There is one form of expression of protest, associated particularly (though not solely) with slaves, which deserves to be singled out: the fable. Phaedrus, a slave and freedman of the Emperor Augustus, who wrote in Latin in the first half of the first century of the Christian era,[10] made great use of collections of the fables of Aesop, another ex-slave, who probably lived in the early sixth century B.C.[11] Phaedrus has a fascinating passage in the Prologue to his Third Book, lines 33-40. He says he will explain why the fable was invented: it was to enable the slave to give expression in a disguised form to sentiments which he dared not speak out aloud for fear of punishment! And it was not only slaves whom Phaedrus had in mind as the disguised heroes of fables. One of his pieces, about a frog dreading a fight between two bulls, is introduced with the words, 'The lowly are in trouble when the powerful quarrel' (*humiles laborant ubi potentes dissident,* I.30.1). And at the end of the Epilogue to his Third Book he quotes Ennius: 'It is sacrilege for a common man [a *plebeius*] to mutter in public' (III. *Epil.* 34). Another fable, intended to demonstrate 'how sweet liberty is', speaks of the wolf who is on the point of being persuaded by the dog to serve his master when he notices that the dog's neck has been galled by a chain; realising what this means, he refuses to join the dog in servitude (III.7; cf. Babrius 100; *Fabulae Aviani* 37). The fable I like best of all is explicitly concerned not merely with slaves but with the poor in general (the *pauperes*): Phaedrus introduces it with the words, 'A change in the person who controls the State [if I may so translate *in principatu commutando*] brings to the poor no change in their situation but a change of master' (*nil praeter dominum* – if that is the correct reading). This fable (I.15) is about a timid old man, pasturing a donkey in a meadow, when suddenly a hostile army approaches. The old man begs the donkey to flee with him, to avoid capture. But the donkey merely enquires if the enemy will make him carry two packs at once; and when his owner says he does not suppose they will, refuses to move. 'What does it matter to me whose servant I am,' he asks, 'so long as I carry only one pack at a time?' Gerrard Winstanley expressed much the same point of view in 1650, in his *Appeal to All Englishmen*, when he said of the poor in England that if they should fight and conquer a foreign enemy, 'they are like to be slaves still, for the gentry will have all . . . For, say they, "We can as well live under a foreign enemy working for day wages as under our own brethren"': see the collection by Hill and Dell (cited in VII.ii n.13 below) 387.

'Aesopic' fables were a literary genre simple enough to appeal to those who lacked the elaborate literary education needed for a proper understanding of a large part of Greek and Latin literature; and even those with no education at all could grasp them immediately. Quintilian, writing in the nineties of the first century the standard Latin handbook on rhetoric (*Institutio Oratoria*), remarks that *fabellae* have a special appeal to country boors and the uneducated (*ducere animos solent praecipue rusticorum et imperitorum,* V.xi.19). He would certainly have said the same about the Parables of Jesus. But the governing classes of antiquity were clever enough to take over this weapon of their subjects and turn it sometimes to their own advantage. We all know the fable of Menenius Agrippa, from the *Coriolanus* of Shakespeare (I.i.53-169), if not from Plutarch's *Life of Coriolanus* (6.3-5) or from Livy (II.xxxii.8-12). However fictitious its attribution to the consular in question and the year 494 B.C., it is the most famous of all those fables that were appropriated by the ruling class. Among other fables intended to keep workers in their place is the amusing one in which the donkeys appeal to Zeus for relief from their labours: its moral is that what each individual must endure cannot be cured (it is *atherapeuton*).[12]

It was not a slave but a learned man, the Hellenistic scholar Daphitas (or Daphidas) of Telmessus, who not only reviled the Attalid kings as 'filings of the treasury of Lysimachus, who rule Lydia and Phrygia', but addressed them directly as 'purple weals' (*porphyrioi mōlōpes*, Strabo XIV.i.39, p.647). He can only have been likening the kings to the marks of a whip on a man's back. This was well understood by Tarn, who shows exceptional awareness of social realities in the Greek East; but several other scholars have failed to grasp the fact that for Daphitas the kings, as oppressors, *are* 'purple weals' on men's backs, and they have supposed the verse to be pretending that the Attalids were once slaves themselves, 'purpled with bruises' or 'with stripes' (Hansen, and the Loeb translator, H. L. Jones); 'they had purple backs then too, or should have had' (Fontenrose).[13] Daphitas, by the way, is said to have paid for his *lèse-majesté* with his life: according to Strabo, he was crucified on Mt. Thorax, near Magnesia on the Maeander.

A few direct and open attacks on emperors, necessarily anonymous, are recorded here and there. In V.iii above I mentioned the bitter verses put up in the hippodrome at Constantinople in the early sixth century, addressing Anastasius as 'world-destroying emperor' and accusing him of 'money-grubbing' (John Lydus, *De magistrat*. III.46).

★　★　★　★　★　★

I must conclude this section with a short discussion of the religious issues which bulked so large in men's minds in the Christian Roman empire of the fourth, fifth, sixth and seventh centuries, in order to make it clear that in my view the religious questions were very largely unconnected with men's class positions, except in one or two special cases, of which Donatism in North Africa is the only conspicuous one. In this book I have been concentrating upon class, because I believe that in the long run it is the production of material necessities and the economic and social structures through which this is accomplished that have the most powerful effect upon men's behaviour and even thinking, rather than any incidental religious beliefs they may hold. But in the short run religion may play a decisive role in influencing men's actions and the nature of the groups into which they divide; and so it was in the Christian Roman empire, when political class struggle was a rare phenomenon (cf. Chapter VIII below) but religious strife was widespread and intense.

I agree with A. H. M. Jones that it is a serious mistake to see the doctrinal controversies which so agitated the early Christian churches as the expression either of 'nationalist feeling'[14] or of 'social protest'. His article, 'Were ancient heresies national or social movements in disguise?', in *JTS* n.s.10 (1959) 280-98 (reprinted in his *RE*, ed. Brunt, 308-29), and his *LRE* II.964-70 (with III.326-7 nn.61-70), are absolutely decisive. I must, however, point out that Jones's attack is concentrated against the view that certain heresies were essentially 'national'; the word 'social' in the title of his article is relevant only to his discussion of the social aspects of Donatism[15] – which of course was always rightly regarded as a schism rather than a heresy, until the Catholics had the ingenious idea that the Donatist belief in the necessity for re-baptising Catholics admitted to their fold could be regarded as a heretical belief, sufficient to bring the Donatists within the scope of the stringent laws passed against heresy in the late fourth century and the early fifth (see *CTh* XVI.vi.4.*pr.*). While admitting in his book that Donatism was 'associated with a social struggle' (possessing, indeed, 'some features of a class war'), Jones insists that its social aspects were far from being the essence of Donatism; and he is clearly right. (See, however, VIII.iii below, on the Circumcellions.)

Another area in which religious 'nationalism' has been seen by some historians is Egypt; but I know of no specifically religious material from that country, comparable with the anti-Roman propaganda of the 'Acts of the Pagan Martyrs' of Alexandria, referred to above, which, as we saw, were evidently produced by members of the Alexandrian upper classes. However, some of the literature emanating from Egyptian monastic circles is worth a mention here for its denunciation of the oppression of the peasantry. It was of course essentially religious, and its social character was purely secondary and due to the fact that during the Later Empire paganism – outside Alexandria, at any rate – became increasingly confined to the upper classes. The outstanding representative of this trend is the monk Shenute (whose name is also rendered Shenoute, Schenute, Shenudi, Schenoudi, Schnoudi, Chenoude, Chenoute; in Latin it is Sinuthius). His works, written in Coptic (Bohairic), but showing knowledge of Greek literature, seem not to be well known to ancient historians, although they have been edited in Coptic and translated into Latin and some modern languages. Shenute was abbot of the White Monastery at Atripe in the desert of the Thebaid (Upper Egypt), where he is said to have lived for more than eighty years from the 380s onwards and to have died at well over a hundred, perhaps as late as 466. For my purposes the most useful document, especially for English readers, is Shenute's open letter to a wealthy pagan landowner, Saturnus of Panopolis, edited in the original Coptic more than once and translated complete into English by John Barns, SHS (1964).[16] Shenute himself was of peasant origin and, as Barns says, 'his sympathy lay with a stratum of society normally too inarticulate to express itself in Greek', and a 'fanatical fearlessness made this formidable monk an outspoken champion of the oppressed Egyptian peasant before the highest authorities' (SHS 155, 152). He delighted in open attacks on 'the paganism lingering among the propertied class' (ibid. 155). We hear of the pillaging of more than one of the few pagan temples which had somehow managed to survive into the fifth century, and of raids on the house of the pagan landlord mentioned above, which Shenute regarded as defiled not only by the presence of pagan cult objects and of magical papers and potions, but also of baths, built by the forced labour of the peasants on the estate and maintained by contributions exacted from them (see Barns, SHS 154–5 and n.17, 158). Baths, as Shenute insisted, were something that peasants did not need. Later Roman peasants could indeed be greatly impressed by what has been cynically called 'the odour of sanctity' in its more extreme forms. The young St. Theodore of Sykeon (not far from the modern Ankara) made a very great impression when he came out of the cave in which he had been living in religious isolation for two years: 'His head was covered with sores and pus, his hair was matted and an indescribable number of worms were lodged in it; his bones were all but through the flesh and the stench was such that no one could stand near him' (*Vita S. Theod. Syk.* 20, in the English translation by Elizabeth Dawes and N. H. Baynes, *Three Byzantine Saints* 101).

Shenute's letter to Saturnus, vigorous and highly abusive, mentions a number of indignities and injustices allegedly inflicted by Saturnus on his dependent peasants: carrying off their property (including cattle and carts), the imposition of forced labour, and compelling the peasants to buy meat and wine from him at unreasonable prices. Here we do see a leading cleric acting as protector of the poor; but one is bound to wonder whether Shenute's attitude to a pious Christian landlord who was similarly oppressive might not perhaps have been very different. And as Barns says, 'If any hoped that the final triumph of Christianity would mean the rectification of social evils and a less bitter spirit in the population of Egypt, that hope was to be disappointed. With the passing of the pagan landlord the tyranny of the great estate only became more absolute; and once paganism was as good as dead the resentment of the governed – by now an inveterate habit of mind – made differences of Christian doctrine its excuse for disaffection from the governing power and schism from its established Church' (SHS 156); cf. VIII.iii below and its nn.32-8.

I wish I had been able to give a systematic account of a few other religious figures who are recorded as acting, or at least speaking, on the side of the humble against their oppressors. They fall into very different categories. Sometimes, as with Shenute in the incident just described, they are simply standing up for Christians against powerful pagans – or for members of their own sect against 'heretics' or 'schismatics'. Some of them are bishops exercising their ecclesiastical authority to prevent acts of obvious injustice (for example against the *coloni* on Church estates), like Pope Gregory the Great and St. Theodore of Sykeon, as described at the end of IV.ii above. (There are other examples of Gregory's concern for the peasants on Church lands.) A particularly interesting group are those 'holy men' whose authority – the Romans would have called it *auctoritas* as opposed to *potestas* (see VI.vi above and its n.8 below) – is not of a political or even ecclesiastical nature but is derived from the force of their own personality, often heightened by the respect engendered by the extreme rigour and asceticism of their lives. They have been studied in particular by Peter Brown, in an article in *JRS* 61 (1971) 80-101 (limited almost entirely to Syria and Asia Minor) which has some fascinating material but is marred by blindness to the realities of the class struggle in the Later Roman Empire (see e.g. IV.ii nn.24 and 42 below). Defiance of 'lawful' political authority is very rare, since the Christian Churches – mindful of the instruction of St. Paul – preached absolute obedience to the State and its organs except when it was believed to be offending against religion (see the latter part of VI.vi above and its nn.77-98 below, with my ECAPS 14 and n.41). But intercession with the powerful on behalf of the humble is recorded on several occasions, often as a simple plea for justice or for mercy and forgiveness.

*   *   *   *   *   *

It is difficult for most people nowadays to understand the great importance attached to religion in the ancient Greek world, above all in the Christian period, when dogma could assume a central role, even in the minds of those who very imperfectly understood the subtle theological issues involved. I have often been struck, when reading the Fathers and the ecclesiastical historians, by the way the spiritual leaders of those times dominated their communities and received their unquestioning loyalty; the priest as well as the layman almost invariably believed what his particular bishop told him he ought to believe, except of course when that bishop was a man who did not hold the traditional beliefs of his community but had been foisted upon it against its will, by imperial decree for instance. (The institution of a Catholic patriarch in Monophysite Alexandria after the Council of Chalcedon – for which the use of troops was necessary – and his subsequent murder by a Monophysite mob provide only the most famous example of this kind of imperial interference and its unhappy results.)[17] Among many examples that could be given of the steadfast loyalty of congregations, whether 'catholic' or 'heretical', to their bishop, one of the best is that of Cyzicus (on the north coast of Asia Minor) in the second half of the fourth century. In 367 its bishop, Eleusius, who seems always to have been a member of the 'Semi-Arian' sect led by Macedonius, was induced by the threats of the Emperor Valens to abandon his particular doctrines and subscribe to the emperor's own brand of Arianism. Eleusius soon repented of his apostasy, and on his return to Cyzicus he announced to his flock that he no longer felt worthy to hold his bishopric. His congregation, however, refused to accept his resignation, and insisted on his remaining their bishop. When Eudoxius, the Arian patriarch of Constantinople, supported by the emperor, sent Eunomius to replace Eleusius, they built themselves a new church outside the city, where they could continue their form of worship under Eleusius; and they persisted until Eunomius withdrew.[18] Eleusius himself, it is worth remarking, was no mean persecutor: he had destroyed pagan temples in his city before the accession of Julian in 361 (Soz., *HE* V.15.4–5); he had also demolished a church in Cyzicus belonging to the Novatian sect, which Julian compelled him to rebuild (later exiling him);[19] and he did his best to harry and drive out those whom Socrates calls 'the Christians', meaning of course the Catholics.[20]

A set of beliefs, once acquired, was indeed not easily eradicated: what made most of the German peoples so stubbornly Arian for so long was simply the fact that Arianism was the form of Christianity they had originally adopted; to them it was the true Catholic faith, and Catholicism was heresy. The Armenians, who had to make valiant efforts to preserve a certain independence from both Rome and Persia, were untouched by the Christological controversies during the fifth century (they were not represented at the Councils of Ephesus or Chalcedon) and became acquainted with them only in the early sixth century, from Mesopotamian Monophysites fleeing from persecution by Persian authorities who supported Nestorianism in that area. The Armenians consequently condemned Nestorianism and adopted a Monophysite form of Christianity, which they retain to this day. The Egyptians, as Jones says, 'were in turn homoousians and monophysites partly because they had been taught no other doctrine, but mainly because these were the faiths of their great popes Alexander and Athanasius, Cyril and Dioscorus'; and the fact that the Council of Chalcedon not only condemned Dioscorus but also gave precedence in the East, above

Alexandria, to Constantinople, 'the upstart see whose pretensions the patriarchate of Alexandria had always resented and often successfully crushed', was an important factor in making Chalcedon detestable to the Egyptians (*LRE* II.966-7). Even quite small 'pockets' of eccentric belief of one kind or another might persist for a long time in particular areas, as in the village in Numidia, part of St. Augustine's diocese of Hippo, where all the inhabitants were Abelites/Abelonii, practising a strange variety of continence and perpetuating their community by adoption, until they were brought to see the error of their ways by St. Augustine (*De haeres*. 87, in *MPL* XLII.47). Such peculiar communities were far less likely to exist for long inside cities; but we hear, for example, of a congregation of 'Tertullianists' at Carthage who worshipped separately in churches of their own and only gave up the last one to the Catholic bishop of Carthage at the end of the fourth century or in the early fifth (Aug., *De haeres*. 86, in *MPL* XLII.46).

Religion in those days was universally regarded as a matter of enormous importance, and it was generally believed by Christians that holding the 'wrong' dogma, and sometimes even practising the 'wrong' ritual, might involve eternal damnation – a position which is far from extinct today, of course, although it is very much less widespread than in the Later Roman Empire. The niceties of doctrine could obsess very ordinary minds. Gregory of Nyssa has a delightful sketch of the passionately theological atmosphere of Constantinople in the late fourth century, which has often been cited but is still worth repeating. 'If you enquire about your change, you will get a piece of philosophising about the Begotten and the Unbegotten,' he warns. 'If you ask the price of a loaf of bread, the reply is "The Father is greater and the Son inferior". And if you say, "Is the bath ready?", the answer is that the Son is from nothing' (*Orat. de Deit. Fil.*, in *MPG* XLVI.557). This is part of a passionate denunciation of ignorant, insane, deranged, illogical and incomprehensible philosophising on the part of amateur dogmatic theologians who are all slaves, rogues, runaways from servile employments, tradesmen, money-changers or purveyors of clothing or food. (I have rearranged the elements of the invective slightly, but every expression I have used comes directly from the text.) These are pleasantries of a type to which many of the Fathers of the Church were addicted when denouncing other Christians belonging to a rival sect. Gregory is saying that Constantinopolitan theologising is what we might call a mere mouthing of slogans; and so indeed it is likely to have been on the part of most laymen and even many clerics and monks, who were simply persevering, faithfully but blindly, like human trams, in the truths – as they saw them – which they had received from their spiritual leaders. This passage is often cited by itself, out of context, and those who quote it usually fail to observe the essential fact that the formulae which Gregory so abhorred were detestable not because they were mindless slogans, but because they were Arian slogans. I have never come across in any of the Fathers any protest against a repetition of what the Father concerned regarded as Catholic slogans – those embodying the tenets of his own particular sect. I cannot refrain from mentioning here the famous theological poem called *Thalia* which Arius the heresiarch is said to have composed in a racy metre for the edification of his followers: St. Athanasius gives extracts which I shrink from reproducing, since they must seem little better than gibberish to anyone not versed in the niceties of the Arian controversy.[21] The *Thalia* would have been rather strong meat for the uneducated. But the ecclesiastical historian Philostorgius, who was himself an Arian (and therefore survives only in fragments), mentions without disapproval that Arius also wrote, and set to catchy tunes, popular theological ballads in the form of work-songs for the mill and travel-songs for journeys by sea and land (*HE* II.2). Another theologian who is credited with the same kind of activity is Apollinaris of Laodicea (the father of the heresiarch of that name), who, in the second half of the fourth century, is said to have had his poems (which were all 'for the praise of God') sung by men not only on convivial occasions but also at their work, and by women at the loom (Soz., *HE* VI.25.5).

Many of us may find much unconscious humour, even absurdity, in the writings of some of the Fathers and in many of the supersubtle theological controversies in which they indulged. The devout Christian, however, may see such things in a very different light. To avoid giving unnecessary offence, therefore, I shall confine myself to a single example, coming from the Arians, whose heresy is surely now extinct. We hear from Socrates (V.23) of a dispute which agitated the Arians from about A.D. 385 onwards, for some thirty-five years in Constantinople and in other cities even longer. Believing as they did that the Son was 'created out of nothing', the Arians fell into controversy as to whether the Father was such, and ought to be called 'Father', before the Son existed. When the party of Dorotheus, which took the negative view, gained the upper hand, the followers of Marinus, who answered the question in the affirmative, insisting that the Father had always been the Father even when the Son did not exist, built separate churches for themselves and worshipped apart from the others. Socrates adds that the latter section of the Arians were nicknamed 'Psathyrians', after one of their number, Theoctistus, who was said to have been a cake-seller, *psathyropōlēs*. The nice theological issue between the two groups was never actually settled, and the division between the two parties in Constantinople was healed only when both sides entered into a self-denying ordinance never to allow the question to be raised again.[21a]

Apart from sarcastic jests at the expense of one's religious adversaries (such as the use of the term 'Psathyrians' in the way I have just described) deliberate humour is a commodity that is scarce enough – perhaps appropriately – in the ecclesiastical writers. Socrates does devote one whole chapter (*HE* VI.22) to the witty sayings of Sisinnius; and this is all the more remarkable in that Sisinnius presided over the schismatic Novation sect at Constantinople (395-407).[22] But pure theological humour is exceedingly rare. I have come across in the early Christian centuries only one example of a real joke which is both strictly theological and not made up for the purpose of ridiculing someone of a different dogmatic persuasion. (It is a strictly Greek joke, which cannot easily be reproduced in another language.) At the service of dedication of the first church of St. Sophia in Constantinople on 15 February 360, the Arian Eudoxius, who was patriarch of Constantinople from 360 to 370, startled the congregation by opening his dedicatory sermon with the words 'The Father is impious [*asebēs*], the Son pious [*eusebēs*]'. A great commotion immediately arose at this apparently blasphemous statement, but Eudoxius quelled it with the explanation, 'The Father is impious because he worships [*sebei*] no one; the Son is pious because he worships the Father.' The joke went down well, and according to Socrates it was still remembered in his own day (the second quarter of the fifth century), although he himself remarks gravely that with such sophistries the heresiarchs rent the Church asunder (*HE* II.43.10-14,15; cf. Soz., *HE* IV.26.1).[23]

In the West, theological controversy was couched in far less subtle terms than in the Greek East (its profundities could be debated more intricately in Greek, and some of them could scarcely be expressed in Latin), but it was equally vigorous in some places, especially Africa and Rome itself. When Constantius II in 358 issued an order that the Roman bishopric should be shared between the two rival popes, Liberius and Felix, the people assembled in the Circus are said to have responded with unanimous and indignant shouts of 'One God, one Christ, one bishop' (Theod., *HE* II.17.6). The fierce fighting between the supporters of the next pair of rival popes, Damascus and Ursinus, in 366, we are told by Ammianus, left 137 corpses in a single day on the floor of a Roman basilica (Amm. XXVII.iii.12-13); another contemporary source gives a figure of 160 victims.[24] One could cite many similar examples of violent strife and massacre on the part of enthusiastic Christians of the fourth and following centuries, in the East even more than the West. Those who enjoyed the support of the state (usually, but by no means always, the Catholics) were seldom reluctant to use force, even armed force, against their religious adversaries. According to Socrates and Sozomen, Macedonius, the Arian patriarch of Constantinople in the 350s, sent four units (*arithmoi, tagmata*) of troops of the regular army to ensure the conversion to Arianism of the exceptionally large congregation of the Novatian sect at the little town of Mantinium in Paphlagonia (in northern Asia Minor). Arming themselves with sickles and axes and whatever else came to hand, the peasants defeated the soldiers and killed nearly all of them in a bloody battle in which they themselves suffered heavy losses (Socr., HE II.38.27[bis]-29; Soz., *HE* IV.21.1-2).[25]

These and other such atrocities may make us sympathise with Ammianus when he endorses the opinion of the Emperor Julian that 'no wild beasts are such enemies to mankind as are most of the Christians [*plerique Christianorum*] in their deadly hatred of one another' (XXII.V.3-4). This statement should surprise only those who have not studied the original sources for the history of early Christianity in detail but have relied upon modern textbooks. It is essential to understand that the Christians, racked by heresy and schism – of which we can see the beginnings even in New Testament times[26] – were never anything like a single, united body, and that each sect (by no means only those who had the best right to call themselves 'Catholics') had an unpleasant habit of denying membership of 'the Church' and indeed the very name of Christian to all 'heretics' and 'schismatics' – that is to say, to all those who were not within its communion – and of persecuting them in one way or another whenever it could, as sinners outside 'the Church'. For the Christian 'ecclesiastical historians' by whom the history of early Christianity has mainly been written, 'persecution' is essentially what is done *to* 'the Church' (in the restricted sense I have just explained), either by pagans or by 'heretics' or 'schismatics'; they have usually forgotten the persecutions *by* 'the Church' (i.e. what they consider to be the orthodox or 'Catholic' church) of pagans, Jews, heretics or schismatics. Anyone who has not discovered this for himself may derive some amusement from a glance at the two entries under 'Persecution' in that often excellent and very scholarly work,

The Oxford Dictionary of the Christian Church[2] (1974): one deals solely with the persecution *of* the early Christians and the other reads merely, 'Persecution: see Toleration' – and when we look under 'Toleration' we find only a very brief reference to the persecutions conducted *by* the early Christians (with hardly more than the remark, 'St. Augustine went so far as to demand corporal punishment for heretics and schismatics'), and we then jump straight to the Middle Ages! In an unpublished *rapport* delivered to the International Colloquium on Ecclesiastical History held at Oxford in September 1974 (a revised version of which I shall publish shortly), I tried to explain the earlier stages in the process of persecution by the Christian churches which 'made of organised Christianity, over more than a millennium and a half, a persecuting force without parallel in the world's history'.

*　*　*　*　*　*

I doubt if a better means could have been devised of distracting the victims of the class struggle from thinking about their own grievances and possible ways of remedying them than representing to them, as their ecclesiastical leaders did, that religious issues were infinitely more important than social, economic or political ones, and that it was heretics and schismatics (not to mention pagans, Manichees, Jews and other 'lesser breeds without the Law') upon whom their resentment could most profitably be concentrated. Of course I am not saying that leading ecclesiastics magnified the importance of theological questions with the deliberate aim of distracting the common herd from their temporal grievances: they themselves quite sincerely held that only adherence to the 'right' dogma and the 'right' sect could ensure salvation and escape from the frightful prospect of eternal damnation. But there is no doubt that the effects of religious enthusiasm were as I have described them. Not many humble folk in the Christian Roman empire were likely to become obsessed with reforming the world of their day, or (for that matter) to achieve much unity among themselves, if they accepted what they were taught (as the vast majority did) and believed that life here and now is insignificant compared with the infinite stretches of eternity, and that their real enemies were those enemies of God and his Church who, if they were not suppressed, would endanger men's immortal souls and bring them to perdition. 'Heretics' and 'schismatics', as well as 'unbelievers', were an entirely new kind of internal enemy, invented by Christianity, upon whom the wrath of 'right-thinking people' could be concentrated, for in paganism the phenomena of 'heresy' and 'schism', as of 'unbelief', were inconceivable: there was no 'correct' dogma in which it was necesary to believe in order to avoid anathema in this world and damnation in the next, and to secure eternal life; and there was nothing remotely resembling a single, universal Church. We may reflect by contrast upon the good fortune of the mass of Greeks in the Classical period, who had no such beliefs instilled into them, to prevent them from recognising who their real internal enemies were, and to persuade them that democracy was a useless if not an impious aim, since 'the powers that be are ordained of God' (see the preceding section of this chapter).

VIII

The 'Decline and Fall' of
the Roman Empire: an Explanation

(i)
Intensified subjection and exploitation of the lower classes
during the first three centuries of the Christian era

In this last chapter I shall again show how a Marxist analysis on class lines can help to *explain*, and not merely to *describe*, a historical process: in this case the disintegration of large portions of the Roman empire, part of a process which seemed to Gibbon 'the greatest, perhaps, and most awful scene in the history of mankind' (*DFRE* VII.325).

I have demonstrated in V.iii above and Appendix IV below how Greek democracy, in the course of the class struggle on the political plane, was attacked with increasing success from the late fourth century B.C. onwards by the Greek propertied classes, their Macedonian overlords and eventually their Roman conquerors. As we have seen, democracy, when it worked, could play an important role by protecting the lower classes to some extent against exploitation and oppression by the powerful. Democracy still led a precarious existence in some places in the last century B.C., but during the first century of the Christian era it was gradually stifled and during the next century it virtually disappeared; certainly before the end of the third century it had, for all practical purposes, sunk without trace. (Democracy in the Latin West had never existed on anything like the same scale, and I know of no real sign of its existence after the first century.)

As we saw in IV.iii above, the great age of slavery in the Roman world, especially in Italy and Sicily, was the last two centuries B.C.: the advent of the Principate in the last generation B.C. and the marked decrease in the number of wars producing large slave-hauls gradually brought about a new economic situation: slaves now had to be bred far more extensively than before, if their number was not to decline drastically; and for the reasons given in IV.iii (§§ 6ff.) above this was bound to result in an attempt to increase the rate of exploitation of humble free men, in order to make up for a reduced return overall from slaves. An exploiting class, except in so far as it can be forced or persuaded (like some capitalist classes in the modern world) to abate its claims in order to facilitate its own survival (an eventuality which of course did not arise in the Graeco-Roman world), will use whatever means may lie to its hand.

In order to tighten the economic screw more effectively on the lower classes among the free population, it was obviously desirable to restrict to an absolute minimum not merely their political but also their legal and constitutional rights and privileges. Until the second and even (to some small extent) the early third century of the Christian era these rights and privileges might vary greatly, in the Greek world under Roman rule, both in theory and (to a less extent) in practice, according to whether a man was (*a*) a Roman citizen (*civis Romanus*),[1] (*b*) a citizen of a 'free' Greek city, a *civitas libera* (occasionally also *foederata*), which enjoyed greater powers of local jurisdiction than other municipalities,[2] (*c*) a citizen of a Greek city which was not technically 'free' (and was therefore more completely subject to the control of the Roman provincial governor), or (*d*) an ordinary provincial, like the great mass of the population (especially the peasantry), whose juridical rights were few and ill-defined and, in so far as they existed at all, were enjoyed largely on sufferance. Free men who were not Roman citizens, for example, were not usually tortured during the Roman Republic or early Principate (see e.g. Garnsey, *SSLPRE* 143 and ff.). Pliny tortured only two female slaves among the Pontic Christians he tried (see his *Ep.* X.96.8). But I know of no binding general rule to this effect, except for Roman citizens, and I cannot see how any *peregrinus* (non-Roman) who was tortured by order of a Roman governor could have had any hope of redress, except through the intervention of some influential patron.

By degrees, by a process – never yet, to my mind, adequately described – which certainly began in practice in the first century of the Christian era and was mainly 'institutionalised' and given explicit legal formulation in the second century and the early third,[3] especially in the Antonine period (A.D. 138-93), the legal rights of the poorer classes were gradually whittled away, and by the Severan period (A.D. 193-235) had been reduced to vanishing point. Possession of local citizenship came to mean nothing, except for those who belonged to the 'curial order': that is to say, the members of the city Councils and their families (cf. V.iii above and Section ii of this chapter), who gradually became a hereditary local governing class. It was possession of the Roman citizenship which had long been the source of the most important juridical privileges, but the citizenship came to mean less and less, as a new set of social and juridical distinctions – which, as I shall show, were essentially, in the main, class distinctions – gradually developed, cutting right across that between *cives* and *peregrini*, so to speak. By the so-called *Constitutio Antoniniana* (the *CA* for short) of the emperor we usually call Caracalla or Caracallus (his real name was M. Aurelius Antoninus), the traditional (and almost certainly the actual) date of which is A.D. 212,[4] the citizenship was extended to all, or virtually all, the free inhabitants of the empire.[5] But this fact is very much less remarkable than it appears at first sight. The only contemporary expression of opinion about the purpose of the *CA* which survives is that of a leading Graeco-Roman historian who lived through the reign of Caracalla as a senator and consular and was in almost as good a position as anyone to understand imperial policy: Dio Cassius (LXXVII [LXXVIII].ix, esp. 5). Dio says explicitly that Caracalla's purpose was to increase his revenue by making former *peregrini* liable to certain taxes paid only by Roman citizens, the most important of which was the 5 per cent inheritance tax (*vicesima hereditatium*).[6] Dio of course detested Caracalla, and some historians have felt able to reject the alleged motive for the *CA*. I myself would not care to deny that a desire to raise additional revenue is likely to have played a major part in the emperor's mind, especially if we accept, as I think we must, the opinion of J. F. Gilliam that the inheritance tax affected estates of much lower value than has generally been assumed and applied even to quite small fortunes,[7] so that a very large number of people would have been subjected to it as a result of the *CA*. Whatever the unbalanced Caracalla's motives may have been for issuing his edict, I would say that by far the most important fact in the background, which made the *CA* both possible and unremarkable, was precisely the 'new set of social and juridical distinctions' I am just about to describe, which by now had replaced the distinction between *civis* and *peregrinus* for most important purposes and had made its continued existence unnecessary and irrelevant – a point to which I shall return presently.

The 'new set of social and juridical distinctions' is not easy to describe in a few sentences, and I know of no satisfactory and comprehensive treatment of it, although there have been very useful studies by Cardascia (ADCHH) and Garnsey (*SSLPRE* and LPRE). Here I can do no more than give a brief and over-simplified summary, in numbered paragraphs, to make cross-reference easier.

1. (*a*) The value to a 'Greek' of possessing the Roman citizenship in the early Principate is admirably illustrated by the story (in Acts XXI.26 to XXVI.32; cf. XVI.37-9) of St. Paul, a Jew of good education (XXII.3) who must have belonged to a fairly well-to-do family and could claim (XXI.39) to possess not only the Roman citizenship but also that of Tarsus, the principal Greek city of Cilicia in southern Asia Minor – a privilege not enjoyed, incidentally, by the linen-workers (*linourgoi*) of that city, as we know from Dio Chrysostom (XXXIV.21-3; cf. Appendix IV § 3B below). Now the technical legal consequences which should be drawn from the story of Paul's 'appeal to Caesar' are by no means certain in all respects, and Garnsey has recently argued that Festus, the Procurator of Judaea, was not bound to send Paul to Rome.[8] But it would be a mistake for us to concentrate only on Paul's appeal to be tried by the emperor. More important is the fact that at an earlier stage in the proceedings it was beyond question Paul's insistence upon his Roman citizenship which first rescued him from an 'inquisitorial' flogging in the barracks at Jerusalem and subsequently induced the commander there, the military tribune Claudius Lysias, to take elaborate precautions to send him to Caesarea, the provincial capital, a little over 100 kilometres away, under strong military escort, thereby saving him from being murdered by a band of Jewish conspirators (see Acts XXII.25-9; XXIII.10,12-22,23-33; esp. XXII.26,29; XXIII.23-7). Whether or not Festus was legally obliged to allow Paul's appeal to the emperor, the fact is that he did allow it; and even Garnsey is prepared to agree that Paul's citizenship played a part in making up his mind (*SSLPRE* 76). If no such appeal had been possible, Paul would doubtless have been tried by Festus at Jerusalem (see Acts XXV.9,20), necessarily with a *consilium* of leading Jews who would have been strongly prejudiced against him[9] – if indeed he was not murdered on the road from Caesarea to Jerusalem, as we are told the Jews had planned (Acts XXV.1-4). Had he not been able to claim Roman citizenship, then, Paul would never even have reached Caesarea and the provincial governor's court; or if he had, he would have been finished off by the Jews fairly easily. I should perhaps add that I in general accept the story in Acts, even if some of it, which can only come ultimately from Paul himself, is almost too good to be true. (Most of us, when first arrested as Paul was at Jerusalem, would have shouted out, at an early stage

in the proceedings, 'You can't do this to me. I'm a Roman citizen.' Paul waits until the last possible moment, when the centurion in charge of the flogging party is just about to give the order to begin; and he is studiously polite and detached.)

(b) Almost at the end of the Antonine period, in the early 180s in fact, the peasants of the Saltus Burunitanus in the province of Africa, at the modern Souk el-Khmis, describing themselves in very humble terms as 'miserrimi homi[nes]' and 'homines rustici tenues', could feel entitled to complain to the emperor because the head lessee of the imperial estate on which they were tenants (*coloni*) had had some of them flogged, 'even though they were Roman citizens'.[10] (I suspect that flogging administered by a magistrate, rather than a private individual, might by then have been something the peasant would have had to take, so to speak, more or less in his stride!) And even in the Severan period Ulpian, in a famous passage included in the *Digest* (XLVIII.vi.7; cf. 8 and Paulus, *Sent.* V.xxvi.1), could speak of the *Lex Julia de vi publica* (of Augustus) as forbidding the execution, flogging or torture of any Roman citizen *adversus provocationem* – that is to say, in defiance of any right of appeal to which the person in question might be entitled.

(c) It is an exaggeration when Garnsey, in the penultimate paragraph of his book (*SSLPRE* 279-80), asserts that 'at no stage in the period under survey was citizenship as such a source of privilege'. (The period in question is 'from the age of Cicero to the age of the Severan Emperors: that is, from the mid-first century B.C. to the early third century A.D.': *SSLPRE* 3.) There is an important element of truth in what Garnsey goes on to say, that citizenship merely 'bestowed certain formal rights on its holders as full members of the Roman community, but provided no guarantee of their exercise'. There was no cast-iron guarantee, certainly. Citizens of even the most advanced modern states are sometimes the victims of illegality and injustice. But the example of St. Paul is sufficient to prove that citizenship could be a 'source of privilege' of the very greatest possible value, which might indeed make all the difference between life and death. And it is interesting to remember here that Greek cities – Rhodes and Cyzicus in particular – could be deprived of their 'free' status for having taken it upon themselves to execute Roman citizens.[11] As we shall see, Garnsey minimises the *changes* (mainly during the second century) which *substituted* for the purely political qualifications of the citizenship, as a source of privilege, a social qualification which was ultimately dependent very largely upon economic position – upon class.

2. (a) For all practical purposes the constitutional rights to which an inhabitant of the Graeco-Roman world was entitled by at any rate the early third century (let us say, by A.D. 212, the date of the *CA*) depended hardly at all upon whether he was a Roman citizen, but, broadly speaking, on whether he was a member of what I shall call 'the privileged groups': namely, senatorial, equestrian and curial families,[12] veterans and their children, and (for some purposes) serving soldiers.[13]

(b) The many relevant legal texts from the second and early third centuries sometimes give privileges to undefined groups, designated by a variety of terms, the most common of which is *honestiores* (often opposed to *humiliores*), although there are many others, not merely *honestiore loco natus, in aliquo honore positus, in aliqua dignitate positus, honoratus, qui in aliquo gradu est* (all equivalents which show the close connection between privileged status and official rank), but also *splendidior persona, maior persona, altior*. The *humilior* may also be a *humilis persona, humilis loci, humiliore loco positus, qui humillimo loco est, qui secundo gradu est, plebeius* (particularly common), *sordidior, tenuior,* and (in the Later Empire) *inferior persona, vilior persona,* even *pessimus quisque.* (My lists are not intended to be exhaustive.) The Roman lawyers, curiously enough, were chary of giving precise definitions: as Javolenus Priscus put it, 'Every definition is dangerous in civil law' (*Dig.* L.xvii.202). But in this case there was a perfectly good reason why they preferred to leave their terms undefined: all these texts relate to cases involving judicial procedure, where it was very desirable to leave it to the individual judge to determine who was and who was not included. (This has been well brought out by Cardascia, ADCHH 335.) Would the brother of a man who had just entered the Senate, the wife of the Praetorian Prefect, or the bosom friend of the Prefect of Egypt be considered a *humilior*, just because he or she did not happen to have the technical qualification for membership of a privileged group? I cannot believe it.[14] Exalted rank could be expected to shed its lustre upon a man's relatives: in a papyrus of the early third century (*P. Gen.* 1) we find a petty official in Egypt advising some other such officials to be very careful how they behave towards the relatives of a man belonging to only the third and lowest equestrian grade (a *vir egregius*) who happened to enjoy the confidence of the Emperor Caracalla (cf. now Millar, *ERW* 114 and n.32).

(*c*) Much of the discussion of the emergence of the privileged groups – Cardascia's excellent article (ADCHH), for instance – has concentrated on the largest group of texts, which establishes different penalties for offences committed by the two categories, using for them some of the undefined expressions I have just been discussing. There are many texts, however, which are quite precise in their terminology and give privileges to perfectly well-defined groups: senators, equestrians, decurions, veterans, and in one case the *eminentissimi* and *perfectissimi* who formed the highest grades of the equestrian order, with certain members of their families (*CJ* IX.xli.11.*pr.*).

3. Again oversimplifying, I shall now summarise the legal, constitutional differences which developed mainly during the second century (and certainly before A.D. 212) between the privileged groups and those below them. The latter I can call without hesitation 'the lower classes': virtually all of them would fall outside what I have defined as 'the propertied class' (see III.ii above), and they would include virtually all those free men and women who were not members of that class. I have avoided speaking of the privileged groups as 'the upper classes' or 'the propertied classes', because they included for many purposes veterans (and even serving soldiers), who might be men of modest fortune; but I would insist that veterans (and soldiers) were given the privileges they received because of the unique importance of the army (which of course included a large part of the imperial civil service)[15] in the life of the empire and the necessity of turning discharged soldiers into contented property-owners: failure to do this had been a major cause of the downfall of the Republic (see VI.v above). The privileges of veterans were explicitly patterned on those of decurions; as the late Severan jurist Marcianus says, 'The same honour is attributed

to veterans and the children of veterans as to decurions' (*Dig.* XLIX.xviii.3). Now the decurions (see Section ii of this chapter) were always, broadly speaking, the class of principal local landowners who were not *honorati* (not members of the senatorial and equestrian aristocracy), and as time went on they became ever more nearly identical with that class. I would emphasise, therefore, that the 'privileged groups', apart from veterans and soldiers, had by the third century become almost identical (at least 90 per cent and perhaps even more nearly identical) with my 'propertied class', just as the non-privileged are virtually my 'lower classes', below the propertied class. Isolated exceptions such as imperial freedmen are too few to damage my case, especially when we remember that being a freedman is strictly a one-generation status (see III.v above) – and anyway some of these freedmen received equestrian status, and one or two even quasi-senatorial rank.[16]

(*a*) The most conspicuous and best attested difference between our two groups (often in this connection referred to as *honestiores* and *humiliores*) is '*the dual penalty system*', in which the privileged groups receive a lighter penalty than the lower classes: decapitation, for instance, instead of one of the *summa supplicia* (crucifixion, burning to death, or the beasts), and general exemption from condemnation to the mines or forced labour (*opus publicum*), often inflicted on the lower classes. There is an interesting controversy between Cardascia and Garnsey about the emergence of the dual penalty system from a matter of practice, according to the discretion of judges, to definite rules of fixed law: here Cardascia's review of Garnsey's book seems to me decisive,[17] and I would see an important change as taking place in the Antonine and Severan age, rather than in the first century. I must not omit to mention one statement in the *Digest*, by the Severan lawyer Aemilius Macer, that slaves were punished 'according to the example of the *humiliores*' (*exemplo humiliorum, Dig.* XLVIII.xix.10.*pr.*). As Garnsey aptly comments, 'The sequence might have been reversed. When one examines the forms of punishment used on *humiliores*, one is struck by the connection with, and the derivation from, typical slave punishments' (*SSLPRE* 127).

(*b*) *Flogging*, during the Republic and early Principate, was not supposed to be used on citizens, whose right of appeal against it, given by a law of the early second century B.C., was confirmed by the *Lex Julia de vi publica* of Augustus.[18] Probably humble citizens were often subjected to flogging by over-zealous magistrates during the investigation of cases – compare the modern 'third degree'. But as we saw above, St. Paul was immediately rescued from an inquisitorial flogging by his assertion of citizenship, and as late as the 180s humble African peasants could formally protest against the flogging – by their landlord, as we saw in 1(*b*) above – of those of their number who were citizens. The whole situation had changed drastically, however, by the early third century. The precise chronology is far from clear, but no one can deny that well before the end of the second century, citizens belonging to the lower classes could legally and properly be flogged for a wide variety of reasons, while their superiors were given legal exemption. (The most interesting texts are perhaps *CJ* II.xi.5, of A.D. 198, and Callistratus in *Dig.* XLVIII.xix.28.2,5, the last showing that the exemption of decurions was a central fact.) Interest in this process has too often concentrated on the exemptions, to which our evidence mainly relates, and as a result the really important development, which is the *introduction* of beating for the great mass of humble citizens, has tended not to receive much attention. Unfortunately, I do not think it is possible to decide precisely how long before the end of the second century the flogging of humble citizens became fully 'institutionalised'. (As I shall show in Section ii of this chapter, decurions in the fourth century lost their general immunity from flogging.)

(c) '*Torture* traditionally was reserved for slaves, but free men of low rank were not immune in the second and third centuries', and 'Torture of *honestiores* was not permitted in the Antonine and Severan periods': these perfectly correct statements by Garnsey are characteristic of what is to be found in most writings on the subject.[19] They conceal the fact that a striking *change* took place in the second century, very probably in the Antonine period. A curiously limited constitution of Marcus Aurelius which excused certain descendants of the two highest grades of the equestrian order (*eminentissimi* and *perfectissimi*) 'from the punishments of plebeians or from tortures' (*plebeiorum poenis vel quaestionibus, CJ* IX.xli.11.*pr.*) has more than once been discussed without the really remarkable thing about it being stressed: that it shows that most Roman citizens had now come to be officially regarded as legally liable to torture! Whether it was ever considered necessary to give legal exemption to such exalted creatures as *eminentissimi* and *perfectissimi* themselves may well be doubted; but, since the privileges of the equestrian order were more strictly personal than those of senators, Marcus obviously thought it desirable to give specific exemption to members of their families within certain degrees.[20] (Compare what I have said above on the lustre shed by exalted rank upon a man's relatives. The circle of relatives automatically entitled to such benefit might well need formal legal definition on occasion; no doubt a governor could always extend it.) As with flogging, so with torture: the exemption of decurions was the essential thing; it may always have been the practice, and a rescript of Antoninus Pius shows that by the time of that emperor (138-61) it had become settled law (*Dig.* L.ii.14; cf. XLVIII.xviii.15.1 = 10.*pr.*; 16.1; and, for the Severan period, Ulpian's statement quoted in *CJ* IX.xli.11.1).[21] This equally shows that there had been an important change in legal practice in the second century, and that there was now nothing legally objectionable in the torture of lower-class citizens. Pliny, when persecuting the Christians in *c.* 111, had tortured only slaves (see above), and we can believe that many officials still preferred not to torture free men of any sort if they could avoid it.[22] But the application of torture in court to accused persons was soon extended even to witnesses of humble condition; and by about the end of the third century the lawyer Arcadius Charisius, in his book *On witnesses* cited in the *Digest* (XXII.v.21.2), could actually advise that 'If the nature of the case is such that we are obliged to admit a *harenarius* or some such person [*vel similis persona*] as a witness, no credence ought to be attached to his testimony without the infliction of torture [*sine tormentis*].' (A *harenarius*, strictly a man who took part in combats in the amphitheatre, was regarded with special contempt by the Roman upper classes;[23] but the words 'vel similis persona' might, I think, be held to apply to almost any propertyless individual who earned a precarious living at the bottom of the social ladder.) There is a tendency to prohibit the torture of slaves in order to procure evidence against their owners, former owners and even possessors, and the near relatives of such people (see Buckland,

RLS 86–91, esp. 88–9). This, however, is due to concern for slaveowners, not slaves. As Cicero had put it, in his speech for Milo, torturing a slave to get evidence against his master is 'more ignominious to the master than death itself', *domini morte ipsa tristius* (*Pro Milone* 59). I should perhaps add that in cases of treason, *maiestas*, all rules relating to exemption from torture could go by the board, as indeed did most other rules.

(*d*) In various other ways members of the lower classes who were charged with crimes were at a disadvantage compared with the propertied classes: for example, they would find it much harder to escape imprisonment pending trial – to get out on bail, as we might say (see esp. *Dig.* XLVIII.iii.1,3). And ancient prison conditions could be very unpleasant for humble people: see Section iii of this chapter, *ad fin.*

(*e*) More important is the fact that evidence given in court by members of the lower classes, whether in criminal or civil cases, was accorded less weight than that of their social superiors. The key text is a passage from Callistratus in the *Digest* (XXII.v.3.*pr.*), explaining the principles on which evidence is to be evaluated: of the criteria mentioned the first concerns the witness's social status (*condicio*) and is 'whether he is a decurion or a commoner' (*decurio an plebeius*), and the third is 'whether he is rich or poor' (*locuples vel egens*). Callistratus proceeds to quote a series of rescripts of Hadrian, some of which illustrate the kind of discrimination he records (ibid. 3.1-2,6). The satirist Juvenal, writing in the early second century, had complained that at Rome a witness was valued according to his wealth (his *census*): the number of his slaves, the extent of his land, the size and quality of his dinner-service. His character and behaviour (his *mores*) came last; he received credit in proportion to the number of coins in his cash-box (*Sat.* III.140-4, ending 'quantum quisque sua nummorum servat in arca, Tantum habet et fidei'). This was closer to the reality, even in Juvenal's day, than I fancy most modern readers of Juvenal appreciate, and by the time of Callistratus (*c.* 200) it was almost the literal truth.

(*f*) In the field of private law, we find that torts committed against a member of the upper classes by a member of the lower classes are regarded as more serious: such a wrong may become automatically an *atrox iniuria*, to the assessment of damages for which special rules applied.[24] And the *actio doli*, or *de dolo malo*, the action for fraud, might be refused to members of the lower classes against at any rate particularly distinguished members of the upper classes. This, however, was of much less importance to a humble plaintiff than one might suppose from reading the recent accounts of Cardascia and Garnsey,[25] who fail to quote the continuation of *Dig.* IV.iii.11.1, showing that the injured man could still have a remedy by bringing an action *in factum*, not involving an accusation of fraud. (Such a plaintiff would lose nothing in most cases; but the great man would suffer less if he lost the action, since he would not have the same liability to *infamia*.)

We need not be surprised to find evidence from the Greek East as well as the Latin West that when distributions of money (*sportulae*, in Latin) or food were made in cities by gracious benefactors, decurions often received more than ordinary citizens;[26] but this of course is a social and not a legal fact.

*   *   *   *   *   *

The very summary and simplified account I have given of some of the principal ways in which the lower classes of the Graeco-Roman world were placed – in most respects increasingly – at a disadvantage compared with their social superiors, during the first two or three centuries of the Christian era (the changes coming about principally in the second and early third centuries), will at least have shown that the propertied classes now found it easier than ever before to exploit those humble free men upon whose labour they were becoming more directly dependent for their surplus, now that slavery was somewhat less fruitful than in the last two centuries B.C. I dare say that the deterioration in the legal position of the lower class was not the result of a deliberate and conscious effort by the propertied class to subject those beneath them to a higher degree of exploitation, with less chance of meeting effective resistance; but that must certainly have been the effect of the whole process. My own inadequate account can be supplemented by Garnsey's book (*SSLPRE*), a very rich source of information and showing awareness of many of the social evils in the Graeco-Roman world over which too many ancient historians have felt able to pass lightly. If I have expressed disagreement with Garnsey on one or two specific points, it must not be taken as a disparagement of his very interesting and valuable book. I should also like to recommend at this point an informative article by Garnsey which should be easily intelligible to those unacquainted with Roman history and even with Latin: 'Why Penal Laws become Harsher: The Roman Case', in *Natural Law Forum* 13 (Indiana, U.S.A., 1968) 141-62.

★ ★ ★ ★ ★ ★

I hope it is already clear that what I have been describing in this section is essentially the replacement of one set of juridical distinctions, largely unrelated to class, by another set which was directly so related. The earlier set had no direct connection with class in my sense: its categories were purely political, with citizenship as the determining element. But although such things as execution, flogging, torture, criminal punishment in general, the evaluation of evidence, and the treatment of individuals by the authorities might vary greatly *in practice* according to class position, as Garnsey's book seems to me to have demonstrated, *in constitutional theory* they differed according to the possession or the lack of citizenship alone. Now from the early Principate onwards, through the grant of the citizenship to *peregrini* who had completed their full twenty-five years' service in the non-citizen auxiliary regiments or the fleet (down to A.D. 140, with their children),[27] the possession of citizenship came to correspond less and less closely with membership of the upper classes. And from Caesar's time Roman citizenship spread widely through the foundation outside Italy of citizen colonies and Roman municipalities, although much more so in the West than in the Greek world.[28] A recent writer has remarked, with greater shrewdness than perhaps he realised, that in the West wholesale extension of the citizenship 'must have led to some practical limitation of *a right which would have become a nuisance when universalised*'![29] The new set of distinctions corresponded very closely with class position, as we have seen, except for soldiers and veterans, who had to be placed collectively among the privileged groups for many purposes because of their great importance in maintaining the whole fabric of the empire, against potential internal rebellion and discontent as well as against external enemies. Eventually, by 212, citizenship was perceived to be an *unnecessary category*, and we may see its sudden general extension in 212 equally as its *disappearance*, when it had become *superfluous*: the propertied classes (with soldiers and ex-soldiers) now had all the constitutional privileges they needed, quite apart from the citizenship, partly by tradition but mainly by specific imperial enactments, only some of which can be identified today.

The whole process is indeed an interesting illustration of the way in which class can assert itself against purely juridical categories which do not correspond with its realities. Of course the important differences that existed at the latest by the Severan period (193-235) between the constitutional rights of the upper and lower classes reflected in part the differences in the practical treatment of the two groups in earlier generations; but they were now the subject of settled law and were much sharper, and they had to be strictly observed by provincial governors and other magistrates. To understand this, we have only to ask ourselves what would have happened to St. Paul had he lived, say, a hundred and fifty years later than he did, at about the time of the *CA*. Unless he could have claimed (as I am sure he could not) to be a member of the city Council of Tarsus, a decurion, he would have been subjected to an unpleasant inquisitorial flogging, and he would probably have been finished off by the Jews soon afterwards. He might or might not have got as far as the governor's court, but he would certainly not have been able to appeal successfully to be sent for trial by the emperor in Rome, and the odds would have been heavily against him at a trial in Judaea, where the governor would have had a *consilium* of leading Jews at his elbow (see n.9 again).

It is naturally impossible for me to prove that the deterioration in the position of humble citizens – and indeed of poor free men in general – during the first two centuries of the Christian era was due to the deliberate desire of the upper classes to reduce their legal rights, with the aim of making them less able to defend themselves against increased exploitation; but that was, I suggest, the direct effect of the changes I have described. Similarly, the exploitation of the humbler citizens of Greek cities must have been similarly facilitated by the process I have described in V.iii above: the gradual extinction of the remaining democratic features of the city constitutions.

*   *   *   *   *   *

I would invite comparison of the picture I have been drawing with that given by Finley, *AE* 84 ff., who notes the 'decline' of slavery and adds that this 'requires explanation' (cf. IV.iii n.18 above). Accepting the hypothesis that 'the employers of labour in the later Empire were not making the efforts needed to maintain a full complement of slave labour', he produces his 'explanation for their behaviour', which is 'a structural transformation within the society as a whole'. He now comes very near to saying something valuable, when he declares that 'the key lies not with the slaves but with the free poor', and he adds that he believes the elements can be 'pinpointed'. Alas! all we get is a 'trend', visible from the beginning of the Principate, 'to return to a more "archaic" structure, in which orders again became functionally significant, in which a broader spectrum of statuses gradually replaced the classical bunching into free men and slaves' – roughly, that is to say, the process which I have been at pains to describe in this section, but conceived from a superficial point of view, in terms of status, serving to conceal its mainspring and its essential character. What I see as primarily a development that would facilitate exploitation is to Finley 'a cumulative depression in the *status* of the lower classes among the free citizens' (*AE* 87, my italics). But how does the 'trend' described by Finley *explain* the changeover (described in IV.iii above) from slave production to what I would call mainly serf production? (Finley prefers to speak of 'tied *tenants*'; but see III.iv and IV.iii above.) The 'explanation' should be precisely the other way round: it was *because* slavery was not now producing as great a surplus as it did in Rome's palmiest days that the propertied classes *needed* to put more pressure on the free poor. On p.93 Finley comes very near to getting it right. But 'exploitation' is not a concept he is prepared to use: for him, ' "exploitation" and "imperialism" are, in the end, too broad as categories of analysis. Like "state", they require specification' (*AE* 157) – which they never receive from him. But the historian who debars himself from using exploitation and imperialism as categories of analysis will hardly make more sense of the ancient than of the modern world.

★ ★ ★ ★ ★ ★

To conclude this section I shall briefly review the much-discussed theory of the 'decline and fall' of the Roman empire advanced by Rostovtzeff in his great work, first published in 1926, *The Social and Economic History of the Roman Empire*, one of the few books on ancient history which the historian of some other period, if not the 'general reader', will not only have heard of but may actually have read, or at least dipped into, and which every Greek and Roman historian consults often. It was somewhat altered for the better in translations into German and Italian, and it was re-edited in a much-improved second English edition by P. M. Fraser in 1957 (*SEHRE*²). As is well known, Rostovtzeff refused to give a complete answer, let alone a single answer, to the question why the Roman empire 'declined and fell', contenting himself with a summary criticism of certain theories which he thought false or inadequate (*SEHRE*² I.532–41). I shall comment presently on an interesting remark in his very last paragraph. At this point I wish to mention the interpretation which Rostovtzeff himself offers of the period in which the 'decline' first became apparent: roughly from the death of Marcus Aurelius to the accession of Diocletian, A.D. 180–284 (I.491–501, cf. 532–41). Rostovtzeff recognises that the civilisation of the Roman empire was essentially urban (the empire, he says, was 'urbanised to excess', I.346), and that the privileged upper class of the cities – 'hives of drones', Rostovtzeff actually calls them (I.380, cf. 531) – lived in some luxury off the backs of the working population, urban and rural, above all the peasantry who formed the bulk of that population (cf. I.iii and IV.ii above).[30] So far, many Roman historians would find nothing to quarrel with. But Rostovtzeff, who had himself experienced the Russian revolution, went on to find the explanation of the upheavals of the third century in a deliberate and class-conscious attack by the exploited peasantry, using as its spearhead that large army which was recruited mainly from its ranks, upon the 'city bourgeoisie' (as Rostovtzeff calls it) – a purely destructive attack, which could bring no lasting gain to the semi-barbarous victors (I, ch.xi, especially 491–501). This theory has been taken on trust by many who do not know the sources for the

Middle and Later Roman Empire at first hand, and has often been cited with approval, although rarely (as Rostovtzeff himself realised: see I.494-5) by Roman historians. In fact, none of the evidence cited by Rostovtzeff supports his theory. Its principal and fatal defect has been exposed several times, notably in a review and an article by Norman Baynes, published in 1929 and 1943 respectively:[31] the contemporary sources reveal that the soldiers, far from being regarded by the peasants as their representatives, or even as allies, were actually their constant terror. (This, indeed, Rostovtzeff himself realised: see his *SEHRE*[2] I.487 for a passage beginning, 'The instruments of oppression and exaction were soldiers . . . They were a real terror to the population'!) Rostovtzeff speaks again and again of 'classes', even (in I.501) of 'the terrible class war' of the third century – a serious misconception, as I shall explain in Section iii of this chapter. Yet although his analysis of the class forces of the Roman empire sometimes verges on one which would be acceptable to many Marxists, he himself always repudiated Marxism, and his concept of classes and their struggle is erratic and wayward. (I find it extraordinary that even so good a historian as Baynes should have regarded Rostovtzeff as a kind of Marxist.)[32] We must purge his theory about the third-century crisis of its eccentric features and strip it down, so to speak, to what is fundamental and true in it: that there was massive exploitation by an urban propertied class of what Rostovtzeff himself twice refers to as 'the working-class' of the empire: the rural population (free or otherwise) and the artisans, retail-traders and slaves in the towns (see esp. I.35, 345-6). When we develop this, we begin to see the reasons for the renewed decline in the Later Empire (a period with which Rostovtzeff seems to have been less familiar), after the heroic revival of the age of Diocletian and Constantine. The Later Empire, especially in the West, was rather less a specifically urban civilisation, but it was if anything even more a regime in which the vast majority were exploited to the very limit for the benefit of a few. (Rostovtzeff seems to have realised this: see *SEHRE*[2] I.527-31.) Among those few, the indifference to the public good as something that concerned only other people, bemoaned by Tacitus (*Hist*. I.1: *inscitia rei publicae ut alienae*), had greatly increased; and the mass of the population, as their behaviour shows (see especially Section iii of this chapter), had no real interest in the preservation of the empire.

The other element in Rostovtzeff's explanation of the 'decline' on which I wish to comment is the very end of his last paragraph. 'Is it possible,' he asks despondently, 'to extend a higher civilisation to the lower classes without debasing its standard and diluting its quality to the vanishing point? Is not every civilisation bound to decay as soon as it begins to penetrate the masses?' To this I think we can reply in the words of Gordon Childe: the cultural capital accumulated by the civilisations of antiquity

> was no more annihilated in the collapse of the Roman empire than smaller accumulations had been in the lesser catastrophes that interrupted and terminated the Bronze Age. Of course, as then, many refinements . . . were swept away. But for the most part these had been designed for, and enjoyed by, only a small and narrow class. Most achievements that had proved themselves biologically to be progressive and had become firmly established on a genuinely popular footing by the participation of wider classes were conserved . . . So in the Eastern Mediterranean, city life, with all its implications, still continued. Most crafts were still plied with all the technical skill and equipment evolved in Classical and Hellenistic times.[33]

Here I agree with Childe. The material arts are never the exclusive preserve of a governing class. When a civilisation collapses, the governing class often disintegrates, and its culture (its literature and art and so forth) often comes to a full stop; and the society which succeeds has to make a fresh start. This is not true of the material arts and crafts: luxury trades of course may disappear, and particular techniques may die out as the demand for them ceases, but in the main the technological heritage is transmitted more or less intact to succeeding generations. This has been the experience of the last five thousand years and more in the Far Eastern, Near Eastern, Mediterranean and Western societies. Each society can normally begin in many material respects where its predecessor left off; and that does matter. It appears, therefore, that it was above all in the degree to which it *had* (to use Rostovtzeff's phrase) 'penetrated the masses' that the legacy of Graeco-Roman civilisation remained continuously alive. When Europe once more began to advance, as it very soon did once the effects of the 'barbarian invasions' had spent themselves, the old techniques, handed down from father to son and from craftsman to apprentice, were still available for the mediaeval world to build on. The 'economic decline' of the Roman empire was essentially a deterioration in the economic organisation of the empire rather than in its techniques, which deteriorated little, except in so far as the lack of any widespread effective demand for certain luxury goods and services eventually dried up their supply. Methods of production, such as they were, seem to have held their own even when the artistic value of the work produced became poorer. It has been said by the American historian Lynn White,[34] and I agree, that 'There is no proof that any important skills of the Graeco-Roman world were lost during the Dark Ages even in the unenlightened West, much less in the flourishing Byzantine and Saracenic Orient' (TIMA 150; cf. II.i n.14 below). Indeed, as White has claimed, 'From the twelfth and even from the eleventh century there was a rapid replacement of human by non-human energy wherever great quantities of power were needed or where the required motion was so simple and monotonous that a man could be replaced by a mechanism. The chief glory of the later Middle Ages was not its cathedrals or its epics or its scholasticism: it was the building for the first time in history of a complex civilisation which rested not on the backs of sweating slaves or coolies but primarily on non-human power' (TIMA 156). That 'primarily' is an exaggeration, but there is an important truth in White's statement, and we could certainly say that by the later Middle Ages there was a real prospect of building 'a complex civilisation which rested *less* on the backs of sweating slaves or coolies and *more* on non-human power'.

(ii)
Pressure on the 'curial class'

In the last section I showed how the propertied classes of the Graeco-Roman world as a whole were able during roughly the first two and a half centuries of the Principate (let us say, from the time of Augustus to the end of the Severan period in A.D. 235) to tighten their grip on those below them and place themselves in an even more commanding position than they had previously been, by reducing the political and constitutional rights of those members of the lower classes who were Roman citizens. I must now describe briefly how and why the governing class of the empire, the men of conspicuous wealth, came to put increasing pressure upon *the lower section of the propertied class itself*: namely, what I am calling the curial class (defined below). I do not need to give a general account of the curial class, as the whole subject has been dealt with by A. H. M. Jones, with great penetration, in several different works.[1] This pressure upon the curials began well before the end of the second century and was already far advanced in the early third; in the fourth century it was intensified, the pressure continued in the fifth, and by the sixth century the curial class had been greatly weakened and had lost nearly all its former prestige.

When I speak of the 'curial class' I mean those members of the propertied class (with their families) who made up the Councils of the cities (*poleis*) of the Greek East (and of course the corresponding Western *civitates*) and filled all the important magistracies, to which they were originally (in the Classical and Hellenistic periods) elected by the Assembly but came eventually (mainly during the first two centuries of the Christian era) to be nominated by the Council itself or enrolled by officials appointed by it (cf. V.iii above and Appendix IV below). As councillors they were called in Latin *decuriones*, in Greek *bouleutai*, and they are often referred to in English as 'decurions'; but the term 'curials' (*curiales*) was often used of decurions and members of their families by the early fourth century,[2] and as I wish to speak of a 'class' I find the adjectival form 'curial' convenient. The word is derived from *curia*, the Latin word for a senate house, which also came to be used – as did the term *ordo* (*ordo decurionum*) – for the collective councillors of a particular city. In the Latin West the *ordo decurionum* of a substantial town could be expected to number about a hundred members; in the Greek East it might sometimes be a great deal larger.[3] I may add that in some areas of the Greek world where city life had been slow to develop we may find occasional exceptions to the general rules I am stating here: see for example the end of § 2 of Appendix IV below for an inscription (*IGBulg.* IV.2263) relating to a Macedonian community which in A.D. 158 had citizens, an *ekklēsia*, and an annual magistrate (*a poleitarch*), but apparently no Council. Nevertheless, the picture I am presenting here is true in the vast majority of cases.

In strictness it might well be preferable to describe the decurions and their families as the 'curial *order*' rather than 'curial *class*', for of course a man became a decurion only when he actually held that position and not merely because he owned property of a sufficient value (*census*) to qualify him for it – perhaps, in substantial towns in the Latin West in the early second century, something in the neighbourhood of HS 100,000 (the figure at Comum in the early second century: Pliny, *Ep.* I.xix.2), one quarter of the equestrian census and one tenth of the senatorial; but the figure might vary very greatly, according to the size and importance of the city concerned (see Jones, *LRE* II.738-9; Duncan-Jones, *EREQS* 82-8, 147-8). However, by the time my story in this section really opens, in the later second century, the class of men financially qualified to become decurions (and not able to achieve the more exalted position of *honorati*, through membership of the senatorial or equestrian order) was beginning to coincide to some degree with the actual curial order. Curial status had always been desirable as an honour, and from the first half of the second century onwards it involved important legal privileges (discussed in Section i of this chapter), so that most men qualified for it would naturally try to obtain it. It is true that in the early second century there was already, in Bithynia-Pontus and doubtless in most other parts of the Greek world, a general feeling among the upper classes (which Pliny evidently shared) that decurions ought to be chosen from families already of curial status – from *honesti homines* rather than *e plebe*, as Pliny puts it (*Ep.* X.79.3). But being a decurion, desirable as it was in itself, was beginning by the second half of the century to involve financial burdens which the less affluent found it increasingly difficult to discharge. An inscription from Galatia dated to 145 can refer to a citizen as having been a councillor *gratis* (*proika bouleut*[*ou*]); but this need mean no more than that he had been adlected into the *ordo*, as an honour, without being made to pay the fee normally exacted in such cases.[4] However, from the later second century pressure was intensified on financially qualified men who were still *plebeii* to become members of their *ordo*. An interesting papyrus of the early third century, as restored with reasonable probability, speaks of men possessing a curial rating (*bouleutikē axia*) who are not yet enrolled on the curial register (*bouleutikon leukōma*), and says that they must not evade both 'the services imposed on the common people' (*dēmotikai hypēresiai*) on the ground that they possess curial means (*?poroi? bouleutikoi*), and also curial liturgies (*bouleutikai leitourgiai*) on the ground that they are not yet entered on the curial register (*SB* III.ii.7261).[5] Even in the fourth century men who were qualified to become decurions could occasionally be found,[6] but it seems likely that by the end of the Severan period (A.D. 235) they were already fairly rare, and that what I have called curial class and curial order very nearly coincided. What looks at first sight like an order turns out to be essentially a class. It is of great interest that although the post of decurion might involve considerable financial and supervisory responsibilities, Diocletian could actually provide in 293 that even illiteracy was not to be allowed to prevent a man from shouldering the burdens associated with being a decurion (*CJ* X.xxxii.6: *expertes litterarum decuriones munera peragere non prohibent iura*).[7] Illiterate decurions sometimes turn up in the papyri.[8] As we saw in III.iii above, the vast majority of decurions in all the major cities (except a few, like Ostia and Palmyra, which were particularly 'commercial' in character) were primarily landowners. In smaller and poorer cities, where the least wealthy of the decurions might be men of very moderate property, more of them would be likely to go in for manufacture. In a real one-horse-town like Abthugni in Byzacena,[9] in 303, we find that Caecilian, who is actually a *duovir* (a magistrate), is a working weaver, who takes his dinner with his workmen, whether slaves or wage-labourers (*cum operarios* [sic]: Optatus, Append. II, f. 27b; cf. 25ab, 29a, in *CSEL* XXVI, ed. C. Ziwsa). And Augustine mentions a 'poor *curialis*' named Curma, who had been *duumvir* of the *municipium Tulliense* near Hippo: he calls him 'a simple peasant', *simpliciter rusticanus* (*De cura gerenda pro mortuis* 15, in *CSEL* XLI.644).

* * * * * *

The reasons for the tightening of the screw upon the curial class are not far to seek. Let us glance at the condition of those poor free men who were below them in the social scale, peasants above all. I strongly suspect that those who were lessees had always been made to pay as much rent as their landlords could get out of them. The position of small peasant freeholders would vary a great deal, according to whether harvests were good, whether conditions in their neighbourhood were peaceful and free from brigandage (or 'barbarian' irruptions), whether the smallholders were subjected to unusual fiscal extortion or oppression by powerful neighbours (cf. IV.ii above), and so forth. All in all, I would expect that as the returns from chattel slavery declined, additional exploitation of the free poor, even when facilitated by the depression of their legal status, would hardly redress the balance.

By the time of the Emperor Marcus Aurelius (161-80) the Roman empire as a whole had not suffered any great calamity since the beginning of the Principate, apart from the civil wars of 68-9 and one or two local revolts of which the most serious was probably that led by C. Julius Civilis in Lower Germany and north-west Gaul in 69-70. Wars, even in the reigns of Domitian and Trajan, were not ruinously expensive, if we allow for the considerable booty obtained in some of them, especially Trajan's last campaign in Dacia in 106. Most of the sums óf money transmitted in our literary sources for public expenditure and receipts are unreliable, and the figure of HS 40,000,000,000 which Vespasian is said by Suetonius (*Vesp.* 16.3) to have thought necessary to meet immediate requirements at his accession in 69-70 ('the largest sum of money mentioned in antiquity', according to Tenney Frank, *ESAR* V.45) has no better credentials than the rest; but Vespasian evidently did take the very unusual step of raising the amount of imperial tribute, perhaps substantially (Dio Cass. LXVI.viii.3-4; Suet., *Vesp.* 16.1). It was in the reign of Marcus Aurelius that things began to go badly wrong. The Parthian war that opened in 162 must have been very costly, and when it ended successfully in 165-6 the armies brought back with them a dreadful plague, which raged for some years in many parts of the Roman world.[10] The Germans now became a real menace. A German irruption across the Danube between 166 and 171 (perhaps 170 or 171), which even reached Italy, was followed by a series of bitter wars against the German Marcomanni and Quadi and the Sarmatian Iazyges which occupied a good many of the later years of Marcus's reign.[11] In 170 or 171 a raid by the Costoboci actually penetrated as far as Attica; and in 171 Baetica (southern Spain) was attacked by Moorish rebels from north Africa (see Birley, *MA* 225-9; IIRMA 222 etc.). Among internal revolts, the most serious may have been that of the *Boukoloi* in Egypt, in the early 170s, led by a priest, Isidore, which was crushed with some difficulty by Avidius Cassius: we have no more than a brief mention of it, by Dio Cassius (LXXI.iv) and the *Historia Augusta* (*Marc. Aurel.* 21.2; *Avid. Cass.* 6.7).[12]

There are stories that Marcus sold the crown jewels and his other treasures by auction (perhaps in 169) to raise money for his wars,[13] and that he once refused his soldiers' demand for a donative with the significant assertion that anything they got beyond the traditional amount would be 'wrung from the blood of their kith and kin' (Dio LXXI.iii.3). It is also said that of the surplus in the Treasury of HS 2,700,000,000 left to Marcus by his predecessor Antoninus Pius in 161, a mere HS 1 million remained in 193, after his reign and the disastrous one of his unbalanced son Commodus (Dio LXXIII[LXXIV].viii.3, with v.4). Then, from 193 to 197, there was another burst of civil wars, about which we are not well informed but which are said by a contemporary historian to have involved some bloody battles with great loss of life (see Dio Cass. LXXIV.viii.1; LXXV.vi.1 and vii.1-2): this is the beginning of the Severan period.

Different views have been expressed[14] about the extent to which the cost of paying[15] and maintaining the Roman armies, certainly the largest single item of imperial expenditure, was increased during wartime. I will only add what seems to me a conclusive argument in favour of the view that large-scale campaigns must have necessitated far greater military spending. There was not much fighting in Hadrian's reign (117-38) and very little indeed under his successor, Antoninus Pius (138-61). It was surely this long period of relative peace that enabled Pius to leave in the Treasury at his death (as we saw above) the enormous sum of HS 2,700 million; and it can only have been the major wars undertaken during the reign of Marcus (especially its early years) which drained away the reserves (see the two preceding paragraphs). Marcus was certainly no spendthrift. It is true that he made some costly distributions to the Roman *plebs urbana*; he also reduced some taxes, and shortly before the end of his reign he remitted all arrears of taxes and other debts due to the Treasury over a period of forty-five years (Dio Cass. LXXI[LXXII].32.2). But he did not increase army pay or indulge in any extensive building programmes. I see no alternative to the conclusion that major wars necessitated much larger military expenditure.

It can be misleading to pay too much attention to Roman state finance, for it was quite possible for the bulk of the Roman governing class to prosper even though the Treasury was virtually bankrupt. But in spite of signs of individual prosperity in many of the cities of the Greek East, as of the West, it does seem that by the third quarter of the second century the wealth of the propertied class was not as securely based as it had seemed to be in the last few generations. And it is precisely in the 160s, during the joint reigns of Marcus Aurelius and Lucius Verus (the *divi fratres*, 161-9), that the first certain evidence appears[16] both of regular financial pressure upon the curial class and of reluctance and even inability on the part of many poorer decurions to sustain the burdens that were now being increasingly put upon them. The whole subject is exceedingly complicated, but an admirable recent survey by Garnsey (ADUAE) has under-lined some of the details in the general picture already established by Jones and others, and has demonstrated the significance in this connection of some of the passages in the *Digest*, notably three which refer to pronouncements of the *divi fratres*. One of these speaks explicitly of 'those who perform a magistracy under compulsion' (*Dig.* L.i.38.6); another, as Garnsey says, 'demonstrates the existence of a sharp cleavage between rich and poor in the council' (L.iv.6.*pr.*; cf. vii.5.5); and a third refers to 'those who are left in debt as a result of an administrative office' (L.iv.6.1). Before this there had been signs of the trouble that was to come: some men had shown reluctance to perform liturgies, or magistracies involving heavy expense; exemptions from such duties had been curtailed; those who had promised voluntarily to undertake public works had sometimes had to be forced to carry them out; fees had begun to be demanded from new councillors; and so on. There are unmistakable signs that (to quote Garnsey, ADUAE 241) 'the Antonine age was a period of prosperity for the *primores viri* and ruin for the *inferiores* within the councils'. (The Latin terms are those used by Hadrian in a rescript to Clazomenae in Asia Minor: *Dig.* L.vii.5.5.) When we remember the extent to which our literary tradition concerning Classical antiquity is dominated by writers whose outlook is essentially that of the propertied class, and the fact that ancient historians in the modern

Western world have either been members of that class or have thoroughly shared its outlook, we need feel no surprise that the Antonine period should still be remembered as a kind of Golden Age. I can think of no statement by an ancient historian about the Roman world that has been quoted more often than Gibbon's:

> If a man were called to fix the period in the history of the world during which the condition of the human race was most happy and prosperous, he would, without hesitation, name that which elapsed from the death of Domitian to the accession of Commodus (*DFRE* I.78) –

that is to say, the years from 96 to 180.

Under the Severan dynasty (193-235), as is well known, compulsion was more and more stringently applied to the curial class. There is no need to go into detail: public services of all kinds were demanded of magistrates and decurions, some of them, which came to be known as *munera personalia*, imposing primarily personal service, and others, *munera patrimonii*, the expenditure of money; in time *munera mixta* were recognised, which involved both personal and pecuniary service.[17] Even *munera personalia*, however, might involve considerable incidental expense. There was an elaborate series of provisions giving immunity, set out at length in the *Digest* L.v-vi and often alluded to elsewhere: these were revised again and again by the emperors, usually in such a way as to restrict or withdraw the immunity and make the service ever more general.

A natural result of the pressure on the curial class which I have just described, increasing from the Antonine age into the Severan, was a marked fall in expenditure by 'public-spirited' (or ambitious and self-advertising) men on civic buildings and on 'foundations' to provide benefits for their fellow-citizens and sometimes others. (The decline in the number of the latter is evident to the eye from the diagrams in Bernhard Laum, *Stiftungen in der griechischen und römischen Antike* [Leipzig, 1914] I.9.) We need not be surprised to find that from about the middle of the third century onwards the cities, in setting up honorific inscriptions, tend to concentrate their praises on the provincial governor rather than on local grandees.[18]

I have said hardly anything so far to explain how the curial class came to be steadily depleted and ultimately reduced to a mere shadow of itself, especially in the East. It used to be customary for historians to express great sympathy with the *curiales* and shed tears over their sad fate; but in recent years it has been realised, largely owing to the researches of A. H. M. Jones (see n.1 above), that we need to look at the whole question in a very different light. Characteristic of the earlier tendency is the picture presented by Jules Toutain, in whose book, *The Economic Life of the Ancient World*, we are told that the people who suffered most from the economic decline of the third century were 'the wealthy and middle classes – the landowners, manufacturers and merchants, *to whom economic prosperity really owed its being*' (p.325, my italics). Now the landowners, at any rate, were precisely the people who had appropriated and monopolised what prosperity there was in the Graeco-Roman world. To say that prosperity 'owed its being' to them is a grotesque distortion of the truth. In the third century, the *curiales* must have represented a high proportion of the propertied landowning class, in the sense of those members of my propertied class who were able to live by their land without having to spend any appreciable time on working it. But the *curiales*, although I often refer to them as a class, when contrasting them with the imperial aristocracy (the senators and equestrians) on the one hand, and the poor free men, *coloni* and slaves on the other, were a class with a considerable 'spread', those at the very lowest end of the scale hardly falling within my 'propertied class', while those at the top end might be very rich and might hope to become members of the imperial aristocracy themselves. And the key to the understanding of the position of the curial class in the fourth and fifth centuries is the realisation of two facts. First, the richer the decurion, the more likely he was to be able to escape upwards into the ranks of the imperial *honorati*, or to obtain by influence or bribery some position (in the imperial civil service in particular)[19] which exempted him from curial duties, thereby increasing the burden on the poorer members of the order who were left, sometimes to the point of actual ruin and loss of property. And secondly, curial burdens, far from being distributed in proportion to wealth, tended to fall more heavily on the poorer decurions in a given Council.

In view of the inherently hierarchical tendencies of the Roman world, no one will be surprised to find the curial order developing an inner ring of privilege within itself which in due course receives legal recognition.[20] I have deliberately said nothing of the *decemprimi* who begin to appear in Italian and Sicilian towns in the late Republic as the leading members of the *ordo decurionum*, or of the *dekaprōtoi*, the 'first ten men' (sometimes *eikosaprōtoi*, the 'first twenty'), who are known in the Greek world from just after the middle of the first century of the Christian era until the beginning of the fourth and are always decurions, responsible for a fiscal liturgy.[21] Although the *dekaprōtoi/eikosaprōtoi* are often mentioned as such in honorific inscriptions (and their function was therefore a dignified one), there is no sign that they, any more than the *decemprimi* in the West, enjoyed any special privileges or powers as such. Legal privilege does, however, appear in the fourth century onwards in connection with the leading decurions known as *principales*, a term which first appears in the Codes as early as 328 (*CTh* XI.xvi.4). In the second half of the fourth century we often hear of these *principales*, who are probably identical with a new kind of *decemprimi* now appearing in various parts of the empire (see Jones, *LRE* II.731; Norman, GLMS 83–4). By the early fifth century, constitutions of Honorius, directed towards stamping out Donatism in north Africa (for which see VII.v above), reveal by the difference in the size of the pecuniary penalties they prescribe the large gap which by now had opened up between the leading decurions and the others: a constitution of 412 which punishes senators with a fine of 30 lb. gold rates the *principales* at 20 lb. gold and other decurions at only 5 lb. (*CTh* XVI.v.52.*pr.*); and in another law, of 414 (id. 54.4), we find senators assessed at 100 lb. silver, the *decemprimi curiales* at 50 lb. and the remaining decurions at 10 lb. (For *coloni*, by the way, both laws prescribe merely flogging: 52.4; 54.8.) Norman has well emphasised that by the latter part of the fourth century the great division in the curiae is 'horizontal, based purely on economic differences, and the few great families have deliberately cut themselves off not only from the commons but also from the humbler members of the order . . . The rapacity of the wealthier and more influential *principales* was increasingly directed against the poorer decurion for their own financial gain' (GLMS 83–4). The class struggle proceeded apace even within the curial order!

The longest of all the titles in the *Theodosian Code* of 438 is XII.i, *De decurionibus*: it contains 192 laws, from Constantine's reign to 438; and other laws affecting decurions appear elsewhere in the *Code*; there are still others again in Justinian's *Code* (X.xxxii and elsewhere). By far the most important consideration, in the eyes of the emperors, was to prevent decurions from evading their obligations, for example by escaping into the army, or into one of the more profitable branches of the imperial civil service, or into the Church. The whole story has been well told in detail (see n.1 above), and I need not recapitulate it here. I will say only that the evidence shows all too well the extent to which the richer members of the order were able to escape from their obligations to their *curia* by doing the very thing the emperors were so anxious to prevent, sometimes by obtaining honorary *codicilli* (letters patent), granting them some rank which conferred exemption from curial duties, sometimes by actually obtaining some post which carried such rank. The constant repetition of some of these laws shows how inefficient they were: patronage (*suffragium*: see my SVP) could often procure the evasion of a law; and the Councils themselves tended to be reluctant to coerce defaulters, partly (as Councils would claim) because it was so difficult for them to operate effectively against a man who had obtained high rank and because it might be dangerous to incur his enmity, and partly also through sheer corruption and the hope of favours to come from the ex-decurion (see esp. Jones, *LRE* I.409; II.754-5). As Norman has said, curial decline in the late fourth century 'could certainly never have proceeded with such speed had there not been powerful support for it from inside the Curiae themselves, not merely that manifested by evasion and subterfuge, but that also provided by the wealthy *principalis*' (GLMS 84).

The desire of decurions to obtain senatorial rank illicitly, even if it meant selling much of their property in order to procure the necessary bribe, was by no means motivated only by the wish to escape their financial obligations – which might, indeed, be increased by senatorial status (see Jones, *LRE* II.544-5, 748 ff.). The sheer prestige was itself a major consideration, in a society intensely conscious of rank and order; but perhaps most important of all was the desire of the decurion to obtain personal security against the maltreatment which in the fourth century was being increasingly meted out to curials by provincial governors and other imperial officials, but which they would not dare to inflict upon men of senatorial status.

One interesting sign of the gradual deterioration in the position of the curial class during the fourth century is the fact that whereas all decurions are still specifically exempted from all flogging by imperial constitutions of 349 or 350 and 359 (*CTh* XII.i.39,47), by 376 the use of the *plumbata*, the leaded scourge, is permitted upon all except the leading decurions (the *decemprimi*), although the emperors express the pious hope that this will be inflicted upon them in moderation! (*habeatur moderatio*, IX.xxxv.2.1). Although constitutions of 380 and 381 again forbid the *plumbata* for any decurion (XII.i.80,85), by 387 the use of the dreadful weapon is permitted again in fiscal cases, and this time even a principal decurion (*principalis*) is not immune (XII.i.117, cf. 126, 190). It is not surprising, then, that we find Libanius, in the late fourth century, insisting that it was above all the frequent flogging of decurions which had driven so many of them to seek the rank of senator (which alone would give secure immunity),[22] even at the cost of paying a very large price for the privilege, and that in this way the ranks of the councillors had become depleted. The severity of Later Roman floggings is brought out by several literary passages, notably in St. Athanasius, suggesting (even if we allow for the man's habitual exaggeration) that in the mid-fourth century a flogging, even without the use of the *plumbata*, could easily result in death (*Hist. Arian*. 60; cf. 12, 72).

In the mid-fourth century, a touching picture of the relationship between a local Council and the general population, as a leading member of the local propertied class liked to imagine it, is given by Libanius: the relationship is that of parents to children! (*Orat*. XI [*Antiochikos*] 150 ff., esp. 152).²³ The Emperor Majorian in 458 could still, in a charming phrase, state it as an undoubted fact that the decurions were 'the sinews of the commonwealth and the vitals of the cities', *curiales nervos esse rei publicae ac viscera civitatum nullus ignorat* (*Nov. Maj*. VII.*pr*.). In the East it seems to have been early in the sixth century, in the reign of Anastasius (491-518), that the city Councils finally ceased to matter very much in the local decision-making process, and perhaps even to meet. The decurions were now reduced to little more than minor local officials responsible for tax-collection and the performance of other public duties. (In the West the position was not very different, even if there is evidence of city Councils meeting as late as the early seventh century: see Jones, *LRE* II.757-63.)

The whole process brings out admirably the complete control exercised over the whole Graeco-Roman world by the very highest class, of senators and equestrians – who had merged into a single order by at least the beginning of the fifth century (see VI.vi above, *ad fin*.). There were now more grades within the senatorial order: the lowest were *clarissimi*, then came *spectabiles* and finally *illustres*; by the mid-fifth century the most illustrious were *magnificentissimi* and even *gloriosissimi*. The utter lack of any kind of real power below the highest class left even men of some property and local distinction helpless subjects of the great, except in so far as the emperors chose to protect them, as they were obliged to do to some extent, if the empire was to be kept going (cf. VI.vi above). The screw, having already been tightened at the bottom of the social scale by landlords and tax-collectors about as far as it would safely go, and indeed further, had from the later second century onwards (as the situation of the empire became less favourable), and regularly during the third, to be put on the curial class, as the only alternative to the increased taxation of the really rich, which they would never have endured. As soon as the curials began to change even to a small extent from the beneficiaries of the system into its victims (as those below them had always been), they made indignant protests, which used to receive unduly sympathetic attention from historians. There is plenty of evidence that they did not allow themselves to suffer until they had squeezed the very last drop out of those beneath them, in particular their *coloni*. The priest Salvian, writing in Gaul in the second quarter of the fifth century, could exclaim, 'What else is the life of *curiales* but injustice?' (*iniquitas*: *De gub. Dei* III.50). We are often reminded that Salvian was prone to exaggeration (cf. Section iii of this chapter); and indeed in the same passage he can see in the lives of business men (*negotiantes*) only 'fraud and perjury', of officials 'false accusation' (*calumnia*), and of soldiers 'plunder' (*rapina*). But lest we be tempted to dismiss entirely his strictures upon curials, we should look at what is, to my mind, perhaps the most extraordinary of all the constitutions ever promulgated by the Roman emperors: one issued by Justinian in 531 (*CJ* I.iii.52.*pr.*, 1), which strictly prohibits all *curiales* from ever becoming bishops or priests, on the ground that it is 'not right for a man who has been brought up to indulge in extortion with violence, and the sins that in all likelihood accompany this, and is fresh from deeds of the utmost harshness as a *curialis*, suddenly to take holy orders and to admonish and instruct concerning benevolence and poverty'! (With the *curiales* [*bouleutai*], Justinian brackets *cohortales* [*taxeōtai*], members of the staff of a provincial governor, on whom see Section iv of this chapter.)

★　★　★　★　★　★

I have seldom had occasion so far to notice movements of revolt or resistance on the part of the lower classes in the ancient world. I shall have a certain amount to say on this subject in the last two sections of this chapter. But since I shall be dealing there mainly with the Middle and Later Roman Empire, and of course this book is concerned with the Greek East rather than the West, I shall have little or nothing to say about a number of local revolts against Roman rule, almost entirely in the West and during the Republic and early Principate, which have been discussed recently in two articles by Stephen L. Dyson, with the praiseworthy aim of applying to them knowledge available today about movements against modern colonialism.[24]

(iii)
Defection to the 'barbarians', peasant revolts, and indifference to the disintegration of the Roman empire

The fable of the donkey which receives with indifference the news of a hostile invasion (see VII.v above) may help us to achieve a better understanding of the quite considerable body of evidence from both Eastern and Western parts of the Roman empire that the attitude of the lower classes towards 'the barbarians' (as I can hardly help calling the Germanic and other invaders, the *barbari*) was by no means always one of fear and hostility, and that incursions of 'the barbarians' (destructive as they could be, especially to property-owners) were often received with indifference and even on occasion positive pleasure and co-operation, in particular by poor men unendurably burdened by taxation. (As we shall see later, even men of some property who had been the victims of injustice and legal corruption are known to have defected to the barbarians.) There is a considerable body of evidence from the second century to the seventh of flight or desertion to 'the barbarians', or of appeals to them or even help given to them, which has never, as far as I know, been fully presented, in English at any rate. I cannot claim to have made anything like a complete collection of the material, but I will mention here the main texts I have come across.

It is convenient to mention also in this section some evidence for peasant revolts, especially in Gaul and Spain, which has been very well discussed by E. A. Thompson (PRLRGS = *SAS*, ed. Finley, 304-20). It is not my intention, however, to try to give anything like a full list of the internal rebellions and dissensions which broke out in various parts of the Greek and Roman world during the Principate and Later Empire: for most of these episodes the evidence is bad and it is unclear whether there was any significant element of revolution from below or even of social protest. Sometimes our only source is of such poor quality or so enigmatic that we are not able to rely on it. For example, it is only in a speech of Dio Chrysostom (XXXII.71-2), which has been variously dated, between 71 and the reign of Trajan,[1] that we hear of a serious disturbance (*tarachē*) in Alexandria, necessitating the use of armed force by the prefect of Egypt to suppress it. There is a mysterious reference in a mid-second-century Spartan inscription to *neōterismoi* (disturbances, revolutionary movements), which may conceivably be connected with a *rebellio* in Greece mentioned in the *Historia Augusta* as having been put down by the Emperor Antoninus Pius (A.D. 138-61). And again, it is only in the *Historia Augusta* that we have a reference to 'something resembling a slave revolt' (*quasiquoddam servile bellum*) in Sicily during the sole reign of Gallienus (260-8), taking the form, it is said, of widespread banditry (*latronibus evagantibus*).[2] Banditry or brigandage is often, of course, a symptom of social protest (cf. V.iii above), but we also come across certain alleged brigand chiefs who are likely to have begun with a following consisting largely of peasants, herdsmen, runaway slaves and other humble folk, but who became local despots: for instance, the adventurer and alleged bandit, Cleon of Gordioucome, in the last century B.C.[3] Sometimes, as in the movement in the area of Carthage, early in 238, which led to the proclamation as emperor (and the exceedingly brief reign) of the aged Gordian I, a rich land-owner who was then proconsul of Africa, it is evident that there was no 'popular' or 'peasant' uprising but that the whole impetus came from the upper classes – in the African example I have just mentioned, from a group of 'well-born and rich young men', who resented recent increases in taxation and the severity with which they were applied by the procurator of the Emperor Maximin, and were able to mobilise their dependants in the countryside and bring them into Carthage (Herodian VII.iv.3-4, with iii.5 ff.).[4] In some cases – even events of real importance – almost everything is uncertain: for instance, the role of Mariades (or Mareades) and of the lower classes of Antioch in the taking of that city by Shapur I of Persia, in 256 or thereabouts.[5] Sometimes the respective roles played in a rebellion by the upper and lower classes are not made clear by our sources and are very variously interpreted by different historians – the rebellion of Firmus in north Africa in 372/3 to 374/5 is a case in point; of other African revolts hardly any details are known: they appear to me to have been essentially tribal movements.[6]

I wish to say with all possible emphasis that in all cases known to me in which there were contests for the imperial throne there is no sign that class struggle ever played any significant part. This is true of the competition for the principate on the death of Nero in 68, of the next series of armed conflicts from 193 to 197, and also of the half-century from the end of the Severan dynasty in March 235 to the accession of Diocletian late in 284, when the succession was virtually always settled by force, and the only emperor who lived to count the years of his reign in double figures was Gallienus, joint ruler from 253 to 260 with his father Valerian and sole emperor from 260 to 268. Nor can any of the few subsequent civil wars in the fourth century be seen as a class war, even where (as I shall explain in Section iv of this chapter) we do find a certain number of men driven desperate by heavy taxation and a highly oppressive administration taking the side of a pretender: Procopius in 365-6 – their support was but a minor and incidental feature of his rebellion. All competition for the imperial dignity was entirely between members of the governing class, attempting to seize or retain power for themselves, and the contests were all decided by at least the threat, and often the use, of armed force.

At the very beginning of the second century we hear of deserters to Decebalus, the Dacian chief. According to Dio Cassius (as preserved in our surviving excerpts) Decebalus gave a reluctant undertaking to surrender to the Romans both 'the deserters' (*hoi automoloi*) and 'his arms and his military machines and artificers' (*mēchanēmata* and *mēchanopoioi*; cf. Herodian III.iv.7-9, mentioned on the next page). Decebalus also promised for the future 'not to receive any deserter or to employ any soldier from the Roman empire'; and Dio adds, 'for it was by seducing men from there that he had been obtaining the majority of his forces, and the best of them' (LXVIII.ix.5-6).[7] On other occasions too we hear of 'deserters', and sometimes the numbers given are so strikingly large as to suggest that there must have been civilian defectors as well as military deserters whom the Romans were anxious to reclaim. (The expression *aichmalōtoi*, 'captives', certainly included civilian as well as military prisoners: see Dio LXXI.xiii.3.) Dio speaks on several occasions of deserters to the Quadi, Marcomanni and others between the late 160s and the 180s. We hear that the Quadi in *c.* 170 promised to surrender 'all the deserters and the captives: 13,000 at first, and the rest later' (Dio LXXI.xi.2,4), a promise they did not fulfil (xiii.2). About five years later the Sarmatian Iazyges, according to Dio, gave back '100,000 captives they still had, after many had been sold [as slaves] or had died or escaped' (xvi.2). When describing the treaties of peace made by Commodus, shortly after his accession in 180, first with the Marcomanni and then with the Buri, Dio mentions the Roman demand to the Marcomanni for the return of 'the deserters and captives' (LXXII.ii.2) and then speaks of 15,000 captives given back to the Romans (by whom, is not clear – by the Alans, perhaps), in addition to 'many' returned by the Buri (iii.2). I think there is reason to suspect that large numbers of civilians may have gone over to the barbarians in these cases of their own free will. In 366, proof that many of those alleging they had been captured by the barbarians were suspected of having gone off voluntarily is furnished by the constitution of that date mentioned below, providing for an inquisition in such cases, whether the man concerned had been 'with the barbarians voluntarily or by compulsion' (*voluntate an coactus: CTh* V.vii.1 = *CJ* VIII.1.19).

Just before the end of the Antonine age, somewhere between 186 and 188, came the revolt in Gaul and Spain led by Maternus, a military deserter, for which I need do no more than refer to Thompson's account (in *SAS*, ed. Finley, 306-9). As he points out, the revolt foreshadowed the first recorded movement of the Bacaudae a century later, described below. Our sources for this revolt fail to reveal much about its character. It is referred to in the *Historia Augusta* as a 'war of deserters' (*bellum desertorum: Commod.* 16.2), 'countless numbers of whom were then plaguing Gaul' (*Pesc. Nig.* 3.4). Although discontented soldiers may have formed its nucleus, it may well have involved many members of 'the submerged classes of Gaul and Spain', as Thompson suggests. Maternus was soon betrayed, captured and beheaded, and his forces broke up.

At the end of the civil war of 193–4 between Septimius Severus and Pescennius Niger many of the soldiers of the defeated Niger fled across the Tigris to the Parthian sphere. This, a consequence of a contest for the imperial throne which lacked any characteristic of a social movement, would be hardly worth mentioning here but for the fact that Herodian (III.iv.7-9) makes much of it, rightly or wrongly, on the ground that the deserters included many craftsmen (*technitai*), who not only gave the barbarians valuable instruction on how to use weapons in hand-to-hand combat but also taught them how to make such weapons. (Herodian seems to have had spears and swords in mind.) At this time and in the years between 194 and 199 we must put the activities of Ti. Claudius Candidus, which we know only from a cryptic reference in an inscription, *ILS* 1140:[8] he conducted military operations 'by land and sea against rebels and public enemies' (*terra marique adversus rebelles hh. pp.*) in the provinces of Asia, Noricum and Hither Spain. In each case, however, Candidus will doubtless have been operating mainly, and perhaps entirely, against the adherents of Severus' two rivals for the imperial throne: Pescennius Niger and Clodius Albinus. Another inscription, *ILS* 1153, records the activities of C. Julius Septimius Castinus, with detachments of four legions of the Rhine army, apparently *c.* 208 or shortly afterwards, 'against deserters and rebels' (*adversus defectores et rebelles*), who must have been Gauls or Germans.

It is at about the same time or a little earlier that we hear of that 'Robin Hood' figure, Bulla or Felix, who is said to have plundered parts of Italy for about two years, with a robber band of 600 men (including, strange to say, a number of imperial freedmen, who had been receiving little pay or none at all), until he too was captured, and thrown to the beasts (see Thompson, in *SAS* 309-10). A contemporary source, Dio Cassius, our main authority for Bulla (LXXVI.x.1-7; cf. Zonar. XII.10), preserves two of his sayings. The first is a message sent to the authorities through a captured centurion: 'Feed your slaves, to stop them becoming brigands.' The other is Bulla's answer to a question at his interrogation by the great jurist Papinian, then praetorian prefect: 'Why did you become a brigand?' Bulla replied tersely, 'Why are you prefect?' (Here one is irresistibly reminded of the dialogue between Alexander the Great and a captured pirate which rounds off a brief but powerful chapter, IV.iv, of St. Augustine's *City of God*.) It appears from Dio that Bulla received much information from country folk in the neighbourhood of Rome and Brundisium; and this may remind us of the statement of Ulpian in the *Digest* that a bandit (*latro*) cannot carry on his operations in concealment for long without local sympathisers (*receptores*, I.xviii.13.*pr.*) – an opinion which applies equally well to modern guerilla movements.

After this, until late in the third century (for the history of which our sources are very defective), I know of only one piece of evidence that is of real value for our present purposes. A Christian bishop in mid-third-century Pontus (in northern Asia Minor), St. Gregory Thaumaturgus (the 'Wonder-Worker') of Neocaesarea, sternly rebukes his flock in his *Canonical Letter*, written perhaps in 255, for going over openly to the invading Goths, helping them to murder their fellow-citizens, and pointing out to the 'barbarians' the houses most worth plundering[9] – actions which we shall find paralleled in Thrace in 376-8 (see below). The failure of the inhabitants of many of the cities of Asia Minor, and even of their garrisons, to offer any resistance to the Gothic invasions of the mid-third century is an indication of the low state of morale at this time: see especially Zosimus I.xxxii–xxxv. Zosimus also speaks of assistance given to the Goths in *c.* 256 by fishermen of eastern Thrace, enabling them to cross the Bosphorus (I.xxxiv.2; cf. 1, for co-operation by captives and traders).

It is in *c.* 284, in the reign of Carinus, that we first hear of the Bacaudae,[10] a name of unknown origin, given to participants in a whole series of peasant rebellions in Gaul and Spain which continued intermittently until *c.* 456 (see Thompson again, in *SAS* 311-20). Their first revolt was easily crushed by Maximian in 285. For the fourth century there is virtually no direct evidence about Bacaudae; but our literary sources are always reluctant to discuss military operations against lower-class rebels; and when Ammianus, writing of the early years of the reign of Valentinian I (364-75), alludes darkly to 'many battles fought in various parts of Gaul' which he thinks 'less worthy of narration' than those against German barbarians, and goes on to say that 'it is superfluous to describe them, both because their outcome led to nothing worth while, and because it is unbecoming to prolong a history with ignoble details', we may suspect (as Thompson shrewdly observes) that Valentinian was suppressing further movements of Bacaudae – and without any resounding and complete success.[11] The most important risings of Bacaudae were in the earlier fifth century: in Gaul in 407-17, 435-7 and 442, and perhaps 448, and in Spain in 441, 443, 449, 454 and 456. On several of these occasions imperial armies operated against them, led by commanders who included the *magistri militum* Flavius Asturius and Merobaudes.[12] These uprisings, coming as they did at a time when the Roman world was facing unparalleled pressure on its western frontiers, may have played an important part in bringing about the disintegration of a considerable part of the Western empire. I have space for only two of the many small scraps of evidence that have survived regarding these revolts. First, the eminent senator Rutilius Namatianus, describing in his poem *De reditu suo* a journey he took from Rome to his native Gaul towards the end of 417 (see VI.vi n.104 below), praises the activity of his relative Exuperantius in restoring 'law and order' in Armorica, the main centre of Bacaudic activity, a large district around the mouth of the Loire. Exuperantius, he says, is now teaching the area 'to love the return of peace from exile' (he uses a highly technical term, *postliminium*); 'he has restored the laws and brought back liberty, and he does not allow the Armoricans to be slaves to their own domestics' (*et servos famulis non sinit esse suis*, I.213-16) – a clear indication of the class war which had been taking place in north-west Gaul. Secondly, in a comedy called the *Querolus*,[13] by an unknown author writing apparently in the early years of the fifth century, there is a disparaging reference to life 'beside the Loire' (surely under the regime of the Bacaudae), where men live under the *ius gentium*, another name for which is 'woodland laws' (*iura silvestria*), and where *rustici* speechify and capital sentences are pronounced under an oak tree and recorded on bones; and indeed *ibi totum licet*, 'there anything goes' (*Querolus*, pp.16-17 ed. R. Peiper: see Thompson, in *SAS* 316-17).

There is no explicit evidence of peasant revolutionaries in Britain in the fourth century; and Collingwood put his case too strongly when he claimed that because 'the same legal and administrative system, the same distinction between rich men in great villas and poor men in village huts, and the same barbarian invasions, were present towards the end of the fourth century in Britain' as in Gaul, 'it is hardly to be doubted that effects were identical too; and that the wandering bands which Theodosius saw in Britain [the reference is to Amm. Marc. XXVII.viii.7, A.D. 368] included large numbers of Bacaudae'.[14] However, Thompson has recently made quite a good case for seeing the revolt in 409, in Britain and 'the whole of Armorica and in other provinces of Gaul', described by Zosimus VI.v.2-3, as a movement of a type akin to the revolts of the Gallic Bacaudae.[15] We do not know enough about the social situation in Britain in the early fifth century or about the details of the revolt itself to make a positive affirmation, but Thompson's interpretation is not contradicted by any ancient source and is probable enough in itself.

Apart from the material I have been discussing there are for the time of Constantine onwards many small scraps of evidence and one or two particularly striking passages. References to the flight of slaves to the barbarians are only to be expected, and I will mention but two examples. *CJ* VI.i.3, a constitution issued by Constantine between 317 and 323, prescribes as a penalty for such desertion amputation of a foot or consignment to the mines. (Mutilation as a punishment for crime had rarely been inflicted by the Romans until now, except in special cases under military discipline; but in the Christian Empire it gradually became more frequent, and in the seventh and eighth centuries it was quite common.)[16] Secondly, it could be said that during the first siege of Rome by Alaric the Visigoth, in the winter of 408-9, virtually all the slaves in Rome, totalling 40,000, escaped to the Gothic camp (Zos. V.xlii.3). It is hardly significant, too, that the ecclesiastical historian Eusebius should speak of Christians fleeing to the barbarians during the 'Great' persecution (of 303 and the years following) and being well received and allowed to practise their religion (*Vita Const.* II.53). It is more interesting to find an edict of Constantine in 323 demanding the burning alive of anyone who affords to barbarians an opportunity to plunder Romans, or shares in the spoils (*CTh* VII.i.1), and another edict, of 366, ordering enquiry to be made, whenever anyone claims that he had been captured by barbarians, to discover whether he had gone off under compulsion or 'of his own free will' (*CTh* V.vii.1 = *CJ* VIII.l.19, quoted above). Ammianus, telling the story of the Persian invasion of Roman Mesopotamia in 359, mentions a former Gallic trooper he himself encountered, who had deserted long ago, to avoid being punished for a crime, and who had been well received and trusted by the Persians and often sent back into Roman territory as a spy – he of course was executed (XVIII.vi.16). In 369 Count Theodosius disbanded the *arcani* (perhaps a branch of the imperial civil service), who had given secret information to the 'barbarians' (Amm. XXVIII.iii.8).

From the years 376-8 we have some extraordinarily interesting evidence from Ammianus about the behaviour of many members of the lower classes in the Balkan area, which we may compare with the tirade of St. Gregory Thaumaturgus in the 250s, mentioned above. Under Fritigern and other chiefs the Visigoths, who had been allowed by the Emperor Valens to cross the Danube into Thrace in 376 (see Appendix III § 19*b* below), but had been very badly treated by the Roman commanders, began to ravage Thrace. Fritigern advised his men to leave the cities alone (he 'kept peace with walls', he told

them!) and plunder the country districts. Those who surrendered to the 'barbarians' or were captured by them, says Ammianus, 'pointed out the rich
villages, especially those where ample supplies of food were said to be available'.
In particular, certain gold-miners, 'unable to bear the heavy burden of taxation',
did the 'barbarians' great service by revealing to them hidden reserves of food
and the secret hiding-places and storehouses of the local inhabitants (Amm.
XXXI.vi.4-7). Roman soldiers who deserted to the Goths also gave them much
valuable information (id. vii.7; cf. xv.2). Even after the disastrous battle of
Adrianople in 378, we hear of 300 Roman infantry going over to the Goths, only
to be massacred (XXXI.xv.4); some guardsmen (*candidati*) who tried to help the
Goths to capture the city of Adrianople soon afterwards were detected and
beheaded (id. 8-9). Yet information was still given to the Goths by deserters:
according to Ammianus it was so detailed, concerning Perinthus (the modern
Eregli) and neighbouring cities, that the Goths 'knew about the interior of the
very houses, not to mention the cities' (id. xvi.1).

Dealing with the year 380, Zosimus speaks of 'every city and every field'
in Macedonia and Thessaly being filled with lamentation and appeals from
everyone to the 'barbarians' to come to their help: it is just after he has mentioned
that instructions had been given for the rigorous exaction of taxes from these
areas, in spite of the serious damage recently inflicted upon them by marauding
Goths (IV.xxxii.2-3). Nicopolis in Thrace seems to have gone over to the Goths
about this time (Eunapius fr. 50).[17] A constitution of 397 threatens with death
anyone entering into a criminal conspiracy with soldiers, private citizens or
'barbarians', to kill some great man or a member of the imperial civil service
(*CTh* IX.xiv.3.*pr.*). A large number of men described by Zosimus as 'slaves'
(*oiketai*) and 'outcasts' joined the army of Tribigild the Ostrogoth in 399 and
participated in the plundering of Phrygia and Lydia (Zos. V.xiii.3-4); and a year
or two later we hear of 'runaway slaves [*oiketai*] and military deserters' plundering the countryside of Thrace, until they were crushed by the Gothic *magister
militum* (and consul in 401) Flavius Fravitta (Zos. V.xxii.3), who is also credited
with having earlier 'freed the whole East from Cilicia to Phoenicia and Palestine
from the scourge of bandits' (or pirates, *lēistai*, xx.1). In the first decade of the
fifth century St. Jerome complains that Pannonians have joined the 'barbarians'
invading Gaul: 'O lugenda res publica,' he exclaims (*Ep.* 123.15.2). There is a
fascinating passage in the *Eucharisticos* of Paulinus of Pella (written in 459),
referring to his presence in the city of Vasates (the modern Bazas, south-east of
Bordeaux) during its unsuccessful siege by the Goths under Athaulf in 415-16.
Paulinus speaks of an ineffectual armed revolt by 'a body of slaves [*factio servilis*],
combined with the senseless fury of a few young men', who were actually of
free birth, and he says it was aimed deliberately at the slaughter of the leading
citizens (the *nobilitas*), including Paulinus himself, whose 'innocent blood', with
that of his fellows, was saved only by divine intervention.[18] Two or three years
later, in 418, we hear of a 'rebellio' in Palestine, put down by the Goth Plinta,
comes and *magister militum* of Theodosius II, and in 431 of a revolt in the West, by
the Nori, suppressed with armed force by Aëtius; but we know nothing of the
details in either case.[19] Soldiers in the army sent by Justinian for the conquest of
Italy in the 540s seem to have deserted wholesale: Procopius can even make
Belisarius complain to the emperor that 'the majority' have deserted (*Bell.* VII =

Goth. III.xii.8; cf. VIII = *Goth.* IV.xxxii.20; and see the next paragraph below).

Other sources too, both Greek and Latin, speak of the inhabitants of the Roman empire as actually desiring the coming of the 'barbarians'. The fact that the panegyric delivered to the Emperor Julian by Claudius Mamertinus on 1 January 362 includes a phrase to this effect may be of little or no significance (*Paneg. Lat.* XI.iv.2, ed. E. Galletier: *ut iam barbari desiderarentur*). And I would ignore the conceit in Libanius, *Orat.* XLVII.20 (of *c.* 391), imagining that a city which is in some way disadvantaged (or put to the worse, *elattoumenē*) by another might call in neighbouring *barbaroi* 'as its allies'. But I would be inclined to take more seriously the statement of Themistius to the Emperor Valens in 368 that 'many of the nobles who have held office for three generations made their subjects long for the barbarians' (*Orat.* VIII.115c): the orator had just been speaking of the tremendous burden of taxation, which he represents as having been doubled in the forty years before the accession of Valens in 364, but now halved by Valens (113abc). Similarly Orosius, writing of the irruption of Germans into Gaul and Spain early in the fifth century, could say that some Romans preferred to live among the 'barbarians', poor but in liberty, rather than endure the anxiety of paying taxes in the Roman empire (VII.41.7: *inter barbaros pauperem libertatem quam inter Romanos tributariam sollicitudinem sustinere*). Here again, as so often, it is the burden of taxation which outweighs all other considerations. Procopius too, after describing the vicious behaviour of the army of Justinian in Italy in the early 540s, could admit that the soldiers made the Italians prefer the Ostrogoths (*Bell.* VII = *Goth.* III.ix.1–4; cf. iv.15–16); and in this case also we hear of unjust extortion practised by Alexander the logothete, whom Justinian sent to Ravenna in 540, and a little later by Bessas at Rome in 545-6.[20]

A particularly eloquent complaint is that of Salvian, a Christian priest in Southern Gaul, who probably wrote in the early 440s. Making some very severe strictures on the wealthy class of Gaul in his day, whom he compares to a pack of brigands, he says that the oppressed poor (and not only they) used to flee for refuge to the 'barbarians' (*De gub. Dei* V.21-3, 27-8, 36-8) or to the Bacaudae (V.22, 24–6; cf. Section iv of this chapter). Salvian stresses above all the oppressiveness of Roman taxation, which allows the wealthy to get off lightly but burdens the poor beyond endurance (IV.20-1, 30-1; V.17-18, 25-6, 28-32, 34–44). I decline to follow Jones in discounting almost entirely the evidence of Orosius (VII.41.7: see the preceding paragraph) as 'suspect' and that of Salvian as 'biassed and unreliable'.[21]

Although of course I recognise that Salvian is prone to rhetorical exaggeration, like the great majority of later Latin and Greek writers, I agree with Ernst Stein that his *De gubernatione Dei* is 'la source la plus révélatrice sur la situation intérieure de l'Empire d'Occident, la seule qui nous laisse voir directement toute la misère du temps dans sa réalité atroce' (*HBE* I².i.344). Stein devotes more than three pages to describing some of Salvian's strictures on the oppressiveness of Roman rule in the West in his day, and he points out that some of these are reflected in an exactly contemporary edict, of Valentinian III (*Nov. Val.* X.*pr.*, and 3, A.D. 441: see Stein, ibid. 347). To this I would add another edict, issued seventeen years later by the Emperor Majorian, which I have summarised in Section iv of this chapter (*Nov. Maj.* II, A.D. 458).

Although, as I have already made clear (in VII.v above), I regard Donatism as being primarily a religious movement and not an expression of social protest, there is no doubt that it contained a strong element of such protest, simply because the class of large landowners in north Africa (including Numidia, where the concentration of Donatists was highest) was overwhelmingly Catholic. The role of the Catholic Church in north Africa in the Later Roman Empire has been admirably described in the great book on Vandal Africa by Christian Courtois (*VA* Part I, ch.ii, § 4, esp. 132, 135-44). As he says, 'L'Afrique du Ve siècle ne demeure romaine que par le double appui de l'aristocratie foncière et de l'Eglise catholique qui s'accordent pour assurer à l'État le minimum de puissance indispensable à la leur' (132, cf. 144). The Circumcellions,[22] the militant wing of the Donatists (sometimes appearing, if we are not seriously misinformed, as a kind of lunatic fringe, bent on religious suicide), waged open war on occasion not only upon the Catholic Church in Africa but also upon the class of large landowners from which that Church derived its main support. The war-cry of these men, *Deo laudes* ('Praise be to God': it often appears on Donatist tombstones), was more to be feared, according to St. Augustine, than the lion's roar (*Enarr. in Ps.* 132.6, in *CCL*, Ser. Lat. XL [1956] 1930). But these fanatics, barbarous as they might seem to the landlord class, were anything but a terror to the poor, for we hear of them threatening to punish moneylenders who exacted payment from the peasants, and forcing landlords to dismount from their carriages and run before them while their slaves drove, or to do slaves' work at the mill (Optat. III.4; Aug., *Ep.* 108 [vi] 18; 185 [iv] 15; cf. 88.8 etc.).

There are clear indications that the regime the Vandals set up on their conquest of Roman north Africa in 429 and the years following was less extortionate than the Roman system existing there, from the point of view of the *coloni*.[23] Constitutions issued by Justinian in 552 and 558, many years after his reconquest of north Africa in 533-4, show that during the Vandal period many *coloni* must have achieved some kind of freedom by escaping from the estates where they were in the condition of serfs: see *Corp. Iur. Civil.* III [*Nov. Just.*] 799-803, Append. 6 and 9.[24] (There is also reason to think that in other Germanic kingdoms humble Greeks and Romans may have found themselves better off.)[25] Although the Ostrogoths, for example, could sometimes – like other 'barbarians' – behave with great savagery to the inhabitants of captured towns, even indulging in general massacre and enslavement,[26] their rule might sometimes seem at least no worse than that of the Roman landowners, as it evidently did in Italy in the 540s during the reign of Totila the Ostrogoth (541-52), who in the areas under his control treated the peasants particularly well (Procop., *Bell.* VII = *Goth.* III.xiii.1; cf. vi.5), in strong contrast with those (apart perhaps from Belisarius) who commanded the Roman army sent by Justinian.[27] Totila made the peasants pay their rents as well as their taxes to himself.[28] He also accepted into his army a considerable number of slaves who had belonged to Roman masters, and he firmly refused to hand them over.[29] He is also credited with representing most successfully to the peasants of Lucania, who had been organised into a military force against him by the great landowner Tullianus (see IV.iv n.7 below), that if they returned to the cultivation of their fields the property of their landlords would become theirs (*Bell.* VII = *Goth.* III.xxii.20-1). All this material comes from Procopius, who was personally present as a member of the staff of Belisarius. In the light of this information, it is easy to understand the particularly venomous way in which Totila is referred to by Justinian in his so-called 'Pragmatic Sanction' of 554,[30] which (among other things) ordered everything done by Totila, including his 'donations', to be abrogated (§ 2), confiscated property to be restored (13-14), marriages between free persons and slaves to be dissolved at the wish of the free party (15), and slaves and *coloni* who had passed into the possession of others to be returned to their original masters (16). The statement by Jones that 'the mass of the Africans and Italians welcomed the armies of Justinian' is far from being justified even by the few passages he is able to quote from Procopius, a witness who would naturally have been glad to find evidence of friendliness towards the armies of which he himself was a member.[31]

At the very end of the sixth century we find Pope Gregory the Great writing of Corsicans and Campanians defecting to the Lombards (*Ep.* V.38 and X.5, ed. L. M. Hartmann, I.ii.324-6 and II.ii.240-1).

In the seventh century we hear from the *Chronicle* of Bishop John of Nikiu of Egyptians deserting to the Arabs.[32] The conquest by the Arabs, first of Palestine, Syria, Mesopotamia and part of Armenia (not to mention the Persian empire), and then of Egypt, was accomplished with astonishing speed within a decade: Syria etc. between 634 and 640, and Egypt by 642. This startling process was no doubt facilitated by the previous large-scale Persian attacks (under their King Chosroes II) on the eastern provinces of the Roman empire in the quarter-century beginning in 604:[33] they overran Mesopotamia, Syria and Palestine; between 611 and 626 they devastated many parts of Asia Minor; and in 617-18 they conquered Egypt and held it for some ten years. These lands were not entirely freed from the Persian danger until 629, the year after Chosroes was murdered in a coup. Although the surviving sources for all these events are very unsatisfactory and some of the dates are only approximate, the general outline is reasonably secure; but it is impossible to say how far the Arab victories during the next few years were due to the discouragement, exhaustion, damage and loss of life caused by the Persian invasions. The Arab conquests certainly deserve much more space than I can give them here, since they were evidently due in large part to the old internal weaknesses of the Later Roman Empire, especially of course class oppression, and including now religious strife and persecution. Not only did the exploitation of the many for the benefit of the few continue as before (if not on quite the same scale as it had done in the West); the hostility between the various Christian sects, especially now between the Monophysites of Syria and Egypt (the Jacobites and the Copts) and the Chalcedonian 'Orthodox', seriously reduced the will to resist the Arabs on the part of the populations of Syria and Egypt, which were predominantly Monophysite and had suffered much persecution on that account. Michael the Syrian, the Patriarch of Antioch at the end of the twelfth century, speaking on behalf of his Jacobite brethren about the Arab conquest, says, 'It was no small advantage to us to be delivered from the cruelty of the Romans [the Byzantines], their wickedness, their fury, their implacable zeal against us, and to find ourselves at peace' (*Chron.* XI.3 *fin.*).[34] The same statement was made in the thirteenth century by Bar Hebraeus (Gregory Abû'l Faraj, or Abulpharagius), another Syrian Jacobite historian, who used Michael as one of his principal sources (*Chron. Eccles.*, Sectio I.50).[35] I feel I should emphasise here that for the seventh century in particular Syriac sources are often essential for the Roman historian: for those who (like myself) do not read Syriac, translations are often available, into Latin or a modern language. There is fortunately an excellent account of all the main editions and translations by S. P. Brock, 'Syriac sources for seventh-century history', in *Byzantine and Modern Greek Studies* 2 (1976) 17-36.

I know of no good evidence that the Syrian Christians actually helped the Arab invaders, whom they naturally feared and hated as infidels until they discovered that the Muslims were prepared in general to allow them to practise their own particular form of Christianity (as the Byzantines were not), provided they paid a poll-tax for the privilege. As for the Egyptian Copts, most of them seem also to have regarded their conquerors at first with aversion and horror. Duchesne was clearly right to say that their sentiments were hostile to the 'empire persécuteur' rather than favourable to the infidel invader.[36] But some of them soon came to regard the rule of the Muslims, who as a rule were far more tolerant towards their subjects in religious matters, as a lesser evil than that of the persecuting Orthodox – the 'Melkites', or 'Emperor's men', as they called them. Even A. J. Butler, who in his history of the Arab conquest of Egypt (still a 'standard work') is eager to defend the Copts against any unfair charge of treachery and desertion to the Arab side, is obliged to admit that from 641 onwards the Copts did on occasion give assistance to the Arabs, notably when the brief Byzantine reoccupation of Alexandria in 645-6 was forcibly terminated – and the whole of Egypt was lost to the Greek world for ever.[37] Butler also records the comments of Bar Hebraeus (*Chron. Eccles.,*. Sectio I.50)[38] on the temporary restoration to the Mesopotamian and Syrian Monophysites in the early seventh century, by the Persian King Chosroes II, of the churches which had been taken from them and handed over to the Orthodox by the persecuting Chalcedonian Bishop Dometianus of Melitene (for whom see n.34 again: Bar Hebraeus was here reproducing Michael the Syrian, *Chron.* X.25). Michael and Bar Hebraeus regarded the Persian conquest of Mesopotamia (605, maintained until 627-8) as a divine punishment on the Chalcedonians for their persecution of the Jacobites – in their eyes, of course, the Orthodox. And Butler adds, 'It is the old story of Christians sacrificing country, race, and religion in order to triumph over a rival sect of Christians' (see n.37 again).

It was not only towards rival sects within Christianity that the Christians gave vent to their religious animosity. The restitution to Jerusalem in 630 of what was believed to be the 'True Cross', carried off by the victorious Persians in 614 and now taken back from them by the Emperor Heraclius, was followed by a severe persecution of the Jews, who were accused of participating in the massacre of Christians at Jerusalem which had followed its capture by the Persians in 614. The consequences were soon to be unfortunate for the Roman empire, for when the Arabs attacked Syria and Palestine in the 630s the Jews evidently received them favourably and in some places gave them significant support.[39]

★ ★ ★ ★ ★ ★

A large number of 'barbarians', mainly Germans, achieved high positions in the Roman world through service in the army in the fourth century and later. As early as the mid-fourth century Arbitio, who had enlisted as a common soldier (*gregarius miles*), reached the most exalted of all military ranks, that of *magister equitum*, and in 355 even became consul, an honour rarely conferred on upstarts (see *PLRE* I.94-5). The vast majority of these 'barbarian' military commanders were completely loyal to Rome, and it is rare indeed to hear of them being guilty of treachery, like the Alamannic chief Hortar, appointed by Valentinian I to a Roman army command but tortured and burnt to death about 372 for treasonable correspondence with his former compatriots.[40] With hardly an exception, these men came to regard themselves as Romans and thoroughly accepted the outlook of the Roman ruling class, of which they had become members, however much they might be despised by some for their 'barbarian origin'. Their situation is admirably illustrated by the story of Silvanus, especially as it is told by Ammianus Marcellinus XV.v.2-33.[41] Silvanus was apparently a 'second-generation immigrant', since Ammianus speaks of his father Bonitus as 'a Frank, it is true', but one who had fought loyally for Constantine (ibid. 33). After rising to very high military office, as *magister peditum* (in 352/3), Silvanus became in 355 the subject of an entirely unjustified accusation of treason, which he knew Constantius II was only too likely to accept; and in the circumstances he was virtually obliged to have himself proclaimed emperor, at Cologne – in which capacity he survived only twenty-eight days before being put to death. Silvanus had thought at first of deserting to his kinsmen the Franks, but he was persuaded by another Frankish officer, Laniogaisus, that the tribesmen would simply murder him or sell him to the Romans (ibid. 15-16) – an interesting indication that many Germans had no use for those of their own number who had gone over to Rome. During a debate on the Silvanus affair in the Consistory (the state Council) of Constantius II at Milan, another officer of Frankish origin, Malarich, the commander of the *Gentiles*, made an indignant protest that '*men devoted to the empire* ought not to be victimised by cliques and wiles' (ibid. 6). Before turning back to the behaviour of ordinary Greeks and Romans, I must emphasise once more that the prominent military men I have been discussing in this paragraph, although of 'barbarian' *origin*, had become above all members of the Roman ruling class and were no more likely than other Romans to prove disloyal to the empire that was now coming to be called *Romania* – an expression the earliest surviving use of which dates from *c.* 358 (Athan., *Hist. Arian. ad monach.* 35; cf. Piganiol, *EC*[2] 458 n.3).

★   ★   ★   ★   ★   ★

Against all the evidence set out above for discontent, rebellion, and defection to the 'barbarians' on the part of humble Greeks and Romans, I have come across very little sign of spontaneous resistance to 'barbarian' incursions on the part of either peasants or townsmen. References to such activities in the countryside, which I have listed in IV.iv (and its n.6) above, almost always attribute the initiative to prominent local landowners, who organise forces *ad hoc*, the nucleus of which is provided by their own *coloni* and slaves (see IV.iv nn.6-7). I know of even fewer examples of the vigorous defence of cities by their own inhabitants, especially without the assistance of garrisons of professional soldiers.[42] This may be due partly to the fact that 'barbarian' ravaging was naturally focussed on the countryside. Walled cities, even if not strongly defended, could present a difficult problem, for few 'barbarian' groups were capable of mounting proper sieges. Fritigern in 376, when advising his Visigoths to concentrate on the best and most fruitful country areas, is said by Ammianus to have remarked that he 'kept peace with walls' (XXXI.6.4). Many other passages testify to the inability of 'barbarians' to capture towns and their consequent preference for the ravaging of rural areas. Besides, many towns were garrisoned. But in the article published in 1977 which I have already utilised above (see nn.10,12,15), Thompson has emphasised the rarity of recorded civilian resistance of any kind to 'barbarian' attacks. As he says, we hear much in the valuable *Chronicle* of Hydatius of the ravaging of north-western Spain by the Suevi, and in the *Life of Severinus* (who died in 482) by Eugippius[43] (511) of the depredations of the Rugi in Noricum Ripense (part of modern Austria), but we never hear of any organised resistance by the provincial population. And he continues,

> Eugippius makes it clear that the Noricans, even when there were imperial troops stationed among them, and still more when there were none, were incapable of making any collective effort to check the ravages of the invaders. They never tried to ambush them, or to sink their boats as they crossed the Danube, or to launch punitive raids across the great river into the territory of those who were tormenting them. One or two forts in Galicia [in north-west Spain] took up an aggressive defence against the Sueves and inflicted some losses upon them;[44] but in general the picture there was one of helplessness and despair, just as in Noricum.[45]

It was not only the very poor who became defectors to the 'barbarians'. At the very highest level of society, needless to say, any outright treasonable conduct, betraying the empire to a 'barbarian' ruler, was almost unknown. I cannot add to the only two cases known to Jones: in 469 Arvandus, praetorian prefect of the Gauls in 464-8, and soon afterwards Seronatus, who was either governor of Aquatanica Prima or vicar of the Gallic diocese of the Septem Provinciae. Both these men – no doubt, as Jones says, 'despairing of the Empire' – were condemned (and Seronatus executed) for collaboration with the Visigothic King Euric.[46] We also hear of a few by no means lowly men who defected to the 'barbarians'. One or two of these evidently acted for reasons of personal advantage. Craugasius, for instance, a leading man of Nisibis in Mesopotamia, who fled to Persia in 359, seems to have been motivated mainly by affection for his beautiful wife, who had been captured by the Persians, and by the prospect of being handsomely treated by the Persian king, Shapur II.[47] And the bishop of Margus on the Danube, who in 441 betrayed his city to the Huns (who immediately destroyed it), seems to have been behaving in a scandalous manner, robbing Hun graves in breach of a treaty of 436: he probably handed over his city to escape being himself surrendered to the vengeance of the exasperated Huns (Priscus fr. 2). But there seems to be no good reason to think that there was any treachery on the part of Bishop Ephraemius of Antioch just before the capture and sack of that city by King Chosroes I of Persia in 540 (Procop., *Bell.* II = *Pers.* II.vi.16-25; vii.14-18, esp. 16-17). The bishop of Bezabde in Mesopotamia also came under suspicion of having betrayed his city to the Persians in 360; but Ammianus, although he admits there was a *prima facie* case against the man, did not believe the accusation, and we must treat it as at best 'not proven' (Amm. XX.vii.7-9). But even men of some substance could be driven to defect, like the poor, by injustice and maltreatment. There is an instructive story in Ammianus about a very able man living in the Greek East named Antoninus, who, after becoming a rich merchant, had taken a position as accountant on the staff of the military governor (the *dux*) of the province of Mesopotamia, and had finally received the honorary rank of *protector*. Certain men of power (*potentes, potiores*) were able through their command of patronage to victimise him and to compel him to acknowledge a debt, the right to enforce payment of which was by collusion transferred to the imperial treasury;[48] and when the Count of the Treasury (the *comes sacrarum largitionum*) pressed him hard, Antoninus defected suddenly to Persia in 359, taking with him the fullest possible details of the Roman army and its resources and dispositions, and becoming the right-hand-man of King Shapur II, who was planning to invade Roman Mesopotamia (Amm. XVIII.v.1-3,8; vi.3,19; vii.10; viii.5-6; x.i; XIX.i.3; ix.7-8; XX.vi.1). At a later parley with the Roman general Ursicinus (the patron of Ammianus), Antoninus protested vehemently that he had not deserted the Graeco-Roman world voluntarily, but only because he had been persecuted by his iniquitous creditors, whom even the great Ursicinus had been unable to hold in check. At the end of their colloquy Antoninus withdrew in the most respectful manner, 'not turning around but facing Ursicinus and deferentially walking backwards until he was out of sight' (XVIII.viii. 5-6) – a touching revelation of his reluctance to abandon the society in which he had lived, and his veneration for its leading men.

At least two men of some quality, one a doctor and the other a merchant, actually took refuge among – of all barbarian peoples – the Huns. A mid-fifth-century Gallic chronographic source laconically records under the year 448 that a doctor named Eudoxius, 'clever but perverse' (*pravi sed exercitati ingenii*), after being involved in a revolt of the Bacaudae, fled to the Huns (*Chron. Min.* I.662). The other man is the subject of the fascinating story told by the historian and diplomat Priscus (fr. 8)[49] of his meeting, during his embassy to the camp of Attila in 448 or 449, with an unnamed man from Greece who had once prospered as a merchant at Viminacium on the Danube (the modern Kostelacz) and married a very rich wife there, but had been captured by the Huns when they took the city in 441 and had then fought for the Huns, even against the Romans. Although freed by his captors, he had by preference stayed to live among the Huns. His scathing description of Graeco-Roman class society is reported by Priscus, a firm believer in the established order, with a grave, incredulous disapproval which makes the testimony all the more valuable. The Greek said that things were bad enough in war-time, but in peace they were even worse, because of heavy taxation; 'and unprincipled men inflict injuries, because the laws are not valid against everyone . . . A transgressor who is one of the very rich is not punished for his injustice, while a poor man, who doesn't understand business, pays the legal penalty – that is, if he doesn't die before the hearing, so long is the course of lawsuits protracted, and so much is the money that is spent on them. The climax of misery, perhaps, is to have to pay in order to obtain justice. For no one will give a hearing to an injured man unless he pays money to the judge and his assistants'.

This was all too true. The Greek seems to have been thinking primarily of civil litigation. We must not expect to find many references to long-drawn-out civil suits, but we do hear of one which seems to have lasted for eighteen years, from A.D. 226 to 244, and another that was ended by the personal intervention of King Theodoric the Ostrogoth (who ruled in Italy from 493 to 526), after dragging on allegedly for thirty years.[50] The position in criminal cases was even worse, for the accused, if they had neither honorific status themselves nor a sufficiently influential patron, might spend long periods in prison, sometimes in appalling conditions. In a speech of Libanius, giving a distressing picture of prison life at Antioch, we hear of a case in which a group of villagers, suspected (perhaps without good cause) of murdering a local landowner, spent many months in prison, where five of them actually died before the case was fully heard (*Orat.* XLV, esp. §§ 8-13, 25-6: see Jones, *LRE* I.521-2). Indeed, 'Roman criminal justice was in general not only brutal but inefficient' (id. 520-1).[51] The Greek was justified, too, in what he said about the venality of officials: all officials in the Later Roman Empire expected to be handsomely tipped, even – and perhaps especially – tax collectors. In a typically emotional edict Constantine says, 'Let the grasping hands of the officials refrain; let them refrain, I say, for unless after this warning they do refrain, they shall be cut off by the sword' (*CTh* I.xvi.7, of 331). And he goes on to forbid their illicit tips, *sportulae* as they were called, a term which extended to many other types of payment, both forced and voluntary, including those made by patrons to their clients, or by benefactors to their fellow-townsmen or others (cf. V.iii above). It was an empty threat, however, as the officials must have known only too well. Only about twenty-five years after Constantine's death, in the reign of Julian, an inscription found at Timgad, recording the order of precedence at official functions in the province of Numidia (roughly the modern Algeria), actually lays down an official tariff of the tips which could be legally demanded by the officials of that province: they are expressed in terms of *modii* of wheat, from two to a hundred *modii* – say from a quarter of a bushel to about twelve bushels.[52] One civil servant of the sixth century who had literary pretensions, John Lydus (John the Lydian), tells us that during his first years as an *exceptor* in the department of the praetorian prefecture, quite a minor post (although in an important department), he actually earned *sōphronōs* ('without sailing too close to the wind', perhaps) as much as a thousand solidi, thanks to the solicitude of his great patron, the Praetorian Prefect Zoticus (*De magistr.* III.26-7). As an ordinary *exceptor*, his nominal initial salary would probably have been only around nine solidi,[53] and although various additional fees and perquisites would have been available, he would not, without powerful backing, have come near earning a thousand solidi, unless he was prepared to indulge in corrupt practices to which the word *sōphronōs* would have been most inappropriate. John also mentions in the same passage that when he wrote a panegyric in verse in honour of his illustrious patron, the great man generously rewarded him with a gold solidus for every line of the poem – although perhaps 'generously' is not quite the right word, for the money was paid out of public funds!

(iv)

The collapse of much of the Roman empire in the fifth, sixth and seventh centuries

After the murder of Alexander Severus in 235 there ensued fifty years of unparalleled disaster for the empire, with a series of futile civil wars between rival claimants to the imperial position, barbarian invasions, and a plague which broke out in 251 and raged for some fifteen to twenty years, with even more disastrous consequences than the pestilence of the 160s.[1] Only in 284-5, with the accession of the very able emperor Diocletian (late 284), was the situation temporarily stabilised;[2] and it was not until 324 that the empire entered upon a long period of internal peace, with Constantine's victory over Licinius and the unchallenged supremacy of the Constantinian house. Even after this there were occasional short periods of internecine warfare, due again in every case to contention for the imperial throne. As I insisted in Section iii of this chapter, the civil wars of the third and fourth centuries, like those of the first and second, were all fought out between the respective claimants and their armies; not once is there any clear sign of an alignment of class forces corresponding to the opposition between the armies, and we must regard all these struggles, ferocious as they sometimes were, primarily as attempts by individuals and factions within the governing class to acquire or retain control of the supreme power in the empire.

No doubt men driven desperate by oppression could sometimes be led to hope that a change of emperor might result in some improvement in their situation, and it need not surprise us, therefore, if we occasionally come across statements about the support given by humble men to some pretender to the imperial throne. Writing probably in the late 360s, the unknown author of a curious little treatise, known today as the Anonymus *De rebus bellicis*, addressed to the reigning emperors (who, at that date, must be Valentinian I and Valens), speaks with vehement disapproval of the greed of the rich, whose store of gold, he says (II.2-3),

> meant that the houses of the powerful [*potentes*] were crammed full and their splendour enhanced to the destruction of the poor, the poorer classes of course being held down by force [*tenuioribus videlicet violentia oppressis*]. But the poor were driven by their afflictions into various criminal enterprises, and losing sight of all respect for the law, all feelings of loyalty, they entrusted their revenge to crime. For they often inflicted the most severe injuries on the empire, laying waste the fields, breaking the peace with outbursts of brigandage, stirring up animosities; and passing from one crime to another they supported usurpers (I have used the English version of E. A. Thompson, *RRI* 110).

The word here translated 'usurpers' is *tyranni*, the standard term for a would-be emperor who did not succeed in establishing his rule firmly and achieving recognition (cf. VI.vi above). Certainly, the worse the situation of the poor under a given emperor, the more likely they might be, *a priori*, to support some new pretender to the throne. But we must not be too impressed by the allegations we occasionally meet with in literary sources that the followers of a particular pretender were – or at least included – the scum of the earth: such statements are part of the normal armoury of ancient political propaganda. However, on one occasion in particular I would be prepared to take such statements seriously. We hear from Ammianus and Zosimus that many humble men joined in the rebellion of Procopius, in 365-6;[3] and there is a good reason why discontent should have been greater than ever at this very time: taxation was especially severe. Taxation had always been recognised by the Roman government as the prime necessity for the maintenance of peace itself, as the Romans understood that term. In the words Tacitus puts into the mouth of the Roman general

Petilius Cerealis in 70, 'Without arms there can be no peace among peoples [*quies gentium*], nor can there be arms without pay, or pay without taxation' (*tributa*: *Hist*. IV.74). And in the ludicrously optimistic picture of a coming Golden Age, put into the mouth of the Emperor Probus (276-82), the cessation of any need for soldiers leads directly to a world in which taxation can disappear (*Hist. Aug., Prob*. 20.3-6 and 22.4-23.3, esp. 20.6, 23.2). Taxation, under the new system inaugurated by Diocletian, had steadily increased during the fourth century, and even Julian, who in Gaul is said to have reduced the tax on each *caput* from 25 solidi to 7 (Amm. Marc. XVI.v.14-15), evidently made no reduction in the East during the short time he ruled there in 361-2. According to Themistius, address-ing the Emperor Valens in March 368, imperial taxation had doubled during the forty years before the accession of Valens in 364; and although Valens proceeded to halve it, he did so only in his fourth year, 367-8 (the year after the revolt of Procopius), keeping it unchanged until then (*Orat*. VIII.113ab,c). Furthermore, Valens' father-in-law Petronius[4] (in what office, we are not told) had made himself widely hated by his ruthless exaction of arrears of taxes, accompanied by torture, and going back, according to Ammianus, to the reign of the Emperor Aurelian (270-5), nearly a hundred years earlier! (XXVI.vi.7-9). Ammianus attributes partly to detestation of Petronius the adhesion to Pro-copius of many of the common people (*populus, vulgus*: ibid. 17). Similarly, Zosimus ascribes the widespread support in Africa for Firmus (who rebelled in 372 or 373) to the exactions of Romanus, the *comes Africae*, in Mauretania (IV.xvi.3).[5] I shall return shortly to the subject of taxation.

One of the many futile civil wars, between Constantius II and the 'usurper' Magnentius, led to a major battle in 351 at Mursa (near to the confluence of the Drave with the Danube) which may well have been 'the bloodiest battle of the century', as Stein has called it, with a total loss of life said – no doubt with much exaggeration, as usual – to have been 54,000.[6] And there were innumerable wars on and over the frontiers, not only against 'barbarians' like the Germans and Sarmatians in the north, and in the fifth century the Huns, as well as against the nomads of the desert who often attacked Egypt, Cyrenaica and the other north African provinces,[7] but also against the Persians, who could be considered a civilised state comparable with the Roman empire itself, and who became much more menacing in the Sassanid period from 224 onwards (see IV.iv above). Julian's disastrous expedition against Persia in 363 involved perhaps the largest army ever assembled by a Roman emperor for a campaign across the frontiers,[8] and the resulting losses in manpower and equipment, although they cannot be even approximately estimated, must have been catastrophic. Ordinary cam-paigns on the frontiers may not have resulted in a greater drain on the resources of the empire than occurred during peace time, for no doubt the prisoners and booty captured will have roughly balanced out the losses. Even war with Persia may have yielded a good profit on occasion, as for example in 298; but in general the long series of conflicts in the East must have greatly strained the economy of the empire. And of course when Roman territory from which recruits were customarily obtained was lost to 'barbarian' invaders, as happened above all in the West in the early years of the fifth century, permanent damage was inflicted on the military strength of the empire (see esp. Jones, *LRE* I.198).

It is indeed hard to estimate how much waste of resources occurred during wars: the army itself was a very great burden on those resources, if less in time of peace than during wars (cf. Section ii of this chapter, with its nn.14-15). One thing we can say with confidence: the army was now considerably enlarged beyond what it had been in the early Principate. The total paper strength of the army may have been about 400,000 or more, even in the Antonine period.[9] When Septimius Severus raised three new legions for his campaign against the Parthians in 197, he was increasing the legionary army by about ten per cent. Estimating the numbers of the armed forces is a very difficult task, especially as regards the auxiliary regiments (*auxilia*), which evidently outnumbered the legions; and all I feel able to say is that Diocletian and Constantine must have greatly increased the size of the army, to perhaps well over half a million men. It is no wonder that Diocletian also began a thorough-going reform of the whole system of taxation, which was apparently far more effective in extracting from the working population – the peasantry above all, of course – the much greater resources needed to enable the government to sustain its military and administrative machine. Further expansion of the army may have brought it up to more than 600,000 before the end of the fourth century. We happen to possess two sets of figures for total army strength, the nature of which may inspire more confidence than we can usually feel in such cases, because they are not in the usual very round numbers and therefore look as if they may go back ultimately to genuine army lists, whether they represent them accurately or not. Very detailed – and not at all implausible – figures which add up to 435,266 are given in the mid-sixth century by John Lydus (*De mens.* I.27) for the reign of Diocletian. (I would guess that they are from the earlier rather than the later part of that reign, during which I think the army grew considerably.) Agathias, writing perhaps *c.* 580, speaks of the army as numbering 645,000 'under the emperors of former times' (*hypo tōn palai basileōn: Hist.* V.13-17), a phrase which must refer back to the time before the division of the empire in 395.[10] All the figures I have given are likely, of course, to represent 'paper strength'; but even if the lists were inflated (as seems very likely) by quite a large number of fictitious soldiers, whose pay and rations were simply appropriated by the officers responsible for the lists, it is the 'paper strength' which matters, as Jones has insisted (see n.10 again), for it would have been those figures on which the actual issues of pay and allowances were based.

It was not only the army which grew under Diocletian and his successors: the civil service too was enormously enlarged, the greatest single expansion coming when Diocletian virtually doubled the number of provinces, to over a hundred. (For the provincial reorganisation, see esp. Jones, *LRE* III.381-9.) At the time of the *Notitia Dignitatum*, drawn up (in the form in which we have it) at the time of the division of the empire in 395 and revised in its Western section during the first quarter of the fifth century, there were, according to my calculation, 119 provinces.[11] Now the total numbers of men employed in the imperial civil service were not really excessive, when we take into account the vast area of the empire and the number of *officia* (bureaux) concerned – those not only of provincial governors, but of the 'palatine ministries' (those serving the emperor directly), the praetorian prefects and their vicars of the civil dioceses, the two urban prefects (of Rome and Constantinople), the *magistri militum* and others. I would agree with Jones, whose knowledge of the evidence has never been equalled, that 'the grand total of regular officials was not much in excess of 30,000, not an extravagant number for an empire which stretched from Hadrian's Wall to beyond the Euphrates'.[12] But, as we shall see, the burden of the civil service upon the economy of the Roman world was out of all proportion to its numbers.

Even before the great growth in the numbers of the Christian clergy (which I deal with below) the army and the civil service represented a tremendous drain upon the resources of the Graeco-Roman world. In a sense many of the men concerned were performing essential functions in defence or administration. But they were all *withdrawn from the productive process*, and they had to be maintained by those who remained within the process, above all of course the peasants and slaves. Some of them – a high proportion of the superior officials, in particular – would already be members of the propertied class, who if they had not been involved in the administration would have been gentlemen of leisure, and to that extent an equal burden on the economy. But there is an essential fact here which it would be easy to overlook. Had civil servants been ordinary gentlemen of leisure, they would have been a burden, certainly, upon their own *coloni* and slaves. What made many of the civil servants an exceptionally heavy weight upon the economy as a whole was that they were able to extort, by means of their official position, a far greater surplus from the working population than they would have been able to do as mere private individuals. Their opportunities for extortion naturally varied very greatly, and the higher a man's position the more he could make. It was not so much the nominal salaries which were the lucrative part of top appointments: indeed, the fixed official salaries, largely owing to the great inflation of the third and fourth centuries, seem to have been distinctly lower in the Later Empire than in the Principate,[13] even if the highest recorded salary in the Later Empire, the 100 pounds of gold paid annually to the Praetorian Prefect of Africa in Justinian's reign, is no less than eight hundred times that of an ordinary clerk.[14] Officials enriched themselves primarily from extra-legal exactions of all kinds. As we saw in Section iii of this chapter, John the Lydian in his first year as a fairly humble clerk (though in a palatine ministry at Constantinople) boasted of having earned quite legally a sum which must have been something like a hundred times his nominal salary. This will have been altogether exceptional, because it was due to the patronage of one of the highest officials of the day, and no doubt the ordinary civil servant would have had to be content with much less, or else resort to questionable or even illegal means of extortion. But 'extra-legal' profits were evidently made from top to bottom of the administrative machine. In the fifth and sixth centuries it looks as if would-be governors of at least some provinces might be willing to spend on a bribe (*suffragium*) that would procure them the office as much as or more than the salary it would bring them – a clear indication of the additional profits to be made out of the post (see Jones, *LRE* I.391–401, esp. 398-9).

The officials who were probably in the very best position of all to extract bribes, namely the *cubicularii*, the eunuchs who, as slaves or freedmen, ministered to the 'sacred bedchamber' of the emperor or empress, could sometimes make enormous fortunes. (I have said something about their influence and the wealth they could acquire in III.v above.) The corps of *cubicularii* being closed to ordinary men, it was the other 'palatine' offices which were most sought after, and in some cases we hear not only of limits being placed on the number of men who could be admitted, called *statuti*, but also of *supernumerarii*, who either worked without salary or waited to step into dead or retired men's shoes; we even find grades being established among these supernumeraries.[15] At the lowest level, that of the officials of the provincial governors, known as *cohortales* (over 10,000 in number), salaries were very low (see Jones, *LRE* II.594) and legal perquisites relatively small; this was the only part of the civil service which in theory a man could not leave and in which his sons were also bound to serve (see Jones, *RE* 413). The lack of adequate official rewards may have driven many *cohortales* to forms of extortion which the law either did not sanction or positively forbade. I can best illustrate this by referring again to the astonishing law of Justinian in 531, applying to *cohortales* (*taxeōtai* in Greek) as well as *curiales*, which I had occasion to mention in regard to *curiales* at the end of Section ii of this chapter. As we saw there, Justinian's reason for prohibiting *cohortales* and *curiales* from becoming bishops or priests was that they would have become habituated to the practice of extortion with violence and cruelty (*CJ* I.iii.52.*pr.*, 1).

The civil service, then, did not merely extract a surplus from the working population (and others); it appropriated a far larger amount than its relatively modest numbers might suggest. Army and civil service together were a fearful burden on the Graeco-Roman economy. Given that the Roman empire was to be stabilised and strengthened, without any fundamental change in its nature, it was fortunate indeed in most of its rulers from Diocletian to Theodosius I (284–395). What men could do, within their lights, they did. Sometimes, they appear in quite a heroic role. But, ironically enough, the very measures they took, necessary as they were if the system was to be maintained, helped to break up the empire, for the increases in army and civil service involved the extraction of an increased surplus from the already overburdened peasantry. Diocletian, as we have seen, thoroughly reorganised the system of taxation. Constantine added two entirely new taxes, one on senators, the *follis* or *collatio glebalis* (at rates which were relatively very low indeed),[16] the other, the *collatio lustralis* or *chrysargyron*, on *negotiatores*, who included for this purpose not only traders but urban craftsmen who sold their own products, fishermen, moneylenders, brothel-keepers and prostitutes. (For the distress allegedly caused by the *collatio lustralis*, see IV.vi above and its n.7 below.) In the East, the former tax was abolished by Marcian in the early 450s (*CJ* XII.ii.2), the latter by Anastasius in 498 (*CJ* XI.i.1, dated by Josh. Styl., *Chron.*31).

* * * * * *

In the preceding paragraph I have characterised the majority of the Roman emperors from Diocletian to Theodosius I as men who performed their functions as effectively as circumstances allowed, and even with some heroism. It is an ironic reflection that most of the Later Roman emperors who served the empire most loyally were men who had risen from a lowly station in life. Diocletian himself was born a Dalmatian peasant, and his three colleagues in the Tetrarchy (of 295 ff.) were also of Balkan peasant stock,[17] including Constantius I, the father of Constantine, whose dynasty lasted until the death of Julian in 363. Valentinian I, who founded the next dynasty in 364, was the son of a Pannonian soldier of humble origins, who had risen from the ranks;[18] and there were later emperors who were also of peasant stock, notably Justin I and his nephew Justinian I.[19] Libanius, in a lament for Julian written about 365, could say that there had been 'not a few emperors of no mean intelligence who had lacked distinguished ancestry, and although they understood how to preserve the empire were ashamed to speak of their parentage, so that it was quite a task for those who delivered encomia of them to alleviate this *trauma*'! (*Orat.* XVIII.7). Members of the Roman upper class would apply to such men, and to leading generals and officials who could boast of no illustrious ancestors, contemptuous terms deriding their rustic origin, such as *agrestis, semiagrestis, subagrestis, subrusticus*.[20] The first two of these words are used by (among others) the epitomator Aurelius Victor, a self-confessed *parvenu*, the son of a poor and uneducated man (*Caes.* 20.5), who nevertheless admits that all the members of the Tetrarchy, although enjoying little enough *humanitas* (culture) and inured to the hardships of rural life and military service, were of great benefit to the state (39.26). The senators on the other hand, he says, 'gloried in idleness and at the same time trembled for their wealth, the use and the increase of which they accounted greater than eternal life itself' (37.7). The Roman upper classes, indeed, could sometimes save themselves only by raising individual members of the most exploited class, the peasantry, to ruling positions, often because of their military competence and ability to command in campaigns. Needless to say, they took care to select only those whom they expected (usually with reason) to promote the interests of the upper classes, while maintaining their exploitation of the remainder. It was a form of 'social mobility' which involved no real danger to the ruling class.

*   *   *   *   *   *

Since the subject of this book is the Greek world, I ought perhaps to say something about individual Greeks who became Roman emperors. The first clear case[21] of a 'Greek' emperor was the young Syrian, Elagabalus (or Heliogabalus), born Varius Avitus Bassianus at Emesa in Syria, who in his teens ruled for four years (218-222) as M. Aurelius Antoninus under the auspices of his formidable mother, Julia Soaemias, until both were murdered by the praetorian guard. The Emperor Philip (M. Julius Severus Philippus, 244-9) came from what the Romans called 'Arabia': he has been aptly described as 'the son of an Arab sheikh from the Trachonitis', south of Damascus (W. Ensslin, in *CAH* XII.87). For the next century and a half the emperors were all primarily Westerners, whose first language was Latin; and the setting up of a permanent Greek-speaking court at Constantinople came only with the lasting division of the empire into Eastern and Western parts on the death of Theodosius I in 395. After a succession of emperors in the East who may genuinely be described as Greek, another dynasty originating in the West ruled at Constantinople from 518 onwards, and under Justinian I (527-65) reconquered much of the Western empire. Nowadays little account is taken of the 'Latin' origins of Justin I, Justinian I and Justin II (518-78); but in the eyes of some later historians who wrote in Syriac, namely Michael the Syrian at the end of the twelfth century and (following him closely) Bar Hebraeus in the thirteenth, all the Roman emperors from Augustus to Justin II (565-78) were 'Franks' (meaning Germans), and their armies too; and these Syriac historians conceive a new 'Greek' Empire as beginning only with Tiberius Constantine (574/8-582).[22]

* * * * * *

From the second decade of the fourth century onwards a new economic burden suddenly appeared, of a kind no one could previously have expected. With the adoption of Christianity as the official religion of the Graeco-Roman world, by Constantine and his successors, the economy had to support an increasingly large body of clerics, monks and nuns, the vast majority of whom were not engaged in any economically productive activity and therefore – whatever their spiritual value to the community – must be counted, from the economic point of view, as so many 'idle mouths'. In the pagan world there had been very few professional, full-time priests, outside Egypt. Now, a vast and steadily growing number of Christian 'religious' had to be supported at public expense, in one form or another. It is true that most of the bishops, many of the priests and deacons and some of the minor clergy and monks were or had been wealthy men, who had never done any productive work and whose labour was consequently not an additional loss; but a good many of the monks and minor clergy came from the poorer classes and their labour was therefore withdrawn from production. Some of the monasteries were maintained by the labour of the monks themselves, but it is unlikely that more than a handful (mainly those in Egypt organised under the Pachomian rule) produced a surplus beyond what they themselves consumed, and of course it was above all producers of a surplus that the Graeco-Roman economy needed, if it was to preserve its existing class structure. The number of monks and full-time clerics by the mid-fifth century must already have been many hundreds of thousands. In the sixth century, in the territory of Constantinople, there seem to have been over eighty monasteries,[23] and, in the Great Church of Constantinople alone, many more than the full establishment of 525 miscellaneous clerics (from priests to cantors and door-keepers) to which the emperor then wished the numbers to be reduced (*Nov.J.* III.i.1, of 535). These figures, for the capital city of the empire, are of course exceptional; but other substantial ones could be produced, above all for Egypt, where the monastic and eremitic movements flourished most of all.[24]

I need scarcely dilate on the immense wealth of the one and only empire-wide organisation that existed apart from the imperial administration itself: I refer of course to the Christian Church. (I have pointed out in VII.iii above that the historian, as distinct from the theologian, ought really to speak of the Christian *churches*, in the plural; but in this case the singular is harmless enough.) The income of the Church came largely from endowments provided by benefactors (nearly always, of course, in the form of landed estates), but also from regular contributions made by the state and from the offerings of the faithful.[25] Of all the churches, Constantine and his successors made that of Rome the richest. Particulars given in the *Liber Pontificalis* (xxxiv-xxxv) enable us to calculate that the estates settled on the Roman Church in the reign of Constantine alone brought in an annual income of well over 30,000 solidi (more than 460 pounds of gold).[26] It is hardly surprising that according to St. Jerome the genial philo-sophic[26a] pagan, Vettius Agorius Praetextatus (who died in 384, when consul designate), remarked ironically to Pope Damasus, 'Make me bishop of Rome, and I'll become a Christian at once.'[27] By the time of Pope Gregory the Great

(590-614) the estates of the Roman Church (by far the most important part of the *patrimonium Petri*) were widespread and enormous in their extent, not only in many different parts of Italy but also in Sicily, Sardinia, Corsica, Africa, Gaul, Dalmatia and probably Illyria; earlier we also hear of estates in the Greek area, in Greece itself, Syria (Antioch, Tyre, Cyrrhus), Cilicia (Tarsus) and Alexandria in Egypt.[28] The incomes of the bishops, of whom there were by the fifth century well over a thousand, were sometimes larger than that of any provincial governor. We happen to hear of one bishop in the mountain country of Isauria in the early sixth century who claimed – as a defence to a charge of lending money at usury – to be receiving less than six solidi per year,[29] two-thirds the pay of a minor civil service clerk (see Section iii of this chapter). But even a small-town bishop like St. Theodore of Sykeon is said to have received for his household expenses as bishop of Anastasiopolis the yearly sum of 365 solidi.[30] And a great prelate like the metropolitan bishop of Ravenna, at about the beginning of Justinian's reign, received 3,000 solidi,[31] a little more than the highest paid provincial governor under the scale of salaries laid down by Justinian a little later:[32] this was the Augustal prefect and *dux* of Egypt, who received forty pounds of gold, or 2,880 solidi (Justin., *Edict*. XIII.3, probably of A.D. 538-9).[33] Even in Merovingian Gaul, just before the middle of the sixth century, Bishop Iniuriosus of Tours is said by Gregory of Tours to have left more than 20,000 solidi (*Hist. Franc*. X.31.xvi).[34] St. John the Almsgiver, Patriarch of Alexandria in the early seventh century, declared in his will, according to his biographer, that when he was appointed to his see he found in the bishop's house about 8,000 pounds of gold (well over half a million solidi), and that his revenues from Christ-loving persons 'almost exceeded human calculation'.[35] To sum up, I can endorse the opinions expressed by A. H. M. Jones, who made much the most thorough investigation of Church finances that I have been able to discover. By the sixth century, if we make the very reasonable assumptions that 'every city had a bishop, who received on the average the salary of a provincial governor', and that metropolitan bishops of provinces were, as the known figures suggest, 'paid on the scale of vicars [the deputies of the praetorian prefects] of [civil] dioceses', then 'the episcopate must have cost the empire far more than the administration'. Turning to the remainder of the clergy, and ignoring the numerous monks, we can say that 'if the figures we have for the numbers of the lower clergy are at all typical, they must have far outnumbered the civil service . . . The staffing of the Church absorbed far more manpower than did the secular administration and the Church's salary bill was far heavier than that of the empire' (*LRE* II.933-4, cf. 894-912).

We must not exaggerate: the Church was not nearly such a heavy burden on the empire as might be assumed if we isolate the facts about its wealth which I have just mentioned. Against all this we must remember that the Church, unlike pagan associations and individuals, certainly spent very large sums on charity – perhaps roughly a quarter of the income of its endowment.[36] (From the time of Constantine it was used by the emperors as the vehicle of charitable distributions to the clergy and the poor.)[37] It is also true that the vast agricultural areas of which the Church was landlord would have paid roughly the same amounts in rent had the lands been owned by secular landlords. But this cannot alter the fact that the Church did create a large number of economically 'idle mouths' which had to be supported by the overloaded Graeco-Roman agricultural economy. Whether the Church gave a good return for what it exacted is a question I shall not enter into. It must be obvious that I believe it did not.

I have referred near the end of VII.v above to some of the many deplorable episodes in the bitter strife among rival groups of Christians which so disfigures the history of the Christian Roman Empire. Such events seem to many of us to cast thorough discredit upon the claim of Christianity to constitute a divine revelation. This verdict can hardly be met except by recourse to the machinations of a Devil, or by the specious claim – made repeatedly by Christians on all sides in antiquity (see VII.v above), but disastrous in its consequences – that there is only one real Christian Church and that all other men and women who may regard themselves as Christians are heretics or schismatics who cannot be accounted Christians at all. If we are to decide whether Christianity strengthened or weakened the Roman empire we must set off the social cohesion it undoubtedly produced *within* individual sects against the discord *between* the sects. The former was surely stronger than anything known in paganism; the latter was unknown to paganism. I find it hard to make a comparative evaluation of the two countervailing tendencies of Christianity that I have just mentioned; but I believe that the latter (the production of discord) was far more powerful than most historians have realised (or at least have been willing to admit) and that over the centuries it was probably the stronger of the two. Religious strife continued sporadically, not only within the Byzantine empire (most noticeably during the Iconoclast controversy in the eighth and ninth centuries) but between Rome and Constantinople. In 1054 the intermittent schism between Pope and Patriarch became effectively final. An attempt to heal it was made by the Byzantine Emperor John VIII and his leading bishops, who submitted to Rome at the Council of Florence in 1439, in the vain hope of obtaining Western help against the now serious threat from the Ottoman Turks. But even the emperor and his bishops were unable on their return to overcome the deep hatred of Rome in the Byzantine world, and the reunion collapsed. The last Byzantine emperor, Constantine XI, made a desperate but fruitless attempt to heal the breach at the end of 1452, a few months before Constantinople finally fell to the Turks. The historian Ducas records with disapproval the opinion expressed in Constantinople in 1453 by a most distinguished man (who shared the later views of Gennadius) that it would be better to have the Sultan's turban in Constantinople than the Pope's mitre (XXXVII.10).[38]

* * * * * *

It was, I suggest, the combination of unlimited economic power and political power in the hands of the propertied class, their emperor and his administration which ultimately brought about the disintegration of the Roman empire. There was nothing to restrain the greed and ambition of the rich, except in so far as the emperor himself might feel it necessary to put a curb on certain excesses in order to prevent a general or local collapse, or simply in order that the population of the empire, under a just regime, might be prosperous enough to be able to pay their taxes promptly – a motive which can be seen clearly in numerous imperial constitutions (cf. below).

For the peasant, it was the tax collector who was the cause of the greatest dread.

What a terrifying individual he could be is nicely illustrated in one of those Lives of Saints from which so much of our information about the lives and outlook of the poor in the Later Roman Empire is derived: the *Life of St. John the Almsgiver*, from which I have quoted above. If we want to characterise a cruel and merciless person, we sometimes say, 'He's like a wild beast'. Well, the Saint is represented as thinking about the dreadful monsters he may meet after death, and the only way he can adequately express the appalling ferocity of these wild beasts is to say that they will be 'like tax-collectors'![39] Certainly, tax collection from the poor in Roman times was not a matter of polite letters and, as a last resort, a legal action: beating-up defaulters was a matter of routine, if they were humble people. A casual remark of the fifth-century ecclesiastical writer Theodoret shows us what the procedure of tax-collection was likely to be in a Syrian village: 'At this time,' he says, 'collectors (*praktores*) arrived, who compelled them to pay their taxes and began to imprison some and maltreat others' (*Hist. relig.* 17; cf. Eunapius, fr. 87). In Egypt the same brutal procedure can be seen at work: local officials would seize taxpayers whom they alleged (rightly or wrongly) to be in default, imprison and ill-treat them, and, with the aid of soldiers and local levies, burn down their houses. After quoting a particular example of such a procedure, from the reign of Justinian, Sir Harold Bell (a leading papyrologist and historian of Graeco-Roman Egypt) remarked, 'Such, to judge by other evidence, were regular accompaniments to the process of collecting arrears of taxes from an Egyptian village in the sixth century' (EVAJ 34). According to Ammianus, an Egyptian in the late fourth century would blush for shame if he could not show on his back scars inflicted by the tax-collector's whip (*erubescit apud eos, si quis non infitiando tributa plurimas in corpore vibices ostendat*: XXII.xvi.23). And it is worth repeating here the statement of Ammianus which I quoted near the end of V.iii above, that the Emperor Julian realised it was no good granting remissions of tax arrears in Gaul in the 350s, because this would only benefit the rich; the poor would have been made to pay immediately and in full (XVI.v.15). There must have been many occasions, too, on which hapless peasants were forced to pay their taxes twice over, whether because the tax had first been extracted from them by the agents of a 'usurper' (cf. VI.vi above), or because their landlord, after collecting the tax, became insolvent before paying it over to the authorities (or the persons to whom he was responsible). There is an example of the latter situation in a letter of Pope Gregory the Great, written in 591, from which we learn that the *rustici* on an estate of the Roman Church in Sicily had been compelled to pay their *burdatio* twice to the head lessee, Theodosius, now almost insolvent. Gregory, an exceptionally conscientious landlord, orders that the 57 solidi concerned are to be repaid to the peasants as a prior claim against Theodosius' estate (*Ep.* I.42).

It will be objected that the appalling situation I have been describing is characteristic only of the Later Empire, and that things were surely very different under the Principate, especially in the first two centuries of the Christian era. Certainly, taxation became much heavier in the fourth century onwards (cf. above, and Section iii of this chapter). But there is no reason to think that defaulting taxpayers who were poor men, especially peasants, would be much better treated in the first century than in the fourth, although, until certain of the privileges of the Roman citizenship became in practice limited to the upper classes, during the second century (see Section i of this chapter), the Roman citizen who was a person of no consequence might occasionally be able to assert his legal rights. (St. Paul did so, as we have seen – but of course he was far from being an uneducated peasant.) The native villager, especially if he was not a Roman citizen (as very few villagers were in the Greek-speaking part of the empire before 212), would have had little chance of escaping any brutal treatment which soldiers or officials cared to inflict upon him. There is a certain amount of evidence pointing in this direction, of which I will single out one text, quoted by several modern writers.[40] Philo of Alexandria writes of events which he represents as having taken place 'recently' (and therefore presumably during the reign of Tiberius, 14–37), apparently in Lower Egypt,[41] as a result of the activity of a rapacious and cruel tax-collector:

> When some who appeared to be defaulting merely through sheer poverty took to flight, in dread of severe punishment, he forcibly carried off their women and children and parents and other relatives, beat them, and subjected them to every kind of outrage. Although they were unable either to reveal the fugitive's whereabouts or (because of their own destitution) to pay what was due from him, he persisted, torturing them and putting them to death in a cruel manner. Others committed suicide to avoid such a fate. When there were no relatives left, he extended his outrages to neighbours and sometimes even to villages and towns, which were rapidly deserted by the flight of their inhabitants to places where they hoped to escape detection (*De spec. leg.* III.158–63).

Even if we make the necessary allowance for Philo's characteristic exaggeration, a grim picture emerges; and, as Bell has said, 'records found in Egypt have brought us proof that there is substantial truth in Philo's statements' (*EAGAC* 77–8). We must admit, with Philo, that such outrages, not only against the property but against the bodies and even the lives of those unfortunates who are seized in substitution for the actual debtors are only too likely when the annual collection of taxes is in the hands of 'men of barbarous nature, who have never tasted of human culture and are obeying tyrannical orders' (ibid.).

Some of the numerous complaints about taxation in the literary sources for the Later Roman Empire are of course over-coloured; their exaggerations are often traceable to political or religious spite, or to a desire to flatter the current emperor by damning his predecessors. However, anyone who is inclined to discount the admittedly very rhetorical evidence of the literary sources should read some of the imperial legislation. A particularly interesting specimen is the *Second Novel* (issued on 11 March 458) of the last great Western emperor, the young Majorian, of whom Stein said that we could 'admire in him without reserve the last figure possessing a real grandeur in the history of the Roman West' (*HBE* I².i.375). Although this Novel was issued only in the West, the situation it depicts, *mutatis mutandis*, prevailed also in the Greek East, where the oppression of the vast majority was effected in ways that were basically similar, even if it did not reach quite the same degree of intensity. The Novel is well worth reading as a whole; but it is long, and I can do no more than summarise parts of it. (There is a full translation in Pharr, *TC* 551–3.) The Novel is entitled 'On the remission of arrears [of tax]', *De indulgentiis reliquorum*. It begins by stressing the woes of the provincials, whose fortunes are said to have been enfeebled and worn down, not only by the exaction of the various forms of regular tribute but also by extraordinary fiscal burdens (*extraordinaria onera, superindictitii tituli*), and the necessity of purchasing deferments – by bribing officials. A nice abstract phrase, *sub impossibili devotione*, characterises the plight of the landowner (*possessor*), drained of resources (*exhaustus*) and unable to discharge his arrears of tax, when confronted with yet another demand that 'dutiful as he is, he cannot fulfil'. With the exception of one minor tax in kind, a general remission of arrears is granted (§ 1), explicitly for the benefit of the landowners (*possessores*), who are conceived as responsible for all taxes. Even if payment has been undertaken by someone else (no doubt at a high rate of interest), perhaps on the faith of a solemn promise by *stipulatio* by the taxpayer, the latter is still to have relief (cf. *Nov. Marc.* II.2). The Novel goes on to boast (§ 2) that the emperor has 'put an end to the harshness of the ferocious tax collectors'. There is a bitter complaint that the staffs of the highest officials of the state (those of the praetorian prefects are singled out) range around the provinces, and 'by enormous exactions terrorise the landowner and the decurion', accounting for only a small proportion of the taxes they collect and, greedy and swollen with power as they are, extorting twice as much or more by way of commission (*sportulae*) for themselves (cf. Jones, *LRE* I.468). In the good old days, Majorian adds, tax collection had been carried out, through the local councils, by the office staff of the provincial governor, who were fairly humble men and whom the governor could keep in order. But now the collection was in the hands of emissaries of the central 'palatine' administration, described by the emperor as 'terrible with the prestige of their exalted official rank, raging against the vitals of the provincials, to their ruin', and able to snap their fingers at a mere provincial governor. (Majorian was not by any means the first emperor, or the last, to complain about the intervention of central government officials in provincial taxation procedures.) Because of the oppression of these high officials, the emperor goes on, the cities have been despoiled of their councillors and can provide no qualified decurion; and the landowners, terrified by the atrocious behaviour of the financial officials, are deserting their country estates, as they are faced not merely with the loss of their fortunes but with 'severe imprisonment and cruel tortures' inflicted upon them by the merciless officials for their own profit, with military aid. The collection of taxes must be entrusted once more to the provincial governors, and there must be no more interventions by palatine officials and the military, except to encourage governors to do their duty. The emperor stresses again (§ 3) that he is making this ordinance as a remedy for the landowner (*pro remedio possessoris*). He proceeds to complain also (§ 4) of 'the men of power' (*potentes personae*), whose agents throughout the provinces neglect to pay their taxes, and who remain contumaciously on their estates, secure against any summons in the fear inspired by their arrogance. The agents and overseers of those families which are 'senatorial or powerful' must submit themselves to the jurisdiction of the provincial governors (as they had not been doing), and so must the local agents in charge of estates belonging to the imperial household. Moreover (§ 5), provincial govenors must not be subjected to molestation by false accusations from the staffs of the great officers of state, who will be furious at having enormously profitable spoils wrested from their own fraudulent grasp.

Some other laws of the fifth and sixth centuries unloose similar streams of righteous indignation at much the same objectives: see, for example, Valentinian III's Novel I.3 § 2 (of 450), followed in § 3 by an ingenuous remark which reveals the main reason for the emperor's solicitude for the *possessores*: 'A landowner who has been made poor is lost to us; one who is not overburdened is useful to us'! There are several similarly revealing laws, notably, for the East, the long *Eighth Novel* of Justinian, of A.D. 535, on which I have remarked elsewhere (SVP 47-8). Justinian too is concerned lest excessive exploitation by the great men, and their imposition of extraordinary burdens, should impair the ability of his subjects to pay their regular taxation, which he calls not only 'accustomed and legal' but also 'pious' (*eusebeis phoroi, Nov.J.* VIII. *Praef., pr.*). Similarly, the anxiety shown by Justinian in a series of three *Novels* in 535 to protect the free peasants of the praetorian prefecture of Illyricum and the provinces of Thracian Haemimontus and Moesia Secunda against moneylenders (*Nov.J.* XXXII-IV) is very likely to have been due in large part to anxiety to preserve them as an important source of recruitment for the army, as we know they were in his reign.[42]

The laws I have been describing nicely illustrate the most fundamental reason why it was necessary to have an emperor in the first place – a subject I have briefly discussed in VI.v-vi above. The Principate was accepted (if at first with some grumbling) by the Roman (and Greek) propertied classes because on the whole they realised that their own privileged position might be imperilled if too many individuals among their number were allowed, as in the Late Republic, to plunder the empire too freely. If that happened, civil wars (accompanied, as they could well be, by proscriptions and confiscations) and even perhaps revolutions from below might destroy many of them. The situation could hardly be put better than in Machiavelli's statement, which I have quoted, about the necessity for having, 'where the material is so corrupt, . . . besides laws, a superior force, such as appertains to a monarch, who has such absolute and overwhelming power that he can restrain excesses due to ambition and the corrupt practices of the powerful' (see VI.vi above, referring to the *Discourses on the First Decade of Livy* I.55; and cf. Machiavelli's diatribe against landed *gentiluomini*, quoted in III.iii above, *ad init.*). In the Later Empire, the *potentes, potentiores* or *dynatoi*, the men of power, became harder to control and often defied or circumvented the emperors with impunity.[43] Senators, at once the richest and the most influential group in the empire, were more easily able than anyone to delay or avoid payment of their taxes and the fulfilment of their other liabilities. This was true even in the Eastern part of the empire. In 397, for example, an edict of the Emperor Arcadius, addressed to the praetorian prefect of the East, complained that in some provinces half of the taxes due from senators were in arrear (*CTh* VI.iii.4). In the West, where the senators were even richer and more powerful, this situation was worse. In the very same year, 397, when the revolt of Gildo in Africa had imperilled the corn supply of Rome itself, three very significant laws were issued in the West, where the young Emperor Honorius was dominated by his able *magister militum* Stilicho. The first, in June, ordered that not even imperial estates should be exempted from the obligation to supply recruits in person (*CTh* VII.xiii.12). The second and third, in September and November, weakly conceded, in response to senatorial objections, that senators alone (even if head lessees of imperial estates) should have the right to commute their liability to supply recruits and pay in gold instead (ibid. 13-14).[44] And as late as the early sixth century we find an edict drafted by Cassiodorus for Theodoric the Ostrogoth, then king of Italy, deploring the fact that Roman senators, who 'ought to be setting an example', had paid virtually none of the taxes due from them, thus leaving the poor (the *tenues*) to bear an intolerable burden (Cassiod., *Var.* II.24-25).

The texts I have been quoting illustrate very well how the 'government' was continually frustrated in such attempts as it did make (for whatever reasons) to protect the peasantry by the fact that the more important of the officials on whom it was obliged to rely to carry out its orders were themselves members of the upper class, and of course felt an instinctive sympathy with its other members and often connived at their malpractices, and indeed were guilty of much extortion themselves. The rulers of the empire rarely if ever had any real concern for the poor and unprivileged as such; but they sometimes realised the necessity to give some of them some protection (as we have just seen), either to prevent them from being utterly ruined and thus become useless as taxpayers, or to preserve them as potential recruits for the army. Try as they would, however, the emperors had no choice but to act through the officials I have just characterised as members of the exploiting class. No text that I know speaks more eloquently of the defects of this system than a Novel of the Emperor Romanus II issued between 959 and 963: 'We must beware lest we send upon the unfortunate poor the calamity of law-officers, more merciless than famine itself.'[45]

Over all, no one I think will doubt that the position of humble folk in the Graeco-Roman world became distinctly worse after the early Principate. I have described in Section i of this chapter how their *Rechtsstellung* deteriorated during the first two centuries; and in Section ii I have shown how even the lower ranges of the curial order (falling only just inside, and sometimes perhaps even a little below, my 'propertied class') were subjected to increasing fiscal oppression from the second half of the second century onwards, and during the latter part of the fourth century lost at least one of their most valuable privileges: exemption from flogging. It need not surprise us when we are told that in the numerous papyri of the Later Roman Empire from the Oxyrhynchus area the use of the Greek word *doulos*, once the standard technical term for 'slave', is almost confined to occasions on which humble members of the free population are referring to themselves when addressing people of higher standing (see IV.ii n.41 below).

I hope it is now clear how I would explain, through a class analysis, the ultimate disintegration of a large part of the Roman empire – although of course a Greek core, centred above all in Asia Minor, did survive for centuries. I would keep firmly in view the process of exploitation which is what I mean primarily when I speak of a 'class struggle'. As I see it, the Roman political system (especially when Greek democracy had been wiped out: see V.iii above and Appendix IV below) facilitated a most intense and ultimately destructive economic exploitation of the great mass of the people, whether slave or free, and it made radical reform impossible. The result was that the propertied class, the men of real wealth, who had deliberately created this system for their own benefit, drained the life-blood from their world and thus destroyed Graeco-Roman civilisation over a large part of the empire – Britain, Gaul, Spain and north Africa in the fifth century; much of Italy and the Balkans in the sixth; and in the seventh, Egypt, Syria and Mesopotamia, and again north Africa, which had been reconquered by Justinian's generals in the sixth century.[46] That, I believe, was the principal reason for the decline of Classical civilisation. I would suggest that the causes of the decline were above all economic and social. The very hierarchical political structure of the Roman empire, of course, played an important part; but it was precisely the propertied class as such which in the long run monopolised political power, with the definite purpose of maintaining and increasing its share of the comparatively small surplus which could be extracted from the primary producers. By non-Marxist historians this process has normally been described as if it were a more or less automatic one, something that 'just happened'. If one wants to find a terse, vivid, epigrammatic charac-terisation of something that happened in the Roman world, one naturally turns first to Gibbon. And indeed, in the excursus at the end of his 38th chapter, entitled 'General observations on the Fall of the Roman empire in the West', there occurs the expressive sentence, 'The stupendous fabric yielded to the pressure of its own weight.' In Peter Brown's sometimes brilliant little book, *The World of Late Antiquity* (1971), there is a metaphor of a rather different kind, which equally expresses the basic idea of something that was essentially either inevitable or else fortuitous: 'Altogether, the prosperity of the Mediterranean world seems to have *drained to the top*' (34, my italics) – Brown is speaking of the fourth century, and he has just mentioned that in the western part of the empire, in that century, the senatorial aristocracy was 'five times richer, on the average, than the senators of the first century'. (In the Greek East, things were not so very different, although the senatorial class was not quite so extravagantly opulent as in the West.) If I were in search of a metaphor to describe the great and growing concentration of wealth in the hands of the upper classes, I would not incline towards anything so innocent and so automatic as drainage: I should want to think in terms of something much more purposive and deliberate – perhaps the vampire bat. The burden of maintaining the imperial military and bureaucratic machine, and the Church, in addition to a leisured class consisting mainly of absentee landowners, fell primarily upon the peasantry, who formed the great bulk of the population; and, ironically enough (as I have already explained), the remarkable military and administrative reorganisation effected by a series of very able emperors from the late third century to the end of the fourth (from Diocletian and Constantine to Theodosius I) succeeded in creating an even greater number of economically 'idle mouths' and thus increased the burdens upon an already overburdened peasantry. The peasants were seldom able to revolt at all, and never successfully: the imperial military machine saw to that. Only in Gaul and Spain did the Bacaudae cause serious if intermittent trouble over several generations (see Section iii of this chapter). But the merciless exploitation of the peasants made many of them receive, if not with enthusiasm at least with indifference, the barbarian invaders who might at least be expected – vainly, as it usually turned out[47] – to shatter the oppressive imperial financial machine. Those who have been chastised with scorpions may hope for some-thing better if they think they will be chastised only with whips.[48]

Appendix I

The contrast between slave and wage-labourer
in Marx's theory of capital (see II.iii above)

We can begin with *Cap*. II.36–7 (cf. 83): in any social form of production, 'labourers and means of production' are separate elements which must unite in some way in order for production to take place. 'The specific manner in which this union is accomplished' is vitally important – so much so that it 'distinguishes the different epochs of the structure of society from one another'. Slave labour and free wage-labour, therefore, remain fundamentally different, even when they happen to coexist in one society.

We can turn next to the passages in which Marx deals with the labour of production as a social process. The labour power of the free worker (purchased by the employer for wages) is here carefully distinguished, in many passages, as 'variable capital', from the 'constant capital' comprising the means of production, themselves divided (when Marx, as in *Cap*. I.178–81; II.164–5, wishes to draw the quite different distinction between 'fixed capital' and 'circulating capital') into (*a*) the 'subjects of labour', such as raw materials and auxiliary materials like coal, gas or manure (which are 'circulating capital'), and (*b*) all 'instruments of labour' (which are 'fixed capital'), including land, buildings, plant, railways, canals, working animals (for the last, see *Cap*. II.163, 165; cf. *Grundrisse*, E.T. 465, 489) and, quite specifically, slaves (*Cap*. II.483; III.804), who, in contrast with free labourers, 'form part and parcel of the means of production' (*Cap*. I.714). In addition to the passages already cited it will be sufficient to refer to *Cap*. I.177–81, 208–9; II.160–8, 221–3, 440–1; III.814–16.

It is true that Marx often refuses, when he is being vigilantly accurate, to apply to the ancient world the terminology ('capital' etc.) which is strictly appropriate only to capitalist society: capital is 'not a thing, but rather a definite social production relation, belonging to a definite historical formation of society' (*Cap*. III.814). Now 'direct forced labour was the foundation of the ancient world' (*Grundrisse*, E.T. 245), and 'wealth confronts direct forced labour not as capital, but rather as a relation of domination [*Herrschaftsverhältnis*]' (*Grundrisse*, E.T. 326; cf. 513, and see also 464–5, and 465 on the serf). 'So long as slavery is predominant the capital relationship can only be sporadic and subordinate, never dominant' (*TSV* III.419). And so, in *Cap*. II.164–5, after recalling the division of 'means of production' (made in *Cap*. I.178–81) into 'instruments of labour' and 'subjects of labour', which he sees 'in every labour-process, regardless of the social conditions in which it takes place', Marx goes on to say that both instruments of labour and subjects of labour 'become capital only under the capitalist mode of production, when they become "*productive* capital"' (cf. *Cap*. II.170–1, 196, 208, 210, 210–11, 229–31); and he adds that the distinction between them 'is reflected in a new form: the distinction between fixed capital and circulating capital. It is only then that a thing which performs the function of an instrument of labour becomes fixed capital'.

Nevertheless, having closed the front door of any pre-capitalist society against 'capital' (in the strict sense of productive capital), Marx opens the back door to what he calls 'money capital' (for which see *Cap*. I.146 ff.; cf. II.57, 482–3 etc.): he can also say that 'in the slave system, the *money-capital* invested in the purchase of labour-power *plays the role of* the money-form of *fixed capital*' (*Cap*. II.483, my italics). In other words, the slaveowner buys labour-power in the slave in a capitalised form, exactly as with working animals. The slave system, for Marx, of course resembles the capitalist system in forcing the direct producer to do unpaid labour; but his master purchases *him* instead of his *labour power*.

I may add that the analysis I have given here does not depend in any way upon the distinction (first worked out in detail by Marx, although it had appeared earlier in a less clear form and with different terminology in Ramsay: see *Cap.* II.394, 440-1) between 'variable capital' and 'constant capital'. The distinction between the free wage-labourer and the slave labourer, as drawn by Marx, can equally well be conceived in terms of the distinction between those familiar categories of Classical political economy: 'circulating capital' and 'fixed capital'. This is so, whether or not we include in our definition of circulating capital the raw materials and auxiliary materials used in the productive process, as Marx and Adam Smith did (see *Cap.* II.168, 204; and especially 297-9, where Marx distinguished between 'the variable and the constant part of circulating capital', as against 'fixed capital'), although others did not, in particular George Ramsay (see *Cap.* II.231, 394, 440-1). What is used in purchasing the labour-power of the free wage-labourer is certainly circulating capital (see e.g. *Cap.* II.168); but, as we have seen, the slave, as an 'instrument of labour' (just like a working animal), is purchased with fixed capital and himself becomes fixed capital.

Appendix II

Some evidence for slavery (especially agricultural) in the Classical and Hellenistic periods (see III.iv above)

There is more than enough evidence to show that in Attica agricultural slave labour was widespread in the Classical period. For large slave households see Xen., *Oecon.* VII.35; IX.5; and XII.2 to XV.5 on slave bailiffs (esp. XII.2-3,19; XIII.6-10; XIV.6,9; XV.3-5), showing that these men were indeed slaves and were intended primarily for supervising agricultural operations. These passages refer, it is true, to an exceptionally rich man, Ischomachus; but elsewhere too we find agricultural slavery taken for granted, e.g. in Aristophanes. In the *Plutus*, Chremylus the farmer, who is specifically described as a πένης (line 29) and is one of the τοῦ πονεῖν ἐρασταί of line 254, owns several slaves (lines 26, 1105), not only the Carion who is one of the main characters in the play. Jones, *AD* 12 and 138 n.54, treats Carion as just a stock comic figure; but the other slaves are certainly not that: they are not necessary figures and indeed would have spoilt the dramatic picture (in which Chremylus' poverty is an essential element) had they not been characteristic. See also Ar., *Plut.* 510-21 and *Eccles.* 651; *Peace* 1138-9, 1146-8; Ps.-Dem. XLVII.52-3; LIII.6; Dem. LV.31-2 (cf. 35); and other texts. I cannot accept the general assumptions of Ehrenberg, *PA*²165-91 (ch.vii), about the unimportance of slaves in Athenian economic life: they seem to me to be in direct conflict with the evidence he himself has produced. But perhaps the most telling argument for the importance of slaves in Athenian agriculture is the negative one: that hired labour, the only alternative way in which Athenian landowners could have made appreciable incomes out of their property (as we know they did), or indeed any profit at all (apart from leasing), was evidently rare and confined mainly to the seasons of harvest, vintage and olive-picking. (I have listed in III.vi n.16 below the only passages I have been able to discover on the use of hired labour in Athenian agriculture.) Even the overseer or manager (ἐπίτροπος, occasionally ἐπιστάτης, οἰκονόμος, οἰκονομικός) of an estate in Attica (or elsewhere) would normally be a slave or a freedman: see Xen., *Mem.* II.viii, esp. 3-4 (noticed in III.vi above); *Oecon.* XII-XV, esp.

the passages singled out in the second sentence of this Appendix. Slaves and freedmen predominated also in other managerial capacities: see e.g. Xen., *Mem.* II.v.2; Aeschin. I.97; Dem. XXVII.19, 22, and XXIX.5, 25-6, 29-32 etc.; Ps.-Dem. XXXVI.28-30 and 43-4, with XLV.33; Ps.-Arist., *Oecon.* I.5, 1344ᵃ25-6; cf. Cittus in Isocr. XVII.11-16, 21, 27, 49 (contrast 14, 51); and the foreigners in *IG* II².1673.57-9. In Isaeus VI (*Philoct.*) 20-1 the woman Alce, who 'managed' Euctemon's house in the Cerameicus (whether in theory as leasehold tenant or not) was a slave or freedwoman; and her unnamed former owner who had similarly run a brothel in Euctemon's house in Peiraeus (§ 19), apparently as his tenant, was also a freedwoman. When Xen., *De vect.* IV.22, contemplates Athenians as well as foreigners taking managerial posts supervising slaves working in the mines, he is again not describing an existing situation – and anyway the managers would be working for the state, not private employers. (I have dealt with Xen., *Oecon.* I.4 in III.vi above.) See also Gert Audring, 'Über den Gutsverwalter (*epitropos*) in der attischen Landwirtschaft des 5. und des 4. Jh. v.u.Z.', in *Klio* 55 (1973) 109-16.

A text that is often misquoted is Thuc. VII.27.5: '*more than* 20,000 slaves' escaped from Attica during the Spartan occupation of Deceleia. This is far too often represented as '20,000 slaves', as recently by Finley (*AE* 72, contrast 24) and even Dover. The latter (in Gomme, *HCT* IV.401-2) first gets it right on p.401, and then twice speaks merely of '20,000 slaves'; on p.402 he flatly contradicts Thucydides by saying '20,000 was the *total* number of deserters', and on p.401 he actually speaks of 'a precise number', which 'implies that he [Thucydides] has a certain point of time in mind'! If I have laboured this point, it is because I wish to emphasise that Thucydides was obviously giving a *rough estimate*: he could not possibly have known, even within wide limits, how many slaves had escaped, and his 'more than 20,000 slaves' – more precisely, 'more than two myriads' (πλέον ἢ δύο μυριάδες) – indicates that he believed 20,000 to be a *minimum* (which may conceivably have been greatly exceeded); the *maximum* in his mind can hardly be put at very much less than 30,000, for the next step in the natural progression after 'more than two myriads' is either 'three myriads' or at least 'nearly three myriads'. And, as I have said in my review of Westermann, *SSGRA*, in *CR* 71 = n.s. 7 (1957) 54 ff., at 56, the statement that follows, 'and of these the greater part were χειροτέχναι', makes it unlikely that, as so many scholars have supposed, Thucydides is referring mainly to mine-slaves. The only other time Thucydides uses the word (VI.72.3) it means 'experts' – in war, as it happens. And that the artisans were indeed *skilled* men best suits Thucydides' meaning here, as the emphatic καὶ τούτων indicates: the loss was all the more keenly felt because the deserters were mainly skilled workmen – no doubt including agricultural specialists such as vine-dressers, who would have better opportunities for running away than e.g. mine-slaves. (The argument here is not affected if, with some scholars, we read πολὺ μέρος in VII.27.5, with most MSS, instead of τὸ πολὺ μέρος, with B: we then merely translate 'a great part' instead of 'the greater part'.)

I must add here that I know of only one recent treatment of Athenian agriculture in the Classical period which gives slavery its proper role and presents the essential evidence concisely and accurately: this is Michael H. Jameson's important article, 'Agriculture and slavery in Classical Athens', in *CJ* 73 (1977-8) 122-45, which I read only after Chapter III and this Appendix had been finished. I am glad to find that we are in substantial agreement; but of course there is much good material in Jameson's paper, going well beyond what I have been able to deal with in this book.

* * * * * *

We can now leave Athens and look at the rest of the Greek world. For the fifth and fourth centuries see e.g. Thuc. III.73 (Corcyra: evidently many slaves in the countryside); VIII.40.2 (Chios: more οἰκέται than in any other Greek state except Sparta; they knew the country and must have been predominantly rural slaves, nor did Chios have any very developed industry); Xen., *HG* III.ii.26 (Elis: very many slaves, ἀνδράποδα, captured from the countryside); IV.vi.6 (Acarnania: numerous slaves, ἀνδράποδα, captured in 389; many of those not engaged in the production of crops may have been herdsmen); VI.ii.6 (Corcyra again: many slaves, ἀνδράποδα, captured from the countryside in *c.* 374; cf. §§ 15, 23, 25); VII.v.14–15 (Mantinea, 362: the ἐργάται are clearly slaves, as they are contrasted with others τῶν ἐλευθέρων). We sometimes hear of besieged cities arming slaves and using them to defend their walls: this happened, for example, at Cyzicus in 319 (Diod. XVIII.51.3) and at Rhodes in 305-4 (XX.84.3; 100.1), but we do not know how many of these slaves were agricultural.

Various passages in Polybius either explicitly mention, or suggest the presence of, considerable numbers of slaves in the countryside of the Greek world in the late third century B.C. It is true that in Polybius the mention of σώματα, without qualification, as booty (or potential booty) can apply indifferently to slave and free (see e.g. II.vi.6; lxii.10; IV.xxix.6). But τὰ δουλικὰ σώματα were evidently an important part of the booty obtained by the Illyrians on the capture of the not very important city of Phoenice in Epirus *c.* 230 B.C. (II.vi.6); in at least one other case, Megalopolis, we hear of σώματα, some of which are specifically described as δουλικά and others as ἐλεύθερα (II.lxii.10); and when we are told of a raid by brigands on the fortified farmhouse 'known as Chyron's' in Messenia we find slaves, this time unmistakable as οἰκέται, forming a significant part of the booty (IV.iv.1). The large-scale plundering expedition launched by the Aetolians into Laconia around 240 B.C. (see Walbank, *HCP* I.483; cf. Will, *HPMH* I.305), which according to Polybius caused the enslavement of 'the perioecic villages' (IV.xxxiv.9), is said by Plutarch to have resulted in the carrying off of 50,000 slaves (*Cleom.* 18.3) – and even if this figure is greatly exaggerated it is likely to include a considerable number of men and women who were already slaves, for the Perioeci had no Helots and the captured Perioeci themselves could hardly have numbered anything like so many. We also hear of cities in Asia Minor under siege promising freedom to their slaves, to induce them to join in their resistance (Abydus at the Hellespont, Polyb. XVI.xxxi.2; Selge in Pisidia, V.lxxvi.5). In the light of these texts, and of Xenophon's statement quoted above about the many slaves in the countryside of Elis (at the very end of the fifth century), it seems very likely that when Polybius speaks of Elis in the late third century as being thickly populated and abounding in σώματα (IV.lxxiii.6; cf. lxxv.1-2, 7), he must have slaves as well as free in mind. Python of Abdera had a very large slave household in 170 B.C., if he is rightly credited with arming and using in defence of his city (until he decided to betray it) '200 slaves and freedmen of his own' (Diod. XXX.6). In 146 B.C. there is a mention in Polybius of an order sent to the cities of the Achaean League by the general Diaeus to free and arm no fewer than 12,000 slaves of military age, 'among those who had been born and bred at home' (οἰκογενεῖς καὶ παράτροφοι, Polyb. XXXVIII.xv.3; cf. my discussion in IV.iii § 4 above).

For the Hellenistic period in general, see (on agricultural and sometimes other slaves) Rostovtzeff, *SEHHW* I.178, 203, 207 (with III.1366-7 n.32), 243, 517, 537-8; II.778-85 (with III.1514-16 nn.47-51), 806 (with III.1521-2 n.76, and Rostovtzeff's article, NEPPK, esp. 377-9, 382-3), 942, 1106, 1111, 1116, 1158-9 (but cf. I.523-4), 1182-96, 1258-63; III.1435 n.260, 1502 n.4. For Egypt, see id. I.321-2, with III.1393-4 n.119, and II.1099; also various works by I. Bieżuńska-Małowist, esp. *EEGR* I (cf. III.iv n.32 below).

Such a large proportion of the texts illustrating the employment of rural slaves relate to their capture during an enemy invasion that we need not be surprised at finding so little evidence either way for most places.

As early as 400 B.C. we find a wealthy Persian, Asidates, who was possessed of an estate on the plain near Pergamum, in north west Asia Minor, employing slaves in quite large numbers (Xen., *Anab.* VII.viii.12,16,19). Xenophon, in the plundering expedition which he describes (without the least sense of shame) at the very end of his *Anabasis*, refers to these men as *andrapoda* even before their capture, and they must surely have been slaves in the Greek sense, rather than dependent peasants. Some two hundred were captured and carried off (§ 19). Again, we happen to know of this set of slaves only because they became the object of a military expedition and are mentioned in one of our narrative sources. Except where special circumstances obtained, for instance at Heraclea Pontica, where the Mariandynoi formed a sort of quasi-serf population which could be profitably used by the Greek settlers (see III.iv and its n.3), I see no reason to doubt that Greeks who settled in new areas of Asia or Syria and became landowners would immediately buy slaves to work their farms, as in their homelands. Nothing prevented them from doing this, and since many slaves had been brought to Greece itself from districts in Asia Minor (especially perhaps Caria, Lydia and Phrygia) and Syria, slaves would probably not be exceptionally dear there. When Romans began to move into the East in considerable numbers (see e.g. Broughton, RLAM, and in *ESAR* IV), they too would certainly want to use agricultural slaves, except perhaps where a local peasant population could be severely exploited, to almost the same degree as slaves.

I have not tried to collect the material, and I will mention just three interesting pieces of evidence, the only ones I happen to have come across in which prices are given for the initial purchase of slaves on capture in bulk in the Classical and Hellenistic periods – far below the price at which they would eventually be sold, of course, in order to allow the dealers a profit. The first is Thuc. VIII.28.4: on the taking of Iasus in Caria by the Spartans in the winter of 412/411, the inhabitants, slave and free (and surely including women and children), were sold off to Tissaphernes at an agreed price of 1 daric stater per head (equivalent to between 25 and 26 Attic drachmae). The second piece of evidence is provided by II Macc. viii.11 (cf. I Macc. iii.41) and Jos., *AJ* XII.299, where the Seleucid army commander Nicanor in 165 B.C. announces that he will sell all the Jews he expects to capture in his forthcoming campaign at the rate of 90 per talent, or 66²/₃ drachmae each. The third piece of evidence is in Plut., *Lucull.* 14.1 and App., *Mith.* 78: Lucullus' campaign against Mithridates of Pontus in 72/1 B.C. was so successful that slaves were sold in his camp for as little as 4 drachmae each – a suspiciously low figure, but perhaps not impossible, if there were large numbers of prisoners, for the slaves might have to be transported some way before they could be sold profitably in bulk. (I do not feel able to give any figure for the price of the Thebans sold off as slaves on the sack of Thebes by Alexander in 335: Diod. XVII.14.1,3 gives 440 talents for 'more than 30,000' Thebans; but his figure may well be a conventional one, and his probable source, Cleitarchus, *FGrH* 137 F 1, *ap.* Athen. IV.148de, gives the same figure, 440 talents, for the total sum realised on the sack of the city.)

I conclude with a general argument for the great importance of slave labour in agriculture in the lands bordering on the Aegean and in the islands of that sea. In an article published in 1923 (NEPPK 377-8) Rostovtzeff pointed out that although the only treatises on agriculture to survive from the ancient world are by Latin writers, their authors undoubtedly based their work on Greek sources, many of whom are actually named, in particular by Varro, who speaks of 'more than fifty' Greek writers on different aspects of agriculture (*RR* I.i.7-10) and proceeds to give a long list of them. The majority, as Rostovtzeff remarked, 'were natives not of the mainland of Greece . . . , but of the large and fertile islands (Thasos, Lemnos, Chios, Rhodos), of Asia Minor (Pergamon, Miletus, Cyme, Colophon, Priene, Soli, Mallos, Nicaea, and Herakleia), and of the Thracian coast (Maroneia and Amphipolis). Most of them belong to the Hellenistic period.' As Rostovtzeff says, 'we do not know the content of these treatises, but it seems evident that it did not differ very much from that of the treatises of Varro, Columella, and Pliny'; and he goes on to infer from this similarity that 'the main foundation of agriculture in the East, and especially of viticulture, horticulture, and cattle-breeding, was slave labour'. Rostovtzeff deals with the same subject in his *SEHHW* II.1182-96 (with III.1616-19): here he admits the lack of evidence concerning methods of cultivation in the Greek East, apart from Egypt, and is very cautious in drawing conclusions. I would accept the statement which appears on p.1196, following the admission that to various questions he has asked

no satisfactory answer can be given. No direct evidence is available. It is, however, certain that some of the landowners in the Seleucid Empire and in Asia Minor instead of renting their estates, large or small, in parcels to local farmers, cultivated them by means of slave labour and hired hands. We may conjecture that this was the method of cultivation adopted by the Attalids on some of their estates. There is evidence of the same practice on the estates of some rich landholders in the city territories (for example Priene), and it may be assumed to have prevailed on the holdings – *cleroi* – of foreign settlers in the κατοικίαι and cities created by the Hellenistic kings, when these *cleroi* were not rented to local tenants . . . What was the influence of these progressive farms on their surroundings, on the peasant economy of their neighbours? No answer can be given to this question. The general impression left on the student is that the estates managed in the Greek manner remained scattered islands in the Oriental sea of small peasant holdings and larger estates, whose native owners had their own traditional methods of exploitation or cultivation.

Rostovtzeff is concerned here with the whole vast subject of the overall aspect of agriculture in Asia. I of course admit that the great bulk of agricultural production there, as in most parts of the ancient world at nearly all times (cf. esp. IV.i-iii above), was the work of small peasants, whether freeholders, leasehold tenants, or serfs in various kinds of dependence. But I have been concerned to investigate *how the propertied classes of the Greek world extracted their surplus*; and when we ask this question (a very different one), we can see that a very important part was played by slavery, not to mention debt bondage, e.g. that of the *obaerarii* (or *obaerati*) mentioned by Varro as still existing in his day in large numbers in Asia, and in Egypt and Illyricum (see III.iv above under its heading III, and its n.66).

Appendix III

The settlement of 'barbarians' within the Roman empire
(see IV.iii § 19 above)

I give here as complete a list as I have been able to compile, with fairly full source references and a little modern bibliography, of those settlements of 'barbarians' within Roman territory which seem to me reasonably well authenticated, from the first century to the late sixth. I have felt obliged to take into account, as far as I could, settlements in the Western as well as the Eastern part of the empire, because I am interested in these settlements not from the cultural but from the economic point of view (see IV.iii §§ 17 and 19 above), and from that aspect their effects might be felt far outside their immediate area. I have to admit, however, a very inadequate treatment of Africa, where the literary sources are nothing like as abundant as for Europe and Asia (above all the provinces on or near the Rhine and Danube frontiers), and the epigraphic and archaeological evidence is often very hard to interpret and may sometimes refer to the control of nomads or semi-nomads or transhumants rather than to permanent new settlements inside the frontiers. Apart from §§ 22 and 32 below, all I can do here is to refer to an impressive article which I saw only after this Appendix had been written: P. D. A. Garnsey, 'Rome's African empire under the Principate', in *Imperialism in the Ancient World*, edited by Garnsey and C. R. Whittaker (1978) 223-54, at 231-3 (with 346-7 nn.39-49).

I have begun at *c.* 38 B.C. and have disregarded some earlier settlements, for example the removal of no fewer than 40,000 Ligurians and their installation on public land in Samnium in 180 B.C., a transplantation which, unlike the vast majority of the settlements I am going to mention, was against the will of the Ligurians (Livy XL.38.3-7). I have ignored a few texts which seem to me irrelevant or of no value: this applies particularly to the later period (after no. 23 below), for which the evidence is often unclear. I have also ignored various treaties in the fifth century by which parts of the Roman empire were ceded outright to external powers, e.g. the surrender of part of the diocese of Africa to the Vandals in 435. Many of the literary texts were first collected by Zumpt (1845) and Huschke (see Clausing, *RC* 44–9, 57–61, 77–89), but I know of no work which sets out the essential literary material and adds some of the epigraphic and archaeological evidence, as I try to do here. (The fullest collection I know is that of Seeck, *GUAW* I⁴.ii.591-3, with i.407-8.) I may say that, for convenience only, I shall usually speak of 'barbarians' without the inverted commas which I normally employ. The whole subject seems to me to have much more importance than is commonly realised: see IV.iii §§ 17 and 19 above (with its nn.28-36 below), where the subject is discussed and further bibliography will be found.

1. Octavian's general, M. Vipsanius Agrippa, probably in 38 B.C., transferred the German Ubii (at their request) to the left bank of the Rhine and settled them there, as a complete *civitas*: Strabo IV.iii.4, p.194 (and presumably VII.i.3, p.290); cf. Tac., *Ann.* XII.27.1-2; XIII.57.4; *Germ.* 28.5. See Hermann Schmitz, *Colonia Claudia Ara Agrippinensium* (Cologne, 1956).

2. In 8 B.C. the future Emperor Tiberius, as general of Augustus, received the submission of the Suevi and Sugambri and settled 40,000 of them on lands west of the Rhine: Suet., *Aug.* 21.1, with *Tib.* 9.2; Eutrop. VII.9; and cf. Augustus, *Res Gestae* 32.1. The number of 40,000 (*Germani*) appears also in Oros. VI.xxi.24.

3. It was almost certainly during the first few years of the first century C.E. that Sextus Aelius Catus settled 50,000 'Getae' south of the Danube, in what was later known as Moesia: Strabo VII.iii.10, p.303. These people were in fact Dacians: see A. Alföldi, 'Dacians on the south bank of the Danube', in *JRS* 29 (1939) 28-31. He publishes a supposed military diploma of 7/8 November 88, of the auxiliary soldier *Gorio, Stibi f., Dacus*, from Nicopol in Bulgaria (which has since been shown to be a forgery, by H. Nesselhauf, in *CIL* XVI Suppl. [1955] p.216), and refers to one or two similar documents (esp. *CIL* XVI.13). On the chronology of this settlement, see R. Syme, in *JRS* 24 (1934) 113-37, at 126-8 = *Danubian Papers* (Bucharest, 1971) 53-5.

When the German chieftains Maroboduus and Catualda were settled in A.D. 19 at Ravenna and Forum Julii respectively, the personal retainers (*comitatus*) of each were settled outside Roman territory, beyond the Danube, to prevent them from creating disturbances in pacified provinces (Tac., *Ann.* II.63, esp. § 7).

4. In A.D. 50, or soon after, Vannius, on ceasing to be king of the Quadi, was settled by order of the Emperor Claudius in Pannonia, with his *clientes*: Tac., *Ann.* XII.29-30, esp. 30.3. (See Mócsy, *PUM* 40-1,57-8, 371 n.13.)

5. (a) In the 60s, in the reign of Nero, Ti. Plautius Silvanus Aelianus claimed to have brought over into his province of Moesia and obliged to pay tribute 'more than 100,000 *Transdanuviani*, with their wives and children and chiefs or kings': *ILS* 986 = *CIL* XIV.3608. The most recent treatment I have seen is by T. Zawadski, in *La parola del passato* 160 = 30 (1975) 59-73.

(b) It is possible, as argued by Zawadski (op. cit. 72-3), that L. Tampius Flavianus (*PIR*¹ III.294 no.5), the legate of Pannonia in 69-70 (and perhaps earlier), performed a feat resembling that of Plautius Aelianus (see the preceding paragraph), since *ILS* 985 = *CIL* X.6225, lines 6-8, as re-edited by Alföldi and Reidinger and reproduced by Zawadski (id. 73), lines 7-9, is probably to be restored '[multis] opsidibus a Tran[sdanuvi/anis acceptis, lim]itibus omnibus ex[ploratis / hostibus(?) ad vectig]alia praestanda [traductis]'.

6. Some Celtic Cotini and perhaps Osi (cf. Tac., *Germ.* 43.1-2) were apparently given land in Pannonia at some time during the first century: see Mócsy, *PUM* 57-60; and cf. § 7 c below.

There is then a long gap, until the reign of Marcus Aurelius (161-180). Appian, *Praef.* 7, refers to ambassadors from barbarian peoples whom he claims actually to have seen at Rome, 'offering themselves as subjects', but refused by the emperor on the ground that they would be of no use to him. This passage must have been written under Antoninus Pius, while 'a long period of secure peace' (as Appian calls it) still prevailed, and it seems to refer only to requests for annexation: nothing is said about entering into territory already Roman.

7. Various settlements of German barbarians are recorded, or can be inferred, during the reign of Marcus Aurelius. They will mostly have been made during the 170s.

(a) According to Dio Cassius LXXI.xi.4-5, various barbarians (who will certainly have included Quadi) received land from Marcus in Dacia, Pannonia, Moesia, Germany (i.e. the two provinces of that name) and Italy itself. (This may have happened as early as 171: see Birley, *MA* 231-2.) When an uprising took place at Ravenna, Marcus sent the barbarians out of Italy and brought no more in there. (For the depopulation of Italy by the plague of A.D. 166 ff., see Oros. VII.xv.5-6; xxvii.7; and cf. VIII.ii above and its n.10 below.)

(b) Dio Cass. LXXI.xii.1 ff., esp. 2-3: the 'Astingoi' (= Asding Vandals) were promised land if they fought against the enemies of Rome. (This also may have taken place in 171: see Birley, *MA* 232-3.)

(c) Further Cotini (cf. § 6 above) must also have been established in eastern Pannonia, apparently around Mursa and Cibalae: see Mócsy, *PUM* 189-91, 199, 248; cf. *CIL* VI.32542 *d*. 3-4; 32544 *g*; Dio Cass. LXXI.xii.3; Tac., *Germ.* 43 (cf. Seeck, *GUAW* I⁴.ii.583-5). These settlements may also have occurred in 171.

(d) Dio Cass. LXXI.xvi.2 (A.D. 175): the Sarmatian Iazyges gave to Marcus 8,000 horsemen, of whom he sent 5,500 to Britain. According to Dio, these men were provided under treaty (§ 1), as the contribution of the Iazyges to their alliance, ἐς συμμαχίαν, and (I should have thought) one might therefore have expected them to be treated as *foederati*, rather than as an auxiliary unit of the Roman army, especially as we are not told that they were to receive land within the empire. But the subsequent evidence concerning men who are generally (and probably rightly) considered to be among the descendants of these Iazyges suggests that they did in fact receive land for settlement and that they joined the regular Roman army, in the units known as *numeri*. A well-known inscription of A.D. 238-44, from Ribchester, the ancient Bremetennacum (probably Bremetennacum Veteranorum), refers to a *n(umerus) eq(uitum) Sarm(atarum) Bremetenn(acensium)*, under a *praep(ositus) n(umeri) et r(egionis)*: *RIB* 583 = *CIL* VII.218; cf. *praep. n. et regi.* in *RIB* 587 = *CIL* VII.222. The unit (presumably of a few hundred men) is referred to as an *ala Sarmatarum* on two tombstones, *RIB* 594, 595 = *CIL* VII.229, 230, and in the early fifth century it still existed as a *cuneus Sarmatarum* (*Not. Dig., Occ.* XL.54). The whole subject has been discussed in detail in an able article by I. A. Richmond, 'The Sarmatae, *Bremetennacum Veteranorum* and the *Regio Bremetennacensis*', in *JRS* 35 (1945) 15-29. Richmond points out that this area (part of the Fylde, in the Ribble valley) is particularly well suited for maintaining the large horses needed for these 'cataphract cavalry', and that the original batch of Iazyges is likely to have been settled here in bulk, on retirement from their service (doubtless in a whole group of *numeri*) about A.D. 200 (loc. cit. 22-3). How many were actually settled in the Fylde is not known. They may well have been set to drain and clear the land, as we know happened to veterans settled elsewhere, e.g. at Deultum Veteranorum in Thrace (Pliny, *NH* IV.45; cf. Richmond, op. cit. 22) and probably in eastern Pannonia (see the preceding paragraph, and 14 b below); cf. also Tac., *Ann.* I.17.5; and *CJ* XI.lx.3 (cited by Richmond, op. cit. 23) = *Nov. Theod.* XXIV.4, where the words 'universis cum paludibus omnique iure' suggest something better than 'marshes' (Jones, *LRE* II.653, translates 'water meadows'); also *CJ* VII.xli.3.1 = *Nov. Theod.* XX.3.

(e) Dio Cass. LXXI.xxi: 3,000 Naristae received land, which must have been in

Pannonia (cf. *CIL* III.4500, from Carnuntum: see again Seeck, as cited in § c above). The date may be 179: see Birley, *MA* 285-6.

(f) According to the *Historia Augusta*, Marcus settled *infinitos ex gentibus* on Roman soil (*Marc.* 24.3), and in particular he brought to Italy a large number of surrendered Marcomanni (22.2). Cf. 14.1: various *gentes* driven on by other barbarians were threatening to make war on the empire, *nisi reciperentur*.

8. It was presumably in 180, the year in which Commodus became sole emperor, that C. Vettius Sabinianus Julius Hospes, as governor of the Tres Daciae (*AE* [1920] 45: see Wilkes, *Dalmatia* 447), promised land in Roman Dacia to 12,000 Dacians who had been driven out of their own land: see Dio Cass. LXXII.iii.3.

There is then another long gap, until the 250s, apart from the minor settlement mentioned in § 9 below.

9. The Emperor Severus Alexander (222-235) is said by Herodian VI.4.6 (cf. Zonar. XII.15) to have settled in villages in Phrygia, to farm the land there, 400 exceptionally tall Persians who had been sent on a mission to him by the Persian king. This must have been in A.D. 231-2.

10. The Emperor Gallienus is said to have given part of Pannonia to the Marcomannic King Attalus, for settlement: [Vict.], *Epit. de Caes.* 33.1, with Victor, *Caes.* 33.6; and see Mócsy, *PUM* 206-7, 209, who dates this 258-60 (in the joint reign of Valerian and Gallienus).

11. There are general statements by Zos. I.xlvi.2 and *Hist. Aug., Claud.* 9.4, that the Emperor Claudius II Gothicus (268-70) settled many Goths as farmers in Roman territory.

12. The Emperor Aurelian (270-5) is also said to have settled some defeated Carpi: Victor, *Caes.* 39.43; cf. *Hist. Aug., Aurel.* 30.4; Lact., *De mort. pers.* 9.2. This was presumably in Thrace. The allegation in *Hist. Aug., Aurel.* 48.1-4, that Aurelian planned to buy uncultivated land in Etruria and settle there *familiae captivae*, to produce free wine for the Roman people, can doubtless be ignored.

13. The Emperor Probus (276-282) evidently settled many barbarians in Roman territory: see Zos. I.lxviii.3 (Burgundians and Vandals in Britain); lxxi.1 (Bastarnae in Thrace); lxxi.2 (Franks; cf. *Paneg. Lat.* IV[VIII].xviii.3); *Hist. Aug., Prob.* 18.1 (100,000 Bastarnae); 18.2 (many Gothic Gepids and Greuthungi, and Vandals). Unlike Günther (*ULGG* 311-12 and nn.3-4), I do not think we can make use of the fictitious letter of Probus to the Senate in *Hist. Aug., Prob.* 15 (esp. §§ 2 & 6) as intended to refer to the settlements just mentioned, since (a) the author does not give them until *Prob.* 18.1-2 and seems to put them later (in 280 ff.), whereas the letter to the Senate seems to belong, in the author's mind, to 277-8; also (b) *Prob.* 14.7 (whatever its historical worth) shows that the author cannot have meant 15.2-6 to refer to the settlements described in 18.1-2, but must be thinking in 15.2 (*omnes iam barbari vobis arant* etc.) of barbarians made tributary, and in 15.6 (*arantur Gallicana rura barbaris bubus* etc.) of booty taken from the Germans. (Zos. I.lxviii.3, however, seems to put the settlement of Burgundians and Vandals in Britain in 277-8.)

14. There is clear evidence of many barbarian settlements made by Diocletian and the Tetrarchs (285-306):

(a) For Gaul (and Thrace), see especially a document of particular value because of its early date (1 March 297): *Paneg. Lat.* IV [VIII]. The most important passages are:

(i) i.4: 'tot excisae undique barbarae nationes, tot translati sint in Romana cultores.'

(ii) viii.4: 'omnes [barbari] sese dedere cogerentur et . . . ad loca olim deserta transirent, ut, quae fortasse ipsi quondam depraedando vastaverant, culta redderent serviendo.'

(iii) ix.1–4: 'captiva agmina barbarorum . . . atque hos omnes provincialibus vestris ad obsequium distributos, donec ad destinatos sibi cultus solitudinum ducerentur . . . Arat ergo nunc mihi Chamavus et Frisius . . . et cultor barbarus laxat annonam . . . Quin etiam si ad dilectum vocetur, accurrit et obsequiis teritur et tergo cohercetur et servire se militiae nomine gratulatur.'

(iv) xxi, esp. 1: 'itaque sicuti pridem tuo, Diocletiane Auguste, iussu deserta Thraciae translatis incolis Asia complevit, sicut postea tuo, Maximiane Auguste, nutu Nerviorum et Trevirorum arva iacentia Laetus postliminio restitutus et receptus in leges Francus excoluit, ita nunc per victorias tuas, Constanti Caesar invicte. quidquid infrequens Ambiano et Bellovaco et Tricassino solo Lingonicoque restabat, barbaro cultore revirescit.'

All the settlements in Gaul referred to in *Paneg.* IV must have taken place between 293 – the date of the victory over the Chamavi and Frisii (see ix.3), who had been allies of Carausius – and early 297, the date of *Paneg.* IV. We must note from xxi.1 that whereas the settlement of the Franks is new (the *Francus* is *receptus in leges*), that of the *laeti* must have been earlier, for the *laetus* is *postliminio restitutus*. If the word *laetus* here has the sense commonly attributed to it (see IV.iii § 19 above and its n.29 below), then this is the earliest known use of the word in that sense. There is nothing to show when the original settlement of these *laeti* took place: it may have been one of the cases referred to above. Nothing seems to be known of Diocletian's settlement of Asiatics in Thrace (xxi.1).

Another early document is *Paneg. Lat.* VII[VI].vi.2 (of 310): 'Quid loquar rursus intimas Franciae nationes . . . a propriis ex origine sui sedibus atque ab ultimis barbariae litoribus avulsas, ut in desertis Galliae regionibus collocatae et pacem Romani imperii cultu iuvarent et arma dilectu?'. This passage is sometimes taken to refer to a settlement of Salian Franks in Batavia by Constantius I, *c.* 297 (thus Jullian, *HG* VII.85–6, 146 n.2, 198–9); but that settlement has also been attributed to Constans in 341 (see id. 86 n.5, 146 n.2) or to the usurpation of Magnentius in 350–3 (Piganiol, *EC*[2] 135–6).

It seems very likely that a famous lead medallion of Lyons depicts one of the various settlements just mentioned: see Maria R. Alföldi, 'Zum Lyoner Bleimedaillon', in *Schweizer Münzblätter* 8 (1958) 63–8, who suggests that it is the Emperors Maximian and Constantius I who are shown as receiving men, women and children in 296. In the lower scene on the medallion the migrants are also depicted as crossing a bridge over the Rhine, *Fl(umen) Renus*, from *Castel(lum)*, the modern Kastel, to *Mogontiacum* (Mainz).

(b) More Carpi were settled in eastern Pannonia in 295–6: Amm. Marc. XXVIII.i.5; Victor, *Caes.* 39.43; Eutrop. IX.25.2; Oros. VII.xxv.12; cf. *Paneg. Lat.* IV[VIII].v.2 (where 'illa ruina Carporum' is very recent); and see Mócsy, *PUM* 272. The date, 295, is given by Euseb. (Hieron.), *Chron.*, p.226 (ed. R. Helm, 1956); *Cons. Constant.*, in *Chron. min.* I.230. Possibly drainage and clearance works were carried out by the settlers: see Victor, *Caes.* 40.9–10, with Mócsy, *PUM* 272.

(c) Bastarnae and Sarmatians are also said to have been settled on Roman soil in large numbers: Eutrop. IX.25.2; Oros. VII.xxv.12; cf. Lact., *De Mort. Pers.* 38.6, with the commentary of Jacques Moreau, *SC* 39 (1934) II.411–12, dating the Sarmatian settlement to 303. For the Bastarnae (295), see Euseb. (Hieron.), *Chron.,* loc. cit.

15. The Emperor Constantine is said to have distributed 'over 300,000 Sarmatians in Thrace, Scythia, Macedonia and Italy': *Anon. Vales.* 6.32; cf. Euseb., *Vita Constant.* IV.vi.1–2; Amm. Marc. XVII.xii.17–19; Zos. II.xxii.1; Publilius Optatianus Porfyrius, *Carm.* VII.20–2 (with 32). This is dated to A.D. 334: Euseb. (Hieron.), *Chron.*, p.233 (ed. Helm); *Cons. Constant.*, in *Chron. min.* I.234. The statement of Jordanes, *Get.* 22/115, that Constantine also installed Vandals in Pannonia, should probably be rejected: see Courtois, *VA* 34–5.

16. The Emperor Constantius II (337–361) seems to have made more than one settlement of barbarians in the empire:

(a) Liban., *Orat.* LIX.83-5 (of A.D. 348-9): in Thrace.

(b) Amm. Marc. XVII.xii.17-20 and XIX.xi.1-7 (esp. 6: 'tributariorum onera . . . et nomen'); cf. 8-15: Sarmatian Limigantes, A.D. 358-9. Cf. perhaps Auson., *Mosell.* 9, who speaks of Sarmatian *coloni* in the region of Tabernae (the modern Rheinzabern), on the left bank of the Rhine – the journey in question was perhaps in 368. But since Ausonius speaks of the *coloni* as 'recently' (*nuper*) planted, the settlement may have been a later one, effected by Valentinian I.

(c) It was presumably *c.* 348 that a certain number (perhaps not large) of Christian Visigoths, fleeing from persecution under the leadership of Ulfila, were settled by Constantius II near Nicopolis in Moesia Inferior: Philostorg., *HE* II.5 (πολὺν . . . λαόν); Jordanes, *Get.* 51/267 (*populus immensus*); Auxentius, *Epist. de fide, vita et obitu Wulfilae* 59-60, p.75 ed. Friedrich Kauffmann, *Aus der Schule des Wulfila = Texte u. Untersuch. zur altgerman. Religionsgesch.* I (Strassburg, 1899); cf. E. A. Thompson, *VTU* 96-7, with xi.

17. Julian in 358, while still Caesar, allowed the Salian Franks to remain where they had settled on Roman territory, near Tongres: Amm. Marc. XVII.viii.3-4 (cf. XX.iv.1); Liban., *Orat.* XVIII.75; XV.32 (cf. Jul., *Ep. ad Athen.* 280b); cf. Eunap. fr. 10; Zos. III.vi.3.

18. Valentinian I, *c.* 370, settled Alamanni (captured by the *magister equitum* Theodosius, father of the emperor of that name) as *tributarii* in the Po area in north Italy: Amm. Marc. XXVIII.v.15.

19. (a) The Emperor Valens in 366, after crushing the revolt of Procopius, is said to have disarmed a contingent of Goths, which had been sent to help Procopius (and which probably numbered *c.* 3,000, as stated by Amm. Marc. XXVI.x.3, rather than the 10,000 of Zos. IV.vii.2, with x.1), and then to have distributed the Goths throughout the cities (of the Danube area), to be held ἐν ἀδέσμῳ φρουρᾷ or φυλακῇ; they were received by the cities ἐς τὰς οἰκίας: see Eunap. fr. 37; Zos. IV.x.1-2 (clearly relying on Eunapius). Some of these Goths will doubtless have been turned into slaves, others perhaps into *coloni*.

(b) Valens in 376-7 settled very large numbers of Visigoths in Thrace: Amm. Marc. XXXI.iii.8; iv.1-11 (and cf. v ff.); Eunap. frr. 42-3; Socr., *HE* IV.34.2-5; Soz., *HE* VI.37.2-6; *Cons. Constant.*, in *Chron. min.* I.242; Philostorg., *HE* IX.17; Jordan., *Get.* 25/131-3; Zos. IV.xx.5-6; xxvi.1; Isid., *Hist. Goth.* 9, ed. T. Mommsen, in *MGH, Auct. Antiquiss.* XI = *Chron. min.* II.271. For the whole story, see Seeck, *GUAW* V.i.99-103.

20. (a) Under Gratian in 377, his general Frigerid settled Visigoths and Taifali, to farm lands in the territories of three cities in Italy (Mutina, Regium and Parma), just south of the Po: Amm. Marc. XXXI.ix.4.

(b) Ausonius, *Grat. Actio* ii § 8 (end of 379), speaks of a *traductio* of Alamanni captured by Gratian, and of Sarmatians 'conquered and pardoned'.

(c) Gratian in 380 (with the subsequent concurrence of Theodosius I: Jordan., *Get.* 28/142) concluded a treaty with the Goths, allowing them to settle in Pannonia and Upper Moesia: Zos. IV.xxxiv.2; xl.1-2; Jordan., *Get.* 27-8/141-2; cf. Procop., *Bell.* VIII (*Goth.* IV).v.13. See Seeck, *GUAW* V.i.129-30, 141-2. Contrast Demougeot, MEFB 147-50. And see 21 b below.

21. Major settlements were made by the Emperor Theodosius I:

(a) In 381 the Visigothic chief Athanaric (who immediately died) and some of his followers were received into the eastern part of the empire: Zos. IV.xxxiv.3-5; Socr., *HE* V.10.4; Themist., *Orat.* XV.190c-1b; Jordan., *Get.* 28/142-5; *Cons. Constant.*, in *Chron. min.* I.243; Prosper Tiro, *Epit. chron.* 1177, in id. 461; Hydatius 6, in *Chron. min.* II.15; Marcellinus Comes, *s.a.* 381 § 2, in id. 61. See Seeck, *GUAW* V.i.130.

(b) By a treaty dated 3 October 382 (*Cons. Constant.*, in *Chron. min.* I.243) Theodosius installed a very large number of Visigoths in the Balkans, especially the lower Danube area. The number may have been at least 20,000: see Jordan., *Get.* 28/144-5. For the other sources see Seeck, *GUAW* V.ii.495; Stein, *HBE* I².ii.521 nn.14–16; Jones, *LRE* III.29 n.46; Demougeot, MEFB 153. Note esp. Themist., *Orat.* XVI.211-12; *Paneg. Lat.* XII[II].xxii.3 (Pacatus, A.D. 389). The Goths were allowed to remain under the command of their own leaders and count as Roman *foederati*: this was perhaps the first time such a status had been conferred on barbarians settled within the empire; but a precedent may already have been set by the treaty of 380 (on which see 20 c above). For critical verdicts on this procedure, see e.g. Jones, *LRE* I.157-8; Piganiol, *EC²* 235; contrast Demougeot, MEFB 152-7 (and cf. 147-50).

(c) Theodosius also settled some Ostrogoths and Greuthungi in Phrygia, presumably after the defeat of the Ostrogothic attempt to cross the Danube in 386 (Zos. IV.xxxv.1, with the doublet in xxxviii-ix; Claudian, *De IV Cons. Honor.* 623-36): see Claudian, *In Eutrop.* II.153-5. These men went marauding in central Asia Minor under Tribigild in the spring of 399: see Stein, *HBE* I².ii.521 n.17; Seeck, *GUAW* V.i.306-11. It must have been this alarming revolt in particular that provoked the passionate outburst against wholesale use of non-Roman troops in chapters 14-15 of the speech *On kingship* delivered by Synesius of Cyrene to the Eastern Emperor Arcadius at Constantinople in 399 (*MPG* LXVI.1053 ff., at 1088-97; there is an English translation by Augustine FitzGerald, *The Essays and Hymns of Synesius of Cyrene* [1930] I.108 ff., at 133-9). Calling the Goths Σκύθαι (with Herodotus in mind), Synesius attacks not only their settlement on Roman soil by Theodosius (ibid. 1097AB = 138) but also the general dependence of the empire on non-Roman soldiery. But, as Gibbon says, 'the court of Arcadius indulged the zeal, applauded the eloquence, and neglected the advice of Synesius' (*DFRE* III.247).

22. *CTh* XIII.xi.10, issued by the Western Emperor Honorius in 399, speaks of the necessity to give *terrae laeticae* to persons of many nations entering the Roman empire. (For the *laeti* and their lands, see IV.iii above and its nn.29 and 33 below. *Laeti* are also referred to incidentally in *CTh* VII.xx.12.*pr.*, of 400; and cf. VII.xviii.10, of the same year.) I would not infer from Claudian, *Stil.* I.222-3 (A.D. 400), with Günther (ULGG 312), a recent settlement of Franks and Sygambri in Gaul. Claudian's words are too vague; and see Cameron, *Claudian* 96-7, 346-7, on Claudian's tendency to use well-known names indiscriminately, sometimes even resurrecting extinct ones from Tacitus (cf. *De IV cons. Honor.* 446-52).

A constitution of Honorius, of 409, *CTh* VII.xv.1, addressed to the vicar of Africa, mentions areas of land granted by the *antiqui* to *gentiles* for the defence of the frontier (cf. XI.xxx.62, of 405, to the proconsul of Africa, mentioning the *praefecti* of the *gentiles*). I know of no evidence as to when these land grants were originally made, but the third century is quite possible: see Jones, *LRE* II.651-2, with III.201 nn.103-4. The term *gentiles* in these texts seems to be the equivalent of *barbari*, as in *CTh* III.xiv.1, of *c.* 370 (contrast XVI.v.46, where *gentiles* are those commonly called *pagani*, pagans). For the specialised use of *Gentiles* for a crack regiment of the imperial bodyguard and field army, from at least the time of Constantine if not Diocletian, see Jones, *LRE* I.54, 120; II.613-14, with III.183-4 nn.11-13.

In 409 Alaric, the chief of the Visigoths, made two successive demands of Honorius. The first was that both provinces of Venetia, as well as Noricum (also then divided into two provinces) and Dalmatia, be handed over to him (Zos. V.xlviii.3-4). When this and other demands were refused, Alaric made a more moderate one, for both provinces of Noricum, a good part of which the Visigoths seem already to have occupied; but this demand too was rejected (Zos. V.l.3; li.1). In the following year, 410, Rome was sacked by Alaric, but the Goths moved away from Noricum.

23. Under Theodosius II, by *CTh* V.vi.3, of 12 April 409 (addressed to, and no doubt originated by, the Praetorian Prefect Anthemius), the captured Scyrae (Sciri) are to be distributed to landowners *iure colonatus*, tied to their fields, with a twenty-year exemption from conscription. They are to be settled in 'transmarine provinces', not Thrace or

Illyricum. Sozomen himself saw many Sciri farming in different places in Bithynia, near the Mysian Mount Olympus, south of Prusa; he also says that some of the Sciri had been sold off cheaply (and even given away) as slaves (*HE* IX.v.5-7).

24. Under the Emperor Honorius more than one settlement of barbarians took place in the years between 411 and 419:

(a) Between 411 and 418 there were several movements of Alans, Asding and Siling Vandals, Burgundians, Suevi and Visigoths into various parts of Spain (Gallaecia, Lusitania, Baetica): Hydatius 49, 60, 63, 67, 68, in *Chron. min.* II.18-19; Prosper Tiro, *Epit. chron.* 1250, in *Chron. min.* I.467; Oros. VII.xliii.1.

(b) Visigoths under Wallia, returning from Spain to Gaul, were settled, mainly in Aquitaine, in 418-19: Hydat. 69, in *Chron. min.* II.19; Prosper Tiro, *Epit. chron.* 1271, in *Chron. min.* I.469; Philostorg., *HE* XII.4; Isid., *Hist. Goth.* 22, in *Chron. min.* II.276.

25. During the reign of Valentinian III there were large settlements in Gaul of Alans in 440 and 442 (*Chron. Gall., ann.* 452, §§ 124, 127, in *Chron. min.* I.660) and of Burgundians in 443 (ibid., § 128).

26. In the reign of the Eastern Emperor Marcian (450-7), after the death of Attila in 453 and the disintegration of his empire, many Germanic, Hunnic and other peoples were given lands for settlement in devastated areas near the Danube from eastern Austria to Bulgaria, and in Gaul. Among other peoples, we hear of Ostrogoths, Sarmatians, Huns, Scyri, Alans and Rugians, and Burgundians. Our information comes mainly from Jordanes, *Get.* 50/263-6, 52/268; cf. *Chron. Min.* II.232, *s.a.* 456; I.305, *s.a.* 457.

27. In 473-4 the Emperor Leo I settled in Macedonia a large group of Ostrogoths under Theodemir (the father of the great Theodoric): Jordanes speaks of seven cities being handed over to them, nearly all of which they had occupied already (*Get.* 56/285-8). The Ostrogothic occupation of the area, however, seems to have been brief.

28. In 483 the Emperor Zeno settled some of the Ostrogothic followers of Theodoric in Dacia Ripensis and Lower Moesia (mainly northern Bulgaria): see Marcellinus Comes, *s.a.* 483, in *Chron. min.* II.92.

29. (a) In 506, while Anastasius I was reigning in the East and Theodoric the Ostrogoth was ruling Italy (with the principal title of *rex*), Theodoric took under his protection a large body of Alamanni who had been defeated and driven south by Clovis the Frank, and settled them in Raetia, in an area which might perhaps still be considered part of the Roman empire (Ennodius, *Paneg.* 72-3, in *MGH, Auct. Antiq.* VII [1885] 212, ed. F. Vogel; Cassiod., *Var.* II.41; Agath. I.6.3-4; and see Stein, *HBE* II.147 and n.1).

(b) In 512, still under Anastasius I, there was a settlement of Heruls in Roman territory (presumably in northern Yugoslavia): see Procop., *Bell.* VI = *Goth.* II.xiv.28-32; Marcellinus Comes, *s.a.* 512 (11), in *Chron. min.* II.98 ('in terras atque civitates Romanorum'). Cf. perhaps Cassiod., *Var.* IV.2 (perhaps of A.D. 511); and see Bury, *HLRE*[2] II.300 ('No people quite so barbarous had ever yet been settled on Roman soil'); Stein, *HBE* II.151, 305.

30. Several settlements were made by the Emperor Justinian I (527-565):

(a) Early in 528, on the conversion to Christianity of the Herul king and his chiefs, Justinian gave the Heruls better lands in eastern Pannonia, in the neighbourhood of Singidunum (Belgrade): Procop., *Bell.* VI = *Goth.* II.xiv.33 ff.; VII = *Goth.* III.xxxiii.13 (cf. xxxiv.37), and other sources given by Bury, *HLRE*[2] II.300 and n.2, and Stein, *HBE* II.305 (cf. 151, 156).

(b) In 534 Justinian settled 'in the Eastern cities' a number of Vandals who had surrendered to Belisarius after his capture of Carthage in the previous year and had been formed into five cavalry squadrons, the *Vandali Iustiniani*, to serve on the Persian frontier: see Procop., *Bell.* IV = *Vand.* II.xiv.17-19. (There must have been at least 2,000 of these Vandals; 400 deserted and sailed back to Africa.)

(c) It must have been during the 540s (probably 546) that Justinian settled Lombards (under their king, Audoin) in western Pannonia and Noricum, giving them territory which included the town of Noreia (Neumarkt): Procop., *Bell.* VII = *Goth.* III.xxxiii.10-11.

(d) Justinian settled in Thrace, apparently in 551, some 2,000 Kotrigurs (a Hunnic people), with their families: see Procop., *Bell.* VIII = *Goth.* IV.xix.6-7.

Conquests made by the Frankish King Theudebert (533/4-547) of portions of Roman territory in Liguria, Venetia, the Cottian Alps, Raetia and Noricum (see Stein, *HBE* II.526-7) were apparently never recognised by Justinian: see Procop., *Bell.* VIII = *Goth.* IV.xxiv.11,15, 27-9 etc., against VII = III.xxxiv.37.

There is a very interesting passage, *Bell.* VII = *Goth.* III.xxxiv.36, in which Procopius makes some Gepid ambassadors tell Justinian in 549 that his empire has such a superfluity of cities and territory that he is actually looking for opportunities to give away parts of it for habitation!

31. In 578, after Maurice (who became emperor four years later) had conducted a very successful campaign against the Persians in their Armenian province of Arsanene (on the upper Tigris), the Emperor Tiberius Constantine (578-582) settled large numbers of the population of that area in Cyprus: see John of Ephesus, *HE* VI.15, cf. 27 *fin.*, 34; Evagr., *HE* V.19, p.215.16-26 ed. Bidez/Parmentier; Theophylact Simocatta III.xv.15, ed. C. de Boor, 1887. A later settlement of Armenians in Thrace, said to have been planned by the Emperor Maurice in 602, never took place: see Sebeos XX, pp.54-5 in the French translation by Frédéric Macler, Paris, 1904.

32. It appears from Greg. Magn., *Ep.* I.73, of 591, that there had been a recent settlement of barbarian 'daticii' (surely *dediticii*) on the estates of the Roman Church in Africa.

33. It must have been in the 590s that the Emperor Maurice settled some Bulgars in Upper and Lower Moesia and Dacia (in the area of Belgrade in Yugoslavia and northern Bulgaria), devastated by the Avars in the reign of Anastasius: see Michael the Syrian, *Chron.* X.21, in the French translation from the twelfth-century Syriac by J. B. Chabot, Vol.II (Paris, 1901-4) 363-4. (I am grateful to Michael Whitby, who has been studying Theophylact, for drawing my attention to this material and some of that in § 30 above.)

Later transfers of population (although mainly those of peoples already inhabiting one region of the Byzantine empire to another such region) are listed by Peter Charanis, 'The Transfer of Population as a Policy in the Byzantine Empire', in *CSSH* 3 (1960-61) 140-54. He also mentions some (by no means all) of the settlements I have listed above.

* * * * * *

Relevant here are a number of entries in the *Notitia Dignitatum* (*Part. Occid.*), including the following , which I give according to the edition by Otto Seeck (Berlin, 1876): *Occ.* XLII.33-44 (various *praefecti laetorum*); 46-63 and 66-70 (various *praefecti Sarmatarum gentilium*); 65 (a *praefectus Sarmatarum et Taifalorum gentilium*). All these are found in the prefecture of the Gauls (in the provinces of Lugdunensis Senonia, Lugdunensis II and III, Belgica I and II, Germania II, and Aquitania I), except nos.46-63, which are in Italy. See also ch.xiii of the *Verona List* (ed. Seeck in the same volume, at pp.251-2). I know of no corresponding entries in that part of the *Notitia* dealing with the *partes Orientis*, although a few names of units there are those of Alamanni, Franks, Sarmatians, Taifali, Vandili etc.

Many of the barbarian peoples settled in Gaul have left their mark in various geographical names (mainly of villages) in modern France: Burgundians, Sarmatians, Alans, Taifali, Franks, Alamanni, perhaps Goths (see e.g. A. Grenier, in Frank, *ESAR* III.598-9; also his *Manuel d'archéol. gallo-romaine* I [Paris, 1931] 398-402; and R. Kaiser, *Untersuch. zur Gesch. der Civitas und Diözese Soissons in römischer und merowingischer Zeit* [Bonn, 1973], as cited by Günther, ULGG 315 and nn.29-30). The same is also true of modern Italy: Sarmatians, Alamanni, Suevi, Taifali (see e.g. Stein, *HBE* II.42 n.2). I have not been able to investigate the growing body of archaeological evidence (in part concerning what is sometimes called the Late Roman 'Reihengräberkultur' in northern and north-eastern Gaul), for which see the convenient summary by Günther, ULGG, and the many recent works there cited.

I should perhaps mention here that I agree with A. H. M. Jones in rejecting the commonly held theory that in the Later Empire the *limitanei*, or some *limitanei*, were 'a kind of hereditary peasant militia', who occupied heritable lands and performed military duties as a sideline: see Jones, *LRE* II.649-54, with III.200-2 nn.97-109. The *limitanei* make their first appearance in the 360s, in *CTh* XII.i.56 (of 363 or 362) and Festus, *Brev.* 25 (perhaps 369-70; but cf. B. Baldwin, 'Festus the historian', in *Historia* 27 [1978] 197-217). Only in the fifth century do we find *limitanei* as such with lands to cultivate: *CJ* XI.lx.3.*pr.* = *Nov. Theod.* XXIV.4, of 443; cf. *CTh* VII.xv.2, of 423, referring to *castellorum loca* or *territoria*, to be occupied only by the *castellanus miles*; and see Jones, *LRE* II.653-4.

* * * * * *

Some further bibliography on some of the subjects dealt with in this Appendix will be found in IV.iii §§ 17-19 above and its notes below, esp. 28-9; and see 34a on *hospitium/hospitalitas*.

Appendix IV
The destruction of Greek democracy in the Roman period

This Appendix is intended to be read as a supplement to Chapter V Section iii above.

The evidence for this subject is so scattered and fragmentary and difficult to interpret that in the text above (V.iii) I have given only a bare outline of what happened to democracy in the Greek world as a whole in the Hellenistic and Roman periods. There is a good deal of evidence which seems not to have been properly collected together yet, and I cannot pretend to have examined more than a part of it myself, although I think I have looked at enough to be satisfied that the picture I give below is correct in its broad outlines. I shall present here a series of not very well connected observations, with some of the most important references to the sources and a little modern bibliography, in the hope that others will soon undertake the task of marshalling all the available evidence and drawing general conclusions from it, with as much detail and as much chronological and topographical precision as the evidence allows. The mass of epigraphic material which has been accumulating during the past few decades needs to be combined with the previously published epigraphic texts and the literary evidence, into a significant whole, with variations and exceptions noticed. The volumes of *SEG* (27 up to 1980) and of *AE*; the critical summary by J. and L. Robert of the year's epigraphic publications which has appeared regularly as a 'Bulletin épigraphique' in *REG*; the many epigraphic papers by various scholars, especially by L. Robert in *Hellenica* (13 volumes up to 1965) and elsewhere; and a number of new publications of inscriptions (including a few relevant ones in Latin) – all these provide much material for a new synthesis. Of existing works, I have found most useful Jones, *GCAJ* (1940) and *CERP*[2] (1971), which can be supplemented, for Asia Minor, by Magie *RRAM* (1950, a gigantic collection of source material and bibliography, seldom exhibiting much historical insight),[1] three admirable articles in *REG* 1895-1901 by Isidore Lévy (EVMAM I-III), Victor Chapot's *La province romaine proconsulaire d'Asie* (1904), esp. its pp.148-279, and other works; but even Jones does not give a complete conspectus in one place, and I have not been able to discover any general work dealing comprehensively with the subject as a whole. I have of course made use of the fundamental work of Heinrich Swoboda, *GV = Die griechischen Volksbeschlüsse. Epigraphische Untersuchungen* (Leipsig, 1890), and of other standard works, such as W. Liebenam, *Städteverwaltung im römischen Kaiserreiche* (Leipzig, 1900). I am also most grateful to A. R. R. Sheppard for allowing me to read his Oxford B.Litt. thesis, *Characteristics of Political Life in the Greek Cities ca. 70-120 A.D.* (1975).

I warmly agree with Barbara Levick that there is an urgent need for at least a catalogue or concordance of the inscriptions of Asia Minor: see her short paper, 'Greek and Latin epigraphy in Anatolia: progress and problems' in *Acta of the Fifth International Congress of Greek and Latin Epigraphy, Cambridge 1967* (Oxford, 1971) 371-6. The four volumes of Indexes (down to 1973) to the Roberts' invaluable 'Bulletins épigraphiques' (in *REG*, from 1938 onwards), prepared by L'Institut Fernand Courby and published in Paris between 1972 and 1979, have made it much easier to discover material published by the Roberts between 1938 and 1973; but they represent only a first step. I must mention also the analytical index by Louis Robert to the five volumes of M. Holleaux's *Études d'épigr. et d'hist. grecques* (ed. L. Robert), in Vol.VI of the *Études*(1968).

* * * * * *

In Rome's relations with other states even in Italy itself there are many indications that she would naturally favour the powerful and the propertied (provided of course they were not anti-Roman, on patriotic or other grounds), and help to suppress revolutions. I will give the clearest examples. In the revolt of the Latins and Campanians in 341-0 B.C., the Campanian *equites*, to the number of 1,600, kept aloof from the rest, and were duly rewarded by Rome, when the revolt was suppressed, with Roman citizenship and a pension to be paid them by their countrymen (Livy VIII.xi.15-16; cf. xiv.10). Similarly, after Capua in 216 had gone over to Hannibal, 300 Campanian *equites* who had been serving in Sicily came to Rome and were given the citizenship (XXIII.xxxi.10-11); and in 213 another 112 *equites nobiles* from Capua deserted to the Romans and were duly received by them (XXIV.xlvii.12-13). For the Campanian *equites*, see Toynbee, *HL* I.333-6, 401-3. At Arretium in 302 B.C. Rome intervened in favour of the *gens Cilnia*, the richest local family, who were in danger of being driven out, and reconciled them with their *plebs* (Livy X.iii.2; v.13; and see Harris, *REU* 63-5, 115). In 296 Livy records the suppression among the Lucanians (who had entered into a treaty with Rome in 299-8: X.xi-xii) of 'seditiones a plebeiis et egentibus ducibus ortas', by Q. Fabius Maximus, to the great delight of the Lucanian *optimates* (xviii.8). At Volsinii in 265-4 Rome helped to suppress an insurrection of the serfs against their Etruscan masters: Livy, *Per.* 16; Florus I.16, ed. P. Jal (=I.21); Zonar. VIII.7; Oros. IV.v.3-5; *De vir. illustr.* 36; John of Antioch fr. 50 (in *FHG* IV.557), etc.; and see Harris, *REU* 115-18, cf. 83-4, 91-2. Another such insurrection in Etruria in 196, called by Livy a 'coniuratio servorum' and evidently serious (according to Livy it made 'Etruriam infestam prope'), was ruthlessly put down by a Roman army under M'. Acilius Glabrio, who scourged and crucified some of the rebels and returned others to their *domini* (Livy XXXIII.xxxvi.1-3). Etruscan society was deeply divided between a ruling class, described by expressions such as *principes, nobiles, ditissimi, domini*, δυνατώτατοι, κύριοι, and a subject class or classes, described as *servi*, οἰκέται, πενέσται. The precise condition of the latter is uncertain, but was probably a form of serfdom (see III.iv above and its n.4 below; and cf. Harris, *REU* 142: in the rising of 196 'the rebels were clearly members of the local serf class'). There has been much dispute about Rome's attitude towards the Etruscans, but I have no doubt that Harris is right: except when Etruscan *principes* showed disloyalty to Rome, as occasionally during the Hannibalic war (218-203), the Romans supported them against their subjects; 'there was no alternative . . . which would not involve radical social change' (*REU* 129-44, at p.143).

There are other examples of the same Roman policy during the Hannibalic war. The defection of Croton to Hannibal in 215 is described in most explicit terms by Livy in XXIV.ii-iii, after two brief anticipatory passages: XXII.lxi.12 and XXIII.xxx.6-7. He explains that '*all* Italian cities were as if infested with a single disease': *plebes* and *optimates* were on opposite sides, with the *senatus* favouring Rome in each case and the *plebs* Carthage (XXIV.ii.8). Under the leadership of Aristomachus, the *princeps plebis* of Croton, the city was surrendered to the Bruttians, allies of Carthage (and represented in XXIV.i.1 as hated by the Greek cities!), while the *optimates* retired into the citadel, which they had fortified in advance (ii.10-11). The situation was much the same in Nola in

216–214. Here again the local senators, especially their *primores*, were faithful to Rome, while the *plebs* were 'wholly for Hannibal', and, 'as usual, wanted revolution', with some advising defection to Hannibal (XXIII.xiv.7; cf. Plut., *Marc.* 10.2 ff.). The senators, by cleverly dissimulating, managed to delay a revolt (Livy XXIII.xiv.8–9). A little later the *principes* were again alarmed at preparations by the *plebs* for betraying the city (xv.7; xvi.2,5–6). In 215 the *plebs* were inclining towards Rome (xlvi.3) but by 214 Livy can describe them as 'for a long time disaffected towards Rome and hostile to their own Senate' (XXIV.xiii.8). The situation at Locri in 216–215 is a little more complicated. As in the case of Croton, the revolt, described more fully in XXIV.i.2–13, is anticipated in two earlier passages: XXII.lxi.12 and XXIII.xxx.8, the latter asserting briefly that the *multitudo* were betrayed by their *principes*, a statement not borne out by the more detailed later narrative: see especially XXIV.i.5–7, where the *principes Locrensium* are said to have convoked an Assembly because they themselves were 'overcome by fear', and there is emphasis on the fact that '*levissimus quisque novas res novamque societatem mallent*'; the decision to go over to Hannibal is represented as being virtually unanimous. In 205 we discover for the first time that there were Locrian *principes* with the Romans at Rhegium: they had been 'driven out by the opposite faction' which had surrendered Locri to Hannibal (XXIX.vi.5). When Rome had regained control of the city the Locrian ambassadors naturally tried to pretend that the defection to Hannibal was '*procul a publico consilio*' and their return to the Roman fold due in no small measure to their own personal efforts (xvii.1–2).

According to E. Badian, 'It is difficult to make out whether Livy's account of class divisions in Italy during the [Hannibalic] war (with the upper classes favouring Rome and the lower classes Hannibal) truthfully represents a state of affairs due to political affinity and collaboration or is a second-century myth, invented to uphold oligarchy in Italy'; and he adds, 'the latter seems more likely' (*Foreign Clientelae* 147–8). Giving examples in which he thinks 'Livy occasionally contradicts his own main thesis', Badian cites, for Locri, only XXIII.xxx.8, ignoring the much more detailed narrative at the beginning of Book XXIV, summarised above. I cannot, therefore, accept Locri as an example in favour of Badian's conclusion; and he seems to me to go well beyond the evidence when he claims that 'at Arpi (XXIV.xlvii.6) and apparently at Tarentum (xiii.3) the People favoured Rome'. As for Arpi, all that Livy says in XXIV.xlvii.6 is that during a successful Roman assault on their town certain individual Arpini complained that they had been kept in a state of subjection and oppression by a few and handed over to Hannibal by their *principes*. What else would one expect them to say, in their desire to exculpate themselves to the victorious Romans? And as for Tarentum, XXIV.xiii.3 is a mere report of a statement allegedly made to Hannibal by five young Tarentine nobles, that the *plebs* of Tarentum, who ruled the city, were 'in potestate iuniorum', a large part of whom (§ 2) favoured Hannibal. In the subsequent narrative of the capture of the city by Hannibal (XXV.viii–x) and its recapture by Q. Fabius Maximus (XXVII.xv–xvi; cf. Plut., *Fab.* 21–2) I see no sign of any pro-Roman feeling on the part of the common people. At Syracuse, certainly, the common people were overwhelmingly hostile to Rome, while certain *nobilissimi viri* (Livy XXV.xxiii.4) were pro-Roman and defected in 214 to Marcellus: see Livy XXIV.xxi to XXV.xxxi, in particular XXIV.xxiii. 10–11; xxvii.1–3, 7–9; xxviii (esp. 9); xxxii.2, 9; XXV.xxiii.4, with xxxi.3,6,8. We have less information about other Sicilian cities in which hostility to Rome was strong, and pro-Roman factions may have been lacking in some of them; but Plutarch tells an entertaining story (from Poseidonius) about Nicias, the leading citizen of Engyum who was also the main advocate of the Roman cause there and was duly rewarded by Marcellus for his services (*Marc.* 20.5–11).

Badian cites no other evidence in favour of his thesis, and I know of none. He does not mention the cases of Arretium and Volsinii, which I have quoted above, and he qualifies the Livian passage concerning Lucania with an 'if true'. He does admit, however, that in 174 the Roman Senate intervened in an internal dispute at Patavium in Venetia (*seditio . . . intestinum bellum*, Livy XLI.xxvii.3), of course on the side of the ruling class. I cannot see why Livy's general statement about the nature of Italian class divisions during the Hannibalic war should be part of a 'second-century myth, invented to uphold oligarchy in Italy', or how such a myth would serve its alleged purpose; and to say that if two or three of the examples given are not true, 'they strongly suggest that before the war there had been little Roman interference on behalf of oligarchic governments' seems to me a *non sequitur*.

The tendency of upper classes to incline towards Rome is a very general phenomenon. We even hear from Appian (*Lib.* 68.304–5) that in the early second century B.C. there was a party at Carthage which ἐρρωμάϊζον, distinguished from those who ἐδημοκράτιζον (and another group which favoured Masinissa). Appian (*Illyr.* 23) also distinguishes between the respective attitudes of the πρωτεύοντες and the δῆμος of the Pannonian town of Siscia (the Segesta) when Octavian demanded its surrender in 35 B.C. The former group (the δυνατοί of Dio Cass. XLIX.37.2) wished to comply with Octavian's demands for the installation of a garrison and the giving of hostages; but the common people would not receive the garrison, and they fought the Romans energetically until they were compelled to surrender. Certainly in their relations with the Greek states the Romans always and everywhere *preferred* to support the propertied classes, although, in their hard-headed way, they were quite prepared to depart from this policy when practical considerations made it necessary for them to do so (see § 2 below). Dealing with the year 192, just before the war with Antiochus III, Livy says it was generally agreed that the *principes, optimus quisque*, in each state were pro-Roman and were pleased with the present state of affairs, while the *multitudo et quorum res non ex sententia ipsorum essent* wanted a general revolution (XXXV.xxxiv.3; cf. xxxiii.1 on the Aetolians). In 190, during the war with Antiochus, we hear that the *multitudo* or *plebs* in Phocaea wished to stand by Antiochus, while the *senatus et optimates* wished to stand by Rome (Livy XXXVII.ix.1–4; cf. Polyb. XXI.vi.1–6). And in 171, at the outset of the Third Macedonian War, we find that in most free Greek states the *plebs* inclined towards Perseus, while the *principes* (and 'the best and most prudent section') preferred Rome (Livy XLII.xxx.1–7). Attempts have recently been made, in particular by Gruen, to belittle this evidence, but without success.[2]

* * * * * *

I suspect that greater influence than has been generally realised may have been exercised upon the political life of some Greek cities by the bodies (*conventus*) of Roman residents established in many places throughout the Greek world: οἱ Ῥωμαῖοι or Ῥωμαίων οἱ ἐπιδημοῦντες or (more often) πραγματευόμενοι or (most commonly) κατοικοῦντες. The political influence of these resident Romans would be most in evidence when they participated in the administration of justice, as we know they did in Sicily and Cyrenaica (see §§ 1 and 5 below) and as they doubtless did elsewhere. Since we hear more about these resident Romans in Asia Minor than anywhere else I will give references for them in § 3 below. The standard book on Italian businessmen operating in the Greek East is still the admirable and comprehensive work of Jean Hatzfeld, *Les Trafiquants Italiens dans l'Orient Hellénique* (*BEFAR* 115, Paris, 1919).

1. Sicily etc.

It is easy to overlook the fact that a province containing many Greek cities was first acquired by Rome during the second half of the third century B.C., before she took over any part of Greece itself. This of course was Sicily, which, as Cicero put it, was the first foreign country to be given the name of a *provincia*, an 'ornament of empire'. 'She first,' Cicero goes on, 'taught our ancestors how excellent a thing it is to rule over foreign peoples' (*II Verr.* ii.2).

Sicily, with its several dozen Greek cities, came under Roman control and became a Roman province by stages, from 241 to 210 B.C. Differences of status among the Greek cities of Sicily do not concern us here. Most of our very scanty information about constitutional details comes either from inscriptions (which I have not been able to examine thoroughly) or from Cicero's *Verrines,* esp. *II Verr.* ii.120-5. Constitutional changes were introduced in various places at different times: the most important were those made by the *Lex Rupilia* (regulations imposed by P. Rupilius in 131 B.C., at the end of the 'First Sicilian Slave War') and those introduced by Augustus.

The Sicilian cities, as inscriptions show, evidently retained their Assemblies for some generations after the Roman conquest; but evidently their Councils soon came to play an increasingly important part under Roman rule, with the powers and functions of their Assemblies steadily waning. By the time of Verres' governorship (73-71 B.C.), at any rate, the Councils seem to have been at least partly reorganised on a model nearer to that of the Roman Senate. Our principal source here is Cicero, *II Verr.* ii.120-1 (general), 122 (Halaesa), 123 (Agrigentum), 125 (Heraclea). We hear of a property qualification for councillors (*census,* § 120) and of Verres personally appointing men 'ex loco quo non liceret' (§ 121). It is a problem, especially in view of the use of the word *suffragium* twice over in § 120, whether some form of election of councillors by the Assemblies may not have survived, at least in some cities; but Cicero's regular use of the word *cooptare* for the appointment of councillors in §§ 120 (general, twice), 122 (Halaesa, twice), 123 (Agrigentum) and 125 (Heraclea) suggests to me that councillors were chosen, in most cases anyway, not by popular election for a year at a time, but for life (this would be the most important change), and in one or more of three ways: (1) what we should call 'co-optation' proper: namely, choice by the collective councillors themselves; (2) nomination by magistrates filling the role of the Roman *censores*; and (3) automatically, upon being elected to certain magistracies. What we know of Roman practice in Italy and in Bithynia-Pontus (see § 3A below) makes me inclined to think that in constitutional theory there existed a combination of the second and third methods rather than the first. Cicero himself could certainly use *cooptatio* of appointments made by censors (see *De leg.* III.27: *sublata cooptatione censoria).*[3] In order to make *cooptare/cooptatio* seem more appropriate, we might have been tempted to wonder whether, if Sicilian councillors were enrolled by magistrates of censorial type (my second alternative), such magistrates were elected by the councils themselves; but against any such supposition is Cic., *II Verr.* ii.131-3, 136-9 (especially *comitia isto praetore censorum ne simulandi quidem causa fuerunt*, at the end of § 136). I would guess that in practice, as distinct from theory, magistrates performing censorial functions would be bound to a considerable extent, in their choice of recruits for their Council, by the views of its dominant section. This would make the use of the term *cooptatio* for censorial nomination peculiarly appropriate.

One remembers how insistent the Athenian democracy had been on the principle of public accountability: that every magistrate should be subjected to *euthyna* at the end of his term of office (see V.ii § D above). At Syracuse by the late 70s, on the other hand, *euthynai* were being conducted by the Council (a practice which had evidently been going on for some time); and this could even be done in secrecy (see Cic., *II Verr.* iv.140). And the procedure adopted by the Syracusan Council at the same period is indicative of an oligarchical atmosphere: the order in which speeches was delivered was according to 'age and prestige' (*aetas* and *honor*), and the *sententiae* of the leading men, the *principes,* were entered in the public records (id. 142-3).

In spite of the fact that Halaesa was in the small privileged category of *civitates sine foedere liberae et immunes,* I cannot agree with Gabba (SCSEV 312-13) that at Halaesa, unlike Agrigentum and Heraclea, the Assembly retained the right of electing councillors even in Cicero's time, for Cicero, recording the petition of Halaesa to the Roman Senate in 95 B.C. to settle its controversies 'de senatu cooptando', specifically mentions (at the end of ii.122) that the city had asked that its choice of councillors should be made 'ne suffragiis quidem': probably elections had taken place down to 95 B.C. in the Assembly, but were now, by the new regulations given to Halaesa by C. Claudius Pulcher in 95, to be effected by the Council itself.

At Halaesa, at any rate, there was not only a property qualification (*census*) and a minimum age of thirty for being a councillor; men practising a trade (a *quaestus*), e.g. auctioneers (*praecones*), were also debarred (ii.122). Similar provisions had earlier been included in the rules prescribed for the Council of Agrigentum by Scipio (§ 123, perhaps L. Cornelius Scipio, praetor in Sicily in 193 B.C.: see Gabba, SCSEV 310), and probably in those laid down by Rupilius for Heraclea Minoa (§ 125).

It is in Sicily, I think, that we have the earliest evidence for the body of resident Roman citizens (*conventus civium Romanorum*) providing the judges in certain lawsuits, according to the *Lex Rupilia*; but precisely which suits were involved is not clear from Cic., *II Verr.* ii.32 (*ceterorum rerum selecti iudices civium Romanorum ex conventu*). Cf. ii.33,34,70 (*e conventu Syracusano*), iii.28 (*de conventu*). It is very likely that these judges would be chosen only from the wealthier residents, as we find later at Cyrene, where we know that in the time of Augustus the system was working badly (see § 5 below).

Among minor points, we may note that in a lawsuit between an individual and his city, according to the *Lex Rupilia*, it was the 'senatus' of some other city in Sicily which appointed the judges (*II Verr.* ii.32). It is also worth noticing the *quinque primi* of Agyrrhium, in iii.73, who had been summoned by Verres, with the magistrates of that city, and with them had reported back to their 'senatus' at home.

Of the subsequent constitutional changes in the Sicilian towns I do not think we can be more specific than to say that they must have followed the general pattern observable elsewhere.

I see no reason to treat the σύγκλητος which is equated with *senatus* in a bilingual inscription from Naples, and which appears beside the Assembly (ἀλία or δῆμος) in inscriptions, certainly at Acragas and Malta, and (later on as πρόσκλητος) at Naples, and probably also at Syracuse, as anything but the Council of these cities; the ἔσκλητος which appears once at Rhegium beside both ἀλία and βουλά is unique (*SIG*³ 715 = *IG* XIV.612): see G. Forni, 'Intorno alle constituzioni di città greche in Italia e in Sicilia', in Κωκαλός 3 (1957) 61-9, who gives the epigraphic evidence and bibliography. Robert K. Sherk, *The Municipal Decrees of the Roman West* (= *Arethusa* Monographs, no.2, Buffalo, N.Y., 1970) 1-15, is a useful sketch of 'The Senate in the Italian communities'.

2. Mainland Greece (with Macedon and some of the Aegean islands)

Roman influence upon the political life of Old Greece, and Greek resistance to it, around the time of the Roman conquest, have recently been treated extensively in two monographs: Johannes Touloumakos, *Der Einfluss Roms auf die Staatsform der griechischen Stadtstaaten des Festlandes und der Inseln im ersten und zweiten Jhdt. v. Chr.* (Diss., Göttingen, 1967); and Jürgen Deininger, *Der politische Widerstand gegen Rom in Griechenland 217-86 v. Chr.* (Berlin, 1971). The first is essentially an exhaustive collection of the evidence: see the review by F. W. Walbank in *JHS* 89 (1969) 179-80. The second attempts much more in the way of interpretation, but its understanding of the political and social situation in Greece is gravely defective: see the critical reviews by G. W. Bowersock, in *Gnomon* 45 (1973) 576-80 (esp. 578); P. S. Derow, in *Phoenix* 26 (1972) 303-11; and especially John Briscoe, in *CR* 88 = n.s.24 (1974) 258-61; and see also Brunt, RLRCRE 173. The best modern treatment of the subject is by Briscoe, 'Rome and the class struggle in the Greek states 200-146 B.C.', in *Past and Present* 36 (1967) 3-20, reprinted in *SAS* (ed. Finley) 53-73. His view of Rome's policy in the first half of the second century B.C. can best be summarised in his own words: 'The natural preference of the Senate and its representatives was for the upper classes and for forms of government in which the upper classes were dominant. Other things being equal, it was to this end that Roman policy was directed.' On the other hand, 'in this turbulent period [200-145] it is only rarely that other things were equal. Rome's object was to win the wars in which she was engaged and to maintain the control over Greek affairs which her military successes bestowed on her. To this end the Senate was glad to accept support from those who were willing to give it to her, irrespective of their position in the internal politics of their own states' (*SAS* 71-2). But 'under the Roman Empire the picture is very different. There was now no question of a struggle for leadership in the Mediterranean world – Rome's mastery was unchallenged. It is not surprising that under these conditions Rome's natural preferences came to the fore, and that both in Italy and in the provinces it was the richer classes who were dominant . . . The result of Rome's victory was indeed to stem the tide of democracy and the ultimate victory belonged to the upper classes' (*SAS* 73).

In the Hellenistic period, according to Alexander Fuks, although the Greek upper classes might have very different attitudes towards Rome, 'the *multitudo, plebs, demos, okhlos* was always and everywhere anti-Roman and reposed its hopes of a change in the social and economic situation in all who manifested opposition to Rome (Antiochus III of Asia, Perseus of Macedon)': see Fuks, 'Social revolution in Greece in the Hellenistic age', in *La parola del passato* 111 (1966) 437-48, at p.445; and cf. 'The *Bellum Achaicum* and its social aspect', in *JHS* 90 (1970) 78-79. This forthright statement, which does go slightly beyond the available evidence, has recently been attacked by Gruen in relation to the events of the Third Macedonian War of 171-168 B.C. (see n.2 again). By carefully isolating the events in question, and by doing his utmost to play down inconvenient passages such as Livy XLII.xiii.9 (cf. App., *Maced.* 11.1; Diod. XXIX.33); xxx.1-7; Polyb. XXIV.ix.3-7; x.14; XXVII.ix.1; x.1,4; and Sherk, *RDGE* 40 (= *SIG*[3] 643 = *FD* III.iv.75), lines 22-4, Gruen feels able to deny altogether for this period any 'attested connection between social conflict and attitudes toward or by the major powers' (op. cit. in n.2, p.47). In spite of the defects in his arguments,[4] the general conclusions in his last two paragraphs are largely unobjectionable *for this particular war*: 'There seems to have been little genuine commitment to the side of either Rome or Perseus . . . The populace was not eager to fight and die in a cause not their own. Attitudes fluctuated with the fortunes of war . . . Security and survival were the dominant motives, not class consciousness' (op. cit. 48). I of course would say that anti-Roman *feeling* on the part of the masses in general would very often not be able to display itself in *action*, as it would tend to be overborne by other considerations, especially sheer prudence and recognition of the futility and even danger of outright opposition to Rome – which might have fearful consequences, as the fate of Haliartus in 171 showed (Livy XLII.lxiii.3-12). The Roman siege of Haliartus ended with massacre, general enslavement, and the total destruction of the city. That was in *the first year of the war*. The catastrophe at Haliartus would have been a most powerful deterrent against actually joining in anti-Roman activity, even for those who were most hostile in their hearts to Roman dominance. Earlier in 171, when the news spread throughout Greece of a Macedonian victory in a cavalry engagement with the Romans (for which see Livy XLII.58-61), the inclinations of οἱ πολλοί, οἱ ὄχλοι in Greece towards Perseus, hitherto mainly concealed, had 'burst out like a fire', according to Polybius XXVII.ix.1; x.1,4. The whole passage (ix-x) is fascinating: Polybius felt that Greece had suffered at the hands of the Macedonian kings but had received real benefits from Roman rule (x.3), and he is anxious to exculpate his fellow-countrymen from the charge of ingratitude to Rome. (Gruen of course attempts to discount the use by Polybius of the terms οἱ πολλοί, οἱ ὄχλοι; but see nn.2 and 4 again.) Roman power could indeed inspire awe. A leading pro-Roman opposed to an incipient revolt might call attention not only to the benefits of peace but to the *vis Romana*: he could warn the young men of the danger of opposing Rome and instil fear into them – as Julius Auspex of the Remi does in Tacitus' narrative of the events in Gaul early in A.D. 70 (*Hist.* IV.69).

In the final struggle against Rome in 146 B.C. in particular we find great emphasis laid on the participation of the lower classes in the anti-Roman movement: in particular, Polybius speaks of the crucial meeting of the Achaean League at Corinth in the spring of 146, which declared war, as being attended by 'such a crowd of workmen and artisans [ἐργαστηριακῶν καὶ βαναύσων ἀνθρώπων] as had never assembled before' (XXXVIII.xii.5).

The first known example of Roman interference with the constitutions of the cities of Old Greece is from 196 to 194 B.C., when T. Quinctius Flamininus, in his settlement of Thessalian affairs after the end of the Second Macedonian War, imposed property qualifications for councillors (probably federal ones) and judges and did his best to strengthen the control of the cities by (as Livy puts it) 'that part of the citizen population to whom it was more expedient to have everything secure and tranquil' (XXXIV.li.4-6; cf. Plut., *Flamin.* 12.4) – the propertied class, of course. (We are not told that Flamininus imposed outright oligarchy by insisting on limitation of the right to attend the Assemblies.) By 192, Livy tells us, it was generally realised among the Aetolians and their allies that the leading men of the cities were pro-Roman and rejoiced in the present condition of affairs, while the multitude wished for revolution (XXXV.xxxiv.3). According to Justin XXXIII.ii.7, Macedonia received from L. Aemilius Paullus in 168 'the laws which it still uses' (cf. Livy XLV.xviii and xxix-xxx, esp. xviii.6: 'ne improbus vulgi adsentator aliquando libertatem salubri moderatione datam ad licentiam pestilentem traheret'!). After crushing the revolt of the Achaean League and its allies in 146 B.C., L. Mummius (who incidentally destroyed Corinth and sold its population into slavery) is said by Pausanias to have 'put down democracies and established property qualifications for holding office' (VII.xvi.9). Polybius XXXIX.5 speaks of the *politeia* and *nomoi* given to the Greek cities (in 146-5 B.C.; and cf. Paus. VIII.xxx.9). In V.iii I have mentioned the letter of Q. Fabius Maximus to Dyme in Achaea, after a revolutionary outbreak there towards the end of the second century B.C.: this refers twice to the *politeia* given to the Achaeans by Rome (*SIG*[3] 684 = A/J 9, lines 9-10, 19-20). Nevertheless, we must understand the statement of Pausanias which I have just quoted in a very qualified sense, as far as the destruction of democracy is concerned, for there is ample evidence of the continuing existence of constitutions at least nominally democratic in these cities: see e.g. Touloumakos, op. cit. 11 ff. In many cities all over the Greek world a system had already become fairly generally established before the Roman conquest whereby proposals had to be approved by some body of magistrates, even before being submitted to the Council and Assembly: see Jones, *GCAJ* 166 (with 337 n.22), 168-9 (with 338 n.26). This practice may have been extended (and it will at least have been encouraged) by the Romans: see ibid. 170 (with 338 n.28), 178-9 (with 340-1 nn.43-4), where most of the examples, as it happens, are from Asia.

Throughout the cities of mainland Greece and the Aegean islands, in the early Roman period, there is surprisingly little in the way of identifiable constitutional change that we can confidently attribute to deliberate action on the part of Rome. When, for example, we find from a famous inscription of Messene of the last century B.C. (*IG* V.i.1433, lines 11, 38) that some of those called τεχνῖται and all those called χειροτέχναι were outside the tribes composing the citizen body, and therefore cannot have been citizens at all in the proper sense, we need not suppose that the disfranchisement of these artisans was due to any outside pressure. (On this inscription and id. 1432, see the exhaustive commentary of A. Wilhelm, 'Urkunden aus Messene', in *JOAI* 17 (1914) 1-119, esp. 54-5, 69-70.) I believe that what we see if we take a very broad and general view of the political life of these cities is essentially a continuation of the process – sketched in V.iii above – that had already gone quite far under the Hellenistic kings: behind a usually democratic façade, with Council and Assembly passing decrees as in old times, the real power is in the hands of the propertied class; the common people rarely show any capacity to assert themselves or even to exercise influence. The Hellenistic kings had mainly been content to leave the cities alone, so long as they gave no trouble; but of course the very existence of the kings, dominating the eastern Mediterranean world, was a threat to democracy, which the kings at best tolerated, unless exceptional circumstances made them positively encourage it (like Alexander in the act of conquering Asia) or at any rate pretend to favour it or evince what could be interpreted – without any real justification – as sympathy towards the lower orders (like Perseus of Macedon, and Mithridates VI Eupator of Pontus). Rome too was quite prepared to tolerate Greek democratic constitutions as long as the Greeks kept quiet; but it must soon have become obvious that she would intervene to protect her 'friends' among the leading citizens if they were threatened from below – as, needless to say, they rarely were now. And this naturally led to a further concentration of power in the hands of the propertied class. After 146 B.C., when Rome was very much the mistress of the Mediterranean world, we hardly ever hear of any upsurge from below. The most remarkable, in Old Greece, was the Athenian revolutionary regime of 88-86 B.C., led by Athenian and Aristion, who of course are depicted as villainous tyrants in our surviving accounts.[5] And this movement could hardly have occurred but for the anti-Roman activities of Mithridates of Pontus in Asia Minor, which made many Greeks hope, vainly as it turned out, for an end to Roman dominance. The sack of Athens by Sulla and his army at the beginning of March 86, which put an end to the revolutionary movement,[6] must have had a severely discouraging effect on any other potential 'trouble-makers'. Yet there are indications of another upheaval at Athens in about A.D. 13. A good account of this neglected episode has recently been given by Bowersock, who sums up admirably: 'The leaders were executed; the affair is described variously as *res novae, stasis,* and *seditio*. These descriptions are perfectly compatible: when an anti-Roman faction gains the upper hand, *stasis* becomes revolt' (*AGW* 105-8, at 107). One wonders what action was taken in Thessaly when a man named Petraeus was burnt to death, probably during the principate of Augustus (Plut. *Mor.* 815d; and see C. P. Jones, *PR* 40-1 and n.7). In the *Historia Augusta* (*Ant. Pius* 5.5) there is a bare mention of an alleged *rebellio* in Greece in the reign of Pius: see VIII.iii above and its n.2 below.

Some oligarchic modifications may have been introduced into the constitution of Athens at the very end of the second century B.C. (see Bowersock, *AGW* 101-2, esp. 101 n.3), and it was perhaps this regime which Sulla restored after crushing the revolt of 88-86, for it is said that he made laws for Athens that were 'substantially the same as those previously established by the Romans' (App., *Mith.* 39: see Bowersock, *AGW* 106 n.2). There were further constitutional changes at Athens in the late Republic and early Principate (see Geagan, *ACS*); but a certain democratic façade was preserved, and the Assembly continued to meet and pass decrees until at least the late Severan period – one of the latest known is from *c.* 230: an honorific decree in favour of M. Ulpius Eubiotus Leurus (see V.iii above and its n.25). The Areopagus, however, had become the main political force, and there is no sign during the Principate of any real political activity in the Assembly, any more than in most other Greek states. At Athens, as elsewhere, we find much evidence of direct interference by the imperial power, through the provincial governor or even the emperor himself, yet sometimes we can see democratic institutions still permitted to function, as when a decree of Hadrian concerning oil production in Attica provides that certain breaches of the regulations there laid down are to be dealt with in the first place by trials in the Council if they involve no more than 50 amphorae and otherwise in the Assembly (*SEG* XV.108 = *IG* II².1100 = A/J 90, lines 46-9: see Oliver, *RP* 960-3; Day, *EHARD* 189-92); cf. A/J 91 = *IG* II².1103 (perhaps also Hadrianic), lines 7-8, providing for trial by the Areopagus of offences against certain commercial regulations. An interesting specimen of an imperial directive (whether it is an edict or a letter) from the Emperor Marcus Aurelius to the city of Athens (to be dated between 169 and 176) was published in 1970, with translation and commentary, by J. H. Oliver, *Marcus Aurelius: Aspects of Civic and Cultural Policy in the East* (= *Hesp.,* Suppl. 13). It has already excited a good deal of discussion and reinterpretation. I will only mention the improved restorations and translation by C. P. Jones, in *ZPE* 8 (1971) 161-83, of the largest plaque of the inscription (II = E), dealing mainly with judicial matters, and two subsequent articles: by Wynne Williams, in *ZPE* 17 (1975), at 37-56 (cf. *JRS* 66 [1976] 78-9), and by Simone Follet, in *Rev. de phil.* 53 (1979) 29-43, with a complete text and French translation of the same portion. Marcus expresses his great 'concern for the reputation of Athens, so that she may recover her former dignity' (or 'grandeur', σεμνότης). Although he feels obliged to allow the sons of freedmen born after their fathers' manumission – not freedmen themselves – to become ordinary councillors (lines 79-81, 97-102), he insists that members of the Areopagus must have both parents born in freedom (lines 61-6); and he expresses the fond wish that it were possible to reinstate the 'ancient custom' whereby Areopagites had to have not only fathers but also grandfathers of free birth (lines 57-61). Obsession of this kind with the status of members of the local Athenian governing class may excite our derision when its professed object is to enable Athens to 'recover her former σεμνότης'!

The Athenian constitution under the Roman Principate presents many puzzles, and there are several questions I feel obliged to leave open, merely referring to the recent discussion by Geagan (*ACS*), the useful review of that work by Pleket, in *Mnem.*[4] 23 (1970) 451-3, and the monograph by Oliver (with modifications) mentioned in the preceding paragraph. It may be that (as undoubtedly at Alexandria: *C. P. Jud.* II.153.53-7; 150.3-4; and see Fraser, *PA* I.76-8) participation in the ephebia, available of course only to the well-to-do, had become an essential qualification for membership of the category of fully privileged citizens who alone were qualified for the Council (now much more capable of independent action than in the Classical period) and perhaps the courts (see pp.64-5 of Oliver's monograph), and who may (as tentatively suggested by Geagan, *ACS* 86-7) have been the same group as those who alone were entitled to speak in the Assembly as well as attend its sessions and vote in them (cf. the treatment of Tarsus in § 3B of this Appendix); the latter group may be the same as those referred to as οἱ ἐκκλησιάζοντες κατὰ τὰ νομ[ιζόμενα] in line 18 of a letter to Athens from Marcus and Commodus, now best read as Oliver's inscription no.4, pp.85 ff. (cf. the ἐκκλησιασταί in two Pisidian cities, mentioned in § 3B below). There may have been a property qualification for those entitled to become councillors; but equally it may have been felt that no quantitative assessment was necessary, having regard to the fact that going through the ephebia (if that was indeed a necessary qualification for the exercise of full political rights) would be possible only for the sons of men of some property. There is unfortunately some uncertainty about all these matters: the epigraphic texts are not absolutely decisive, and it is hard to say how much of the intriguing evidence provided by Lucian (e.g. in *Deor. conc.* 1, 14-19; *Iupp. trag.* 6, 7, 18, 26; *Demon.* 11; *Gall.* 22; *Nec.* 19-20; *Navig.* 24; *Bis. accus.* 4, 12) we can treat as accurately reflecting contemporary practice.[7]

In many other Greek cities some of the old constitutional forms were preserved, even when they had become an empty shell. The Council of Carystus on Euboea was actually chosen annually by lot as late as the reign of Hadrian: see *IG* XII.ix.11. In Sparta, surprisingly enough at first sight, there was at least one change in a direction opposite to what we might have expected: the traditional Gerousia, consisting of men over 60 who were elected for the rest of their lives, seems to have become transformed, apparently by at least the last century B.C., into a Council of normal Greek type (sometimes actually called ἁ βουλά), consisting of men elected annually, with re-election possible: see W. Kolbe in *IG* V.i, p.37 (commentary on nos. 92-122); K. M. T. Chrimes, *Ancient Sparta* (Manchester, 1949) 138-48. But I think Chrimes may well be right in ascribing the change to Cleomenes III, in the 220s B.C. According to Pausanias III.xi.2, the Gerousia in his day was the συνέδριον Λακεδαιμονίοις κυριώτατον τῆς πολιτείας.

City Assemblies long continued, but there is no reliable literary evidence of genuine political activity on their part during the Principate (as there is for some of the cities of Asia Minor), and nearly all the inscriptions which survive record honorific decrees. The latest definitely datable decree from Greece or the islands known to Swoboda, when he published *Die griechischen Volksbeschlüsse* in 1890, was the one now republished as *IG* XII.vii.53, from Arcesine on the island of Amorgos, which was passed on 11 December 242, in the reign of Gordian III, an honorific *psēphisma* of the *dēmos* of that city (Swoboda, op. cit. 185, was mistaken in referring this decree to Aigiale, another city of Amorgos). I know of no definitely datable later material from the area with which I am concerned here; but there are one or two known meetings of Greek Assemblies half a century later, from Asia Minor (as we shall see in § 3B below) and Egypt (cf. V.iii above).

I must add a word about the Balkans, an area in which city life was slow to develop except in a few centres. There is at least one Macedonian community which is proved by a very interesting inscription dated as late as A.D. 194 to have had an ἐκκλησία, πολεῖται, and at least one magistrate (with a title often found in Macedonian cities), a πολειτάρχης, but almost certainly no βουλή – for the Assembly was summoned by the *poleitarch*; instructions for carrying out the decree (the operative part of which begins ἔδοξε τῶι τε πολειτάρχηι καὶ τοῖς πολείταις ὁμογνωμονοῦσι) are given to the *poleitarch*; and he and a number of others are listed by name at the end of the decree; but there is no sign of a Council. The inscription, first published in 1880, was republished in a much improved form by A. M. Woodward in *JHS* 33 (1913) 337-46, no.17. (It has not, I think, been republished since.) The community is not identifiable, but it may, as suggested by Woodward, be Erattyna, perhaps the place called Eratyra by Strabo VII.vii.8, p.326. In spite of the 'citizens' and their *poleitarch* (proved by lines 24-5 to be an annual magistrate), I am not entirely satisfied that this community was a proper *polis*, as assumed by Woodward and others (including Rostovtzeff, *SEHRE*² II.651 n.97). The alternative is to regard it either as a smaller political unit within the *ethnos* (referred to in line 33 in connection with an embassy to the provincial governor, to obtain his authorisation of the decree), as believed by Larsen and others (see Frank, *ESAR* IV.443-4), or as the *ethnos* itself. As Rostovtzeff says of Macedonia, 'The impression one gains is that the economic backbone of the country continued to be the native tribes and the numerous villages, particularly the mountain villages, of peasants and shepherds' (*SEHRE*² I.253). I wonder if perhaps the community on the site of the modern Sandanski in Bulgaria, in the valley of the Strymon (now the Struma), also in Macedonia, was not yet a full *polis* in A.D. 158, the date at which Antoninus Pius sent a letter to it, part of which was recently found in an inscription, *IGBulg*. IV.2263 (referred to in V.iii above and its n.26). It has been assumed that Pius was merely authorising an increase in the number of councillors (lines 8-12); but may he not have been referring to the creation of a Council, as part of the formal inception of a true *polis*? At any rate, the inscription published by Woodward should warn us to be prepared for possible variations from the usual pattern of *polis* development, as late as the beginning of the Severan period: that is why I have devoted some attention to it.

In the section of this Appendix dealing with Asia Minor (§ 3B below) I shall have occasion to refer to a distinction, in the Roman period, between citizens who were entitled to participate fully in the general Assembly of a city, and who in at least two cases, Pogla and Sillyum in Pisidia, are called ἐκκλησιασταί (cf. perhaps οἱ ἐκκλησιάζοντες κατὰ τὰ νομ[ιζόμενα] at Athens, mentioned above), and an inferior category who evidently did not enjoy full rights in the Assembly, although at the two Pisidian cities they are called πολεῖται. The existence of these grades in Asia may help us to understand an inscription of the Antonine period from Histria in the Dobrudja, where Aba, an outstanding female benefactor of the city (who may remind us of Menodora of Sillyum: see the main text of III.vi above, just after its n.35, and § 3B below), bestows a series of gifts on various different categories of inhabitants. Councillors, members of the Gerousia and certain other groups head Aba's list: they receive 2 denarii each and must also have shared in the distribution of wine (οἰνοπόσιον) which was to be given to various less dignified categories, including 'those in the tribes (φυλαί) who are organised in groups of fifty (πεντηκονταρχίαι)'. In subsequent lines of the inscription (37-43) which cannot be restored with any confidence there are references to ὁ δῆμος and τὸ πλῆθος. The inscription was published by Em. Popescu, in *Dacia* n.s.4 (1960) 273-96; but it is best read in the slightly revised edition by H. W. Pleket, *Epigraphica* II (= *Textus Minores* XLI, Leiden, 1969), no.21, making use of the observations of J. and L. Robert in *REG* 75 (1962) 190-1, no.239. I am inclined to agree with the acute observations of Pleket, in his review of Duncan-Jones, *EREQS*, in *Gnomon* 49 (1977) 55-63, at pp.62-3, that 'those organised in *phylai* in groups of 50' are perhaps to be identified with the category of privileged citizens who have the right to participate fully in the Assembly at Tarsus, at Pogla and Sillyum, and possibly at Athens, and who are distinguished, in the two Pisidian cities, from plain πολῖται. (Pleket goes on to compare the Histrian *phylai* with the African *curiae* discussed by Duncan-Jones and others.)

3. Asia Minor

An episode of the very greatest interest to the historian is a revolt which took place in western Asia Minor at the very time when it began to pass under Roman rule. Attalus III, the last king of Pergamum, died in 133 B.C., leaving his kingdom by will to Rome. The gift was accepted by the Roman Senate. Aristonicus, a bastard son of King Eumenes II, claimed to be the heir of Attalus, and led a large-scale revolt which was not crushed until 129. This subject has been much discussed in recent years, and very different views have been put forward concerning the character of the revolt. There is still no general agreement on how far it should be considered primarily as a movement of the poor, with the slaves and serfs, a protest against the existing social order (and even 'a slave revolt'), how far it was a 'nationalist' or anti-Roman rising, and what precisely was the role of Aristonicus himself. I have nothing new to say on the subject, the best account of which seems to me the most recent one, that of Vladimir Vavřínek, 'Aristonicus of Pergamum: pretender to the throne or leader of a slave revolt?', in *Eirene* 13 (1975) 109-29. Vavřínek, who had himself produced a book on the revolt in French nearly twenty years earlier (*La Révolte d'Aristonicos*, Prague, 1957), gives an excellent review of the whole range of theories, including those of Börner, Carrata Thomes, Dumont, and Vogt.[8] Those who cannot easily obtain Vavřínek's article and wish for a brief account of this subject would perhaps do best to read Rostovtzeff, *SEHHW* II.805-26, especially 807-11 (with III.1521-8 nn.75-99), and Vogt (as cited in n.8). I will only add, for the specialist, a very useful article by C. P. Jones, 'Diodoros Pasparos and the Nikephoria of Pergamon', in *Chiron* 4 (1974) 183-205, demonstrating that the activities of Diodorus Pasparus of Pergamum were associated not (as used to be believed) with the war of Aristonicus but rather with the Mithridatic wars from the eighties to the sixties B.C.

I have already referred, in the introductory part of this Appendix and in its § 1 (and shall revert in § 5 below) to the bodies of Roman residents in various Greek cities. It is particularly in Asia Minor, and above all in the province of Asia itself, that we know of their presence and activities, mainly through inscriptions. The evidence for Asia Minor, and much of the modern literature, is given by Magie, *RRAM* I.162-3 (with II.1051-3 nn.5-13), 254-6 (with II.1129-30 nn.51-6); II.1291-2 n.44; and see II.1615-16 for a list of some forty cities in Asia Minor where *conventus civium Romanorum* were known down to 1950. Among much further information that has come to light since Magie wrote is a decree of Chios referring to οἱ παρεπιδημοῦντες ʿΡωμαίων (line 20), to be dated hardly later than 188 B.C. (or just afterwards), and thus much earlier than any of Magie's examples: see Th. Ch. Sarikakes, 'Οἱ ἐν Χίῳ παρεπιδημοῦντες ʿΡωμαῖοι', in Χιακὰ Χρονικά (1975) 14-27, with text p.19; Ronald Mellor, Θεὰ ʿΡώμη. *The Worship of the Goddess Roma in the Greek world* (= *Hypomnemata* 42, Göttingen, 1975) 60-1; on the date, cf. also J. and L. Robert, in *REG* 78 (1965) 146-7 no.305 (the decree 'doit dater d'après la paix d'Apamée'); F. W. Walbank, in *JRS* 53 (1963) 3; W. G. Forrest, cited in *SEG* XVI.486 as advocating a late-third-century date.

A. *Bithynia-Pontus*

Here we have to take account above all of the *Lex Pompeia*, known mainly from Pliny's correspondence with Trajan in *c.* 110-12 (Pliny, *Ep.* X.79. 1,4; 112.1; 114.1-3; 115; cf. Dio Cass. XXXVII.xx.2), which was still in force in the early second century, as slightly modified by Augustus. The *Lex Pompeia* embodied the settlement effected by Pompey in 64–3 B.C. after his victory over Mithridates of Pontus. (For its nature, see Sherwin-White, *LP* 669–73, 718, 720, 721, 724–5; Jones, *CERP*² 156–62.) For our present purposes, the most important provisions of the *Lex Pompeia* were that there was to be a minimum age of 30 for holding a magistracy or becoming a councillor; that councillors were to achieve that status by being enrolled by officials whom Pliny calls *censores* (the actual title in Greek was τιμηταί); and that ex-magistrates must automatically be enrolled, although eligibility was not confined to them. Augustus reduced the age for certain minor magistracies to 22. Pliny reports to Trajan a local opinion, which he seems to share (it must have been the opinion of the leading families, with whom he would associate), that it was 'necessary' to continue a practice that had grown up, of enrolling some young men aged between 22 and 30 as councillors, even though they had held no magistracy. And he adds a remark of great interest, giving the reason for this opinion: that it is 'much better to choose the sons of members of the upper classes for the Council rather than men from the lower orders' (*honestorum hominum liberos quam e plebe, Ep.* X.79.3). From this statement three conclusions inevitably follow: (1) the young men whom it was considered desirable to enrol as councillors were already members of what we may now begin to call 'curial families' (those which had members serving on the Council); (2) but these young men were reluctant to fill one of the magistracies which would automatically have led to a seat on the Council, surely because of the expense involved; and (3) there were men of sufficient means outside the circle of curial families who could have filled a magistracy and thereby qualified themselves for a seat on the Council, had the local curial families not objected to this broadening of their circle. (Trajan, incidentally, told Pliny that no one under 30 ought to become a member of a local Council, except through holding a magistracy.) In this connection I must also mention another letter of Pliny's, referring to the issue of invitations for certain entertainments to 'the whole Council and even no small number from the lower classes' (*totam bulen atque etiam e plebe non exiguum numerum*): here again we see the emergence of a group of families of curial status, distinguished from the *plebs* (*Ep.* X.116.1) – an early stage in the development of a fundamental division soon to be given constitutional recognition in various ways (see VIII.i–ii above).

There is no proof of a property qualification for councillors (or magistrates) in the *Lex Pompeia*, but some would infer the existence of one from Pliny, *Ep.* X.110.2; cf. 58.5 and I.19.2 (see Sherwin-White, *LP* 720).

The *censores* (τιμηταί) charged with the task of enrolling the councillors of the cities of Bithynia and Pontus (Pliny, *Ep.* X.79.3; 112.1,2; 114.1) are officials who do not seem to have turned up yet elsewhere in Asia Minor, except as τιμηταί at Aphrodisias and Pergamum and as βουλογράφοι at Ancyra (see section B below). We find τιμηταί in Bithynia, at Prusa (LB/W 1111), Prusias ad Hypium (*SEG* XIV.773.13–14 and 774.8; *IGRR* III.60.13, 64.6, 66.7; *BCH* 25 [1901] 61–5 no.207.10), Dia (*BCH* 25 [1901] 54–5 no.198.6), and a βουλογράφος at Nicaea (*IGRR* III.1397.11, of A.D. 288–9, as restored by L. Robert in *BCH* 52 [1928] 410–11).

As always, we must be prepared to find exceptional procedures on occasion, as when Trajan allowed Prusa to elect no fewer than 100 councillors, evidently in the Assembly (Dio Chrys. XLV.3,7,9–10).

We know of no special rules in the *Lex Pompeia* regarding the Assemblies or the courts of the Greek cities; and this subject can be treated for Asia Minor as a whole under *B* below, where I shall also occasionally deal with matters that affect the whole area, such as obtaining the provincial governor's authorisation of certain decrees, and his power to suspend Assemblies.

B. *The rest of Asia Minor*

As early as Cicero's speech for Flaccus in 59 B.C. it seems that the Councils of some Greek cities in the province of Asia were already permanent bodies, the members of which were enrolled for life: Cicero actually speaks only of Temnus, in the Hermus valley, but the form of words he uses may suggest that the kind of Council he had in mind was not limited to that city (*Pro Flacc.* 42-3). Jones goes too far, however, when he generalises for this period from Temnus to 'the Asiatic cities' collectively (*CERP*² 61); and he himself realises that the Councils of some 'free cities', in particular Rhodes and its former dependency Stratonicea in Caria, and also Mylasa, long continued to change periodically – those at Rhodes and Stratonicea every six months. For the evidence, it will be sufficient to refer, for Rhodes and Stratonicea, to Magie, *RRAM* II.834 n.18; for Mylasa, see LB/W 406; *BCH* 12 (1888) 20-1 no.7. I know of no literary evidence for such a system, except perhaps Dio Chrys. XXXIV.34-6, from which it appears that the *prytaneis* at Tarsus in Dio's day served for six months only.

The evidence for the growth in Asia Minor of a 'curial order' (which by at least the early third century was substantially a curial *class*: see VIII.ii above), is almost purely epigraphic, apart from Pliny's correspondence with Trajan concerning Bithynia-Pontus, noticed in *A* above. The inscriptions concerned rarely enable us to generalise, even for a particular area, and I shall make no attempt to summarise them here. Perhaps it will be sufficient if I select one batch of inscriptions from Lycia, which show that during the second century the common folk, δημόται, were a recognisably distinct category from the βουλευταί (as at Sidyma, A.D. 185-92: *TAM* II.176 = *IGRR* III.597-8, with *TAM* II.175), or from οἱ φ' at Oenoanda (*IGRR* III.492), doubtless the same as οἱ πεντακόσιοι at nearby Termessus Minor, who receive 10 denarii each at a distribution when the δημόται get only 2 denarii each (*BCH* 24 [1900] 338-41 no.1.25-7). At Xanthus we encounter claims to descent from a father, grandfather and other ancestors who are described as βουλευταί (*TAM* II.305; and 303 = *IGRR* III.626; *TAM* II.308 refers to a father who was βουλευτής at Pinara too). It seems to be the same category, of councillors, which is referred to at Bubon as the τάξις of the πρωτεύοντες of the city (*IGRR* III.464), at Balbura as τάξις ἡ πρωτεύουσα or οἱ πρῶτοι ἐν πό[λει] (*CIG* III.4380e,f) and at Phaselis as τὸ πρῶτον τάγμα τῆς πόλεως (*TAM* II.1202; and 1200 = *IGRR* III.764). At Xanthus, too, an athlete who is being honoured in *TAM* II.301 = *IGRR* III.623 is described in lines 3-7 as the son of an ἀνδρὸς ἐπισήμου βουλευτοῦ τελέσαντος ἀρχάς, δημοτικὴν μὲν μίαν, βουλευτικὰς δὲ πάσας (cf. Jones, *GCAJ* 180, with 342 n.47). And in other parts of Asia Minor we discover references to a curial order, as at Iotapa in Cilicia in the 170s (*IGRR* III.833 b.4-5: βουλευτι[κ]ο[ῦ τάγματ]ος; cf. a.2: [τάγματ]ος [βουλευτικοῦ]). Sometimes we find men boasting of descent from ancestors who were not merely councillors but magistrates (see Jones, *GCAJ* 175).

Outside Bithynia-Pontus (see *A* above) evidence does not seem to have come to light of Councils being enrolled by the Greek equivalent of Roman *censores*, except at Ancyra in Galatia, where the officials concerned are called βουλογράφοι (*AE* [1937] 89; *IGRR* III.206, and 179 = *OGIS* II.549), and at two cities in the province of Asia, where (as in Bithynia-Pontus) they are τιμηταί: Aphrodisias (*REG* 19 [1906] 274-6 no.169.2: τοῦ τειμητοῦ) and Pergamum (*IGRR* IV.445-6; *Ath. Mitt.* 32 [1907] 329 no.60). Elsewhere they probably came to be elected more and more generally by the Council itself, by co-optation (cf. § 1 above on Sicily). The statement by Hadrian, in a much-quoted letter of A.D. 129 to Ephesus, asking it to elect his *protégé* L. Erastus as a councillor, is sometimes taken to provide evidence of popular election there, because when the emperor promises to pay the fee required from a new councillor on election he says he will pay it [τῆς ἀρχαι]ρεσίας [ἕ]νεκα (*SIG*³ 838 = A/J 85, line 14). However, since the letter is addressed not to the Demos of Ephesus but to the magistrates and Council only (line 5), I would infer that there was no real participation by the Assembly in the election. Nowhere, as far as I am aware, do we hear of a property qualification for membership of a Council; but, especially as being a magistrate and councillor came more and more to involve the expenditure of money, the non-propertied were automatically excluded in practice (cf. VIII.i-ii above).

It would, I think, be universally agreed that election of councillors and of magistrates from below had ceased everywhere, or virtually everywhere, before the end of the second century, and that those Councils which were not enrolled by 'censors' appointed their own members by co-optation. Where the Assembly joins in, it is merely to ratify a *fait accompli*: I would thus explain the inscription from Smyrna, apparently of the early third century, which refers to the election of a principal ταμίας and his (six) colleagues κατὰ τὴν τοῦ δήμου χειροτονίαν (*CIG* II.3162, lines 16-19).

For admission to the Assembly, at least as a full member, property qualifications were evidently sometimes imposed in one way or another. The example most frequently quoted is Tarsus, where a fee of 500 drachmae was exacted – too large, according to Dio Chrysostom (XXXIV.21-3), for the linen-workers who formed a substantial section of the lower classes but remained (as Dio puts it) 'as it were outside the constitution' (ὥσπερ ἔξοθεν τῆς πολιτείας, § 21), being regarded as foreigners (δοκοῦντες ἀλλότριοι, § 22) and suffering some form of ἀτιμία (§ 21), which apparently did not extend to dyers, shoe-makers or carpenters as such (§ 23). From the way Dio speaks (§ 21), it seems that the linen-workers were permitted to be present at the Assembly: we must surely suppose, however, that, as non-citizens, they could neither speak nor vote there. In two cities of Pisidia, namely Pogla (A/J 122 = *IGRR* III.409) and Sillyum, men known as ἐκκλησιασταί are distinguished from ordinary πολεῖται (as well as from βουλευταί), and at Sillyum they receive far larger sums than πολεῖται under the foundation of Menodora (*IGRR* III.800-1, cf. 802). Presumably the officials referred to as πολιτογράφοι in inscriptions had the duty of keeping the necessary registers (for examples, see Magie, *RRAM* II.1503 n.26). Here again (cf. the portions of § 2 of this Appendix dealing with Athens and Histria) we have examples of the division of the permanent residents in a Greek city into graded categories, with only a limited number entitled to exercise even the right of participating fully in the general Assembly.

Sometimes we find decrees passed not only by a Council and Assembly but also by the body of resident Roman citizens. At Phrygian Apamea (in the province of Asia), for example, a number of honorary decrees open with the words ἡ βουλὴ καὶ ὁ δῆμος καὶ οἱ κατοικοῦντες Ῥωμαῖοι ἐτείμησαν (*IGRR* IV.779, 785-6, 788-91, 793-4); in one case the words ἀγομένης πανδήμου ἐκκλησίας are added (id. 791.5-6). In other cities too we find ὁ δῆμος joined with οἱ πραγματευόμενοι Ῥωμαῖοι, e.g. at Assus (*IGRR* IV.248), Cibyra (id. 903-5, 913, 916-19), and elsewhere.

The Assembly had ceased by at any rate the middle of the second century to have any political importance. It is now convoked and presided over by magistrates without whose consent nothing can be proposed and who usually appear as the authors of motions, with some such phrase as πρυτανέων (or στρατηγῶν) γνώμη, and with the concurrence of the Council. I agree with Isidore Lévy that we have to recognise 'l'efface-ment de la notion des droits du peuple souverain. L'affaiblissement de l'ecclesia, ou plutôt son annihilation, tel est, à l'époque Antonine, le phénomène capital de la vie constitution-nelle de la cité grecque. L'assemblée populaire est non seulement impuissante, mais résignée à l'impuissance, devant les usurpations de tout genre qui achèvent de la dépouiller' (EVMAM I.218, concluding the best account I have found of the degenera-tion of the Assemblies of the Greek cities of Asia, ibid. 205-18).

I would also draw attention to an excellent passage in Jones, *GCAJ* 179 (cf. 340-1 n.44), containing much interesting evidence):

> Under the Principate the formal mover of a decree, if put on record at all, is almost invariably a magistrate or group of magistrates, and private members of the Council are stated merely to 'introduce the proposal' and to 'request a vote' on it, processes which were apparently pre-liminary to the formal motion: in a number of cases the introducer and his seconder, if he may be so called, are alone recorded, but in these it is probably assumed that the magistrates moved. Decrees of the people moved by private persons are recorded only at Athens and Delphi, both free cities . . . The evidence thus points strongly to the conclusion that it was the universal practice,

outside a few free cities where democratic tradition was strong, that magistrates should propose decrees, and that private members of the Council should confine themselves to introducing proposals. This uniformity of practice, however, hardly justifies the assumption that magistrates alone had the right of moving decrees.

Isidore Lévy, writing in 1895, could find no single example in the second century of that hallmark of activity initiated in the Assembly itself: an amendment of a decree (EVMAM I.212), and I know of no evidence discovered since Lévy's time.

I think it would be safe to say that by the third century, even when decrees still use traditional formulae like ἔδοξεν τῆι βουλῆι καὶ τῶι δήμωι, the Assembly of no Greek city should be regarded as having played any greater part than merely assenting by acclamation to decisions taken by the magistrates and/or the Council. From about the middle of the second century onwards, inscriptions recording decisions in which an Assembly participates will sometimes use a word signifying merely 'acclamation': e.g ἐπεφώνησαν (Tyre), ἐβόησαν (Chalcis), ἐξεβόησαν; and cf. OGIS 515 (= A/J 133), an inscription of about A.D. 210 from Mylasa in Caria, where in line 55 we find the corresponding Latin term 'succlam(atum) est'. In the long series of inscriptions from Rhodiapolis in Lycia, recording the munificence of Opramoas, we find e.g. ἡ κρατίστ«η» τοῦ ἔθνους βουλὴ ἐπεβοήσατο τὸ ψήφισμα διαγραφῆναι (TAM II.905, § 45, XII B.3–5 [= IGRR III.739]); cf. ἐπιβόησις (in the singular and plural) in e.g. ibid. § 16, IV G.13; § 43, XII A.2. And see Jean Colin, op. cit. (in V.iii n.41 below) 112-16, for 'les divers vocables grecs de l'ἐπιβόησις'. For a long list of similar expressions in Latin, see W. Liebenam, *Städteverwaltung im römischen Kaiserreiche* (Leipzig, 1900) 248 n.1.

And in the very latest record of a decree of a Greek Assembly that I have been able to discover (with the possible exception of the one from Oxyrhynchus, in P.Oxy. I.41, quoted in V.iii above), from Antioch in Pisidia, we again find, written in Latin in the middle of a Greek inscription (unfortunately very fragmentary), the words 'suclam(atum) [est]' (fr. i.5). This inscription must record a decree of the Assembly, since it almost certainly refers to a ψ[ήφισμα] (fr. i.11), entered in the Minutes (ὑπομνημάτων, fr. f.12), with a copy deposited in the archives ([ἀν]τιγράφου ἀποκειμένου, fr. f.13), and in fr. a.2 we have [κ]αὶ δήμω[ι] and in fr. f.11 [τ]ῆς βουλῆς καὶ τ[οῦ δήμου]. Anderson, who published the inscription in *JRS* 3 (1913) 284-7, no.11, takes the appearance of the word [Κ]αίσαρες in fr. h.3 as an indication of a date 'not much earlier than about A.D. 295'. I think we can indeed date the document during the Tetrarchy, in the years following March 293. (I owe my knowledge of this inscription to Barbara Levick, whose interest in Pisidian Antioch is well shown in her book, *Roman Colonies in Southern Asia Minor*, 1967.)

Evidently in some cases it was essential for a city to have a decree of its Council and/or Assembly ratified by the provincial governor. J. H. Oliver, 'The Roman governor's permission for a decree of the polis', in *Hesp.* 23 (1954) 163-7, has discussed this question, citing six decrees (four from Ephesus and one each from Sidyma and Smyrna) which bear on this question; cf. Magie, *RRAM* I.641-2; II.1504 n.29, 1506 n.32. Among other decrees, I would add the one published by Woodward in 1913, discussed near the end of § 2 above. Plutarch, in a passage I have quoted in V.iii above, deplored the practice of referring to the governor even minor matters, for which the governor's approval was clearly not a constitutional necessity: he points out that this obliges the governors to become the δεσπόται of the cities beyond the degree they themselves desire.

Revolutionary activity, of course, was almost inconceivable: it could have no chance of success, and I do not even know of any surviving evidence that it was attempted, although we do occasionally hear of food riots, as in Dio Chrysostom's Bithynia (see V.iii above), and of an occasional unexplained outbreak of violence, as when Petraeus was burnt alive in Thessaly (see § 2 above). An inscription like that of Cibyra in honour of Q. Veranius Philagrus (mentioned in V.iii above), with its mysterious reference to the suppression of a very harmful 'conspiracy', may or may not betoken active discontent on the part of the non-privileged; it may equally well refer to some factional struggle involving mainly the interests of a dissatisfied element among the local propertied class.

4. Cyprus

Cyprus was first annexed by Rome in 58 B.C. and attached to the province of Cilicia. (The letters written by Cicero during his governorship of the joint province in 51-50 B.C., some of which relate to Cyprus, are among our most informative sources for Roman provincial administration during the late Republic.) From 48 onwards Cyprus was put under client rulers of the Ptolemaic royal house, but after Actium it was again annexed, and it was made a province on its own in 22 B.C. (Dio Cass. LIII.xii.7; LIV.iv.1) or perhaps rather 23 B.C. (see Shelagh Jameson, '22 or 23?' in *Historia* 18 [1969] 204-29, at p.227).

I know of only two clear pieces of evidence about innovations in the constitution of any Cypriot city which can with confidence be attributed to Roman influence. Both are inscriptions referring to men who had occupied the position of τιμητής (*censor*; cf. § 3*A* above). One, from Cyprian Salamis, of the reign of Nero, describes its honorand as τιμητεύσα[ς]: see T. B. Mitford and I. K. Nicolaou, *Salamis,* Vol.6: *The Greek and Latin Inscriptions from Salamis* (Nicosia, 1974), 24-6, no.11, line 5. In the other inscription, from Soli, also of the first century, the honorand is described as τιμητεύσας, τὴν βουλὴν [κατα]λέξας: see T. B. Mitford, in *BSA* 42 (1947) 201-6 no.1, lines 9-10 (rather than *IGRR* III.930).

It seems to me quite possible that it was Augustus who provided for the enrolment of councillors in Cyprian cities by an official corresponding to the Roman *censor*. This innovation cannot be dated, but it may conceivably be connected with the sending to Cyprus by Augustus, for a second and extraordinary proconsulship (probably in the last two decades B.C.) of P. Paquius Scaeva, 'procos. iterum extra sortem auctoritate Aug. Caesaris et s.c. missus ad componendum statum in reliquum provinciae Cypri' (*ILS* 915 = *CIL* IX.2845).

5. Cyrenaica (and Crete)

I have already mentioned (in V.iii above; and see its n.8) the very interesting constitution dictated to Cyrene by Ptolemy I, probably in 322/1 B.C. For the subsequent very chequered history of Cyrenaica down to its organisation as a Roman province I will merely refer to Jones, *CERP*[2] 356-60, with 496-7 nn.10-14. (This part of *CERP*[2] was revised with the help of Joyce M. Reynolds.) Before Rome took over there was evidently a good deal of interference by the Ptolemaic rulers (see id. 358, with 497 n.13; add Jean Machu, in *RH* 205 [1951] 41-55). Although bequeathed to Rome by the will of Ptolemy Apion (a bastard son of Ptolemy VII Euergetes II), who died in 96 B.C., Cyrenaica was not organised as a Roman province until at least 75-74 and perhaps even later (see the works cited in Jones, *CERP*[2] 497 n.12; contrast W. V. Harris, *War and Imperialism in Republican Rome 327-70 B.C.* (1979) 154,267). After further changes, it finally became part of the province of Crete and Cyrenaica under Augustus.

There is hardly any evidence for political conditions in the cities, apart from a brief statement by Strabo, preserved by Josephus (*AJ* XIV.114-15), to the effect that Cyrene itself contained four categories of inhabitants: citizens, farmers (γεωργοί),[9] metics and Jews (a privileged class of metics).[10] From this we can infer that in the early years of the first century the old native rural population did not enjoy the citizenship of Cyrene (and see Rostovtzeff, *SEHRE*[2] I.309-10). I myself do not believe that it had ever done so, as I cannot accept the theory that the περίοικοι of Hdts IV.161.3 were native Libyans, in spite of the advocacy of this theory by such scholars as A. H. M. Jones (*CERP*[2] 351, 359; cf. 497 n.13 *ad fin.*), Busolt, and Larsen. See the discussion by F. Chamoux, *Cyrène sous la monarchie des Battiades* (Paris, 1953) 221-4, and the interesting suggestions made more recently by L. H. Jeffery, 'The pact of the first settlers at Cyrene', in *Historia* 10 (1961) 139-47, at 142-4.

There are a few scraps of information from inscriptions found on the sites of other cities in Cyrenaica. In *SEG* XVIII.772, a proxeny decree of 350-320 B.C. from Euhesperides, we find the Ephors and Gerontes introducing a proposal to the Council, evidently the ruling body, for the decree opens with the words, ἐφόρων καὶ γερόντων ἐπαγόντων, ἆδε τᾶι βωλᾶι, and there is no sign of a general Assembly. Similarly, we have a recently published decree, almost certainly of the second or the fairly early first century B.C., from the modern Tocra (Taucheira or Teucheira, known in the Ptolemaic period as Arsinoe), which was passed by the Gerontes and Council (there being 109 votes in favour), with a mention of other magistrates (Ephors and Tamiai) but not of an Assembly: see Joyce M. Reynolds, 'A civic decree from Tocra in Cyrenaica', in *Arch. Class.* 25/26 (1973/74) 622-30; cf. L. Moretti, 'Un decreto di Arsinoe in Cirenaica', in *RF* 104 (1976) 385-98, esp. 389 (on πόλιας in line 13). I would draw attention to lines 11-14 of the Tocra inscription, praising the honorand for the way he had conducted himself ποτὶ τὸς ὄχλος [κ]αι πόλιας, and the words ἐπὶ τῶν ὄχλων σωτηρίαν in lines 53-4: here we find a non-pejorative use of the term ὄχλος (in the plural because, presumably, the man's generosity had not been confined to Tocra), which occurs also in some village inscriptions of Asia Minor and Syria: see IV.ii above and its n.35 below. Even if, with Moretti, we keep πόλιας in line 13 (as I think we probably should), and still more if, with Reynolds, we emend to πολίτας, we shall be justified in finding in Cyrenaica, as in other areas, a privileged class of full citizens, contrasted with a larger number of others (the ὄχλοι) who had no political rights, or only very limited ones.

In the period of Roman rule one famous series of documents stands out: the inscription recording five edicts of Augustus dating from 7/6 to 4 B.C.: E/J²311 = *FIRA*² I no.68 = *SEG* IX.8; cf. XIV.888; XVI.866; XVIII.728; and see esp. F. De Visscher, *Les édits d' Auguste découverts à Cyrène* (Louvain, 1940); cf. the long review by L. Wenger, in *ZSS*, Röm. Abt., 62 (1942) 425-36; and De Visscher's later article, 'La justice romaine en Cyrénaïque', in *RIDA*³ 11 (1964) 321-33; also Jolowicz and Nicholas, *HISRL*³ 71-4. For our present purposes it is the first and fourth of these edicts which are relevant. Both demonstrate the participation of resident Romans in lawsuits at Cyrene. The first shows that when Roman judges had been chosen, they had been taken only from Romans with a census of at least 2,500 denarii, of whom there were 215 in Cyrenaica in 7/6 B.C. The same edict also affords evidence of complaints by the local Greeks of unjust behaviour on the part of Roman judges. Augustus gives to Greeks accused on capital charges the right to choose whether to be tried by Roman judges or by an equal number (twenty-five each) of Romans and Greeks, both Romans and Greeks to be drawn from those with a census of at least 7,500 denarii, or, if there are too few men with such a qualification, then at least half that figure. The fourth edict leaves it to the provincial governor to decide whether to take capital cases himself or to have them tried as specified in the first edict, and adds that in non-capital cases the judges are to be Greeks unless a defendant or accused prefers to have Romans. (I omit some minor provisions.)

★ ★ ★ ★ ★ ★

I do not propose to treat Crete separately. However, there is one passage of exceptional interest which we cannot afford to miss: Strabo X.iv.22, p.484. At the end of his very muddled and inadequate account of Cretan institutions, derived mainly from Ephorus (and therefore very much out of date), Strabo adds that not many of these νόμιμα still exist, but that Crete is 'mainly administered by the διατάγματα of the Romans, as happens in the other provinces'! (It is with this text that Swoboda, *GV* 176, opens the ninth chapter of his book on the decrees of Greek Assemblies: 'Veränderungen unter dem Einflusse der Römer'.)

6. Massalia

Of Massalia it is only necessary for me to say that the famous 'aristocratic' constitution, as we know it from the early Principate, was not a product of Roman influence but an indigenous growth.[11] In the time of Aristotle, who wrote a *Constitution of Massalia* (see his fr. 549), it was not a democracy: two passages in the *Politics*, taken together, show that an extreme oligarchy had merely become more moderate (V.6, 1305^{b}2-10; VI.7, 1321^{a}26-31). By 197 B.C., as we know from an inscription of Lampsacus of that date (*SIG*^{3} II.591, lines 43-5, 47-9), the directing body at Massalia was already the Council of Six Hundred described by Strabo (IV.i.5, p.179, very probably from Poseidonius) as consisting of τιμοῦχοι, who sat for life – and were presumably appointed by co-optation, as we hear of no general Assembly at Massalia, and two passages in Cicero, *De republica*, quoted below, would seem to exclude its existence. This constitution was much admired by Strabo; and several Roman writers, including Cicero (*Pro Flacc.* 63), Livy, Valerius Maximus (II.vi.7) and Silius Italicus, speak well of it, using terms like *gravitas* and *disciplina*. However, Cicero in the *De republica*, although prepared to say that Rome's 'clients' the Massiliots 'per delectos et principes cives summa iustitia reguntur', yet admits that 'inest tamen in ea condicione populi similitudo quaedam servitutis' (I.27/43); and a little later he compares this 'paucorum et principum administratio' with the rule of the Thirty at Athens (28/44)!

By the second half of the second century of the Christian era, the constitution of Massalia (now Massilia) had evidently become thoroughly romanised, with 'decuriones' and the usual Roman municipal magistrates (*duumviri* etc.).[12]

7. *Mesopotamia and beyond*

We have only a few scraps of information about the constitutions and political life of the various Greek cities of Mesopotamia and farther east. The most easterly of all these cities about whose internal political affairs we have any evidence that is relevant for our present purposes is Seleuceia on the Tigris, an exceptionally large town with a population put by Pliny the Elder at 600,000 (*NH* VI.122, on what authority we do not know) and believed by Strabo to be comparable with that of Alexandria and rather larger than that of Antioch (XVI.ii.5, p.750). Seleuceia was for a time the main Seleucid capital. It must have been a flourishing city in the late third century B.C. if it is true that Hermeias, the chief administrator of Antiochus III, could impose on it a fine of a thousand talents (reduced by the king to 150 talents) for having taken part in the revolt of Molon in 222-220 B.C. (Polyb. V.54.10-11). From just after the middle of the second century B.C. Seleuceia was nearly always within the Parthian rather than the Seleucid or Roman sphere of dominance, but was evidently allowed a considerable measure of independence and self-government. We hear of its being under a tyrant, Himerus, probably in the 120s B.C. (Poseidonius, *FGrH* 87 F 13). According to Plutarch, writing of Crassus' campaign against the Parthians in 54-3, Seleuceia had always been ill-disposed towards the Parthians (*Crass.* 17.8).

In relation to the year A.D. 36 Tacitus speaks of faction at Seleuceia between the common people (the *populus* or *plebs*) and the three hundred members of the Council, described enigmatically as 'chosen for their wealth or their wisdom to be a Senate' (*opibus aut sapientia delecti ut senatus*), a form of words which may indicate that the members of the Council sat for life. Factious disorder was particularly likely to occur in this city, because either party in a *stasis* might call in the Parthians, as Tacitus notes in the same passage (*Ann.* VI.xlii.1-3,5). Before 36 the Parthian King Artabanus III had put the commons under the *primores* (presumably the Council of 300); in that year the situation was reversed by the pretender Tiridates, who had the backing of the Emperor Tiberius and was welcomed by the populace of Seleuceia but soon fled back to Roman Syria. Artabanus' successor Vardanes reduced Seleuceia in 42 (*Ann.* XI.viii.4 to ix.6), and that may well have been the end of popular government in Seleuceia – brought about not by the Romans, be it noted, but by the Parthians. Seleuceia now became increasingly orientalised, and we hear no more of it except in connection with Rome's Parthian wars: it was briefly taken over by the Romans at the end of Trajan's reign, and sacked and partly destroyed by Verus' general Avidius Cassius in 165 (see Magie, *RRAM* II.1531 n.5). Dio Cassius in two passages in his narrative of the campaign of Crassus in 54–53 stresses the Hellenic character of Seleuceia (XL.xvi.3; xx.3), and in the first of these he speaks of the city as an existing *polis* still thoroughly Hellenic in his own day (πλεῖστον τὸ Ἑλληνικὸν καὶ νῦν ἔχουσα); but this statement may have little foundation – there is certainly no evidence that Dio himself was ever in or even near Mesopotamia (see Millar, *SCD* 13–27).

For the history of the city, see *OCD*² 971 (with bibliography); add M. Streck in *RE*² II.i (1921) 1149–84.

* * * * * *

Another Mesopotamian city about which a good deal is known is Edessa (the modern Urfa in Turkey, not far from the Syrian border), which is always known by that name rather than the one given to it as a Seleucid foundation: Antioch by Callirhoe. The most recent book is by J. B. Segal, *Edessa. 'The Blessed City'* (1970). See also E. Meyer, in *RE* V.ii (1905) 1933–8. For what is known of the constitution, see C. B. Welles, in A. R. Bellinger and Welles, 'A third–century contract of sale from Edessa in Osrhoene', in *YCS* 5 (1935) 95–154, at 121–42. I have no legitimate reason for mentioning it here, but there is a remarkable exchange of letters (bogus, of course) between Jesus and the then dynast of Edessa, Abgar, in Eus., *HE* I.xiii. (Eusebius, who thought the letters genuine, says he had them translated from the originals in Syriac in the public archives of Edessa, § 5.) The Edessenes firmly believed that Jesus had made a promise to Abgar that their city would never be captured by an enemy (Josh. Styl., *Chron.* 5, 58, 60, ed. in the original Syriac, with an English translation, by W. Wright, Cambridge, 1882). It was in fact captured more than once by the Sassanids, and in 638 by the Arabs.

Notes

[I.ii]

1. It is astonishing how few maps show this very important linguistic division. It does appear in e.g. *Westermanns Atlas zur Weltgeschichte* (Berlin etc., 1965) 42. For the situation in the Later Empire, see Jones, *LRE* II.986. In support of my division of north Africa between the Greek and Latin worlds I would cite p.9 of Louis Robert's book on gladiators in the Greek East (see VII.1 n.3 below): 'La Cyrénaïque fait partie de l'Orient grec, et j'ai laissé à l'Occident la Tripolitaine.'
2. For the cities which were newly founded, or achieved the status of cities, only from the time of Alexander onwards, see e.g. *Westermanns Atlas* (n.1 above) 22-3; *CAH* VII, Map 4; Bengtson, *GG*[5], Map 9.
3. Norman Baynes, who had said in 1930 that 'the reign of Heraclius marks the beginning of Byzantine history', later came to feel that 'Byzantine history begins with Constantine the Great' (*BSOE* 78 and n.2). For the Byzantine historian Ostrogorsky it was in 'the age of Heraclius' (610-41) that 'the Roman period ended and Byzantine history properly speaking began' (*HBS*[2] 106). For Arnold J. Toynbee 'ancient Greek or Hellenic historical thought . . . came to an end when Homer yielded precedence to the Bible as the sacred book of a Greek-speaking and Greek-writing *intelligentzia*. In the series of historical authors [that] event occurred between the dates at which Theophylactus Simocatta and George of Pisidia produced their repective works' – that is to say, during the reign of Heraclius (*Greek Historical Thought from Homer to the Age of Heraclius*, 1952 and repr., Introduction, p.ix).
4. For English-speaking readers the most convincing statement of this view is by Baynes, *BSOE* 1-82. Different as my own position is from his in some ways, I find him entirely convincing on this particular topic.
5. Nicholas [I] Papa, *Ep.* 8, in J. D. Mansi, *Sacr. Conc. nova et ampl. coll.* XV (1770) 186-216, at 191, repr. as *Ep.* 86 in *MPL* CXIX.926-62, at 932.

[I.iii]

1. See Jones, *LRE* II.841-5 (with the notes, III.283); Brunt, *IM* 703-6 (who notes that 'Jones has much the clearest conception of the general conditions that obtained for the food supply').
2. See esp. the references that follow in the main text above to Jones, *LRE* and *RE*. Among many other discussions of ancient transport, see e.g. Duncan-Jones, *EREQS* 366-9; also C. A. Yeo, 'Land and sea transportation in Imperial Italy', in *TAPA* 77 (1946) 221-44; and of course the indexes to Rostovtzeff, *SEHHW* and *SEHRE*[2], s.v. 'Transportation' etc. On any question of navigation or sea transport, see Lionel Casson, *Ships and Seamanship in the Ancient World* (Princeton, 1971). There is a great deal of miscellaneous information about travel and journeys by land and sea in the first two centuries C.E. in Ludwig Friedländer's massive work, *Darstellungen aus der Sittengeschichte Roms in der Zeit von August bis zum Ausgang der Antonine*[9-10] (Leipzig, 1919-21) I.316-88, esp. 331-57.
3. The fragments of Diocletian's Price Edict known down to 1938-9 were published (with an English translation) by Elsa R. Graser, in Frank, *ESAR* V (1940) 305-421; there are some further relevant fragments in her article, 'The significance of two new fragments of the Edict of Diocletian', in *TAPA* 71 (1940) 157-74. An edition by Siegfried Lauffer, *Diokletians Preisedikt* (Berlin, 1971) was complete down to 1970; another edition (with Italian translation) by Marta Giacchero, *Edictum Diocletiani et Collegarum de pretiis rerum venalium* (Genoa, 1974), includes several fragments found subsequently, and is now the most useful single text. A number of

fragments of the Edict found at Aezani in Phrygia, on the upper Rhyndacus, make up the most complete Latin version yet available from a single source. These fragments (including a clear price of 72,000 denarii for the pound of gold and 6,000 for the pound of silver) have been incorporated in Giacchero's edition. On the publication of the Aezani fragments by R. and F. Naumann in 1973, see Joyce Reynolds, in *JRS* 66 (1976) 251-2 (with Hugh Plommer) and 183, with the works cited in the latter passage, nn.117-19. I give here, for convenience, a few particularly important prices from the Edict (in denarii) which can now be regarded as certain: (1) the pound of gold: 72,000 (Giacchero 28.1a,2); (2) the pound of silver: 6,000 (G. 28.9); (3) an ordinary slave aged 16-40: male 30,000, female 25,000 (G. 29.1a,2; Lauffer 31.1a,2); (4) the daily wage of an agricultural worker: 25 plus food (G. and L. 7.1a; cf. IV.iii above and its n.1 below); (5) the 'castrensis modius': of wheat 100, of barley 60 (G. and L. 1.1a,2). The last section of all in the Edict, dealing with sea and river transport charges, is no.35 in G. and 37 in L.; the section dealing with land transport charges is no.17 in each. The best attempt to solve the complicated problem of the size of the *castrensis modius* (probably 1½ ordinary modii) is by R. P. Duncan-Jones, 'The size of the *modius castrensis*', in *ZPE* 21 (1976) 53-62, cf. 43-52.

4. For a high degree of literacy among the Athenians of the Classical period, see the admirable article by F. D. Harvey, 'Literacy in the Athenian democracy', in *REG* 79 (1966) 585-635. Athens was no doubt exceptional, in this as in so many other ways. Illiteracy was very common in Hellenistic and Roman Egypt, especially among women: see H. C. Youtie, *Scriptiunculae* (Amsterdam, 1973) II.611-27, 629-51 (nos. 29 and 30), reprinting (with minor additions) two articles, ''Αγράμματος: an aspect of Greek society in Egypt', in *HSCP* 75 (1971) 161-76; and 'Βραδέως γράφων: between literacy and illiteracy', in *GRBS* 12 (1971) 239-61. Sufficient bibliography will be found there. Even a village clerk, a κωμογραμματεύς, who of course was supposed to be literate, might not be so, or only minimally. Two known cases are mentioned in *P. Petaus* 11 and 31: see the articles by Youtie mentioned above, and his no.34 in *Scriptiunculae* II.677-95, a reprint of 'Pétaus, fils de Pétaus, ou le scribe qui ne savait pas écrire', in *CE* 41 (1966) 127-43.

5. The best account of this fundamental opposition between town and country in the Greek East is in Jones, *GCAJ* 259-304 (Part V, 'The achievement of the cities'), esp. 285 ff. Another major work by Jones, *CERP* (frequently cited in *GCAJ*), has been reissued in a second edition, *CERP²* (1971), with additions, a few of them substantial. A recent work, limited to the Late Republic and the Principate, is MacMullen, *RSR*: the first chapters of this (I. 'Rural', and II. 'Rural-Urban', pp.1-56) have much well-chosen illustrative material – of an antiquarian rather than historical character, since this book (like the rest of MacMullen's work) is not supported by any consistent structure of theory or method, and therefore lacks any principle of organisation and is seldom or never able to furnish explanations. For the opinions of a great scholar who knew the archaeological as well as the literary evidence particularly well, see Rostovtzeff, *SEHRE²*, e.g. I.255-78 (with II.654-77), 344-52, 378-80, 505. For a similar situation in the West, see I.33, 59-63, 203-6 (Italy); 252 (Thrace). I should perhaps add that I know of no parallel to Strabo's classification into *agroikoi, mesagroikoi* and *politikoi* (XIII.i.25, p.592): it may be no more than a reflection of Plato, *Laws* III.677-81, which he had quoted.

6. Galen, Περὶ εὐχυμίας καὶ κακοχυμίας 1.1-7 = *De bonis malisque sucis*, ed. G. Helmreich, in *Corp. Medic. Graec.* V.iv.2, Galenus (Leipzig/Berlin, 1923) 389-91 = *De probis pravisque alimentorum succis*, ed. C. G. Kühn, in Galenus VI (Leipzig, 1823) 749-52, with Latin trans.

7. As Brunt says (*IM* 703), 'comprehensive examination is still needed' of ancient famines. His own brief treatment of the subject is admirable and gives a few references to other works, among which I would single out MacMullen, *ERO* 249-54 (an appendix devoted entirely to famines), and H. P. Kohns, *Versorgungskrisen und Hungerrevolten im spätantiken Rom* (= *Antiquitas* I.6, Bonn, 1961).

8. See esp. D. Sperber, 'Angaria in Rabbinic literature', in *AC* 38 (1969) 164-8, at 166, citing R. Hanina b. Hama. As Sperber indicates, 'angaria' as used by the rabbi in question has the general meaning of extortion and oppression. And see P. Fiebig, in *ZNW* 18 (1917-18) 64-72. For *angariae* in general in the Greek (and Roman) world, see Rostovtzeff, 'Angariae', in *Klio* 6 (1906) 249-58; *SEHRE²* I.381-4 (with II.703 nn.35-7), 519-20, II.723 n.46; F. Oertel, *Die Liturgie* (Leipzig, 1917) 24-6, 88-90. For the incidence of *angariae* falling on the peasant and not the well-to-do landowner, see Liebeschuetz, *Ant.* 69 (on Liban., *Orat.* L, *De angariis*), quoted in the text above. For the very wide incidence of transport services of various kinds in the Roman empire, organised by the Roman government as the *vehiculatio*, later the *cursus publicus*,

see Stephen Mitchell, 'Requisitioned transport in the Roman Empire: a new inscription from Pisidia' [Sagalassus], in *JRS* 66 (1976) 106-31, esp. the list of 21 documents (111-12). A text in the *Digest* that is seldom noticed mentions a rescript to the effect that ships belonging to veterans *angariari posse* (XLIX.xviii.4.1, Ulpian). In a papyrus we even find the word ἀνεγγάρευτος (*SB* I.4226).

9. There is an up-to-date bibliography on this subject, for the Western as well as the Eastern part of the Roman empire, in P. A. Brunt, RLRCRE = 'The Romanisation of the local ruling classes in the Roman empire', in *Assimilation et résistance à la culture gréco-romaine dans le monde ancien = Travaux du VI*ᶜ [Madrid, 1974] *Congrès International d'Études Classiques* (Bucarest/Paris, 1976) 161-73, at 170-2. I should perhaps add Jones, *CERP*² 228-30 and *GCAJ* 288-95 (partly but not entirely replaced by *LRE* II.966, 968-9, 991-7); Rostovtzeff, *SEHRE*² II.626-7 n.1, 666 n.36. J. C. Mann, 'Spoken Latin in Britain as evidenced in the inscriptions', in *Britannia* 2 (1971) 218-24, although dealing mainly with Britain, may suggest a way in which research might be conducted in other areas.

10. On Lystra, see Barbara Levick, *RCSAM* 51-3, 153-6, 195-7.

11. The revenue of the reigning Ptolemy is given in respectable ancient sources as 14,800 talents of silver and 1½ million artabae of wheat in the second quarter of the third century B.C. (Jerome, *In Daniel*. XI.5), and in the last century B.C. as 12,500 talents (Cic., *ap*. Strab. XVII.i.13, p.798) or 6,000 talents (Diod. XVII.52.6): see Rostovtzeff, *SEHHW* II.1150-3, with III.1607 n.86. The total population of late Ptolemaic Egypt (*c*. 60 B.C.) is given as 7 million by Diod. I.31.8 (with the emendation now commonly accepted: τούτων for τριακοσίων). That of Roman Egypt in the Flavian period is given by Jos., *BJ* II.385, as 7½ million, apart from Alexandria. These figures may be approximately correct. We should perhaps allow a million or so for Alexandria: cf. Fraser, *PA* I.90-1; II.171-2 n.358.

12. Cf. Rostovtzeff, *SEHHW* II.878-914; Jones, *CERP*² 302-11.

13. For example, Claude Vandersleyen, 'Le mot λαός dans la langue des papyrus grecs', in *CE* 48 (1973) 339-49, argues that the expressions λαός, λαοί, when occurring in the papyri in reference to Egypt, should be taken to be describing a particular section of the native Egyptian population, indeed a superior section, 'couche supérieure de la population égyptienne, existant aussi bien a l'époque pharaonique qu'à l'époque ptolémaïque' (cf. another work of Vandersleyen, which I have not been able to read: *Les Guerres d'Amosis* [1971], esp. 182-4 on the Rosetta Stone), and not the general mass of the native population. Rostovtzeff, like many other scholars, will then have misinterpreted the words λαοί, λαός in such documents as the Rosetta Stone (*OGIS* 90.12: see *SEHHW* II.713-15) and in the papyrus he describes in *SEHHW* II.883-4 – he fails to give the reference, which is *BGU* VIII (1933) 1768 (W. Schubart and D. Schäfer, *Spätptolemäische Papyri aus amtlichen Büros des Herakleopolites = Aegyptische Urkunden aus den staatlichen Museem zu Berlin, Griechische Urkunden* VIII, Berlin [1933], no.1768, pp.47-9). However, Vandersleyen's conclusions do not appear to be securely established: contrast W. Clarysse, in *Anc. Soc.* 7 (1976) 185 ff., at 195 and nn.22-6 (pointing out that Vandersleyen takes into account only the noun λαός and not the adjective λαικός, for which see e.g. Préaux, *ERL* 224 and n.2); and Heinz Heinen, ibid. 127 ff., at 144 n.32, who declares himself unconvinced; cf. Heinen in *Anc. Soc.* 8 (1977) 130 n.21.

14. Eurip., *Electr.* 31-53, 207-9, 247-57, 302-9, 362-3, 404-5. Ar., *Clouds* 46-72 is irrelevant here, since Strepsiades, however boorish by origin, is obviously conceived as well-to-do and does not fall within my definition of a peasant (see IV.ii above).

15. Cf. *IGRR* IV.1087, from Cos, for a distinction between τοὶ κατοικεῦντες ἐν τῷ δάμῳ τῶν Ἀλεντίων καὶ το[ὶ] ἐνεκτημένοι καὶ τοὶ γεωργεῦντε[ς] ἐν Ἀλεντι καὶ Πέλη, τῶν τε πολειτᾶν καὶ Ῥωμαίων καὶ μετοίκων. (I can see no justification for lining-up the two sets of inhabitants in parallel and making the κατοικεῦντες the citizens, the ἐνεκτημένοι the Romans, and the γεωργεῦντες the metics, with Rostovtzeff, *SEHRE*² II.654 n.4.) I may add that there is some evidence from the Latin West for the extension of distributions to include inhabitants of a city who are not its citizens (*municipes*, or *coloni*) but *incolae* (see below, and Duncan-Jones, *EREQS* 259 n.3, 279 n.5). This unfortunately raises a thorny question about the meaning of the expression *incolae*. They clearly are people who do not have citizen rights in the *civitas* or πόλις in which (or in the territory of which) they reside. But are they (1) simply residents with a *domicilium* in the city who have an *origo* elsewhere, or are they (2) primarily the population of territory subject to the city, who have no local citizen rights, whether or not they are officially its *attributi* (or *contributi*)? The former is the standard view (see e.g. Berger in *RE* IX.ii.1249-56), the latter that

of Rostovtzeff, *SEHRE*² II.632 n.33, cf. 687 n.97. I agree with Brunt, *IM* 249: 'Though the term "incolae" in my view denotes no more than "residents without local citizen rights", and is not a technical term designating members of a subject population, it is wide enough to embrace such a class.' Two legal texts seem to me to show a development between the second and third centuries. Pomponius, in *Dig.* L.xvi.239.2, writing in about the second quarter of the second century, equates *incola* with Greek πάροικος and includes in his definition of *incolae* not only those who reside *in oppido* but also those who have farmland (*agrum*) within the boundaries of the town which is in some sense their home (such I take to be the meaning of 'ut in eum se quasi in aliquam sedem recipiant'). But around the second quarter of the third century Modestinus does not count as an *incola* ὁ ἐν ἀγρῷ καταμένων, on the ground that a man who makes no use of the ἐξαίρετα (*commoda*, conveniences, benefits) of a city is not to be considered its *incola* (*Dig.* L.i.35, in Greek). By then, at any rate, it seems that *attributi* and the like were no longer considered to be *incolae* – an important exclusion, for since about the third quarter of the second century *incolae* had become equally liable with local *cives* for *munera publica* (Gaius, in *Dig.* L.i.29). I find it interesting that in *ILS* 6818 (of the third quarter of the second century), from Sicca Veneria in Numidia, the *incolae* who are to benefit, with *municipes*, from the foundation there established are restricted to those living 'in the buildings included in our colony'. And in Italian cities many foundations, where they extend to the lower classes, are specifically limited to the *urban* population: see e.g. Duncan-Jones, *EREQS* nos. 638, 644 (= 1165), 697, 947, 962, 976, 990, 1023, 1066, 1079m.

16. This is well borne out by Libanius, *Orat.* XI.230: the 'large populous villages' in the territory of Antioch exchanged their products with each other at their fairs (πανηγύρεις) and 'had little use for the city because of their exchange among themselves'.
17. Cf. Rostovtzeff, *SEHHW* II.1106-7.
18. Contrast the official view, expressed by Ulpian in *Dig.* L.i.30, that the *patria* of a man who originated in a village is the city (*res publica*) to which the village belongs.
19. Jones, I am sure, meant much the same as I would when he used the expression 'too narrow a class foundation'; but for him 'class' – a term he used quite often – was not something that needed to be defined, or even, for that matter, thought about. I hesitate to give equal prominence to the final sentence of the paragraph in question ('The great mass of the population, the proletariat of the towns, and still more the peasants of the countryside, remained barbarians'), as it not only uses again the inappropriate expression 'proletariat' but ends with a word which the 'general reader' is likely to misunderstand unless he realises that it is very much a Classical scholar's quasi-technical term, almost the equivalent of the Greek word *barbaroi*, not necessarily meaning more than 'non-Greek'.

[I.iv]

1. There are very few exceptions, the main one being E. A. Thompson: see e.g. his *A Roman Reformer and Inventor* (an edition of the *Anonymus De rebus bellicis*, 1952), esp. pp.31-4, 85-9; and other works, including *A History of Attila and the Huns* (1948), *The Early Germans* (1965) and *The Visigoths in the Time of Ulfila* (1966). Benjamin Farrington has also made use of Marxist concepts, e.g. in his *Greek Science* (Pelican, 1953 and repr.) and his collection of essays, *Head and Hand in Ancient Greece* (London, 1947). For George Thomson and Margaret O. Wason, see II.i above and its nn.19-20 below.
2. I shall merely record the 'Select bibliography on Marxism and the study of antiquity', by R. A. Padgug, pp.199-225. If I have retained in this book much that is in my *Arethusa* article, it is because not many people in Britain have easy access to a library containing the periodical in question.
3. I should like to record in particular Maurice Dobb, *On Economic Theory and Socialism* (1955 and repr.); and *Political Economy and Capitalism* (1937 and repr.); Ronald L. Meek, *Studies in the Labour Theory of Value*² (1973); and the 'Penguin Special' by Andrew Glyn and Bob Sutcliffe, *British Capitalism, Workers and the Profits Squeeze* (1972).
4. I have benefited particularly from Godelier, *RIE*: Dupré and Rey, RPTHE; and Meillassoux, 'From reproduction to production. A Marxist approach to economic anthropology', in *Economy and Society* 1 (1972) 93-105; 'Are there castes in India?' in *Economy and Society* 2 (1973) 89-111; and 'Essai d'interprétation du phénomène économique dans les sociétés traditionelles d'auto-

subsistance', in *Cahiers d'études africaines* 4 (1960) 38-67. A paper by Terray, 'Classes and class consciousness in the Abron Kingdom of Gyaman', appears in *Marxist Analyses and Social Anthropology*, ed. Maurice Bloch (= *ASA Studies* 2, 1975) 85-135; and the bibliographies at the end of that paper and of the others in the same volume refer to further works by Terray and the other Marxist anthropologists I have mentioned.

5. See Jerzy Topolski, 'Lévi-Strauss and Marx on history', in *History and Theory* 12 (1973) 192-207, for a demonstration of the great superiority of Marx to Lévi-Strauss in understanding of the historical process.

6. This lecture, already published separately, is in the *Procedings of the Brit. Acad.* 58 (1972) 177-213 (published early in 1974). It has been reprinted in *Marxist Analyses and Social Anthropolgy* (see n.4 above) 29-60.

7. An example is E. Ch. Welskopf, *Die Produktionsverhältnisse im alten Orient und in der griechisch-römischen Antike* (Berlin, 1957). There are of course a number of other works published in the German Democratic Republic and by Italian and French Marxists which are less alien to the bulk of Western scholars. Among the German publications, the one that is most obviously relevant to the subject of this book is the collective work, *Hellenische Poleis. Krise - Wandlung - Wirkung*, ed. E. Ch. Welskopf (4 vols, pp.2296, Berlin, 1974); but I have not often found it useful for my particular purposes. Among other German articles and monographs, I would single out several by Heinz Kreissig, including *Die sozialen Zusammenhänge des judäischen Krieges. Klassen und Klassenkampf im Palästina des 1 Jahrh. v.u.Z. = Schriften zur Gesch. u. Kultur der Antike* 1 (Berlin, 1970); other works by Kreissig are cited in III.iv nn.33 etc. below. Translations into German from Russian (which very few Western Classical scholars can read: I am ashamed to say I cannot) are also being published in the DDR, e.g. E. M. Schtajerman [Štaerman], *Die Krise der Sklavenhalterordnung im Westen des römischen Reiches* (Berlin, 1964). German translations from the Russian have also begun to appear in the German Federal Republic, e.g. E. M. Štaerman, *Die Blütezeit der Sklavenwirtschaft in der römischen Republik* (Wiesbaden, 1969); T. V. Blavatskaja, E. S. Golubcova and A. I. Pavlovskaja, *Die Sklaverei in hellenistischen Staaten im 3.-1. Jh. v.Chr.* (Wiesbaden, 1972); and see below for an Italian translation of a Russian work. The *Bibliographie zur antiken Sklaverei*, ed. Joseph Vogt (Bochum, 1971), lists many Russian and East European works, with titles usually transliterated as well as being translated into German. There has been some hostile discussion in German of some of the Soviet material: see e.g. Friedrich Vittinghoff, 'Die Theorien des historischen Materialismus über den antiken "Sklavenhalterstaat". Probleme der Alten Geschichte bei den "Klassikern" des Marxismus und in der modernen sowjetischen Forschung', in *Saeculum* 11 (1960) 89-131; cf. his 'Die Bedeutung der Sklaven für den Übergang von der Antike ins abenländische Mittelalter', in *Hist. Ztschr.* 192 (1961) 265-72, with a *résumé* in *XIe Congrès International des Sciences Historiques* [Stockholm, 1960], *Résumés des Communications* (Göteborg etc., 1960) 71-3. The latest such work that I have seen is G. Prachner, 'Zur Bedeutung der antiken Sklaven- und Kolonenwirtschaft für den Niedergang des römischen Reiches (Bemerkungen zur marxistischen Forschung)', in *Historia* 22 (1973) 732-56. (And see Finley, *AE* 182 n.39.) These anti-Marxist works have a rather narrow scope and are directed against Marxist (or 'would-be Marxist') interpretations of ancient history significantly different from mine: they are largely irrelevant to the arguments I advance in this book. Much more objective and instructive are some studies by Heinz Heinen of Soviet (and Polish) material on (mainly) ancient slavery, of which I have seen (1) 'Neuere sowjetische Monographien zur Geschichte des Altertums', in *Historia* 24 (1975) 378-84; (2) & (3) 'Neuere sowjet. Veröffentlichungen zur ant. Sklaverei', in *Historia* 25 (1976) 501-5, and 28 (1979) 125-8; (4) & (5) 'Zur Sklaverei in der hellenistichen Welt' I and II, in *Anc. Soc.* 7 (1976) 127-49 and 8 (1977) 121-54 (these last with much more detailed discussion). See also Heinen's review of L. Iraci Fedeli, *Marx e il mondo antico* (Milan, 1972), in *Riv. stor. dell'antich.* 5 (1975) 229-33; and his article, 'Sur le régime du travail dans l'Égypte ptolémaïque au IIIe siècle av. J.-C., à propos d'un livre recent de N. N. Pikus', in *Le Monde Grec. Hommages à Claire Préaux* (Brussels, 1975) 656-62. See also Paul Petit, 'L'esclavage antique dans l'historiographie soviétique', in *Actes du Colloque d'hist. soc. 1970* = *Annales littéraires de l'Univ. de Besançon* 128 (Paris, 1972) 9-27. The only work I know in English that gives a general review of Soviet work on ancient history from the Revolution down to the 1950s is the article by H. F. Graham, 'The significant role of the study of Ancient History in the Soviet Union', in *Class. World* 61.3 (1967) 85-97. I greatly regret that it has not been possible for me as yet to examine carefully more than a little of the

large quantity of Italian Marxist material on ancient (mainly Roman) history which I know exists. I can only mention some works which I was not able to do more than glance at until after this book had been substantially finished: Mario Mazza's valuable article, 'Marxismo e storia antica. Note sulla storiografia marxista in Italia', in *Studi storici* 17.2 (1976) 95-124, with much bibliography; Mazza's book, *Lotte sociali e restaurazione autoritaria nel III sec. d.C.* (republished in Rome, 1973); and an Italian translation, *La schiavitù nell'Italia imperiale I-III sec.* (Rome, 1975), of a book published in Russian in 1971 by E. M. Štaerman and M. K. Trofimova, with a most useful 37-page Preface by Mazza discussing Russian and other modern Marxist work on ancient (mainly Roman) history. Unfortunately, I have not been able to read *Annalisi marxista e società antiche* (= *Nuova biblioteca di cultura* 178, *Atti dell' Istituto Gramsci*), ed. Luigi Capogrossi and others (Rome, 1978). Much interesting work from a Marxist standpoint has been published in Italy on ancient literature and archaeology, subjects with which I am not directly concerned here, and I will mention only the most relevant of those I know: Vittorio Citti, *Tragedia e lotta di classe in Grecia* (Naples, 1978). Among recent French works on ancient history written by Marxists I would single out those of Pierre Briant, mentioned in III.iv above and its nn.26,33 below.

8. *MECW* II.584-5; 572-4 (with 620 n.248) = *MEGA* I.ii.480-1, 478-9. And see Johannes Irmscher, 'Friedrich Engels studiert Altertumswissenschaft', in *Eirene* 2 (1964) 7-42.

9. *MESC* 495-7, 498-500, 500-7 (esp. 503, 504-5, 507), 540-4, 548-51. (The last letter is now known to have been written to W. Borgius, not H. Starkenburg as once believed.)

10. See the five-volume *Selected Works of Mao Tse-tung* (in English) I (Peking, 1965 and repr.) 311-47, at 336; or the one-volume *Selected Readings from the Works of Mao Tse-tung* (Peking, 1967) 70-108, at 94.

11. Katherine and C. H. George, 'Roman Catholic sainthood and social status', in Bendix-Lipset, *CSP²* 394-401, a revised reprint of an article in *Jnl of Religion* 5 (1953-5) 33 ff. For the effect of economic status on voting in the Western democracies, see S. M. Lipset, in Bendix-Lipset, *CSP²* 413-28 (cf. II.iv n.12 below).

12. The only recent paper of value on this subject that I happen to have seen is E. J. Hobsbawm, 'Karl Marx's contribution to historiography', in *Ideology in Social Science*, ed. Robin Blackburn (Fontana paperback, 1972) 265-83.

13. The distinction (which, as I say in the main text above, I do not propose to discuss in this book) between the economic 'basis' of society and its ideological 'superstructure' was already formulated in Part I of the *German Ideology*, written jointly by Marx and Engels in 1845-6 (see *MECW* V.89), and it is most clearly stated by Marx himself in a famous passage in the *Preface to a Contribution to the Critique of Political Economy* of 1859 (*MESW* 181), on which see II.ii above. Although this idea lies behind much of what Marx writes (a good example is the criticism of Sir Frederic Eden, in *Cap*. I.615-16, esp. 615 n.2; but there are scores of similar passages), I have found few other explicit references to it by Marx himself. See however the early letter to P. V. Annenkov, of 28 December 1846 (*MESC* 39-51, esp. 40-1, 45), and the passage in the third chapter of *The Eighteenth Brumaire of Louis Bonaparte* in which Marx writes, 'Upon the different forms of property, upon the social conditions of existence, rises an entire superstructure of different and distinctly formed sentiments, illusions, modes of thought and views of life. The entire class creates and forms them out of its material foundations and out of the corresponding social relations' (*MECW* XI.128). It seems that when in later life Marx was supervising the French translation of the 1859 *Preface*, he toned down the statement that 'the mode of production of material life *bedingt . . . überhaupt* the social, political and intellectual life process', by choosing to represent the German words I have quoted by 'domine en général': see Prawer, *KMWL* 400-1, apparently in agreement with Rubel. The other standard discussions of this topic are by Engels, in particular in the letters cited in n.9 above and his speech at the graveside of Marx on 17 March 1883 (*MESW* 429-30). Few recent discussions of the subject that I have seen have been illuminating, apart from two useful papers in which Gerald A. Cohen successfully demolishes objections raised by H. B. Acton and John Plamenatz to Marx's notion of basis and superstructure: 'On some criticisms of historical materialism', in *Proceedings of the Aristotelian Society* (Suppl. Vol.) 44 (1970) 121-41; and 'Being, consciousness and roles: on the foundations of historical materialism', in *Essays in Honour of E. H. Carr*, ed. Chimen Abramsky (1974) 82-97. And see now Cohen's book, *Karl Marx's Theory of History, A Defence* (1978, repr. 1979).

14. See Hobsbawm's excellent Introduction to his *KMPCEF*, esp. 11, 17 and n.2, 19-21, 27-38, 49-59, 61-5.
15. I regard Perry Anderson, *LAS* 462-549, as conclusive against retaining the conception of an Asiatic/Oriental mode of production. He makes good use of other recent work, notably an excellent article by Daniel Thorner (MAIMP), who shows in particular that the English translation of *Das Kapital* I in 1887, which was supervised by Engels, makes at one point a significant departure from the German text (now best read in *MEW* XXIII.354 n.24), which speaks of small-scale peasant agriculture and independent handicrafts as forming the basis not only of 'the feudal mode of production' but also of 'the Classical communities at their best, after the primitive Oriental form of ownership of land in common had disappeared, and before slavery had seized on production in earnest', by omitting the word 'Oriental' (MAIMP 60). And in his *Origin of the Family*, published in 1884 (the year after Marx's death), Engels never refers to an Asiatic/Oriental mode of production; cf. esp. *MESW* 581. Marx showed little interest in a specifically Asiatic/Oriental mode in his last years (see esp. Thorner, MAIMP 63-6), although he occasionally makes passing references to it: see *Cap.* I.77-8 n.1, 79; cf. 334 n.3, 357-8; and see also *TSV* III.417, 434, 435. Cf. also, on the question of the Asiatic/Oriental mode, Hobsbawm, *KMPCEF* 11, 17 n.2, 19, 25, 32-8, 51, 58, 61, 64. Those who are able to take a greater interest than I can in would-be Marxist discussions of the Asiatic mode of production and bibliographical accounts of such discussions (especially in the U.S.S.R.) may consult a series of articles in *Eirene*: J. Chesneaux, in 3 (1964) 131-46; J. Pečírka, in ibid. 147-69; 6 (1967) 141-74; P. Skalnick and T. Pokora, in 5 (1966) 179-87. English readers may find useful A. M. Bailey and J. R. Llobera, 'The Asiatic mode of production. An annotated bibliography', appearing in four parts in *Critique of Anthropology*. I have seen only two parts: 'I. Principal Writings of Marx and Engels', in no.2 of that periodical (Autumn 1974) 95-103; and 'II. The Adventures of the Concept from Plekhanov to Stalin', in nos.4/5 (Autumn 1975) 165-76.
16. Such criticisms of Marx are often as ill-founded as the ridiculing by Dahrendorf (*CCCIS* 22) of an isolated passage in *Cap.* III.436-8 relating to joint-stock companies. This happens to be one of those places at which Marx perhaps over-indulges his taste for paradox (e.g. 'the abolition of capital as private property within the framework of capitalist production itself'). The passage becomes fully comprehensible only when read with an earlier one: *Cap.* III.382-90. (I mention this in order to refute one set of Dahrendorf's objections to Marx's theory of class.)

[II.i]

1. 'The history of the concept of class in sociology is surely one of the most extreme illustrations of the inability of sociologists to achieve a minimum of consensus even in the modest business of terminological decisions,' says Dahrendorf, *CCCIS* 74. He then mentions nine authors who have given 'versions and perversions of the concept of class' during the last half-century, including Pitirim Sorokin, who in his *Contemporary Sociological Theories* (1928) 'counted thirty-two variations of the concept'! He proceeds to give half a dozen recent definitions, but none of them bears any resemblance to the one I adopt in this book.
2. I have seen a number of rather half-hearted attempts to bring order out of the confusion created by Marx's varying usage of the term class, none of which seems to me adequate. A characteristic example, useful as far as it goes but neither comprehensive nor profound, is Bertell Ollman, 'Marx's use of "class"', in *Amer. Jnl of Sociol.* 73 (1968) 573-80. I have not myself found much illumination in Ossowski, *CSSC*, or his 'Les différents aspects de la classe sociale chez Marx', in *Cahiers internationaux de sociologie* 24 (1958) 65-79.
3. This passage is reproduced in many anthologies compiled from Marx's writings, the most useful of which are perhaps those of Bottomore/Rubel, *KM*; and Jordan, *KMECSR*.
4. Just as in the capitalist world, with its highly developed law of property, so also in the Greek (and the Roman) world, control over the conditions of production was exercised above all by property ownership, and there is no necessity for me to consider any other possible methods whereby such control might be exercised. The passage in the text leaves open the possibility that such other methods might exist – for instance, in a society without a developed property law, in which actual possession of the means of production (especially land) would be the decisive factor; cf. Claude Meillassoux, 'Are there castes in India?', in *Economy and Society* 2 (1973) 89-111, at p.100.

5. G. W. Bowersock, in *Daedalus* (1974) 15-23, at 17-18. For a very interesting and acute appraisal of Rostovtzeff as a historian (much the best I know), see Meyer Reinhold, 'Historian of the Classic world: a critique of Rostovtzeff', in *Science and Society* 10 (1946) 361-91. There is a large bibliography of Rostovtzeff's writings (444 items) by C. B. Welles in *Historia* 5 (1956) 358-81; and there is also a biography by Welles in *Architects and Craftsmen in History. Festschr. für Abbott Payson Usher* (Tübingen, 1956) 55-73.
6. See esp. the opening section of the *Grundrisse* (E.T. 83-100); cf. the translation by David McLellan, *Marx's Grundrisse* (1971) 16-33.
7. There are some useful remarks on the different ways in which these expressions can be used by Marx and Engels, in Ronald L. Meek, *Studies in the Labour Theory of Value*[2] (1973) 19 n.2, 151-2. If it is not invidious to pick out a handful of examples from a large number of passages, perhaps I could mention *Cap.* I,.509; III.776, 814-16, 831, 881; and the 1859 *Preface* (*MESW* 181). See also Section iii of this chapter.
8. I use the term 'primitive society' in the economic and indeed mainly technological sense. In what I am calling 'primitive societies' there may be an elaborate and sophisticated kinship structure and quite a complicated ideology; but that is entirely beside the point.
9. I make this reservation to allow for observations like those of the Siane of New Guinea by R. F. Salisbury, *From Stone to Steel* (1962); cf. Godelier, *RIE* 273 ff.
10. 'The creation of surplus-value (including rent) always has its basis in the relative productivity of agriculture; the first real form of surplus-value is surplus of agricultural produce (food), and the first real form of surplus-labour arises when one person is able to produce the food for two' (Marx, *TSV* II.360: 'the true physical basis of Physiocracy', according to Adam Smith).
11. H. W. Pearson, in Polanyi, *TMEE* 320-41 (esp. 322-3), a chapter (xvi) entitled 'The economy has no surplus: critique of a theory of development'. (It would be superfluous to cite other literature in this field: enough of it is discussed by Godelier, *RIE* 249-319.) Pearson finds a sense in which 'an institutional [as opposed to a 'biologically determined'] concept of specific surpluses – their creation and employment – may be fruitfully applied to the analysis of economic development' (ibid. 322). But in his argument he is thinking not of the *actual division* of the products of human labour but of *society's needs*. Criticising others' use of the term 'surplus', he says, 'There is a level of subsistence which once reached provides a measure – so to speak the dam over which the surplus flows. This surplus which is *beyond needs however these happen to be defined* [my italics] is then in some sense available: it may be traded abroad, or used to support the existence of craftsmen, a leisure class or other nonproductive members of the society' (ibid.). Having committed himself to this unfortunate definition, Pearson then discusses whether 'subsistence needs' are 'biologically determined' or 'socially defined'. Rejecting the first alternative, he concludes, 'If it is held that subsistence needs are not biologically but socially defined, there is no room for the concept of absolute surplus, for then the distribution of economic resources between subsistence and other requirements is determined only within the *total* context of needs thus defined . . . If the concept of surplus is to be employed here at all, it must be in a relative or constructive sense. In brief: A given quantity of goods or services would be surplus only if the society in some manner set these quantities aside and declared them to be available for a specific purpose' (ibid. 323). My 'surplus' is not that which 'the *society* in some manner sets aside' as in some way surplus to '*its* needs', but that which workers yield up, for the benefit of others, at first perhaps voluntarily in return for useful services, but later (the stage at which exploitation begins) without an adequate return, and under the influence of persuasion and compulsion.
12. Godelier, *RIE* 275-6. See also Lévi-Strauss, *SA* 338-40.
13. See IV.iv above, esp. the reference to Hilton, *BMMF* 131.
14. The very great advances in technology in the modern world do not need documentation here; but I will mention two passages I have come across which emphasise the immense increase in agricultural productivity: Jerome Blum, *The End of the Old Order in Rural Europe* (Princeton, 1978) 136 and n.56; and V. Gordon Childe, *Progress and Archaeology* (1944), who quotes (p.24) the report of an American national Committee on Technological Trends and National Policy, 1937, to the effect that 'in 1787 the surplus produced by nineteen farmers was required to support one city-dweller; now nineteen farmers produce on the average sufficient to support fifty-six city-dwellers and ten foreigners'. I cannot give a detailed bibliography here on Greek and Roman technology. For general surveys, see H. W. Pleket, 'Technology in the Greco-Roman world: a general report', in *Talanta* 5 (1973) 6-47; M. I. Finley, 'Technical innovation

and economic progress in the ancient world', in *Econ. Hist. Rev.*[2] 18 (1965) 29–45; Finley's review-article, 'Technology in the ancient world', in id. 12 (1959) 120–5; R. J. Forbes, *Studies in Anc. Technology*, especially (on sources of energy) II[2] (1965) 80–130, or Forbes' chapter xvii in *History of Technology* II, ed. Chas. Singer and others (1956). For the advances in the Middle Ages, see esp. Lynn White's brilliant article, TIMA (1940), which, although not entirely correct in some details and superseded at several points by more accurate recent work (some of it his own), remains very well worth reading, as one of the best summary statements of the technological advances made in the Middle Ages. It is not open to as many damaging criticisms as his most recent book, *MTSC* (1962): for some of these criticisms, see the review-article by R. H. Hilton and P. H. Sawyer, 'Technical determinism: the stirrup and the plough', in *Past & Present* 24 (1963) 90–100. See also White's contribution to *Scientific Change*, ed. A. C. Crombie (1963) 272–91, cf. 311–14, 327–32; and most recently White's chapter on 'The expansion of technology 500-1500', in *FEHE: MA* = the Fontana *Econ. Hist. of Europe, I. The Middle Ages*, ed. Carlo M. Cipolla (1972) 143–74, including a useful bibliography (172–4). I have not yet mentioned the fullest recent account known to me in a single book of the developments in technology during the Roman Empire: Franz Kiechle, *Sklavenarbeit u. technischer Fortschritt im römischen Reich (Forsch. zur ant. Sklaverei* 3, Wiesbaden, 1969). This is a compilation of much useful information, arranged conveniently under different headings; but it is unfortunately presented as a polemic against 'the Marxist' position, which is assumed to be that the existence of slavery was responsible for a lack of technological progress in antiquity. Some historians writing from a Marxist point of view have held this opinion, but so too have some non-Marxist historians; and if the horse that Kiechle is flogging is not quite a dead one, it is not a genuinely Marxist one either. In his Introduction Kiechle begins by quoting a famous letter of Engels (which, incidentally, he cites at second hand and dates to 15 January 1895 instead of 25 January 1894; he is also unaware that it was written to W. Borgius and not H. Starkenburg), although this does not mention slavery (see *MEW* XXXIX.205–7 = *MESC* 548–51). Kiechle continues with a quotation of a well-known footnote in *Das Kapital* (*MEW* XXIII.210 n.17 = *Cap.* I.196 n.1), which certainly does stress factors that 'make production by slave labour such a costly process', such as heavier agricultural implements than are otherwise necessary, but says nothing about slavery hindering inventiveness. Marx is here writing about American slavery and using the very best sources then available: F. L. Olmsted, *A Journey in the Seaboard Slave States* (1856), and J. E. Cairnes, *The Slave Power* (1862). I myself know of nothing in Marx to justify the belief that he thought slavery necessarily a hindrance to technical progress. Nor does Engels say so in his *Origin of the Family*, although in his preparatory notes for *Anti-Dühring* he did call slavery 'an impediment to more developed production' and say that 'Greece too perished on account of slavery' (Eng. trans. 413–14, Moscow 1947 & repr.; London 1975); and in the body of that work we find the statement that slavery was 'one of the chief causes of the decay' of those peoples among whom it was 'the dominant form of production' (ibid. 216). Yet Engels then proceeds at once to emphasise the important progressive role that slavery played in the Greek and Roman world: 'Without slavery, no Greek State, no Greek art and science; without slavery, no Roman Empire. But without the basis laid by Greek culture and the Roman Empire, also no modern Europe.' Kiechle's work has of course been welcomed by anti-Marxists. For example, W. Beringer, reviewing it (or rather, summarising its contents) in *Gnomon* 44 (1972) 313–16, regards it as an ample refutation of what he calls '*the Marxist assertion* that the institution of slavery hindered scientific-technical progress in the Roman Empire' (313); cf. '*the Marxist view* that the availability of slaves rendered technical innovations unnecessary', and 'contrary to *Marxist assertions* that slaves always do their worst' (314, my italics – Cairnes and Olmsted would have been astonished by such statements). A much more critical notice of Kiechle's book, written from a Marxist point of view but making points quite different from mine, is that of K.-P. Johne, in *Klio* 54 (1972) 379–83. I think I should add that in an *obiter dictum* in an early article, published in 1847 as part of his polemic against Karl Heinzen, Marx used the words 'the *slave-economy*, which caused the downfall of the republics of antiquity'; but he was clearly not thinking in terms of technology, as his sentence continues, 'the slave-economy, which will provoke the most fearful conflicts in the southern States of republican North America' (*MECW* VI.325, part of 'Moralising criticism and critical morality' = 'Die moralisierende Kritik und die kritisierende Moral').

15. See Joseph Needham, *Science and Civilisation in China* IV.ii (1965) 258–74; Lynn White, TIMA 147 and n.4.

16. See Kiechle, op. cit. 155-62, and other works cited in n.14 above. For China, see Needham, op. cit. 304-30.
17. On all aspects of ancient ships and sailing see Lionel Casson, *Ships and Seamanship in the Anc. World* (Princeton, 1971).
18. See Kiechle, op. cit. (in n.14 above) 115-30, and Forbes, as cited in n.14.
19. George Thomson, *Stud. in Anc. Greek Society, II. The First Philosophers* (1955) 249 ff., at 252.
20. Margaret O. Wason, *Class Struggles in Anc. Greece* (1947) 82, 36 n.1, 143; cf. 95, 96, 98, 99, 134, 144 etc.
21. Ernst Badian, *Publicans and Sinners* (Dunedin, 1972) 42; cf. many other passages, e.g. 49, 50, 51, 84-5, 91, 93, 98, 116 ('a partnership in exploitation' between governing élite and Equites). The most illuminating works on the Equites are (a) P. A. Brunt, 'The Equites in the Late Republic', in *Deuxième Conférence Internat. d'hist. écon.* [Aix-en-Provence, 1962], Vol.I. *Trade and Politics in the Anc. World* (Paris, 1965) 117-49, with Comment by T. R. S. Broughton, ibid. 150-62, both repr. in *The Crisis of the Roman Republic*, ed. Robin Seager (1969) 83-115, 118-30; and (b) Claude Nicolet, *L'Ordre équestre à l'époque républicaine (312-43 av. J.-C.)* = *BEFAR* 207, esp. Vol.I. *Définitions juridiques et structures sociales* (Paris, 1966), on which see Brunt in *Annales* 22 (1967) 1090-8; Vol.II is *Prosopographie des chevaliers romains* (Paris, 1974). Cf. also Benjamin Cohen, 'La notion d' "ordo" dans la Rome antique', in *Bull. de l'Assoc. G. Budé*, 4ᵉ Série, 2 (1975) 259-82, at 264-5; Finley, *AE* 49-50. It appears from an incidental remark in *Cap.* III.596-7 that in the eyes of Marx the characteristic Eques was 'the usurer, who becomes a landed proprietor or a slaveholder himself'. Some Equites may well have made their pile in this way, but most of them will always have been primarily landowners. And see VI.iii above.
22. The use of the term 'caste' should perhaps be confined to India. For a recent short introduction by a leading sociologist, with brief bibliography, see Bottomore, *Sociology*² 189-94. A book which has been greeted with an almost universal chorus of praise in the West is Louis Dumont, *Homo Hierarchicus*, which first appeared in French in 1966 and in an English tranlation in 1970; but it is most unsatisfactory to a historian. For a Marxist view of caste in India by a French anthropologist with African experience, see Meillassoux, op. cit. in n.4 above.

[II.ii]

1. Marx makes it clear in several places that *capital* too is 'not a thing, but rather a definite social production *relation*' (*Cap.* III.814); it is 'essentially the command over unpaid labour' (*Cap.* I.534).
2. See *Cap.* III.385 ('exploitation, the appropriation of the unpaid labour of others') and many similar passages.
3. Here I take a fundamentally different view from e.g. Dahrendorf, who wishes to understand class in political rather than economic terms, and for whom 'control over the means of production is but a special case of authority' (*CCCIS*, esp. 136); cf. Section v of this chapter.
4. 'Most commonly', but not always: my definition allows for e.g. control being exercised by directors of a limited company who are not also majority shareholders. Cf. Marx, *Cap.* III.382-90 (and I.iv above, n.16).
5. E.g. the treatment of barbarians in Amm. Marc. XVI.xi.9; XVII.viii.3-4; xiii.13-20; XIX.xi.14-15; XXIV.iv.25; XXVIII.v.4-7; XXX.v.14; vii.8; and above all XXXI.xvi.8; also the assassination in XXVII.x.3-4, with XXX.vii.7. Ammianus describes without a shudder the atrocities (mutilation or burning alive) repeatedly inflicted by Count Theodosius (father of the Emperor Theodosius I, and described as exceptionally able by Amm. XXIX.v.4) on traitors and rebels in Africa: XXIX.v.22-4 (where Ammianus warmly approves the action, with a quotation from Cicero about 'wholesome severity'), 31, 43, 48-9, 50.
6. The massacre of no fewer than 700 members of the *dēmos* of Aegina at the end of the revolution led by Nicodromus in the early fifth century (Hdts VI.88-91) is said to have been the work of 'the wealthy men' (οἱ παχέες, 91) and was no doubt the product of class conflict between rich and poor. At Corcyra in 427 (Thuc. III.70-81) we hear again and again of the *dēmos* on one side, some of them burdened with debt (81.4), and on the other of the ὀλίγοι (74.2), some of whom were 'very rich' (70.4); in 410 (Diod. XIII.48) we have the *dēmos* against 'the most influential people' (48.5) – class conflict again. (Here my opinion differs from that of A. Fuks, in *AJP* 92 [1971] 48-55.)

[II.iii]

1. See esp. Marx's letter to Weydemeyer of 5 March 1852: 'No credit is due to me for discovering the existence of classes in modern society or the struggle between them. Long before me bourgeois historians had described the historical development of this class struggle and bourgeois economists the economic anatomy of the classes' (*MESC* 86; the continuation is very interesting). It is hard to name the 'bourgeois historians' in question: certainly they include Augustin Thierry, whom Marx calls 'the father of the "class struggle" in French historiography' (*MESC* 105, 27 July 1854), and who is also mentioned in the letter of 5 March 1852 already referred to, with Guizot and John Wade; probably also Mignet, mentioned, with Thierry and Guizot and 'all the English historians up to 1850', in a letter of Engels of 25 January 1894 (*MESC* 550). In addition to Thierry, Guizot, Wade and Mignet, we should perhaps add Saint-Simon; and I have also seen named in this connection Linguet (on whom see Marx's letter to Schweitzer of 24 January 1865, *MESC* 192), Sismondi, Thiers, and even Macaulay, whom Marx despised as a 'systematic falsifier of history' (*Cap.* I,717 n.1; cf. 273-4 n.2). For the emergence of class terminology in England, see Asa Briggs, 'The language of "class" in early nineteenth-century England', in *Essays in Labour History* I, ed. Asa Briggs and John Saville (rev. edn., 1967) 43-73. The expressions 'higher' and 'middle' classes are known to have appeared in the eighteenth century, 'the working classes' only in 1813. W. A. Mackinnon in 1828 defined his 'upper', 'middle' and 'lower' classes in terms of income.
2. For convenience, I will cite only one work for all three groups: (a) *Cap.* III.249-50, 257, 263-4, 884; (b) 266, 440; (c) 812.
3. See I.iv and its n.10 above. Mao, in his essay 'On contradiction', dating from August 1937 (see I.iv n.10 above), speaks of 'the contradiction between the exploiting and exploited classes' (discovered, he says, by Marx and Engels): he sees it as needing to develop to a certain stage before it 'assumes the form of open antagonism'. There is some very acute discussion in this essay of the principles that should guide a Marxist confronted with the kind of revolutionary situation in which Mao found himself in 1937.
4. The German originals are *MEGA* I.v.410 = *MEW* III.417, and *MEW* XXV.399.
5. See *MEGA* I.iii.71, 72, 77 = *MECW* III.262, 263, 267.
6. See e.g. *MEGA* I.v.386-92 (= *MEW* III.393-9) = *MECW* V.408-13; *MEW* XXIII.309, 419, 743 = *Cap.* I.292, 397, 715; *MEW* XXIV.299-300, 306 = *Cap.* II.300, 308; *MEW* XXV.51, 147, 151, 207, 232, 243 = *Cap.* III.41, 139, 142, 196-7, 220, 232.
7. *MEGA* I.i.i.565 = *MECW* III.141; and see esp. *MEW* XXIII.743 = *Cap.* I.715 (*Ausbeutung, ausbeuteten,* and *kapitalistische Exploitation,* all occurring close together); *MEW* XXIV.42 = *Cap.* II.37 (*Ausbeutung der Arbeitskraft*); *MEW* XXV.623 = *Cap.* III.609 (*eine sekundäre Ausbeutung*).
8. My own translation is very literal. For a more readable one, see Bottomore/Rubel, *KM* 99-100. I have felt obliged to turn one abstract German expression, 'Herrschafts- und Knechtschaftsverhältnis' ('relationship of domination and subjection'), into a more concrete English one, 'relationship between those who dominate and those who are in subjection'.
9. Carl N. Degler, 'Starr on slavery', in *JEH* 19 (1959) 271-7, criticising C. G. Starr, 'An overdose of slavery', in *JEH* 18 (1958) 17-32. Degler's excellent article has unfortunately been omitted from the massive *Bibliographie zur antiken Sklaverei,* ed. Joseph Vogt (Bochum, 1971). For another critique of Starr's article, less effective than Degler's, see P. Oliva, 'Die Bedeutung der antiken Sklaverei' in *Acta Ant.* 8 (1960) 309-19, at 310-15.
10. In *AE* 186 nn.30-1 Finley reveals his reliance upon what he mistakenly calls the 'brilliant analysis' of Ossowski, *CSSC*; and in n.32 he also refers with approval to a work by Vidal-Naquet which I criticise farther on in the main text above.
11. I agree with most of what J. A. Banks says in *Marxist Sociology in Action* (1970) 25-8, except that I would treat 'the relationships which labourers have *with other labourers* in a co-operative system' not as part of 'the material forces of production' but as part of 'the relations of production'. I am unhappy about the way the first paragraph on *MSA* 27 is phrased, but I warmly agree again with Banks that class struggles are 'to be seen not simply as a history of conflict between property owners and the propertyless, as such, but as an inevitable consequence of the division of society along the lines of a relationship in which the products of one class are appropriated, at least in part, by the other. In brief, however exploitation is achieved, whether through force or through socially approved methods of legal justification, the

distinction between social classes is to be drawn along the lines of the manner in which the products of labour are distributed'.

12. Arist., *Eth. Nic.* VIII.13, 1161^{b}4; *Pol.* I.4, 1253^{b}32, with 27 ff.; cf. *Eth. Eud.* VII.8, 1241^{b}23-4. And see Varro, *RR* I.xvii.1: *instrumentum vocale*.

13. See pp.9-10 of the Pelican paperback edition, 1968 (and repr.), a reissue of the original edition of 1963.

14. E. J. Hobsbawm, 'Class consciousness in history', in *Aspects of History and Class Consciousness*, ed. Istvan Mészaros (1971) 5-21, at 6. The italics are mine.

15. By R. Archer and S. C. Humphreys, as 'Remarks on the class struggle in Ancient Greece', in *Critique of Anthropology* 7 (1976) 67-81.

16. Charles Parain, 'Les caractères spécifiques de la lutte de classes dans l'Antiquité classique', in *La Pensée* 108 (April 1963) 3-25. The distinction seems to be a feature of French neo-Marxist thought.

17. Contrast *OPW* 90: I would now express myself differently.

18. Here I recommend the third chapter in Stampp, *PI* (86-140), entitled 'A troublesome property', which gives much interesting evidence from the Old South. R. W. Fogel and S. L. Engerman, *Time on the Cross* (1974), maintain, rightly or wrongly, that Stampp overestimates the role of punishment in the treatment of American slaves, and that he has not allowed sufficiently for rewards; but see the chapter (II) by H. Gutman and R. Sutch in *Reckoning with Slavery*, ed. Paul A. David and others (New York, 1976) 55-93. In antiquity, of course, an even more valuable reward was available than anything Southern slaveowners were normally willing to offer: manumission, the prospect of which must have been a very powerful inducement to the slave to ingratiate himself with his master. Cf. III.v above.

19. This particular passage (*MECW* V.432) is part of one of the comparatively few really important and excellent portions of Parts II and III of Volume I of the *German Ideology* (*MECW* V.97-452), on which see McLellan, *KMLT* 148-51, who is rightly critical. But I warmly agree with his totally different verdict on Part I of the same work, which he calls 'one of the most central of Marx's works ... a tremendous achievement ... Marx never subsequently stated his materialist conception of history at such length and in detail. It remains a masterpiece today'.

20. Among other examples of the use of the expression 'free men' in reference to a situation of class struggle against slaves, where 'slaveowners' would have been preferable, see the article by Engels in the *Neue Rheinische Zeitung* for 1 July 1848, *MECW* VII.153.

21. It is interesting to compare a statement made in a book published in 1836 by Eduard Gans, a progressive Hegelian whose lectures on law Marx attended in the late 1830s at the University of Berlin, and who had been influenced by Saint-Simon and his followers. 'Once,' said Gans, 'there was the opposition between master and slave, then between patrician and plebeian, and later still between feudal lord and vassal; now we have the idle rich and the worker.' (I quote from Werner Blumenberg, *Karl Marx* [trans. by Douglas Scott, London, 1972] 44-6.)

22. There was an excellent review of this book in the *Times Literary Supplement* no.3729 (24 August 1973) 965-6.

23. I have not been able to read a book which has recently appeared: Frederick A. Johnstone, *Class, Race and Gold. A Study of Class Relations and Racial Discrimination in South Africa* (London, 1976).

24. In particular, it would be impossible, on the principles adopted by Castles and Kosack, to treat a slave χωρὶς οἰκῶν (see III.iv above and its n.9 below) as belonging to a different class from the poor free craftsman, whom he would resemble in all relevant respects except that he was an unfree man, whose relatively privileged status (for a slave) was infinitely precarious.

[II.iv]

1. The most convenient text of the *Politics* is that of W. D. Ross (*OCT*, 1957). The most useful English translation is that of Ernest Barker, *The Politics of Aristotle* (1946 and repr.); but there are occasional mistranslations, e.g. of περίοικοι as 'serfs' (cf. III.iv above). The very detailed commentary of Newman, *PA* = W. L. Newman, *The Politics of Aristotle* (4 vols, 1887-1902), makes the same error but is not often marred by similar ones.

2. I shall give no detailed references here: see the penultimate paragraph of my AHP = 'Aristotle on history and poetry (*Poetics* 9, 1451^{a}36-^{b}11)', in *The Ancient Historian and his Materials* (Essays in Honour of C. E. Stevens), ed. Barbara Levick (1975), 45-58. The most useful recent book dealing

with the 'political' and historical writings of Aristotle is Weil, *AH* = Raymond Weil, *Aristote et l'histoire* (Paris, 1960).

3. Plut., *Numa* 1.6 = Diels-Kranz, *FVS*[6+] II.330, no.86 B 3 = *FGrH* 6 F 2 (in I.157; cf. 477). The Greek is τῶν Ὀλυμπιονικῶν . . . ὧν τὴν ἀναγραφὴν ὀψέ φασιν Ἱππίαν ἐκδοῦναι τὸν Ἠλεῖον, ἀπ' οὐδενὸς ὁρμώμενον ἀναγκαίου πρὸς πίστιν. For a change in Jacoby's view, see his *Atthis* (1949) 353 n.3. See also *Atthis* 58-9, 297 n.6, and *FGrH* III b (Suppl., 1954) i.381.

4. See my AHP (n.2 above) 52-3 and 58 n.49, citing esp. H. Bloch's admirable article, published in 1940.

4a. I have not been able to take account of an article by Alexander Fuks, published posthumously as 'Plato and the social question: the problem of poverty and riches in the *Laws*', in *Anc. Soc.* 10 (1979) 33-78.

5. According to Plato, *Theaet.* 174e, a common Greek view was that a man was εὐγενής if his family had been rich for seven generations. Some other relevant passages are quoted by J. D. Denniston in his edition of Euripides, *Electra* (1939), at pp.80-2, cf. 95. For some fifth/fourth-century attacks on εὐγένεια, see W. K. C. Guthrie, *History of Greek Philosophy* III (1969) 152-5 = *The Sophists* (paperback, 1971) 152-5,

6. For some examples, see my *OPW* 35 nn.66, 68; and to n.68 add esp. Plato, *Rep.* IV.422e-3a.

7. Arist., *Pol.* IV.11, 1296[a]22 ff., esp. 36-8. My own view is that the unnamed 'one single man' in a position of authority who set up a mixed constitution (1296[a]38-40) can only be Solon: cf. *Pol.* II.12, 1273[b]27-4[a]21.

8. See my ECAPS 10 and nn.29-32. Newman, *PA* IV.332 (on *Pol.* V.4,1304[b]1), gives a list of passages in the *Politics* in which ὁ δῆμος (in the sense of the lower classes) is contrasted with οἱ πλούσιοι, οἱ εὔποροι, οἱ τὰς οὐσίας ἔχοντες, οἱ γνώριμοι, οἱ ἐπιεικεῖς, or even οἱ ὁπλῖται.

9. In *Pol.* IV.4, 1290[b]15, some recent editors have substituted ὀλιγαρχία for δῆμος, without any MS authority. Actually, either reading can be made to fit both the immediate context (1290[a]30-[b]20) and III.8, 1279[b]16-80[a]6 (esp.1279[b]20-6), because the example of Colophon that follows (1290[b]15-17) and the imaginary case in 1290[a]33-7 (which seems to me precisely similar, and incidentally contains a negation of *democracy*) are *exceptions* which do not fit the definition of democracy and oligarchy given in 1290[b]17-20. But it is perfectly clear from III.8, 1279[b]17-19 and 1279[b]34-80[a]6 (esp. 1279[b]39-80[a]3), not to mention various other passages, that in Aristotle's mind oligarchy is above all the rule of the propertied class, democracy the rule of the poor, so that δῆμος is the more relevant word in 1290[b]15. If, however, with Newman (*PA* IV.161), we interpret 1290[b]14-15 as saying emphatically '[*not because of their wealth but*] simply because they are more numerous', there is perhaps some justification for reading ὀλιγαρχία.

10. Cf. *Pol.* III.9, 1280[a]27-31; V.3, 1303[b]6-7.

11. For all this, see my *OPW* 35-7 (and, on Ps.-Xen., *Ath. Pol.* in general, *OPW* 307-10, Appendix VI).

12. This is widely admitted, however painful the fact may be to many Western ideologists. It should be sufficient to refer to S. M. Lipset, 'Elections: the expression of the democratic class struggle', in Bendix/Lipset, *CSP*[2] 413-28, repr. from pp.230-78 of the 1963 Anchor edition (New York) of Lipset, *Political Man* (1960).

13. I know of no work containing a fully adequate study of the concept of the 'mixed constitution', from its first appearance in Thuc. VIII.97.1-2 down to the Roman period. The most recent works I have seen are by Kurt von Fritz, *The Theory of the Mixed Constitution in Antiquity* (New York, 1954), who concentrates on Polybius, and G. J. D. Aalders, *Die Theorie der gemischten Verfassung im Altertum* (Amsterdam, 1968), who discusses the early appearances of the concept but has not sufficiently grasped the fact, made so clear by Aristotle above all, that oligarchy *was* the rule of the propertied class. A very useful brief survey is that of Walbank, *HCP* I.639-41.

14. See my CFT. As I shall explain elsewhere (and see V.ii and its nn.30-1 below), I see nothing to make me alter my views in the article by P. J. Rhodes, in *JHS* 92 (1972) 115-27, which contains not a single valid new argument.

15. See e.g. von Fritz, op. cit. (in n.13 above) 78-81.

16. Arist., *Pol.* IV.8-9, 1293[b]31-94[b]41; cf. 11, 1295[b]1-96[a]40; 13, 1297[a]38-[b]1.

17. See e.g. Cic., *De rep.* I.45, 54, 69; II.41, 57 etc.

18. Jones, *AD* 50-4; M. H. Hansen, '*Nomos* and *Psephisma* in fourth-century Athens', in *GRBS* 19 (1978) 315-30; and 'Did the Athenian *Ecclesia* legislate after 403/2 B.C.?', in ibid. 20 (1979) 27-53. I wish to mention here some other recent articles by Hansen which have made a useful contribution to our knowledge of the working of the Athenian democracy: 'How many

Athenians attended the *Ecclesia*?', in ibid. 17 (1976) 115-34; 'How did the Athenian *Ecclesia* vote?', in ibid. 18 (1977) 123-37; 'How often did the *Ecclesia* meet?', in ibid. 43-70; '*Demos, Ecclesia* and *Dicasterion* in Classical Athens', in ibid. 19 (1978) 127-46; and 'The duration of a meeting of the Athenian *Ecclesia*', in *CP* 74 (1979) 43-9; cf. also *The Sovereignty of the People's Court in Athens in the Fourth Century B.C. and the Public Action against Unconstitutional Proposals* = *Odense Univ. Class. Stud.* 4 (1974).

19. See e.g. *Pol.* III.4, 1277^{b}3; IV.11, 1296^{a}1-2; 12, 1296^{b}29-30; 14, 1298^{a}31; V.10, 1312^{b}5-6 (where ἡ δημοκρατία ἡ τελευταία is a τυραννίς), 35-6; 11, 1313^{b}32-3; VI.5, 1320^{a}17. The word τελευταία is used partly because the 'extreme' form of democracy is also the last to develop, ἡ τελευταία τοῖς χρόνοις, IV.6, 1293^{a}1.

20. For Aristotle's conception of the relation between νόμος and ψήφισμα, see his *EN* V.10, 1137^{b}13-32 (esp. 13-14, 27-32); cf. *Pol.* IV.4, 1292^{a}4-13, 23-5, 30-7.

21. The main passages, given by Hansen on p.44 of his 1979 article (n.18 above), are *Pol.* IV.4, 1292^{a}4-13 (esp. 5-7, 10), 23-5, 32-4, 35-7; 6, 1292^{b}41 ff., esp. 1293^{a}9-10; 14, 1298^{b}13-15; V.5, 1305^{a}32; 9, 1310^{a}2-4; cf. VI.2, 1317^{b}28-9.

22. Cf. Hansen's two articles (n.18 above). I am not sure myself whether Aristotle would have thought of the Athenian constitution as reaching the form of 'extreme democracy' in 462/1, or after the death of Pericles, or only with the introduction of Assembly pay after 403.

23. Arist., *Pol.* IV.3, 1289^{b}27-90^{a}13.

24. For the distinction between ἔμποροι and ναύκληροι, see M. I. Finkelstein [Finley], in *CP* 30 (1935) 320-36.

25. Cf. *Pol.* IV.12, 1296^{b}24-31; and VI.4, 1318^{b}6-19^{b}4; also IV.4, 1291^{b}17-28, where the categories are muddled: they overlap. Two other passages, IV.4, 1291^{b}30-2^{a}13, and 6, 1292^{b}23-3^{a}10, are technical, like those cited in the next note on types of oligarchy. Another passage, mentioned in the text above, viz. IV.4, 1290^{b}38-1^{a}8 with 1291^{a}33-^{b}13, is general and applies indifferently to oligarchy and democracy, although mainly more relevant to democracy.

26. *Pol.* IV.5, 1292^{a}39-^{b}10; 6, 1293^{a}12-34; VI.6, 1320^{b}18-1^{a}4. These texts may be compared with the two cited in the preceding note (1291^{b}30-2^{a}13, 1292^{b}23-3^{a}10) relating to democracy.

27. I feel I must emphasise here that I have said 'non-citizens' and not 'metics', because although I made my position perfectly clear in *OPW* 265 (and n.59) and 393 ff., two of my Oxford colleagues, reviewing that book, accused me of believing that 'Greek trade was largely in the hands of metics' (G. L. Cawkwell, in *CR* 89 = n.s. 25 [1975], at 259) or of 'relying heavily on the modern theory that trade was largely in the hands of metics' (Oswyn Murray, in *Greece & Rome*² 20 [1973], at 205)!

28. D. J. McCargar, 'The relative date of Kleisthenes' legislation', in *Historia* 25 (1976) 385-95, at 394-5. He refers to some of the works I have in mind; one could add e.g. R. Sealey, 'The origins of *Demokratia*', in *CSCA* 6 (1973) 253-95; and *A History of the Greek City States ca. 700-338 B.C.* (Berkeley etc., 1977), the very unsatisfactory nature of which is well brought out in the review by Paul Cartledge, in *JHS* 98 (1978) 193-4.

29. 'Aristotle's analysis of the nature of political struggle', in *AJP* 72 (1951) 145-61, repr. in *Articles on Aristotle 2. Ethics and Politics*, ed. Jonathan Barnes and others (1977) 159-69.

30. Virtually all occurrences of the word τιμή in Aristotle divide into two main groups, according in almost every case to whether the word is being used in the singular or the plural. (1) In the plural, τιμαί, the examples come almost entirely from the *Politics*, where τιμαί = ἀρχαί = offices, magistracies: this is made specific in III.10, 1281^{a}31-2. Among other passages are II.8, 1268^{a}20-3 (where τιμαί in 21 = ἀρχαί in 23; contrast 1268^{a}8 for τιμή in the singular: cf. below); III.5, 1278^{a}37-8; 13, 1283^{b}14; IV.4, 1290^{b}11-14; 13, 1297^{b}6-8 (where τιμαί = τὸ ἄρχειν in V.8, 1308^{b}35); V.6, 1305^{b}2-6 (where τιμαί in 4 = ἀρχαί in 3); 8, 1308^{b}10-14. (2) in the *singular*, τιμή is honour, esteem, something highly subjective, in the sense that different people may well see it very differently: it is the vital element in Weber/Finley 'status' ('soziale Einschätzung der Ehre': Weber, as quoted in translation in the main text above). The examples are almost entirely from the ethical works, e.g. (in addition to the passages quoted in the main text above, and some others) *EN* VIII.14, 1163^{b}1-11; *EE* III.5, 1232^{b}10-19. See also *Rhet.* I.5, 1361^{a}27-1^{b}2. In the *Politics* there are only one or two casual mentions of τιμή in the singular, e.g. II.8, 1268^{a}8 (contrast 21, in the plural: see above); III.12, 1283^{a}14 (athletics); and V.2, 1302^{a}32-2^{b}2, with 3, 1302^{b}10-14 (τιμή as a cause of στάσις). There are of course a few peculiar usages, e.g. *Pol.* I.7, 1255^{b}36 (= almost 'duty'), and VII.16, 1335^{b}16 (= function of being in charge of); and on a few other occasions the word means something like 'valuation' (e.g. *Rhet.* II.2, 1378^{b}30-1; 16, 1391^{a}1-2).

31. Ernest Barker, *From Alexander to Constantine* (1956), gives a fair selection in translation, which reveals the shallowness and futility of nearly all this stuff. Little of it seems to me to reach even the modest standard of Cicero's *De republica*. Others may be able to find more of value than I can in Ernest Barker's other anthology, published a year later: *Social and Political Thought in Byzantium from Justinian I to the Last Palaeologus* (1957).

[II.v]

1. On 'functionalism', see e.g. Bottomore, *Sociology*² 42-5, 57-9, 62, 201-2, 299-300; Bendix/Lipset, *CSP*² 47-72 (extracts from essays by Kingsley Davis and Wilbert Moore, Melvin M. Tumin, Włodzimierz Wesołowski, and Arthur L. Stinchcombe); Ralf Dahrendorf's Inaugural Lecture at Tübingen, 'On the origin of inequality among men', in *Essays in the Theory of Society* (1968) 151-78, repr. in *Social Inequality*, ed. André Béteille (1969 and repr.) 16-44, at pp.28 ff.; Leonard Reissman, in *Sociology: An Introduction*, ed. Neil J. Smelser (1967) 225-9. For an eloquent protest by a distinguished anthropologist against what he could describe in the Marett Lecture for 1950 as 'the functional theory dominant in English anthropology today' (the situation is rather different now), see E. E. Evans-Pritchard, *Essays in Social Anthropology* (1962, paperback 1969), 18-28 (the phrase quoted is from p.20), 46-65.
2. The passage quoted comes from 'The rise and fall of the manorial system: a theoretical model', in *JEH* 31 (1971) 777-803, at p.778. The earlier article by North and Thomas is 'An economic theory of the growth of the western world', in *Econ. Hist. Rev.*² 23 (1970) 1-17, and the later book is *The Rise of the Western World* (Cambridge, 1973).
2a. Brenner's article has been criticised in many different ways, e.g. in a series of papers of very uneven value in *Past & Present* 78 (1978) 24-37, 37-47, 47-55, by M. M. Postan and John Hatcher, Patricia Croot and David Parker, Heide Wunder, and 79 (also 1978) 55-9, 60-9, by E. Le Roy Ladurie, and Guy Bois; but I have seen nothing there or elsewhere to weaken Brenner's arguments against the position adopted by North and Thomas.
3. See p.5 n.1 of their 1970 article, cited in n.2 above.
4. See 'The trend of modern economics', in Dobb's *Political Economy and Capitalism* (1937, repr. 1940) 127-84 (esp. 170-80), which has been conveniently reprinted in *A Critique of Economic Theory*, ed. E. K. Hunt and J. G. Schwartz (Penguin, 1972) 39-82, esp. 71-8. (I owe my knowledge of this work of Dobb's to Jeffrey James.)
5. There is a *Schriftenverzeichnis* of Weber's publications in German on pp.755-60 of the biography of Weber by his widow, Marianne Weber, *Max Weber. Ein Lebensbild* (repr. 1950). The most recent 'Max Weber Bibliographie', by Dirk Käsler, assisted by Helmut Fogt, can be found in *Kölner Zeitschr. für Soziologie u. Sozialpsychologie* 27 (1975) 703-30, following an article on pp.663-702 by Friedrich H. Tenbruck, 'Das Werk Max Webers'. The flow of contemporary writing on Weber shows no sign of abating. The *Hist. Ztschr.* 201 (1965) devoted a hundred pages (529-630) to three articles on Weber, by Alfred Heuss, Wolfgang J. Mommsen, and Karl Bosl, of which the first relates specifically to the ancient world: Heuss, 'Max Webers Bedeutung für die Geschichte des griechisch-römischen Altertums', pp.529-56. Bendix, *MWIP* vii-x, gives a useful short list of Weber's main works in German, with English translations. Weber, *CIB* 311-13, has a list of English translations of Weber, with some modern works on him in English; there is also a bibliography of important works in English by Weber and others in Eldridge, *MWISR* 291-5. More recent than any of the editions and translations mentioned in this note is the unsatisfactory English translation by R. I. Frank, with the inappropriate title, *The Agrarian Sociology of Ancient Civilizations* (1976), of Weber's *AA* (see my Bibliography). I might also mention the criticisms of Weber in Polanyi, *PAME* 135-8, cf. 124.
6. Max Weber, *Die römische Agrargeschichte in ihrer Bedeutung für das Staats- und Privatrecht* (Stuttgart, 1891).
7. See Rostovtzeff, *SEHRE*² II.751 n.9.
8. Weber's 'Die sozialen Gründe des Untergangs der antiken Kultur', delivered in 1896 at Freiburg and published originally in the magazine, *Die Wahrheit* (Stuttgart, 1896), was reprinted in Weber's collected essays, *Gesammelte Aufsätze zur Sozial- und Wirtschaftsgeschichte* (Tübingen, 1924) 289-311. An English translation by Christian Mackauer, under the title quoted in the text above, was published in *The Journal of General Education* 5 (1950) 75-88, and reprinted in

Eldridge, *MWISR* 254-75, and in *The Slave Economies*, Vol.I. *Historical and Theoretical Perspectives*, ed. Eugene D. Genovese (New York/London etc., 1973) 45-67; there is a different one in Weber, *ASAC* 389-411. See IV.iii above, § 13(a).

9. That he could write in his *AA* 151 of 'die kaufmännische [Oligarchie] von Chios' and 'die kaufmännischen Oligarchien Korinths und Kerkyras' (contrast my *OPW* 266-7, 396) may show no more than that he took over some current 'standard views', however groundless; but in general he reveals no thorough acquaintance with the original sources for Greek history in this work or in his *WG* or elsewhere.

10. For some interesting and justified observations on the difficulty of Weber's German, and of translating it into English, see the Preface to Gerth/Mills, *FMW* vi-vii.

11. Most useful are Weber, *ES* (3 vols), *TSEO*, and *GEH* (the last less well translated); Gerth/Mills, *FMW*; Eldridge, *MWISR*.

12. See Guenther Roth, 'The historical relationship to Marxism', in *Scholarship and Partisanship: Essays on Max Weber*, ed. Reinhard Bendix and Roth (paperback 1971) 227-52, at p.228; and see Gerth/Mills, *FMW* 46-50, 63.

13. See e.g. Weber, *MSS* 103, reprinted in Eldridge, *MWISR* 228. Cf. the essay cited in the last note, at p.240.

14. See Eldridge, *MWISR* 205 (I have altered the translation slightly). Weber's lecture, 'Der Sozialismus', is printed in his *Gesammelte Aufsätze zur Soziologie und Sozialpolitik* (1924) 492-518: see 504-5.

15. The two passages are: (1) *WuG*⁵ I.177-80 (= *ES* I.302-7 = *TSEO* 424-9); and (2) *WuG*⁵ II.531-40 (= *ES* II.926-39, mainly reprinted from Gerth/Mills, *FMW* 180-95). And see the passages quoted in the next two notes. But I agree with W. G. Runciman, *Relative Deprivation and Social Justice* (1966) 37, reprinted in the Penguin *Social Inequality* (ed. André Béteille, 1969 and repr.) 46, that it is not entirely clear what Weber meant by his 'class, status and power'!

16. See Gerth/Mills, *FMW* 300-1, translated from *Archiv für Sozialwiss.* 41 (1915), reprinted in Weber's *Gesammelte Aufsätze zur Religionssoziologie* I.237 ff., at 273-5.

17. See Gerth/Mills, *FMW* 405, again trans. from an article in the *Archiv* (1916), and reprinted in Weber's *GAzRS* II.41-2.

18. According to Runciman, *RDSJ* (n.15 above) 37-8, reprinted in *SI* (n.15 above) 47, 'A person's "class"-situation, in Weber's sense, is the location which he shares with those who are similarly placed in the processes of production, distribution and exchange'; and he adds, 'This is close to the Marxist definition of class.' This seems to me not an entirely correct description of Weber's position.

19. Weber, *WuG*⁵ I.180 (= *ES* I.306 = *TSEO* 428); cf. *WuG*⁵ II.535 (= *ES* II.932 = *FMW* 187).

20. Weber, *WuG*⁵ II.534 (= *ES* II.932 = *FMW* 186-7); cf. *FMW* 405.

21. Weber, *WuG*⁵ II.537 (= *ES* II.935-6 = *FMW* 191).

22. Weber, *WuG*⁵ II.538 (= *ES* II.937 = *FMW* 193).

23. This work originated in two articles, 'Die protestantische Ethik und der "Geist" des Kapitalismus', in *Archiv für Sozialwiss.* 20 (1904) and 21 (1905), repr. in Weber's *Gesammelte Aufsätze zur Religionssoziologie* I.17-206. There is a good English trans. by Talcott Parsons, with a Foreword by R. H. Tawney (1930 and repr.). For the controversy aroused by this work, see *Protestantism and Capitalism. The Weber Thesis and its Critics*, ed. Robert W. Green (Boston, 1959), which includes extracts from a number of authors, including Ephraim Fischoff, Albert Hyma, and H. M. Robertson. [A second edition of Parsons's translation (1976) has a useful Introduction by Anthony Giddens and further bibliography.]

23a. A German correspondent of mine (who is far from being a Marxist) correctly identified a basic element in Finley's outlook when he wrote, in a letter to me, that 'in der *Ancient Economy* Finley von den Bewusstseinsstrukturen ausgeht'.

24. Weber, *WuG*⁵ II.534-5 (= *ES* II.932).

25. Finley's 'spectrum' or 'continuum' of statuses seems to have appeared for the first time in his paper, *WGCBSL*, a lecture delivered in 1958 and published in 1959 and since reprinted more than once, e.g. in *SCA*, ed. Finley, 53-72 (see esp. p.55). It can also be found in several of his other works, e.g. *AE* 67-8, 87; *SSAG* 186; *BSF* 247, 248. And see J. Pečírka, 'Von der asiatischen Produktionsweise zu einer marxistischen Analyse der frühen Klassengesellschaften', in *Eirene* 6 (1967) 141-74, at p.172.

26. Lys. XII.19: 120 slaves, probably including domestics as well as those who worked in the brothers' shield-factory. We hear of three Athenians who allegedly possessed even larger numbers of slaves: Nicias 1,000, Hipponicus 600, and Philemonides 300 (Xen., *De vect.* IV.14-15); but these figures are hardly reliable: see Westermann, *ASA* 461 = *SCA* (ed. Finley) 83.

27. See J. Pečírka, _The Formula for the Grant of Enktesis in Attic Inscriptions_ (_Acta Univ. Carolinae, Philos. et Hist. Monographia_ XV, Prague, 1966). The 'Conclusions' are on pp.137–49. See also Pečírka's 'Land tenure and the development of the Athenian polis', in ΓΕΡΑΣ. _Studies Pres. to George Thomson_, ed. L. Varcl and R. F. Willetts (Prague, 1963) 183–201.

28. I admit that I have not thoroughly investigated this question, of which I have seen no comprehensive treatment, and I will merely give references to two very recent works: I. S. Svencickaja, in _Eirene_ 15 (1977) 27–54, at 28–9, 30–1; and M. H. Crawford, in _Imperialism in the Ancient World_, ed. P. D. A. Garnsey and C. R. Whittaker (1978), at 195–6 and 332 n.14.

29. There is a large bibliography on metics, of which it will be sufficient to mention H. Hommel, in _RE_ XV.ii (1932) 1413–58; Busolt-Swoboda, _GS_ I.292-303; M. Clerc, _Les métèques athéniens_ (Paris, 1893, limited to Athens); A. R. W. Harrison, _The Law of Athens_ I (1968) 187–99; and, most recently, Philippe Gauthier, _Symbola. Les étrangers et la justice dans les cités grecques_ (Nancy, 1972), an unnecessarily verbose book of uneven quality, with a long chapter (iii, pp.107–56) devoted largely to metics at Athens. (I do not know whether it is carelessness, or a lack of sufficient familiarity with the English language, which led Gauthier, op. cit. 180, to give a gross misrepresentation of opinions I expressed in my NJAE I. His statement that I 'voyait en tout et pour tout dans les δίκαι ἀπὸ συμβολῶν des litiges d'ordre commercial, portant sur des biens' pretends that I hold views which in fact I was at pains to refute at length: see esp. NJAE I.95-6, 101-3, 108-10.) See also now David Whitehead, _The Ideology of the Athenian Metic_ (= Camb. Philol. Soc., Suppl. Vol.4, 1977).

30. Thus in _Dig._ L.xvi.239.2, Pomponius can equate Roman _incola_ with Greek πάροικος. For πάροικος (or κάτοικος) as the standard Hellenistic word for what we usually call a 'metic', see Welles, _RCHP_, pp.353, 345.

31. See n.1 above: the passage in question is in n.20, _ETS_ 173 = _SI_ 37, where Dahrendorf is explaining his 'substantial revision' of his previously published views. Cf. Dahrendorf's _CCCIS_ 204, where he says that by 'class' he means here 'complex groups that are generated by the differential distribution of authority in imperatively coordinated associations' (cf. id. 138 etc.). His 'imperatively coordinated association' is Weber's _Herrschaftsverband_ (id. 167).

32. It will be sufficient to refer to the objections to Dahrendorf's position raised by Frank Parkin, _Class Inequality and Political Order_ (1971; Paladin paperback, 1972) 44–6. I agree with Parkin that 'to some extent, . . . to conceive of stratification in terms of power may simply be another way of conceptualising the distribution of class and status advantages. That is, to speak of the distribution of power could be understood as another way of describing the flow of rewards . . . In other words, power . . . can be thought of as a concept or metaphor which is used to depict the flow of resources' (ibid. 46). And Parkin, himself particularly concerned with 'social stratification', has no occasion to notice that Dahrendorf's arguments against Marx are partly based on the mistaken assumption that Marx was seeking to account for stratification (cf. the main text of this section).

33. See George Sarton, in _Isis_ 24 (1935) 107-9, quoting a letter of Newton to Robert Hooke (of 5 February 1675/6), and also Bernard of Chartres, as cited by John of Salisbury, _Metalogicon_ III.iv, 900c (see the edition by C. C. I. Webb, 1929); and cf. Raymond Klibansky, in _Isis_ 26 (1936) 147(-9).

[II.vi]

1. To my astonishment, some friends to whom I showed a draft of this section objected to the use of the word 'production' in reference to human beings, and said that treating 'reproduction' as a form of 'production' is a kind of pun. In fact, of course, neither _word_ is essential for my argument. By 'production' (see the second of the five propositions set out in II.i above) I mean all those basic activities needed both to _sustain human life_, providing the necessities it requires (and if possible, of course, luxuries too), and to _keep the species in being_ by bearing offspring and rearing it to maturity. 'Production' happens to be the most convenient single word covering both these sets of fundamental activities. I see nothing in the least objectionable in saying that farmers produce food, that at Cowley they produce motor cars, that both I and my publisher (in different senses) produce books, and that women, with some co-operation from men, produce children.

1a. The book, published after this chapter was finished, is David Schaps, _Economic Rights of Women in Ancient Greece_ (Edinburgh, 1979), a very scholarly work.

2. It does not matter very much, for the ancient Greek world, whether it is women in general or wives whom we regard as a class, for virtually all Greek women married (see later statements in the text above). But of course this question may need to be decided in relation to other societies.

3. The fundamental general work is L. Mitteis, *Reichsrecht und Volksrecht in den östlichen Provinzen des römischen Kaiserreichs* (1891, reprinted with a Preface by L. Wenger, Leipzig, 1935). See also Crook, *LLR* 336 n.173; Jolowicz and Nicholas, *HISRL*³ 74, 346-7, 469-73 (esp. 470).

4. See A. R. W. Harrison, *The Law of Athens, I. The Family and Property* (1968) 1 ff. On the whole subject of Athenian marriage, see now the admirable article by E. J. Bickerman, 'La conception du mariage à Athènes', in *BIDR* 78 (1975) 1-28.

5. See Harrison, op. cit. 30-2, 43, 123 n.2 (on p.124); Claire Préaux, in *Recueils de la Soc. Jean Bodin XI. La Femme* (Brussels, 1959) 127-75, at 128, 163-4.

6. See Harrison, op. cit. 10-12, 132-8, 309-11.

7. See the bibliography in Rostovtzeff, *SEHHW* II.623-4 (with III.1465 nn.23-5), 892 (with III.1547 n.170); *SEHRE*² II.738 n.15. The reference that follows in the main text above to Poseidippus is to his fr. 11, in Kock, *CAF* III.338-9, *ap.* Stob., *Anthol.* IV.xxiv.c.40 (ed. O. Hense, IV.614). See also (mainly for Italy) Brunt, *IM* 148-54. [Only after this book was finished did I see the article by Donald Engels, 'The problem of female infanticide in the Greco-Roman world', in *CP* 75 (1980) 112-20, which is obviously based on greater knowledge of modern demography than most ancient historians possess. Engels' conclusion is that 'a rate of 10 percent of female births killed per year would be highly improbable, and the rate almost certainly never exceeded more than [*sic*] a few percent of female births in any era' (120). I of course regard the rate as impossible to estimate. My sole concern has been to show that a girl child had less chance of being reared by its own parents than a boy.]

8. The only study of this kind known to me that comes anywhere near being adequate is Herbert Preisker, *Christentum und Ehe in den ersten drei Jahrhunderten* (= *Neue Studien zur Gesch. der Theol. und Kirche* 23, Berlin, 1927).

9. There was a strong tendency among religious Jews to limit sexual intercourse even between husband and wife to the procreation of children only: see Jos., *C. Apion.* II.199; Baron, *SRHJ* II².218-19, with 408 n.2. I find it rather surprising that Paul lays down no such specific restriction.

10. Among the other 'Pauline' passages that are relevant here (most of them referred to later on in the main text) are I Cor.xi.3-15; xiv.34-5, 37; II Cor. xi.3; Coloss. III.18-19; Ephes. V.22-33 (esp. 22-4, 33); I Tim. ii.11-15; v.11-12; Tit. II.4-5. See also I Pet. iii.1-7.

11. I suppose it could be said that such passages as I Tim. ii.15 and v.14 recognise that the primary function of marriage for the woman is to produce children.

12. See Robin Scroggs, 'Paul and the eschatological woman', in *Jnl of the Amer. Acad. of Religion* 40 (1972) 283-303; and 'Paul and the eschatological woman: revisited', ibid. 42 (1974) 532-7. The concept is rightly rejected as a contradiction in terms by Elaine H. Pagels, 'Paul and women: a response to recent discussion', ibid. 538-49 – who is nevertheless, in my opinion, far too indulgent both to Paul and to Scroggs.

13. I believe that the virgin of verse 25, like the virgin of verses 36-7, may be a *subintroducta*; but the subject is too complicated to be dealt with here. (Among various texts in the Early Fathers dealing with *subintroductae* see John Chrysostom, *Adversus eos qui apud se habent virgines subintroductas*, in *MPG* XLVII.495-514.

14. Anyone who wants to pretend that ὑποτάσσεσθαι is less strong than ὑπακούειν (used e.g. of children obeying their parents in Ephes. VI.1; Coloss. III.20) should read I Pet. iii.5-6, where the two words are equated in regard to women, and compare Ephes. VI.5 and Coloss. III.22, where the word used for the obedience of slaves to their masters is ὑπακούειν, with Tit. II.9 and I Pet. ii.18, where it is ὑποτάσσεσθαι. I must add here that only in one small respect can I admit that St. Paul improved on the attitudes to marriage existing in his day: see David Daube, 'Biblical landmarks in the struggle for women's rights', in *Juridical Review* 23 (1978) 177 ff., at 184-7 (esp. 185-6). But what Daube calls 'an enormous step forward' (an exaggeration, to my mind) is such by comparison only with Jewish ideas about marriage. (Note, by the way, Daube's correction of the article, 'Pauline privilege', in *ODCC*² 1054.) Of course forms of ὑποτάσσειν are used of wives by pagan Greek writers, e.g. Plut., *Praec. coniug.* 33 = *Mor.* 142e (ὑποτάττουσαι), who applies to the husband's role not only such terms as ἡγεμονία καὶ προαίρεσις (139d) but also κρατεῖν (as soul to body) and ἄρχειν (142e). Plutarch's ideal of woman's behaviour is οἰκουρία καὶ σιωπή (142d).

15. In I Cor. vii.10(-11), where Paul presumably had in mind sayings of Jesus such as those contained

in our Synoptic Gospels (Mk X.2-12, esp. 11-12; Mt. V.31-2 and XIX.3-12, esp. 9; Lk. XVI.18), he felt able to say specifically, 'Unto the married I command [παραγγέλλω], [yet] not I but the Lord.' Yet in verse 12 it is 'To the rest speak I, not the Lord'; in verse 6 he says, 'But I speak this by way of permission and not of commandment' (κατὰ συγγνώμην, οὐ κατ᾽ ἐπιταγήν), meaning that he is allowing, on his own authority, an exception from what he regards as God's general rule; and in verse 25 he remarks, 'I have no commandment [ἐπιταγή] from the Lord concerning virgins' – a text on which I have already commented in the main text above. In verse 40, however, at the very end of the chapter, he says (replying perhaps to those who claimed divine inspiration along different lines), 'I think I also have the Spirit of God.' And at the end of another chapter, immediately after giving instructions to women to be silent in church, he says (specifically replying again to anyone else who might claim to speak with special prophetic or spiritual gifts), 'The things that I write unto you are the commandment [ἐντολή] of the Lord' (xiv.37).

16. For example, I Cor. xiv.34-6; Coloss. III.18; I Tim. ii.11-14; Tit. II.5; and above all, of course, Ephes. V.22-4, 33.

17. Stephen Bedale, 'The meaning of κεφαλή in the Pauline Epistles', in *JTS* n.s.5 (1954) 211-15. Good examples illustrating his thesis are Coloss. I.18; II.10, 19; Ephes. IV.15.

18. In the Old Testament the Hebrew word *rosh*, primarily 'head' in the anatomical sense, can also be used for a ruler, chief, captain, commander etc. In that sense the LXX commonly translates ἄρχων, ἀρχή, or ἀρχηγός (also ἡγούμενος, ἀρχίφυλος, ἀρχιπατριώτης), but occasionally it uses κεφαλή: e.g. in Ps. XVIII.43; Isai. VII.8-9; Judg. XI.11; and cf. the head/tail metaphor in Deut.XXVIII.13 and 44, and Isai. IX.14. I suspect that Ps. CXVIII (CXVII in LXX).22, εἰς κεφαλὴν γωνίας (also translating *rosh*), may have been a particularly influential passage with those early Christians who (like St. Paul) knew the Hebrew as well as the LXX text, for it is quoted no fewer than five times in the New Testament: Mt. XXI.42 = Mk XII.10 = Lk. XX.17; Acts IV.11; I Pet. ii.7; cf. I Pet. ii.6 (and Ephes. II.20), where ἀκρογωνιαῖος comes from the LXX of Isai. XXVIII.16. Scroggs, op. cit. (in n.12 above), concentrates on the fact that *rosh* in the sense of rule or lordship is rarely translated κεφαλή in the LXX – he thinks that when it is, the translator was being 'wooden-headed or sleepy'! (op. cit. [1974] 534-5 n.8). He fails to realise the significance of the fact that *rosh*, the main Hebrew word for 'head', is very often used in a sense which demands translation by the Greek words I have mentioned that signify rule or authority, and that this, for those familiar with the Hebrew O.T. as well as the LXX, would of itself tend to endow the Greek word for 'head', κεφαλή, with the authoritarian sense in which we find it used a few times in the LXX and by St. Paul.

19. Bedale, op. cit. (in n.17 above) 214-15, at 215.

20. Op. cit. 214. It even 'includes the "sonship" of the Christ himself': in I Cor. xi.3 God is the 'head' of Christ. And it comes in very nicely to explain the relationship of Christ to the Church in Ephes. V.23-4. But of course in Ephes. I.22, κεφαλὴν ὑπὲρ πάντα τῇ ἐκκλησίᾳ, it is *purely* the authority of Christ, his 'overlordship', which is being stressed, as Bedale half admits (214).

21. As for example Scroggs has done, op. cit. (in n.12 above), esp. (1972) 298-9 n.41, where he can even misrepresent Bedale as interpreting κεφαλή 'to refer to source or origin, *not lordship*' (my italics). Scroggs makes some outrageous statements, to the effect that Paul is 'the only certain and consistent spokesman for the liberation and equality of women in the New Testament', and 'the one clear voice in the New Testament asserting the freedom and equality of women in the eschatological community'! (op. cit. [1972] 283 and 302).

22. I know of nothing similar in pagan literature, except the religious reason (the prestige of Isis) given by Diod. Sic. I.27.1-2 for the supposed fact that in Egypt the queen 'has greater power and honour than the king, and that among private individuals the wife has authority over her husband' – where Diodorus uses the same verb, κυριεύειν, as the LXX version of Gen. III.17 (16) for the husband's authority over the wife!

22a. The article by Averil Cameron, 'Neither male nor female', has now been published in *Greece & Rome*² 27 (1980) 60-8.

23. It is true that no woman could be a *paterfamilias*, but his dominance extended to his whole family, including even grown-up sons, whereas his wife, unless married on condition of passing into his *manus*, would still be under the *potestas* of her own father as long as he lived. All juristic systems have made children up to a certain age legally incapable of many things, e.g. entering into contracts and making wills. Roman law simply extended this situation farther than other systems – in the absence of *emancipatio*, to the death of the father (or grandfather).

24. Cf. Levit. XVIII.19. The Hebrew word used in XX.18 normally signifies execution or expulsion from the community, and it is represented in the LXX by ἐξολοθρευθήσονται. Levit. XV.24 (like its whole context) had no occasion to specify any penalty, apart from 'uncleanness'.

25. See my 'Herodotus', in *Greece & Rome*² 24 (1977) 130-48, at 146-7 and 148 n.24.

26. For Dionysius 'the Great' of Alexandria, see the Second Canon in his Letter to Basileides of Pentapolis (Cyrenaica), in the standard edition of his works by C. L. Feltoe, *The Letters and other Remains of Dionysius of Alexandria* (1904) 102-3; and *MPG* X.1281. The English translation by Feltoe, *St. Dionysius of Alexandria. Letters and Treatises* (1918) 81, delicately omits this part of the letter and the following sections, with the words, 'Three rulings follow on points which it is not necessary to set out here.' There is, however, a full English translation of the letter by S. D. F. Salmond, in Vol.XX of the *Ante-Nicene Christian Library* (Edinburgh, 1871) 196-201. This letter was subsequently included in the standard Byzantine collections of Canon Law: see G. A. Rallis and M. Potlis, Σύνταγμα τῶν θείων καὶ ἱερῶν κανόνων . . . IV (Athens, 1854) 7, where the comments of Zonaras and Balsamon are also printed (7-9). For the letter of Timothy, Answer 7, see Rallis and Potlis, op. cit. IV.335; and *MPG* XXXIII.1300. For Canon 2 of the Council *in Trullo*, maintaining Dionysius's canons, see Hefele-Leclercq, *HC* III.i (1909) 563; J. D. Mansi, *Sacrorum Conciliorum Nova et Amplissima Collectio* XI (1765) 939-42. (I am grateful to my former pupil in ancient history, Dr Kallistos Ware, for help with some of the references in this note.)

27. Jerome, *Contra Helvid.* (esp. 2, 21, 24); *Contra Vigilant.* (with *Epist.* CIX, esp. 1, 2); *Contra Jovinian.* I (esp. 40); *Vita Pauli* 3; *Vita Malchi* 6; *Epist.* XXII (esp. 7); LII.2-3; LV.3-4; LXXIX (esp. 10); CVII (esp. 11); cf. XIV.10 ('He that is once washed in Christ needs not to wash again' – a very forced interpretation of Jn XIII.10); CVIII.15; CXXIII; CXXVIII; CXLVII. It is very interesting to find, from the casual allusion in *Cap.* I.103 n.1, that Marx had read Jerome, *Epist.* XXII.7, 30. Those who wish to read a scholarly account by a Christian of Jerome's attitude to sexuality, marriage and virginity should begin with J. N. D. Kelly, *Jerome. His Life, Writings, and Controversies* (1975) 98-9, 100-3, 104-7, 171-2, 180-91, 273-5, 312-13. The comment on p.183 is particularly interesting: 'It was St. Paul whom he [Jerome] made his chief oracle, twisting the famous texts of I Corinthians 7 and I Timothy to wrest from them an even greater aversion to marriage and second marriages than they contain.'

28. In addition to Hense's introduction to his text and the article by Lutz, see A. C. van Geytenbeek, *Musonius Rufus and Greek Diatribe*, rev. edn., translated by B. L. Hijmans (Assen, 1963), esp. ch.iii, pp.51-77; and M. P. Charlesworth, *Five Men* (= Martin Classical Lectures, Vol.VI, Cambridge, Mass., 1936) 33-62.

29. The references to the passages I have quoted from Musonius are as follows (according to Lutz's edition): (1) fr. XIIIA, pp.88-9; (2) fr. XIV, pp.94-5; (3) frr. IV, pp.44-5, and XII, pp.86-7 and 88-9; (4) fr. XIV, pp.90-7; (5) frr. IV, pp.42-9, and III, pp.38-43. It is true that in fr.XII, p.86.4-8, Musonius sees the only purpose of sexual intercourse as the begetting of children, and regards it as 'unjust and unlawful when it is mere pleasure-seeking, even in marriage'; but this was an attitude taken up by many Christians, and to many of us today it seems less objectionable than the Pauline conception of marriage as a second-best to complete virginity and an unfortunately necessary way of sanctifying what would otherwise be sinful lust.

30. I have not thought it necessary to give much bibliography in this section. There is a 'Selected bibliography on women in antiquity' in *Arethusa* 6 (Spring 1973) 125-57, by Sarah B. Pomeroy, whose book, *Goddesses, Whores, Wives, and Slaves. Women in Classical Antiquity* (New York, 1975), also gives on pp.251-9 a long bibliography to which many additions could already be made, e.g. two important articles by E. Bickerman: the one mentioned in n.4 above, and 'Love story in the Homeric Hymn to Aphrodite', in *Athenaeum* n.s. 54 (1976) 229-54. For anyone tempted to accept the ridiculous idea, advocated in recent times by some admirers of Plato, that Plato was a 'feminist' should read the excellent article by Julia Annas, 'Plato's *Republic* and feminism', in *Philosophy* 51 (1976) 307-21, which, in spite of its title, is not limited to the *Republic* but glances at other works by Plato, including the *Timaeus* (of which in particular 42bc and 90e-91a are too rarely noticed in this connection: see ibid. 316) and the *Laws* (esp. VI.780d-1b; XI.917a: see ibid 317). The main qualification I would make is that the very bad position in which Plato would leave women in the *Laws* is very like their condition at Athens but should not be described as 'the position of fourth-century *Greek* women' (ibid. 317, my italics), since even then there were Greek states which gave women a much better status in regard to property etc. than did Athens: see above, n.1a and my OPRAW. It should surprise

no one to find Plato choosing an unpleasant and repressive alternative when there were more progressive ones in the world around him. [After this book was in proof there appeared the best single article I have seen on the position of women in Classical Athens: John Gould, 'Law, custom and myth: aspects of the social position of women in Classical Athens', in *JHS* 100 (1980) 38-59.]

[III.i]

1. I have written a very full technical analysis of the Solonian τέλη, which I hope to publish shortly.
2. See Ulrich Wilcken, *Griechische Ostraka aus Aegypten und Nubien* (Leipzig/Berlin, 1899) I.506-9; *Grundzüge und Chrestomathie der Papyruskunde* (Leipzig, 1912) I (Hist. Teil) i.342-3.
3. The theory is that of Rudi Thomsen, *Eisphora. A Study of Direct Taxation in Ancient Athens* (Copenhagen, 1964), my review of which is in *CR* 80 = n.s.16 (1966) 90-3. Cf. Jones, *RE* 154 n.21, describing Thomsen's book as 'a baseless phantasy'. My own views on the eisphora are given in ''Demosthenes' τίμημα and the Athenian eisphora in the fourth century B.C.', in *Class. et Med.* 14 (1953) 30-70. I gladly accept the small modification suggested by Davies, *APF* 126-33, at 131.

[III.ii]

1. Among much modern writing on ancient sport, see esp. H. W. Pleket, 'Zur Soziologie des antiken Sports', in *Mededelingen van het Nederlands Instituut te Rome* 36 (1974) 57-87; and 'Games, prizes, athletes and ideology. Some aspects of the history of sport in the Greco-Roman world', in *Stadion* 1 (1976) 49-89, esp. 71-4.
2. Heracl. Pont., fr. 55, in Fritz Wehrli, *Herakleides Pontikos²* (= *Die Schule des Aristoteles* VII, 2nd edn, Basel, 1969), from Athen. XII.512b.
3. In Classical Athens I have come across only one certain example of a man who is said to have owned more than one ship: Phormio, the former slave of Pasion (Ps.-Dem. XLV.64).
4. *AE* 40-1. A similar mistranslation of πρὸς ἄλλον ζῆν ('that he does not live under the restraint of another') appears also in two other articles by Finley, WGCBSL 148 = *SCA* 56; and BSF 239.
5. See e.g. Arist., *EN* IV.3, 1124ᵇ31-5ᵃ2 (a fascinating passage); *EE* III.7, 1233ᵇ34-8. Aristotle uses a slightly different form of words for exactly the same idea in *Metaph*. A.2, 982ᵇ24-8, where he describes the ἄνθρωπος ἐλεύθερος as ὁ αὑτοῦ ἕνεκα καὶ μὴ ἄλλου ὤν. See also *Pol*. III.4, 1277ᵇ3-7; VIII.2, 1337ᵇ17-21.
6. I have treated the Peloponnesian League at length in my *OPW*, ch.iv (esp. 101-24), also 333-42. For the Delian League and Athenian Empire, see V.ii above and its nn.26-7 below; cf. my *OPW*, esp. 34-49, 298-307, 310-14, 315-17. For the Second Athenian Confederacy, see V.ii n.35 below.
7. We are told by Xenophon (*HG* III.i.28) that the wealth in the family treasury was sufficient to provide pay for an army of 8,000 men for 'nearly a year' – a statement which looks to me like a genuine attempt to give an estimate of the real value of the treasure. Now we may take mercenary pay at this date for land troops to have been 25 drachmae per month or a little more for the ordinary soldier; double that sum might be given to the junior officer and four times as much to a senior commander (see e.g. Xen., *Anab.* VII.ii.36; iii.10; vi.1). If we understand 'nearly a year' as ten or eleven months, we can estimate the wealth in the treasury as somewhere in the neighbourhood of 350 talents.
8. See M. Dandamayev, 'Achaemenid Babylonia', in *Ancient Mesopotamia, Socio-Economic History*, ed. I. M. Diakonoff (Moscow, 1969) 296-311, esp. 302.
9. On the 'King's friends', see E. Bikerman, *Institutions des Séleucides* (Paris, 1938) 40-6; C. Habicht, 'Die herrschende Gesellschaft in den hellenistischen Monarchien', in *Vierteljahrschrift für Sozial- und Wirtschaftsgeschichte* 45 (1958) 1-16; Rostovtzeff, *SEHHW* I.517-18; II.1155-6 etc. The wealth of these men would of course be mainly in land, but Dionysius, the Secretary of Antiochus IV, could produce no fewer than 1,000 slaves carrying fine silver plate as a contribution to the magnificent procession organised by Antiochus at Daphne near Antioch in 166: see Athen. V.194c-5f, at 195b = Polyb. XXX.xxv.16.
10. See e.g. Rostovtzeff, *SEHHW* II.805-6 (with III.1521-2 n.76); 819-26 (with III.1527-8 n.98);

1143-9 etc.; *SEHRE*² I.149-51, with II.601-2 n.13; 563 n.20, etc.; Tarn, *HC*³ 108-13. As far as I know, the largest fortune attributed to a Greek during the late Republic and Principate is the HS 100 million (well over 4,000 talents) credited by Suetonius, *Vesp.* 13, to Ti. Claudius Hipparchus (the grandfather of Herodes Atticus). Among the others are Pythodorus of Tralles, the friend of Pompey, who is said by Strabo (XIV.i.42, p.649) to have had over 2,000 talents (= HS 48 million); and Hiero of Laodicea-on-the-Lycus, who is said by Strabo again (XII.viii.16, p.578) to have bequeathed to his city over 2,000 talents.

11. Christian Habicht, 'Zwei neue Inschriften aus Pergamon', in *Instanbuler Mitteilungen* 9/10 (Deutsches Archäologisches Institut, Abteilung Istanbul, 1960) 109-27, at pp.120-5. See also Levick, *RCSAM* 103-20.

12. See C. S. Walton, 'Oriental senators in the service of Rome: a study of Imperial policy down to the death of Marcus Aurelius', in *JRS* 19 (1929) 38-66; P. Lambrechts, 'Trajan et le recrutement du Sénat', in *Ant. Cl.* 5 (1936) 105-14; Mason Hammond, 'The composition of the Senate, A.D. 68-235', in *JRS* 47 (1957) 74-81; *The Antonine Monarchy* (Rome, 1959) 249 ff., esp. 251-4; and the standard prosopographical works (some of them very out of date) by S. J. de Laet (28 B.C. - A.D. 68), B. Stech (69-117), P. Lambrechts (117-192), and G. Barbieri (193-285), describing the composition of the Roman senatorial order in the Principate, which (with the work of P. Willems on the Republican Senate, 1883-5) are conveniently listed in *OCD*² 975, in the article 'Senatus' by A. Momigliano.

13. Levick, *RCSAM* 111-19, gives an excellent appraisal of the main senatorial families of Pisidian Antioch, esp. the Caristanii and Flavonii. For Attaleia etc., see esp. *RCSAM* 127 and its nn.3-4.

14. See Jones, *LRE* II.554-7, 781-8, cf. 710-11.

15. Tarius Rufus is no.15 in Duncan-Jones's list of great private fortunes under the Principate (*EREQS* 343-4, App.7), and his reputed wealth is the same as that of the richest Greek in that list, Ti. Claudius Hipparchus, for whom see n.10 above.

16. Justinian is said to have spent 4,000 lb. gold on his games at Constantinople when he became consul for the first time in 521, in the reign of Justin (*Chron. Min.* II.101-2, remarking upon the sensation this caused – the figure was extraordinary for Constantinople). Olympiodorus fr. 44 speaks of 1,200 lb. gold being spent by Probus, son of Olybrius, on his praetorian games (this will have been in Rome, *c.* 424), and 2,000 lb. gold by Symmachus on his son's praetorian games (at Rome in 401); he also refers to the expenditure of 4,000 lb. gold on praetorian games which must be those given at Rome in the praetorship (in 410 or a year or two later) of Petronius Maximus, who became emperor in the West for a few weeks in 455: see Chastagnol, *FPRBE* 283. On the 'games' in general, see Jones, *LRE* II.1016-21.

17. J. O. Maenchen-Helfen, *The World of the Huns* (1973) 459, regards Olympiodorus' statements as of 'questionable value'. He believes that 'most figures in Olympiodorus are dubious and some are outright fantastic'. But to my mind the figures in n.16 above (including the first, from the sixth-century *Chronicle* of Marcellinus Comes), some at least of which would probably be matters of common knowledge, are consistent with those given in the text above – although of course they cannot be taken to confirm them. On Olympiodorus, see also E. A. Thompson, 'Olympiodorus of Thebes', in *CQ* 38 (1944) 43-52; J. F. Matthews, 'Olympiodorus of Thebes and the history of the West', in *JRS* 60 (1970) 79-97.

[III.iii]

1. Amphis, fr. 17.2-3, in Kock, *CAF* II.241, from Stobaeus, *Anthol.* IV.ii, cap. xv.4, ed. O. Hense (Berlin, 1909), IV.377. Cf. other passages included in the same chapter (xv, pp.376-88).

2. The best short account in English of Xenophon's life and writings is by G. L. Cawkwell in his Introduction (pp.9-48) to the reissue of the Penguin Classics translation of Xenophon's *Anabasis*, by Rex Warner: *Xenophon. The Persian Expedition* (1972).

3. The last passage is Xen., *Oecon.* VI.8-9. Other relevant portions of the same work are IV.4-17, 20-5; V.1-20 (esp. 1); VI.1-11; XII.19-20; XV.3-12 (esp. 4, 10, 12); XVIII.10; XIX.17; XX.1,22; XXI.1. And see IV.iv n.5 below.

4. Fronto, *Epist. ad M. Caes.* IV.vi.1 (a letter from Marcus to Fronto), p.63 ed. M. P. J. van den Hout, 1954; cf. *Hist. Aug., Ant. Pius* 11.2. In § 2 of the same letter Marcus tells Fronto how he and his father had afterwards enjoyed themselves, listening to 'the yokels (*rustici*) chaffing one another' in the oil-press room.

5. For both these passages see Cicero, as quoted immediately in the main text above; also e.g. Pliny, *NH* XVIII.18-20; Val. Max. IV.iii.5 (Curius); iv.7 and Livy III.26.6-10 (Cincinnatus). According to Livy III.26.8, Cincinnatus had only 4 *iugera* (*c.* 2½ acres); cf. Val. Max. IV.iv.7, where he has 7 *iugera* (less than 5 acres) but loses 3 which are given in suretyship for a friend and forfeited – a characteristic moralising touch; cf. Plut., *Sol.* 2.1, quoted in the main text above. M. Atilius Regulus (consul 267 and 256) is another such figure: in the most detailed version of his story, that of Val. Max. IV.iv.6, he is said to have written to the Senate in 256-5, asking to be relieved of his command in Africa, on the ground that the overseer (*vilicus*; cf. Pliny, *NH* XVIII.39) of his farm of 7 *iugera* had died and a hired man (*mercennarius*; cf. Senec., *Dial.* XII = *Ad Helv.* xii.5; and the *mercennarii* in Livy, *Per.* XVIII) had decamped with his stock, so that his family were in danger of destitution unless he returned to them. (In Col., *RR* I.iv.2, Regulus is described as the cultivator of a *pestilentis simul et exilis agri* at Pupinia, for which cf. Varro, *RR* I.ix.5.) I agree with Brunt: the story of Regulus 'can hardly be true of a noble and a magistrate even in the third century, but illustrates what must have been the plight of many common soldiers in the foreign wars' (*IM* 642-3).

6. See the Pelican Classics edition by Bernard Crick, *Machiavelli: The Discourses* (1970) 245-6, 247. The translation is a revision of that by Leslie J. Walker, *The Discourses of Niccolò Machiavelli*, 2 vols (London, 1950), from *Tutte le opere storiche e letterarie di Niccolò Machiavelli*, ed. Guido Mazzoni and Mario Casella (Florence, 1929) 127.

7. In Lutz's edition, of 1947 (in *YCS* 10: see II.vi above), this is fr. XI, pp.80-5, from Stobaeus. Lutz's translation is 'without violating one's dignity or self-respect'. There may be some reflection of Musonius' attitude towards farming in Dio Chrysostom, who was said to have been influenced by him: see Brunt, ASTDCS, esp. 13.

8. The passage in question is part of 'New Fragment 21', published by M. F. Smith, *Thirteen New Fragments of Diogenes of Oenoanda* = Österreich. Akad. der Wiss., Philos.-hist Klasse, Denkschr. 117 (Ergänzungsbände zu den *Tituli Asiae Minoris* 6, Vienna, 1974) 21-5; and see p.8 for a full bibliography, including C. W. Chilton, *Diogenis Oenoand. Fragmenta* (Leipzig, 1967); and *Diogenes of Oenoanda. The Fragments, a Trans. and Comm.* (London etc., 1971).

9. See P. Graindor, *Un milliardaire antique, Hérode Atticus et sa famille* (Cairo, 1930); John Day, *An Economic History of Athens under Roman Domination* (New York, 1942) 235-6; K. Münscher, in *RE* VIII.i (1912) 923; Rostovtzeff, *SEHRE²* I.151.

10. Frank, *ESAR* V.208-9, at 209; cf. his *Economic History of Rome²* (1927) 227-31, at 230-1; and Helen J. Loane, *Industry and Commerce of the City of Rome (50 B.C. - 200 A.D.)* = *Johns Hopkins Univ. Stud. in Hist. and Pol. Science* LVI.2 (Baltimore, 1938) 101-5; also T. P. Wiseman, 'The potteries of Vibienus and Rufrenus at Arretium', in *Mnemos.*[4] 16 (1963) 275-83.

11. I have seen so far only Tapio Helen, *Organisation of Roman Brick Production in the First and Second Centuries A.D. An Interpretation of Roman Brick Stamps* = *Annales Academiae Scientiarum Fennicae Dissertationes Humanarum Litterarum* 5 (Helsinki, 1975); and Päivi Setälä, *Private Domini in Roman Brick Stamps of the Empire. A Historical and Prosopographical Study of Landowners in the District of Rome* = id. 10 (Helsinki, 1977). Their views seem to be gaining general acceptance: see e.g. the review of Setälä's monograph by A. M. Small, in *Phoenix* 33 (1979) 369-72, who says Helen has convinced him 'that *figlinae* are clay districts and not brick works. A *dominus figlinarum* did not on this definition necessarily involve himself in brick production, though he exploited his land by renting it out to *officinatores* of a lesser order. This interpretation radically affects some current ideas about the nature of the involvement of the Roman aristocracy in industry' (370).

12. There is a good discussion of the original meaning of the Latin word *negotiator* and of the later change in its meaning in Rougé, *ROCMM* 274-91, 293-4, 302-19. For the earlier phase, see Jean Hatzfeld, *Les trafiquants Italiens dans l'Orient Hellénique* (Paris, 1919), Part II, pp.193 ff. (esp. 193-6, 234-7).

13. Moesia Inferior, because the law is addressed to Florus, who was praetorian prefect of the East, and Moesia Inferior, in the Thracian diocese, was in that prefecture, whereas Moesia Superior was in the Dacian diocese and the praetorian prefecture of Illyricum.

14. The Latin is 'nobiliores natalibus et honorum luce conspicuos et patrimonio ditiores perniciosum urbibus mercimonium exercere prohibemus, ut inter plebeium et negotiatores facilius sit emendi vendendique commercium'. I have adapted the translation of Jones, *LRE* II.871, merely trying to give effect to the comparative adjectives (*nobiliores, ditiores*), which in texts of this period are often used as mild forms of the superlative, both in legal texts and in

literary authors such as Ammianus.

15. *SIG*³ II.880 = *IGRR* I.766 = A/J 131. There is an Eng. trans. in *ARS* 224, no.274. See Jones, *CERP*² 22-3 (rev. G. Mihailov).

16. On the *navicularii*, see Jones, *RE* 57-9, 399-401; *LRE* II.827-9 (with III.272-4); Rougé, *ROCMM* 233-4, 239-43, 245-9, 263-5, 431-5, 471-2, 480-3.

17. Cardascia, *ADCHH* 329; followed by Garnsey, *SSLPRE* 258 n.1. (The use of the word *negotiantes* in the sense of *negotiatores* is anyway unique to *Dig.* XLVII.xi.6.*pr.*) I would point out that *CTh* XIII.v.16.2 specifically emphasises that other *negotiatores* will not be allowed to obtain *immunitas* by the fraudulent pretence of being *navicularii*. Cf. above and *Dig.* L.vi.1.*pr.*

18. There is a useful brief sketch in Jones, *RE* 54-5, with references, e.g. to Frank, *ESAR* V.236-52; F. H. Wilson; and R. Meiggs, *Roman Ostia* (there is now a 2nd edn., 1973), one of our best books on any Roman town. For Puteoli, see J. H. D'Arms, 'Puteoli in the second century of the Roman Empire: a social and economic study', in *JRS* 64 (1974) 104-24, with ample references to the earlier literature.

19. For Lugdunum and Arelate, see Jones, *RE* 52-4. The situation was the same at Narbo. This does not emerge sufficiently from Rostovtzeff's account in *SEHRE*², e.g. I.166-7, 218, 223, 225; II.607 n.21, 611-13 n.27. Cf. Broughton, in Seager (ed.), *CRR* 127-8, 129-30.

20. On Palmyra, see Jones, *CERP*² 219, 231, 265-6 (with 458-9 nn.51-2), 563-4; *RE* 55-7, 145; Rostovtzeff, *SEHRE*² I.95 (with II.575 n.15), 157 (with II.604-7 nn.19-20), 171-2 (with II.614-15 n.34), 267-9 (with II.662-3 nn.28, 31); *The Caravan Cities* (1932); 'Les inscriptions caravanières de Palmyre', in *Mél. G. Glotz* (Paris, 1932) II.793-811; I. A. Richmond, 'Palmyra under the aegis of Rome', in *JRS* 53 (1963) 43-54; J. P. Rey-Coquais, 'Syrie romaine de Pompée à Dioclétien', in *JRS* 68 (1978) 44-73, esp. 51, 54-6, 59-61.

21. On Petra, see Jones, *CERP*² 290-3 (with 467-8 n.88), 568; *RE* 57, 141, 143, 144, 150; Rostovtzeff, *SEHRE*² I.94-5 (with II.575 n.14, 596-7 n.4), 157; *The Caravan Cities* (1932). Recent bibliography on Petra will be found in G. W. Bowersock's article, 'A Report on Arabia Provincia', in *JRS* 61 (1971) 219-42. As for Edessa and Nisibis, both important centres of commerce, I know of no evidence of rich merchants in their curial class. See e.g. J. B. Segal, *Edessa, 'The Blessed City'* (1970) 136-8, cf. 29-31. It is significant that in 498, when Anastasius abolished the *chrysargyron/collatio lustralis* in the East, Edessa had been paying at the rate of 140 lb. gold every four years, or 2,520 solidi per annum – yet the tax in question included all *negotiatores* in the widest sense (see the main text above, at n.12): Josh. Styl., *Chron.* 31, from whom our information comes, dilates on the general enthusiasm caused by the abolition of the tax, which evidently affected a very large number of people. At Batnae in Anthemusia (in Osrhoene) we hear of many *mercatores opulentes*, but only at the annual fair in early September, at which articles traded from India and China were sold, among other things (Amm. Marc. XIV.iii.3).

22. See Arist., fr. 549, ap. Athen. XIII.576ab; Justin XLIII.iii.4-13; Livy V.34.7-8, for the main accounts of the foundation of Massilia. Aristotle says the Phocaeans founded the city 'in the course of trade' (ἐμπορίᾳ χρώμενοι); but cf. Justin, loc. cit., esp. iii.5-8, with Hdts I.163-7 (esp. 163.1; 166.1: piracy).

23. H. W. Pleket, 'Economic history of the ancient world and epigraphy: some introductory remarks', in *Akten des VI. Internationalen Kongresses für Griechische u. Lateinische Epigraphik = Vestigia* 17 (1972) 243-57, at 253-4.

24. See Rostovtzeff, *SEHRE*² II.655 n.5, for a much better text of *IGRR* IV.186 (the epitaph of Myrinus) – which, by the way, is misinterpreted in Ziebarth's n.1 to *SIG*³ 1229 = *IGRR* IV.841, the interesting inscription of Flavius Zeuxis, of Hierapolis in Phrygia, who claimed to have made 72 voyages around Cape Malea to Italy.

[III.iv]

1. Cf. Finley, who speaks of 'dependent (or involuntary) labour', an expression he uses to include 'everyone who worked for another not because of membership in the latter's family, as in a peasant household, and not because he had entered a voluntary, contractual agreement (whether for wages, honoraria or fees), but because he was bound to do so by some pre-condition, birth into a class of dependents or debt or capture or any other situation which, by law or custom, automatically removed some measure of his freedom of choice and action, usually for a long term or for life' (*AE* 69).

2. See Arist., *Ath. Pol.* 2.2, 6.1, 9.1; Plut., *Sol.* 15.2, and other texts; and cf. V.i above. I cannot accept Finley's interpretation, in SD 168-71, of the Solonian debt-situation, of which I hope to publish an examination shortly. (The article by A. Andrewes and himself, which Finley promises in SD 169 n.39, has not yet appeared.)

3. For all these 'unfree' peoples, see the Index to Lotze, *MED*, *s.vv.* For the Spartan Helots and Thessalian Penestai, see the main text of this section under the heading 'II. Serfdom', and nn.18-19 (Helots) and 20 (Penestai) below. For the Klarotai and Mnoïtai of Crete, see Lotze, *MED* 4-25, 79; for the Mariandynoi of Heraclea Pontica, id. 56-7, 74-5, 79; Magie, *RRAM* II.1192 n.24; Vidal-Naquet, RHGE 37-8; also nn.35 and 52 below; and for the Killyrioi, cf. Dunbabin, *WG* 111, 414. For the Bithynians in the territory of Byzantium, see the main text of this section and n.17 below. For some interesting provisions forbidding the sale of certain serfs, see the same text and nn.35-6 below.

4. On the condition of the 'Penestai' of Etruria, see esp. W. V. Harris, *REU* 114-29 (esp. 121-2), cf. 31-40, 142. For a more recent account of social and economic developments in Etruria, with ample bibliography, see M. Torelli, 'Pour une histoire de l'esclavage en Etrurie', in *Actes du Colloque 1973 sur l'esclavage = Annales littéraires de l'Univ. de Besançon* 182 (Paris, 1975) 99-113. And see Arnold Toynbee, *Hannibal's Legacy* (1965) II.541-4. To illustrate the variety of terminology that we encounter more than once where serfs or serf-like peoples are concerned, it is perhaps worth mentioning that Diodorus, when dealing with the Etruscans in V.40 (perhaps utilising Poseidonius), can speak of οἱ θεραπεύοντες ὄχλοι (§ 1), of τῶν διακονούντων οἰκετῶν οὐκ ὀλίγος ἀριθμός who dress more elaborately ἢ κατὰ δουλικὴν ἀξίαν (§ 3), and of οἱ θεράποντες who are evidently distinct from οἱ ἐλεύθεροι (§ 4).

5. Juv., *Sat.* XIV.145-51; cf. *P. Merton* 92 (A.D. 324); Plut., *Mor.* 170a (= *De Superstit.* 10); Seneca, *Epist.* XC.39. In his *Orat.* XLVI.7 (dating perhaps from the early 80s), Dio Chrysostom thinks it worth while to boast that none of his neighbours can complain of having been evicted by him, *justly or unjustly*. Cicero charges M. Crassus in *Parad.* VI.46 with 'expulsiones vicinorum', probably a common accusation. For a collection of passages illustrating the violence often offered to the poor and humble by the rich and powerful in the ancient world, see the first chapter of MacMullen, *RSR*, esp. 1-12 (with the notes, pp.147 ff.). MacMullen speaks of 'the existence of extralegal kinds of power to a degree quite surprising' (id. 7). And see VI.v above and its n.22 below.

6. The *only* example I have been able to find of an influential man exercising patronage at Athens in such a way as to interfere with the course of justice is the story of Alcibiades and Hegemon of Thasos, the parodist, in Athen. IX.407bc, from the very uncritical fourth/third-century writer, Chamaeleon of Heraclea Pontica. (Thuc. VIII.48.6 is very relevant here.) Contrast, for the Roman world, my SVP, esp. 42-5.

7. Among many other works, see esp. Gunnar Landtman, *The Origin of the Inequality of the Social Classes* (1938) 227-86, esp. 228-9; and H. J. Nieboer, *Slavery as an Industrial System* (1900). In my opinion, W. L. Westermann insisted much too strongly on certain 'rights' which he believed ancient slaves possessed: see his *SSGRA*, and the bibliography of his own works, id. 172-3.

8. We have a certain amount of information, mainly in small scraps, about the slaves in the silver (and lead) mines of Laurium in Attica: see the comprehensive work of Siegfried Lauffer, *Die Bergwerkssklaven von Laureion* I and II = *Abhandl. der Akad. der Wiss. u. der Lit. in Mainz, Geistes- u. sozialwiss. Klasse*, 1955 no.12, pp.1101-1217 = 1-117, and 1956 no.11, pp.883-1018 and 1*-20* = 119-274. (For the revolts there in ?135-3 and ?104-0 B.C. see id. II.912-14 = 148-50 and 991-1015 = 227-51. The principal sources for the first revolt are Diod. XXXIV.2.19 and Oros. V.9.5, and for the second revolt Poseid., *FGrH* 87 F 35, *ap.* Athen. VI.272ef.) Lucret. VI.806-15 describes with sympathy the lot of the slaves in the gold mines of the Pangaean area ('Scaptensula', the Skaptē Hulē of Hdts VI.46.3). A horrifying description of the lethal effects of mining, in this case in the quicksilver mines at Pimolisa near Pompeiopolis in Paphlagonia (west of the River Halys, in northern Asia Minor), is given by Strabo XII.iii.40. p.562. Diodorus has two particularly sympathetic accounts of the terrible conditions in the gold mines in Egypt (III.12.1 to 14.5) and the silver mines in Spain (V.35.1 to 38.3): see Benjamin Farrington, *Diodorus Siculus* (Inaugural Lecture at Swansea in 1936, published 1937) = *Head and Hand in Ancient Greece* (1947) 69-70; also J. G. Davies, in *JHS* 75 (1955) 153, who produces arguments for the validity of Diodorus' picture, including some parallel passages in the *Letters* of St. Cyprian. The source of the first of these two passages in Diodorus (on the Egyptian gold mines) is Agatharchides of Cnidus, who wrote a work *On the Erythraean Sea* in the late second century B.C.: for the text of the excerpts made (independently

of Diodorus' version) by Photius, see *Geogr. Graeci Minores*, ed. C. Müller, I (Paris, 1855) 123-9, frr. 23-9. On Agatharchides, see Fraser, *PA* I. 173-4, 539-50 (esp. 543). According to Strabo III.ii.10, pp.147-8, Polybius wrote of the silver mines near Nova Carthago in Spain that 40,000 men were employed there and that the Roman State received a revenue of 25,000 drachmae (over 4 talents) per day. According to Pliny, *NH* XXXIII.97, the Spanish silver mines in Hannibal's time (the late 3rd century B.C.) had produced 300 lb. silver per day.

9. Among the literary passages referring to the χωρὶς οἰκοῦντες are Andoc. I.38; Aeschin. I.97; Theophr., *Char.* XXX.15; Menand., *Epitrep.* 378-80 ed. F. H. Sandbach = 202-4 ed. A. Koerte (all referring to the ἀποφορά paid to the masters); and presumably Ps.-Xen., *Ath. pol.* I.11 (where the masters become 'slaves to their slaves'!); cf. Teles fr. IVb (pp.46-7, ed. O. Hense, 1909), *ap.* Stob., *Anthol.* V. p.786 (ed. Hense, 1912). In Ps.-Dem. XLVII.72 the slave who χωρὶς ᾤκει is a freedwoman; Dem. IV.36 must refer mainly if not entirely to freedmen; and *Anecd. Gr.* I.316.11-13 (ed. I. Bekker) defines χωρὶς οἰκοῦντες as freedmen or slaves. Lampis, mentioned again and again in Ps.-Dem. XXXIV, is described both as a 'shipowner' (ναύκληρος, § 6) and as a 'slave' of Dion (οἰκέτης in § 5; § 10 puts him among the παῖδες of Dion); if a slave, he might be considered a χωρὶς οἰκῶν, but I think he was much more probably a freedman, as believed by Sandys (see his note in F. A. Paley and J. E. Sandys, *Select Private Orations of Demosthenes* I³ [1898] 5n.). From the χωρὶς οἰκοῦντες we must in principle distinguish slaves *hired out* to others (and referred to by some such expression as ἀνδράποδα μισθοφοροῦντα), as in Ps.-Xen., *Ath. pol.* I.17; Xen., *De vect.* IV.14-15, 19, 23; Isae. VIII.35; Ps.-Dem. LIII.20-1; Dem. XXVII.20-1, with XXVIII.12; Theophr., *Char.* XXX.17; *Anecd. Gr.* I.212.12-13 (ed. Bekker); cf. Plaut., *Asin.* 441-3. I know of no completely satisfactory treatment of this subject. See most recently Elena Perotti, 'Esclaves χωρὶς οἰκοῦντες', in *Actes du Colloque 1972 sur l'esclavage* (Centre de Recherches d'histoire ancienne, Vol.11) = *Annales littéraires de l'Université de Besançon* 163 (Paris, 1974) 47-56; and 'Contribution à l'étude d'une autre catégorie d'esclaves attiques: les ἀνδράποδα μισθοφοροῦντα', in *Actes . . . 1973* (. . . Vol.18) = *Annales . . .* 182 (Paris, 1976) 179-91, cf. 192-4. See also, for Graeco-Roman Egypt, I. Bieżuńska-Małowist, 'Les esclaves payant l'ἀποφορά dans l'Égypte gréco-romaine', in *JJP* 15 (1965) 65-72; 'Quelques formes non typiques de l'esclavage dans le monde ancien', in *Antichnoe Obshchestvo* [= *Ancient Society*] (Moscow, 1967) 91-6, the latter with a reference (92 and n.1) to an evidently useful article in Russian (which I do not read) by Emily Grace Kazakevitch, in *VDI* (1960 no.3) 23-42.

10. Among several passages recommending the care of sick slaves, see e.g. Xen., *Mem.* II.iv.3; x.2; *Oecon.* VII.37. Cato's heartless advice is in his *De Agric.* ii.4,7.

11. Varro, *RR* I.xvii.2-3; cf. Plut., *Crass.* 2.7, where Crassus is said to have taken great care of his slaves as living tools of his household economy – an echo of Arist., *EN* VIII.11, 1161ᵇ4 (cf. *Pol.* I.4, 1253ᵇ32). The Columella passages are *RR* I.vii.4 (lands with a severe climate or barren soil), 6-7 (distant estates).

12. F. L. Olmsted, *Journey in the Seaboard Slave States* (1856, reissued 1904) II.192-3; *The Cotton Kingdom* (1861; ed. A. M. Schlesinger, 1953) 214-15.

13. The imperial *dispensatores* of the Principate, although always of slave (and not even freedman) status, are ranked by P. R. C. Weaver (the main authority on the *familia Caesaris*) as officials 'of intermediate grade' in the imperial bureaucracy: see his paper in *SAS* (ed. Finley), at 129-32; cf. his article, '*Vicarius* and *vicarianus* in the *Familia Caesaris*', in *JRS* 54 (1964) 117 ff., at 118-20; and his *Familia Caesaris* (1972) 201-6, 251-2 etc.

13a. In an interesting and useful but very one-sided and sometimes inaccurate article which appeared when this book was in the press ('Rural labour in three Roman provinces', in *Non-Slave Labour in the Greco-Roman World*, ed. Peter Garnsey = Camb. Philol. Soc., Suppl. Vol.6 [1980] 73-99, at 77) C. R. Whittaker has committed precisely this error: he can actually speak of slaves recorded in inscriptions in managerial posts as 'concerned with estate supervision, collection of revenue ['or domestic service', irrelevant here] *but not production*' (my italics) – as if 'production' took place only at the lowest levels of work! On the next page he can say, with some exaggeration (referring to Gsell, ERAR, mentioned a little earlier in the main text above), that 'Gsell's celebrated catalogue of rural slaves in Roman Africa can without violence be almost entirely reduced to supervisory and domestic staff'. This ignores, for example, the large slave-worked estate of Pudentilla near Oea in Tripolitania in the mid-second century, which we happen to know about only because of the existence of a unique literary text, the *Apology* of Apuleius. Whittaker does give the briefest possible reference to *Apol.* 93 in his n.27, but without mentioning the large number of slaves (400 or more) or another passage in the same speech, § 87, showing that at least a large part of the estate was run with slave labour. There is nothing to suggest that this situation was exceptional, and there may have been an appreciable number of such slave-worked estates in north Africa, even if the bulk of the agricultural population was much as Whittaker describes it. It is a serious error of method always to press what little evidence we have in one direction, and to pretend that we can *know* slave labour was almost non-existent in areas for which the evidence is both deficient and largely epigraphic. And Whittaker's handling of the texts is sometimes misleading. He can say, for example, that in Diod. XIV.77.3 'the 200,000 Libyans who rebelled against Carthage in 396 B.C. were termed "slaves" ', wrongly (78; cf. '200,000 slaves and others', on p.338 of his article in *Klio* 60, 1978). In fact Diodorus, far from speaking of 200,000 'slaves', says that Carthage's *allies* formed an army and *then* were *joined* by *'free men and* slaves'; the slaves are not emphasised and receive no further mention. Whittaker clearly knows far more about Africa and Gaul than Asia. He would not have been so confident about the alleged 'overwhelming predominance of *laoi* on the land of the Hellenistic kingdoms' (77) if he had collected all the surviving references to *laoi*, which in fact are few, and limited as a rule to a specific locality, and do not often allow us to draw any conclusion about the condition of these people except that they are non-hellenised 'natives' without political rights. Whittaker is also mistaken in supposing that the terms *paroikoi* and *katoikountes* 'can generally be accepted as referring . . . to peasants *in various forms of dependency*' (77, my italics): for the meaning of *paroikos*, equated in the Roman period with *incola* (which carried no suggestion of 'dependence'), see I.iii n.15 and II.v n.30 above, including a reference to Welles, *RCHP*, pp.353, 345. It is misleading to say that in the Ephesian inscription, *SIG*³ 742, the *paroikoi* are 'ranked alongside temple servants and freedmen' (83), without also mentioning the *isoteleis* (a *privileged* category of non-citizens) whom they are equally 'ranked alongside' (in line 44)! And Whittaker is again wrong in denying (against J. Strubbe, 'A group of Imperial estates in central Phrygia', in *Anc. Soc.* 6 [1975] 229-50, at 235) that Soa (the Soenoi) had become a *polis* by the time of *IGRR* IV.605: that decree is by the βουλή as well as the δῆμος, a clear sign of a *polis*, unparalleled (as far as I know) for a mere village, in Asia Minor or Syria at any rate; cf. Jones, *CERP*² 69, 393 n.64, and, on the general question, IV.ii above and its n.36 below.

14. See Jones, *LRE* II.788-91, esp. 790 (with III.254 n.48). Jerome, *Comm. in Epist. ad Tit.* I.7 (*MPL* XXVI.566), assumes that the contemporary *vilicus* will be a slave.

15. The bibliography on ancient slave revolts is very large. The best single treatment for English readers is Vogt, *ASIM* (in English translation) 39-92, with 213-14, giving sufficient references to other work. See also e.g. Toynbee, *HL* II.313-31. On the revolts in the Athenian silver mines in the second half of the second century B.C., see n.8 above; and for the war of Aristonicus in Asia Minor in 133-129 B.C., see Appendix IV above, § 3 *ad init.* and its n.8. I need waste no time on the 'revolt of Saumacus' in the Bosporan area in the late second century B.C., as there is no reason to suppose that Saumacus was a slave. [In support of this view I can now cite Zeev Wolfgang Rubinsohn, 'Saumakos: ancient history, modern politics', in *Historia* 29 (1980) 50-70, an article which appeared after this book was finished. It includes an English translation of the Diophantus inscription from Chersonesus, *SIG*³ 709 = *IOSPE* I².352.]

16. For the identification of *originarii/originales* and *adscripticii*/ἐναπόγραφοι, see Jones, in *SAS* (ed. Finley) 298-9 ff. = *RE* 302-3 ff.; and *RE* 417. The law of *c.* 370, of Valentinian I and his co-emperors, is *CJ* XI.xlviii.7.*pr.*: 'Quemadmodum originarios absque terra, ita rusticos censitosque servos vendi omnifariam non licet'. (It must be dated between the creation of Gratian as Augustus in 367 and the death of Valentinian I in 375.) This measure was repealed (probably by Theodoric II in the 450s/460s, for Visigothic Gaul: see Jolowicz and Nicholas, *HISRL*³ 468) by § 142 of the *Edictum Theoderici* (in *FIRA*² II.683-710) – which apparently also reversed a prohibition even more restrictive upon the master's right to deal with his slaves than the constitution just mentioned: see Marc Bloch, in *CEHE* I².252. In 327 Constantine had ordained that slaves entered in the census lists (*mancipia ascripta censibus*) should be sold only inside the same province: *CTh* XI.iii.2, addressed to the Comes Macedoniae (could the law perhaps have been intended for the diocese of Macedonia only?). In *CTh* II.xxv.1 (perhaps 334) Constantine had protested against the unnecessary breaking up of slave families when estates of the imperial household in Sardinia had been recently divided among individual proprietors, and had forbidden such things for the future. (In the *CJ* version, III.xxxviii.11, references to *coloni adscripticii* and *inquilini* have been interpolated.) But although Constantine

here speaks in general terms of the undesirability of breaking up families, the actual terms of the law, even in its broader *CJ* form, would apply only to the division of estates. In 349 Constantius II, contemplating that in some (unspecified) circumstances serving soldiers might be given imperial permission to have their households (*familiae*) with them, specifically limits this to their 'wives, children, and slaves bought with their *peculium castrense*', and excludes their 'slaves enrolled on the census lists' (*servos . . . ascriptos censibus*): *CTh* VII.i.3 = *CJ* XII.xxxv.10.

17. Cf. Polyb. IV.lii.7, where the λαοί handed back to the Byzantines by Prusias I are no doubt the Bithynian serfs. See Walbank, *HCP* I.507.

18. Thuc. I.101.2. (Cf. II.v above, at p.93.) Thucydides says that *most* of the Helots were Messenians, and this was why they *all* came to be called 'Messenians'. He does speak twice of 'Messenians and Helots' (V.35.6; 56.2), and once of 'Messenians and the other Helots' (35.7) – who are joined with 'deserters from Laconia' (perhaps some Perioikoi as well as Laconian Helots), but in 56.3 are simply 'the Helots from Cranii'. But he refers more than twenty times to all those who went to Naupactus as 'Messenians', and that was what those settled at Naupactus called themselves (M/L 74.1). Doubtless those who survived in the revolt of 465/4 ff. were mainly Messenians. Diod. XI.63–64, 84.7–8 is very unreliable (note esp. the exaggerations in 63.1,4). Although the earthquake occurred in Laconia, indeed at Sparta itself, and one might therefore expect the Laconian Helots to seize their opportunity and revolt first (as indeed some of them must have done), Diodorus gives the main role to the Messenians (64.1,2), and it is only at a late stage that he writes of 'the [Laconian] Helots' as revolting 'all together' (πανδημεί, which must be an exaggeration) and joining 'the Messenians' (64.4). Again, in 84.7–8 it is only the Messenians who are allowed to go from Ithome to Naupactus; the Spartans, says Diodorus, punished (with death, obviously) those of 'the Helots' who had been the authors of the revolt, and 'enslaved' the rest – perhaps a misunderstanding by Ephorus (almost certainly the source of Diodorus here) of the language of Thucydides, who calls all those settled at Naupactus 'Messenians' (see above).

19. Arrian, *Ind.* 10.9 (written in the mid-second century), speaks of the Spartan Helots as if they still existed in his day; but this need cause us no worry, for Arrian is simply transcribing here his source, Megasthenes, who wrote around 300 B.C. (P. A. Brunt, whose knowledge of Arrian is unsurpassed, and who is preparing a new edition of the second volume of Arrian for the Loeb series, tells me that he regards such carelessness as characteristic of Arrian.) Perhaps some of the Helots who remained after Nabis's time obtained their freedom and others became outright slaves. For a sufficient refutation of theories advanced by Chrimes and Robins, see B. Shimron, 'Nabis of Sparta and the Helots', in *CP* 61 (1966) 1–7.

20. Among the most interesting texts on the Penestai of Thessaly are Dem. XXIII.199, with XIII.23 (Menon the Thessalian brings 200 or 300 of his Penestai to Athens, to serve under him as cavalrymen); Archemachus, *FGrH* 424 F 1, *ap.* Athen, VI.264ab; Xen., *HG* VI.i.11; Theopomp., *FGrH* 115 F 81, *ap.* Athen. VI,259f–60a. I know of no further reference to the Penestai in a credible historical context after the fourth century B.C. See also Lotze, *MED* 48–53, 79. For the fact that the Penestai could not be sold off the land, see n.35 below.

21. See Eleanor Searle, *Lordship and Community: Battle Abbey and its Banlieu, 1066-1538* (Toronto, 1974) 167, 174–5, 183, 194, 267–337 (esp. 268–9, 272–86).

22. For some examples of such gifts by Persian kings and even satraps, see my *OPW* 38–40. We must not add the gift by Pharnabazus to Alcibiades, alleged by Nepos, *Alcib.* 9.3, a crude error by Nepos or his source: see Hatzfeld, *Alc.*² 342 n.3.

23. For the unfair treatment of Ahab which we must expect from the authors of Kings, see my 'Herodotus', in *Greece and Rome*² 24 (1977) 130–48, at 132–3 and n.3. In their present form, of course, Kings I and II are appreciably later than the reign of Ahab (*c.* 850); but I regard the picture of Israelite land tenure in the Naboth story as very likely to be historical.

24. I need cite only Tod, *SGHI* II.185, esp. line 11, where Alexander claims the χώρα as his – with the important consequence that it remained liable to φόροι, as the next sentence shows. One can see such a claim foreshadowed in Xenophon's *Hellenica*, where the property of the under-satrap Mania (III.i.12) is treated as the property of her master Pharnabazus, and is consequently regarded as having passed to the conquerors of Pharnabazus (§ 26). Of course even a satrap, in Greek eyes, was but a 'slave' of the Great King (see Xen., *HG* IV.i.36: ὁμοδούλους); cf. the alleged letter of Darius I, M/L 12, addressed to Γαδάται | δούλωι (lines 3–4), where the king speaks of [τ]ὴν ἐμὴν . . . [γ]ῆν. Fourth-century Greeks and Macedonians did not distinguish as clearly as we do between sovereignty and ownership, and I am not clear what the position

really was in Achaemenid Persia.

25. The year is described as 'the 59th year' (of the Seleucid era): that is, 254/3 B.C. See Welles, *RCHP*, pp.95-6 (commentary on no.18.8-10).

26. I am thinking particularly of recent articles by Pierre Briant, esp. RLER = 'Remarques sur les "Laoi" et esclaves ruraux en Asie Mineure hellénistique', in *Actes du Colloque 1971 sur l'esclavage* = *Annales littéraires de l'Université de Besançon* 140 (Paris, 1972) 93-133, at 103-5. Briant believes it is 'certain' that the λαοί of the Laodice inscription (Welles, *RCHP* 18.8,12,26) were not sold with the land: he thinks Laodice received only the revenues of the land! This mistake seems to be founded on two misconceptions. First, Briant places great emphasis on the fact, pointed out by Bikerman (which I also accept), that the peasants are bound to their village rather than to individual plots: they are *adscripti vico* rather than *adscripti glebae*. (So were some Later Roman peasants: see IV.iii §§ 20-1 above.) But unless we are to pretend, gratuitously, that the Greek does not *mean* what it *says*, we must admit that the village itself was certainly conveyed to Laodice; and this gives no ground for denying that its peasants also passed to the ex-queen, as our document indeed specifically says. Secondly, Briant has apparently misunderstood lines 7-13 of the inscription (which are correctly translated by Welles). I fancy that he may have been misled by the reference in lines 9-10 to 'the revenues of the 59th [Seleucid] year' (cf. n.25 above), and may have failed to realise that this point is specified merely to make it clear exactly at what time Laodice is to take over the revenues – here *RCHP* 70.9 is relevant.

27. Now republished as *C. Ord. Ptol.* 21-2. This document has been discussed again and again since its original publication over 40 years ago by H. Liebesny, 'Ein Erlass des Königs Ptolemaios II Philadelphos über die Deklaration von Vieh u. Sklaven in Syrien u. Phönikien', in *Aeg.* 16 (1936) 257-91. It will be sufficient to cite Rostovtzeff, *SEHHW* I.340-6 (with III.1400 n.135), and the latest treatment, which is exceptionally clear and sensible, by Bieżuńska-Małowist, *EEGR* I (1974) 20 ff., esp. 24-5, 29-31.

28. Bieżuńska-Małowist, *EEGR* I.25; Rostovtzeff, *SEHHW* I.342-3.

29. See Pippidi, PMOA, in *PTGA* (ed. M. I. Finley), at 75-6. He refers to 'paysans dépendants' and compares them with the Cretan κλαρῶται or ἀφαμιῶται.

30. For other evidence, not otherwise discussed here, which may indicate the presence of native serfs, see e.g. Athen. XV.697d, where Attalus I of Pergamum appoints a δικαστὴς . . . βασιλικῶν τῶν περὶ τὴν Αἰολίδα (unless we should read δικαστὴς βασιλικός, with Atkinson, SGCWAM 39 n.32); Plut., *Eumen.* 8.9 (σώματα in the territory of Celaenae, *c.* 321 B.C.); *SIG*³ 282. 14-15 and Welles, *RCHP* 8 B.3 ff. (Pedieis at Priene); *OGIS* 215 and 351 (= *Inschr. von Priene* 18 and 39: σώματα); *SIG*³ 279.4-5 and Michel, *RIG* 531.27 = *SGDI* III.ii.5533 *e*.6 (Zeleia); Strabo XII.ii.9, p.539 (the kings of Cappadocia had possessed σώματα in the area of Mazaca). Agatharch. Cnid., *FGrH* 86 F 17, *ap.* Athen. VI.272d, is mentioned in the text above. A non-technical term which it is generally safest to translate 'dependants' (its Latin equivalent is *clientes*) is πελάται: see e.g. *CIRB* 976 = *IOSPE* II.353, line 5 (an inscription of Rhoemetalces, A.D. 151, from the 'Bosporan kingdom'); Plut., *Crass.* 21.7 (Parthians); cf. the προσπελάται of the Illyrian 'Ardiaioi', who were surely serfs and could be compared by Theopompus with the Spartan Helots (see the main text above, just after the reference to n.17).

31. The inscription of Mnesimachus was first published by W. H. Buckler and D. M. Robinson, in *AJA* 16 (1912) 11-82, and later in their edition of the inscriptions of Sardis, *Sardis* VII.i (Leiden, 1932), no.1. It has recently been republished with an English translation and reinterpretation by K. M. T. Atkinson, 'A Hellenistic land conveyance: the estate of Mnesimachus in the plain of Sardis', in *Historia* 21 (1972) 45-74, whose analysis in general I accept. (The relevant lines are I.11, 14-15, 16; II.5.) Her most important conclusion (which is certainly correct) is that the original transaction was what English lawyers would call a 'conveyance' and not a 'mortgage'. See also the earlier article by the same author, SGCWAM, esp. (on the estate of Mnesimachus) 37, 40. I also agree with her that Mnesimachus could not have owned the property in freehold: his tenure is quite different from that given to e.g. Laodice and Aristodicides (Welles, *RCHP* 18-20 and 10-13). I must say, I am not happy about treating the οἰκέται here as slaves, since the word κατοικοῦντες, applied to them in I.16, is not in my experience used for slaves.

32. The best brief general description I know is that of Rostovtzeff, *SEHHW* I.277 ff. (esp. 277-80); II.1196-1200, etc. I have also found very instructive the thorough monograph by Iza Bieżuńska-Małowist, *EEGR* I, on the Ptolemaic period; I did not see Vol.II, on the Roman period, until this section was finished. Much interest has been shown in this subject in recent years by Soviet scholars, but as I do not read Russian I was not able to examine any of the

works I am now going to mention until this part of my book was virtually finished. The main works that have come to my knowledge are as follows:

(1) The 36-page monograph in Russian by N. N. Pikus (Pikous), the French title of which would be *Agriculteurs royaux [produceurs immédiats] et artisans dans l'Egypte du 3ᶜ siècle av. n. è.* (Moscow, 1969), with the review by Heinz Heinen in *CE* 45 (1970) 186-8.

(2) The contribution by Pikus to the *Actes du Xᶜ Congrès internat. de Papyrologues* (Warsaw/ Cracow, 1961), ed. J. Wolski (Warsaw etc., 1964) 97-107, entitled 'L'esclavage dans l'Égypte hellénistique'.

(3) A book in Russian of 244pp. by K. K. Zelyin (and M. K. Trofimova), the French title of which would be *Les formes de dépendance dans la Méditerranée orientale à l'époque hellénistique* (Moscow, 1969). This consists of three separate studies, of which the first, by Zelyin, 'Les formes de dépendance à l'époque hellénistique' (pp.11-119), sounds particularly interesting, in the review by I. F. Fikhman, in *CE* 45 (1970) 182-6, at 183-4.

(4) Zelyin's article in *VDI* (1967 no.2) 7-31, in Russian with an English summary, the English title of which is 'Principles of morphological classification of forms of dependence'.

(5) A book originally published in Russian by T. V. Blavatskaia, E. S. Golubtsova and A. I. Pavlovskaia (Moscow, 1969), and subsequently translated into German, as *Die Sklaven in hellenistischen Staaten im 3.-1. Jh. v. Chr.* (Wiesbaden, 1972), the original third part of which, by Pavlovskaia, was reviewed by Iza Bieżuńska-Małowist in French in *CE* 46 (1971) 206-9.

(6) An article by Pavlovskaia in *VDI* (1976 no.2) 73-84, in Russian with an English summary, the English title of which is 'Slaves in agriculture in Roman Egypt'.

In my opinion too much emphasis may have been placed by some scholars on the fact that the known leases (from very limited areas), in the early Ptolemaic period especially, appear to be 'free contracts'. The peasants were strictly controlled in many of their agricultural activities (see e.g. Rostovtzeff, *SEHHW* I.279-80, 317, 320). Those engaged in the production of vegetable oils were supervised and regulated to an extraordinary degree: see id. 302-5, based mainly on *P. Rev. Laws*, partly re-edited in W. *Chr.* 258 (cols. 1-22), 249 (36-7), 299 (38-58), 181 (73-8); and in Hunt and Edgar, *SP* II.10-35, no.203 (cols. 38-56). I regard the question of the role played by slaves in Egyptian economic life as still partly an open one. As regards the use of slaves in agriculture in the Ptolemaic period, I agree with the opinion recently expressed by Bieżuńska-Małowist (concurring with Claire Préaux) that 'le problème ne peut être défini-tivement résolu dans l'état actuel des sources' (*EEGR* I.59). Although she can say later in the same work that it seems justifiable to conclude that slavery 'n'avait que fort peu d'importance comme forme de travail dans les domaines fondamentaux de la production' (id. 139, cf. 82), she can nevertheless also affirm, 'au moins eu égard aux villes grecques, que l'esclavage du type classique avait une assez grande importance, et que le nombre des esclaves devait dépasser les chiffres modestes que l'on admet parfois dans la littérature du sujet' (id. 105). Even for the Egyptian χώρα she has well demonstrated that slave ownership in Ptolemaic Egypt was by no means confined to the rich but went a good way down the social scale: it became 'très répandu dans les maisons des gens peu aisés' (ENMM 159, cf. 158 and esp. the first paragraph on 161, on 'le rôle des esclaves dans les modestes maisons égyptiennes'). See also on this topic her *EEGR* I.134-6, 138-9, and two articles (already cited in n.9 above): 'Les esclaves payant l'ἀποφορά dans l'Égypte gréco-romaine', in *JJP* 15 (1965), at 70-2; and 'Quelques formes non typiques de l'esclavage dans le monde ancien', in *Antichnoe Obshchestvo* [= *Ancient Society*] (Moscow, 1967), at 92-4, 96. If even those of middling wealth used slaves, surely the really rich would be even more likely to do so. If the propertied class as a whole made no great use of slave labour in Egypt, except for domestic purposes and in workshops in the few cities (see esp. *Bell. Alexandr.* 2.2), then I would suppose that the condition of the free poor (peasants, artisans, hired labourers and others) was so abject as to make legal enslavement superfluous. I suspect, however, that unfree labour may have played a greater part *in providing the propertied classes with their surplus* than most Egyptologists have been interested in revealing, concerned mainly as they have been with such matters as the share of slaves in economic life in general, rather than their role in providing a fairly small class of property-owners with a surplus. In particular, forms of debt bondage, including the more burdensome varieties of *paramonē* (see n.73 below), may have been more important than is generally allowed. And even chattel slavery may bulk larger than in many modern accounts if we see it in the way I am advocating, as a means of providing the propertied classes with their surplus, and if we are therefore not dismayed by the fact that the ordinary free Egyptian owned no slaves, any more than the ordinary poor man in the rest of the Greek and Roman world – who possessed at most one or two slaves who normally worked beside him, like (for example) the poor Athenian (see Xen., *Mem.* II.iii.3). It may well be, however, that the pressures, economic and non-economic, to which the humble free Egyptian was subjected, and the fact that it seems to have been cheaper to maintain life there than anywhere else in the Graeco-Roman world (see Diod. Sic. I.80.5-6), were so effective that a greater surplus could be extracted from the free population in Egypt than in the rest of the Mediterranean world, and there was consequently the less need to bring in slaves.

33. Its significance is hardly appreciated to the full even by the two Marxist scholars who have most recently produced interesting discussions of Hellenistic land tenure in the East: Heinz Kreissig and Pierre Briant. For their main works in this field, see esp. Briant, RLER (in French) and DDAHA (in German), and Kreissig, LPHO (in English): the notes to these articles cite all other material of importance, except the works of A. H. M. Jones, which are strangely ignored. As I may not have occasion to refer to it elsewhere, I will mention here a useful recent article by a Soviet scholar, I. S. Svencickaja, 'Some problems of agrarian relations in the province of Asia', in *Eirene* 15 (1977) 27-54, which of course deals with the Roman peiod. This cites much epigraphic evidence and deals very sensibly with the problems on which it concentrates. Two earlier articles by the same author in Russian are known to me only through their English summaries, 'The condition of the λαοί in the Seleucid kingdon', in *VDI* (1971 no.1) 16, and 'The condition of agricultural workers on the imperial domains in the province of Asia', in *VDI* (1973 no.3) 55, where the author's name appears in the anglicised form 'Sventsitskaya' in both cases. [Only when this book was in the press did I become aware of the book by Kreissig, *Wirtschaft und Gesellschaft im Seleukidenreich: Die Eigentums- und die Abhängigigkeitsverhältnisse* (Berlin, 1978), which has a useful list of Kreissig's relevant articles and monographs to 1975 on p.129; add the article in *Klio* 1977 mentioned in the next note.]

34. Those unacquainted with the subject of ἱεροδουλία could well begin with the good little article by F. R. Walton, 'Hierodouloi', in *OCD*² 514. See also Pierre Debord, 'L'Esclavage sacré: État de la question', in *Actes du Colloque 1971 sur l'esclavage = Annales litt. de l'Univ. de Besançon* 140, Paris, 1972) 135-50, with extensive bibliography; Hepding, 'Hierodouloi', in *RE* VIII.ii (1913) 1459-68; Bömer, *URSGR* II.149-89; III.457-70 (= 215-28). For the hierodules of Asia Minor, see Broughton, in *ESAR* (ed. Frank) IV.636, 641-5, 684. For Asia Minor and Syria, see H. Kreissig, 'Tempelland, Katoiken, Hierodulen im Seleukidenreich', in *Klio* 59 (1977) 375-80. For Egypt, see esp. Rostovtzeff, *SEHHW* I.280-4 (with III.1383-4 n.90), 321-3; and W. Otto, *Beiträge zur Hierodoulie im hellenistischen Ägypten* (= *Abhandl.*, Bayer. Akad. d. Wiss., Philos.-hist. Klasse, Munich, n.F. 29, 1950). [Only after this chapter was in proof did I see the article by K.-W. Welwei, 'Abhängige Landbevölkerungen auf Tempelterritorien im hellenistischen Kleinasien und Syrien', in *Anc. Soc.* 10 (1979) 97-118.]

35. For the Helots of Sparta, see Ephorus, *FGrH* 70 F 117, *ap.* Strab. VIII.v.4, p.365; Myron of Priene, *FGrH* 106 F 2, *ap.* Athen. XIV.657cd; Plut., *Inst. Lac.* 41 = *Mor.* 239e (where ἐπάρατον should be compared with ἐν τῷ ἄγεϊ ἐνέχεσθαι in Hdts VI.56; cf. my *OPW* 149-50). For the Penestae of Thessaly, see Archemachus of Euboea, *FGrH* 424 F 1, *ap.* Athen. VI.264ab. For the Mariandynois of Heraclea Pontica, see Poseidonius, *FGrH* 87 F 8, *ap.* Athen. VI.263d; Strabo XII.iii.4, p.542.

36. For the best and most complete text of all the relevant inscriptions from Commagene, see Helmut Waldmann, *Die kommagenischen Kultreformen unter König Mithradates I, Kallinikos und seinem Sohne Antiochos I = Études Préliminaires aux Religions Orientales dans l'Empire Romain* 34 (Leiden, 1973), where the following pages are relevant: (1) pp.59-79 (*IGLS* I.1 = *OGIS* I.383 = Laum, *Stift.* II.148-53 = Michel, *RIG* 735), esp. 68 (lines 171-86); (2) pp.123-41 (*IGLS* I.47), esp. 125 (lines 30-2) and 127 (lines 89-101); (3) pp.33-42 (*IGLS* I.51), esp. 34 (lines 10-24); (4) pp.80-122, esp. 84 (lines 66-9) and 87 (lines 151-65).

37. The two best examples of the form of ἱεροδουλία in which I am interested, apart from the six mentioned in the main text above (and in the preceding note), are (1) the κωμόπολις of Ameria, in the territory of Cabeira in Pontus (Strabo XII.iii.31, p.557); and (2) Albania = Azerbaijan (Strabo XI.iv.7, p.503).

38. E.g. (1) Pessinus in Galatia (Strabo XII.v.3, p.567); (2) Aezani in Phrygia (*IGRR* IV.571 = *OGIS* II. 502 and *AE* [1940]44); (3) the temple of Zeus Abrettenus in Mysia (Strabo XII.viii.9, p.574); (4) the temple of Zeus of Olba in Cilica (XIV.v.10, p.672); (5) the temple of Anaïtis in Acisilene, and elsewhere in Armenia (XI.xiv.16, p.532); and (6) the temple of Zeus (Baal) of Baetocaece in Northern Phoenicia, the subject of a set of documents (known for over 200

years) inscribed on the north gate of its *peribolos*, the publication of which as *IGLS* VII (1970) 4028 (with a good commentary) has superseded all others (e.g. A/J 147; *OGIS* 262; *IGRR* III.1020; Welles, *RCHP* 70). The Seleucid grant 'for all time' of the κώμη ἡ Βαιτοκαι[κη]νή to the god, σὺν τοῖς συνκύρουσι καὶ καθήκουσι πᾶσι, must have included its peasantry. The village seems to have been in the territory of Aradus rather than Apamea: see H. Seyrig, 'Antiquités syriennes 48. Aradus et Baetocaecé', in *Syria* 28 (1951) 191–206. I agree with Kreissig, LPHO 20, that the grant gave the temple full ownership of the land. Further bibliography on the subject of temple lands in Asia can be found in Magie, *RRAM* II.1016–21, nn.62–6.

39. Examples are (1) the temple of the Mothers at Engyum in Sicily (Diod. IV.80.4–5; cf. 79.6–7); and (2) the temple of Aphrodite at Eryx in Sicily: Strabo mentions only the large number of sacred prostitutes in earlier times (ἱερὸν . . . ἱεροδούλων γυναικῶν πλῆρες τὸ παλαιόν, VI.ii.6, p.272); but in the 70s B.C. there were 'permulti Venerii' there (Cic., *Pro Cluent.* 43; and see Scramuzza, WVSS, and in Frank, *ESAR* III.317-18). See also n.34 above for bibliography on the subject of ἱεροδουλία.

40. For Comana Pontica, see Strabo XII.iii.36, p.559; for Corinth, VIII.vi.20, p.378 ('more than a thousand ἱερόδουλοι ἑταῖραι), cf. XII.iii.36, p.559; for Eryx, see the previous note. The girls in Hdts I.93.4; 94.1; 199, and Strabo XI.xiv.16, p.532, are in a different category: their status was temporary.

41. See e.g. Kreissig, LPHO, esp. 6, 26 ('Oriental'); Briant, RLER, esp. 118 ('Asiatic'), and DDAHA; with the many works by themselves and others cited in their three articles. Briant's emphasis is different from Kreissig's: he concentrates on the peasant *village*, and he refuses to use the term 'serf', evidently under the mistaken impression that serfdom involves 'feudalism' and a 'feudal mode of production' (see esp. RLER 105-7, 118); he therefore prefers to use a vague term such as 'dépendants' (ibid. 106).

42. For the Pedieis of Priene, see *SIG*³ 282 (= *IP* 3).14-15; Welles, *RCHP* 8 (= *IP* 16).B.2,3; *OGIS* 11 (= *IP* 14).5-6. Rostovtzeff seems to me over-confident in *SEHHW* I.178-9, with III.1355 n.44 (where the reference to Rostovtzeff, *SGRK* ['*Kolonat*'] should presumably be to p.260). Cf. n.46 below. The ἀνδράποδα of whom Pythius the Lydian of Celaenae boasted to Xerxes in 480 may well have been serfs (Hdts VII.28.3; cf. Plut., *Eum.* 8.9, quoted in n.30 above).

42a. Particularly instructive here is a text discussed in Appendix II above: Xen., *Anab.* VII.viii.8-19, esp. 12,16,19. This shows a wealthy Persian, Asidates, as early as 400 B.C., employing on his fine estate on the plain near Pergamum a large number of slaves, of whom, after some had escaped (§ 12), Xenophon captured some 200 (§ 19). 'Barbarian' grandees were often only too ready to adopt Greek practices.

43. For both these processes, see above all Jones, *GCAJ* and *CERP*²; and V. Tscherikower [elsewhere usually Tcherikover], *Die hellenistischen Städtegründungen von Alexander dem Grossen bis auf der Römerzeit = Philologus*, Suppl. XIX.1 (1927).

44. These two examples are of transfers to Aristodicides (*RCHP* 10-13 = *OGIS* 221) and to Laodice (*RCHP* 18-20 = *OGIS* 225+). The best discussion of these transactions is by Atkinson, SGCWAM. I accept the view of Kreissig, LPHO 19-20 (cf. 18-19), that the Hellenistic kings were prepared to make absolute hereditary grants of land in Asia, in what we call freehold, not only (a) to cities (see the two examples given in the main text above, immediately after the reference to this note), (b) to temples (see no.6 in n.38 above), and (c) to individuals, accompanied by the right to join the land to the territory of a recognised city (as in the two examples given at the beginning of this note), but also (d) to individuals, without any such accompanying right: see (1) the inscription from near Scythopolis in Palestine, published by Y. H. Landau, 'A Greek inscr. found near Hefzibah', in *IEJ* 16 (1966) 54-70, lines 22-3 (§ IVa), which has been re-edited, with bibliography, by T. Fischer, in *ZPE* 33 (1979) 131-8 (§ F); and (2) Welles, *RCHP* 51, lines 20-1; cf. *SIG*³ 332 (esp. lines 9-15, 18-23) and *SEG* XX.411 (esp. line 33). I cannot follow Kreissig (LPHO 17, 20), however, in including *IGRR* III.422, as it is of Roman date. Nevertheless, perhaps these grants, of my type (d), although 'hereditary' in the sense that they did not revert automatically to the king on the death of the holder, like cleruchic land, might still be revoked if the holder were held guilty by the king of some offence – as they would not be (or would be much less likely to be) if in the category of type (c) above; hence one of the advantages of that type of grant.

45. See Rostovtzeff, *SEHHW* I.509 (with III.1441 n.285 and the references there given, esp. Rostovtzeff, *SGRK* 261-3), and in *CAH* VII.182-3; Welles, *RCHP* pp.96-7; Tarn, *HC*³ 134-8.

46. Welles (*RCHP* p.53) states the 'accepted interpretation' of *RCHP* 8 as being that the king

concerned 'had permitted such of the Pedieis as applied within 30 days to become πάροικοι . . . of Priene, for them an advantage in that as βασιλικοὶ λαοί they were little better than serfs, while through connection with a Greek city they acquired a good deal of freedom'. Kreissig accepts this, merely emphasising that those who did not apply 'remained λαοί. Both possibilities existed' (LPHO 24). Against this, I would point out not only that there is no reference in the inscription to λαοί (cf. Atkinson, SGCWAM 38) but that we have to take παροικεῖν in a sense, namely 'to *become* a πάροικος', which I have never observed elsewhere.

47. Atkinson, SGCWAM 38-9, is wrong in calling this document 'the Will of Attalus III'; but she has some useful things to say about this inscription and the general question I have been dealing with (ibid. 37-42, 53-7).

48. The clearest case, to my mind, is at Hasta in Spain, where an inscription of 189 B.C., ILS 15 = FIRA I².51, records a decision by L. Aemilius Paullus that 'quei Hastensium servei in turri Lascutana habitarent leiberei essent', and should continue to possess and hold, at the pleasure of the 'poplus senatusque Romanus', their 'agrum oppidumqu.'. I think Haywood (TSCD 146-7) is probably right in emphasising that the possession of land by the so-called 'servi' (even though it did not amount to ownership) shows that they are more likely to have been serfs than slaves; and here I would compare the condition of the German 'servus quasi colonus' (if I may call him that), described by Tac., *Germ.* 25.1 (see IV.iii above, § 12). The use of the technical word 'servi' seems to me to show that the Lascutani were not being made 'liberi' *merely* in the sense that they were being 'taken from under the control of the Hastenses' (as A/J, p.250, note on its no.2). My second example is particularly interesting, as the 'sole instance of temple serfs in Italy' (Frank, *ESAR* I.293-4): Cicero, *Pro Cluent.* 43-5, accuses Oppianicus of treating as 'free and Roman citizens' the Martiales of Larinum in Italy, whom he describes as 'ministri publici Martis' and 'in Martis familia' and compares to the Venerii of Eryx in Sicily (my third example, below), adding that Oppianicus' action caused great resentment among 'the decurions and all the citizens of Larinum', who brought an action against Oppianicus at Rome. We are not told who won the case, but it seems likely that it was Oppianicus, for it would have been in Cicero's interest to mention any condemnation of Oppianicus (see Haywood, TSCD 145-6). My third example is the Venerii of Sicilian Eryx, about whose status in Verres' time there seems to have been some dispute: see esp. Cic., *Div. in Caec.* 55-7, for the curious case of Agonis of Lilybaeum, described by Cicero as a 'liberta Veneris Erycinae' who had become 'copiosa plane et locuples', and who had claimed under pressure that 'se et sua Veneris esse', with the result that she was reduced to slavery again by Verres' quaestor, Q. Caecilius Niger, but was apparently reinstated in freedom by Verres himself (see Scramuzza, WVSS, and in Frank, *ESAR* III.317-18).

49. See the Indexes to these works and, in Newman, *PA*, esp. III.394; IV.304. Aristotle refers to περίοικοι in *Pol.* II.9, 1269ᵇ3; 10, 1271ᵇ30, 1272ᵃ1,18; V.3, 1303ᵃ8 (cf. Plut., *Mor.* 245f); VII.6, 1327ᵇ11; 9, 1329ᵃ26; 10, 1330ᵃ29. There are some good remarks on Aristotle's use of the term περίοικοι in Finley, SSAG 176; and see Lotze, *MED* 8-9.

50. On the Spartan περίοικοι, see also my *OPW* 93, 331-2, 372. For general treatments, see Busolt[-Swoboda], *GS* II.663-6; J. A. O. Larsen, s.v. *Perioikoi*, in *RE* XIX.i (1937) 816-33, at cols. 816-22; Pavel Oliva, *Sparta and her Social Problems* (Prague, 1971) 55-62.

51. See Larsen, op. cit. 822-4, 825-32. For Argos, see W. G. Forrest, 'Themistocles and Argos', in *CQ* 54 = n.s.10 (1960) 221-41, at 221-9; Lotze, *MED* 53-4; K. W. Welwei, *Unfreie im antiken Kriegsdienst, I. Athen und Sparta* (= *Forsch. zur ant. Sklaverei* 5, Wiesbaden, 1974) 182-92. For the περίοικοι of Cyrene (Hdts IV.161.3), see Appendix IV, § 5. I have not yet been able to make full sense of the very complicated social and economic structure of Crete and will merely refer to Lotze, *MED*, esp. 4-25, 79.

52. See e.g. Arist., *Pol.* V.6, 1305ᵇ5, 11, 36. Plato also refers to the Mariandynoi in *Laws* VI.776cd, where they are compared with the Helots and Penestai.

53. German usage of these words varies somewhat. According to Busolt[-Swoboda], *GS* II.670 n.4, 'Hörigkeit und Leibeigenschaft lassen sich zwar begrifflich nicht scharf unterscheiden, im allgemeinen versteht man aber *unter Leibeigenschaft den höchsten Grad der Hörigkeit* [my italics], der sich von der Sklaverei nur dadurch unterscheidet, dass der Leibeigene nicht einfach als Sache betrachtet, sondern sein Personalcharakter bis zu einem gewissen Grade anerkannt wird.' He had just ended his discussion of the Helots by designating them as 'Hörige', adding 'Im Umfange des allgemeinen Begriffes der Hörigkeit gehörten sie zu den Grundhörigen und zwar zu den *leibeigenen Bauern*, denn sie waren unter Schmälerung ihrer

persönlichen Freiheit an die Scholle gebunden und den Grundherren zu bestimmten Abgaben, sowie zu persönlichen Dienstleistungen verpflichtet' (ibid. 670). The whole paragraph is excellent.

54. There is an unsatisfactory discussion of Menand., *Hero* 20-40 (and its *Hypoth.* 3-4), in A. W. Gomme and F. H. Sandbach, *Menander. A Commentary* (1973) 385, 390-2.

55. Gomme and Sandbach, op. cit. 390, are certainly wrong in taking Isocr. XIV (*Plat.*) 48 to refer to Plataeans *at Athens* as seeing their children enslaved for petty debts (etc.). The Plataean speakers are represented as having just arrived in Athens as suppliants (§ 1 etc.); they have not yet been received at Athens as in 427 (cf. § 51) and indeed are still 'wanderers and beggars' (§ 46), their families broken up (§ 49). This is so, whether the speech is to be taken as written for a particular occasion in 371 or as a later piece of rhetoric.

56. On the Matthaean texts which I have referred to, and on other matters dealt with here, see the mainly admirable article by Dieter Nörr, 'Die Evangelien des Neuen Testaments u. die sogenannte hellenistische Rechtskoine', in *ZSS* 78 (1961) 92-141, at 135-8 ('Vollstreckung'), 140-1 ('Zusammenfassung'). Cf. 'Griechisches und orientalisches Recht im Neuen Test.', Nörr's contribution to the *Actes du Xe Congrès internat. de Papyrologues* (Warsaw etc., 1964) 109-15.

57. See Bieżuńska-Małowist, *EEGR* I.29-49 (a very clear analysis), 99-100; Préaux, *ERL* 312-17, 537-43, and cf. 308-12. In the interest of the royal administration, restrictions were placed upon 'personal execution' against e.g. the βασιλικοὶ γεωργοί and ὑποτελεῖς: see *P. Tebt.* 5.221-30 (= M.*Chr.* 36).

58. For this statement and the one at the end of the previous sentence in the text above it should be sufficient to refer to Weiss, *GP* 510 ff. (esp. 514-19); Nörr, op. cit. (in n.56 above) 137; and (for Egypt) Bieżuńska-Małowist, loc. cit. (n.57 above). The last-named puts it very well: 'Il est certain que la politique de l'État tendait visiblement à restreindre et peut-être même à abolir l'esclavage définitif sanctionnant les débiteurs privés insolvables. Le *PSI* 549 [for which see id. 28-9, 47] paraît bien témoigner qu'à la fin de l'époque ptolémaïque l'asservissement des hommes libres était prohibé, l'esclavage temporaire [which I would call 'debt bondage'] restant vraisemblablement admis' (id. 48). For debt bondage in fifth-century Gortyn in Crete, see *Inscr. Cret.* IV.72 = R. F. Willetts, *The Law Code of Gortyn* (= *Kadmos*, Suppl. I, Berlin, 1967) 39-40: Col. I.56 to II.2 (with Eng. trans.); and see Willetts, *Aristocratic Society in Ancient Crete* (1955) 36, 54-6. I must also mention at this point Dio Chrys. XV.20, saying that παρὰ πολλοῖς καὶ σφόδρα εὐνομουμένοις fathers can sell their sons: debt is not mentioned, and Dio adds that the fathers can also put their sons to death. This presumably refers to Roman law; but on the sale of children see a later passage in the main text above and nn.74-5 below.

59. Among many treatments of *nexum*, see the brief one in Jolowicz and Nicholas, *HISRL*[3] 164-6 (cf. 189-90), which gives some bibliography and the text of Varro, *LL* VII.105.

60. Contrast Frederiksen, who thinks that 'by the Empire it is clear that real attempts were made to enforce in the provinces the Roman principle that bondage or imprisonment should not happen without a court order' (*CCPD* 129-30), and that the imperial government 'introduced for debt forms and procedures that were milder and more lenient than anything the provinces had known' (*CCPD* 141). I cannot see that his explicit invocation (*CCPD* 130 n.14) of the authority of Mitteis is justified: I need only cite on the Principate the paragraph in *RuV* 450 ending 'Mann kann daher von der Annahme ausgehen, dass in den ersten Jahrhunderten der Kaiserzeit die Personalexecution im ganzen Reiche ein durchaus praktisches Institut gebildet hat'; it is even attested in Italy itself. Cf. also the 'Lex Rubria', *FIRA* I[2].174-5, no.19, xxi.19; xxii.46 (Roman law applied to Cisalpine Gaul in the 40s B.C.); 'Lex Ursonensis', id. 179, no.21, lxi. 1-3, 6 (Caesar's citizen colony, Colonia Genetiva Julia, 44 B.C.). Only in the Later Empire, says Mitteis (*RuV* 451), do we find that 'die spätrömischen Kaiser die Personal-execution auf das bestimmteste perhorresciren', from A.D. 388 in fact (*CTh* IX.xi.1); and on the next page he contrasts 'der Rechtsstandpunkte' with 'die thatsächlichen Verhältnisse', showing subsequently that 'Personalexecution' remained alive until Justinian's time. Here it may be appropriate to cite Schulz, *CRL* 214: *cessio bonorum* (for which see the next paragraph but two of the main text above and the next four notes below) 'was regarded as an exceptional privilege and not as the starting-point of a new development in the law of execution. Execution on the person still seemed too important to allow it to be restricted any further'.

61. For *bonorum venditio*, *cessio* and *distractio*, see Buckland, *TBRL*[3] 402-3, 643-5, 672-3; Jolowicz and Nicholas, *HISRL*[3] 217-18, 445; Crook, *LLR* 172-8. I should also like to recommend an

ingenious and entertaining article on a subject ('decoctio') closely allied to *cessio bonorum*: J. A. Crook, 'A study in decoction', in *Latomus* 26 (1967) 363-76; cf. his *LLR* 176-7.

62. See Frederiksen, CCPD 137-41, who makes quite a good case for attributing the law to Caesar rather than Augustus.

63. On *cessio bonorum* in general von Woess, PCBRR, is still unsurpassed (but see n.64 below): he gives references to the earlier works of Lucien Guénoun, *La cessio bonorum*, and M. Wlassak, in *RE* III.ii (1899) 1995-2000. The best summary account in English that I know is given in a single paragraph in de Zulueta, *Inst. of Gaius* II.136. A convenient work which utilises the papyrological evidence from Egypt in describing 'personal execution' and *cessio bonorum* is Chalon, *ETJA* 114-22, 187. See also n.61 above.

64. The account of *cessio bonorum* by von Woess, PCBRR, needs to be modified here: see Frederiksen, CCPD 135-6 (but cf. n.60 above). Chalon, *ETJA*, is well worth consulting: see esp. 117 n.33*bis*, in which he quotes and discusses *P. Ryl.* II.75 and *P. Vind. Boswinkel* 4.

65. Cf. Schulz, *CRL* 214, 402-5; also 44, 281, 302, 459-60, 511. See also Jolowicz and Nicholas, *HISRL*³ 187-90, 215-16, 401, 444-5; Buckland, *TBRL*³ 618-23, 634, 642-6, 671-2; de Zulueta, *Inst. of Gaius* II.242-7; Crook, *LLR* 170-8; Frederiksen, CCPD 129-30, 135-6, 141; and cf. P. A. Brunt's long and valuable review of Westermann, *SSGRA*, and two other books on ancient slavery, in *JRS* 48 (1958) 164-70, at 168. Anyone tempted to explain away an incident such as that described by Livy VI.xiv.3 ff. (385 B.C.), on the ground that it occurred before the Lex Poetelia (cf. Livy VIII.xxviii.1-9), should note Livy XXIII.xiv.3, where in 216 B.C. we hear of the freeing for military service, during an emergency, of those accused of capital crimes *and of judgment debtors* (evidently numerous) who were being kept in chains ('qui pecuniae iudicatae in vinculis essent'). It is significant that Livy, whose outlook here is typical of the Roman propertied classes, regards the liberation of these debtors as an 'ultimum prope desperatae reipublicae auxilium, cum honesta utilibus cedunt', to which the Dictator M. Junius Pera 'descendit'! Val. Max. VII.vi.1, summarising Livy, calls the debtors 'addicti' and records his own sense of shame ('aliquid ruboris habeant').

66. See Varro, *LL* VII.105 (*obaeratus*); *RR* I.xvii.2-3 (*obaerarii*, in Asia Minor, Egypt and Illyricum). The word *obaeratus*, of course, is also sometimes used in the ordinary, simple sense of 'debtor', as e.g. in Livy XXVI.xl.17, and Suet., *Div. Jul.* 46 (where Caesar is *tenuis adhuc et obaeratus*). For rent in arrear as debt, see IV.iii above, and n.67 below.

67. In addition to the examples which follow in the text, see e.g. Caes., *BG* I.iv.2 and VI.xiii.1-2 (pre-Roman Gaul); Tac., *Ann.* III.xl.1 and xlii.1-2 (Roman Gaul in A.D. 21). Colum., *RR* I.iii.12 is very relevant here; also Sall., *Cat.* 33.1. And see Mt. XVIII.23-34; V.25-6; Lk. XII.58-9, mentioned in the text earlier. The very unreliable *Historia Augusta* speaks of Hadrian as abolishing 'ergastula servorum *et liberorum*' (*Hadr.* 18.9). *CJ* IV.lxv.11 (A.D. 244) shows that attempts had 'often' been made to prevent tenants who were in arrear with their rents from leaving the farms they had leased, a practice which Hadrian, more than a century earlier, had found it necessary to deplore, as an 'inhumanus mos', in regard to leases of public land (*Dig.* XLIX.xiv.3.6). Cf. also Rostovtzeff, *SEHRE*² I.178-9 (with II.619-22 nn.42-5), 190-1, 471-2; Jones, *LRE* II.835-7, 858.

68. The latest and best edition of the edict of Tiberius Julius Alexander (*OGIS* 669 = *IGRR* I.1263) is by Chalon, *ETJA*. There are English translations, including that of A. C. Johnson, in *ESAR* (ed. Frank) II.705-9. The relevant lines of the edict are 15-18: for Chalon's commentary see his *ETJA* 110-22 (esp. 114-19 and n.33*bis*); and cf. line 37, with Chalon's commentary, *ETJA* 187-8, where I think Chalon is probably right in refusing to see a reference to *cessio bonorum*. And see von Woess, PCBRR 492-3 and n.4; also 525 n.1 on *M.Chr.* 71 = *P. Lips.* Inv. 244, lines 7-8.

69. See Garnsey, *SSLPRE*, esp. 99-100, 277-80.

70. Olivia Robinson, 'Private prisons', in *RIDA*³ 15 (1968) 389-98, at 391, seems to take *CJ* VII.lxxi.1 as applying to *iudicati* in general, whereas in fact it deals only with those who have been allowed to make a *cessio bonorum*, for which see above and nn.61-4.

71. Mitteis, *RuV* 450-8, cites some interesting evidence, including that of St. Ambrose for Italy.

72. See e.g. Schulz, *CRL* 214-15. One may doubt whether provincial practice changed much for the better.

73. For παραμονή see esp. A. E. Samuel, RPCAD, including a discussion of modern theories (221-8); Bertrand Adams, *Paramoné u. verwandte Texte, Stud. zum Dienstvertrag im Rechte der Papyri* (= *Neue Kölner rechtswiss. Abhandl.* 35, Berlin, 1964); W. L. Westermann, 'The *paramone* as general service contract', in *JJP* 2 (1948) 9-50 (not reliable); the bibliography in Nörr,

SRBFAR 89 n.107; and Crook, *LLR* 192-3, 200-2, 246-7.

74. The actual term *sanguinolenti* occurs in the title of *CTh* V.x and in *CJ* IV. xliii.2.*pr.* (= *CTh* V.x.1.*pr.*).

75. For the main laws referring to sale of children and other free persons (including self-sale, a difficult subject, treated by Buckland, *RLS* 427-33) see esp., in addition to the three constitutions quoted in the text above, *Dig.* XLVIII.xv (on the Lex Fabia *de plagiariis*); *CJ* VII.xvi.1 (Caracalla, 211-17), 10 (293); IV.xliii.1 (294); VII.xvi.39 (294); *Fr. Vat.* 33 (313); *CTh* IV.viii.6 (323); cf. Paul., *Sent.* V.i.1; *Dig.* XL.xii.33. Enslavement of free provincials as a result of Roman exactions is said to have occurred in the late Republic and early Principate: see e.g. Plut., *Lucull.* 20.1-4; App., *BC* IV.64; Tac., *Ann.* IV.lxxii.4-5. For the literary sources and papyri from the Later Roman Empire see Jones, *LRE* II.853-4 (with III.287 n.71): the clearest are Zos. II.38.1-3; Liban., *Orat.* XLVI.22-3; Rufinus, *Hist. Monach.* 16 (in *MPL* XXI.436) = *Hist. Monach. in Aeg.* 14.5-7, ed. A. J. Festugière (Brussels, 1961); Cassiod., *Var.* VIII.33 (see the main text above, just below n.73); *P. Cairo* 67023; add Evagr., *HE* III.39 (cf. IV.vi above). I must add a word here about one type of *liber homo bona fide serviens* (a condition which could arise in several different ways: see e.g. Berger, *EDRL* 562), namely the man who has allowed himself to be sold into slavery *in order to share the price*. So many legal texts deal with this situation that it must have been common – and not only in the Later Empire or even the Severan period, especially if the reference to a ruling of Hadrian on the matter in *Dig.* XL.xiv.2.*pr.* is not an interpolation. I would suppose that a man who allowed himself to be sold in order to obtain part of the price would normally do so with the aim of rescuing his family, if not himself, from starvation. (I have read nothing more recent than Buckland, *RLS* [1908] 427-33. For further bibliography see e.g. Kaser, *RP* I² [1971] 241 n.49, 302 n.8.) [It was only after this chapter was finished that my attention was drawn to the article by Theo Mayer-Maly, 'Das Notverkaufsrecht des Hausvaters', in *ZSS* 75 (1958) 116-55.]

76. There is a good treatment of this subject by Isaac Mendelsohn, *Slavery in the Ancient Near East* (New York, 1949). I would also like to draw attention to the brief remarks on this subject in Finley, *SD* 178, and the article by J. Bottéro, 'Désordre économique et annulation des dettes en Mésopotamie à l'époque paléo-babylonienne', in *JESHO* 4 (1961) 113-64, which is mainly about the famous edict of King Ammi-ṣaduqa of Babylon (the fourth successor of Hammurabi).

77. See Th. Mommsen, *Röm. Strafr.* 949-55. Two major examples from the reign of Nero are (*a*) Suet., *Nero* 31.3, where the emperor orders convicts from all parts of the empire to be sent to Italy to take part in building his projected canal from Lake Avernus to Ostia, and (*b*) Jos., *BJ* III.540, with Suet., *Nero* 19.2, where Vespasian sends 6,000 young men from among the Jews captured at Tarichaeae in September 67, to work on the canal through the isthmus of Corinth which had just been begun by Nero in person.

78. For the confessors sent to the copper mines of Phaeno, see Euseb., *HE* VIII.13.5; *Mart. Pal.* 5.2; 7.2-4; 8.1,13; for those in the porphyry mines opposite the Thebaid, *Mart. Pal.* 8.1; 9.1; for those sent to the Cilician mines, *Mart. Pal.* 11.6, with 8.13; 9.10.

79. See Fulvio Canciani, 'Lydos, der Sklave?', in *Antike Kunst* 21 (1978) 17-20; G. Neumann,, 'Zur Beischrift auf dem Kyathos', ibid. 21-2. This painter cannot be the same as the famous Lydos, who signs o Λυδος.

80. The epitaph is reprinted in *Anthol. Lat.* II.ii = *Carm. Lat. Epigr.*, ed. F. Bücheler (Leipzig, 1897) 468, no.1015.

[III.v]

1. Dionysius adds that he has known Romans who have freed all their slaves at their death, thus providing an impressively large train of mourners: this practice he deeply deplores (*AR* IV.24.6); it was restricted by Augustus (see Buckland, *RLS*, ch.xxiii, esp. 546-8).

2. Of the large literature I will cite only Max Kaser, *RP* I² (1971) 298-301 (§ 70: 'Freigelassene und Patronat'), with II² (1975) 585, and Kaser's article, 'Die Geschichte der Patronatsgewalt über Freigelassene' in *ZSS* 58 (1938) 88-135; and a work I have not seen, J. Lambert, *Les operae liberti. Contribution à l'histoire des droits de patronat* (Paris, 1934).

3. See the bibliography in M. I. Finley's article, 'Freedmen', in *OCD²* 447-8; and in Berger, *EDRL* 564 (s.v. *libertus*) and 609 (s.v. *operae liberti*). Add P. R. C. Weaver, *Familia Caesaris: a Social Study of the Emperor's Freedmen and Slaves* (1972); and see Weaver's article repr. in *SAS* (ed. Finley) 121-40. Roman manumission is dealt with at great length in most of the second half of

Buckland, *RLS* (437 ff.). The beginner might well start with that lively work, Crook, *LLR*, esp. 41, 50-5, 60, 191-2. Most historians I think would agree that manumission was much more common among Romans than Greeks: see e.g. Géza Alföldy's article, 'Die Freilassung von Sklaven u. die Struktur der Sklaverei in der römischen Kaiserzeit', in *Riv. stor. dell' Ant.* 2 (1972) 97-129, at 97 ff.

4. For the disabilities of the freedman himself, see Duff, *FERE*, ch.iii, iv, vii; and the bibliography in Berger, *EDRL* 609, s.v. *operae liberti*. There is a brief summary in Crook, *LLR* 51.

5. The only explicit authority for this is *Hist. Aug., Pertinax* 1.1; cf. *PIR*² IV.63-7, H no.73.

6. See in particular Mary L. Gordon, 'The freedman's son in municipal life', in *JRS* 21 (1931) 65-77; and most recently Garnsey, DFLP (mainly, but by no means entirely, on Beneventum); also e.g. J. H. D'Arms, 'Puteoli in the second century of the Roman Empire: a social and economic study', in *JRS* 64 (1974) 104-24, esp. 111-13.

7. For Licinus, see *PIR*² IV.iii (1966) 228-9, I no.381. For his misbehaviour in Gaul, see esp. Dio Cass. LIV.21.2-8; Suet., *Div. Aug.* 67.1; Senec., *Apocol.* 6. His wealth is spoken of as if it were comparable with that of Pallas (Juv. I.109; cf. below and n.9), and as late as the 470s he is mentioned in the company of seven other notorious imperial freedmen (including Pallas and Narcissus) by Sidonius Apollinaris, *Ep.* V.vii.3. He appears as no.7 in Duncan-Jones, *EREQS* 343-4, App.7: 'The size of private fortunes under the Principate.'

8. Plut., *Crass.* 2.3, says that Crassus' own assessment of his property in 55 B.C. (after he had made vast gifts) was 7,100 talents (a little over HS 170 million); and according to Pliny, *NH* XXXIII.134, he had land worth HS 200 million (over 8,000 talents). His famous remark is quoted by Pliny, loc. cit., as referring to the annual upkeep of a legion (estimated by Frank, *ESAR* I.327, at *c.* 1 million denarii and by Crawford at 1½ million for the period: see VIII.iv n.10 below); but in Cic., *De offic.* I.25, it refers to an 'exercitus', and in Cic., *Parad.* VI.45, this is made more explicit: Crassus actually spoke of an *exercitus* of six legions with auxiliary horse and foot, which would surely have cost something in the neighbourhood of HS 30-60 million a year.

9. For Narcissus, see Dio Cass. LX(LXI).34.4 (100 million drachmae = HS 400 million); for Pallas, Tac., *Ann.* XII.53.5 (HS 300 million), and Dio LXII.14.3 (100 million drachmae).

10. I base this figure on the fact that in 43 B.C. Cicero (*XIII Phil.* 12, cf. 10, and *II Phil.* 93) could say that the Senate had promised Sextus Pompey HS 700 million, as compensation for the confiscation of his father's property. Cf. App., *BC* III.4: in 44 B.C. Sextus had been offered 50 million drachmae = denarii (HS 200 million). In 39 B.C. the figure seems to have been put at HS 70 million (Dio XLVIII.36.5: 17,500,000 drachmae).

11. The standard view that this took place only or mainly from the reign of Hadrian onwards has been controverted by Weaver, in the works mentioned in n.3 above: see briefly *SAS* (ed. Finley) 137-9.

12. See Jones, *LRE* II.567-70; M. K. Hopkins, 'Eunuchs in politics in the Later Roman Empire', in *PCPS* 189 = n.s.9 (1963) 62-80. [This article has now been reprinted, with a few changes, as ch.iv, 'The political power of eunuchs', in the book by Hopkins mentioned in n.18 below.]

13. For the letter of Epiphanius, see *Acta Conc. Oec.*, ed. E. Schwartz, I.iv.3.222-5, §§ 293-4. The subject is also treated by Pierre Batiffol, 'Les présents de Saint Cyrille à la cour de Constantinople', in his *Études de liturgie et d'archéol. chrét.* (Paris, 1919) 154-79. The list of bribes paid to Chryseros is on p.224 of the *Acta*, lines 14-20. Mansi V (1761) 987-9 gives the letter of Epiphanius but omits the schedule of Cyril's bribes at the end (§ 294 in the *Acta Conc. Oec.*). See also Nestorius, *The Bazaar of Heracleides*, Eng. trans. from Syriac by G. R. Driver and L. Hodgson (Oxford, 1925), 272, 279-82, 286 and esp. 349-51; cf. xxii-iii, xxx. (Only the Syriac translation of the Greek original survives: it was edited by Paul Bedjan in 1910.) It seems not to be clear whether Chryseros (whose name used to be given as Chrysoretus or Chrysoretes) was the *praepositus* of the Emperor Theodosius II or of the pious Empress Pulcheria. For a summary of the main *benedictiones* or *eulogiae* given by St. Cyril, see Jones, *LRE* I.346. The gifts were so expensive that Cyril is said by his archdeacon to have borrowed 1,500 lb. gold from the Comes Ammonius, after having stripped his Church of everything (*ecclesia Alexandrina nudata*: see the *Acta*, p.223, lines 31-3, § 293.6). St. Cyril was a most remarkable character: he is caustically described by the great historian Ernst Stein (himself a Roman Catholic) in his *HBE* I².i.276.

14. See e.g. Stein, *HBE* II.356-60, 381, 454, 597-617 etc.

15. Westermann, *ASA* 457 n.2 = *SCA* (ed. Finley) 79 n.2, rejects the figures for slaves and small animals; but P. A. Brunt, 'Two great Roman landowners', in *Latomus* 34 (1975) 619-35, argues

that Isidorus is not likely to have exceeded the limits of credibility, although he also admits that the MS figures may not have been transmitted accurately.

16. Cf. Duncan-Jones, *EREQS* 238-48. The well-known essay by P. Veyne, 'Vie de Trimalcion', in *Annales* 16 (1961) 213-47, has much excellent material, but perhaps does not fully bring out the extravagance of some of the exaggerations in the *Cena Trimalchionis*.

17. Cf. *IGRR* III.802.19-26, where οἰυνδικτάριοι and ἀπελεύθεροι again appear together (line 25), but the πάροικοι are omitted, as are (doubtless by mistake) the πολεῖται who appear next to the ἐκκλησιασταί in 801.19 and 800.9-10. In 800 the οἰυνδικτάριοι do not appear. See also Section vi of this chapter after its n.35.

18. What I have said applies, in my opinion, even to the material examined in the very interesting and able article by Géza Alföldy mentioned in n.3 above, with which I need not concern myself here, as it deals only with Rome and Italy, Spain, and the Danubian area, and not with my 'Greek world'. [Cf. now Keith Hopkins, *Conquerors and Slaves. Sociological Stud. in Roman Hist.* I (1978) 115 n.30 and 127 n.63, which I read after this section was finished. I am glad to find that we are in broad agreement about Alföldy's conclusions.]

19. See n.2 above; also e.g. W. W. Buckland, *TBRL*[3] 88-90, or, much more briefly, Duff, *FERE* 43-4; Crook, *LLR* 53.

[III.vi]

1. This section naturally concentrates on Greek rather than Roman wage labour; but, as I shall not have an opportunity to give more than occasional bibliographical references for Roman *mercennarii* (and the law relating to them, which I shall have to touch upon), I will mention here some standard works that deal in a general way with Roman hired labour and the law relating thereto: Remo Martini, *'Mercennarius'. Contributo allo studio dei rapporti di lavoro in diritto romano* (Milan, 1958); and a series of works by F. M. De Robertis: the two mentioned in n.36 below; also *Il diritto associativo romano* (Bari, 1938); *Il fenomeno associativo nel mondo romano, dai collegi della Repubblica alle corporazioni del Basso Impero* (Naples, 1955); *Storia delle corporazioni e del regime associativo nel mondo romano* (2 vols, Bari, 1971). See also nn.36 and 39-40 below. [Only when this chapter was in proof did I see the article by P. A. Brunt, 'Free labour and public works at Rome', in *JRS* 70 (1980) 81-100, of which the author kindly showed me an early draft. I accept much of what he says about Rome; but note his statement (p.84) that he is 'not claiming that what is true for Rome holds for other towns in the empire'.]

2. Cf. Aeschin. I.105, where the forms of property envisaged are dwelling house and tenement house (*oikia* and *synoikia*: for the distinction, see § 124), land, slaves, and money invested in loans.

3. See L. A. Moritz, 'Alphita – a note', in *CQ* 43 (1949) 113-17; *Grain-Mills and Flour in Classical Antiquity* (1958), esp. 149-50.

4. The law was evaded by decurions' taking over a head-lease of the property they were going to manage, so that they could legally claim to be *conductores*, not *procuratores*; but this practice too was forbidden by Theodosius II and Valentinian III in 439, by *Nov. Theod.* IX.1, which even goes on to forbid decurions acting as sureties for lessees (§ 4).

5. Aristotle speaks of hired labour as a form of μισθαρνία (*Pol.* I.11, 1258[b]25-7), or μισθαρνικὴ ἐργασία or τέχνη (VIII.2, 1337[b]13-14; *Eth. Eud.* I.4, 1215[a]31; cf. Ps.-Arist., *Oecon.* I.2, 1343[a]29), and uses the verb μισθαρνεῖν (*Pol.* IV.12, 1296[b]28-30). He never uses λατρεία for hired labour.

6. The six main passages in Aristotle are *Pol.* I.11, 1258[b]25-7; 13, 1260[a]36-[b]1; III.5, 1278[a]21-5; IV.4, 1290[b]39-1[a]8; VI.7, 1321[a]5-6; *Rhet.* I.9, 1367[a]28-32. For other passages on the *thēs* and his activities, see Arist. *Eth. Eud.* VII.12, 1245[b]31; fr.485; the texts cited in n.5 above in which μισθαρνεῖν and its cognates appear; and *Pol.* III.5, 1278[a]11-13, 17-18, 20-1; VI.1, 1317[a]24-6; 4, 1319[a]26-8; VII.9, 1329[a]35-8 (to be understood in the light of 8, 1326[a]21-5, 1328[b]2-4); VIII.2, 1337[b]19-21; 6, 1341[b]13-14; 7, 1342[a]18-21; *Eth. Nic.* IV.3, 1125[a]1-2.

7. Among other passages, see Arist., *Pol.* II.8, 1269[a]34-6 (τὴν τῶν ἀναγκαίων . . . σχολήν); IV.4, 1291[b]25-6; VII.9, 1329[a]1-2; 14, 1333[a] 33-6; 15, 1334[a]14-16; with the admirable paper by J. L. Stocks, 'ΣΧΟΛΗ', in *CQ* 30 (1936) 177-87. On *otium* (the Latin word most nearly – although often not very nearly – corresponding to σχολή) there is a large recent book of no fewer than 576 pages, by Jean-Marie André, *L'otium dans la vie morale et intellectuelle romaine des origines à l'époque augustéenne* (= Publ. de la Fac. des lettres et sciences humaines de Paris, Série 'Recherches', XXX, Paris, 1966).

8. Arist., *Pol.* IV.4, 1290^{b}38-1^{a}8, 1291^{a}33-^{b}13; VI.7, 1321^{a}5-6; cf. VI.1, 1317^{a}24-6; 4, 1319^{a}26-8; VII.9, 1329^{a}35-8.

9. Cf. the discussion of the two passages in question in II.iv above, from which it should be evident that although it is only the one in Book VI which sets out to deal with the μέρη of the πλῆθος specifically, yet the first four μέρη in IV.4 turn out in the end not to include the εὔποροι, the propertied class, and therefore are in effect divisions of the πλῆθος.

10. Unlike most editors, I would delete the οἱ in line 24, for in my opinion it would be absurd to suppose that Aristotle can be saying that *most* of the τεχνῖται are rich – especially in the oligarchies of which Aristotle is here speaking! I would suppose, by the way, that τεχνῖται who became rich did so by employing slave labour, like Cyrebus and the others mentioned in the second of Xenophon's dialogues summarised above – the one with Aristarchus (*Mem.* II.vii), where indeed all the men concerned are specifically stated to have made their pile by using slaves. Such men as the fathers of Isocrates and Demosthenes would certainly fall into this category. On the other hand, I feel sure that when Aristotle speaks of οἱ χερνῆτες (*Pol.* III.4, 1277^{a}38-^{b}1) and τὸ χερνητικόν (IV.4, 1291^{b}25-6) he is thinking primarily of hired workers: note the δούλου εἴδη of 1277^{a}37 and the μὴ δύνασθαι σχολάζειν of 1291^{b}26.

11. For another statement treating wage-labour and slavery as very much alike, see the late Peripatetic work, Ps.-Arist., *De virtut.* 7, 1251^{b}10-14 (esp. βίος θητικὸς καὶ δουλοπρεπὴς καὶ ῥυπαρός, φιλοτιμίας καὶ ἐλευθερίας ἀλλότριος).

12. Other passages in Homer in which θῆτες appear are *Iliad* XXI.441-57 (where Poseidon and Apollo serve Laomedon of Troy for hire for a year, but are cheated of their pay – probably a very common experience for the θής); *Odyss.* IV.643-4 (where θῆτες and household servants are envisaged as the likely source for rowers); XIV.101-2 (herdsmen); XVIII.356-61 (farm work); cf. *Iliad* XVIII.550, 560, where the ἔριθοι are presumably also hired labourers.

13. *IG* II^2.1672.28-30, 32-4, 45-6, 60-2, 125-6, 158-9, 292-5, 299; 1673.4, 28-9, 44-5, 58-9 (μισθωτοί). Some additional restorations have been made by Kevin Clinton, 'Inscriptions from Eleusis', in Ἀρχαιολογικὴ Ἐφημερίς (1972) 81-136, at 83-8.

14. *IG* II^2.1672.4-5, 42-3, 117-18, 141-2; 1673.39 (δημόσιοι). And see n.13 above.

15. 'Κολωνὸς μίσθιος: labour exchange in Classical Athens', in *Eranos* 49 (1951) 171-3. (This Kolonos was not a deme, like Kolonos Hippios, the deme of the poet Sophocles; it was in the deme Melite.)

16. I give here all the passages I know from Athens relating to hired labour in agriculture: Solon fr. 1.47-8 and Ps.-Dem. LIII.20-1 (cited in the text above); Ar., *Wasps* 712; Dem. XVIII.51; LVII.45; Theophr., *Char.* IV.3; Menand., *Agric.* 46-7; *Dysc.* 330-1; cf. Xen., *Hiero* VI.10.

17. In the 1,651 pages of text and notes in Rostovtzeff, *SEHHW*, there are few specific references to wage-labour outside Delos (the situation in which is discussed in Tarn's chapter mentioned in n.18 below; cf. Larsen in Frank, *ESAR* IV.408-12). Perhaps the most useful statement is one in *SEHHW* III,1601 n.53: 'The average remuneration of technical service (with few exceptions) was about 1 dr. a day, sometimes less, sometimes a little more. The salary of a 'foreman' (for example, a ἡγεμών in the military service) was no more than double the salary of a common *technitēs*, which was 'little more than a living wage, while the unskilled or half-skilled hired hands earned a little less than this living wage.'

18. In *The Hellenistic Age*, by J. B. Bury and others (1923) 108-40. Tarn gives no references, but many of them can easily be discovered with the aid of Tarn, *HC*^{3} (esp. ch.iii); Rostovtzeff, *SEHHW*; and Larsen's 'Roman Greece', in Frank, *ESAR* IV.259-496.

19. In the whole of Rostovtzeff, *SEHRE*^{2}, there are hardly any references to hired labour which are supported by the production of evidence. And I know of nothing at all to compare with the Mactar inscription, mentioned in the text above, just after the passage to which the present note relates. I see no reason to give a string of uninformative references and will content myself with two. First, there is *IG* XII.v.129, lines 14-20, where the Parians, in the second century B.C., congratulate their *agoranomos* for having dealt justly both with hired men and with their employers, and for having obliged the hired men to go to work and the employers to pay their wages without litigation. I agree with Buckler, LDPA 28 (see esp. his n.3), that the men are more likely to have been agricultural labourers than industrial workers. The second text is Dio Chrys. VII.11, one of very few which speak of free men serving as herdsmen for hire. Perhaps I should add that the most interesting of the documents set out and discussed in Buckler, LDPA (36-45, 47-50), namely the declaration by the collective building workers of Sardis dated 27 April 459, has nothing to do with hired labour in the technical sense (see IV.vi below). I think we can generalise the statement Rostovtzeff makes on Egypt (I^2.471): 'We can hardly presume the existence of a specific wage-earning class of labourers in Egypt. The majority of wage-earners worked occasionally and had another permanent occupation (most of them being peasants); moreover, women and children worked along with the men. The position of labour

in industry is almost unknown.' This can surely be taken to be broadly true of the whole empire. There was certainly a good deal of hired labour in agriculture, of a purely seasonal nature (cf. MacMullen, *RSR* 42 and 162 nn.43–8; White, *RF* 347–50, with Brunt's review in *JRS* 62 [1972], at 158; Jones, *LRE* II.792–3). A very exceptional construction programme which offered high rates of pay, such as the building at great speed by Anastasius in 505–7 of a new frontier fortress city at Dara (renamed Anastasiopolis) near Nisibis in Mesopotamia, might attract large numbers of workers while it lasted, and many of them might be μισθωτοί/ *mercennarii* (see Jones, *LRE* II.858); cf. Procop., *Bell.* III (*Vand.* I).xxiii.19–20 for Belisarius at Carthage in 533 offering generous pay to τοῖς τε περὶ τὴν οἰκοδομίαν τεχνίταις καὶ τῷ ἄλλῳ ὁμίλῳ, to repair the city wall and surround it with a ditch and a wooden stockade. I think that Procopius' distinction between the τεχνῖται and the ἄλλος ὅμιλος is a genuine one: the latter would be mainly unskilled wage-labourers.

20. For Epidaurus, see Burford, *GTBE* 57–9, 88–118, 131, 138–58, 159–66, 184–91, 191–206; *EGTB*, esp. 24–5, 27–30, 31. For Delos, see P. H. Davis, 'The Delos building contracts', in *BCH* 61 (1937) 109–35; still useful too is G. Glotz, 'Les salaires à Délos', in *Jnl des Savants* 11 (1913) 206–15, 251–60. [It was not until after this book was finished that I was able to look at Gabriella Bodei Giglioni, *Lavori pubblici e occupazione nell' antichità classica* (Bologna, 1974).]

21. *IG* II².1672–3. For the μισθωτοί in these documents, see n.13 above; for the δημόσιοι, n.14; for the tithe corn, 1672.263–88, cf. 292–3. Among various other accounts from Athens, I must mention those for the Erechtheum from the last decade of the fifth century: see *IG* I².372–4 and II².1654–5, with additions in *SEG*, esp. X.268–301; and L. D. Caskey, in *The Erechtheum* (1927), ed. J. M. Paton and others, ch.iv. These latter accounts are usefully, if not very acutely, analysed by R. H. Randall, 'The Erechtheum workmen', in *AJA* 57 (1953) 199–210. I have referred to wages by the day: these are at least once called καθημερίσια (*IG* I².373.245–6; cf. [καθεμερ]ισιείας restored in *IG* I².363.32, 39: see *SEG* III.39); but it is often made clear that the rate is by the day, and even the salary of the architect at Athens, Epidaurus and elsewhere is usually at so much per day. Wages paid (if not calculated) by the month, καταμήνια, are mentioned several times in fifth-century Athenian inscriptions, e.g. *IG* I².339.30; 346.67 (where they are perhaps distinct from the μισθώματα in line 63); 352.37; 363.48–9, where I think we can hardly separate καταμε[νίον] from μισθομά[τον].

22. My position is very different from that of Burford, *GTBE* 109 ff., esp. 112, where the statement that 'The accounts for the repair of the Erechtheion record "day-wages" (μισθώματα) paid to "hired workers" (μισθωτοί)' is far from justified by the evidence: the word μισθωτός never appears in fifth-century Athenian inscriptions, as far as I know, and certainly not in *IG* I², and the word μισθώματα occurs only in one context in the surviving portion of the Erechtheum accounts, in *IG* I².373.245 (cf. 261), quoted in the text above towards the end of the paragraph containing the reference to this note (22). The unnamed 'men', numbering between 19 and 33, who in the Erechtheum accounts for 407/6 (*IG* I².374.404–17) were paid 1 dr. each on various days and were presumably 'hired by the day' (Randall, op. cit. 200), were very probably μισθωτοί in the strict sense but are not so called in the lines surviving, nor is their pay called μισθός, a term which in the Erechtheum accounts seems to be reserved for the pay of the architect and under-secretary (374.108–12), apart from a possible appearance in line 122. I would particularly emphasise, too, that in *IG* I².352.34–5 [μι]σθός is paid in 434/3 B.C. to the sculptors of the pediment-reliefs of the Parthenon, who would be anything but mere μισθωτοί. Μισθός is also given in the Eleusinian accounts to other men who appear to be skilled artisans, contractors: see e.g. *IG* II².1672.67–8, 110–11, 144–5, 189–90; 1673.14, 22–3, 36 and esp. 65 to near the end, where μισθός appears again and again as given for the use of yokes of oxen in transporting the tambours of the columns, usually in sums of a few hundred drachmae at a time. And here again, of course, the architect and other figures of reputable status receive μισθός. Given by the State, μισθός is unobjectionable. I do not want to go into too much detail about the peculiarities of the building inscriptions I have mentioned and others, but I think I should add three points. First, we occasionally find payments described as σιτία (provisions, rations) to building workers, which we may translate 'ration money', as in *IG* II².1672.6–8 (Eleusis, 329/8), where the payment is at the rate of 7 obols per day each to a number of men of unknown status, who have been carving inscriptions. Secondly, we hear – although never, as far as I know, in inscriptions – of men referred to as ἐπισίτιοι, whose work is said to be remunerated not in money but in food only: see Athen. VI.246f–7a, citing esp. Plato *Rep.* IV.420a and Eubulus. Thirdly, it is sometimes specifically recorded that particular payments

have been made to workers described as οἰκόσιτοι (literally, 'eating at home'), evidently signifying that they supply their own food (e.g. *IG* II². 1672.28, 29, 32, 33, 46, 62, 111, 160, 178); but I feel certain that the use of the word in question has no significance, and that men not described as οἰκόσιτοι did not receive in addition rations or money therefor. (It seems clear that there is no difference in rates of money pay according to whether the word οἰκόσιτος is used or not; and of course, if not being οἰκόσιτος had involved additional remuneration in money or kind, then the relevant expenditure would have had to appear in the accounts – and it does not.) I may add that the recipients of pay who are described as οἰκόσιτοι are sometimes μισθωτοί (1672.29, 33, 46, 62), and that only one payment to an οἰκόσιτος is actually called μισθός (line 111). The word οἰκόσιτος occurs only in 1672 and not in the preserved portions of 1673.

23. In the surviving parts of the Erechtheum inscriptions (see n.21 above) only one man seems actually to be called a μισθωτής: the metic Dionysodorus, in *IG* I². 374.99-100, 264-7. Later, however, the word is used more freely, and in the Eleusis accounts (see n.21 again) it is often applied to contractors. But I do not myself see any real economic significance in the terminological variations in the different inscriptions. Outside Athens, as I said earlier in the main text above, other terms may be used for the contractor, and at Epidaurus, for instance, he is merely said to have 'undertaken' the work.

24. See Meiggs, *AE* 132 ff., esp. 139-40 (an excellent passage), showing that it would be a mistake to accept Plut., *Per.* 12 as necessarily founded on a good contemporary source (as has so often been assumed); also A. Andrewes, 'The opposition to Perikles', in *JHS* 98 (1978) 1-8, at 1-5 (esp. 3-4), going further and plausibly arguing that the passage is worthless and must derive from a late source, perhaps a composition produced by 'a student in some post-classical school'. See also A. Burford, 'The builders of the Parthenon', in *Parthenos and Parthenon* (= *Greece & Rome*, Suppl. to Vol.10, 1963) 23-35, esp. 34.

25. See esp. Burford, *EGTB* 30-4; also Francotte, *IGA* II.83-4.

26. The silence of Isocr. II (*Ad Nicocl.*) is particularly significant here, since the passage in §§ 15-16 that begins μελέτω σοι τοῦ πλήθους advocates particular concern for the masses. Perhaps I should just add that it would of course be wrong to pretend that when Demades spoke of τὰ θεωρικά as the 'glue of the democracy' (κόλλα τῆς δημοκρατίας: fr. II.9 Sauppe, *ap.* Plut., *Mor.* 1011b) he could have been referring to the public works which were paid for out of the theoric fund (see the passages listed in my review of J. J. Buchanan, *Theorika*, in *CR* 78 = n.s.14 [1964] 191), since it is clear that it was the *distributions* of theoric money for certain festivals (τὰς διανομάς in the passage quoted) to which Demades was referring. To suppose the contrary would be to assume, without the slightest reason, that Plutarch was misunderstanding Demades; and it would anyway be ridiculous to imagine that some very minor public works could be called the 'glue of the democracy'.

27. See Zvi Yavetz, 'Plebs sordida', in *Athen.* n.s. 43 (1965) 295-311; cf. 'Levitas popularis', in *Atene e Roma* n.s. 10 (1965) 97-110. On the generally neglected question how the poor at Rome were accommodated (mainly in overcrowded and unsafe tenement-houses, *insulae*) see, for the Late Republic, Yavetz, 'The living conditions of the urban plebs in Republican Rome', in *Latomus* 17 (1958) 500-17, repr. in *CRR* (ed. Seager) 162-79, and, for the early Principate, B. W. Frier, 'The rental market in early Imperial Rome', in *JRS* 67 (1977) 27-37. As Brunt has noticed (see *SAS*, ed. Finley, 90 n.49), there is evidence from a Late Republican jurist, C. Trebatius Testa, of patrons providing free tenancies for their own or their wives' *liberti et clientes: Dig.* IX.iii.5.1.

28. See J.-P. Waltzing, *Étude historique sur les corporations professionnelles chez les Romains* I (Louvain, 1895) 346-7. Cf. H. J. Loane, *Industry and Commerce of the City of Rome 50 B.C.-200 A.D.* (= *Johns Hopkins Univ. Stud. in Historical and Political Science* LVI.2, Baltimore, 1938) 64-5 etc.

29. P. A. Brunt, in *JRS* 63 (1973) 250, referring to his *SCRR* (see its Index, 164, *s.v.* 'public works'); cf. Brunt in *SAC* (ed. Finley) 87-91. [And see now Brunt's 1980 article, mentioned at the end of n.1 above.]

30. See Walbank, *HCP* I.692-4 on the whole subject. He cites (692) Livy XXIV.18.13 for the use of the Latin term *plebs* in the same sense as Polybius uses the Greek word πλῆθος in VI.17.3.

31. Having regard to the context, and Polyb. IV.50.3, I believe that Walbank (ibid. 694) is right in taking ταῖς ἐργασίαις ταῖς ἐκ τούτων to mean 'the *profits from* the contracts' rather than 'the *business consequential on* the contracts' (Brunt, as cited in n.29 above).

32. Only after this chapter was finished did I see the interesting article by Lionel Casson, 'Unemployment, the building trade, and Suetonius, *Vesp.* 18', in *BASP* 15 (1978) 43-51, giving another interpretation of that text. I shall say nothing about this here, as P. A. Brunt will

shortly be dealing with the subject fully. [See again now his 1980 article.]

33. Ramsay MacMullen, 'Roman Imperial building in the provinces', in *HSCP* 64 (1959) 207-35, is a mine of information on its subject. For the role of the army, see esp. ibid. 214-22.

34. See Denis van Berchem, *Les distributions de blé et d'argent à la plèbe romaine sous l'empire* (Geneva, 1939); and cf. now J. R. Rea, *P. Oxy.* XL (1972), pp.8-15.

35. The evidence is most plentiful for Italy and Africa: this has been collected and well analysed by Duncan-Jones, *EREQS* 80-2 (Africa) and 132-44 (Italy); see esp. 139, 141-3 for social discrimination. The only exception I have come across to the rule that where distributions are graded, the grading is strictly according to social rank, is where a freedman at Ostia gives more to Augustales (themselves of course freedmen) than to decurions (*CIL* XIV.431 = Duncan-Jones, *EREQS* no.674 = 772, pp.176-7, 187). See in general A. R. Hands, *Charities and Social Aid in Greece and Rome* (1968), esp. 89-92 and, among his translated documents, D 41 (Menodora) and D 40, 42-3 (Italy).

36. Crook, *LLR* 191-8, with ample references, 320-1 nn.59-96. I would add Th. Mayer-Maly, *Locatio Conductio* (= *Wiener rechtsgeschichtliche Arbeiten* IV, 1956), esp. 123-7; and Dieter Nörr, SRBFAR = 'Zur sozialen und rechtlichen Bewertung der freien Arbeit in Rom', in *ZSS* 82 (1965) 67-105, which is partly a review of F. M. De Robertis, *Lavoro e lavoratori nel mondo romano* (Bari, 1963); cf. De Robertis, *I rapporti di lavoro nel diritto romano* (Milan, 1946). My one objection to Crook's material is his citation of Cic., *Ad Att.* XIV.iii.1 (44 B.C.), as evidence that 'the workers on a building contract for Cicero at Tusculum . . . went off to do harvesting in April' (*LLR* 195). A similar reading of the passage appears in White, *RF* 513 n.33. This interpretation of the words 'ad frumentum' in that letter is absolutely ruled out, however, both by the time of year (the men had returned by early April) and by the continuation of Cicero's sentence, to the effect that the men had 'returned empty-handed, reporting a strong rumour that all the grain in Rome was being taken to Antony's house'. The phrase 'ad frumentum' must mean 'to buy grain'. I may remark that Brunt's interpretation of the same passage (in *SAS*, ed. Finley, 90) would require not 'ad frumentum' but e.g. 'ad frumentationem'; and it also does not suit the continuation of the sentence.

37. For the usage of the expressions 'Aramaic' and 'Syriac' in the early centuries, see F. Millar, in *JRS* 61 (1971) 1 ff., at pp.2-8.

38. We must not, however, go so far as to imagine that the wage-labourer was legally assimilated to the slave in Roman law, as some scholars have been tempted to suppose. The *mercennarius* certainly did not form part of the *familia*, for instance: nothing in *Dig.* XLIII.xvi.1.16-20 or elsewhere justifies such an assumption. And in *Dig.* XLVII.ii.90 and XLVIII.xix.11.1 the relationship of the *mercennarius* to his employer can no more be equated with that of the slave to his master than with that of the freedman or the client to his *patronus*; nor can 'loco servorum' in *Dig.* VII.viii.4.*pr.* and XLIII.xvi.1.18 be intended to apply to ordinary *mercennarii*: for all this, see R. Martini, op. cit. (in n.1 above) 62 ff., esp. 69-72. [Better still is Brunt, in § 5, pp.99-100, of the 1980 article cited at the end of n.1 above.]

39. For the bibliography, see n.36 above, also Crook, *LLR* 192-8 (with 320-1 nn.59-96). I think I have found most illumination from the article by J. A. C. Thomas, '*Locatio* and *operae*', in *BIDR* 64 (1961) 231-47. I agree with Crook that Schulz, *CRL* 542-4 is over-legalistic in belittling the distinction I am describing. Among the earliest passages in Latin referring to *locatio conductio operarum* I would pick out Plaut., *Trinumm.* 843-4, 853-4.

40. See very briefly Berger, *EDRL* 567 (*s.v. locatio conductio operarum*); Buckland, *TBRL*[3] 503-4. I agree with the account given by Crook, *LLR* 203-5, following Thomas, op. cit. 240-7.

41. Except in an inferior MS reading of *Dig.* XXXVIII.i.26.*pr.*

42. Thomas, op. cit. (in n.39 above) 239, says he finds 'no legal use of *operas locare/conducere* before the time of Hadrian'; but Petronius, *Sat.* 117.11-12, cited in the text above, shows that it was well known *in ordinary speech* by the mid-first century.

43. See esp. Dio Chrys. XL.5-9; XLV.12-16; XLVI.9; XLVII.12-21; XLVIII.11-12.

44. It will be sufficient to refer to Finley, *AE* 81, with 194 n.58.

45. I take it that in the sentence, 'Demosthenes' guardians did not claim that they had sold off the products of his factory cheap, owing to the alleged glut, but that they did not sell them at all, or alternatively suspended the slaves' work', Jones is referring to Dem. XXVII.20-2. But his conclusions are not justified; Demosthenes is giving a set of possible alternatives which he thinks Aphobus might propose, and we can have little idea what the real situation was: see Davies, *APF* 126-33, for an admirably sceptical account of Demosthenes' assertions.

46. Davies' *APF* 127-33, is excellent on the estate of Demosthenes' father. I accept his modification, p.131, of the theory I put forward in *Class. et Med.* 14 (1953) 30-70: it is clearly an improvement.
47. Jones, SAW 190-1 = *SCA* 6-7, begins his section III with a praiseworthy attempt to distinguish between free craftsmen and hired labourers. But then, when he is ostensibly dealing with hired labour, after asserting that 'We do not know what the practice of private employers was, but the Athenian State, as the temple building accounts prove, paid the same rate . . . to free workers or hired slaves', he makes a reference to the Erechtheum accounts, where there are no specifically *hired* labourers such as the μισθωτοί of *IG* II².1672-3 (see n.13 above) but the payments for work done are (in my opinion) given to those I am calling 'contractors', apart from the groups of unspecified 'men' in *IG* I².374.404-17, mentioned in n.22 above, whom I take to be in fact μισθωτοί, although they are not so called.
48. I find it hard to decide between the position adopted by Keith Thomas, 'The Levellers and the franchise', in *The Interregnum. The Quest for Settlement 1646-1660*, ed. G. E. Aylmer (1972) 57-78, and that of C. B. Macpherson, *The Political Theory of Possessive Individualism, Hobbes to Locke* (1962), e.g. 107, 282-6; and *Democratic Theory. Essays in Retrieval* (1973) 207-23, whose views are at least partly shared by Christopher Hill, *Puritanism and Revolution* (1958) 307, and by Pauline Gregg, in her delightful book on the most important of the Levellers, *Free-born John. A Biography of John Lilburne* (1961) 215, 221-2, 257, 353-4. Thomas is certainly right in emphasising the wide differences of opinion among the Levellers, and on the whole he seems to me to have the better of the argument.
49. There has been some dispute how far 'alms-takers' should be distinguished from 'beggars', and also on the question how wide the category of 'servants' was, and how far it included wage-earners who were not household servants. See the works cited in the preceding note.
50. For the first definition, see (*a*) *The Oceana of James Harrington and his Other Works*, ed. John Toland (1700) 83, from *Oceana* (of 1656), and (*b*) ibid. 436, from *The Art of Lawgiving* (1659), Book III, chapter i (servants have not 'wherewithal to live of themselves'); and for the second, see ibid. 496, from *A System of Politics* (1661) I.13-14. (The page references are the same as above in the two editions of 1737, published separately in London and Dublin.) On Harrington, the most recent work seems to be by Charles Blitzer, *An Immortal Commonwealth. The Political Thought of James Harrington* (= *Yale Stud. in Pol. Science* 2, New Haven, 1960). The latest edition of *Oceana* (with notes) is by S. B. Liljegren, *James Harrington's Oceana* (Heidelberg, 1924). See also Hill, op. cit. (in n.48 above), esp. 299-313; R. H. Tawney, 'Harrington's interpretation of his age', in *PBA* 27 (1941) 199-223; and the Inaugural Lecture as Harmsworth Professor delivered at Oxford (and published) in 1976 by Jack P. Greene, *All Men Are Created Equal*, esp. 17-23, with 37-9 nn.66-88. [Only after this section was finished did I become aware of *The Political Works of James Harrington*, ed. J. G. A. Pocock (1977).]
51. My quotations are from the excellent summary of the political ideas of Kant in *Kant's Political Writings*, ed. (with Introduction and notes) by Hans Reiss and translated by H. B. Nisbet (1970) 78 & note, 139-40. The references to the German text in each case will be found on pp.193 and 197 of the book.
52. Mt. XX.1-16 (where ἐργάται from the ἀγορά, hired to work in a vineyard by its owner, receive μισθός from an ἐπίτροπος); Mk I.20 (μισθωτοί on a ship); Lk. X.7 (the ἐργάτης is worthy of his μισθός), XV.17,19 (μίσθιοι); Jn IV.36 (a harvester receives μισθός), X.12-13 (a μισθωτός who is not the regular ποιμήν does not look after the sheep properly); James V.4 (keeping back by fraud the μισθός of the ἐργάται who have been harvesting or mowing). Cf. Lk. III.14 (ὀψώνια of soldiers); II Cor. xi.8 (Paul received ὀψώνια from churches); II Pet. ii.15 and Rom. VI.23 (μισθός and ὀψώνια used metaphorically).

[IV.i]

1. H. I. Bell, in *JHS* 64 (1944), at p.36. The metaphors, of course, come from I Kings xii.14.
2. See Jones, *RE* 151-86, 'Taxation in antiquity', rightly described by the editor of the volume, P. A. Brunt, as 'a valuable and indeed unique introduction to the subject'..
3. There is a useful short summary in Jones, *RE* 153. The longest account of Athenian taxation available in English is that of A. M. Andreades, *A History of Greek Public Finance* I (Eng. trans. by Carroll N. Brown, Cambridge, Mass., 1933) 268-391, but it is not well written and is already in many ways out of date. It is still worth going back to the great work of August

Böckh, *Die Staatshaushaltung der Athener*[3] (1886).
4. See Rostovtzeff, *SEHHW* I.241–3 (with III.1374–5 nn.71–2); Andreades, op. cit. 150–4.
5. See S. L. Wallace, *Taxation in Egypt from Augustus to Diocletian* (1938), an unnecessarily difficult book on an admittedly very difficult subject. H. C. Youtie, *Scriptiunculae* II.749 n.1 (= *AJP* 62 [1941] 93 n.1), reviewing Wallace's book, conveniently gives references to other reviews, by Bell, Ensslin, Naphtali Lewis, Préaux, Rostovtzeff, and Westermann. I agree with Brunt's remark appended to Jones, *RE* 158 n.34: 'The marvellously lucid account of taxation in Ptolemaic and Roman Egypt in U. Wilcken, *Gr. Ostraka* I (1899), though in parts antiquated, remains perhaps the best introduction.' Claire Préaux, *ERL*, makes as much sense as anyone can hope to make of the Ptolemaic taxation system.
6. Cf. V.iii above and its n.26 below; and Appendix IV § 2 *ad fin.* The words τοῖς σώμασι τοῖς ἐλευθέροις seem reasonably certain. Those of them who have to pay the poll-tax are defined only as ἅ [δι]ὰ χρόνου φόρον διδόασιν.
7. See Jones, *RE* 82–9, 'Over-taxation and the decline of the Roman Empire'; and *LRE* I.411–69 (esp. 462–9). And cf. Section vi of this chapter and its n.7, also VIII.iii–iv above.
8. See, for 428, Thuc. III.16.1; for 406, Xen., *HG* I.vi.24; for 376, *HG* V.iv.61. For 362, see Ps.-Dem. L.6–7, 16. After that, see Isocr. VIII.48 (delivered *c.* 355); Dem. IV.36 (delivered 351 or just after); III.4 (referring to late 352); Aeschin. II.133 (referring to 346); perhaps Tod II.167.59–65 (346, but it is not certain that conscription was involved here). Contrast passages referring to the years before 362, e.g. Thuc. VI.31.3; Lys. XXI.10; Dem. XXI.154.5.

[IV.ii]

1. There is a corresponding American volume: *Peasant Society: A Reader*, ed. J. M. Potter, M. N. Diaz and G. M. Foster (Boston, 1967).
2. The paper was originally printed in the Proceedings, *Deuxième* [1962] *Conférence internat. d'hist. écon.* (Paris, 1965) II.287–300. See also Thorner's article, 'Peasantry', in *International Encyclopedia of the Social Sciences* 11 (1968) 503–11.
3. See *The Complete Letters of Vincent van Gogh* (3 vols, London, 1958) II.370 (Letter 404).
4. *The Complete Letters* (see the preceding note) II.375 (Letter 406); cf. 367, 372, 384 (Letters 402, 405, 410).
5. Cf. Hilton, *EPLMA* 16, quoted in the main text of VII.i above, just after its n.7.
6. See e.g. Rostovtzeff, *SEHHW* I.284–7, 427 with 482–9 (esp. 487–9) and 497–501; contrast II.645–8, 727–9, 890–1.
7. There are bibliographies in the articles on *emphyteusis* by Barry Nicholas, in *OCD*[2] 382–3, and Berger, *EDRL* 452; and see Kaser, *RP* II[2] (1975) 308–12. But for the historian, as distinct from the Roman lawyer, the most useful account I know is that of Jones, *LRE* I.417–19; II.788–9, 791.
8. And see the reference to the article by Bottéro in III.iv n.76 above.
9. Among many accounts of the practice, see e.g. Rostovtzeff, *SEHHW* II.898–9 (with III.1549 n.179); also I.291, 339, 411 (with III.1419 n.208); II.647; *SEHRE*[2] I.274, 298 (with II.677 n.52), 405–6 (with II.712–13 n.15), 409; Préaux, *ERL* 492–3, 500–3, 508–9, 511, 519–20, 544; MacMullen, *RSR* 34 (with 158 n.24). The practice can be traced far back into the Pharaonic period: see Georges Posener, 'L'ἀναχώρησις dans l'Égypte pharaonique', in *Le Monde Grec. Hommages à Claire Préaux* (Brussels, 1975) 663–9. The term ἐκχώρησις is also used, more in the sense of 'migration' to another district.
10. I know of (A) only one collection which has texts of all four of these inscriptions in a single volume: A/J (in the order in which they appear in the main text above) nos. 111, 141, 139, 142; and of (B) only one book containing English translations of all four: Lewis and Reinhold, *RC* II (in the same order) 183–4, 453–4, 439–40, 452–3. Among similar inscriptions which I cannot take time to discuss is A/J 143 (= Keil and Premerstein, op. cit. in n.14 below, pp.24–9, no.28), from Mendechora in the territory of Philadelphia in Lydia, of the early third century (probably 198–211).
11. Cf. n.10 above. This inscription (A/J 111) is also *FIRA*[2] I.495–8 no.103 = *CIL* VIII (ii) 10570 and (Suppl.) 14464. There are other English translations, e.g. *ARS* 219–20 no.265. For other evidence relating to imperial estates in Africa, see the works cited by Millar, *ERW* 179 n.20.
12. Cf. n.10 above. The text in *ESAR* IV.659–61 reproduces the best one: that of Rostovtzeff,

*SEHRE*² II.741-2 n.26. This inscription (A/J 141) is also *OGIS* 519 = *IGRR* IV.598 = *CIL* III (Suppl. 2) 14191; cf. *FIRA*² I.509-10 no.107.

13. Cf. n.10 above. This inscription (A/J 139) is also *SIG*³ 888 = *IGRR* I.674 = *CIL* III (Suppl. 2) 12336; cf. *FIRA*² I.507-9 no.106.

14. Cf. n.10 above: the inscription is A/J 142. The original publication was by Josef Keil and A. von Premerstein, 'Bericht über eine dritte Reise in Lydien . . . ', in *Denkschr. der Kais. Akad. der Wiss. in Wien*, Philos.-hist. Klasse 57.1 (1914) 37-47 no.55. See also Magie, *RRAM* I.678-81, with II.1547-9 nn.34-5.

15. *Penuria* always means 'scarcity' rather than 'poverty', at any rate in Classical Latin: see the new *Oxford Latin Dictionary*, fasc. VI (1977) 1326. The nearest parallel I know to Pliny, *Ep*. III.19.7 is Cic., *II Verr*. iii.125-8, where the *aratorum penuria* which occurs four times in §§ 126-7 certainly means 'scarcity'; cf. 'incolumis *numerus* manebat dominorum atque aratorum' and 'nunc autem *ne . . . quisquam reperiretur* qui sine voluntate araret, *pauci essent reliqui*' in § 125; the emphasis on '*reliquos aratores*' in § 126; and '*reliquos aratores colligit*' in § 128.

16. John Percival's main article is 'Seigneurial aspects of Late Roman estate management', in *Eng. Hist. Rev.* 84 (1969) 449-73. See also '*P. Ital*. 3 and Roman estate management', in *Hommages à Marcel Renard* II (= *Coll. Latomus* 102, Brussels, 1969) 607-15. One of the few mediaevalists to take a real interest in this problem is P. J. Jones: see his valuable 'L'Italia agraria nell'alto medioevo: problemi di cronologia e di continuità', in *Settimane di studio del Centro italiano di studi sull' alto medioevo, XIII. Agricoltura e mondo rurale in Occidente nell'alto medioevo* (Spoleto, 1966) 57-92, at 83-4; and the discussion with Vercauteren, ibid. 227-9.

17. For example, Colum., *RR* I.vii.1 ('avarius opus exigat quam pensiones'), on the interpretation of which I agree with M. I. Finley, *Studies in Roman Property* (1976) 119-20.

18. The inscriptions are: (1) *FIRA*² I.484-90 no.100 = A/J 74 = *CIL* VIII (Suppl. 4) 25902 (Henchir Mettich, Villa Magna Variana, Mappalia Siga), of A.D. 116-17; (2) *FIRA*² I.495-8 no.103 = A/J 111 = *ILS* 6870 = *CIL* VIII (ii) 10570 + (Suppl. 1) 14464 (Souk el-Khmis, Saltus Burunitanus), of A.D. 180-3 (on which see also n.11 above); (3) *CIL* VIII (Suppl. 1) 14428.A (Gasr-Mezuar), of A.D. 181. The 12 days in the third inscription may conceivably be something imposed on the *coloni*, about which they are complaining, rather than a legitimate exaction. I have no occasion here to comment on the two other inscriptions, which, with the three I have just cited, make up an important group of five: they are (4) *FIRA*² I.490-2 no.101 = A/J 93 = *CIL* VIII (Suppl. 4) 25943 (Ain el-Jemala, Saltus Blandianus et Udensis), of A.D. 117-38; (5) *FIRA*² I.493-5 no.102 = *CIL* VIII (Suppl. 4) 26416 (Ain Wassel, same Saltus), of A.D. 198-212: both refer (like no.1) to 'tertias partes fructuum', no.4 (like no.1) to the Lex Manciana, and no.5 (like no.2) to the Lex Hadriana. For nos. 1, 2, 4 and 5, see R. M. Haywood, in Frank, *ESAR* IV.89-101 (texts, Eng. trans. and comm.); and for further English translations (apart from those mentioned in nn.10-11 above) see *ARS* 221 no.268 (my no.5); Lewis and Reinhold, *RC* II.179-83 (my nos.1 and 4-5).

19. There is a possible example in Horace's Sabine *agellus* – if indeed we can take literally his *Epist*. I.xiv.1-3, with *Sat*. II.vii.117-18 (cf. his *Od*. III.xvi.29-30). See Heitland, *Agricola* 215-17, 235, and Percival's first article cited in n.16 above, p.451 and n.1 (with a ref. to Fustel de Coulanges).

20. This of course has often been realised. I cannot begin to give a bibliography, which, if it was to be really useful, would need to specify individual contributions to some collective works which are of very unequal value, such as the two volumes edited by M. I. Finley, *Stud. in Roman Property* (1976) and *Problèmes de la terre en Grèce ancienne* (= *Civilisations et Sociétés* 33, Paris, 1973). Although it may seem invidious to single out a few particular works, I should like to mention V. N. Andreyev, 'Some aspects of agrarian conditions in Attica in the fifth to third centuries B.C.', in *Eirene* 12 (1974) 5-46, which summarises, with some corrections and supplements, the contents of eight earlier papers published by Andreyev between 1958 and 1972 and listed in its n.1; and a series of four articles by R. T. Pritchard on agrarian matters in Sicily in the first century B.C., in *Historia* 18 (1969) 545-56; 19 (1970) 352-68; 20 (1971) 224-38; and 21 (1972) 646-60. In *Antiquités africaines* 1 (1967) there are two particularly useful articles dealing almost entirely with north Africa: Henriette d'Escurac-Doisy, 'Notes sur le phénomène associatif dans le monde paysan à l'époque du Haut-Empire' (59-71), and Claude Lepelley, 'Déclin ou stabilité de l'agriculture africaine au Bas-Empire? À propos d'une loi de l'empereur Honorius [*CTh* XI.xxviii.13]' (135-44).

21. The most important passage is one of 200 pages in *Cap*. III.614-813 (Part VI, ch.xxxvii-xlvii = *MEW* XXV.627-821); cf. *TSV* II.15-160, 161-3, 236-372; III.399-405, 472, 515-16 etc.;

MECW III.259-70 (the *Econ. and Philos. MSS*), 427-30; VI.197-206.

22. This famine is sometimes thought to be the famous one in Rev. VI.6, where the prices given work out at about 8 denarii/drachmae for one modius (one sixth of a medimnos) of wheat or three of barley. See e.g. Magie, *RRAM* I.581, with II.1443-4 nn.38-9; Rostovtzeff, *SEHRE*² II.599-600 (part of the very useful n.9 on food-supply and famines).

23. I know of no entirely satisfactory and complete account of the famine of 362-3; but see Downey, *HAS* 383-4, 386-91, and 'The economic crisis at Antioch under Julian', in *Studies in Roman Economic and Social History in Honor of A. C. Johnson*, ed. P. R. Coleman-Norton (Princeton, 1951) 312-21; Paul Petit, *LVMA* 109-18; P. de Jonge, 'Scarcity of corn and cornprices in Ammianus Marcellinus', in *Mnemos.*⁴ 1 (1948) 238-45.

24. Soz., *HE* III.xvi.15; cf. Pallad., *Hist. Laus.* 40, ed. C. Butler (1904) p.126. That the shortage of food was due largely to the greed of the rich men of Edessa does not emerge at all in the treatment of this incident by Peter Brown, 'The rise and function of the Holy Man in Late Antiquity', in *JRS* 61 (1971) 80-101, at 92: he is interested only in the fact that (as he puts it) 'It was as a "stranger" that Ephraim was able to administer food supplies in Edessa during a famine, for none of the locals could trust one another'. That is not how our sources put it (inadequate as they are): they speak of mutual distrust not on the part of 'the locals' but specifically of 'the rich'; and the very lame excuse they give (meekly accepted by Brown) is that of the same rich folk! In a footnote (143) on the same page Brown alludes to the famine at Aspendus, mentioned by Philostratus, *Vita Apollon.* I.15 (see I.iii above), and again he is interested only in the fact that 'Apollonius of Tyana did the same [as Ephraim], and, also, as a total "stranger", "dissociated" by the Pythagorean vow of silence'. This is characteristically subtle, but again it conceals by far the most important fact: that it was οἱ δυνατοί who had got possession of the corn. (They are clearly the rich landowners, for they have hidden away the corn on their country estates, even if Apollonius' written message to them addresses them as σιτοκάπηλοι – surely a deliberate slight.)

25. This date has been proposed by J. R. Palanque, 'Famines à Rome à la fin du IVᵉ siècle', in *REA* 33 (1931) 346-56; cf. Chastagnol, *FPRBE* 198.

26. I accept the chronology of Palanque (see the preceding note) and Chastagnol, *FPRBE* 223, against Seeck's dating of Symm., *Ep.* II.7 to 383 (see Seeck's Introd., pp.cxix-cxx and n.601, to his edition of Symm. in *MGH, Auct. Antiquiss.* VI.i, 1883). Against some interpretations suggested by De Robertis and Ruggini (equally unacceptable to me), see Edgar Faure, 'Saint Ambroise et l'expulsion des pérégrins de Rome', in *Études d'hist. du droit canonique dédiées à Gabriel Le Bras* (Paris, 1965) I.523-40, esp. 526, 530, 536-9.

27. Cf. Liban., *Orat.* I.226 ff.; X.25. See Norman, *LA* 213-14 (on *Orat.* I.225 ff.); Downey, *HAS* 420-1. Guards stationed at the city gates prevented the peasant (τὸν γεωργόν) from taking out more than two loaves (Liban., *Orat.* XXVII.14; cf. L.29).

28. The standard edition of Joshua, by the best Syriac scholar of his day, W. Wright (Cambridge, 1882), has an English translation.

29. For the severe famine in 538 in much of north and central Italy, from Venetia and Aemilia to Tuscia and Picenum, see esp. Procop., *Bell.* VI (*Goth.* II) xx.15-33: he was an eye-witness in Picenum (§ 22), and he speaks of reports of many tens of thousands dying of starvation.

30. Cf. Procop., *Bell.* VII (*Goth.* III) xvii.1 ff., esp. 9-19; xix.13-14; xx.1, 26. On corn prices in this period, see Stein, *HBE* II.582-3 n.1.

31. See the edition by H. Delehaye, *Les Saints Stylites* (= *Subsidia Hagiographica* 14, Brussels/Paris, 1923, repr. 1962) 195-237, at 201-2.

32. For some other terms for 'village', see A/J p.22; Broughton, in *ESAR* IV.628-9.

33. See H. Swoboda, κώμη, in *RE* Suppl. IV (1924) 950-76; Jones, *GCAJ* 272-4, 286-7; and see 391, Index, *s.v.*; *CERP*² 137-46, 281-94; and see 595, Index, *s.v.* (add e.g. 67-8, 80, 233); *LRE* III.447, Index, *s.v.*; G. M. Harper, 'Village administration in the Roman province of Syria', in *YCS* 1 (1928) 103-68; Broughton, in *ESAR* IV.628-47, 671-2, 737-9; and see 950, Index, *s.v.*; Rostovtzeff, *SEHHW* III.1747, Index, *s.v.*; *SEHRE*² II.821, Index, *s.v.* (esp. 656-7 nn.6-7, 661-6 nn.23-35); Magie, *RRAM* II.1660, Index, *s.v.* (esp. I.143-6, with II.1022-32 nn.69-77, and the passages cited in n.14 above; also I.64, with II.862-3 n.41). Some impressive recent books in French, by Tchalenko and others, have given us much valuable information about villages in Roman Syria: see n.50 to Section iii of this chapter; and cf. Liebeschuetz, *Ant.* 68-73.

34. This is a subject which would surely repay detailed investigation. I have seen no illuminating reference to it other than the one quoted in the main text above. Of course, by the fifth and

sixth centuries village life had apparently developed along ever more hierarchical lines, as in the cities; but evidence seems almost non-existent, except for Egypt.

35. See e.g. the works cited in n.33 above, esp. Jones, *GCAJ* 272-4 (with 364 n.18); *CERP²* 284-7; also 'The urbanisation of the Ituraean principality', in *JRS* 21 (1931) 265-75, esp. 270; Harper, op. cit. (in n.33 above) 142-3 (against 143-5, see Jones, *CERP²* 286-7). The ὄχλος as the Assembly of the village is certain in *IGRR* III.1192 = LB/W 2136 [not 2138, as in *IGRR*], from Saccaea in Syria (later Maximianopolis, from *c.* 300: see Jones, *CERP²* 285, with 465 n.82), where we have ὄχλου γενομένου τῆς κώμης ἐν τῶι θεάτρωι. In some villages of Asia Minor, e.g. in the territories of Cibyra and Ormela, we find inscriptions in which so-and-so gives a donation 'in honour of the ὄχλος' (usually ἐτίμησε τὸν ὄχλον): see e.g. *CIG* III.4367*a*; and E. J. S. Sterrett, 'An epigraphical journey [1883-4] in Asia Minor', in *Papers of the Amer. School of Class. Stud. at Athens* 2 (1888) nos.47-50 (= *IGRR* IV.892), 72-5. But I have not noticed anything in these inscriptions which justifies inferring the existence of an actual Assembly *called* the ὄχλος. A few villages are recorded as having an ἐκκλησία (*contra* Jones, *RE* 31-2), e.g. Castollus near Philadelphia (*OGIS* 488); the Panamareis, a federation of villages in Caria (Michel, *RIG* 479); and Orcistus, on the borders of Asia and Galatia, which had an [ἐκ]κλησία . . . πάνδημος (see W. H. Buckler, in *JHS* 57 [1937] 1-10, esp. 9 on B.3; and cf. Jones, *CERP²* 67-8 and 392 n.63).

36. See Jones, *CERP²* 286-7; *RE* 32; and pp.272-3 of his article (of 1931) cited in the preceding note.

37. E.g. at Orcistus and Castollus: see *IGRR* IV.550; *OGIS* 488.

38. On αὐτοπραγία see Stein, *HBE* I².i.246, 278-9 (with ii.563-4 n.135); Bell, *EAGAC* 119-25; Gelzer, *SBVA* 89-96, and in *Archiv f. Pap.* 5 (1913) 188-9, 370-7; Rouillard, *ACEB²* 13-15, 58-60, 202-3; Hardy, *LEBE* 54-9. Virtually all the evidence comes from Egypt; but *CTh* XI.vii.12 (A.D. 383, the earliest piece of evidence I know for the existence of what was later called *autopragia*) is addressed to the vicar of the Pontic diocese; and XI.vii.15 (which must surely be understood in the light of XI.xxii.4) is addressed to Messala, who in 399-400 was praetorian prefect of Italy (including of course Africa and Pannonia: see esp. I.v.12). Αὐτοπραγία and its cognates do not seem to appear before the fifth century; but see *IG* IX.i².137, line 20, for the use of αὐτοπραξία in the second century B.C., at Calydon in Aetolia, apparently for the right of personally exacting a fine.

39. Our information about Aphrodito comes from a large group of papyri which have found their way to Cairo, London, Florence, Geneva and Ghent: see esp. R. G. Salomon, 'A papyrus from Constantinople (Hamburg Inv. No. 410)', in *JEA* 34 (1948) 98-108. Aphrodito was fortunate in that Dioscorus (mentioned later in the main text above) was prepared to busy himself on behalf of the village and even to journey to Constantinople to solicit help from highly-placed bureaucrats there. The village had obtained its autopract status in the third quarter of the fifth century, in the reign of Leo I, 457-74 (*P. Cairo Masp.* I.67019, lines 1-6), but it constantly suffered arbitrary treatment at the hands of successive pagarchs of Antaeopolis, and in order to gain imperial protection it had had itself enrolled as part of the household (οἶκος, οἰκία) of Justinian's wife, the Empress Theodora (ibid., lines 11-12; cf. ibid. 67283), whose household at her death in 548 was amalgamated with the other part of the imperial ('sacred', or 'most sacred') household, that of the emperor himself (see Salomon, op. cit. 102 n.6). For the troubles of Aphrodito in *c.* 548-51, see Bell, *EVAJ*; Salomon, op. cit.; and the summary in Jones, *LRE* I.407-8. On Aphrodito see also Hardy, *LEBE* 55, 57-8, 137-8, 146-7. The most important documents are *P. Cairo Masp.* I.67002 (part of which is given in the main text above), 67029, 67024; *P. Hamb. Inv.* no.410 (of which Salomon gives a text), and *P. Genev. Inv.* no.210 (see Salomon, op. cit. 98 and nn.1-2). Among other relevant papyri from Aphrodito are *P. Cairo Masp.* I.67283; *P. Lond.* V.1674, 1677, 1679. On pagarchs, see W. Liebeschuetz, 'The pagarch: city and imperial administration in Byzantine Egypt', in *JJP* 18 (1974) 163-8; 'The origin of the office of the pagarch', in *Byz. Ztschr.* 66 (1973) 38-46.

40. For Dioscorus, see esp. J. Maspero, 'Un dernier poète grec d'Égypte: Dioscore, fils d'Apollôs', in *REG* 24 (1911) 426-81.

41. As I. F. Fikhman points out, 'In the papyri of Byzantine Oxyrhynchus "doulos" was used almost exclusively by people of free status for themselves when addressing people of higher standing and very seldom about slaves' ('Slaves in Byzantine Oxyrhynchus', in *Akten des XIII* [1971] *Internat. Papyrologenkongr.*, ed. E. Kiessling and H.-A. Rupprecht [1974] 117-24, at 119).

42. I have given the essential bibliography in my *SVP* 45 n.2. Add now the edition of Liban., *Orat.* XLVII, with an excellent Eng. trans., by A. F. Norman, in the Loeb Libanius Vol.II (1977); and two works by Louis Harmand, of which full details are given in n.50 to Section iii

of this chapter: the very full edition of the same speech, with text, French trans. and comm., *Libanius, Discours sur les patronages* (1955), and *Le patronat sur less collectivités publiques des origines au Bas-Empire* (Paris, 1957), esp. 421-87 on the Later Empire. A totally different picture from mine of the role of rural patronage in Syria in the Later Empire can be found in Peter Brown's article on the 'Holy Man' (see n.24 above), at 85-7. Brown, who has never grasped the realities of the class struggle in the ancient world, can see only the good side of patronage, and his bland account of that institution gives only a fraction of the real picture, in spite of those flashes of insight which Brown shows intermittently, as always. Of course it was an advantage for villagers to have someone to arbitrate in their disputes *among themselves*, especially since legal process in the Roman world was so unsatisfactory and open to abuse. But that was not what was mainly expected of the patrons I have referred to: they were brought in by the peasants to protect them against oppression, in particular by landlords and tax-collectors, and of course the patrons always exacted a price for services of that sort (see *CTh* XI.xxiv.2; *CJ* XI.liv.1.*pr., 2.pr.*), and probably often a heavy one. Even the story of how the 'holy man' Abraham became patron of a village (apparently near Emesa) looks rather different when we discover that Brown's 'when the tax collector came' stands for Theodoret's 'now *praktores* arrived, who compelled them [the villagers] to pay their taxes and began to imprison some and maltreat others' (*Hist. relig.* 17, in *MPG* LXXXII.1421A).

43. See the Eng. trans. by Elizabeth Dawes and N. H. Baynes, *Three Byzantine Saints* (1948) 139-40 (ch.76). The standard edition of the Life (or Lives) of St. Theodore is now A. J. Festugière, *Vie de Théodore de Sykéôn* (= *Subsidia Hagiographica* 48, 2 vols, Brussels, 1970): see esp. I.63-4; II.66-7. And see Derek Baker, 'Theodore of Sykeon and the historians', in *SCH* 13 (1976) 83-96.

44. The passage translated by Stevens is from John Chrysostom, *Hom. in Matth.* 61.3 (*MPG* LVIII.591-2); cf. *Expos. in Psalm.* 48.17, esp. § 8 (*MPG* LV.510-12). *Hom. in Act. Apost.* 18.4-5 (*MPG* LX.147-50) is interesting in its belief that building a church on an estate will help to keep the peasants quiet.

[IV.iii]

1. For slave prices at Athens in the Classical period, see first W. K. Pritchett, 'The Attic stelai, Part II', in *Hesp.* 25 (1956) 178 ff., at 276-81, esp. 276-8. (The reader should beware the extraordinary error on p.281, where two rich Athenian citizens, Menecles and Stratocles, in Isae. II [*Menecl.*] 29, 35, and XI [*Hagn.*] 42, who owned property to the value of 7,000 dr and 5½ talents respectively, are taken to be slaves, entirely without justification.) See also, for slave prices, Jones, SCA, in *SAS* (ed. Finley) 1-15, esp. 5 & 7 (fifth/fourth-century Athens); 7, 9-10, 13 (Roman world, Republic to Late Empire); *LRE* II.852 (with III.286 n.68); De Martino, *SCR²* IV.i (1974) 26 nn.66-7, 339-40 n.6; Westermann, *SSGRA* 14-15, 36, 71-2, 100-1; Duncan-Jones, *EREQS* (concerned almost entirely with the West) 11-12, 40, 50, 243-4, and esp. 348-50. Recently Duncan-Jones has made a bold attempt to estimate the cost of slaves in terms of wheat values in seven separate contexts over a period of some 1,500 years, from the late fifth century B.C. onwards: see his 'Two possible indices of the purchasing power of money in Greek and Roman antiquity', in the proceedings of a conference at the French School in Rome in November 1975, published as *Les 'Dévaluations' à Rome, Époque républicaine et impériale* (*Coll. de l'École française de Rome* 37, Rome, 1978) 159-68, at 162-6, 168. The Edict of Diocletian on maximum prices, of 301, is the only document I know from the whole of antiquity that gives both prices for slaves and the wages of various different workers. (For recent editions of that Edict, see I.iii n.3 above.) Its prices in denarii (now much depreciated, of course) for ordinary slaves aged 16-40 are 30,000 for a male and 25,000 for a female; the wage of an unskilled farm worker is 25 denarii per day 'with food' (*pasto*) – an addition which cannot be fixed precisely, but to which Duncan-Jones (ibid. 161) plausibly allots a 'wheat value' of an additional third, or about another 1.1 litres, making with the 3.3 litres 'wheat value' of the 25 denarii a total of 4.4 litres. The 'wheat value' of the slave price of 30,000 denarii is given by Duncan-Jones (loc. cit.) as 3,938 litres, or 895 times the total daily wage – I would call it three full years' pay.

I am not entirely happy about the prices of slaves in the legal sources, from Gaius to the *Corpus Iuris Civilis* of Justinian. Duncan-Jones (*EREQS* 50 n.2, 348-9) accepts a standard figure of HS 2,000 as the price of slaves for 'legal purposes'. There is one very good piece of evidence for this, which (unfortunately for my purposes in this book) comes from Africa Proconsularis: *CIL* VIII (Suppl. 4) 23956, a fragmentary inscription dated A.D. 186, from Henchir Snobbeur, where a slave 'ex forma censoria' seems to be valued at 500 denarii (line 14), which of course is HS 2,000. (Cf. A. H. M. Jones, SAW, in *SCA*, ed. Finley, 10, for a range of actual prices during the Principate indicating that 'a normal price for an unskilled adult' was about 500–600 denarii.) Apart from the one inscription I have quoted, however, the figure of HS 2,000 as the 'legal value' of a slave depends on some slave prices or valuations in aurei or solidi in Justinian's *Corpus*, with the aureus and solidus assumed to be equivalent to HS 100: these are either 20 aurei (*Dig.* IV.iv.31, Papinian; V.ii.8.17, Ulpian; V.ii.9, Paulus cited by Modestinus, but interpolated; *CJ* VII.iv.2, perhaps Caracalla) or 20 solidi (*Dig.* XL.iv.47.*pr.*, Papinian; *CJ* VI.i.4.*pr.*, of 317; and VII.vii.1.5, of 530, with VI.xliii.3.1, of 531, where the figures vary between 10 and 70 solidi, 20 being the basic one). Now it is true that from the time of Julius Caesar onwards the aureus was always regarded as equivalent to 25 denarii, or HS 100, and that this continued to be the official ratio at least until the time of Dio Cassius (see T. V. Buttrey, 'Dio, Zonaras and the value of the Roman aureus', in *JRS* 51 [1961] 40-5) – although by Dio's time there must have been a black market in aurei, as Jones has pointed out (*RE* 195); and in the disastrous half-century (235–284) between the end of the Severan dynasty and the accession of Diocletian there can hardly have been any realistic ratio. (It may be useful at this point to recall that under Augustus the pound of gold made up 42 aurei, under Nero 45, under Caracalla about 50, and under succeeding emperors even more; under Diocletian it was at first 70; at the time of the Price Edict the figure was 60, and the theoretical value of the aureus was therefore 1,200 depreciated denarii – 1/60th of 72,000: see I.iii n.3 above. From Constantine onwards the solidus was struck at 72 to the pound.)

In the legal sources listed in the last paragraph the aureus has often (as by Mommsen and Duncan-Jones) been taken to represent HS 100, so that 20 aurei are HS 2,000. However, the article by Kübler published in 1900 (SCRK 566-79), which I have praised in § 13(*c*) of the main text of this section, seems to me to have modified this picture. I shall extract two relevant conclusions: (1) except in a particular case where the contrary can perhaps be proved, a figure given in Justinian's *Corpus* in aurei or solidi which replaces a sum expressed in sesterces in the Classical law-books must be taken to equate the aureus or solidus with HS 1,000, not 100; and (2) this, and examination of the few prices and valuations of slaves in sesterces which survive from the Classical lawyers, seem to justify the conclusion that the standard valuation of a slave in the legal writers was HS 10,000. Certainly *Inst.J.* III.vii.3 explicitly equates the aureus (which had now, like the sesterce long ago, become a pure term of account) with HS 1,000, and this is borne out by four passages in that work which correspond closely with parallel passages in the *Institutes* of Gaius, dating from the mid-second century. Three of these (*Inst.J.* II.xx.36; III.xix.5; and III.xxvi.8, derived respectively from Gai., *Inst.* II.235; III.102; and III.161) have nothing to do with slaves; but *Inst.J.* IV.vi.33d substitutes 10 aurei for the HS 10,000 valuation of the slave in Gai., *Inst.* IV.53d, equating the aureus therefore with HS 1,000. The only certain slave prices I know which are left in sesterces in the *Digest* are the HS 10,000 and 5,000 in XXI.i.57.1 (Paulus), and – unless we should read 'mihi' for 'milia' – the 'quinque milia' (HS, of course) in X.iii.25 (Julianus), which is represented as half the value of the slave at 'aureorum decem' earlier in the same passage. A post-Classical compilation, *Epit. Ulp.* II.4 (*FIRA*[2] II.266), deals with the manumission of a slave who pays for that privilege 'decem milia': that is to say, HS 10,000. It is worth noticing here that Dig. XXIX.v.25.2 (from Gaius) has a penalty of 100 aurei corresponding to one of HS 100,000 in Paulus, *Sent.* III.v.12a; and that in two other texts in the *Digest* specifying penalties (L.xvi.88, Celsus; XXXII.97, Paulus) the curious phrase 'centiens (or 'centies') aureorum' must surely replace the familiar 'centies sestertium' (HS 10 million) in the original texts. In very many passages in the *Digest* the valuation of a slave, or the price he has to pay for manumission, is given simply as 'decem', meaning undoubtedly 10 aurei (the noun sometimes appears): see e.g. XL.vii, where phrases such as 'si decem dederit, liber esto' occur in at least 26 different sections (cf. 'denos aureos' in 3.13). Most of the legal texts containing slave prices or valuations may perhaps be expected to give exceptionally high figures, as they are normally dealing with slaves who are purchasing their freedom or are thought worthy of being freed by will, as in *Dig.* XL.vii, and (as throughout that particular title, which relates to *statuliberi*) the figures are often notional anyway. Only in a few prescriptive constitutions such as *CJ* VI.xliii.3.1; VII.vii.1.5 are we entitled to expect completely realistic figures. I would add that the 'gold value' of an unskilled adult male slave works out according to the Edict of Diocletian at ⁵/₁₂ lb. gold, a fraction under 30 Diocletianic aurei or exactly 30 Constantinian solidi.

2. I have not found these inscriptions listed in full anywhere, and I will therefore give those I have been able to identify, including some which were published too late to be taken into account in Westermann's analysis, referred to in the main text above: *FD* III.i (1929) 565-72; ii (1909-13) 212-47; iii (1932-43) 1-60, 130-41, 174-6, 205-6, 208-11, 258, 262-96/7, 300-37, 339-41, 346-9, 351-8, 362-77, 385-441; iv (1930-76) 70-3, 78, 479-509; vi (1939) 5-58, 62-95, 97-110, 112-40/2; and cf. the selection in *SGDI* II.iii-v (1892-6) 1684-2342; vi (1899) 2343. Some of these refer to dates later than *c*. 53 B.C., where Westermann's analysis and mine end.

2a. See now Keith Hopkins, *Conquerors and Slaves. Sociological Studies in Roman History* I (1978) 133-71, published after this chapter was finished. His figures take account of rather more inscriptions than Westermann knew, but the results are not significantly different, for my purposes (see esp. 141 n.15: Westermann's figures are 'very slightly different' from those of Hopkins).

3. See my review of Westermann's book, in *CR* 71 = n.s.7 (1957) 54-9, and the review by Brunt cited in III.iv n.65 above. See also n.5 below.

4. I have not seen anything more recent on this question than G. Daux, *Delphes au IIe et au Ier siècle* (Paris, 1936) 490-6.

5. The objections of Westermann, *SSGRA* 32 n.53 can be disregarded. As so often in that book he has misinterpreted the text: it does not say that the men were actually enlisted, but only that they were demanded by Diaeus. That is not inconsistent with the actual total force of 14,000 infantry and 600 cavalry recorded by Paus. VII.xv.7. Westermann actually believed that this passage (in Greek) is preserved in the Latin historian Orosius! – see *SSGRA* 32. (I think he must have misunderstood the heading in the Loeb edition of Polybius, Vol.VI, p.423, which of course refers to ch.xiv.3 only.)

6. Livy, *Per.* 96-7; App., *BC* I.117-20.

7. Over 400,000, according to Vell. Pat. II.47.1. Plut., *Caes.* 15.5, and App., *Celt.*2, say that Caesar took a million prisoners.

8. It will be sufficient to refer to Fogel and Engerman, *TC* I.15-16, 20-2, 41-3, 89-94, and 245-6 ('Most U.S. cotton was consumed not in the U.S. but abroad' *c.* 1850). But Gavin Wright has shown that Fogel and Engerman have not made sufficient allowance for the effect of the world demand for cotton on the Southern economy *c.* 1820-50: see his chapter vii (pp.302-36) in *Reckoning with Slavery*, by Paul A. David and others (1976).

9. Hopkins adds that his 'upper limit of life expectancy is, however, tentative, in the sense that the determinants of the demographic revolution in Western Europe are even now only dimly understood. Nevertheless it seems to me that the burden of proof is firmly on those who wish to assert that the Roman population in general had a lower mortality than other pre-industrial populations with similar technical achievements or towns; they must show that there were present in the Roman empire factors which would have led to a general diminution of mortality' (*PASRP* 263-4). Brunt agrees with Hopkins that the Roman expectation of life must have been 'below 30 with infant mortality above 200 per 1,000'; but he is doubtful about Hopkins's lower limit for expectation of life of 20, as far as the free population of Republican Italy is concerned (*IM* 133). [And see now the article by Donald Engels cited at the end of II.vi n.7 above.]

10. The θρεπτοί are a difficult subject, and I shall mention only the good discussion of Pliny, *Ep.* X.lxv-lxvi, lxxii, by Sherwin-White, *LP* 650-1, 653-4, 659, which gives references to other recent work, including that of Cameron (1939).

11. See briefly Jones, *LRE* II.853, with the references in III.286 n.70 – although I think the Visigothic law is not dealing specially with infants who had been *sold* by their parents, as is e.g. *CJ* IV.xliii.2.

12. *Leg. Visigoth.* IV.iv.3 is ed. K. Zeumer, in *MGH, Leges* I.i (1902) 194. I can find no specific figure in earlier laws, such as the Constantinian *CTh* V.x.1.pr. (*pretium quod potest valere exsolvat*); cf. *CJ* IV.xliii.2.1; *Leg. Visigoth.* IV.iv.1-2.

13. The subject is appallingly complicated: see Jones, *LRE* I.30-1, 64-5, 448-9 ff., with the notes; also *RE* 8-9, 169-70 (esp. n.96). For *immunitas* and the *ius Italicum*, see also E. Kornemann, in *RE* IV.i (1900) 578-83; H. M. Last, in *CAH* XI.450-1, 454-6.

14. E. J. Jonkers, *Economische en sociale toestanden in het romeinsche Rijk blijkende uit het Corpus Iuris*

(Wageningen, 1933) 113 lists 152 legal texts referring to *partus ancillarum* or to *vernae*, and of these only four are said to cite Republican or Augustan jurists: see Brunt, *IM* 707-8. Of the four cited by Brunt, only three certainly fulfil this specification: VII.i.68.*pr.*; IX.ii.9.*pr.*; XXIV.iii.66.3 (XLI.x.4.*pr.* seems to come from Neratius rather than Trebatius); but add XXIII.iii.18. See also Brunt, *IM* 143-4 (esp. 144 n.1). Perhaps I should add at this point that there seems to be little or no information about slave sex-ratios anywhere at any time in antiquity. (I do not regard the relative frequency of manumissions as informative on this question.) As I say in the main text above, § 10, Cato never mentions female slaves, apart from the *vilica*, and I may add that much the same is true of Varro, who, apart from the passages cited in the main text above (between nn.14 and 15), refers to female slaves (I think) only in *RR* I.xviii.1,3 (the *vilica*), and in II.x.2, where he makes Cossinius remark that 'in fundis non modo pueri sed etiam puellae pascant'. In Columella, on the other hand, female slaves often appear, and he too can find employment not only for slave boys (II.ii.13; IV.xxvii.6; XI.ii.44) but for children of both sexes (XII.iv.3) and for an *anus sedula vel puer* (VIII.ii.7). M. I. Finley may be right in advocating that one should 'avoid inferences' from changes in the practices or institutions reflected in Cato, Varro and Columella, or in *Digest* excerpts from Severan as compared with Republican or early Imperial jurists; and he does admit that the differences between them '*may* reflect institutional changes'. But he exaggerates absurdly in saying that 'the presumption is *too strong* that *nothing more* than "literary history" lies behind them' (*SRP* 4, my italics; cf. 104). There is no such 'presumption'. The examples I have used are not the *basis* for 'inferences', but they do provide corroborative evidence.

14a. After this chapter was finished I saw the interesting article by David Daube, 'Fashions and idiosyncrasies in the exposition of the Roman law of property', in *Theories of Property*, ed. A. Parel and T. Flanagan (Waterloo, Ont., Canada, 1979) 35-50, at 35-7, discussing the rule that a Roman usufructuary did not acquire a right to a slave woman's offspring, which was not considered to be *fructus*.

15. The word *uxor* was applied by the leading Antonine jurist, Q. Cervidius Scaevola, to what was surely the consort of a slave *actor*, *Dig.* XXXIII.vii.20.4; and it is similarly used in Paul, *Sent.* III.vi.38; contrast II.xix.6; Ulp., *Reg.* V.5. See also Constantine's law, *CTh* II.xxv.1.*pr.* And as Paulus put it, in *Dig.* XXXVIII.x.10.5, the technical terms of *cognatio* (such as *parentes, filii, fratres*) were sometimes used in relation to slaves, although *serviles cognationes* were not legally recognised (*sed ad leges serviles cognationes non pertinent*).

16. Gelasius fr. 28, in *Epist. Roman. Pontif. genuin.*, ed. Andreas Thiel (1867-8) 499-500.

17. Pelagius I, *Ep.* 84, ed. P. M. Gassó and C. M. Batlle, *Pelagii I Papae Epist. quae supersunt* (Montserrat, 1956) 205-6.

18. M. I. Finley, *AE* 83 ff., seems to me to misunderstand Weber's position. In an attempt to explain the 'decline' of slavery, on which I have commented in VIII.i above, he asks, 'What happened, and why? . . . What motivated the upper classes, in particular the owners of large estates, to change over from slave gangs to tied tenants?' The only explanation he mentions, before producing his own, is one that he calls – without attributing it to anyone in particular – 'a simple cost-accounting explanation': that after the great age of Roman conquest was over, insufficient new slaves were brought on to the market to replace the stock. By far the best treatment of the problem on these lines that I can think of is Weber's, in the essay which I have just outlined in the main text above. Finley unjustly depreciates this, accusing Weber (with other writers) of asserting 'that slave labour is inefficient, at least in agriculture, and ultimately unprofitable' (*AE* 83, with 195 n.64) – which in fact Weber does not do in any work that I have read, and certainly not in the passage referred to in Finley's note. Allowing 'an obvious element of truth' in the interpretation he is criticising, Finley attacks it with three arguments, none of which has any real force, since (1) much more evidence is needed than from one single estate (*AE* 196 n.74); (2) no assumption about the unsatisfactory character of Germans as slaves is necessarily involved, or usually made; nor (3) is there any necessary 'assumption that a reduction in the supply of captive or imported slaves cannot be met by breeding' – the correct assumption is only that breeding is *more costly* to slave owners in general than the mass appropriation of captives or the purchase at very cheap rates of slaves produced outside the economy (cf. the main text of this section).

19. See Pliny, *Ep.* V.xiv.8; VII.xxx.3; VIII.ii.1-8; IX.xvi.1; xx.2; xxxvi.6; xxxvii.1-3; X.viii.5-6. It may be convenient if I list here other passages in Pliny's letters concerning his (and others') estates. The most important is III.xix.1-3,4,5-7,8; see also I.xx.16; xxiv.1-4; II.iv.3;

xv.1-2; V.vi, e.g. 2-4, 9-12; VI.iii.1-2; VII.xi.1,5-7; xiv.1-2; VIII.xv.1-2. It appears from X.viii.5 that Pliny derived an annual income of more than HS 400,000 from his estates at Tifernum Tiberinum, all of which were apparently let to tenants. I may add that I am not impressed by the opinion of M. I. Finley that there is 'no significant managerial difference, for absentees, between tenancies and slave-operated estates under *vilici*' (*SRP* 117). Of the letters of Pliny to which he appeals, X.viii.5-6 refers to some new lettings (doubtless after 5 years) and the possibility of a reduction in rents due to an exceptional series of bad harvests; in IX.xxxvii.3, again, new leases are necessary (for the usual 5 years, § 2); and in III.xix.2 Pliny is simply asking for a friend's advice whether he should buy an adjoining estate. Caecina, when he 'rationes a colono accepit', was making the round of his estates (Cic., *Pro Caec*. 94). That tenancies were indeed regarded as involving less supervision is perfectly clear in Col., *RR* I.vii.5-7. And see the continuation of the main text above.

20. See e.g. Xen., *Oecon*. XII.20; XXI.9-11; Colum., *RR* I.*praef*.12-15, 20 etc.; I.vii.3-5,6; XII.*praef*.8-10; Pliny, *NH* XVIII.35 (Mago), 43.

21. A very early passage I have not seen quoted in this connection is Terence, *Adelph*. 949 (produced 160 B.C.), where Demea reminds Micio that he has a little farm near the city which he is in the habit of renting out (*agellist hic sub urbe paulum quod locitas foras*); Micio only seems surprised at hearing it called a 'little' farm (*paulum id autemst?*). Even if this comes directly from the original by Menander, the use of the frequentative verb, *locito* (which I have not encountered elsewhere), surely suggests that Romans in the mid-second century B.C. were used to regular farm-lettings.

22. Wilkes, *Dalmatia* 234-6, 392; cf. 149, 197, 243, 276, 280-1; Géza Alföldy, *Noricum* 190-3 (esp. Table 6 on p.191), cf. 128-32.

23. K. D. White, 'Latifundia', in *BICS* 14 (1967) 62-79 is right in saying that the term *latifundia* is 'post-Augustan, and virtually limited to a narrow period, that of Pliny the Elder, Petronius and Seneca', although he missed the earliest passage, in Valerius Maximus, which I have quoted in the main text above. He gives a most useful collection of early source material referring to large estates.

24. See *Corp. Agrimens. Rom.*, ed. C. Thulin (Leipzig, 1913) I.i.45, lines 16-22, replacing the older work, *Die Schriften der röm. Feldmesser* I, ed. F. Blume, K. Lachmann and A. Rudorff (Berlin, 1848) 84-5. Cf. the much-quoted statement of the Elder Pliny (*NH* XVIII.35) that Nero executed six landowners who 'possessed half of Africa', and whose holdings would have been confiscated and become imperial property.

25. I am very dissatisfied with A. E. R. Boak, *Manpower Shortage and the Fall of the Roman Empire in the West* (Ann Arbor, 1955), for the reasons set out in my review, in *Population Studies* 10 (1956) 118-20; cf. M. I. Finley's review-discussion of the same book in *JRS* 48 (1958) 156-64.

26. See A. M. Honoré, 'The Severan lawyers: a preliminary survey', in *SDHI* 28 (1962) 162-232, at 212-13.

26a. After the main text of this book was in page proof, I received from Tony Honoré an opinion which is of course far weightier than mine and indeed on such a matter is the most authoritative I could obtain. He believes that the words 'sine praediis quibus adhaerent' are undoubtedly an interpolation by the compiler of this part of the *Digest*, whom he identifies as Tribonian (see Honoré, *Tribonian* 261). Bequests of *inquilini* (or *coloni*) were of course void in law, but the very fact that Marcianus dealt with them in a textbook for students shows that they were not infrequent, and by the late 170s the emperors were apparently prepared to construe such legacies as bequests of the *rent* involved, if that seemed to fulfil the testator's intention: *aestimatio* would then be necessary. I am grateful to Tony Honoré for this view of *Dig.* XXX.112.*pr.*, which must be preferred to the alternatives I have offered in the main text above. It is substantially the same as the combination of the views of Saumagne and Fustel de Coulanges that will be found on p.246 above.

27. The mistake of thinking that the text of Marcianus refers to all *inquilini* (and indeed all *coloni*) is made by Norbert Brockmeyer, *Arbeitsorganisation und ökonomisches Denken in der Gutswirtschaft das römischen Reiches* (Diss., Bochum, 1968) 274, who says, 'Im 3.Jh. wurden die Kolonen, insbesondere die Inquilinen, bereits so sehr mit dem Gut identifiziert, dass Marcian sagte, sie könnten ohne ihre Parzelle nicht vermacht werden.'

28. Seeck's theory has been accepted in particular by Stein, *HBE* I².i.17, 22, 29-30, 55; ii.409 n.6 (Seeck 'à mon avis n'a été réfuté ou dépassé par aucune publication postérieure'), etc.; also by De Martino, *SCR²* IV.i (1974) 347; Ganshof, SPCBE 263-4 (cf. n.37 below); Heitland,

Agricola 340 and n.3, 360-1; and others. Jolowicz and Nicholas, after saying that the *colonus* in the Later Empire 'was already in fact an appurtenance of the land and could, in some cases at least, be bequeathed along with it', cite our passage from Marcianus in a note, adding, 'The text speaks of *inquilini*, and they were perhaps German prisoners who had been settled in the empire', with a reference to Seeck (see their *HISRL*[3] 435-6 and n.9). Seeck's theory has been rejected by Bolkestein (*CRO* 40-5) and Clausing (*RC* 190 ff., esp. 195-7), and by Piganiol and Saumagne (see the main text above). Fustel de Coulanges, in his essay on the Roman colonate mentioned in § 13(*b*) above (and published 25 years before Seeck's interpretation appeared), does at least offer a sensible suggestion as to how the testator in question may have conceived himself as able to bequeath his *inquilini*: what the testator really had in mind, says Fustel, was a bequest of the *rents* paid by the *inquilini* (65 n.1). This, I may say, would have been one of those laymen's errors to which Roman testators were prone. The man would not have realised that if he made no specific bequest of the land itself (ownership of which of course included the right to receive the rents) it would simply pass to the heir, with what we should call the residuary estate. But I cannot follow Fustel in believing that Marcianus 'veut dire: Si un testateur lègue un *inquilinus* avec la terre où il est attaché, ce legs est valable', in the sense that it is the land which is bequeathed. In fact the bequest of a free tenant, with or without the land he occupied, was simply null and void in law, as indeed Fustel realised (see the earlier part of the same note). Nor does Fustel explain how Marcianus could use the surprisingly strong term *adhaerent* of the *inquilini*. For another way in which Fustel's note may be usefully applied, see the main text above, near the end of § 18.

29. On the alleged connection between the *laeti* (and *gentiles*) and the so-called 'Reihengräberkultur', I have been convinced by the admirably clear arguments of Rigobert Günther, 'Laeti, Foederati und Gentilen in Nord- und Nordostgallien im Zusammenhang mit der sogenannten Laetenzivilisation', in *Ztschr. für Archäol.* 5 (1971) 39-59; 'Die sozialen Träger der frühen Reihengräberkultur in Belgien und Nordfrankreich im 4./5. Jahrh,', in *Helinium* 12 (1972) 268-72; and ULGG = 'Einige neue Untersuch. zu den Laeten u. Gentilen in Gallien im 4. Jahrh. u. zu ihrer hist. Bedeutung', in *Klio* 58 (1976) 311-21. On the *laeti* (and *gentiles*), in addition to the works referred to in §§ 18-19 of the main text of this section, in Appendix III, and in n.28 above, see e.g. Émilienne Demougeot, 'Àpropos des lètes gaulois du IVe siècle', in *Beiträge zur Alten Gesch. u. deren Nachleben. Festschr. für F. Altheim* (Berlin, 1970) II.101-113; 'Laeti et Gentiles dans la Gaule du IVe siècle', in *Actes du Colloque d'hist. sociale 1970 = Annales litt. de l'Univ. de Besançon* 128 (Paris, 1972) 101-112; MEFB = 'Modalités d'établissement des fédérés barbares de Gratien et de Théodose', in *Mélanges d'hist. anc. offerts à William Seston* (Paris, 1974) 143-60; cf. *De l'unité à la division de l'Empire romain 395-410. Essai sur le gouvernement impérial* (Paris, 1951) 23, 200-1, 223-5, cf. 80; Jones, *LRE* II.620, with III.186-7 n.26. Some of the barbarian settlements are also noticed by Ramsay MacMullen, 'Barbarian enclaves in the northern Roman Empire', in *Ant. Class.* 32 (1963) 552-61. Among other relevant recent works which I have seen but have not been able to digest properly are László Várady, *Das letzte Jahrh. Pannoniens, 376-476* (Amsterdam, 1969), e.g. 154-9, 384-91, 462-7; and Dietrich Hoffmann, *Das spätröm. Bewegungsheer u. die Notitia Dignitatum = Epigraph. Stud.* 7 (Düsseldorf) I (1969), II (1970), esp. e.g. I.139-41, 148-55; II.48-54. I did not see Pavel Oliva, *Pannonia and the Onset of Crisis in the Roman Emp.* (Prague, 1962, an Eng. trans. of the original Czech version of 1957) until this chapter was finished. For additions to the bibliography, see its 86-7, 303-5 (esp. 304-5 n.139, mentioning various works in Czech, Russian, Hungarian etc.). [Only when the main text of this chapter was in page proof did I read two important articles by E. A. Thompson which materially increase our understanding of the relations between the Roman rulers and the 'barbarians', the Visigoths in particular: 'The settlement of the barbarians in southern Gaul', in *JRS* 46 (1956) 65-75; and 'The Visigoths from Fritigern to Euric', in *Historia* 12 (1963) 105-26. Another interesting paper by Thompson which has just appeared, 'Barbarian invaders and Roman collaborators', in *Florilegium* [Carleton Univ., Ottawa] 2 (1980) 71-88, discusses some of the material dealt with in VIII.iii above.]

30. See *P. Ital.* I, pp.472-3 n.1, 474 n.7 (from the commentary on *P. Ital.* 24), where references will be found. One of the texts is *CIL* V.ii.7771, of A.D. 591, from Genoa: see the improved restoration in *P. Ital.* I, p.473 n.1

31. I feel that this distinction may be reflected, for example, in *CTh* VII.xiii.16 (Honorius, 406), which contemplates the recruitment of slaves of *foederati* and of *dediticii*.

32. E.g., in particular, in Appendix III, nos.4, 10, 17, 21(*a*) and (*b*), 26, 27.

33. E.g., in Appendix III, nos. 14(a) and (b), 19(a), and 32. I would understand *CTh* XIII.xi.10 (no. 22 in that Appendix) to be referring to imperial grants or sales of *terrae laeticae* to well-to-do Romans who would become the freehold owners of such lands and benefit from the tenancy of their *laeti*.

34. See, in Appendix III, nos. 5(a) and (b), 16(b), 18.

34a. I have not dealt in this book with the system of *hospitium/hospitalitas*, terms which in the fifth century came to be applied to the division of the landed property of individual Romans with 'barbarians' on fixed terms, as a development of standard Roman practice in billeting (for which see *CTh* VII.viii.5 = *CJ* XII.xl.2, of A.D. 398). My main reason for neglecting this subject, apart from its extreme complexity, is the fact that we know of its existence only in the West (in Italy, Gaul and Spain, among the Visigoths, Ostrogoths, Burgundians and perhaps Alans) and only at a late date: the earliest certain references are for 440 and 443, although the system may well have been applied first on the settlement of the Visigoths in Aquitaine in 418, mentioned in Appendix III § 24 (b) above. I need do no more than refer to the standard treatment of the subject, by F. Lot, 'Du régime de l'hospitalité', in *RBPH* 7 (1928) 975-1011; and to Jones, *LRE* I.248-53, with III.45-7 nn.26-37 (also 29 n.46, 39 n.66); and Thompson's two articles of 1956 and 1963, mentioned at the end of n.29 above.

35. See esp. Thompson, *EG* 3-9, 15-18, 25-8, 51-3, 57; *VTU* 25-8, 32-3.

36. Tacitus wrote the *Germania* in A.D. 98 or just after, the *Histories* presumably in the first and the *Annals* in the late second and/or the early third decade of the second century.

37. The views of A. H. M. Jones on the Later Roman colonate can be found mainly in three different works: (1) 'The Roman colonate', in *Past & Present* 13 (1958) 1-13, which can also be read in Jones, *RE* 293-307 or (better still) in *SAS* (ed. Finley) 288-303, with improvements in the notes by Dorothy Crawford (see its p.x); (2) *LRE* II.767-823, esp. 795-812 (with the notes, III.247-70, esp. 257-64 nn.62-99); and (3) *RE* 86-8, 232-3, and esp. 405-8 and 416-17. A good deal of the earlier work on the Later Roman colonate can be considered out of date since Jones's magisterial treatment of the subject. For a selective bibliography of books and articles published down to 1923, see Clausing, *RC* (1925) 318-23. Of these the modern reader may find most useful H. Bolkestein, *CRO* = *De colonatu romano eiusque origine* (Amsterdam, 1906), and Rostovtzeff, *SGRK* (1910). An important work not noticed by Clausing is Matthias Gelzer, *SBVA* (1909), of which the most relevant part is pp.64 ff. (esp. 69-77). The main value of Clausing's book lies in its account of earlier views: he seems to me to have nothing important to say himself that is both new and valid. Among the works on the Later Roman colonate published since 1925 are Ch. Saumagne, ROC = 'Du rôle de l'*origo* et du *census* dans la formation du colonat romain', in *Byz.* 12 (1937) 487-581; F. L. Ganshof, SPCBE = 'Le statut personnel du colon au Bas-Empire. Observations en marge d'une théorie nouvelle', in *Ant. Class.* 14 (1945) 261-77 (successfully criticising part of Saumagne's paper); Angelo Segrè, 'The Byzantine colonate', in *Traditio* 5 (1947) 103-33; Maurice Pallasse, *Orient et Occident à propos du Colonat Romain au Bas-Empire* (= *Bibl. de la Fac. de Droit de l'Univ. d'Alger* 10, Lyons, 1950, 93pp.); Claire Préaux, 'Les modalités de l'attache à la glèbe dans l'Égypte grecque et romaine', in *Recueils de la Soc. Jean Bodin II*². *Le Servage* (2nd rev. edition, Brussels, 1959) 33-65; Paul Collinet, 'Le colonat dans l'Empire romain', in ibid. 85-120, with a *Note complémentaire* by M. Pallasse, 121-8; F. M. De Robertis, *Lavoro e lavoratori nel mondo romano* (Bari, 1963) 339-417; Marc Bloch, Chapter VI, 'The rise of dependent cultivation and seignorial institutions', in *CEHE* I² (1966) 235-90 (repr. from 1st edition, 1941). I will add here a reference to the informative second chapter of *CEHE* I² (1966) 92-124, 'Agriculture and rural life in the Later Roman Empire', by C. E. Stevens, with 755-61, a revised version by J. R. Morris of the bibliography in *CEHE* I¹.

38. Land or house, perhaps, to allow for the *inquilinus*, who in some passages in the Codes seems to be the tenant of a house, as he certainly is in most passages in the *Digest* (cf. § 18 of the main text of this section).

39. See esp. *CTh* X.xii.2.4 (*c.* 370); XI.xxiv.6.3 (of 415, relating to Egypt); and the papyri cited in n.40 below.

40. See esp. *P. Cairo Isid.* 126 (of 308-9), also 128 (of 314), and *P. Thead.* 16-17 (of 332), with Jones, *RE* 406; cf. Jones's article in *SAS* (ed. Finley) 293-5. The conclusion appears to be justified that peasants who did own land in freehold would not in any event appear on the returns of landlords from whom they happened also to lease land; although the only specific evidence I know for this is in *CTh* XI.i.14 = *CJ* XI.48.4.*pr.*, 1 (of 371).

41. The word first occurs in a speech by the Emperor Marcian to the Council of Chalcedon in 451: *Acta Conc. Oecum.*, ed. E. Schwartz, II.i.2 (1933) 157, § 17 (ἐναπόγραφος). For a list of occurrences in the papyri, from 497 onwards, see Jones, *LRE* III.260 n.74.

42. I have ignored some texts using words like 'inservire', which do not necessarily refer to any form of slavery at all, although in certain cases they may do so. For instance, in 371 Valentinian I, Valens and Gratian said of the *coloni* and *inquilini* of Illyricum, 'Inserviant terris . . . nomine et titulo colonorum', adding that if they ran away they might be brought back in chains and punished (*CJ* XI.liii.1.1). By itself, *inservire* in late Latin (as always in Classical Latin) normally means 'serve the purposes of', 'care for', 'minister to', (see e.g. *CJ* III.xii.2; *CTh* VIII.v.1, and more than a score of other legal texts); and even in *CTh* XIV.xvii.6 (of 370) the words 'sub vinculis' had to be added to make it clear what 'pistrino . . . inserviat' there implies; only in *CTh* XV.xii.1 (of 325) do the words 'metallo . . . inservire' themselves remind us of the traditional phrase 'servi poenae'.

43. See Jones, *LRE* II.798 ff., esp. 802-3. A long list of such leases, dated between 285 and 633, is given by A. C. Johnson and L. C. West, *Byzantine Egypt: Econ. Stud.* (Princeton, 1949) 80-93.

44. *P. Ital.* 1 is ed. by J.-O. Tjäder, *Die nichtliterarischen lateinischen Papyri Italiens aus der Zeit 445-700* (Lund, 1955) I.172-8 (with German trans.), cf. 398-405 (*Kommentare*). The rents payable ('quid annua . . . singuli conductores dare debent') are listed in lines 57 ff.; for the 756 solidi payable for the Massa Enporitana, see line 59.

45. See above and n.16; also Jones, *LRE* II.791 (with III.254-5 n.49).

46. Pelag. I, *Ep.* 64, ed. Gassó and Batlle, pp.167-70 (cf. n.17 above). Cf. Cassiod., *Var.* II.18: some men regarded as *curiales* by their local Council were claimed as slaves by the Church.

47. See the *MGH* edition of the letters of Pope Gregory, in four parts: *Epist.* I.i (1887) by P. Ewald, and I.ii (1891), II.i (1893), ii (1895) and iii (1899), by L. M. Hartmann (Berlin). On the *patrimonium Petri*, see Jones, *LRE* I.90; II.770, 781-2, 789; III.250 n.31, 252-3 nn.45-6; René Aigran, 'Le temporel des églises occidentales' = ch.xvi of *Histoire de l'Église*, ed. A. Fliche and V. Martin, Vol.5, *Grégoire le Grand, les états barbares et la conquête arabe (590-757)*, by Louis Bréhier and R. Aigran (Paris, 1947) 543-53, with bibliography (543-4 n.1); F. Homes Dudden, *Gregory the Great. His Place in Hist. and Thought*, 2 vols (1905) I.295-320, esp. 296-9; and cf. VIII.iv above and its nn.26 and 28 below.

48. See the *MGH* edition (n.47 above) I.i.133-9, at 134-5.

49. Among the relevant laws issued in the West are *CTh* I.xi.1 (397), 2 (398); II.xxx.2 and xxxi.1 (422); V.vii.3 (408-9); X.iii.2 (372); iv.3 (370-3); v (396-8); xxvi.1 and 2 (426); XI.xvi.5 (343), 12 (380); XIV.iii.19 (396); XVI.v.40.7 (407), 52.1 (412), 54.5 and 6 (414); vi.4.1 (405); *Const. Sirmond.* 16 (408); *Nov. Val.* VI.i.1 (440); ii.1 (443); *Nov. Major.* VII.i.1 (458); *CJ* XI.lxvi.3 (376-7); lxxi.3-4 (early Arcadius and Honorius); lxxi.5.6-7 (?429). Cf. the Papal documents of the late fifth and mid-sixth centuries quoted by Jones, *LRE* III.254 n.49. Too much emphasis has sometimes been placed on the absence from *CTh* of a title corresponding to *CJ* IV.lxv: *De locato et conducto*. For *conductores* in the Later Empire in general, see Jones, *LRE* II.788-92, esp. 791.

50. See above all Jones, *LRE* II.773-81, 809, with the notes. Here again I must disagree with Finley, *AE* 196 n.73, who is demonstrably mistaken about the peasants referred to in Libanius, *Orat.* XLV (*De patrociniis*). They fall into two quite distinct groups, to only the second of which Finley's statements apply. The first group, described in §§ 4-10, consists specifically of peasant freeholders; and in these sections we find none of the terms (οἰκέται, δοῦλοι and σώματα, subject to a δεσπότης) which are taken by Finley as indications that the men concerned are not 'free landowning peasants'. (In § 4, of course, δεσπόται designates the peasants themselves, as owners. I cannot see, incidentally, that σώματα is used at all.) Moreover, the people harmed by the patronage which the peasants of the first group obtain from the *dux* are not landlords but 'those who collect the taxes' (τὸν φόρον, 7 ff.), i.e. the decurions as such – who would not have been involved in tax-collection from these people had they been *coloni* (their landlords would then have been responsible for their taxes): it is only the second group, dealt with in §§ 11-16, who are *coloni* (and with whom Libanius is obviously much more concerned in this speech): it is their landlords who are described in § 11 as their δεσπόται (and κύριοι), and it is these landlords as such who are harmed by the patronage of which Libanius is complaining. (The terms δεσπότης and κύριος, by the way, occur again in §§ 19, 21-3, where they will refer to the same people as before.) The account given by Liebeschuetz, *Ant.* 61-73 (esp. 67), which Finley criticises, is perfectly sound. See also Louis Harmand, *Libanius. Discours sur les Patronages*

(Publ. de la Fac. des Lettres de l'univ. de Clermont, 2ᵉ Série, Fasc. 1, Paris, 1955), esp. 124–40 on the two groups I have distinguished; cf. Harmand's larger work, *Le Patronat sur les collectivités publiques des origines au Bas-Empire* (Publ. de . . . Clermont, 2ᵉ Série, Fasc. 2, Paris, 1957) 449–61. Liebeschuetz, *Ant.* 68–73, ably presents the evidence for independent peasants in the area of Antioch, making use of the important recent books in French which have provided so much new information about certain parts of Roman Syria: G. Tchalenko, *Villages antiques de la Syrie du nord. Le Massif du Bélus à l'époque romaine* (3 vols, Paris, 1953, 1958); R. Mouterde and A. Poidebard, *Le 'Limes' de Chalcis, organisation de la steppe en haute Syrie romaine* (Paris, 1945); and J. Lassus, *Sanctuaries chrétiens de Syrie* (Paris, 1944), and *Inventaire archéologique de la région au nord-est de Hama* (Damascus, 1935). As in Liban., *Orat.* XLV, so in Theodoret, *Hist. relig.* (*MPG* LXXXII), we find both *coloni* and freehold peasants in northern Syria: for the former, see ch.14 (col. 1412–13, esp. 1413AB); for the latter, ch.17 (col. 1421–4, esp. 1421A). For the possible role of *emphyteusis* in promoting the prosperity of small and middling peasants in the area dealt with by Tchalenko (not discussed by Liebeschuetz; but see his *Ant.* 72 n.2), see Tchalenko, op. cit. I.414–17.

51. In this very summary account of the Later Roman colonate I have had to ignore many complications and peculiarities. For example, I cannot understand the situation depicted in Cassiod., *Var.* XII.9 (of A.D. 533–7), where an African *peregrinus*, claiming under a special ancestral custom to inherit the land of a fellow-countryman who has died without heirs, will (if his claim succeeds) become a *possessor* and a Roman citizen, liable to pay *tributa*, but inferior to other *domini* in being unable to alienate the property. It is *captivitas* which is responsible for making it possible for the man to enjoy *Romana civitas* as well as *Afrorum privilegia* – was he perhaps claiming to succeed the deceased as a freedman? But the inability to alienate remains inexplicable. Nor have I said anything in this section about labour services, which could have been dismissed as playing no important role in the Greek or Roman world but for a piece of evidence from mid-sixth-century Italy which I have mentioned in Section ii of this chapter.

52. The legacy of a 'fundus instructus' seems to have been slightly broader than that of a 'fundus cum instrumento': see Berger, *EDRL* 505 (*s.v.* 'instructum domus [fundi]' and 'instrumentum fundi [domus]', with brief bibliography), and 540 (*s.v.* 'legatum instrumenti').

53. See Sherwin-White, *LP* 504, where the reference in the penultimate line should be to VIII (not VII) 2n. (on p.449).

54. As e.g. in *CTh* IV.xii.5 (A.D. 362); VII.xviii.2.*pr.*,1 (379); XII.i.179.4 (415); cf. *Nov. Maj.* VII.i.4 (458). Sometimes the nature of the penalties threatened against such men suggests that they are likely to be slaves, as e.g. in *CTh* VII.xviii.4.1; IX.xxix.2.

55. The Latin *Life of St Melania the Younger* was edited by C. de Smedt and others in *AB* 8 (1889) 16–63; cf. its §§ 15, 21. I have not been able to read the more complete edition by Cardinal Rampolla, *Santa Melania Giuniore senatrice romana* (Rome, 1905). The best edition of the Greek Life is now that by Denys Gorce, *Vie de Sainte Melanie* = *SC* 90 (Paris, 1962): see esp. its §§ 1, 9–12, 15, 17–22, 37. If we can trust the two *Lives* (partly confirmed by Pallad., *Hist. Laus.* 61), Melania and her husband owned estates in Italy, Sicily, Africa (including Numidia and Mauretania), Spain, Gaul and Britain. And see P. Allard, in *RQH* 81 (1907) 5–30.

56. See e.g. Jones, *LRE* I.251–2; II.781, 787, 793–5, 810 (slaves of *coloni*), 815, 818, 932, with the notes.

57. A. H. M. Jones, P. Grierson and J. A. Crook, 'The authenticity of the "Testamentum S. Remigii"', in *RBPH* 35 (1957) 356–73, while regarding the longer version as 'beyond salvation' (357 n.5), have made an excellent case for accepting the shorter one as authentic. It is edited by B. Krusch, *Vita S. Remigii* 32, in *MGH, Scr. rer. Merov.* III (1896) 336–40.

58. See esp. op. cit. 371–3; Jones, *LRE* II.785, 793–4.

59. This is a very difficult question. I do not wish to deny that hired labour, especially at peak periods of agricultural activity, may have been more important than our surviving evidence suggests: see e.g. Brunt's review of White, *RF*, in *JRS* 62 (1972), at 158 – although in my opinion the *vindemiatores* of Col., *RR* III.xxi.6 are mainly the owner's slaves, working under the supervision of other such slaves as *antistitores*; it is only if too many vines ripen at once that it may be necessary to hire additional workers (*pluris operas . . . conducere*, § 10). The elaborate calculations of 'man-days' (*operae*) given in particular by Columella (see e.g. *RR* II.xii; and XI.ii passim, esp. 17, 46) are surely intended to help the landowner to decide whether he will need hired hands to supplement the labour of his slaves; and if so, how many. Like *operae*, the term *operarii* can refer to the landowner's slaves or to hired men – but we must never forget that even hired hands may often be slaves belonging to other landowners. Some of the workers

mentioned by Cato, *De agri cult.*, may well be free men (see Heitland, *Agricola* 171-3); but some of his *operarii* must be slaves, e.g. those in x.1, xi.1 and surely xxiii.2; there are also hired *operarii*, e.g. in i.3 (stressed by Pliny, *NH* XVIII.28; cf. 300), iv (*locabis . . . conduces*), v.4, cxlv.1. Varro refers very occasionally to hired workers, e.g. the *mercennarii* in *RR* I.xvii.2-3; the hired *anniversarii . . . vicini* of I.xvi.4 are not agricultural labourers but doctors and artisans; the *operarii* of I.xviii.4 must be slaves. Hired workers are conspicuously absent from Columella, *RR* I.vii.1,4,7 (cf. I.iii.12; ix.4); and indeed I have found no clear mention of hired agricultural workers in the whole of Columella, *RR,* except in III.xxi.10 (cited above) and I.*praef.*12, although the *operae* in II.ii.12 and IV.vi.3 may be (or at least include) those of hired men, even if elsewhere they are often clearly those of slaves, as e.g. in XII.xiii.1. *Operarii* in other writers are often clearly slaves, as e.g. in Phaedr., *Fab. Aesop.* IV.v.23. As I have not had an opportunity to mention it before, I will record here the useful article by K. D. White, 'Roman agricultural writers I: Varro and his predecessors', in *ANRW* I.iv (1973) 439-97.

[IV.iv]

1. The opinion that conscription was widely resorted to in the Principate is perhaps not yet the 'standard view'; but see P. A. Brunt, 'Conscription and volunteering in the Roman Imperial army', in *Scripta Classica Israelica* 1 (1974) 90-115.
2. The best general account of ancient Iran is by R. N. Frye, *The Heritage of Persia*[2] (1976). Frye is a specialist on the Sassanid period but deals well with the Achaemenid and Parthian eras.
3. See Jones, *LRE* II.668-70 (contrast 614-19). Against some recent objections, see John F. Haldon, *Recruitment and Conscription in the Byzantine Army c. 550-950. A Study on the Origins of the Stratiotika Ktemata* (= *Sb* 357, Österreichische Akad. der Wiss., Philos.-hist. Klasse, Vienna, 1979) 20-8.
4. Ostrogorsky's views on this subject, which will be found in greater detail in his *HBS*[2] (e.g. 133-7, 272-6, 280-2, 286-8, 294-5, 305-7, 320-3, 329-31, 331-2, 371-2, 391-4, 481-3), are summarised in his excellent chapter in *CEHE* I[2] (1966) 205-34 (esp. 207-8, 215-18, 219, 220-2). See also his article, 'The peasant's pre-emption right', in *JRS* 37 (1947) 117-26. Since the reign of Heraclius is within the period covered by this book, I must record the fact that there has been much criticism of Ostrogorsky's attribution to Heraclius of thoroughgoing reforms of the administration, including in particular the creation of the 'theme'-system visible in later times. In this field Ostrogorsky's picture is clearly overdrawn, although it seems probable that Heraclius did begin the military reorganisation which attained its full development in the tenth century. In my opinion the best account is the most recent one: that of Haldon, op. cit. 28-40. As for the Middle Byzantine period, I am referring to it by way of illustration only, and I must do no more than cite Haldon, op. cit. 17-19, 41 ff., and an article by Rosemary Morris, 'The powerful and the poor in tenth-century Byzantium: law and reality', in *Past & Present* 73 (1976) 3-27, both with full bibliography. What for me is essential about the conflict between 'the powerful' and 'the poor' (which I of course see as a class struggle) is that over all 'the powerful' were essentially large landowners, however they may happen to be characterised in legal documents, e.g. the famous Novel V of 934 (935) of Romanus Lecapenus, in J. and P. Zepos, *Jus Graecoromanum* (Athens, 1931; repr. Aalen, 1962) I.205-14 (esp. 209.1-9, concentrating on rank and office-holding: see Morris, op. cit. 14). In discussing the motivation of the imperial legislation on behalf of 'the poor' against 'the powerful', some historians may prefer to concentrate on the desire of the emperors to curb the dangerously disruptive and centrifugal activities of their most 'over-mighty subjects'. Near the end of VIII.iv above, while emphasising that few if any of the Roman emperors had much concern for the poor and unprivileged as such, I have stressed two motives for the legislation in the Later Roman Empire designed to protect the peasantry which in the long run seem to me even more important: the preservation of the ability of the peasants to pay taxes, and to serve as recruits for the army. (It is not irrelevant to add that the largest expenditure of money raised by taxation was precisely on the army.)
4a. Needless to say, this did not escape the notice of Marx – or of Francis Bacon, from whose *The History of the Reign of King Henry VII* (1622) Marx quotes to good effect in *Cap.* I.719-20: see esp. 720 n.2, beginning, 'Bacon shows the connexion between a free, well-to-do peasantry and good infantry'.

4b. I have altered the translation by Frank H. Knight slightly, to make it closer to the German text.
5. Xen., *Oecon.* V.4-5, 13-15; VI.9-10 etc.; Ps.-Arist., *Oecon.* I.2, 1343ᵇ2-6; Cato, *De agric.*, Praef. 4; Pliny, *NH* XVIII.26; Veget., *De re milit.* I.3.
6. I give some examples here. (*a*) In the early 260s Odenathus, a magnate of Palmyra, organised a large body of country folk into an army which beat off the Persians: see Festus, *Brev.* 23, and other sources given in J. W. Eadie's edition (1967), pp.144-5. (*b*) In 399 Valentinus of Selge in Pamphylia successfully raised a large force of slaves and peasants (οἰκετῶν πλῆθος καὶ γεωργῶν) against Tribigild the Ostrogoth and his marauding army (Zos. V.xv-xvi, esp. xv.5). Zosimus, no doubt realising how rare such exploits were, remarks on the fact that the men concerned were all habituated to such clashes by long experience of armed resistance to neighbouring marauders. (*c*) The men in Spain who in 408 were armed, ineffectually, by Didymus and Verinian (relatives of the Emperor Honorius) against the invading army of Constans, son of the usurper Constantine, were doubtless mainly their own *coloni* and slaves: see Zos. VI.iv.3 (πλῆθος οἰκετῶν καὶ γεωργῶν), with V.xliii.2; VI.i.1, iv.1, v.1-2; Soz., *HE* IX.11.4 (πλῆθος ἀγροίκων καὶ οἰκετῶν); Oros. VII.40.5-8 ('servulos tantum suos ex propriis colligentes ac vernaculis alentes sumptibus'). (*d*) For Cyrenaica, see Synes., *Ep.* 107, 108, 122 (where in the early fifth century the priests of the village of Axomis organise the peasants to resist the nomad raiders), 125; *Catast.*, in *MPG* LXVI.1568d (women also bear arms); *De regno* 14. (I would draw attention to *Ep.* 78 as showing that on some occasions at any rate the number of raiding barbarians must have been quite small: a mere 40 Hunnic auxiliaries had already won victories, and Synesius was confident that another 160, making the total up to 200, would end the menace of the Ausurians. Cf. *Ep.* 62 for a quick and decisive victory by the *dux* Marcellinus.) For surviving traces of the defence of the countryside of Cyrenaica, see R. G. Goodchild, 'Mapping Roman Libya', in *Geog. Jnl* 118 (1952) 142-52, at 147-8, 150, 151. (*e*) From the brief notice of Hydat. 91 (in *Chron. Min.* II.21) it appears that when the Suevi ravaged part of Gallaecia (in north-west Spain) in 430, the common people (the *plebs*), *quae castella tutiora retinebat*, resisted them most successfully. Cf. Hydat. 186 (in *Chron. Min.* II.30) for the equally praiseworthy resistance of a single fortified place to the Goths *c*. 457. (*f*) According to Sidon. Apoll., *Ep.* III.iii.3-8 (esp. 7), Ecdicius, the brother-in-law of Sidonius, collected a small military force in the early 470s in Auvergne, *privatis viribus*, to defend Clermont Ferrand against incursions by the Visigoths: see Stein, *HBE* I².i.393; C. E. Stevens, *Sidonius Apollinaris and his Age* (1933) 141-9. (*g*) Procop., *Bell.* III (*Vand.* I).x.22-4 mentions that Pudentius of Oea in 532 raised forces which ejected the Vandals from his province, Tripolitana. I have not made use here of Jerome, *Ep.* 123.15.4 (*CSEL* LVI = 123.16, *MPL* XXII), since I think it is probably the spiritual 'merits' of Exsuperius to which the salvation of Toulouse is being attributed. Sometimes *coloni* and slaves were organised by their masters into armed bands for less patriotic purposes: see e.g. Herodian VII.iv.3-4 (with *Hist. Aug., Gord.* 7.3-4), cf. v.3 and ix.4 (the proclamation of the aged Gordian as emperor in 238: we hear of the participation of countrymen, armed with clubs and axes, obeying 'the orders of their masters', δεσπόται: see VIII.iii n.4 below); also *Hist. Aug., Firm.* etc. 12.2 ('it is said' that when Proculus made himself emperor in the 270s he armed 2,000 of his slaves); and Procop., *Bell.* V (*Goth.* I).xii.50-1 (Theudis the Ostrogoth raised a force of about 2,000 men from the estate of his rich Roman wife in Spain, *c*. 525). I can do no more than mention Procop., *Anecd.* 21.28: how much truth there is in it we have no means of telling. In VIII.iii and its n.42 I give examples of the defence of *cities* by their inhabitants. For defection to the barbarians, peasant revolts etc., see VIII.iii and its notes.
7. Tullianus, a leading landowner of Lucania-Bruttium, organised a large force of peasants against Totila in 545-6 (Procop., *Bell.* VII [*Goth.* III].xviii.20-2; xxii.1-5). Totila also raised an army of country folk, which was defeated (id. xxii.4-5). But Totila was able to procure the desertion of Tullianus' peasants, by making their masters (who were now in his power) order them to return to their lands (id. xxii.20-1). For Totila, see also VIII.iii and its nn.27-30.
8. Brunt is arguing specifically against MacMullen, *RSR* 35 (with 158-9 n.26). I agree in general with Brunt's view of *Digest* XLVIII.vi.1 ff. (DIRDS 262-4) rather than e.g. that of Jones, *LRE* III.343 n.54.
9. See M. T. [sic] Rostovtseff, 'Συντέλεια τιρώνων' in *JRS* 8 ((1918) 26-33, esp. 29-30.
10. Fergus Millar, *SCD* 109, suggests that the reference to brigands is 'a clear reference to what ensued when Septimius Severus ended the recruitment of Italians into the praetorian cohorts' – Dio himself says later that young Italians were driven to become brigands (LXXIV.ii.5-6).
11. By *CTh* VII.xiii.13-14, of 397, senators alone were allowed to commute in gold for the recruits

they should have furnished; and cf. Veget., *De re milit.* I.7.
12. For the Roman army, see the bibliography in *OCD*² 121; add Jones, *LRE* II.607-86.
13. Anyone who is tempted by the brilliant colouring by Tacitus in the speech of Percennius to suppose that Tacitus had any sympathy with the mutineers should read the trenchant remarks by Erich Auerbach in the second chapter of his *Mimesis,* 1946 (esp. 36-7, also 39-40, 41, and cf. 52, in the English translation by W. R. Trask, Princeton, 1953 and repr.).

[IV.v]

1. Jones, *CERP*² 38-9 ('what may be conveniently if inaccurately called a feudal system' – apparently because 'villages were owned by lords; the villagers were serfs, bound to the soil'. Later we have 'a feudal aristocracy', 'the feudal system', and temples as 'feudal landlords'). A glance at the Index to Rostovtzeff's *SEHHW* will reveal many references to allegedly 'feudal' structures, aristocracies etc.; and see his *SGRK* 377. For Syme, see his *RR* 11-12 (the Roman Republic 'a feudal order of society'). See also D. W. S. Hunt, 'Feudal survivals in Ionia', in *JHS* 67 (1947) 68-75; Tarn, *HC*³ 134-5; and many other works. Bikerman, in his *Institutions des Séleucides* at any rate, seems to reserve expressions like 'la structure féodale', 'chefs féodaux', and 'serfs' for 'Haute-Asie': that is to say, Asia excluding Asia Minor (see his *IS* 172-6).
2. I will refer at this stage only to F. L. Ganshof, *Feudalism* (3rd edn. of the Eng. trans. by Philip Grierson, 1964, of the work originally published in French in 1944, *Qu'est-ce que la féodalité?*); Marc Bloch, *Feudal Society*² (Eng. trans. in 2 vols, by L. A. Manyon, 2nd edn., 1962, of *La société féodale,* 2 vols, Paris, 1939-40); also Bloch's chapter in *CEHE* I², cited subsequently in the text; and the discussion by Lynn White, *Medieval Technology and Social Change* (1962) 2-14, 135-6, of the theories of H. Brunner and J. R. Strayer regarding the inception of feudalism.
3. Elizabeth A. R. Brown, 'The tyranny of a construct: feudalism and historians of Medieval Europe', in *Amer. Hist. Rev.* 79 (1974) 1063-88. The quotation is from the last page.
4. *Feudalism in History,* ed. Rushton Coulborn (1956). The editor's essay is on pp.185 ff. There is a review-article on this book by Owen Lattimore, 'Feudalism in history', in *Past & Present* 12 (Nov. 1957) 47-57.
5. As by Jones and Rostovtzeff: see n.1 above. Rostovtzeff, in his *SGRK,* and Wilcken, *Chrest.* I.i.280-4, both speak of 'Lehnsland'.
6. Frederick Pollock and F. W. Maitland, *History of English Law* I².66-7 (ed. S. F. C. Milsom, 1968).
7. Ganshof, *Feudalism*³ (see n.2 above) xv n.1.
8. R. A. Crossland, 'Hittite society and its economic basis', in *BICS* 14 (1967) 106-8, at 106. Crossland gives references to the relevant literature, including Sedat Alp, 'Die soziale Klasse der NAM.RA-Leute und ihre hethitische Bezeichnung', in *Jahrb. für kleinasiat. Forsch.* 1 (1951) 113-35; and K. Fabricius, 'The Hittite system of land tenure in the second millenium B.C.', in *Acta Orientalia* 7 (1929) 275-92.

[IV.vi]

1. The one recent book in English on ancient craftsmen, Alison Burford, *CGRS = Craftsmen in Greek and Roman Society* (1972), has some real merits, but is not wholly reliable. Among many other works that are still worth consulting are Henri Francotte, *IGA = L'industrie dans la Grèce ancienne,* 2 vols (Brussels, 1900-1); Paul Guiraud, *La main-d'oeuvre industrielle dans l'ancienne Grèce* (Paris, 1900); Gustave Glotz, *Le travail dans la Grèce ancienne* (Paris, 1920), Eng. trans. as *Ancient Greece at Work* (1926); and 'Industrie u. Handel', in *RE* IX (1916) 1381-1439 (Greek, by H. Francotte) and 1439-1535 (Roman, by H. Gummerus).
2. Being a leading architect in fifth/fourth-century Athens is not likely to have brought large financial rewards. We hear of at least one such man, Philon son of Execestides, who in the fourth century was a member of the trierarchic class (see Davies, *APF* 555-6); and another architect, Demomeles, of the late fifth century, may well have been the father of two rich Athenians of the first half of the fourth century: Demosthenes (the father of the statesman) and Demon (ibid. 113-14). But there is no proof, and no likelihood, that such men obtained their wealth by the practice of their profession. Certainly the state salaries paid to architects in all recorded cases are small, e.g. 1 drachma per day for the Erechtheum in the late fifth century

(*IG* I².374, lines 2-3, 109-10, 256-8) and 2 dr. at Eleusis in 329/8 (*IG* II².1672.11-12); cf. the 350-3 dr. per year paid to Theodotus, the architect of the temple of Asclepius at Epidaurus *c*. 370 B.C. (*IG* IV².i.102: see Burford, *GTBE* 212-17; and cf. 138-45, with references for Delphi and Delos – I agree with her here, against Glotz and Lacroix). According to Vitruvius, in order to become a first-rate architect one needed an extensive education from childhood (I.i, esp. 1-4, 7, 10-15), such as he himself had received (VI *praef.* 4) – yet he could admit that this was not true of many practising architects of his day (id. 6-7). Vitruvius boasted that his own objective had not been to make money out of his profession (id. 5).

3. The most recent monograph in English, by Louis Cohn-Haft, *The Public Physicians of Ancient Greece* (= *Smith Coll. Stud. in Hist.* 42, Northampton, Mass., 1956), is limited to 'the Greek city-states of the period down to the founding of the Roman Empire', and is therefore obliged to set aside the large volume of evidence for later periods; but it is thorough as far as it goes. (One may feel that the author has spent too much time lamenting the deficiencies of earlier writers.) For the Hellenistic period, see esp. Rostovtzeff, *SEHHW* II.1088-94 (with III.1597-1600 nn.45-8). Further bibliography will be found in *OCD*² 664. Add Thomas, LO (1961) 241-3, on doctors and Roman law.

4. A good bibliography on Galen is given in L. Edelstein's all-too-brief article on him in *OCD*² 454-5. George Sarton, *Galen of Pergamon* (Lawrence, Kansas, 1954), includes a list of Galenic texts available in English translation (Appendix III. pp.101-7).

5. See M. I. Finkelstein [Finley], "Ἔμπορος, Ναύκληρος and Κάπηλος: a prolegomena to the study of Athenian trade', in *CP* 30 (1935) 320-36. I am saying virtually nothing in this book about Greek merchants; but my former graduate pupil, Charles M. Reed, hopes to produce a book on Greek maritime traders in the near future.

6. I am reluctant (cf. III.v above) to make any use of the figures scattered over the *Satyricon* of Petronius, since they are sometimes wildly exaggerated (for an example, see Duncan-Jones, *EREQS* 239 n.4, *init.*). Thus in *Sat.* 76 Petronius gives Trimalchio a profit of HS 10 million on a single voyage, after a disastrous one in which he lost three times as much; and cf. 117 for another loss by shipwreck of more than HS 2 million! But I think it is significant that after Trimalchio has made his 'ten million' he gives up merchanting himself and goes in for staking his freedmen (76); he now thinks in terms of landed property (76, 77; cf. 53).

7. See Jones, *RE* 35-6; *LRE* I.110, 148 (with III.27 n.28), 431-2 (with III.108-9 nn.52-3), 464-5; II.853-4, 871-2 (with III.292 nn.116-18). See esp. Liban., *Orat.* XLVI.22-3; Zos. II.38.1-3; Evagr., *HE* III.39, for the distress allegedly caused by the tax.

8. On the *collegia* of the Roman world and their Greek equivalents, see the comprehensive work of J.-P. Waltzing, *Étude historique sur les corporations professionnelles chez les Romains*, I-IV (Louvain, 1895-1900). For other works on Greek 'Vereinswesen', by Ziebarth (1896), Oehler (1905), Poland (1909) and others, see the bibliography by M. N. Tod, 'Clubs, Greek', in *OCD*² 254-5. Cf. also Rostovtzeff, *SEHRE*² I.178-9, with II.619-20 nn.43-4 ('The treatment of the corporations in existing works is wholly inadequate, being merely systematic and not historical', n.43).

9. E.g. συνέδριον, συντεχνία, συνέργιον, σύστημα, συμβίωσις, συνεργασία, ἐργασία, ὁμοτέχνον, στατίων, στόλος, πλατεῖα, κοινόν, οἶκος, even ἡ ἱερὰ φυλή. There is a handy collection of the evidence for such organisations in Asia Minor in the Roman period by Broughton, in Frank, *ESAR* IV.841-6. For the 'guilds' of the Later Roman Empire, see Jones, *LRE* II.858-64.

10. For the continuation of this passage, mentioning Anacreon, Philemon and Archilochus, and for much other interesting material, see Brunt's excellent note, *ASTDCS* 15 n.1: Anacreon and Archilochus at least 'were regarded as men of bad character' – and Archilochus, I may add, was said to be the son of a slave girl. I must also say here that we need to be careful in interpreting Plutarch's frequent references to the indulgence by great men in artistic pursuits, for their implications are not always obvious. For example, in one story, which Plutarch thought so admirably illustrative that he used it in no fewer than four separate treatises, we hear of the harper whose playing was criticised by Philip of Macedon, and who responded by expressing the hope that the king would never sink so low as to acquire a greater knowledge of playing the harp than he had himself (*Mor.* 67f-68a, 179b, 334cd, 634d). But only in two of these (67f-68a, and esp. 634d) does Plutarch reveal the lesson he wishes us to draw from the incident: that the harper was cleverly and covertly rebuking the king's impertinence in fancying that he knew better than a professional.

11. See, briefly, Burford, *CGRS* 164-83, 207-18, with the notes, 243-5, 249-50, giving a selection of

the evidence. Rostovtzeff, *SEHRE*² I.166-7, and esp. II.611-12 n.27, should not be neglected, although dealing with the Latin West, and specifically with the Moselle region. See also Crook, *LLR* 193, with 320 nn.65-7. For a useful collection of epigraphic material, see Ida Calabi Limentani, *Studi sulla società romana: il lavoro artistico* (= Biblioteca storica universitaria, Serie II Monografie, Vol.IX, Milan, 1958) 151-80 ('Iscrizioni', 224 in number, mainly in Latin, but some in Greek). [After this section was finished I saw the article by J. F. Drinkwater, 'The rise and fall of the Gallic Iulii: aspects of the development of the aristocracy of the three Gauls under the Early Empire', in *Latomus* 37 (1978) 817-50: see esp. 835-46.]

12. Cf. the fullers of *IG* I².436, 642 + 491 (= *DAA* 49), and 751 (= *DAA* 342).
13. For another family of Greek woodcutters, proud of their calling, see the charming epitaph, *Anth. Pal.* VII.445.
14. For *IG* II².10051, see Siegfried Lauffer, *Die Bergwerkssklaven von Laureion* II (= *Abh.* der Akad. der Wiss. u. der Lit. in Mainz, Geists- u. sozialwiss. Klasse, 1956 no.11) 198-205 (= 962-9), cf. 132-3 (= 896-7). Atotas may or may not have come to Attica as a slave; when he died he was almost certainly no slave or even underground worker (see Lauffer, op. cit. 132-3, 199-200): I would guess that he may have been in charge of smelting operations in an ἐργαστήριον, in which capacity there may have been much scope for display of τεχνή. I take this opportunity of mentioning further bibliography for the *Selbstbewusstsein* of craftsmen, in H. W. Pleket's article in *Talanta* 5 (1973) 6-47, at 9-10 nn.16-18 (see II.i n.14 above). And see MacMullen, *RSR* 119-20.
15. *IGRR* I.810 = G. Kaibel, *Epigrammata Graeca ex lapidibus conlecta* (Berlin, 1878) 841 = Calabi Limentani, op. cit. (in n.11 above) 165, no.107.
16. *IG* V.i.823 = Jeffery, *LSAG* 200, no.32.
17. A brief but masterly summary will be found in J. D. Beazley, 'Potter and painter in Ancient Athens', in *Proc. Br. Acad.* 30 (1944) 87-125, at 107 ff. (also published separately, at 25 ff.), where information is also given about inscriptions on marble by potters, mainly from the Athenian Acropolis (ibid. 103-7 = 21-5), and about representations on vases and votive plaques of potters at work or at leisure (ibid. 87-103 = 5-21).

[V.i]

1. The most recent edition of Hesiod, *Works and Days*, is by M. L. West (1978).
2. Hes., *WD*, esp. 176-7, 302-19, 376-80, 381-2; cf. 637-40, 717-18.
3. That Hesiod has the freeholder rather than the tenant-farmer in mind is clear from *WD* 341.
4. Hes., *WD* 459, 470, 502-3, 559-60, 573, 597 ff., 602-3, 607-8, 765-6.
5. Ibid. 602.
6. It will be sufficient to refer to Brunt, *IM* 140-1, who cites not only the lines of Hesiod to which I have referred (*WD* 376 ff.) and a fascinating eighteenth-century passage from Gaetano Filangieri of Naples, but also Polyb. XXXVI.xvii.5-8. That famous text attributes the depopulation of Greece by the second century B.C. to a disinclination to rear children, and in particular to a general desire not to split up an estate among more than one or two children (see esp. § 7 *fin.*), with the result that many families became extinct. Musonius Rufus complains of similar motivation for the exposure of children of the rich in the early Principate: see his fr. XV, ed. Hense or Lutz (cf. II.vi and its nn.28-9 above): τὰ ἐπιγενόμενα τέκνα μὴ τρέφειν, ἵνα τὰ προγενόμενα εὐπορῇ μᾶλλον. I would add that there is some excellent material in Brunt, *IM* 131-55 (ch.xi, 'Reproductivity in ancient Italy'), much of which is applicable to the Greek world. [Cf. now the addition to II.vi n.7 above.]
7. Witold Kula, *An Economic Theory of the Feudal System* (1976), ch.3.3, esp. p.72 & n.66, citing some interesting eighteenth-century material. This book reads remarkably well, although translated into English (by Lawrence Garner) from an Italian translation from the original Polish edition of 1962. A leading French historian, Fernand Braudel, in his introduction, describes the book as 'an example of a Marxist problematic mastered, assimilated and elevated to the level of a lucid and intelligent humanism, and a broad explanation of the evolution of the collective destiny of men', and as 'an effort of objective and patient reflection, of unusual intellectual honesty, . . . an important event for historians . . . a milestone in our common research' (ibid. 8).
8. Hes., *WD* 38-9, 220-1, 248-51, 263-4.

9. In support of the early date (which I favour) see M. L. West, in *Studies in Greek Elegy and Iambus* = *Untersuch. zur antiken Lit. u. Gesch.* 14, ed. H. Dörrie and P. Moraux (Berlin/New York, 1974), ch.iv, 'The life and times of Theognis', pp.65-71. See esp. 70: Theognis' 'poetic and political career began in the 630s at the latest, and apparently extended over several decades. It may have reached into the sixth century, overlapping Solon's'. I have used the Teubner edition of Theognis by E. Diehl, in *Anthol. Lyrica Graeca* II³ (1950); there is a more recent text by M. L. West, in *Iambi et Elegi Graeci* I (1971). There is also a text (much less reliable) with an English translation in the Loeb *Elegy and Iambus* I (1931 and repr.), by J. M. Edmonds. On Theognis, see the article by C. M. Bowra, in *OCD*² 1056-7 (with bibliography), and Bowra's book, *Early Greek Elegists* (1935, repr. 1960) 139-70.

10. Theogn. 341-50, cf. 1197-1202.

11. See my ECAPS 9-11 (with its nn.29-32); cf. my *OPW* 358 ff., esp. 371-6.

12. Cf. Solon frr. 1.33; 4.9; 23.21; 24.18. For Solon I have used the Teubner edition of E. Diehl, in *Anthol. Lyrica Graeca* I³ (1949). There is a more recent edition (unfortunately with yet another re-numbering of the fragments) by M. L. West, in *Iambi et Elegi Graeci* II (1972). There is also a text (much less reliable) with an English translation in the Loeb *Elegy and Iambus* I (see n.9 above).

13. Cf. Theogn. 193-6, 1112 etc.

14. Alcaeus, fr. Z 24, in E. Lobel and D. Page, *Poetarum Lesbiorum Fragmenta* (1955); and see Denys Page, *Sappho and Alcaeus* (1955) 169 ff., 235-40. Cf. the κακόπατρις in Theogn. 193.

15. See the commentary of Newman, *PA* IV.432-3.

16. Cf. Theogn. 53-60, 233-4 etc.

17. There is a vast literature on this topic. The best introduction for the 'general reader' is still Andrewes, *GT*. Forrest, *EGD*, is valuable in that it carries the story on, beyond the point (roughly 500 B.C.) at which Andrewes stops, to show the subsequent evolution of Greek political forms down to the democracy of late-fifth-century Athens. H. W. Pleket, 'The Archaic tyrannis', in *Talanta* 1 (1969) 19-61 (for the specialist), is confined mainly to the tyrants in Athens, Corinth and Lesbos, with very full references to modern work. The most complete work on the Greek tyrants in general (going down to the fourth century) is Helmut Berve, *Die Tyrannis bei den Griechen* (Munich, 1967, two vols, some 800 pages).

18. The longest known tyranny is that of the Orthagorids (including Cleisthenes) of Sicyon, which is said by Arist., *Pol.* V.12, 1315^b11-14, to have lasted a century.

19. Cf. the role of the rich Plebeians in the Roman 'Conflict of the Orders', briefly discussed in VI.ii above.

20. E.g. Peisistratus of Athens. Cypselus of Corinth is said to have had a mother belonging to the ruling Bacchiad aristocracy, who was lame and had therefore been married off to a commoner: see Andrewes, *GT* 45-9 (with 154 n.34).

21. Polyaen. V.i.1: see e.g. Dunbabin, *WG* 315. (There is an Eng. trans. of the Polyaenus passage on pp.274-5 of the book by P. N. Ure mentioned in the next note.)

22. P. N. Ure, *The Origin of Tyranny* (1922).

23. Cf. my *OPW* 360. But in late-fifth-century Athens there were at least 1,000 Hippeis at any given time, and it has been suggested to me that I would have done better to speak of 'Jaguar owners' rather than 'Rolls-Royce owners' as the equivalent of the Hippeis at that time.

24. The French original of this book, *La Cité grecque* (Paris, 1928), was reissued a few years ago in a new edition (Paris, 1968) with supplementary notes and bibliography.

25. I use Diehl's edition and numbering of the fragments: see n.12 above. The most relevant fragments are 1, 8, 10, 27, and esp. 3-5 and 23-5. I know of no complete account of Solon's outlook and activity that seems to me really satisfactory; but see Andrewes, *GT* 78-91; Forrest, *EGD* 143-74.

26. See esp. Solon frr. 5.1-6; 23.1-21; 24.18-25; 25.1-9 Diehl.

27. The main sources for Solon's laws on debt are of course Arist., *Ath. Pol.* 6.1 (cf. 9.1, 10.1, 11.2); Plut., *Sol.* 15.2, 5-6 (the account by Androtion, given in 15.3, is certainly to be rejected).

28. See esp, Thuc. VI.54.5-6; cf. Hdts I.59.6; Arist., *Ath. Pol.* 16.2-9.

29. I hope to explain this elsewhere shortly.

30. See my *OPW* 37-40.

31. Even Peisistratus employed mercenaries in 546 (see Hdts I.64.1 etc.), but he also had considerable support among the citizens: see esp. Hdts I.62.1.

32. Cf. Arist., *Pol.* VI.7, 1321^a11-21, esp. 19-21, cited in Section ii of this chapter, at the end of § 5. I am sure this would not have been true before the late fifth century.

33. Cartledge gives very full bibliography. The article by A. M. Snodgrass, 'The Hoplite reform and history', is in *JHS* 85 (1965) 110-22. I cannot see that Cartledge's conclusions are at all weakened by J. Salmon's article, 'Political hoplites?', in *JHS* 97 (1977) 84-101, which however adds some interesting archaeological details. I am tempted to suggest that some useful results might be achieved, here as elsewhere, by comparative studies of comparable phenomena in other societies. (Great caution, of course, would be necessary, as always in such cases.) The most obvious parallel is the rise of the *signorie* in the Italian towns in the late Middle Ages (thirteenth to fifteenth centuries); but the situation there was totally different: see esp. P. J. Jones, 'Communes and despots: the city state in Late Medieval Italy', in *TRHS* (1965) 71-96. The history of the Italian towns, however, can in some respects illustrate the history of the Classical world: see in particular the admirable article by E. J. Bickerman, 'Some reflections on early Roman history', in *RFIC* 97 (1969) 393-408, esp. 402-5. I particularly like his wise remark on p.406: 'The value of analogies is not probative, but illustrative, and, thus, heuristic. They can make us recognise aspects of facts which would otherwise remain hidden from us.'
34. I have in mind such passages as Hdts I.59.4; 60.3-5 (and parallels in later sources).

[V.ii]

1. King Darius I of Persia abandoned his support for Greek tyrants in 494, in theory, but they continued to appear in the Asiatic Greek cities and Aegean islands: see my *OPW* 37 ff.
2. Perhaps the best general book on fifth-century Greece is now Édouard Will, *Le Monde grec et l'Orient, I. Le Ve siècle, 510-403* (Paris, 1972).
3. I have not been able to read the recent book by J. K. Davies, *Democracy and Classical Greece* (1978). Those who have not already studied the subject thoroughly would certainly benefit by beginning with Jones, *AD*, chapters III (esp. pp.41-62) and V, describing respectively the ideology of the democracy and its practical working. See also Forrest, *EGD* (cf. V.i n.17 above).
4. Anyone looking for an ancient definition of the aims of Classical Greek δημοκρατία might begin with Arist., *Pol.* V.9, 1310^{a}28-36 (note the hostile ending), and VI.2, 1317^{a}40-^{b}17, both emphasising freedom and the ability to 'live as you wish'; cf. VI.4, 1319^{b}27-32 (hostile again); also *Rhet.* I.8, 1366^{a}4, where the objective, the τέλος, of democracy is ἐλευθερία, as wealth of oligarchy etc. See also, of course, Thuc. II.37-40 (esp. 37.2-3; 39.1; 40.2). 'Living as you wish' as a definition of personal freedom later became a commonplace, which we often find in literature, e.g. in Cic., *De offic.* I.70 (*vivere ut velis*); *Parad.* V.i.34 (*potestas vivendi ut velis*, occurring in a passage taking as its text the Stoic maxim that 'the wise man alone is free'), and Epict., *Diss.* IV.i.1; Diog. Laert. VII.121 (ἐξουσία αὐτοπραγίας).
5. Jones, *AD*, ch.V (pp.99-133, with the notes, 153-60), is still unsurpassed as a brief description of how the Athenian democracy worked in practice: it is a masterpiece of compression.
6. It seems indeed that slaves may have been better treated in a democracy (at Athens anyway) than elsewhere: see the quotation from Plato, *Rep.* VIII, in the next paragraph of the main text above; and cf. Ps.-Xen., *Ath. Pol.* I.10-12 (a striking passage); Xen., *HG* II.iii.48 (where οἱ δοῦλοι may, I think, be an echo of the gift of citizenship to some of the slaves who fought for the Athenian democracy in 403); and other texts, e.g. those showing that a γραφὴ ὕβρεως could be brought by any Athenian (not only the master) against anyone who injured a slave (Aeschin. I.15-17; Dem. XXI. 45-9; Athen. VI.266f-7a, citing also Hypereides and Lycurgus), and that the slave at Athens might obtain some protection against ill-treatment by taking asylum in a temple (the Theseum, and perhaps the shrine of the Semnai) and requesting to be sold to another owner (see Busolt-Swoboda, *GS* II.982-3).
7. See, in addition to the passages cited in the text and in n.4 above, Thuc. VI.39; VII.69.2; Eur., *Suppl.* 349-53, 404-8, 438-41; *Ion* 670-5; *Hippol.* 421-3; Ps.-Lys. II.18-19, 55-7, 64-6, 68; Dem. XX.106 (contrast with Sparta); and many hostile ones in Isocrates, Plato and others, e.g. Isocr. VII.20; XII.131; Plato, *Rep.* VIII.557ab, 560e; IX.572e; *Laws* III.701ab, etc.
8. The most recent treatment I have seen of παρρησία is by G. Scarpat, *Parrhesia. Storia del termine e delle sue traduzioni in Latino* (Brescia, 1964). The word first appears in the late fifth century, e.g. in Eur., *Hippol.* 422, *Ion* 672, 675, *Phoen.* 391; it is also found in Democr., DK 68 B 226. (Cf. Section iii of this chapter and its n.57.) I cannot follow here the later history of the word and will merely refer to the works cited by Peter Brown in *JRS* 61 (1971), at 94 and nn.171-2.

9. Aristotle often recognises a connection between democracy and political equality. He takes it for granted that οἱ δημοτικοί seek τὸ ἴσον for τὸ πλῆθος (*Pol.* V.8, 1308ᵃ11-12; cf. V.1, 1301ᵃ26-31). In a passage critical of democracy which I have cited in n.4 above (*Pol.* V.9, 1310ᵃ28-36) he sees democrats as assuming that equality is just and identifying it with the sovereignty of τὸ πλῆθος. He notes the opinion held by some that ἰσότης as well as ἐλευθερία can be attributed most of all to democracy (IV.4, 1291ᵇ34-5). In several passages, of which perhaps the most interesting is VI.2-3, 1317ᵃ40-18ᵇ5, he demonstrates how his own concern for the minority of property-owners prevents him from accepting the equality demanded by democrats.

10. See many of the passages cited in nn.4 & 7 above. I am not fully satisfied with any of the treatments of ἰσονομία I have seen, the most recent of which are by Bořivoj Borecký, 'Die politische Isonomie', in *Eirene* 9 (1971) 5-24; and H. W. Pleket, 'Isonomia and Cleisthenes: A Note', in *Talanta* 4 (1972) 63-81. There is an admirably thorough discussion of the origin and meaning of the word by Martin Ostwald, *Nomos and the Beginnings of the Athenian Democracy* (1969) 96-136 (cf. 137 ff.), which nevertheless seems to me to seek for a greater precision than I would suppose possible. I accept Ostwald's view that *isonomia* is 'not a form of government but a political principle' (111, cf. 97, 116), 'the principle of political equality . . . not a constitutional form' (113), and I have therefore described democracy in the main text above as '*characterised by* ἰσονομία'. Ostwald rightly remarks that 'ἰσονομία comes closer than any other Greek word to expressing the modern notion of "rights" in the sense in which we speak of the "rights of man", "rights of a citizen", "Bill of Rights", etc.' (113 n.1). Interesting later uses of ἰσόνομος include App., *BC* I.15/63; Marcus Aurel., *Medit.* I.14; for ἰσονομία and ἰσομοιρία see e.g. Dio Cass. XLI.17.3; XLIV.2.1. The best treatment I know of ἰσηγορία is by G. T. Griffith, 'Isegoria in the Assembly at Athens', in *Ancient Society and Institutions: Studies presented to Victor Ehrenberg* (1966) 115-38; and see A. G. Woodhead, "Ἰσηγορία and the Council of 500', in *Historia* 16 (1967) 129-40.

11. This is a feature of democracy which its critics were naturally not fond of emphasising. Aristotle does not use the term ὑπεύθυνος, though he does refer to εὔθυναι in (for instance) *Pol.* II.12, 1274ᵃ15-18; III.11, 1281ᵇ32-4, 1282ᵃ12-14,26-7; VI.4, 1318ᵇ21-2. Hdts III.80.6 speaks of ὑπεύθυνος ἀρχή as a characteristic feature of that πλῆθος ἄρχον which has 'the fairest name of all', ἰσονομίη. (This is part of the so-called 'Persian debate', the earliest surviving discussion in any language of alternative forms of political constitution, which must be a literary fiction, originating, I believe, in the late sixth century or the early fifth.) Cf. VI.vi above, *ad init.*, for the reflections of Dio Chrysostom on the fact that a monarch (such as the Roman emperor) is ἀνυπεύθυνος.

12. This subject is well treated in brief by Jones, *AD* 50-4, and more recently it has been examined thoroughly by Hansen, in the valuable articles cited in II.iv n.18 above. For the elaborate procedure necessary in fourth-century Athens to alter fundamental laws, see C. Hignett, *A History of the Athenian Constitution to the End of the Fifth Century B.C.* (1952) 299-305. For Athens, against such passages as those referred to in II.iv n.21 above, see e.g. Aeschin. I.4 = III.6; Lyc., *C. Leocr.* 3-4; Dem. XXIV.5, 75-6 etc. (cited by Jones, *AD* 50-3). For the importance of *written* laws, enabling the poor to deal on terms of equality with the rich, see esp. Eur., *Suppl.* 433-7. I see no reason, by the way, why any Greek democrat should not have subscribed to the impassioned advocacy of the supremacy of the laws in Cic., *Pro Cluent.* 146.

13. Perhaps I should just mention here *Pol.* V.6, 1306ᵃ12-19, where Aristotle envisages a situation in which there is an inner ring within an oligarchical *politeuma*, to the members of which certain offices are reserved. A good example is the Ptolemaic constitution of Cyrene, for which see Section iii of this chapter and its n.8 below.

14. See Arist., *Pol.* III.9, 1280ᵃ22-32; VII.8, 1328ᵃ33 ff.

15. By far the best book I know on the history of ideas about property is Richard Schlatter, *Private Property. The History of an Idea* (1951). [*Ad Att.* I.xix.4 best reveals Cicero's attitude.]

16. The standard book in English on Greek mercenaries is H. W. Parke, *GMS = Greek Mercenary Soldiers from the Earliest Times to the Battle of Ipsus* (1933); and see also G. T. Griffith, *The Mercenaries of the Hellenistic World* (1935).

17. See the main text of II.iv, esp. the first part of the paragraph containing n.10.

18. See my *OPW* 37-43, 98-9, 144, 157, 160-1. I take this opportunity of mentioning a neglected source which provides an intriguing little picture of the stasis in some of the Aegean islands – in this case, Paros and Siphnos – in 394 and the years following: Isocr. XIX (*Aegin.*) 18-20, 38-9.

(This speech is the only genuine one we possess from the Classical period which was actually written for delivery to a court or assembly outside Athens, apart from Ps.-Herodes, *Peri politeias*, mentioned in my *OPW* 35 n.65, if indeed that speech is not just a literary composition.)

19. See esp. Tod, *SGHI* II.100, with its notes, giving the literary material and much bibliography. (There is an Eng. trans. by Austin and Vidal-Naquet, *ESHAG* 271-3, no.70.) Add *IG* II².2403; and *SEG* XII (1955) 84 = Daphne Hereward, 'New fragments of *IG* II².10', in *BSA* 47 (1952) 102-117.

20. Lys. VII.10 (from the 390s) shows a piece of land in Attica let out to a freedman, Alcias, at the turn of the century. In Lys. XII.8 ff. (esp. 18-19) Lysias and his brother Polemarchus, both metics, are in possession of three houses, one containing a large workshop. The dialogue in Plato's *Republic* takes place at the house of Polemarchus in the Peiraeus: see *Rep.* I.328b.

21. An important reason for this (perhaps indeed the principal reason, although modern scholars seldom notice it) was that if a citizen held an office in which state funds passed through his hands (as they did in many cases) it was thought desirable that he should have sufficient property to make it possible for any funds he embezzled to be recovered from him. The only magistracy for which we know that a necessary qualification was membership of the highest property-class, the Solonian Pentacosiomedimnoi, was that of the Treasurers of Athena (Arist., *Ath. Pol.* 8.1), who had charge of all the offerings made to the goddess, many of them in gold or silver.

22. There is an excellent and clear description of the democratic organisation of the deme in the Inaugural Lecture by R. J. Hopper at Sheffield University in 1957, *The Basis of the Athenian Democracy* (Sheffield, 1957) 14-19, with 23-4 nn.86-152. For the specialist, a very full account of the demes, tribes etc. is given by J. S. Traill, *The Political Organisation of Attica. A Study of the Demes, Trittyes and Phylai, and their Representation in the Athenian Council* = Hesp., Suppl. XIV (1975).

23. Sufficient information, with the necessary references, is given by Jones, *AD* 5-6 (with 136-7 nn.3-14), 17-18, 49-50 (with 145 nn.36-44), 80-1 (with 150 nn.19-23). On pay for magistrates, see M. H. Hansen, 'Misthos for magistrates in Classical Athens', in *Symbolae Osloenses* 54 (1979) 5-22.

24. Against Finley's assertion that political pay was given only by Athens, as a consequence of her empire, I adduced in my PPOA a whole series of passages from Aristotle's *Politics*, proving beyond doubt that in the fourth century B.C. political pay was not only given at Rhodes (specifically mentioned in *Pol.* V.5, 1304ᵇ27-31) but was a *characteristic* feature of Greek democracies; and I also showed that political pay continued at Rhodes into the Roman period and existed in Hellenistic times in at least one other city, Iasus. In his chapter on the Athenian empire in *Imperialism in the Ancient World*, ed. P. D. A. Garnsey and C. R. Whittaker (1978) 103-26, 306-10, Finley misconceives this evidence and tries to brush it aside. 'That Rhodes *occasionally* paid for some *offices* in the late fourth century and perhaps in the Hellenistic period [*sic*: Dio Chrysostom scarcely belongs to the Hellenistic period], and Hellenistic Iasos, too, and that Aristotle *made some general remarks* on the subject of pay in the *Politics*, completely misses the force of my argument', he says (310 n.53, my italics). Arguments flatly contradicted by the evidence are unimpressive, however much 'force' their authors may imagine them to have. That Aristotle 'made some general remarks on the subject of pay' is an ingenious under-statement of what Aristotle says, amounting to misrepresentation. In particular, as I showed in PPOA, Aristotle makes it perfectly clear in a whole series of passages that in his day political pay, *for Assembly and courts*, was characteristic of what he sometimes calls 'extreme' demo-cracies (cf. II.iv and its n.19 above): '*many*', he says, had already been overturned by the unfortunate methods they had been driven to adopt in order to provide the necessary funds, and so on; at least two passages do not reflect the situation at Athens. (My point remains valid even if we regard 'many' as a probable exaggeration and prefer to think in terms of 'some'.) Moreover, since in PPOA I tried not to be too severe on Finley's mistake, I did not emphasise, as perhaps I should have done, that one of the two *major* types of political pay at Athens, that for attending the Assembly, was *first introduced* only after the fall of the empire, and was subsequently increased several times. Attacking Jones (*AD* 5-10), Finley says that he 'tried to falsify' the proposition Finley himself supports 'by pointing to the *survival* of pay for *office* after the loss of empire, and he has been gleefully quoted by scores of writers' (ibid. 310 n.54, my italics). This is inexcusably misleading. Finley suppresses the force of Jones's argument when he speaks of him as pointing to the *survival* of pay after the loss of empire: Jones's actual words

(*AD* 5) refer not to 'survival' but to '*a new and important form* of pay, that for attendance in the Assembly' (cf. M. H. Hansen, in *GRBS* 17 [1976], at 133). To represent Jones as speaking of 'survival' is disingenuous – but of course it is essential to Finley's argument, in the second half of his n.54, that there should be mere 'survival'. Incidentally, Finley speaks again and again of 'pay for *office*' (four times, ibid. 122 and 310 nn.53–4) and of nothing else. But pay for what is usually meant by 'office' was relatively unimportant (see Hansen, as cited in n.23 above): what mattered was pay for attending the courts and Assembly, and the Council. Athens may well have been the first Greek democracy to make this bold innovation, and her imperial revenues will of course have made the introduction of pay for courts and Council less of a burden than it would otherwise have been; but it is certain both that she herself, after the fall of her empire (when she was in a relatively much worse financial position), continued the existing forms of political pay and introduced a major new one (for attending the Assembly), and that a number of other democracies followed her example, at any rate in the fourth century.

25. A recent work on this subject is W. R. Connor, *The New Politicians of Fifth-Century Athens* (1971). It is astonishing to find Claude Mossé repeating the contemporary allegations that 'Cléon est tanneur, Hyperbolos, fabricant de lampes, Cléophon, luthier', without contradicting them (in Édouard Will, Claude Mossé and Paul Goukowsky, *Le Monde grec et l'Orient, II. Le IVe siècle et l'époque hellénistique* [Paris 1975] 105).

26. I need not discuss the Athenian empire in this book, as I have already expressed my views about it in *OPW* 34–49 (also 298–307, 308, 60 with 315-17); cf. my CAE and NJAE. The 'standard work' on the empire is now Russell Meiggs, *AE* = *The Athenian Empire* (1972), a major book of well over 600 pages. I have seen only one more recent book on the subject: Wolfgang Schuller, *Die Herrschaft der Athener im Ersten Attischen Seebund* (Berlin/New York, 1974). On this I should perhaps record the judgment of D. M. Lewis, in his review in *CR* 91 = n.s.27 (1977) 299-300: 'I have learnt virtually nothing from it, and he very seldom comes to a different conclusion on an issue from that already reached by Meiggs.' Schuller's subsequent (and quite short) monograph, *Die Stadt als Tyrann – Athens Herrschaft über seine Bundesgenossen* (Konstanz, 1978), seems to me to have mainly bibliographical value. A great deal that has been written against the position I have adopted rests either upon misrepresentation (usually quite innocent) of the little evidence we have or upon dismissal or suppression of it. There is a nice example of the former tendency in a recent article, 'The commons at Mytilene', in *Historia* 25 (1976) 429–40, by H. D. Westlake, a scholar who has made several useful contributions to fifth-century history. In *OPW* 40-1 I emphasised that in the case of Mytilene in 427, as in many others, we can see 'a marked difference of attitude towards the imperial city between the ruling Few and the mass of lower-class citizens'. Commenting on the mutiny of the Mytilenaean demos (in Thuc. III.27.2 to 28.1), I pointed out that 'it would be very simple-minded to interpret their one immediate demand (for a general distribution of the little remaining food) as the sum total of what they wanted. The fact that the Mytilenaean oligarchs did not see fit to comply with their very reasonable request but incontinently surrendered at discretion . . . is a sufficient indication that they took the first demand of the demos at more than its face value, and realised that the lower classes could not be relied upon to fight, even if that first demand were met.' Westlake, who otherwise ignores what I have written about the revolt, does refer briefly at one point to the first sentence I have just quoted about the mutiny from *OPW* (suppressing the second, which explains and justifies it); but he blandly dismisses it with the words, '*According to Thucydides*, they rose because they were hungry' (432 & n.12, my italics). In reality, that the demos took the step they did *because they were hungry* is precisely what Thucydides does *not* say, although of course he could easily have done so, had it been a fact! (cf. only III.27.1). What he does say is that the demos *told the men in power* that they wanted the remaining corn to be shared out among everyone, *or else* they would themselves come to terms with Athens and hand over the city. Westlake's misquotation of Thucydides (for that is what it is) begs the essential question at issue: it assumes gratuitously that what I would see as a perfectly natural *first move* on the part of the demos represented its *sole objective*. Now the demos, which could have had no earlier opportunity to organise itself, had just become able to act in concert (note the κατὰ συλλόγους in 27.3) for the first time. It very sensibly put forward two alternative demands, surely representing the main objectives of two groups: those who were mainly concerned about their own hunger, and those who actually desired a surrender to Athens. The narrative of Thucydides gives a clear indication that it was the second group that really mattered. We can be sure of this, for two different reasons. First, the ultimatum of the

demos did not just say, as one might have expected, 'Divide up the food, *or we won't fight*'; the alternative was very much stronger: '*or we shall betray the city*'. And secondly, the oligarchs could perfectly well have solved the immediate problem by complying with the first alternative (a very reasonable one in itself, as the demos were now being asked to fight), had they not realised, as they evidently did, that the initial demand was only an opening move, and that it was the second alternative alone which would satisfy the dominant section of the demos. Confronted with two alternatives, they did not comply, as they could have done, with the *far less unpleasant* first one; they realised they had to accept the second alternative, terrifying as it was to their leading members (28.1). It does seem to me 'simple-minded' not to recognise that this is exactly what Thucydides intended to convey: I find no ambiguity in it. In *OPW* I was concerned to make the valid point that on this occasion (as on so many others we know about) 'there were two distinct groups, with two very different attitudes to revolt: one was determinedly hostile to Athens, the other uninterested in fighting for a "freedom" which would benefit not themselves but their rulers' (cf. II.iv above). Westlake has pointed out that there are several cases in which Thucydides 'omits to provide any clear guidance on a question of some substance': his favoured explanation is a lack of information on Thucydides' part. So it may often be, and so it may be even in this case. But Thucydides' silences are sometimes due to his justifiably assuming in his contemporary readers knowledge which may not always be immediately apparent to everyone nowadays. (An excellent example of this is his failure to specify the Peloponnesian route into Attica in 431, on which see my *OPW* 7 n.7.) Thucydides shows throughout his work an awareness of the cleavage within many cities of the Athenian empire between upper classes who were deeply opposed to Athenian dominance and others who either preferred it (mainly, I believe, because of the democracy it might make possible for them) or were at least indifferent about it and disinclined to resist it. He knew perfectly well that this was common knowledge among the educated Greeks of his day, who would not need to have the situation spelt out for them on every occasion. He could well afford, therefore, to make Cleon give what his readers would perceive as a misrepresentation of the facts about Mytilene (III.39.6), since he had sufficiently countered Cleon's statement in advance (27.2 to 28.1) and was to reinforce his narrative with an even more explicit passage in the speech of Diodotus (47.2-3). I must add that Westlake's article is at least very much better than those of Bradeen, Legon and Quinn, to which he refers in his nn.1, 12 etc. The best treatment of the revolt of Mytilene is still that of Gillis, cited in *OPW* 34 n.64, 40 n.77. [It seems convenient to add a reference here to a very courageous and thought-provoking article by Gillis, which I saw only after this section was finished: 'Murder on Melos', in *Istituto Lombardo (Rend. Lett.)* 112 (1978) 185-211.]

27. Sir Moses Finley, in his disappointing chapter (5), 'The fifth-century Athenian Empire: a balance-sheet', in *Imperialism in the Ancient World*, ed. P. D. A. Garnsey and C. R. Whittaker (1978) 103-26, says, 'The puzzle is that we are unable to specify how the upper classes could have been the chief beneficiaries. Apart from the acquisition of property in subject territories, I can think of nothing other than negative benefits' (123): he seems to have in mind principally freedom from high taxation. But here, as so often, a glance at the fourth-century evidence can be illuminating. For example, (1) Aeschin. I.107 alleges that Timarchus had secured the post of archon in Andros (doubtless during the 'Social War' of 357-5) by means of a bribe of 30 minae, a sum which he had borrowed at 18 per cent. This may of course be a baseless slander, but it suggests that the Athenian archon of a large island even in the mid-fourth century (when Athenians could hardly 'throw their weight about' as much as in the fifth) might expect to make a substantial profit, and that a jury would not think it unreasonable if this were estimated at well over half a talent. And (2) in Tod, *SGHI* II.152, Androtion (the Atthidographer and politician), who had been Athenian archon of Arcesine on Amorgos during the same war, gains the valuable privilege of becoming hereditary Athenian proxenos of Arcesine, a post which might be both financially lucrative and politically advantageous: see esp. S. Perlman, 'A note on the political implications of Proxenia in the fourth century B.C.', in *CQ* 52 = n.s.8 (1958) 185-91. This was his reward for lending Arcesine money, free of interest, with which to pay the garrison (almost certainly voted, incidentally, by the allied *synedrion*: see lines 24-5, with 156, lines 9-12). Other Athenian governors and phrourarchs, in the fifth century as well as the fourth, may well have taken the opportunity to lend money to the cities they governed, at a handsome rate of interest. Androtion had also 'not made a nuisance of himself to citizens or visiting foreigners': this was unusual enough to attract comment, and reward! I must add that

what Thuc. VIII.48.6 has in mind is evidently in particular (because of the words ποριστὰς ὄντας καὶ ἐσηγητὰς τῶν κακῶν τῷ δήμῳ) motions proposed and carried in the Assembly by the καλοὶ κἀγαθοί he is making Phrynichus refer to – surely including such things as appointments of each other as archons, phrourarchs, ambassadors etc. This makes it unlikely that 'the acquisition of property in subject territories' referred to by Finley (see the beginning of this note) was *in Thucydides' mind* when he wrote VIII.48.6. But of course such acquisitions may nevertheless have greatly benefited individual Athenians. (Here I hold to the suggestions I made in *OPW*, in spite of the comments of Finley, op. cit. 308 n.37, who gives a false page reference to that book: 245 instead of 43–4.) Since the list in 'Table B: property abroad sold by Poletai' by W. K. Pritchett in *Hesp.* 25 (1956) 271 is necessarily incomplete, I give here for convenience a list of all the passages concerned that I have been able to identify in the 'Attic Stelai' published by Pritchett in *Hesperia* 22 (1953) 240–92: Stelai nos. II.177-9, 311-14; IV.17-21/2; VI.53-6, 133; VII.78; VIII.3-5, 5-7 and probably 8-9; X.10-11 and conceivably also 33-6. The quantity of property on Euboea owned by proscribed Athenians, at Lelanton, Diros, and Geraistos (II.177-9, 311-14; IV.17-21/2), mostly by Oionias son of Oionochares of Atene, may be due to the *epigamia* between Athens and Euboea mentioned by Lys. XXXIV.3. Other items of property outside Attica, belonging to the proscribed, were at Abydos, Ophryneion, Thasos and Oropus.

28. See Plut., *Arist.* 13 (480-79); Thuc. I.107.4 (458 or 457); Arist., *Ath. Pol.* 25.4 and other sources (462/1). The conspiracy of 480-79 will be dealt with by David Harvey, 'The conspiracy of Agasias and Aischines', an article to be published shortly in *Phoenix*. (I am grateful to him for kindly allowing me to read a draft of this paper before publication.)

29. This is made clear by Arist., *Pol.* V.4, 1304ᵇ7 ff., esp. 11-15, a passage which is all the more important in that the account in Aristotle's *Ath. pol.* 29-33 is totally different. The *Politics* passage, treating the case of the Four Hundred as a classic example of revolution procured by deceit and maintained by force, is surely based upon Thucydides (whom Aristotle never once quotes by name but had of course read; cf. my AHP), for although Thucydides does not say in so many words that Peisander & Co. did not reveal, on their return to Athens in the spring of 411, that they knew there was now no hope of obtaining money for the war from the King and Pharnabazus and Tissaphernes, Alcibiades having proved to be a broken reed, he clearly takes this for granted, also that the existence of the Spartan-Persian treaty concluded in about April 411 (VIII.58) was not known at Athens. The *Ath. pol.* account, on the other hand, has only a brief mention (in 29.1) of an Athenian expectation 'that the King would fight with them rather [than the Spartans], if they put their constitution into the hands of a few'. I would suppose that it was reading the speech of Antiphon in his own defence (so much admired by Thucydides: see VIII.68.1-2) and/or the *Atthis* of Androtion (son of Andron, a leading member of the Four Hundred) which made Aristotle change his mind about the coming to power of the Four Hundred. (The belief that Alcibiades might be able to swing Persian financial assistance over to the Athenian side was evidently by no means as foolish at the time as it may now appear to us, for even the highly intelligent Thrasybulus held it: see Thuc. VIII.81.1; and cf. 52, lines 29-30 *OCT*, where Thucydides represents Tissaphernes as very ready to be persuaded by Alcibiades to become the friend of Athens.)

30. This is indeed a cardinal fact. I did not bring it out sufficiently in my CFT, the argument of which it supports. (It is also very damaging to the theory of Rhodes, mentioned below, as I shall explain.) There are two vitally important passages in the admirable account, in Thuc. VIII.53-4, of the Assembly to which Peisander presented his proposals on the first of his two visits to Athens in 412-11: the one in (probably) January 411. In 53.3 Thucydides makes Peisander speak of 'a more moderate form of constitution' and 'committing to a few the offices' (the ἀρχαί) – not, I would point out, the franchise. Thucydides then represents Peisander as saying that 'Later on it will be *possible for us to change back again*, if we are not completely satisfied' (53.3 still); and in 54.1, speaking in his own person, Thucydides says that the demos, although at first they did not at all like what was proposed about an oligarchy, nevertheless gave in eventually, being assured by Peisander that there was no other means of salvation, 'and being in a state of fear, and at the same time expecting too that there would be *a change back again*'. The μεταθέσθαι in 53.3 and μεταβαλεῖται in 54.1 show that the Athenian masses imagined that if things went badly they would be able to vote the democracy back into existence again: they failed to realise that the oligarchs' plan was to deprive them of the franchise altogether – as happened at Colonus: Thuc. VIII.67.3, with Arist., *Ath. Pol.* 29.5. In

fact it took another revolution to get rid of the Four Hundred, in which 'many of those from Peiraeus' played a part, with the bulk of the hoplites: see my CFT 9. P. J. Rhodes, 'The Five Thousand in the Athenian revolutions of 411 B.C.', in *JHS* 92 (1972) 115-27, at 121 and 123-4, prefers his own fancies to the narrative of Thucydides: he suggests that Thucydides 'ought not to be regarded as infallible', that Thucydides 'may have been wrong' – and of course Thucydides *has* to be very wrong if Rhodes's picture is to stand. Given the choice between Thucydides and Rhodes, we must unhesitatingly prefer Thucydides. It is a pity that Rhodes paid no attention at all to the passages I have emphasised in Thuc. VIII.53-4, which show clearly the mood of the demos at the beginning of the events in 411, seen again in the narrative in VIII.92.4-11, 93, 97.1. I would again emphasise that in the decisive episode in the struggle against the oligarchs, namely the destruction of the wall at Eëtioneia, 'the hoplites and many of those from the Peiraeus' quite naturally spoke of their objective as the coming to power of the Five Thousand rather than full democracy simply from prudence and the fear that 'the Five Thousand' (still unknown and actually non-existent) might be able to take power and frustrate them (92.10-11). They were 'afraid', says Thucydides (92.11, line 7 OCT), 'that the Five Thousand really existed' and that anyone they spoke to might be a member of that body. Thucydides evidently had no doubt that those who were resisting the Four Hundred, or at any rate the great bulk of them, had no hankering for another oligarchy, even if it consisted of 5,000 and was therefore more broadly based than the existing narrow oligarchy of the Four Hundred.

31. See my CFT. In the preceding note I have mentioned one reason why the attempt of Rhodes to substitute a different picture for that of Thucydides is a failure. I may be able to deal with the subject elsewhere rather more fully. Here I will only add that there is a patent fallacy in Rhodes's attempt to explain away Thuc. VIII.97.2. He admits (122) that I am right in saying that 'in contexts of this kind the Many are not any kind of numerical majority but specifically the lower classes' (cf. II.iv above); but he then tries at once to evade the disastrous consequences of this admission. Although he rejects my general interpretation, he carefully refrains from giving his own translation of VIII.97.2; and he ends up with a curious picture of a constitution having 'one feature characteristic of constitutions giving power to the Few' (in that there was, as he thinks, 'a property qualification for active citizenship': the hoplite census), and 'one characteristic of constitutions giving power to the Many', which he proceeds to identify as '*real sovereignty* in the hands of the assembly rather than the *boulē*' (123, my italics). This reveals the fatal weakness in Rhodes's position. The first feature, the 'characteristic of constitutions giving power to the Few' (that is, the alleged property qualification for the exercise of political rights), would be perfectly all right, if it were a fact. (Of course I do not believe there was a property qualification *for the franchise itself*, the exercise of bare political rights, although I agree that being at least a hoplite was a qualification for exercising *effective day-to-day control* of the operation of the political system, of τὰ πράγματα: Thuc. VIII.97.1.) But Rhodes's 'characteristic of constitutions giving power to the Many' is completely bogus in this context. The vital fact, which wrecks his interpretation (but is liable to escape anyone who does not scrutinise the argument carefully), is that the Assembly, on the 'real sovereignty' of which he lays stress, is, on his picture, a straight *oligarchic* Assembly, *completely excluding all the Thetes* who on any interpretation (even his own) must form at least the bulk of the Many! In reality, then, on his interpretation, the Many (or at any rate the bulk of the Many) get *nothing whatever*. Of course, it could be said that an oligarchy which allows all the oligarchs some say is 'more democratic', at least in a Pickwickian sense, than one which sets up a *boulē* (like the Four Hundred) as an all-powerful minority ruling within the *politeuma*. But this involves a refusal to think in terms of Thucydides' Few and Many, and a determination to substitute different categories: oligarchy and democracy, which of course Thucydides might have used in 97.2, but did not. There is much more to be said on this question, in particular about the significance of the word σύγκρασις; but this must wait for another occasion.

32. See my OPW 144, 157, 343. The decisive passage, showing that Lysander was able to force the Athenians to set up the Thirty by threatening to punish them (doubtless by mass enslavement) for breaking the peace terms, by not pulling down the Long Walls and the Peiraeus walls in time, is Lys. XII.71-6, esp. 74; and cf. OPW 157 n.180.

33. Paul Cloché, *La restauration démocratique à Athènes en 403 avant J.-C.* (Paris, 1915).

34. See Arist., *Ath. pol.* 40.3; Lys. XII.59; Xen., *HG* II.iv.28; Isocr. VII.68; Dem. XX.11-12. The matter is discussed by Cloché, op. cit. 379-83.

35. It was only after this chapter was finished that there appeared an account of Philip II which must now rank as the best and most useful over all, by G. T. Griffith, in N. G. L. Hammond and Griffith, *A History of Macedonia, II. 550-336 B.C.* (1979) 201-646, 675 ff. Griffith was not able to take account of two earlier books: J. R. Ellis, *Philip II and Macedonian Imperialism* (1976), which retains some value, and G. L. Cawkwell, *Philip of Macedon* (1978), representing a point of view very different from my own. The best book on the Second Athenian Confederacy is Silvio Accame, *La lega ateniese del sec. IV a.C.* (Rome, 1941). By far the best recent discussion of the Confederacy is the article by G. T. Griffith, 'Athens in the fourth century', in *Imperialism in the Ancient World* (for which see n.27 above) 127-44 (with the notes, 310-14): this is less inclined than most modern treatments to judge Athens by standards much harsher than those applied to other Greek states (cf. my *OPW* 33-4). For the events that occurred during this period, F. H. Marshall, *The Second Athenian Confederacy* (1905), although out of date, is still of some use, especially if read with Tod, *SGHI* II.

36. I cannot discuss this here, but I may say that I believe it was the appearance of Philip in October 352 at Heraion Teichos (Dem. III.4) that made Demosthenes realise how dangerous he could be to Athens, for he was now much farther to the East than he is known to have taken an army earlier, and he could be seen as a threat to the two bottle-necks on the Athenian corn-route from the Crimea: the Dardanelles and the Bosphorus (see my *OPW* 48). That Demosthenes had not sufficiently recognised the danger of Philip earlier is evident from his speech XXIII, which in its present form seems to date from 353/2.

37. The following is the list of passages concerned. A few of the most important are italicised. (1) B.C. 389-8 (Thrasybulus in the eastern Aegean): Xen., *HG* IV.viii.27-31; Diod. XIV.94.2; 99.4; Lys. XXVIII.1-8,11,12,17; cf. XXIX.1-2,4,9; XIX.11; and cf. Tod, *SGHI* II.114.7-8; *IG* II².24A.3-5; Dem. XX.60. (2) B.C. 375-4 (Timotheus at Corcyra): Xen., *HG* V.iv.66 (cf. VI.ii.1); Isocr. XV. *108-9*; Ps.-Arist., *Oecon.* II.ii.23b, 1350ª30-ᵇ4. (3) B.C. 373 (Timotheus' second Periplous): Xen., *HG* VI.ii.11-12; Ps.-Dem. XLIX.6-8, 9-21 (esp. *9-12, 13, 14-15*). (4) B.C. 373-2 (Iphicrates at Corcyra): Xen., *HG* VI.ii.37 (in spite of 60 talents booty: Diod. XV. 47.7; cf. Xen., *HG* VI.ii.36); cf. Polyaen. III.ix.55 (and 30?). (5) B.C. 366-4 (Timotheus at Samos and in the Hellespont and north Aegean): Isocr. XV. *111-13*; Ps.-Arist., *Oecon.* II.ii.23a, 1350ª23-30; Polyaen. III.x.9, 10 (Samos), 14 and perhaps 1 (Olynthus); Nepos, *Timoth.* 1-2. (6) B.C. 362, September, to 360, February (Apollodorus' trierarchy): Ps.-Dem. L.*7-18, 23-5*, 35-6, *53*, *55-6*. (7) B.C. 356-5 (Chares and Artabazus): Diod. XVI.*22.1-2*, with Plut., *Arat.* 16.3; *FGrH* 105.4; Schol. Dem. IV.19 and III.31; Dem. IV.24; II.28; Aeschin. II.70-3; Isocr. VII.8-10; cf. Dem. XIX.332. (8) B.C. 342-1 (Diopeithes at the Hellespont): Dem. VIII.8-9, 19, *21-8*, 46-7; Ps.-Dem. XII.3. (9) General: Dem. III.20; XVIII.114; XXIII.61, 171; Aeschin. II.71; Xen., *Mem.* III.iv.5.

38. See Rostovtzeff, *SEHHW* I, ch.ii, esp. 92-4, with the notes, III.1327-8 nn.23-6.

39. See Rostovtzeff, *SEHHW* I.94 ff., esp. 104-25, with the notes, III.1328-37 nn.27 ff.

40. Claude Mossé, *La Fin de la démocratie athénienne* (Paris, 1962) 123-32, esp. 127-8. The theory is criticised by Austin and Vidal-Naquet, *ESHAG* 141, but not quite fairly, for Rostovtzeff's evidence is not confined almost entirely, as these authors imply, to pottery: it includes also coins, jewellery, metal-work, tiles, textiles, wine and olive oil.

41. See Parke, *GMS* 227, who very plausibly estimates that 'between 399 and 375 B.C. there were never less than 25,000 mercenaries in service, and later the average number must have remained about 50,000'.

42. See esp. Isocr. IV.146, 168; V.120-3; VIII.24; and cf. the preceding note.

43. Plato, *Laws* I.630b; cf. the next note (44).

44. Isocr. VIII.43-6; cf. V.120-1; *Epist.* IX (*Ad Archid.*) 8-10; Dem. IV.24; XXIII.139.

45. For the social roots of Isocrates' whole attitude, see further on in the main text above and n.53 below.

46. First, the *Olympic Oration* of Gorgias, on *Homonoia*: see Diels-Kranz, *FVS*⁵⁻⁸ II no.82, A 1 § 4 (from Philostr., *VS* I.9), and B 8a. This speech is probably to be dated 392: see Beloch, *GG* III².i.521 & n.3. In an *Epitaphios* delivered at Athens, Gorgias also asserted that 'victories over barbarians demand hymns, but over Greeks, dirges', and stressed Athens' victories over the Persians: *FVS*⁵⁻⁸ II. no.82, A 1 § 5 (from Philostr., ibid.), and B 5b. Secondly, Lys. XXXIII (esp. §§ 6, 8-9), which is dated 388 by Diod. XIV.109.3, but is more probably of 384: see Grote, HG VIII.70, 72 n.2; IX.34 n.1. Isocrates took up this theme in 380, and returned to it again and again until his death in 338. At first, in 380, he wanted Athens and Sparta jointly to

lead the crusade (IV, esp. 3, 15-16, 173-4, 182, 185). In the late 370s he may have had hopes of Jason of Pherae (see V.119; cf. Xen., *HG* VI.i.12). In *c.* 368 he appealed to Dionysius I of Syracuse (*Epist.* I, esp. 7), and in *c.* 356 to King Archidamus III of Sparta (*Epist.* IX, esp. 8-10, 17-19). From 346 onwards he concentrated on King Philip II of Macedon: from that year comes his *Orat.* V (see esp. 9, 12-16, 30-1, 95-7, 120-3, 126, 130); in 342 he wrote his *Epist.* II (see esp. 11), and in 338 *Epist.* III (see esp. 5). Cf. Isocr. XII.163.

47. The best treatment of these events is still G. T. Griffith, 'The union of Corinth and Argos (392-386 B.C.)', in *Historia* 1 (1950) 236-56. More recent articles have added nothing of real value.

47a. At the end of 1979, after this chapter was finished, there appeared what is now the best book on early Sparta: Paul Cartledge, *Sparta and Lakonia. A Regional History 1300-362 BC.*

48. See e.g. Xen., *HG* IV.viii.20; VI.iii.14; VII.i.44; cf. Diod. XV.45.1 etc. For particular examples, see e.g. Xen., *HG* III.iv.7; V.i.34; ii.7, 36; iv.46; VI.iii.8; iv.18; VII.i.43; Diod.XV.40.1-5; 45.2-4; 46.1-3 etc.

49. R. P. Legon, 'Phliasian politics and policy in the early fourth century', in *Historia* 16 (1967) 324-37, at 335-7. Legon simply assumes, without the least justification, that 'the citizens' (οἱ πολῖται) thrice mentioned by Xenophon (*HG* VII.ii.7-8) as successfully repelling an attack by democratic exiles and their allies in 369, were the whole body of Phliasians, whereas of course there is no need to suppose that they were anything but the oligarchic body who were now the only 'citizens' in the full sense (the *politeuma*), set up as a result of the Spartan King Agesilaus' intervention some ten years earlier (cf. Legon, op. cit. 332-4). The oligarchs alone would be armed as hoplites, and they must have numbered over 1,000 (see Xen., *HG* V.iii.17) – more than enough to cope with the small invading force of *c.* 600, even though these were aided (VII.ii.5) by 'traitors' inside the city. I may add that the most recent treatment I have seen of Phliasian politics, namely L. Piccirilli, 'Fliunte e il presunto colpo di stato democratico', in *ASNP³* 4 (1974) 57-70, does not deal with the events of 369, but has a useful bibliography on early fourth-century Phlius.

50. For the evidence concerning Clearchus, see S. M. Burstein, *Outpost of Hellenism: The Emergence of Heraclea on the Black Sea* = *Univ. of California Publications: Class. Stud.* 14 (1976) 47 ff., esp. 49-65 (with 127-34). Among earlier accounts, see T. Lenschau, in *RE* XI.i (1921) 577-9; Helmut Berve, *Die Tyrannis bei den Griechen* (Munich, 1967) I.315-18; II.679-81; Glotz-Cohen, *HG* IV.i.17-19. See also Jacoby, *FGrH* III b (Kommentar, 1955), on the fragments of Memnon, his no.434.

51. Xen., *HG* VII.i.44-6; ii.11-15; iii.2-12; Diod. XV.70.3.

52. *IG* II².448 = *SIG³* 310 (323/2 B.C.) + 317 (318/17 B.C.): see esp. *SIG³* 310 n.7.

53. Isocrates was trierarch at most three times, apparently on each occasion jointly with his son: Isocr. XV.145. See Davies, *APF* 245-8. The two most illuminating treatments of Isocrates in any language are those of Baynes, *BSOE* 144-67; and Minor M. Markle, 'Support of Athenian intellectuals for Philip', in *JHS* 96 (1976) 80-99. See also Fuks, *ISESG.*

54. See, however, Thuc. V.4.2-3 (Leontini, *c.* 422 B.C.).

55. I know of no really satisfactory general treatment of this subject. A. Passerini, 'Riforme sociali e divisioni di beni nella Grecia del IV sec. a.C', in *Athen.* 8 (1930) 273-98, is useful only as a collection of material; cf. his 'I moti politico-sociali della Grecia e i Romani', in *Athen.* 11 (1933) 309-35, where again the interpretation given to some of the sources utilised can be very faulty. There are two good general collections of evidence by David Asheri: *LGPD* and *Distribuzioni di terre nell'antica Grecia* (= *Mem. dell'Accad. delle Scienze di Torino*, ser. IV.10, Turin, 1966). Among the interesting fourth-century texts mentioning both redistribution of land and cancellation of debts are Dem. XXIV.149 (the Athenian heliastic oath); Plato., *Rep.* VIII.565e-6a, 566e; *Laws* III.684de; V.736cd; Isocr. XII.258-9; and Ps.-Dem. XVII.15 (cited in the main text above, at the end of the paragraph following the one from which this note comes). I must not step aside to list the later sources here, but I should like to mention Justin XVI.iv.2 ff. (see above and n.50), and the 'oath of Itanos' in Crete, *SIG³* 526 = *IC* III.iv.8 (see lines 21-4), of the early third century. As late as the Flavian period Dio Chrysostom could congratulate the Rhodians because their laws provided for the most stringent penalties against both the practices I have been mentioning (XXXI.70). For the redistribution of land, see for the fourth century Aristotle, *Pol.* V.8, 1309ᵃ14-17; cf. III.10, 1281ᵃ14-24; V.5, 1305ᵃ5-7; VI.3, 1318ᵃ24-6; *Ath. pol.* 40.3; Ps.-Arist., *Rhet. ad Alex.* (= Anaximenes, *Ars Rhet.*) 2.17, 1424ᵃ31-5; *SIG³* 141.10-11 (from Corcyra Melaina/Nigra). The best-attested cancellation of debts since Solon's, that in 243 B.C. by King Agis IV of Sparta, has recently been discussed by Benjamin

Shimron, *Late Sparta. The Spartan Revolution 243-146 B.C.* (= *Arethusa Monographs* 3, Buffalo, N.Y., 1972), esp. 9-26. Plut., *Cleom.* 17.5 is particularly significant for its mention of the hopes of distribution of land and cancellation of debts raised (and disappointed) in other parts of the Peloponnese by the campaigns of Agis' successor, Cleomenes III, in the 220s. And see Section iii of this chapter and its n.14 for the revolution at Dyme in Achaea in the late second century, and one or two later attempts to destroy evidence of indebtedness by the burning of public archives.

56. Xen., *HG* VII.iii.1. There is quite a good Eng. trans. in the Loeb edition (1923), and a critical edition, *Aeneas on Siegecraft*, by L. W. Hunter, rev. S. A. Handford (1927, with text and commentary; and see the Introduction, pp.ix-xxxvii). See also H. Bengtson, 'Die griechische Polis bei Aeneas Tacticus', in *Historia* 11 (1962) 458-68. In my opinion, the work was most probably written in the early 350s.

57. Aen. Tact. I.3, 6-7; II.1, 7-8; III.3; V.1, 2; X.3, 5-6, 15, 20, 25-6; XI.1-2 (with 3-6, 7-10, 10a-11, 13-15); XIV.1-2; XVII..1 (with 2-4, 5); XVIII.2 ff., 8 ff.; XXII.5-7, 10, 15-18, 19, 20, 21; XXIII.6, 7-11; XXVIII.5; XXIX.3-4 ff.; XXX.1-2. Among other works providing evidence of a similar situation in the fourth century, see Isocr. VI (*Archid.*) 64-8. esp. 67 (dating from *c.* 366).

58. Demosthenes habitually attacks his opponents at Athens and elsewhere, sometimes with justice and sometimes not, as having been bribed by Philip II. Among the passages in question, see I.5; V.6-8; VI.29-36; XIX.10-13, 94, 114, 139, 145, 167-8, 207, 222-3, 229-33, 259-62, 265-8, 294-5, 305-6, 329 etc.; IX 54, 56; XVIII.21, 33-6, 41, 45-8, 50-2, 61, 132-3, 136-7, 295 etc. The reply of Polyb. XVIII.xiii.1 to xv.4 is particularly interesting.

59. See e.g. *Hell. Oxy.* VII[II].2,5.

60. For the relationship, see Davies, *APF* 332-4.

61. Sparta was deliberately excluded. See Arr., *Anab.* I.i.2 and the very significant words of Alexander's dedication to Athena of the spoils of the Granicus in ibid. xvi.7; and cf. my *OPW* 164-6.

62. Cf. what happened at Ambracia (Diod. XVII.3.3 etc.), Elis (Dem. XIX.260, 294; IX.27; Paus. IV.28.4-6; V.4.9; Diod. XVI.63.4-5), and Eretria and Oreus in Euboea (Dem. IX.12, 33, 57-62, 65-6; XVIII.71, 79; Diod. XVI.74.1). In Dem. IX.61, ὁ δῆμος ὁ τῶν Ὠρειτῶν must not be taken to refer to 'the democratic party' at Oreus: it is the technical expression for the [democratic] State of Oreus.

[V.iii]

1. See e.g. Isocr. VII.12, 14-15, 16-18, 20-8, 31-5, 37-42, 44-5, 48-9, 51-5, 57, 60-1, 70, 83; VIII.13-14, 36-7, 50-6, 64, 75-6, 122-31, 133. Among many other passages in Isocrates see e.g. XV.159-60 (quoted in V.ii above), also 232-5, 313-19.

2. I know of no up-to-date, thorough and illuminating account of the 'Lamian war' and its immediate consequences. Narratives can be found in Ferguson, *HA* 14-28; Glotz-Cohen, *HG* IV.i.266-75; A. W. Pickard-Cambridge, *Demosthenes* (1914) 473-86; Grote, *HG* X.247-66; and see Piero Treves, *Demostene e la libertà greca* (Bari, 1933) 173-98. More recent treatments, e.g. by Will, *HPMH* I.27-30, and Claude Mossé, *Athens in Decline 404-86 B.C.* (Eng. trans. by Jean Stewart, London/Boston, 1973) 96-101, are brief, and the latter does not even think it worth while to mention the very important class division inside Athens, where the propertied class (οἱ κτηματικοί) were against the war, while τὰ πλήθη (admitted to be the great majority, but represented of course as needing to be incited by demagogues, οἱ δημόκοποι!) were strongly in favour: see esp. Diod. XVIII.10.1; cf. §§ 2-4 for the decree 'giving effect to the impulses of οἱ δημοτικοί' but thought 'inexpedient' by οἱ συνέσει διαφέροντες, which speaks of the common freedom and security of all Hellas. See also Diod. XVIII.18.4 (in particular the statement that it was the poor, disfranchised by Antipater, who had been the ταραχώδεις καὶ πολεμικοί); 18.5, with Plut., *Phoc.* 27.5; 28.7 (the oligarchic constitution: Plutarch's 12,000 for the number of the disfranchised is generally, and probably rightly, preferred to Diodorus' 22,000, a figure which is often emended accordingly); and 66.5 to 67.6 for the bitter resentment of τὸ πλῆθος, ὁ ὄχλος, τὸ πλῆθος τῶν δημοτικῶν against Phocion and his associates in 318, during the temporary restoration of the democracy under the auspices of Polyperchon, while πολλοὶ τῶν σπουδαίων ἀνδρῶν openly sympathised with Phocion. For other evidence for the important role of Phocion (that Pétain-like figure) in the oligarchy of 322-318 and the hatred this had aroused

among the lower classes, see Plut., *Phoc.* 27.6,7 (it was simply the Macedonian *garrison* to which Phocion objected); 30.4,8; 32.1-3; 34.1 to 35.4. Some of the main sources for the Lamian war are given by Will, *HPMH* I.30: add in particular Suid., *s.v.* Demades (οὗτος κατέλυσε τὰ δικαστήρια), and *IG* II².448, esp. lines 43-5, 47, 52-6, 60-1, 62-4 = *SIG*³ 317, lines 9-11, 13, 18-22, 26-7, 28-30 (and cf. *SIG*³ 310, lines 8-13 = *IG* II².448, lines 7-12). There is nothing interesting in Dexippus, *FGrH* 100 F 32-6. It seems unlikely that many of the Athenians disfranchised in 322 accepted Antipater's offer to settle them in Thrace (Diod. XVIII.18.4; Plut., *Phoc.* 28.7, cf. 29.4; and see Ferguson, *HA* 26-7); but we hear that many Athenians – doubtless drawn from those disfranchised again in 317 – went to Cyrenaica to join in the abortive expedition of Ophellas in 309/8 (Diod. XX.40.6-7). I do not myself believe (with e.g. Jones, *AD* 31 and 142 n.50) that 2,000 dr. was the technical qualification for the Athenian hoplite/zeugite: I shall argue elsewhere that this was not expressed in fixed quantitative terms, in money. The view of Busolt-Swoboda, *GS* II.928 n.1, with 837-8, that the traditional qualification of the Athenian hoplite/zeugite was 1000 dr. is founded on a serious mis-understanding of Poll. VIII.130.

3. See Ferguson, *HA* 36-94 (esp., on the position of Demetrius, 47 & n.3); Will, *HPMH* I.43-5. An inscription of 186 B.C. from Seleucia in Pieria (*SEG* VII.62 = Welles, *RCHP* 45) provides the earliest known instance of a royal governor described as an ἐπιστάτης in a Greek city in the Seleucid area (line 24): see esp. M. Holleaux, in *BCH* 57 (1933) 6-67, repr. in his *Études d'épigr. et d'hist. grecques* III (Paris, 1942) 199-254, at 216-20 and 253-4.

4. The best account is the very brief one given by Jones, *GCAJ* 95-112. There is a vast bibliography in Magie, *RRAM* II.822 (n.10) ff. A useful work on the newly founded cities is by V. Tscherikower (elsewhere usually Tcherikover), as cited in III.iv n.43 above.

5. For the 'exiles decree', see E. Bikerman (elsewhere usually Bickerman), 'La lettre d'Alexandre le Grand aux bannis grecs', in *Mél. Radet* = *REA* 42 (1940) 25-35; J. P. V. D. Balsdon, 'The "divinity" of Alexander', in *Historia* 1 (1950) 363-88, at 383-8; E. Badian, 'Harpalus', in *JHS* 81 (1961) 16-43, at 25-31.

6. I find views such as those of Zancan, Lenschau, Tarn, Heuss and Magie (for which see Magie, *RRAM* II.825 ff., esp. 827-8) insufficiently realistic. Contrast the sensible picture in Jones, *GCAJ* 111-12, with 319 nn.29-30.

7. Claire Préaux, in *Recueils de la Soc. Jean Bodin* 6 (1954) 69-134, at 87, part of one of the best accounts of Alexander's relations with the Greek cities.

8. *SEG* IX.i.1, with XIII.616; XVII.793, XVIII.726; XX.713. See Jones, *CERP*² 355-6, with 495-6 n.9; and for further bibliography Will, *HPMH* I.34. The fullest discussion in English is by M. Cary, in *JHS* 48 (1928) 222-38.

9. See Fraser, *PA* I.93-6 (with II.173 n.3), also 54 and 70 (on the native Egyptian population), 96-8 (the magistrates), 98-101 (the working of the constitution), 112-15 (the courts). The evidence cited by Fraser conclusively refutes the view of Tarn (see e.g. *HC*³ 148, 145-6) that Alexander's newly founded Alexandrias were not proper Greek *poleis* but mere 'collections of *politeumata*' (cf. ibid. 157). I agree with Fraser's summing-up on early Ptolemaic Alexandria: 'Public institutions and administration of justice alike seem to have maintained the appearance which they had in an independent city-state: ecclesia, boule and dikasteria, the hallmarks of a democratic society, all existed, but all were dominated, indeed controlled by the Crown either directly through superior edicts, or indirectly by reason of the fact that Ptolemy was king, and the Alexandrians were his subjects' (I.115). For a detailed discussion of the situation at Antioch see Downey, *HAS* 112-15; but I myself see little reason to doubt the existence from the first, here and in most if not all the other dynastic foundations, of the normal institutions of a Greek city, even if royal control was ensured by the installation of a superintendent or governor, as for instance at Seleuceia in Pieria (*IGLS* 1183 = Welles, *RCHP* 45 = *SEG* VII.62) and Laodicea ad Mare (*IGLS* 1261). In the case of many new foundations by the kings which at their creation did not have dynastic names, we do not know for certain whether they were originally cities or mere military colonies (*katoikiai*), and here we should do well to follow the example of Rostovtzeff (*SEHHW* I.482; III.1437-8 n.268) and refrain from speculation about their con-stitutions (cf. Jones, *CERP*² 245-6).

10. See Tarn, *HC*³ 147, 157-8, 220-1; W. Ruppel, 'Politeuma', in *Philologus* 82 = n.F. 36 (1927) 268-312, 433-54.

11. The three inscriptions from Magnesia are in Otto Kern, *Inschr. von Magnesia am Maeander* (Berlin, 1900) 92.b.19; 94.14-15; and 92.a.14-16; the decree of Halicarnassus in the Coan

inscription is included in Michel, *RIG* 455, from *BCH* 5 (1881) 211-16 no. 6 = W. R. Paton and E. L. Hicks, *The Inscriptions of Cos* (1891) 13, lines 20-2. Lists of known Hellenistic inscriptions giving recorded votes can be found in the articles by Louis Robert, 'Nouvelles inscriptions d'Iasos', in *REA* 65 (1963) 298-329, at 304-7, and M. H. Hansen, 'How did the Athenian *ecclesia* vote?', in *GRBS* 18 (1977) 123-37, at 131-2; cf. also Busolt[-Swoboda], *GS* I.446 n.3. We have, by the way, little reliable information about actual voting numbers before the Hellenistic period, even at Athens, for which see *IG* II².1641B.30-3, and the literary sources given by Hansen, op. cit. 130-1. Hansen points out (130-2) that there is no clear evidence for votes being actually counted except where they were given by ballot.

12. See Magie, *RRAM* I.59, and II.839-40 n.24, with the works there cited, esp. L. Robert, 'Divinités éponymes', in *Hellenica* 2 (1946) 51-64.

13. For a very interesting specimen of Rome's most enthusiastic 'friends', in a much earlier period (*c.* 180 B.C.), namely Callicrates of Leontium, see Polyb. XXIV.viii-x, esp. viii.9 - ix.7 and x.3-5. Callicrates is very well treated by P. S. Derow, 'Polybios and the embassy of Kallikrates', in *Essays Presented to C. M. Bowra* (1970) 12-23.

14. I need do no more than refer to Alexander Fuks, 'Social revolution in Dyme in 116-114 B.C.E.', in *Scr. Hierosol.* 23 (1972) 21-7, who gives a full bibliography. The inscription is *SIG*³ II.684 = A/J 9 = Sherk, *RDGE* 43; there is an Eng. trans. in *ARS* 35, no.40. See also M. H. Crawford, 'Rome and the Greek world: economic relationships', in *Econ. Hist. Rev.*² 30 (1977) 42-52, at 45-6. Among other boasted burnings of archives, allegedly to destroy evidence of indebtedness, are those at Jerusalem in A.D. 66 (Jos., *BJ* II.425-7) and at Antioch in 70 (VII.55, 60-1: I agree with Downey, *HAS* 204-5, 586-7, against Kraeling).

15. Michael Woloch, 'Four leading families in Roman Athens (A.D. 96-161)', in *Historia* 18 (1969) 503-10; C. P. Jones, 'A leading family of Roman Thespiae', in *HSCP* 74 (1968) 223-55. I wish we knew the identity of the πρῶτοι who appear beside the ἄρχοντες and βουλή in line 12 of the Thespian inscription of A.D. 170-1, published by A. Plassart, in *Mél. Glotz* II (1932) 731-8 (see 737-8).

16. Among many similar passages, see esp. Cic., *De rep.* I.44, 67-8 (reproducing Plato); III.23. The complaint was made by members of the propertied class in antiquity that the boasted 'freedom' of full democracy, in which the lower classes participated, has a natural tendency to degenerate into license: *libertas* becomes *licentia* (cf. VI.v above), and δημοκρατία turns into ὀχλοκρατία. This line of argument, of which of course Plato was one of the main ancestors, was fully developed in the Hellenistic period, when the term ὀχλοκρατία was coined: it appears in Polyb. VI.iv.6,10; lvii.9; cf. Stob., *Anthol.* II.vii.26, ed. C. Wachsmuth (1884) II.150, line 23 (and see Walbank, *HCP* I.640-1, and n.50 below). I fancy that a similar attitude to democracy lies behind the opinions expressed in the last paragraph of a series of six articles in *Athenaeum* n.s. 9-11 (1931-3), under the general title, 'Studi di storia ellenistico-romana', by an Italian Fascist, Alfredo Passerini. See 11 (1933) 334-5 (the last sentences of the series): 'Ma ora l'Italia e Roma stessa rinunciavano alla libertà democratica per sottomettersi alla superiore idea imperiale. Di simile la Grecia non aveva nel suo passato nulla: e fu ben giusto, che anch'essa si acconciasse ad ubbidire'!

17. For the chronology of Plutarch's works, see C. P. Jones, 'Towards a chronology of Plutarch's works', in *JRS* 56 (1966) 61-74; and the chronological table in Jones, *PR* 135-7. Jones's date for the *Praec. ger. reip.* is 'after 96, before 114'. Of this work there is a recent edition with commentary (which I have not been able to consult): *Plutarco, Praecepta gerendae reipublicae*, by E. Valgiglio (= *Testi e documenti per lo studio dell'Antichità* 52, Milan, 1976).

18. The κάλτιοι of *Mor.* 813e are the senatorial shoes of the proconsul, not military boots, as they are sometimes taken to be: see Oliver, *RP* 958 and n.27; and C. P. Jones, *PR* 133.

19. An expression of Plutarch's views about 'equality', bound up with the theory of 'geometrical proportion' (for which see VII.i above and its nn.10-11 below), can be found in *Mor.* 719bc, partly given in VII.i above.

20. On Plutarch's attitude to Rome, see esp. C. P. Jones, *PR*, with whom I basically agree. The reader of such passages in Polybius as XXIV.xi-xiii may well feel a similarity between Plutarch's attitude and that of Polybius, notably in the latter's preference for the policy advocated by Philopoemen over that of Aristaenus, without strongly criticising the second: see xiii.2,4 (with its protest against behaving 'like prisoners of war', καθάπερ οἱ δοριάλωτοι), 5-6, and esp. 8.

21. Rostovtzeff, *SEHRE*² II.586-7 n.18, with many references.

22. Dio Chrys. XXXII (Alexandria; for the date, see VIII.iii n.1 below); XXXIII-IV (Tarsus); XLV-VI and XLVIII (Prusa); and I would add XXXI (Rhodes). See esp. XXXI.105-6, 111-14, 125, 149-51, 159-60; XXXIV.48, 51 (cited in the main text above); XXXII.71-2 (the recent ταραχή: see VIII.iii n.1 again); XXXIII.37 (testifying to the continuance of manual voting in Assemblies and voting by ballot in courts); XXXIV.7-8 (the patronage of Augustus; cf. § 25 and XXXIII.48), 9 (accusations against provincial governors; cf. § 42), 16-21 (discord between Assembly, Council, Gerousia etc.), 21-3 (partial disfranchisement of despised linen-workers; figure of 500 dr. fee for enrolment as a citizen), 31 (political importance of those who perform liturgies), 33 (hostile attitude of common people, cf. § 39), 35-6 (offices held for six months only), 38 (delicate situation *vis-à-vis* Rome, cf. §§ 40, 48, 51), 39 (danger of losing right of free speech, παρρησία; cf. XLVIII.2-3, 15); XL.22, with XLI.9 (see the main text above); XLV.6 (order from provincial governor regarding city finance), 7 (100 councillors at Prusa), 15 (provincial governor convenes Assembly); XLVI.6 (people threaten to stone Dio and burn his property; cf. §§ 1, 4, 11-13), 8 (Dio claims he is not to blame for the famine; cf. §§ 9-10), 14 (threat of intervention by provincial governor); XLVIII.1 (provincial governor had restored the right to hold Assemblies, evidently withdrawn as a consequence of the disturbances; cf. §§ 2-3, 9-10, 14-15 etc.), 11 (fees for enrolment in Council, βουλευτικά); LVI.10 (most demagogues will introduce ἀπροβούλευτα ψηφίσματα . . . εἰς τὸν δῆμον).

23. See e.g. Magie, *RRAM* I.474 (with 477) and 503 (Cyzicus, twice); 530 (Lycians); 548 and 569 (Rhodes, twice); 569 (probably Samos); 570 (probably Cos); with the references, II.1337 n.21, 1339-40 n.27, 1387 n.50, 1406-7 n.24; 1427-9 nn.9-10. And see VIII.i n.11 below. For Cos, see now Susan M. Sherwin-White, *Ancient Cos* (= *Hypomnemata* 51, 1978) 145-52.

24. There is a useful collection of the evidence in the Oxford B.Litt. thesis by J. R. Martindale, *Public Disorders in the Late Roman Empire, their Causes and Character* (1961).

25. The inscription is *IG* II².1064, with additions (cf. *SEG* XXI.506, and 505): see now J. H. Oliver, *The Sacred Gerusia* = *Hesp.*, Suppl. 6 (1941) 125-41 no.31 (text, trans. and comm.), with 142 · no.32; Oliver, 'On the Athenian decrees for Ulpius Eubiotus', in *Hesp.* 20 (1951) 350-4, as corrected by B. D. Meritt, in *Hesp.* 32 (1963) 26-30 no.27.

26. See also *SEG* XIV.479; cf. XVI.408; XXIV.619. (And cf. § 2 of Appendix IV above, *ad fin.*).

27. There is an up-to-date account of the Gerousia, with immense bibliography, in Magie, *RRAM* I.63 (with II.855-60 n.38). For the Epheboi and Neoi, see ibid. I.62 (with II.852-5 nn.36-7); add H. W. Pleket, '*Collegium Iuvenum Nemesiorum*. A note on ancient youth-organisations', in *Mnemos.*⁴ 22 (1969) 281-98.

28. I know of no firm evidence for political pay at Athens in the Hellenistic period. Without making an exhaustive search among the inscriptions, the latest evidence I can quote for any kind of major compensation for state service is the so-called καθέσιμον paid to members of the Council in years around the middle of the second century B.C., and this was evidently a special distribution made for the festival of the Thesea and is not to be seen as political pay of the old kind: *IG* II².956.14-15 (161/0 B.C.), 957.9-10 (*c.* 158/7), 958.12-13 (*c.* 155/4), 959.11-12 (*c.* 150 or a little later).

29. There is a useful discussion of the precise meaning of Cicero's words *peregrini iudices* by J. A. O. Larsen, '"Foreign judges" in Cicero *Ad Atticum* vi.i.15', in *CP* 43 (1948) 187-90.

30. Asclepiades etc.: Sherk, *RDGE* 22 = *IGRR* I.118 = *CIL* I.² 588. There is an Eng. trans. in Lewis and Reinhold, *RC* I.267-9, and in the Loeb *Remains of Old Latin* IV.444-51. Seleucus: Sherk, *RDGE* 58 = E/J² 301 [= *IGLS* III.i.718], ii, § 8. There is an Eng. trans. in Lewis and Reinhold, *RC* I.389-91. And see the article in two parts by F. De Visscher, 'Le statut juridique des nouveaux citoyens romains et l'inscription de Rhosos', in *Ant. Class.* 13 (1944) 11-35; 14 (1945) 29-59.

31. E.g. (1) A/J 36 = Sherk, *RDGE* 67 = E/J² 312 = *SIG*³ 780 = *IGRR* IV.1031 (Cnidus); (2) A/J 121 = *IG* V.i.21 (Sparta); (3) A/J 90 = *IG* II².1100, lines 54-5 (Athens); (4) A/J 119 = *IGRR* IV.1044 (Cos). The literary evidence of course includes the case of St. Paul (cf. VIII.i above). Security might be demanded for a reference to the emperor's court, even from a city: see e.g. J. H. Oliver in *Hesp.* Suppl. 13 (1970), at p.38 and n.20.

32. The existence of the provincial governor's court (held in the principal cities of the province) is too well known to need citation of evidence, and I will merely mention as specimens some letters in Pliny, *Ep.* X: nos.29-32, 56-60, 72, 81, 84, 96-7, 110-11.

33. As e.g. in (1) Rhodes (see my PPOA; add Epict., *Diss.* II.ii.17 for a private suit at Rhodes before δικασταί, probably in about the first decade of the second century); (2) Chios: *SEG* XXII.507

= Sherk, *RDGE* 70 (= A/J 40 = E/J² 317 = *SIG*³ 785 = *IGRR* IV.943); lines 17-18 are particularly interesting, as they subject Romans in Chios to the city laws (see A. J. Marshall, 'Romans under Chian law', in *GRBS* 10 [1969] 255-71); and (3) *IGBulg*. IV.2263, an interesting and recently discovered inscription (cf. n.26 above); here, presumably, cases involving more than 250 denarii (lines 12-14) went to the provincial governor's court.

34. But see, e.g. for Athens, (1) *SEG* XV.108 = *IG* II².1100 = A/J 90: Hadrian's oil law (mentioned a little later in the text above and in Appendix IV, § 2), where lines 45-50 provide for trials in the Council or (in certain cases) the Assembly; (2) A/J 91 = *IG* II².1103, lines 7-8: the Areopagus; (3) the edict of Marcus Aurelius, of 169-76 (see Appendix IV above, § 2), Plaque II = E, lines 8, 68, 75, where the last two references must surely be to the Areopagus: see Oliver, in *Hesp.*, Suppl. 13 (1970), at p.65.

35. As in (very probably) Sicily in the Republic and (certainly) Cyrenaica in the late Republic and early Principate (see Appendix IV above, §§ 1,5), and no doubt in many other places. It has been suggested that in Roman Athens δικασταί were drawn only from those qualified to become Councillors (see Appendix IV, § 2), and by the second quarter of the second century perhaps only from Areopagites: see Oliver, op. cit. (in n.34) 64-5.

36. E.g. (1) Plut., *Mor.* 815a; and (2) A/J 122 = *IGRR* III.409 (Pogla in Pisidia: for the interpretation of τοπικὰ δικαστήρια ἔτεσιν κοινω[νίας], see Jones, *CERP*² 142-3).

37. See e.g. Magie, *RRAM* I.113 (with II.963-4 n.81), 525 (with II.1382-3 n.36), 648 (with II.1517-18 n.49). Cf. Larsen, as cited in n.29 above.

38. In the early Principate Apamea was the centre of one of the *conventus* of the province of Asia: see Jones, *CERP*² 64-91, at 69-73; cf. Magie, *RRAM* I.171-2 and Index, *s.v.* 'Dioceses (judiciary districts)'. The main point made by Dio XXXV.14-17 is that the holding of the courts 'brings together a mass of people without number' to Apamea (§ 15 *init.*); and therefore the δικάζοντες ought not to be local people, or anyway not entirely. Apart from the two alternative interpretations of δικάζοντες suggested in the main text above, there is a third which I suppose is just possible: that there existed at Apamea in Dio's time a system of jury-courts such as we find in the first and fourth of the Cyrene Edicts of Augustus (see Appendix IV § 5 above). I know of no trace of such a system anywhere in Asia Minor in the Roman period, and I regard this alternative as unlikely in the extreme.

39. See J. Touloumakos, 'Δικασταί = *Iudices*?', in *Historia* 18 (1969) 407-21.

40. In MacMullen, *ERO*, there are attacks in the text and notes on would-be Marxist accounts, partly justified but partly misconceived. As elsewhere, MacMullen cites a great deal of good material but fails to make much use of it, owing to the serious inadequacy of his conceptual equipment. A. Momigliano, reviewing MacMullen, *RSR*, in *Riv. stor. ital.* 86 (1974) 405-7, ends with the words, 'Ma la stratificazione di una società complessa come quella dell'impero romano non può essere esaminata con categorie pre-weberiane'. I wish I knew which *Weberian* categories Momigliano had in mind! I cannot think that a *merely* Weberian analysis would have materially helped MacMullen to *explain* the phenomena he so ably *describes*. The article by Léa Flam-Zuckermann, 'À propos d'une inscription de Suisse (*CIL* XIII, 5010): étude du phénomène du brigandage dans l'Empire romain', in *Latomus* 29 (1970) 451-73, which has a very large number of source references and much modern bibliography, aims at giving 'le contribution fertile que peut apporter une analyse sociologique du phénomène du brigandage' (id. 451); but pp.470-2 are very muddled on the question whether acts of brigandage ought to be regarded as class struggles, and there is a most misguided attempt on p.471 to characterise the Roman social hierarchy as consisting not of 'classes sociales' but of 'groupes sociaux'! (The inscription mentioned in her title can most conveniently be consulted as *ILS* 7007.)

41. Jean Colin, *Les villes libres de l'Orient gréco-romain et l'envoi au supplice par acclamations populaires* (= *Coll. Latomus* 82, Brussels, 1965), has a collection of evidence in this field, but is very unreliable, especially on constitutional questions. See also Millar, *ERW* 369-75. I have not been able to study Traugott Bollinger, *Theatralis Licentia. Die Publikumsdemonstrationen an den öffentlichen Spielen im Rom der früheren Kaiserzeit und ihre Bedeutung im politischen Leben* (Diss., Basel, 1969), which, as its title indicates, is confined to Rome.

41a. There is a favourable review of Cameron's *Circus Factions* by W. Liebeschuetz, in *JRS* 68 (1978) 198-9, and another in *CR* 93 = n.s. 29 (1979) 128-9, by Cyril Mango. I can only concur with most of the negative side of Cameron's thesis, rightly denying the identification of the factions as long-term representatives of particular economic or religious groups and indeed having some of the characteristics of political 'parties'. This side of his book is most valuable and entirely convincing. But I am not convinced by his virtual denial (see esp. his CF 271-96, ch.x) of all political significance to the factions. Cf. the review by Robert Browning in *TLS* 3902 (24 December 1976) 1606. On this subject I feel that I have profited from discussions with Michael Whitby.

42. On Roman policy towards clubs etc., see (very briefly) Sherwin-White, *LP* 607, 608-9, 688-9.

43. For a long list of occasions on which we hear of the stoning of prominent men or the burning of their houses (or of threats to commit these acts), see MacMullen, *RSR* 171 nn.30, 32.

44. For the food supply of Antioch, see Petit, *LVMA* 105-22; Liebeschuetz, *Ant.* 126-32.

45. See Thompson, *HWAM* 60-71; Petit, *LVMA* 107-9; Downey, *HAS* 365-7.

46. Cf. the cryptic statement in Amm. Marc. XV.xiii.2: at the subsequent investigation by the Praetorian Prefect of the East, certain *divites* involved in the assassination of Theophilus merely had their property confiscated, while some *pauperes* were condemned (to death, undoubtedly) although they had not even been present.

47. For δημοκρατία in the Hellenistic period, see Jones, *GCAJ* 157 ff.; J. A. O. Larsen, 'Representation and democracy in Hellenistic federalism', in *CP* 40 (1945) 65-97, at 88-91; Walbank, *HCP* I.221-2 (on Polyb. II.38.6), 230, 478. For the Roman period, see Jones, *GCAJ* 170 ff.

48. *IGRR* I.61 = *IG* XIV.986 = *OGIS* 551 = *ILS* 31. For the date, see e.g. Magie, *RRAM* II.954-5 n.67. Among other inscriptions that might be quoted, see the Pergamene one of 46-44 B.C., where the δῆμος hails the proconsul of Asia, P. Servilius Isauricus, as 'saviour and benefactor' and records that he had restored to the city τοὺς πατρίους νόμους καὶ τὴν δημοκρατίαν ἀδούλωτον: A/J 23 = *OGIS* 449 = *IGRR* IV.433 = *ILS* 8779.

49. As in (1) Plut., *On Monarchy, Democracy and Oligarchy* (see esp. *Mor.* 826ef), where monarchy is preferred (827bc, cf. 790a etc.); (2) Dio Chrys. III.45-9 (dating perhaps from the early years of the second century), where δημοκρατία, as distinguished from ἀριστοκρατία, is disparaged in favour of monarchy (democracy, says Dio, actually expects σωφροσύνη and ἀρετή from the δῆμος, so as to obtain a κατάστασιν ἐπιεικῆ καὶ νόμιμον – as if that were practicable!); (3) App., *BC* IV.133, where it is the common soldiers, formerly in Julius Caesar's army, who serve Brutus and Cassius ὑπὲρ δημοκρατίας, and (to show exactly what sort of democracy is meant in this case) a sneering comment follows: ὀνόματος εὐειδοῦς μέν, ἀλυσιτελοῦς δὲ αἰεί; (4) Philostr., *VA* V.34, where δημοκρατία must have its original meaning, as it is distinguished not only from τυραννίδες but also from ὀλιγαρχίαι and ἀριστοκρατία. (In V.33, however, it is the Roman Republic to which both δημοκρατεῖσθαι and τὸ τοῦ δήμου κράτος refer; and V.35 is one of the three passages I give, further on in the main text above, where the Principate itself is a democracy, a δῆμος – the three chapters, V.33-5, certainly illustrate the possible variations in meaning of δημοκρατία and its cognates in a single author, even within a single passage.)

50. As in Dio Cassius XLIV.2.3; LIII.8.4; cf. ὄχλου ἐλευθερία in LII.14.5; and perhaps ὅμιλος in 14.3 and possibly 5.4. There is a curious reference to the ὄχλος at Rome in Dio Cass. LXVI.12.2. Evagrius, writing at the very end of the sixth century, could describe the Late Roman Republic, out of which Julius Caesar's μοναρχία emerged, as an ὀχλοκρατία: *HE* III.41, p.142 ed. J. Bidez and L. Parmentier. On ὀχλοκρατία, see also n.16 above. In an oratorical work by (or attributed to) a Greek rhetorician of the late third century C.E., Menander of Laodicea on the Lycus, we find ὀχλοκρατία replaced by λαοκρατία: see *Rhetores Graeci* III.359-60, ed. L. Spengel (1856). I know of no other occurrence of the words λαοκρατία, λαοκρατεῖσθαι. There is a rather nice late use of ὀχλοκρατεία in Evagr., *HE* VI.1 (p.223 ed. Bidez and Parmentier), for the rule of the passions, which the Emperor Maurice (582-602) thrust out of his mind, establishing there as ἀριστοκρατία of reason.

51. Out of scores of possible examples I will give only App., *BC* IV.69, 97, 138 etc. (for his *Praef.* 6, see later on in the main text above, and VI.vi); Dio Cass. XLIV.2.1-4; XLV.31.2; 44.2; XLVII.20.4; 39.1-5; 40.7; 42.3-4; L.1.1-2; LII.1.1; 9.5; 13.3; LIII.1.3; 5.4; 11.2,4-5; 16.1; 17.1-3,11; 18.2; 19.1; LIV.6.1; LV.21.4; LVI.39.5; 43.4 (where alone the Principate is a mixture of μοναρχία and δημοκρατία); LX.1.1; 15.3; LXVI.12.2; Herodian I.1.4 (the Roman δυναστεία changed into a μοναρχία under Augustus; cf. δυναστεῖαι in Dio Cass. LII.1.1). The verb δημοκρατεῖσθαι and the adjective δημοκρατικός (for which see esp. Dio Cass. LV.4.2) are often used in the same sense as δημοκρατία. Dio can even use δημοτικώτατος (meaning 'most republican') in XLIII.11.6 of the arch-reactionary, Cato. I have said nothing here of Philo, the leading Alexandrian Jew who wrote (and thought) in Greek in the first half of the first century, since his use of the word δημοκρατία, in six different works, is a notorious puzzle: (1) *De Abrahamo* 242, (2) *Quod Deus sit immut.* 176, (3) *De spec. leg.* IV.237 (cf. § 9, δημοκρατικός), (4)

De virtut. 180, (5) *De agric.* 45, (6) *De confus. ling.* 108. In three of those texts (nos. 4, 5, 6) δημοκρατία is the opposite of ὀχλοκρατία, in one (no.1) it is the opposite of tyranny, in two (nos.3, 4) it is εὐνομωτάτη, and in four (nos.1, 2, 3, 5) it is ἀρίστη. All this would incline one to think that in Philo's mind the term δημοκρατία would fit the Roman Republic. Yet his δημοκρατία is also characterised by ἰσότης (nos.3, 6). I feel there may be something in the suggestion which has been made that in his conception of δημοκρατία Philo was much influenced by a unique passage in Plato, namely *Menex.* 238bc-9a, taking it to be serious praise of the Athenian constitution instead of a reproduction – in Plato, deeply ironical – of what Athenian democrats themselves said. (I have not seen any more recent treatment of this question than that of F. H. Colson, in the Loeb edition of Philo, Vol. VIII [1939] 437-9.)

52. See e.g. Dio Cass. XLI.17.3; XLVI.34.4; XLVII.39.2; LII.1.1; 6.3; 13.2 (δυναστεῦσαι too); 17.3. Cf. App., *Praef.* 6: Gaius [= Julius] Caesar δυναστεύσας made himself μόναρχος. In Dion. Hal., *De antiq. orator.* 3 (written under Augustus), the Roman leaders are οἱ δυναστεύοντες.

53. See C. G. Starr, 'The perfect democracy of the Roman Empire', in *AHR* 58 (1952-3) 1-16. This article is quite a useful collection of material but shows no understanding of Greek democracy in its great days or of the process (described earlier in the main text above) by which, during the Hellenistic period, the term had 'come in practice to be applicable to any government which was not openly monarchical' (ibid. 2).

54. Ael. Arist., *Orat.* XXVI (ed. B. Keil), esp. 60, 90; cf. 29, 36, 39, 64, 65, 107 etc. (The key phrase in § 60 is καθέστηκε κοινῇ τῆς γῆς δημοκρατία ὑφ' ἑνὶ τῷ ἀρίστῳ ἄρχοντι καὶ κοσμητῇ, and in § 90 δημοκρατίαν νομιεῖ καὶ οὐδὲν ἐνδεῖν πλὴν ὧν ἐξαμαρτάνει δῆμος.) The date of the speech is usually given nowadays as A.D. 143, or anyway between about 143 and 156, and thus during the reign of Antoninus Pius. There is an edition, with Eng. trans. and comm., by J. H. Oliver, *RP*; but Oliver is often ready to take Aristeides' panegyric at too near its face value. De Martino, *SCR*² IV.i (1974) 383 n.44, lists ten reviews of Oliver's edition, with other literature. Rostovtzeff, *SEHRE*² II.544 n.6, thinks the speech 'wonderful'!

55. There is a good recent abridged Eng. trans. by C. P. Jones (Penguin Classics, 1970), with an Introd. by G. W. Bowersock: this includes nearly all the most important parts of this interesting work. There is also a complete Loeb edition in 2 vols (with Eng. trans.) by F. C. Conybeare (1912).

56. For an account of this literary debate (Dio Cass. LII.ii.1 to xiii.7, and xiv.1 to xl.2) see Millar, *SCD* 102-118. (I certainly cannot accept his view that the speech of Maecenas was actually delivered by Dio before the Emperor Caracalla – at Nicomedia late in 214, as he suggests, or at any other place and time. That would have been a foolhardy act, and it would have been highly unlikely to have any effect on a despot like Caracalla.) There are some interesting features in Agrippa's speech which I cannot discuss here, but I must not fail to draw attention to the use of ἰσονομία in LII.4.1.

57. See n.8 to Section ii of this chapter. One of the later specimens of our Greek treatises *On kingship* (A.D. 399), by Synesius, later to become bishop of Cyrene, can still praise παρρησία in its opening paragraph, as something that ought to be fostered by emperors (*MPG* LXVI.1056), and make a claim to exercise it (ibid. 1056-7, §§ 2, 3).

57a. After this chapter was finished I read the discussion of 'Longinus', *De sublim.* 44, by Gordon Williams, *Change and Decline. Roman Literature in the Early Empire* (= Sather Classical Lectures 45, Berkeley/London, 1978) 17-25. This is well worth reading and makes some good points, but an important part of the argument is vitiated by Williams's demonstrably false belief that 'it seems unlikely . . . that a Greek of the Empire would use the word δημοκρατία of the Roman Republic' (21 n.33), and that 'Greek writers do not seem to have been politically conscious of the change from republic to principate in the way that, for instance, Roman Stoics in the early Empire were' (18). As I show in the main text above (and n.51), δημοκρατία is applied to the Roman Republic from the late first century, if not earlier, and is a standard term for it in the Greek historians of the second and third centuries. This is perfectly natural in view of the degeneration in the meaning of the word which had already taken place in the Hellenistic period: see the main text and nn.47-9 above.

58. *'Longinus' On the Sublime*, ed. with an Introd. and Comm. by D. A. Russell (1964). See also *Ancient Literary Criticism*, ed. D. A. Russell and M. Winterbottom (1970) 460-1, 501-3.

59. I suppose I must mention here Tac., *Dial.* (esp. 1.1, 27.3, 38.2, 40.2-4, 41.1-4), although of course it is solely concerned with oratory, and 'Longinus' does not limit himself to that. For an earlier Roman view of the dependence of oratory on the enjoyment of peace, leisure and a good

616 *Notes on V.iii (pp.325-326)*

constitution, see Cic., *Brut.* 45-6, part of a long passage, 25-51, in which other interesting remarks occur in 26, 39, and esp. 49-51, maintaining that *eloquentia* was at first peculiar to Athens and unknown to Thebes (except perhaps for Epaminondas), Argos, Corinth, and above all Sparta, but that oratory later spread to all the islands and the whole of Asia, with unfortunate consequences except at Rhodes.

60. Expressly or by implication our author shows some enthusiasm (if qualified in a few cases) for some 16 writers (Aeschylus, Archilochus, Demosthenes, Euripides, Herodotus, Homer, Hypereides, Pindar, Plato, Sappho, Simonides, Sophocles, Stesichorus, Theocritus, Thucydides, and Xenophon), of whom only one, Theocritus, is Hellenistic, and only four others (Archilochus, Homer, Sappho, and Stesichorus) do not come from the fifth or fourth century. Of the eight Hellenistic writers he mentions, only one, Apollonius, receives praise and no reproach; on three (Aratus, Eratosthenes, and Timaeus) his verdict is mixed; and four (Amphicrates, Cleitarchus, Hegesias, and Matris) are harshly criticised. A curious omission is Menander, who is never mentioned. Perhaps I should add that our author is the only Greek I have come across who mentions (with admiration, in 9.9) Genesis I.3 – perhaps not from direct acquaintance with the LXX: cf. the wording here and in Gen. I.9.

61. The only references I can find in Hippolytus (or elsewhere) to these 'democracies' are indeed in *De Antichr.* 27, ed. Hans Achelis, in *GCS* I.ii (1897) 19: καὶ τῶν δέκα δακτύλων τῆς εἰκόνος εἰς δημοκρατίας χωρησάντων, and *Comm. in Dan.* II.xii.7, ed. G. N. Bonwetsch, in *GCS* I.i (1897) 68, and Maurice Lefèvre, in *Hippolyte Commentaire sur Daniel = SC* 14 (Paris, 1947) 144: εἶτα δάκτυλοι ποδῶν, ἵνα δειχθῶσιν αἱ ... δημοκρατίαι αἱ μέλλουσαι γίγνεσθαι. At this point we must take account of the 'beast' with ten horns in Dan. VII (7, 20), interpreted there as ten βασιλεῖς (verse 24), since Hippol., *Comm. in Dan.*, equates the ten toes of the image in Dan. II.41-2 with the ten horns of the 'beast' (IV.vii.5), and identifies the ten horns as ten kings (IV.xiii.3); and similarly in *De Antichr.* 27 he speaks of the ten horns of the 'beast' as ten kings. Cf. the 'beast' of Rev. XIII.1 ff. and XVII.3 ff., which also has ten horns (XIII.1; XVII.3,7), interpreted as ten βασιλεῖς (XVII.12-17). The δημοκρατίαι are a real problem to me. I cannot understand how Géza Alföldy, 'The crisis of the third century, as seen by contemporaries', in *GRBS* 15 (1974) 89-111, at 99 and n.35, can say that 'Irenaeus, Hippolytus and Tertullian were already so impressed by the political crisis after Commodus' death that they predicted, as did Lactantius later, that one day the end of the Empire would come through its disintegration into ten "democracies"', and can cite in support of this Iren., *Adv. haeres.* V.26.1; Hippol., *Comm. in Dan.* IV.vi and *De Antichr.* 28; Tert., *De resurr.* 24.18; and Lact., *Div. inst.* VII.16.1 ff. As I have said, the only two texts that seem to me relevant are the two quoted at the beginning of this note, and not any of those cited by Alföldy. In each of his passages we certainly find the ten horns = ten kings (except *Comm. in Dan.* IV.vi; but see e.g. IV.xiii.3).

62. See H. A. Drake, 'When was the "de laudibus Constantini" delivered?', in *Historia* 24 (1975) 345-56 (esp. 352-6), who prefers 336 to 335 and thinks the actual day is likely to have been 25 July in that year. It was only after this section was finished that I saw Drake's subsequent book, *In Praise of Constantine: A Historical Study and New Translation of Eusebius' Tricennial Orations* (Univ. of California Publications: Class. Stud. 15, Berkeley/London, 1976).

63. Euseb., *Triacont.* (or *Orat. de laud. Constant.*) III.6, ed. I. A. Heikel, in *GCS* 7 (1902). There is an Eng. trans. of this speech (or speeches) in *Eusebius = NPNF* I (1890 & repr.) 561-610, a revision by E. C. Richardson (on the basis of F. A. Heinichen's second edition of the Greek text in 1869) of the anonymous Eng. trans. published by Samuel Bagster and Sons in London in 1845, from the seventeenth-century Greek text by Valesius (see *NPNF* I.52, 405, 466-7, 469). The new English translation by H. A. Drake (see the preceding note) is made from the improved text by Heikel. I need not enter here into the question whether *Triacont.* 1-10 and 11-18 should be treated as a unity or as a conflation of two separate addresses: the latter seems far more probable (see Drake, as cited in the preceding note, and J. Quasten, *Patrology* III [1960] 326-8).

64. The earliest examples I happen to have come across are in the correspondence between the two patriarchs, Atticus of Constantinople and Cyril of Alexandria, concerning the rehabilitation of John Chrysostom, in the second decade of the fifth century: see Cyril, *Ep.* 75 (by Atticus), in *MPG* LXXVII.349CD and esp. 352A (ὥστε μὴ ... ἐθισθῆναι εἰς δημοκρατίαν τὴν πόλιν). There are several examples in John Malalas (mid-sixth century), *Chronographia*, ed. L. Dindorf (*CSHB*, Bonn, 1831), e.g. pp.244.15-17 (Book X, Caligula: the Green faction, given παρρησία by the emperor, ἐδημοκράτησεν in Rome and other cities); 246.10-11 (Book X, Claudius); and esp. 393.5-6 (Book XVI, Anastasius: the Green faction at Antioch δημοκρατοῦν

ἐπήρχετο τοῖς ἄρχουσιν), and 416.9-10 and 21 to 417.1 (Book XVII, Justin I: the Blue faction rioted at Constantinople until the Praefectus Urbi Theodotus κατεδυνάστευσε τῆς δημοκρατίας τῶν Βυζαντίων; at Antioch the Comes Orientis Ephraemius also ἠγωνίσατο κατὰ τῶν δημοκρατούντων Βενέτων, etc.). There are some particularly good examples in Theophanes (early ninth century), *Chronographia*, ed. C. de Boor (Leipzig, 1883): I.166.26 (A.M. 6012: ἐδημοκράτησε τὸ βένετον μέρος), 181.17-18 (A.M. 6023: καὶ ἐγένοντο κοσμικαὶ δημοκρατίαι καὶ φόνοι), and 492.27 (A.M. 6303: ἡ δημοκρατίαν ἐγεῖραι Χριστιανοῖς). See Cameron, *CF* 305-6, improving on G. I. Bratianu, 'Empire et "Démocratie" à Byzance', in *Byz. Ztschr.* 37 (1937) 86-111, at 87-91.

65. I ought perhaps to have said more in this section about the *staseis* and revolutions in Greek cities in the Hellenistic age: some were clearly forms of political class struggle to a greater or less degree. But our sources are usually defective or biased, and the movements in question are rarely very significant. I shall merely refer to a comprehensive set of articles by A. Fuks: the main one, 'Patterns and types of social-economic revolution in Greece from the 4th to the 2nd century B.C.', in *Anc. Soc.* 5 (1974) 51-81, lists the others, p.53 n.6.

[VI.i]

1. For a good brief statement of what made Roman law (virtually the *ius civile* in the sense in which I am using the term) 'the most original product of the Roman mind', see Barry Nicholas, *IRL = An Introduction to Roman Law* (1962) 1-2. That book (of xv + 281 pages) is the bestelementary introduction to the subject in English, and is a model of clarity. More comprehensive, and dealing also with public law, is H. F. Jolowicz, *HISRL*[3] = *Historical Introduction to the Study of Roman Law*, 3rd edn, revised by Barry Nicholas (1972). Other works are referred to in the text above. Those unacquainted with Roman law who wish to see how it actually functioned in Roman society will find their best 'way into' the subject through Crook, *LLR* (1967), a book which, in the most praiseworthy manner, avoids the unnecessary technicalities that make so many of the writings of modern specialists in Roman law scarcely intelligible to anyone except another such specialist. Crook, however, takes a far more indulgent view than I could of the class nature of the Roman legal system and the way it helped to fortify the position of the Roman propertied class.

2. See my WWECP, in *SAS* (ed. Finley) 218-20, with references (esp. n.53), cf. 249 n.170.

3. To the references given in my article cited in n.2 above add Jolowicz and Nicholas, *HISRL*[3] 175, 397-8; Kaser, *RZ* (1966) 339-40, § 66: 'Wesen und Arten der Kognitionsverfahren' (see 339 for the 'Sammelbegriff Kognitionsprozess'); *RP* II² (1975) 16-17.

4. This was by no means a late development in Roman law: see Garnsey, *SSLPRE* (referred to several times in VIII.i above); J. M. Kelly, *Roman Litigation* (1966); Rudolf von Ihering, *Scherz und Ernst in der Jurisprudenz* (8th edn, Leipzig, 1900) 175-232 (Abt. II.iii: 'Reich und Arm im altrömischen Civilprozess').

5. Cf. now Brunt, LI 175-8.

6. See Brunt, LI 159.

7. See esp. Polyb. I.iii.6,7,9-10 (and cf. 4); vi.3; lxiii.9; III.ii.2; IX.x.11; XV.ix.2 (cf. 4-5); x.2. Cf. also I.vi.6; x.5 ff.; xx.1-2; II.xxi.9; xxxi.8; III.iii.9; V.civ.3; VI.ii.3; l.6. (Cf. n.6 to Section iv of this chapter.)

8. Brunt, LI 162. The proof of this follows, LI 162-72.

9. The bestial savagery of Yahweh was of course depicted by his zealous worshippers as extending not only to foreign peoples but also to disobedient Israelites. As my concern at this point is only with the former, I give but one reference to the fate imagined for the latter: Deuteronomy XXVIII, where, after 14 verses describing the blessings of the obedient, there are 54 verses containing an awe-inspiring list of curses upon transgressors – including the only biblical reference I know to placentophagy (verse 57).

10. The archaeological record is not yet absolutely clear; but (*a*) although Hazor was a considerable city which could have been destroyed by the Israelites under 'Joshua' in the late thirteenth century B.C., yet (*b*) it seems almost certain that the destruction of the major city of Ai took place more than a thousand years earlier and that Ai could not possibly have been a place of any size or importance in 'Joshua's day'; also (*c*) the great days of Jericho were also much earlier,

and the place was in a poor way after the mid-sixteenth century and in the time of 'Joshua' was small and unimportant and probably unwalled. But I am concerned here not so much with what actually happened as with what the Israelites wished to believe about their own past and the role played by their God.

11. I understand from Zvi Yavetz that the earliest surviving passage mentioning the advocacy of genocide *of* the Jews is Diod. XXXIV/XXXV.1.1,4 (the friends of Antiochus VII).

12. See in particular Num. XXV.8-9, 10-13; I Chron. ix.20; Ps. CVI.30. In Ecclus. XLV.23-5 Phineas is celebrated along with Moses and Aaron. He is also cited with admiration by some Christian writers seeking Old Testament justification for persecution, e.g. Optat. III.5,7; VII.6.

[VI.ii]

1. E. J. Bickerman, 'Some reflections on early Roman history', in *Riv. di filol.* 97 (1969) 393-408.

2. Among many recent works dealing with the problem of the *secessiones*, see esp. Kurt von Fritz, 'The reorganisation of the Roman government in 366 B.C. and the so-called Licinio-Sextian laws', in *Historia* 1 (1950) 3-44, at 21-5.

3. See Lily Ross Taylor, 'Forerunners of the Gracchi', in *JRS* 52 (1962) 19-27, at 20, with nn.11-12.

4. I make this qualification because those taking *effective* part in the *secessiones* (mentioned in the main text above) are not likely to have included the poorest citizens, who at this date would not have been serving in the main army.

5. A. W. Lintott, 'The tradition of violence in the annals of the Early Roman Republic', in *Historia* 19 (1970) 12-29; cf. Lintott's book, *Violence in Republican Rome* (1968) 55-7 etc. There are at least four passages in Cicero mentioning all three men (Cassius, Maelius and Manlius): *Pro domo ad pontif.* 101; *II Phil.* 87 and 114; *De rep.* II.49. Among other Ciceronian texts referring to one or more of them are *Lael.* 28 and 36; *De senect.* 56; *Pro Mil.* 72; *I Cat.* 3; *I Phil.* 32. Cassius and Manlius are depicted as Patricians and consulars, Maelius as a rich Plebeian who had distributed corn to the poor. Livy says that Manlius was 'primus omnium ex patribus *popularis* factus' (VI.11.7); and note his unconsciously ironical comment (VI.20.14) that Manlius would have been 'memorabilis' if he had not been born 'in libera civitate'! Cf. II.41.2 (on Cassius). Among other narratives, I would draw attention to that of Cn. Genucius, tribune of the plebs in 473: Livy II.54-55 (esp. 54.9-10); Dion. Hal., *AR* IX.37-38 (esp. 38.2-3); X.38.4-5.

[VI.iii]

1. (Or descendants of consular tribunes or dictators.) Gelzer's *Die Nobilität der römischen Republik* (1912) was repr. in his *Kleine Schriften* I (Wiesbaden, 1962) 1-135 and is now easily available in a good Eng. trans. by Robin Seager, as *The Roman Nobility* (1969) 1-139. Cf. H. Strasburger, in *RE* XVII.i (1936) 785-91, *s.v.* 'Nobiles', and 1223-8, *s.v.* 'Novus homo'; E. Badian, in *OCD²* 736, 740, *s.v.* 'Nobilitas', 'Novus homo'; Syme, *RR* 10 ff.; H. H. Scullard, *Roman Politics 220-150 B.C.* (1951) 10-11; and see A. Afzelius, 'Zur Definition der römischen Nobilität vor der Zeit Ciceros', in *Class. et Med.* 7 (1945) 150-200.

2. Thus we encounter phrases such as *equestri loco natus* or *ortus* (Cic., *De rep.* I.10; *De lege agr.* I.27; Nepos, *Att.*19.2, cf. 1.1; Vell. Pat. II.128.1-2; cf. 88.2). And see VI.vi n.102.

3. See e.g. Badian, *PS* 100, 107, 111-12.

4. See II.i n.21 above for this and other works, by Nicolet, Cohen, etc.

5. For Atticus, see Nepos, *Att.*, esp. 1.1, 6.1-5, 11.5, 13.6, 19.2, 20.5. For Maecenas, see esp. Vell. Pat. II.88.2. For Annaeus Mela, see Tac., *Ann.* XVI.17.3. Cf. *Hist.* II.86 on Cornelius Fuscus, who in his youth 'senatorium ordinem exuerat' in order to enter the imperial service. The MS, giving his motive, has 'quietis cupidine'; some editors prefer 'inquies' or 'quaestus' to 'quietis'.

6. See esp. B. Cohen, op. cit. in II.i n.21 above.

7. See e.g. H. Strasburger, *Concordia Ordinum. Eine Untersuchung zur Politik Ciceros* (Diss. [at Frankfurt], Leipzig, 1931).

8. I accept the view that the *comitia tributa* were identical with the *concilium plebis* (cf. Section ii of this chapter), except that they (*a*) also included Patricians (who of course were few in number even in the Middle Republic), and (*b*) were presided over by a consul (or praetor) instead of a tribune. The most recent book in English on the Roman Assemblies is by Lily Ross Taylor, *Roman Voting Assemblies from the Hannibalic War to the Dictatorship of Caesar* (Ann Arbor, 1966).

See also E. S. Staveley, *Greek and Roman Voting and Elections* (1972). G. W. Botsford, *The Roman Assemblies from their Origin to the End of the Republic* (New York, 1909), is still worth consulting. Further bibliography will be found in the article, 'Comitia', by A. Momigliano, in *OCD*² 272-3. And see the next note.

9. The latest work I have seen on the subject is R. Develin, 'The third-century reform of the comitia centuriata', in *Athenaeum* n.s. 56 (1978) 346-77.

10. I must add here that the origin of the word *suffragium* has been admirably explained in the article by M. Rothstein (1903) cited in my *OPW* 348 n.2, which I did not come across until after my SVP was published.

11. Among various editions, see *FIRA*² I.62. Another section, V.8 (*FIRA*² I.41), refers to patronage, but over freedmen only.

12. Cf. Livy VI.18.6; Plut., *Rom.* 13.3 *fin.*, 5, 7-8. [On the origin and early development of the *clientela*, see now the recent works cited by H. Strasburger, *Zum antiken Gesellschaftsideal = Abhandl.* der Heidelberger Akad. der Wiss., Philos.-hist. Klasse (1976 no.4) 104 n.731, which I saw only after this chapter was finished. To my mind, the dissent expressed in P. A. Brunt's review of that work, in *Gnomon* 51 (1979) 443 ff., at 447-8, is justified only if a narrow interpretation is adopted, and we think purely in terms of cases in which the *cliens/patronus* relationship existed formally and is made explicit.]

13. W. V. Harris, *War and Imperialism in Republican Rome 327-70 B.C.* (1979), which I read only after this section was finished, has an excellent note, 135 n.2, pointing out that 'Massilienses nostri clientes' in Cic., *De rep.* I.43, is a reference to the *clientela* of Scipio Aemilianus, not of Rome, and also that the first clear use of the 'client' metaphor by a Roman writer for Rome's relationship with some of its subjects is in *Dig.* XLIX.xv.7.1 (Proculus, mid-first century C.E.).

14. See Gelzer, *The Roman Nobility* (n.1 above) 63 and nn.55-9; and on the whole subject E. Badian, *Foreign Clientelae 264-70 B.C.* (1958).

14a. I have used the Loeb edition, by J. W. and A. M. Duff (1934).

15. In my *RRW* I refer in a note (69 n.26) to Augustine, *De civ. Dei* IV.31-2; cf. 27 (against Scaevola) and VI.10 (against Seneca); also Cic., *De leg.* II.32-3 (contrast *De div.*, esp. II.28-150); Livy I.19.4-5; and Dio Cass. LII.36.1-3. As the sincerity of the religious opinions expressed by members of the Roman governing class, and in particular Cicero himself, is often doubted (with how much cause it is very hard to say), I must add here Cic., *De leg.* II.16, stressing the *practical usefulness* of inculcating a general adherence to religion: it secures respect for oaths, and 'the fear of divine punishment has reclaimed many from crime' (cf. II.30). Without *pietas* towards the gods, Cicero says elsewhere (*De nat. deorum* I.4), 'fides etiam et societas generis humani et una excellentissima virtus, iustitia' may well disappear. For the general attitude to religion in the Roman world, especially that of the ruling classes, see also my *WWECP* 24-31, repr. in *SAS* (ed. Finley) 238-48; and cf. now Brunt, LI 165-8.

16. As when in 327 B.C. the appointment of M. Claudius Marcellus as dictator was declared invalid by the augurs: see Livy VIII.23.14-17. Cf. now the examples (not including the one just given) set out in J. H. W. G. Liebeschuetz, *Continuity and Change in Roman Religion* (1979) 309 (Appendix).

17. As when the laws of M. Livius Drusus in 91 B.C. were cancelled by the Senate, one of the grounds being disregard of auspices (Cic., *De leg.* II.31, a fascinating passage; Ascon. 61, *In Cornelian.*, ed. A. C. Clark, p.69.6-7). Cf. perhaps the utilisation of sinister omens by the haruspices to stop the agrarian bill of Sex. Titius, tribune in 99 B.C. (Cic., *De leg.* II.14, 31, and other sources given in Greenidge and Clay, *Sources*² 113, and in Broughton, *MRR* II.2): the laws of Titius could be said to be *contra auspicia latae*. And see A. W. Lintott, *Violence in Republican Rome* (1968) 134-5.

18. The references to the six passages I have quoted are Cic., *In Vat.* 23; *De har. resp.* 58; *In Pis.* 9; *Post red. in sen.* 11; *In Vat.* 18; *Pro Sest.* 33. Sufficient bibliography on these laws is given by H. H. Scullard in *OCD*² 601, *s.v.* 'Leges: Aelia (1): *Aelia et Fufia*'; and Lintott, op. cit. 146-7.

[VI.iv]

1. The fullest account that I know is by Gaston Colin, *Rome et la Grèce de 200 à 146 av. J.-C.* (Paris, 1905). A particularly interesting recent work, giving a critical general survey of the earlier literature, is E. Badian, *Titus Quinctius Flamininus. Philhellenism and Realpolitik* (Louise Taft

Semple Lecture, Cincinnati, 1970). A recent very scholarly general work with good bibliographies is Will, *HPMH* I and II (1966-7). And see n.5 below.

2. See e.g. L. Homo, *Primitive Italy and the Beginnings of Roman Imperialism* (Eng. trans., 1927) 264-70, for this and some similar examples of Roman brutality towards conquered peoples. Badian, op. cit. 56 n.50, gives the sources for the Epirot episode in full, and refers in this connection to Paullus's approval of a massacre in Aetolia (Livy XLV. xxviii.6 ff.; xxxi.1 ff.), adding, 'Flamininus appears resplendent by comparison.' H. H. Scullard, 'Charops and Roman policy in Epirus', in *JRS* 35 (1945) 58-64, does his best to defend Paullus, in my opinion unsuccessfully. For 'the Roman method of conducting war', see also Rostovtzeff, *SEHHW* II.606.

3. The facts and sources are given very fully by Magie, *RRAM* I.199 ff. (esp. 216-17), with the notes in II.1095 ff. (esp. 1103 nn.36-7). See also Brunt, *IM* 224-7.

4. T. R. S. Broughton, in *ESAR* (ed. Frank) IV.590. For the details, see ibid. 516-19, 525-6, 562-8, 571-8, 579-87 (and 535 ff.). Cf. Jones, *RE* 114-24.

5. See W. V. Harris, 'On war and greed in the second century B.C.', in *AHR* 76 (1971) 1371-85, and M. H. Crawford, 'Rome and the Greek world: economic relationships', in *Econ. Hist. Rev.*[2] 30 (1977) 42-52, both modifying the picture presented in Badian, *RILR*[2], a mine of information in compact form which is perhaps most likely to be consulted by students gaining their first acquaintance with Roman expansion in the last two centuries of the Republic. And see Brunt, LI 170-5. [Only after this section was finished did I see the interesting books by Harris (mentioned in n.13 to Section iii of this chapter) and Michael Crawford, *The Roman Republic* (Fontana Hist. of the Anc. World, 1978).]

6. I must add that I cannot follow those writers who have supposed that the policy of Augustus and most of his successors was fundamentally defensive and eschewed further conquests. My own views are much the same as those of P. A. Brunt, in his review of H. D. Meyer, *Die Aussenpolitik des Augustus und die augusteische Dichtung* (Cologne, 1961), in *JRS* 53 (1963) 170-6, and A. R. Birley, 'Roman frontiers and Roman frontier policy: some reflections on Roman imperialism', in *Trans. of the Archit. and Archaeol. Soc. of Durham and Northumberland* n.s.3 (1974) 13-25. The existence during the Principate of a strong current of opinion in favour of further expansion is something that should not be entirely ignored when we are considering Roman imperialism in the Late Republic (cf. Section i of this chapter and its nn.5-7). For a scathing criticism of Roman 'frontier policy' in the Principate, see the impressive article by J. C. Mann, 'The frontiers of the Principate', in *ANRW* II.i (1974) 508-33 (with a bibliography).

7. Cf. M. P. Nilsson, *Gesch. der griech. Religion* II[2] (1961) 177: 'Dieser Kult hat denselben Sinn und Zweck wie der Herrscherkult.' There are two recent comprehensive treatments of the Greek cult of Rome, by Ronald Mellor, Θεὰ ʿΡώμη. *The Worship of the Goddess Roma in the Greek World* (= *Hypomnemata* 42, Göttingen, 1975); and a work I have not seen: Carla Fayer, *Il culto della Dea Roma. Origine e diffusione nell'Impero* (*Collana di Saggi e Ricerche* 9, Pescara, 1976) – see the review of both works by I. C. Davis, in *JRS* 67 (1977) 204-6. I agree with Mellor (21 and n.50) on the absence of any 'religious dimension' (in the modern sense) in the cults of rulers and of Rome.

8. J. A. O. Larsen, 'Some early Anatolian cults of Rome', in *Mélanges d'archéol. et d'hist. offerts à André Piganiol* (Paris, 1966) III.1635-43. The list of cults of Roma in Asia Minor known down to the 1940s in Magie, *RRAM* II.1613-14, has now been superseded by the much longer list of all known Greek cults of Roma given by Mellor, op. cit. 207-28.

9. The cult of Flamininus was still being celebrated at Gytheum in Laconia in the reign of Tiberius (see E/J[2] 102.11-12) and at Chalcis in Euboea in Plutarch's time (Plut., *Flam.* 16.5-7; cf. *IG* XII.ix.931.5-6). On the whole subject see Nilsson, op. cit. (in n.7 above) 178-80; Kurt Latte, *Römische Religionsgesch.* (1960) 312-13.

10. The best book I know on ancient Persia is R. N. Frye, *The Heritage of Persia*[2] (1976). See also R. Ghirshman, *Iran* (1951; Eng. trans., 1954).

11. For the history of Edessa see J. B. Segal, *Edessa, 'The Blessed City'* (1970); E. Kirsten, 'Edessa', in *RAC* 4 (1959) 552-97.

12. See esp. C. B. Welles, 'The Population of Roman Dura', in *Stud. in Roman Econ. and Soc. Hist. in Honor of A. C. Johnson,* ed. P. R. Coleman-Norton (Princeton, 1951) 251-74; and J. B. Ward-Perkins, 'The Roman West and the Parthian East', in *PBA* 51 (1965) 175-99 (with Plates). For further bibliography (including the excavation reports) see *OCD*[2] 422, s.v. 'Europus'.

13. Sherwin-White, *RC*[2] 38-58 (cf. 200-14), 245, 271-2, 293, 295-306, 311-12, 334-6, 382 (with 336), citing most of the modern literature. See also Jolowicz and Nicholas, *HISRL*[3] 71-4.

[VI.v]

1. I cannot accept the position taken up by F. G. B. Millar, in *CR* 82 = n.s.18 (1968) 265–6; and *JRS* 63 (1973) 61–7, which may perhaps be summarised as the belief that, in the time of Augustus, expressions such as 'res publica restituta' are 'not likely to have meant that the Republic was restored', and that Augustus never even claimed to have 'restored the Republic'. Millar is quite justified in pointing out that in some statements about a restoration of the 'res publica' that term must be translated '"the State" or "the condition of public affairs"': in addition to passages such as Livy III.20.1 (which he quotes), see Aug., *RG* 1.1,3; and 2, where the Greek equivalents are worth noticing. But Augustus himself, in *RG* 34.1, claims to have transferred the *res publica* (surely, '*control* of the state') from his own *potestas* into the *arbitrium* of the Roman Senate and People – and what is this but a claim to have done precisely what people mean nowadays when they speak of 'a restoration of the Republic': that is to say, of the state in its pre-Triumviral constitutional and political form? The Greek version of *RG* 34.1 speaks of a transfer of κυρυῄα, mastery, from his own ἐξουσία to that of the Roman Senate and People; and in a famous deceitful statement in 34.3 Augustus shows that after the transfer just mentioned he wished to appear not to have complete *potestas* or ἐξουσία. I cannot see in what other form of words Augustus could have made a clearer claim to have 'restored the Republic' in the very sense which the phrase normally bears today. That the regime was now a monarchy in all but name was of course widely recognised from the first; but in theory it was not a monarchy. I see not the least reason to take the words of Vitruv., *De architect.* I, *praef.* 1-2, and other passages quoted by Millar, as a disproof of the claim to have 'restored the Republic'. Velleius speaks specifically of the *form* of the state (as a *republic*, therefore) in a much-quoted passage that ends with the words, 'Prisca illa et antiqua rei publicae forma revocata' (II.89.3). And there is a passage I should like to cite (written in the 30s, under Tiberius) which is not usually quoted in this connection: Val. Max. IX.xv.5, 'postquam a Sullana violentia Caesariana aequitas rempublicam reduxit', where *rempublicam* (if that is the right reading: it is that of the Teubner editor, C. Kempf, 1888, accepted by P. Constant, Paris, 1935) can only mean 'the Republic'. In spite of the chronological difficulty, *Caesariana* can only refer to Augustus (as in I.i.19), rather than Julius Caesar, because of ibid., *Ext.* 1 (*eodem praeside reipublicae, cum cohortis Augusti*) and 2 (opening with *idem*, and dealing with events after the execution of Ariarathes by Mark Antony in 36).

1a. A. Momigliano was not justified in remarking, in his review of Syme's *Tacitus* (in reference to Syme's *RR*), that 'Ohne Namier als Vorgänger ist Syme nicht zu denken': see *Gnomon* 33 (1961) 55, repr. in Momigliano's *Terzo Contributo alla storia degli studi classici e del mondo antico* (Rome, 1966) 739. When he wrote *The Roman Revolution*, Syme had not yet read Namier.

2. See esp. Brunt's fundamentally important article, ALRR = 'The army and the land in the Roman revolution', in *JRS* 52 (1962) 69–86; also his acute review, in *JRS* 58 (1968) 229–32 (esp. III, 230-2), of Christian Meier, *Res Publica Amissa* (Wiesbaden, 1966). Relevant here too is another article by Brunt, '"Amicitia" in the Late Roman Republic', in *PCPS* 191 = n.s.11 (1965) 1-20, repr. in *CRR* (ed. Seager) 199–218. For the 'general reader', Brunt's most useful article in this field is 'The Roman mob', in *Past & Present* 35 (1966) 3-27, repr. (with an addendum) in *SAS* (ed. Finley) 74-102. Those with at least a little further knowledge will also profit from Z. Yavetz, *Plebs and Princeps* (1969) 1-37; and Helmuth Schneider, *Die Entstehung der römischen Militärdiktatur. Krise und Niedergang einer antiken Republik* (Cologne, 1977). I am sorry to say that I cannot cite any other recent books or articles that share the same general position as mine: otherwise, we must go back to Beesly (see n.5 below).

3. For a good brief statement about Optimates and Populares, see Brunt, *SCRR* 92-5. Nearer to the current standard view (which is not mine), but better than some other recent statements, is E. Badian's article, 'Optimates, Populares', in *OCD*² 753-4. He cites two recent works on the Populares, by K. Rübeling and C. Meier; add H. Strasburger, in *RE* XVIII.i (1939) 773-98, *s.v.* 'Optimates'. The *locus classicus* for the distinction between Optimates and Populares, from the Optimate point of view, is of course Cic., *Pro Sest.* 96-105 (note esp. 105 on the Populares), 136-40.

4. I do not mean to imply that the plebs cared much about the treatment of provincials: no doubt the majority of them wanted their share of the spoils of empire. But we should not forget that most of the few attempts to improve provincial administration, including the Gracchan jury bill and Caesar's important law of 59, were promoted by recognisably 'popularis' figures.

5. I should like to take this opportunity of recommending the book by E. S. Beesly, *Catiline, Clodius, and Tiberius* (1878; repr., New York, 1924), a series of four brilliantly written and highly entertaining lectures delivered at the Working Men's College at St. Pancras. Beesly (1831-1915) was Professor of History at University College London. He was not just an

ancient historian; he also published a book on Queen Elizabeth, and wrote many articles on contemporary affairs. Although a Comtian Positivist rather than a Marxist, Beesly was chairman of the inaugural meeting at St. Martin's Hall, London, on 28 September 1864 of the International Workingmen's Association (the 'First International'). Several letters from Marx to Beesly in 1870-1 have been published in *MEW* XXXIII. See Royden Harrison, 'E. S. Beesly and Karl Marx', in *IRSH* 4 (1959) 22-58, 208-38; and 'Professor Beesly and the working-class movement', in *Essays in Labour Hist.*, ed. Asa Briggs and John Saville (rev. edn, 1967) 205-41. Marx described Beesly in a letter to Kugelmann on 13 December 1870 as 'a very capable and courageous man', despite some 'crotchets' deriving from his adherence to Comte; and in a letter to Beesly of 12 June 1871 he told Beesly that although he himself was very hostile to Comte's ideas, he considered Beesly as 'the only Comtist either in England or France who deals with historical "crises" not as a sectarian but as an historian in the best sense of the word' (*MEW* XXXIII.228-30). Harrison (see above) mentions several letters from Beesly to Marx which have not yet been published. The two always remained good friends: see the statement by Beesly quoted by Harrison, op. cit. (1959) 32 & n.3.

6. A particularly remarkable action of Ti. Gracchus was procuring the deposition by the *concilium plebis* of his fellow-tribune, M. Octavius, who in 133 by interposing his veto was threatening to defeat the popular will (Plut., *Ti. Gr.* 11.4 to 12.6, etc.). For Saturninus and Glaucia certain laws passed by the popular Assembly, prescribing the taking of oaths by magistrates and/or senators to obey them (see nos. 1 and 4-6 below), have sometimes been held to be relevant; and I would add Caesar's agrarian laws in 59 (nos. 2 and 3). Unfortunately, the dates of some of these laws (nos.4-6) are uncertain. It has moreover been claimed that oaths by *magistrates* to obey laws were not new or necessarily 'popularis' measures: this I think is true, even if we draw (as we must) a firm distinction – not sufficiently recognised by G. V. Sumner, in *GRBS* 19 (1978) 211-25, at 222-3 n.52, or A. N. Sherwin-White, in *JRS* 62 (1972) 83-99, at 92 – between (a) the very general oath to obey the laws, which apparently had to be taken by every magistrate within five days of entering upon office and is known from 200 B.C. (Livy XXXI.50.6-9), and (b) oaths to obey a specific law, such as those mentioned in nos.1-6 below. In spite of the opinions expressed by A. Passerini, in *Athen.* n.s.12 (1934), esp. 139-43 and 271-8, and G. Tibiletti, in id. 31 (1953) 5-100, at 57-66, I would accept (1) the oath by every senator which was prescribed by the agrarian law of Saturninus (App., *BC* I.29-31; Plut., *Mar.* 29.2-11; cf. Cic., *Pro Sest.* 37, 101, etc.) as something objectionable to the senators not merely because they considered the law to have been passed illegally. Cf. (2) Caesar's first agrarian law in his consulship in 59 (App., *BC* II. 12/42; Plut., *Cat. min.* 32.5-11; Dio Cass. XXXVIII.7.1; cf. Cic., *Pro Sest.* 61, etc.), which also imposed an oath on senators, and (3) Caesar's subsequent law on the *ager Campanus*, which contained a new kind of oath, for candidates for magistracies (Cic., *Ad Att.* II.xviii.2): there is reason to think that both these provisions were detested by Optimates, apart from the fact that the laws were stigmatised as having been passed illegally. Another law, (4), ordering oaths to be taken both by magistrates and by senators, is most probably (although not certainly) of the last year or two of the second century: the *Lex Latina tabulae Bantinae, FIRA*² I.82-4, no.6, §§ 3-4, lines 14-23 and 23 ff. (5) The *Fragmentum Tarentinum*, first published by R. Bartoccini in *Epigraphica* 9 (1947, published 1949) 3-31, and re-edited by Tibiletti, op. cit. 38-57 (cf. 57-66, 73-5), contains in lines 20-3 an oath by magistrates; but it cannot be securely dated (contrast Tibiletti, op. cit. 73-5; H. B. Mattingly, in *JRS* 59 [1969] 129-43, and 60 [1970] 154-68; Sherwin-White, op. cit., and Sumner, op. cit.). The last of these texts is (6) the 'Pirate Law', of which one version was discovered at Delphi in the 1890s and another has recently been found at Cnidus: see the article by M. Hassall, M. Crawford and J. Reynolds, in *JRS* 64 (1974) 195-220, where there are combined texts and translations (201-7, 207-9). But even the Delphic version, which has an oath for certain magistrates (*FIRA*² I.121-131, no.9, C.8-19), provides no evidence that the law was 'popularis' or in any way anti-senatorial: see (esp. on the crucial question of the date, for which I would accept 99 or the last days of 100 rather than 101-100) A. Giovannini and E. Grzybek, in *Mus. Helv.* 35 (1978) 33-47; Sumner, op. cit. To sum up – I regard only the oaths in nos. 1, 2 and 4 (the ones by senators, and perhaps that by magistrates in no.4) and the one in no.3 as significantly 'popularis' in character; in this context, no.6 is almost certainly and no.5 is possibly irrelevant.

7. See farther on in the main text above, and nn.8-10 below, for the feelings of the plebs and the honours they paid to the memories of Ti. and C. Gracchus, Saturninus, Marius Gratidianus,

Catiline, Clodius and Caesar. It is very interesting to find Cicero feeling obliged to offer insincere praise to the Gracchi when addressing the People in a *contio*, as in the *De lege agr.* II.10, 31, 81 (contrast I.21, in the Senate!) and *Pro Rabir. perd. reo* 14–15. His real opinions about the Gracchi were very different: see e.g. *De offic.* I.76, 109; II.43; *Lael.* 40; *De rep.* I.31; *De leg.* III.20; *Tusc. disp.* III.48; IV.51; *De fin.* IV.65; *De nat. deor.* I.106; *Brut.* 212 (cf. 103, 125–6, 128, 224); *De or.* I.38; *Part. or.* 104, 106; *I Cat.* 29 (cf. 3); *IV Cat.* 13; *Pro domo ad pontif.* 82; *De har. resp.* 41; *Pro Sest.* 140 (cf. 101, 103); *De prov. cons.* 18; *Pro Planc.* 88; *Pro Milon.* 14, 72; *In Vat.* 23; *VIII Phil.* 13–14. Several of these passages show that Cicero thoroughly approved the killing of both the Gracchi. The most recent treatment I have seen of this subject, by Jean Béranger, 'Les jugements de Cicéron sur les Gracques', in *ANRW* I.i.732–63, comes at the end to conclusions about Cicero's attitude which seem to me gravely mistaken and contradicted by much of the evidence Béranger himself cites. I cannot understand how anyone can say, as he does, 'Jamais il n'y a d'outrance, de dénigrement systématique ou d'acrimonie. Même s'il déplore leur action, Cicéron rend justice aux Gracques' (762). Even Cicero could hardly deny that the Gracchi were great orators and leading men! For Catiline, see also Sall., *Cat.* 35.3; 36.5; and esp. 37.1–2 (contrast 48.1–2); 61.1–6. It would be interesting to know whether Mark Antony really claimed to resemble Catiline, as Cicero alleged (*IV Phil.* 15).

8. Cicero must have had particularly in mind the man referred to in our sources (uniformly hostile to him) as L. Equitius, who in the last years of the second century B.C. aroused great excitement among the lower classes at Rome by representing himself as a son of Tiberius Gracchus, and who was killed in 100 immediately on his election to the tribunate. The main sources are only partly given in Greenidge & Clay, *Sources*[2] 96–7, 102, 108: add Cic., *Pro Rab. Perd.* 20; Val. Max. III.viii.6; IX.vii.2 (incomplete in *Sources*[2]); xv.1; App., *BC* I.32, 33. Particularly interesting on the popular enthusiasm aroused by Equitius are the passages just cited from Val. Max. (for whom Equitius was a *portentum*, a *monstrum*), and App., *BC* I.32.

9. Cic., *De offic.* III.80; Seneca, *De ira* III.18.1; Pliny, *NH* XXXIII.132; XXXIV.27.

10. On the whole question of Caesar's great popularity with the masses see Z. Yavetz, *Plebs and Princeps* (1969), esp. 38–82. It is fascinating to observe how Augustus, while styling himself 'divi filius' and making full use of the appeal he possessed for the masses by being Caesar's heir, eventually dissociated himself from Caesar. This has been admirably brought out by Syme, *RPM* 12–14, showing how Augustan propaganda preferred to play down and as far as possible to forget Caesar. In Horace, as Syme puts it, 'Julius Caesar is not quite referred to as a person' (see only the 'Iulium sidus' of *Od.* I.xii.47 and the 'Caesaris ultor' of I.ii.44). In the *Aeneid*, Vergil ignores Caesar except in VI.832–5, where it is Caesar and not Pompey who is exhorted to throw down his arms first. Livy, as we know from Seneca (*NQ* V.xviii.4), professed to be uncertain whether the birth of Caesar had benefited the state, or whether it would not have been better for it had he not been born; and according to Tacitus (*Ann.* IV.34.4) Augustus used to call Livy a 'Pompeianus'. As Syme comments, 'These men understood each other. Livy was quite sincere; and the exaltation of Pompeius, so far from offending Caesar Augustus, fitted admirably with his policy' (*RPM* 13). Finally, although Pompey's image was carried in the funeral procession of Augustus, with those of other great generals, Caesar's was not. It could of course be said that Caesar had been deified and therefore was not to be considered a mortal man (see Dio Cass. LVI.34.2–3); but I would take the omission, as Syme does, as yet another piece of evidence that (as Syme puts it) 'It was expedient for Augustus to dissociate himself from Caesar . . . He exploited the divinity of his parent and paraded the titulature of "*Divi filius*". For all else, Caesar the proconsul and dictator was better forgotten' (*RPM* 13–14). [Syme's *RPM* is now repr. in his *Roman Papers* (1979) I.205–17: see esp. 213–14.]

11. These events are described, and the sources given, in several modern works, among which I will mention only T. Rice Holmes, *The Roman Republic* (1923) II.166 and n.1. But cf. the book by E. S. Beesly, cited in n.5 above.

12. Cicero (*Ad Att.* IV.i.3–5) makes out that on his return from exile (decreed by a special meeting of the *comitia centuriata*) in August–September 57 he was greeted with unanimous enthusiasm both on his journey from Brundisium to Rome and in the city itself. This would be a surprising exception to the general rule, if it were true. It is of course easy to believe that 'everyone of every order' *whose name was known* to Cicero's *nomenclator* came out to meet him as he reached Rome (§ 5), and that all the *boni* and *honestissimi* welcomed him (§§ 3, 4). But we may expect Cicero to exaggerate, especially at such a time, and indeed in § 6 of the same letter he happens to mention that agitators 'egged on by Clodius' had demonstrated against him three days after

his arrival in Rome. There are several indications of Cicero's unpopularity with the *plebs urbana*: see e.g. Dio Cass. XXXVII.38.1-2. He himself was well aware of it: see e.g. *Ad Att.* VIII.iii.5; xiD.7 (both from 49 B.C.); and *VII Phil.* 4 (43 B.C.), where Cicero boasts that he has 'always opposed the rashness of the multitude'; cf. Ascon., *In Milonian.* 33 (p.37, ed. A. C. Clark, *OCT*).

13. Yavetz, in the bibliography of his book cited in n.2 above, mentions George Rudé, *The Crowd in the French Revolution* (1959; there is now a paperback, 1967), and *The Crowd in History. A Study of Popular Disturbances in France and England 1730-1848* (1964). See also Rudé, *Paris and London in the Eighteenth Century. Studies in Popular Protest* (1970, a collection of essays published between 1952 and 1969); E. J. Hobsbawm and G. Rudé, *Captain Swing* (1969, Penguin 1973); Hobsbawm, *Bandits* (1969); *Primitive Rebels*[3] (1971).

14. An admirable paper which is perhaps not as well known as it should be is Z. Yavetz, 'Levitas popularis', in *Atene e Roma* n.s.10 (1965) 97-110; and see Yavetz, 'Plebs sordida', in *Athenaeum* n.s.43 (1965) 295-311; and 'The living conditions of the urban plebs in Republican Rome', in *Latomus* 17 (1958) 500-17, repr. in *CRR* (ed. Seager) 162-79. And see n.3 above. It is interesting to see how Cicero, in a speech delivered to the populace in a *contio*, could pretend to be shocked when recalling how his opponent, Rullus, had referred to the urban plebs as if he were speaking *de aliqua sentina, ac non de optimorum civium genere* (*De lege agr.* II.70).

15. For the Roman census figures, the most authoritative work is now Brunt, *IM*.

16. The facts and figures are mostly presented (not in a very easily assimilable way) in Frank, *ESAR* I. A useful selection will be found in A. H. M. Jones's contribution, 'Ancient empires and the economy: Rome', to the papers of the *Third International Conf. of Econ. Hist.* at Munich in 1965, Vol. III (1969) 81-104, at 81-90, repr. in Jones, *RE* 114-24.

17. See Benjamin Farrington, *Diodorus Siculus: Universal Historian* (Inaugural Lecture, at Swansea, 1936, published 1937) = *Head and Hand in Ancient Greece* (1947) 55-87.

18. In such passages as Varro, *RR* III.iii.10; xvii.2, 3, 5-8, 8-9; Pliny, *NH* IX.167-72, we find among the owners of famous fishponds Q. Hortensius, M. and L. Licinius Lucullus, a Licinius Murena, and a Marcius Philippus. For Vedius Pollio, see Syme, *RR* 410 and n.3.

19. See e.g. Cic., *Ad fam.* XV.i.5 (an official despatch to the Senate, from Cicero's province of Cilicia); *Pro lege Manil.* 65; *Div. in Caec.* 7; *II Verr.* iii.207; v.126 (cf. *De offic.* II.73); *Ad Att.* V.xvi.2.

20. The *manubiae* or *manibiae*: see P. Treves, in *OCD*[2] 644, with brief bibliography. Cf. Jones, *RE* 116-17, with nn.16-17. (The reference to Pompey's donative in n.16 should be to p.115 n.6.) And see the reference to Brunt, *IM* 394, in the main text above, a few lines on.

21. The temporary interruption of the corn supply from Sicily as a consequence of the First Sicilian Slave War of 135 ff. B.C. must have had a serious effect on the urban poor at Rome, by raising the price of bread, their staple diet; and this may have helped to precipitate Ti. Gracchus' agrarian bill: see H. C. Boren, 'The urban side of the Gracchan economic crisis', in *AHR* 63 (1957/8) 890-902, repr. in *CRR* (ed. Seager) 54-66.

22. And see III.iv above, & its n.5.

23. See Brunt, *ALRR* 69 (the excellent opening para.), 79-80, 83, 84; and cf. his *IM*.

24. It will be convenient if I mainly give references to Syme, *RR*. The cases I have in mind are in B.C. 44 (*RR* 118), 43 (*RR* 178-9, and see esp. 180-1), 41 (*RR* 209, and App., *BC* V.20/79-80), and 40 (*RR* 217).

25. E.g. in B.C. 39 (Syme, *RR* 221), when they were successful in forcing on their leaders the 'Peace of Puteoli' or 'Treaty of Misenum'; and in 38 (*RR* 230: see App., *BC* V.92/384).

26. See e.g. Lily Ross Taylor, 'Forerunners of the Gracchi', in *JRS* 52 (1962) 18-27. I myself feel that the passing of the ballot laws, *leges tabellariae* (of which Cicero so deeply disapproved), deserves more emphasis than it usually receives, for ballot voting of course makes it much more difficult, perhaps impossible, for leading men to ensure that their clients, or those they have bribed, vote in the 'right' way. Of the *leges tabellariae*, the two most important were before 133: the Lex Gabinia of 139 for elections, and the Lex Cassia of 137 for trials other than for *perduellio*. The main sources are all in Cicero: *De leg.* III.33-9 (esp. 34, 35, 39); *Lael.* 41; *Pro Sest.* 103; *Pro Planc.* 16; *Brut.* 97, 106; cf. *De lege agr.* II.4; *Pro Cornel., ap.* Ascon., p.78.2-3,5-8 (ed. A. C. Clark, *OCT*). See, briefly, Brunt, *SCRR* 65-6; E. S. Staveley, *Greek and Roman Voting and Elections* (1972) 158-9, 161, 228-9, 253 n.302. For C. Flaminius, who appears to have been the most notable pre-Gracchan *popularis*, and was tribune in 232 and consul in 223 and 217, see Z. Yavetz, ' The policy of C. Flaminius and the Plebiscitum Claudianum. A reconsideration', in *Athenaeum* n.s.40 (1962) 325-44.

27. Anyone who wishes to read an account of the Gracchi, and of the period that followed, totally different from the one given here might try R. E. Smith, *The Failure of the Roman Republic* (1955). This is well summarised in the opening words of the review by G. E. F. Chilver, in *JRS* 46 (1956) 167: 'The story Professor Smith tells is of the destruction of a close-knit and harmonious society by the irresponsibility of two brothers, young men in a hurry, who tried to apply philosophical learning to the handling of a political structure peculiarly ill adapted to absorb it. The result was disintegration, not only of politics, but of morals, religion, taste; and the work of the Gracchi was not undone until Augustus imposed the harmony which Rome might otherwise have reached through peaceful change.' Another account of Ti. Gracchus, totally different again from mine and exhibiting that obsession with the prosopography of the ruling Roman families which has been so common in recent years, is D. C. Earl, *Tiberius Gracchus* (1963), on which see the review by P. A. Brunt, in *Gnomon* 37 (1965) 189-92 – attacked, unsuccessfully in the main, by Badian, TGBRR 674-8 etc. (Badian's article is however a mine of bibliographical information, supplementing his 'From the Gracchi to Sulla (1940-1959)', in *Historia* 11 [1962] 197-245.) Another recent account of the fall of the Republic which seems to me deeply mistaken in its conception of the attitude of the Roman lower classes, but has had considerable influence, especially in Germany, is Christian Meier, *Res Publica Amissa* (Wiesbaden, 1966): see the review by Brunt, in *JRS* 58 (1968) 229-32, with which I am wholly in agreement. The best part of Meier's book is perhaps his criticism of the modern overemphasis on supposedly enduring political factions based to a considerable extent on the ties of kinship, intermarriage and *amicitia*. On this and other matters see also Brunt's article, 'Amicitia' (1965), cited in n.2 above; and T. P. Wiseman's very short article, 'Factions and family trees', in *Liverpool Classical Monthly* I (1976) 1-3.

28. See the review of Meier's book by Brunt (1968), mentioned in the preceding note, at 231-2, giving many references, esp. from Sallust. Of these, I would stress particularly *Hist.* I.12; *Cat.* 38-39.1; *BJ* 40.3; 41.2-8 (esp. 5); 42.1. I would also add *Hist.* III.48 (*Oratio Macri*).27-8; *Cat.* 20.11-14; 28.4 with 33.1; 35.3; 37.1-4 (contrast 48.1); 37.7; 48.2; *BJ* 16.2; 31.7-8,20; 73.6-7; 84.1.

29. See the works cited in VI.iv n.2 above.

30. The most interesting passages in the sources are App., *BC* III. 86/353-6 and 88/361-2 (whether referring to two successive embassies or duplicating a single one); Dio Cass. XLVI.42.4 to 43.5. The words παρρησία and παρρησιάζεσθαι appear in App., *BC* III.88/362. Some initiative is attributed to the legions by App., *BC* III.86/353, 356; 88/361, 363; contrast Dio Cass. XLVI.42.4, with 43.1; cf. 43.5, where a senator asks whether the men have been sent by the legions themselves or by Octavian.

31. For early 43 B.C., see Cic., *Ep. ad Brut.* I.xviii.5 (fraudulent returns by the recalcitrant *boni viri*); cf. Dio Cass. XLVI.31.3 to 32.1. For the further taxation on land and houses later in 43, see Dio Cass. XLVII.14.2: the owner of a house in Rome or Italy had to pay a sum equal to the annual rent if it were let, and half that amount if he occupied it himself; owners of land had to pay half its produce in tax. For the tax on land and slaves in 42 B.C., see Dio Cass. XLVII.16.1 to 17.1, esp. 16.5 on under-assessment. For 39 B.C., see App., *BC* V.67; Dio Cass. XLVIII.34.2,4. For 32 B.C., see Dio Cass. L.10.4-6; Plut., *Ant.* 58.2.

32. App., *BC* IV.32-34; Val. Max. VIII.iii.3.

33. Birley, TCCRE 263 n.2, traces the changes in the taxes that fed the *aerarium militare*, to A.D. 38.

34. For the attempts in 22 B.C. to induce Augustus to become dictator, consul every year, and a sort of censor for life, see Aug., *RG* 5.1,3; Vell. Pat. II.89.5; Suet., *Aug.* 52; Dio Cass. LIV.1.2-5 (esp. 3) and 2.1; cf. 6.2 (21 B.C.) and 10.1 (19 B.C.).

35. I think this is certainly the meaning of τό τε τοῦ δήμου σφίσιν ὄνομα προτείνοντος in Dio Cass. LX.15.3. For the name, see *PIR*², A no.1140.

36. It is widely held that under the Principate the provinces were much better governed. There is some truth in this, but serious abuses continued: see esp. Brunt, CPMEP = 'Charges of provincial maladministration under the Early Principate', in *Historia* 10 (1961) 189-227, and Section vi of this chapter.

37. 'Obscuro loco natus', of course, was a taunt that became familiar in the Late Republic. See esp. the fourth chapter of T. P. Wiseman, *New Men in the Roman Senate 139 B.C. - A.D. 14* (1971) 65-94. Perhaps I could also mention here again the useful little article by Wiseman, cited at the end of n.27 above; and the large book by Israel Shatzman, *Senatorial Wealth and Roman Politics* (*Coll. Latomus* 142, Brussels, 1975), which however is marred by a number of errors, pointed out by reviewers. See also Maria Jacynowska, 'The economic differentiation of the Roman nobility at the end of the Republic', in *Historia* 11 (1962) 486-99.

38. See the list given by Millar, in *JRS* 63 (1973), at 63 n.92.

39. Pliny, *Paneg.* 63.2; 77.7; 92.1,2,3; 93.1; cf. 77.1; 93.2.

40. On patronage, see also Lily Ross Taylor, *Party Politics in the Age of Caesar* (Berkeley etc., 1949, repr. 1961) 41-9, 174-5 and *passim*. Further bibliography will be found in A. Momigliano's articles, 'Cliens' and 'Patronus', in *OCD*² 252, 791.

41. Less attention has been paid to this subject than it deserves, even in two useful recent books, J. M. Kelly, *Roman Litigation* (1966), and Peter Garnsey, *SSLPRE* (1970).

42. For a good brief account of the whole subject (including *destinatio, commendatio* and *nominatio*, and the *Tabula Hebana*), see Staveley, op. cit. (in n.26 above) 217-23, with 261-3 nn.423-48, where sufficient bibliography will be found. [After this section was finished, there appeared an interesting paper by A. J. Holladay, 'The elections of magistrates in the Early Principate', in *Latomus* 37 (1978) 874-93.]

43. Eunap., *VS* VII.iii.9 to iv.1, pp.476-7 (Boissonade), ed. Joseph Giangrande, Rome, 1956. The passage can also be found on pp.440-3 of the Loeb edition of Philostratus and Eunapius, by W. C. Wright, 1921 and repr. For Maximus, see *PLRE* I.583-4.

44. There is an excellent study of *amicitia* in the Late Republic, by P. A. Brunt: see n.2 above. Vatinius was of course joking when he said he was writing to Cicero (*Ad fam.* V.ix.1) as if a *cliens* to his *patronus*. As for the term *amicus*, it could sometimes be used in rather a surprising way, as when Quintus Cicero tells his brother that he is pleased at the prospect of Tiro's manumission, so that he can be an *amicus* rather than a *servus* (*Ad fam.* XVI.xvi.1).

45. Cf. Dio Cass. LVII.vii.6.

46. Another leading Roman historian, who kindly read a draft of this section, objected to my saying that the presence of Tiberius 'prevented' these unjust judgments from being given: 'No,' he said, 'that was the *intention*.' But again, the Latin is perfectly clear: the 'consulitur' belongs to the next sentence; 'multa . . . constituta' can only mean that decisions *were actually given* 'adversus ambitum et potentium preces'.

47. This passage is also not noticed by Walter Jens, 'Libertas bei Tacitus', in *Hermes* 84 (1956) 331-53.

48. Momigliano is certainly right about Wirszubski's view: see his *LPIR* 3-4, 4-5, 7-9, 14 & *passim*. But against a too close identification of *libertas* with *civitas* see Ernst Levy, 'Libertas und Civitas', in *ZSS* 78 (1961) 142-72.

49. Wirszubski speaks of Cicero's 'moral idealism' (*LPIR* 87), and his sympathies are strongly with Cicero's thoroughly oligarchical position: see e.g. his *LPIR* 71-4 (with the second paragraph of 52) and other passages. He can even say, 'Tacitus knew that at its best the Republican constitution provided genuine political freedom'! (*LPIR* 163).

50. Cf. V.iii and its n.16 above.

51. For the main facts, see Walter Allen, 'Cicero's house and *libertas*', in *TAPA* 75 (1944) 1-9. Wirszubski refers to Cic., *De dom.* 110 & 131, but only in a footnote, to justify his statement that 'Clodius must have also posed as liberator' (*LPIR* 103 n.4). He does not even mention the temple of Libertas.

52. I must not pursue this issue further here, as it is not sufficiently relevant to my main theme. It will be enough to refer mainly to one author, Sallust: see his *Cat.* 20.14 (from the speech of Catiline to his associates; cf. 58.8,11, and, for the spirit animating the rebels, 61); 33.4 (from the speech of C. Manlius); *Hist.* III.48.1-4, 12-13, 19, 26-8 (from the speech of C. Licinius Macer in 73 B.C.). Wirszubski pays little attention to such texts, although he refers to some in footnotes and gives the ironical Sall., *Hist.* III.48.22 as an example of the 'misuse' of the expression *libertas* (*LPIR* 103). I should also like to draw attention to a couple of expressions in Livy (already mentioned in n.5 to Section ii of this chapter), which bring out particularly well the highly oligarchical sense of *libertas* (of Cicero's and Wirszubski's *libertas*): Livy II.41.2, where Spurius Cassius is said to 'periculosas libertati opes struere' by giving the plebs the land they so sorely needed (cf. § 5: *servitutem*); and VI.20.14, remarking that M. Manlius, who was put to death on a trumped-up charge (see n.5 to Section ii of this chapter) of aiming at *regnum*, would have been *memorabilis* had he not been born *in libera civitate*!

53. The phrase occurs e.g. in *Pro Sest.* 98; *Ad fam.* I.ix.21.

54. Perhaps the most accessible recent scholarly discussion, for the English reader, is Wirszubski, 'Cicero's *cum dignitate otium*: a reconsideration', in *JRS* 44 (1954) 1-13, which is reprinted in *CRR* (ed. Seager) 183-95. The most important of the relevant passages in Cicero is perhaps *Pro Sest.* 98.

55. See the recent article by K. E. Petzold, 'Römische Revolution oder Krise der römischen

Republik?' in *Riv. stor. dell' Ant.* 2 (1972) 229-43, whose outlook is very different from mine. He discusses a number of different views.

56. Cf. Fronto, *Princip. hist.* 17 (pp.199-200, ed. M. P. J. van den Hout, Leiden, 1954): 'ut qui sciret populum Romanum duabus praecipue rebus, annona et spectaculis, teneri' etc.

57. The letter (never actually despatched) was written in French, at the end of 1877, to the editor of a Russian journal: see *MESC* 379; *MEW* XIX.111-12. The words '*mob*' and 'poor whites' are in English in the original. Cf. Marx's reference to 'the Roman plebs at the time of bread and circuses' (*Grundrisse*, E.T. 500 = Hobsbawm, *KMPCEF* 102).

58. J. P. V. D. Balsdon, 'Panem et circenses', in *Hommages à Marcel Renard* II (= *Coll. Latomus* 102, Brussels, 1969) 57-60; *Life and Leisure in Anc. Rome* (1969) 267-70.

59. Even in the Late Republic it was possible for Cicero to say that the Roman people made clear their point of view (their *iudicium ac voluntas*) not only in *contiones* and *comitia* (for the difference, see Section ii of this chapter) but also at the games and gladiatorial shows (*Pro Sest.* 106-27: for the games etc. see 115 ff., esp. 115, 124).

60. Sall., *BJ* 73.4-7 writes rather as if the election of Marius as consul was due to the *opifices agrestesque*; but this can hardly be so, since the consular elections were held in the *comitia centuriata*; and it was no doubt the support of the equestrians and the well-to-do non-nobles which was decisive (cf. ibid. 65.4-5).

[VI.vi]

1. This appears as early as the 'Persian Debate' in Hdts (III.80.6), for which see V.ii n.11 above.

2. See esp. J. A. O. Larsen, *Representative Government in Greek and Roman History* (= Sather Classical Lectures 28, Berkeley etc., 1955); and *Greek Federal States. Their Institutions and History* (1968); also F. W. Walbank, 'Were there Greek federal states?', in *Scr. Class. Israelica* 3 (1976/7) 27-51, which rightly upholds the genuinely federal character of some of the Greek confederations, against A. Giovannini, *Untersuchungen über die Natur u. die Anfänge der bundesstaatlichen Sympolitie in Griechenland* = *Hypomnemata* 33 (Göttingen) 1971, who argues that they were unitary states, not 'Bundesstaaten' or 'Staatenbünde'.

3. Diocletian's *dies imperii* is now known to have been 20 November 284: see *P. Beatty Panop.* (1964) 2, lines 162-3 etc. (with p.145).

4. See, briefly, J. P. V. D. Balsdon, in *OCD*[2] 877-8, *s.v.* 'Princeps'. The most comprehensive treatment that I have seen is the article by Lothar Wickert, 'Princeps (civitatis)', in *RE* XXII.ii (1954) 1998-2296. See also Wickert's survey of recent work on the Principate, in *ANRW* II.i (1974) 3-76; his useful article, PF = 'Der Prinzipat und die Freiheit', in *Symbola Coloniensia Iosepho Kroll Sexagenario . . . oblata* (Cologne, 1949) 111-41; and his less interesting 'Princeps und βασιλεύς', in *Klio* 36 = n.F. 18 (1944) 1-25; also De Martino, *SCR*[2] IV.i.263-308. Wickert's article in *RE*, and Jean Béranger, *Recherches sur l'aspect idéologique du Principat* (= *Schweizer. Beitr. z. Altertumswiss.* 6, Basle, 1953), are reviewed at length by W. Kunkel, in his third 'Bericht über neuere Arbeiten zur römischen Verfassungsgesch.', in *ZSS* 75 (1958) 302-52. I have found scarcely anything that is both new and illuminating in the recent article by D. C. A. Shotter, 'Principatus ac libertas', in *Anc. Soc.* 9 (1978) 235-55.

5. I must not discuss here the official titles of the Princeps, even the most important, 'Augustus', which 'connotes no magisterial powers at all, and is yet the highest that the Princeps bears' (Jolowicz and Nicholas, *HISRL*[3] 343). Although the title of Augustus was often applied to Tiberius, he never officially assumed it, nor did Vitellius in 69.

6. Aug., *RG* 13; 30.1; 32.3; and in Suet., *Aug.* 31.5; cf. e.g. Ovid, *Fasti* II.142; Tac., *Ann.* I.i.3; 9.6. The usual Greek translation of *princeps* is ἡγεμών – a word which could also stand for *dux* (cf. Aug., *RG* 25.2; 31.1). Among various editions of the *Res Gestae*, the best and fullest is that by Jean Gagé, *Res Gestae Divi Augusti*[2] (Paris, 1950). Non-specialists will find useful the Latin text (following, with 'minor changes of punctuation', that of E/J[2], ch.I, where the Greek text will also be found), with English translation, introduction and commentary, by P. A. Brunt and J. M. Moore, *Res Gestae Divi Augusti. The Achievements of the Divine Augustus* (1967).

7. Anyone who uses one of the older editions of the *Res Gestae*, such as the Loeb (1924, printed at the end of the history of Velleius Paterculus), should beware of the Latin version of 34.3: *dignitate* (translated 'in rank'), in place of *auctoritate*, in reliance on the Greek, ἀξιώματι, known from the version discovered at Ancyra, where the Latin word cannot be read. The Greek word

was thought (not unreasonably) to justify the restoration of *dignitate*, until the discovery of the version at Pisidian Antioch (published in 1927), which has [*a*]*uctoritate*.

8. See e.g. De Martino, *SCR*² IV.i.278-85 (on *auctoritas*), 285-9 (on *potestas*).

9. Seneca, *De clem.*, uses *rex* in a good sense or couples *rex* and *princeps* (in singular or plural) in I.iii.3; iv.3; II.i.3; v.2; he uses *rex* as a synonym for *princeps* in e.g. I.vii.4; xiii.1, with 5; xvi.1-2; xvii.3, with 2, and for *imperator* in I.iv.2, with 1; cf. iii.4; and he uses *rex* for the emperor himself in e.g. I.viii.1,6,7, with ix.1; xix.1-3, 5-6.

10. Occasionally *rex* and *regnum* might be employed in 'philosophical' treatises for the *good* king and his rule, as by Cicero, *De rep.* I.42-3, 69; II.43, 48-9.

11. Miriam Griffin, *Seneca* (1976) 133 ff., esp. 141-8, cf. 194-201.

12. It is perhaps worth mentioning here that Tacitus never refers to an emperor as *rex* or (I think) uses *regno*, *regius* or even *rego* of an emperor, although he writes of men calling the Augustan house *domus regnatrix* (*Ann.* I.4.4). When he describes Antonius Felix, the procurator of Judaea, as exercising *ius regium* (*Hist.* V.9), he is presumably representing him as governing like one of the petty Oriental kings (to some of whom Felix was related by marriage); and when he speaks of the prefects of Egypt as acting *loco regum* (I.11), he may only be thinking of the Ptolemies – although the prefects of Egypt, like the procurators of Judaea, were of course subordinates of the emperor. Yet in a fourth such passage Tacitus can say of Pallas, the freedman *a rationibus* of Claudius and Nero, that he *velut arbitrium regni agebat* (*Ann.* XIII.14.1); and of course Pallas was a pure imperial functionary at Rome. While prudently refraining from applying monarchical terminology to even 'bad emperors', Tacitus evidently felt less hesitation in castigating their subordinates openly for the way they exercised the quasi-regal powers they derived directly from their imperial masters. *Rego* (especially in its present participial form) is occasionally used of emperors from the early Principate onwards, as when Valerius Maximus (writing in the 30s) speaks of *divi quidem Augusti etiam nunc terras regentis excellentissimum numen* (IX.xv.2); and I think it might be possible to find earlier parallels even to such a statement as that of Mamertinus, *Paneg. Lat.* II.xi.2-3 (A.D. 289), congratulating Diocletian and Maximian because they 'rule the state with one mind' (*rem publicam una mente regitis*), and referring to their *maiestas regia*, increased by their *geminatum numen*, while at the same time they preserve by their unity the advantage of single command (*imperium singulare*). I ignore Statius and Martial here: for them see n.68 below. Examples of the use of the words referred to in this note and similar ones – *rex*, *rego*, *regno*, *regnum*, *regnator*, *regius*, *regalis*, and *regina* for an empress – are given by Wickert at cols.2108-18 of his article in *RE* cited in n.4 above.

13. This statement by Claudian was quoted with great approval in the seventeenth century, notably by Ben Jonson, as Alan Cameron has recently demonstrated (*Claudian* 434-7).

14. The date of *Anth. Pal.* X.25 depends on a proconsulate of Asia for L. Calpurnius Piso (cos. 15 B.C.), probably in 9/8 B.C.: see Sir Ronald Syme's brilliant article, 'The Titulus Tiburtinus', in *Akten des VI. Internat. Kongr. für Griech. u. Latein. Epigraphik, München 1972 = Vestigia* 17 (1973) 585-601, at 597.

15. E.g. by H. J. Mason, *Greek Terms for Roman Institutions. A Lexicon and Analysis = Amer. Stud. in Papyrology* 13 (Toronto, 1974) 117-21, at 120.

16. Josephus speaks of the Roman emperors as βασιλεῖς in *BJ* III.351; IV.596; V.563. In V.58 he even calls Titus ὁ βασιλεύς (cf. § 60), although Titus was as yet only Caesar (and of course Vespasian was still alive when Josephus was writing). Josephus also speaks of the βασιλεία of Vespasian (V.409) and uses the verb βασιλειᾶν in I.5 and IV.546 of aspirants to the imperial throne in A.D. 68-9. As far as I can see, Josephus does not use comparable language in his other works. Could this be because the *Jewish War* was originally written in Aramaic? (See *BJ* I.3; but of course the *BJ* is much more than a mere translation and probably incorporates extensive rewriting.)

17. Of the Orations of Dio Chrysostom, nos. I-IV are entitled *On kingship*, and no. LVI *Agamemnon, or On kingship;* no. LXII is *On kingship and tyranny;* and cf. VI, *Diogenes, or On tyranny*. In several of these the rule of the Roman emperor is clearly seen as a form of βασιλεία, and e.g. in LXII.1 the words βασιλεύειν . . . ὥσπερ σύ are directly addressed to the emperor, surely Trajan. In VII.12 (the 'Euboean Oration') the peasant is made to refer to the emperor as ὁ βασιλεύς.

18. For the date of Dio Chrys. XXXI, see A. Momigliano, in *JRS* 41 (1951) 149-53. The reference in XXXI.150 is to Nero (contrast § 110: τῶν αὐτοκρατόρων τις), as is that in LXXI.9.

19. E.g. Jn XIX.15; I Tim. ii.2; I Pet. ii.13 (cf. 14), 17; and esp. Rev. XVII.10.

20. Dio Cassius (most of whose History was written in the first quarter of the third century) habitually uses αὐτοκράτωρ for an emperor; but Herodian (writing about the middle of the third century) and Dexippus (*FGrH* IIA 100, writing mainly in the 260s-270s) regularly call the emperor βασιλεύς. Particularly interesting is Dio LIII.17.

21. It is perhaps worth adding a reference to *IG* V.i.572, lines 4-5, from Sparta, where Gordian III is τὸν θεοειδέστατον βασιλέα αὐτοκράτορα Καίσαρα (A.D. 239-44). ˙

22. See Ostrogorsky, *HBS*² 106-7; Averil Cameron, 'Images of authority [etc.]', in *Past & Present* 84 (1979) 3-35, at 16 & n.58.

23. For John Lydus see, briefly, A. Momigliano, in *OCD*² 630, *s.v.* 'Lydus'; and Jones, *SRGL* 172-4; *LRE* II.601-2 etc. The standard edition is the Teubner, by R. Wuensch (Leipzig, 1903). There is an English translation by T. F. Carney (Lawrence, Kansas, 1971).

24. The longest account we have of the murder of Gaius and the accession of Claudius is Jos., *AJ* XIX.37-273 (see esp. 115, 158, 162, 187-9, 224-5, 227-8, 229-33, 235, 249-50, 255, 259-61, 263); cf. *BJ* II.204-14 (esp. 205); Suet., *Claud.* 10.3-4; Dio Cass. LX.i, esp. §§ 1,4. Jos., *AJ* XIX.187-8, speaks of the Republic as a δημοκρατία (cf. 162, and contrast *BJ* II.205: ἀριστοκρατία), and of the Principate (from the point of view of the senators) as a τυραννίς and its opposite as τὸ ἀβασίλευτον; in id. 227-8 the emperors are τύραννοι and their rule δουλεία, again in the Senate's opinion. (The passage that follows, on the attitude of the δῆμος, is quoted in the text of Section v of this chapter, just after the reference to n.34.)

25. E.g. κελεύω, line 58 (in Edict III); κωλύω, lines 54-5 (in Edict II); ἀρέσκει (lines 67, 70 in Edict IV). The edicts are translated into English by Lewis and Reinhold, *RC* II.36-42, no.9.

26. Lines 13-14, cf. 36-7 (in Edict I). I must say, I would regard merely as another piece of tactfulness, calculated to gratify all members of the Senate, the oath taken at their accession by all (or nearly all) emperors from Nerva to Septimius Severus, not to put senators to death: see A. R. Birley, 'The oath not to put senators to death', in *CR* 76 = n.s.12 (1962) 197-9.

27. See Jones, *LRE* I.132-4, 144, 331-2; II.527-8, 554-6.

28. See Jones, *LRE* I.24-5, 48-9. I have not been able to read Lukas de Blois, *The Policy of the Emperor Gallienus* (Leiden, 1976).

29. Contrast H. W. Pleket, 'Domitian, the Senate and the provinces', in *Mnem.*⁴ 14 (1961) 296-315, esp. 301-3, 314-15. A less hostile view of the reign of Domitian than used to be customary has also been taken by other recent writers, e.g. T. A. Dorey, 'Agricola and Domitian', in *G&R* 7 (1960) 66-71; K. Christ, 'Zur Herrscherauffassung u. Politik Domitians. Aspekte des modernen Domitianbildes', in *Schweizer. Ztschr. für Gesch.* [Zürich] 12 (1962) 187-213; B. W. Jones, 'Domitian's attitude to the Senate', in *AJP* 94 (1973) 79-91.

30. See e.g. Jones, *LRE,* Index, *s.v.* 'defensor civitatis', especially I.144-5, 279-80 (with III.55 n.25), 479-80 (with III.134 n.20), 517 (with III.148 n.108); II.726-7 (with III.229 nn.31-2), 758-9 (with III.242 nn.104-5). See also, more briefly, Stein, *HBE* I².i.180 (with ii.512 n.123), 224-5, 376-7. The most interesting texts are *CTh* I.xxix.1-8; XI.viii.3; XIII.xi.10; *Nov. Major.* III; *CJ* I.lv.1-11. (The *vindices* introduced by Anastasius I probably represent a similar policy.) I must add that some time before Valentinian and Valens made the office of *defensor civitatis* a general one, *defensores* are found in some eastern provinces; and we happen to possess a remarkably detailed record of some proceedings before the *defensor civitatis* of Arsinoe in Egypt in A.D. 340: *SB* V (1955) 8246 = *P. Col. Inv.* 181-2; a full text with an Eng. trans. and notes is given by C. J. Kraemer and N. Lewis, 'A referee's hearing on ownership', in *TAPA* 68 (1937) 357-87.

31. Thus Cardascia, ADCHH 310 n.1.

32. With Sall., *BJ* 41.8, cf. Caes., *BG* VI.22.3 (the Germans seek to prevent *potentiores* driving *humiliores* from their lands). And see NG. TRANS. AND NOTES IS GIVEN BY C. J. Kraemer and N. Lewis, 'A referee's hearing on ownership', in *TAPA* 68 (1937) 357-87.

31. Thus Cardascia, ADR, IN THE REIGN OF Tiberius); Tac., *Ann.* XV.20.1 (*ut solent praevalidi provincialium et opibus nimiis ad iniurias minorum elati*); Pliny, *Ep.*IX.v.2-3 (*gratiae potentium*); *Dig.* I.xviii.6.2, for the *Opiniones* (probably of the 220s-230s) attributed to Ulpian (it should be a matter of conscience for the provincial governor to see to it *ne potentiores viri humiliores iniuriis adficiant*); cf. also the δυνατοί in Ael. Arist., *To Rome* 65, and Dio Cass. LII.37.6-7.

33. One of the earliest Greek texts discussing monarchy, namely the very end of Xenophon's *Oeconomicus* (XXI.12), says that to procure willing obedience a man must have divine qualities: it is θεῖον τὸ ἐθελόντων ἄρχειν, while τὸ ἀκόντων τυραννεῖν results in a life like that of Tantalus, of whom it was said that he spends eternity in Hades, dreading a second death.

34. Mommsen's view is well summarised by Jolowicz and Nicholas, *HISRL*³ 342-4, with

references. Constitutional lawyers are naturally more inclined than most historians to take seriously the proclaimed principles of a constitution, however bogus they may be in practice. Thus a leading Roman lawyer, Fritz Schulz, could say that the restoration by Augustus of 'the free State, the *libera res publica* (in contradistinction to the absolute monarchy, the *dominatio*) . . . was not a foolish attempt to delude the people, but, looked at juristically, the literal truth' (*PRL* 87-8). According to Schulz, again, 'the Roman state under the Principate was a free communal body, for the Principate was not a Dominate' (*PRL* 141); but in support of this claim Schulz proceeds to cite isolated passages from Pliny's *Panegyricus* (141 n.2), while noting that 'Pliny in his letters addresses Trajan simply as *dominus*', a term he is 'careful to avoid' in the *Panegyricus*! Cf. also Schulz's statement that 'to him who has no feeling for juristic distinctions the Romans must ever remain incomprehensible; the Romans' assertions, honest enough, but limited to their meaning in law, must seem to him to be nothing but canting hypocrisy' (*PRL* 144). Although an ex-lawyer myself, I can feel no sympathy for Schulz's outlook.

35. For those who wish to examine later monarchical thought in the Latin West there is an ample literature. A. J. Carlyle, *A History of Mediaeval Political Theory in the West* I² (1927) is still a mine of useful information. A recent book dealing briefly but well with the early mediaeval period is Walter Ullmann, *A History of Political Thought in the Middle Ages* (Pelican Hist. of Pol. Thought, Vol. 2, 1965, improved repr. 1970).

36. The same is true, as Brunt points out, of the so-called 'Tabula Hebana' (E/J² 94a), which calls itself a *rogatio* (line 14 etc.) but is also cast in the form of a *senatus consultum*.

37. Cf. Inst.J. I.ii.5; Ulpian, in *Dig.* I.iii.9. Pomponius – solemnly, or with his tongue in his cheek? – also attributes the institution of the Principate itself to the difficulty the Senate had in attending properly to everything: *nam senatus non perinde omnes provincias probe gerere poterat* (*Dig.* I.ii.2.11).

38. This raises some much-disputed questions, on which see e.g. Jolowicz and Nicholas, *HISRL*³ 359-63; Zulueta, *Inst. of Gaius* II.20-3; Berger, *EDRL* 681.

39. In Dio Cass. LIII.18.1 the historian is clearly thinking of the Latin words, 'legibus solutus est'. And he adds that the emperors have all things appertaining to kings except the empty title.

40. Dio Cass. LXVIII.2.1 does not bother to mention any *lex*.

41. For the appearance of hippodromes in the Greek East, later than is often realised, see Cameron, *CF* 207-13.

42. We must notice, of course, that Baynes refers, not to 'election' by the people but only to their 'acclamation'. He does, however, speak of 'the people' – hardly an appropriate term for the insignificant fraction of 'the people' who might be assembling, in the Circus perhaps, on a particular occasion. (A twentieth-century market researcher would not be satisfied to call them even a 'random sample' of 'the people'.)

43. It will be sufficient to refer to Amm. Marc. XVI.xii.64; XX.iv.14-18; XXV.v.1-6; XXVI.i-ii; XXVII.vi.10-16; XXX.x.4-5; cf. XV.viii.1-18; also v.15-16; XXVI.vi.12-18; vii.17.

44. 'Sententiam militum secuta patrum consulta.' Cf. XI.25.1, where a senatorial decision obediently 'followed the *oratio principis*'.

45. R. Syme, *Emperors and Biography* (1971) 242-3, thinks this invitation a fiction.

46. The most plausible account seems to me that of Bury, *HLRE*² II.16-18, followed in effect by Jones, *LRE* I.267-8. See also Stein, *HBE* II.219-20; A. A. Vasiliev, *Justin the First* (Cambridge, Mass., 1950) 68-82. The power of the Senate at Constantinople had perhaps begun to revive by the seventh century, as shown especially by its deposition of Heraclonas and Martina in 641 (see Ostrogorsky, *HBS*² 114-15); but by then we are near the limit of this book. It is worth mentioning here the stress, as early as the 560s, on the senators' role on the accession of Justin II, as described in Corippus' poem on that subject (mentioned farther on in the main text above and at the beginning of n.79 below), II.165-277: see the excellent commentary in Averil Cameron's edition (n.79 below) 165-70, with full references to the modern literature.

47. See e.g. Jolowicz and Nicholas, *HISRL*³ 341-4. There is much useful material in the chapter on succession to the Principate by De Martino, *SCR*² IV.i.403-31.

48. Cf. Tac., *Hist.* II.55 (Vitellius).

49. Cf. Liban., *Orat.* XXV.57, where βασιλεία, although the greatest of all offices, is subject to law; and other passages.

50. Among many other examples of the stock theme that the emperors have made themselves (or ought to make themselves) subject to the laws is Claudian, *De IV Cons. Honor. Aug.* 296-302, from a panegyric delivered in 398, on which see Cameron, *Claudian* 380 ff.

51. Among other imperial constitutions stigmatising disobedience to the imperial will as *sacrilegium* are *CTh* VI.v.2 (= *CJ* XII.viii.1); xxiv.4 (= *CJ* XII.xvii.1); VII.iv.30 (= *CJ* XII.xxxvii.13); and other examples given by Jones, *LRE* III.60 n.1.

52. Thus Robert Browning, *Justinian and Theodora* (1971) 69, part of a passage (65-9) which is the best introduction I know for the non-Byzantinist to the extraordinary story of Theodora. But Gibbon is at his best in *DFRE* IV.212 ff., esp. n.26. [See also now Alan Cameron, 'The house of Anastasius', in *GRBS* 19 (1978), at 271, making an interesting point about *CJ* V.iv.23, and referring (in n.30) to an article by David Daube, emphasising how 'every detail of the law is tailored to the particular dilemma of Justinian and Theodora'.]

53. *Dig.* I.iii.31; XXXII.23; *Inst.J.* II.xvii.8; *CJ* VI.xxiii.23 are all in the context of marriage or testamentary laws.

54. Cf. other parts of the same article: NH 14, 32-3 = *RE* 62, 80. I am not impressed by the reply made to Jones by C. H. V. Sutherland, 'The intelligibility of Roman Imperial coin types', in *JRS* 49 (1959) 46-55, on which see M. H. Crawford, in Jones, *RE* 81 (the first para.).

55. John of Ephesus, *HE* III.14: see *The Third Part of the Eccl. Hist. of John, Bishop of Ephesus* (Eng. trans. from the Syriac by R. Payne Smith, 1860) 192, and the Latin trans. of the same work, *Ioannis Ephesini Hist. Eccles., Pars Tertia* = *Corp. Script. Christ. Orient., Ser. Syri* 55, ed. E. W. Brooks (Louvain, 1936, repr. 1952) 104.

56. P. M. Bruun, *The Roman Imperial Coinage* (ed. C. H. V. Sutherland and R. A. G. Carson) *VII, Constantine and Licinius A.D. 313-337* (1966) 33 n.3.

57. See the *Catalogue of the Byzantine Coins in the Dumbarton Oaks Collection and in the Whittemore Collection* II.i, by Philip Grierson (Washington, D.C., 1968) 95. The coins are illustrated in the same *Catalogue* I (1966), by A. R. Bellinger, Plate XLIX nos. 1-8b (see pp.198-200), and Plate LX nos. 2-7.4 (see pp.266-9). Among various literary passages that yield evidence of the interest of rulers in antiquity in stamping their coins with their own names and/or portraits is Procop., *Bell.* VII (= *Goth.* III).xxxiii.5-6. Perhaps I should just mention a rather ridiculous passage in the *Chronicle* (cxvi.3) of John of Nikiu (for which see VIII.iii n.32 below). According to this, some said that the death of the Emperor Heraclius in 641 was due to his having stamped the gold coinage with the figures of the three emperors, himself and his two sons (as in fact he did), thus leaving no room for 'the name of the Roman empire'; after the death of Heraclius the three figures were removed. I find this absurd and unintelligible: the 'name of the Roman empire' did not in fact appear on the Roman coinage, but there would have been plenty of room for it on the reverse side of Heraclius' coins, even if the obverse were entirely used up!

58. See N. J. E. Austin, 'A usurper's claim to legitimacy: Procopius in A.D. 365/6', in *Riv. stor. dell' Ant.* 2 (1972) 187-94, at 193, with all necessary references.

59. I cannot give a proper bibliography here. Anyone not already acquainted with the subject could begin with that masterpiece, A. D. Nock's chapter, 'Religious developments from the close of the Republic to the death of Nero', in *CAH* X (1934) 465-511, esp. 481-503. The imperial cult is of course dealt with in the standard works on Greek and Roman religion, e.g. Kurt Latte, *Römische Religionsgeschichte* (Munich, 1960) 312-26; M. P. Nilsson, *Gesch. der griech. Religion* II² (Munich, 1961) 384-95, with 132-85 on the Greek background. There is a great deal of material in L. Cerfaux and J. Tondriau, *Le culte des souverains dans la civilisation gréco-romaine* (Tournai, 1957). The most recent work is *Le culte des souverains dans l'Empire romain = Entretiens sur l'antiquité classique* 19, Fondation Hardt (Vandoeuvres/Geneva, 1973); cf. the review by T. D. Barnes, in *AJP* 96 (1975) 443-5.

60. It might be a nice point to determine how far the 'families' extended for this purpose. See e.g. the prudent edict of Germanicus, *SP* II no. 211, lines 31-42.

61. Christian Habicht, in *Entretiens Hardt* 19 (1973) 33 (see the end of n.59 above).

62. I know of no text which brings out this difference properly, although a Greek writer may employ slightly different terminology when referring to appeals to the gods and the emperors respectively: e.g. Ael. Arist. XIX (*Ep. de Smyrn.*) 5, who uses εὐχόμεθα of prayers to the gods and δεόμεθα of requests to the θειότατοι ἄρχοντες – but then goes on at once to use δεῖσθαι of appeals for benefits 'from gods and from men'.

63. Tac., *Hist.* IV.81, cf.82; Suet., *Vesp.* 7.2-3; Dio Cass. LXVI.8.1.

64. Cf. Nock, *DJ* 118 n.28 = *ERAW* II.838 n.28: 'Sarapis miracles were a commonplace at Alexandria.'

65. In Lucian, *Philops.* 11 (probably written in the late 160s), the sick man who has been miraculously healed picks up his pallet and carries it off: this too reminds us of the miracles of Jesus, in Mk

II.3-12 = Mt. IX.2-7 = Lk. V.18-25 (Galilee), and Jn V.2-16 (Jerusalem), where in every case the man who is healed walks off with his κράβαττος / κλίνη / κλινίδιον.

66. I would draw attention to Dio Cass. LV.10.9, where the 'Games' (ἀγὼν ἱερός: Strabo V.iv.7, p.246) set up at Neapolis in Campania in 2 B.C. (or A.D. 2), in honour of Augustus, and held every four years, are described by Dio as nominally in gratitude for the restoration of the city by Augustus after an earthquake, but in reality because they were 'trying to emulate, in a way, Greek customs' (cf. LX.6.2). Dramatic competitions were included: Suet., *Claud.* 11.2 records that the Emperor Claudius produced a play there. One of the last acts of Augustus himself was to preside over these Games (Dio Cass. LVI.29.2; Vell. Pat. II.123.1; Suet., *Aug.* 98.5). Known as Ἰταλικὰ Ῥωμαῖα Σεβαστὰ ἰσολύμπια, they were famous, and evidently very influential in the spread of such customs in the West: see G. Wissowa, *Religion u. Kultus der Römer*[2] (Munich, 1912) 341-2 n.10, 465 n.1; R. M. Geer, 'The Greek games at Naples', in *TAPA* 66 (1935) 208-21 (advocating a foundation date of A.D. 2). I should also like to mention here the very useful chapter, 'Provincial assemblies in the western provinces of the Roman Empire', in Larsen, *RGGRH* 126-44, which is too often overlooked.

67. It should be sufficient merely to refer to W. Ensslin, in *CAH* XII.358-9, where references will be found. Perhaps I could also mention *ILS* 629, in which Diocletian and Maximian are addressed as 'Diis genitis et deorum creatoribus dd. nn.'! Latin inscriptions and municipal coin-legends, of course, sometimes call the emperor 'deus' outright: for some early examples, see e.g. E/J[2] 106 (= *ILS* 9495), 107 (the Roman *municipium* of Stobi), 107a (a coin of the Roman *colonia* of Tarraco).

67a. After this chapter was finished I read the lively and readable chapter by Keith Hopkins, in his *Conquerors and Slaves* (1978): 'Divine Emperors or the symbolic unity of the Roman Empire' (pp.197-242). This is not sufficiently well informed and is marred by several errors and misconceptions. Hopkins contradicts (p.227) the opinion I have expressed in the text above: he refers to Millar's article (ICP) but shows inability to refute it. On the same page he even quotes Tertullian, *Apol.* 10.1, thereby helping to demolish his own case, for the charge Tertullian mentions is not directly concerned with 'emperor worship' at all: the Romans are represented as saying to the Christians, 'You do not *worship* the gods; you do not offer *sacrifice for* the emperors.' Thus Hopkins's next sentence is a *non sequitur*. And his lack of acquaintance with Greek history has led to his presenting 'emperor worship' out of focus, by forgetting its origin in the cult of benefactors and always thinking in terms of 'ruler-cult'. That 'Augustus and his immediate successors . . . allowed temples and priests to be established in their honour, but *only* in association with an established deity, usually Roma' (ibid. 203-4) reveals a serious misconception, and confuses the limited number of cults at the provincial level with cults by cities and other bodies. And see now T. D. Barnes, in *AJP* 96 (1975) 443-5.

68. 'Jupiter': Mart. IV.8.12; IX.86.8; 91.6. 'Our Thunderer': VI.10.9; VII.56.4; cf. IX.39.1; 86.7. The passage in Statius is *Silv*. IV.3.128-9. For Statius on Domitian, see Kenneth Scott, 'Statius' adulation of Domitian', in *AJP* 54 (1933) 247-59. For the adulation of Domitian by both poets, see Franz Sauter, *Der römische Kaiserkult bei Martial u. Statius* (= *Tübinger Beitr. zur Altertumswiss.* 21, Stuttgart/Berlin, 1934). For Martial's very different attitude to Domitian after the latter's death, see e.g. Mart. X.72 (esp. 3, 8).

69. Suet., *Dom*. 13.2; Dio Cass. LXVII.4.7; 13.4; cf. Mart. V.8.1; IX.66.3, etc.

70. On the orations of Dio Chrysostom concerned with kingship (and tyranny), see n.17 above. Of these, the most interesting are I and III. For present purposes, see e.g. I.36; LXII.1; and III.50 ff., where Dio expresses great satisfaction with the present state of affairs, as 'happy and divine' (esp. §§ 61, 85-9. 111, 133 etc.).

71. I. A. Richmond, *Archaeology and the After-Life in Pagan and Christian Imagery*, a Riddell Memorial Lecture at the University of Durham (Oxford, 1950) 16-17. The most recent publication of the Arch of Beneventum, with excellent photographs and bibliography, is by F. J. Hassel, *Der Trajansbogen in Benevent: ein Bauwerk des römischen Senates* (Mainz, 1966): see esp. Tafeln 14-15. Hassel's conclusions, especially in regard to the date of completion of the Arch, are discussed in a long review by F. A. Lepper, in *JRS* 59 (1969) 250-61. Among many other works dealing with the iconography of the Arch, see Jean Beaujeu, *La religion romaine à l'apogée de l'Empire, I. La politique religieuse des Antonins 96-192* (Paris, 1955) 71-80 (esp. 73-6), 362, 431-7 (esp. 432). Some tricky problems arise. For example, is the scene between Trajan and Jupiter to be interpreted as an *adventus*, in which case the handing over of the thunderbolt (if that is what it is) must be a general concession of power, or is it a *profectio*, in which event the thunderbolt might perhaps symbolise no more than military power over external 'barbarians'?

72. Coins, especially in the third century, often display some god, most commonly Jupiter, handing the emperor a globe, the symbol of his power over the world: see W. Ensslin, in *CAH* XII.360-1, with references.

72a. It was only after this chapter was virtually finished that I saw J. Rufus Fears, *Princeps a diis electus: The Divine Election of the Emperor as a Political Concept at Rome* (= *Papers and Monographs of the American Academy in Rome* 26, 1977). It has not changed my views, expressed in the main text above. I am grateful to Peter Brunt for showing me a draft of his review, which has since appeared in *JRS* 69 (1979) 168-75. He too is unconvinced.

73. Cf. Cassiod., *Var.* VIII.xiii.5, where Trajan says to an orator, 'Sume dictationem, si bonus fuero, pro re publica et me, si malus, pro re publica in me.' Cassiodorus calls this 'dictum illud celeberrimum Traiani'.

74. The work in English with the most promising-sounding title is K. M. Setton, *Christian Attitude towards the Emperor in the Fourth Century* (= Columbia Univ. *Stud. in Hist., Economics and Public Law* 482, New York, 1941), but it is very disappointing: see e.g. the review by N. H. Baynes, in *JRS* 34 (1944) 135-40 (partly repr. in *BSOE* 348-56). In particular, as Baynes puts it, Setton 'treats Eusebius very scurvily' (ibid. 139).

75. I cannot give a bibliography here and will refer only to Baron, *SRHJ*² I.63-6, and esp. 91-3 ('Antimonarchical trends'), with the notes; and Roland de Vaux, *Ancient Israel, Its Life and Institutions* (Eng. trans. by John McHugh, 1961) 94-114 (esp. 98-9), with the bibliography, 525-7.

76. Constantine's letter to Aelafius, a particularly interesting document, is preserved in Optatus, Append. III, ed. C. Ziwsa (*CSEL* 26, 1893), re-ed. by C. H. Turner, *Eccles. Occid. Monumenta Iuris Antiq.* I.ii.1 (1913) 376-8. It is no.14 (pp.16-18) in the admirable collection of sources for the origin of Donatism: *UED*² = *Urkunden zur Entstehungsgesch. des Donatismus*² (= *Kleine Texte für Vorlesungen u. Übungen* 122), ed. Hans von Soden, 2nd edn by Hans von Campenhausen (Berlin, 1950). There are several English translations, e.g. by J. Stevenson, *A New Eusebius* (1957) 318-20, no.273; and P. R. Coleman-Norton, *Roman State and Christian Church* I (1966) 54-6, no.19. See A. H. M. Jones, *Constantine and the Conversion of Europe* (1948) 110-11, where Jones calls the passage part of which I have quoted in the text above 'the key to Constantine's whole religious position'.

77. Read at least Euseb., *Triakont.* I.6; II.4,6; III.4,6; V.4; VI.1-2; VII.12; X.6,7; XI.1; XVI.4-6. The most important passages are perhaps I.6 *fin.*; III.6; X.7. The most profitable work in English on the subject of the *Triakontaëtērikos* is Baynes, *BSOE* 48, 168-72. And see the last paragraph of V.iii and its nn.62-3 above. In the text above I have concentrated on Eusebius alone and have not tried to collect other material from the early fourth century which has been adduced in recent times as influencing his outlook or at least presenting parallels to it, such as Athan., *Contra Gentes* 38.2-4; 43.3-4 (probably written as early as 318), from which the existence and necessity of monarchy in this world, bringing about universal harmony (for 'the rule of more than one' would be 'the rule of none'), is used as an argument for a single God, and vice versa.

78. The constitution *Deo auctore* is printed in the standard edition of the *Digest* (= *Corpus Iuris Civilis* I.ii.8-9), and with it the constitutions known as *Omnium* and *Tanta*. All are well translated by C. H. Munro, *The Digest of Justinian* I (1904) xiii ff. My own version will appear shortly in the translation of the whole *Digest*, edited by Alan Watson, which is about to be published by the Harvard University Press. The study of the *Corpus Iuris Civilis* has been materially advanced by the publication in 1978 of Tony Honoré's book, *Tribonian*.

79. Flavius Cresconius Corippus, *In laudem Iustini Augusti minoris*, ed. Averil Cameron (1976). The commentary has much material that is of interest to anyone concerned with the Roman Principate and Later Empire. I can only mention briefly here some other relevant texts, such as (1) the *Ekthesis* of Agapetus (*Expositio capitum admonitoriorum*, in *MPG* LXXXVI.1164-85), for which see Patrick Henry, 'A mirror for Justinian: The *Ekthesis* of Agapetus Diaconus', in *GRBS* 8 (1967) 281-308; and briefly Dvornik, *ECBPP* II (1966) 712-15; there are extracts in Eng. trans. by Ernest Barker, *Social and Political Thought in Byzantium from Justinian I to the Last Palaeologus* (1957) 54-63; and (2) the anonymous work, Περὶ πολιτικῆς ἐπιστήμης (*De scientia politica*), ed. A. Mai, *Scriptorum veterum nova collectio* II (Rome, 1827) 590-609 (with a new fragment., ed. C. Behr, 'A new fragment of Cicero's *De republica*', in *AJP* 95 [1974] 141-9); and see Barker, op. cit. 63-75 for a summary in English: this work may or may not be the same as (*a*) the lost treatise, Περὶ πολιτείας (or Περὶ πολιτικῆς), mentioned by Photius, *Bibl.* 37, in *MPG* CIII.69, and/or (*b*) the lost treatise, Περὶ πολιτικῆς καταστάσεως, by Peter the Patrician, mentioned in the Suidas *Lexicon*, s.v. Πέτρος ὁ ῥήτωρ, ὁ καὶ Μάγιστρος (ed. A. Adler, IV [1935]

117): see V. Valdenberg, 'Les idées politiques dans les fragments attribués à Pierre le Patrice', in *Byzantion* 2 (1925) 55-76 (who follows Mai in attributing the anonymous work to Peter, probably without justification); and briefly Dvornik, *ECBPP* II.706-11. I only wish I could have found some parallel to a work written just before the middle of the sixth century by John Philoponus, *De opific. mundi* VI.16 (p.263, ed. W. Reichardt, Leipzig, 1897): this very brief passage is unique (as far as I can discover) in the literature that survives from the Christian writers of the Late Empire in rejecting the usual extravagant glorification of kingship and in treating it explicitly as human in origin and as something that is not φυσικόν but only θέσει. The pagan historian Zosimus, writing at some time in the two decades following 498 (see esp. the Introd. to François Paschoud's Budé edition of Books I-II, pp.XII-XX [esp. XVII], 132-3 n.13), certainly has an outright denunciation of the Principate from Augustus onwards – to him, of course, an absolute monarchy – as a form of government (I.v.2-4); he objects in particular to the immeasurable character of its authority (its ἄλογος ἐξουσία, § 3 fin.). 'I challenge you to find so strong a condemnation of monarchy as a constitutional form in itself in any other ancient author,' says Lellia Cracco Ruggini, 'The Ecclesiastical Historians and the Pagan Historiography: Providence and Miracles', in *Athenaeum* n.s.55 (1977) 107-26, esp. 118-24, at 120. The best recent treatment that I have seen of Zos. I.v.2-4 is by Fr. Paschoud, 'La digression antimonarchique du préambule de l'*Histoire nouvelle*', in *Cinq études sur Zosime* (Paris, 1975) 1-23. The best general treatment of Zosimus is now that of Paschoud, 'Zosimus (8)', in *RE²* X.A (1972) 795-841, and in his Introd. to Vol. I of his Budé edition, cited above.

80. See Cameron, op. cit. (in n.79 above) 188.

81. In what follows, for convenience, I shall confine my references in the main to two powerful articles published (with very full bibliography) in 1978 and 1979, the outlook of which I find congenial: Averil Cameron, 'The Theotokos in sixth-century Constantinople', in *JTS* n.s.29 (1978) 79-108; and 'Images of authority: elites and icons in late sixth-century Byzantium', in *Past & Present* 84 (August 1979) 3-35.

82. The Virgin's role may remind us of Athena Promachos at Athens in the fifth century B.C.: see Cameron, art. cit. (1978) 103 n.4.

83. See Cameron, art. cit. (1978) 84, 96-103, 104; and (1979) 11, 18 (& nn.70-3), 19-24, 32-5. Of course 'the Byzantine emperor had always been seen in a religious context'; but it has been argued that the reign of Justin II represents 'something of a turning-point in imperial ideology', and that from now on at least it is often difficult to separate the 'imperial' from the 'religious' (ibid. [1979] 15 and n.54).

84. Cameron, art. cit. (1978) 81-2, cf. 99-105, 108; also (1979) 4-5, 22-8, 30-1.

85. See Averil Cameron, art. cit. in n.81 above (1979) 15, with its n.53.

86. Averil Cameron, art. cit. (1978) 99, with nn.2-3 (cf. 106-7), 108.

87. I quote from an analysis (as a whole, over-generous, as it seems to me) of the political thought of St. Augustine, by Norman H. Baynes, *The Political Ideas of St. Augustine's De Civitate Dei* (= Historical Assocn. Pamphlet no.104, London, 1936) 9: 'In the original intention of God man was not created to exercise domination over man: this is the starting point for Augustine: but that original intention had been thwarted by man's sin: it is this changed condition with which God is faced, and to meet sin coercive government has a place as at once punitive and remedial. As a reaction against sin even the earthly State has a relative justification; it beareth not the sword in vain. Ultimately God's ways are beyond our understanding: He chooses such rulers for man as man deserves. Thus a tyrant, such as Nero, the traditional example of the worst type of ruler, is appointed by divine Providence. Because rulers are chosen by divine Providence, the servants of Christ are bidden to tolerate even the worst and most vicious of States, and that they can do by realising that on earth they are but pilgrims, and that their home is not here but in Heaven.' (This passage is repr. in Baynes, *BSOE* 295-6.) It is a pity we cannot ask Augustine to explain, given that divine Providence really chose Hitler as a ruler, whether there is any point, outside the sphere of religion, beyond which resistance to his more vicious orders (e.g. for the extermination of the Jews) could be justified.

88. The first scholar, as far as I know, to attach importance to the idea of νόμος ἔμψυχος as an element in Hellenistic theories of monarchy was E. R. Goodenough, 'The political philosophy of Hellenistic kingship', in *YCS* 1 (1928) 55-102, esp. 59-61. His view that the treatises on kingship by Diotogenes and a couple of other Pythagoreans were composed in the early Hellenistic period has been accepted by several other scholars, including e.g. Tarn; Francis Dvornik, *ECBPP, passim*, esp. I.245-52; and Holger Thesleff, *An Introduction to the Pythagorean*

Writings of the Hellenistic Period (Åbo, 1961) 50 ff., esp. 65–71. But I know of no certain evidence for the existence of these treatises earlier than the quotations from them by Stobaeus (probably early fifth century): for 'Diotogenes' on this subject, see Stob., *Anthol.* IV.vii.61 (ed. Hense, IV.263, 265). Apart from Diotogenes, and Philo and Justinian (quoted in the text above), the main references are Musonius Rufus, fr. 8 Hense (and Lutz: see II.vi above & its nn.28-9), *ap.* Stob., *Anthol.* IV.vii.67 (ed. Hense, IV.283); Plut., *Mor.* 780c; Themist., *Orat.* V (*Ad Jovian.*) 64b; XVI (*Charist.*) 212d. Fritz Taeger, *Charisma* I (Stuttgart, 1957) 80 & n.114, 398–401; II. (1960) 622-5; and 'Zur Gesch. der spätkaiserzeitlichen Herrscherauffassung', in *Saeculum* 7 (1956) 182-95, at 189 ff., would date Diotogenes and the others as late as the mid-third century; Louis Delatte, *Les Traités de la Royauté d'Ecphante, Diotogène et Sthénidas* (Liège, 1942), makes quite a good case for the first or perhaps the second century. (For a convenient summary of Delatte's conclusions in English, see M. P. Charlesworth's review, in *CR* 63 [1949] 22-3.) For the view that the notion of νόμος ἔμψυχος became important in political thought, as *lex animata*, only in the Middle Ages, see Artur Steinwenter, 'Νόμος ἔμψυχος: Zur Gesch. einer polit. Theorie', in *Anz. Ak. Wien*, Phil.-hist. Klasse, 83 (1946) 250–68.

89. There is nothing comparable in the *Digest*. Contrast e.g. the statement of Marcian about praetorian law: 'Nam et ipsum ius honorarium viva vox est iuris civilis' (I.i.8).

90. See esp. Millar, *ERW* 594-5, ending with the admission, 'It is clear that some third party had informed him of the situation.' There are some omissions and errors in Millar's narrative: e.g. he does not notice the role – highly significant, surely – of the imperial official Philumenus (presumably *magister officiorum*) at the Council of Nicaea, revealed by a fragment (discovered only this century) of the Arian historian Philostorgius, *HE* I.9a; and he says that 'at Nicaea ... Eusebius of Nicomedia, Theognis of Nicaea and their followers, as well as Arius himself, were exiled by imperial command' (*ERW* 598), whereas it is sufficiently clear not only from Philostorgius (*HE* I.9, 9c, 10) but also from the letter of Constantine to the Nicomedians (in Gelas., *HE* III App. I.13 ff., esp. 16 = Theod., *HE* I.xx.5 ff., esp. 9), and from Theodoret (*HE* I.vii.15-16; viii.17-18), Sozomen (*HE* I.xxi.3, cf. 5; III.xix.2), and even Socrates (*HE* I.ix, esp. 4, against viii.33-4), that the exile of Eusebius and Theognis took place later – probably three months later, as stated by Philostorgius, *HE* I.10. The fact that Constantine did indeed exile these bishops some time after the Council of Nicaea, at which they had escaped condemnation by formally subscribing to the creed endorsed by the Council, is something that naturally disconcerts some 'orthodox' modern ecclesiastical historians: see e.g. I. Ortiz de Urbina, *Hist. des Conciles Oecuméniques* (ed. Gervais Dumeige), *Nicée et Constantinople* (French trans., Paris, 1963) 118.

91. Cf. the apt remark of Gibbon, 'The name of Cyril of Alexandria is famous in controversial story, and the title of *saint* is a mark that his opinions and his party have finally prevailed' (*DFRE* V.107).

91a. Two admirable works by Klaus M. Girardet, which I read only after this chapter was in proof, express quite a different view, which seems very close to my own: 'Kaiser Konstantius II. als "Episcopus Episcoporum" und das Herrscherbild des kirchlichen Widerstandes', in *Historia* 26 (1977) 95-128; and esp. *Kaisergericht und Bischofsgericht* (= *Antiquitas* I.21, Bonn, 1975).

92. Constantine says himself, in the letter to the Nicomedians mentioned in n.90 above, that at Nicaea he single-mindedly pursued the aim of securing ὁμόνοια for all (Gelas., *HE*, App. I.13 = Theod., *HE* I.xx.5). There is much other evidence to the same effect, e.g. the end of Constantine's letter to Aelafius, of 313-14, mentioned in n.76 above; the end of his letter to Domitius Celsus, of 315-16 (Optat., Append. VII = *UED*² no.23); and of course many passages throughout the letter to Bishop Alexander and Arius (Euseb., *Vita Constant.* II.64-72) mentioned in the text above.

93. For those who are not already acquainted with the source material, the best account of Constantine's relations with the Christian churches is A. H. M. Jones's book on Constantine (for which see n.76 above). A fundamental work is Norman H. Baynes's Raleigh Lecture on History in 1930, *Constantine the Great and the Christian Church* (1931), which can now be read in a second edition, with a Preface by Henry Chadwick (1972).

94. See B. Altaner, *Patrology* (1960, Eng. trans. from the fifth German edition, of 1958) 418; *ODCC*¹ 797, *s.v.* 'St. Leo I', corrected in the second edition (1970) to 'his [the Pope's] legates spoke first at the Council of Chalcedon' (p.811). Cf. G. Bardy, in *Histoire de l'Église*, ed. A. Fliche and V. Martin, IV (Paris, 1948) 228 ('On décida enfin que Paschasinus de Lilibée présiderait le concile, ainsi que l'avait demandé le pape'), with 229 n.1.

95. The Latin text can be found in *CSEL* XXXV.ii.715–16. There is an Eng. trans. in Coleman-Norton, *RSCC* III.987–8, no.561.
96. There is a good English translation of the works of Athanasius in *NPNF*, 2nd Series, IV (1892), ed. Archibald Robertson, where the letter of Ossius will be found on pp.285–6.
97. The letter of Pope Gelasius I to the Emperor Anastasius I, of 494, is *Ep.* XII (see esp. § 2), ed. A. Thiel, *Epist. Roman. Pontif. Genuin.* I.1 (1867) 349–58; it is also ed. E. Schwartz, *Publizistische Sammlungen zum Acacianischen Schisma = Abhandl.* der bayer. Akad. der Wiss., Philos.-hist. Abt., n.F. 10 (Munich, 1934), where *Ep.* XII is no.8, pp.19–24, at 20. For the view that the letter of Gelasius is not such a new departure as many modern scholars have believed, see F. Dvornik, 'Pope Gelasius and Emperor Anastasius I', in *Byz. Ztschr.* 44 (1951) 111–16. Cf. also Gaudemet, *EER* 498–506.
98. Those who are disinclined to spend much time on Lucifer will find a useful summary of his attacks on Constantius II in Setton, op. cit. (in n.74 above) 92–7.
99. See T. D. Barnes, 'Who were the nobility of the Roman Empire?', in *Phoenix* 28 (1974) 444–9. The theory of Gelzer (which prevailed for so long), that in the Principate it was only descendants of Republican consuls who were called *nobiles*, was finally refuted by H. Hill, 'Nobilitas in the Imperial period', in *Historia* 18 (1969) 230–50.
100. Thus Dio Cass. LIV.26.3; Suet., *Aug.* 41.1 gives HS 1,200,000.
101. Among the known examples are Tac., *Ann.* II.37–38 (esp. 37.2, where Augustus gives HS 1 million to M. Hortensius Hortalus; and 38.8, where Tiberius gives HS 200,000 to each of the man's four sons); I.75.5–7 (Tiberius gives HS 1 million to Propertius Celer); XIII.34.2–3 (Nero gives a pension of HS 500,000 *per year* to M. Valerius Messalla Corvinus, *quibus paupertatem innoxiam sustentaret*, and similarly gives pensions, the amounts of which are not stated, to Aurelius Cotta and Haterius Antoninus, *quamvis per luxum avitas opes dissipassent*); cf. XV.53.2. See also Vell. Pat. II.129.3; Suet., *Nero* 10.1; *Vesp.* 17; Dio Cass. LVII.10.3–4; *Hist. Aug., Hadr.* 7.9. Even Caracalla is said to have given Junius Paulinus HS 1 million: Dio Cass. LXXVII.11.1[2] (ed. Boissevain III.384–5).
102. See the texts cited in VI.iii n.2 above. For the Principate, see *ILS* 1317, where a three-year-old deceased is described by his father in his funerary inscription as 'eq(uiti) R(omano)'; and *ILS* 1318, where a man setting up a funerary inscription to his son describes himself as 'natus eques Romanus'.
103. See on the whole subject Jones, *LRE* II.525–30. The statement by Hopkins (*SAC*, ed. Finley, 105) that 'under Constantine . . . the equestrian and senatorial orders were fused', in a 'new expanded order (*clarissimi*)' should have read 'began to be fused'. Certain posts held in the late third century by equestrians were now made, it is true, to carry senatorial rank (with the title of *clarissimus*), but the principal equestrian grade, that of *perfectissimus*, continued to be quite common until at least the last decade or two of the fourth century (when it was divided into three grades: *CJ* XII.xxiii.7, of 384). For the details, see Jones, *LRE* II.525–8, with the notes, esp. III.150 n.9 and 151 n.12.
104. For this date, see Alan Cameron, 'Rutilius Namatianus, St. Augustine, and the date of the *De reditu*', in *JRS* 57 (1967) 31–9.

[VII.i]

1. See my ECAPS 16 n.46, refuting the view of Buckland and others that the slaves in such cases were merely tortured and not executed. It could even be said that slaves ought to be punished if their master committed suicide in their presence and they failed to stop him when they could have done so (*Dig.* XXIX.v.1.22, Ulpian; cf. *Sent. Pauli* III.v.4, speaking only of the torture of such slaves). I may add that when Afranius Dexter, a suffect consul of A.D. 105, died in mysterious circumstances, Pliny describes the debate in the Senate as to what should be done with the *freedmen* of the dead man (*Ep.* VIII.xiv.12–25). My reading of the letter is that the freedmen were relegated to an island (see § 21 *init.*, 24, 25–6); and I would infer that the slaves were executed.
2. See e.g. Diod. Sic. XXXIV/V.ii.22; XXXVI.ii.6; iii.6; x.2–3. Cf. Symm., *Ep.* II.46, for the mass suicide of 29 Saxon prisoners promised to Symmachus by the emperor as gladiators in 393 (see Jones, *LRE* II.560–1).
3. See Louis Robert, *Les gladiateurs dans l'Orient grec* (Paris, 1940, repr. Amsterdam, 1971), with a few corrections in *REG* 53 (1940) 202–3, and considerable supplements in a series of articles

entitled 'Monuments de gladiateurs dans l'Orient grec', in *Hellenica* 3 (1946) 112-50; 5 (1948) 77-99; 7 (1949) 126-51; 8 (1950) 39-72; and cf. the 1971 reprint of the book, pp.1-2 of the Preface. See also Georges Ville, 'Les jeux de gladiateurs dans l'empire chrétien', in *MEFR* 72 (1960) 273-335. There is some further bibliography in J. P. V. D. Balsdon's article, 'Gladiators', in *OCD*² 467; add his *Life and Leisure in Ancient Rome* (1969) 248-52, 267-70, 288-302, part of a useful chapter on the games etc. A particularly interesting literary passage, relating to Athens, is Dio Chrys. XXXI.121-2. I should perhaps have mentioned that the Seleucid King Antiochus IV Epiphanes exhibited gladiatorial games in the Greek East as early as 175 B.C. (Livy XLI.20.11-13); but this was an isolated occasion (see Robert's book cited above, pp.263-4).

4. My quotations are from p.263 of Robert's book mentioned in the preceding note, and from Mommsen's *Römische Geschichte* I⁹.337 (near the end of Book II Ch.iv). For a relief from Halicarnassus showing two women gladiators, fighting with swords and shields, see Robert's book, pp.188-9, no.184; there is a reproduction of the relief in A. H. Smith, *A Catalogue of Sculpture in the Department of Greek and Roman Antiquities, British Museum* II (1900) 143, no.1117, where the names of the gladiators are given: Amazon and Achillia. References to female gladiators are given by Smith and by Robert, locc. citt.

5. Aristoxenus fr. 35, in F. Wehrli, *Aristoxenus von Tarentum*² (Stuttgart, 1967) 18 = fr. 18 in *FHG* II.278, ap. Stob., *Ecl.* IV.i.49. Cf. Xen., *Mem.* I.ii.10; *Cyrop.* III.i.28; VIII.ii.4; Plato, *Phileb.* 58ab.

6. See A. Spawforth, 'The slave Philodespotos', in *ZPE* 27 (1977) 294, based on *IG* V.i.147.16-18; 153.31-2; and 40.6-7 (cf. *SEG* XI.482). The eunuch in Diod. XVII.66.5 describes himself to Alexander as φύσει φιλοδέσποτος. *Philodespotos* is also the title of several Attic comedies: see LSJ⁹, *s.v.*, for this and other examples of the word.

7. Genovese, *RB* 33, an interesting essay (repr. from *Jnl of Social Hist.* I.4, 1968) entitled 'Materialism and idealism in the history of Negro slavery in the Americas', which would be particularly instructive to anyone inclined to believe that a Marxist approach to history involves 'economic determinism'.

8. See e.g. Arist., *Pol.* V.1, 1301ᵃ31-3; 12, 1316ᵇ1-3; and esp. VI.3, 1318ᵃ18-20 (cited in II.iv above).

9. For the *Republic* this is so well known as hardly to need illustration, but see e.g. *Rep.* II.369bc-71e on the composition of the citizen body, and III.412b-15d on who are to rule (and nothing else). In the *Laws*, the citizens have their own farms (worked by slaves, VII.806d) but are forbidden to engage in arts or crafts or any other occupation: see esp. V.741e, 742a; VII.806d; VIII.842d, 846d-7a; XI.919d. From the involved arguments in the *Politicus* it is difficult to pick out particular passages, but see *inter alia* 259cd, 267abc, 267de-8d, 292b-3c, 294abc, 298b-302a, 302e-3c, and esp. 289e-90a, 308c-9a. The ludicrous unreality of much of this dialogue comes out best, perhaps, in the notion of the true βασιλεὺς καὶ πολιτικός who rules with the voluntary assent of all his subjects (276de).

10. F. D. Harvey, 'Two kinds of equality', in *Class. et Med.* 26 (1965) 101-46, with the corrections and addenda in id. 27 (1966) 99-100. All the important source material is cited in full.

11. Elaine Fantham, '*Aequabilitas* in Cicero's political theory, and the Greek tradition of proportional justice', in *CQ* 67 = n.s.23 (1973) 285-90, at p.288. (This article was evidently written without knowledge of Harvey's, cited in n.10 above.) And see C. Nicolet, 'Cicéron, Platon, et le vote secret', in *Historia* 19 (1970) 39-66, cited by Fantham.

12. Cf. Plato, *Polit.* 291e-2a: under democracy, τὸ πλῆθος rules over the owners of property either βιαίως or ἑκουσίως.

[VII.ii]

1. See esp. Plato, *Rep.* V. 469bc, 470bcd (note πολεμίους φύσει); cf. *Laws* VI.777cd (where the advice to have slaves of different nationalities and speaking different languages implies that most if not all will be barbarians); *Meno* 82ab (where the slave who 'is Greek and speaks Greek' is born in the house, οἰκογενής. In *Polit.* 262cde Plato is making the purely theoretical point that it is not profitable to separate off one very small category of humans as 'Hellenes' and lump together as 'barbarians' all the rest, who differ greatly from each other; and Schlaifer (GTSHA 170 = Finley [ed.], *SCA* 98) goes much too far in saying that Plato here 'reversed the position he had earlier taken in the *Republic* and adopted Antiphon's theory' (denying any difference in φύσις between Greeks and barbarians).

2. Plato, *Polit.* 309a; cf. *Laws* VI.777e-8a, and other passages. And see Morrow, *PLS* 35 etc.
3. Vlastos, SPT, repr. in Finley (ed.), *SCA* 133-48, cf. 148-9.
4. As Vlastos puts it (SPT 289 = *SCA* 133), 'A formal discussion of slavery is nowhere to be found in Plato. We must reconstruct his views from a few casual statements.' Particularly interesting is the way in which, after emphasising in *Laws* VI.776b-7c that slavery is a very tricky problem, Plato shies away from the subject after making a few rather obvious remarks (777c-8a). And see Vlastos, 'Does slavery exist in Plato's *Republic*?', in *CP* 63 (1968) 291-5, who decides that 'the case for the affirmative must be reckoned conclusive'.
5. See esp. Arist., *Pol.* I.2, 1252ª30-4, 1252ᵇ5-9; 4, 1254ª14-15; 5, 1254ª17-5ª3; VII.14, 1333ᵇ38-4ª2, etc. Schlaifer, GTSHA 196 (= *SCA* 124), tries to give Aristotle's view, purged of its inconsistencies. But see below and n.10.
6. Arist., *Pol.* I.4, 1254ᵇ14-15; 5, 1254ª17-20, 1254ᵇ16-5ª3 (esp. 1254ᵇ19-21, 1255ª1-3); 6, 1255ᵇ6-9, 12-14; III.6, 1278ᵇ33-4; cf. VII.14, 1333ᵇ38-4ª2.
7. Arist., *Pol.* I.6, 1255ª5-11, 1255ᵇ5 (accepting Susemihl's insertion of ἀεί).
8. Arist., *Pol.* I.5, 1254ᵇ19-20; 1255ª3; 6, 1255ᵇ6-7.
9. Arist., *Pol.* I.2, 1252ᵇ7-9 (citing Eurip., *Iph. Aul.* 1400); 6, 1255ª29-35. (Surely the same view lies behind Plato, *Rep.* V.469bc.)
10. Arist., *Gen. An.* I.19, 727b29-30. See my AHP, where I have discussed at length Aristotle's use of the concept of τὸ ὡς ἐπὶ τὸ πολύ (an important subject, badly neglected by philosophers) and have given many examples of its use, including the one just mentioned.
11. Arist., *Pol.* VII.10, 1330ª25-31; cf. 9, 1329ª24-6, where no preference is expressed between the two alternatives.
12. George Fitzhugh, *Sociology for the South, or the Failure of Free Society* (Richmond, Va., 1854) 179. On Fitzhugh, see Harvey Wish, *George Fitzhugh, Propagandist of the Old South* (Baton Rouge, La., 1943). Fitzhugh lived from 1806 to 1881.
13. 'I am sure there was no man born marked of God above another; for none comes into the world with a saddle on his back, neither any booted and spurred to ride him' (Richard Rumbold). See *The Good Old Cause. The English Revolution of 1640-1660, Its Causes, Course and Consequences*². Extracts from contemporary sources, ed. Christopher Hill and Edmund Dell, 2nd edn, revised (London, 1969), 474.
14. Arist., *Pol.* VII.10, 1330ª32-3; otherwise there is only Ps.-Arist., *Oecon.* I.5, 1344ᵇ14-17. Cf. Xen., *Oecon.* V.16.
15. E.g. Arist., *Pol.* I.13, 1260ª36-ᵇ6.
16. Arist., *Pol.* I.6, 1255ª25-6, and other passages.
17. See my OPW 45. For statements in the more negative form, that slavery is 'not according to nature' (οὐ κατὰ φύσιν), see e.g. Chrysippus, *Fragm. moral.* 351-2, in H. von Arnim, *Stoic. Vet. Fragm.* III.86: the slave is a *perpetuus mercennarius* (fr. 351, from Seneca, *De benef.* 3.22.1), and no one is a slave ἐκ φύσεως, but masters should treat those they have bought not as slaves but as μισθωτοί (fr. 352, from Philo). Probably the Middle as well as the Old Stoa rejected the 'natural slavery' theory: see Griffin, *Seneca* 257, 459-60.
18. This subject is not directly relevant for my purposes, and it will be sufficient to refer to Guthrie, *HGP* III.153.
19. There is a good recent text, with French translation, of the *Contra Symmachum* in Vol. III of the Budé edition of Prudentius, ed. M. Lavarenne (3rd edn., 1963): see its p.186 and the introduction, 85 ff., esp. 104. No one should feel surprise at the persistence of such an attitude, in spite of Coloss. III.11 and Gal. III.28: see Section iii of this chapter.
20. See Hanke, *AAI* 14. Hanke is my main source for what follows.

[VII.iii]

1. The distinction between φύσις and τύχη in this connection is drawn e.g. by Dion. Hal., *Ant. Rom.* IV.23.1; cf. Dio Chrys. XV.11. Latin writers make the same distinction, between *natura* and *fortuna*.
2. *Conc. Illib.*, Can. 5, in Hefele-Leclercq, *HC* I.i.224-5. This Canon was incorporated in Gratian's *Decretum*, as Dist. L, Can. 43: see *Corp. Iuris Canon.* I².195, ed. E. Friedberg (Leipzig, 1879).
3. It will be sufficient to mention one Gallic episcopal synod, that of Narbo in 589. Canon 15, dealing with those who refuse to work on a Thursday (for pagans, sacred to Jupiter), sentences

the *ingenuus aut ingenua* to one year's excommunication, the *servus aut ancilla* to a whipping (*flagellis correcti*); and Canon 4 punishes anyone who works on a Sunday with a fine of 6 solidi if free or 100 lashes (*centum flagella*) if a slave: see J. D. Mansi, *Sacr. Conc. nova et ampl. coll.* IX (1763) 1015-18.

4. Among other passages in Augustine relating to slavery are *De civ. Dei* IV.3 (cited in the first paragraph of the main text of this section); *Quaest. in Hept.* II.77 (cited at the end of the second paragraph of the main text of this section) and esp. I.153 (both in *CSEL* XXVIII.iii.3.142 and 80, and *CCL* XXXIII.107 and 59); *Enarr. in Psalm.* XCIX.7 (in *CCL* XXXIX.1397: Christian slaves should not seek manumission) and CXXIV.7 (in *CCL* XL.1840-1); *Epist.* CLIII.(vi).26 (in *CSEL* XLIV.426-7; *Tract. in Ep. Ioann. ad Parthos* VIII.14 (in *MPL* XXXV.2044); *De serm. Dom. in monte* I.(xix).59 (in *MPL* XXXIV.1260); *De mor. eccl. cathol.* 30.63 (in *MPL* XXXII.1336). I have merely noted a few passages I happen to have come across; no doubt there are many others.

5. See Stampp, *PI* 198, 340-9. Some may object that the Old South was Protestant and that in slave societies which were Roman Catholic things were different. There is some truth in this (see the convenient summary in S. M. Elkins, *Slavery*[2] 52 ff., esp. 63-80); but the contrast between North American and Latin American slavery in this respect must not be exaggerated: see Davis, *PSWC* 98-106, 223-61; and three essays in Genovese, *RB* 23-52, 73-101, and 158-72. It is also worth mentioning here a curious and little-known work, *Slavery and the Catholic Church* (sub-titled *The history of Catholic teaching concerning the moral legitimacy of the institution of slavery*), by a Roman Catholic priest, J. F. Maxwell (published by Barry Rose Publishers, Chichester/London, in association with the Anti-Slavery Society for the Protection of Human Rights, 1975, complete with 'Imprimatur'), which considers 'the common Catholic teaching on slavery', right down to the time when it 'was officially corrected by the Second Vatican Council in 1965', to have been a 'disaster' (10-12), and ends by regretfully pointing out 'how very slender and scarce is the Catholic anti-slavery documentation since 1888 as compared with the very large volume of Catholic pro-slavery documentation right up to the time of the Second Vatican Council' (125). There is a nice appreciation of the fact that 'The few members of the Society of Friends (Quakers) in the early eighteenth century who appear to have been open to the direction of the Holy Spirit concerning slavery exercised an enormous influence, first on their fellow Quakers, and then on all North American Protestants', while 'On the other hand, the graces received by most of the eighteenth- and nineteenth-century Catholic laity from the traditional Latin prayer and liturgy were apparently insufficient to awaken their consciences [etc.]' (20). One wonders how the author accounts for the fact that the Holy Spirit preferred to vouchsafe its direction so much more generously to those his Church regards as heretics, in preference to Catholics. 'God moves in a mysterious way his wonders to perform', perhaps?

6. Suet., *Claud.* 25.2; *CJ* VII.vi.1.3; *Dig.* XL.viii.2. Other imperial legislation in favour of slaves is given by Buckland, *RLS* 36-8; Griffin, *Seneca* 268-74.

7. See *Inst.J.* I.viii.2; *Dig.* I.vi.1.2, and vi.2; *Mos. et Rom. leg. coll.* III.iii.1-2, cf. 5-6. Cf. Diod. XXXIV/XXXV.2.33; also the passages from Seneca cited by Griffin, *Seneca* 263, and those from Poseidonius and Seneca in ibid. 264-5. [Cf. p.383 above, first paragraph.]

8. For this and what follows, see Jones, *LRE* II.920-2 (with III.315 nn.126-30), mentioning a minor modification by Justinian. See also Gaudemet, *EER* 136-40.

9. *Dig.* L.xvii.32 is an extraordinary text if taken too literally. Slaves are considered *pro nullis* for the purposes of the *ius civile*, 'but not also by *ius naturale*, because, in so far as pertains to *ius naturale*, all men are equal' (*omnes homines aequales sunt*).

10. Among many publications of this text, see *Documents of American History*[5], ed. H. S. Commager (New York, 1949) 37-8, no.26. And see Davis, *PSWC* 308-9.

11. See e.g. the letter of the Jesuit missionary, Francisco de Gouveia, to the king of Portugal in 1563, quoted by Boxer, *PSE* 102-3: he asserted 'that experience had shown that these Bantu were barbarous savages, who could not be converted by the methods of peaceful persuasion . . . Christianity in Angola . . . must be imposed by force of arms.' And Boxer continues, 'This was, and for long remained, the general view among Portuguese missionaries and laymen alike.' And this attitude was by no means peculiar to the Portuguese: 'The vast majority of Europeans, if they thought about the matter at all, saw nothing incongruous in simultaneously baptising and enslaving negroes, the former procedure often being advanced as an excuse for the latter' (Boxer, *PSE* 265).

12. See Davis, *PSWC* 63–4, 97–8, 217, 316–7, 451–3 (Ham and Canaan); 171, 236, 326, 459 (Cain); also Boxer, *PSE* 265.

[VII.iv]

1. Cf. Cic., *De rep*. III.22/33, 6th edn, by K. Ziegler (Leipzig, 1964), pp.96–7.
1a. For the very different early Christian position at its best, see the advice to the rich widow Olympias by John Chrysostom, *ap*. Soz., *HE* VIII.ix.1–3 (esp. 3).
2. For the history of Palestine in the late Hellenistic and early Roman period, see the new English version, by Geza Vermes and Fergus Millar, *The History of the Jewish People in the Age of Jesus Christ (175 B.C. – A.D. 135)*, of Emil Schürer's *Geschichte des jüdischen Volkes im Zeitalter Jesu Christi* (3rd/4th edn, 1901–9), of which Vol. I (Edinburgh, 1973) has already appeared. The events of 63 B.C. to A.D. 44 are dealt with on pp.237–454. [Vol. II appeared in late 1979.]
3. The latest treatment I have seen of this question is by J. A. Emerton, 'The problem of vernacular Hebrew in the first century A.D. and the language of Jesus', in *JTS* n.s.24 (1973) 1–23 (with bibliography, 21–3).
4. To the bibliography in ECAPS 4 n.8 add Shimon Applebaum, 'Hellenistic Cities of Judaea and its vicinity – some new aspects', in *The Ancient Historian and his Materials* (Essays in Honour of C. E. Stevens), ed. Barbara Levick (1975), 59–73. [See now Schürer (n.2 above) E.T. II, 1979.]
5. See my ECAPS 4 n.10, and add the best modern treatment of the subject: V. A. Tcherikover, 'Was Jerusalem a "Polis"?', in *IEJ* 14 (1964) 61–78.
6. Many attempts have been made to prove that Jesus himself was in fact a leader of an anti-Roman political movement, but they all rest almost entirely on guesswork. The Gospels, virtually our only sources for the life of Jesus, are most unsatisfactory as historical documents (which of course they were not intended to be); but if we suppose Jesus to have been a political activist, a 'Zealot', then we must convict them of such wholesale and deliberate falsification that their evidence becomes almost entirely worthless: see my review, in *Eng. Hist. Rev*. 86 (1971) 149–50, of S. G. F. Brandon, *The Trial of Jesus of Nazareth* (1968), one of the most scholarly of the recent works which take the line I am criticising. On the other hand, the results of N.T. scholarship are such that the positive value of the Gospels as historical sources for the life of Jesus (apart from his teaching) can only be seen as very restricted. The attempt of Sherwin-White, *RSRLNT* 192 n.2 (on p.193), to adduce the *Acta Martyrum* as a useful parallel to the Gospels and as a reason for taking them seriously as historical sources founders on the fact that all the best scholars who have dealt with the martyr-acts have begun by rigorously excluding from them, as a mark of hagiographical inauthenticity, all miraculous elements – a procedure which, if applied to the Gospels, would reduce them to something very different from what Sherwin-White wants to make of them.
7. See Schürer (Vermes/Millar), op. cit. (in n.2 above) I.358 and n.22.
7a. Only twice in the Gospels are 'Greeks' mentioned in connection with Jesus – as if contacts with them were something out of the ordinary. In Mk VII.26 a 'Syrophoenician woman', described as a Ἑλληνίς, approaches Jesus when he is within 'the borders [ὅρια] of Tyre [and Sidon]'; and in Jn XII.20 an approach is made to him – with what success is not clear – through Philip the apostle by Ἕλληνές τινες, who are in fact Hellenised Jews coming to celebrate the Passover at Jerusalem.
8. Particularly interesting is the article by C. H. Roberts, 'The Kingdom of Heaven (Lk. XVII.21)', in *HTR* 41 (1948) 1–8, showing that the much-disputed expression ἐντὸς ὑμῶν in Lk. XVII.21 is most likely to mean that the kingdom is 'within your power' ('It is a present reality if you wish it to be so', p.8) rather than 'within you' or 'among you'.
9. For a different approach from mine, see Joseph Vogt, *ASIM* (in Eng. trans.), ch.viii (pp.146–69): 'Ecce Ancilla Domini: the social aspects of the portrayal of the Virgin Mary in antiquity'. (For the German original, see ECAPS 14 n.39.)
10. See B. Lifshitz, 'The Greek documents from Nahal Seelim and Nahal Mishmar', in *IEJ* 11 (1961) 53–62, at p.55, Papyrus no.1, line 7: Ταπεινὸς ἀ[δελφός].
11. See, for a brief bibliography, ECAPS 24 n.78. The most comprehensive work is Paul Christophe, *L'usage chrétien du droit de propriété dans l'écriture et la tradition patristique* = Collection *Théologie, Pastorale et Spiritualité*, no.14 (Paris, 1964).
12. See esp. ECAPS 30 n.104, on Ambr., *De offic. minist*. I.130–2 (with Cic., *De offic*. I.20–2).
13. For a brief bibliography on allegory, see ECAPS 35 n.128. I will add here a quotation from the

article by Henry Chadwick, 'Origen, Celsus, and the Stoa', in *JTS* 48 (1947) 34–49, at p.43: 'The allegorical method of interpretation was . . . an inheritance from the Alexandrian tradition. In passing, it is instructive to notice how Origen, an allegorist *par excellence*, will not allow the validity of the method when applied to Homer (*C. Cels.* 3.23); and Celsus and Porphyry deny the right of Christians to allegorise the Old Testament, although they use the method freely themselves to interpret Homer.'

14. See August., *Ep.* 93.5; 173.10; 185.24; 208.7; *C. Gaudent.* I.28. I have dealt with this question in the paper on persecution by the Christian churches mentioned near the end of Section v of this chapter.

15. See Duncan-Jones, *EREQS* 17-32 (esp. 18 n.4, 32 n.6); and App. 7 on p.343, where Pliny is no.21.

16. The hymn is 'All things bright and beautiful', by Mrs Cecil Frances Alexander (1818–95), *née* Humphreys, who in 1850 married William Alexander, bishop of Derry (afterwards of Armagh).

17. For John Ball, see Froissart's *Chronicles* 73-4 (ECAPS 37 n.132). For Torres, see *Revolutionary Priest. The Complete Writings and Messages of Camilo Torres*, ed. John Gerassi (1971, paperback in *Pelican Latin American Library*, 1973).

[VII.v]

1. Woodhouse, *PL²*1-124, gives a modern text of the Debates (followed by the Whitehall Debates and much other material), from the Clarke MSS, Vol. 67 (at Worcester College, Oxford), first printed in an edition by C. H. Firth, *The Clarke Papers*, Vol. I (1891), published by the Camden Society, Westminster (Vol. 155 [154] = n.s.49). I have already referred to the Levellers in III.vi above and its nn.48-9.

2. Cf. Woodhouse, *PL²* 26-7, 50, 52-5, 57-8, 60, 62-3, 69, for further opinions by Ireton on the all-important subject of property.

3. See K. W. Welwei, *Unfreie im antiken Kriegsdienst, I. Athen und Sparta* (= *Forsch. zur ant. Sklaverei* 5, Wiesbaden, 1974). I have not been able to use here Vol. II of this work (1977).

4. On the Book of Daniel, it will be sufficient to refer to Otto Eissfeldt, *The Old Testament, An Introduction* (Eng. trans., 1965, from the third German edn, 1964) 512-29, esp. 520-2. No honest and reputable scholar now denies that at least the bulk of Daniel dates from the persecution of Yahwism in Judaea by Antiochus IV Epiphanes which began at the end of 167 B.C. The persecution has been admirably elucidated in the past few decades, esp. by the work of E. J. Bickerman and V. Tcherikover: see Will, *HPMH* II.275-89, with the essential bibliography; also pp.35-44 of Pierre Vidal-Naquet's useful Introduction (of more than 100 pages) to Pierre Savinel's French translation, *Flavius Josèphe, La guerre des Juifs* (Paris, 1977). It is an interesting and well-known fact that the correct dating of Daniel was established in Book XII of Porphyry's major work, *Against the Christians*, written in Greek at the end of the third century or the beginning of the fourth (see the able article by T. D. Barnes, 'Porphyry *Against the Christians*: date and the attribution of fragments', in *JTS* n.s.24 [1973] 424-42, with very full bibliography). For Jerome's uncomfortable reaction to Porphyry, in his *Commentary on Daniel*, published in 407, see J. N. D. Kelly, *Jerome. His Life, Writings, and Controversies* (1975) 298-302. There is one point I must add here, which applies also to much of the literature I shall be mentioning in the remainder of the paragraph in the text above from which this note comes. As scholars have often emphasised, the Book of Daniel, for all its immediate appeal to simple folk, was itself very much the product of the most characteristic type of Jewish learning: saturation with the texts of the earlier Jewish Scriptures. Daniel himself is represented as a man of wisdom and learning, and so are some of the other authors or heroes of Jewish pseudepigraphic literature. Daniel & Co., then, are anything but humble peasants, but that would not prevent them from being an inspiration to such people.

5. See esp. P. A. Brunt, 'Josephus on social conflicts in Roman Judaea' in *Klio* 59 (1977) 149-53. Cf. Shimon Applebaum, 'The Zealots: the case for revaluation', in *JRS* 61 (1971) 155-70; Heinz Kreissig, *Die sozialen Zusammenhänge des judäischen Krieges. Klassen u. Klassenkampf im Palästina des 1 Jahrh. v.u.Z.* = Schriften zur Gesch. u. Kultur der Antike, no.1 (Berlin, 1970); with Vidal-Naquet, op. cit. (in n.4 above) 65-73 and 86 ff. (esp. 95-109), who gives a good up-to-date selective bibliography. I have felt obliged to pay virtually no attention in this book, either to external wars or to internal rebellions within the empire, that took place before about the middle of the second century of the Christian era (see VIII.iii-iv; cf. the last paragraph of VIII.ii and its n.24). I have therefore had to ignore not only the Jewish revolt of 66-70 (or rather,

66–73/4), but also the other two major Jewish rebellions: in Egypt, Cyrenaica and Cyprus, and even to a small degree in Palestine, at the end of Trajan's reign (115–17); and the great uprising in Palestine under Hadrian (132–5). I can do no more than refer to Vol. I.529–57 of the revised English version of Schürer's great work, cited in VII.iv n.2 above, which has ample bibliography.

6. There is an edition of all the relevant papyri·known some 25 years ago, with Eng. trans. and commentary, by H. A. Musurillo, *The Acts of the Pagan Martyrs. Acta Alexandrinorum* (1954). See also *C. P. Jud.* II..154–9 for those *Acta* with a direct bearing on Jews.

7. For these works, see esp. S. K. Eddy, *The King is Dead. Studies in the Near Eastern Resistance to Hellenism 334-31 B.C.* (Lincoln, Nebraska, 1961), Index, *s.vv.*; also J. J. Collins, 'Jewish apocalyptic against its Hellenistic Near Eastern environment', in *BASOR* 220 (Dec. 1975) 27–36; Harald Fuchs, *Der geistige Widerstand gegen Rom in der antiken Welt* (Berlin, 1938, repr. 1964); and MacMullen, *ERO*. MacMullen denies the existence of anything *he* is prepared to call 'class struggle' (199–200 etc.), because he uses the expression in the narrowest possible sense, limiting it to occasions when there is conscious class feeling as such; and cf. the review by Oswyn Murray in *JRS* 59 (1969) 261–5. For the 'Sibylline Oracles', see esp. Fuchs, op. cit. 7–8, with 30–6; and Fraser, *PA* I.708–13 (on *Orac. Sibyll.* III); II.989–1000 nn.217–49 (of which n.217 gives a full bibliography on the *Oracles*), with the Addendum on p.1116; see also n.8 below. For the 'Oracle of the Potter', see L. Koenen, 'The prophecies of a potter: a prophecy of world renewal becomes an apocalypse', in *Proc. XII* [Michigan] *Internat. Congr. of Papyrology = Amer. Stud. in Papyrol.* 7 (Toronto, 1970) 249–54; for the most recent edition of the Oracle, see Koenen, 'Die Prophezeiungen des "Töpfers" ', in *ZPE* 2 (1968) 178 ff.; the text is on pp.195–209. And see Fraser, *PA* I.683–4. For the 'Demotic Chronicle', see Fraser, *PA* I.682; II.951–2 nn.31–4; C. C. McCown, 'Hebrew and Egyptian apocalyptic literature', in *HTR* 18 (1925) 357–411, at pp.387–92 (with some translation, pp.388–9). For the 'Oracle of Hystaspes', see H. Windisch, *Die Orakel des Hystaspes* (Amsterdam, 1929); McMullen, *ERO* 147–8, with 329–30 n.19. Lactantius calls Hystaspes 'a most ancient king of the Medes' and thinks his name was the origin of that of the River Hydaspes! (*Div. Inst.* VII.xv.19; cf. xviii.2; *Epit. Div. Inst.* 68 [73]). For the 'Bahman Yasht', see Eddy, op. cit., esp. 15–32, and the translation in the Appendix, pp.343–9.

8. There is a good, scholarly English translation of *Orac. Sibyll.* III–V by H. N. Bate, *The Sibylline Oracles Books III-V* (S.P.C.K., 1918), and another by H. C. O. Lanchester, in *Apocrypha and Pseudepigrapha of the O.T.*, ed. R. H. Charles, II (1913) 368(377)–406. The three most recent editions of the *Sibylline Oracles* that I have seen (all worth consulting) are by A. Kurfess, *Sibyllinische Weissagungen* (1951, with German trans.); J. Geffcken, *Oracula Sibyllina* (= *GCS* 8, 1902); and A. Rzach, *Oracula Sibyllina* (Vienna etc., 1891). And see J. Schwartz, 'L'historiographie impériale des *Oracula Sibyllina*', in *Dialogues d'hist. anc. 1976* (= Centre de recherches d'hist. anc. 21 = *Annales littéraires de l'Univ. de Besançon* 188, Paris, 1976) 413–20. On the three 'false Neros', see MacMullen, *ERO* 143–6, with 328–9 nn.15–17; Levick, *RCSAM* 166–8; R. Syme, *Tacitus* (1958) II.518. The latest piece I have seen on the 'false Neros' is P. A. Gallivan, 'The false Neros: a re-examination', in *Historia* 22 (1973) 364–5. Among the Christians who wrote of 'Nero redivivus' is Commodian, a Latin author whom I have no occasion to mention elsewhere: in my opinion he was probably an African of the 260s or a little later (his dates have been much disputed). For his chiliastic fantasies, see his *Carm. Apol.* 791–1060, esp. (for Nero) 823–936, and (for disasters to Rome) 809–22, 891–926 (ed. B. Dombart, in *CSEL* XV, 1887; there is a less good Teubner text by E. Ludwig, 1877). Commodian's attitude to Rome can be ferociously hostile, not only in the *Carmen Apologeticum* but also in the *Instructiones*: see e.g. *Instruct.* I.xli (esp. 12: 'Tunc Babylon meretrix «erit» incinefacta favilla'). Lactantius may well have had Commodian in mind among others when in *De Mort. Pers.* 2.8 he rejected the notion of Nero returning as precursor of Antichrist: see the edition by Jacques Moreau, *Lactance. De la mort des persécuteurs* (= *SC* 39, Paris, 1954) II.201–4. See also Frend, *MPEC* 561, 567–8 nn.146–9 (with references to J. P. Brisson, *Autonomisme et Christianisme dans l'Afrique romaine*, Paris, 1958). A good general account of Commodian's works can be found in P. Monceaux, *Hist. litt. de l'Afrique chrét.* III (1905) 451–89.

9. Caes., *BG* VII.77, esp. §§ 9, 15–16 (Critognatus the Gaul, 52 B.C.); Tac., *Ann.* I.59.2–7 (the German Arminius, A.D. 15); II.9.3 to 10.3 (dialogue, Arminius and Flavus, A.D. 16), and 15.2–4 (Arminius); XII.34.2–3, 37.1–4 (Caratacus the Briton, A.D. 50); XIV.35, and Dio Cass. LXII.3–6 (Boudicca the Briton, A.D. 61); Tac., *Hist.* IV.14, 17, 32 (the German Julius Civilis, A.D. 69) and 64 (Tencteri, A.D. 70). I ought also to mention here what has been called 'perhaps the most famous justification of Roman imperialism' (Birley, *TCCRE* 264): the

speech put by Tacitus into the mouth of Petilius Cerialis in 70, to the Treveri and Lingones (*Hist.* IV.73-4).

10. On Phaedrus and his work, see Perry, *BP* = B. E. Perry's Loeb volume, *Babrius and Phaedrus* (Cambridge, Mass., 1965) lxxiii-cii.

11. See Perry, *BP* xxxv-xlvi. On the ancient collections of Aesopic fables, see Perry, *BP* xi-xix; and on the fable in general, xix-xxxiv. The most illuminating recent treatment of the Aesopic fable that I have seen is by the Italian Marxist, Antonio La Penna, 'La Morale della favola esopica come morale delle classi subalterne nell' antichità', in *Societa* 17.2 (1961) 459-537, which I was not able to read until this chapter was finished. For Aesop himself, see Johannes Sarkady, 'Aisopos der Samier. Ein Beitrag zur archaischen Geschichte Samos'', in *Acta Classica* (Univ. Scient. Debrecen.) 4 (1968) 7-12. Meuli, *HWF*, gives an interesting general survey, with bibliography (esp. 5 n.1, 9 n.1, 11 n.1), and mentions many relevant literary passages, e.g. Hdts I.141.1-3; Arist., *Rhet.* II.20, 1393^{b}23-4^{a}2, 1394^{a}2-9; *Pol.* III.13, 1284^{a}15-17 (on this last, see Perry, *BP* 512-13, no.450; Newman, *PA* III.243). It is interesting to find that the earliest known collection of Aesopic fables was made in the late fourth century B.C. by Demetrius of Phalerum: see Diog. Laert. V.81 (with Meuli, *HWF* 11). Of course, we cannot identify any fable as having been composed, by Aesop or anyone else, while still a slave, and the lament of David Daube is perfectly correct: 'We do not possess a single work composed by a slave while in slavery. When you consider the enormous ratio of slaves in the ancient world and the talent that must have existed among them, you begin to realise the tragedy, the horror, of this datum' ('Three Footnotes on Civil Disobedience in Antiquity', in *Humanities in Society* 2 [1979] 69-82, at 69). For Hebrew fables, see Daube, *Ancient Hebrew Fables* (1973, Inaugural Lecture of Oxford Centre for Postgraduate Hebrew Studies).

12. This fable is summarised in Perry's Loeb edition of Babrius and Phaedrus (see n.10 above) 456-7 no.185, where references are given to various texts, specified at 420-2.

13. For Tarn, see his *HC*^{3} 164; contrast E. V. Hansen, *The Attalids of Pergamon*^{2} (= *Cornell Stud. in Class. Philol.* 36, 1971) 144; H. L. Jones in Vol. VI.251 of the Loeb edition of Strabo; Joseph Fontenrose, 'The crucified Daphidas', in *TAPA* 91 (1960) 83-99, at p.85.

14. For an interesting general treatment of 'nationalism' in the Roman world, see F. W. Walbank, 'Nationalism, as a factor in Roman history', in *HSCP* 76 (1972) 145-68; cf. Walbank's 'The problem of Greek nationality', in *Phoenix* 5 (1951) 41-60.

15. See pp.294-5 of Jones's article (= *RE* 324-5), and *LRE* II.969-70. Cf. W. H. C. Frend, *The Donatist Church* (repr., 1971), esp. 172-6, 190-2, 208-10, 222, 226, 233-5, 257-8, 260, 265, 272, 291-2, 298-9, 326-32. Jones in his article, p.282 n.1 (= *RE* 310 n.3), says he differs 'only in some points of emphasis and interpretation' from Frend's book. There are also some very interesting remarks on the Donatist as having deep inside him 'quelque chose qui disait non à l'Empire', in Courtois, *VA* 135-52 (my quotation is from p.148, which merits special attention). The best short survey of the problem of Donatism and the proffered solutions that I have seen is by R. A. Markus, 'Christianity and Dissent in Roman North Africa: changing perspectives in recent work', in *SCH* 9 (1972) 21-36.

16. John Barns, SHS (1964) is brief. For bibliography on Shenute, see Otto Bardenhewer, *Gesch. der altkirklichen Lit.* IV^2 (1924) 98-100; and esp. J. Quasten, *Patrology* III (1960) 185-7. The 'standard work' on Shenute is Johannes Leipoldt, *Schenute von Atripe und die Entstehung des national ägyptischen Christentums* = *Texte u. Untersuch.* XXV.1 = n.F. X.1 (Leipzig, 1903). For those who do not read Coptic, there are Latin translations by Hermann Wiesmann of the three volumes in Coptic ed. by Leipoldt and W. E. Crum, *CSCO, Scr. Copt.*, Series 2, Vols II, IV and V (= Sinuthius i, iii and iv): these translations are (in corresponding order) *CSCO* 129 = *Scr. Copt.* 16 (Louvain, 1951), containing the interesting Life of Shenute by his pupil Besa; also *CSCO* 96 = *Scr. Copt.* 8 (Paris, 1931, repr. Louvain, 1965), and *CSCO* 108 = *Scr. Copt.* 12 (Paris, 1936, repr. Louvain, 1952), containing works by Shenute. The letter of Shenute translated by Barns, SHS 156-9, can also be found in Wiesmann's Latin version (almost complete) in *CSCO* 96 = *Scr. Copt.* 8 (see above) 43-7. The texts and translations by E. Amélineau, *Les Oeuvres de Schenoudi* (2 vols in parts, Paris, 1907-14), are said to be much less reliable. One or two other editions are mentioned by Barns, SHS 152; Quasten, op. cit. 186. To Quasten's bibliography I need add only Stein, *HBE* I^2.298-300; R. Rémondon, 'L'Egypte et la suprême résistance au Christianisme (V^e-VIIe siècles)', in *Bull. de l'Inst. français d'archéol. orientale* 51 (1952) 63-78.

17. I shall have much to say about the Council of Chalcedon and its consequences in my discussion of persecution *by* the Christian Churches, referred to near the end of this section.

18. I have preferred the version of Socr., *HE* IV.6.3 to 7.11, and Soz., *HE* VI.8.3-8 (cf. 26.1, 6-7) to that of Theod., *HE* II.27.4, 20-1; 29.1-10 (where the replacement of Eleusius by Eunomius takes place during the reign of Constantius II). See also Philostorg., *HE* IX.13.

19. Socr., *HE* II.38.28 (contrast III.11.3); Soz., *HE* IV.21.1; V.5.10. It appears from Soz., *HE* V.xv.4-7, that whereas the Cyzicene embassy to Julian asking for the restoration of pagan temples must have emanated from the Council and therefore from the curial class, Eleusius drew support for his anti-pagan activities mainly from the large number of humble workers in the State wool-manufactory and the mint.

20. Socr., *HE* II.38.28; Soz., *HE* IV.20.2-3. But Eleusius did not go in for the enormities described by Socr., *HE* II.38.6-13, as characteristic of the activities of Macedonius.

21. The fragments of the *Thalia* have been collected and analysed by G. Bardy, *Recherches sur Saint Lucien d'Antioche et son école* (Paris, 1936) 246-74, virtually a republication of his article, 'La Thalie d'Arius', in *Rev. de philol.* 53 = 3ᵉ série 1 (1927) 211-33. The latest treatment I have seen of the *Thalia* is by G. C. Stead, 'The *Thalia* of Arius and the testimony of Athanasius', in *JTS* n.s.29 (1978) 20-52, with a partial reconstruction in verse (48-50): 7 lines from Athan., *Orat. c. Arian.* I.5, and 42 lines from *De synod.* 15, with commentary. See also Aimé Puech, *Hist. de la litt. grecque chrét.* III (1930) 59-63. The principal fragments are from Athan., *De synod.* 15; *Orat. c. Arian.* I.5-6, 9 (cf. 2 and esp. 4); *Ep. ad episc. Aegypt. et Lib.* 12. (The best text of *De synod.* 15 is now that of H. G. Opitz, *Athanasius Werke* II.i [1941] 242-3.)

21a. It appears from Philostorgius, *HE* II.15, that Theognis, Arian bishop of Nicaea in the reign of Constantine and just afterwards, had had similar thoughts half a century earlier: he took the same view as Marinus. And cf. Socr., *HE* I.vi.9.

22. Soz., *HE* VIII.1.9 ff. repeats roughly the same material as Socrates. Sozomen too admired Sisinnius: see the passage just cited, and VII.12.3-6.

23. Eudoxius, as a major Arian figure, is of course execrated by Catholic writers, e.g. Theod., *HE* II.25.1, describing him as ravaging the Lord's vineyard like a wild boar during his earlier tenure of the bishopric of Antioch.

24. *Coll. Avell.* I, § 7, in *CSEL* XXXV.i.3, ed. O. Guenther, 1895. The most recent treatment I have seen of the Damascus-Ursinus strife is the admirable brief article by M. R. Green, 'The supporters of the Antipope Ursinus', in *JTS* n.s.22 (1971) 531-8. There is an Eng. trans. of the relevant part of the *Coll. Avell.* passage by S. L. Greenslade, *Schism in the Early Church*² (1964) 15-16. Greenslade's attitude to 'the Church' and to schism and heresy should be compared with the position adopted here. It is highly theological and, in my opinion, does not take sufficient account of historical reality, in particular the fact (which I have stressed in the next paragraph of the main text above) that the early Christians normally denied the very name of Christians to those they regarded as heretics or schismatics.

25. Socrates says that he got the story from a Paphlagonian peasant (*agroikos*) who claimed to have been present at the battle (it was a long time ago!), and that his account was confirmed by many other Paphlagonians (*HE* II.38.30).

26. Among New Testament passages which refer to or foreshadow the rise of heresy or schism, see esp. Act. Apost. XX.29-30 (note the λύκοι βαρεῖς!); Rom. XVI.17-18 (those causing τὰς διχοστασίας καὶ τὰ σκάνδαλα παρὰ τὴν διδαχήν); I Cor. i.10 (σχίσματα)-12; iii.3-4, xi.18 (σχίσματα), 19 (αἱρέσεις); Galat. I.6-9 (ἀνάθεμα against anyone preaching ἕτερον εὐαγγέλιον); V.20 (διχοστασίαι, αἱρέσεις); Tit. III.10-11 (reject the αἱρετικὸς ἄνθρωπος after two admonitions); II Pet. ii.1-3 (ψευδοδιδάσκαλοι, bringing in αἱρέσεις ἀπωλείας); Rev. II.6 & 15 (the hateful ἔργα and διδαχή of the Nicolaïtai), also 14 (the διδαχή of Balaam). Cf. also Act. Apost. XV (esp. 1-2, 5, 24); II Cor. xi.3-4, 12-13, 14-15; Galat. II.11-14; I Tim. i.19-20; vi.3-5, 20-1; II Tim. ii.16-18; iii.5-9; iv.3-4; Tit. I.9-14 (esp. 10-11).

[VIII.i]

1. The standard work on the Roman citizenship is Sherwin-White, *RC*² (1973). It will be obvious that my views are very different from his in some ways.

2. For the position in the Greek cities generally, see Jones, CLIE; *GCAJ* 117-20, 131-2; and V.iii above, with Appendix IV. 'Freedom' was precarious and could be taken away for alleged misconduct: see V.iii n.23 above, and n.11 below.

3. It is here that I find myself in disagreement with Garnsey (*SSLPRE* and *LPRE*): see below.

4. If not 212, the date must be 213 (as advocated by E. Bickermann in 1926, and by Z. Rubin, in *Latomus* 34 [1975] 430-6), and apparently early in that year (see D. Hagedorn, in *ZPE* 1 [1967] 140-1). But Simone Follet, *Athènes au IIᵉ et au IIIᵉ siècle. Études chronologiques et prosopographiques* (Paris, 1976) 64-72, makes a good case for the traditional date of publication at Rome between March and July 212. The principal study of the *CA* is by Chr. Sasse, *Die Constitutio Antoniniana* (Wiesbaden, 1958), which sets out all the relevant evidence and concludes with three biblio- graphies, the third of which alone, containing 'Die Spezialliteratur' on the *CA*, runs to no fewer than ten pages and 145 items. A certain amount of relevant literature has appeared since, some of which is noticed in A. N. Sherwin-White's article, 'The *tabula* of Banasa and the *CA*', in *JRS* 63 (1973) 86-98; cf. Sherwin-White, *RC*² 312, 382, and esp. 336 and 393-4. (For a useful comment on the relevance of that inscription to the *CA*, see also Brunt's addition to Jones, *RE* 5 n.11.) For full particulars of the literature up to 1965, see Sasse, 'Literaturübersicht zur Constitutio Antoni- niana', in *JJP* 14 (1962) 109-49; 15 (1965) 329-66. I should say that I accept *P. Giss.* 40.I = *FIRA*² I.445-9, no.88 = M. *Chr.* 426, no.377, as very probably representing the text of the *CA*. I have not been able to study the dissertation of 536 pages in two volumes by Hartmut Wolff, *Die Constitutio Antoniniana und Papyrus Gissensis 40.I* (Cologne, 1976). My knowledge of Byzantine papyri is not sufficient to enable me to form a definite opinion on the extent to which Roman imperial legislation was actually the law in Late Roman Egypt, a problem which has been the subject of much controversy since Mitteis, *RuV* (1891); and I shall therefore merely give a reference to one recent work (which has very full bibliography): A. Arthur Schiller, 'The fate of Imperial legislation in Late Byzantine Egypt', in *Legal Thought in the U.S.A. Under Contemporary Pressures*, ed. John N. Hazard and Wenceslas J. Wagner (Brussels, 1970). On the wider question of the enforcement of Roman law in the empire generally, cf. now V. Nutton, in *Imperialism in the Anc. World*, ed. P. D. A. Garnsey and C. R. Whittaker (1978), at 213-15 and 340-1 nn.33-41.

5. There has always been a dispute whether certain words of *P. Giss.* 40.I, 'except the *deditici*', are an exception to the main clause or to the subordinate clause (the genitive absolute) that follows. I am inclined to favour the latter view, having regard to the usage of the papyri, as established by Sasse: see Sherwin-White, *RC*² 381-2, and pp.97-8 of his article cited in the preceding note. Contrast Brunt's addition to Jones, *RE* 5 n.11. Perhaps we should leave the question open. But whatever our decision on this point, the *deditici* will be such a small proportion of the total population of the empire that it must be correct to see the *CA* as giving the citizenship (as I have put it in the main text above) to 'all, or virtually all, the free inhabitants of the empire'.

6. The *vicesima libertatis* was another such tax, but the one on inheritances was surely much more important. Some if not all of Caracalla's extensions of these taxes, including his doubling of the rate to 10 per cent, were cancelled some five years later by Macrinus: see Dio Cass. LXXVII[LXXVIII].ix.4-5; LXXVIII[LXXIX].xii.2.

7. See J. F. Gilliam, 'The minimum subject to the *vicesima hereditatium*', in *AJP* 73 (1952) 397-405. The lower limit of HS 100,000 which is often assumed seems wildly exaggerated: Gilliam shows from the evidence of *P. Mich.* 435 + 440 that the tax probably went down below 2,000 drachmae. If he is right, to say that 'it is highly probable that by the time of Caracallus the majority of the great fortunes of the empire were already within the fold' (Sherwin-White, *RC*² 281) is a weak argument against accepting Dio's statement. Gilliam is inclined to accept Dio's opinion, as some other leading scholars have been: see recently Jones, *SRGL* 140.

8. Garnsey, *SSLPRE* 75-6; and in *JRS* 56 (1966) 167-89, at 184-5; cf. *JRS* 58 (1968) 51-9.

9. See on this Sherwin-White, *RSRLNT* 64, 67.

10. Full references to texts and English translations of this famous inscription are given in IV.ii n.11 above (*FIRA*² I, no.103 etc.). The specific passages referred to here are col. iii, lines 1-2, 19-20; and col. ii, lines 13-14.

11. Rhodes was deprived of its freedom in A.D. 44 by Claudius, for executing Roman citizens (Dio Cass. LX.24.4); Cyzicus in B.C. 21 by Augustus, for the same reason (Dio Cass. LIV.7.6). When Cyzicus was deprived of its freedom for a second time, by Tiberius, one of the charges against it was of maltreating Roman citizens (Tac., *Ann.* IV.36.2-3; Suet., *Tib.* 37; Dio Cass. LVII.24.6). According to Dio Cass. LX.17.3 (A.D. 43), the reason why Claudius deprived the Lycians of their freedom was that they had been στασιάσαντες and had killed some Romans; but contrast Suet., *Claud.* 25. Cf. V.iii n.23 above.

12. To speak of 'families' in all these cases is a gross oversimplification; but I must not go into detail. On the whole I agree with Garnsey, *SSLPRE* 235-51. Membership of the senatorial order went down to the third generation of agnatic descendants and their wives (ibid. 237 and n.2).

For equestrian status, see VI.vi above, *ad fin.*: it was not hereditary in the same sense as that of senators; but see *CJ* IX.xli.11.*pr.* for a specific case of privilege for *eminentissimi* and *perfectissimi* extending to the third generation. Garnsey may well be right in saying that equestrians of lower grade were 'perhaps protected only to the first generation', as was the case with curial families (ibid. 242).

13. The position of soldiers is peculiar and disputed: see Garnsey, *SSLPRE* 246-51; Cardascia, ADCHH 328.

14. Cf. Cardascia's review of Garnsey, *SSLPRE*, in *Iura* 21 (1970) 250-6.

15. See Jones, RCS 44 ff. = *SRGL* 161 ff.

16. Narcissus received *quaestoria insignia* from the Senate in 48 (Tac., *Ann.* XI.38.5), Pallas *praetoria insignia* in 52 (ibid. XII.53.2-5: the *SC*, which also contained a gift to Pallas of HS 15,000,000, was moved by Barea Soranus; cf. ibid. XVI.21.2!).

17. Cardascia, op. cit. in n.14 above, esp. 253-4.

18. See Garnsey, *SSLPRE* 136-41, esp. 139 and nn.6-7. But Garnsey does not make it sufficiently clear how the situation *changed*, as it did, during the second century.

19. Garnsey, *SSLPRE* 104, 141; cf. 141-7, 213-16, 224, 242-3.

20. Cf. Garnsey, *SSLPRE* 146, 166. In case anyone wishes to delete 'vel quaestionibus' from *CJ* IX.xli.11.*pr.*, as an interpolation, I would point out that the text forms part of the *CJ* title *De quaestionibus*. That does not absolutely rule out interpolation, I suppose, but to my mind it makes it unlikely. Marcus' ruling was presumably taken by Diocletian and Maximian, when issuing their constitution (*CJ* IX.xli.11.*pr.* and 1), from Ulpian's *Disputationes* (ibid. 1), indeed Book I thereof (see *Dig.* L.ii.2.2). Of course we cannot rule out the possibility that they may have interpolated the words 'vel quaestionibus'; but why should we make any such unnecessary assumption?

21. Of these texts, *Dig.* L.ii.14 is decisive. Pius ruled that a decurion was not to be tortured even if he had been condemned – to a penalty, evidently, which involved loss of his status as a decurion, as would result even from *relegatio* (Ulpian, in *Dig.* L.ii.2.*pr.*, etc.), which did not involve loss of citizenship, as did *deportatio*. The second sentence of L.ii.14 may be Paulus' comment rather than the decision of Pius; but for what it is worth it proves conclusively that, at least in the eyes of Paulus, it was the condemned man's former status *as a decurion* (not as a citizen, or a free man) that prevented him from being tortured.

22. Perhaps I should mention that before the persecution of Decius in 250-1 there are few reliable references to the judicial torture of Christians. Some Christian slaves were certainly tortured (see e.g. Pliny, *Ep.* X.96.8), and some of the others who are said to have been tortured (see e.g. the mid-second-century *Passio Polycarpi* 2.2-3,4; Eus., *HE* IV.xv.4-5) will have been slaves or *peregrini*. If the martyrdom of Carpus and Papylus is Decian in date, as seems likely, then I think that only one of the Christians alleged to have been tortured before the Decian persecution can be positively identified as a Roman citizen: Attalus, in the persecution at Lyons in *c.* 177 (Eus., *HE* V.i.43-4, 50-2, cf. 17, 37). It will be useful to refer here to a recent book on the records of early Christian martyrdoms which is exceptionally well-informed and accurate: Giuliana Lanata, *Gli atti dei martiri come documenti processuali* (Milan, 1973), esp. 113-14, cf. 68 n.108. Some early Christian authors write as if the torture of accused Christians were usual: see e.g. Tert., *Apol.* (*c.* 197 A.D.) 2.5, 10-11, 13, 15, 19; *Ad Scap.* (after *c.* 210) 4.2-3; Minuc. Fel., *Octav.* 28.3. The last-mentioned work is almost certainly to be dated in the latter part of the Severan period – 'the first third of the third century', according to G. W. Clarke, *The Octavius of Marcus Minucius Felix* (New York, 1974) 5-12, 136-9.

23. Cf. e.g. *CJ* III.xxviii.11; Maecianus, in *Dig.* XXXVI.i.5.

24. See Cardascia, ADCHH 317-19, preferable to Garnsey, *SSLPRE* 200-3, 234-5, 251-2, who hardly takes sufficient account of the corruption of the text of Paulus, *Sent.* V.iv.10.

25. Cardascia, ADCHH 310, 466-7; Garnsey, *SSLPRE* 182-5.

26. For the Greek East, see Jones, *GCAJ* 180 (with 342 n.46); and for Italy and north Africa, Duncan-Jones, *EREQS* 81-2, 138-44. See also III.vi and its n.35 above.

27. I need only refer to J. C. Mann's article, 'The frontiers of the Principate', in *ANRW* II.i (1974) 508-33, at 516-17 (with its n.5), which explains the reason for the change.

28. There were scarcely three dozen Roman citizen colonies in the Greek East and only three Roman *municipia*: see Jones, *RE* 90-1.

29. Sherwin-White, *RC*² 273 (my italics).

30. Rostovtzeff, *SEHRE*² I.343-52, 378-81; cf. 35, 117 (with II.586-7 n.18), 191, 192-4, 263 and 266 (with II.660-1 nn.20-5), 273-98 (on Egypt), 334, 381-5, 413, 430-1, 477-80, 503. In most of

these passages (and others like them) Rostovtzeff shows himself well aware of the existence of what I am calling 'the class struggle'. For a good general critique of Rostovtzeff's work, a biography, and a very full bibliography (of 444 items), see II.i n.5 above.

31. N. H. Baynes, review of Rostovtzeff, *SEHRE*[1], in *JRS* 19 (1929) 224-35, at 229-33, repr. in *BSOE* 307-16; and 'The decline of the Roman power in Western Europe: some modern explanations', in *JRS* 33 (1943) 29-35, repr. in *BSOE* 83-96 (esp. 92-3).

32. See Baynes, *BSOE* 309, 93.

33. V. Gordon Childe, *What Happened in History* (Pelican, 1942 and repr.) 250. Childe's earlier work, *Man Makes Himself* (1936; 3rd ed. 1956 and repr.), has also, deservedly, been read by many who are neither archaeologists nor historians. A detailed description of Childe's great contributions to archaeology and history was announced as I was completing this section: Bruce G. Trigger, *Gordon Childe: Revolutions in Archaeology* [published 1980].

34. For the important contributions of Lynn White (and of R. J. Forbes) to the history of mediaeval technology, see II.i n.14 above, where I have mentioned that White's article (TIMA) quoted in the main text of this section, although open to criticism at some points, is still well worth reading, although it is largely replaced by his chapter in Vol. I of the Fontana *Economic History of Europe*.

[VIII.ii]

1. Jones, *RE* 11-19 (a masterly summary over the whole period from the first to the sixth century); *RE* 396-418, esp. 396-9, 401, 413-16, 418; *LRE* II.724-63 (esp. 737-57), with the notes in III.228-43, and other passages (some of them important) given in the Index, *s.v.* 'decurions (curiales)'; *GCAJ* 179-210 (with the notes, 342-8), not entirely superseded by *LRE*. Among other recent articles, Garnsey, ADUAE, is particularly well worth reading and has a useful bibliography at the end.

2. Among the early occurrences of the word *curialis* in this sense are (i) *CTh.* XII.i.6 = *CJ* V.v.3.1 (*civitati cuius curialis fuerat*), probably A.D. 318 rather than 319 (if 'Aquileia' is correct); (ii) *FIRA* I[2].462, no.95 (= *MAMA* VII.305 = A/J 154), col.i.19, A.D. 325-6; (iii) *CTh*.XII.i.19 (*init.*), A.D. 331; (iv) *CTh.* XII.i.21 (*init.*), probably A.D. 334 rather than 335. Characteristic of the neglect of Later Roman history by Classical scholars until recently is the fact that Lewis and Short's *Latin Dictionary* (the one most used in the English-speaking world) is most misleading *s.v. curiales*, making out that the word means 'in late Latin, *belonging to the imperial court*': the three references which follow from Ammianus all refer quite clearly to local councillors!

3. See Liebenam, *SRK* 229-30 and n.5; Jones, *GCAJ* 176, with 340 n.40; *LRE* II.724-5, with III.228 n.26 (corrected as regards *ILA* 266 by Duncan-Jones, *EREQS* 283 n.7). For the West, see Duncan-Jones, *EREQS* 283-7, and in *PBSR* 31 (1963) 159-77, at 167-8.

4. *IGRR* III.154 = *CIL* III.282, line 49. For payment of *summa honoraria, honorarium decurionatus*, on becoming a decurion in a Greek city, see e.g. Pliny, *Ep.* X.xxxix.5 and cxii-xiii; Dio Chrys. XLVIII.11; *SIG*[3] 838 = A/J 85, line 14; *IGBulg*. IV.2263, lines 9-12. Much more is known about the corresponding payments in the Latin West: see e.g. Duncan-Jones, *EREQS* 82-8 (Africa) and 147-55 (Italy); here too adlections *gratis* are recorded (ibid. 148 and n.2). Cf. Garnsey, as cited by Duncan-Jones; and Pleket, in *Gnomon* 49 (1977) 59-60.

5. For *SB* III.ii (1927) 7261, see H. B. van Hoesen and A. C. Johnson, 'A papyrus dealing with liturgies', in *JEA* 12 (1926) 118-19.

6. See Jones, *GCAJ* 204-5 (with 347 n.96), who could give only three examples after Constantine: *CTh* XII.i.53, 96, 133. (In Clyde Pharr's translation of the *CTh* there is a serious error in XII.i.96; contrast Jones's correct translation, *GCAJ* 205.) I would add ibid. 72, 124.

7. Even if the explicit purpose of the law was to prevent illiterates who were already decurions from escaping curial burdens, it shows that there were now illiterate decurions. And although of course some illiterates who had made money might be pleased to join their *ordo*, it is at least as likely that the well-to-do illiterates Diocletian had in mind had been obliged to become decurions because of their financial usefulness to their *curia*; it may have been attempts on the part of some of them to claim that their illiteracy made the performance of *munera* impossible for them which called forth Diocletian's edict.

8. An interesting example is *P. Oxy.* I.71, col.i.11 (A.D. 303): the man had been chief priest at Arsinoë and superintendent of the corn supply (col.i.2, 15-16).

9. This is the correct form of the name (often given as Aptungi): see *CIL* VIII, Suppl. iv (1916), no.23085, and p.2338.

10. The best account is that of J. F. Gilliam, 'The plague under Marcus Aurelius', in *AJP* 82 (1961) 225-51, who rightly warns against exaggerating its dimensions and its effects – as is only too common with ancient plagues (an example is the recent book by W. H. McNeill, *Plagues and Peoples,* 1977). See also A. R. Birley, *MA* (1966) 202-5, 212, 214, 217-18. Dio Cass. LXXII[LXXIII].14.3-4 is particularly interesting: he mentions a disease in about 189 of which '2,000 people often died at Rome in a single day'; and Dio describes this as 'the greatest disease' he knew of – yet he had probably been born in 163-4 (see F. Millar, *SCD* 13), just before the outbreak of the great plague under Marcus. One of Gilliam's arguments against exaggerating the plague of the 160s, based on the passage from Dio I have just quoted, is rejected by Millar (ibid. n.4, endorsed by Birley, IIRMA 217 n.8), on the ground that the infant Dio 'no doubt failed to notice' when Verus' plague-stricken army returned through his home town of Nicaea in 166. But Millar mistranslates Dio, who refers to the plague of the 160s as the greatest he 'knew of', not the greatest he 'had experienced'.

11. See the very well informed discussion of the chronology by A. R. Birley, IIRMA (with full bibliography, esp. in 214 nn.1-3).

12. Βουκόλοι should mean 'herdsmen', but the name may be derived rather from the district where the rebels operated, known as τὰ βουκόλια (W. *Chr.* 21.6,19-20), where there had been a rising some twenty years earlier, in the reign of Antoninus Pius, as shown by W. *Chr.* 19 = A/J 175; *Hist. Aug., Ant. P.* 5.5; Malalas XI, p.280.16-17, ed. W. Dindorf; cf. the very full discussion by Alexander Schenk, Graf von Stauffenberg, *Die römische Kaisergesch. bei Malalas* (Stuttgart, 1931) 307-9, 312-13. [See also Pavel Oliva, *Pannonia and the Onset of Crisis in the Roman Emp.* (Prague, 1962) 119-20; and J. C. Shelton, in *Anc. Soc.* 7 (1976) 209-13; which I saw only after this chapter was finished.]

13. *Hist. Aug., Marc.* 17.4-5; 21.9; Eutrop. VIII.13.2 (the auction lasted for two months). Cf. the probable fragment of Dio Cassius preserved by Zonaras XII.1 and the *Excerpta Salmasiana* 117, printed in Boissevain's standard edition of Dio, Vol. III, p.280, and in Vol. IX of the Loeb edition, p.70. See Birley, *MA* 218-19.

14. Contrast, recently, M. H. Crawford, 'Finance, coinage and money from the Severans to Constantine', in *ANRW* II.ii (1975) 560-93, at 591-2, with Birley, TCCRE 260 n.1, who rightly points out that 'vast sums would be required during campaigns for equipment (arms, armour, *matériel* of all kinds), road and bridge building, repair of enemy damage, remounts etc.'. There is no doubt some truth in Crawford's argument that army units were often under strength in time of peace; although if that was so, then the increased expenditure in wartime would have been even greater.

15. There is a convenient brief summary by G. R. Watson, in *OCD*² 1014, with bibliography, to which add M. Speidel, 'The pay of the Auxilia', in *JRS* 63 (1973) 141-7, and other works cited by Birley, TCCRE 267 and nn.6-7.

16. I am ignoring that famous passage, Pliny, *Ep.* X.113, because I think the text is too uncertain to bear the weight of the argument usually based upon it: namely, that we have here the earliest evidence of men being compelled to become councillors (see Jones, *GCAJ* 343-4 n.64; cf. Garnsey, ADUAE 232 and nn.11-12; F. A. Lepper, in *Gnomon* 42 [1970], at 570-1). It may well be that we should read 'invitati' instead of 'inviti', with Mynors (in the *OCT*, 1963) and Sherwin-White, *LP* 722-4; but I regard the question as still open.

17. The distinction between *munera personalia* (or *personae*) and *patrimonii* is not clearly explained by the Severan lawyers (cf. Rostovtzeff, *SEHRE*² II.714-15 n.18), although it often appears in their surviving writings (as in Ulpian, *Dig.* L.vi.4, and Papinian, L.v.7); but it is stated in detail by Hermogenian (*Dig.* L.iv.1), probably in the late third century. The only formal statement about *munera mixta* is by Arcadius Charisius, a little later (probably in the last years of the third century or the first years of the fourth), in *Dig.* L.iv.18, esp. *pr.* and 26-8. A very useful recent work is Naphtali Lewis, *Inventory of Compulsory Services in Ptolemaic and Roman Egypt* (= *Amer. Stud. in Papyrology* 3, 1968), an essential supplement to F. Oertel, *Die Liturgie. Studien zur ptolemäischen und kaiserlichen Verwaltung Ägyptens* (Leipzig, 1917).

18. See the interesting chapter by V. Nutton, 'The beneficial ideology', in *Imperialism in the Ancient World,* ed. P. D. A. Garnsey and C. R. Whittaker (1978) 209-21, at 219-20, with 342 nn.64-8, utilising esp. L. Robert, 'Epigrammes relatives à des gouverneurs', in *Hellenica* 4 (1948) 35-114.

19. There is a nice example in Symm., *Rel.* XXXVIII.2,5: Venantius, a decurion in Apulia, had managed to obtain the minor post of *strator* in the department of the *magister officiorum* (§ 4) –

illegally, since he was proved to be a decurion. The possible conflict of authority between the provincial governor and the *vicarius urbis Romae* on the one hand and the *magister officiorum* on the other made Symmachus feel it necessary to refer the case to the emperor himself. See Jones, *LRE* I.518.

20. In the text and in the notes below I have been very sparing with references to modern works and have cited only Jones (*LRE* and *GCAJ*), Norman (GLMS), Rostovtzeff (*SEHRE²*), and Turner (n.21 below). Norman, GLMS, is a particularly good summary, but I must also mention here his most useful long review, in *JRS* 47 (1957) 236-40, of two important books by Paul Petit (of which one especially, *LVMA*, is a mine of information), including much that is relevant to the curial class, especially of course of Antioch.

21. See E. G. Turner, 'Egypt and the Roman Emp.: the δεκάπρωτοι', in *JEA* 22 (1936) 7-19; Jones, *GCAJ* 139 (with 327 n.85), 153 (with 333 n.106); Rostovtzeff, *SEHRE²* I.390-1 (with II.706-7 nn.45, 47), 407 (with II.715 n.19).

22. See Jones, *LRE* II.544, and 750 (with III.240 n.88). Most interesting is Liban., *Orat.* XXVIII.4 ff., esp. 21-2 (see Jones, *LRE* II.750). See also *Nov. Theod.* XV.2.1 for some extraordinary behaviour by a decurion of Emesa, who had obtained the honorary rank of *illustris*; and note the very mild punishment he received.

23. See Liban., *Orat.* XI.133 ff. for the Council, 150 ff. for the *dēmos*. In § 150 the demos is to follow the Council as a chorus follows its leader (*koryphaios*).

24. Stephen L. Dyson, 'Native revolts in the Roman Empire', in *Historia* 20 (1971) 239-74; and 'Native revolt patterns in the Roman Empire', in *ANRW* II.iii (1975) 138-75.

[VIII.iii]

1. C. P. Jones, 'The date of Dio of Prusa's Alexandrian oration', in *Historia* 22 (1973) 302-9, suggests A.D. 71-2. In § 72 he would emend Κόνων to Κόλων = L. Peducaeus Colonus, Prefect of Egypt *c.* 70-2. But J. F. Kindstrand, same title, in *Historia* 27 (1978) 378-83, agrees with H. von Arnim, *Leben und Werke des Dio von Prusa* (Berlin, 1898) 435-8, in preferring the reign of Trajan. I cannot deal in this book with several disturbances at Alexandria, recorded in sources of very varying value, but I will at least mention the article by S. J. Oost, 'The Alexandrian seditions under Philip and Gallienus', in *CP* 56 (1961) 1-20, which has very full references.

2. The Spartan inscription is *AE* (1929) 21, first published by A. M. Woodward in *BSA* 27 (1925-6) 234-6, where line 7 has ἔφορος ἐπὶ τῶν νεωτερισμῶν; cf. perhaps ἐπὶ [τῶν γενομένων | ν]ξωτερισμῶν in *IG* V.i.44.9-10. Some have brought Lucian, *De morte Peregr.* 19 (*init.*) into this context. The two *Historia Augusta* references are *Pius* 5.5 and *Gallien.* 4.9. (For the Egyptian rebellion which is also mentioned in *HA, Pius* 5.5, see VIII.ii n.12 above.)

3. Cleon is probably the Medeius of Dio Cass. LI.ii.3. He is said to have earned the favour of Antony by organising resistance to the tax-collectors of Q. Labienus (acting as commander of a Parthian force in 40-39 B.C.) and to have been rewarded first by Antony with the priesthood of Zeus Abrettenus in Mysia and a local principality in Morene, and then, when he changed sides in the civil war, to have been rewarded by Octavian with the important high priesthood of Comana in Pontus (Strabo XII.viii.8-9, pp.574-5). As for the activities of the ex-slave Anicetus and his followers in the Pontic region in A.D. 69 (Tac., *Hist.* III.47-8), there is evidently no need to take seriously Tacitus' contemptuous description of their suppression as a *bellum servile*.

4. This picture is not affected by other references to participation in the revolt by the lower classes: Herodian VII.iii.6; *Hist. Aug., Gord.* 7.3-4. Note that the landowners are described as δεσπόται, giving orders to obedient country folk – who are likely to have been mainly their tenants, with some peasant freeholders too. Cf. Whittaker's note on Herodian VII.iv.3, in the Loeb Herodian, Vol. II. I have not been able to digest the long article by Frank Kolb, 'Der Aufstand der Provinz Africa Proconsularis im Jahr 238 n. Chr. Die wirtschaftlichen u. sozialen Hintergründe', in *Historia* 26 (1977) 440-78, which I saw only after this section had been completed; but it seems evident from his last paragraph on p.477 that Kolb's main conclusion is not different from mine.

5. See Downey, *HAS* 254-8, 261, 311, 587-95 (esp. 590-2). Note esp. Petr. Patric. fr. 1, discussed by Downey, *HAS* 256. Against the view, put forward by Jean Gagé, that Mariades was a leader of a circus faction, see Cameron, *CF* 200-1.

6. On the revolt of Firmus, see Thompson, *HWAM* 90-2, 129-30, and Frend, *DC* 72-3, 197-9; contrast J. F. Matthews, 'Mauretania in Ammianus and the *Notitia*', in *Aspects of the Notitia Dignitatum*, ed. R. Goodburn and P. Bartholomew (= *British Archaeological Reports*, Suppl. Series 15, Oxford, 1976) 157-86, at 177-8. Matthews is surely right in denying that the rebellion of Firmus was in any real sense 'one of the lower orders of town or country against the landed aristocracy of the Roman cities' and that 'the Donatist schism contributed at all significantly to the rebellion'. That other African revolts were mainly tribal movements seems to me to be true even of such notable risings as those of Faraxen and the 'Fraxinenses' and the Quinquegentanei in the late 250s, and of the Quinquegentanei in the last decade of the third century, suppressed by Maximian. For these and other north African revolts, see Seston, *DT* I.115-28; Rostovtzeff, *SEHRE*² I.474 (with II.737 n.12); Mazza, *LSRA*² 659 n.4; and the article by Matthews cited above.

7. Cf., for the deserters, Dio Cass. LXVIII.x.3; xi.3; and see Petr. Patric. fr. 5. The Romans were particularly keen to stop the desertion of craftsmen: see e.g. for shipbuilders *CTh* IX.xl.24 = *CJ* IX.xlvii.25 (A.D. 419).

8. See Géza Alföldy, *Noricum* (1974) 168-9, with 335 nn.58-64; *Fasti Hispanienses* (Wiesbaden, 1969) 43-5.

9. Greg. Thaumaturg., *Epist. Canon.* 7, in *MPG* X.1040. The best edition I know is by J. Dräseke, 'Der kanonische Brief des Gregorios von Neocäsarea', in *Jahrb. für prot. Theol.* 7 (1881) 724-56, at 729-36. Dräseke's date is 254, which may be right. There was an even bigger Gothic invasion in *c.* 256, but I know of no evidence that this penetrated so far east. (The chronology of the Gothic invasions of Asia Minor in the 250s and 260s is notoriously in a state of confusion.)

10. There is no reason to see a reference to the Bacaudae in *Paneg. Lat.* V.iv.1, ed. E. Galletier (= IX[IV].iv.1, ed. Baehrens or Mynors), referring to A.D. 269-70: see Thompson, PRLRGS, in *SAS* (ed. Finley) 315 n.41; also 'Britain, A.D. 406-410', in *Britannia* 8 (1977) 303-18, at 312 n.36. The groundless emendation by Lipsius, 'Bagaudicae', appears in the editions of the *Panegyric* just referred to by e.g. Baehrens and Mynors but not Galletier.

11. The main passage in Ammianus, XXVII.ii.11, may be compared with Anon., *De rebus bellicis* II.3, ed. Thompson, and the evasive language of *Paneg. Lat.* II.iv (esp. 4); vi.1; III.v.3; VI.viii.3, ed. Galletier.

12. For all the known details, and the sources, see Thompson, in *SAS* 312-13, 316-18; and in his article of 1977 (mentioned in n.10 above), esp. 310-13. (See also Thompson's article in *JRS* 1956, mentioned at the end of IV.iii n.29 above.)

13. I have used the Teubner edition, *Aulularia sive Querolus*, by Rudolf Peiper (1875). Much recent bibliography will be found in the article by Luigi Alfonsi, 'Il "Querolo" e il "Dyskolos"', in *Aeg.* 44 (1964) 200-5, esp. 200 n.1, where references are given to the most recent editions of the play, by G. Ranstrand (Göteborg, 1951) and F. Corsaro (Bologna, 1965).

14. In Collingwood and Myres, *RBES*² 304, cf. 284-5, 302; contrast Applebaum, in *AHEW* I.ii.236. Nor do I think there is any good ground for supposing (with Applebaum, loc. cit. and 32) that an insurrection in Britain some eighty years earlier, *c.* 284, in the reign of Carinus, may have involved a peasant uprising comparable to that of the Bacaudae (who are first heard of at this very time in Gaul), even if Carinus (A.D. 283-5) did take the title 'Brittannicus Maximus' (*ILS* 608), based no doubt upon some activity by one of his generals in Britain. Applebaum seems (ibid. 32 n.2) to have taken Eutrop. IX.20.3 to be referring to Carinus: in fact Eutropius is speaking there of Diocletian.

15. Thompson, 'Britain, A.D. 406-410' (already cited in nn.10 and 12 above), esp. 304-9 on the chronology.

16. See e.g. Mommsen, *Röm. Strafr.* 981-3; Ostrogorsky, *HBS*² 159-60. In ibid. 114 we are told that the cutting off of the nose of Heraclonas in 641 was 'the first time that the oriental custom of mutilation by cutting off the nose is met with on Byzantine soil'. (The Empress Martina's tongue was also cut off at the same time.) But I have noticed that in Michael the Syrian, *Chron.* IX.3 (ed. J. B. Chabot, II.412: see n.34 below), the Emperor Heraclius is said to have ordered that anyone in Syria not accepting Chalcedonian orthodoxy was to have his nose and ears cut off and his property confiscated: this was presumably in A.D. 621, when Heraclius was at Mabboug/Hierapolis. I do not know whether Michael's report is true, or is simply the anti-Heraclian propaganda of a Jacobite. It is repeated by Bar Hebraeus, *Chron. Eccles.* I. col.274 (see n.35 below).

17. Is this perhaps the sort of situation referred to by Orientius, *Commonit.* II.173-4 (*CSEL* XVI.i.234, ed. R. Ellis)?

18. Paulinus of Pella, *Eucharist*. 328 ff., esp. 333-6, in *CSEL* XVI.i.304, ed. G. Brandes; and in Vol. II of the Loeb Ausonius, ed. H. G. Evelyn White, with Eng. trans.

19. For the revolt in Palestine, see Marcellinus Comes *ad a*. 418, in *Chron. Min*. II.73. (Plinta was consul in 419, perhaps partly as a reward for suppressing the rebellion.) For the revolt of the Nori, see Hydatius 95, in *Chron. Min*. II.22.

20. For Alexander, see Procop., *Bell*. VII = *Goth*. III.i.28-33; xxi.14. For Bessas, see ibid. xvii.10-14, 15-16; xix.13-14; xx.1,18,26.

21. Jones, *LRE* II.1060-1. He does admit that 'some victim of extortion may have fled in desperation' (note the singular case!). We can hardly include among Salvian's humble refugees the two sons of Paulinus of Pella, who went off to settle among the Goths at Bordeaux, inspired by 'libertatis amor' (*Eucharist*. 498-502).

22. The controversy about the real nature of the Circumcellions still continues. I am inclined to accept the general view of W. H. C. Frend, as expressed in his book, *The Donatist Church* (for which see VII.v and its n.15 above), and in two articles: 'The *cellae* of the African Circumcellions', in *JTS*, n.s.3 (1952) 87-90, and 'Circumcellions and monks', in id. 20 (1969) 542-9, where references will be found to all the recent literature, by Brisson, Calderone, Diesner, Saumagne, and Tengström. See also MacMullen, *ERO* 200-3 (with 353-4 n.10).

23. See e.g. Procop., *Bell*. III = *Vand*. I.v.11-17 (esp. 14); xix.3 (cities not friendly to Belisarius' army); xxiii.1-6 (peasants hostile to it); and IV = *Vand*. II.iii.26 and esp. viii.25; cf. Courtois, *VA* 286, 311-13, with 131 ff., 144 ff.

24. I accept the interpretation of these laws given by Stein, *HBE* II.558-9, with 321-2 and I² (1959) i.327.

25. See e.g. A. Dopsch, in *CEHE* I².204, with 182.

26. See e.g. Procop., *Bell*. VI = *Goth*. II.xxi.39, Milan; VII = *Goth*. III.x.19-22, Tibur.

27. See Procop., *Bell*. VII = *Goth*. III.i.8-10, 23-4; iv.15-16; ix.1-4; xi.1-3; and see the main text and n.20 above. My 'perhaps' allows for the possibility that there may be a little more truth than is generally allowed in the vicious criticisms made of Belisarius in Procop., *Anecd*. I.10 to V.27.

28. See Procop., *Bell*. VII = *Goth*. III.vi.5; xiii.1.

29. Ibid. xvi.14-15, 25.

30. Justinian's *Pragmatic Sanction*, of 13 August 554, can be found in *Corp. Iuris Civil*. III (*Nov. Just.*) 799-802, Appendix 7. It was issued after the collapse of the Ostrogothic kingdom in Italy and the expulsion of the invading Franks and Alamans. Cf. also ibid. 803, Appendix 8 (soon after 554); and see Stein, *HBE* II.613-17; also, on the agrarian policy of Totila, ibid. 569-71, 573-4, 579, 585-6, 613-14. For abuse of Totila see *Nov. Just.*, Append. 7.2,5,6,7,8,15,17,24 (Totila the *tyrannus*, who is *nefandissimus*, is guilty of *tyrannica ferocitas*, and is of *sceleratae memoriae*). Totila is also *nefandissimus tyrannus* in an inscription set up by Narses near Rome in 565: *ILS* 832.

31. Jones, *LRE* II.1022, with III.338 n.79. Contrast the passages I have cited in the main text and in nn.23-4, 27-30 above, and in IV.iv, n.7. Some of the passages Jones cites either prove little or tell against him, e.g. Procop., *Bell*. V. = *Goth*. I.xiv.4-5, where the principal reason for the decision by the inhabitants of Rome to hand their city over to Belisarius is their fear of sharing the fate of many of the Neapolitans (see ibid. x.29 ff. for the slaughter that took place on the capture of Neapolis, until it was stopped by Belisarius).

32. *The Chronicle of John, Bishop of Nikiu*, trans. from Zotenberg's Ethiopic text by R. H. Charles (Text and Trans. Soc., London, 1916) cxi.12; cxiii.2; cxiv.1,3,9,10; cxix.1-2; cxxi.10-11; cf. cxi.2; cxviii.3; cxx.4, and esp. cxv.9, where we are told that 'When the Moslems saw the weakness of the Romans and the hostility of the people to the Emperor Heraclius, because of the persecution wherewith he had visited all the land of Egypt in regard to the orthodox faith, at the instigation of Cyrus the Chalcedonian patriarch [cf. cxxi.2], they became bolder and stronger in the war'. See the interesting remarks about John of Nikiu (who 'wrote his *Chronicle* to show that the Arab conquest was God's judgment on the heresy of the empire in accepting Chalcedon') in Henry Chadwick's article on John Moschus, in *JTS* n.s.25 (1974) 41-74, at 70-1 (esp. 71 n.1). John wrote near the end of the seventh century. His work, composed originally in Greek (partly in Coptic), survives only in an Ethiopic version of an Arabic translation. Therefore, if we read it in English (or in Zotenberg's French, 1883), we are taking it at fourth hand. The *Chronicle*, although a valuable source for the conquest of Egypt by the Arabs, contains much superstitious and other rubbish, and it exhibits a hostility to Hypatia (one of the most eminent of all the victims of Christian bloodthirstiness) which is unique among the surviving sources that refer to the murder of that philosopher (lxxxiv.87-102, esp. 87-8, 100-3).

33. Of the whole twenty-five years' *war between Rome and Persia* I know of no single full and reliable account. One of the most useful outlines I have seen is that by Louis Bréhier, in *Histoire de l'Église*, ed. A. Fliche and V. Martin, V (Paris, 1947) 72-5, 80-5, 88-101, with much citation of original sources and modern bibliography (for the sources etc., see 8-10, 14-16, 55-6, 79-88). For the Persian occupation of Egypt, see A. J. Butler's book (in its second edition, by P. M. Fraser), cited in n.37 below, 69-92, 498-507, with parts of the 'Additional Bibliography', xlv ff., esp. lviii-ix. For Asia Minor, Clive Foss, 'The Persians in Asia Minor and the end of Antiquity', in *Eng. Hist. Rev.* 90 (1975) 721-47, cites the essential modern work by N. H. Baynes (1912-13), A. Stratos (now 3 vols) and the numismatists and archaeologists. There are only very brief accounts of the Persian wars in such standard works as Arthur Christensen, *L'Iran sous les Sassanides*[2] (Copenhagen, 1944) 447-8, 492-8; Ostrogorsky, *HBS*[2] 85, 95, 100-4; and Ch. Diehl, *Hist. générale, Histoire du Moyen Age III. Le Monde oriental de 395 à 1081*[2] (Paris, 1944) 140-50. I have not come across any examples for this period (contrast, for the fourth century, the main text above and nn.46-7, 49 below) of assistance being given to the Persians (or of flight to them) except on the part of the Jews (see the main text above and n.39 below). As for the exceedingly obscure subject of the *Arab conquests*, there is again a useful outline by Louis Bréhier, op. cit. V.127-30, 134-41, 151-60. Fraser's second edition of Butler's book (n.37 below) is essential, with its 'Additional Bibl.', esp. lxiii-iv, lxviii-lxx, lxxii-iii. For modern works in English on the subject of the Arab conquests in general, see Philip K. Hitti, *Hist. of the Arabs from the Earliest Times to the Present*[10] (1970) 142-75; Franceso Gabrieli, *Muhammad and the Conquests of Islam*, Eng. trans. by V. Luling and R. Linell (1968) 103 ff., esp. 143-80, with the Bibliography, 242-8.

34. See the very scholarly French trans. by J. B. Chabot, *Chronique de Michel le Syrien, Patriarche Jacobite d'Antioche (1166-1199)*, Vol. II.iii (Paris, 1904) 412-13. Of all the persecuting Chalcedonian clerics, the one who was remembered most bitterly by the Syrian Christians was Dometianus of Melitene, in the last years of the sixth century, in the reign of Maurice (himself a zealous Chalcedonian): see e.g. Michael the Syrian, *Chron.* X.23, 25 (ed. Chabot, II.372-3, 379, 381); cf. R. Paret, 'Dometianus de Mélitène et la politique religieuse de l'empereur Maurice', in *REB* 15 (1957) 42-72, who shows that the persecution by Dometianus took place from late 598 until well into 601. For what seems to have been a murderous persecution of Monophysites (rather than Jews) at Antioch in 608-9, under Phocas, by the *comes Orientis* Bonosus, see Louis Bréhier, op. cit. (in n.33 above) V.73-5.

35. *Gregorii Barhebraei Chronicon Ecclesiasticum*, ed. J. B. Abbeloos and T. J. Lamy (3 vols, Louvain, 1872/4/7), Vol. I, col.274: Syriac, with Latin trans. This work is Part II of the *Chronography* of Bar Hebraeus. Part I is translated into English by E. A. Wallis Budge, *The Chronography of Gregory Abû'l Faraj . . . commonly known as Bar Hebraeus* I (1932), which also gives a biography of Bar Hebraeus and a discussion of his works (pp.xv-xxxi, xxxii-vi; and see xliv-lii). For Michael as a principal source of Bar Hebraeus, see ibid. I, p.1. J. Pargoire, *L'Église byzantine de 527 à 847* (Paris, 1905) 147-9, has a good little section (ch.II, § 4) entitled 'Cause politico-religieuse des succès de l'Islam' citing Bar Hebraeus only, as he was writing before the definitive publication of Michael's *Chronicle* by Chabot (see the preceding note). For Egypt, Pargoire uses John of Nikiu.

36. L. Duchesne, *L'Église au VI*[e] *siècle* (Paris, 1925) 423. Cf. Bréhier, op. cit. (in n.33 above) 134-41, 151-5.

37. A. J. Butler, *The Arab Conquest of Egypt and the Last Thirty Years of the Roman Dominion*, 2nd edition by P. M. Fraser (1978), is not merely a reprint of the original edition of 1902 but has in addition two essays published as pamphlets by Butler and a most valuable 'Additional Bibliography' of 39 pages (xlv-lxxxiii) by Fraser. For Copts assisting the Arabs or failing to resist them, see esp. 278-9, 285, 318-19, 337-8, 355-7, 443, 445-6, 471, 474, 478-80; contrast 211-12, 295-6 n.1, 357, 363-4, 442, 472. The quotation that follows in the main text above is from 158 n.2 (on 159). For the persecution of the Copts by Cyrus (Al Muḳauḳas), see Butler, *ACE*[2] 183-93, 252, 273-4, 317, 443-6.

38. Vol. I, col.264-8, in the edition cited in n.35 above.

39. For a modern account of Heraclius' persecution of the Jews which will not be suspected of anti-Christian bias, see Bréhier, op. cit. (in n.33 above) 108-111. I do not sufficiently know the sources for Jewish hostility to Byzantine rule in the first half of the seventh century; but see (for the capture of Jerusalem by the Persians in 614) ibid. 81-2, 88-9; Butler, *ACE*[2] 59-61, 133-4; and (for Jewish attitudes to the Arabs) Bréhier, op. cit. 110-11. A particularly fascinating

contemporary source that is very revealing on Jewish attitudes in the second quarter of the seventh century is the *Doctrina Jacobi nuper baptizati*, published (with an Introduction) by N. Bonwetsch, in *Abh*. Göttingen, Philol.-hist. Klasse, n.F. XII.3 (Berlin, 1910). Among the passages illustrating Jewish hostility to the Byzantine empire are IV.7; V.12, 16-17 (pp.69, 81-2, 86-8). I must also mention at this point that the persecution of the Samaritans of Palestine from 527 onwards (*CJ* I.v.12, 13, 17-19), culminating in Justinian's edict ordering the destruction of their synagogues, drove them to break out into a fierce revolt in 529, soon mercilessly crushed, with the massacre and enslavement of large numbers of Samaritans (Procopius and Malalas speak of many tens of thousands; cf. Theoph., A. M. 6021, p.179.1-4), fled to Persia to number 50,000 (by Malalas, p.455.14-15; cf. Theoph., A. M. 6021, p.179.1-4), fled to Persia and offered help to King Cavadh if he attacked Palestine: see Stein, *HBE* II.287-8, cf. 373-4, on another revolt of Samaritans (and Jews) at Caesarea in 555.

40. Amm. Marc. XXIX.iv.7. Treachery was suspected in 354 on the part of three other Alamans: Latinus (*comes domesticorum*), Agilo (*tribunus stabuli*), and Scudilo (commander of the Scutarii, a *schola palatina* of the imperial bodyguard); but evidently nothing was proved (see Amm. XIV.x.7-8). In the whole of Ammianus' history I know of no other examples of treachery by soldiers of 'barbarian' origin, even quite humble men, unless they had become liable to punishment for some offence, like the men in XVI.xii.2 and XVIII.vi.16. See also perhaps Evagr., *HE* VI.14, where Sittas is said to have betrayed Martyropolis to the Persians *c.* 589.

41. For the other sources for Silvanus, see *PLRE* I.840-1.

42. A recent statement that 'from the late third century on, . . . there is abundant evidence from all over the empire (though especially from the eastern provinces) of ordinary people defending their towns and cities against invaders and brigands' (Cameron, *CF* 110) is an exaggeration, as anyone will discover who looks up all the references given by the authors there referred to. There is certainly much evidence for the building of walls and fortifications; but we may take it that these were mainly for the benefit of military garrisons (whose installation would be more likely in a fortified town), or simply as a natural deterrent to attackers (see the main text above for 'barbarian' reluctance to assault walled cities), so rare is the evidence for whole-hearted participation by ordinary citizens in their defence. Of course I would not deny that there must have been many more examples of this sort of activity than the cases for which evidence happens to survive; but I think it is worth emphasising how few such cases there are. (My list is as full as I can make it: I dare say it is far from complete.) The earliest recorded evidence that I know is for the organising of a group of armed men at ELATEA in Phocis (in central Greece) by the Olympic victor Mnesibulus, against the Costoboci who raided Greece in 170-1 (Paus. X.34.5). Another episode in the resistance to this Costobocan raid is revealed by an inscription from THESPIAE in Boeotia, discussed by A. Plassart, in an article cited in V.iii n.15 above. The inhabitants of a few cities are said to have made a stout resistance to Gothic sieges during the invasions of the 250s/260s (the precise chronology is very doubtful): in particular THESSALONICA, perhaps in 254 and (with CASSANDREIA/POTIDAEA: Zos.I.43.1) 268 (Zos. I.29.2; 43.1; Euseb., *FGrH* II A 101 F 1 and perhaps 2; Amm. Marc. XXXI.5.16; Zonar. XII.23, 26; Syncell., p.715); MARCIANOPOLIS, perhaps in 248 (Dexippus, *FGrH* II A 100 F 25; but contrast Jordanes, *Get.* 16/92, 17/94, where the enemy are bribed to depart) and, with TOMI, in *c.* 268 (Zos. I.42.1), although Marcianopolis may have been sacked by the Goths in 250-1 (see A. Alföldi, in *CAH* XII.145-6); PHILIPPOPOLIS, in 250-1 (Dexippus. F 26; but the city was then captured: Dexippus, F 22; Amm. Marc. XXXI.5.17; Zos. I.24.2; Jordanes, *Get.* 18/101-3), and probably in *c.* 268 (Dexippus, F 27: for the date, see Alföldi in *CAH* XII. 144 n.7, 149); SIDE, perhaps 268-9 (Dexippus, F 29). One or two other cities should perhaps be added: NICOPOLIS and ANCHIALUS in 268-9 (*HA, Claud.* 12-4; but contrast Amm. Marc. XXXI.5.16; Jord., *Get.* 20/108-9), and perhaps at the same time CYZICUS (Amm. Marc. XXXI.5.16; Zos. I.43.1; Syncell., p.717; cf. *HA, Gallien.* 13.8). But in several of these cases the role played by civilians as distinct from members of a garrison is far from clear. For recent literature on the whole subject, see F. Millar, in *JRS* 59 (1969) 12-29, esp. 24-9, who adds a couple of examples from the Latin West (AUTUN, A.D. 269, and SALDAE in Africa, p.29). There now seems to be a long gap in the evidence. The principal magistrate of ADRIANOPLE in 376 organised a force of 'the lowest of the people', with the workers in the imperial arms factory (*fabricenses*), in order to exert pressure on the Visigoths to leave the city, with disastrous results (Amm. Marc. XXXI.6.2-3). In 399, according to Zosimus (V.xvi-xvii, esp. xvi.4), many of the town-dwellers of PAMPHYLIA and PHRYGIA (οἱ τῶν πόλεων

οἰκήτορες, xvi.4), inspired by the example of Valentinus of Selge (for whom see IV.iv n.6 above), offered armed resistance to Tribigild the Goth and his marauding army; but they were betrayed by the machinations of Gainas. It appears from Paulinus of Pella, *Eucharist.* 311-14, that BURDIGALA (Bordeaux) surrendered without resistance (line 312) to Athaulf and his Visigoths in 414; contrast the resistance of nearby VASATES (Bazas: see above and n. 18). The inhabitants of ASEMUS (if that is the right name) are said by Priscus fr. 5 (Dindorf or Mueller) to have taken effective action against their Hun attackers in *c.* 443. Alone among the towns of Auvergne (Sidon. Apoll., *Ep.* VII.v.3), the men of CLERMONT FERRAND (*civitas Arvernorum*; during the Principate, Augustonetum), apparently assisted by a small Burgundian garrison, held out stoutly against annual plundering expeditions and some rather half-hearted attempts at blockade by bands of Visigoths during the early 470s, until the place was abandoned to Euric and the Visigoths by a treaty made by Nepos in 475: see Sidon. Apoll., *Ep.* III.i-iv; VII.vii.3-5 etc.; and note the reference in *Ep.* III.ii.2 to internal dissensions (*civitatem non minus civica simultate quam barbarica incursione vacuatam*). In this case the Roman general Ecdicius provided some help and encouragement (see IV.iv n.6 above), but his forces were evidently very small (see Sidon, Apoll., *Ep.* III.iii, esp. 3); and perhaps Sidonius himself, as well as the priest Constantius (*Ep.* III.ii), played a prominent part. Many young men of ANTIOCH, who had been 'accustomed to riot against each other in the hippodromes', joined bravely with the garrison in a vain defence of the city against Chosroes I, the Persian king, in 540 (Procop., *Bell.* II = *Pers.* II.viii.11, 17, 28-34; ix.5: see Alan Cameron, *CF* 108, 110, 125, 273). When JERUSALEM fell to the Persians in 614, we hear from Sebeos of 'young people of the city' organising an unsuccessful revolt (Sebeos XXIV, p.68, in the French trans. by Frédéric Macler, Paris, 1904). As Cameron has said, the analogy of the 'young men' of Antioch in 540 may perhaps suggest that in Jerusalem too the people concerned were circus partisans (*CF* 109). All too often, it seems, everything depended on the garrison. I suspect that in face of a serious attack what happened at DAMASCUS in 636 may have been characteristic: 'Abandoned by the Byzantine garrison, the civilian population of Damascus capitulated' (P. K. Hitti, *Hist. of the Arabs*[10] 150). And the behaviour of a garrison might depend on the quality of its commander: for example, we hear from Zosimus (I.32-33.1) that at PITYUS, on the eastern shore of the Black Sea, the garrison first drove off the Goths (apparently in 254) under its capable commander Successianus; but shortly afterwards, when Successianus was promoted to the praetorian prefecture by Valerian, the garrison offered no resistance to a renewed Gothic attack, and the town fell at once. (Cf. the behaviour of Gerontius at TOMI, *c.* 386, in Zos. IV.40.) Only occasionally would there have been a substantial number of veteran soldiers settled nearby, who might hurry to the defence of a threatened town, as at AUTUN in 356 (Amm. Marc. XVI.2.1). No doubt there are other examples I should have quoted, but the sources, in the other cases I have found, are too poor to be worth using. A good example is NISIBIS, where the inhabitants showed such great distress when handed over to Persia by the treaty made by the Emperor Jovian in 363 (see, among other sources, Amm. Marc. XXV.vii-ix, esp. viii.13 and ix.2-8; Zos. III.33-4) that it is not difficult to believe they had taken part with the garrison in defending the city during at least some of the many sieges they had endured since becoming a Roman *colonia* under Septimius Severus (*c.* 195) – in particular three unsuccessful sieges by Shapur II, in 337 or 338, 346, and 350. Too many of the surviving narratives, even when they reproduce some good material, mix it with credulous rubbish: see e.g. Theodoret, *HE* II.30. Apart from a few scraps like Julian, *Orat.* II.64C (I have not been able to consult Ephraim Syrus), I know of no useful evidence for the general participation of citizens in the defence; and see J. Sturm, in *RE* XVII.i (1936) 741 ff. esp. 744-6. Again, we may easily be misled by the desire of a writer to glorify his native place by giving its population a greater role in defending their city than they had displayed in reality. I suspect that this is true, for instance, of two passages in that ardent Constantinopolitan, the ecclesiastical historian Socrates (*HE* IV.xxxviii.3-5; V.i.2-5; cf. Soz., *HE* VI.xxxix.3; VII.i.1-2), giving the people of CONSTANTINOPLE an important role in resisting the Visigoths in the summer of 378 that is missing in Amm. Marc. XXXI.xi.1; xvi.4-7, and may well be exaggerated.

One incident that seems to have been universally accepted in modern times, at least since Gibbon (*DFRE* I.265-6), I would unhesitatingly reject as a probable fiction: the supposed exploit by the elderly Athenian historian Dexippus in 267, in organising a successful attack upon the Heruls (often referred to in the sources as 'Goths' or 'Scythians') after they had sacked ATHENS. (The fullest recent account, taking it for granted that the exploit actually occurred and can be attributed to Dexippus, is that of F. Millar, in *JRS* 59 [1969] 12-29, esp. 26-8; cf. *PIR²* IV.72-3, H 104, etc.) The reasons for my scepticism are as follows. (1) The speech, *FGrH* II A 100 F 28a §§ 1-6 (translated by Millar, 27-8), is commonly assumed to be the historian's record of a speech of his own; and in § 7 Dexippus says that the speaker was then accepted by the Athenians as their leader. However, although in F 28*d* Dexippus *is* named as the speaker ('to the Hellenes'), I see no evidence whatever in the fragments (or the *testimonia*) of Dexippus or anywhere else to suggest that the speaker in F 28*a* is the historian himself: this has simply been assumed. (2) The *only* source representing Dexippus as the leader of an Athenian force which actually overcame the Heruls is a very unreliable one: *HA, Gallien.* 13.8. The only other references to a successful Athenian attack on the Heruls are by (*a*) the early-ninth-century writer George Syncellus, *Chronograph.*, ed. W. Dindorf, I (Bonn, 1829) 717.15-20, in which there is no word of Dexippus, and (*b*) the twelfth-century historian Zonaras, *Epit. hist.* XII.26, ed. Dindorf, III (1870) 150.23-151.5, who has a totally different story, again ignoring Dexippus, and attributing the rout of the Heruls to 'Cleodemus an Athenian', who successfully attacked the Heruls 'from the sea with ships'; cf. the 'Cleodamus and Athenaeus, Byzantines', appointed by Gallienus to restore and fortify the cities in the Balkan area, who overcame the 'Scythians' in a battle 'circa Pontum' (*HA, Gallien.* 13.6), apparently at about the same time as the naval victory of Venerianus (ibid. 13.7) and the alleged exploit of Dexippus (13.8). (3) In the inscription set up to Dexippus by his sons, *IG* II².3669 = *FGrH* 100 T 4 (which, as Millar says, op. cit. 21, 'we can be certain . . . is subsequent to the Herulian invasion'), there is not the least hint of Dexippus' supposed exploit. (The opening word, ἀλκῆ, appropriately Homeric, is simply part of a description of the famous men of the land of Cecrops.) (4) The fact that no later Greek writer mentions the brilliant exploit of Dexippus is extraordinary unless (as I believe) it is a modern myth, deriving from the *Historia Augusta* and a misunderstanding of Dexippus F 28*a*. Zosimus in particular, although he records the sack of Athens on the occasion in question, does not mention Dexippus (or any Athenian counter-attack); and Eunapius (the main source of Zosimus' earlier books), who thought highly enough of Dexippus to begin his own history at the point where Dexippus left off (and cf. Eunap., fr. 1, Dindorf or Mueller), speaks of Dexippus purely as a man of culture and oratorical ability (*Vitae Sophist.* IV.iii.1 [457 Didot], p.10.14-16 ed. J. Giangrande, Rome, 1956). Nor does the Souda have anything to say about Dexippus except as a ῥήτωρ (*FGrH* 100 T 1). Nothing is to be gained by consulting the source of F 28: Constantine Porphyrogenitus, *Excerpta hist.*, ed. U. P. Boissevain etc., IV. *Excerpta de sentent.* (1906) 234-6 (Dexippus 24). (5) The speech in F 28a refers to Athens as 'in the hands of the enemy' (§ 3), and adds a mysterious reference to 'those who have been forced against their will to fight alongside the enemy'; cf. the πταῖσμα of the city in § 5. If this is indeed 267, then the Heruls have already captured Athens. That would surely make Dexippus' exploit an even more remarkable one: cities might sometimes drive off their besiegers, but I know of hardly an occasion on which they are reliably said to have pursued their attackers after their withdrawal. I would need much stronger evidence than we have, before accepting, on the strength of the *Historia Augusta* alone, a daring and successful piece of military activity against fierce professional fighters, led by a man of letters who must have been in his sixties and had almost certainly had no previous experience of warfare.

In IV.iv above, and its n.6, I have given examples of resistance to 'barbarians' etc. in the countryside. The attitude of the peasantry, I think, must often have depended on that of the city of whose territory they formed part. I find it easy to believe the Arab historian Abu Yūsuf, when he says of the villages and rural areas of Edessa and Harran (in 637-8) that after the surrender of the cities, no resistance was attempted. 'In every district, once the seat of government had been conquered, the country people said, "We are the same as the people of our town and our chiefs" ' (*Kitāb al-Kharāj* 39-41, translated by Bernard Lewis, in his *Islam from the Prophet Muhammad to the Capture of Constantinople,* I [1974] 230-1).

43. The valuable *Vita Severini* of Eugippius has appeared (since *MPL* LXII.1167-1200) in several modern scholarly editions, by H. Sauppe (*MGH*, 1877), P. Knoell (*CSEL*, 1886), Th. Mommsen (*Scr. Rerum German.*, 1898), and most recently R. Noll, *Eugippius, Das Leben des heiligen Severin* (Berlin, 1963), with German translation and commentary. There are English translations by Ludwig Bieler and Ludmilla Krestan (Washington, D.C., 1965), and by G. W. Robinson (Harvard Translations, Cambridge, Mass., 1914). Géza Alföldy, *Noricum* (1974) 347 n.36, refers to various recent studies of Eugippius and St. Severinus, and gives much information about Noricum in the fifth and sixth centuries (ibid. 213-27).

44. Thompson must be referring to Hydat. 91, noticed in IV.iv n.6 § (e) above.
45. My quotation is from Thompson's 1977 article (see n.10 above) 313-14.
46. Jones, *LRE* II.1059. For Arvandus, see Sidon. Apoll., *Ep.* I.vii (esp. 5, 10-12); Stevens, *SAA* 103-7. For Seronatus, see Sidon. Apoll., *Ep.* II.i (esp. 3); VII.vii.2; Stevens, *SAA* 112-13. (For Sidonius' extreme detestation of Serenatus, see also his *Ep.* V.xiii.)
47. Amm. Marc. XVIII.x.1-3; XIX.ix.3-8; XX.vi.1.
48. This would surely have been illegal after 422, at any rate in the West, because of *CTh* II.xiii.1 = *CJ* II.xiii.2.
49. Priscus fr. 8 Dindorf (*HGM* I.305-9) and Mueller (*FHG* IV.86-8). There is an English translation by C. D. Gordon, *The Age of Attila* (Ann Arbor, 1960) 85-9. See esp. Thompson, *HAH* 184-7, with ch.v.
50. *FIRA*² III.510-13, no.165; and Malalas XV, p.384, ed. Dindorf (*CHSB*, 1831).
51. Cf. Jones, *LRE* I.472-7, 484-94, 494-9, 502-4, 518-20.
52. *FIRA*² I.331-2, no.64. There is an English translation in *ARS* 242-3, no.307.
53. At any rate, it would have been the equivalent of 9 solidi in the same department (*ab actis*) in the praetorian prefecture of Africa: see *CJ* I.xxvii.1.26.

[VIII.iv]

1. The full story of the plague can never be reconstructed. A. Alföldi, in *CAH* XII.228 n.1, gives the essential source references. Add Zos. I.46.
2. The very marked improvement brought about by the victories of Diocletian and his colleagues is celebrated in a most remarkable document, which no one should miss: the Preface to the 'Edict on Maximum Prices' issued in 301. For the recent editions of the Edict as a whole, see I.iii n.3 above. The Preface is more easily available in *ILS* 642, and there is also a text with an English translation by E. R. Graser in Frank, *ESAR* V.310-17. The *Panegyrics* of the years 289-321 (*Paneg. Lat.* II-X, ed. E. Galletier, with French trans.) are often ludicrously optimistic.
3. Amm. Marc. XXVI.vi.9, 17-18; vii.1, 7, 14; viii.14; cf. x.3; Zos. IV.v.5; vii.1-2. The latest treatment of the revolt of Procopius that I have seen is by N. J. E. Austin, in the article cited in VI.vi n.58 above.
4. He is Petronius 3 in *PLRE* I.690-1.
5. See B. H. Warmington, 'The career of Romanus, Comes Africae', in *Byz.* 49 (1956) 55-64.
6. Stein, *HBE* I².i.140. He lists the sources in ii.490 n.51.
7. A useful recent work is G. W. Clarke, 'Barbarian disturbances in north Africa in the mid-third century', in *Antichthon* 4 (1970) 78-85.
8. See Jones, *LRE* I.59-60, 97-100; II.679-80. I know of only one larger army ever marshalled by Rome for a foreign expedition: that which Antony took through Armenia against the Parthians in 36 B.C., for which see Plut., *Ant.* 37.4; W. W. Tarn, in *CAH* X.73 ff.
9. For this I shall merely refer to A. R. Birley, *TCCRE* 267-8, where the figure of 'some 400,000 or more in a population of about fifty million' is partly based on the article by Eric Birley, 'Septimius Severus and the Roman army', in *Epigr. Studien* 8 (1969) 63-82. Further bibliography is given by A. R. Birley.
10. What I have said in the main text above about Roman army numbers is based primarily on Jones, *LRE* II.679-86 (cf. 1035-8), with the notes in III.209-11; and see III.379-80 (Table XV). Of the total cost of Roman military expenditure under the Empire there is no way of making even an informed guess. M. H. Crawford, *Roman Republican Coinage* (1974) II.696-7, estimates the annual cost of a single legion at 600,000 denarii down to 124 B.C., 1,500,000 den. from 123 onwards (contrast Frank, *ESAR* I.327: 1 million), and 3,000,000 den. after Caesar's doubling of legionary pay; but these figures can only be regarded as intelligent guesses. For the Principate and Later Empire, estimates become impossibly difficult, even apart from the fact that *auxilia* and other non-legionary forces now played an ever larger part.
11. Jones, *LRE* III.341 n.44, has 113 + 3 = 116 provinces; but his list on pp.382-9 has 119, and I believe that to be the true figure, if we allow for one or two errors in the *Notitia* – for example, the deletion by a clerk of the Pannonian province of Valeria instead of the Italian Valeria (see Jones, *LRE* III.351). Cf. the list of provinces in J. W. Eadie, *The Breviarium of Festus* (London, 1967) 154-71: 126 names are given, but we must deduct 7 (nos. 8, 23, 35, 62, 78, 119, 123). I have not been able to study properly the very scholarly recent work by Dietrich Hoffmann, *Das*

spätrömische Bewegungsheer u. die Not. Dign. = *Epigr. Stud.* 7 (2 vols, Düsseldorf, 1969-70): this has the most useful map I have seen of the Roman provinces at the time of the *Not. Dign.* (loose, in Vol. II), and see the three maps for *c.* 400 following II.326-7.

12. Jones, *LRE* II.1057; and see III.341-2 n.44, concluding with a table. Jones omits all 'domestic palace staff (*cubicularii* and *castrensiani*)'.

13. See Jones, *LRE* I.396-9; *RE* 209-11.

14. See *CJ* I.xxvii.1.22-39, with Jones, *LRE* II.590-1. As Jones says, three-quarters of the staff received not more than 9 solidi or its equivalent in kind (1 *annona* = 5 solidi, 1 *capitus* = 4 solidi). And the 16 lowest of the 40 clerks in the four financial *scrinia* received only 7 solidi each (*CJ* I.xxvii.1).

15. See Jones, *LRE* II.571 (*castrensiani*, with graded supernumeraries), 585 (*largitionales*), 597-8 (*magistriani*), 604.

16. For the *collatio glebalis, gleba* or *follis*, see Jones, *LRE* I.110, 219, 431 (with III.106-8 n.51), 465. Since the new lowest rate of tax introduced by Theodosius I in 393 was only 7 solidi (*CTh* VI.ii.15), I have no difficulty in accepting Jones's figures of (in effect) *c.* 40, 20 and 10 solidi for the original rates (*LRE* I.431; Jones's article on the *follis* is now repr. in his *RE* 330-8; but see R. P. Duncan-Jones, in *JRS* 66 [1976] 235).

17. So were Flavius Valerius Severus (Augustus 306-7) and Maximin Daia (Augustus *c.* 309-13), both from Illyricum, as well as Licinius, a Dacian of peasant origin.

18. In Amm. Marc. XXX.vii.2 he is 'ignobili stirpe', in *Epit. de Caes.* 45.2 'mediocri stirpe'.

19. Marcian (451-7) was apparently of humble origin: see Evagr., *HE* II.1. Leo I (457-74), a Dacian soldier, may well have been of peasant stock. Zeno (474-91) was originally an Isaurian named Taracodissa; but he seems to have been a local chief.

20. For *agrestis*, see Victor, *Caes.* 40.17, 41.26; for *semiagrestis*, 39.17 (of Maximian). For *subagrestis*, see Amm. Marc. XIV.xi.11; XV.v.10; XVIII.iii.6; XXI.x.8; XXX.iv.2; XXXI.xiv.5, the last passage referring to Valens, who is also *subrusticus* in XXIX.i.11.

21. For the view that the family of the three Gordians (238-44) originated in Asia Minor, see Birley, *TCCRE* 277 and n.1. This may well be right, but there is nothing specifically 'Greek' in what we know of the Gordians, I, II and III: they were thoroughly westernised.

22. Michael the Syrian, *Chron.* X.xi (*init.*), ed. Chabot II.316; and Bar Hebraeus, *Chronogr.* I.ix, ed. Charles p.81. (For the editions concerned, see VIII.iii nn.34-5 above.)

23. *Acta Conc. Oec.* III, ed. E. Schwartz (Berlin, 1940) 260-1 (A.D. 536).

24. See e.g. Jones, *LRE* II.931-2, with III.318 n.154.

25. The best treatment of the whole subject of Church finance is by Jones, *LRE* II.894-910, with III.301-11 nn.51-95; and 'Church finance in the fifth and sixth centuries', in *JTS* n.s.11 (1960) 84-94 = *RE* 339-49.

26. Very full details are given in the *Liber Pontificalis Ecclesiae Romanae*. The most useful edition of this work is by L. Duchesne, *Le Liber Pontificalis,* second edition (Paris) I and II (1955), III (1957); the first edition, in two vols, was published in 1886-92. There is also a text by Th. Mommsen, in *MGH, Gest. Pontif. Roman.* I (1898). And see n.28 below.

26a. I must add a reference to a work I saw only after this chapter was finished: Alan Cameron, 'Paganism and literature in late fourth-century Rome', in *Entretiens sur l'ant. class.* 23 (Fondation Hardt, Vandoeuvres-Geneva, 1977) 1 ff., at 16-17, making the point that Praetextatus was the real 'heavyweight among late Roman pagans, . . . leader of the pagan intelligentsia of late fourth-century Rome . . . It is easy to see why the death of Praetextatus was such a blow to the pagan party. Not only was he a man of enormous authority and determination; he was their one intellectual. He was a philosopher.'

27. Jerome, *C. Johann. Hierosol.* 8; cf. Amm. Marc. XXVII.iii.14-15.

28. The main sources are the *Liber Pontificalis* (see n.26 above) xxxiv (Silvester, 314-35), xxxv (Marcus, 336), xxxix (Damasus, 366-84), xlii (Innocent, 401-17), xlvi (Xystus, 432-40), all in Vol. I, ed. Duchesne; and the letters of Gregory the Great, as cited in IV.iii n.47 above (with bibliography).

29. The bishop was Musonius of Meloe: Severus Ant., *Ep.* I.4 (with 23), ed. E. W. Brooks, *The Select Letters of Severus of Antioch,* II.i (London, 1903) 25. See Jones, *LRE* II.905-6.

30. *Vita S. Theod. Syk.* 78: see the excellent Eng. trans. by Elizabeth Dawes and N. H. Baynes, *Three Byzantine Saints* (1948) 141. (Cf. IV.ii n.43.)

31. See the *Liber Pontif. Eccles. Ravenn.* 60, in *MGH, Scr. Rer. Langobard.* 265-391, at 319, ed. O. Holder-Egger (1878), for the *Constitutum Felicis* (Pope Felix IV, A. D. 526-30), also in *MPL* LXV.12-16, at 12C, revealing that one quarter of the *patrimonium* of the Church of Ravenna

was 3,000 solidi. (In Italy, a quarter of the revenues of a church normally went to its bishop; cf., for Ravenna, Jones, *RE* 346-7; *LRE* II.902, 905.)

32. The list of salaries is conveniently reproduced in Jones, *LRE* III.89-90 n.65.

33. Gertrude Malz, 'The date of Justinian's *Edict* XIII', in *Byz.* 16 (1942-3) 135-41, argues for A.D. 554; but I would accept the traditional date, 538-9: see Roger Rémondon, 'L'Édit XIII de Justinien a-t-il été promulgué en 539?', in *Chr. d'Ég.* 30 (1955) 112-21.

34. *MGH, Scr. Rer. Meroving.* I².533, ed. B. Krusch and W. Levison (1951). There is an excellent Eng. trans. of this work (with commentary) by O. M. Dalton, *The Hist. of the Franks by Gregory of Tours* (2 vols, 1927): for this passage, see II.475. According to Gregory (loc. cit.), the next bishop, Baudin, distributed the 20,000 + solidi among the poor.

35. *Vita S. Ioann. Eleemos.* 45, ed. H. Delehaye, in *AB* 45 (1927) 5-74, at 65-6. See Dawes and Baynes, op. cit. (in n.30 above) 256.

36. See Jones, *RE* 340-9; *LRE* II.899-902.

37. See Jones, *LRE* II.898-9, with III.304 n.66 (cf. II.697, with III.216 n.20 *fin.*). The most interesting passage is Theodoret, *HE* I.xi.2-3, with IV.iv.1-2.

38. Ducas, *Hist. Turcobyzantina* XXXVII.10, p.329.11-12, ed. V. Grecu (Bucarest, 1958) = *CHSB*, ed. I. Bekker (Bonn, 1834) p.264.14-16: κρειττότερόν ἐστιν εἰδέναι ἐν μέσῃ τῇ πόλει φακιόλιον βασιλεῦον Τούρκων ἢ καλύπτραν Λατινικήν.

39. *Vita S. Ioann. Eleemos.* 41: see Dawes and Baynes, op. cit. (in n.30 above) 248, 249.

40. E.g. Naphtali Lewis, 'Μερισμὸς ἀνακεχωρηκότων', in *JEA* 23 (1937) 63-75, at 64-5 and n.6; Bell, *EAGAC* 77-8; MacMullen, *RSR* 36-7.

41. Philo's words are πρώην τις ἐκλογεὺς φόρων ταχθεὶς παρ' ἡμῖν (§ 159). The last two words should mean 'in our area'. MacMullen (see the preceding note) takes this to be Judaea. Certainly the text seems to exclude Alexandria (see § 162). But I think we must take it that Philo is speaking of some area in Lower Egypt.

42. See Jones, *LRE* II.781, with 667-8. It seems to me obvious that most if not all these peasants were freeholders, for otherwise they would not have been driven out of their lands, as each of the three laws says they were.

43. A valuable (and, I think, rather neglected) work on 'the over-powerful' can be found among the 'Études de droit byzantin' (the sub-title of which makes them a 'méditation' on *CJ* IV.lxv.34) published by H. Monnier in *Nouvelle revue historique de droit français et étranger* 24 (1900) in three parts, the relevant section for our purposes being pp.62-107 (Ch.vi: 'Généralités sur les Puissants'; vii: 'Des Puissants à l'époque classique'; viii: 'Quelques exemples des entreprises des Puissants au Bas-Empire'; and ix: 'Le *patrocinium potentiorum*'). This is the richest collection of material on the subject that I have found.

44. Cf. Symm., *Ep.* VI.58, 62, 64, on which see Jones, *LRE* I.365.

45. For the Novel in question see J. and P. Zepos, *Jus Graecoromanum* (8 vols, Athens, 1931; repr. Aalen, 1962) I.240-2, at 242. The translation is that of G. Ostrogorsky, 'The peasant's pre-emption right: an abortive reform of the Macedonian emperors', in *JRS* 37 (1947) 117-26, at 122. The Greek is καὶ χρὴ διευλαβεῖσθαι ἡμᾶς, μὴ λιμοῦ βιαιότεραν ἀνάγκην κριτοῦ τοῖς ἀθλίοις ἐπιστήσομεν πένησι (§ 2).

46. The conquest of Syria, Mesopotamia, Egypt and north Africa by the Arabs was extraordinarily rapid. Particularly striking is the virtual disappearance of Christianity from large parts of that area, especially the lands west of Syria and Egypt. This is all the more remarkable in that, as Mommsen said (if with some exaggeration), 'In the development of Christianity Africa plays the very first part; if it arose in Syria, it was in and through Africa that it became the religion for the world' (*Provinces of the Roman Empire* [1886] II.343).

47. In the case of the Arab conquest of Egypt, this situation existed also in the great city of Alexandria. See e.g. Butler, *ACE²* 337-8, for the view that in the submission of the Alexandrians to the Arabs in 641 the expectation of lighter taxation may have been an important element. He continues, 'This promise of reduced taxation may count for a great deal in all the Muslim conquests. In the case of Alexandria it may have been the determining factor, although it is known that the hope of financial relief was bitterly disappointed.' (Cf. also ibid. 349, 365, 451-6; but see lxxxiii.) For the forced labour which was also exacted by the Arabs later, see ibid. 347-8, 363. I may add that I know of no scholarly treatment of the problems of Arab taxation in the Roman provinces they conquered more recent than D. C. Dennett, *Conversion and the Poll-Tax in Early Islam* (= *Harvard Historical Monographs* 22, 1950); and Frede Løkkegaard, *Islamic Taxation in the Classic Period* (Copenhagen, 1950). Dennett is particularly successful in bringing out the differences in the treatment by the Arabs of the various areas.

48. See IV.i above and its n.1.

[Appendix IV]

1. A good example of Magie's conventional right-wing views and inability to think deeply about his material is the passage in *RRAM* I.114–15: 'It is true that under the influence of the Romans, whose general policy it was to *ensure a greater stability* by entrusting government to the *wealthier and more responsible citizens*, there was a growing tendency to lessen the power of the Assembly in favour of the Council' (my italics). Cf. I.214 (those who received Mithridates with enthusiasm in 88 were 'the less responsible element among the citizens'), 640 ('the wealthier and presumably more responsible class'), 600 etc.

2. See E. S. Gruen, 'Class conflict and the Third Macedonian War', in *AJAH* 1 (1976) 29–60. His attempt to discredit Livy fails. First, he is inclined to treat Livy's statements about divisions on class lines in second-century Greece and in Italy during the Second Punic war as a mere 'common Livian device' (op. cit. 31). But the comparison with the narrative of the Second Punic war only serves to weaken his case, for reasons that will be clear from the introductory part of this Appendix. Secondly, he makes too much of minor differences which certainly exist between Livy and Polybius: e.g. between Livy XLII.xliv.3–5 and Polyb. XXVII.i.7–9 in regard to the Boeotian assembly at Thebes in 171 (45). Livy's *turba* and *multitudo* (§ 4) are quite natural expressions in view of συνδεδραμηκότες in Polybius (§ 8); and Livy's 'constantia principum . . . victa tandem multitudo' (§ 4) is also understandable in the light of Polybius' statement of a massive change in the attitude of the πλῆθος (§ 9) – by which Polybius probably meant here simply 'the majority'. Contrary to Gruen's statement (op. cit. 58 n.154), there may well have been much Polybian material available to Livy which is lost to us: Gruen here forgets that we do not have, for example, the Polybian original of Livy XLII.xliii.6–10. Thirdly, Gruen pays insufficient regard to the evidence of continued anti-Roman feeling at Coronea and especially Haliartus (Livy XLII.xlvi.7–10; lxiii.3–12), which must have been overwhelming at the latter place, in view of its heroic resistance to the siege by greatly superior Roman forces. In the light of what actually happened later, may not Livy's account of the assembly at Thebes convey a rather more realistic picture than that of Polybius? I would add, in reply to the treatment by P. S. Derow, in *Phoenix* 26 (1972) 307, of Livy XXXVII.ix.1–4 and Polyb. XXI.vi.1–6, on the events at Phocaea in 190, that Livy's account, although using different language from that of Polybius, need not be seen as a distortion: in Polybius the Phocaeans ἐστασίαζον (§ 1) and, as distinct from οἱ ἄρχοντες (§ 2), οἱ πολλοί are represented as in a disturbed condition because of famine (§§ 2,6), as well as the activities of the 'Antiochistai'. There is nothing here to convict Livy of any significant misrepresentation, and again the subsequent lost narrative of Polybius may well have contained further particulars of the situation at Phocaea, justifying Livy's rather more sharply drawn picture. (Derow, I may say, tells me that his conclusions on the question of class attitudes in Greece towards Rome are much nearer to those of Briscoe and Fuks – for which see the main text of this Appendix, § 2, *ad init.* – than to those of Gruen.)

   Only after V.iii and this Appendix had been virtually finished did I read Doron Mendels, 'Perseus and the socio-economic question in Greece (179–172/1 B.C.). A study in Roman propaganda', in *Anc. Soc.* 9 (1978) 55–73. This is a much better analysis than Gruen's: it is virtually limited to proving (as it does successfully) that Perseus never (so to speak) 'played the *popularis*'. Mendels realises, however (see esp. his pp.71–3), that on the eve of the Third Macedonian War 'the masses in the free states were inclined towards Perseus', as were some of the leading men (cf. Livy XLII.xxx.1–8, esp. 1, 4), and although at first their sympathy for Perseus remained passive, when he won a battle they began to have high hopes of him (see Polyb. XXVII.ix.1; x.1,4, cited in the main text above; also Diod. XXX.8; Livy XLII.lxiii.1–2), which of course were disappointed.

3. Cicero also uses *cooptare/cooptatio* of men who can be represented as owing their position to the efforts of an individual, whether as Roman senators (*De div.* II.23: [*Caesar*] *ipse cooptasset*) or as members of a priestly college (e.g. *Brut.* 1; *XIII Phil.* 12; *Ad fam.* III.x.9; *Lael.* 96).

4. See n.2 again. Although Gruen cites Livy XLII.xxx.1–7 and quotes phrases from it (op. cit. 31, and 49 nn.17–18) he fails to mention that of the two groups into which Livy divides those taking the side of Perseus the first is 'quos aes alienum et desperatio rerum suarum, eodem manente statu, praecipites ad novanda omnia agebat' (xxx.4; cf. v.7 on Aetolia, Thessaly and Perrhaebia). He would shrug off the whole 'antithesis between *plebs* and *principes*, the one anti-Roman, the other pro-Roman', as 'a common Livian device'; but see n.2 above. And in relation to Livy XLII.v.7 he even tries to obscure the basic class nature of indebtedness (op. cit.

35) – in the way that used to be so common (before the publication of Brunt, ALRR) in regard to the demand for *novae tabulae* in the Catilinarian affair of 63 B.C. In regard to Sherk, *RDGE* 40 (= *SIG*[3] 643 = *FD* III.iv.75), lines 22-4, Gruen claims that there is no warrant for inserting, with Colin and Pomtow, τὸ πλῆθος or τὰ πλήθη θεραπεύων (line 22 or 23). But the document (an official Roman letter to Delphi) does have διαφθείρων τοὺς προεστηκό[τας] in line 23, [κ]αὶ νεωτερισμοὺς ἐποίει in line 24, and ὅλον τὸ ἔθνος εἰς ταρα[χάς] in line 21; and this language surely suggests actions against some ruling groups in favour of others who were disfranchised or under-privileged, rather than mere support of factions of *principes* against similar factions in the party struggles which were certainly rife at this period in some areas of Greece, including Aetolia (contrast Gruen, op. cit. 36 and 53 nn.66-7). Even a 'party struggle', which Gruen would dismiss as such and no more (n.67), might have strong class determinants: the extreme bitterness of the one in question (Livy XLI.xxv.3-4) may well have been due to its having that character. (However, since reading the article by Mendels cited at the end of n.2 above, I would agree with him that the statements I have quoted from the inscription must be treated with extreme distrust, as Roman propaganda which *may* have little or no basis in fact.)

5. The fullest narrative in English is still that of Ferguson, *HA* 440-59; but the reader should begin with 435 ff., describing the oligarchy which preceded the uprising. See, however, Day, *EHARD* 109-10, esp. n.346 for a modification of Ferguson's chronology. Cf. also Silvio Accame, *Il dominio romano in Grecia dalla guerra acaïca ad Augusto* (Rome, 1946) 163-71, and the bibliography in Magie, *RRAM* II.1106 n.42. The principal sources are Poseidonius, *FGrH* 87 F 36 (ap. Athen. V. 211d-15b); App., *Mith.* 28-39; Plut., *Sulla* 11-14. Other sources are given in Greenidge and Clay, *Sources*[2] 169-70, 178, 181-2. It is interesting to find Plutarch singling out Aristion, with Nabis and Catiline, as the most pestilential type of politician (*Praec. ger. reip.* 809e).

6. For the damage done to Athens (and in Attica generally) by Sulla, see the material conveniently collected by A. J. Pappalas, in Ἑλληνικά 28 (1975) 49(-50) n.3.

7. Cf. Josef Delz, *Lukians Kenntnis der athenischen Antiquitäten* (Diss., Basel, 1950).

8. In F. Bömer's monumental work in four parts dealing with the religion of Greek and Roman slaves, *URSGR*, the relevant portion is III (1961) 396 (154) to 415 (173). The book by Fr. Carrata Thomes is *La rivolta di Aristonico e le origini della provincia romana d'Asia* (Turin, 1968): see the review by John Briscoe, in *CR* 86 = n.s. 22 (1972) 132-3. J. C. Dumont's article, 'À propos d'Aristonicos', is in *Eirene* 5 (1966) 189-96. Joseph Vogt's treatment of the subject appeared originally in his *Struktur der antiken Sklavenkriege* (= *Abh.* d. Akad. d. Wiss. u. d. Lit. in Mainz, Geistes- u. sozialwiss. Klasse, 1957, no.1), and has been republished in his *Sklaverei und Humanität*[2] (= *Historia* Einzelschr. 8, 1972), at 20-60, with the brief paper, 'Pergamon und Aristonikos' (61-8), first published in the *Atti del terzo congresso internaz. di epigrafia greca e latina* (Rome, 1959) 45-54. See now Vogt, *ASIM* (in Eng. trans.) 39-92, 93-102 (with 213-14). For further discussion and bibliography see Magie, *RRAM* I.144, 148-54, with II.1034-42 nn.2-25; Will, *HPMH* II.352-6.

9. These are perhaps the same category as e.g. (a) the λαοί of *SEG* XVII.817 (second quarter of the third century B.C.), from Apollonia, mentioned beside the πτολίεθρα in line 4 of the poem (cf. Joyce Reynolds, in *Apollonia*, Suppl. Vol. of *Libya Antiqua* [1977], 295-6, no.2); and (b) τὰ κατὰ τὰν χώραν ἔθνεα mentioned in *SEG* XX.729, line 4, beside Cyrene itself καὶ τὰς ἄλλας πόλιας.

10. *SEG* XVI.931 (cf. *IGRR* I.1024), of the last century B.C., is a decree of the [ἄρ]χοντες and πολίτευμα of the Jewish community at Berenice (lines 12-13), earlier Euhesperides and now Benghazi. Some Jews evidently became full citizens of Cyrene: see e.g. *SEG* XX.737 (A.D. 60-1), a list of νομοφύλακες of Cyrene (line 5), which includes Elazar son of Jason (line 8), and id. 741 (A.D. 3-4), a list of ephebes which includes some Jewish names, e.g. Elaszar son of Elazar (a.II.48), Julius son of Jesous (a.I.57; cf. 740.a.II.8); and see Atkinson, *TCEA* 24.

11. The most recent work that gives a full discussion of the pre-Roman constitution is the long article by Monique Clavel-Lévêque, 'Das griechische Marseille. Entwicklungsstufen u. Dynamik einer Handelsmacht', in *Hellenische Poleis*, ed. E. Ch. Welskopf (Berlin, 1974), II.855-969, at 893, 902-7 (with 957-9 nn.446-82), 915 (with 963 nn.555-7). The article in question has since been expanded into a monograph of 209 pages (with maps and plates): *Marseille grecque. La dynamique d'un impérialisme marchand* (Marseilles, 1977). The relevant portions are 93, 115-24, 128-9 (with 146), 137 (with 149). See also Michel Clerc, *Massalia* I (Marseilles, 1927) 424-43; Camille Jullian, *Hist. de la Gaule* I[4].433-7; H. G. Wackernagel, in *RE* XIV.ii (1930) 2139-41; Busolt, *GS* I.357-8.

12. See Clerc, *Massalia* II (1929) 292-8; Jullian, op. cit. VI.314-19.

Bibliography (and Abbreviations)

Part I lists, usually *without the name of an author or editor*, works such as periodicals and collections of inscriptions or papyri, cited in this book normally by the initial letters of their titles, or by other customary abbreviations.

Part II is a very selective list of works recorded *under the names of authors or editors*. Many of these are cited by the initial letters of their titles (see the Preface, pp.x–xi), books in italics, articles not; and these are always placed first in each case (and in alphabetical order) under the names of their respective authors or editors, before works cited without abbreviation.

Abbreviations of *modern works* (including periodicals) not included here are either obvious or can be easily identified with the aid of such lists of abbreviations as those in *LSJ*[9] I.xli–xlviii, *OCD*[2] ix–xxii, *ODCC*[2] xix–xxv, or any recent number of *L'Année philologique*.

The identification of *ancient sources* will usually be obvious enough to those able to profit by consulting them. In case of doubt, reference can be made to *LSJ*[9] I.xvi–xli or (for Latin authors) to Lewis and Short's *Latin Dictionary* vii–xi. The best available editions are used. Those less acquainted with Early Christian sources (cited wherever possible from *GCS, CSEL* or *SC* editions, otherwise commonly from *MPG* or *MPL*), or with Later Roman ones, will find particularly helpful the lists in Jones, *LRE* III.392–406; Stein, *HBE* I[2].ii.607–20 and II.847–61; and of course the Patrologies, by B. Altaner, J. Quasten, and O. Bardenhewer, given in Part II below.

In a few cases I have cited books not under the author's name but under that of a reviewer whose opinions seem to me valuable. (In all such cases sufficient particulars of the books concerned are given.) Books and articles which I believe I have adequately noticed above are sometimes not given again here. And I have omitted here many works which seem to me valueless or irrelevant; but the inclusion of a book or article in this Bibliography is not necessarily to be taken as a recommendation. Greek titles are transliterated here, though not (as a rule) in the Notes above.

I hope that the entries for Karl Marx and Max Weber will be found particularly helpful.

Part I

(A star indicates that references are to the numbers of the inscriptions or papyri, rather than to pages, except where the contrary is stated. References here to papyri are mainly limited to those cited in the main text rather than the Notes. Standard abbreviations are used: all can be identified with the aid of a work of reference such as Orsolina Montevecchi, *La Papirologia* [Turin, 1973], if not in the convenient short list at the end of Bell, *EAGAC*, for which see Part II below.)

AB	= *Analecta Bollandiana*
AC (or *Ant. Class.*)	= *L'Antiquité Classique*
Acta Ant.	= *Acta Antiqua* (Budapest)
AE★	= *L'Année épigraphique*
Aeg.	= *Aegyptus*
AHEW I.ii	= *The Agrarian History of England and Wales*, I.ii, ed. H. P. R. Finberg (1972)
AHR	= *American Historical Review*

A/J★	=	F. F. Abbott and A. C. Johnson, *Municipal Administration in the Roman Empire* (Princeton, 1926)
AJA	=	*American Journal of Archaeology*
AJAH	=	*American Journal of Ancient History*
AJP	=	*American Journal of Philology*
AJS	=	*American Journal of Sociology*
Anc. Soc.	=	*Ancient Society*
ANRW	=	*Aufstieg und Niedergang der römischen Welt*, ed. Hildegard Temporini (Berlin/New York, 1972 ff.)
Ant. Class.: see under AC above
Arch. Class.	=	*Archeologia Classica*
Arch.f.Pap.	=	*Archiv für Papyrusforschung*
ARS	=	*Ancient Roman Statutes*. A Translation, with Introduction, Commentary etc., by A. C. Johnson and others (Austin, Texas, 1961)
ASNP	=	*Annali della Scuola Normale Superiore di Pisa, Classe di lettere e filosofia*
Athen.	=	*Athenaeum*
BASOR	=	*Bulletin of the American Schools of Oriental Research*
BASP	=	*Bulletin of the American Society of Papyrologists*
BCH	=	*Bulletin de Correspondance hellénique*
BEFAR	=	*Bibliothèque des Écoles françaises d'Athènes et de Rome*
BGU★	=	*Berliner Griechischer Urkunden (Aegyptische Urkunden aus den königlichen Museen zu Berlin*, 1895 ff.)
BICS	=	*Bulletin of the Institute of Classical Studies*, London
BIDR	=	*Bullettino dell'Istituto di diritto romano*
BJS	=	*British Journal of Sociology*
BSA	=	*Annual of the British School at Athens*
Byz.	=	*Byzantion*
Byz. Ztschr.	=	*Byzantinische Zeitschrift*
CAF	=	*Comicorum Atticorum Fragmenta*, ed. Theodore Kock, 3 vols (Leipzig, 1880-8)
CAH	=	*Cambridge Ancient History*, 12 vols
CCL	=	*Corpus Christianorum, Series Latina* (1935 ff.)
CE (or Chr. d'Ég.)	=	*Chronique d'Égypte*
CEHE I²	=	*Cambridge Economic History of Europe*, Vol. I, 2nd edn (1966)
Chr. d'Ég.: see under CE above
CIG★	=	*Corpus Inscriptionum Graecarum* (1825-77)
CIL★	=	*Corpus Inscriptionum Latinarum* (1863 ff.)
CIRB★	=	*Corpus Inscriptionum Regni Bosporani*
CJ	=	*Classical Journal*
C. Ord. Ptol.★	=	M. T. Lenger, *Corpus des ordonnances des Ptolémées* (Brussels, 1964)
CP	=	*Classical Philology*
C.P.Jud.★	=	*Corpus Papyrorum Judaicarum*, 3 vols (1957-64)
CQ	=	*Classical Quarterly*
CR	=	*Classical Review*
CRR: see Part II under Seager, R. (ed.)
CSCA	=	*California Studies in Classical Antiquity*
CSCO	=	*Corpus Scriptorum Christianorum Orientalium* (1903 ff.)
CSEL	=	*Corpus Scriptorum Ecclesiasticorum Latinorum* (Vienna, 1866 ff.)
CSHB	=	*Corpus Scriptorum Historiae Byzantinae* (Bonn, 1828-78)
CSSH	=	*Comparative Studies in Society and History*
DAA★	=	*Dedications from the Athenian Akropolis*, ed. A. E. Raubitschek, with the collaboration of L. H. Jeffery (Cambridge, Mass., 1949)
DOP	=	*Dumbarton Oaks Papers*
Econ. Hist. Rev.	=	*Economic History Review*

E/J²★ = *Documents Illustrating the Reigns of Augustus and Tiberius*, collected by V. Ehrenberg and A. H. M. Jones, 2nd edn (1955)
Eng. Hist. Rev. = *English Historical Review*
ESAR: see Part II under Frank, Tenney
ESHAG: see Part II under Austin, M. M., and P. Vidal-Naquet
FD★ = *Fouilles de Delphes*
FGrH = *Die Fragmente der griechischen Historiker*, ed. F. Jacoby (1923 ff.)
FHG = *Fragmenta Historicorum Graecorum*, 5 vols (1841 ff.)
*FIRA*² = *Fontes Iuris Romani Antejustiniani*, 3 vols, 2nd edn, ed. S. Riccobono etc. (Florence, 1940-3)
GCS = *Die griechischen christlichen Schriftsteller der ersten drei Jahrhunderte* (Berlin, 1897 ff.)
G. & R. = *Greece and Rome*
GRBS = *Greek, Roman and Byzantine Studies*
Hesp. = *Hesperia* (Journal of the American School of Classical Studies at Athens, 1932 ff.)
HGM = *Historici Graeci Minores*, 2 vols, ed. L. Dindorf (Leipzig, 1870-1)
Hist. Ztschr. = *Historische Zeitschrift*
HSCP = *Harvard Studies in Classical Philology*
HTR = *Harvard Theological Review*
IEJ = *Israel Exploration Journal*
IG★ = *Inscriptiones Graecae* (Berlin, 1873 ff.)
IGBulg.★ = *Inscriptiones Graecae in Bulgaria repertae*, ed. G. Mihailov (1956 ff.)
IGLS★ = *Inscriptions grecques et latines de la Syrie*, ed. L. Jalabert etc. (1929 ff.)
IGRR★ = *Inscriptiones Graecae ad res Romanas pertinentes* I, III, IV, ed. R. Cagnat etc. (1906-27)
ILS★ = *Inscriptiones Latinae Selectae*, ed. H. Dessau, 3 vols in 5 (Berlin, 1892-1916)
IOSPE★ = *Inscriptiones Antiquae Orae Septentrionalis Ponti Euxini*, ed. B. Latyshev (1885-1901); I² = Vol. I, 2nd edn (1916)
IRSH = *International Review of Social History*
Istituto Lombardo = *Istituto Lombardo, Accademia di Scienze e Lettere, Rendiconti, Classe di*
(Rend. Lett.) *Lettere*
JEA = *Journal of Egyptian Archaeology*
JEH = *Journal of Economic History*
JESHO = *Journal of the Economic and Social History of the Orient*
JHI = *Journal of the History of Ideas*
JHS = *Journal of Hellenic Studies*
JJP = *Journal of Juristic Papyrology*
JOAI = *Jahreshefte des Oesterreichischen archäologischen Instituts in Wien*
JPS = *Journal of Peasant Studies*
JRS = *Journal of Roman Studies*
JTS = *Journal of Theological Studies*
LB/W★ = P. Le Bas and W. H. Waddington, *Voyage archéologique en Grèce et en Asie Mineure: Inscriptions . . .* III (Paris, 1870)
*LSJ*⁹ = Liddell and Scott, *Greek-English Lexicon*, 9th edn (1925 ff.)
MAMA★ = *Monumenta Asiae Minoris Antiqua*, 8 vols (1928-62)
M.Chr.★ = Ludwig Mitteis, *Grundzüge und Chrestomathie der Papyruskunde* II.ii (Leipzig/Berlin, 1912)
MEFR = *Mélanges d'archéologie et d'histoire: École française de Rome*
MGH = *Monumenta Germaniae Historica*
M/L★ = R. Meiggs and D. M. Lewis, *A Selection of Greek Historical Inscriptions to the End of the Fifth Century B.C.* (1969)
Mnemos. = *Mnemosyne*
MPG = *Patrologia Graeca*, ed. J.-P. Migne

MPL	=	*Patrologia Latina*, ed. J.-P. Migne
NPNF	=	*Nicene and Post-Nicene Fathers*
NRHDFE	=	*Nouvelle revue historique de droit français et étranger*
OCD²	=	*Oxford Classical Dictionary*, 2nd edn (1970)
OCT	=	*Oxford Classical Texts*
ODCC²	=	*Oxford Dictionary of the Christian Church*, 2nd edn (1974)
OGIS★	=	*Orientis Graeci Inscriptiones Selectae*, 2 vols (1903-5)
PBA	=	*Proceedings of the British Academy*
PBSR	=	*Proceedings of the British School at Rome*
PCPS	=	*Proceedings of the Cambridge Philological Society*
P. Hibeh★	=	*The Hibeh Papyri*, ed. with trans. and notes by B. P. Grenfell and A. S. Hunt (1906 ff.)

P. Ital.: see Part II, under Tjäder, J.-O.

PIR	=	*Prosopographia Imperii Romani*, Saeculi I, II, III, ed. E. Klebs and H. Dessau (1897-8); 2nd edn by E. Groag and A. Stein (1933 ff.)
PLRE I	=	*The Prosopography of the Later Roman Empire, Vol. I. A.D. 260-395*, by A. H. M. Jones, J. R. Martindale and J. Morris (1971)
P. Oxy.★	=	*The Oxyrhynchus Papyri* (1898 ff.)
PSI★	=	*Papiri greci e latini, pubbl. della Società Italiana . . .* (Florence, 1912 ff.)

PTGA: see Part II under Finley, M. I. (ed.)

RAC	=	*Reallexikon für Antike und Christentum* (Stuttgart, 1950 ff.)
RBPH	=	*Revue Belge de Philologie et d'Histoire*
RCHP★	=	*Royal Correspondence in the Hellenistic Period. A Study in Greek Epigraphy*, by C. Bradford Welles (1934)
RE	=	Pauly-Wissowa, *Real-Encyclopädie der classischen Altertums-wissenschaft* (Stuttgart, 1893 ff.)
REA	=	*Revue des études anciennes*
REB	=	*Revue des études byzantines*
REG	=	*Revue des études grecques*
Rev. de phil.	=	*Revue de philologie*
RFIC	=	*Rivista di filologia e di istruzione classica*
RHDFE	=	*Revue historique de droit français et étranger*
RIDA	=	*Revue internationale des droits de l'antiquité*

Riv. stor. dell'Ant.: see under *RSA* below

RQH	=	*Revue des questions historiques*
RSA	=	*Rivista storica dell'Antichità*

RSCC: see Part II under Coleman-Norton, P. R. (ed.)

SAS: see Part II under Finley, M. I. (ed.)

Sb	=	*Sitzungsberichte* (of various German-speaking academic institutions)
SB★	=	*Sammelbuch griechischer Urkunden aus Aegypten*, ed. F. Preisigke etc. (1915 ff.)
SC	=	*Sources chrétiennes* (Paris, 1940 ff.)

SCA: see Part II under Finley, M. I. (ed.)

SCH	=	*Studies in Church History*
Scr. Hierosol.	=	*Scripta Hierosolymitana* (Jerusalem)
SDHI	=	*Studia et Documenta Historiae et Iuris*
SEG★	=	*Supplementum Epigraphicum Graecum* (1923 ff.)
SGDI★	=	*Sammlung der griechischen Dialekt-Inschriften*, ed. H. Collitz etc. (Göttingen, 1884-1915)
SGHI II★	=	M. N. Tod, *A Selection of Greek Historical Inscriptions, II. From 403 to 323 B.C.* (1948)
SIG³★	=	*Sylloge Inscriptionum Graecarum*, ed. W. Dittenberger, 4 vols, 3rd edn by F. Hiller von Gaertringen (Leipzig, 1915-24)
SP★	=	A. S. Hunt and C. C. Edgar, *Select Papyri* [Loeb] I (1932), II (1934)

SRP: see Part II under Finley, M. I. (ed.)

TAPA = *Transactions of the American Philological Association*
TLS = *Times Literary Supplement* (London)
TRHS = *Transactions of the Royal Historical Society*
UED²: see Part II under Soden, Hans von
VDI = *Vestnik Drevnei Istorii*
W.Chr.* = Ulrich Wilcken, *Grundzüge und Chrestomathie der Papyruskunde* I.ii (Leipzig/Berlin, 1912)
YCS = *Yale Classical Studies*
ZNW = *Zeitschrift für die neutestamentliche Wissenschaft*
ZPE = *Zeitschrift für Papyrologie und Epigraphik*
ZSS = *Zeitschrift der Savigny-Stiftung für Rechtsgeschichte, romanistische Abteilung*

Part II

(Names beginning with 'de' [though not 'De'], 'van' or 'von' are usually given under the next word in the name – so, e.g., my own name appears under 'Ste.' [= 'Sainte'] but De Martino under 'De'. 'Mc' is treated as 'Mac'.)

Aalders, G. J. D., *Die Theorie der gemischten Verfassung im Altertum* (Amsterdam, 1968)
Accame, Silvio, *Il dominio romano in Grecia dalla guerra acaïca ad Augusto* (Rome, 1946)
——, *La lega ateniese del sec. IV a.C.* (Rome, 1941)
Adams, Bertrand, *Paramoné und verwandte Texte. Studien zum Dienstvertrag im Rechte der Papyri* (= *Neue Kölner rechtswiss. Abhandl.* 35, Berlin, 1964)
Alföldy, Géza, 'The crisis of the third century, as seen by contemporaries', in *GRBS* 15 (1974) 89-111
——, *Fasti Hispanienses* (Wiesbaden, 1969)
——, 'Die Freilassung von Sklaven und die Struktur der Sklaverei in der römischen Kaiserzeit', in *Riv. stor. dell'Ant.* 2 (1972) 97-129
——, *Noricum* (1974)
Alfonsi, Luigi, 'Il "Querolo" e il "Dyskolos"', in *Aeg.* 44 (1964) 200-5
Allen, Walter, 'Cicero's house and *libertas*', in *TAPA* 75 (1944) 1-9
Altaner, B., *Patrology* (1960, Eng. trans. from the 5th German edn of 1958)
Anderson, J. G. C., 'Festivals of Mên Askaênos in the Roman Colonia at Antioch of Pisidia', in *JRS* 3 (1913) 267-300, esp. 284-7
Anderson, Perry, *LAS = Lineages of the Absolutist State* (1974)
——, *PAF = Passages from Antiquity to Feudalism* (1974)
Andreades, A. M., *A History of Greek Public Finance* I (Eng. trans. by Carroll N. Brown, Cambridge, Mass., 1933)
Andrewes, A., *GT = The Greek Tyrants* (1956 & repr.)
——, in Gomme, *HCT* IV (*q.v.*)
——, 'The opposition to Perikles', in *JHS* 98 (1978) 1-8
Andreyev, V. N., 'Some aspects of agrarian conditions in Attica in the 5th to 3rd centuries B.C.', in *Eirene* 12 (1974) 5-46
Annas, Julia, 'Plato's *Republic* and feminism', in *Philosophy* 51 (1976) 307-21
Applebaum, Shimon, 'Hellenistic cities of Judaea and its vicinity – some new aspects', in *The Ancient Historian and his Materials* (Essays in Honour of C. E. Stevens), ed. Barbara Levick (1975) 59-73
——, 'Roman Britain', in *AHEW* I.ii.1-277
——, 'The Zealots: the case for revaluation', in *JRS* 61 (1971) 155-70
D'Arms, J. H.: see under D
Arnim, H. von, *Leben und Werke des Dio von Prusa* (Berlin, 1898)
Asheri, David, *LGPD = Leggi greche sul problema dei debiti* (= *Studi Classici e Orientali* 18, Pisa, 1969)
——, *Distribuzioni di terre nell'antica Grecia* (= *Mem. dell'Accademia delle Scienze di Torino*, ser. IV.10, Turin, 1966)

Atkinson [Chrimes], K. M. T., SGCWAM = 'The Seleucids and the Greek cities of western Asia Minor', in *Antichthon* 2 (1968) 32-57

——, TCEA = 'The third Cyrene edict of Augustus', in *Ancient Society and Institutions. Studies presented to Victor Ehrenberg* (1966) 21-36

——, 'A Hellenistic land conveyance: the estate of Mnesimachus in the plain of Sardis', in *Historia* 21 (1972) 45-74

Audring, Gert, 'Über den Gutsverwalter (*epitropos*) in der attischen Landwirtschaft des 5. und des 4. Jh. v.u.Z.', in *Klio* 55 (1973) 109-16

Austin, M. M., and P. Vidal-Naquet, *ESHAG = Economic and Social History of Ancient Greece. An Introduction* (1977), an improved Eng. trans. of the French original, *Économies et sociétés en Grèce ancienne* (Paris, 1972, 1973). [See pp.64-5 above]

——, Austin, N. J. E., 'A usurper's claim to legitimacy: Procopius in A.D. 365/6', in *Riv. stor. dell'Ant.* 2 (1972) 187-94

Badian, Ernst, *PS = Publicans and Sinners. Private enterprise in the service of the Roman Republic* (Dunedin, 1972)

——, $RILR^2$ = *Roman Imperialism in the Late Republic*, 2nd edn (1968)

——, TGBRR = 'Tiberius Gracchus and the Beginning of the Roman Revolution', in *ANRW* I.i (1972) 668-731

——, *Foreign Clientelae 264-70 B.C.* (1958)

——, 'From the Gracchi to Sulla (1940-59)', in *Historia* 11 (1962) 197-245

——, *Titus Quinctius Flamininus. Philhellenism and Realpolitik* (Louise Taft Semple Lecture, Cincinnati, 1970)

Bailey, A. M., and J. R. Llobera, 'The Asiatic Mode of Production. An annotated Biliography', in *Critique of Anthropology* 2 (Autumn, 1974) 95-103 ('I. Principal writings of Marx and Engels'), and 4/5 (Autumn, 1975) 165-76 ('II. The adventures of the concept from Plekhanov to Stalin')

Bailey, Cyril, 'Karl Marx on Greek Atomism', in *CQ* 22 (1928) 205-6

Balsdon, J. P. V. Dacre, 'The "divinity" of Alexander', in *Historia* 1 (1950) 363-88

——, *Life and Leisure in Ancient Rome* (1969)

——, 'Panem et circenses', in *Hommages à Marcel Renard* II (= *Coll. Latomus* 102, Brussels, 1969) 57-60

Banks, J. A., *MSA = Marxist Sociology in Action* (1970)

Bardenhewer, Otto, *Geschichte der altkirchlichen Literatur*, 5 vols (Freiburg im Breisgau), I^2 (1913), II^2 (1914), III (1912), IV (1924), V (1932)

——, *Patrology* (Freiburg im Breisgau, 1908; Eng. trans. from the 2nd German edn)

Barker, Ernest, *AC = From Alexander to Constantine. Passages and Documents Illustrating the History of Social and Political Ideas 336 B.C. - A. D. 337* (1956)

——, *Social and Political Thought in Byzantium from Justinian I to the Last Palaeologus* (1957)

——, *The Politics of Aristotle* (1946 & repr.: Eng. trans., with Introd. and notes)

Barnes, T. D., 'The date of Vegetius', in *Phoenix* 33 (1979) 254-7

——, 'Porphyry *Against the Christians*: date and the attribution of fragments', in *JTS* n.s. 24 (1973) 424-42

——, 'Who were the nobility of the Roman Empire?', in *Phoenix* 28 (1974) 444-9

——, Review, in *AJP* 96 (1975) 443-5, of *Le Culte des Souverains dans l'Empire Romain = Entretiens Hardt* 19 (1973)

Barns, John, *SHS* = 'Shenute as a historical source', in *Actes du Xe Congrès International* [Warsaw etc., 1961] *de Papyrologues* (Warsaw etc., 1964) 151-9

Baron, S. W., *SRHJ* I^2 & II^2 = *A Social and Religious History of the Jews* I and II, 2nd edn (1952 & repr.)

Baynes, Norman H., *BSOE = Byzantine Studies and Other Essays* (1955)

——, *Constantine the Great and the Christian Church*, 2nd edn (1972), with a Preface by Henry Chadwick

——, *The Political Ideas of St. Augustine's De Civitate Dei* (= Historical Assocn Pamphlet no.104, London, 1936)

——, 'The decline of the Roman power in Western Europe: some modern explanations', in *JRS* 33 (1943) 29-35, repr. in *BSOE* (above) 83-96

——, Review of K. M. Setton, *Christian Attitude* . . . (*q.v.*), in *JRS* 34 (1944) 135-40, partly repr. in *BSOE* (above) 348-56

Beazley, J. D., 'Potter and painter in Ancient Athens', in *PBA* 30 (1944) 87-125 (also published separately)

Bedale, Stephen, 'The meaning of *kephalē* in the Pauline Epistles', in *JTS* n.s. 5 (1954) 211-15

Beesly, E. S., *Catiline, Clodius, and Tiberius* (1878; repr., New York, 1924). [See pp.621-2 n.5 above]

Bell, Harold Idris, *EAGAC = Egypt from Alexander the Great to the Arab Conquest* (1948)

——, *EVAJ* = 'An Egyptian village in the age of Justinian', in *JHS* 64 (1944) 21-36

Bellinger, A. R.: see under Welles, C. Bradford

Beloch, K. J., *GG III²* = *Griechische Geschichte III².i & ii*, 2nd edn (1922, 1923)

Bendix, Reinhard, *MWIP* = *Max Weber. An Intellectual Portrait* (1959 & repr.)

Bendix, Reinhard, and S. M. Lipset, *CSP²* = *Class, Status, and Power. Social Stratification in Comparative Perspective*, 2nd edn (1966/7)

Bendix, Reinhard, and Guenther Roth, *Scholarship and Partisanship: Essays on Max Weber* (1971)

Bengtson, H., *GG⁵* = *Griechische Geschichte*, 5th edn (1977)

Béranger, Jean, 'Les jugements de Cicéron sur les Gracques', in *ANRW* I.i (1972) 732-63. [See p.623 n.7 above]

Berchem, Denis van, *Les distributions de blé et d'argent à la plèbe romaine sous l'Empire* (Geneva, 1939)

Berger, Adolf, *EDRL = Encyclopedic Dictionary of Roman Law*, in *Transactions of the American Philosophical Soc.*, n.s. 43, Part 2 (1953), pp.333-809

Berve, Helmut, *Die Tyrannis bei den Griechen*, 2 vols (Munich, 1967)

Béteille, André (ed.), *SI = Social Inequality* (Penguin Modern Sociology Readings, 1969 & repr.)

Bickerman, E. J. [also Bikerman, Bickermann], *APT* = '*Autonomia*. Sur un passage de Thucydide (I, 144,2)', in *RIDA³* 5 (1958) 313-44

——, *IS = Institutions des Séleucides* (Paris, 1938)

——, 'La conception du mariage à Athènes', in *BIDR* 78 = ser. III.17 (1975) 1-28

——, 'Love story in the Homeric Hymn to Aphrodite', in *Athenaeum*, n.s. 54 (1976) 229-54

——, 'Some reflections on early Roman history', in *RFIC* 97 (1969) 393-408

Bieżuńska-Malowist, Iza, *EEGR* I & II = *L'Esclavage dans l'Égypte gréco-romaine* (Warsaw etc.) *I. Période Ptolémaïque* (1974), and *II. Période romaine* (1977). [See p.566 above, n.32, *ad init.*]

——, *ENMM* = 'Les esclaves nés dans la maison du maître (*oikogeneis*) et le travail des esclaves en Égypte romaine', in *Studii Clasice* 3 (Bucharest, 1961) 147-62

——, 'Les esclaves payant l'*apophora* dans l'Égypte gréco-romaine', in *JJP* 15 (1965) 65-72

——, 'Quelques formes non typiques de l'esclavage dans le monde ancien', in *Antichnoe Obshchestvo* [= *Ancient Society*] (Moscow, 1967) 91-6

Birley, Anthony R., *IIRMA* = 'The invasion of Italy in the reign of Marcus Aurelius', in *Provincialia. Festschrift für Rudolf Laur-Belart*, ed. Elisabeth Schmid and others (Basel/ Stuttgart, 1968) 214-25

——, *MA = Marcus Aurelius* (1966)

——, *TCCRE* = 'The third century crisis in the Roman empire', in *Bull. of the John Rylands Univ. Library of Manchester* 58 (1976) 253-81

——, 'The oath not to put senators to death', in *CR* 76 = n.s. 12 (1962) 197-9

——, 'Roman frontiers and Roman frontier policy', in *Transactions of the Architectural and Archaeological Soc. of Durham and Northumberland*, n.s. 3 (1974) 13-25

Blavatskaja, T. V., E. S. Golubcova and A. I. Pavlovskaja, *Die Sklaverei in hellenistischen Staaten im 3.-1. Jh. v.Chr.* (Wiesbaden, 1972: German trans. from Russian)

Bloch, Marc, *Feudal Society*[2] (Eng. trans. in 2 vols, by L. A. Manyon, 2nd edn, 1962, of *La société féodale*, 2 vols, Paris, 1939-40)

———, 'The rise of dependent cultivation and seignorial institutions' (Ch. vi), in *CEHE* I[2] (1966) 235-90 (repr. from 1st edn, 1941)

Bloch, Maurice (ed.), *Marxist Analyses and Social Anthropology* (= *ASA* Studies 2, 1975)

Blum, Jerome, *The End of the Old Order in Rural Europe* (Princeton, 1978)

Blumenberg, Werner, *Karl Marx* (Eng. trans. by Douglas Scott, 1972)

Bodei Giglioni, Gabriella, *Lavori pubblici e occupazione nell'antichità classica* (Bologna, 1974)

Böckh, August, *Die Staatshaushaltung der Athener*[3], 2 vols, 3rd edn (Berlin, 1886, ed. Max Fränkel)

Bömer, Franz, *URSGR* = *Untersuchungen über die Religion der Sklaven in Griechenland und Rom*, I-IV, in Mainz Akad., *Abhandlungen* der geistes- und sozialwiss. Klasse, Wiesbaden, 1957 no.7 (I), 1960 no.1 (II), 1961 no.4 (III), 1963 no.10 (IV)

Bolkestein, H., *CRO* = *De colonatu romano eiusque origine* (Diss., Amsterdam, 1906)

Borecký, Bořivoj, 'Die politische Isonomie', in *Eirene* 9 (1971) 5-24

Bottéro, J., 'Désordre économique et annulation des dettes en Mésopotamie à l'époque paléo-babylonienne', in *JESHO* 4 (1961) 113-64

Bottomore, T. B., *Sociology*[2] = *Sociology. A Guide to Problems and Literature*, 2nd edn (1971)

Bottomore, T. B., and Maximilien Rubel, *KM* = *Karl Marx. Selected Writings in Sociology and Social Philosophy* (1956 & repr.)

Bowersock, G. W., *AGW* = *Augustus and the Greek World* (1965)

———, 'A report on Arabia provincia', in *JRS* 61 (1971) 219-42

———, Review, in *Gnomon* 45 (1973) 576-80, of Jürgen Deininger, *Der politische Widerstand . . . (q.v.*, below)

Bowman, Alan K., *PRIH* = 'Papyri and Roman Imperial history, 1960-75', in *JRS* 66 (1976) 153-73

Boxer, C. R., *PSE* = *The Portuguese Seaborne Empire 1415-1825* (1969; Pelican, 1973)

Bratianu, G. I., 'Empire et "Démocratie" à Byzance', in *Byz. Ztschr.* 37 (1937) 86-111

Bréhier, Louis, ch. ii-vi (pp.55-179) of *Histoire de l'Église*, ed. A. Fliche and V. Martin, V (Paris, 1947)

Brenner, Robert, 'Agrarian class structure and economic development in pre-industrial Europe', in *Past & Present* 70 (1976) 30-75

Briant, Pierre, *DDAHA* = 'Dörfer und Dorfgemeinschaften im achämenidischen und hellenistischen Asien', in *Jahrbuch für Wirtschaftsgeschichte* (1975) 115-33

———, *RLER* = 'Remarques sur les "laoi" et esclaves ruraux en Asie Mineure hellénistique', in *Actes du Colloque 1971 sur l'esclavage* (= *Annales littéraires de l'Université de Besançon* 140, Paris, 1972) 93-133

———, 'Villages et comunautés villageoises d'Asie achéménide et hellénistique', in *JESHO* 18 (1975) 165-88

Briggs, Asa, 'The language of "class" in early nineteenth-century England', in *Essays in Labour History* I (see the next item) 43-73

Briggs, Asa, and John Saville (eds), *Essays in Labour History* I (rev. edn, 1967)

Briscoe, John, 'Rome and the class struggle in the Greek states 200-146 B.C.', in *Past & Present* 36 (1967) 3-20, repr. in *SAS*, ed. Finley (*q.v.*) 53-73

———, Review, in *CR* 88 = n.s. 24 (1974) 258-61, of Jürgen Deininger, *Der politische Widerstand . . . (q.v.*)

Brock, S. P., 'Syriac sources for seventh-century history', in *Byzantine and Modern Greek Studies* 2 (1976) 17-36

Broughton, T. R. S., *MRR* II = *The Magistrates of the Roman Republic, II. 99 B.C.-31 B.C.* (1952)

———, *RLAM* = 'Roman landholding in Asia Minor', in *TAPA* 65 (1934) 207-39

———, 'Roman Asia Minor' = Part IV of *ESAR* (ed. Tenney Frank) IV (1938) 499-950

Brown, Peter, *The World of Late Antiquity* (1971)

———, 'The rise and function of the Holy Man in Late Antiquity', in *JRS* 61 (1971) 80-101

Browning, Robert, *Justinian and Theodora* (1971)

——, Review, in *TLS* 3902 (24 December 1976) 1606, of Alan Cameron, *Circus Factions* (*q.v.*)

Brunt, P. A., ALRR = 'The army and the land in the Roman revolution', in *JRS* 52 (1962) 69–86

——, ASTDCS = 'Aspects of the Social Thought of Dio Chrysostom and of the Stoics', in *PCPS* n.s. 19 (1973) 9–34

——, CPMEP = 'Charges of provincial maladministration under the Early Principate', in *Historia* 10 (1961) 189–227

——, DIRDS = 'Did Imperial Rome disarm her subjects?', in *Phoenix* 29 (1975) 260–70

——, ELR = 'The Equites in the Late Republic', in *Deuxième Conférence Internat. d'hist. écon.* [Aix-en-Provence, 1962], Vol. I. *Trade and Politics in the Anc. World* (Paris, 1965) 117–49, repr. in *CRR*, ed. Seager (*q.v.*) 83–115

——, IM = *Italian Manpower 225 B.C. - A.D. 14* (1971)

——, LI = 'Laus imperii', in *Imperialism in the Anc. World*, ed. P. D. A. Garnsey and C. R. Whittaker (1978) 159–91, 319–30

——, RLRCRE = 'The Romanisation of the local ruling classes in the Roman empire', in *Assimilation et résistance à la culture gréco-romaine dans le monde ancien = Travaux du VIe* [Madrid, 1974] *Congrès International d'Études Classiques* (Bucarest/Paris, 1976) 161–73

——, SCRR = Social Conflicts in the Roman Republic (1971)

——, '"Amicitia" in the Late Roman Republic', in *PCPS* n.s. 11 (1965) 1–20, repr. in *CRR*, ed. Seager (*q.v.*) 199–218

——, 'Conscription and volunteering in the Roman Imperial army', in *Scripta Classica Israelica* 1 (1974) 90–115

——, 'Free labour and public works at Rome' in *JRS* 70 (1980) 81–100

——, 'Josephus on social conflicts in Roman Judaea', in *Klio* 59 (1977) 149–53

——, 'Lex de imperio Vespasiani', in *JRS* 67 (1977) 95–116

——, 'The Roman mob', in *Past & Present* 35 (1966) 3–27, repr. (with an addendum) in *SAS*, ed. Finley (*q.v.*) 74–102

——, 'Two great Roman landowners', in *Latomus* 34 (1975) 619–35

——, 'What is ancient history about?', in *Didaskalos* 5 (1976) 236–49

——, Review, in *Gnomon* 37 (1965) 189–92, of D. C. Earl, *Tiberius Gracchus* (1963)

——, Review, in *JRS* 69 (1979) 168–75, of J. Rufus Fears, *Princeps a diis electus* [see p.633 n.72a above]

——, Review, in *JRS* 58 (1968) 229–32, of Christian Meier, *Res Publica Amissa* (1966)

——, Review, in *JRS* 53 (1963) 170–6, of H. D. Meyer, *Die Aussenpolitik des Augustus und die augusteische Dichtung* (1961)

——, Review, in *JRS* 48 (1958) 164–70, of W. L. Westermann, *SSGRA* (*q.v.*), and two other books on ancient slavery

——, Review, in *JRS* 62 (1972) 153–8, of K. D. White, *Roman Farming* (1970)

Brunt, P. A., and J. M. Moore, *Res Gestae Divi Augusti. The Achievements of the Divine Augustus* (1967; includes Latin text, trans., introd. and comm.)

Bruun, P. M., *The Roman Imperial Coinage* [ed. C. H. V. Sutherland and R. A. G. Carson], *VII. Constantine and Licinius A.D. 313-337* (1966)

Buckland, W. W., RLS = *The Roman Law of Slavery* (1908)

——, TBRL³ = *A Text Book of Roman Law from Augustus to Justinian*, 3rd edn, rev. by Peter Stein (1963)

Buckler, W. H., LDPA = 'Labour disputes in the province of Asia', in *Anatolian Studies pres. to Sir W. M. Ramsay*, ed. W. H. Buckler and W. M. Calder (1923) 27–50

Burford, Alison, CGRS = *Craftsmen in Greek and Roman Society* (1972)

——, EGTB = 'The economics of Greek temple building', in *PCPS* n.s. 11 (1965) 21–34

——, GTBE = *The Greek Temple Builders at Epidaurus* (1969)

——, 'The builders of the Parthenon', in *Parthenos and Parthenon* (= *Greece & Rome*, Suppl. to Vol. 10, 1963) 23–35

Burstein, S. M., *Outpost of Hellenism: The Emergence of Heraclea on the Black Sea* (= *Univ. of California Publications: Class. Stud.* 14, 1976)

Bury, J. B., *HLRE*² = *History of the Later Roman Empire from the Death of Theodosius I to the Death of Justinian (A.D. 395 to A.D. 565)*, 2 vols (1923). [I have not used in this book what is sometimes regarded as a first edition of the same work: *A History of the Later Roman Empire from Arcadius to Irene, 395 A.D. to 800 A.D.*, 2 vols, 1889]

Bury, J. B., E. A. Barber, Edwyn Bevan, and W. W. Tarn, *The Hellenistic Age* (1923)

Busolt, Georg (or Busolt-Swoboda), *GS* = *Griechische Staatskunde*, 2 vols (Munich), I (1920), and II (1926, ed. H. Swoboda, whose contribution begins at p.881).

Butler, A. J., *ACE*² = *The Arab Conquest of Egypt and the Last Thirty Years of the Roman Dominion*, 2nd edn by P. M. Fraser (1978) [See p.652 n.37 above]

Buttrey, T. V., 'Dio, Zonaras and the value of the Roman aureus', in *JRS* 51 (1961) 40-5

Calabi Limentani, Ida, *Studi sulla società romana: il lavoro artistico* (= Biblioteca storica universitaria, Serie II Monografie, Vol. IX, Milan, 1958)

Calderini, Aristide, *La manomissione e la condizione dei liberti in Grecia* (Milan, 1908)

Cameron, Alan, *CF* = *Circus Factions. Blues and Greens at Rome and Byzantium* (1976)

——, *Bread and Circuses: the Roman Emperor and his People* (Inaugural Lecture, King's College London, 1973)

——, *Claudian. Poetry and Propaganda at the Court of Honorius* (1970)

——, 'The house of Anastasius', in *GRBS* 19 (1978) 259-76

——, 'Rutilius Namatianus, St. Augustine, and the date of the *De Reditu*', in *JRS* 57 (1967) 31-9

Cameron, Averil, *Flavius Cresconius Corippus, In laudem Iustini Augusti minoris* (1976: text, Eng. trans., and comm.)

——, 'Images of authority: elites and icons in late sixth-century Byzantium', in *Past & Present* 84 (August 1979) 3-35

——, 'Neither male nor female', in *Greece & Rome*² 27 (1980) 60-8

——, 'The Theotokos in sixth-century Constantinople', in *JTS* n.s. 29 (1978) 79-108

——, 'Early Byzantine *Kaiserkritik*: Two case histories', in *Byzantine and Modern Greek Studies* 3 (1977) 1-17

Cardascia, G., *ADCHH* = L'apparition dans le droit des classes d'"*honestiores*" et d'"*humiliores*"', in *RHDFE*⁴ 27 (1950) 305-37 and 461-85

——, 'La distinction entre *honestiores* et *humiliores* et le droit matrimonial', in *Studi in memoria di Emilio Albertario* II (1951) 655-67

——, Review, in *Iura* 21 (1970) 250-6, of Garnsey, *SSLPRE* (*q.v.*)

Carlyle, A. J., *A History of Mediaeval Political Theory in the West* I² (1927)

Cartledge, Paul, 'Hoplites and heroes', in *JHS* 97 (1977) 11-27

——, *Sparta and Lakonia. A Regional history 1300-362 B.C.* (1979)

——, Review, in *JHS* 98 (1978) 193-4, of R. Sealey, *A History of the Greek City States ca. 700-338 B.C.* (1977)

Casson, Lionel, *Ships and Seamanship in the Ancient World* (Princeton, 1971)

——, 'Unemployment, the building trade, and Suetonius, *Vesp.* 18', in *BASP* 15 (1978) 43-51

Castles, Stephen, and Godula Kosack, *Immigrant Workers and Class Structure in Western Europe* (1973)

Cawkwell, G. L., Introduction to 1972 reissue of Penguin Classics Eng. trans. of Xenophon's *Anabasis* by Rex Warner, as *Xenophon. The Persian Expedition*

Cerfaux, L., and J. Tondriau, *Le culte des souverains dans la civilisation gréco-romaine* (Tournai, 1957)

Chabot, J. B., *Chronique de Michel le Syrien, Patriarche Jacobite d'Antioche (1166-1199)*, 4 vols (Paris, 1899-1924, repr. Brussels, 1963), esp. II (French trans.)

Chadwick, Henry, *The Early Church* (Pelican History of the Church, Vol. I, 1967)

——, 'John Moschus and his friend Sophronius the sophist', in *JTS* n.s. 25 (1974) 41-74

——, 'Origen, Celsus, and the Stoa', in *JTS* 48 (1947) 34-49

Chalon, Gérard, *ETJA* = *L'Édit de Tiberius Julius Alexander. Étude historique et exégétique* (Bibl. Helvet. Romana, Olten/Lausanne, 1964)

Chamoux, François, *Cyrène sous la monarchie des Battiades* (Paris, 1953)

Chapot, Victor, *La province romaine proconsulaire d'Asie* (Paris, 1904)

Charanis, Peter, 'The transfer of population as a policy in the Byzantine Empire', in *CSSH* 3 (1960–61) 140–54

Charlesworth, M. P., VRE = 'The Virtues of a Roman emperor: propaganda and the creation of belief' (the 1937 Raleigh Lecture on History), in *PBA* 23 (1937) 3–31 (also published separately). [See p.374 above]

——, Review, in *CR* 63 (1949) 22–3, of Louis Delatte, *Les Traités de la Royauté d'Ecphante, Diotogène et Sthénidas* (Liège, 1942)

Chastagnol, André, FPRBE = *Les Fastes de la Préfecture de Rome au Bas-Empire* (Paris, 1962)

Childe, V. Gordon, *What Happened in History* (Pelican, 1942 & repr.)

——, *Man Makes Himself* (1936; 3rd edn, 1956 & repr.)

Chrimes [Atkinson], K. M. T., *Ancient Sparta* (1949)

Christensen, Arthur, *L'Iran sous les Sassanides*² (Copenhagen, 1944)

Christophe, Paul, *L'Usage chrétien du droit de propriété dans l'Écriture et la tradition patristique* (= Collection *Théologie, Pastorale et Spiritualité*, no. 14, Paris, 1964)

Citti, Vittorio, *Tragedia e lotta di classe in Grecia* (Naples, 1978)

Clarke, G. W., 'Barbarian disturbances in north Africa in the mid-third century', in *Antichthon* 4 (1970) 78–85

Clausing, Roth, *The Roman Colonate. The Theories of its Origin*, with an Introd. by Vladimir G. Simkhovitch (*Studia Historica* 17, New York, 1925; repr. Rome, 1965)

Clavel-Lévêque, Monique, *Marseille grecque. La dynamique d'un impérialisme marchand* (Marseilles, 1977), an expansion of 'Das griechische Marseille. Entwicklungsstufen und Dynamik einer Handelsmacht', in *Hellenische Poleis*, ed. E. Ch. Welskopf (Berlin, 1974) II.855–969

Clerc, M., *Les métèques athéniens* (Paris, 1893)

Cloché, Paul, *La restauration démocratique à Athènes en 403 avant J.-C.* (Paris, 1915)

Cohen, Benjamin, 'La notion d'"ordo" dans la Rome antique', in *Bulletin de l'Association G. Budé*, 4ᵉ Série, 2 (1975) 259–82

Cohen, G. A., *Karl Marx's Theory of History, A Defence* (1978; repr., with corrections, 1979)

——, 'On some criticisms of historical materialism', in *Proceedings of the Aristotelian Soc.* (Suppl. Vol.) 44 (1970) 121–41

——, 'Being, consciousness and roles: on the foundations of historical materialism', in *Essays in Honour of E. H. Carr*, ed. Chimen Abramsky (1974) 82–97

Coleman-Norton, P. R., RSCC I–III = *Roman State and Christian Church. A Collection of Legal Documents to A.D. 535*, 3 vols (1966). [Particularly useful indexes at end of Vol. III]

Coleman-Norton, P. R. (ed.), *Studies in Roman Economic and Social History in Honor of A. C. Johnson* (Princeton, 1951)

Colin, Gaston, *Rome et la Grèce de 200 à 146 av. J.-C.* (Paris, 1905)

Collinet, Paul, 'Le colonat dans l'Empire romain', in *Recueils de la Société Jean Bodin* II². *Le servage* (2nd rev. edn, Brussels, 1959) 85–120, with a 'Note complémentaire' by M. Pallasse, 121–8

Collingwood, R. G., and J. N. L. Myres, RBES² = *Roman Britain and the English Settlements*, 2nd edn (*Oxford History of England*, Vol. I, 1937 & repr.)

Collins, J. J., 'Jewish Apocalyptic against its Hellenistic Near Eastern environment', in *BASOR* 220 (December, 1975) 27–36

Connor, W. R., *The New Politicians of Fifth-Century Athens* (1971)

Coulborn, Rushton (ed.), *Feudalism in History* (1956). [See above, pp.267 and 596 n.4]

Courtois, Christian, VA = *Les Vandales et l'Afrique* (Paris, 1955)

Crawford, Dorothy, 'Imperial estates', in *Studies in Roman Property*, ed. M. I. Finley (1976) 35–70

Crawford, Michael H., *Roman Republican Coinage*, 2 vols (1974)

——, *The Roman Republic* (Fontana History of the Ancient World, 1978)

——, 'Finance, coinage and money from the Severans to Constantine', in *ANRW* II.ii (1975) 560–93

——, 'Republican denarii in Romania: the suppression of piracy and the slave-trade', in *JRS* 67 (1977) 117-24

——, 'Rome and the Greek world: economic relationships', in *Econ. Hist. Rev.*² 30 (1977) 42-52

Crook, J. A., *LLR = Law and Life of Rome* (1967)

Crossland, R. A., 'Hittite society and its economic basis', in *BICS* 14 (1967) 106-8

Dahrendorf, Ralf, *CCCIS = Class and Class Conflict in Industrial Society* (1959 & repr.), a revised and expanded version by the author himself of the German original, *Soziale Klassen und Klassenkonflikt in der industriellen Gesellschaft* (1957)

——, *ETS = Essays in the Theory of Society* (1968), including 'In praise of Thrasymachus', pp.129-50; and 'On the origin of inequality among men', pp.151-78, repr. also in Béteille (ed.), *SI* (see above) 16-44

Dandamayev, M., 'Achaemenid Babylonia', in *Ancient Mesopotamia, Socio-Economic History. A Collection of Studies by Soviet scholars*, ed. I. M. Diakonoff (Moscow, 1969) 296-311

Danilova, L. V., 'Controversial problems of the theory of precapitalist societies', in *Soviet Anthropology and Archaeology* 9 (1971) 269-328

D'Arms, J. H., 'Puteoli in the second century of the Roman Empire: a social and economic study', in *JRS* 64 (1974) 104-24

Daube, David, *Ancient Hebrew Fables* (1973, Inaugural Lecture of Oxford Centre for Postgraduate Studies)

——, 'Biblical landmarks in the struggle for women's rights', in *Juridical Review* 23 (1978) 177-97

——, 'Fashions and idiosyncrasies in the exposition of the Roman law of property', in *Theories of Property*, ed. A. Parel and T. Flanagan (Waterloo, Ontario, Canada, 1979) 35-50

David, Paul A., and others, *Reckoning with Slavery* (1976 & repr.), with an Introduction by Kenneth M. Stampp ('A humanist perspective', 1-30), and including Gavin Wright, 'Prosperity, progress, and American slavery', 302-36

Davies, J. K., *APF = Athenian Propertied Families 600-300 B.C.* (1971)

——, *Democracy and Classical Greece* (1978). [See p.600 n.3]

Davis, David Brion, *PSWC = The Problem of Slavery in Western Culture* (Ithaca, N.Y., 1966)

Davis, P. H., 'The Delos building contracts', in *BCH* 61 (1937) 109-35

Dawes, Elizabeth, and N. H. Baynes, *Three Byzantine Saints* (1948: Eng. trans. of the lives of Daniel the Stylite, Theodore of Sykeon, and John the Almsgiver, of Alexandria, with Notes)

Day, John, *EHARD = An Economic History of Athens under Roman Domination* (New York, 1942)

Debord, Pierre, 'L'esclavage sacré: État de la question', in *Actes du Colloque 1971 sur l'esclavage* (= *Annales littéraires de l'Univ. de Besançon* 140, Paris, 1972) 135-50

Degler, Carl N., 'Starr on slavery', in *JEH* 19 (1959) 271-7

Deininger, Jürgen, *Der politische Widerstand gegen Rom in Griechenland 217-86 v. Chr.* (Berlin, 1971). [See p.523]

Delatte, Louis, *Les Traités de la Royauté d'Ecphante, Diotogène et Sthénidas* (Liège, 1942) [And see above under Charlesworth]

Delehaye, H., *Les Saints Stylites* (= *Subsidia Hagiographica* 14, Brussels/Paris, 1923, repr. 1962)

Delz, Josef, *Lukians Kenntnis der athenischen Antiquitäten* (Diss., Basel, 1950)

De Martino, Francesco, *SCR² = Storia della costituzione romana*, 2nd edn (Naples, 1972-5): I² (1972), II² (1973), III² (1973), IV².i (1974) and ii (1975), V² (1975)

Dennett, D. C., *Conversion and the Poll-Tax in Early Islam* (= *Harvard Historical Monographs* 22, 1950)

Demougeot, Émilienne, MEFB = 'Modalités d'établissement des fédérés barbares de Gratien et de Théodose', in *Mélanges d'histoire ancienne offerts à William Seston* (Paris, 1974) 143-60

——, 'À propos des lètes gaulois du IVe siècle', in *Beiträge zur alten Geschichte und deren Nachleben. Festschrift für F. Altheim* (Berlin, 1970) II. 101-13

——, 'Laeti et Gentiles dans la Gaule du IVe siècle', in *Actes du Colloque d'histoire sociale 1970 (= Annales littéraires de l'Univ. de Besançon* 128, Paris, 1972) 101-12

——, *De l'unité à la division de l'Empire romain 395-410. Essai sur le gouvernement impériale* (Paris, 1951)

De Robertis, F. M., *Il diritto associativo romano* (Bari, 1938)

——, *Il fenomeno associativo nel mondo romano, dai collegi della Repubblica alle corporazioni del Basso Impero* (Naples, 1955)

——, *Lavoro e lavoratori nel mondo romano* (Bari, 1963)

——, *I rapporti di lavoro nel diritto romano* (Milan, 1946)

——, *Storia delle corporazioni e del regime associativo nel mondo romano*, 2 vols (Bari, 1971)

Derow, P. S., 'Polybios and the embassy of Kallikrates', in *Essays Presented to C. M. Bowra* (1970) 12-23

De Visscher, F., *Les édits d'Auguste découverts à Cyrène* (Louvain, 1940)

——, 'La justice romaine en Cyrénaïque', in *RIDA*³ 11 (1964) 321-33

——, 'Le statut juridique des nouveaux citoyens romains et l'inscription de Rhosos', in *Ant. Class.* 13 (1944) 11-35; and 14 (1945) 29-59

Diakonoff, I. M. (ed.), *Ancient Mesopotamia, Socio-Economic History. A Collection of Studies by Soviet Scholars* (Moscow, 1969)

Dobb, Maurice, *On Economic Theory and Socialism* (1955 & repr.)

——, *Political Economy and Capitalism* (1937 & repr.)

Dover, (Sir) Kenneth J., *GPM = Greek Popular Morality in the Time of Plato and Aristotle* (1974)

——, in Gomme, *HCT* IV (*q.v.*)

Downey, Glanville, *HAS = A History of Antioch in Syria from Seleucus to the Arab Conquest* (Princeton, 1961)

——, 'The economic crisis at Antioch under Julian', in *Studies in Roman Economic and Social History in Honor of A. C. Johnson*, ed. P. R. Coleman-Norton (Princeton, 1951) 312-21

Drake, H. A., 'When was the "de laudibus Constantini" delivered?', in *Historia* 24 (1975) 345-56

——, *In Praise of Constantine: A Historical Study and New Translation of Eusebius' Tricennial Orations (= Univ. of California Publications: Class. Stud.* 15, Berkeley/London, 1976)

Dräseke, J., 'Der kanonische Brief des Gregorios von Neocäsarea', in *Jahrbuch für protestantische Theologie* 7 (1881) 724-56

Duchesne, Louis, *L'Église au VIe siècle* (Paris, 1925)

——, *Le Liber Pontificalis*, 2nd edn (Paris) I and II (1955), III (1957); the first edition, in two vols, was published in 1886-92

Dudden, F. Homes: see under Homes Dudden, F.

Duff, A. M., *FERE = Freedmen in the Early Roman Empire* (1928; repr., with corrections and additions, 1958)

Dumont, Louis, *Homo Hierarchicus. The Caste System and its Implications* (1970, Eng. trans. from the French original of 1966)

Dunbabin, T. J., *WG = The Western Greeks. The History of Sicily and South Italy from the Foundation of the Greek Colonies to 480 B.C.* (1948)

Duncan-Jones, Richard P., *EREQS = The Economy of the Roman Empire: Quantitative Studies* (1974)

——, 'Two possible indices of the purchasing power of money in Greek and Roman antiquity', in *Les 'Dévaluations' à Rome, Époque républicaine et impériale (Collection de l'École française de Rome* 37, Rome, 1978) 159-68

——, 'The *choenix*, the *artaba* and the *modius*', in *ZPE* 21 (1976) 43-52; and 'The size of the *modius castrensis*', ibid. 53-62

——, 'The price of wheat in Roman Egypt under the Principate', in *Chiron* 6 (1976) 241-62

——, 'Pay and numbers in Diocletian's army', in *Chiron* 8 (1978) 541-60

Dupré, Georges, and Pierre-Philippe Rey, RPTHE = 'Reflections on the pertinence of a theory of the history of exchange', in *Economy and Society* 2 (1973) 131-63 (Eng. trans. by Elizabeth Hindess from the French original, in *Cahiers internationaux de sociologie* 46 [1968] 133-62)

Dvornik, F., *ECBPP* = *Early Christian and Byzantine Political Philosophy: Origins and Background*, 2 vols (1966)

——, 'Pope Gelasius and Emperor Anastasius I', in *Byz. Ztschr.* 44 (1951) 111-16

Dyson, Stephen L., 'Native revolts in the Roman Empire', in *Historia* 20 (1971) 239-74; and 'Native revolt patterns in the Roman Empire', in *ANRW* II.iii (1975) 138-75

Eadie, J. W., *The Breviarium of Festus* (1967)

Eddy, S. K., *The King is Dead. Studies in the Near Eastern Resistance to Hellenism 334-31 B.C.* (Lincoln, Nebraska, 1961)

Ehrenberg, Victor, *PA²* = *The People of Aristophanes*, 2nd edn (1951)

Eisenstadt, S. N., *Max Weber on Charisma and Institution Building* (1968)

Eldridge, J. E. T., *MWISR* = *Max Weber: The Interpretation of Social Reality* (1971; paperback repr., 1972)

Emerton, J. A., 'The problem of vernacular Hebrew in the first century A.D. and the language of Jesus', in *JTS* n.s. 24 (1973) 1-23

Engels, Donald, 'The problem of female infanticide in the Greco-Roman world', in *CP* 75 (1980) 112-20

Engels, Friedrich/Frederick, *OFPPS* = *The Origin of the Family, Private Property and the State* (Eng. trans. from *Der Ursprung der Familie, des Privateigenthums und des Staats*, of 1884), cited here from pp.449-583 of *MESW* (see below, under Marx [and Engels])

——, 'The peasant question in France and Germany', cited here from *MESW* 623-40 (Eng. trans. from the German original of 1894)

——, Travel notes, 'From Paris to Berne' (1848, published in German 1898-9), cited here from *MECW* (see below, under Marx [and Engels]) VII.507-29 (Eng. trans.)

Enzensberger, Hans Magnus, [*Selected*] *Poems* (cited from Penguin Modern European Poets edn, 1968)

Evans-Pritchard, E. E., *Essays in Social Anthropology* (1962; cited from paperback edn, 1969)

Fantham, Elaine, '*Aequabilitas* in Cicero's political theory, and the Greek tradition of proportional justice', in *CQ* 67 = n.s. 23 (1973) 285-90

Farrington, Benjamin, *Diodorus Siculus: Universal Historian* (Inaugural Lecture, Swansea, 1936, published 1937) = *Head and Hand in Ancient Greece* (1947) 55-87

Faure, Edgar, 'Saint Ambroise et l'expulsion des pérégrins de Rome', in *Études d'histoire du droit canonique dédiées à Gabriel Le Bras*, 2 vols (Paris, 1965) I.523-40

Fears, J. Rufus, *Princeps a diis electus: The Divine Election of the Emperor as a Political Concept at Rome* (= *Papers and Monographs of the American Academy in Rome* 26, 1977). [See p.633 n.72a above]

Ferguson, W. S., *HA* = *Hellenistic Athens* (1911)

Fiebig, P., '*Angareuō*', in *ZNW* 18 (1917-18) 64-72

Fikhman, I. F., 'On the structure of the Egyptian large estate in the sixth century', in *Proc. XII Internat. Congress of Papyrology* = *American Stud. in Papyrology* 7 (Toronto, 1970) 127-32

——, 'Slaves in Byzantine Oxyrhynchus', in *Akten des XIII* [*1971*] *Internat. Papyrologenkongr.*, ed. E. Kiessling and H.-A. Rupprecht (1974) 117-24

——, 'Quelques données sur la genèse de la grande propriété foncière a Oxyrhynchus', in *Le Monde Grec. Hommages à Claire Préaux*, ed. J. Bingen and others (1975) 784-90

Finkelstein [Finley], M. I., '*Emporos, nauklēros* and *kapēlos*: a prolegomena to the study of Athenian trade', in *CP* 30 (1935) 320-36

Finley (Sir) Moses I., *AE* = *The Ancient Economy* (1973)

——, BSF = 'Between slavery and freedom', in *CSSH* 6 (1964) 233-49

——, SD = 'La servitude pour dettes', in *RHDFE*[4] 43 (1965) 159-84

——, SSAG = 'The servile statuses of Ancient Greece', in *RIDA*[3] 7 (1960) 165-89

——, WGCBSL = 'Was Greek civilisation based on slave labour?', in *Historia* 8 (1959) 145-64, repr. in *SCA*, ed. Finley (see below) 53-72

——, 'Athenian demagogues', in *Past & Present* 21 (1962) 3-24, repr. in *SAS*, ed. Finley (see below) 1-25

——, 'The fifth-century Athenian Empire: a balance sheet', in *Imperialism in the Ancient World*, ed. P. D. A. Garnsey and C. R. Whittaker (1978) 103-26, 306-10. [See above, pp.602-3 n.24, and 604-5 n.27]

——, 'Technical innovation and economic progress in the Ancient World', in *Econ. Hist. Rev.*[2] 18 (1965) 29-45

——, 'Private farm tenancy in Italy before Diocletian', in *Studies in Roman Property*, ed. Finley (see below) 103-21, 188-90

——, Review, in *JRS* 48 (1958) 156-64, of A. E. R. Boak, *Manpower Shortage and the Fall of the Roman Empire in the West* (1955)

——, *Ancient Slavery and Modern Ideology* (1980) [I did not see this book before mine was finished]

Finley, M. I. (editor), *PTGA = Problèmes de la terre en Grèce ancienne* (Paris, 1973)

——, *SCA = Slavery in Classical Antiquity. Views and Controversies* (1960)

——, *SAS = Studies in Ancient Society* (1974)

——, *SRP = Studies in Roman Property* (1976)

Firth, (Sir) Raymond, 'The sceptical anthropologist?', in *PBA* 58 (1972) 177-213, repr. in *Marxist Analyses and Social Anthropology*, ed. Maurice Bloch (1975); also published separately

Fitzhugh, George, *Sociology for the South, or The Failure of Free Society* (Richmond, Virginia, 1854)

Flam-Zuckermann, Léa, 'À propos d'une inscription de Suisse (*CIL* XIII, 5010): étude du phénomène du brigandage dans l'Empire romain', in *Latomus* 29 (1970) 451-73

Fliche, A., and V. Martin (editors), *Histoire de l'Église* (Paris) III (1947), IV (1948), V (1947)

Flusser, David, 'Blessed are the poor in spirit', in *IEJ* 10 (1960) 1-13

Fogel, R. W., and S. L. Engerman, *TC or TC I = Time on the Cross. The Economics of American Negro Slavery* I (1974)

Follet, Simone, *Athènes au II*[e] *et au III*[e] *siècle. Études chronologiques et prosopographiques* (Paris, 1976)

——, 'Lettre de Marc-Aurèle aux Athéniens (*EM* 13366): nouvelles lectures et interprétations', in *Rev. de phil.* 53 (1979) 29-43

Forbes, R. J., *Studies in Ancient Technology* II[2] (1965), esp. 80-130

——, Chapter xvii in *History of Technology* II (1956), ed. Charles Singer and others

Forni, G., 'Intorno alle costituzioni di città greche in Italia e in Sicilia', in Κωκαλός 3 (1957) 61-9

Forrest, W. G., *EGD = The Emergence of Greek Democracy. The Character of Greek Politics 800-400 B.C.* (1966)

——, 'Themistocles and Argos', in *CQ* 54 = n.s. 10 (1960) 221-41

Foss, Clive, 'The Persians in Asia Minor and the end of Antiquity', in *Eng. Hist. Rev.* 90 (1975) 721-47

Francotte, H., *IGA = L'Industrie dans la Grèce ancienne*, 2 vols (Brussels, 1900-1)

——, 'Industrie und Handel' [Greek], in *RE* IX (1916) 1381-1439

Frank, Tenney, editor and part author of *ESAR* I-V = *Economic Survey of Ancient Rome*, 5 vols (and Index)

Fraser, Peter M., *PA = Ptolemaic Alexandria*, 3 vols (1972)

Frederiksen, Martin W., *CCPD = 'Caesar, Cicero and the problem of debt', in *JRS* 56 (1966) 128-41

——, 'The contribution of archaeology to the agrarian problem in the Gracchan period', in *Dialoghi di Archeologia* 4-5 (1970-71) 330-57 (with 358-67)

Frend, W. H. C., *DC* = *The Donatist Church* (1952; improved repr., 1971)

——, *EC* = *The Early Church* (1965)

——, *MPEC* = *Martyrdom and Persecution in the Early Church* (1965)

——, 'The *cellae* of the African Circumcellions', in *JTS* n.s. 3 (1952) 87–90

——, 'Circumcellions and monks', in *JTS* n.s. 20 (1969) 542–9

Friedländer, Ludwig, *Darstellungen aus der Sittengeschichte Roms in der Zeit von August bis zum Ausgang der Antonine*, 4 vols, 9th/10th edns (Leipzig, 1919–21)

Frier, B. W., 'The rental market in early Imperial Rome', in *JRS* 67 (1977) 27–37

Fritz, Kurt von, *The Theory of the Mixed Constitution in Antiquity. A Critical Analysis of Polybius' Political Ideas* (New York, 1954)

——, 'The reorganisation of the Roman government in 366 B.C. and the so-called Licinio-Sextian laws', in *Historia* 1 (1950) 3–44

Frye, R. N., *The Heritage of Persia*, 2nd edn (1976)

Fuchs, Harald, *Der geistige Widerstand gegen Rom in der antiken Welt* (Berlin, 1938, repr. 1964)

Fuks, Alexander, *ISESG* = 'Isocrates and the social-economic situation in Greece', in *Anc. Soc.* 3 (1972) 17–44

——, *PSQ* = 'Plato and the social question: the problem of poverty and riches in the *Republic*', in *Anc. Soc.* 8 (1977) 49–83

——, 'Plato and the social question: the problem of poverty and riches in the *Laws*', in *Anc. Soc.* 10 (1979) 33–78. [See above, p.550 n.4a]

——, 'The Bellum Achaicum and its social aspect', in *JHS* 90 (1970) 78–89

——, '*Kolōnos misthios*: labour exchange in Classical Athens', in *Eranos* 49 (1951) 171–3

——, 'Patterns and types of social-economic revolution in Greece from the fourth to the second century B.C.', in *Anc. Soc.* 5 (1974) 51–81

——, 'Social revolution in Greece in the Hellenistic age', in *La parola del passato* 111 (1966) 437–48

——, 'Social revolution in Dyme in 116–114 B.C.E.', in *Scripta Hierosolymitana* 23 (1972) 21–7

Fustel de Coulanges, 'Le colonat romain', in his *Recherches sur quelques problèmes d'histoire* (Paris, 1885) 1–186

Gabba, Emilio, *SCSEV* = 'Sui senati delle città siciliane nell'età di Verre', in *Athenaeum* n.s. 37 (1959) 304–20

Gabrieli, Francesco, *Muhammad and the Conquests of Islam*, Eng. trans. by V. Luling and R. Linell (1968)

Gagé, Jean, *Res Gestae Divi Augusti*, 2nd edn (Paris, 1950)

Gallivan, P. A., 'The false Neros: a re-examination', in *Historia* 22 (1973) 364–5

Ganshof, F. L., *SPCBE* = 'Le statut personnel du colon au Bas-Empire. Observations en marge d'une théorie nouvelle', in *Ant. Class.* 14 (1945) 261–77

Garnsey, Peter D. A., *ADUAE* = 'Aspects of the decline of the urban aristocracy in the Empire', in *ANRW* II.i (1974) 229–52

——, *DFLP* = 'Descendants of freedmen in local politics: some criteria', in *The Ancient Historian and his Materials* (Essays in Honour of C. E. Stevens), ed. Barbara Levick (1975) 167–80

——, *LPRE* = 'Legal privilege in the Roman Empire', in *Past & Present* 41 (1968) 3–24, repr. in *SAS*, ed. Finley (1974) 141–65

——, *PARS* = 'Peasants in Ancient Roman society', in *Jnl of Peasant Studies* 3 (1976) 221–35

——, *SSLPRE* = *Social Status and Legal Privilege in the Roman Empire* (1970)

——, 'The criminal jurisdiction of governors', in *JRS* 58 (1968) 51–9

——, 'The *Lex Iulia* and appeal under the Empire', in *JRS* 56 (1966) 167–89

——, 'Introduction' (pp.1–5) and 'Non-slave labour in the Roman world' (pp.34–47), in *Non-Slave Labour in the Greco-Roman World* (= Cambridge Philol. Soc., Suppl. Vol. 6, 1980), ed. Garnsey

——, 'Rome's African empire under the Principate', in *Imperialism in the Anc. World*, ed. Garnsey and C. R. Whittaker (1978) 223–54, 343–54

——, 'Where did Italian peasants live?', in *PCPS* n.s. 25 (1979) 1-25

——, 'Why penal laws become harsher: the Roman case', in *Natural Law Forum* 13 (Indiana, 1968) 141-62

Garnsey, Peter (ed.), *Non-Slave Labour in the Greco-Roman World* (1980: see under Garnsey above)

Garnsey, P. D. A., and C. R. Whittaker (editors), *Imperialism in the Ancient World* (1978)

Gaudemet, Jean, *EER = L'Église dans l'empire romain (IVᵉ-Vᵉ siècles)* (Paris, 1958)

——, 'Constantin et les Curies municipales', in *Iura* 2 (1951) 44-75

——, 'La décision de Callixte en matière de mariage', in *Studi in onore di Ugo Enrico Paoli* (Florence, 1955) 333-44

Geagan, Daniel J., *ACS = The Athenian Constitution after Sulla* (= *Hesperia* Suppl. XII, 1967)

Gellner, Ernest, 'The Soviet and the savage', in *TLS* 3789 (18 October 1974) 1166-8

Gelzer, Matthias, *SBVA = Studien zur byzantinischen Verwaltung Ägyptens* (= *Leipziger historische Abhandlungen* XIII, Leipzig, 1909)

——, 'Altes und Neues aus der byzantinisch-ägyptischen Verwaltungsmisere', in *Archiv f. Pap.* 5 (1913) 346-77, esp. 370-7; cf. 188-9

——, *The Roman Nobility* (1969), Eng. trans. by Robin Seager from *Die Nobilität der römischen Republik* (1912), repr. in Gelzer, *Kleine Schriften* I (Wiesbaden, 1962) 1-135

Genovese, Eugene D., *PES = The Political Economy of Slavery. Studies in the Economy and Society of the Slave South* (U.S.A., 1965 & repr., cited from the First Vintage Books paperback edn, 1967)

——, *RB = In Red and Black: Marxian Explorations in Southern and Afro-American History* (U.S.A., 1968 & repr., cited from the First Vintage Books paperback edn, 1972)

——, *RJR = Roll, Jordan, Roll. The World the Slaves Made* (U.S.A. 1974; London, 1975)

George, Katherine and C. H., 'Roman Catholic sainthood and social status', in Bendix-Lipset, *CSP²* (*q.v.*, above) 394-401, a revised repr. from *Jnl of Religion* 5 (1953-5) 33 ff.

Gerth, H. H., and C. Wright Mills (editors), *FMW = From Max Weber: Essays in Sociology*, trans. and ed. with Introd. by Gerth and Mills (1946 & repr., cited from the O.U.P. paperback edn, 1958 & repr.)

Giacchero, Marta, *Edictum Diocletiani et Collegarum de pretiis rerum venalium*, 2 vols (= *Pubbl.* dell'Istituto di storia antica e scienze ausiliare dell' Università di Genova VIII, Genoa, 1974)

Gibbon, Edward, *DFRE = The Decline and Fall of the Roman Empire* (1776-88), cited from the standard edn in 7 vols by J. B. Bury (1896-1900 & repr.)

——, *Memoirs of my Life*, ed. G. A. Bonnard (1966)

Giglioni, Gabriella Bodei: see under Bodei Giglioni

Gilliam, J. F., 'The minimum subject to the *vicesima hereditatium*', in *AJP* 73 (1952) 397-405

——, 'The plague under Marcus Aurelius', in *AJP* 82 (1961) 225-51

Gillis, Daniel, 'Murder on Melos', in *Istituto Lombardo, Rend. Lett.* 112 (1978) 185-211

——, 'The Revolt at Mytilene', in *AJP* 92 (1971) 38-47

Girardet, Klaus M., *Kaisergericht und Bischofsgericht* (= *Antiquitas* I.21, Bonn, 1975)

——, 'Kaiser Konstantius II. als "Episcopus Episcoporum" und das Herrscherbild des kirchlichen Widerstandes', in *Historia* 26 (1977) 95-128

Glotz, Gustave, *GC = The Greek City and its Institutions* (Eng. trans., 1929, from *La Cité grecque*, Paris, 1928) [And see p.599 n.24 above]

——, 'Les salaires à Délos', in *Jnl des Savants* 11 (1913) 206-15, 251-60

——, *Mélanges Gustave Glotz*, 2 vols (Paris, 1932)

Glotz, Gustave, P. Roussel and R. Cohen, *HG* IV.i = *Histoire grecque* IV.i (Paris, 1938)

Godelier, Maurice, *RIE = Rationality and Irrationality in Economics* (1972), trans. Brian Pearce from *Rationalité et irrationalité en économie* (Paris, 1966)

Gogh, Vincent Van: see under Van Gogh

Golubcova, E. S.: see under Blavatskaja, T. V.

Gomme, A. W., *HCT* IV = *A Historical Commentary on Thucydides*, by A. W. Gomme, A. Andrewes and K. J. Dover, Vol. IV (Books V.25-VII) (1970)

Gomme, A. W., and F. H. Sandbach, *Menander. A Commentary* (1973) [See p.571 nn.54–5]

Goodenough, E. R., 'The political philosophy of Hellenistic kingship', in *YCS* 1 (1928) 53–102

Gordon, C. D., *The Age of Attila* (Ann Arbor, 1960)

Gordon, Mary L., 'The freedman's son in municipal life', in *JRS* 21 (1931) 65–77

Gould, John, 'Law, custom and myth: aspects of the social position of women in Classical Athens', in *JHS* 100 (1980) 38–59

Graham, H. F., 'The significant role of the study of Ancient History in the Soviet Union', in *The Classical World* 61 (1967) 85–97

Graindor, P., *Un milliardaire antique, Hérode Atticus et sa famille* (Cairo, 1930)

Green, Robert W. (ed.), *Protestantism and Capitalism. The Weber Thesis and its Critics* (Boston, 1959)

Greene, Jack P., *All Men are Created Equal. Some Reflections on the Character of the American Revolution* (Inaugural Lecture as Harmsworth Professor, Oxford, 1976)

Greenidge, A. H. J., and A. M. Clay (editors), *Sources*² = *Sources for Roman History 133–70 B.C.*, 2nd edn, rev. by E. W. Gray (1960)

Greenidge, C. W. W., *Slavery* (1958)

Greenslade, S. L., *Schism in the Early Church*, 2nd edn (1964)

Gregg, Pauline, *Free-Born John, A Biography of John Lilburne* (1961)

Griffin, Miriam, *Seneca* (1976)

Griffith, G.T., 'Athens in the fourth century', in *Imperialism in the Ancient World*, ed. P. D. A. Garnsey and C. R. Whittaker (1978) 127–44, 310–14

——, Pp.201–646, 675 ff, of N. G. L. Hammond and Griffith, *A History of Macedonia, II.550–336 B.C.* (1979), on Philip II

——, 'Isegoria in the Assembly at Athens', in *Anc. Society and Institutions: Studies Pres. to Victor Ehrenberg* (1966) 115–38

——, *The Mercenaries of the Hellenistic World* (1935)

——, 'The union of Corinth and Argos (392–386 B.C.)' in *Historia* 1 (1950) 236–56

Grote, George, *HG* = *History of Greece*, 10 vols (New edn, 1888)

Gruen, E. S., 'Class conflict and the Third Macedonian War', in *AJAH* 1 (1976) 29–60 [See above, pp.524, 659–60 nn.2,4]

Gsell, Stéphane, *ERAR* = 'Esclaves ruraux dans l'Afrique romaine', in *Mélanges Gustave Glotz* (Paris, 1932) I.397–415

Günther, Rigobert, *ULGG* = 'Einige neue Untersuchungen zu den Laeten und Gentilen in Gallien im 4. Jahrhundert und zu ihrer historischen Bedeutung', in *Klio* 58 (1976) 311–21

——, 'Laeti, foederati und Gentilen in Nord- und Nordostgallien im Zusammenhang mit der sogenannten Laetenzivilisation', in *Ztschr. für Archäologie* 5 (1971) 39–59

——, 'Die sozialen Träger der frühen Reihengräberkultur in Belgien und Nordfrankreich im 4./5. Jahrhundert', in *Helinium* 12 (1972) 268–72

Guiraud, Paul, *La main-d'oeuvre industrielle dans l'ancienne Grèce* (Paris, 1900)

Gummerus, H., 'Industrie und Handel' [Roman], in *RE* IX (1916) 1439–1535

Guthrie, W. K. C., *HGP* III = *History of Greek Philosophy* III (1959)

Habicht, Christian, 'Die herrschende Gesellschaft in den hellenistischen Monarchien', in *Vierteljahrschrift für Sozial- und Wirtschaftsgeschichte* 45 (1958) 1–16

——, 'Zwei neue Inschriften aus Pergamon', in *Instanbuler Mitteilungen* 9/10 (Deutsches Archäologisches Institut, Abteilung Istanbul, 1960) 109–27

Haldon, John F., *Recruitment and Conscription in the Byzantine Army c. 550–950. A Study on the Origins of the Stratiotika Ktemata* (= *Sb* 357, Österreichische Akad. der Wiss., Philos.-hist. Klasse, Vienna, 1979)

Hammond, N. G. L., and G. T. Griffith: see under Griffith

Hands, A. R., *Charities and Social Aid in Greece and Rome* (1968)

Hanke, Lewis, *AAI* = *Aristotle and the American Indians. A Study in Race Prejudice in the Modern World* (1959)

Hansen, Mogens Herman, '*Demos, ecclesia* and *dicasterion* in Classical Athens', in *GRBS* 19 (1978) 127-46

———, 'Did the Athenian *ecclesia* legislate after 403/2 B.C.?', in *GRBS* 20 (1979) 27-53

———, 'The duration of a meeting of the Athenian *ecclesia*', in *CP* 74 (1979) 43-9

———, 'How did the Athenian *ecclesia* vote?', in *GRBS* 18 (1977) 123-37

———, 'How often did the Athenian *dicasteria* meet?' in *GRBS* 20 (1979) 243-6

———, 'How often did the *ecclesia* meet?' in *GRBS* 18 (1977) 43-70

———, 'How many Athenians attended the *ecclesia*?', in *GRBS* 17 (1976) 115-34

———, '*Misthos* for magistrates in Classical Athens', in *Symbolae Osloenses* 54 (1979) 5-22

———, '*Nomos* and *psephisma* in fourth-century Athens', in *GRBS* 19 (1978) 315-30

———, 'Perquisites for magistrates in fourth-century Athens', in *Classica et Mediaevalia* 32 (1980) 105-25

———, 'Seven hundred *archai* in Classical Athens', in *GRBS* 21 (1980) 151-73

———, *The Sovereignty of the People's Court in Athens in the Fourth Century B.C. and the Public Action against Unconstitutional Proposals* (= *Odense Univ. Classical Studies* 4, 1974)

Hardy, E. R., *LEBE* = *The Large Estates of Byzantine Egypt* (= Columbia Univ. *Studies in History, Economics and Public Law* no.354, New York, 1931)

Harmand, Louis, *Libanius, Discours sur les Patronages* (= Publ. de la Faculté des Lettres de l'Univ. de Clermont, 2ᵉ Série, Fasc. 1, Paris, 1955)

———, *Le Patronat sur les collectivités publiques des origines au Bas-Empire* (= Publ. de . . . Clermont, 2ᵉ Série, Fasc. 2, Paris, 1957)

Harper, G. M., 'Village administration in the Roman province of Syria', in *YCS* 1 (1928) 103-68

Harrington, James, *The Political Works of James Harrington*, ed. J. G. A. Pocock (1977)

———, *The Oceana of James Harrington and his Other Works*, ed. John Toland (1700)

Harris, Marvin, *The Rise of Anthropological Theory* (1969 & repr.)

Harris, W. V., *REU* = *Rome in Etruria and Umbria* (1971)

———, *War and Imperialism in Republican Rome 327-70 B.C.* (1979)

———, 'On war and greed in the second century B.C.', in *AHR* 76 (1971) 1371-85

Harrison, A. R. W., *The Law of Athens, I. The Family and Property* (1968)

Harrison, Royden, 'E. S. Beesly and Karl Marx', in *IRSH* 4 (1959) 22-58, 208-38

———, 'Professor Beesly and the working-class movement', in *Essays in Labour History*, ed. Asa Briggs and John Saville (rev. edn, 1967) I.205-41

Harvey, F. David, 'Two kinds of equality', in *Classica et Mediaevalia* 26 (1965) 101-46, with the corrections and addenda in id. 27 (1966) 99-100

———, 'Literacy in the Athenian democracy', in *REG* 79 (1966) 585-635

Hassall, Mark, Michael Crawford, and Joyce Reynolds, 'Rome and the eastern provinces at the end of the second century B.C. The so-called "Piracy Law" and a new inscription from Cnidos', in *JRS* 64 (1974) 195-220

Hatzfeld, Jean, *Alc.*² = *Alcibiade. Étude sur l'histoire d'Athènes à la fin du Vᵉ siècle*, 2nd edn (Paris, 1951)

———, *Les trafiquants Italiens dans l'Orient Hellénique* (*BEFAR* 115, Paris, 1919)

Haywood, R. M., *TSCD* = 'Some traces of serfdom in Cicero's day', in *AJP* 54 (1933) 145-53

Hefele, C. J., and H. Leclercq, *HC* = *Histoire des Conciles d'après les documents originaux* (Paris), I.i (1907) and III.i (1909)

Heinen, Heinz, 'Neuere sowjetische Monographien zur Geschichte des Altertums', in *Historia* 24 (1975) 378-84

———, 'Neuere sowjetische Veröffentlichungen zur antiken Sklaverei', in *Historia* 25 (1976) 501-5, and 28 (1979) 125-8

———, 'Zur Sklaverei in der hellenistischen Welt I & II', in *Anc. Soc.* 7 (1976) 127-49, and 8 (1977) 121-54

———, Review, in *Riv. stor. dell'Antich.* 5 (1975) 229-33, of L. Iraci Fedeli, *Marx e il mondo antico* (Milan, 1972)

———, 'Sur le régime du travail dans l'Égypte ptolémaïque au IIIᵉ siècle av. J.-C., à propos d'un livre recent de N. N. Pikus', in *Le Monde Grec. Hommages à Claire Préaux* (Brussels, 1975) 656-62

Heitland, W. E., *Agricola* (1921)

Held, Wieland, 'Das Ende der progressiven Entwicklung des Kolonates am Ende des 2. und in der ersten Hälfte des 3. Jahrhunderts im Römischen Imperium', in *Klio* 53 (1971) 239-79. [I did not see this article until after this book was finished]

Helen, Tapio, *Organisation of Roman Brick Production in the First and Second Centuries A.D. An Interpretation of Roman Brick Stamps* = *Annales Academiae Scientiarum Fennicae Dissertationes Humanarum Litterarum* 5 (Helsinki, 1975)

Henry, Patrick, 'A mirror for Justinian: the *Ekthesis* of Agapetus Diaconus', in *GRBS* 8 (1967) 281-308

Hicks, (Sir) John, *TEH* = *A Theory of Economic History* (1969). [See pp.83-4 above]

Hill, Christopher, and Edmund Dell (editors), *The Good Old Cause. The English Revolution of 1640-1660, Its Causes, Course and Consequences*, 2nd edn, revised (1969)

Hilton, Rodney H., *BMMF* = *Bond Men Made Free. Medieval Peasant Movements and the English Rising of 1381* (1973)

——, *EPLMA* = *The English Peasantry in the Later Middle Ages* (1975)

——, *DSME* = *The Decline of Serfdom in Medieval England* (1969)

——, *TFC* = *The Transition from Feudalism to Capitalism* (Foundations of History Library, London, 1976, with Introduction by Rodney Hilton)

Hilton, Rodney H., and P. H. Sawyer, 'Technical determinism: the stirrup and the plough', in *Past & Present* 24 (1963) 90-100

Hinton, William, *Fanshen. A Documentary of Revolution in a Chinese Village* (1966 & repr.)

Hitti, Philip K., *History of the Arabs from the Earliest Times to the Present*, 10th edn (1970)

Hobbes, Thomas, *Leviathan* (1651; there are several modern editions)

Hobsbawm, E. J., *KMPCEF* = *Karl Marx. Pre-Capitalist Economic Formations*, Eng. trans. by Jack Cohen, with Introduction by Hobsbawm (1964 & repr.)

——, 'Karl Marx's contribution to historiography', in *Ideology in Social Science*, ed. Robin Blackburn (1972) 265-83

——, 'Class consciousness in history', in *Aspects of History and Class Consciousness*, ed. Istvan Mészáros (1971) 5-21. [And see p.624 n.13 above]

Hoesen, H. B. van, and A. C. Johnson: see under van Hoesen below

Hoffmann, Dietrich, *Das spätrömische Bewegungsheer und die Notitia Dignitatum*, 2 vols (= *Epigraphische Studien* 7, Düsseldorf, 1969-70). [See p.657 n.11 above]

Homes Dudden, F., *Gregory the Great. His Place in History and Thought*, 2 vols (1905)

——, *The Life and Times of St. Ambrose*, 2 vols (1935)

Hommel, H., 'Metoikoi', in *RE* XV.ii (1932) 1413-58

Homo, L., *Primitive Italy and the Beginnings of Roman Imperialism* (Eng. trans., 1927)

Honoré, A. M./Tony, *Tribonian* (1978)

——, 'The Severan lawyers: a preliminary survey', in *SDHI* 28 (1962) 162-232

Hopkins, Keith, *EMRE* = 'Elite mobility in the Roman Empire', in *Past & Present* 32 (1965), repr. in (and cited here from) *SAS*, ed. Finley (1974) 103-20

——, *PASRP* = 'On the probable age structure of the Roman population', in *Population Studies* 20 (1966) 245-64

——, *Conquerors and Slaves. Sociological Studies in Roman History*, Vol. I (1978)

Hopper, R. J., *The Basis of the Athenian Democracy* (= Inaugural Lecture, Sheffield Univ., 1957)

Hunt, Richard N., *The Political Ideas of Marx and Engels, I. Marxism and Totalitarian Democracy, 1818-1850* (Pittsburgh, 1974; London, 1975)

Ihering, Rudolf von, *Scherz und Ernst in der Jurisprudenz*, 8th edn (Leipzig, 1900), esp. 175-232

Institut Fernand Courby: Indexes to L. and J. Robert's 'Bulletins épigraphiques' in *REG* (etc.), from 1938 onwards, 4 vols (Paris, 1972-9)

Irmscher, Johannes, 'Friedrich Engels studiert Altertumswissenschaft', in *Eirene* 2 (1964) 7-42

Jacynowska, Maria, 'The economic differentiation of the Roman nobility at the end of the Republic', in *Historia* 11 (1962) 486-99

Jameson, Michael H., 'Agriculture and slavery in Classical Athens', in *CJ* 73 (1977-8) 122-45. [See p.506 above]

Jeffery, L. H., *LSAG* = *The Local Scripts of Archaic Greece* (1961)

——, 'The pact of the first settlers at Cyrene', in *Historia* 10 (1961) 139-47

Johnson, A. C., *Roman Egypt* = *ESAR* (ed. Tenney Frank) II (1936)

[——,] *Studies in Roman Economic and Social History in Honor of A. C. Johnson*, ed. P. R. Coleman-Norton (Princeton, 1951)

Johnson, A. C., and L. C. West, *Byzantine Egypt: Economic Studies* (Princeton, 1949)

Jolowicz, H. F., and Barry Nicholas, *HISRL*³ = *Historical Introduction to the Study of Roman Law*, 3rd edn (1972)

Jones, A. H. M., *AD* = *The Athenian Democracy* (1957)

——, *CERP*² = *The Cities of the Eastern Roman Provinces*, 2nd edn, revised (1971; the 1st edn was in 1937)

——, CLIE = 'Civitates liberae et immunes in the East', in *Anatolian Studies pres. to W. H. Buckler*, ed. W. M. Calder and Josef Keil (1939) 103-17

——, *GCAJ* = *The Greek City from Alexander to Justinian* (1940)

——, *LRE* = *The Later Roman Empire 284-602*, 3 vols, plus a vol. of maps (1964)

——, NH = 'Numismatics and History', in *Essays pres. to Harold Mattingly*, ed. R. A. G. Carson and C. H. V. Sutherland (1956), repr. in Jones, *RE* (see below) 61-81 (with addendum by M. H. Crawford)

——, RC = 'The Roman Colonate', in *Past & Present* 13 (1958) 1-13, repr. in Jones, *RE* (see below) 293-307, and in *SAS* (ed. Finley) 288-303 (with improvements in the notes by Dorothy Crawford: see *SAS* p.x)

——, RCS = 'The Roman civil service (clerical and sub-clerical grades)', in *JRS* 39 (1949) 38-55, repr. in Jones, *SRGL* (see below) 151-75, 201-13

——, *RE* = *The Roman Economy. Studies in Ancient Economic and Administrative History*, ed. P. A. Brunt (1974)

——, SAW = 'Slavery in the Ancient World', in *Econ. Hist. Rev.*² 9 (1956) 185-99, repr. in *SCA* (ed. Finley) 1-15

——, *SRGL* = *Studies in Roman Government and Law* (1960)

——, 'Ancient empires and the economy: Rome', in *Third Internat. Conf. of Econ. Hist.* [Munich, 1965] III (1969) 81-104, repr. in Jones, *RE* (see above) 114-39

——, 'Church finance in the fifth and sixth centuries', in *JTS* n.s. 11 (1960) 84-94, repr. in Jones, *RE* (see above) 339-49

——, *Constantine and the Conversion of Europe* (1948)

——, 'The Greeks under the Roman Empire', in *DOP* 17 (1963) 3-19, repr. in Jones, *RE* (see above) 90-113

——, 'The Hellenistic Age', in *Past & Present* 27 (1964) 3-22

——, 'Taxation in Antiquity', in *RE* (see above) 151-85

——, 'The urbanisation of the Ituraean principality', in *JRS* 21 (1931) 265-75

——, 'Were ancient heresies national or social movements in disguise?', in *JTS* n.s. 10 (1959) 280-98, repr. in Jones, *RE* (see above) 308-29

Jones, A. H. M., P. Grierson and J. A. Crook, 'The authenticity of the "Testamentum S. Remigii"', in *RBPH* 35 (1957) 356-73

Jones, C. P., *PR* = *Plutarch and Rome* (1971)

——, 'Towards a chronology of Plutarch's works', in *JRS* 56 (1966) 61-74

——, 'Diodoros Pasparos and the Nikephoria of Pergamon', in *Chiron* 4 (1974) 183-205

——, 'A leading family of Roman Thespiae', in *HSCP* 74 (1968) 223-55

——, 'A new letter of Marcus Aurelius to the Athenians', in *ZPE* 8 (1971) 161-83

Jones, Philip J., 'Communes and despots: the city state in Late Medieval Italy', in *TRHS* (1965) 71-96

——, 'L'Italia agraria nell'alto medioevo: problemi di cronologia e di continuità', in *Settimane di studio del Centro italiano di studi sull'alto medioevo, XIII. Agricoltura e mondo rurale in Occidente nell'alto medioevo* (Spoleto, 1966) 57-92, cf. 227-9

——, Chapter VII ('Medieval agrarian society in its prime'), § 2 ('Italy'), in *CEHE* I² (1966) 340-431

Jonge, P. de, 'Scarcity of corn and cornprices in Ammianus Marcellinus', in *Mnemos.*⁴ 1 (1948) 238-45
Jordan, Z. A., *KMECSR* = *Karl Marx: Economics, Class and Social Revolution* (1971)
Jullian, Camille, *HG* = *Histoire de la Gaule* (Paris), esp, I⁴ (1920) and VII (1926)

Kant, Immanuel: see under Reiss, Hans
Kaser, Max, *RP*² I-II = *Das römische Privatrecht* (Munich) I² (1971) and II² (1975)
——, *RZ* = *Das römische Zivilprozessrecht* (Munich, 1966)
——, 'Die Geschichte der Patronatsgewalt über Freigelassene', in *ZSS* 58 (1938) 88-135
——, 'Partus ancillae', in *ZSS* 75 (1958) 156-200
Kelly, J. M., *Roman Litigation* (1966)
Kiechle, Franz, *Sklavenarbeit und technischer Fortschritt im römischen Reich* (= *Forschungen zur ant. Sklaverei* 3, Wiesbaden, 1969) [See p.546 n.14 above]
Kock, Theodore, *CAF*: see under *CAF* in Part I of this Bibliography
Koenen, L., 'The prophecies of a potter: a prophecy of world renewal becomes an apocalypse', in *Proceedings, XII* [Michigan] *Internat. Congress of Papyrology* = *American Studies in Papyrology* 7 (Toronto, 1970) 249-54
——, 'Die Prophezeiungen des "Töpfers"', in *ZPE* 2 (1968) 178 ff. (text, 195-200)
Kohns, H. P., *Versorgungskrisen und Hungerrevolten im spätantiken Rom* (= *Antiquitas* I.6, Bonn, 1961)
Kolb, Frank, 'Der Aufstand der Provinz Africa Proconsularis im Jahr 238 n.Chr. Die wirtschaftlichen und sozialen Hintergründe', in *Historia* 26 (1977) 440-78 [See p.649 n.4 above]
Kraemer, C. J., and N. Lewis, 'A referee's hearing on ownership', in *TAPA* 68 (1937) 357-87
Kreissig, Heinz, LPHO = 'Landed property in the "Hellenistic" Orient', in *Eirene* 15 (1977) 5-26
——, *Die sozialen Zusammenhänge des judäischen Krieges. Klassen und Klasenkampf im Palästina des 1. Jahrhunderts v.u.Z.* (= *Schriften zur Geschichte und Kultur der Antike* 1, Deutsche Akad. der Wiss. zu Berlin, 1970)
——, 'Zur sozialen Zusammensetzung der frühchristlichen Gemeinden im ersten Jahrhundert u.Z.'. in *Eirene* 6 (1967) 91-100
——, *Wirtschaft und Gesellschaft im Seleukidenreich* (= *Schriften . . . der Antike* 16, Deutsche Akad., 1978), giving on p.129 a list of other relevant works of Kreissig, to which should be added:
——, 'Zur antiken und zur altorientalischen Komponente im sog. Hellenismus (anstelle eines Nachworts)', in *Klio* 60 (1978) 217-19
——, 'Tempelland, Katoiken, Hierodulen im Seleukidenreich', in *Klio* 59 (1977) 375-80
Kübler, Bernhard, SCRK = 'Sklaven und colonen in der römischen Kaiserzeit', in *Festschrift Johannes Vahlen* (Berlin, 1900) 561-88
Kula, Witold, *ETFS* = *An Economic Theory of the Feudal System. Towards a Model of the Polish Economy* (translated by Lawrence Garner from an Italian translation of the Polish 1962 original, London, 1976)
Kunkel, W., 'Bericht über neuere Arbeiten zur römischen Verfassungsgeschichte, III', in *ZSS* 75 (1958) 302-52, a review of L. Wickert's article, 'Princeps', in *RE* (see under Wickert below), and Jean Béranger, *Recherches sur l'aspect idéologique du Principat*, Basle, 1953)

Lambton, Ann K. S., *Landlord and Peasant in Persia* (1953; enlarged repr., 1959)
Landau, Y. H., 'A Greek inscription found near Hefzibah', in *IEJ* 16 (1966) 54-70
Landtman, Gunnar, *The Origin of the Inequality of the Social Classes* (1938)
La Penna, Antonio, 'La Morale della favola esopica come morale delle classi subalterne nell'antichità', in *Società* 17.2 (1961) 459-537
Larsen, J. A. O., *RGGRH* = *Representative Government in Greek and Roman History* (= Sather Classical Lectures 28, 1955)

——, *Greek Federal States. Their Institutions and History* (1968)

——, 'Roman Greece', = Part III of *ESAR* (ed. Tenney Frank) IV (1938) 259–496

——, 'Perioikoi', in *RE* XIX.i (1937) 816–33

——, 'Representation and democracy in Hellenistic federalism', in *CP* 40 (1945) 65–97

Latte, Kurt, *Römische Religionsgeschichte* (Munich, 1960)

Lattimore, Owen, 'Feudalism in history', in *Past & Present* 12 (November 1957) 47–57

Lauffer, Siegfried, *Die Bergwerkssklaven von Laureion* I–II = *Abhandlungen* der Akad. der Wiss. und der Lit. in Mainz, Geistes- und sozialwiss. Klasse, 1955 no.12, pp.1101–1217 = 1–117, and 1956 no.11, pp.883–1018 and 1*–20* = 119–274

Laum, Bernhard, *Stiftungen in der griechischen und römischen Antike*, 2 vols (Leipzig, 1914)

Legon, R. P., 'Phliasian politics and policy in the early fourth century', in *Historia* 16 (1967) 324–37. [See above, pp.296 and 608 n.49]

Lepper, Frank, Review, in *JRS* 59 (1969) 250–61, of F. J. Hassel, *Der Trajansbogen in Benevent: ein Bauwerk des römischen Senates* (Mainz, 1966)

——, Review, in *Gnomon* 42 (1970) 560–72, of Sherwin-White, *LP* (see below)

Levick, Barbara, *RCSAM* = *Roman Colonies in Southern Asia Minor* (1967)

Levick, Barbara (editor), *The Ancient Historian and his Materials* (Essays in Honour of C. E. Stevens, 1975)

Lévi-Strauss, Claude, *SA* = *Structural Anthropology*, Eng. trans. by Claire Jacobson and B. G. Schoepf (U.S.A., 1963, cited here from the Penguin University Books edn of 1972), from the French original of 1958 (a collection of papers written 1944–57)

Levy, Ernst, RPGL = 'Vom römischen Precarium zur germanischen Landleihe', in *ZSS* 66 (1948) 1–30. [See pp.253–5 above]

——, *WV* = *Weströmisches Vulgarrecht. Das Obligationenrecht* (= *Forschungen zum römischen Recht*, 7. Abhandlung, Weimar, 1956). [See pp.253–5 above]

——, 'Libertas und Civitas', in *ZSS* 78 (1961) 142–72

Lévy, Isidore, EVMAM = 'Études sur la vie municipale de l'Asie Mineure sous les Antonins', I, in *REG* 8 (1895) 203–50; II, in id. 12 (1899) 255–89; III, in id. 14 (1901) 350–71

Lewis, Bernard, *Islam from the Prophet Muhammad to the Capture of Constantinople* I (1974)

Lewis, Naphtali, 'Merismos anakechōrhēkotōn', in *JEA* 23 (1937) 63–75

Lewis, Naphtali, and Meyer Reinhold, *RC* I–II = *Roman Civilization. Selected Readings, I. The Republic* (New York, 1951); and *II. The Empire* (1955), ed. with Introductions and notes

Liebenam, W., *SRK* = *Städterverwaltung im römischen Kaiserreich* (Leipzig, 1900)

Liebeschuetz, W./J. H. W. G., *Ant.* = *Antioch. City and Imperial Administration in the Later Roman Empire* (1972)

——, 'The origin of the office of the pagarch', in *Byz. Ztschr.* 66 (1973) 38–46

——, 'The pagarch: city and imperial administration in Byzantine Egypt', in *JJP* 18 (1974) 163–8

Liebesny, H., 'Ein Erlass des Königs Ptolemaios II Philadelphos über die Deklaration von Vieh und Sklaven in Syrien und Phönikien', in *Aeg.* 16 (1936) 257–91

Lifschitz, B., 'The Greek documents from Nahal Seelim and Nahal Mishmar', in *IEJ* 11 (1961) 53–62

Limentani, I. Calabi: see under Calabi Limentani

Lintott, A. W., *Violence in Republican Rome* (1968)

——, 'The tradition of violence in the annals of the Early Roman Republic', in *Historia* 19 (1970) 12–29

Lipset, S. M., 'Elections: the expression of the democratic class struggle', in Bendix and Lipset, *CSP*² (see under Bendix above) 413–28

Llobera, J. R.: see under Bailey, A. M., and Llobera

Løkkegaard, Frede, *Islamic Taxation in the Classic Period* (Copenhagen, 1950)

Lot, F., 'Du régime de l'hospitalité', in *RBPH* 7 (1928) 975–1011

Lotze, Detlef, *MED* = *Metaxy eleutherōn kai doulōn* [in Greek]. *Studien zur Rechtsstellung unfreier Landbevölkerungen in Griechenland bis zum 4. Jahrhundert v.Chr.* (= Deutsche Akad. der Wiss. zu Berlin, Schriften der Sektion für Altertumswiss. 17, Berlin, 1959)

Lutz, Cora E., 'Musonius Rufus, "The Roman Socrates"', in *YCS* 10 (1947) 3-147 (also published separately)

[Mc is treated as Mac]
McCown, C. C., 'Hebrew and Egyptian apocalyptic literature', in *HTR* 18 (1925) 357-411
Machiavelli, Niccolò, *The Discourses [on the First Decade of Livy]*, cited here from the Eng. trans. with Introd. by Bernard Crick (Penguin Classics, 1970)
——, *The Discourses of Niccolò Machiavelli*, trans. and ed. by Leslie J. Walker, 2 vols (1950)
——, *Tutte le opere storiche e letterarie di Niccolò Machiavelli*, ed. Guido Mazzoni and Mario Casella (Florence, 1929)
McLellan, David, *KMLT = Karl Marx, His Life and Thought* (1973)
MacMullen, Ramsay, *ERO = Enemies of the Roman Order: Treason, Unrest, and Alienation in the Empire* (Cambridge, Mass., 1967)
——, NRS = 'A Note on Roman strikes', in *CJ* 58 (1962-3) 269-71
——, *RSR = Roman Social Relations 50 B.C. to A.D. 284* (1974)
——, 'Barbarian enclaves in the northern Roman empire', in *Ant. Class.* 32 (1963) 552-61
——, 'Roman Imperial building in the provinces', in *HSCP* 64 (1959) 207-35
Macpherson, C. B., *The Political Theory of Possessive Individualism, Hobbes to Locke* (1962)
——, *Democratic Theory. Essays in Retrieval* (1973)
Maenchen-Helfen, J. O., *The World of the Huns* (1973)
Magie, David, *RRAM* I-II = *Roman Rule in Asia Minor to the End of the Third Century after Christ*, 2 vols (Princeton, 1950)
Mann, J. C., 'The frontiers of the Principate', in *ANRW* II.i (1974) 508-33
——, 'Spoken Latin in Britain as evidenced in the inscriptions', in *Britannia* 2 (1971) 218-24
Mansi, J. D. (ed.), *Sacrorum Conciliorum nova et amplissima collectio* (1759 ff): VI (1761), IX (1763), XI (1765), XV (1770)
Mao Tse-tung, *Selected Works of Mao Tse-tung,* 5 vols (Peking): I-III (1965), IV (1961), V (1977)
——, *Selected Readings from the Works of Mao Tse-tung* (1 vol., Peking, 1967)
Markle, Minor M., 'Support of Athenian intellectuals for Philip', in *JHS* 96 (1976) 80-99
Markus, R. A.,'Christianity and Dissent in Roman North Africa: changing perspectives in recent work', in *SCH* 9 (1972) 21-36
Marshall, A. J., 'Romans under Chian law', in *GRBS* 10 (1969) 255-71
Martindale, J. R., *Public Disorders in the Late Roman Empire, their Causes and Character* (Oxford University B.Litt. thesis, 1961)
Martini, Remo, *'Mercennarius'. Contributo allo studio dei rapporti di lavoro in diritto romano* (Milan, 1958)
Martino, Francesco De: see under De Martino
Marx, Karl [with F. Engels, where so stated]
——, *Cap.* I-III = *Capital* I and II (London, 1970), and III (London, 1972). The German text, *Das Kapital*, occasionally cited as such, is that of *MEW* (see below) XXIII—XXV. (The German volumes are well indexed. Vol. I of the latest English edition, cited here, lacks an index. Readers may therefore sometimes find useful the earlier English edition, London, 1946, which has quite good Indexes, pp.863-86.)
——, *Grundrisse* [German text] = *Grundrisse der Kritik der politischen Ökonomie (Rohentwurf)*, published by Dietz Verlag, East Berlin (1953)
——, *Grundrisse,* E.T. = *Grundrisse. Foundations of the Critique of Political Economy (Rough Draft)*, Eng. trans. with a Foreword by Martin Nicolaus (Pelican Marx Library, 1973). The section on 'Pre-Capitalist Economic Formations' ('Formen die der kapitalistischen Produktion vorhergehen'), on pp.471-514 (German edn, 375-413), is the main part of Hobsbawm, *KMPCEF* (see above), where it appears in a different translation, with an excellent Introduction, some supplementary texts, and an Index
——, *MECW* (Marx/Engels) = Karl Marx and Frederick Engels, *Collected Works,* an English edn in 50 vols (Moscow/London/New York, 1975 ff.), Vols I-XIV appeared in 1975-80

——, *MEGA* (Marx/Engels) = Karl Marx and Friedrich Engels, *Gesamtausgabe* (1st edn), I.i.1 (Frankfurt, 1927); I.i.2-I.vi (Berlin, 1929-32); I.vii (Moscow, 1935); III.i-iv (Berlin, 1929-31). No more published. I have not been able to use the 2nd edn (Dietz Verlag, East Berlin, 1975 ff.), now in course of publication

——, *MESC* (Marx/Engels) = Karl Marx and Frederick Engels, *Selected Correspondence* (Moscow and London, 1956). For the German texts etc., see p.24 above

——, *MESW* (Marx/Engels) = Karl Marx and Frederick Engels, *Selected Works*, in one vol. (London, 1970)

——, *MEW* (Marx/Engels) = Karl Marx and Friedrich Engels, *Werke* I-XXXIX (Dietz Verlag, East Berlin, 1961-8)

——, *TSV* I-III = Karl Marx, *Theories of Surplus Value* I-III (London, 1969-72), an Eng. trans. of *Theorien über den Mehrwert* = Marx-Engels *Werke* (above) XXVI.i-iii

——, *WPP* = *Wages, Price and Profit* (an address given by Marx in English in June 1865 to the General Council of the First International), cited here from *MESW* (see above) 185-226

——, *Karl Marx on Colonialism and Modernization*, ed. with an Introd. by Shlomo Avineri (Anchor Books, New York, 1969)

——, *The Ethnological Notebooks of Karl Marx*, ed. Lawrence Krader (Assen, 1972)

Mason, H. J., *Greek Terms for Roman Institutions. A Lexicon and Analysis* (= *American Studies in Papyrology* 13, Toronto, 1974)

Matthews, John F., 'Mauretania in Ammianus and the *Notitia*', in *Aspects of the Notitia Dignitatum*, ed. R. Goodburn and P. Bartholomew (= *British Archaeological Reports*, Suppl. Series 15, Oxford, 1976) 157-86

——, *Western Aristocracies and Imperial Court A.D. 364-425* (1975)

Maxwell, J. F., *Slavery and the Catholic Church. The History of Catholic Teaching concerning the Moral Legitimacy of the Institution of Slavery* (Chichester/London, 1975: see p.639 n.5 above)

Mazza, Mario, *LSRA*² = *Lotte sociali e restaurazione autoritaria nel III sec. d.C.* (re-published, Rome, 1973)

——, 'Marxismo e storia antica. Note sulla storiografia marxista in Italia', in *Studi storici* 17.2 (1976) 95-124

——, Preface to Italian trans., *La schiavitú nell'Italia imperiale I-III sec.* (Rome, 1975), of a book in Russian in 1971 by E. M. Staerman and M. K. Trofimova

Mazzarino, Santo, *EAW* = *The End of the Ancient World*, Eng. trans. by George Holmes (London, 1966) from the Italian, *La fine del mondo antico* (1959)

——, *Aspetti sociali del quarto secolo. Ricerche di storia tardo-romana* (Rome, 1951)

Meek, Ronald L., *Studies in the Labour Theory of Value*, 2nd edn (1973; the 1st edn was in 1956)

Meier, Christian, *Res Publica Amissa* (Wiesbaden, 1966). [See the review by P. A. Brunt, given above]

Meiggs, Russell, *AE* = *The Athenian Empire* (1972)

——, *Roman Ostia*, 2nd edn (1973)

Meikle, Scott, 'Aristotle and the political economy of the polis', in *JHS* 99 (1979) 57-73. [I have not had occasion to mention this article above, but it is a very interesting contribution by a Marxist philosopher]

Meillassoux, Claude, 'Are there castes in India?', in *Economy and Society* 2 (1973) 89-111

——, 'Essai d'interprétation du phenomène économique dans les sociétés traditionelles d'auto-subsistance', in *Cahiers d'études africaines* 4 (1960) 38-67

——, 'From reproduction to production. A Marxist approach to economic anthropology', in *Economy and Society* 1 (1972) 93-105

Mellor, Ronald, *Thea Rhōmē* [in Greek]. *The Worship of the Goddess Roma in the Greek World* (= *Hypomnemata* 42, Göttingen, 1975)

Mendels, Doron, 'Perseus and the socio-economic question in Greece (179-172/1 B.C.). A study in Roman propaganda', in *Anc. Soc.* 9 (1978) 55-73

Mendelsohn, Isaac, *Slavery in the Ancient Near East* (New York, 1949)

Meuli, Karl, *HWF = Herkunft und Wesen der Fabel* (Basle, 1954)

Millar, Fergus G. B., *ERW = The Emperor in the Roman World* (1977)

——, ICP = 'The Imperial cult and the persecutions', in *Le culte des souverains dans l'Empire romain* (= *Entretiens sur l'antiquité classique* 19, Fondation Hardt, Vandoeuvres/ Geneva, 1973) 143-165/175

——, *SCD = A Study of Cassius Dio* (1964)

——, 'P. Herennius Dexippus: the Greek world and the third-century invasions', in *JRS* 59 (1969) 12-29

——, 'Paul of Samosata, Zenobia and Aurelian: the Church, local culture and political allegiance in third-century Syria', in *JRS* 61 (1971) 1-17

——, See also under Schürer, Emil, below

Mitchell, Stephen, 'Requisitioned transport in the Roman Empire: a new inscription from Pisidia', in *JRS* 66 (1976) 106-31

Mitteis, Ludwig, *RuV = Reichsrecht und Volksrecht in den östlichen Provinzen des römischen Kaiserreichs* (1891; repr., with a Preface by L. Wenger, Leipzig, 1935)

Mócsy, András, *PUM = Pannonia and Upper Moesia. A History of the Middle Danube Provinces of the Roman Empire* (1974, trans. from the German)

Mommsen, Theodor, *Röm. Staatsr. = Römisches Staatsrecht* (Leipzig), 3 vols: I-II, 3rd edn (1887), III (1888); repr., Tübingen (1952)

——, *Röm. Strafr. = Römisches Strafrecht* (Leipzig, 1899; repr. by Akademie-Verlag, Berlin, Darmstadt, 1955)

Monceaux, P., *Histoire littéraire de l'Afrique chrétienne depuis les origines jusqu'à l'invasion arabe*, 7 vols (Paris, 1901-23, repr. 1966)

Monnier, H., 'Études de droit byzantin', in *NRHDFE* 24 (1900), esp. 62-107 [see p.658 n.43 above]

Moritz, L. A., *Grain Mills and Flour in Classical Antiquity* (1958)

Morris, Rosemary, 'The powerful and the poor in tenth-century Byzantium: law and reality', in *Past & Present* 73 (1976) 3-27

Morrow, Glenn R., *PLS = Plato's Law of Slavery in its Relation to Greek Law* (= *Illinois Studies in Language and Literature* XXV.3, Urbana, Illinois, 1939)

——, 'Plato and Greek slavery', in *Mind* 48 = n.s. 190 (1939) 186-201

Mouterde, R., and A. Poidebard, *Le 'Limes' de Chalcis, organisation de la steppe en Haute Syrie romaine* (Paris, 1945)

Münzer, F., *Römische Adelsparteien und Adelsfamilien* (Stuttgart, 1920)

Murray, Oswyn, Review, in *JRS* 59 (1969) 261-5, of MacMullen, *ERO* (*q.v.* above)

Needham, Joseph, *Science and Civilisation in China*, esp. IV.ii (1965)

Newman, W. L., *PA I-IV = The Politics of Aristotle*, 4 vols (1887-1902)

Nicholas, Barry, *IRL = Introduction to Roman Law* (1962)

——, See also under Jolowicz, H. F., above

Nicolet, Claude, *L'Ordre equestre à l'époque républicaine (312-43 av. J.-C.)*, I. *Définitions juridiques et structures sociales* (Paris, 1966); II. *Prosopographie des chevaliers romains* (Paris, 1974) = *BEFAR* 207

Nieboer, H. J., *Slavery as an Industrial System* (1900)

Nilsson, M. P., *Geschichte der griechischen Religion*, 2 vols (Munich): I² (1955), II² (1961)

Nock, A. D., DJ = 'Deification and Julian', in *JRS* 47 (1957) 115-23, repr. in Nock, *ERAW* (below) II.833-46

——, EDC = 'The emperor and his divine *comes*', in *JRS* 37 (1947) 102-110, repr. in Nock, *ERAW* (below) II.653-75

——, *ERAW = Essays on Religion and the Ancient World*, ed. Zeph. Stewart, 2 vols (1972)

——, 'Religious developments from the close of the Republic to the death of Nero', in *CAH* X (1934) 465-511

Nörr, Dieter, SRBFAR = 'Zur sozialen und rechtlichen Bewertung der freien Arbeit in Rom', in *ZSS* 82 (1965) 67-105

——, 'Die Evangelien des Neuen Testaments und die sogenannte hellenistische Rechts-koine', in *ZSS* 78 (1961) 92-141

——, 'Griechisches und orientalisches Recht im Neuen Testament', in *Actes du Xe Congrès internat. de Papyrologues* (Warsaw etc., 1964) 109-15

Norman, A. F., GLMS = 'Gradations in later municipal society', in *JRS* 48 (1958) 79-85

——, *LA = Libanius' Autobiography (Oration I)*, ed. with Introd., trans. and notes (1965)

——, Review, in *JRS* 47 (1957) 236-40, of Paul Petit, *LVMA* (*q.v.* below) and *Les Étudiants de Libanius* (1957)

North, D. C., and R. P. Thomas, 'The rise and fall of the manorial system: a theoretical model', in *JEH* 31 (1971) 777-803; and 'An economic theory of the growth of the western world', in *Econ. Hist. Rev.*[2] 23 (1970) 1-17; also *The Rise of the Western World* (1973): see p.83 above

Nutton, V., 'The beneficial ideology', in *Imperialism in the Ancient World*, ed. P. D. A. Garnsey and C. R. Whittaker (1978) 209-21, 338-43

Oertel, F., *Die Liturgie. Studien zur ptolemaïschen und kaiserlichen Verwaltung Ägyptens* (Leipzig, 1917)

Oliva, Pavel, *Pannonia and the Onset of Crisis in the Roman Empire* (Prague, 1962; from the Czech, 1957)

——, 'Die Bedeutung der antiken Sklaverei', in *Acta Ant.* 8 (1960) 309-19

——, *Sparta and her Social Problems* (Prague, 1971)

Oliver, J. H., *RP = The Ruling Power. A Study of the Roman Empire in the Second Century after Christ through the Roman Oration of Aelius Aristides* (= *Trans. Amer. Philos. Soc.* n.s. 43.4, Philadelphia, 1953) 871-1003. [See p.615 n.54 above]

——, *Marcus Aurelius: Aspects of Civic and Cultural Policy in the East* (= *Hesperia* Suppl. 13, 1970)

——, *The Sacred Gerusia* (= *Hesperia* Suppl. 6, 1941)

——, 'The Roman governor's permission for a decree of the polis', in *Hesp.* 23 (1954) 163-7

——, 'A new letter of Antoninus Pius', in *AJP* 79 (1958) 52-60

Ollman, Bertell, 'Marx's use of "class"', in *Amer. Jnl of Sociology* 73 (1968) 573-80

Olmsted, F. L., *The Cotton Kingdom* (1861; ed. A. M. Schlesinger, 1953)

——, *Journey in the Seaboard Slave States* (1856; reissued 1904, 2 vols)

Oost, S. J., 'The Alexandrian seditions under Philip and Gallienus', in *CP* 56 (1961) 1-20

Ossowski, Stanislaw, *CSSC = Class Structure in the Social Consciousness* (Eng. trans. by Sheila Patterson, 1963 & repr.)

——, 'Les différents aspects de la classe sociale chez Marx', in *Cahiers internationaux de sociologie* 24 (1958) 65-79

Ostrogorsky, Georg, *HBS*[2] = *History of the Byzantine State*, 2nd edn of the Eng. trans. by Joan M. Hussey (1968, from the 3rd German edn, *Geschichte des byzantinischen Staates*, 1963)

——, 'Agrarian conditions in the Byzantine Empire in the Middle Ages' = chapter v of *CEHE* I[2] (1966) 205-34, with bibliography, 774-9

——, 'The peasant's pre-emption right', in *JRS* 37 (1947) 117-26

Ostwald, Martin, *Nomos and the Beginnings of the Athenian Democracy* (1969)

Otto, W., *Beiträge zur Hierodoulie im hellenistischen Ägypten* (= *Abhandlungen,* Bayer. Akad. der Wiss., Philos.-hist. Klasse, Munich, n.F. 29, 1950)

Padgug, R. A., 'Select bibliography on Marxism and the study of Antiquity', in *Arethusa* 8 (1975) 199-225

Page, Denys (L.), *SA = Sappho and Alcaeus* (1955)

Palanque, J. R., 'Famines à Rome à la fin du IVe siècle', in *REA* 33 (1931) 346-56

Pallasse, Maurice, *Orient et Occident à propos du Colonat Romain au Bas-Empire* (= *Bibl. de la Faculté de Droit de l'Univ. d'Alger* 10, Lyons, 1950)

Parain, Charles, 'Les caractères spécifiques de la lutte de classes dans l'Antiquité classique', in *La Pensée* 108 (April 1963) 3-25

Paret, R., 'Dometianus de Mélitène et la politique religieuse de l'empereur Maurice', in *REB* 15 (1957) 42-72

Pargoire, J., *L'Église byzantine de 527 à 847* (Paris, 1905)

Parke, H. W., *GMS = Greek Mercenary Soldiers from the Earliest Times to the Battle of Ipsus* (1933)

Parkin, Frank, *Class Inequality and Political Order* (1971 & repr.)

Paschoud, François, *Cinq études sur Zosime* (Paris, 1975), including 'La digression anti-monarchique du préambule de l'Histoire nouvelle', pp.1-23

——, 'Zosimus (8)', in *RE*² X.A (1972) 795-841

Passerini, Alfredo, 'I moti politico-sociali della Grecia e i Romani', in *Athen.* n.s. 11 (1933) 309-35

——, 'Riforme sociali e divisioni di beni nella Grecia del IV sec. a.C.', in *Athen.* n.s. 8 (1930) 273-90

——, Six articles in *Athen.* n.s. 9-11 (1931-3) under the general title, 'Studi di storia ellenistico-romana': see p.611 n.16 above

Patlagean, Evelyne, *Pauvreté économique et pauvreté sociale à Byzance 4ᵉ-7ᵉ siècles* (Paris, 1977). [I did not see this work until my book was finished and in page proof]

Pečírka, J., *The Formula for the Grant of Enktesis in Attic Inscriptions* (= *Acta Univ. Carolinae, Philos. et Hist. Monographia* XV, Prague, 1966)

——, 'Land tenure and the development of the Athenian polis', in *Geras* [Greek]. *Studies pres. to George Thomson*, ed. L. Varcl and R. F. Willetts (Prague, 1963) 183-201

Pelham, H. F., *ERH = Essays* (1911) [On the spine: *Essays on Roman History*]

Penna, Antonio La: see under La Penna

Percival, John, 'Seigneurial aspects of Late Roman estate management', in *Eng. Hist. Rev.* 84 (1969) 449-73

——, '*P. Ital.* 3 and Roman estate management', in *Hommmages à Marcel Renard* II (= *Coll. Latomus* 102, Brussels, 1969) 607-15

Perlman, S., 'A note on the political implications of Proxenia in the fourth century B.C.', in *CQ* 52 = n.s. 8 (1958) 185-91

Petit, Paul, *LVMA = Libanius et la vie municipale à Antioche au IVᵉ siècle après J.-C.* (Paris, 1956)

——, 'L'esclavage antique dans l'historiographie soviétique', in *Actes du Colloque d'histoire sociale 1970* (= *Annales littéraires de l'Univ. de Besançon* 128, Paris, 1972) 9-27

Petzold, K. E., 'Römische Revolution oder Krise der römischen Republik?', in *Riv. stor. dell'Ant.* 2 (1972) 229-43

Pharr, Clyde, *TC = The Theodosian Code and Novels and the Sirmondian Constitutions*, Eng. trans., with commentary etc. (Princeton, 1952)

Piganiol, André, *EC² = L'Empire chrétien (325-395)*, 2nd edn, by André Chastagnol (Paris, 1972)

Pippidi, D. M., *PMOA = 'Le problème de la main-d'oeuvre agricole dans les colonies grecques de la Mer Noire', in *PTGA* (ed. M. I. Finley) 63-82

Pleket, H. W., 'The Archaic Tyrannis', in *Talanta* 1 (1969) 19-61

——, '*Collegium iuvenum Nemesiorum*. A note on ancient youth-organisations', in *Mnemos.*⁴ 22 (1969) 281-98

——, 'Domitian, the Senate and the provinces', in *Mnem.*⁴ 14 (1961) 296-315

——, 'Economic history of the ancient world and epigraphy: some introductory remarks', in *Akten des VI Internationalen Kongresses für Griechische und Lateinische Epigraphik = Vestigia* 17 (1972) 243-57

——, 'Games, prizes, athletes and ideology. Some aspects of the history of sport in the Greco-Roman world', in *Stadion* 1 (1976) 49-89

——, 'Zur Soziologie des antiken Sports', in *Mededelingen van het Nederlands Instituut te Rome* 36 (1974) 57-87

——, 'Technology in the Greco-Roman world: a general report', in *Talanta* 5 (1973) 6-47

——, Review, in *Gnomon* 49 (1977) 55-63, of Duncan-Jones, *EREQS* (above)

Pleket, H. W. (editor), *Epigraphica, I. Texts on the Economic History of the Greek World* (= *Textus Minores* 31, Leiden, 1964), and *II. Texts on the Social History of the Greek World* (= *Textus Minores* 41, Leiden, 1969)

Pocock, J. G. A.: see under Harrington, James

Polanyi, Karl, *PAME* = *Primitive, Archaic and Modern Economies. Essays of Karl Polanyi*, ed. George Dalton (Boston, 1968)

——, *TMEE* = *Trade and Market in the Early Empires. Economies in History and Theory*, ed. K. Polanyi, C. M. Arensberg and H. W. Pearson (Glencoe, Illinois, 1957)

Pomeroy, Sarah B., 'Selected bibliography on women in antiquity', in *Arethusa* 6 (Spring, 1973) 125-57

——, *Goddesses, Whores, Wives, and Slaves. Women in Classical Antiquity* (New York, 1975)

Potter, J. M., M. N. Diaz and G. M. Foster (editors), *Peasant Society: A Reader* (Boston, 1967)

Prawer, S. S., *KMWL* = *Karl Marx and World Literature* (1976)

Préaux, Claire, *ERL* = *L'Économie royale des Lagides* (Brussels, 1939)

——, 'Le statut de la femme à l'époque hellénistique, principalement en Égypte', in *Recueils de la Société Jean Bodin XI: La Femme* (1959) 127-75

——, 'Les villes hellénistiques, principalement en Orient. Leurs institutions administratives et judiciaires', in *Recueils de la Soc. Jean Bodin* VI (1954) 69-134

——, 'Institutions économiques et sociales des villes hellénistiques, principalement en Orient', in *Recueils de la Soc. Jean Bodin* VII (1955) 89-135

——, 'Sur les causes de décadence du monde hellénistique', in *Atti dell'XI* [1965] *Congresso Internazionale di Papirologia* (Milan, 1966) 475-98

——, 'Sur la stagnation de la pensée scientifique à l'époque hellénistique', in *Essays in Honor of C. Bradford Welles* = *American Studies in Papyrology* 1 (1966) 235-50

——, 'Les modalités de l'attache à la glèbe dans l'Égypte grecque et romaine', in *Recueils de la Soc. Jean Bodin II²*. *Le Servage* (2nd edn, revised and enlarged, Brussels, 1959) 33-65

Preisker, Herbert, *Christentum und Ehe in den ersten drei Jahrhunderten* (= *Neue Studien zur Geschichte der Theologie und Kirche* 23, Berlin, 1927)

Prinz, Arthur M., 'Background and ulterior motive of Marx's "Preface" of 1859', in *JHI* 30 (1969) 437-50

Pritchard, R. T., 'Land tenure in Sicily in the first century B.C.', in *Historia* 18 (1969) 545-56; 'Cicero and the *Lex Hieronica*', in id. 19 (1970) 352-68; 'Gaius Verres and the Sicilian farmers', in id. 20 (1971) 224-38; 'Some aspects of first century Sicilian agriculture', in id. 21 (1972) 646-60

Pritchett, W. K., 'The Attic Stelai': I (texts etc.), in *Hesperia* 22 (1953) 225-99; II (commentary), in id. 25 (1956) 178-317/328

Quasten, J., *Patrology*, 3 vols (Utrecht, 1950-60)

Rallis, G. A., and M. Potlis, *Syntagma tōn theiōn kai hierōn kanonōn* . . . [in Greek: the Canon Law of the Orthodox Church], esp. IV (Athens, 1854): see p.557 n.26 above

Randall, R. H., 'The Erechtheum Workmen', in *AJA* 57 (1953) 199-210

Rea, J. R. (editor), *The Oxyrhynchus Papyri* [*P. Oxy.*] XL (1972)

Reinhold, Meyer, 'Historian of the Classic World: a critique of Rostovtzeff', in *Science and Society* 10 (1946) 361-91

——, See also Lewis, Naphtali, and Reinhold

Reiss, Hans, *Kant's Political Writings*, ed. Hans Reiss, and trans. by H. B. Nisbet (1970)

Rémondon, Roger, 'L'Édict XIII de Justinien a-t-il été promulgué en 539?', in *Chr. d'Ég.* 30 (1955) 112-21

——, 'L'Égypte et la suprème résistance au Christianisme (Vᵉ-VIIᵉ siècles)', in *Bull. de l'Inst. français d'archéol. orientale* 51 (1952) 63-78

Rey, Pierre-Philippe: see under Dupré, Georges, and Rey

Reynolds, Joyce M., 'A civic decree from Benghazi' [Berenice], in *Fifth Annual Report of the Society for Libyan Studies* (1973-4) 19-24

——, 'A civic decree from Tocra in Cyrenaica', in *Arch. Class.* 25/26 (1973/74) 622-30

——, 'The inscriptions of Apollonia', in *Apollonia*, Suppl. Vol. of *Libya Antiqua* (1977) 293-333

———, 'The cities of Cyrenaica in decline', in *Thèmes de recherches sur les villes antiques d'Occident* (= *Colloques internationaux du Centre National de la recherche scientifique*, no. 542, Strasbourg, 1971, published at Paris, 1977) 53-8

———, 'Roman inscriptions 1971-5', in *JRS* 66 (1976) 174-99

———, 'Aphrodisias: a free and federate city', in *Akten des VI. Internationalen Kongresses für Griechische und Lateinische Epigraphik* (Munich, 1972) = *Vestigia* 17 (1973) 115-22

Rhodes, P. J., 'The Five Thousand in the Athenian revolutions of 411 B.C.', in *JHS* 92 (1972) 115-27. [See pp.605-6 nn.30-1 above]

Richmond, I. A., *Archaeology and the After-Life in Pagan and Christian Imagery* (1950)

———, 'Palmyra under the aegis of Rome' in *JRS* 53 (1963) 43-54

———, 'The Sarmatae, *Bremetennacum Veteranorum* and the *Regio Bremetennacensis*', in *JRS* 35 (1945) 15-29

Robbins, Lionel (Lord), *An Essay on the Nature and Significance of Economic Science*, 2nd edn (1935; the first edn was in 1932). [See pp. 84-5 above]

Robert, Louis, 'Divinités éponymes', in *Hellenica* 2 (1946) 51-64

———, *Les gladiateurs dans l'Orient grec* (Paris, 1940; repr. Amsterdam, 1971); with corrections and supplements in the articles in *REG* and *Hellenica* given in n.3 on pp.636-7 above

———, 'Nouvelles inscriptions d'Iasos', in *REA* 65 (1963) 298-329

———, Numerous other articles (some with J. Robert) in *Hellenica, REG, BCH* etc.

Robertis, F. M. De: see under De Robertis, F. M.

Roberts, C. H., 'The Kingdom of Heaven (Lk. XVII.21)', in *HTR* 41 (1948) 1-8

Robinson, Joan, *Essay in Marxian Economics*, 2nd edn (1966; the first edn was in 1942)

Robinson, Olivia, 'Private prisons', in *RIDA*[3] 15 (1968) 389-98

Rostovtzeff, M., NEPPK = 'Notes on the economic policy of the Pergamene kings' in *Anatolian Studies pres. to Sir W. M. Ramsay*, ed. W. H. Buckler and W. M. Calder (1923) 359-90

———, *SEHHW* = *Social and Economic History of the Hellenistic World*, 3 vols (1941)

———, *SEHRE*[2] = *Social and Economic History of the Roman Empire*, 2nd edn, rev. by P. M. Fraser, 2 vols (1957; the first edn was in 1926)

——— [Rostowzew], *SGRK* = *Studien zur Geschichte des römischen Kolonates* (= Beiheft I, *Archiv für Papyrusforschung*, Leipzig/Berlin, 1910)

———, 'Angariae', in *Klio* 6 (1906) 249-58

———, *The Caravan Cities* (1932)

———, 'Les inscriptions caravanières de Palmyre', in *Mél. Gustave Glotz* (Paris, 1932) II.793-811

Roth, Guenther, 'The historical relationship to Marxism', in *Scholarship and Partisanship: Essays on Max Weber*, ed. Reinhard Bendix and Roth (1971) 227-52

Rothstein, M., 'Suffragium', in *Festschrift zu Otto Hirschfelds 60tem Geburtstage* (1903) 30-3

Rougé, Jean, ROCMM = *Recherches sur l'organisation du commerce maritime en Méditerranée sous l'empire romain* (Paris, 1966)

———, edition of the *Expositio totius mundi et gentium* (SC 124, Paris, 1966)

Rouillard, Germaine, ACEB[2] = *L'administration civile de l'Égypte byzantine*, 2nd edn (Paris, 1928)

Rubinsohn, Zeev Wolfgang, 'Saumakos: ancient history, modern politics', in *Historia* 29 (1980) 50-70

Rudé, George, *The Crowd in the French Revolution* (1959 & repr.); *The Crowd in History. A Study of Popular Disturbances in France and England 1730-1848* (1964); and *Paris and London in the Eighteenth Century. Studies in Popular Protest* (1970): see p.624 n.13 above

Ruggini, Lellia Cracco, *Economia e società nell' "Italia annonaria". Rapporti fra agricoltura e commercio dal IV al VI secolo d.C.* (Milan, 1961)

———, 'The ecclesiastical historians and the pagan historiography: Providence and miracles', in *Athen.* n.s. 55 (1977) 107-26

Runciman, W. G., RDSJ = *Relative Deprivation and Social Justice* (1966)

Ruppel, W., 'Politeuma', in *Philologus* 82 = n.F. 36 (1927) 268-312, 433-54

Ste. Croix, G. E. M. de, AGRML = 'Ancient Greek and Roman maritime loans', in *Debits, Credits, Finance and Profits* [Essays in Honour of W. T. Baxter], ed. Harold Edey and B. S. Yamey (1974) 41-59

——, AHP = 'Aristotle on History and Poetry (*Poetics* 9, 1451ª36-ᵇ11)', in *The Ancient Historian and his Materials* [Essays in Honour of C. E. Stevens], ed. Barbara Levick (1975) 45-58

——, CAE = 'The character of the Athenian Empire', in *Historia* 3 (1954/5) 1-41

——, CFT = 'The constitution of the Five Thousand', in *Historia* 5 (1956) 1-23

——, ECAPS = 'Early Christian attitudes to property and slavery', in *SCH* 12 (1975) 1-38

——, GRA = 'Greek and Roman accounting', in *Studies in the History of Accounting*, ed. A. C. Littleton and B. S. Yamey (1956) 14-74

——, KMHCA = 'Karl Marx and the history of Classical Antiquity', in *Arethusa* 8 (1975) 7-41

——, NJAE I and II = 'Notes on jurisdiction in the Athenian Empire', in *CQ* 55 = n.s. 11 (1961) 94-112 and 268-80

——, OPRAW = 'Some observations on the property rights of Athenian women', in *CR* 84 = n.s. 20 (1970) 273-8; cf. 387-90

——, OPW = *The Origins of the Peloponnesian War* (1972)

——, PPOA = 'Political pay outside Athens', in *CQ* 69 = n.s. 25 (1975) 48-52

——, RRW = 'The religion of the Roman world', in *Didaskalos* 4 (1972) 61-74

——, SVP = 'Suffragium: from vote to patronage', in *British Jnl of Sociology* 5 (1954) 33-48

——, WWECP = 'Why were the early Christians persecuted?', in *Past & Present* 26 (1963) 6-38, repr. in *SAS* (ed. M. I. Finley) 210-49; cf. 256-62

——, 'Aspects of the "Great" persecution', in *HTR* 47 (1954) 75-113

——, 'Demosthenes' *timēma* and the Athenian *eisphora* in the fourth century B.C.', in *Classica et Mediaevalia* 14 (1953) 30-70

——, 'Herodotus', in *Greece & Rome*² 24 (1977) 130-48

——, Review, in *Population Studies* 10 (1956) 118-20, of A. E. R. Boak, *Manpower Shortage and the Fall of the Roman Empire in the West* (1955)

——, Review, in *Eng. Hist. Rev.* 86 (1971) 149-50, of S. G. F. Brandon, *The Trial of Jesus of Nazareth* (1968)

——, Review, in *CR* 78 = n.s. 14 (1964) 190-2, of J. J. Buchanan, *Theorika. A Study of Monetary Distributions to the Athenian Citizenry during the Fifth and Fourth Centuries B.C.* (1962)

——, Review, in *CR* 80 = n.s. 16 (1966) 90-3, of Rudi Thomsen, *Eisphora. A Study of Direct Taxation in Ancient Athens* (1964)

——, Review, in *CR* 71 = n.s. 7 (1957) 54-9, of W. L. Westermann, *The Slave Systems of Greek and Roman Antiquity* (1955)

Salomon, R. G., 'A papyrus from Constantinople (Hamburg Inv. No. 410)', in *JEA* 34 (1948) 98-108

Samuel, A. E., RPCAD = 'The role of Paramone clauses in ancient documents', in *JJP* 15 (1965) 221-311

Sarkady, Johannes, 'Aisopos der Samier. Ein Beitrag zur archaischen Geschichte Samos", in *Acta Classica* (Univ. Scient. Debrecen.) 4 (1968) 7-12

Sasse, Christoph, *Die Constitutio Antoniniana* (Wiesbaden, 1958)

——, 'Literaturübersicht zur Constitutio Antoniniana', in *JJP* 14 (1962) 109-49; 15 (1965) 329-66

Saumagne, Charles, ROC = 'Du rôle de l'*origo* et du *census* dans la formation du colonat romain', in *Byzantion* 12 (1937) 487-581

Scarpat, G., *Parrhesia. Storia del termine e delle sue traduzioni in Latino* (Brescia, 1964)

Schaps, David, *Economic Rights of Women in Ancient Greece* (1979)

——, 'The woman least mentioned: etiquette and women's names', in *CQ* 71 = n.s. 27 (1977) 323-30

Schiller, A. Arthur, 'The fate of Imperial legislation in late Byzantine Egypt', in *Legal Thought in the U.S.A. Under Contemporary Pressures*, ed. John N. Hazard and Wenceslas J. Wagner (Brussels, 1970) 41–60

Schlaifer, Robert, GTSHA = 'Greek theories of slavery from Homer to Aristotle', in *HSCP* 47 (1936) 165–204, repr. in *SCA* (ed. Finley) 93–132

Schlatter, Richard, *Private Property. The History of an Idea* (1951)

Schneider, Helmuth, *Die Entstehung der römischen Militärdiktatur. Krise und Niedergang einer antiken Republik* (Cologne, 1977)

Schürer, Emil, *Geschichte des jüdischen Volkes im Zeitalter Jesu Christi*, 3rd/4th edn (1901-9)

——, New English version of the same book, by Geza Vermes and Fergus Millar, *The History of the Jewish People in the Age of Jesus Christ (175 B.C. - A.D. 135)*, of which two volumes have appeared: I (Edinburgh, 1973), and II (1979)

Schuller, Wolfgang, *Die Herrschaft der Athener im Ersten Attischen Seebund* (Berlin/New York, 1974); and *Die Stadt als Tyran–Athens Herrschaft über seine Bundesgenossen* (Konstanz, 1978)

Schulz, Fritz, *CRL = Classical Roman Law* (1951)

——, *PRL = Principles of Roman Law*, Eng. trans. by Marguerite Wolff (1936), from a text revised and enlarged by the author from his *Prinzipien des römischen Rechts*, 2nd edn (1934)

Schwartz, Eduard (editor), *Acta Conc. Oec. = Acta Conciliorum Oecumenicorum*, I [Ephesus, 431] i–v (Leipzig/Berlin, 1921-9); II [Chalcedon, 451] i–vi (1932-8)

Scramuzza, Vincent, WVSS = 'Were the *Venerii* in Sicily serfs?', in *AJP* 57 (1936) 326–30

Scroggs, Robin, 'Paul and the eschatological woman', in *Jnl of the American Acad. of Religion* 40 (1972) 283–303; and 'Paul and the eschatological woman revisited', in id. 42 (1974) 532-7. [See pp.104, 105-6 above]

Seager, Robin (editor), *CRR = The Crisis of the Roman Republic. Studies in Political and Social History* (1969). And see under Gelzer above

Seeck, Otto, *GUAW = Geschichte des Untergangs der antiken Welt*, 5 vols (in 10 parts): I⁴.i–ii (Stuttgart, 1921-2) III².i–ii (1921), IV-V (no date), VI.i–ii (1920-1)

——, *RKP = Regesten der Kaiser und Päpste für die Jahre 311 bis 476 n.Chr.* (Stuttgart, 1919; repr. Frankfurt, 1964)

——, 'Colonatus', in *RE* IV.i (1900) 483–510

Segal, J. B., *Edessa, 'The Blessed City'* (1970)

Segrè, Angelo, 'The Byzantine colonate', in *Traditio* 5 (1947) 103–33

Seston, William, *DT* I = *Dioclétien et la Tétrarchie* I (1946: no more published)

Setälä, Päivi, *Private Domini in Roman Brick Stamps of the Empire. A Historical and Prosopographical Study of Landowners in the District of Rome* (= *Annales Academiae Scientiarum Fennicae Dissertationes Humanarum Litterarum* 10, Helsinki, 1977)

Setton, K. M., *Christian Attitude towards the Emperor in the Fourth Century* (= Columbia Univ. *Studies in History, Economics and Public Law* 482, New York, 1941)

Seyrig, Henri, 'Antiquités syriennes 48. Aradus et Baetocaecé', in *Syria* 28 (1951) 191-206

Shanin, Teodor (editor), *PPS = Peasants and Peasant Society* (Penguin, 1971)

Sheppard, A. R. R., *Characteristics of Political Life in the Greek Cities ca. 70-120 A.D.* (Oxford B.Litt. thesis, 1975)

Sherk, Robert K., *RDGE = Roman Documents from the Greek East. Senatus Consulta and Epistulae to the Age of Augustus* (Baltimore, 1969)

Sherwin-White, A. N., *LP = The Letters of Pliny* (1966)

——, *RC² = The Roman Citizenship*, 2nd edn (1973)

——, *RSRLNT = Roman Society and Roman Law in the New Testament* (1963). [See p.640 n.6 above]

——, 'The *tabula* of Banasa and the *Constitutio Antoniniana*', in *JRS* 63 (1973) 86–98

Sherwin-White, Susan M., *Ancient Cos* (= *Hypomnemata* 51, 1978)

Shimron, Benjamin, *Late Sparta. The Spartan Revolution 243-146 B.C.* (= *Arethusa* Monographs 3, Buffalo, N.Y., 1972)

——, 'Nabis of Sparta and the Helots', in *CP* 61 (1966) 1-7

Small, A. M., Review, in *Phoenix* 33 (1979) 369-72, of Tapio Helen on Roman brick production (see above under Helen, Tapio)

Smelser, Neil J. (editor), *Sociology. An Introduction* (1967)

Snodgrass, A. M., 'The hoplite reform and history', in *JHS* 85 (1965) 110-22

Soden, Hans von (editor), *UED*² = *Urkunden zur Entstehungsgeschichte des Donatismus* (= *Kleine Texte für Vorlesungen und Übungen* 122), ed. Hans von Soden, 2nd edn by Hans von Campenhausen (Berlin, 1950)

Sorokin, Pitirim, *Contemporary Sociological Theories* (1928)

Spawforth, A., 'The slave Philodespotos', in *ZPE* 27 (1977) 294

Speidel, M., 'The pay of the Auxilia', in *JRS* 63 (1973) 141-7

Sperber, D., 'Angaria in Rabbinic literature', in *Ant. Class.* 38 (1969) 164-8

Štaerman, E. M. [Schtajerman], *Die Blütezeit der Sklavenwirtschaft in der römischen Republik*, German trans. from Russian (Wiesbaden, 1969)

——, *Die Krise der Sklavenhalterordnung im Westen des römischen Reiches*, German trans. from Russian (Berlin, 1964)

Štaerman, E. M., and M. K. Trofimova, *La schiavitù nell'Italia imperiale I-III sec.*, Italian trans. from Russian of 1971 (Rome, 1975), with Preface by Mario Mazza (see p.543 n.7 above)

Stampp, Kenneth M., *PI = The Peculiar Institution. Slavery in the Ante-Bellum South* (New York, 1956; London, 1964)

Starr, Chester G., 'An overdose of slavery', in *JEH* 18 (1958) 17-32. [See p. 54 above]

——, 'The perfect democracy of the Roman Empire', in *AHR* 58 (1952-3) 1-16

Stauffenberg, Alexander Schenk, Graf von, *Die römische Kaisergeschichte bei Malalas* (Stuttgart, 1931)

Staveley, E. S., *Greek and Roman Voting and Elections* (1972)

Stead, G. C., 'The *Thalia* of Arius and the testimony of Athanasius', in *JTS* n.s. 29 (1978) 20-52

Stein, Ernst, *HBE* I².i-ii and II = *Histoire du Bas-Empire* I [A.D. 284-476], 2nd edn, in 2 parts, ed. J. R. Palanque (Paris, 1959), an improved French version of Stein's *Geschichte des spätromischen Reiches, I. 284-476 n.Chr.* (Vienna, 1928); and II [A.D. 476-565], written in French and published posthumously by Palanque (Paris, 1949)

Stevens, C. E., *SAA = Sidonius Apollinaris and his Age* (1933)

——, 'Agriculture and rural life in the Later Roman Empire', in *CEHE* I² (1966) 92-124, with bibliography rev. by John Morris, 755-61

——, See also Levick, Barbara (ed.)

Stevenson, J., *A New Eusebius. Documents illustrative of the history of the Church to A.D. 337* (1957 & repr.)

Stocks, J. L., *'Scholē'* [in Greek], in *CQ* 30 (1936) 177-87

Strasburger, Hermann, *Concordia Ordinum. Eine Untersuchung zur Politik Ciceros* (Diss., Leipzig, 1931)

——, 'Nobiles', in *RE* XVII.i (1936) 785-91

——, 'Optimates', in *RE* XVIII.i (1939) 773-98

Strubbe, J., 'A group of Imperial estates in central Phrygia', in *Anc. Soc.* 6 (1975) 229-50

Svencickaja, I. S. [Sventsitskaya], 'Some problems of agrarian relations in the province of Asia', in *Eirene* 15 (1977) 27-54. (And see p.568 n.33 above)

Swoboda, H., *GV = Die griechischen Volksbeschlüsse. Epigraphische Untersuchungen* (Leipzig, 1890)

——, *'Kōmē'* [in Greek], in *RE* Suppl. IV (1924) 950-76

Syme, (Sir) Ronald, *RPM = A Roman Post-Mortem. An Inquest on the Fall of the Roman Republic* (= Todd Memorial Lecture no. 3, Sydney, 1950) repr. in Syme's *Roman Papers* (1979: see below) I.205-17

——, *RR = The Roman Revolution* (1939 & repr.)

——, *Danubian Papers* (Bucharest, 1971)

——, *Emperors and Biography* (1971)

——, *Roman Papers*, 2 vols, ed. E. Badian (1979)

——, *Tacitus*, 2 vols (1958)

——, 'The Titulus Tiburtinus', in *Akten des VI. Internat. Kongr. für Griech. und Latein. Epigraphik*, Munich 1972 (= *Vestigia* 17 [1973] 585–601)

Taeger, Fritz, *Charisma* I-II (Stuttgart, 1957, 1960)

——, 'Zur Geschichte der spätkaiserzeitlichen Herrscherauffassung', in *Saeculum* 7 (1956) 182–95

Tarn, W. W., *HC*[3] = *Hellenistic Civilisation*, 3rd edn, rev. by the author and G. T. Griffith (1952 & repr.)

——, 'The social question in the third century [B.C.]', in *The Hellenistic Age*, by J. B. Bury and others (1923) 108–40: see pp.186 and 578 n.18 above

Taylor, Lily Ross, 'Forerunners of the Gracchi', in *JRS* 52 (1962) 19-27

——, *Party Politics in the Age of Caesar* (Berkeley etc., 1949, & repr.)

——, *Roman Voting Assemblies from the Hannibalic War to the Dictatorship of Caesar* (Ann Arbor, 1966)

Tchalenko, G., *Villages antiques de la Syrie du Nord. Le Massif du Bélus à l'époque romaine*, 3 vols (Paris, 1953, 1958)

Tcherikover, V. [Tscherikower], *Hellenistic Civilization and the Jews* (Philadelphia/ Jerusalem, 1959)

——, 'Was Jerusalem a "polis"?', in *IEJ* 14 (1964) 61-78

——, *Die hellenistischen Städtegründungen von Alexander dem Grossen bis auf der Römerzeit* (= *Philologus*, Suppl. XIX.1, 1927)

——, 'Prolegomena' [on the position of the Jews in Egypt in the Ptolemaic, Early Roman, Late Roman and Byzantine periods] to *C.P.Jud.* I = *Corpus Papyrorum Judaicarum* I (1957) 1–111

Thesleff, Holger, *An Introduction to the Pythagorean Writings of the Hellenistic Period* (Åbo, 1961)

Thomas, J. A. C., LO = 'Locatio and operae', in *BIDR* 64 (1961) 231-47

——, NM = 'The nature of *merces*', in *Acta Juridica* (1958) 191-9

Thomas, Keith, 'The Levellers and the franchise', in *The Interregnum. The Quest for Settlement 1646-1660*, ed. G. E. Aylmer (1972) 57-78

Thompson, E. A., EG = *The Early Germans* (1965)

——, HAH = *A History of Attila and the Huns* (1948)

——, HWAM = *The Historical Work of Ammianus Marcellinus* (1947)

——, PRLRGS = 'Peasant revolts in Late Roman Gaul and Spain', in *Past & Present* 2 (1952) 11-23, repr. in *SAS* (ed. M. I. Finley) 304-20

——, RRI = *A Roman Reformer and Inventor*, being a new text of the Treatise *De Rebus Bellicis*, with a Translation and Introduction by Thompson and a Latin Index by Barbara Flower (1952)

——, SEG = 'Slavery in Early Germany', in *Hermathena* 89 (1957) 17-29, repr. in *SCA* (ed. M. I. Finley) 191-203

——, VTU = *The Visigoths in the Time of Ulfila* (1966)

——, 'Barbarian invaders and Roman collaborators', in *Florilegium* [Carleton Univ., Ottawa] 2 (1980) 71-88

——, 'The barbarian kingdoms in Gaul and Spain', in *Nottingham Mediaeval Studies* 7 (1963) 3-33

——, 'Britain, A.D. 406–410', in *Britannia* 8 (1977) 303-18

——, 'Christianity and the northern barbarians', in *Nottingham Mediaeval Studies* 1 (1957) 3-21, repr. in *The Conflict between Paganism and Christianity in the Fourth Century*, ed. A. Momigliano (1963) 56-78

——, 'Olympiodorus of Thebes', in *CQ* 38 (1944) 43-52

——, 'The settlement of the barbarians in southern Gaul', in *JRS* 46 (1956) 65-75

——, 'The Visigoths from Fritigern to Euric', in *Historia* 12 (1963) 105-26

Thompson, Edward P., *The Making of the English Working Class* (1963 & repr., cited from the Pelican edn, 1968 & repr.)

Thorner, Daniel, MAIMP = 'Marx on India and the Asiatic mode of production', in *Contributions to Indian Sociology* 9 (1966) 33-66

——, 'Peasant economy as a category in economic history', in *Deuxième* [1962] *Conférence internationale d'histoire économique* (Paris, 1965) II.287-300

——, 'Peasantry', in *International Encyclopedia of the Social Sciences* 11 (1968) 503-11

Tjäder, J.-O., *Die nichtliterarischen lateinischen Papyri Italiens aus der Zeit 445-700*, 2 vols (Lund, 1955)

Topolski, Jerzy, 'Lévi-Strauss and Marx on history', in *History and Theory* 12 (1973) 192-207

Torelli, M., 'Pour une histoire de l'esclavage en Etrurie', in *Actes du Colloque 1973 sur l'esclavage = Annales littéraires de l'Univ. de Besançon* 182 (Paris, 1975) 99-113

[Torres, Camilo] *Revolutionary Priest. The Complete Writings and Messages of Camilo Torres*, ed. John Gerassi (1971 & repr.)

Touloumakos, Johannes, *Der Einfluss Roms auf die Staatsform der griechischen Stadtstaaten des Festlandes und der Inseln im ersten und zweiten Jhdt. v.Chr.* (Diss., Göttingen, 1967)

Toynbee, Arnold J., *HL = Hannibal's Legacy. The Hannibalic War's Effects on Roman Life*, 2 vols (1965)

——, *Greek Historical Thought from Homer to the Age of Heraclius* (1952 & repr.)

Traill, J. S., *The Political Orgnaisation of Attica. A Study of the Demes, Trittyes and Phylai, and their Representation in the Athenian Council = Hesperia* Suppl. XIV (1975)

Treves, Piero, *Demostene e la libertà greca* (Bari, 1933)

Trigger, Bruce G., *Gordon Childe: Revolutions in Archaeology* (1980)

Turner, E. G., 'Egypt and the Roman Empire: the *dekaprōtoi*', in *JEA* 22 (1936) 7-19

Ullmann, Walter, *A History of Political Thought in the Middle Ages* (Pelican Hist. of Pol. Thought, Vol. 2, 1965; improved repr., 1970)

Valdenberg, V., 'Les idées politiques dans les fragments attribués à Pierre le Patrice', in *Byzantion* 2 (1925) 55-76

Vandersleyen, Claude, 'Le mot *laos* dans la langue des papyrus grecs', in *Chr. d'Ég.* 48 (1973) 339-49

Van Gogh, Vincent, *The Complete Letters of Vincent Van Gogh*, 3 vols (London, 1958)

van Hoesen, H. B., and A. C. Johnson, 'A papyrus dealing with liturgies', in *JEA* 12 (1926) 118-19

Várady, László, *Das letzte Jahrhundert Pannoniens, 376-476* (Amsterdam, 1969)

Vasiliev, A. A., *Justin the First* (Cambridge, Mass., 1950)

Vaux, Roland de, *Ancient Israel, Its Life and Institutions*, Eng. trans. by John McHugh (1961)

Vavřínek, Vladimir, 'Aristonicus of Pergamum: pretender to the throne or leader of a slave revolt?', in *Eirene* 13 (1975) 109-29

——, *La Révolte d'Aristonicos* (Prague, 1957)

Vermes, Geza, *Jesus the Jew. A Historian's Reading of the Gospels* (1973)

——, See also under Schürer, Emil, above

Vernant, J.-P., 'Remarques sur la lutte de classe dans la Grèce ancienne', in *Eirene* 4 (1965) 5-19; Eng. trans. by R. Archer and S. C. Humphreys, 'Remarks on the class struggle in ancient Greece', in *Critique of Anthropology* 7 (1976) 67-81. [See p.63 above]

Veyne, P., 'Vie de Trimalcion', in *Annales* 16 (1961) 213-47

——, *Le Pain et le cirque. Sociologie historique d'un pluralisme politique* (Paris, 1976)

Vidal-Naquet, Pierre, RHGE = 'Réflexions sur l'historiographie grecque de l'esclavage', in *Actes du Colloque 1971 sur l'esclavage = Annales littéraires de l'Univ. de Besançon* 140 (Paris, 1972) 25-44

——, 'Les esclaves grecs étaient-ils une classe?', in *Raison présente* 6 (1968) 103-12. [See pp.63-5 above]

——, 'Introduction to Pierre Savinel's French translation, *Flavius Josèphe. La guerre des Juifs* (Paris, 1977)

——, See also under Austin, M. M., and Vidal-Naquet

Ville, Georges, 'Les jeux de gladiateurs dans l'empire chrétien', in *MEFR* 72 (1960) 273-335

Visscher, F. De: see under De Visscher, F.

Vittinghof, Friedrich, 'Die Bedeutung der Sklaven für den Übergang von der Antike ins abendländische Mittelalter', in *Hist. Ztschr.* 192 (1961) 265-72

——, 'Die Theorien des historischen Materialismus über den antiken "Sklavenhalterstaat". Probleme der Alten Geschichte bei den "Klassikern" des Marxismus und in der modernen sowjetischen Forschung', in *Saeculum* 11 (1960) 89-131

Vlastos, Gregory, SPT = 'Slavery in Plato's thought', in *Philosophical Review* 50 (1941) 289-304, repr. in *SCA* (ed. M. I. Finley) 133-48; cf. 148-9

——, 'Does slavery exist in Plato's Republic?', in *CP* 63 (1968) 291-5

Vogt, Joseph, *ASIM* = *Ancient Slavery and the Ideal of Man* (1974), an Eng. trans. by Thomas Wiedemann of *Sklaverei und Humanität. Studien zur antiken Sklaverei und ihrer Erforschung*[2] = *Historia* Einzelschrift 8 (1972)

Vogt, Joseph (editor), *Bibliographie zur antiken Sklaverei* (Bochum, 1971)

Walbank, F. W., *HCP* = *A Historical Commentary on Polybius*, 3 vols (1957-79)

——, *The Awful Revolution. The Decline of the Roman Empire in the West* (1969)

——, 'Nationalism as a factor in Roman history', in *HSCP* 76 (1972) 145-68

——, 'The problem of Greek nationality', in *Phoenix* 5 (1951) 41-60

——, 'Were there Greek federal states?', in *Scripta Classica Israelica* 3 (1976/7) 27-51

Waldmann, Helmut, *Die kommagenischen Kultreformen unter König Mithradates I, Kallinikos und seinem Sohne Antiochos I* = *Études Préliminaires aux Religions Orientales dans l'Empire Romain* 34 (Leiden, 1973)

Wallace, S. L., *Taxation in Egypt from Augustus to Diocletian* (1938). (For reviews, see p.581 n.5 [on IV.i] above)

Walton, C. S., 'Oriental senators in the service of Rome: a study of Imperial policy down to the death of Marcus Aurelius', in *JRS* 19 (1929) 38-66

Waltzing, J.-P., *Étude historique sur les corporations professionnelles chez les Romains*, 4 vols (Louvain, 1895-1900)

Ward-Perkins, J. B., 'The Roman West and the Parthian East', in *PBA* 51 (1965) 175-99

Warmington, B. H., 'The career of Romanus, Comes Africae', in *Byzantion* 49 (1956) 55-64

Watson, G. R., 'Stipendium', in *OCD*[2] 1014 (with bibliography)

Weaver, P. R. C., *Familia Caesaris: a Social Study of the Emperor's Freedmen and Slaves* (1972)

——, 'Social mobility in the early Roman Empire: the evidence of the Imperial freedmen and slaves', in *Past & Present* 37 (1967), repr. in *SAS* (ed. M. I. Finley) 121-40

——, '*Vicarius* and *vicarianus* in the *Familia Caesaris*', in *JRS* 54 (1964) 117-28

Weber, Marianne, *Max Weber. Ein Lebensbild* (Tübingen, 1926; repr. Heidelberg, 1950)

Weber, Max, *AA* = *Agrarverhältnisse im Altertum*, from *Handwörterbuch der Staatswissenschaften*[3] (1909), republished in (and cited in this book from) *Gesammelte Aufsätze zur Sozial- und Wirtschaftsgeschichte* (Tübingen, 1924) 1-288

——, *ASAC* = *The Agrarian Sociology of Ancient Civilizations*, Eng. trans. with Introd. by R. I. Frank (1976) of (1) *AA* (above), pp.37-386, and (2) the German original of *SCDAC* (below), pp.389-411

——, *CIB* = *On Charisma and Institution Building* (Selected papers, ed. with an Introd. by S. N. Eisenstadt, 1968)

——, *ES* = *Economy and Society. An Outline of Interpretive Sociology*, 3 vols, ed. Guenther Roth and Claus Wittich (New York, 1968), an Eng. trans. mainly from *WuG*[4] (1956; cf. *WuG*[5] below). [There is now an edn of *ES* in 2 vols, 1978, with a new Preface and some additional bibliography]

——, *FMW* = *From Max Weber. Essays in Sociology*, trans. and ed. with an Introd. by H. H. Gerth and C. Wright Mills (1946; paperback 1958 & repr.)

——, *GAzRS* = *Gesammelte Aufsätze zur Religionssoziologie*, 3 vols (Tübingen: I[2], 1922; II, 1921; III, 1921)

——, GEH = General Economic History, trans. by F. H. Knight (New York, 1961, a partial trans. of WG, below)

——, MSS = The Methodology of the Social Sciences, trans. and ed. by Edward A. Shils and Henry A. Finch (New York, 1949) from three essays published in 1917, 1904 and 1905, and repr. in Weber's Gesammelte Aufsätze zur Wissenschaftslehre (now in a 3rd edn, by Johannes Winckelmann, Tübingen, 1968)

——, RA = Die römische Agrargeschichte in ihrer Bedeutung für das Staats- und Privatrecht (Stuttgart, 1891)

——, SCDAC = 'Social causes of the decline of ancient civilisation', Eng. trans. in Jnl of General Education 5 (1950) 75-88, repr. in Eldridge, MWISR (q.v., above) 254-75 and elsewhere, with a different trans. by R. I. Frank in ASAC (above) 389-411. The original German article, 'Die soziale Gründe des Untergangs der antiken Kultur', was first published in Die Wahrheit in 1896 and repr. in Gesammelte Aufsätze zur Sozial- und Wirtschaftsgeschichte (above) 289-311

——, TSEO = The Theory of Economic and Social Organization, Eng. trans. by A. M. Henderson and Talcott Parsons (1947 & repr.) of Part I of WuG (below)

——, WG³ = Wirtschaftsgeschichte. Abriss der universalen Sozial- und Wirtschaftsgeschichte. Aus der nachgelassene Vorlesungen, ed. S. Hellman and M. Palyi, 3rd edn, rev. J. F. Winckelmann (Berlin, 1958)

——, WuG⁵ = Wirtschaft und Gesellschaft = Grundriss der verstehenden Soziologie, 5th edn, ed. Johannes Winckelmann, 3 vols (Tübingen, 1976). This is a later edn of the work of which ES (above) is a trans.

——, Gesammelte Aufsätze zur Soziologie und Sozialpolitik (Tübingen, 1924), including Weber's lecture to the Austro-Hungarian officer corps in July 1918, 'Der Sozialismus' (492-518): see pp.87 & 553 n.14 above

——, The Protestant Ethic and the Spirit of Capitalism, Eng. trans. by Talcott Parsons, 2nd edn, with Introd. by Anthony Giddens (1976)

Weil, Raymond, AH = Aristote et l'histoire. Essai sur la 'Politique' (Paris, 1960)

Weiss, Egon, GP = Griechisches Privatrecht I (Leipzig, 1923)

Welles, C. Bradford, RCHP: see Part I of this Bibliography

——, Bibliography of M. Rostovtzeff, in Historia 5 (1956) 358-81

——, Biography of M. Rostovtzeff, in Architects and Craftsmen in History. Festschrift für A. P. Usher (Tübingen, 1956) 55-73

——, 'The population of Roman Dura', in Studies in Roman Economic and Social History in Honor of A. C. Johnson, ed. P. R. Coleman-Norton (Princeton, 1951) 251-74

——, 'III. The Constitution of Edessa', in A. R. Bellinger and Welles, 'A third-century contract of sale from Edessa in Osrhoene', in YCS 5 (1935) 95-154, at 121-42

Welskopf, E. Ch., Die Produktionsverhältnisse im alten Orient und in der griechisch-römischen Antike (Berlin, 1957). [See pp. 23 & 542 n.7 above]

Welskopf, E.Ch. (editor), Hellenische Poleis. Krise - Wandlung - Wirkung, 4 vols (Berlin, 1974)

Welwei, K.-W., 'Abhängige Landbevölkerungen auf "Tempelterritorien" im hellenistischen Kleinasien und Syrien', in Anc. Soc. 10 (1979) 97-118

——, Unfreie im antiken Kriegsdienst, I. Athen und Sparta (= Forschungen zur antiken Sklaverei 5, Wiesbaden, 1974); and II. Die kleineren und mittleren griechischen Staaten und die hellenistischen Reiche (= Forschungen zur antiken Sklaverei 8, Wiesbaden, 1977)

West, M. L., 'The life and times of Theognis', ch. iv (pp.65-71) of Studies in Greek Elegy and Iambus = Untersuchungen zur antiken Literatur und Geschichte 14, ed. H. Dörrie and P. Moraux (Berlin/New York, 1974)

Westermann, W. L., ASA = 'Athenaeus and the slaves of Athens', in Athenian Studies presented to W. S. Ferguson = HSCP, Suppl. (1940) 451-70, repr. in SCA (ed. M. I. Finley) 73-92

——, SSGRA = The Slave Systems of Greek and Roman Antiquity (= Memoirs of the American Philosophical Society 40, Philadelphia, 1955)

White, K. D., RF = Roman Farming (1970)

——, 'Latifundia', in *BICS* 14 (1967) 62-79

——, 'Roman agricultural writers, I. Varro and his predecessors', in *ANRW* I.iv (1973) 439-97

White, Lynn, *MTSC* = *Medieval Technology and Social Change* (1962)

——, TIMA = 'Technology and invention in the Middle Ages' in *Speculum* 15 (1940) 141-59

——, 'The expansion of technology 500-1500', ch.4 (pp. 143-74) of *The Fontana Economic History of Europe, I. The Middle Ages*, ed. C. M. Cipolla (1972)

——, 'What accelerated technological progress in the Western Middle Ages?', in *Scientific Change*, ed. A. C. Crombie (1963) 272-91, cf. 311-14, 327-32

Whitehead, David, *The Ideology of the Athenian Metic* (= Cambridge Philological Soc., Suppl. Vol. 4, 1977)

Whittaker, C. R., 'Rural labour in three Roman provinces', in *Non-Slave Labour in the Greco-Roman World*, ed. Peter Garnsey (= Cambridge Philol. Soc., Suppl. Vol. 6, 1980) 73-99. [See pp.563-4 n.13a above]

——, See also under Garnsey, P. D. A., and Whittaker (editors)

Wickert, Lothar, PF = 'Der Prinzipat und die Freiheit', in *Symbola Coloniensia Iosepho Kroll Sexagenario . . . oblata* (Cologne, 1949) 111-41

——, 'Princeps (civitatis)', in *RE* XXII.ii (1954) 1998-2296; with *ANRW* II.i (1974) 3-76

Wilcken, Ulrich, *W.Chr.*: see Part I above

——, *Gr. Ostr.* = *Griechische Ostraka aus Aegypten und Nubien*, 2 vols (Leipzig/Berlin, 1899)

Wilhelm, Adolf, 'Urkunden aus Messenien', in *JOAI* 17 (1914) 1-119

Wilkes, J. J., *Dalmatia* (1969)

Will, Édouard, *HPMH* = *Histoire politique du monde hellénistique (323-30 av. J.-C.)*, 2 vols (Nancy, 1966-7)

——, *Le Monde grec et l'Orient, I. Le Ve siècle, 510-403* (Paris, 1972)

Will, Édouard, Claude Mossé, and Paul Goukowsky, *Le Monde grec et l'Orient, II. Le IVe siècle et l'époque hellénistique* (Paris, 1975)

Willetts, R. F., *The Law Code of Gortyn* (= *Kadmos*, Suppl. 1, Berlin, 1967)

——, *Aristocratic Society in Ancient Crete* (1955)

Williams, Wynne, 'Formal and historical aspects of two new documents of Marcus Aurelius', in *ZPE* 17 (1975) 37-56

Windisch, H., *Die Orakel des Hystaspes* (Amsterdam, 1929)

Wirszubski, Ch., LPIR = *Libertas as a Political Idea at Rome during the Late Republic and Early Principate* (1950). [See pp.367-9 above]

——, 'Cicero's *cum dignitate otium*: a reconsideration', in *JRS* 44 (1954) 1-13

Wiseman, T. P., *New Men in the Roman Senate 139 B.C. - A.D. 14* (1971)

——, 'Factions and family trees', in *Liverpool Classical Monthly* 1 (1976) 1-3

Woess, Friedrich von, 'Personalexekution und cessio bonorum im römischen Reichsrecht', in *ZSS* 43 (1922) 485-529

Wolff, Hartmut, *Di Constitutio Antoniniana und Papyrus Gissensis 40.I*, 2 vols (Diss., Cologne, 1976)

Woloch, Michael, 'Four leading families in Roman Athens (A.D. 96-161)', in *Historia* 18 (1969) 503-10

Woodhouse, A. S. P., PL² = *Puritanism and Liberty, Being the Army Debates (1647-9) from the Clarke MSS with Supplementary Documents*, 2nd edn (1950)

Woodward, A. M., 'Inscriptions from Thessaly and Macedonia', in *JHS* 33 (1913), at 337-46

Wright, Gavin, 'Prosperity, progress, and American slavery', Chapter Seven (pp.302-36) of *Reckoning with Slavery*, by Paul A. David and others (1976 & repr.)

Yavetz, Zvi, 'Levitas popularis', in *Atene e Roma* n.s. 10 (1965) 97-110

——, 'The living conditions of the urban plebs in Republican Rome', in *Latomus* 17 (1958) 500-17, repr. in *CRR* (ed. Seager) 162-79

——, *Plebs and Princeps* (1969)

——, 'Plebs sordida', in *Athen.* n.s. 43 (1965) 295–311

Yeo, C. A., 'Land and sea transportation in Imperial Italy', in *TAPA* 77 (1946) 221–44

——, 'The development of Roman plantation and marketing of farm products', in *Finanzarchiv* 13 (Tübingen, 1952) 321–42; and 'The economics of Roman and American slavery', in id. 445–85

Youtie, H. C., *Scriptiunculae*, 2 vols (Amsterdam, 1973)

Zepos, J. and P., *Ius Graecoromanum*, 8 vols (Athens, 1931; repr. Aalen, 1962)

Zulueta, Francis de, *Inst. of Gaius* = *The Institutes of Gaius*, 2 vols: *Part I, Text with critical notes and trans.* (1946); *Part II, Commentary* (1953)

Index

References to passages of special interest or importance are sometimes placed in italics, and occasionally then by themselves at the beginning of an entry. Greek words are transliterated. As a rule, I have not mentioned separately here those passages in the Notes which can easily be found by consulting the relevant part of the main text (or appendices) where references are given to the notes concerned.

I had intended to provide an Index of Sources, but the task proved an impossible one, owing to the vast number and range of the sources cited above. I have tried to make up for this to some extent by giving in this Index, under the names of the authors concerned, references to passages in which I have written (or mentioned) a discussion of some texts of special interest; and the same applies to some modern works that are either important or at least well known.

Aalders, G. J. D.: 550 n.13
Abdera: 228, 507
Abelites/Abelonii: 449
Abgar, dynast of Edessa: 537
Abrettenus: see under 'Zeus'
Abthugni: 467
Abulpharagius (Gregory Abû'l Faraj, Syrian Jacobite historian): see under 'Bar Hebraeus'
Abu Simbel: 182
Abydus: 507
Acarnania: 507
Accame, Silvio: 607 n.35, 660 n.5
acclamation (epiboēsis, succlamatum est, etc.), measures passed by: 533
accountability of magistrates in democracy: see under 'euthyna'
accounting, ancient: 114, 346-7
Achaea, Achaeans, Achaean League: 163, 230, 304, 307, 524-5
Achan, fate of: 332
Achilles: 185
Acisilene (in Armenia): see under 'Anaïtis'
Acragas: 280, 523. And see under 'Agrigentum'
actio doli, or de dolo malo: 460
Actium, battle of: 8, 360, 361, 363
actor (pragmateutēs): 132
Adaarmanes (Persian): 319
Adam and Eve, myth of, as buttress of male 'superiority': 107
Adams, Bertrand: 572 n.73
adoratio: 384
Adrianople: 480, 653 n.42
adscripticii (enapographoi, also originarii, originales, tributarii): 148 (with 564-5 n.16), 159, 250, 252-3, 255
Aegean islands, in Later Roman census: 250
Aegina: 41, 120, 271, 547 n.6
Aegospotami, battle of: 74
Aelafius (vicar of Africa), Constantine's letter to: 399
Aemilia (district in north Italy): 11
Aemilius Rectus: see under 'Rectus'
Aeneas Tacticus: 298 (with 609 nn.56-7)
aerarium militare: 358, 362
Aeschines: 299, 604 n.27

Aeschylus: 24; Marx on: 24
Aesop: 444
Aëtius, Flavius: 480
Aetolians: 525
Aezani, in Phrygia: 538-9 n.3 (on I.iii), 568 n.38
Africa, Roman north: 6, 97, 120, 125-6, 132, 144-5 (with 563-4 n.13a), 215-16 and 218 (with 582 n.18), 240, 242, 265, 313, 356, 370, 382, 391, 403, 434-5, 445-6, 475, 482, 490, 492, 496, 502-3, 582 n.20
Africanus, Caecilius: see under 'Caecilius'
Aga Bey Köy (village in Lydia): 216
Agag, king of the Amalekites: 332
Agatharchides of Cnidus: 150, 562-3 n.8
Agennius Urbicus: 242
Agesilaus II, king of Sparta: 190, 295
Agis IV, king of Sparta: 118-19, 215, 608-9 n.55
Agonis of Lilybaeum: 570 n.48
agrestis: 494
'agribusiness': 210
agricultural writers, Roman (based on Greek sources): 234-5. See also under 'Cato', 'Columella', 'Mago', 'Pliny the Elder'
Agrigentum: 522-3. And see under 'Acragas'
Agrippa, M. Vipsanius: 193, 265, 323; speaker in Dio Cassius LII: 265, 323, 615 n.56
Agrippa II, king of Judaea: 192
Agyrrhium: 523
Ahab, king of Israel: 151 (with 565 n.23); name used as a term of abuse: 405
Ahenobarbus, Domitius: 213
Ai, Israelite claim of massacre at: 332 (with 617 n.10)
Aigiale (on Amorgos): 527
Alamanni, Alamans (a major German people): 249, 514, 517 etc.
Alans: 476, 516, 517
Alaric, Visigothic king: 479
Albania, ancient (Azerbaijan): 568 n.37
Albania, modern: 7
Albinus, Clodius: 477
Alcaeus: 279
Alcibiades: 291, 415, 562 n.6, 565 n.22, 605 n.29
Alexander 'the Great': 10, 12-13, 19, 74, 97, 118, 119, 150, 151, 155, 172, 186, 260, 270, 292, 295, 299, 301, 302, 304-5, 325, 477, 525

Alexander Isius, of Aetolia: *118*
Alexander, Ti. Julius, prefect of Egypt: 163, 167 (with 572 n. 68)
Alexander the logothete: 481
Alexander, bishop of Alexandria: *403*, 448
Alexander Severus (Roman emperor): 390, 488, 512
Alexandreia in the Troad: 119
Alexandria: 12-13, 128-9, 132, 162, 305, 319, 396, 403, 405, 437, 448, 475, 484, 496; population of: 540 n.11; rich merchants at: 129; public corn-dole at: *195-6*; its suspension: 196
Alfenus Varus, Roman lawyer: see under '*Digest*'
Alföldy, Géza: 242, 574 n.3, 575 n.18, *616 n.61*, 650 n.8, 655 n.43
Algeria: see under 'Numidia'
Alis (woman of Oxyrhynchus): 103
allegory: *437*
Allen, Walter: 626 n.51
almsgiving, Christian: *433-5, 438*, 496; its expiatory character: 434-6; its Jewish roots: 434-5, 438; Optatus on: 434-5; Clement of Alexandria on: 435; Ambrose on: 435-6
Alypius: 366-7
Amalekites, Israelite massacre of: 332
Amaseia, in Pontus: 153
Ambracia: 609 n.62
Ambrose, St.: *220, 421,* 435-6
Ameria (part of Pontic Cabeira): 568 n.37
American Old South (antebellum South): *54-5*, 122, 142, 143-4, 148, 200-1, 227, 229, 232-3, 234, 421, 424, 549 n.18
   slaves and free in: *54-5*
   Christianity as a method of social control in: 424
   family life of slaves in (including break-up of): 148
   slave marriages never legally recognised in: 148
   'break-even' point in rearing slaves in: *232-3*
   prices of slaves in: 227
   free hired labour in: 200-1; hired labour of slaves in: 227
   expanding markets of, for cotton: 227 (with 232 & 587 n.8); for tobacco and sugar: 232
amicitia and *amici* (of emperor and others): 365-6 (with 626 n.44)
Amisus: 309
Ammianus Marcellinus: 11, 48 (with 547 n.5), 128, 220, 247, 258, 321, 341, 378-9, 387-8, 390-1, 394, 451, 478-80, 485, 485-7, 489-90, 498, 513-14
   regards Christians as worse than wild beasts to each other: *451*; records injustice or cruelty to 'barbarians' without disapproval: 48 (with 547 n.5)
Amorgos: 527
Amorites, Israelite massacre of: 332
Amphipolis: 292
Amphis: 120-1
amphitheatres: 318
Ampliatus (slave of Roman Church): 238, 254
Amyclae, temple of Apollo at: 275
Amyot: 354
anachōrēsis (secessio): 215 (with 581 n.9)
Anaïtis, of Acisilene and elsewhere in Armenia: 568 n.38; of Zela in Pontus: 154
Anastasiopolis (in Galatia): 225-6, 496
Anastasius I (Roman emperor): 272, 318-19, 404-5, 406, 445, 473, 493, 561 n.21, 577 n.19
Anaximenes (=Ps.-Arist., *Rhet. ad Alex.*): 191, 285
Anchialus: 653 n.42
Anchises (in *Aeneid*): 327
Ancyra (Ankara): 530, 531, 627 n.7
Anderson, Perry: 155, 269, *544 n.15*
Andrewes, Antony: 189 (with 578 n.24), 193, 282

Andreyev, V. N.: *582 n.20*
Andros: 604 n.27
Androtion: 604 n.27, 605 n.29
angariae (angareiai): *14-16* (with 539-40 n.8), 135, 205-6, 227-8, 287
Anicetus (ex-slave and rebel): 649 n.3
Annas, Julia: 557-8 n.30
Anonymus, De rebus bellicis: 394, *489*
Anonymus Valesianus: 513
Anoup (Egyptian tenant): 223
Antaeopolis, nome of: 222
Antalcidas, Peace of ('King's Peace'): 295
Antichrist, as a term of abuse: 405
Antigonus (Egyptian): 223
Antinoöpolis: 17, 196
Antioch, Pisidian: 119 (with 559 n.13), 154, 219, 533, 628 n.7
Antioch (in Syria): 12, 15, 187, 196, 219-20, 305, 319, 320-1, 365, 405, 475, 488, 496
   public corn-dole at, suspended after 'riot of the statues' (387): *196*
   famine at (in 362-3): *219-20*; famine at (in 384-5): *220*
   merciless treatment of peasants by landowners of: *226*
   '1-2000 slaves' of some Antiochene landowners (John Chrysostom): 242
   Jews of: 305
   capture by Shapur I (c.256): 475; sack by Chosroes I (540): 486, 654 n.42
   persecution in 608-9 of Monophysites (Jews?) by Bonosus, under Phocas: 652 n.34
Antiochus I, king of Commagene: *154*
Antiochus I, Seleucid king: 157
Antiochus II, Seleucid king, sale of land by, to ex-Queen Laodice: 152 (with *566 nn.25-6*)
Antiochus III, Seleucid king: 521, 536
Antiochus IV Epiphanes, Seleucid king: 558 n.9
Antipater (Macedonian general): *292, 301, 304*
Antipater of Sidon: 48
Antipater of Thessalonica: *38*, 24, 377
'antiquarians', and antiquarian research: 81-2
anti-Semitism and its literature: 442
Antisthenes: 130
Antistius Rusticus, L.: *219*
Antonine Age/period (A.D. 138-193): 13, 174, 236, 323, 454, 458, 459, 468-9, 470, 476, 491; often depicted as a Golden Age: 470
Antoninus (Roman defector to Persia, A.D. 359): *486-7*, 128
Antoninus Pius, Roman emperor: see under 'Pius'
Antonius, C. (consul with Cicero, 63 B.C.): 354
Antonius Labeo, M. (Roman lawyer): see under 'Labeo, M. Antonius'
Antony, Mark (M. Antonius): 354-5, 361
Antony, St. (hermit): *408*
Anytus: 124-5
Apamea/Celaenae, in Phrygia (Bithynia): 312, 317 (with 613 n.38), 532
Apamea in Syria: 568-9 n.38
apartheid, Gibeonites as Scriptural justification for: 332
Apelles: 270
Aphrodisias: 530, 531
Aphrodite: 18, 154, 393; 'Kallipygos': *18*; temple of, at Eryx in Sicily: 154 (with 569 nn.39-40)
Aphrodito (Egyptian village): 213, *222,* 223-4
Apion family at Oxyrhynchus: *169*, 223
Apocalyptic literature, Jewish and Christian: 6, *440,* 442-3. For 'The Apocalypse' = the last book of the

N.T., see 'Revelation, Book of'. See also 'Daniel, Book of', 'Sibylline Oracles', 'Oracle of the Potter', 'Oracle of Hystaspes'
Apollinaris of Laodicea: 450
Apollonius of Tyana: 14, 129, 323; his conversation with a tax-collector at Zeugma: 129
Appian: 24, 202, 208, 235, 323, 353, 359, 361, 362, 378, 409, *511*, 521, 526, 614 nn.49, 51
apprentices and servants: 203
Apuleius: 186, 563-4 n.13a
Apulia (district of Roman Italy): 254
aqueducts, Roman: 193
Aquitanica Prima (Gallic province): 486
Arabia, Arabs (Muslims) and their conquests: 6-7, 8, 265, 400, 401, *483-4* (with *651-2 nn.32-7*), 537
    regarded by Jacobite and Coptic Christians as a 'lesser evil' than the persecuting Chalcedonian Catholics: *484*
    their poll-tax on Christians: 484
Aradus (in Phoenicia): 569 n.38
Arague (village in Phrygia): *216*
Aramaic: 427, *579 n.37*; the language of Jesus' preaching: 427
Arbitio (Magister Militum and consul): 484-5
Arcadius (Eastern Roman emperor): 252, 501
arcani: 479
Arcesilaus (sculptor): 270
Arcesine (on Amorgos): *527*, 604 n.27
Archelaus, king of Cappadocia: 119
Archelaus, priest of Ma at Pontic Comana: 154
Archelaus of Chersonesus: 18
architects, Greek: 596-7 n.2
Architeles (Corinthian): 132
Archytas of Tarentum, on geometric and arithmetical proportion: *413-14*
'Ardiaioi' (of Illyria): 149
Arelate (Arles): 128 (with *561 n.19*)
Areobindus: 264
Areopagus: see under 'Athens'
Arginusae, battle of: 441
Argos: 139, 160, 295-6; 'skytalismos' at (in 370): 296
Arian heresy, Arians (including Semi-Arians): 403, 448-51 (esp. *450*). And see under 'Arius'
Aristarchus (character in dialogue by Xenophon): *180-1*
Aristeides, Aelius: 309, *323* (with *615 n.54*), 386; his picture of Rome as the ideal *dēmokratia* (same refs, except first)
Aristion (Athenian 'tyrant' c.87 B.C.): *526* (with *660 n.5*)
Aristion, Claudius (of Ephesus): 312
aristocracy, hereditary: 278-9
Aristodicides of Assos (*RCHP* 10-13): *157* (with *569 n.44*)
Aristonicus of Pergamum: *345, 529*
Aristophanes (Attic comedian): 41, 104, 124-5, 144, 163, 185, 206, 290, 292, 413, 441, 505
Aristophanes of Byzantium: 139
Aristotle (and Ps.-Arist.): *4*, 24, *35*, 53, *55-6*, *69-80*, *113*, *116-17*, *129-30*, *140*, 149, *182-5*, 229, *282-3*, *285*, *286-8*, *289-90*, *305-6*, *416-18*, 422, *600-1 nn.4*, *9*, *602-3 n.24*, 100, 115, 131, 142, 146, 148, 150, 160, 189, 190-1, 197-8, 279, 323, 353, 359, 402, 413-14, 423-4, 437, 440, 441, 536, 575 n.11, 605 n.29
    his influence on (and similarity of thought to) Marx: *55-6*, *69 ff*. (esp. *74*, *77-80*)
    his analysis of hired labour: *182-5*
    his insistence on the necessary minimum of political rights: *74-6*
Aristoxenus of Tarentum: 411
Arius (heresiarch): *403*. And see under 'Arian heresy',
'Thalia'
Armenia, Armenians: 345, 483, 517; Roman province: 345; Monophysitism of: 448
armies (and fleets):
    military efficiency sometimes essential, in face of external threats, relevance here of economic, social and political factors: *260*, *261-2*; necessity to base army on vigorous peasantry: *5*, *261*, 501
    light-armed and naval crews recruited from non-propertied: 207; slaves occasionally used as rowers: 207, 213
    until 362 B.C., conscription applied to Athenian Thetes (sub-hoplites) in emergencies only: *207* (with 581 n.8, on IV.i)
    Greek hoplite armies: 115, 280
    Roman army: 25, 29-30, 261-2, 469, 491, 501 etc.; its size: *491*; cost of maintaining it: *469*, *491*; discipline in Roman army under Empire: *264-6*
    soldiers in Roman Empire among the 'privileged groups': *456-8*, *461-2*
    conscription (mainly Roman): *207-8*, 4, 6, 44, 206, 261, 335, 373, 501-2; Marx on Roman conscription: 335. And see under 'hoplites'
Armorica (in Gaul): 478-9
Arpi: 520
Arretium: 519
Arrian: 119, 186, 565 n.19
Arsaces, king of Parthia, letter of Mithridates VI of Pontus to (in Sallust): *443*, 356
Arsames (Persian satrap): 118
Artabanus III, king of Parthia: 536
Artemis, temple and cult of, at Ephesus: 164, 270, 313
artisans, craftsmen (*technitai*, *cheiro-technai* etc.): *33*, *182-4*, *197-9*, *205*, *269-75*, *372*, 4, 52, 77, 78, 114-15, 116, 117, 126-7, 128, 130-1, 133, 186, 190-3, 199, 200, 201-2, 203, 524, 525
    'assets and credit embodied in their hands' (Sallust): *271*, *372*
    basic distinction between skilled craftsman (*technitēs* etc.) and hired labourer: *182-4*, *197-9*
    misleading to say 'the ancient Greeks' despised craftsmen: *274-5*
artists (painters, sculptors): 270, 274. And see under 'Polygnotus', 'Praxiteles', and esp. 'Pheidias' and 'Polycleitus'
Arvandus (Praetorian Prefect): 486
Asclepiades of Clazomenae: *316*
?Asemus: 654 n.42
Asheri, David: 162-3, 608 n.55
Asia (continent): 8, 10, 147, 153-8, 160, 172, 299-300
Asia (Roman province): 309, 316, 318, 347, 356, 365, 370
Asia Minor (modern Turkey): 8, 11, 12, 117-19, 150-8, 172, 187, 196, 221-2, 227-8, 250, 283, 300, 345, 365, 447, 477, 483-4, 508-9, 529-33; wealth of: *117-19*
Asiatic/Oriental mode of production: see under 'production'
Asidates (Persian, farming in 400 B.C. near Pergamum): *507-8*, *569 n.42a*
Aspendus: 14 (with *583 n.24*)
Assyria (Roman province): 345
Asturius, Flavius (Magister Militum): 478
Athanasius, St., bishop of Alexandria: 404-5, 448, 449-50, 473, 485
Athanasius, priest of Alexandria: *146*
Athanasius, Flavius . . . (Patrician and prefect of Thebaid), petition of villagers of Aphrodito to: *223-4*
Athaulf (Visigothic chief): 480
Athenaeus: 18, 24, 113, 131, 132, *140*, 146, 202, etc.
Athenion (Athenian 'tyrant' c.87 B.C.): *526* (with *660 n.5*)

Athens, Athenians, Attica: *70-1, 76, 137, 141, 147, 163,*
174-5, 185-6, 188-90, 196, 206, 227, 257, 284-5, 289-
93, 295-9, 301-2, 316, 345-6, 526-7, 562 n.8, 576 n.16,
603-4 n.26, 613 n.35, 654-5 n.42, 11, 78, 92, 100-3,
117-18, 144, 146, 162, 193-4, 201, 212-13, 215, 231,
271, 275, 289, 309, 310, 313, 528-9, 532, 558 n.3 (on
III.ii)
    upholder of democracy in other cities: 288, 294, 296
    why slavery developed most in democratic
Athens: *141-2*
    Athenian laws minimising women's property
rights, and their effects: *101-2*
    Athenian 'empire' (in 5th c.): 290 (with *603-4*
n.26), 293, 294, *345-6*; unique among past empires in
relying on support of lower classes: 290
    naval imperialism a consequence of need to secure
supply-routes: 293; difficulty in financing naval
activities: *292-3* (with *607 n.37*)
    how leading Athenians profited most from the
empire (Thuc. VIII.48.6): 604-5 n.27
    Second Athenian Confederacy (in 4th c.): *292-3*
(with 607 n.35)
      Aeropagus in Roman Principate: *174-5, 526-7*
      And see under 'Aristion (Athenian)', 'Athenion'
etc.
athletics, importance of: 96, 115
Atkinson [Chrimes], K. M. T.: 566 n.31, 569-70 nn.44-7
Atotas the Paphlagonian (miner): 274
Atrestidas (Arcadian): 298-9
Attaleia in Pamphylia: 119
Attalids of Pergamum: 119, 345, 445, 529; Attalus III:
345, 529; Daphitas' epigram: *445*
Atticus, Ti. Claudius (father of Herodes Atticus): 124
Atticus, T. Pomponius (friend of Cicero): 12, 235, 340,
348-9, 356, 370; his use of home-born slaves: 235
Atticus, bishop of Constantinople: *616 n.64*
Attila (the Hun): 260, 265, *487*
auctoratus: 167-8
auctoritas (and *potestas, potentia*): 376, 362, 363, 447
Audring, Gert: 506
Augustan History: see under *Historia Augusta*
Augusta Traiana (in Thrace): 127
Augusta Treverorum (Trier): 128
Augustine, St.: *366-7, 419-21, 437,* 226, 258, 343, 407,
409, 434, 436, 449, 467, 477, 482
Augustus/Octavian (Roman emperor): 8, 120, 166,
175, 181, 194, 304, 313, 354, 356, *360-2, 363-4, 369-*
71, 381, 385, 391-2, 393, 395-6, 494, 510, 521, 529-
30, 534, 535
    his *Res Gestae:* 362, 376, 387, 391; his 'restoration
of the Republic': *350* (with *621 n.1*), 375, cf. 380; his
remark quoted by Macrobius: *360-1* (with *375*); his
attitude to Julius Caesar: *623 n.10*
Aurelian (Roman emperor): 128, 129, 388, 396, 490
Aurelius, Marcus: see under 'Marcus Aurelius'
Aurelius Victor: see under 'Victor, Aurelius'
Ausonius: 12, 221, 514
Auspex, Julius (of the Remi): 524
auspices (*auspicia*): 343-4
Austin, M. M. (with P. Vidal-Naquet): 23, *64-5, 77-8*
autokratōr, as Greek term for emperor, corresponding
to Latin *imperator:* 377-8, 392
automation, as the only imaginable alternative to
slavery in antiquity: *113, 140*
autonomia ('autonomy'): 303
autopragia: 222
Autun: 653 & 654 n.42
Auxentius (Late Latin writer): 514
auxilia (Roman) and fleet: 461, 491; difficulty of esti-

mating size: 491; gift of Roman citizenship to
members on discharge (and the change A.D. 140): *461*
Avars: 400-1
Avidius Cassius: 537
Avitus (Western Roman emperor): 407
Axomis (village in Cyrenaica): 595 n.6

Babrius: 18
Bacaudae (peasant rebels in Gaul and Spain): *478-9* (esp.
478), *481,* 476, 487, 503, 650 nn.10, 14
Bacon, Francis: *594 n.4a* (Bacon quoted by Marx)
Badian, Ernst: 42, 165, 339, 345-6, 351, 359, 520-1,
619-20 n.1
Baetica, Roman province of: 309, 468
Baetocaece (in territory of Aradus in Phoenicia): see
under 'Zeus'
'Bahman Yasht': 443 (with 642 n.7)
Bailey, A. M., and J. R. Llobera: *544 n.15*
Bailey, Cyril: 23
Baker, Derek, 585 n.43
bakers, bakeries: 170, 273
Balbinus (Roman emperor): 388
Balbura (in Lycia): 531
Balfour, Lord: *375*
Balkans (Greek and Roman): 6, 242, 502-3, 528-9
Ball, John: 440
Balsdon, J. P. V. Dacre: 371 (with *627 n.58*), 610 n.5
bandits, banditry: see under 'brigands or bandits'
Banks, J. A.: 548-9 n.11
baptism of slave, refusal of, without master's consent:
420
'barbarians':
    'barbarian' and Hellene or Roman: *17*; Greeks and
natives in Egypt: 17
    'barbarians' as 'natural slaves': *416-17*
    injustice or cruelty to, recorded without dis-
approval by Ammianus: 48 (with 547 n.5)
    desertion to, help to, etc.: *7, 474, 476-84, 486-7*
    settlement of (much more extensive in West than
East), within Roman empire, economic and military
consequences of: *243-4, 247-9, 509-18,* 5, 7; two main
types distinguished: 247-8 [Many of the particulars
are not recorded in this Index. The settlements are
listed in chronological order]
Bardy, G.: *325*
Bar Hebraeus (Syrian Jacobite historian = Abul-
pharagius or Gregory Abû'l Faraj): *483-4* (with *652
n.35*), 494
Barker, Ernest: 160, 402, 549 n.1, *552 n.31*
Barnabas, St.: 16
Barnabas, Epistle of: 419-20
Barnes, T. D.: 351, 632 n.67a, 636 n.99, 641 n.4
Barns, John: 446-7
Baron, S. W.: 106, 555 n.9, 633 n.75
Barthes, Roland: 20
Basil 'the Great', St.: 435
Basil II 'the Bulgar-Slayer' (Byzantine emperor): 262-3
basileus (king), as Greek term for Roman emperor: *377-8*
basilikoi: 158. And see under 'King's land'
'Basis and Superstructure' in Marx: 28-9 (with 543 n.13)
baths, dislike of, by Christian ascetics: 446-7
Batiffol, Pierre: 574 n.13
Batnae (in Osrhoene): 561 n.21
Baynes, Norman H.: 386, *400,* 402, *464,* 538 nn.3-4 (on
I.ii), 608 n.53, 634 n.87, 635 n.93. And see under
'Dawes, Elizabeth, and Baynes'
Beazley, J. D.: 598 n.17
Bebel, August, Marx's letter to: 47
Bedale, Stephen: *105-6 (with 556 nn.17-21)*

Beesly, E. S.: *621-2 n.5*
beggars (and apprentices and servants): 203
Belisarius: 263, 319, 480-2, 577 n.19, 651 n.27
Bell, Harold Idris: 206, *223-4, 498-9,* 584 nn.38-9
Belloc, Hilaire: 36
Belshazzar, king of Babylon, name used as a term of abuse: 405
Bendix, Reinhard: 31, *87-8,* 550 n.12
benefactions, 'foundations': *18,* 196-7, 221, 426, 470, 495; 'foundations' not 'charitable': *196-7* (with *579 n.35*), *426*; to Christian Church: 495
'beneficium' (as favour): 342
Beneventum, Arch of (Trajan's): 397
Bengtson, Hermann: 609 n.56
Berchem, Denis van: 579 n.34
Berger, A.: 573 n.75, 573-4 nn.3-4
Berlin: 47, 48
Bernard of Chartres: 98
Berve, Helmut: 599 n.17
Bessas (Justinian's commander in Rome): 221, 481
'Bewusstseinsstrukturen': *553 n.23a*
Bezabde (in Mesopotamia): 486
'Bible', The, veneration of by Early Christians, as 'inspired': 103, 106. And see under 'Daniel, Book of', 'Gospels', 'New Testament', 'Old Testament', 'Parables of Jesus', 'Revelation, Book of', etc.
Bickerman(n)/Bikerman, E. J.: *303, 333-4* (with 618 n.1, on VI.ii), *555 n.4,* 557 n.30, 558 n.9, *600 n.33*
Bieżuńska-Małowist, Iza: 152 (with 566 nn.27-8), 563 n.9, *566-7 n.32,* 571 nn.57-8
billeting soldiers, in Cyprus in Late Republic and in Cyrenaica in Late Empire: 346
Birley, A. R.: 357, 511-12, *620 n.6, 648 nn.11,* 14, 656 n.9
Bithynia (and Bithynia-Pontus): 157, 309, 312, 319-20, 529-30
Bithynians subject to Byzantium: 139, 149
'Black Death': 210, 217
Blake, Robert (Lord): 212, *360-1, 375*; his definition of a British Conservative: *375* (with *360-1*)
Bloch, Marc: 15, 136, 138, 238, *267-8,* 591 n.37, *596 n.2*
'Blues' and 'Greens': see under 'circus factions'
Blum, Jerome: 545 n.14
Blumenberg, Werner: 549 n.21
Bocchoris (Pharaoh): 162
Bodei Giglioni, Gabriella: 577 n.20
Böckh, August: 580-1 n.3
Boeotia: 278
Bolkestein, H.: 591 n.37
Bolte, F., Marx's letter to: *62*
Bolus 'Democritus' of Mendes: *234*
Boniface VIII, Pope, his Bull, *Unam sanctam*: 404
Bonitus (Frank), father of Silvanus: 485
Bonosus (Comes Orientis): 652 n.34
Bosphorus: 478
Bottéro, J.: 573 n.76
Bottomore, T. B.: 21, *43,* 80, 547 n.22
Bottomore, T. B., and M. Rubel: 544 n.3, 548 n.8
bottomry: see under 'maritime loans'
Boukoloi: 468, 648 n.12
boulographoi, at Ancyra and Nicaea: 530-1
'bourgeoisie': 60-1, 463
Bowersock, G. W.: 34, 526, 561 n.21
Bowman, Alan: 129
Boxer, C. R.: *424, 639-40 nn.11-12*
'brainwashing': 411
'bread and circuses': *371-2*
Brecht, Bertolt: 433
Bréhier, Louis: *652 nn.33* (two separate refs), *34, 36, 39*
Brenner, Robert: *83*

Briant, Pierre: 155-6, 566 n.26, 568 n.33, 569 n.41
bricks, brick-stamps, brickyards, and the conclusions of T. Helen and P. Setälä on names of owners of *praedia* or *figlinae* appearing on Roman brick-stamps: *126* (with *560 n.11*)
brigandage, brigands or bandits (*latrones*): *265, 317-18, 475-80,* 489. And see under '*receptores*'
Briggs, Asa (Lord): *548 n.1*
Briscoe, John: *523-4*
Britain, Roman, and Britons: 6, 97, 120, 229, 478-9, 502
Britain and British (modern): 331, *347-8*; British assumption of moral superiority: 331; Marx on British rule in India: *347-8*
Brock, S. P.: *484*
Broughton, T. R. S.: 197, 216, 345, 583 n.33, 597 n.9, 620 n.4
Brown, Elizabeth A. R.: 267 (with 595 n.3)
Brown, Peter: 447, *503, 583 n.24, 585 n.42,* 600 n.8
Browning, Robert: *614 n.41a,* 631 n.52
Brundisium: 477
Brunt, P. A.: *31, 41-2* (with *547 n.21*), *122, 331, 333-7, 339, 351-2, 355, 357-8, 370, 385, 540 n.9, 572 n.65, 594 n.1,* 11, 193, 195, 234, 236, 241, 264-5, 541 n.15, 555 n.7, 575 n.1, 578 n.29, 620 n.6, 625 n.27, 641 n.5
Bruttium: 254, 263
Brutus, M. Junius: 370
Bubon (in Lycia): 531
Buckland, W. W.: 329, 571-3 nn.61, 65, 75, 573-4 nn.1, 3, 575 n.19
Buckler, W. H.: *273*
Bulgaria: 7, 8, 207, 314, 528. And see under 'Parthicopolis'
Bulgars: 517
Bulla or Felix ('brigand'): 318, 477
Bunyan, John, his Christian and the pious pagan: 34-5
burdatio: 498
Burdigala (Bordeaux): 480, 654 n.42
Burford, Alison, 171, 270, *577 n.20,* 22, 578 nn.24-5, 596 n.1 (on IV.vi), *597-8 n.11*
burgarii: 264
Burgundians: 512, 516, 517
Buri: 476
Burstein, S. M.: 608 n.50
Bury, J. B.: 8, 630 n.46
Busolt, Georg (and Busolt-Swoboda): 41, 138, *570-1 n.53,* 600 n.6
Butler, A. J.: 484, *652 n.37,* & 33
Buttrey, T. V.: 586 n.1
Byzantium (city): 8, 138. And see under 'Constantinople'
Byzantine empire: *262-3,* 400, 497; Byzantines called themselves '*Rhomaioi*': 400; successes against many attackers from 7th to 11th cc.: *262-3*

Cabeira (in Pontus): 568 n.37
Caecilian, duovir of Abthugni: 467
Caecilius Africanus, Sextus (Roman lawyer): 165
Caecilius Classicus: see under 'Classicus, Caecilius'
Caecilius Isidorus, C.: see under 'Isidorus, C. Caecilius'
Caesar, C. Julius: 166, 213, 230, 353-4, 358, 361, 362, 363, 369-70, 371; his mass enslavements in Gaul: 230; attitude of Augustus towards his memory: *623 n.10*
Caesarea Paneas (Caesarea Philippi): 428-30
'Caesaro-Papism': *403*
Cain, negro as inheritor of God's curse on: 424
Cairnes, J. E.: 546 n.14
Calabi Limentani, Ida: 598 n.11
Calaris (Cagliari): 405. And see under 'Lucifer'
Calderini, A.: 175
Calestrius Tiro: 309

Calgacus (British chieftain), speech of, in Tacitus: *443*
Caligula (Roman emperor): see under 'Gaius'
Calixtus III, Pope: 424
Callicrates of Leontium: 611 n.13
Callisthenes, Pythian victor-list of Aristotle and: *69*
Callistratus (Roman freedman, in Martial): 178
Callistratus, Roman lawyer: see under '*Digest*'
Callistus (Roman Imperial freedman): 176-7
Calpurnius Flaccus (Roman rhetorician): *167*
Calvisius Taurus: see under 'Taurus'
Cameron, Alan: *318* (with *613-14 n.41a*), *371-2*, *392*, 401, 515
Cameron, Averil: 107 (with 556 n.22a), *399*, *633-4 nn.79-86*
Camillus Scribonianus, L. Arruntius: see under 'Scribonianus'
Campania, Campanians: *483*, 519
Canaan, negro as inheritor of Noah's curse on: 424
Candidus, Ti. Claudius (*ILS* 1140): 477
capital, a 'social production relation' (Marx): *504*, *547 n.1*; fixed/circulating and constant/variable: 58, 504-5
capitalism, an advance, in contrast with earlier systems of unfree labour: 112; development of, from feudal regimes: 259; development in England: 262
capital levies (*eisphora, tributum*): 114
capite censi at Rome: see under '*proletarii*'
Capitolinus, M. Manlius: *337* (with *618 n.5* on VI.ii)
Cappadocia: 119, 157, 321
Capua (in Campania): 196, 519
Caracalla (Roman emperor: M. Aurelius Antoninus): 380, 389, 390, *454-5*
Cardascia, G.: 128, 455, 457-8, 460
Carinus (Roman emperor): 478
Carpi: 512, 513
Carthage: 192, 196, 270-1, 360, 449, 475, 521, 577 n.19
Cartledge, P. A.: *282*, *608 n.47a*, *551 n.28*
Carystus (on Euboea): *527*
casarii (and *servi casati*): 238
Cassander, son of Antipater (Macedonian general): *301*, *304*
Cassandreia (Potidaea): 653 n.42
Cassiodorus: 169, 221, 254, 263-4, 502, 516, 592 n.46, 593 n.51
Cassius, C. (Roman senator and lawyer): *409*
Cassius Dio: see under 'Dio Cassius'
Cassius, Spurius: 337 (with 618 n.5, on VI.ii)
Casson, Lionel: *538 n.2* (on I.iii), *578-9 n.32*
caste: 42, 547 n.22
Castinus, C. Julius Septimius (*ILS* 1153): 477
Castles, Stephen, and Godula Kosack: 21, *67-8* (with *549 n.22*)
castrense peculium: see under '*peculium castrense*'
categories: see under 'concepts', and 'Historical Materialism'
Catiline (L. Sergius Catilina): 89, *352*, *352-3*, 368, *410*, *621-2 n.5*, *622-3 n.7*, *626 n.52*
Cato ('the Censor'): 142, 186, 235, 236, 263, 344, 593-4 n.59
Cawkwell, G. L.: 551 n.27, *559 n.2*
Celaenae (in Phrygia): see under 'Apamea'
censores = timētai: 522, 530, 531, 534
census records: 257
Cephisodotus, son of Praxiteles: 270
Ceramon (Athenian): 180
Cercidas of Megalopolis: 18
Certus, Publicius (Roman senator): *382*
Cervidius Scaevola, Q.: see under '*Digest*'
Chabot, J. B.: editor of Michael the Syrian, *q.v.*
Chadwick, Henry: *405*, *430*, *635 n.93*, *640-1 n.13*, 651 n.32

Chaeronea, battle of (338 B.C.): 292, 298
Chalcedon, Council of: see under 'Councils of the Christian Churches'
Chalcedonians, Chalcedonian 'Orthodox' or 'Catholic': *483-4*
Chalcis (on Euboea): 533
Chalcis (in Syria): 220
Chalon, Gérard: 572 n.68
Chamaeleon of Heraclea Pontica: *562 n.6*
Chamavi (a German people): 248, 513
Chamoux, F.: 534
Chapot, Victor: 518
Charanis, Peter: 517
Charaxus, son of Scamandronymus (and brother of Sappho), of Lesbos: 131
charity: see under 'almsgiving' and 'benefactions'
Charlemagne: 238
Charles V, Emperor: *418*
Charlesworth, M. P.: 374, 392, 397
Charon (in Aristophanes): 441
Chastagnol, A.: 583 nn.25-6 etc.
Chayanov, A. V.: 98
Chersonesus (Greek city in Crimea): 564 n.15
Childe, V. Gordon: 21, *464-5* (with *647 n.33*), 545 n.14
China (modern), People's Republic of, its Agrarian Reform Law: 212; peasants of: 212; meeting of peasants at Li Village Gulch: *212*; Chinese Communists called 'bandits': *318*; wheelbarrow in: 38
Chios: 131, *506*, *529*, 553 n.9 (with 85), *612-13 n.33*
chōris oikountes (slaves and freedmen): *142* (with *563 n.9*), 171, 180, 549 n.24
Chosroes I, king of Persia: 486; sacks Antioch (540): 486
Chosroes II, king of Persia: 483-4; his toleration of Syrian Jacobites, persecuted by Dometianus of Melitene: see under 'Dometianus'
Chremes (character in Comedy): 122
Chremylus (character in Aristophanes, *Plutus*): 144
Christianity, Christian Churches, Christians: 4, *6*, 209, *396-405*, *419-25*, *425-41*, *445-52*, 477, *481-2*, *483-4*, *495-7*;
  'the Christian Church/churches': *420*, 6, 495
  'Pauline Christianity': *105*, 433, 439, 440
  Christian ideology reinforcing Imperial authority: *396-402*; and procuring submissiveness of slaves and lower classes: 209, 398, 401-2, 419-20 (and see under 'Paul, St., doctrine')
  role of Catholic Church in north Africa: *482*
  clergy/clerics: 29, 495; bishops and priests: 365, *474 & 493*, 495-6; large salaries of some bishops: *496*; deacons and minor clergy: 495
  monks and monastic movement: 365, 495; 'Holy Men': *446-7*, 365
  attitude to slavery: *419-25*; to property ownership, of Jesus: *431-3*; of Early Churches: *433-8*
  attitude to women, marriage, sex, virginity etc.: *103-10*
  Rome, Church of: *495-6*, 497; Constantinople, Great Church of: *495-6*, 497; vast wealth of these and other churches: *495-6*; churches as landlords: 225-6, 383, *495-6*
  heresy and schism: *445-52* (esp. *452*), 497, 403-5; a new Christian phenomenon: *452*; N.T. beginnings of: *644 n.26*
  persecutions *of* Christians: 170, 396, 450; persecutions *by* Christians (of each other, pagans, Jews, Manichees etc.): *403-5*, 445-6, 448-52 (esp. *451*)
  And see under e.g. 'Almsgiving', 'Arian heresy' and 'Arius', 'Councils of the Christian Churches', 'Donatism', 'Jesus Christ', 'Parables of Jesus', 'Paul, St., doctrine', 'women' etc.
Chronica Minora (ed. Mommsen, *MGH*), including

Cons. Constant.; Hydatius; Isid., *Hist. Goth.*; Marcellinus Comes; Prosper Tiro, etc.: 513, 514, 516
chrysargyron: see under 'taxation . . . , *collatio lustralis*'
Chryseros (Grand Chamberlain of Theodosius II): 177 (with *574 n.13*)
Chrysippus: *419*
Chrysostom, St. John: *226*, 242, *320*, 555 *n.13*, 585 *n.44*, 616 n.64
Church, churches: see under 'Christianity'
Cibyra: 307-8, 532, 533
Cicero, M. Tullius: *12*, 71, 74, 75 (with 550 n.17), *121-2*, 146-7, 163, 166, 198-9, 234, 235, 241, *286*, 309, *310*, 312, 316, 322, 324, 327, *331*, 335, 337-49 (esp. *344*, *346-7*), 352-7, 359, 366, *368-70*, 372, 376, 414, 417-18, 426, 440, 460, 521-3, 530-1, 534, 536, 611 n.16, 618 n.5 (on VI.ii), *623 n.7*;
   on Ptolemaic revenue (*ap.* Strab.): 540 n.11
   his Latin trans. of Xenophon, *Oeconomicus*: 234
   his belief that States exist primarily to protect private property rights: *286*
   his abuse of Greek Assemblies, in *Pro Flacco*; *310*
   his awareness of the abuses of Roman imperialism: *331* (with *624 n.19*)
   his attitude to the Gracchi: *623 n.7*
Cicero, Quintus Tullius (brother of Marcus): 309
Cilicia (Roman province): 12, 170, 316, *346-7*, *356*, 480, 496
Cincinnatus, L. Quinctius: 121 (with *560 n.5*)
Circumcellions (Donatists): *481-2* (with *651 n.22*)
circus (hippodrome): *318-19*, 320, *451*; at Rome: *451*
circus factions (esp. 'Blues' and 'Greens'): *318* (with *613-14 n.41a*), *401*
citizenship (of Greek cities and of Rome):
   'Rechtsstellung' as a factor that may help to determine class: *42*, *43-5*, *68*
   citizenship of Greek city/cities: 10, 13, 19, 64-5, 94-5, 141, 189-90 etc.; included exclusive access to freehold land ownership, but broadened in Hellenistic period: 94-5, *288-9*; effect of citizenship on 'class': 95
   isopoliteia, with prominent men becoming citizens and even councillors of other cities in Roman period (and Roman legislation on this): 95
   metics (resident foreigners: *metoikoi*, *paroikoi*, etc.): *95-6* (with 554 n.29), *289*, 79, 92, 141, 189-90, 197, 289, 551 n.27; at Athens (and presumably most other cities) they could lease land: 94-5, 289
   Roman citizenship: 61, 95, 96, 350, 454-6, *461-2*; finally perceived as a superfluous distinction which could virtually (in effect) disappear: *462*
   'dual citizenship': 348-9; '*civitas sine suffragio*': 349
   incolae: *540-1 n.15*, *554 n.30*
   attributi: 540-1 n.15
   And see under '*paroikoi*'
Citti, Vittorio: *543 n.7*
'Civil Service', Roman Imperial: *29-30*, *491-2*; total numbers of, in Later Roman Empire: *491-2*; represented a burden on the Roman economy out of proportion to its numbers: *492-3*
   'palatine' bureaux of: 491, 492, *500*
civil wars in Graeco-Roman world: 265-6, *475-6*, *488-9*; in 3rd c., contests for Imperial throne were not class struggles: *475-6*, *489*, cf. 265-6
Civilis, C. Julius, revolt of (69-70): 468
Clarentius (son of a slave of the Roman Church): *254*
clarissimi: 406, 473
Clarke, G. W.: 646 n.22, 656 n.7
class, classes, class struggle/conflict, class society, class consciousness:
   definitions: *42-5*, cf. *31-2*, 37, *40-2* etc.; class as a

relationship: *32*, *43*; as also is *capital*: *547 n.1*
   distinctions between historical and sociological problems in definition of classes: *40-2*
   'explosiveness' of the concept of class, and its 'threatening' nature: *31*, *45*, cf. 22
   membership of more than one class: *44-5*
   slaves as a class: *63-5*; women (or married women) as a class: *98-103*
   Marx's failure to complete a definition of class: 32, 59
   why the 1859 *Preface* contains no reference to class struggle: *46-7*
   emergence of the concept of class struggle in Marx's thought: *55-7*
   class *consciousness* not a necessary element in class: *44*, 3, 57, 62-3
   class struggle may be on political plane or not: *44*, 3, 46, 57, 58
   class struggle on ideological plane: *409-52*, 6, 66
   behaviour (and morality) of classes, compared with States and individuals: *47-9*
   importance of control of the State in class struggle: *286-8* (cf. *96-7*, *279-81*, 333, 336, etc.)
   class and status distinctions contrasted: *63-6*, *86-94*; they are sometimes confused, even by Marx and Engels: 66
   Marx's concept of, never discussed by Max Weber: 88-90
Classicus, Caecilius (governor of Baetica): *382*
Claudia Bassa: 132
Claudia (Late Latin poet): 377, 515
Claudius [I], Roman emperor: 143, 176, *322*, 362, 372, 392
Claudius [II] Gothicus, Roman emperor: 383
Claudius, Appius: 304
Claudius Pulcher, C.: 522
Clausing, Roth: 240, 243, 510, 591 n.37
Clavel-Lévêque, Monique: 660 n.11
Clazomenae: 316, 469
Clearchus, tyrant of Heraclea Pontica: *296-8*
Cleisthenes (Athenian lawgiver): 289
Clement, Epistle of (= *I Clement*): 170
Clement of Alexandria, *Quis dives salvetur* of: *434*, 435, 437
Cleomenes III, king of Sparta: 288
Cleomis, tyrant of Mytilene: 297
Cleon (Athenian 'demagogue'): 41, *124-5*, *290* (with 603 n.25), 604 n.26
Cleon of Gordioucome: 475
Cleophon (Athenian 'demagogue'): *124-5*, 603 n.25
Clerc, Michel: 554 n.29
Clermont Ferrand: 595 n.6, 654 n.42
cleruchies, military: 213 § 2 (with 581 n.6, on IV.ii), 268, 569 n.44
clientela, *clientes* (Roman), and patronage: 175, 334, *341-3*, 362, *364-7*, 372; includes relationship of freedman to former master: 341; increased in importance in Principate: *342*, *364-5*; Roman 'client States': 341-2, 536
'client kingdoms', Roman: 228
Cloché, Paul: 291 (with 606 nn.33-4)
Clodius (P. Clodius Pulcher): *344*, *352-4*, *368-9*
cognitio (*extraordinaria*): *328-9*
Cohen, Benjamin: 547 n.21
Cohen, G. A.: xi, *543 n.13*
cohortales = *taxeōtai*: *474*, *493*
coin-types (and legends): 392-4
Colin, Jean: 533 (with 613 n.41)
collatio glebalis (*follis*): see under 'taxation'
collatio lustralis: see under 'taxation'

Collectio Avellana: 404, 644 n.24 (with 451)
collegia ('guilds'): 273 (with 597 nn.8–9)
Collinet, Paul: 591 n.37
Collingwood, R. G.: 478–9
colonate and (serf) *coloni* of Later Roman Empire:
  colonus, different meanings of the word: *159*
  the Later Roman colonate: *158-60, 249-55*, 173,
  373–4; a form of serfdom: 5, 83, 136, 148, 155
  Later Roman *coloni* bound either to a village or to a
  particular plot of land: *158-9*; but were always technically free: 159, *252-3*; although they (or some of
  them) could be 'regarded as slaves of the land' (etc.):
  159-60, 173, *252*
    position of Later Roman *coloni* differed in different
  areas: *250*
    term '*colonatus*' from second quarter of 4th c.:
  251-2, 159, 173
    coloni homologi: 251; *adscripticii* (*enapographoi*, also
  originarii, originales, tributarii): 148 (with 564–5 n.16),
  159, 250, 252-3, 255
colonia partiaria: see under 'share-croppers'
Colonus (place in Attica): 291 (with 605 n.30)
Colophon: 550 n.9
Columella: 122, 142, 187, *234, 235-6, 239, 241, 256, 593
n.59*
Comana in Cappadocia: 154; in Pontus: 154
Commagene: *153-4* (with *568 n.36*)
commerce: see under 'traders'
'commercial cities' (so-called): see under 'Alexandria',
  'Arelate', 'Augusta Treverorum', 'Lugdunum',
  'Narbo', 'Ostia', 'Palmyra', 'Petra'
'commercial' aristocracies etc. in Ancient Greece, a
  misconception: *41*
Commodian (African Christian writer); 642 n.8
Commodus (Roman emperor): 139, 215, 244, 380, 389,
  468, 476. And see under 'Marcus Aurelius'
'communism' (so-called) of Apostolic community: 433
compulsion, in Thucydides and Marx: 27-8
concepts and categories, and their use: *33-5, 43-6*. And
  see under 'Historical Materialism'
concordia ordinum: 340
Connor, W. R.: 603 n.25
Conservatism, British: 27; definition of, by Lords
  Balfour and Blake: *375*
Constans, son of 'usurper' Constantine: 595 n.6
Constantine I (Roman emperor): 8, 128, 159, 170, 196,
  224, 250-1, 257, 272, 313, 351, 365, 373, 393, *398-9,
  403-4*, 407, 464, 479, 485, 488, 491, 493, *495*, 496,
  503, 538 n.3 (on I.ii), 564–5 n.16, *635 n.92*
  his letter to Aelafius: *399*; his letter to Bishop
  Alexander of Alexandria and Arius: *403*
  his new taxes: 493
Constantine XI (last Byzantine emperor): 497
Constantine, 'usurper': 595 n.6
Constantinople (Byzantium): 8, 9, 124, 127, 132, 272,
  273, 393, 400, 445, 448-51, 492, 495, 497, 654 n.42,
  559 n.16
  Senate of: 124, 381, 388, 407
  public food dole at (from 332): 195; suspension of:
  196
  'Oecumenical' Church Council of, in 381, and
  'Quinisext' Council 'in Trullo' in 692: see under
  'Councils of the Christian Churches'
Constantius I (Roman emperor): 248, 493
Constantius II (Roman emperor): 177, 247, 258, 379,
  387, 390, *403-5*, 451, 485, 490, 565 n.16
  his entry into Rome, described by Ammianus: 379
  his letter to Persian King Shapur II: 379
Constitutio Antoniniana (A.D. 212): 328, *454-62*

'contiones' at Rome, importance of: *335-6*
'contractors': *188-9* (with 578 n.23), 193, 194, 273;
  other terms for (apart from *misthōtai*) include
  '*ergolabos*', '*ergōnēs*' (in Greek): 188-9; and '*redemptor*',
  '*manceps*': 193, 194
'contradictions', role of, in relation to class and class
  struggle: 49-50; sometimes 'conflict', 'opposition',
  'antagonism' preferable: 50, cf. 56; difference
  between French and English usage: 63
convict labour ('forced labour' in Slavery Conventions
  of 1926 and 1956): 134-5, 170
coöptare, coöptatio: 522
Coptic Church (Egyptian, Monophysite): *483-4* (with
  652 n.37)
Coptos (in Egypt): 129
Corax (character in Petronius): 199
Corcyra (Corfu): 12, 296, 506-7, 547 n.6, 553 n.9 (with
  85)
Corinth: 41, 120, 132, 154, 190, 288, 295-6, 299, 344,
  524, 525, 553 n.9 (with 85)
Corippus, Flavius Cresconius (Late Latin poet), his
  poem in praise of Justin II: *399-400*
Cornificius (Roman rhetorician), on *licentia* as equiva-
  lent of Greek *parrhēsia*: 368
Corsica (Roman province), Corsicans: 356, *483*, 496
Cos: 206, 305, 612 n.23
Costoboci: 468, 653 n.42
Cotini: 510, 511
Cotta Maximus, M. Aurelius (consul, A.D. 20): *178*
Coulborn, Rushton (ed.), 596 n.4
Councils of the Christian Churches: *401, 403*
  Elvira (Illiberis, late 3rd or early 4th c.), Canon V:
  420
  Nicaea (325): *401, 403*
  Constantinople (381): *401*
  Ephesus I (431): 177 (with *574 n.13*), 401, 448
  Ephesus II (449, 'Latrocinium'): 401
  Chalcedon (451): *145-6, 401, 403-4*, 448-9, 592 n.41
  Constantinople (692, 'Quinisext' Council *in
  Trullo*): 109
  Florence (1439): 497
  Narbo (589): *638-9 n.3*
  Justinian gives force of law to Canons of the 'Four
  General Councils': *401*
  Only the emperor could summon a General
  Council of the Church and decide who should
  preside over it: *403*
Courby, Institut Fernand: see under 'Institut . . .'
Courtois, Christian: *482*
Crassus, M. Licinius: *176* (with *574 n.8*), 194
Crates (Attic comedian): 113
Craugasius of Nisibis: 486
Crawford, Dorothy: 257
Crawford, Michael H.: 230, 345, 554 n.28, 611 n.14,
  620 n.5, 648 n.14, *656 n.10*
Crete, Cretans: 139, 150, 160 (with *570 n.51*), 345, 535
Crimea (Pontic kingdom): 130, *292*, 294, 607 n.36
Cromwell, Oliver: 441
Crook, John: 197, 571-3 nn.61, 65, 73, 574 n.3, *617 n.1*
Cross (The 'True Cross'), captured by Persians and
  recaptured by Heraclius: 400, 484
Crossland, R. A.: *269*
Croton: 41, 519
Crusade, Fourth: 9
cubicularii: *143*, 176-7 (with *574 n.13*), 492
cults of the living: 74, *348*; the earliest certain ones those
  of Lysander at Samos (404 B.C.) and Alexander the
  Great: 74; of Hellenistic kings and other benefactors:
  348; of the City of Rome at Smyrna from 195 B.C.

onwards: 348; of individual Roman generals and proconsuls, from Flamininus onwards: 348; of Verres at Syracuse (the *Verria*): 348

cuneiform documents: 170 (with 573 n.76)

curiales, curial class/order, decurions (city councillors): 7, *126-7*, 197, *257*, *308*, *454*, *456-7*, *457-60*, *530-3*, and esp. *466-73 & 473-4* (with 493), 254, 313-14, 365, 462, 561 n.21, 592 n.46, 644 n.19, 647 n.2
    size and census of: *466*
    illiterates not excluded: *467*
    pressure on curials from Antonine period: *467 ff.*;
    class struggle within curial order: *471*
        maltreatment of, by provincial governors etc.: *472-3*; flogging of (and exemptions): *472-3*
        received larger share from many benefactions: *197*
        assumed by Constantine to have both urban and rural slaves: *257*
        forbidden by Justinian to become bishops or priests, because 'too wicked': *474*, 493

Curius Dentatus, M.: 121

cursus publicus: see under 'post, imperial/public'

Cylon (Athenian): 282

Cyprian, St.: 240

Cyprus (Roman province): 345, 346, 356, *534*

Cyrebus (Athenian): 180

Cyrene, Cyrenaica: 7, 8, 160, 265, 304, 316, 345, 346, 349, 381, 490, 523, *534-5*, *595 n.6*, 610 n.2; Simon of: 15

Cyril, St. (bishop of Alexandria): 177, 448, 616 n.64 (with 326); lavishes bribes on court officials of Theodosius II: *177* (with *574 n.13*); Gibbon's comment on his sanctity: 635 n.91

Cyrrhus (in Syria): 496

Cyrus (Persian prince): 121

Cyzicus: *448* (with *644 n.19*), 456, 507, 653 n.42

Dacia, Dacians: 476, 510-12

Daedalus: 113, 140

Dahrendorf, Ralf: *59-62*, *96-7*, 31 (with 544 n.1), *82*, 544 n.16, 554 n.31; on functionalism, and Plato's Socrates as the first functionalist: *82*

Dalmatia (Roman province): 242, 362, 496

Damascus: 654 n.42

Damasus, Pope: *451*, *495*

Danube, River (and its basin): 8, 230, 249, 258, 266, 479, 486, 487; Republican coin-hoards in Romania etc.: *230*

Daniel, Book of: *325* (with *616 n.61*), *441-2* (with *641 n.4*)

Danilova, L. V.: 98

Daos (character in Menander, *Hero*): *163*

Daphitas (Daphidas) of Telmessus: *445*

Daphne, near Antioch: 558 n.9

Dara (Anastasiopolis), in Mesopotamia: 577 n.19

Dardanians (of Illyria and Thrace): 150

Dardanus (in Troad): 118

Darius I, king of Persia: 207

D'Arms, J. H.: 574 n.6

Daube, David: *555 n.14*, 588 n.14a, *643 n.11*

David, Paul A.: 587 n.8

Davies, J. G.: 562 n.8

Davies, J. K.: 174, 270, *558 n.3* (on III.i), 596 n.2, 600 n.3, 608 n.53

Davis, P. H.: 577 n.20

Dawes, Elizabeth, and N. H. Baynes: 446-7, 585 n.43

'Dead Sea Sect': 432

'debellare superbos': *327-8*

Debord, Pierre: 568 n.34

debt, and debt bondage: *136-7*, *138-9*, *162-70*, *282*, 4, 33, 228, 247, 259, 285-6, 287, 335

    debt bondage defined, and distinguished from enslavement for debt: *136*; Athens exceptional in abolishing both (Solon, 594/3): *137*, *162-3*, *282*; though debt bondage revived in Attica after fall of democracy (in 322/1): *163*
    debt bondage largely superseded enslavement for debt in Hellenistic cities: 165
        often by 'personal execution' as well as legal process: 137, *163*, 164, 165
        slave terminology sometimes applied to: *163*
        sale of debtor's children: 163
    cancellation of debts (*chreōn apokopē*, *novae tabulae*): 137, *162-3*, *190-1*, 215, 288, 298 (with *608-9 n.55*)
    harsh Roman law of debt: *163-70*; *obaerarii*, *obaerati*: *167* (with 572 nn.66-7), 187; *addictus*, *addictio*: 163, *166-8*, *169*, 173, 240; *iudicatus*, *actio iudicati*: 166-8, 240, 247; *manus iniectio*: 165, 166; creditor seizing debtor might well make him work, even without explicit legal right: *168*; *bonorum venditio/cessio/distractio*: 166. And see under '*paramonē*'

Decapolis (in Palestine): *428-9*

Decebalus (Dacian chieftain): 476

Decelea: 147, 291, *506*

decemprimi (leading decurions in Italian and Sicilian towns, from Late Republic): 471; distinguished from later *decemprimi curiales* (probably = *principales*: q.v. below) of 4th c. onwards: *471*, *472*

Decius (Roman emperor): 240

'Decline and Fall of the Roman Empire', the: *497-503*; 6-7, 265

decurions: see under '*curiales*'

defensor (*civitatis* or *plebis*; *ekdikos*, *syndikos*): 317, 383

Degler, Carl N.: 54

Deininger, Jürgen: 523

Deinocrates of Rhodes: *12-13*

Deiotarus, king of Galatia: 119

dekaprōtoi (*eikosaprōtoi*), decurions responsible for certain liturgies, from 1st to early 4th c.: 471

Delos, Delians: 12, 157, 188, 228, 233, 395

Delphi: 229, 332, 532; manumission-inscriptions of (from 201 B.C.): *229* (with *587 nn.2 & 2a*)

Demades (Athenian): 578 n.26, 610 n.2; on the *theōrika* as 'the glue of democracy': *578 n.26*

'demagogues': *125*, *290* (with *603 n.25*), 296

Demaratus, exiled king of Sparta: 117

Demaratids: 118

De Martino, Francesco: 585 n.1, 615 n.54

'deme', as political unit, esp. at Athens: *289* (with *602 n.22*)

Demeas (Athenian): 180

'demesne land', 'home farm': 218, cf. 151

Demetrius of Phalerum: 301

Demetrius, freedman of Pompey: 176

Demetrius Poliorcetes: 174

Democedes of Croton (doctor): 271

democracy: *283-5* (with *600-1* nn.1-12), 5-6, 44, 70-1, 72-7, 80, 96-7, 141, 280; originality of: *284*
    essential characteristics and institutions of: *284-5*; ancient definitions of: *600 n.4*
    important role in protecting poor against exploitation and oppression: *44*, *72-3*, *96-7*, *141*, 206, 213, *284*, *287-8*, 298, 312, *315*, *317*
    freedom (*eleutheria*) its great aim: *284* (with *600 n.4*); including freedom of speech, *parrhēsia*: *284-5*, cf. 323; its *isonomia* and *isēgoria*: *285* (with 601 nn.9-10), cf. 323
    fundamental importance of *euthyna* in: 75, *285* (with *601 n.11*, contrast *372*); its belief in rule of law: *285* (with *601 n.12*)

appointment by lot to minor offices only: 285
position of women and slaves in: *284, 288*
destruction of: *300-26*, with *518-37*, 97, 294, 295-300
devaluation of term *dēmokratia* in Hellenistic and
Roman periods: *321-3, 326*
dēmokratia as the constitution of the Roman
Republic: *322-3* (with *614-15 nn.51-2*)
the Roman Principate as a *dēmokratia*: *323*
dēmokratia finally as mob violence, riot, insurrection: *325-6* (with *616-17 n.64*)
Democritus: 23-4, 24 (cf. 234); Marx's doctoral thesis,
on Democritus and Epicurus: 23-4
dēmos (the word): 72 with *284*, 73, 74, 77, 279, 280-1,
283, 286, 609 n.62
Demosthenes (and Ps.-Dem.): 144, 185, 186, 200, 202,
292 (with *607 n.36*), *299* (with 609 n.58), 302, 505-6,
607 n.37
'Demotic Chronicle': 443 (with 642 n.7)
Demougeot, Émilienne: 514-15, 590 n.29
Dennett, D. C.: 658 n.47
De Robertis, F. M.: 575 n.1, 591 n.37
Derow, P. S.: 611 n.13, 659 n.2
'determinism, economic', alleged in Marx: *26-8*
De Visscher, F.: 535
Dexippus: 653-5 n.42; his supposed exploit against the
Heruls in 267, commonly accepted, on authority of
Historia Augusta only: *654-5 n.42*
Diaeus: *230* (with *587 n.5*), 507
Didache: *419-20*
Didymus (relative of the Emperor Honorius): 595 n.6
Digest (of Justinian): *144*, 239-40, 586-7 n.1, etc.,
including (among others) the following lawyers:
Alfenus Varus: 237
Arcadius Charisius: 459
Callistratus: 126, 128, 168, 240, 458, 460
Florentinus: 423
Gaius: 166, 217
Hermogenianus: 242, 310
Javolenus Priscus: 457
Labeo, M. Antonius: 237
Macer, Aemilius: 458
Maecianus: 378
Marcianus, Aelius: 237, 244-7 (with 589-90
nn.26a-28), 457-8
Modestinus: 541 n.15
Paulus: 168, 236, 237, 238, 242, 308
Pegasus: 237
Pomponius: 385, 541 n.15 with 554 n.30
Proculus: 619 n.13
Salvius Julianus: 168, 236, 237
Scaevola, Q. Cervidius: 237
Tryphoninus: 423
Ulpian: 109, 135, 168, 198, 233, 236-7, 272-3, 308,
318, 385, (the *lex regia* etc.), 423, 456, 459, 477, 540
n.8, 541 n.18, 646 n.21
Venuleius Saturninus: 168
'*dignitas*': 363-4, 370
'dignity of labour', idea absent in antiquity: 201
Dio Cassius (Cassius Dio Cocceianus): 165, 195, 196,
265, 308, 317-18, 323, 361, 362, 363, 367, 372, 386,
444, 454-5, 468-9, 476-7, 511-12, 521, 537, *614-15
nn.51-2*, and esp. *615 n.56*
Dio Chrysostom, of Prusa: *200, 306, 312* (with *612
n.22*), *320, 372, 377*, (with *628 nn.17-18*), *419*, 18,
39-40, 106, 141, 146, 169, 188, 194, 236, 310, 313, 317
(with 613 n.38), 319, 377, 397, 475, 531-3, 560 n.7,
608 n.55, 614 n.49; said to have been influenced by
Musonius Rufus: 560 n.7
Diocletian (Roman emperor): 8, 11-12, 168, 224,
234, 245, 249, 250, 251, 253, 261, 264, 313, 360, *373*,
381, 384, 386, 407, 463, 464, 467, 475, 489, 490, 491,
493, 503
Price-edict of: *538-9 n.3* (with 12), and *656 n.2*;
585-7 n.1
Diodoros Pasparos of Pergamum: 529
Diodorus (Siculus): 79, *162, 301, 355-6, 609-10 n:2*, 24,
119, 151, 165, 191-2, 228, 270-1, 296-7, 302
on equality of property: 79
on Solon's debt-legislation: 162
on late-4th-c. restrictions on Athenian constitution
(322/1 and 317 B.C.): *301*
critical attitude to Italians and Romans: 355-6
on population of Late Ptolemaic Egypt: 540 n.11;
on Ptolemaic revenue: 540 n.11; on low cost of living
in Egypt: 568 n.32; on wife's alleged authority over
husband in Egypt: 556 n.22
on Etruscan serfs etc.: 562 n.4
on 1st Sicilian slave war, gold mines in Egypt and
silver mines in Spain: *562 n.8*
on public works at Syracuse: 191-2, 270-1
on 'spear-won territory': 151
Diodotus (Athenian speaker in Thucydides): 604 n.26
Diogenes Laertius: 130, 131
Diogenes of Oenoanda: 123 (with 560 n.8)
Dionysius, bishop of Alexandria: 109 (with 557 n.26)
Dionysius I, tyrant of Syracuse: 117, 119, 191-2, 270-1
Dionysius of Halicarnassus: 24, 139, *175*, 324-5, 336-7,
341
Dionysius, slave of Cicero: 146-7
Dionysius, secretary of Antiochus IV: 558 n.9
Diophantus (*SIG*³ 709): 564 n.15
Dioscorus, bishop of Alexandria: 146, 404, 448
Dioscorus, *prytanis* of Oxyrhynchus: *314*
Dioscorus, Greek poet in Egypt: 223-4
Dioscuri: 396
dispensatores (Imperial slaves): 143 (with 563 n.13). And see
under 'Musicus Scurranus' and 'Rotundus Drusillianus'
Disraeli, Benjamin, his *Sybil*; 70
divi fratres (Roman emperors Marcus and Verus, 161-9):
469 etc.
Dobb, Maurice: 21, 85
Dobrudja: 528
doctors: 271, 597 n.3; 'public physicians' (of cities and
royal courts): 271; *archiatroi*: 271; Democedes, Galen:
271
Doctrina Jacobi nuper baptizati: *652-3 n.39*
Dometianus, bishop of Melitene: *484* (with *652 n.34*)
'Dominate' opposed to 'Principate', not a useful
notion: *251*
Domitian (Roman emperor): 15-16, 124, 369, 380, *381-
2*, 392, 397
Domitius Afer (and the Domitii): *126* (with *560 nn.10-11*)
Domitius Ahenobarbus: see under 'Ahenobarbus'
Donatism, Donatists: 240, 403, *445-6* (with *643 n.15*),
471, *481-2*
Donatists ingeniously turned by Catholics from
schismatics into heretics: 446
coloni converted by their landlords from Donatism
to Catholicism or vice versa: *240*
And see under 'Circumcellions'
Donatus, bishop of Euroea in Epirus, his miracle: 408
Doricha (Rhodopis): 131
Dorotheus, Arian theologian: 450
Douglass, Frederick (American ex-slave): 143, 410
doulos (standard word for 'slave') used in Later Roman
Egypt by humble free men of themselves in address-
ing superiors: *502*
Dover, (Sir) Kenneth: 9, *506* (on Thuc. VII.27.5)

Downey, Glanville: 583 nn.23, 27
dowries: 101, 103
'drainage' metaphor, for distribution of wealth in Later Roman Empire: 503
Drake, H. A.: 616 nn.62-3
Dresden, bombing of: 48
'drones', 'hives of': Rostovtzeff's description of the upper classes of the Graeco-Roman cities: 463
'dual citizenship': see under 'citizenship'
'dual penalty system': *457-60*; its emergence in Antonine (and Severan) age: *458*
Ducas (Late Byzantine historian): *497*
Duchesne, Louis: 484 (with 652 n.36), 657 n.26
Duff, A. M.: 574 n.4
Dumont, Louis: 547 n.22
Dunbabin, T. J.: 562 n.3
Duncan-Jones, R. P.: 65, 92, 176, 538 n.2 (on I.iii), *539 n.3*, 575 n.16, 579 n.35, *585-6 n.1*
Dupré, G., and P.-P. Rey: 21-2, 37
Dura Europus: 348 (with *620 n.12*)
Durkheim, E.: 22, 43, 82
dux, duces: 224
Dvornik, Francis: 374, 399, 633-4 n.79
Dyme: *307*, 344-5, 525, 611 n.14
dynasteia: see under 'oligarchy'
'dynasts' of the Magnificat and Thomas Hardy: *432-3, 440*
'*dynatoi*': see under 'powerful'
Dyrrhachium (Epidamnus, Durazzo): 7
Dyson, Stephen L.: 474

Eadie, J. W.: 656 n.11
East India Company: 347
Eberhard, Wolfram: 268-9
Ecclesiasticus, Book of' *413, 435*
Ecdicius (relative of Sidonius Apollinaris): 595 n.6
'economic determinism', 'economism': see under 'determinism, economic'
Edessa: *220, 264, 272*, 348, *537*, 561 n.21; famines at (c.373 and 500-1): *220*; *chrysargyron* at (in late 5th c.): *272*; correspondence (bogus) between its dynast and Jesus: *537*
'*Edictum Theodorici*': 246, 564 n.16
Eëtioneia (in Attica): 606 n.30
egregii: 406, 457
Egypt: 6, 8, 10, 17, 114, 118, 119, 129, 130, 131, 153 (with *566-8 n.32*), 154, 163, 165, 167, 169, 170, 187, 215, 220, 221, 222-4, 228, 242, 250, 251, 257, 299, 321, 345, 400, 442, 446-7, 448-9, 468, 483-4, 490, 495, 496, 499, 503, 576-7 n.19
    its Monophysitism: 448-9
    relatively small role of slavery in production: 228, 257 etc.
        Ptolemaic revenue of: 540 n.11; population of Ptolemaic and Roman Egypt: *540 n.11*
        low cost of living in: 568 n.32
        Jews in: 442
        pyramids of, scorned by Frontinus: 193
Eisenhower, President: 420
Eisenstadt, S. N.: 88
eisphora: 114 (with *558 n.3*, on III.i), 206, 290
ekklēsiastai (*ekklēsiazontes*): 197, 527, 528, 532
Elagabalus (Heliogabalus, Roman emperor): 494
Elataea in Phocis: 653 n.42
Eldridge, J. E. T.: 43
Electra (as character in Euripides): 18, 185
Eleusis, building-inscriptions of temple at (in late 4th c. B.C.): *188* (with *577-8 nn.21-2*), 171, 185-6, 201, 597 n.2; unique value of these inscriptions: *188*

Eleusius ('Semi-Arian' bishop of Cyzicus): 448; a persecutor of pagans, Novatians and Catholics: *448*
eleutheria, eleutheros: *284-5* (with 600 nn.4, 7), 312, 319, 323, 324
    eleutheros in the special sense of 'the gentleman', freed from having to earn his own living (Aristotle): 116-17
        And see under 'freedom, liberty', '*libertas*', 'democracy'
Elis: 160, 506-7, 609 n.62
Emesa: 494
eminentissimi: 406, 459
emphyteusis: *214* (with *581 n.7*, on IV.ii), 247, 593 n.50
Empiricus, Sextus: see under 'Sextus Empiricus'
'employment' or 'unemployment' in antiquity: 189-90, 190-1, 192, *201-2*; unemployment in England in 16th c.: 262
energy, sources of ('prime movers'): *38* (animal power, water, wind)
Engels, Donald: 555 n.7
Engels, Friedrich/Frederick [apart from Marx]: *20*, 25, *26*, 28, 50, *59*, 99-100, *162*, 211, 418, 543 nn.9, 13, *544 n.15*, 546 n.14, 548 n.1, 549 n.20. And see under 'Marx, Karl'
Engerman, Stanley L: see under 'Fogel, R. W., and Engerman'
England: unique depression of peasantry by 16th c. (Weber): 262; Reformation in: 279
Engyum (in Sicily): 520
'*enkekrimenoi*', at Prusias ad Hypium in Bithynia: 18
Ennius: 186
Ennodius (Late Latin writer): 516
Enzensberger, Hans Magnus: 20
ephēboi, ephēbia: 315, *527*
Ephesus: 119, 164, 190, 270, 273, 312, 313, 365, 531, 533; Church Councils of (A.D. 431 and 449): see under 'Councils of the Christian Churches'
Ephialtes (Athenian): 289, 291
Ephraemius, bishop of Antioch: 486
Ephraim, St. (Syrian Holy Man): 220
Epictetus (Stoic philosopher, ex-slave): *15*, *142*, 199, *423*
Epicurus: 23-4, 25; Marx's doctoral thesis, on Democritus and Epicurus: 23-4
Epidaurus: 188, 577 n.20, 597 n.2
epiklēros: see under 'women'
Epiphanius, archdeacon of Alexandria, his letter to the bishop of Constantinople, detailing the bribes paid by St. Cyril to officials at the court of Theodosius II: *177* (with *574 n.13*)
Epipolae (Syracuse): 191
Epirus, Epirots: 8, 132, *235*, 344, 360; slaves from, as family units, in Late Republic: *235*
epitaphs of slaves and freedmen e.g. of Narcissus, slave *vilicus* at Venafrum: *174*; and of Zosimus, freedman *accensus* of M. Aurelius Cotta: *178*
equality (*isotēs, aequalitas*): *285* (with *601 n.9*), *309*, *323*; 'nothing more unequal than equality' (Pliny the Younger): *309*
equites, equester ordo: *338-40*, *381*, *406-7*, 41-2, 96, 129, 178, 194, 362, 363, 456 ff., 473
    not a separate 'class': 41-2, 339-40
    census of: *406*, 129, 178, 362
    '*equestri loco natus/ortus*': 618 n.2 (on VI.iii), 636 n.102
    freedmen's sons entering: 178
    penetration of Greeks into: 96
    ultimate fusion with Senate, in late 4th and early 5th cc.: *407*
Equitius, L., represented himself as a son of Ti. Gracchus: *623 n.8*

eranoi (mutual benefit societies): 320
Erastus, L. (protégé of Hadrian, at Ephesus): 531
Eratyra/Erattyna (in Macedonia): 528
Erechtheum (at Athens), building inscriptions of (late 5th c. B.C.): *577-8 nn.21-3*, 171, (189), 201, 596-7 n.2
Eretria: 609 n.62
Eryx (in Sicily), temple of Aphrodite at: 154, 569 n.39
Esau, to *douleuein* to Jacob (in LXX Genesis): 423
'eschatological woman, the': 104 (with 555 n.12)
Essenes: 422, 433; in Philo: 422
Etruria, Etruscans (Tuscany, Tuscans): 139, 158, 238-9, 519; *penestai* (Dion. Hal.) of: 139
Eubiotus Leurus, M. Ulpius (Athenian): 313, 526
Euboea, Euboeans: 18, 605 n.27, 609 n.62
Eubulus (of Antioch): 321
Eudoxius, Arian bishop of Constantinople: 448, *450-1*; his joke: *450-1*
Eudoxius (doctor): 487
Euesperides, Berenice (Benghazi): 305, 535; Jews of: 305
eugeneia: see under 'nobility'
Eugippius, his *Life of Severinus*: 486
Eunapius: 365, 498, 514
Eunomius, Arian bishop of Cyzicus: *448*
eunuchs, Imperial: see under '*cubicularii*'
Eupatrids (Athenian aristocracy): 282
Euphrates, River: 8
Euphron of Sicyon (the Elder): *297-8*
Euphron of Sicyon (grandson of the foregoing): 297
Euric (Visigothic king): 486
Euripides: 18, *73*, 185, *319*, 601 n.12; *Auge* of, *319*
Eurymedon, River, battle of: 311
Eusebia (Roman empress, wife of Constantius II): 177
Eusebius (Christian historian and bishop): *325-6* (with *616 nn.62-3*) and *399* (his *Triakontaëtērikos*), and *537*, 170, 195-6, 393, 402, 403, 479, 513
Eusebius (eunuch, Imperial freedman of Constantius II): 177, 405
Eutherus (character in dialogue of Xenophon): *181, 184*
euthyna (and accountability; also *hypeuthynos, anhypeuthynos*): 75, *285, 372, 522*
Euthyphro (character in Plato): 185
Eutropius (Late Latin epitomator): 513
Eutychianus, Novatian 'holy man': *365*
Evagrius (Christian historian): 196, 258, 272, *319*, 405, 517, *614 n.50*, 653 n.40
Evangelus (slave of Pericles): 132
Eve: see under 'Adam and Eve'
evidence, evaluation of, according to property: *460*
'execution, personal': see under 'personal execution'
expectation of life in antiquity: see under 'mortality'
'explanation' and 'description': 45
exploitation: 3-4, 6-7, 13-15, 42-69 (esp. 43-4, 51-2, 53), 203-4, 205-6, 211-12, 219-21, 226, 231, 269-72, 305, 317, 328, 345-6, 373-4, 453-4, 492-3, 497-503, and *passim*
    definition of: *43*, 3, 37
    'direct individual' and 'indirect collective' exploitation: *44, 205-8*, 4, 33, 135, 203-4, 213, 226; the distinction recognised by Marx: *206*
    scale of, to be taken into account in assessing class: *116*
    origin in control of conditions of production: 44
    metaphors concealing: *503*
    'Ausbeutung' and 'Exploitation' in Marx: *51*
    ways of extracting surplus: *53*, 203-4
    change in forms of, during first three cc. C.E.: 226-59 (esp. *231*)
    alleged change from 'Principate' to 'Dominate' was essentially an intensification of the forms of

exploitation: *373-4*, 6
    Roman tribute likely to increase rate of: 228
exports from Greek and Roman world: 232, 293-4; outflow in cash, esp. gold, in Roman period: *232*
    subsidies to 'barbarian' chiefs: 232
Expositio totius mundi et gentium: 258
exposure of infants: 103; more common in the case of girls than boys: 103, *555 n.7*
Exsuperius (of Toulouse): 595 n.6
Exuperantius: *478*

Fabius Maximus, Q. (proconsul of Achaea): 307, 525
fables: *444-5*, 6, 18, 186; a kind of slave cryptography (Phaedrus): *444*
    of Phaedrus: 444; of Babrius: 18, 444; of Menenius Agrippa: 444-5; *Fabulae Aviani*: 444
    despised by Quintilian: 444
Fabricius Luscinus: 342
'facts', historical: *31*, 34; A.D. Nock on: *31*
'Fall of Man', greater responsibility of the woman for: *107*; role of, in Christian soteriology: 107
family responsibility for crime, in Jewish Scriptures: *108-9*
famines: see under 'food supply'
Fantham, Elaine: *414*
Farrington, Benjamin: 562 n.8
Faure, Edgar: 583 n.26
Favorinus of Arles: 390
Fears, J. Rufus: 633 n.72a
Felix = Bulla: see under 'Bulla'
Felix (procurator of Judaea, Imperial freedman): 176
Felix, Pope (or Anti-Pope): 451
feminism, feminists: 105, 111
Ferguson, W. S.: 301-2 (with 609-10 nn. 2-3), 660 n.5
Festugière, A. J.: 585 n.43
Festus (procurator of Judaea): 455
Festus (Late Latin epitomator): 518, 595 n.6
feudalism: *5, 136, 267-9*; Soviet and Western uses of the term: *268*; frequent misuse of the term in relation to Greek and Roman society: *267* (with *596* n.1, on IV.v)
    'feudal mode of production': 5, 269, *544 n.15*
    'feudalism' and serfdom or *Hörigkeit*: 138, 267
    Marx on Japanese 'purely feudal organisation of landed property': 269
    feudalism as a 'political form' (Marx and Engels): 269
    'feudalism' seen in Japan, China, Ancient Mesopotamia and Iran, Ancient Egypt, India, Byzantine empire and Russia: 267 (with 596 n.4)
    Hittite feudalism: 269 (with 596 n.8)
Feuerbach, Ludwig: 56
Fikhman, I. F.: 584 n.41
Finkelstein [Finley], M. I.: 597 n.5
Finley, (Sir) Moses I.: *58-9, 80* (with *551 n.30*), *86, 91-4, 117* (with *558 nn.4-5*), *141-2, 289-90* (with *602-3 n.24, 604-5 n.27*), *462-3, 553 n.23a*, 4, 62, 122, 136-7, 137-8, 162, 164, 178, 253, 315, 545-6 n.14, 562 n.2, 570 n.49, 588-9 nn.14, 18, 19, 592 n.50
    misunderstanding of 'class' in Marx: 58-9, 91
    his 'spectrum/continuum of statuses (and orders)': 58, 93, 94, 137-8; yet 'vague' concept of status: 92
    dilemma concerning place of slavery in Greek civilisation: 94, 141-2
    'Bewusstseinsstrukturen' as his point of departure: *553 n.23a*
fire-brigades, forbidden by Trajan in Greek East: *319-20*
Firmus (rebel African chief): 475, 490
Firmus (alleged aspirant to Imperial throne): 128-9
Firth, (Sir) Raymond: 22, 45
fiscus, as the belly of the body politic, in Corippus: 400
Fitzhugh, George (Virginian apologist for slavery): 85, 417

'Five Thousand', The: see under 'Four Hundred and Five Thousand'

Flaccus, Calpurnius: see under 'Calpurnius Flaccus'

Flaccus, L. Valerius (governor of Asia): 310

Flamininus, T. Quinctius: 307, 525

Flam-Zuckermann, Léa: 318

flogging: *455-6*, *458-9*, 471, *472-3*, 498-9, 502
  often resulting in death: *473*; use of *plumbata*: 472-3 of *curiales*: 472-3, 502; of *coloni*: 471
  St. Paul's avoidance of: 455-6

Florence, Council of (1439): see under 'Councils of the Christian Churches'

Florentius (praetorian prefect): 272

Flusser, David: 432

foederati. 247, *515*, 590 n.31

Fogel, R. W., and S. L. Engerman: 232, 410, 549 n.18

Follet, Simone: 526, 645 n.4

food supply and famines:
  supply of corn: 11, 13-14, 15-16, 130, 132, 188, 195-6, 219-21, 292, 294-5, 313, 320, 320-1; of wheat: 11, 188, 313; of barley: 188; price of wheat and barley: *188*, 219, *539 n.3*, cf. 585 n.1
  public food doles in Late Republic and early Principate (*frumentationes*): 352; under Roman Empire, at Rome and Constantinople and some other cities: *195-6*; reduced or suspended owing to disturbances: 196; not given in return for labour: 193, 194
  famines: *13-14*, *219-21* (with 583 nn.23-31), *313*; peasants then crowd into cities: *14*, *219-21*

Forbes, R. J.: 546 n.14

'forced labour' in modern sense: 134

Forni, G.: 523

'fornication', Christian attitude to: 104, 109-10

Forrest, W. George: 570 n.51, 599 n.17

Fortunatianus (Roman rhetorician), his *Ars rhetorica*: 167

Foss, Clive: 652 n.33

foundations: see under 'benefactions'

'Four Hundred', The, and the 'Five Thousand' at Athens (411/10 B.C.): *291-2* (with *605-6 nn.29-34*)

France and the French:
  influence of Marx's study of the French Revolution on the development of his thought: 55; influence on Marx of the French working-class movement: 56
  Marx on French peasantry: *58-9*, *60-1*

Francotte, Henri: 188, 596 n.1 (on IV.vi)

Frank, Tenney: 126, 560 n.10, 624 n.16, 656 n.10

Franks: 485, 494, 512-17; their attitude to Silvanus (in 355): 485; term used by Syriac historians for 'Germans': 494

Fraser, Peter M.: 540 n.11, 563 n.8, 610 n.9

Fravitta, Flavius (Goth, Magister Militum): 480

Frederiksen, M. W.: 571-2 nn.60-5

freedmen: *174-9*, 4, 92, 143, 144-5, 158, 176-7, 192, 196-7, 213, 258, 270, 341, 356, 361, 372, 458, 526-7
  Greek and Roman distinguished: *174-5*, 95
  status of, for one generation only: *175*, *179*, 458; freedmen's descendants in municipal life: *175-6* (with *574 n.6*)
  Imperial freedmen: 29, 92, 143, 176-7, 381, 477
  And see under '*cubicularii*', 'manumission'

freedom, liberty: 27-8, 116-17, *284-5*, 303-4, 312, 313, 319, 322, 323, 324, 342, 349, 362, *366-70*, 384, 443
  freedom as 'the understanding of necessity': 27-8;
  Marx on: 28
  Aristotle on (in a special sense): 116-17
  Plato against: *284*; Plutarch on: 312; Sallust on: *443*; Livy on: 626 n.52
  Roman 'free [and federate] States' (*civitates liberae [et foederatae]*): 303-4, 312, 313, 322, 349, 373 etc.

And see under '*eleutheria*', '*libertas*'

French Revolution, working-class movement etc.: see under 'France'

Frend, W. H. C.: 404, 643 n.15, 651 n.22

Friedländer, Ludwig: 538 n.2 (on I.iii)

Frier, B. W.: 578 n.27

Frisians: 248, 513

Fritigern (Visigothic chief): 479-80, 485-6

Fritz, Kurt von: 550 nn.13, 15, 618 n.2 (on VI.ii)

Frontinus, Sextus Julius: 193, 242, 327

Fronto, M. Cornelius: 318, 559 n.4

'*fructus*' of an estate, in Roman law: 236

Frye, R. N.: 594 n.2

Fuks, Alexander: 70, 79, *186* (with *576 n.15*), *524*, *550 n.4a*, *608 n.53*, *611 n.14*, *617 n.65*

functionalism: *82* (with *552 n.1*), 83

Fustel de Coulanges: *239-401*, 246 (with 589-90 n.28, cf. 589 n.26a)

Gabba, Emilio: 522-3

Gadara (in the Decapolis): *429*

Gaetulians: 391

Gaius (Roman emperor, 'Caligula'): 12, 322, 392

Gaius (Roman lawyer), *Institutes* of: 138, 167-8, *385*. And see under '*Digest*'

Galatia: 119, 157, 225

Galba (Roman emperor): 167, 322, 361, 389; his speech in Tacitus, adopting Piso: *389*

Galen: *13-14* (with 539 n.6), 219, 242, 271 (with *597 n.4*)

Galicia (Gallaecia, in north-west Spain): 486

Galilee: 192, *427-33*; part of a 'client kingdom' in Jesus' day: 430

Gallaecia (Galicia, in north-west Spain): 595 n.6

Gallienus (Roman emperor): 196, 381, 475

Gallus (Caesar): 321

games: 120 (with 559 nn.16-17)

Gamoroi of Syracuse: 305

Gans, Eduard: 549 n.21

Ganshof, F. L.: 591 n.37, 596 n.2 (on IV.vi)

Garnsey, Peter D. A.: 122, 128, 217, 454, *455-61* (with *646 n.18*), *469*, 509, 572 n.69 (with 167), 574 n.6, 647 n.1

Gaudemet, Jean: 422, 639 n.8 (with 421)

Gaul, Roman: 6, 12, 97, 120, 144, 163, 176, 370, 474, 476, 477, 478-81, 490, 496, 498, 502, 503

Gauls, Prefecture of the: 247, 250

Gauthier, Philippe: 554 n.29

Geagan, D. J.: 526-7

Gelasius I, Pope: 238, 254, 404-5, 422

Gellius, Aulus: 48-9, 165, 186

Gellner, Ernest: 98

Gelzer, Matthias: 255, 338, 584 n.38, 591 n.37

Gennadius (Late Byzantine, Patriarch of Constantinople from 1454): 497

genocide: practised by the Israelites in their conquest of Canaan, according to their own tradition: *331-2*; of the Jews, advocated by the friends of Antiochus VII: 618 n.11

Genovese, Eugene: 21, 31, 148, 200-1, 229, 410

gentiles/Gentiles: *243*, *247*, *515*, *590 n.29*, 485; *Gentiles* as a crack regiment: 485, 515; *gentiles* as equivalent sometimes of *barbari*, sometimes of *pagani*: 515

Genucius, Cn. (Roman tribune): 618 n.5 (on VI.ii)

George, Katherine and C. H.: *543 n.11* (with 27)

George of Pisidia (Byzantine poet): 402, 538 n.3 (on I.ii)

Gerasa (in the Decapolis): *429*

'Gergesa': 429

Gergis (in the Troad): 118

Germanicus (nephew and adopted son of the Emperor

Tiberius): 327-8
Germans in antiquity: 238, 249, 260, 327-8, 468, 477, 481, 484-5, 490
   slavery among early Germans: *238, 249* (Tacitus); increase of slavery among Alamanni, Marcomanni and Quadi: 249
      traditional Arianism of: 448
      attitude to Roman Empire of those who entered Roman service: *484-5*
      And see under 'Alamanni', 'Chamavi', 'Frisians', 'Goths', 'Marcomanni', 'Ostrogoths', 'Quadi', 'Usipi', 'Visigoths'
Germantown (Pennsylvania), Mennonites of: *423*
gerousia of Greek cities in the Roman period: 314-15; of Sparta in the Roman period: 527
Gerth, H. H., and C. Wright Mills: 86-9
gēs enktēsis: 94-5, 288-9
Gibbon, Edward: *13, 209, 372, 377, 420-1, 453, 470, 503*, 515, *635 n.91*, 654 n.42
Gibeonites, used as Scriptural justification of *apartheid*: 332
gift-exchange: 132
Gildo (rebel African chief), revolt of, in Africa (397): *265, 501-2*
Gilliam, J. F.: *454-5, 648 n.10*
Gillis, Daniel: *604 n.26*
Girardet, Klaus M.: *635 n.91a*
gladiators, exported to Greeks from Rome: *410* (with 636-7 n.3)
Glaucia, C. Servilius: 353
Glaucon (in Plato's *Republic*): 147
gloriosissimi: 473
Glotz, Gustave: *281*, 577 n.20, 596 n.1 (on IV.vi)
Godelier, Maurice: 21-2, 37
Gogh, Vincent van: see under 'Van Gogh'
Gomme, A. W.: 131, 571 nn.54-5
Gongylids: 118
'Good' and 'Bad' in social sense: *279, 283, 355*; Theognis on: *279*; terminology in Greek: *agathoi, beltistoi, epieikeis, gnōrimoi, kaloi kagathoi* etc., against *kakoi, ponēroi, deiloi* etc.: *279, 283, 550 n.8* etc.; for the Romans: 355 (Cicero and Sallust), *360* with *375* (Augustus, quoted by Macrobius), 456-7 etc.
Gordian I (Roman emperor): 475, 657 n.21
Gordion III (Roman emperor): 216, 527, 657 n.21
Gordon, Mary L.: *574 n.6*
Gorgias of Leontini: 295 (with 607 n.46)
Gospels: 164, *427-33*
Goths: 258, 477-8, 512, 514, 517. And see 'Ostrogoths', 'Visigoths'
Gould, John: *558 n.30*
Gracchi, Tiberius and Gaius Sempronius: 337-9, 351-4, 359-60, 368, 376, *622-3 nn.7-8*
Gratian (Roman emperor): 128, 182, 252, 388
Gray, The Rev. Canon Joseph Henry ('Joey'): ix-x
Greece, poverty of (Mainland): 117-18
Greenidge, C. W. W.: 134, 147
Gregory I 'the Great', Pope St.: *225, 254-5* (with 592 nn.47-8), 384, *423*, 447, *483, 495-6*, 498, *517*; his administration of the *patrimonium Petri* in Italy, Sicily, Gaul etc.: *225, 254-5, 495-6, 517*; his proposal for converting Jews to Christianity by offering reduction of rents: *254*
Gregory of Nazianzus: 11, 438
Gregory of Nyssa: 436, *449*
Gregory Thaumaturgus ('the Wonder-Worker'), of Neocaesarea in Pontus, his *Canonical Letter*: 477, 479
Gregory of Tours: 496, 658 n.34
Greuthungi: 512, 515

Griffin, Miriam: 376, 409, 419
Griffith, G. T.: 601 nn.10, 16, *607 n.35, 608 n.47*
Grote, George: 609 n.2
Gruen, E. S.: 521 (with 659-60 nn.2, 4), 524
Gsell, Stéphane: *144-5*
Günther, Rigobert: 512, 515, 517, *590 n.29*
guerrillas (modern): 477
Guiraud, Paul: 596 n.1 (on IV.vi)
Guizot, F.; 548 n.1
Gummerus, H.: 596 n.1 (on IV.vi)
Gymnetes of Argos: 139

Habicht, Christian: *119*, *396*, 558 n.9
habitator, slave, of a house: 237
Hadrian (Roman emperor): 17, 119, 196, 240, 257, 316, 370, 390, 460, 469, 526, 527, 531; his law on Attic olive oil: 257, 316, 526
Haemimontus (Thracian province): 501
Halaesa (in Sicily): 522-3
Haldon, John F.: 594 n.3
Haliartus: *524*
Halicarnassus: 305
Halonnesus: *302*
Hands, A. R.: 579 n.35
Hanke, Lewis: *418*
Hannibal: 519-21
Hansen, Mogens Herman: 76 (with *550-1 nn.18-22*), *602 n.23*, 602-3 n.24
Hardy, E. R.: 169, 584 nn.38-9
harenarius: 459
Harmand, Louis: 592-3 n.50, with 584-5 n.42
Harper, G. M.: 583-4 nn.33, 35
Harpocras (Pliny's Egyptian masseur): 342
Harrington, James: 203
Harris, Marvin: 22
Harris, W. V.: 345, 519, 562 n.4, 619 n.13, 620 n.5
Harrison, A. R. W.: 554 n.29, 555 nn.4-6
Harvey, F. David: *414, 539 n.4*, 605 n.28
Hasta (in Spain): 570 n.48
Hatzfeld, Jean: 521, 560 n.12
Hauran: 19
Haywood, R. M.: 216, 570 n.48
Hazor (in Palestine), Israelite claim of massacre at: 332 (with 617 n.10)
Hebrew, Hebrews: 170, 427, 640 n.3; Hebrew prophets: 440
Hefele, C. J., and H. Leclercq: 557 n.26, 638 n.2 (on VII.iii)
Hefzibah (in Palestine): see under 'Scythopolis'
Hegel, G. W. F.. his dialectic 'standing on its head': 26; Marx's study of: 55, 56
Hegemon of Thasos (5th-c. parodist): *562 n.6*
Helen, Tapio: *560 n.11*
Heliogabalus (Roman emperor): see under 'Elagabalus'
Helots, Spartan, of Laconia and Messenia: 48, *93*, 139-40, 146, *147*, 148-9, *149-50*, 153-4, 160, 173, 227, *286*, 568 n.35; as 'State serfs': *149*; Laconian and Messenian Helots: 149-50 (with 565 n.18)
   ephors' annual declaration of war upon: *149*
   verb *heilōteuein* (etc.) applied to other serf peoples: 139, 148-9, 160
Helvidius (Christian writer): 109-10
Helvidius Priscus (Roman Stoic): 370
Hephaestus: 113, 140
Heraclea Minoa (in Sicily): 522-3
Heraclea Pontica (on southern shore of Black Sea): 136, 150, 156, 160, 296-8, 508. And see under 'Mariandynoi'
Heracleides Ponticus: 115

Heracleides of Temnus: 163
Heracles: 137
Heraclius (Roman/Byzantine emperor, 610–41): *8* (with *538 n.3*, on I.ii), 318, 378, 400–1, *484*, *594 n.4*, 631 n.57, *650 n.16*, 651 n.32, 652 n.39
    his persecution of the Jews, and its consequences: *484* (with *652-3 n.39*)
Heraion Teichos: *607 n.36*
Hermaiscus (Alexandrian): 442
Hermippus (Hellenistic biographer): 130
Hermippus of Temnus (in Cicero): 163
Hermogenianus (Roman lawyer); see under '*Digest*'
Hermopolis (in Egypt): 196
Herod, king of Judaea, and his dynasty: 119, 164, 427; Herod Antipas, the 'tetrarch': 427, 430
Herodes Atticus: 124
Herodian (Greek historian): 323, *387*, *392*, 477, 512, 595 n.6, 649 n.4
Herodotus: 24, 73, *117* (with 293), 129–30, 163, 271, 283, 305, 332, *601 n.11*
Heruls: 516
Hesiod: 24, 130–1, 185, 221, 231, *278*
Hicks, (Sir) John: *83-4*
Hierapolis (in Syria): 220
hierarchy, in Later Roman Empire, projected into the celestial and demonic spheres: *407-8*
Hiero, tyrant of Syracuse: 132
hierodules (temple servants): *153-7* (with 568–9 nn.34–40); often serfs, not slaves: 153, 154
Hignett, C.: 601 n.12
Hilarion (Egyptian): 103
Hill, Christopher: 21; and Edmund Dell: 444, *638 n.13* (with *417*)
Hilton, Rodney: 21, 159, *210-11*, 266, 269
Hinton, William: *212*, 82, 84
Hipparchus, grandfather of Herodes Atticus: 124
hippeis ('knights'): 280 (with 599 n.23)
Hippias of Elis, his alleged Olympic victor list: 69
Hippocrates of Chios (mathematician): 131
hippodrome: see under 'circus'
Hippolytus, Pope (or Anti-Pope): 325; on the toes of Daniel's image as 'democracies': *325* (with *616 n.61*)
Hipponicus (Athenian): 118
hired (wage) labour: *4*, *25*, *29*, *40*, *45*, *53*, *58-9*, *68*, *77*, *112-13*, *117*, *127*, *130*, *145*, *170*, *172*, *179-204*, *217*, *273*, *281*, *419*, *441*, 32, 65, 103, 205, 212, 278, 285, 287
    terminology: in Greek, *misthōtoi* or *thētes*: 179, 182, (with 575 nn.5-6); *ergatai*: 188; *erithoi*: 200, 576 n.12; in Latin, *mercennarii*: 179, 197-9; for hired labour: 575 nn. 5-6
    on public works, in Classical period: 188–92; in Roman period: 192-5
    Marx on mercenary service as earliest known large-scale hired labour: *24-5*, *182*; his contrast between hired labour and slavery and serfdom: 112-13
    working as hired man (even in responsible position, e.g. bailiff) considered 'slavish': *181*, *184*, *185*, *198-9*; his condition generally despised: 185-6, 187-8; except by Solon: 185, and except in service of State: *197*
    Aristotle's analysis of hired labour: *182-5*, cf. 197-8; in Plato and Aristotle, hired men are at bottom of social scale among all free men: *183-4*, *188*
    hired labour generally unskilled: 182-3, 184, 199-200; low pay: 185-6, 186-8
    in Athenian agriculture in Classical period: *576 n.16*
    in Roman period, evidence is mainly for agri-

culture (seasonal) and building (irregular): 187, 192-5
Hiroshima: 48
Historia Augusta: 128-9, 245, 386, 475, 476, 490, 512, 595 n.6, *654-5 n.42*
Historia monachorum: 129
Historical method: 28, 33–5, 55–6, 81-2, 91–4
    of Marx: 28 (with 543 n.12); historical studies and method of Marx: *55-7*
    of Fergus Millar: *81-2*
    of functionalists, and economic historians adopting a kindred method: *82-5*
    of Max Weber: *85-91*; of M. I. Finley: *91-4* (esp. *553 n.23a*)
    contrast between historian and sociologist: 33-5 (esp. 34)
    refusal of many historians to examine their concepts and categories: 33-4
'History', hypostatisation of: 28, 260; 'on the side of . . .': 260
Histria (in the Dobrudja): 528-9, 532
Hobbes, Thomas: 35, 183
Hobsbawm, Eric J.: 21, *28*, 46, 62-3, 355, 544 n.15
Hörigkeit and *Leibeigenschaft*: *161-2*, *570-1 n.53*
Hoffmann, Dietrich: 590 n.29, 656-7 n.11
Holleaux, M.: 519
'holy men': see under 'Christianity'
Homer: 24, 113, 185 (with 576 n.12), 413
Hommel, H.: 554 n.29
honestiores (etc.) and *humiliores* (etc.): *456-62*
honorati, defined: 458
Honoratus (Comes Orientis): 321
Honoré, A. M./Tony: *589 nn.26, 26a*, *633 n.78*
Honorius (Western Roman emperor): 127, 471, 501
Hopkins, Keith: 232 (with 587 n.9), 380, 574 n.12, 587 n.2a, 632 n.67a; alleged conflict between 'the emperor' and the senatorial aristocracy: *380-1*
hoplites: *260*, *280*, *282*, 115–16, 207, 291–2 (with 605-6 nn.30-1)
    role of, in supporting early tyrants: *282*
    hopla parechomenoi (hoplites with cavalry, *hippeis*) perhaps ¹/₅ to ¹/₃ of all citizens in 5th/4th cc.: *283*
Hopper, R. J.: *602 n.22*
Horace: 121, *124*, 240, *241*, 391, 582 n.19
Hormisdas, Pope, Justinian's letter to: *404*
horse-harness, ancient: *38*
Hortar (Alamannic chief): 485
Hosius, bishop: see under 'Ossius'
hospitalitas, hospitium: *591 n.34a*
'human nature', in Thucydides: 27
humiliores (etc.): see '*honestiores*'
Huns: 249, *486-7*, 490, 516–17
Hunt, Richard N.: 57
Hydatius (Late Latin chronicler): 486
Hyperbolus: 603 n.25 (with 290)
Hystaspes: see under 'Oracle of Hystaspes'

Ianouarios (assistant sculptor): 274-5
Iasus (in Caria): 315 (with 602 n.24), 508
Iazyges (Sarmatians): 468, 476, 511
Iberia (modern Georgia): 147, 154
Iconoclast controversy: 497
'ideal types' (Weber): *43*, 74, 86
ideology: 5, 6, 34, 125; of Athenian democracy: *284-5*; of the Roman Principate: *372-408*; of the victims of the class struggle: *441-52*; conscious and unconscious: *34*
Ignatius, St., his *Epistle to Polycarp*: *420*
Ihering, Rudolf von: 617 n.4
illiteracy in antiquity: 13 (with 539 n.4)

illustres: 473
Illyria: 496
Illyricum (large Balkan area): 187, 188, 250, 501, 572 n.66
immigrant workers (modern): 57, 67-8
impartiality: see under 'objectivity'
'*Imperator*' as imperial title: 392. And see '*autokratōr*'
imperial cult: *394-8*
imperialism: 44, *442-4*, 6, 53, 417, 463; protests against: *442-4*; modern Western: 417
imports into Graeco-Roman world: 232; annual drain of cash to India, China and Arabia (Pliny the Elder): *232*
incolae: see under 'citizenship'
India: 89, 90-1, *347-8*; Marx on British rule in: *347-8*
individuals, 'the individual': 47, *439*
inertia of civil population in Roman empire, in face of 'barbarian' incursions: 264 (with 595, n.6), 485 ff. (with 653-5 n.42), 502-3, etc.
inflation of 3rd/4th cc.: 492
inheritance, desirability (or not) of having a single heir: *278*
Iniuriosus, bishop of Tours: 496
inquilini: 244-7 (but see 589 n. 26a), 253
Institut Fernand Courby: 519
instrumentum of a farm: 216-17, 246, 256; '*cum instrumento*' and '*instructus*': 257-8 (with 593 n.52)
Iotapa (in Cilicia): 531
Iran (modern): *150-1*
Irenaeus, St.: 436
Ireton, Henry: *441*
Isaac tells Esau to *douleuein* to Jacob (in LXX Genesis): 423
Isaeus: 185
isēgoria: see under 'democracy'
Isidore (Alexandrian): 442
Isidorus, C. Caecilius (rich freedman): 177 (with 574-5 n.15)
Isocrates: *130*, *295*, *297-8* (with *608 n.53*), *299*, *300*, *301* (with *609 n.1*), *601-2 n.18*, 24, 115, 124, 149, 160, 185, 190, 191, 286, 290, 413, 571 n.55
isonomia, isonomos: see under 'democracy'; add 615 n.56
isotēs: 285 (with *601 n.9*), 309, 323, 615 n.51
Israel, Israelites, ancient: *331-2* (with *617-18 nn.9-12*), 151. And see under 'Jerusalem', 'Jesus Christ', 'Jews', 'Judaea', 'Palestine', etc.
Issachar: 437
Italian Marxist work on ancient history: 543 n.7, 643 n.11 etc.
Italica (in Spain): 370
Italy, Roman: 6, 9, 52, 97, 122, 134, 163, 208, 221, 229, 230, 231, 233, 234, 235, 238-9, 241, 242, 254, 258, 263, 264, 270, 294, 318, 351, 356, 361-2, 370, 373, 480-1, 502-3, 519-21
ius civile, Roman: *328-30*, 426. And see under 'jurisdiction', 'law, laws, lawyers', '*lex/leges*'
ius gentium and *ius naturale*: 422

Jacob (Israelite Patriarch): 437
Jacobite Church (Syrian, Monophysite): 483-4
James, Epistle of: 188, 204, 580 n.52
Jameson, Michael H.: *506*
Jeffrey, L. H.: 534
Jericho, Israelite claim of massacre at: *332* (with *617-18 n.10*)
Jerome, St.: *109-10*, *325*, *430*, 434, 480, 495, 540 n.11, 557 n.27, 595 n.6, 641 n.4
    aversion to sex of: 109-10 (with 557 n.27 – which shows Marx knew his *Ep.* 22)

on Ptolemaic revenue: 540 n.11
    his exegesis of the Book of Daniel inferior to Porphyry's: *325*, *641 n.4*
Jerusalem: 192, 328, 428, 484, 611 n.14, *640 n.5*, 654 n.42; building of Second Temple at: *192*
Jesus Christ: 6, 15, 104-8, 110-11, 164, 366, 396, *419*, *427-33*, 537
    the countryside as the locus of his preaching (no evidence of his ever entering a real *polis*): *427-31*
    central feature of his preaching: see under 'Kingdom of God/Heaven'; his public preaching at Nazareth: 431
    his Parables: see under 'Parables of Jesus'
    his miracles: 396
    executed on the false charge of being a 'Resistance leader': 430 (with 640 n.6)
    minimal contacts with Greeks and Greek culture: *430-1* (with *640 n.7a*)
    attitude to wealth: *431-3*; the 'rich [young] man': *431*; the 'Beatitudes', differences between 'Sermon on the Mount' (in Mt.) and 'on the Plain' (in Lk.): *432* problems of 'Christian origins': 433
Jews, Judaism: 103-9, 192, 228, 254-5, 305, *331-2*, 417, 423, 442, 455, *484* (with *652-3 n.39*), 508, 534, *641-2 n.5*, *652-3 n.39*
    revolts of, against Rome: 192, 228, 442, 641-2 n.5
    Jewish attitude to women, sex and marriage (compared with Christian): *103-7*; 'uncleanness' by contact with menstruating woman: *108-9*
    attempt by Pope Gregory to convert Jewish tenants to Christianity: 254
    persecution of Jews by Christians: 484 (with 652-3 n.39); Jews forbidden to own Christian slaves: 255
    support given by Jews to Arabs in 7th c.: *484*
    ferocity attributed by Jews to Yahweh: *331-2*
    And see under 'Israelites', 'Jerusalem', 'Women', Yahweh'
Jezebel, queen of Israel: 151
John VIII (Byzantine emperor, 15th c.): *497*
John the Almsgiver (Almoner), St., bishop of Alexandria: 496, 498
John Chrysostom, St.: see under 'Chrysostom'
John of Ephesus (Monophysite ecclesiastical historian): 393-4, 517
John Lydus (John the Lydian, Late Greek writer): 378, 406, 445, 488, 490, 491
John of Nikiu (Monophysite historian, in Greek and Coptic): *483* (with *651 n.32*)
Johne, K. P.: 546 n.14
Jolowicz, H. F., and Barry Nicholas: 168, 328, 422, 571 nn.59, 61, 572 n.65
Jones, A. H. M.: *8*, *9*, *13*, *19*, *108*, *126*, *217*, *222* (with *583-4 nn.33-6*), *249-50* (with *591 n.37*), *251*, *252-3*, *254*, *257*, *262*, *264-5*, *302-4*, *328*, *356-7*, *383-4* & *ff.*, *389*, *393-4*, *445-6*, *448-9*, *466*, *469-73*, *481*, *483*, *491-3* (with *656 n.11*), *496*, *515*, *532-3*, *534*, *539 n.5*, *580 n.2*, *600 n.5*, *647 n.1*, *657 n.25*, and *passim*
Jones, C. P.: 309, 526, 529, *611 nn.17, 20*, 649 n.1
Jones, Philip J.: 15, *582 n.16*, *600 n.33*
Jonkers, E. J.: 234
Jordan, Z. A.: 544 n.3
Jordan valley: 19
Jordanes (Late Latin historian): 247, 513, 514, 516
Josephus: 12, 106, *192*, 322, *362*, 377, 534; on population of Roman Egypt: 540 n.11; on the building of the Second Temple at Jerusalem: *192*
Joshua (traditional Israelite leader), alleged massacres by: *332* (with *617-18 n.10*)
'Joshua the Stylite': *220*, *264*, 272, 493, 537, 561, n.24

Judaea: 119, 186, 192, 215, *427-33*. And see under 'Jesus Christ', 'Jews', 'Palestine'
Judaism: see under 'Jews'
Julia Soaemias: see under 'Soaemias'
Julian (Roman emperor): *11*, 127, 128, 177, *219-20*, *320-1*, 365, 379, *387*, 390-1, 434, 448, *451*, 481, 488, *490*, 493, 494, *498*
Julian, bishop of Cingulum: 238
Julianus, Salvius (Roman lawyer): see under *'Digest'*
Julius Caesar, C.: see under 'Caesar'
Jupiter: 322, 397; Capitoline: 322
jurisdiction, courts of law, judges etc.: *96-7, 286-8, 289, 290, 300-1, 306, 315-17, 366-7, 487-8, 525*, 76, 311, 321, 338-9, 364, 523, 526-7, 535
   control of courts gives *dēmos* control of constitution (Aristotle): *290*; and protection: *286-90*
   transfer of cases to court of provincial governor or emperor: 316-17, 535, etc.
   And see under 'law, laws, lawyers', 'pay, political', 'property qualifications'
Justin I (Roman emperor): 388, 494
Justin II: *399-400*, 319, 393, 494
Justin (Latin historian): *292, 296-7*
Justinian I (Roman emperor): *8*, 11, 12, 138, 147-8, *159*, 166, 169, 173, *224*, 233, *252-3, 261*, 263, 264, 319, 321, *391*, 399, 402, 404, 409, *480-3*, 492, 494, 496, *501*, 503, 516-17, *559 n.16*; his *Institutes* (A.D. 533): 138, 328-9; his 'Pragmatic Sanction' (A.D. 554): 482-3
Justin Martyr, St.: 433
'Just War' and bellum iustum, doctrines of *439-40*
Juvenal: *141, 371, 382, 460*

Kallikyrioi/Killikyrioi of Syracuse: see under 'Killyrioi'
'Kallipygoi' of Syracuse: *18*
kalos kagathos: 121, *297*
Kant, Immanuel: 203
Kapiton, sculptor at Perinthus: 274-5
Kaser, Max: 253-4, *573 n.75 & n.2*, *617 n.3*
katoikoi, katoikountes: *157-8*, 564 n. 13a. And see 'metics', 'paroikoi'
katōnakophoroi: see under *'korynēphoroi'*
Kelly, J. M.: *626 n.41*
Kelly, J. N. D.: *557 n.27*
kephalē (Pauline metaphor, applied to husband/wife relationship): 105-6
Kiechle, Franz: *546 n.14*, 547 nn.16, 18
Killyrioi/Kyllyrioi of Syracuse: 139, 305
'Kingdom of God/Heaven', the central feature of Jesus' preaching: *431* (with *640 n.8*)
'King's friends': 119 (with 558-9 nn. 9-10), 156-7. And see 'Aristodicides'
'King's land': 151 etc.
klarōtai (of Crete): 139, 150
'knights': see under *'hippeis'* (Greek) and *'equites'* (Roman)
Kolakowski, L.: xi
Kolonos Agoraios (at Athens): *186*
korynēphoroi/katōnakophoroi of Sicyon: 139
Kosack, Godula: see under 'Castles, Stephen'
Kotrigurs (a Hunnic people): 249, 517
Kreissig, Heinz: *151*, 155-6, 158, *542 n.7*, *568 n.34*, 569 nn.38, 44
'Kreuznacher Exzerpte' (by Marx): 55
Kroeber, A. L.: 98
Kübler, Bernhard: *240, 586-7 n.1*
Kugelmann, L.: Marx's letter to: 68
Kula, Witold: 269, 278, *598 n.7*

Labeo, M. Antonius (Roman lawyer): see under *'Digest'*

labour services. forced/involuntary labour, labour rents: *14-16*, 44, 53, 112, 135, 206-7, 213, 228, 287, 446
   labour rents: *218* (with 582 nn. 16-19, esp. *18*), 53, 113, 151, 160-1, 215-16
Lactantius: 443, 512, 513
Laelius, C. as speaker in Cic., *De Rep.*: 71, 331
laeti: 243, 247, 513, 515, 590 n.29
   Seeck's identification of Marcus's *inquilini* (*Dig.* XXX. 112.*pr.*) with *laeti*: 244-7, with *589 n.26a*
   terrae laeticae: 245, *515*
Lambton, Ann K. S.: *150-1*
Lamian war: 297, *301* (with *609-10 n.2*)
Lampis (freedman or slave): 563 n.9
Lampon (Alexandrian): 442
Lampsacus: 536
Lanata, Juliana: 646 n.22
Landau, H.: 569, n.44
land tenure:
   importance of land as a principal means of production in antiquity: 40, 112, cf. 120-33
   ways of obtaining surplus from land: *53*
   freeholders: 5, 58-9, 136, 155, 213, 214-15, 250; freehold ownership of land in Greek cities at first confined to citizens: see under 'citizenship'
   leaseholders, tenants, lessees: 5, 44, 172, 212-18, 224-6, 238, 239-42, 250; types of: *213-14*; 'head lessees' (*conductores*, who often sub-let to *coloni*): 250, 253-5
   powerful landlord might give protection (not otherwise available) to tenant: 215,216
   rent: *213-19*; Marx on: *219* (with *582-3 n.21*); improper exactions of rent: 225-6; labour rents: *218* (with 582 nn.16-19, esp. *18*), 53, 113, 151, 160-1, 215; arrears of rent (*reliqua*): 239-40, 247, 257; unpleasant consequences of default: 240-1
   slaves often involved when land leased to tenants: *256-9*
   leasing likely to yield smaller surplus than direct cultivation with slaves: 53, 113, 116, 256 ff.; but leasing involved less trouble to landowner than direct cultivation: *241, 258*; and wives might dislike visiting country estates: *241*
   Later Roman colonate (a form of serfdom): *249 ff.*; *'colonatus'* from mid-4th c.: 251-2; earlier use of *'colonus'* for free tenant: 5, 213, 215-16, 217
   slave 'quasi colonus': *237-8*, 44-5, 137, 210, 211, 238, 243
   after Late Republic, rich landowners' estates probably more and more scattered: 241
   the 'pleasures' of farming: 121-2
   farming as a 'sordidum opus': 122
   distribution and redistribution of land (*gēs anadasmos*): 190-1, 282, 288, 298-9 (with 608-9 n.55), 335, 352, 357-8
Landtman, Gunnar: 562 n.7
languages other than Greek and Latin (e.g. Aramaic, Armenian, Egyptian/Coptic, Lycaonian, Syriac): 10, 13, 16 (with *540 n.9*), 17, 197, 220, 300, 348, 446, 537, *579 n.37*
   native languages usually prevailed in *chōra*: 10, 13, 16, 300
Laniogaisus (Roman officer of Frankish descent): *485*
Laodice (Seleucid ex-queen), sale of land to, by King Antiochus II: 152 (with *566 n.26, 569 n.44*)
laokratia: 614n.50
laos, laikos: *151-3* (with *566-8 nn. 26-33*), *157-8*, 540 *n.13*, 564 n.13a; *basilikoi laoi*: 151 (cf. *basilikoi geōrgoi*: 153, with 566-8 n.32)
   somata laika oiketika/eleuthera (*SB* V. 8008): *152-3*

Laos (modern State): 48
La Penna, A.: 643 n.11
Larcius Macedo: see under 'Macedo'
Larinum (in Italy), Martiales of: 570 n.48
Larisa (in Thessaly): 174
Larsen, J. A. O.: 570 n.50, 576 n.18, 614 n.47
Las Casas, Bartolomé de: *418*
Lascutani (at Hasta in Spain): 570 n.48
Lassalle, F.: 24, 47
Lassus, J.: 593 n.50
Last, Hugh M.: 309, 357
latifundia: 242 (with 589 n.23)
Latin America: 234
Latin Panegyrics: 245, 248, 512, 513, 515
Lattimore, Owen: 596 n.4
Lauffer, Siegfried: 538 n.3 (on I.iii), 562 n.8
Laum, Bernhard: 470
Laurium, Athenian silver mines at: 294, 562 n.8
law, laws, lawyers: 76, *285* (with *601 n.12*), *328-30*, *366*, 334-5
    in Aristotle, 'either oligarchic or democratic': 76
    Marx and Engels on history of law: 330
    respect of Greek democrats for laws: 285 (with 601 n.12)
    Romans did not have 'rule of law' in our sense: *328-9*; Roman lawyers: 329-30; Roman law of succession and legacies: 329-30; Roman 'Law and Order': *366*; first publication of laws at Rome: 334-5
    And see under '*Constitutio Antoniniana*', '*ius civile*', '*ius gentium* and *ius naturale*', 'jurisdiction', '*lex/leges*'
Lazarus, Parable of: 110-11
Lechaeum (port of Corinth): 132
Legon, R. P.: *296* (with *608 n.49*)
Leibeigenschaft: see under '*Hörigkeit*'
leisure (*scholē*): *116-17*, *122-3*, *183-4* (with 575 n.7), 36-7, 79, 115, 124-5, 226
Lenin, V. I.: 46, 50, 359
leno (procurer, brothel-keeper): 272-3
Lentulus, Cossus Cornelius (proconsul of Africa): *391*
Lentulus Sura, P. Cornelius: 372
Leo I (Eastern Roman emperor): 143, 272, 657 n.19
Leo I 'the Great', Pope St.: 421-2; on 'servile vileness' polluting the Christian priesthood: *422*
Leo XIII, Pope, his Encyclical, *Rerum novarum* (1931): 440
Leocrates (Athenian): 132
Leontiadas (Theban): 296
Lepcis Magna (in Africa): 370, 391
Leucas: 132
Leuctra, battle of (371 B.C.): 103
Levellers, English: *203*, *441*
Levick, Barbara: 518-19, 533, 559 n.13
Lévi-Strauss, Claude: 22, 32, 36, 542 n.5
Levy, Ernst: 253-4
Lévy, Isidore: *518*, *532-3*
Lewis, Naphtali: 658 n.40
Lewis, Naphtali, and Meyer Reinhold: 174, 216
lex/leges: leges Aelia et Fufia (2nd c. B.C.): *344* (with 619 n.18); *lex Hortensia* (287 B.C.): 333; *lex de imperio Vespasiani*: see under 'Vespasian'; *lex Julia* (of Caesar, 59 B.C.): 346; *lex Julia* (of Augustus): 456, 458; *lex Poetelia* (326 B.C.): 165-6, 572 n.65; *lex Pompeia* (63/ 59 B.C.): 529-30; *lex Rupilia* (131 B.C.): 522-3; *leges tabellariae* (139 ff. B.C.): *624 n.26*
lex animata: see under '*nomos empsychos*'
Libanius: *11-12*, *15-16*, 124, 132, *143 & 145*, 220, 224, 272, 321 365, 390, *472, 473, 488*, 494, 514, *541 n.16*
Liberius, Pope: 451
Liber Pontificalis: 495-6 (with 657 nn.26, 28)

libertas: 366-70 (with 626 nn.48, 51 & esp. *52*); as 'the rule of a class' (Syme): *368*; different kinds of: *368*
    And see under 'eleutheria', 'freedom'
liberty; see under 'eleutheria', 'freedom', 'libertas'
licentia: 366, 368 (with *611 n.16*), *369*
Lichtheim, George: 20
'Licinio-Sextian rogations', tribunes Licinius and Sextius: *336-7*
Licinus (Augustus' *procurator* in Gaul): 176 (with 574 n.7)
Liebenam, W.: 518, 533
Liebeschuetz, W./J. H. W. G.: 15, 132, *196*, *365*, 584 n.39, *592 n.50*, 614 n.44
Liebknecht, Wilhelm, Marx's letter to: *47*
Liguria, Ligurians: 187-8, 221, 509
Lilybaeum: see under 'Agonis'
Limigantes: 514
limitanei: 518
Linguet, S. N. H.: 548 n.1
Lintott, A. W.: 337 (with 618 n.5, on VI.ii)
Lipset, S. M.: 31, 550 n.12
literacy in antiquity: see under 'illiteracy'
Littleton, A. C. (ed.): 114
liturgies (*leitourgiai*, public services): 305-6, 467-74; assimilation of magistracies to: *305-6*; imposition of, on god or hero: *306*; burdens imposed on *curiales*: *467-74*
Li Village Gulch: *212*, 84
Livius Drusus, M.: 619 n.17
Livy (T. Livius): *167*, 303, *304, 307*, 335, *336-7*, 342, 343, 363, 509, *519-21, 524-5, 572 n.65*
Loane, Helen J.: 578 n.28
locatio conductio, locator, conductor:
    locatio conductio rei: 198-9, 238, 239-40, 250, 254-5 (with *592 n.49*), 330
    locatio conductio sui: 198
    locatio conductio operis/operarum: 189, 198-9 (with 579 nn.39-40), 203
Locke, John: 286
Locri: 520
Locris, East: 139
locusts: 220
Lombards: 483, 516
Long Bow village: *212*, 84
Longinus (or Ps.-Longinus), *On the Sublime: 323-5* (with 615-16 nn. 57a-60)
Lotze, Detlef: 136, *138-9*, 148, 149, 562 n.3, 565 n.20, *570 n.51*
Lucania (district of Roman Italy): 169, 254, 263, 482, 519
Lucian of Samosata: 24, *197*, *396*, *527*
Lucifer, bishop of Calaris: 405
Lucilius ('*cedo alteram*'): *266*
'Lucius', editor of Musonius Rufus: 110
Lucretius: *418*
Lucullus, L. Licinius: 270, 410, 508
Lugdunum (Lyons): 128 (with 561 n.19)
Luke the Stylite: 221
Luna (in Etruria): 255
Lupicinus (Roman official): 258
Lusitanians: 360
Lutz, Cora E.: 110
Lycaonia and its language: 16
Lycia, Lycians, Lycian League: 322, 531
Lycurgus (Athenian) 132, 414
Lydia: 216, 480
Lydus, slave and vase painter at Athens: 174 (with 573 n.79)
Lydus, John: see under 'John Lydus'
Lysander and 'Lysandreia': 74, 121, 190, 291, (with 606 n.32), 395

Lysias (Attic orator): 92, 295 (with 607 n.46), 607 n.37
Lysias, Claudius (military tribune at Jerusalem): 455
Lystra: 16

[Mc is treated as Mac]
Ma of Comana in Cappadocia, and Ma (Enyo) of Comana in Pontus: 154
Macarius (emissary of Constans to Africa in 347): 434-5
Macaulay, Lord: 548 n.1
Maccabees I and II: 508
McCargar, D. J.: 79-80
McCulloch, J. R.: 56
Macedo, Larcius (freedman's son and praetor): *409*
Macedon, Macedonians: 5, 8, 97, 151, 260, 291, 292, 293, 295, 298, 299, 301, 309, 314, 344-5, 349, 361, 480, 528, 564 n.16; rise of, from early 350s, with Philip II: 292
Macedonius, Semi-Arian bishop of Constantinople: 448, 451
Machiavelli, Niccolò: *122-3*, *363*, *382*, 55, 501; his *gentiluomini* defined: *122-3*; contrast between his attitude and that of a rich Greek or Roman: *123*
Mackinnon, W. A.: 548 n.1
McLellan, David: 55-6, 347
MacMullen, Ramsay: 187, 273, 318, *539 nn.5*, 7, 562 n.5, 577 n.19, *579 n.33*, *613 n.40*, *614 n.43*
Macrobius: *360-1* (with *375*)
Mactar, inscription from (*ILS* 7457): 187
Maecenas: 340; speaker in Dio Cassius LII: *265*, *308*, *323*, *615 n.56*
Maelius, Spurius: *337* (with 618 n.5, on VI.ii)
Magie, David: 196-7, 302, 518 (with 659 n.1), 529, 569 n.38, 583 n.33
Magnentius (Roman 'usurper'): 387, 490
Magnesia on the Maeander: 305
'Magnificat': *432-3*, *440*
magnificentissimi: 473
Mago (Carthaginian writer on agriculture): 235
maiestas (treason), an exception to all rules: 460
Majorian (Western Roman emperor): 377, 383, 387, 473, 481, *499-500*; his Second Novel: *499-500*
Malachi (Old Testament prophet): 186
Malalas, John (Byzantine historian): *616-17 n.64*
Malarich (commander of Gentiles): *485*
male 'superiority': see under 'Adam and Eve'
Malinowski, B.: 82
Malta: 523
Malthus, T. R.: 29
Mamertinus, Claudius (Late Latin orator): 481
managers: see under 'slaves, slavery'
Mania, widow of Zenis of Dardanus: *118*, *565 n.24*
Mann, J. C.: 540 n.9, *620 n.6*, *646 n.27*
Mannes the Phrygian (woodcutter): 274
'manpower shortage': 244 (with 589 n.25)
Mansi, J. D.: 538 n.5, 557 n.26, 574 n.13, 639 n.3
Mantinea: 296, 507
Mantinium in Paphlagonia: 451
manumission: *174-5*, 135, 169, 233, 238, 255, 417
　　Greek and Roman compared; *174-5*; Dionysius of Halicarnassus on why Romans gave citizenship to freed slaves: *175*
　　Aristotle on: 417; manumission by the city, for services rendered: 174; esp. for military service in emergency: 174, 441 (with 641 n.3); Delphic manumission-inscriptions: see under 'Delphi'
　　contrast with American Old South: 410, 549 n.18
　　And see under 'freedmen'
Mao Tse-tung: 26 (with 543 n.10), 50 (with 548 n.3), 339
Marathon, battle of: 115, 260, 280, 311

Maratocupreni: 48
Marcellus, M. Claudius (cos. IV, 210 B.C.): 342
Marcellus, M. Claudius (dictator 327 B.C.): 619 n.16
Marcian (Eastern Roman emperor): 404, 493, 657 n.19
Marcianopolis: 653 n.42
Marcianus, Aelius: 244-7, with 589 n.26a. And see under '*Digest*'
Marcomanni: 245, 249, 260, 468, 476, 512; Marcomannic wars of Marcus Aurelius: 245, 468, 476
Marcus Aurelius (Roman emperor): 13, 121, 126, 128, 174-5, 244-5, 260, 271, 323, 374, 389, 459, 468-9, 526-7; his *Meditations*: *323*
Marcus Aurelius and L. Verus (joint emperors): 128, 174-5
Marcus Aurelius and Commodus (joint emperors): 244, 527
Margus (on the Danube), betrayed to the Huns by its bishop: *486*
Mariades of Antioch: 475
Mariandynoi of Heraclea Pontica: 139, 149, 150, 153-4, 160 (with 570 n.52), 508
Marinus, Arian theologian: 450
Marinus 'the Syrian' (praetorian prefect): 318-19
maritime loans: 116
Marius, C.: 208, 271, *357-8*, *372*
Marius Gratidianus: *353-4*
Markle, Minor M.: *299*, *608 n.53*
Markus, R. A.: *643 n.15*
marriage: see under 'Christianity', 'Jews, Judaism', 'Musonius Rufus', 'Paul, St.', 'Women'
Marshall, A. J.: 613 n.33
Martial: 178, 238, 397, *406*
Martiales: see under 'Larinum'
Martindale, J. R.: 612 n.24
Martini, Remo: 575 n.1
Marx, Karl (often with F. Engels):
　　life: 23-5, 55-6
　　writings and thought: see separate heading immediately below
　　other references: 3, 4, 5, 19-30, 68, 87, 356-7
　　'Marxism' and 'Marxists' (genuine or not): 20, 41, 57, 78, 94, 155, 259, 268-9, 546 n.14, 549 n.16
　　And see under 'Engels, F.'
Marx, Karl (sometimes with F. Engels), writings and thought: 20, 23, *24-5*, 26, 27, 28-30 (with 543-4 nn.13-16), 32, 35-7, (with 545 nn.6-7, 10), 38-9, 43, 45, 46-7, 49, 49-52, 53-4, 55-7, 58, 59-62, 63-4, 66, 70, 74, 77-80, 86, 89-93, 99, 102, 112, 112-13, 122, 125, 133, 140-1, 155, *159*, *160-2*, *182*, *183*, *206*, *208*, 219 (with *582-3 n.21*), *269*, *283*, *287*, *330*, *335*, *347-8*, *371*, *504-5*, 544 n.15, *546 n.14*, 547 n.21 and nn.1-2, 4, *548 n.1*, *549 n.19*, 557 n.27, *594 n.4a*, *621-2 n.5*
Mary, Virgin: 109-10, 400-1, 408; cult of, as *Theotokos*: *400-1*; church of, at Blachernae (Constantinople): 401. And see 'Magnificat'
Maspero, J.: 584 n.40
Massalia/Massilia (Marseilles): 131, 535-6
'Materialism', and 'Dialectical Materialism': 26
Maternus (leader of a revolt c.187): 476
matrilineality (*Mutterrecht*): 102-3
Matthews, J. F.: 650 n.6
Mauretania (part of Roman north Africa): 258
Maurice (Eastern Roman emperor): 8, 517, 652 n.34
Maximian (Roman emperor): 168, 478, 513
Maximian, bishop of Constantinople, recipient of a letter from Epiphanius of Alexandria, detailing St. Cyril's bribes to court officials: 177 (with 574 n.13)
Maximus of Ephesus (Greek pseudo-philosopher): 365, 379

Maximus (Roman official, c.376-7): 258
Maxwell, J. F.: 639 n.5
Mazza, Mario: 543 n.7, 650 n.6
Mazzarino, Santo: 239
Meek, Ronald L.: 21, 57, 545 n.7
Megacles (of Mytilene): 279
Megalopolis (in Arcadia): 507
Megara, Megarians: 132, 163, 180, 278
Meidias (son-in-law of Mania of Dardanus), his great treasure at Gergis: *118*
Meiggs, Russell: 189 (with 578 n.24), 561 n.18, 603 n.26
Meillassoux, Claude: 21-2, 544 n.4
Mela, M. Annaeus: 340
Melania the Younger, St.: *258*
'Melkites': 484
Mellor, Ronald: 620 nn.7-8
Memmius, C. (Roman tribune): 337, 343-4
Memnon, of Heraclea Pontica (Greek historian): 296-7
Menander (Athenian poet): 122, *163*
Menander of Laodicea (Greek rhetorician), *laokratia* in: 614 n.50
Menas, pagarch: 224
Men Ascaënus, at Pisidian Antioch: 154
Mendels, Doron: 659-60 nn.2, 4
Mendelsohn, Isaac: 573 n.76
Mennonites of Germantown: *423*
Meno (Athenian): 180
Menodora of Sillyum (in Pisidia): 179, 196-7, 528, 532
mercenaries: 24-5, 118, 182, 282 (with 599 n.31), 287, 288, *295*, *558 n.7*, 607 n.41; Marx on: *24-5*, 182
merchants: see under 'traders'
Merobaudes (Magister Militum): 478
Merton, R. K.: 82
mesoi, men of midling wealth: 71-4. And see under 'mixed constitution'
Mesopotamia (Iraq): 8, 128, 220, 345, 400, 483-4, 486-7, 503, 536-7; Roman province of: 128, 345
Messene, Messenians: 93, 149, 160, 286, 507, 525. And see under 'Helots, Spartan'
métayage: see under 'share-croppers'
Metellus, L. Caecilius (governor of Sicily), his rebuke to Cicero for addressing the Council of Syracuse in Greek: *349*
Metellus Celer, Q. Caecilius (cos 60 B.C.): 376
methodology: see under 'concepts and categories', 'functionalism', 'Historical method', 'New Economic History', 'structuralism'
Meyer, Eduard: 41
Meyer, S. (recipient of a letter from Marx): 68
Miccalus of Clazomenae: 186
Michael III (Byzantine emperor), refers to Latin as 'a barbarous Scythian language' in writing to Pope Nicholas I: *9*
Michael the Syrian (Syrian Jacobite historian, Patriarch of Antioch, late 12th c.): *483-4* (with *652 n.34*), 494, 517, 657 n.22
'middle class', not a good translation of '*hoi mesoi*': 71; three developments in Roman Empire: *29-30*; modern managerial: 29
Midianites, Israelite massacre of: 332; Cozbi, Midianite, speared by Phineas: 332
Mignet, F. A.: 548 n.1
Miletus: 131, 157
'military-industrial complex' in U.S.A.: 420
mills: see under 'water-mill', 'windmill'
Mill, James: 56
Millar, Fergus G. B.: *81-2*, 365-6, *375*, *403* (with *635 n.90*), 537, *579 n.37*, *615 n.56*, *621 n.1*, *655 n.42*
Millett, J. F.: 210

Milo, T. Annius: *354*
Mills, C. Wright: see under 'Gerth, H. H., and Mills'
Milton, John: 369
mines (and quarries): 134, 169, 197, 562-3 n.8, 564 n.15; condemnation to: 134, 169, 573 n.78; free hired labour in: 197; slaves in: 134, 169, *562-3 n.8*; slave revolts in: 564 n.15
miracles: 225-6. 396; of Vespasian, and of Jesus: 396 (with 631-2 n.65)
Mishnah, The, tractate *Niddah*: *109*
misthōmata: 189
misthos (pay, salary, rent etc.): 189, 273, cf. 289-90 and 602-3 n.24. And see under 'hired (wage) labour', 'pay, political'
misthōtai (contractors): *188-9*, 578 n.23
misthōtoi (hired labourers): see under 'hired (wage) labour'
Mithridates VI Eupator, king of Pontus (and the 'Mithridatic wars'): 345, 356, 508, 525-6, 529-30; letter of, to Arsaces, in Sallust: 356, *443*
Mitteis, L.: 166-9, *555 n.3*, 571 n.60, 572 n.71
'mixed constitution': 74-6, 291 (with 605-6 nn.29-31), 322-3
Mnason of Phocis: 202
Mnesimachus, inscription of: *153* (with *566 n.31*)
Mnoïtai (of Crete): 139, 150
Mócsy, A.: 510-13
'Moderates': 74
Modestinus (Roman lawyer): see under '*Digest*'
Moesia (Roman province): 510, 511
Moesia Inferior/Secunda (Roman province): 127 (with 560 n.13,), 501, 514, 516-17
Moesia Superior/Prima (Roman province): 514, 517, 560 n.13
Momigliano, A.: 341, 351, *367-8*, *613 n.40*, 621 n.1a
Mommsen, Theodor: 24, *329*, 368, *384*, *387*, 410 (with 637, n.4), 573 n.77 (with 170), 658 n.46; his conception of the Roman Principate: *384*
monarchy and 'tyranny':
   Aristotle on monarchy (*basileia*) and tyranny (*tyrannis*): 282-3
   monarchy (*basileia*): 8, *282-3*, 372-81 etc.; Dio Chrysostom on *basileia* (mainly of the Roman emperors): *372*, *628 n.17*, 614 n.49; the Roman Principate a *basileia*: 372 ff.
   tyranny and tyrants: *279-83*, *296-8*, 5, 71, 190-1, 191-2; tyrants not 'merchant princes': 280; 'most tyrants began as demagogues' (Arist.): 282-3; why tyranny a neccessary stage in Greek political development: *281*; *tyranni/tyrannoi* as unsuccessful usurpers of the Roman Imperial throne: see under 'usurpers'
Monnier, H.: *658-n.43*
Monophysites, Monophysitism: 401, 404, 448, 483-4. And see under 'Coptic Church', 'Jacobite Church'
Montesquieu, C.: 55
morality, Christian, concerned solely with relations between man and man or man and God: *439-41*
Moretti, L.: 535
Morimene (in Cappadocia): 154
Morris, Rosemary: 594 n.4
Moritz, L. A.: 575 n.3
mortality in antiquity, high rates of: 231, *232-3*, 248; low life expectancy and high infant mortality: *232*
Moschus, John: 187, 188, 651 n.32
'Moses and the prophets': 110-11
mos maiorum (ancestral custom): 375
Mossé, Claude: 294, 603 n.25, 609 n.2
Motya (in Sicily): 119

Mousnier, Roland: 69
Mouterde, R., and A. Poidebard: 593 n.50
Münzer, F.: 351
Mummius, L.: 307, 344, 525
Mundus (6th c. military commander): 319
munera personalia/patrimonii/mixta: 470
Murray, Oswyn: 551 n.27, 642 n.7
Mursa, battle of: 490
Musicus Scurranus (Imperial slave): 44, 65, *143*
Muslims: see under 'Arabia, Arabs'
Musonius, bishop of Meloe in Isauria: 657 n.29
Musonius Rufus (Roman equestrian, Stoic philo-
    sopher): *110* (with *557 nn.28-9*), 123, 402; his attitude
    to sex, marriage, and the education of girls: *110* (with
    557 n.29); his views on exposure of children as
    designed to preserve a single inheritance: *598 n.6*;
    influenced Dio Chrysostom: 560 n.7
mutilation as a punishment: 439, *479* (with 650 n.16);
    rare before Constantine and more frequent in
    Christian Empire: 479
Mylasa: 531, 533
Myrina (in Lydia): 174
Myrinus (of Zeleia in Phrygia): 132 (with 561 n.24)
Myro: 48
Mytilene: 119, 279, 297, *603-4 n.26*

Nabis (Spartan king): 149-50 (with 565 n.19), 307, *660
    n.5 (fin.)*
Naboth and his vineyard: *151*
Nagasaki: 48
Nahal Seelim (in Palestine), Jewish sectarian
    community at: 433
Namier, Lewis: 351 (with *621 n.1a*)
Naples (Neapolis): 523. 632 n.66
Narbo (Narbonne): 128 (with 561 n.19)
Narcissus (Roman Imperial freedman): 176, 177
Narcissus (slave at Venafrum): *174*
Naristae: 511-12
'narrative history', Brunt on: *31*
Narses (eunuch and general of Justinian): 177
'nationalism', nationality, Greek and Roman: *445-6,
    643 n.14*
natura/fortuna = nature/fortune = *physis/tychē*: 418
    (with 638 n.1)
Nature: see under 'human nature'
Naucratis: 17, 131
Nausicydes (Athenian): 180
navicularii: 127-8 (with 561 n.16), 132-3
Naxos: 185
Nazareth: *428-31*
Nazarius (Latin orator): 407
Neaera (Ps.-Dem. LIX): 100
negotiatores: 127 (with 560 n.12), 132, 272 (with 597
    n.7), 493
Nehemiah (Hebrew prophet): *164, 215*
Neocaesarea in Pontus: 477
neoi: 315
Nepos, Cornelius: 197, 235, 348, 565, n.22
Nero (Roman emperor): 176, 370, 376, 380, 387, 392,
    443, 475; the 'false Neros': 443
Nerva (Roman emperor): 386, 388
Nestorius, the heresiarch: 177, 574 n.13
'New Economic History', The: 83
Newman, J. H. (Cardinal): *424*
Newman, W. L.: 160, 549 n.1, 550 n.8
'new men' (*novi homines* etc.): 290, 364 (with *625 n.37*)
New Testament (general): 204 (with 580 n.52), 377,
    451 (with 644 n.26). And see under particular books,
    also e.g. 'Jesus Christ', 'Parables of Jesus', 'Paul, St.'

Newton, Isaac: 98
Nicaea (in Bithynia): 530; Church Council of: see under
    'Councils of the Christian Churches'
Nicanor (Seleucid general): 508
Nicholas I, Pope: 9
Nicholas V, Pope: 424
Nicholas, Barry: 168, 329, 617 n.1. And see under
    'Jolowicz, H. F., and Nicholas'
Nicias of Engyum (in Sicily): 520
Nicodromus, Aeginetan: *547 n.6*
Nicolaus, Martin: 183
Nicolet, Claude: 41-2 (with 547 n.21), 340
Nicomedes III, king of Bithynia: 165
Nicomedia (in Bithynia): 319
Nicopolis (in Thrace): 480, 653 n.42
Nieboer, H. J.: 562 n.7
Niebuhr, B. G.: 24
Niger, Pescennius (contender for Imperial throne): 477
Nimrud Dagh (in south-eastern Turkey), inscription
    of Antiochus I of Commagene at: *154*
Nisibis (in Mesopotamia): 486, 654 n.42
Noah, negro as inheritor of his curse on Canaan: 424
nobility (*eugeneia*, *nobilitas*), Greek idea of (*eugeneia*): 71
    (with 550 n.5), 411; '*nobilitas*' in Roman Republic:
    338; in Roman Empire: 406
Nock, Arthur Darby: *31, 395-6,* 398, 399, *631 n.59*
Nörr, Dieter: *571 nn.56, 58, 572-3 n.73*
Nola: 519-20
nomos empsychos (*lex animata*): 402 (with 634-5 nn. 88-9)
Nomus (Magister Officiorum): 146
Nori, Noricans: 480, 486
Noricum (Roman province): 242, 477, 486
Norman, A. F.: 16, *471-2,* 583 n.27, 649 n.20
North, D. C., and R. P. Thomas: *83-4*
North, Thomas, translator of Plutarch: 354
Notitia dignitatum: 247, 491, 517
Nova Carthago (in Spain): 563 n.8
Novatians (Christian sect): 448, 450, 451
novi homines: see under 'new men'
Numidia (modern Algeria): 403, 449, 482, 488
Nutton, V.: 645 n.4, 648 n.18

objectivity and impartiality: 31
ochlokratia: 322 (with 614 n.50), 611 n.16, 614 n.50
ochos, as Assembly of a village: *222* (with *584 n.35*), cf.
    535
Octavian: see under 'Augustus/Octavian'
Odenathus of Palmyra: 595 n.6
Odysseus: 279, 413
Oea (in Tripolitania): 563 n.13a, 595 n.6
Oenoanda: 531. And see under 'Diogenes of Oenoanda'
Oertel, F.: 398
Ofellus (*colonus* in Horace): *241*
'*officium*' (as favour): 342
O'Hagan, Timothy: 50, 62
oiketai (*oiketeia, oiketika*): 152-3 (with 566 n.27), 153
    (with 566 nn.29-31)
Oionias, son of Oinochares (Athenian): *605 n.27*
Olba (in Cilicia): see under 'Zeus'
'Old Oligarch': see under 'Xenophon' (sub-heading,
    'Ps.-Xenophon')
Old South: see under 'American Old South'
Old Testament: 164, 186, 398, 405, 419, 423, 431-2.
    And see under particular books, also e.g. 'Israelites',
    'Jews', 'Yahweh'
oligarchy, Greek: *72-3, 283,* 5, 45, 70, 72, 77, 95, 213,
    227, 280, 281, 287, 288, 291, 304, 308-9; hereditary
    oligarchy = *dynasteia*: 283, 323
    dependence of oligarchy on a property qualifi-

cation: *283*, 45, 72–3, 281
  oligarchic view of justice: *287-8*
  Sparta's role in upholding: 288, 296
Oliva, Pavel: 570 n.50, 590 n.29, 648 n.12
Oliver, J. H.: 526–7, 533, 615 n.54
Olmsted, F. L.: 142 (with *563 n.12*), 546 n.14
Olympiodorus (of Egyptian Thebes, Greek historian): *120* (with 559 n.17)
Olympus, Mysian Mount: 365, 516
Olynthus: 299
Omphale: 137
'operae liberales': 198
Ophellas: 610 n.2
Oppianicus: 570 n.48
Opramoas, of Rhodiapolis in Lycia: 533
Optatianus Porphyrius, Publilius: 513
Optatus, St. (African Christian writer): 399, 467, 482;
  cites Phineas (*q.v.*, below) as justification for
  persecution: *618 n.12*
optimates at Rome: 352–3, 359, 368–9, 370, 426; defined
  by Cicero: *353*
'Oracle of Hystaspes': 443 (with 642 n.7)
'Oracle of the Potter': 443 (with 642 n.7)
orators, Athenian: 185 etc.
Orestes (character in Euripides): 185
Oreus (in Euboea): 609 n.62
'Oriental/Asiatic mode of production': see under
  'production'
'Orientalisation' of the Graeco-Roman world: 9 (with
  538 n.4)
Origen: 109, 425
originales, originarii: see under '*adscripticii*'
Orosius (Late Latin Christian historian): 481, 510, 511,
  513, 516, 595 n.6
Osi: 510
Osrhoene (Roman province): 345, 561 n.21
Ossius (Hosius), bishop of Cordova: *404*
Ossowski, S.: 46, 71, 544 n.2, 548 n.10
Ostia: 128 (with 561 n.18), 467
Ostrogorsky, Georg: *262* (with *594 n.4*), *404*, 538 n.3
  (on I.ii), *658 n.45*
Ostrogoths: 221, 249, 263, 264, 480–3, 502, 515–16.
  And see under 'Theodoric', 'Totila'
Ostwald, Martin: *601 n.10*
Otranto: 12
Otto, W.: 568 n.34
overseers, managers (of slaves and others: *epitropoi,
  vilici, actores* etc.): see under 'slavery, slaves'
Ovid: *425*
'Oxyrhynchus historian': 73, 292, 609 n.59
Oxyrhynchus and its papyri: 17, *103*, 131, *169*, *196*, *223*
  (with *584 n.41*), *314* (with 533), 502

Pachomius (Egyptian abbot), Rule of: 495
paganism, pagans: 9, 18 etc.; pagans as 'Hellenes': *9*
'Pagan Martyrs' (of Alexandria), Acts of the: 442, 446
pagarchs: 224, 584 n.39 (*fin.*); Menas and Theodosius,
  of Antaeopolis: 224
Page, Denys L.: 131
Pagels, Elaine H.: 555 n.12
paidagōgos: 199, 200
Palanque, J. R.: 583 n.25
Palatine Hill at Rome, Cicero's house on: 368–9
Palestine: 119, 152, 164, 170, 250, 251, 427–33, 442,
  480, 483. And see under 'Decapolis', 'Galilee',
  'Jerusalem', 'Jews', 'Judaea'
Paley, F. A., and J. E. Sandys: 563 n.9
Palladius (Greek Christian writer): 220, 258, *408*
Pallas (Roman Imperial freedman): 176–7

Pallasse, Maurice: 591 n.37
Palmyra: *129* (with *561 n.20*), 467, 595 n.6
Pamphylia: 595 n.6, 653–4 n.42
Panaetius of Rhodes (Stoic philosopher): 122, 198
Panegyrici Latini: see under 'Latin Panegyrics'
'*panem et circenses*': see under 'bread and circuses'
Pangaeum, Mount (Thrace): 562 n.8
Pangloss, Dr.: 83
Pannonia (part of Roman Balkans), and Pannonians:
  258, 266, 480, 510–14, 516
Pannoukome (or village of Pannos): 152
Panopeus (in Phocis): 9–10
Pantaleo, notary on Sicilian estate of Roman Church,
  rebuked for using an excessive modius-measure: 225
Paphlagonia: 157
Papinian (Roman lawyer and praetorian prefect), his
  interrogation of the rebel Bulla: 477. And see under
  '*Digest*'
Papirius Carbo, Cn.: 346
papyri: 166, 251, and *passim*, e.g. 539 n.4, 540 n.13, 591
  n.40, 592 n.44. And see 'Oxyrhynchus and its papyri'
Paquius Scaeva, P. (proconsul of Cyprus): 534
Parables of Jesus: 164, 186, 444; of the Great Supper:
  437; of Lazarus: 110–11, 431–2, 436; of the
  Unmerciful Servant: 164; of the Vineyard: 186, 204
Paraetonium: 17
Parain, Charles: 63
paramonē (paramenein): 135, *169*, 170
Paret, R.: 652 n.34
Pargoire, J.: 652 n.35
Parke, H. W.: 601 n.16, 607 n.41
Parkin, Frank: 544 n.32
paroikoi: 95 (with *554 n.30* and 540–1 n.15), 157–8,
  178–9, 197, 564 n.13a
Paros: 601–2 n.18
parrhēsia: *284-5* (with *600 n.8*), *323* (with *615 n.57*), *361*,
  368
Parsons, Talcott: 43, 82, 85–6
Parthenon: 193; building-accounts of: 577 n.22
Parthians: 260–1, 348, 468, 477, 491, 536, 620 n.12
?Parthicopolis (in Roman province of Macedonia; now
  Sandanski in Bulgaria), letter of Antoninus Pius to
  (*IGBulg.* IV.2263): 314, 528
Pasion (Athenian, ex-slave): 174, *558 n.3* (on III.ii)
Passerini, Alfredo: 611 n.16
Patavium (in Venetia): 520
paterfamilias: 556 n.23 (with 108)
Patras: 12
patria potestas: 108 (with 556 n.23)
patrimonium Petri: see under 'Roman Church'
Patron, Egyptian police superintendent: 223
patronage and clientship: see under '*clientela*'
patronage, rural, in Later Roman Empire: 224-5, 343;
  different types of, used as a form of class struggle by
  peasant freeholders or tenants: 224-5; legislation
  against, in East but not West: 224-5
Paul, St., doctrine: *104-8* with 555-6 nn.9-12, 14-18,
  21), *398* with *400* and *432-3*, and *419-20*, 16, 96, 109,
  176, 313, 401, 439, 440, 447
  'Pauline Christianity': 105, 433
  Pauline and 'deutero-Pauline' epistles: 105
  Paul's insistence on his own inspiration by God:
  105 (with *555-6 n.15*)
  'the powers that be are ordained of God': *398*, 400,
  432-3, 439, 440, 447, 452
  Coloss. III.11 and Gal. III.28 compared: 107-8, 419
  attitude to sex, virginity, marriage, second
  marriage: *104-10*; compared with Musonius Rufus:
  110

attitude to slavery: *419-20*
Paul, St., life: 455-6, 458, 462, 498
Paul the Simple (early hermit): *408*
Paulinus of Nola, St.: 435
Paulinus of Pella: 480; 651 n.21, 654 n.42; his *Eucharisticos* (A.D. 459): 480, 654 n.42
Paullus, L. Aemilius: 334, 360
Paulus (Roman lawyer): see under '*Digest*'. (The *Sententiae Pauli*, cited in this book as '*Sent. Pauli*' or '*Paulus, Sent.*' are a compilation of around A.D. 300)
Paulus, son of Vibianus: 406
Pausanias ('the Greek Baedeker'): *9-10*, 301, 525, 527 etc.
'Pax Augusta': 228, 358
pay, political: *289* (with *602 n.23*), *289-90* and *315* (with *612 n.28*); not confined to Athens: *289-90* (with *602-3 n.24*)
pay, rates of ('piece-rates' and 'time-rates'): 189, 199, 201
Peace, 'Augustan': see under 'Pax Augusta'
Pearce Commission (Rhodesia, 1972): 212
Pearson, H. W.: 37 (with 545 n.11)
peasants, peasantry: *4-5, 9-19, 33, 208-26, 261-6* (esp. *263*), *300, 493-4*, 44, 45, 52, 54, 58-9, 98, 114-15, 133, 135, 205, 207-8, 233, 242, 243, 280-1, 349, 357, 372, 456, 463-4, 467-8, 491, 497-503; 'peasant society', 'peasant economy': *208-9*
    definition of peasantry as a class: *210-11*
    categories of (including freeholders): 213-14, 250, 251-2, 253
    Marx on (in *18th Brum.*): *60-1*; and (citing Bacon) *594 n.4a*; Engels on: *211*; Gibbon on: 209; Hinton on: 212
    idealisation of farming: 9, 122, 209
    'the land-and-peasant system' (Hicks etc.): *83-4*
    peasants receiving little benefit from city communities: 213
    inscriptions showing plight of peasants under Roman Empire: *215-16*
    importance of local labour situation: 217
    peasants acting as hired labourers: 186, 217
    problem of relative burdens of rent, compulsory services (*angariae* etc.) and taxation: 243
    'king's peasants' (*basilikoi geōrgoi*): 215
    military recruitment mainly from: 259-67 (esp. *260-3*)
    enserfment of working peasants (incl. freeholders) from end 3rd c.: *249-51*
    revolts by: 474 ff.
    resistance to barbarians (rare): 264 (with 595 nn.6-7), 485
    And see under 'anachoresis', 'Bacaudae', 'villages'
Pečírka, J.: 554 n.27
peculium (*castrense*): 25 (*castrense*: Marx), 44, 254
Pedanius Secundus, execution of all his 400 urban slaves (in A.D. 61): 372, 409
Pedieis (of Priene): 156 (with 569 n.42)
Pegasus (Roman lawyer): see under '*Digest*'
Peiraeus: 12
Peisander (Athenian): 605 nn.29-30
Peisistratus, tyrant of Athens: 190, 271, 282, 283, 353
Pelagius I, Pope: 238, 254
Pelagius, heresiarch (and Pelagian writings): *436-7*
pelatēs (dependant, client): 185
Pelham, H. F.: 226-7
Peloponnesian war, end of: 291
Penestai (of Thessaly): 139, 146, 150 (with 565 n.20), 153-4 (with 568 n.35), 162, 227; term applied also to serfs in Etruria: 139

Penia and Ptocheia in Aristophanes: 431
Pentacosiomedimnoi: see under 'Solon'
Penthelids of Mytilene: 279
'*penuria colonorum*': 217 (with 582 n.15), 257
Percennius (leader of mutiny): 266, 443
Percival, John: *218*
perfectissimi: 406, 459
Pergamum (Pergamon): 119, 151, 158, 178, 219, 242, 345, 529-30, 531
    inscription of 133 B.C. improving civic status of various categories: 158, 178-9
    Galen on number of citizens, with wives and slaves: 242
Pericles: 132, 415
Perinthus: 274-5, 480
Perioikoi: 150, *160* (with 570 nn.49-52), 416-17, 534; of Sparta: 160 (with 570 n.50)
Perlman, S.: 604 n.27
Perotti, Elena: 563 n.9
Perseus, king of Macedon: 521 and 524 (with 659-60 nn.2, 4), 525
Persia, Persians: 384 etc.
    Achaemenid period: 118, 119, 151, 260, 280, 282, 288, 291, 295, 298, 332, 565-6 n.24, 601 n.11, 604-5 n.29
    Sassanid period: 128, 251, 260-1, 319, 348, 400, 401, 479, 483-4 (with 652 n.33), 486-7, 490, 512, 517, 537, 595 n.6; defectors/deserters to Sassanid Persia: *128, 486-7*; Persians in Sassanid period never called 'barbari' by Ammianus: 261
    And see under 'Parthians'
'Persian debate' (in Hdts III.80-83): 601 n.11, 627 n.1
'Persian Gulf: 186
'personal execution': 164, 165-9, 240-1
Pertinax, P. Helvius (Roman emperor): 175
Pescennius Niger: see under 'Niger, Pescennius'
Pessinus (in Galatia): 568 n.38
pestilences: see under 'plagues'
Peter Damian, St. (11th c.): 404
Peter, sub-deacon in Sicily, ordered by Pope Gregory to use modius-measure of not more than 18 *sextarii* for exaction of rents of Roman Church: 255
Petilius Cerealis (Roman general): 489-90
Petit, Paul: 542 n.7, 583 n.23, 614 nn.44-5
Petra: 128 (with 561 n.21)
Petraeus (of Thessaly): 526, 533
Petronius (Roman satirist): 177-8, 199, 236, 597 n.6
Petronius (father-in-law of the Emperor Valens): 490
Petronius Probus, Sextus (praetorian prefect): 341
Petty, Maximilian (Leveller): 203
Phaedrus (Latin poet, of fables): *444*
Phaeno (in Palestine), copper mines at: 170
Phalaris, tyrant of Acragas: 281
Phaleas of Chalcedon: 79
Pharnabazus (Persian satrap): 118, 605 n.29
Pharr, Clyde: 127, 499
Phaselis (in Lydia): 531
Pheidias (Athenian sculptor): 274; Zeus of, at Olympia: 274; 'no young gentleman could want to be Pheidias' (Plut.): 274
Phibion (Egyptian creditor): *167*
Philadelphia (in Lydia): 216
Philagrus: see under Veranius Philagrus, Q.
Philip (Roman emperor: M. Julius Severus Philippus): 216, 240-1, 494
Philip II, king of Macedon: 149, 160, 260, *292, 298, 302*; his 'Fifth Columns' in Greek states: *298-9* (with 609 n.58); his 'League of Corinth': *299*; his professed friendliness for Athens: *299*

Philip V, king of Macedon: 174
Philippopolis (Plovdiv): 8, 653 n.42
Philista (of Tricomia in the Fayum): 223
Philo Judaeus (of Alexandria): *106-7*, 170, *319*, 402, *422-3*, 437, *499*, *614-15* n.*51*
philodespotos/Philodespotos ('master-loving') as adjective: *279*, 411; the proper name: 411
Philoponus, John: *634 n.79*
Philostorgius (Arian ecclesiastical historian): *450*, 514, 516, *635 n.90*
Philostratus (Greek biographer): *14*, 124, *129*, *163*, 219, *323*, *390*, *614 n.49*
Phineas (grandson of Aaron), his murders approved by Yahweh, and used to justify persecution: *332* (with *618 n.12*)
Phlius: 296 (with *608 n.49*)
Phocaea, Phocaeans: 521, 561 n.22
Phocas (Late Roman emperor): 8, 652 n.34
Phocion (Athenian): *609-10 n.2*
Phocis, Phocians: 202
Phoebidas (Spartan): 296
Phoenicia: 154, 186, 356, 480
Phormio (Athenian, former slave of Pasion): 174, *558 n.3* (on III.ii)
Phrygia, Phrygians: 163, 216, 221, 480, 653-4 n.42
Phylarchus (Greek historian): 149
Picenum (Italian district): 11, 120, 346
Piganiol, A.: 246, 485, 513, 515
Pilate, Pontius: 366; used as a term of abuse: 405
Pimolisa (in Paphlagonia), quicksilver mines at: *562 n.8*
Pinara (in Lycia): 531
Pindar: 24, 25
Pinianus, husband of St. Melania the Younger: 258
Pippidi, D. M.: 566 n.29
piracy, involving kidnapping and slave-raiding, suppressed by Pompey (67 B.C.): 230
Pirenne, Henri: 83
'piscinarii': *356*
Pisidia: 313. And see 'Antioch, Pisidian'
Piso, Julius (of Amisus): *309-10*
Pitane: 157
Pittacus of Mytilene, *kakopatridēs* in Alcaeus: 279
Pityus (on east coast of Black Sea): 654 n.42
Pius, Antoninus (Roman emperor): 121, 128, 314, 459, 468-9, 475, 526, 648 n.12
Pius XI, Pope, his Encyclical, *Quadragesimo anno* (1931): 440
Pizus (Thracian emporium): 127
placentophagy, in Deuteronomy: *617 n.9*
plagues, pestilences: 217, 332, 468, 488-9, 511
Plataea, Plataeans: 571 n.55; battle of (479 B.C.): 115, 260, 280, 311
Plato: *70-1*, *82*, *147*, *183*, *284*, 287, *411-14*, *416-17*, *557-8* n.*30*, 72-4, 76, 79, 103, 130, 146, 149, 185 190-1, 271, 287, 295, 297, 299, 322, 359, 423, 440
    arch-enemy of freedom and democracy: *284* (with 70-1), 412
    his 'bald-headed little tinker': *417* (with 71) and 'feminism': *557-8 n.30*
Plebeians, *plebs urbana* etc.: see under 'Rome, Romans'
Pleket, H. W.: 132, 528-9, 545-6 n.14, 558 n.1 (on III.ii), 561 n.23, 598 n.14, 599 n.17, 612 n.27)
Plekhanov, G.: 26, 544 n.15
Plinta (Magister Militum): 480
Pliny the Elder: 120, 143, *176-7*, *217*, *232*, *239*, 263, 270, 330, 511, 536, 563 n.8
Pliny the Younger: 95, *178*, *217*, *238*, *239-40*, 241, *257*, *309-10*, *312*, *319*, 343, *364*, *369*, 377, *381-2*, *389*, 397, *409*, *438*, 454, 459, 467, *529-30*, 531, *648 n.16*; his

estates, slaves and tenants: *217*, *239-40*, 241, *257*, *588-9 n.19*; his slaves not fettered: *238*; his settlement on his old nurse: *178*; his *Panegyric* on Trajan: *364*, *369*, 377, *389*; text of his *Ep.* X.113: *648 n.16*
Plotinus: 123-4
Plutarch (L. Mestrius Plutarchus): 24, 34-5, *48-9*, 69, 118-19, 130, 131, 132, *149*, *163-4*, *189* (with *578 n.24*), 193-4, 194, 195, *199-200*, 235, *274*, 301, 307, *310-13*, 316, 322, *324*, *343*, 345, *353-4*, 359, 360, 402, *414*, 520, 533, 536, 555 n.14, *608-9 n.55*, *609-10 n.2*, *611 nn.17-20*, *614 n.49*, *660 n.5*
Pogla (in Pisidia): 528-9, 532, 613 n.36
Poitiers, battle of (1356): 266
Poland: 278
Polemarchus (brother of orator Lysias): 92
Polemo, king of Pontus: 199
pōlētai (Athenian officials): 189
'*polis*' and '*chōra*': 3, 6, *9-19* (esp. *9-10*), *427-30*
political pay: : see under 'pay, political'
political thought, Greek, in Hellenistic and Roman periods: *80*, *552 n.31*
politographoi: 532
Pollock, Frederick and F. W. Maitland: 267-8
Pollux, Julius (of Naucratis): 185; his *Onomasticon* III.83: 138, *139-40*, 150; *Onomasticon* VIII.130: 610 n.2
Polybius: 74, 118, 140, 163, 171, 194, *230*, *303*, 307, *331* (with *617 n.7*), 342, *343*, *507*, 524-5, 536, 563 n.8, 565 n.17, *611 nn.16, 20*
Polycleitus of Argos (sculptor): *274*; 'no young gentleman could want to be Polycleitus' (Plut.): *274*
Polycrates, tyrant of Samos: 190, 271
Polygnotus (of Thasos and Athens, painter) decorated Stoa Poikile at Athens *gratis*: 274
Polyperchon (Macedonian general): 301, 609 n.2
Pomeroy, Sarah B.: 557 n.30
Pompeiopolis, in Paphlagonia: 562 n.8
Pompey (Cn. Pompeius Magnus): 25, 154, 176, 230, 529-30; the richest known Roman of the Republic: 176 (with 574 n.10)
Pomponius (Roman lawyer): see under '*Digest*'
Pontus (in north-east Asia Minor): 38, 119, 157, 477. And see under 'Bithynia (and Bithynia-Pontus)', also (for the 'Pontic kingdom') under 'Crimea'
'poor' and 'rich' vocabulary: *425-6*; *penētes* and *aporoi*: 53, *144*; contrast Hebrew usage: 431-2
populares (*dēmotikoi*) at Rome: 193, 340-1, *352-4*, 371; common features of their policies: *352*; not 'democrats': 353; defined by Cicero: 353; often revered after death by common people: *353-4*
Porcius Latro: 425
Porphyrius, Publilius Optatianus: see under 'Optatianus'
Porphyry (pagan scholar): *325*; his intelligent interpretation of the Book of Daniel: *325*, *641 n.4*
Portuguese traders and empire, and slavery: *424*
Poseidippus (Athenian comic dramatist): 103 [cf. p. 555 n.7]
Poseidonius of Rhodes (Hellenistic philosopher and historian): 187-8, 536
possessio, in Roman law, leasehold tenant did not have: 172
possessores, emperors' concern for: *499-501*
post, Imperial/public: 11, 539-40 n.8. And see under 'angariae', 'transport'
Postan, M. M.: 83, 268
postliminium: 478
Postumius Terentianus: 324
'Potato Eaters', The: see under 'Van Gogh'

potentiores, potiores: see under 'Powerful'
Potidaea: see under 'Cassandreia'
'Powerful', The (in Greek, *dynatoi*: in Latin, *potentiores, potiores* etc.): 127, *225-6*, 263, *367, 383* (with *629 n.32*), 487, 489, 500, 501, 562 n.5, 583 n.24, 594 n.4, 658 n.43; contrast 141
praedia, urbana and *rustica*: 244
Praetextatus, Vettius Agorius: 495 (with 657 n.26a)
pragmateutēs: see under 'actor'
praktores (tax collectors): 498
Prawer, S. S.: 25
Praxiteles (Athenian sculptor): 270
Préaux, Claire: 303, 555 n.5, 581 n.5, 591 n.37, 610 n.7, 617 n.65
predictability: see under 'probability/certainty'
Preisker, Herbert: 555 n.8
Priene: 155, 156, 158. And see under 'Pedieis'
'Primitive' society: 36
'princeps', for Roman emperor: 350, *375-8*
principales (= *decemprimi* in later sense): 471, 472
Principate, Roman: *372-408*, also 350-72 (esp. 350, 360, 361, 362, 363-4, 369-70); contrast between attitude of senators and *dēmos* to: *362*; relationship between emperor and Senate: *380-1*; supposed change from 'Principate' to 'Dominate': see under 'Dominate'; succession to Principate: *384-7, 387-8, 388-9*, 380; the emperor as a 'military dictator': *392*; ideology of the Principate: *392-4*; and its theology: pagan *394-7*, Christian *398-402*. And see under '*autokratōr*', '*basileus*', '*Imperator*', 'imperial cult', '*rex*'
Prinz, A. M.: 47
Priscus (Late Greek historian): 265, *468-7*
Priscus, Marius (proconsul of Africa): *382*
prison (Roman period): 460, 488
Pritchard, R. T.: 582 n.20
Pritchett, W. K.: 585 n.1, 605 n.27
'privileged groups' (in Roman period, as defined on p. 456): *456-62*
probability/certainty (Thucydides and Marx compared)' 27
Probus (Roman emperor): 490
Probus, Sextus Petronius: see under 'Petronius'
Procopius: 11, 480-3, 486, 514, 516, 517, 577 n.19, 583 nn.29-30, 595 n.6
Procopius ('usurper', 365-6): 394, 475-6, 489, 490
procurators, *procuratio*: 127
production, defined: *35*, cf. 112-14; (social) relations of/forces of: 3, 35 (with 545 n.7), 38-9, 49-50, 58, 548-9 n.11; conditions of: 4, 43; control of conditions of, as foundation of exploitation: *43-4*; ownership of means of production as commonest foundation: 44 (with 547 n.4)
    means of, in antiquity, esp. land and unfree labour: 40, 112
    'the small independent producer': 4, 33, 52, 205 ff.
    'modes of production': *29*, *155-7*; distinguished above all by methods of exploitation: *50-3*
    'Asiatic/Oriental mode of production': *29* (with *544 n.15*), *155-7* (with *569 n.42a*)
'professional' services (of 'sophists', philosophers, doctors, teachers, surveyors): 197, 198-9
proletariat: 56, 60-2
proletarii/capite censi at Rome: 357
Prometheus: 24
propertied classes, the
    qualification for membership, and characteristics: *4, 114-17*, 59, 211, 270, 309, 411-12, 414-15 etc.
    subdivisions of: *116*
    predominance of landed wealth among: *4, 120-33*,

78, 112, 114-20 etc.
    Rome generally favoured, and was favoured by, the Greek propertied classes: 306-12, 315-21, 344-5, 349, 519-33, 535-6
    And see under 'property qualifications'
Propertius: 358
property qualifications (for citizenship, magistracies, attending Assembly, courts, Council or Senate etc.): 114 (with 558 n.3), 129, 178, 289, *301, 305-6, 308, 338-9, 525, 527, 530*, 531, 535; *602 n.21*
'proportion', 'arithmetical' and 'geometric', political use as metaphor: *413-14*, 309
prosopography: 351
prostitutes, *hetairai*: 100, 101, 102, 129, 131, 154, 179-80, 271, 272, 569 n.40; sacred: 154
Proterius, Chalcedonian patriarch of Alexandria, strongly resisted: 196; and eventually murdered: 448
Protis, founder of Massalia: 131
Providentia: 397
provinces of Roman empire, total number apparently 199 around 400 A.D.: 491
provocatio: 352
Prudentius (Late Latin Christian poet): 417
Prusa (in Bithynia): 312, 319, 516, 530
Prusias ad Hypium (Bithynia): 18, 530
Psamtik II, Egyptian Pharaoh, employment of Greek mercenaries by: 182
'Psathyrians' (Arian sect): 450
Ptelea, Athenian deme: 163
Ptolemaic Egypt (and the Ptolemies): 17, 119, 207, 304, 540 n.11, and much in II.iv and IV.iii
Ptolemais (Greek city in Egypt): 17, 304, 315
Ptolemy I Soter (king of Egypt): 304, 534; Ptolemy II Philadelphus: 152, 157; Ptolemy III Euergetes: 223; Ptolemy IV Philopator: 223; Ptolemy Apion: 534
public works: 188-95 (with 577-9 nn.20-33), 200, 201; in Roman provinces: 195 (with 579 n.33)
Publilius Syrus (Late Republican writer): 342
Pudens (friend of Sidonius Apollinaris): 253
Pudentilla (wife of Apuleius): 563-4 n.13a
Pudentius of Oea (in Tripolitana): 595 n.6
Pulcheria, St. (Roman empress, sister of Theodosius II and wife of Marcian): 177, 404
punishment, Roman: 459; increasing harshness of, in Christian Empire: 439. And see 'dual penalty system', 'flogging', 'mutilation', 'torture'
Pupienus (Roman emperor): 388, 392
Puteoli: 196, 395-6, 561 n.18
'Putney debates' (1647): *203, 441*
Pythagoreans: 41, 411. And see 'Archytas of Tarentum'
Python of Abdera: 228, 507

Quadi: 249, 260, 468, 510, 511
Querolus (Late Latin comedy); 478 (with 650 n.13)
Quintilian (and Ps.-Quintil.): 165, 167, 368, 444

Rachel and the mandrakes (Gen. XXX): 437
Radagaisus (Gothic chief): 258
Radcliffe-Brown, A. R.: 22, 82
Rainborough, Col. Thomas (English Leveller): *441*
Rallis, G. A., and M. Potlis: 557 n.26
Ramsay, George: 505
Ramsay, (Sir) William: 153
Randall, R. H.: 577 nn.21-2
rates of pay: see under 'pay, rates of'
Ravenna: 218, 247, 254, 481, 496, 657-8 n.31; Latin papyri from: 218, 247, 254
Rawson, Elizabeth: 240
Rea, J. R.: 196, 579 n.34

Rebus bellicis, De: see under 'Anonymous'
receptores, in the sense of those who assist 'brigands': 477
Rectus, Aemilius (governor of Egypt): 363
Redfield, Robert: 98
'Reformation', in England and elsewhere: 279
Regulus, M. Atilius: 560 n.5
'Reihengräberkultur': 247 (with 590 n.29), 517
Reinhold, Meyer: 545 n.5. And see 'Lewis, Naphtali, and Reinhold'
religion in the service of politics: 209, *343-4*, *396-402*, 452, 619 n.15. And see 'Paul, St.'
religion, great importance in antiquity: *445-52*
Remigius, St., bishop of Rheims, will of: *259*
reproduction, human: 98-9
'Resistance literature' (Books of Daniel and Revelation etc., *q.v.*): 6, 325, *442-3*
responsa prudentium (opinions of legal experts): 385
Revelation, Book of ('The Apocalypse'): 325, *442*, 616 n.61
rex (king), esp. as applied to the Roman emperor: 376-7; as Greek word *rēx*: 378
Rey, P.-P: see under 'Dupré, G., and Rey'
Rey-Coquais, J. P.: 561 n.20
Reynolds, Joyce: 534-5, 539 n.3
Rhegium (in southern Italy): 523
Rheims: 259
Rhine, River and its neighbourhood: 11-12, 266
Rhodes: 174, *196, 289-90*, 306, 315, 316, *317*, 342, 456, 507, 531, *602 n.24*, 612 n.33, 645 n.11; food liturgies at: *196*; political pay at: *289-90* (with *602 n.24*), *317*
Rhodes, P. J.: 550 n.14, 605-6 nn.30-1
Rhodiapolis (in Lycia): 533
Rhodopis: see under 'Doricha'
Rhōmaioi, as the name by which the Byzantines called themselves: 9, 400
Rhosus: 316
Ricardo, David: 29, 35, 56
'rich' and 'poor' vocabulary: see under 'poor' and 'rich'
Richmond, I. A.: 397, *511*, 561 n.20
Rienzi, Cola di: 385
riots in cities: 313, 318-21, 357; the 'Nika riot' (A.D. 532): 319
Robbins, Lionel (Lord): *84-5*
Robert, Louis (sometimes with J. Robert): *410* (with 636-7 n.3), 518-19, 611 nn.11-12, etc.
Roberts, C. H.: *640 n.8*
Roberts, Rhys: 325
Robinson, Joan: 21
Robinson, Olivia: 572 n.70
Roman Church: saints of: 27; *patrimonium Petri*: 254, 496 estates of, in Italy: 255; in Sicily: 225, 254; in Gaul: 254; in general: 495-6, 592 n.47
Romania (ancient term): 485
Romania (modern State): 230
Romans resident in Greek cities: 316, *521, 529*, 532, *535*
Romanus I Lecapenus (10th c. Byzantine emperor): 263
Romanus II (Byzantine emperor): 502
Romanus (*comes Africae*): 490
Rome, Romans, *Rhōmaioi*: 327-408 & ff.
  genius of, in 'ruling': *327-8*; and in *ius civile*: *328-30*
  plebs urbana of: 192 (with 578 n.27), 352-3, 355, 356-7, 358, 361, 372, 409; abused by Cicero: *355*; Plebeian objectives in 'Conflict of Orders': *333-5*, *cf. 336*; *secessiones*: *335*; *provocatio*: 335 etc.; 'Licinio-Sextian rogations': *336-7*; tribunes and their powers: 333-6, 352, 362; 'Twelve Tables': 334-5, 341
  comitia populi Romani and *concilium plebis*: 333, 334, 340 (with 618-19 n.8), 355; importance of *contiones*: *335-6*

Greek city cults of *Roma*: 348
  'restoration of the Republic': 350 ff. (with 621 n.1)
  And see under '*Rhōmaioi*', 'Rome (city)' etc.
Rome (city): 127, 132, 192-6, 220, 477, 479, 481 etc.
  expulsion of *peregrini* from, during famine (A.D. 384): 220
  Church of: see under 'Christianity'
  attacked as 'Babylon': 442
  And see under 'Senate of Rome . . . Senate House'
Roscius, Sextus: 241
Rostovtzeff, M.: *10*, 17, 34, 85, 124, *125-6*, 152-3, 156, 157, 178, 186, 206, 207, 239, 294-5, *507*, *508-9*, 529, 540-1 n.15, *545 n.5*, 555 n.7, 558-9 nn.9-10, 561 nn.19-21, 24, 568 n.34, 569 nn.42, 45, 576 n.17, 576-7 n.19, 583 n.33, 591 n.37, 598 n.11; his theory of the 'Decline and Fall': *463-5*
Rothstein, M.: 619 n.10
Rotundus Drusillianus (Imperial slave): 65, 143
Rougé, Jean: 258, 560 n.12, 561 n.16
Rouillard, Germaine: 584 n.38
Rousseau, J. J.: 55
Rubinsohn, Z. W.: *564 n.15*
Rudé, George: 21, 355
Rufinus, of Pergamum: 132
Rugi, Rugians: 486, 516
'rule of law': see under 'law, laws'
Rumbold, Richard (English radical): 417
Rupilius, P.: 522-3
Russell, D. A.: 324
Russia, South (in antiquity): 294
Rusticus, L. Antistius: see under 'Antistius'
Rutilius Namatianus (Late Latin poet): 407, 478

Sabines, Sabine area in Italy: 187
'*sacrilegium*', as disobedience to Imperial will: 390 (with 631 n.51)
Sagalassus (in Pisidia): 539-40 n.8
saints, of Roman Catholic Church: 27
Saint-Simon, Henri: 548 n.1
Salamis, battle of: 260
Salamis in Cyprus: 534
Saldae (in north Africa): 653 n.42
Salisbury, R. F.: 545 n.9
Sallust: *271*, 337, 338, *344, 352, 355-9, 372, 410, 443*
Salomon, Albert: 86
Salomon, R. G.: 584 n.39
saltus Burunitanus (Souk el-Khmis): 215 (with 581-2 nn.10, 11, 18), 456 (& 458)
Salvian: 216, *225, 473, 481*
Salvius Julianus (Roman lawyer): see under '*Digest*'
Samaria (Sebaste) and the Samareitis: 427-9
Samaritans (religious sect), persecution of, by Justinian, and its consequences: *653 n.39*
Samnites, Samnium: 342, 509
Samos: 74, 271, 291, *395*; 'decarchy' of B.C. 404 ff.: 74
Samosata: 197
Samuel, A. E.: 135
Sappho: 131
Sarapis: 396
Sardinia: 356, 496
Sardis: 121, 153, *273*, 310; builders and artisans make compact with city *ekdikos*: *273*, 576 n.19
Sarmatians: 258, 490, 513, 514, 516. And see under 'Iazyges'
Saturninus, L. Appuleius: 352-4
Saturninus, Venuleius: see under 'Venuleius'
Saul, king of Israel, as a term of abuse: 405
Saumacus, revolt of: *564 n.15*

Saumagne, Charles: 246 (with 591 n.37, and see 589 n.26a)

Say, J. B.: 56

Scaevola, Q. Cervidius (Roman lawyer): see under 'Digest'

Scamandronymus: 131

Scaptensula (Skapte Hyle): 562 n.8

Scaptopara (village in Thrace): 216

Scarpat, G.: 600 n.8

Schaps, David: 100 (with 554 n.1a)

Schiller, A. Arthur: 645 n.4

Schlatter, Richard: 601 n.15

Schmidt, Conrad, letter of Engels to: 20

Schneider, Helmut: 355

Schuller, Wolfgang: 603 n.26

Schulz, Fritz: 108, 166, 329-30, 571 n.60, 572 nn.65, 72

Schwartz, Eduard: 146, 574 n.13, 636 n.97

Sciri: see under 'Scyrae'

Scramuzza, V.: 569-70 nn.39, 48

scribae, more honoured among Greeks, considered mercenarii by Romans (Nepos), except scribae publici: 197

Scribonianus, L. Arruntius Camillus (governor of Dalmatia), revolt of: 362

Scroggs, Robin: 555-6 nn.12, 18, 21 (with 104-6)

Scyrae (Sciri): 515-16

Scythopolis (in Palestine): 569 n.44

Sealey, R.: 551 n.28

Searle, Eleanor: 151

Sebeos (Armenian historian): 517, 654 n.42

'secessio' (in Early Roman Republic): 335 (with 618 nn.2, 4, on VI.ii)

Secunda (under-slave of Musicus Scurranus): 143

Seeck, Otto: 243, 245-6, 252, 510-11, 514-15, 517

Segal, J. B.: 537, 620 n.11

Segesta (in Pannonia): see under 'Siscia'

Segrè, Angelo: 591 n.37

Seleuceia on the Tigris: 305, 536-7; Jews of: 305

Seleucid dynasty: 119, 536

Seleucus of Rhosus: 316

Selge (in Pisidia/Pamphylia): 507, 595 n.6

semiagrestis: 494

Senate of Rome: 333, 338-40, 362-4, 381, 406-7, 355, 385, 387-8, 399-400, 456 (& ff.), 471, 472-3, 494, 501-2
certainly an 'order', may be treated as a 'class': 42
no 'class struggle' between Senate and Equites: 41-2, 339-40
penetration of Greeks into: 96, 119
Olympiodorus on wealth of: 120; Western senators the wealthiest: 119-20
census of: 129, 406
gifts by emperors to 'impoverished' senators: 406 (with 636 n.101)
Senate House burnt down on death of Clodius (52 B.C.): 354

Senate of Constantinople: 124, 381, 388

Seneca, L. Annaeus: 166, 176, 242, 343, 372, 376-7, 409, 419, 421

Seneca, L. Annaeus, 'the Elder': 425

Senex, Julius: 318

Sepphoris (in Galilee): 427, 429

Septem Provinciae (of Gaul): 486

Septimius Severus (Roman emperor): see under 'Severus'

Septuagint (LXX): 105-6 (with 556 n.18), 423, 431, 616 n.60

Sepúlveda, Juan Ginés de: 418

serfdom, serfs: 83-4, 133 ff. (esp. 135-6, 137-40, 146, 147-62), 228, 4, 5, 6, 33, 44, 482-3 etc.; and see under 'colonate and (serf) coloni of Later Roman Empire'

definition of serfdom: 135-6; terminology of: 147-8
serfdom distinguished from, and (for the serf) preferable to, slavery: 147-8; esp. in ability to have family life: 148
no necessary connection between serfdom and feudalism (Engels): 162, cf. 136; objections to applying terms 'serfdom', 'Hörigkeit' etc. outside European feudalism are gratuitous: 138
Marx on serf, slave and wage-labourer: 112-13; on inheritor of entailed estate as a 'serf': 159; on serfdom: 160-2
status of serfs often a result of conquest: 136; often unclear in our sources: 147
no general (only local) terminology for serfs, Greek or Roman, until Late Roman colonate: 138-9, 147-8, 156, 173
enserfment of great part of working agricultural population of Graeco-Roman world from end 3rd c.: 249-51
the expression 'between slave and free' (Poll. III.83) includes forms of serfdom: 138, 139, 150
'quasi-serfs': 5, 136, 172, 250, 255, 261
examples of earlier Greek and Roman serfs: see e.g. under 'Ardiaioi (of Illyria)', 'Bithynians subject to Byzantium', 'Dardanians (of Illyria and Thrace)', 'Helots, Spartan', 'klarōtai (of Crete)', 'Mariandynoi of Heraclea Pontica', 'Mnoītai (of Crete)', 'Penestai (of Thessaly)'
use of Greek word perioikoi, sometimes of serfs: 160
serfdom in Hellenistic Asia etc.: 150-7; in Sicily and Roman area: 158 (with 570 n.48)
tendency of serfdom to disappear on lands owned or dominated by Greeks, hellenised natives, or Romans: 154-5, 156-7, 172; consequences of this process: 157-8

'Sermon on the Mount': 15, 432; 'on the Plain': 432

Seronatus (vicar or provincial governor): 486

'servants and apprentices': see under 'apprentices and servants'

Setälä, Päivi: 560 n.11

settlement of 'barbarians' in Roman empire: see under 'barbarians . . . settlement of'

'Severan period' (A.D. 193-235): 198, 236, 318, 454, 456, 458, 459, 465, 467, 468, 470, 475 etc.

Severinus, St.: 486

Severus, Alexander (Roman emperor): see under 'Alexander Severus'

Severus, Septimus (Roman emperor): 216, 370, 389, 390, 491

sex, Christian and Jewish attitudes to: see under 'Christianity', 'Jews, Judaism', 'women'

Sextus Empiricus: 24

Seyrig, H.: 569 n.38

Shakespeare, William: 254-5, 444

Shanin, Teodor: 98, 208

Shapur I, king of Persia: 261, 475

Shapur II, king of Persia: 379, 486, 487; his letter to Constantius II: 379

share-croppers (coloni partiarii): 214, 216-17, 257

Shenute (Egyptian abbot): 446-7

Sheppard, A. R. R.: 518

Sherk, R. K.: 523

Sherwin-White, A. N.: 95, 238, 341-2, 348, 461 (with 646 n.29), 530, 587 n.10, 614 n.42, 640 n.6

Sherwin-White, Susan M.: 612 n.23

Shimron, B.: 565 n.19, 608-9 n.55

Sibylline Oracles: 442-3 (with 642 nn.7-8)

Sicily: 8, 9, 66, 117, 119, 132, 134, 154, 233, 242, 254, 270, 279, 280, 283, 316, 344, 346, 347, 349, 356, 496,

498, *521-3*, 569 n.39

Sicinnius Clarus, Q. (legate of Thrace): 127

Sicyon (on Corinthian Gulf): 139

Side: 653 n.42

Sidon: 427-9

Sidonius Apollinaris (Late Latin Christian writer and bishop): 144, *253*, 377, 407, 595 n.6, 654 n.42; interesting terminology of letter to Pudens: *253*

Sidyma (in Lycia): 531, 533

Silesia (in 18th c.): 162

Silius Italicus: 536

Sillyum (in Pisidia): *179, 196-7, 528-9, 532*

Silvanus, son of Bonitus (Frank) and Magister Peditum: *485*

Simon of Cyrene: *15*

Siphnos: *601 n.18*

Siscia (Segesta) in Pannonia: *521*

Sisinnius, Novatian bishop of Constantinople, his witticisms: 450

Sismondi, J. C. L. Simonde de: 548 n.1

slavery, slaves: 3-4, 5, 6, *39-40*, *48-9*, *91*, *107-8*, *112-14*, *116*, 133 ff. (esp. *113-5*, *138-47*, *171-4*), *205*, *209*, 226 ff. (esp. *226-43*, *255-9*), *409-11*, *416-25*, *444*, *504-9*
    [Only a few particular issues are selected here]
    slave society/economy: 3-4, *52-3*, *209*, 226; 'direkte Zwangsarbeit' the foundation of the ancient world (Marx, *Grundrisse*): 52, *54*, 133; slavery the dominant form of it in Greek world: 172-3
    absence of evidence for slavery not necessarily to be taken as evidence for absence of slavery: *133-4*, *144-5*; accounts of military campaigns often the only source of evidence for rural slavery: 171, 505-8
    automation the only imaginable alternative to slavery: *113*
    slaves as a 'class': *63-5*; slave/free as a distinction of *status*, slave/slave-owner a distinction of *class*: 40, 64, *66*, 91
    extraordinary cheapness of ancient slaves: 227 (with *585-7* n.1)
    slave vocabulary; 138-9
    slaves necessarily the great majority of managers and overseers (*epitropoi, pragmateutai, vilici, procuratores, actores*): *140*, *144-5* (with 563-4 nn.13a, 14), 172, 173, 181-2, 256, 257-8, 505-7; 'slave—drivers' (*praefecti*), also slaves: 235
    slaves in agriculture generally: 144, with 505-6 (Athens) & 506-9 (elsewhere), 148 etc. (Later Empire)
    merciless treatment of slaves: 409-10; punishment (esp. flogging): 48-9
    slave revolts (mainly in Hellenistic period): 146 (with 564 n.15)
    sale of oneself or one's children into slavery: 163, 169-70; of *sanguinolenti*: 170
    slaves hired out: 179, 186, 200-1, 202, 563 n.9
    slave *quasi colonus*: *237-8*, 44-5, 137, 210, 211, 238, 243
    agricultural slaves eventually bound to the land: *148* (with 564-5 n.16), 246, 255
    slave as *empsychon organon*: 58; as *instrumentum vocale*: 549 n.12; cf. 563 n.11
    planned heterogeneous character of slave households: *146*, 65-6, 93
    public slaves (*dēmosioi*): 158, 186, 205, 307; mine slaves: 134; under-slaves (*vicarii*): 44, 65, 143, 237
    breeding of slaves (*oikogeneis, vernae*): *229-30*, *231-42*, 148 etc.; increase in: 229, 230; sex-ratios: 231, 234 (with 587-8 n.14); abortion and infanticide by slave women: 236, 237
    large slave households in sources, e.g. 202, 228,

242, 258, 558 n.9, *563-4* n.13a
    And see under '*chōris oikountes*', 'freedmen', 'manumission' etc.

Slavery (and Supplementary) Conventions: Slavery Convention (1926) of League of Nations: 134; Supplementary Convention (1956) of United Nations, on abolition of the slave trade, and institutions and practices similar to slavery: 134

Small, A. M.: *560 n.11*

Smikythe (Athenian washerwoman): 274

Smith, Adam: 35, 56, 505

Smith, Ian: 212

Smyrna: 348, 532, 533

Snodgrass, A. M.: 282

Soaemias, Julia: 494

Socrates, as character in Plato: 82, 147, 179, 180; in Xenophon: 123, 179-81

Socrates (Christian ecclesiastical historian): 170, 196, 450-1, 514 etc.

'Sogdian rock', the: 119

Soli (in Cyprus): 534

Solon of Athens: 41, 78, 96, 114, *129-31*, *137*, 162, 164, *185*, *215*, *281-2*, 298, *426*, 441, 550 n.7
    not a 'merchant': *129-31*
    his poems: *281* (with 599 n.25); his not unfavourable treatment of the agricultural labourer: *185*
    his *seisachtheia* and other legislation on debt: *137*, 162, 164, *215*, *281-2*
    his Pentacosiomedimnoi and other *telē*: 114, 610 n.2
    a principal reason for requiring a property qualification for some magistracies: *602 n.21*

sōmata (lit.: 'bodies'): 152-3, 163; *sōmata laika oiketika/ eleuthera* (*SB* V. 8008): 152-3; working with hands = working with the *sōma*: 181

Sophia, St. (Cathedral of Constantinople): *450-1*

Sophocles: 24

Sorokim, Pitirim: 544 n.1

Souk el-Khmis (in Tunisia): see under '*saltus Burunitanus*'

South Africa (modern): 67

'South, Old': see under 'American Old South'

Soviet work on ancient history: 542-3 n.7, 558 n.8, 566-8 nn.32-3, 582 n.20

Sozomen (Christian ecclesiastical historian): 196, 220, 365, 450-1, 514, *516* etc.

Spain, Roman: 6, 12, 97, 120, 254, 370, 474, 476, 477, 478, 481, 486, 502, 503, 516

Spain (16th c.): *418*

Sparta (Lacedaemon): *48*, *102*, *139*, *147*, *149-50*, *288*, *295-6*, *527*, *608 n.47a*, *609 n.61* (with *299*), 75, 100, 117, 118-19, 136, 291, 292, 414, 415, 475
    annual declaration of war by ephors on Helots at: *48*, *149*
    the great upholder of oligarchy: *288*, *296*
    decline in number of citizens at: *102*
    gerousia at: 527
    patrouchos (corresponding to Athenian *epiklēros*) at: 102
    And see under 'Helots', 'Perioikoi'

Spartacus, slave revolt in Italy (73-1 B.C.) led by: 25, 230, 409; resulted in mass killings of slaves: *230*, *409*

'spear-won territory': 151

spectabiles: 473

Speer, Albert: xi

Sperber, D.: 539 n.8

sportulae ('hand-outs'): 196, 460, *488*, *500*; 'tips' to officials, illicit (*sportulae*) and authorised: 488, 500

Sraffa, Piero: 21

Stalin: 544 n.15

Stampp, Kenneth: 39, *55*, 122, 143-4, 148, *227*, 424, 549 n.18

Starr, Chester G.: *54*
stasis (civil commotion), and class struggle: 49, 78-9
Statius: 397
States, 'the State':
 nature and role of 'the State': *286-7*, 205-6 etc.
 the *politeia* 'the soul of the polis': 286; the State the instrument of the *politeuma*: 287; rulers will rule in their personal or class interest (Aristotle): 286-7; control of the State the great prize of political class struggle: 287, 291-2 etc.
 morality and behaviour of a State: *47-8*, 27
status (also 'orders' and 'caste'):
 distinctions of status, compared with class differences: 63-6, 86-94; but sometimes confused (even by Marx and Engels): *66*
 Stände, status groups: 85-6
 status essentially a descriptive and not (like class) a dynamic or explanatory classification: *90-1*, *93-4*, 175 etc.
 'social stratification' according to status: 4, 45, 58; in Max Weber: *85-91*; in M. I. Finley: *58-9*, *91-4*; Marx uninterested in 'social stratification': 86
 social status tends to derive from class position: *45*, cf. *461-2*
 'honour' (*timē*) as Greek equivalent of 'status': *80* (with *551 n.30*)
 Finley's 'spectrum (continuum) of statuses (and orders)': 58, 91-3
 'orders': *42* (cf. 340 for Latin *ordo*, and 332 ff. for the 'Conflict of the Orders' in early Rome), 4, 7
 caste: *42*, 90-1, 544 n.4
Staveley, E. S.: 619 n.8
Stein, Ernst: 196, 255, 258, 319, 481, 490, 499, 515-17, 574 n.14, 583 n.30, etc.
Stevens, C. E.: 226, 591 n.37, 595 n.6
Steward, Austin: 143-4
Stilicho: 381, 501
stipulatio (by a taxpayer): 500
Stobaeus: 110
Stocks, J. L.: 79
Strabo: 12, 24, 38, 131, *147*, *149*, *150*, *153-4*, 156, 158, 187-8, 196, *228*, 301, 322-3, *410*, 445, 510, 534, 535, 536, *539 n.5*, 540 n.11, *562-3 n.8*
Strasburger, H.: 618-19 nn.1, 7, 12
stratification, social: see under 'status'
Stratonicea: 531
Strepsiades (character in Aristophanes): 540 n.14
'strikes' in antiquity: 273
Strubbe, J.: 564 n.13a
Structuralism, structuralists: 22, 36
Strymon, River, and its valley: 292, 314
subagrestis: 494
subintroductae: 555 n.13
subrusticus: 494
Suetonius: 187, 194-5, 304, 313, *381-2*, 510
Suevi: 486, 510, 516, 595 n.6
suffragium (patronage): *224*, *341-3* (with 619 n.10), 365 (with 366-7), 472, 492; '*venale suffragium*': 342, 365
 And see under 'clientela'
Sugambri (Sygambri): 510, 515
Sulla, L. Cornelius: 302, 345, 358, 526 (with 660 n.6)
Sulpicius Galba, Servius: 360
Sulpicius Rufus, P.: 352-3
Sulpicius Severus (Latin Christian writer): 377; his use of *princeps*, *imperator* and *rex* in a single sentence for the Roman emperor: 377
supernumerarii (as opposed to *statuti*): 492-3
superstition (*deisidaimonia*, *supertstitio*): 108-9, 343, 400-1

'superstructure' (and 'basis'): see under 'Basis and Superstructure in Marx'
supplicia: *summa supplicia* (defined) reserved for lower classes: 458
surplus: 35-7 (with 545 n.10), 43-4, 51, 52-3, and many other passages, including 133, 172, 173, 205, 209, 213, 226
 and exploitation: 37
 And see under 'exploitation'
surveyors (*mensores, agrimensores*): 198
Svencickaja [Sventsitskaya], I. S.: 568 n.33
Swoboda, H.: 518, 527, 535, 583 n.33
Sygambri: see under 'Sugambri'
Syme, (Sir) Ronald: 34, *350-1*, 360, *361-2*, 366, *368*, *370*, 510, *623 n.10*, *628 n.14*, 630 n.45
Symmachus, Q. Aurelius (cos. 391, the great orator): *120*, 196, 220, 254, 263, *387-8*, *390*, 407, *648-9 n.19*
Symmachus, L. Aurelius Avianius (father of the foregoing): 320
Synesius of Cyrene, bishop of Ptolemais: 265, *346*, 378, 515, *595 n.6*, *615 n.57*
Syracuse: 117, 119, 132, 191-2, 270, 305, 349, 520, 522-3
Syria, Syrians: 6, 8, 12, 19, 119, 150, 151, 152, 172, 186, 221-2, 224, 227-8, 294, 300, 345, 400, 447, 483-4 (with 652 nn.33-5), 494, 496, 498, 503, 561 n.20; Syrians 'born for slavery' (Cicero): 417

Tacitus, Claudius (Roman emperor): 386, 388
Tacitus, Cornelius (Latin historian): *192*, 229, *238*, *249*, 266, *327-8*, 342, 348, *356*, *361*, *362*, *363*, *366-70*, 372, *387*, *389*, 396, *443-4*, 464, *489-90*, 510-11, 524, 536, 615-16 n.59; on slavery among the Germans: *238*, *249*
Taifali: 514, 517
Tapeinos, member of a sectarian community at Nahal Seelim: 433
Tarentum: 520
Tarius Rufus, L.: 120
Tarn, W. W.: 17, 157-8, *186*, 196, *395*, 445, 569 n.45
Tarracina (in Spain): 196
Tarsus (in Cilicia): *106*, *317*, *455*, 462, 496, 531, *532*; its linen-workers not citizens: *455*, *532*; women veiled in: *106*; home town of St. Paul: 106, 455, *462*
Taurus, Calvisius: 48-9
taxation: *44*, *206-7* (with *580-1 nn.2-7*), 217-18, 222, 224-5, 234, 306, 345-6, 349, 373, 473-4, 481, 487, 488, 489-90, 493, 497-503, 4, 11, 13, 53, 97, 128, 228, 234, 248, 250, 358, 361-2, 363, 475-6
 never in antiquity on money income: *114*
 eusebeis phoroi: 501
 collatio lustralis/chrysargyron: *127*, *272*, 493; abolished in 498 in East: 493; the yield at Edessa: *516 n.21*
 collatio gelbalis (*follis*): 493
 partial tax exemption for veterans: 217-18
 inheritance tax (*vicesima hereditatium*): 361, 362, *454-5* (with *645 nn. 6-7*)
 iugatio/capitatio: 217-18
 requisitions in kind (*indictiones* etc.): *234*
 tributum, *tributum soli/capitis*: 114, *234*
 extraordinaria onera, superindictitii tituli: 500
 immunitas and *ius Italicum*: 234 (with *587 n.13*)
 tax-farming, -farmers (*telōnai, publicani*): *114*, *128*, 157, *165*, *206*, 228, 240, *338-9*, *346*, *430*; other tax-collectors: *129*, *224*, *473*, *488*, 497-8, 499-500
 And see under 'eisphora'
taxeōtai (*cohortales*): 474, 493
Taylor, Lily Ross: 618 n.3 (on VI.ii), n.8 (on VI.iii)
Tchalenko, G.: *593 n.50*
Tcherikover [Tscherikower], V.: *442*, 569 n.43, 634 n.5

Techn'archos: 275

technology: *38* (with *545-7 nn.14-18*). And see under 'automation'

Tegea, Tegeates: 302

telē (Solonian, at Athens): see under 'Solon'

Temnus: 163, 531

temple estates (in Asia): *153-7*. And see under 'hierodules'

temple-servants: see under 'hierodules'

Tennyson, Alfred (Lord): 425

Terence: 103, 122; *locito* (Adelph. 949): *589 n.21*

Termessus Minor: 531

terrae laeticae: see under '*laeti*'

Terray, Emmanuel: 21-2

territorium (chōra): 10, 11

Tertullian: 165, 328, 433

'Tertullianists' (at Carthage): 449

'Tetrarchy' (A.D. 295 ff.): 493, 494

Thagaste (in Africa): 366

Thalassius of Antioch: *124*

Thales of Miletus: 131

Thalia of Arius: *449-50* (with 644 n.21)

Thamugadi (Timgad): 488

theatres: 318-19, 320

Thebes: 292, 296-9, 508; Cadmea of, garrisoned by Sparta (382-79): 296. And see under 'Boeotia'

Themistius: 402, 481, 490, 514, 515

Themistocles: 108

Theoctistus '*psathyropōlēs* (Arian): 450

Theodohad (Ostrogothic king of Italy): 263

Theodora (Roman empress, wife of Justinian): *391* (with *631 n.52*)

Theodore, St. (of Sykeon, bishop of Anastasiopolis): *225-6*, 446-7, 496

Theodoret of Cyrrhus (Greek ecclesiastical historian): 451, 498

Theodoric I ('the Great'), Ostrogothic king: 487-8, 502

Theodoric II, Ostrogothic king: 564 n.16

Theodorus, father of Isocrates: *124*

Theodosius I (Roman emperor): 147, *159*, 170, 251, 252, 390, 493, 494, 503

Theodosius II (eastern Roman emperor): 146, 177, 252, 272, *381*

Theodosius, 'Count' (Magister Equitum, father of the Emperor Theodosous I): 479, 514; his atrocities in Africa: *547 n.5*

Theodosius (6th c. pagarch of Antaeopolis in Egypt): 224, 321

Theodosius of Anastasiopolis (administrator of Church lands): *225-6*

Theodosius, head lessee of land of Roman Church in Sicily: 498

Theodote (*hetaira* at Athens, character in dialogue of Xenophon): 100, *179-80*

Theognis and the *Theognidea*: 78, *278-9* (with *599 n.9*), 411

Theophanes (Byzantine historian): *617 n.64*

Theophilus, governor of Syria: *321*

Theophrastus: 70, *140*

Theophylact Simocatta (7th c. Byzantine historian): 517, *538 n.3* (on I.ii)

Theopompus (Greek historian): 132, 149

'Therapeutia' (in Philo): 422

Thersites, 'agitator' in Homer: *279*, 413

Theseus (in Euripides, *Suppl.*) 73

Thesaurus Linguae Latinae: 252

Thespiae (in Boeotia): *309*, *611 n.15*, 653 n.42

Thessalonica: 653 n.42

Thessaly: 136, 139, 160, 162, 480, *525*, 526. And see

under 'Penestai'

Thetes (plural of *thēs*), as Solonian *telos* at Athens: 207, 281, 291, *606 n.31*; conscription of: 207. And see under 'hired (wage) labour' for *thētes = misthōtoi*

Thierry, Augustin, 'the father of the "class struggle" in French historiography' (Marx): *548 n.1*

'Thirty [tyrants]', The (Athens, 404-3): 180, *291* (with *606 n.32*), *536*; the Athenian democratic resistance to, in 403: *291* (with *606 n.33*)

Thomas, J. A. C.: 240, 597 n.3

Thomas, R. P.: see under 'North, D. C., and Thomas'

Thompson, E. A.: *238*, *249*, *474*, 476-9, *486*, *489*, *541* n.1, *590 n.29* (fin.), *591 n.34a*

Thompson, E. P.: 21, 62

Thomsen, Rudi: *558 n.3* (on III.i)

Thomson, George: 41

Thoranius, C.: 175

Thorax, Mount (near Magnesia on the Maeander): 445

Thorner, Daniel: 98, *155*, 208; *544 n.15*, 581 n.2

Thrace, Thracians: 127, *163*, 216, 227, 250, 294, 478, 479-80 (with 477), 512-15, 517, 610 n.2; provided large proportion of Greek slaves in Classical period: *163, 227*

'Thracian Chersonese': 292

Thrasea Paetus (Roman Stoic): 370

Thrasybulus (Athenian): *605 n.29*

Thrasymachus (of Chalcedon), as opponent (Dahrendorf) of 'functionalist' position of Plato's Socrates: *82*

threptoi, defined: 233; rulings of *leges Visigothorum* and of Justinian on: 233

thrushes (*turdi*), Roman, feeding of: 187

Thucydides: 27, 47, 74, *506*, *603-6 nn. 26-7 & 29-31*, 3, 24, 73, 80, 93, 132, 147, 171, 183, 283, 290-1, 296, 323, 346, 362, 506-7, 508

Thurii (in south Italy): 287

Tiberias (in Galilee): *427*, *429*

Tiberius (Roman emperor): 143, 194, 228, 266, 327, 358, 361, 363, 366-7, 370, 374, 385, 388, 392, 499, 510, 536; mutinies of Danube and Rhine armies at beginning of his reign (A.D. 14): *266*

Tiberius Constantine (late Roman emperor): 393-4, 494-5, 517

Tifernum Tiberinum, Pliny's estate at: 238

Tigris, River: 8, 345

Timaeus (Sicilian Greek historian): 202

Timarchus (Athenian): 604 n.27

timē (Greek word for 'honour', 'office' etc.): 80 (with 551 n.30)

timētai: see under 'censores'

Timgad: see under 'Thamugadi'

Timothy, bishop of Alexandria: 109 (with *557 n.26*)

timouchoi, at Massalia: 536

'tinker', Plato's 'bald-headed little': *412*, 71

Tiridates (Parthian pretender): 536

Tissaphernes (Persian satrap): 605 n.29

Titius, Sextus (Roman tribune): *619 n.17*

Titus (Roman emperor): 328

Tobit, Book of: *435*

Tocra (Taucheira, Teucheira) = Arsinoe in Cyrenaica: 535

Toulouse (Tolosa): 595 n.6

Tolstoy, his Prince Andrey in *War and Peace* on evils of serfdom: *425*

Tomi: 653 and 654 n.42

toparchs: 127

Torelli, M.: *562 n.4*

Torres, Camilo: 440

Torture, Roman: *439*, *454*, *459-60*; more prevalent in Christian Empire: 439; torturing slaves to procure evidence against their masters: 459-60. And see under 'dual penalty system', 'flogging', 'mutilation', 'punishment, Roman'

Totila, Ostrogothic king of Italy: 221, 264 (with 595 n.7), 482-3 (with 651 n.30)

Touloumakos, Johannes: 523, 525

Tours (Turones): see under 'Gregory of Tours' and 'Iniuriosus of Tours'

Toynbee, Arnold: 258, 538 n.3 (on I.ii), 562 n.4, 564 n.15

Trachonitis: 494

Tracy, Destutt de: 56

traders, merchants, shopkeepers: 4, 33, 41, 77-8, (with 551 n.27), 95-6, 120, 205, 340, 52, 78, 114-15, 116, 124-8, 128-9, 129-32, 199, 270, 271, 272, 553 n.9 (with 85), 561 nn.21-2
    emporoi/kapēloi/nauklēroi distinctions: 77 (with 551 n.24)
        tyrants not 'merchant princes': 280
        imaginary 'mercantile aristocracies' of Aegina, Corinth etc.: 41, 120, 553 n.9 (with 85)
        Greek trade not 'largely in the hands of metics': 95-6, 551 n.27 (with 78)
        one certain example of an Athenian (Phormio) owning more than one merchant ship: 558 n.3 (on III.ii)

Traill, J. S.: 602 n.22

Trajan (Roman emperor): 309-10, 319-20, 343, 364, 369, 370, 374, 382, 389, 397, 398, 468, 529-30, 537
    Arch of, at Beneventum: 397
    And see under 'Pliny the Younger' for the Panegyric of Trajan by Pliny
    transport: 11-12, 132, 191-2, 199, 201, 539-40 n.8
        by water (river or sea) much more cheaply than by land: 11-12
    And see under 'angariae', 'post, Imperial/public'

Treveri: 443

Tribigild (Ostrogoth): 480, 595 n.6

tribunes (*tribuni plebis*): see under 'Rome, Romans'

tributarii: see under '*adscripticii*'

tributum: 114, 234

Tridentum: 221

Trimalchio (freedman character in Petronius): 177-8 (with 575 n.16)

Tripolitana (Roman province): 595 n.6

Tscherikower, V.: see under 'Tcherikover, V.'

Tullianus (Lucanian landowner): 482

Turkey (modern): 8

Turks, Ottoman: 8, 9, 497

Tuscany: see under 'Etruria'

'Twelve Tables', Law of the: 165, 334-5

Tymandus (in Pisidia): 313-14

tyranny, tyrants: see under 'monarchy and tyranny'

Tyre: 427-9, 496, 533

Ubii: 510

Ulfila: 514

Ulpian: see under '*Digest*'; for *Epit. Ulp.*, see 586 n.1

Umbria: 187

'uncleanness' of women: see under 'Jews, Judaism', 'women'

'unemployment': see under 'employment or un-employment'

United States of America, Americans: 57, 83, 331, 420
    denial of class struggle in: 57
    assumption of moral superiority: 331
    'military-industrial complex' in: 420

Urbicus, Agennius: see under 'Agennius Urbicus'

Ure, Andrew: 25

Ure, Percy N.: 280 (with 599 n.22)

Ursicinus (Magister Equitum and Peditum): 487

Ursinus (Pope or Anti-Pope): 451

Usipi, mutiny and fate of those serving in a Roman auxiliary cohort (A.D. 83): 229

'usurpers' of the Roman Imperial throne (= '*tyranni*'): 384, 387, 389, 489, 490, 498

Valens (Eastern Roman emperor): 388, 448, 479, 481, 490, 514. And see under 'Valentinian I and Valens'

Valentinian I (Roman emperor): 388, 478, 485, 493, 514

Valentinian I and Valens (Roman emperors): 127, 383, 489, 564 n.16

Valentinian II (Western Roman emperor): 388

Valentinian III (Western Roman emperor): 252, 390, 481, 501

Valentinus of Selge: 595 n.6

Valentinus, Julius (of the Treveri): speech of, in Tacitus: 443

Valerian (Roman emperor): 261, 475

Valerius Maximus (Latin historical compiler, A.D. 30s): 242, 387, 536, 572 n.65, 621 n.1

Valladolid, conference at (A.D. 1550): 418

'vampire bat' metaphor: 503

Vandals: 482 (with 651 nn.23-4), 510, 511-13, 516-17, 595 n.6

Vandersleyen, Claude: 540 n.13

Van Gogh, Vincent: Frontispiece, 209-10 (with 581 nn.3-4, on IV.ii), 278

Vardanes, Parthian king: 536

Varro, M. Terentius: 142, 146, 165, 187, 188, 235, 242, 270, 343, 572 n.66, 594 n.59

Varus, Alfenus: see under 'Alfenus Varus'

Vasates (Bazas): 480, 654 n.42

Vatinius: 147

Vavřínek, Vladimir: 529

Vedius Pollio, P.: 356

Vegetius: 263, 401-2; his date: 263; on poverty of peasant strengthening his military qualities: 263; on the military *sacramentum*: 401-2

vehiculatio: 539-40 n.8

Velleius Paterculus: 361

Venantius (decurion in Apulia): 648-9 n.19

Venasa in Morimene (Cappadocia): see under 'Zeus'

'Venerii', temple-servants of Aphrodite at Eryx in Sicily: 569 n.39, 570 n.48

Venetia: 221

Venuleius Saturninus (Roman lawyer): see under '*Digest*'

Venus Pastoralis: 235

Veranius Philagrus, Q. (of Cibyra): 307-8, 533

Vergil: 327

Verinian (relative of Emperor Honorius): 595 n.6

Vermes, Geza, his book *Jesus the Jew*: 430

Vernant, J. -P.: 63

Verres, C. (governor of Sicily): 346, 348, 349, 354, 522-3; his cult, the 'Verria', at Syracuse: 348

Verus, L. (Roman emperor jointly with Marcus Aurelius, 161-9): 175, 537

Vespasian (Roman emperor): 187, 194-5, 323, 328, 370, 374, 385-6, 396, 468
    'Lex de imperio Vespasiani': 385-6
    miracle of, at Alexandria: 396

veterans (discharged soldiers): 217-18, 456-8, 461-2; members of the 'privileged groups' in the Roman Empire: 456-8 (with 645-6 nn.12-13)

Vettius Agorius Praetextatus: see under 'Praetextatus'

Veyne, P.: 122, 575 n.16

Victor, Aurelius (Late Latin epitomator): 494, 512, 513

Vidal-Naquet, Pierre: 23, 63-5, 77-8, 138, 140, 562 n.3, 641 n.4. And see under 'Austin, M. M., and Vidal-Naquet'

Vietnam (modern): 48

Vigilantius (Christian priest, attacked by St. Jerome): 109–10

vilicus (and *vilica*): 145 (with *563 n.13a*), 234, 235, 257-8

villages (*kōmai*): *10-11*, 19, *221-5*, *300*, 5, 135, 151-2, 157-8 (with 569 n.43), 216, 250, 251; types of: 221
    democratic organisation in: *221-2*; including Assembly (*koinon*, *dēmos*, *ekklēsia*, *syllogos*, *synodos*, *ochlos*): *222*; no Council (*boulē*) in: 222 (with 584 n.36, 564 n.13a)
        kōmarchos of: 222; *gerousia* of: 222
        autopract villages: *222*
        grovelling attitude of Late Roman village in Egypt to powerful man: *223-4*
        village markets and fairs: 19 (with 541 n.6)
        And see under 'pagarchs'

Viminacium: *487*

virginity (female and male), Christian attitude to: 103–4, 109–10
    Virgin Mary: see under 'Mary, Virgin'

virtus of Romans: 330-1

Visigoths: 233, 249, 258, 479–80, 485–6, 514–16, 595 n.6; kingdom in Spain and south-west Gaul: 233; its *Leges Visigothorum*: 233

Vitellius (Roman emperor): 322

Vitruvius: 12–13, 621 n.1

Vlastos, Gregory: *416* (with 638 nn.3-4)

Vogt, A.: 68

Vogt, Joseph: 146, 564 n.15

Volsinii (in Etruria): 519

Vulci: 174

Wade, John: 548 n.1

Walbank, F. W.: 550 n.13, 578 nn.30-1, 643 n.14

Waldmann, Helmut: 568 n.36

Wallace, S. L.: 581 n.5

Walton, C. S.: 559 n.12

Waltzing, J. -P.: 597 n.8

Warmington, B. H.: 656 n.5

Wason, Margaret O.: 41

water-mill: 24, *38-9*

wealth in antiquity: 4, 78, 112–14, 117–20 (with 558-9 nn.10-17), 120-33, and many other passages
    primarily in land: *120-33*, 4, 78, 112, 114–20
    quantified as capital, not income (except in landed produce in kind): *114*
    of *nouveaux riches*: 125-6
    of Asiatic Greeks, in 4th c. B.C.: *117-18*; in Hellenistic and Roman periods: *119-20* (with 558-9 nn.10-17)
    Plutus, god of wealth, in Theognis: 279
    And see under 'propertied classes' etc.

Weaver, P. R. C.: 143, 563 n.13, 573 n.3, 574 n.11 (with 176)

Weber, Marianne: 552 n.5

Weber, Max: *80* (with 551 n.30), *85-91*, *239*, *262*, 4, 22, 41, 43, 74, 92, 93, 231, 259–60, cf. 613 n.40
    attitude to Marx: 86-7; comparison with Marx: *89-91*; failure to discuss Marx's concept of class: 87, 90
    definitions of 'class': 88-9; weakness of these: *90*
    use of 'Stand' and 'ständische Lage': 85-7; status his essential category: *87-8*
        slaves for him not a class but a status group: 89, 91
        lack of organic relationship between his classes and between his status groups: *90-1*; hence his inability to explain social change: *90-1*
        obscurity of: 85
        And see under 'ideal types'

Weiss, Egon: 571 n.58

Welles, C. Bradford: 152, 157–8, *537*, *545 n.5*, 554 n.30, 566 n.26, 569–70 nn.44-6, *620 n.12*

Welwei, K. -W.: 568 n.34, 570 n.51

West, M. L.: *599 n.9*

Westermann, W. L.: *299-30*, 553 n.26, 562 n.7, 572 nn.65, 73, 574 n.15, 585 n.1, 587 nn.2-5

Westlake, H. D.: *603-4 n.26*

wheelbarrow: 38

Wheeler, Marcus: 80

Whitby, Michael: 517, 614 n.41

White, K. D.: 577 n.19, 589 n.23, 593–4 n.59

White, Lynn: *10-11*, 14, *465*, 546 n.14

Whitehead, David: 554 n.29

Whittaker, C. R.: 563–4 n.13a, 649 n.4

Wilcken, Ulrich: 558 n.2 (on III.i), 581 n.5 (on IV.i)

Wilhelm, Adolf: 525

Wilkes, J. J.: 242, 512

Will, Édouard: *600 n.2*, *609 n.2* etc.

Willetts, R. F.: 571 n.58

Williams, Gordon: 615 n.57a

Williams, Wynne: 526

wind (and see under 'windmill'): 38

windmill: 38

Winstanley, Gerrard: *444*

Winterbottom, Michael: 167

Wirszubski, Ch.: *366-8*, 626 n.54

Wiseman, T. P.: *625 nn.27*, 37

Woess, Friedrich von: *165-6*, *330*, 572 nn.63-4, 68

Woikiatai of East Locris: 139

Woloch, Michael: *309* (with 611 n.15)

women (and sex, marriage, divorce, virginity etc.): *98-111*, 4, 17-18, 45, 148, 196-7, 234, 235, 236-7, 256-7, 362
    Marx and Engels on women: 99; on 'latent slavery in the family': 99; on division of labour between men and women: 99; exploitation of: 100
    women (or married women) as a 'class': 4, 45, *98-102*; but membership of the class will vary in importance: 100-1
    restriction of property rights of women (or married women): 101-3; other disabilities of Greek women: 101-2; the *kyrios*: 101; *epiklēros*, *patrouchos*: 101-2
    girl babies in antiquity, less chance of survival of: 103 (with *555 n.7*)
    matrilineality (*Mutterrecht*): 103
    humanistic character of Roman law of husband and wife: 108
    Christian and Jewish attitudes to women, sex, marriage and virginity: *103-10*; subjection of women in Christian and Jewish marriage: *104-7*; contrast attitude of Musonius Rufus: *110*
    irrational ideas about 'uncleanness' of women in paganism, and esp. in Judaism and Orthodox Christianity: *108-9*; other superstitious ideas about women (in Columella and Bolus 'Democritus'): *234*
    slave 'marriages' never recognised even in Christian Roman Empire (or in North American slave States): 148, 236-7, 256-7
    marriages between city men and peasant girls rare: 17-18; Aphrodite Kallipygos: 18; Venus Pastoralis: 235
    special importance of religion to women in antiquity: 107
    women's work in the home: 180-1, 234
    they might receive less from benefactions/foundations: 196-7
    special taxation of women: 362
    And see under 'Adam and Eve', 'Christianity', 'fornication', 'Jerome, St.', 'Jews, Judaism', 'Paul, St.', 'virginity'

Woodhouse, A. S. P.: *203, 441*
Woodward, A. M.: *528, 533*
Wright, Gavin: 587 n.8
Wright Mills, C.: see under 'Gerth, H. H.'

Xanthus: 531
Xenophon (and Ps.-Xen.): 9, 24, *66*, 73, *118* (with *558 n.7*), *121, 123*, 147, 150, 171, *179-82*, 185, 190, 191, 222, *231, 234*, 263, *295-8* (*esp. 296*), 402, 412, *414-15*, 419, *505-6, 506-7*, 607 n.37
    his brilliant and anti-democratic piece in *Mem.*: *414-15*
        Cicero's Latin trans. of his *Oecon.*: 234
        Ps.-Xen., *Ath. Pol.* ('Old Oligarth'): 73 (with 550 n.11)
Xiphilinus: 195

Yahweh, ferocity of: *331-2* (with *617-18* nn.9-12); Christian complicity in ignoring this: *331-2*
Yavetz, Zvi: *335*, 578 n.27, 624 n.14
Youtie, H. C.: *539 n.4*
Yugoslavia: 7, 8

Zela in Pontus: see under 'Anaïtis'
Zenis of Dardanus: *118*
Zeno (Late Roman emperor), edict of, forbidding monopoly: 273
Zeno (founder of Stoicism): 423
Zenodotus (honorary consul): 406
Zeugma (on Euphrates): 129
Zeus: 154, 568-9 n.38
    Zeus Abrettenus in Mysia: 568 n.38, 649 n.3
    Zeus (Baal) of Baeticaece in northern Phoenicia (*IGLS* VII.4028): 568-9 n.38
    Zeus of Olba in Cilicia: 568 n.38
    Zeus of Venasa in Morimene: 154
Zeuxis, Flavius (of Phrygian Hierapolis): 561 n.24
Zimbabwe: 212
Zosimus (Late Greek historian): 11-12, 247, 272, 478-80, 489-90, 512-15, 595 n.6, etc.
Zosimus (freedman of M. Aurelius Cotta Maximus): 178
Zoticus (praetorian prefect): *488*
Zulueta, F. de: 572 nn. 63, 65

Errata

p. viii : *for* Indexes *read* Index
p. 37, para 2, line 31 : *for* producers *read* producers'
p. 69, para 3, line 5 : *read* pre-revolutionary
p. 82, line 15 : *read* summarised
p. 163, para 3, line 3 : *for* Temnos *read* Temnus
p. 309, line 20 : *for* Caelestrius *read* Calestrius
p. 317, para 2, line 10 : *for civitatum read civitatium*
p. 404, para 1, line 9 : *for* Dioscurus *read* Dioscoros
p. 506, para 2, line 2 : *for* Deceleia *read* Decelea
p. 521, para 2, line 6, first word : *for* the *read* then
p. 526, line 8 : *for* Athenian *read* Athenion
p. 535, para 1, line 2 : *for* Euhesperides *read* Euesperides
p. 568, n.33, line 8 : *read* period
p. 616, n.64 : *for* CHSB *read* CSHB
pp. 622-3, running heads : *for pp. read p.*
p. 624, running head : *for IV read VI*
p. 624, n.26, line 1 : *for* 18 *read* 19
p. 628, n.17, line 4 : *read* ὥσπερ
p. 641, n.4 : *add* [And see p. 325 above]
p. 654, line 16 : *for* Sidon, *read* Sidon.